Grade 4 Volume 2

Houghton Mifflin Math

Teacher's Edition

time

HOUGHTON MIFFLIN BOSTON

Printed in the U.S.A.

ISBN-13: 978-0-618-59117-6

ISBN-10: 0-618-59117-6

3 4 5 6 7 8 9 B 14 13 12 11 10 09 08

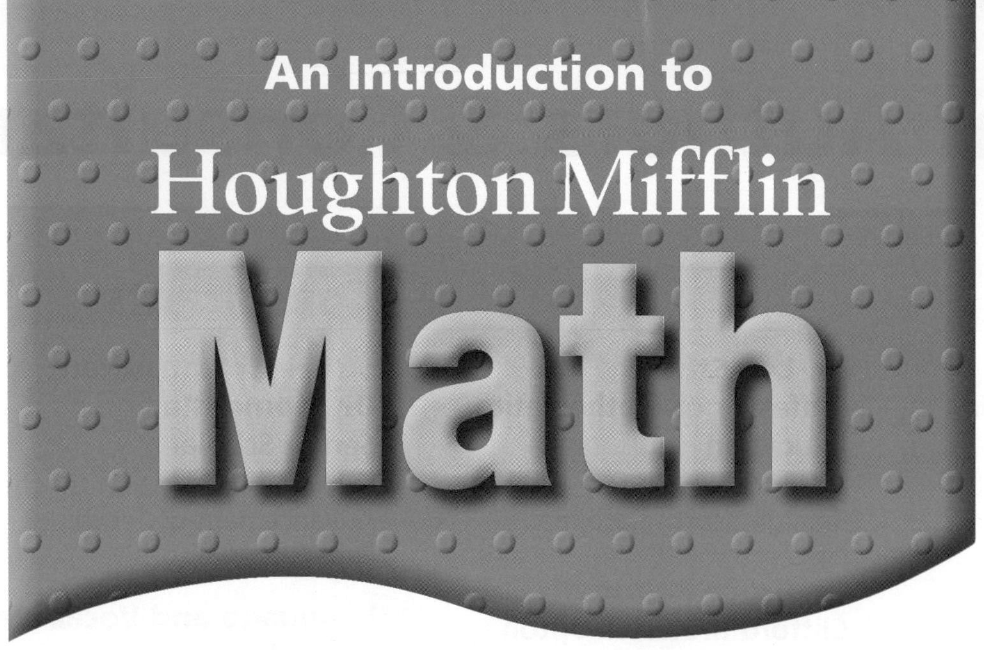

Your Teacher's Edition is a key component for effective and easy teaching of mathematics. This section will give you an overview of Houghton Mifflin Math. You will learn about how the exciting features of the program can help you meet the needs of all your students, prepare students for high-stakes testing, and make lessons fun and engaging for your students and you.

Program Authors & Consultants

Authors

Dr. Carole Greenes
Professor of Mathematics Education
Boston University
Boston, Massachusetts

Dr. Matt Larson
Curriculum Specialist for Mathematics
Lincoln Public Schools
Lincoln, Nebraska

Dr. Miriam A. Leiva
Distinguished Professor of Mathematics Emerita
University of North Carolina
Charlotte, North Carolina

Dr. Jean M. Shaw
Professor Emerita of Curriculum and Instruction
University of Mississippi
Oxford, Mississippi

Dr. Lee Stiff
Professor of Mathematics Education
North Carolina State University
Raleigh, North Carolina

Dr. Bruce R. Vogeli
Clifford Brewster Upton Professor of Mathematics
Teachers College,
Columbia University
New York, New York

Dr. Karol Yeatts
Associate Professor
Barry University
Miami, Florida

Consultants

Strategic Consultant
Dr. Liping Ma
Senior Scholar
Carnegie Foundation for the Advancement of Teaching
Palo Alto, California

Language and Vocabulary Consultant
Dr. David Chard
Professor of Reading
University of Oregon
Eugene, Oregon

Blended Usage Advisor

Houghton Mifflin Math and Math Expressions
Dr. Matt Larson
Curriculum Specialist for Mathematics
Lincoln Public Schools
Lincoln, Nebraska

Teacher Reviewers

Kindergarten

Karen Sue Hinton
Washington Elementary School
Ponca City, OK

Hilda Kendrick
W E Wilson Elementary School
Jefferson, IN

Debby Nagel
Assumption Elementary School
Cincinnati, OH

Jen Payet
Lake Ave. Elementary School
Saratoga Springs, NY

Grade 1

Stephanie McDaniel
B. Everett Jordan Elementary School
Graham, NC

Juan Melgar
Lowrie Elementary School
Elgin, IL

Sharon O'Brien
Echo Mountain School
Phoenix, AZ

Paula Rowland
Bixby North Elementary School
Bixby, OK

Karen Wood
Clay Elementary School
Clay, AL

Grade 2

Sally Bales
Akron Elementary School
Akron, IN

Rose Marie Bruno
Mawbey Street Elementary School
Woodbridge, NJ

Megan Burton
Valley Elementary School
Pelham, AL

Kiesha Doster
Berry Elementary School
Detroit, MI

Kristy Ford
Eisenhower Elementary School
Norman, OK

Marci Galazkiewicz
North Elementary School
Waukegan, IL

Ana Gaspar
Lowrie Elementary School
Elgin, IL

Elana Heinoren
Beechfield Elementary School
Baltimore, MD

Kim Terry
Woodland Elementary School West
Gages Lake, IL

Grade 3

Jenny Chang
North Elementary School
Waukegan, IL

Patricia Heintz
PS 92
Harry T. Stewart Elementary School
Corona, NY

Shannon Hopper
White Lick Elementary School
Brownsburg, IN

Amy Simpson
Broadmoore Elementary School
Moore, OK

Allison White
Kingsley Elementary School
Naperville, IL

Grade 4

Kathy Curtis
Hoxsie School
Warwick, RI

Lynn Fox
Kendall-Whittier Elementary School
Tulsa, OK

Brenda Hancock
Clay Elementary School
Clay, AL

Barbara O'Hanlon
Maurice & Everett Haines
Elementary School
Medford, NJ

Connie Rapp
Oakland Elementary School
Bloomington, IL

Pam Rettig
Solheim Elementary School
Bismarck, ND

Karen Scroggins
Rock Quarry Elementary School
Tuscaloosa, AL

Tracy Smith
Carstens Elementary School
Detroit, MI

Grade 5

Jim Archer
Maplewood Elementary School
Indianapolis, IN

Linda Carlson
Van Buren Elementary School
Oklahoma City, OK

Maggie Dunning
Horizon Elementary School
Hanover Park, IL

Mike Intoccia
McNichols Plaza
Scranton, PA

Jennifer LaBelle
Washington Elementary School
Waukegan, IL

Peg McCann
Warwick Neck School
Warwick, RI

Ellen O'Rourke
Bower Elementary School
Warrenville, IL

Gary Smith
Thomas H. Ford Elementary School
Reading, PA

Grade 6

Robin Akers
Sonoran Sky Elementary School
Scottsdale, AZ

Ellen Greenman
Daniel Webster Middle School
Waukegan, IL

Angela McCray
Abbott Middle School
West Bloomfield, MI

Mary Popovich
Horizon Elementary School
Hanover Park, IL

Debbie Taylor
Sonoran Sky Elementary School
Scottsdale, AZ

Across Grades

Jacqueline Lampley
Hewitt Elementary School
Trussville, AL

Rose Smith
Five Points Elementary School
Orrville, AL

Winnie Tepper
Morgan County Schools
Decatur, AL

Houghton Mifflin

Math

Math...the way you always knew it could be.

Powerful approaches make a difference—right from the start

- Engaging hands-on activities begin each lesson
- Easily managed manipulatives, packaged in special student kits, support understanding
- Unique Write-On, Wipe-Off Workmats help students share strategies and solutions
- Daily homework reinforces and maintains concepts and skills

Powerful teaching support never lets you down

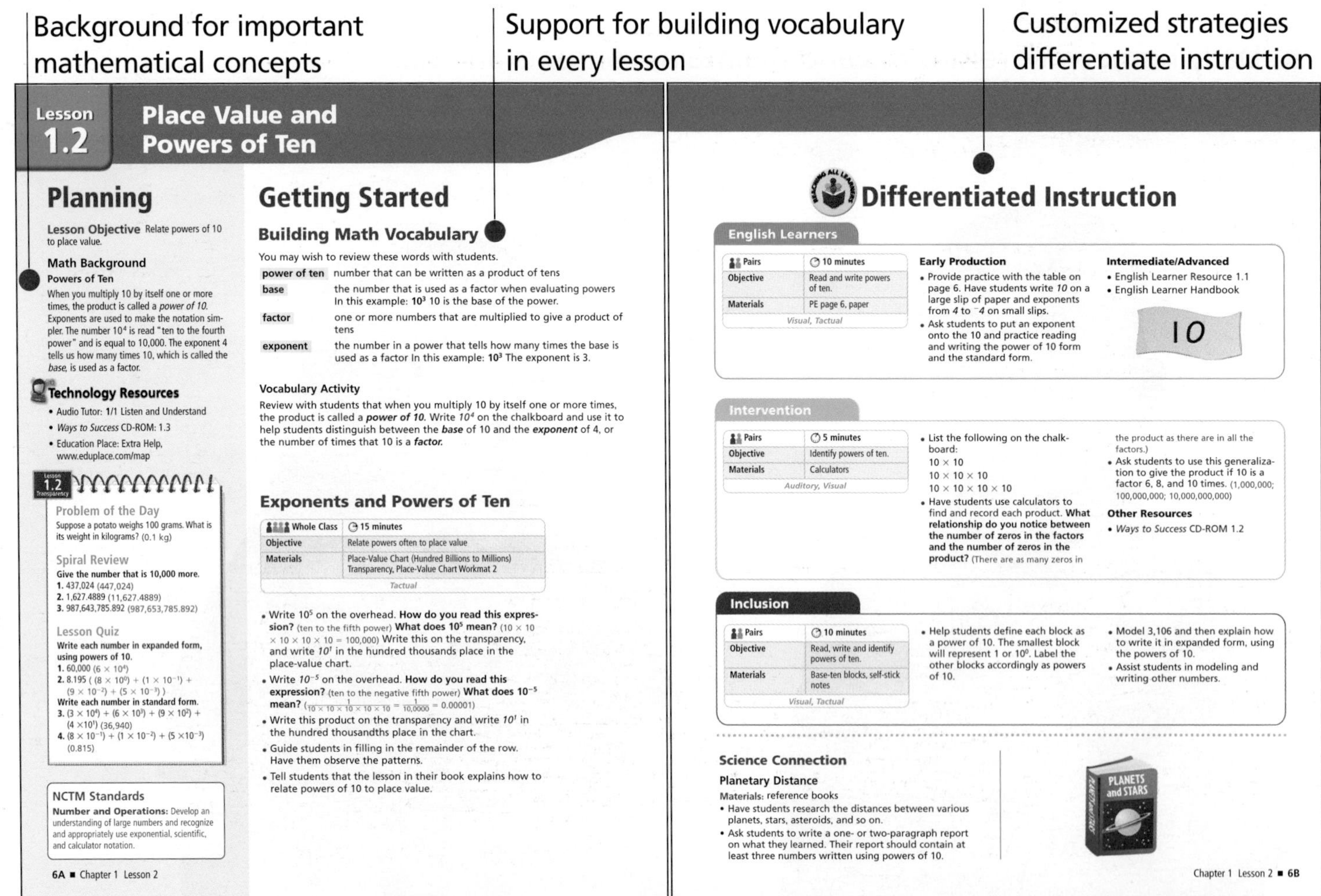
Background for important mathematical concepts
Support for building vocabulary in every lesson
Customized strategies differentiate instruction

Lesson 1.2 **Place Value and Powers of Ten**

Planning

Lesson Objective Relate powers of 10 to place value.

Math Background

Powers of Ten

When you multiply 10 by itself one or more times, the product is called a *power of 10.* Exponents are used to make the notation simpler. The number 10^4 is read "ten to the fourth power" and is equal to 10,000. The exponent 4 tells us how many times 10, which is called the *base,* is used as a factor.

Technology Resources

- Audio Tutor: **1/1** Listen and Understand
- *Ways to Success* CD-ROM: 1.3
- Education Place: Extra Help, www.eduplace.com/map

Lesson 1.2 Transparency

Problem of the Day

Suppose a potato weighs 100 grams. What is its weight in kilograms? (0.1 kg)

Spiral Review

Give the number that is 10,000 more.

1. 437,024 (447,024)
2. 1,627.4889 (11,627.4889)
3. 987,643,785.892 (987,653,785.892)

Lesson Quiz

Write each number in expanded form, using powers of 10.

1. 60,000 (6×10^4)
2. 8.195 ($(8 \times 10^0) + (1 \times 10^{-1}) + (9 \times 10^{-2}) + (5 \times 10^{-3})$)

Write each number in standard form.

3. $(3 \times 10^4) + (6 \times 10^3) + (9 \times 10^2) + (4 \times 10^1)$ (36,940)
4. $(8 \times 10^{-1}) + (1 \times 10^{-2}) + (5 \times 10^{-3})$ (0.815)

NCTM Standards

Number and Operations: Develop an understanding of large numbers and recognize and appropriately use exponential, scientific, and calculator notation.

6A ■ Chapter 1 Lesson 2

Getting Started

Building Math Vocabulary

You may wish to review these words with students.

power of ten	number that can be written as a product of tens
base	the number that is used as a factor when evaluating powers In this example: $\mathbf{10^3}$ 10 is the base of the power.
factor	one or more numbers that are multiplied to give a product of tens
exponent	the number in a power that tells how many times the base is used as a factor In this example: $\mathbf{10^3}$ The exponent is 3.

Vocabulary Activity

Review with students that when you multiply 10 by itself one or more times, the product is called a ***power of 10.*** Write 10^4 on the chalkboard and use it to help students distinguish between the ***base*** of 10 and the ***exponent*** of 4, or the number of times that 10 is a ***factor.***

Exponents and Powers of Ten

Whole Class	15 minutes
Objective	Relate powers often to place value
Materials	Place-Value Chart (Hundred Billions to Millions) Transparency, Place-Value Chart Workmat 2
Tactual	

- Write 10^5 on the overhead. **How do you read this expression?** (ten to the fifth power) **What does 10^5 mean?** ($10 \times 10 \times 10 \times 10 \times 10 = 100{,}000$) Write this on the transparency, and write 10^1 in the hundred thousands place in the place-value chart.
- Write 10^{-5} on the overhead. **How do you read this expression?** (ten to the negative fifth power) **What does 10^{-5} mean?** ($\frac{1}{10 \times 10 \times 10 \times 10 \times 10} = \frac{1}{10{,}0000} = 0.00001$)
- Write this product on the transparency and write 10^1 in the hundred thousandths place in the chart.
- Guide students in filling in the remainder of the row. Have them observe the patterns.
- Tell students that the lesson in their book explains how to relate powers of 10 to place value.

Differentiated Instruction

English Learners

Pairs	10 minutes
Objective	Read and write powers of ten.
Materials	PE page 6, paper
Visual, Tactual	

Early Production

- Provide practice with the table on page 6. Have students write *10* on a large slip of paper and exponents from *4* to $^-4$ on small slips.
- Ask students to put an exponent onto the 10 and practice reading and writing the power of 10 form and the standard form.

Intermediate/Advanced

- English Learner Resource 1.1
- English Learner Handbook

10

Intervention

Pairs	5 minutes
Objective	Identify powers of ten.
Materials	Calculators
Auditory, Visual	

- List the following on the chalkboard:
  10×10
  $10 \times 10 \times 10$
  $10 \times 10 \times 10 \times 10$
- Have students use calculators to find and record each product. **What relationship do you notice between the number of zeros in the factors and the number of zeros in the product?** (There are as many zeros in the product as there are in all the factors.)
- Ask students to use this generalization to give the product if 10 is a factor 6, 8, and 10 times. (1,000,000; 100,000,000; 10,000,000,000)

Other Resources

- *Ways to Success* CD-ROM 1.2

Inclusion

Pairs	10 minutes
Objective	Read, write and identify powers of ten.
Materials	Base-ten blocks, self-stick notes
Visual, Tactual	

- Help students define each block as a power of 10. The smallest block will represent 1 or 10^0. Label the other blocks accordingly as powers of 10.
- Model 3,106 and then explain how to write it in expanded form, using the powers of 10.
- Assist students in modeling and writing other numbers.

Science Connection

Planetary Distance

Materials: reference books

- Have students research the distances between various planets, stars, asteroids, and so on.
- Ask students to write a one- or two-paragraph report on what they learned. Their report should contain at least three numbers written using powers of 10.

PLANETS and STARS

Chapter 1 Lesson 2 ■ 6B

Clear, four-step teaching plans

Audio Tutor assists teachers and learners

Built-in daily test prep

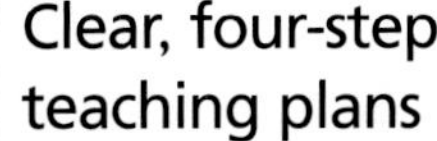

❶ Introduce

Point out to students that we have our number system of 10 because we have 10 digits (fingers) on our hands. Explain that the lesson will teach how this base-ten number system relates to place value.

❷ Teach

Learn About It

- **In any power of 10, what does the exponent indicate?** (the number of times the base, 10, is used as a factor)
- **Look at the table. In any row, how are the power of 10, the standard form of the power of 10, and the fractional form related?** (The values are equivalent.)
- **Compare the fractional forms of 10^2 and 10^{-2}. How are the standard forms of these two numbers different?** ($10^2 = \frac{100}{1}$ and $10^{-2} = \frac{1}{100}$)

Guided Practice

Have students complete **Exercises 1–5** as you observe. Remind them to use the ***Ask Yourself*** questions to help. Give students the opportunity to talk about the question in ***Explain Your Thinking***.

Common Error

- Incorrect expanded form Some students may make mistakes when writing the expanded form of a power of 10.
- Intervention Encourage students to use multiplication and addition to check the expanded form of a number. Explain that the sum of the products in a number in expanded form is the same as the number in standard form.

Lesson 2

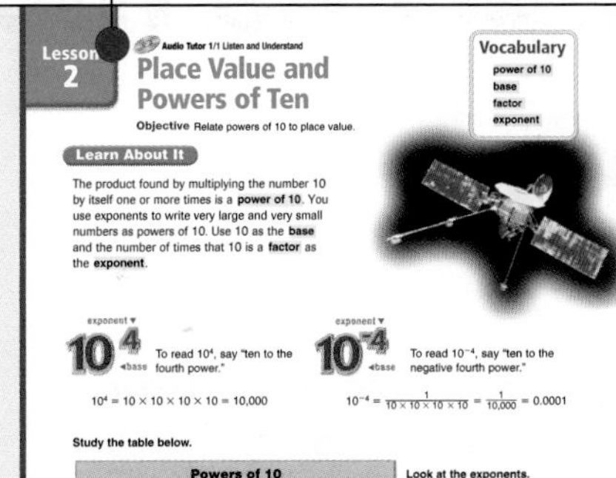

Place Value and Powers of Ten

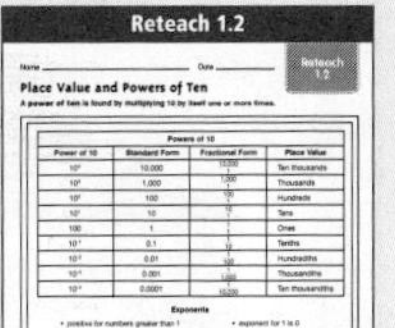

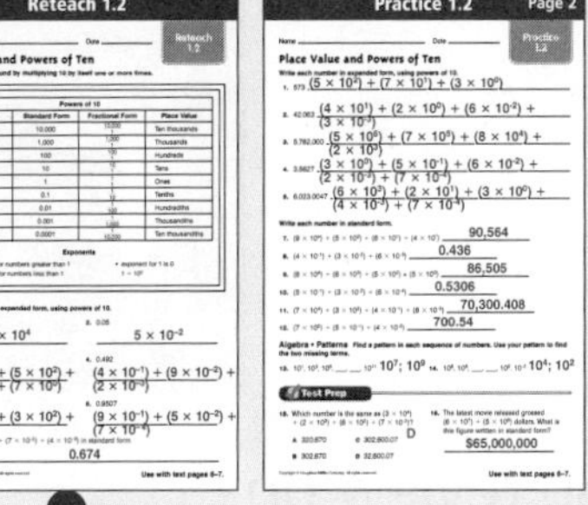

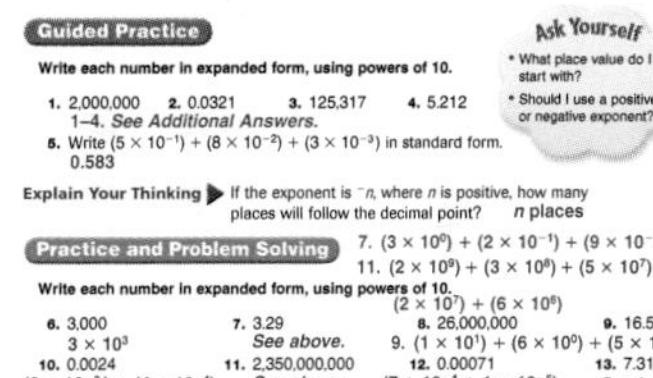

Reteach 1.2

Practice 1.2 Page 2

Enrichment 1.2

Problem Solving 1.2

Homework 1.2 Page 2

❸ Practice

Practice and Problem Solving

Select from **Exercises 6–32** as independent work.

- **Algebra • Patterns for Exercises 19–21:** Students should look for patterns in both the base and exponent.
- **Problem Solving for Problems 22–25:** Have students share their solutions.

❹ Assess & Close

Math Talk in Action

- **Using powers of 10, how would you write 0.037 in expanded form?** ($0.037 = (3 \times 10^{-2}) + (7 \times 10^{-3})$)
- Ask students to explain how they could use exponents to tell if a power of 10 is greater or less than 1. (exponent positive: number > 1; exponent negative: number < 1)

Math Journal Prompt

Display $2{,}003 = (2 \times 10^3) + (3 \times 10^0)$ on the board. Have students explain in writing why powers of 10 for the zeros in the hundreds and tens digits have been omitted from the expanded form of this number.

Lesson Quiz
Use the quiz on Lesson Transparency 1.2.

Lesson 1.2 Transparency

Test Prep & Spiral Review
Use Test Prep Transparency 1.2.

Test Prep 1.2 Transparency

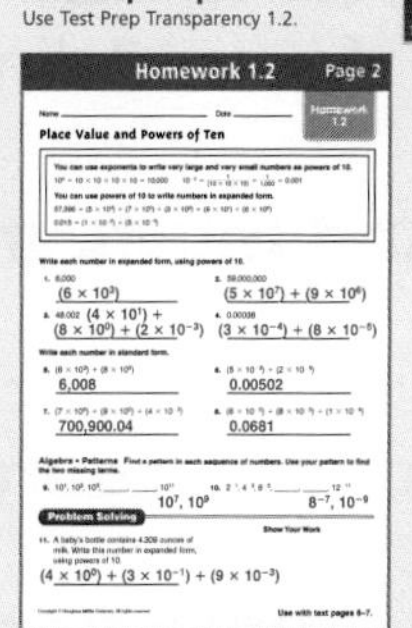

Leveled resources to support all learners

Population Growth of Alaska

Population

Year of Census

Differentiated resources meet the needs of all learners

Teacher Resource Package

Plan instruction, manage your classroom, and organize your time with ready-made resources.

- **Chapter Challenges:** Chapter-based activities and projects for advanced students
- **Teaching Transparencies:** Movable transparencies for modeling mathematical concepts.

And much, much more!

Additional resources include:

- **Audio Tutor:** Extra support and key lesson review on CD
- **Ways to Success Intervention CD-ROM:** Diagnostic reteaching and targeted practice for struggling students
- **Write-On, Wipe-Off Workmats:** Dry-erase mats with workspace and visual supports that link to program activities and help students share their strategies and solutions

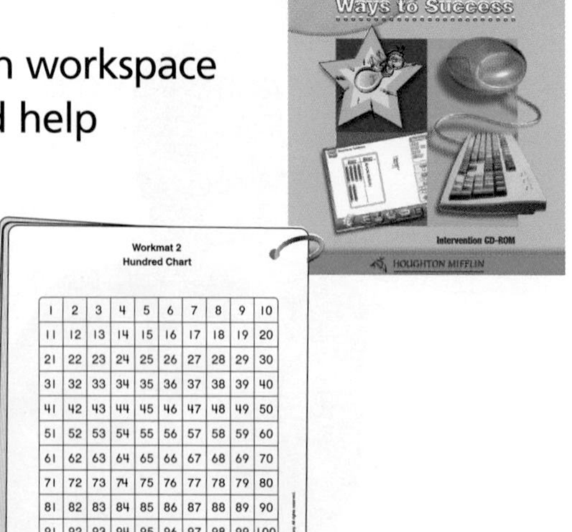

- **Blended Usage Planning Guide:** Three levels of grade-specific support for teachers who use ***Houghton Mifflin Math*** together with the new NSF program ***Math Expressions***

  - **Level One: Math Talk**
    Questions to encourage discussion, and suggestions for incorporating Math Talk and MathBoards from ***Math Expressions*** into ***Houghton Mifflin Math*** lessons

  - **Level Two: Problem Solving and Accessible Algorithms**
    Descriptions of ***Math Expressions*** algorithms and problem-solving approaches, and suggestions for how to incorporate them into ***Houghton Mifflin Math***

  - **Level Three: Replacement Lessons**
    Suggestions for how and when to integrate entire Math Expressions chapters into daily teaching

Houghton Mifflin
Math
Blended Usage Planning Guide
Math Expressions

Math...the way you always knew it could be.

Components

	K	1	2	3	4	5	6
Student Book	●	●	●	●	●	●	●
Student Book, Multi-Volume Set	●	●	●				
Teacher's Edition	●	●	●	●	●	●	●
Write-On, Wipe-Off Workmats	●	●	●	●	●	●	●
Big Book (Student Book in Big Book Format)	●						
Read-Aloud Anthologies, Volumes 1–4	●	●	●				
Trade Book Literature Library	●	●	●	●	●	●	●
Unit Resource Folders	●	●	●	●	●	●	●
Reteach/Practice/ Enrichment	●	●	●	●	●	●	●
Problem Solving/Homework/English Learners		●	●	●	●	●	●
Assessments/Learning Tools	●	●	●	●	●	●	●
Practice Workbook	●	●	●	●	●	●	●
Homework Workbook		●	●	●	●	●	●
English Learners Handbook	●	●	●	●	●	●	●
Building Vocabulary Kit	●	●	●	●	●	●	●
Adequate Yearly Progress		●	●	●	●	●	●
Chapter Challenges	●	●	●	●	●	●	●
Combination Classroom Guide	●	●	●	●	●	●	●
Kindergarten Kit	●						
Busy Bear Puppet	●						
Math Songs for Young Learners	●						
Student Manipulatives Kit	●	●	●	●	●	●	●
Custom Manipulatives Kits	●	●	●	●	●	●	●
Overhead Manipulatives Kit	●	●	●	●	●	●	●
Math Center	●	●	●	●	●	●	●
Lesson Transparencies	●	●	●	●	●	●	●
Daily Routines Flip Chart	●	●	●	●	●	●	●
Teaching Transparencies	●	●	●	●	●	●	●
Test Prep Transparencies		●	●	●	●	●	●
Lesson Planner CD-ROM	●	●	●	●	●	●	●
Ways to Success Intervention CD-ROM		●	●	●	●	●	●
Chapter Intervention Ways to Success Skill Sheets		●	●	●	●	●	●
eMathBook (Student Book on CD-ROM and Online)	●	●	●	●	●	●	●
eTeacher's Edition (Teacher's Edition on CD and Online)	●	●	●	●	●	●	●
Ways to Assess CD-ROM (test and spiral review generator)		●	●	●	●	●	●
Audio Tutor MP3 Audio CD		●	●	●	●	●	●
Houghton Mifflin Assessment System	●	●	●	●	●	●	●
Education Place Web site	●	●	●	●	●	●	●
Houghton Mifflin Math/Math Expressions Blended Usage Planning Guide	●	●	●	●	●	●	

Manipulatives

Program Manipulatives	Suggested Alternatives	K	1	2	3	4	5	6
Algebra Tiles	Bars and squares made from grid paper or construction paper						●	●
Attribute Blocks	Seashells, pasta, buttons	●	●	●				
Balance Scales	Ruler, paper cups, and string	●	●	●	●	●	●	●
Bill Set	Bills made from construction paper and markers	●	●	●	●	●	●	●
Blank Number	Number cards, spinners **Cubes with Labels**	●	●	●	●	●	●	●
Coin Set	Real coins, buttons	●	●	●	●	●	●	●
Connecting Cubes	Paper clips, string and beads or pasta	●	●	●	●	●	●	●
Counting Chips	Buttons, coins, beans	●						
Demonstration Clock	Clockface with two lengths of string fastened to the center for the hands	●	●	●	●	●	●	●
Fraction Tiles	Bars and squares made from grid paper or construction paper				●	●	●	●
Geometric Solids	Cans, boxes, balls, cones, modeling clay shapes	●	●	●	●	●	●	●
Geotool Compass							●	●
Pattern Blocks	Shapes cut out of different-colored construction paper or cardboard	●	●	●	●	●	●	●
Place-Value Blocks/ Base-Ten Blocks	Grid paper cutouts	●	●	●	●	●	●	●
Protractor							●	●
Ruler, inch and centimeter	One-inch or one-centimeter grid paper strips				●	●	●	●
Transparent Spinner	Construction paper, paper clip, and pencil	●	●	●	●	●	●	●
Two-Color Counters	Coins, washers, or beans with one side painted	●	●	●	●	●	●	●

Scope and Sequence

In the Program...

Number and Operations

Addition

	K	1	2	3	4	5	6
Adding decimals				●	●	▲	▲
Adding fractions				●	●	▲	▲
Adding integers and rational numbers					●	●	▲
Adding measurements						●	▲
Adding mixed numbers					●	▲	▲
Adding money	●	●	●	●	▲	▲	
Adding multi-digit numbers	●	●	●	▲	▲	▲	▲
Adding whole numbers	●	●	▲	▲	▲	▲	▲
Basic facts	●	●	▲				
Equations						●	▲
Estimating sums		●	●	▲	▲	▲	▲
Expressions					●	●	▲
Fact families		●	●	●	▲		
Inverse operations	★	●	●	●	●	▲	▲
Mental math		●	●	●	●	▲	▲
Missing addends	●	●	●	▲	▲		
Modeling addition	★	●	●	●	●	●	●
Number sentences	●	●	●	▲	▲		
Problem-solving applications	●	●	●	▲	▲	▲	▲
Properties of addition		●	●	▲	▲	▲	▲
Regrouping to add			●	●	▲	▲	▲
Strategies for adding	●	●	●	▲	▲		
Three or more addends		●	▲				

Comparing and Ordering Numbers

	K	1	2	3	4	5	6
Decimals				●	●	▲	▲
Decimals and fractions				●	●	●	▲
Decimals, fractions, and percents						●	▲
Fractions			●	●	●	▲	▲
Integers					●	▲	▲
Money amounts	●	●	●	●	▲		
Percents						●	▲
Rational numbers						●	●
Using <, >, and = symbols		●	●	●	▲	▲	▲
Using models to compare	●	●	●	●	●	●	●
Whole numbers	●	●	●	▲	▲	▲	▲

Counting, Reading, Writing Numbers

	K	1	2	3	4	5	6
Decimals				●	●	●	▲
Fractions		●	●	●	▲	▲	▲
Integers						●	●
Mixed numbers				●	●	▲	▲
Modeling whole numbers	●	●	●	●			
Money		●	●	▲	▲		
One-to one correspondence	●	▲					
Ordinal Numbers	●	●	●	▲	▲		
Percent						●	●
Powers and exponents						●	●
Rational numbers						●	●
Roman and other numerals			●	●	●	▲	▲
Scientific notation						●	●
Square numbers				●	●	●	●
Square roots							●
Whole numbers	●	●	●	●	●	▲	▲

KEY Teach and Apply ● Practice and Apply ▲ Teacher's Edition Lesson ★

In Level 4...

Number and Operations

Addition

adding decimals 572–575
adding fractions
  like denominators 516–519
  unlike denominators
    using models 528–529
adding integers 345–346, 348, 349
adding mixed numbers 520–521
adding money 70–71
adding whole numbers
  adding greater numbers 76–79
  adding three-digit, four-digit, five-digit numbers 70–71
  adding two-digit numbers 70–71
  estimating sums 64–67
checking by adding in a different order 70–71
checking subtraction with addition 72–73
expressions 112–114
inverse operations 72–73
mental math 62–63
missing addends 73
number sentences 118–124
parentheses 86, 110–111
problem-solvng applications 104
properties of addition 60–61
regrouping to add 70–71, 76–78
strategies for adding 60–61, 70–71

Comparing and Ordering Numbers

decimals
  mixed numbers and decimals 546–548, 558–563
  using a number line 558–563
  using place value 558–563
decimals and fractions 550–552
fractions
  using a model 498–501
  using a number line 498–501
  with like denominators 498–501
  with unlike denominators 498–501
integers 624–626
money amounts 30–33
using <, >, and = symbols 24–25, 66, 78, 86, 116–117, 166, 173, 281, 559, 561, 626
whole numbers 24–25

Counting, Reading, Writing Numbers

base ten, base two, base five 9
Braille numerals 33
decimals 542–545
fractions 490–491
Mayan numbers 155
mixed numbers 508–510
Roman numerals 51
skip-counting to multiply 92–93
square numbers 90, 105, 142
Thai numberals 29
whole numbers 6–8, 14–18

Scope and Sequence

In the Program...

Number and Operations

Mental Math

	K	1	2	3	4	5	6
Addition		●	●	●	●	▲	▲
Division				●	▲	▲	▲
Multiples and powers of 10		●	●	●	▲	▲	▲
Multiplication				●	▲	▲	▲
Patterns	●	●	▲	▲	▲	▲	▲
Problem-solving applications			●	▲	▲	▲	▲
Subtraction		●	●	▲	▲	▲	▲
Use properties		●	●	●	●	▲	▲

Mixed Numbers

	K	1	2	3	4	5	6
Adding mixed numbers					●	▲	▲
Decimals and mixed numbers				●	●	▲	▲
Dividing mixed numbers						●	▲
Meaning of mixed numbers				●	▲	▲	▲
Multiplying mixed numbers						●	▲
Subtracting mixed numbers					●	▲	▲
Using a number line with mixed numbers				●	▲	▲	▲
Writing mixed numbers				●	▲	▲	▲

Multiplication

	K	1	2	3	4	5	6
Arrays			●	▲	▲		
Basic facts		●	●	●	▲		
Drawing a picture to multiply		●	●	▲			
Equations						●	▲
Estimating products				●	●	▲	▲
Expressions					●	▲	▲
Fact families				●	▲		
Horizontal and vertical forms				●	▲		
Inverse operations				●	●	▲	▲
Mental math				●	▲	▲	▲
Missing factors				●	●	▲	▲
Modeling multiplication		●	●	●	●	▲	▲
Multiplication as equal groups	●	●	●	▲			
Multiplication as repeated addition		●	●	●			
Multiplying decimals						●	▲
Multiplying fractions						●	▲
Multiplying integers and rational numbers							●
Multiplying mixed numbers						●	▲
Multiplying money				●	●	▲	▲
Multiplying three factors				●	▲	▲	▲
Multiplying whole numbers		●	●	▲	▲	▲	▲
Number sentences			●	▲	▲		
Problem-solving applications		●	●	▲	▲	▲	▲
Properties of multiplication			●	●	▲	▲	▲
Related facts				●	▲		
Related to other operations			●	●	▲	▲	▲
Skip-counting to multiply	●	●	●	●	▲		
Square numbers				●	▲	▲	▲
Strategies			●	●	▲		

KEY Teach and Apply ● Practice and Apply ▲ Teacher's Edition Lesson ★

In Level 4...

Number and Operations

Mental Math

adding 62–63, 570–571
dividing with multiples of 10, 100, and 1,000 218–219
multiplying with 10, 100, and 1,000 146–147, 172–173
subtracting 62–63, 570–571
using patterns in multiplication 90–91
use properties 61
- breaking apart numbers 62–63
- compensation 62–63

Mixed Numbers

adding mixed numbers 520–521
drawing pictorial representations 508–510
mixed numbers as decimals 546–548
mixed numbers as fractions 508–510
subtracting mixed numbers 520–521
using a number line with mixed numbers 508–510

Multiplication

basic multiplication facts 92–99
estimating products 148–149, 174–175
expressions 146–147
inverse operations 72, 119–120, 240
mental math 146–147, 172–173
missing factors 89, 101
modeling multiplication 92, 94, 150–153, 176–177
money 160–162, 184–185, 187–188
multiplying money amounts 164–167, 186–189
multiplying to check division 214–217
multiplying three factors 100–101
multiplying whole numbers
- multiplying by one-digit numbers
  - four or five digits 164–167
  - three digits 160–163
  - two digits 150–155
- multiplying by two-digit numbers with regrouping
  - four or five digits 186–189
  - three digits 184–185
  - two digits 176–181
- regrouping 152–155

number sentences 118–124
problem-solvng applications 104
properties 84–87, 100–101, 176–177
related facts 88–89
related to other operations 88–89
square number 90–91
strategies 90–97, 146–147, 172–173

Scope and Sequence

In the Program...

Number and Operations

Number Theory

	K	1	2	3	4	5	6
Even and odd numbers	●	●	●	▲	▲	▲	▲
Factor trees					●	▲	▲
Factors			●	●	▲	▲	▲
Figurate numbers, square numbers				●	●	▲	▲
Greatest common factor						●	▲
Least common denominator						●	▲
Least common multiple						●	▲
Multiples				●	●	●	▲
Prime factorization						●	▲
Prime and composite numbers					●	●	▲
Reciprocals						●	▲
Rules for divisibility						●	▲

Place Value

	K	1	2	3	4	5	6
Decimals				●	●	▲	▲
Expanded form			●	▲	▲	▲	▲
Millions and billions					●	●	▲
Money				●	●	▲	▲
Standard form	●	●	●	▲	▲	▲	▲
Using models		●	●	▲	▲		
Using a place-value chart		●	●	●	▲	▲	▲
Whole numbers	●	●	●	▲	▲	▲	▲

Ratio, Proportion, and Percent

	K	1	2	3	4	5	6
Estimation with percents						●	●
Finding a percent of a number						●	●
Graphing proportional relationships						●	●
Indirect measurement					●	●	●
Meaning of percents				●	●	●	●
Modeling					●	●	▲
Pi as a ratio						●	▲
Percents related to circle graphs						●	●
Percents related to fractions and/or decimals				●	●	●	●
Proportional Reasoning				●	▲	▲	▲
Rates				●	●	▲	▲
Reading and writing ratios						●	●
Writing and solving percent equation						●	▲
Writing and solving proportions						●	●

Subtraction

	K	1	2	3	4	5	6
Basic facts	●	●	●	▲			
Checking subtraction		●	●	●	▲	▲	▲
Equations						●	▲
Estimating differences		●	●	●	▲	▲	▲
Expressions						●	▲
Fact families	●	●	●	●			
Inverse operation	★	●	●	●	●	▲	▲
Mental math	★	●	●	▲	▲	▲	▲
Number sentences	●	●	●	▲	▲		
Problem-solving applications	●	●	▲	▲	▲	▲	▲
Properties of subtraction			●	▲	▲	▲	▲
Regrouping to subtract			●	▲	▲	▲	▲

KEY Teach and Apply ● Practice and Apply ▲ Teacher's Edition Lesson ★

In Level 4...

Number and Operations

Number Theory

common multiples 252–253
composite numbers 254–257
factor tree 257
factors 84–87, 252,253
multiples 252–253
prime numbers 254–257
rules for diivisibility 297

Place Value

addition 70–71
decimals
  hundredths 542–543, 546–548
  tenths 542–543, 546–548
  thousandths 544–545
expanded form 6–9, 14–19
hundred thousands 6–7
millions, billions, trillions 14–15, 16–18
short word form 6–9, 14–19
standard form 6–7
subtraction 72–73
using a chart 6–8, 16–17
whole numbers 6–9. 14–19

Ratio, Proportion, and Percent

indirect measurement 312, 320, 322, 325, 344
meaning of percents 553
percents related to fractions and decimals 553
proportional reasoning 126–127, 308–309, 310–311, 312–313, 320–312, 322–323, 326–327, 334–335, 492–493, 498, 553, 584, 598–600
rates—batting averages 549

Subtraction

checking subtraction with addition 72–73
estimating differences
  using clustering 67
  using front-end estimation 67
  using rounding 64–67
inverse operations 72, 119–120, 240
mental math
  breaking apart 62–63
  compensation 62–63
modeling subtraction 517, 518, 530–531, 573
money amounts 72–73
number sentences 118–124
strategies 72–73
subtracting decimals 572–575
subtracting fractions
  with like denominators 516–519
  with unlike denominators
    using models 530–532
subtracting integers 345–346, 348, 349
subtracting mixed numbers 520–521
subtracting whole numbers
  subtracting across zeros 74–75
  subtracting four-digit and five-digit numbers 72–73
  subtracting greater numbers 76–79
  subtracting three-digit numbers 72–73

Scope and Sequence

In the Program...

Number and Operations

	K	1	2	3	4	5	6
Strategies for subtracting	●	●	●	▲	▲		
Subtracting decimals				●	●	▲	▲
Subtracting fractions				●	●	●	▲
Subtracting integers					●	●	▲
Subtracting mixed numbers					●	▲	▲
Subtracting measurements						●	▲
Subtracting money	●	●	●	●	▲	▲	▲
Subtracting whole numbers	●	●	▲	▲	▲	▲	▲
Subtracting with zeros		●	●	●	●	▲	▲

Algebra

Readiness and Applications

	K	1	2	3	4	5	6
Addition and subtraction number sentences	●	●	●	▲	▲		
Analyze change	●	●	●	▲	▲	▲	▲
Fact families		●	●	●	▲		
Inverse operations		●	●	●	▲	▲	▲
Meaning of equality				●	●	▲	▲
Missing addends	●	●	●	▲	▲		
Missing digits			▲	▲	▲	▲	▲
Missing factors			●	●	▲	▲	▲
Missing measurements and units			●	●	●	▲	▲
Missing operations	●	●	●	●	▲	▲	▲
Multiplication and division number sentences			●	●	▲		
Proportional reasoning	●	●	●	●	▲	▲	▲
Symbols showing relationships	●	●	●	▲	▲	▲	▲
Variables			●	●	▲	▲	▲
Venn diagrams		●	●	●	●	▲	▲
Writing and solving number sentences or equations	●	●	●	●	●	●	●

Coordinate Graphs

	K	1	2	3	4	5	6
Distance between points						▲	▲
Graphing an equation						●	▲
Graphing ordered pairs			●	●	▲	▲	▲
Ordered pairs			●	●	▲	▲	▲
Patterns in the coordinate place						●	▲

Equations and Inequalities

	K	1	2	3	4	5	6
Equations with more than one variable						●	●
Graphing an equation						●	▲
Linear equations						●	▲
Modeling equations		●	●	●	▲	▲	▲
Formulas					●	●	▲
Solving addition and subtraction equations						●	▲
Solving equations by using inverse operations						●	▲
Solving multiplication and division equations						●	▲
Writing an equation or number sentence				●	●	▲	▲
Writing and solving proportions						●	▲
Writing and solving percent equations						●	▲

KEY Teach and Apply ● Practice and Apply ▲ Teacher's Edition Lesson ★

In Level 4...

Algebra

Readiness and Applications

- addition and subtraction number sentences 118–124
- analyze change 8, 42, 346, 458, 620–623
- classifying and sorting 408–409, 412–414, 416–417, 464, 466
- fact families 88–89
- inverse operations 72, 119–120, 240
- meaning of equality 24–25, 86
- missing addends 61, 66, 73, 263, 265
- missing digits 8, 28, 78, 87, 163, 289
- missing factors 85–86, 89, 93, 101, 103
- missing measurements and units 308–309, 310–311, 313–314, 320–321, 323–324, 326–327, 335, 338
- multiplication and division number sentences 84–86, 88–89, 90–96
- proportional reasoning
  - better price 233
  - equivalencies in measurement and money 30–32
  - equivalent fractions 492–493, 494–497
  - fraction of a group 490–491
  - map scales/scale drawings 587
  - perecents related to fractions and decimals 553
  - probabilities 596–597, 598–601, 608–610
  - regrouping or trading 56, 70–71, 72–78, 151–154, 160–162, 214–217
- symbols showing relations (inequalities) 24–25, 66, 78, 86, 116–117, 166, 173, 281, 559, 561, 626
- variables 118–124, 222
- Venn diagrams 79, 167, 432, 488
- writing and solving number sentences and equations
  - balance equations 121
- in addition and subtraction 60–61, 66, 73, 118–120, 121, 122–124
- in multiplication adn division 88–89, 92–93, 94–96, 100–101, 118–120, 121, 122–124

Coordinate Graphs

- coordinate plane 627
- graphing functions 620–622, 623, 628–629, 634–635
- graphing ordered pairs 616–619
- graphing a line 620–623
- quadrants 627
- slides in the first quadrant 639
- *x*-coordinate 620–623
- *y*-coordinate 620–623

Equations and Inequalities

- equations
  - balancing equations 118–124
  - meaning of equations 116–117
  - solving equations 118–124
  - variables in equations 118–124
  - writing equations for word phrases 118–124
- formulas
  - area 456–459
  - perimeter 454–455
  - volume 468–469
- inequalities 24–25, 66, 78, 86, 116–117, 166, 173, 281, 559, 561, 626

Scope and Sequence

In the Program...

Algebra

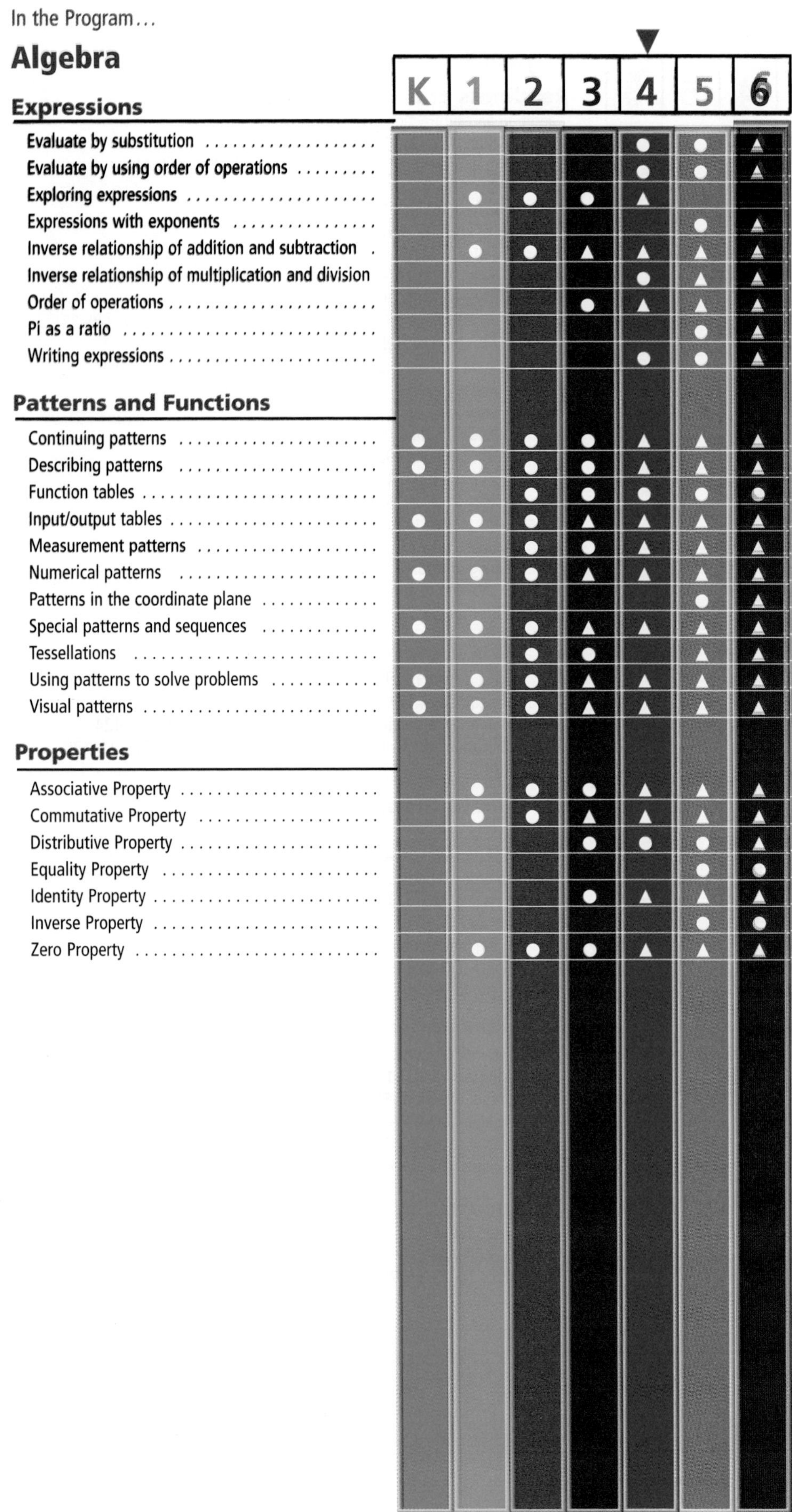

Expressions	K	1	2	3	4	5	6
Evaluate by substitution					●	●	▲
Evaluate by using order of operations					●	●	▲
Exploring expressions		●	●	●	▲		
Expressions with exponents						●	▲
Inverse relationship of addition and subtraction		●	●	▲	▲	▲	▲
Inverse relationship of multiplication and division					●	▲	▲
Order of operations				●	▲	▲	▲
Pi as a ratio						●	▲
Writing expressions					●	●	▲

Patterns and Functions	K	1	2	3	4	5	6
Continuing patterns	●	●	●	●	▲	▲	▲
Describing patterns	●	●	●	●	▲	▲	▲
Function tables			●	●	●	●	●
Input/output tables	●	●	●	▲	▲	▲	▲
Measurement patterns			●	●	▲	▲	▲
Numerical patterns	●	●	●	▲	▲	▲	▲
Patterns in the coordinate plane						●	▲
Special patterns and sequences	●	●	●	▲	▲	▲	▲
Tessellations			●	●		▲	▲
Using patterns to solve problems	●	●	●	▲	▲	▲	▲
Visual patterns	●	●	●	▲	▲	▲	▲

Properties	K	1	2	3	4	5	6
Associative Property		●	●	●	▲	▲	▲
Commutative Property		●	●	▲	▲	▲	▲
Distributive Property				●	●	●	▲
Equality Property						●	●
Identity Property				●	▲	▲	▲
Inverse Property						●	●
Zero Property		●	●	●	▲	▲	▲

In Level 4...

Algebra

Expressions

Patterns and Functions

Properties

KEY Teach and Apply ● Practice and Apply ▲ Teacher's Edition Lesson ★

Scope and Sequence

In the Program…

Geometry

Basic Figures	K	1	2	3	4	5	6
Attributes of plane figures		●	●	●	▲	▲	▲
Basic figures: square, rectangle, triangle, and circle	●	●	●	▲	▲	▲	▲
Classifying and sorting figures and shapes	●	●	●	●	▲	▲	▲
Geometric patterns	●	●	●	▲	▲	▲	▲
Pattern blocks: triangle, square, rhombus, trapezoid, hexagon	●	●	●	●	▲	▲	▲
Real-life objects	●	●	▲	▲			
Sides, vertices		●	●	▲	▲	▲	
Plane Figures and Spatial Sense							
Angles			●	●	▲	▲	▲
Circles	●	●	●	●	▲	▲	▲
Circumference						●	▲
Comparing angles				●	●	▲	▲
Complex figures		●	●	▲	▲	▲	▲
Constructing angles						●	▲
Constructing circles, using a compass						●	▲
Classifying polygons			●	●	●	▲	▲
Congruent figures		●	●	●	▲	▲	▲
Intersecting lines				●	●	▲	▲
Line of symmetry	●	●	●	▲	▲	▲	▲
Line segments				●	▲	▲	▲
Lines				●	▲	▲	▲
Making and drawing polygons		●	●	▲	▲	▲	▲
Making and drawing quadrilaterals		●	●	▲	▲	▲	▲
Measuring angles, using a protractor					●	▲	▲
Orientation						●	▲
Parallel lines				●	▲	▲	▲
Perpendicular lines				●	▲	▲	▲
Polygons			●	●	▲	▲	▲
Points				●	▲	▲	▲
Pythagorean Theorem						●	●
Quadrilaterals			●	●	▲	▲	▲
Radius, diameter, chord					●	●	▲
Rays				●	▲	▲	▲
Relating solid and plane figures	●	●	▲	▲	▲	▲	▲
Right angles			●	●	▲	▲	▲
Sides, angles, and diagonals of polygons				●	●	●	▲
Similar figures				●	▲	▲	▲
Symmetry	●	●	●	▲	▲	▲	▲
Subdividing and combining		●	●	▲	▲	▲	▲
Tiling/Tesselations and tangrams			●	●	▲	▲	▲
Vertex			●	▲	▲	▲	▲
Visual Thinking	●	●	●	▲	▲	▲	▲

KEY Teach and Apply ● Practice and Apply ▲ Teacher's Edition Lesson *

In Level 4…

Geometry

Basic Figures

circles 422–424
identifying, classifying, and describing polygons 412–415
quadrilaterals 412–415
triangles 416–447

Plane Figures and Spatial Sense

angles 408–411
circles 422–424
classifying polygons 412–415
  triangles 416–417
congruent figures 430–433
line segment 404–406, 415
lines 404–406
point 404–406
ray 408–409
relating space figures and plane figures 464–466
similar figures 433
symmetry 440–443
visual thinking 79, 121, 129, 167, 444–446

Scope and Sequence

In the Program...

Geometry

Solid Figures (3-dimensional objects)

	K	1	2	3	4	5	6
Building 3-dimensional objects	●	●	●	▲	▲	▲	▲
Complex figures				●	●	●	▲
Cone	●	●	●	▲	▲	▲	▲
Cube	●	●	●	▲	▲	▲	▲
Cylinder	●	●	●	▲	▲	▲	▲
Face, edge, vertex		●	●	▲	▲	▲	▲
Identifying, classifying, and describing solid figures	●	●	▲	▲	▲	▲	▲
Nets			●	●	●	▲	▲
Prisms	●	●	●	▲	▲	▲	▲
Pyramids		●	●	▲	▲	▲	▲
Relating solid and plane figures	●	●	▲	▲	▲	▲	▲
Sphere		●	●	●	▲	▲	▲

Transformations

	K	1	2	3	4	5	6
Constructions, using a compass to draw arcs						●	▲
Degrees turned						●	▲
Flips (Reflections)	●	●	●	●	●	▲	▲
Slides (Translations)	●	●	●	●	●	▲	▲
Transformations in the coordinate plane						●	●
Turns (Rotations)	●	●	●	●	●	▲	▲

Measurement

Area and Perimeter

	K	1	2	3	4	5	6
Complex figures					●	●	▲
Estimating area, using square units		●	●	▲	▲		
Finding area, using a formula				●	●	●	▲
Finding area, using square units		●	●	▲			
Finding circumference						●	●
Finding perimeter			●	●	▲	▲	▲
Finding perimeter, using a formula				●	●	●	▲
Meaning of area			●	▲	▲	▲	▲
Meaning of perimeter			●	▲	▲	▲	▲
Problem-solving applications			●	●	▲	▲	▲
Pythagorean theorem						●	●
Relating area and perimeter			●	●	●	▲	▲
Surface area						●	▲
Surface area, using a formula					●	●	▲

Capacity

	K	1	2	3	4	5	6
Conversion table		●	●	●	▲	▲	▲
Customary system		●	●	●	▲	▲	▲
Equivalent units		●	●	●	▲	▲	▲
Estimating capacity	●	●	●	▲	▲	▲	▲
Measuring capacity	●	●	●	▲	▲	▲	▲
Metric system		●	●	●	▲	▲	▲
Problem-solving applications	●	●	●	▲	▲	▲	▲

In Level 4...

Geometry

Solid Figures

building 3-dimensional objects 464–467
cone 464–466
cube 464–466
cylinder 464–466
face, edge, vertex 464–466
identifying, classifying, and describing 464–466
making solid figures from nets 464–466
prisms 464–466
pyramids 464–466
relating solid and plane figures 464, 467
sphere 464–466

Transformations

rotations, reflections, and translations 434–435
transformations in the coordinate plane 639

Measurement

Area

estimating 457, 463
finding area 452–453, 460–462
formula
rectangle 456–459
right triangle 459

Perimeter

estimating 463
finding perimeter 452–453, 460–462
formula
rectangle and square 454–455
problem solving 452-453, 460-462

Capacity

choosing the unit
customary 311
metric 323–324
comparing capacity
customary 311
metric 324
converting capacity
customary system 310–311
metric system 322–324
problem solving 306–328, 348–349

KEY Teach and Apply ● Practice and Apply ▲ Teacher's Edition Lesson ★

Scope and Sequence

In the Program...

Measurement

Length

	K	1	2	3	4	5	6
Centimeter		●	●	▲	▲	▲	▲
Choosing appropriate unit		●	●	●	▲	▲	▲
Conversion table			●	●	▲	▲	▲
Customary measurement		●	●	▲	▲	▲	▲
Distance formula							●
Equivalent units			●	●	▲	▲	▲
Estimating length	●	●	●	▲	▲	▲	▲
Fractions and measurement			●	▲	▲	▲	▲
Foot, yard			●	▲	▲	▲	▲
Inch	●	●	▲	▲	▲	▲	▲
Indirect measurement					●	●	●
Kilometer				●	▲	▲	▲
Measuring instruments		●	●	▲	▲	▲	▲
Measuring length	●	●	●	▲	▲	▲	▲
Meter		●	●	●	▲	▲	▲
Metric measurement		●	●	●	▲	▲	▲
Mile				●	▲	▲	▲
Millimeter				●	▲	▲	▲
Problem-solving applications	●	●	●	●	▲	▲	▲

Money

	K	1	2	3	4	5	6
Adding and subtracting money		●	●	●	▲	▲	▲
Comparing amounts			●	●	▲	▲	▲
Consumer applications	●	●	●	▲	▲	▲	▲
Counting coins and bills	●	●	▲	▲	▲		
Counting on with money	●	●	▲	▲	▲		
Decimals, fractions, and money				●	▲		
Equivalent amounts	●	●	●	▲	▲		
Estimating money			●	●	▲		
Identifying coins and bills	●	●	▲	▲			
Making change			●	▲	▲	▲	▲
Multiplying and dividing money				●	●	▲	▲
Place value					●	▲	▲
Problem-solving applications	●	●	●	●	▲	▲	▲
Rounding money				●	▲		
Symbolic notation	●	●	●	▲	▲	▲	▲

Temperature

	K	1	2	3	4	5	6
Celsius scale			●	▲	▲	▲	▲
Estimating temperature				●	▲		
Fahrenheit scale		●	●	▲	▲	▲	▲
Interpreting a thermometer		●	●	▲	▲		
Negative numbers				●	●	▲	▲
Relating Celsius scale to Fahrenheit scale						●	●
Writing temperature			●	●	▲	▲	▲

KEY Teach and Apply ● Practice and Apply ▲ Teacher's Edition Lesson ★

In Level 4...

Measurement

Length

centimeter, millimeter
- choosing the unit 320–321
- equivalencies 320–321
- measuring 318–319

decimeter, meter, kilometer
- choosing the unit 320–321
- equivalencies 320–321

foot, yard, mile

equivalencies 308–309

inch
- equivalencies 308–309
- estimating 306–307
- measuring
  - to the nearest eighth-inch 306–307
  - to the nearest half-inch 306–307
  - to the nearest inch 306–307
  - to the nearest quarter-inch 306–307

indirect measurement—map scales 587

problem solving 306–328, 348–349

Money

adding money 70–71

change
- counting 34–37
- subtracting to find 80
- using fewest coins and bills 32

comparing amounts 30–33

dividing money 234–237

estimating 148–149

mental math 148–149

multiplying money 148–149, 164–167, 186–189

problem solving 161–162, 235–236

subtracting money 72–75

value of money 30–33

writing money amounts 30–33

Temperature

Celsius
- estimating 344–347
- finding the difference between temperatures 344–347
- negative numbers 344–347
- reading temperatures 344–347

Fahrenheit
- estimating 344–347
- finding the difference between temperatures 344–347
- negative numbers 344–347
- reading temperatures 344–347

problem solving 348–349

Scope and Sequence

In the Program...

Measurement

Time

	K	1	2	3	4	5	6
A.M. and P.M.			●	●	▲		
Analog clock	●	●	●	▲			
Calendar concepts	●	●	▲	▲			
Digital clock	●	●	●	▲			
Elapsed time		●	●	▲	▲	▲	▲
Equivalent units			●	▲			
Estimating time	●	●	▲	▲			
Ordinal numbers	●	●	▲	▲			
Problem-solving applications	●	●	●	▲	▲	▲	▲
Schedules		●	●	▲	▲		
Sequencing events	●	●	▲	▲			
Telling time	●	●	●	▲	▲		
Time line				●	●	▲	▲
Time zones					●	●	▲

Volume

	K	1	2	3	4	5	6
Estimating volume			●	●	▲	▲	▲
Finding volume, counting cubic units			●	●	▲	▲	▲
Finding volume, using a formula					●	●	▲
Meaning of volume				●	●	▲	▲
Problem-solving applications				●	●	●	▲

Weight and Mass

	K	1	2	3	4	5	6
Conversion table				●	●	▲	▲
Equivalent units				●	●	▲	▲
Estimating weight and mass	●	●	●	●	▲	▲	▲
Finding weight and mass			●	●	▲	▲	▲
Gram and kilogram		●	●	●	▲	▲	▲
Ounce				●	●	▲	▲
Pound		●	●	▲	▲	▲	▲
Problem-solving applications	●	●	●	●	▲	▲	▲
Ton				●	●	▲	▲

Data Analysis and Probability

Data Analysis

	K	1	2	3	4	5	6
Analyzing and interpreting data	●	●	●	●	▲	▲	▲
Average				●	▲	▲	▲
Bar graphs	●	●	●	▲	▲	▲	▲
Box-and-whisker plots							●
Choosing an appropriate display				●	●	▲	▲
Circle graph			●	●	●	●	▲
Cluster						●	▲
Collecting data	●	●	●	●	▲	▲	▲
Displaying data	●	●	●	●	▲	▲	▲
Double bar graphs					●	▲	▲
Double line graphs						●	▲
Drawing conclusions from data		★	●	●	▲	▲	▲
Frequency tables/tally charts	●	●	●	●	▲	▲	▲
Gap						●	▲

In Level 4...

Measurement

Time

A.M. and P.M. 336–339
century 334–335
decade 334–335
elapsed time 334–335
  on calendar 334–335
  hours and minutes 336–339
equivalent units 334–335
time line 395
time zone 390–391

Volume

cubic centimeter 468–469
estimating volume 468–469
finding volume using a cubic centimeter and a formula 468–469
meaning of volume 468–469
problem solving 470–472

Weight and Mass

choosing the unit 314, 327
comparing 314, 328
converting 312–314
equivalencies 312–314, 326–328
estimating 312, 326–327
gram, kilogram 326–328
ounce, pound, ton 312–314
problem solving 314, 328

Data Analysis and Probability

Data Analysis

average 262–266
choosing an appropriate display 384–386
collecting, organizing, and displaying data 356–359
  in frequency tables—tally charts 356–359
  in graphs 366–367, 368–370, 376–377, 382–383
  in organized lists 604–606
  in tables or charts 356–362
comparing ways of representing data 384–386
displaying data 368–370, 376–377, 378–379, 380–381, 382–383, 387
drawing conclusions from data 368–370, 376–377, 378–379, 380–381, 382–383, 387
formulate questions
designing investigations to address a question 356–359, 385
graphs
  bar graph 40–41
  circle graph 378–379, 534–535
  double bar graph 376–377

KEY Teach and Apply ● Practice and Apply ▲ Teacher's Edition Lesson ★

Scope and Sequence

In the Program...

Data Analysis and Probability

Data Analysis	K	1	2	3	4	5	6
Histogram					●	●	▲
Interpreting data	●	●	●	●	▲	▲	▲
Line graphs		●	●	●	●	▲	▲
Line plots				●	▲	▲	▲
Making tables and charts	●	●	●	▲	▲	▲	▲
Mean				●	▲	▲	▲
Measures of central tendency				●	●	▲	▲
Median				●	▲	▲	▲
Misleading data or graphs						●	▲
Mode				●	▲	▲	▲
Organized lists			●	●	●	●	●
Organizing data	●	●	●	●	▲	▲	▲
Outliers					●	●	▲
Pictographs	●	●	●	▲	▲	▲	▲
Problem-solving applications	●	●	●	▲	▲	▲	▲
Quartiles							●
Range				●	▲	▲	▲
Reading tables and charts	●	●	●	▲	▲	▲	▲
Sampling techniques						●	●
Scatter plot							●
Stem-and-leaf plots					●	●	▲
Surveys	●	●	●	●	▲	▲	▲
Probability							
Calculating probability of simple event				●	●	▲	▲
Compound events					●	▲	▲
Developing and analyzing predictions and inferences	●	●	●	●	▲	▲	▲
Fair or unfair		●	●	▲	▲		
Fundamental Counting Principle							●
Likelihood of an event	★	●	●	▲	▲	▲	▲
Modeling with coins, cubes, or spinners	●	●	●	▲	▲	▲	▲
Permutations and combinations							●
Possible outcomes			●	●	●	▲	▲
Probability experiments	●	●	●	●	▲	▲	▲
Problem-solving applications	●	●	●	▲	▲	▲	▲
Recording outcomes	●	●	●	●	▲	▲	▲
Representing likelihood as a number from 0 to 1					●	●	●
Theoretical probability						●	▲
Using a tree diagram or grid					●	▲	▲
Using coins, cubes, or spinners	●	●	●	▲	▲	▲	▲

KEY Teach and Apply ● Practice and Apply ▲ Teacher's Edition Lesson ★

In Level 4...

Data Analysis and Probability

Data Analysis

Probability

Scope and Sequence

In the Program...

Problem Solving

Applications / Decisions

	K	1	2	3	4	5	6
Addition applications	●	●	●	▲	▲	▲	▲
Building new knowledge	●	●	●	●	●	●	●
Choosing a computation method		●	●	●	●	▲	▲
Choosing an operation	●	●	●	▲	▲	▲	▲
Curriculum connections	●	●	●	●	●	●	●
Data applications	●	●	●	▲	▲	▲	▲
Decimal applications				●	●	▲	▲
Division applications			●	●	▲	▲	▲
Estimated or exact answers			●	●	●	▲	▲
Fraction applications	●	●	●	●	●	▲	▲
Geometry applications	●	●	●	●	●	▲	▲
Integer applications						●	▲
Interpreting remainders				●	●	▲	▲
Measurement applications	●	●	●	●	▲	▲	▲
Money applications	●	●	●	●	▲	▲	▲
Multiplication applications		●	●	▲	▲	▲	▲
Number and operations	●	●	●	●	▲	▲	▲
Percent applications						●	▲
Place-value applications		●	●	●	▲	▲	▲
Probability applications	●	●	●	▲	▲	▲	▲
Ratio applications						●	▲
Solving multi-step problems		●	●	●	●	▲	▲
Subtraction applications	●	●	▲	▲	▲	▲	▲
Time applications	●	●	●	●	▲	▲	▲
Too much information or too little information		●	●	▲	▲	▲	▲
Using a bar graph	●	●	●	▲	▲	▲	▲
Using a diagram					●	▲	▲
Using a formula					●	●	▲
Using a number sentence	●	●	●	▲	▲		
Using a pattern	●	●	●	▲	▲	▲	▲
Using a pictograph	●	●	●	▲	▲	▲	▲
Using a picture, graph, or map	●	●	●	●	▲	▲	▲
Using a table or chart	●	●	●	▲	▲	▲	▲
Using an equation						●	▲
Using estimation			●	●	●	▲	▲
Using functions and graphs					●	●	●

Strategies

	K	1	2	3	4	5	6
Act it out with models	●	●	●	●	▲	▲	▲
Choose a method		●	●	●	▲	▲	▲
Draw a picture or diagram	●	●	●	●	●	▲	▲
Find a pattern	●	●	●	▲	▲	▲	▲
Guess and check	●	●	●	●	▲	▲	▲
Make a model	●	●	●	●	●	●	▲
Make a table or chart	●	●	●	●	▲	▲	▲
Make an organized list			●	●	●	▲	▲
Monitor and reflect on the process	●	●	●	●	▲	▲	▲
Solve a simpler problem				●	●	▲	▲
Use logical reasoning	●	●	●	●	▲	▲	▲
Work backward				●	●	▲	▲
Write a number sentence or equation	●	●	●	●	●	▲	▲

KEY Teach and Apply ● Practice and Apply ▲ Teacher's Edition Lesson ★

In Level 4...

Problem Solving

Applications/Decisions

addition applications 63, 71, 78
building new knowledge 118–124, 186–189, 282–285, 494–497, 520–521, 528–529, 544–545, 572–575, 620–626
choosing a computation method 42, 78, 188, 212, 222, 246, 350, 362, 370, 446, 536
choosing an operation 104–105
curriculum connections 69, 155, 183, 223, 237, 279, 317, 425, 501, 527, 533, 537
data applications 40–41, 356–370, 376–386, 628–630
decimal applications 545, 548–549, 553–556, 559, 562, 576–578
division applications 86, 89, 91, 96, 103–104, 209, 211, 216, 219, 221, 229, 231, 235, 239, 281
estimated or exact answers 66, 68–69, 339
fraction applications 491, 496, 500, 503, 505–506, 518–519, 521, 523, 526, 529, 532
geometry applications 409, 414, 417–410, 425, 443–446
interpreting remainders 210–211, 522–523
measurement applications 306–328, 348–349
money applications 161–162, 235–236
multiplication applications 86, 89, 91, 96, 101, 104, 147, 149, 153, 162, 173, 175, 182–183
place-value applications 8, 17, 18, 25, 28, 32, 36, 42, 189
probability applications 597, 600–610
real-world applications 33, 306–328, 334–351, 404, 409, 417, 425, 549, 631
solving multi-step problems 288–289
statistics applications 364–370
subtraction applications 63, 73, 75, 78
time applications 338–339
too much or too little information 316–317
using a diagram 504–505, 608–610
using a number sentence 118–125
using a pattern 418–420
using a pictograph 386
using a picture, graph, or map 431, 504–505, 628–630
using charts or tables 356–362
using estimation 66, 68–69, 149, 175, 221
using functions and graphs 628–629

Strategies

act it out 436–438
choose a strategy 42, 158, 212, 242, 260, 342, 362, 362, 420, 438, 446, 536
draw a picture or diagram 504–505, 608–610
find a pattern 418–420, 554–556
guess and check 156–159, 340–342
logical thinking 10–13, 43, 167
make a table or chart 360–362
make an organized list 604–606
monitor and reflect upon the process 76–79, 128–129, 182–183
solve a simpler problem 258–260
use formulas 470–472
use mental math 62–63, 147
work backward 240–242
write a number sentence 118–124, 468–469
write an equation 468–469

Scope and Sequence

In the Program…

Reasoning and Proof

Analyzing

	K	1	2	3	4	5	6
Algebraic thinking				▲	▲	▲	▲
Analyzing	●	●	●	●	▲	▲	▲
Checking reasonableness of answers		●	●	●	▲	▲	▲
Classifying	●	●	●	●	●	▲	▲
Creating and solving problems	●	●	●	●	●	●	●
Developing arguments and proof	●	●	●	●	▲	▲	▲
Drawing conclusions		●	●	●	▲	▲	▲
Explaining reasoning	●	●	●	●	▲	▲	▲
Generalizing	●	●	●	●	●	▲	▲
Identifying relationships					●	▲	▲
Identifying relevant information		●	●	▲	▲	▲	▲
Logical thinking	●	●	●	●	▲	▲	▲
Making and investigating conjectures	●	●	●	●	▲	▲	▲
Making decisions	●	●	●	●	▲	▲	▲
Making predictions	●	●	●	●	▲	▲	▲
Number relationships	●	●	●	●	●	▲	▲
Reading mathematics	●	●	●	●	▲	▲	▲
Reasonableness of method and solution		●	●	●	▲	▲	▲
Using logic	●	●	●	●	▲	▲	▲
Using strategies to find solutions	●	●	●	●	▲	▲	▲
Visual thinking	●	●	●	▲	▲	▲	▲

Communication

Analyzing and Evaluating Strategies

	K	1	2	3	4	5	6
Act it out with models	●	●	●	●	▲	▲	▲
Choose a method		●	●	●	▲	▲	▲
Choose an operation	●	●	●	▲	▲	▲	▲
Draw a picture or diagram	●	●	●	●	●	▲	▲
Find a pattern	●	●	●	▲	▲	▲	▲
Guess and check	●	●	●	●	▲	▲	▲
Make a table or chart	●	●	●	●	▲	▲	▲
Make an organized list			●	●	●	▲	▲
Monitor and reflect on the process	●		●	●	▲	▲	▲
Solve a simpler problem				●	●	▲	▲
Use logical reasoning	●	●	●	●	▲	▲	▲
Work backward				●	●	▲	▲
Write a number sentence or equation	●	●	●	●	●	▲	▲

KEY Teach and Apply ● Practice and Apply ▲ Teacher's Edition Lesson ★

In Level 4…

Reasoning and Proof

Analyzing

algebraic reasoning 110–129
Algebraic Thinking 129
analyzing 8, 42, 231, 287. 328, 346, 417, 432, 556
classifying 408–409, 412–415, 464–466
creating and solving problems 166, 241, 358, 535
checking reasonableness of answers 76–79, 182–183
developing arguments and proof 412–417, 430–433, 458
drawing conclusions 40–41
evaluating reasonableness 128–129
explaining reasoning 128–129
formulating and solving problems 166, 241, 358, 535
generalizing 408–409, 412–415, 464–466
identifying relationships 628–630
identifying relevant information 316–317
justifying thinking 128–129
logical thinking 10–13, 43, 167
making decisions
  choosing a graph 376–377, 384–386
  choosing a method 166, 526
  choosing a strategy 42, 158, 212, 242, 260, 342, 362, 420, 438, 446, 536
  choosing an operation 104–105
  determining reasonableness of an answer 76–79, 128–129, 182–183
  estimated or exact answer 66, 68–69, 339
  too much or too little information 316–317
making predictions 602–603
number relationships 63, 90–91, 247, 508–510, 546–548, 550–556
reading mathematics 611
reasonableness of method and solution 76–79, 128–129
solving a simpler problem 258–260
using logic 10–13, 43
using strategies to find solutions 42, 158, 212, 242, 260, 342, 362, 420, 438, 446, 536
visual thinking 444–446

Communication

Analyzing and Evaluating Strategies

act it out with models 153, 209, 436–438
choose a method 166, 526
choose an operation 104–105
draw a picture or diagram 504–505, 608–610
find a pattern 418–420, 554–556
guess and check 156–159, 340–342
make an organized list 604–606
make a table or chart 360–362
monitor and reflect on the process 76–79, 128–129, 182–183
solve a simpler problem 258–260
use logical reasoning 10–13, 43, 167, 247
work backward 240–242
write a number sentence 118–124, 468–469

Scope and Sequence

In the Program...

Communication

Analyzing and Evaluating Thinking

	K	1	2	3	4	5	6
Determining reasonableness of an answer		●	●	●	▲	▲	▲
Estimating or exact answer			●	●	●	▲	▲
Explaining reasoning	●	●	●	●	▲	▲	▲
Identifying relevant information		●	●	▲	▲	▲	▲
Justifying thinking	●	●	●	●	▲	▲	▲
Making predictions	●	●	●	●	▲	▲	▲
Too much or too little information		●	●	▲	▲	▲	▲

Communicating Mathematical Thinking

	K	1	2	3	4	5	6
Clarifying understanding	●	●	●	●	▲	▲	▲
Drawing a picture or diagram	●	●	●	●	●	▲	▲
Talk About It/Write About It		▲	▲	▲	▲	▲	▲
Using manipulatives	●	●	●	●	▲	▲	▲

Organizing and Consolidating Thinking

	K	1	2	3	4	5	6
Classifying	●	●	●	●	●	▲	▲
Drawing conclusions		●	●	●	▲	▲	▲
Generalizing	●	●	●	●	●	▲	▲

Using Mathematical Language

	K	1	2	3	4	5	6
Creating and solving problems	●	●	●	●	●	●	●
Describing problems and solutions	●	●	●	●	▲	▲	▲
Vocabulary		▲	▲	▲	▲	▲	▲

Connections

Building Upon Prior Knowledge

	K	1	2	3	4	5	6
Adding	●	●	●	▲	▲	▲	▲
Dividing			●	●	▲	▲	▲
Multiplying		●	●	●	▲	▲	▲
Subtracting	●	●	●	▲	▲	▲	▲
Using money	●	●	●	●	▲	▲	▲

Recognizing and Applying Mathematics in Context

	K	1	2	3	4	5	6
Curriculum connections	●	●	●	●	●	●	●
Real-life applications	●	●	●	●	●	●	●

Recognizing and Using Connections

	K	1	2	3	4	5	6
Decimals, fractions, and mixed numbers				●	●	▲	▲
Drawing conclusions		●	●	●	▲	▲	▲
Generalizing	●	●	●	●	●	▲	▲
Measurement and time	●	●	●	●	▲	▲	▲
Money		●	●	●	▲	▲	
Patterns	●	●	●	▲	▲	▲	▲
Related facts	●	●	●	●	▲		

KEY Teach and Apply ● Practice and Apply ▲ Teacher's Edition Lesson ★

In Level 4...

Communication

Analyzing and Evaluating Thinking

determining reasonableness of an answer 76–79, 128–129, 182–183
estimating or exact answer 66, 68–69, 339
explaining reasoning 128–129
identifying relevant information 316–317
making predictions 602–603
justifying thinking 128–129
too much or too little information 316–317

Communicating Mathematical Thinking

clarifying understanding See Explain Your Thinking in lessons.
drawing a picture 431, 504–505
Talk About It/Write About It 15, 55, 91, 99, 141, 151, 177, 201, 207, 253, 263, 278, 301, 307, 319, 358, 365, 377, 399, 411, 453, 485, 493, 529, 532, 543, 573, 591, 603, 643
using manipulatives 150–155, 176–177, 206–209, 214–215, 254–255, 262–263, 276–278, 452–453, 498–501, 528–532, 572–573, 596–610

Organizing and Consolidating Thinking

classifying 408–409, 412–415, 464–466
drawing conclusions 40–41
generalizing 408–409, 412–415, 464–466

Using Mathematical Language

Building Vocabulary xxx–1, 56–57, 142–143, 202–203, 302–303, 400–401, 486–487, 592–593
creating and solving problems 166, 241
describing problems and solutions 306–315, 318–329, 344–347, 408–409, 412–417, 422–424, 434–435, 452–453, 456–469, 616–617, 620–623
Vocabulary Wrap-Up 55, 141, 201, 301, 399, 485, 591, 643

Connections

Building upon Prior Knowledge

adding 517–521
dividing 282–285
multiplying 186–189
subtracting 517–521
using money 148–149, 164–167, 186–189, 234–237

Recognizing and Applying Mathematics in Context

curriculum connections 69, 155, 183, 223, 237, 279, 317, 425, 501, 527, 533, 537
real-life applications 33, 306–328, 334–351, 404, 409, 417, 425, 549, 631

Recognizing and Using Connections

decimals, fractions, and mixed numbers 508–510
drawing conclusions 40–41
generalizing 408–409, 412–415, 464–466
measurement 308–309, 312–314, 320–321, 326–328
money 70–75, 148–149, 164–167, 186–189, 234–237
patterns 418–420, 554–556
related facts 88–89, 92–97
time 334–339

Scope and Sequence

In the Program...

Representation

Organizing, Recording, and Communicating Ideas	K	1	2	3	4	5	6
Making a list			●	●	●	▲	▲
Using a bar graph	●	●	●	▲	▲	▲	▲
Using a circle graph			●	●	●	▲	▲
Using a double bar graph				●	●	▲	▲
Using a double line graph						●	▲
Using a line graph			●	●	●	▲	▲
Using a line plot				●	▲	▲	▲
Using a pictograph	●	●	●	▲	▲		
Using a picture or diagram		●	●	●	●	▲	▲
Using a stem-and-leaf plot					●	●	▲
Using a table or chart	●	●	●	▲	▲	▲	▲
Using measurement	●	●	●	●	▲	▲	▲
Using probability	●	●	●	▲	▲	▲	▲
Using symbols	●	●	●	▲	▲	▲	▲
Selecting, Applying, and Translating Among Representations							
In decimals, fractions, and money				●	▲	▲	
In geometry	●	●	●	●	▲	▲	▲
In measurement	●	●	●	●	▲	▲	▲
In percent						●	▲
In time			●	●	▲	▲	▲
Using Representations to Model and Interpret Mathematics							
Algebraic equations	●	●	●	●	●	▲	▲
Arrays			●	●	●	●	▲
Counters, connecting cubes	●	●	●	●	▲	▲	▲
Data	●	●	●	●	▲	▲	▲
Decimal models				●	●	●	▲
Fraction models		●	●	●	▲	▲	▲
Geoboard/dot or grid paper		●	●	●	●	▲	▲
Geometric tools (compass, protractor, straightedge)					●	●	●
Hundreds chart	●	●	●	▲	▲	▲	▲
Integer models				●	●	●	▲
Make a model (act it out)	●	●	●	●	●	●	●
Manipulatives or models	●	●	●	●	▲	▲	▲
Modeling solids	●	●	●	●	●	●	●
Money and coins	●	●	▲	▲	▲	▲	▲
Multiplication table				●	▲		
Number lines	●	●	●	●	●	▲	▲
Part/part whole models		●	●	●	▲	▲	▲
Pattern blocks	●	●	▲	▲	▲	▲	▲
Percent models				●	●	●	●
Pictures/diagrams	●	●	●	●	▲	▲	▲
Place-value models		●	●	▲	▲	▲	▲
Symbols	●	●	●	●	▲	▲	▲
Technology	▲	▲	▲	▲	▲	▲	▲

KEY Teach and Apply ● Practice and Apply ▲ Teacher's Edition Lesson ★

In Level 4...

Representation

Organizing, Recording, and Communicating Ideas

making a list 604–606
using a bar graph 40–41
using a circle graph 379
using a double bar graph 376–377
using a graph 628–630
using a line graph 382–383
using a line plot 366–367
using a pictograph 386
using a picture 431, 504–505
using a stem-and-leaf plot 368–370
using a table or chart 356–362
using mathematical language 306–315, 318–329, 344–347, 408–409, 412–417, 422–424, 434–435, 452–453, 456–469, 616–617, 620–623
using measurement 306–328, 348–349
using probability 602–603, 608–610
using symbols 24–25

Selecting, Applying, and Translating Among Representations

in decimals, fractions, mixed numbers, or percents 546–553, 555–563
in geometry 434–435
in measurement 308–309, 312–314, 320–321, 326–328
in money 30–33
in time 334–339

Using Representations to Model and Interpret Mathematics

algebraic equations and number sentences 118–124, 468–469
arrays 57, 105, 143
counters 105, 254, 262–263, 601
data 40–41, 262–263, 356–370, 376–386, 628–630
decimal models 542–543, 546–548, 550–551, 558
fraction models 490–491, 492–493, 508–510, 550–551
geoboard/dot or grid paper 105, 432, 433, 435, 441, 442, 452–453, 456, 463
geometric tools (protractor) 410–411
hundreds chart 267
integer models 624–625
make a model (act it out) 436–438
modeling solids 464–467
money and coins 359
multiplication table 90–91, 98–99, 252–253
number cards 181
number cubes 217, 602
number lines
  adding and subtracting integers 642
  line plots 366–367
  modeling multiplication and division 92
  to compare and order 24, 26, 558, 560
  to round numbers 38, 39, 568, 569
  to show probability 599
part/part whole bar model 128, 504
pattern blocks 434
pictures/diagrams 121, 418–420, 431, 504–505
place-value (base ten) blocks 150–153, 206–207, 208, 214, 276–278
spinners 601
symbols 24–25
technology 163, 165
thermometers 344–347, 348–349
Venn diagrams 79, 167, 432, 488

Pacing Guide

Grade Four

Houghton Mifflin Math encourages you to customize instruction to meet the needs of your students. As a guide, we have identified lessons as review, core, or extend for typical fourth–grade level content. As these categories may vary based on your local curriculum, consider this chart as a guide to help you plan your teaching year.

Unit	Chapter	Review Lessons	Days	Core Lessons	Days	Extend Lessons	Days	Days to Assess
1	1	1–2	2	3–5	3			1
	2	1–2	2	3–6	4			2
2	3	1, 5–6	3	2–4, 7–8	5			1
	4	1–2	2	3–9	7			1
	5			1–7	7			2
3	6	1	1	2–7	6			1
	7			1–7	7			2
4	8	1–2	2	3–6	4			1
	9			1–6	6			1
	10			1–5	5			1
	11			1–7	7			2
5	12	1	1	2–9	8			1
	13	1–2	2	3–5	3			1
	14	1	1	2–5	4			1
	15			1–4	4	5	1	2
6	16	1	1	2–7	6			1
	17	1	1	2–4	3	5	1	1
	18	1	1	2–7	6			2
7	19	1	1	2–7	6			1
	20	1	1	2–7	6	8	1	1
	21	1	1	2–7	6			1
	22			1–5	5			2
8	23	1	1	2–5	4			1
	24	1	1	2	1	3–5	3	2
Totals		Review	24	Core	123	Extend	6	32

Table of Contents

As you read through the Table of Contents (it begins on the next page), you will see that *Houghton Mifflin Math* is organized into 8 units. Each unit consists of 2–4 chapters related to the big mathematical idea of the unit. Chapters have from 5 through 9 lessons. Chapters begin with an open-ended investigation and opportunity to informally assess students' knowledge of prerequisite skills. Each chapter has a mid-chapter Quick Check and a Chapter Review/Test. At the end of each unit is a Unit Test.

This unit/chapter organization promotes the kind of effective teaching and assessment that will help you reach all the learners in your class. Daily Lesson Quizzes make you aware of which students may be in need of help and which have mastered the material. Quick Checks and Chapter and Unit Tests are all linked to immediate and focused remediation and intervention tools—Reteach Resources and the *Ways to Success* Intervention CD-ROM. Enrichment resources and Chapter Challenges are available for those students who are ready for an extra challenge. If algebra is an important element in your mathematics curriculum, you will find special support for this teaching in those lessons with an Algebra label.

Be sure to look for the Weekly Reader Connection icons—these indicate activities for which students can find additional information by visiting the Weekly Reader™ link at Houghton Mifflin's Education Place Web site (**www.eduplace.com/map**).

Place Value and Money

Algebra Indicates lessons that include algebra instruction.

2 Compare, Order, and Round Whole Numbers and Money

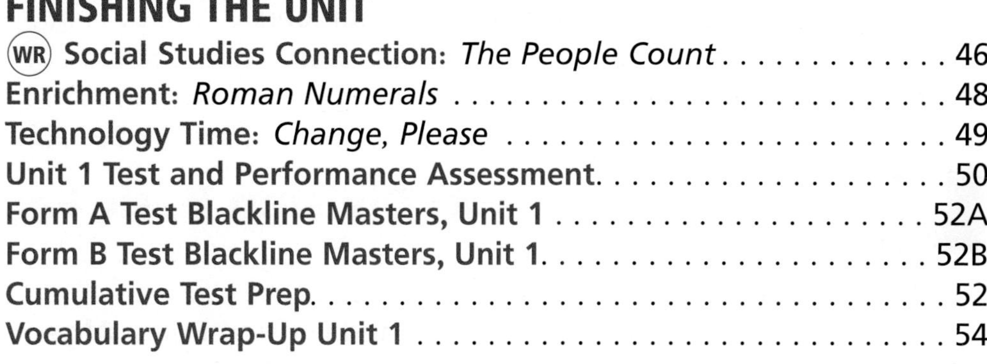

FINISHING THE UNIT

Unit 1 Literature Connection *Beyond Pluto* p. T50

Technology

Ways to Assess Customized Spiral Review and Test Generator CD
Lesson Planner CD-ROM
Ways to Success Intervention CD-ROM
Audio Tutor CD-ROM
Education Place: www.eduplace.com/map
Houghton Mifflin Math eBook CD-ROM
eManipulatives
eGames

(WR) Indicates 

www.eduplace.com/map

Operations and Algebraic Reasoning

Unit 2 Operations and Algebraic Reasoning

STARTING THE UNIT

3 Add and Subtract Whole Numbers

4 Multiplication and Division Basic Facts

Algebra Indicates lessons that include algebra instruction.

5 Algebraic Reasoning

FINISHING THE UNIT

Unit 2
Literature Connection
Kid Camp
p. T51

Technology

Ways to Assess Customized Spiral Review and Test Generator CD
Lesson Planner CD-ROM
Ways to Success Intervention CD-ROM
Audio Tutor CD-ROM
Education Place: www.eduplace.com/map
Houghton Mifflin Math eBook CD-ROM
eManipulatives
eGames

(WR) Indicates WEEKLY WR READER www.eduplace.com/map

Unit 3 Multiplication of Whole Numbers

Multiplication of Whole Numbers

STARTING THE UNIT

6 Multiply by One-Digit Numbers

Algebra Indicates lessons that include algebra instruction.

7 Multiply by Two-Digit Numbers

FINISHING THE UNIT

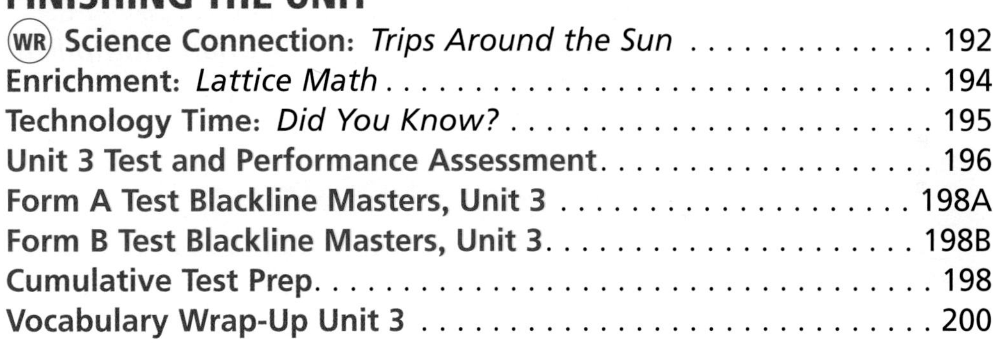

Unit 3 Literature Connection *Gone Prawning* p. T51

Technology

Ways to Assess Customized Spiral Review and Test Generator CD
Lesson Planner CD-ROM
Ways to Success Intervention CD-ROM
Audio Tutor CD-ROM
Education Place: www.eduplace.com/map
Houghton Mifflin Math eBook CD-ROM
- eManipulatives
- eGames

(WR) Indicates WEEKLY WR READER www.eduplace.com/map

Division of Whole Numbers

STARTING THE UNIT

8 Understand Division

9 Divide by One-Digit Divisors

Algebra Indicates lessons that include algebra instruction.

10 Number Theory and Mean

11 Divide by Two-Digit Divisors

Technology

Ways to Assess Customized Spiral Review and Test Generator CD

Lesson Planner CD-ROM

Ways to Success Intervention CD-ROM

Audio Tutor CD-ROM

Education Place: www.eduplace.com/map

Houghton Mifflin Math eBook CD-ROM

eManipulatives
eGames

FINISHING THE UNIT

Unit 4 Literature Connection *But I'm Not Tired* p. T52

(WR) Indicates WEEKLY READER www.eduplace.com/map

Unit 4 Division of Whole Numbers

Measurement and Graphing

STARTING THE UNIT

12 Customary and Metric Measurements

13 Time and Temperature

Algebra Indicates lessons that include algebra instruction.

14 Collect and Analyze Data

15 Graph Data

Technology

Ways to Assess Customized Spiral Review and Test Generator CD

Lesson Planner CD-ROM

Ways to Success Intervention CD-ROM

Audio Tutor CD-ROM

Education Place: www.eduplace.com/map

Houghton Mifflin Math eBook CD-ROM

- eManipulatives
- eGames

Unit 5 Literature Connection *Lengths of Time* p. T53

FINISHING THE UNIT

(WR) Indicates WEEKLY WR READER www.eduplace.com/map

Unit 6 Geometry and Measurement

Geometry and Measurement

STARTING THE UNIT

16 Plane Figures

17 Congruence, Symmetry, and Transformations

Algebra Indicates lessons that include algebra instruction.

18 Perimeter, Area, and Volume

FINISHING THE UNIT

Unit 6 **Literature Connection** ***Dividing the Cheese*** p. T53

Technology

Ways to Assess Customized Spiral Review and Test Generator CD
Lesson Planner CD-ROM
Ways to Success Intervention CD-ROM
Audio Tutor CD-ROM
Education Place: www.eduplace.com/map
Houghton Mifflin Math eBook CD-ROM
- eManipulatives
- eGames

(WR) Indicates  www.eduplace.com/map

Unit 7 Fractions and Decimals

Fractions and Decimals

STARTING THE UNIT

19 Understand Fractions

20 Add and Subtract Fractions

Algebra Indicates lessons that include algebra instruction.

21 Understand Decimals

22 Add and Subtract Decimals

FINISHING THE UNIT

Technology

Ways to Assess Customized Spiral Review and Test Generator CD

Lesson Planner CD-ROM

Ways to Success Intervention CD-ROM

Audio Tutor CD-ROM

Education Place: www.eduplace.com/map

Houghton Mifflin Math eBook CD-ROM

- eManipulatives
- eGames

Unit 7 Literature Connection *Hold the Meat!* p. T54

Unit 7 Fractions and Decimals

(WR) Indicates 

Probability/Algebra and Graphing

Unit 8 Probability/Algebra and Graphing

STARTING THE UNIT

23 Probability

Algebra Indicates lessons that include algebra instruction.

24 Algebra and Graphing

Technology

Ways to Assess Customized Spiral Review and Test Generator CD

Lesson Planner CD-ROM

Ways to Success Intervention CD-ROM

Audio Tutor CD-ROM

Education Place: www.eduplace.com/map

Houghton Mifflin Math eBook CD-ROM

eManipulatives

eGames

Unit 8 Literature Connection *The Perfect Present* pages 654–655

FINISHING THE UNIT

END OF BOOK RESOURCES

(WR) Indicates WEEKLY WR READER www.eduplace.com/map

Notes

UNIT 5

Measurement and Graphing

Standards

Standards

Unit 5 Objectives	Lessons	NCTM Standards	Your State's Standards
5A Estimate, measure, compare, and convert customary and metric units of length, capacity, and weight/mass.	**12.1, 12.2, 12.3, 12.4, 12.6, 12.7, 12.8, 12.9**	**Measurement:** Understand measurable attributes of objects and the units, systems, and processes of measurement. Carry out simple conversions. Understand the need for measuring with standard units.	
5B Determine elapsed time using clocks and calendars.	**13.1, 13.2**	**Measurement:** Select and apply appropriate standard units and tools to time. **Problem Solving:** Solve problems that arise in mathematics and other contexts. **Representation:** Create and use representations to organize, record, and communicate mathematical ideas.	
5C Read, write, and compare temperatures in degrees Fahrenheit and degrees Celsius.	**13.4, 13.5**	**Measurement:** Select and apply appropriate standard units and tools to measure temperature. **Connections:** Recognize and use connections among mathematical ideas.	
5D Collect, organize, and analyze data; find mean, median, mode, and range.	**14.1, 14.3**	**Data Analysis and Probability:** Select and use appropriate statistical methods to analyze data.	
5E Make, read, and interpret line plots, stem-and-leaf plots, bar graphs, circle graphs, and line graphs.	**14.4, 14.5, 15.1, 15.2, 15.4, 15.5**	**Data Analysis and Probability:** Select and use appropriate statistical methods to analyze data. Represent data using tables and graphs such as line plots, bar graphs, and line graphs. Compare different representations of the same data and evaluate representations.	
5F Solve problems using skills and strategies.	**12.5, 13.3, 14.2, 15.3**	**Problem Solving:** Solve problems that arise in mathematics and in other contexts. Apply and adapt a variety of appropriate strategies to solve problems.	

NCTM Process Standards	Sample Lessons or Features	Your State's Standards
Reasoning and Proof: Use various levels and types of reasoning, including formulating proofs, patterns, conjectures, and rules.	Reasoning, Problem Solving, and Algebra Readiness features. For example, see **Lessons 12.4, 12.5, 12.8, 13.2, 13.3, 13.4, 14.2, 14.4, 15.3, 15.5.**	
Communication: Understand vocabulary, organization of processes, and how to communicate and comprehend mathematical concepts and justifications with accuracy.	Hands-On and Problem-Solving lessons, Explain Your Thinking, games, Reading Mathematics, and Create and Solve features. For example, see **Lessons. 12.2, 12.4, 12.6, 13.1, 13.5, 14.1–14.3, 15.1, 15.2, 15.4, 15.5.**	
Connections: Relate mathematics to real-life situations and other subject areas and make mathematical connections.	Connections features, skills lessons, and Problem Solving. For example, see **Lessons 12.4, 12.5, 13.3, 13.4, 13.5, 14.2, 15.3.**	
Representation: Represent mathematical ideas using concrete objects, pictures, and symbols.	Occurs throughout as students use manipulatives, workmats, number lines, drawings, tables, symbols, and number sentences to model or explain. For example, see **Lessons 12.1, 12.2, 12.6, 13.1, 13.3, 13.4, 14.1, 14.2, 14.3, 14.4, 15.1, 15.2, 15.3, 15.5.**	

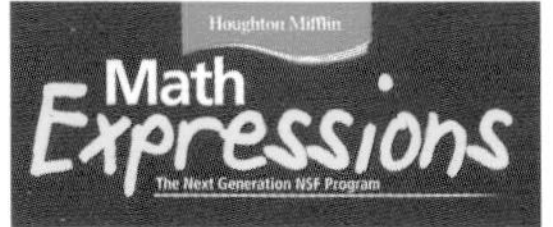

For content corresponding to this *Houghton Mifflin Math* unit, see lessons in *Math Expressions*

- Unit C: The Metric Measurement System
- Unit F: The U.S. Customary System

See also, Unit 1: Basic Multiplication and Division, Unit 4: Multi-Digit Division, and Unit D: Polygons and Circles.

Assessment System

Monitoring Student Progress

Unit Objectives

5A	Estimate, measure, compare, and convert customary and metric units of length, capacity, and weight/mass.
5B	Determine elapsed time using clocks and calendars.
5C	Read, write, and compare temperatures in degrees Fahrenheit and degrees Celsius.
5D	Collect, organize, and analyze data; find mean, median, mode, and range.
5E	Make, read, and interpret line plots, stem-and-leaf plots, bar graphs, circle graphs and line graphs.
5F	Solve problems using skills and strategies.

Classroom-Based Assessment

Prior Knowledge

Use What You Know, PE pp. 305, 333, 355, 375
Chapters 12, 13, 14, 15 Pretests, Unit Resources
Unit 5 Reading Mathematics, PE p. 302–303

Ongoing Assessment

Student Self-Assessment

Explain Your Thinking, PE pp. 309, 311, 313, 321, 323, 327, 334, 337, 345, 367, 371, 378, 383, 386
Mixed Review & Test Prep, PE pp. 309, 311, 314, 321, 325, 329, 335, 339, 371, 379, 383, 387
Quick Check, PE pp. 317, 347, 369, 383
Vocabulary Wrap-up, PE p. 398

Informal Assessment by Teachers

Problem of the Day, First page of every TE lesson
Spiral Review, First page of every TE lesson
Common Error/Intervention, TE pp. 308, 310, 312, 320, 322, 326, 334, 336, 344, 348, 356, 360, 364, 366, 370, 378, 380, 382, 384
Lesson Quiz, First page of every TE lesson

Diagnostic/Intervention

Quick Check, PE pp. 317, 347, 369, 383
Common Error/Intervention, TE pp. 308, 310, 312, 320, 322, 326, 334, 336, 344, 348, 356, 360, 364, 366, 370, 378, 380, 382, 384
Chapter Review/Test, PE pp. 330, 352, 372, 388
Unit 5 Test, PE pp. 394–395

Formal Evaluation

Chapter & Unit Assessment

Chapter Review/Test, PE pp. 330, 352, 372, 388
Chapters 12, 13, 14, and 15 Tests, Unit Resources
*__Unit Test, Form A and Form B,__ Unit Resources
Unit 5 Test, PE pp. 394–395

Performance Assessment & Rubric

Performance Assessment, PE p. 395
Scoring Rubric, TE p. 395

Test Prep

*__Problem-Solving on Tests,__ PE pp. 343, 363
*__Cumulative Test Prep,__ PE pp. 396–397
Test Prep on the Net, on Education Place
www.eduplace.com/map

(Starred tests use standardized test formats.)

Test Generator

The ***Ways to Assess*** **CD-ROM** allows you to create and score customized tests or review pages. You can select items that assess your state's standards, NCTM standards, or lesson objectives of your choosing. The CD-ROM also includes program, chapter, and unit tests for online administration and scoring, or for printing.

Intervention

Ways to Success **CD-ROM** Reteach the lesson objective, provide extra practice, or reteach a required prerequisite skill.
Lessons 12.1–12.9, 13.1–13.5, 14.1–14.5, 15.1–15.5

Audio Tutor For students who need extra support, who were absent, or who have reading difficulties.
Lessons 12.2, 12.5, 12.7, 13.2, 13.4, 14.4, 14.5, 15.2, 15.4

Unit Activities

Unit Project

Individuals	45 minutes
Objective	Collect, organize and analyze data.
Materials	Research materials
Visual, Tactual	

State Data

- Ask students to share what they know about their state or another state. Tell students that they will gather and compare measurements and statistical data about a state for this Unit Project.
- Guide students to organize the data they find in charts, tables, graphs, or illustrations. Students should focus on numerical data and interesting facts.
- Use the activity found on page 398 to wrap up the Unit Project.

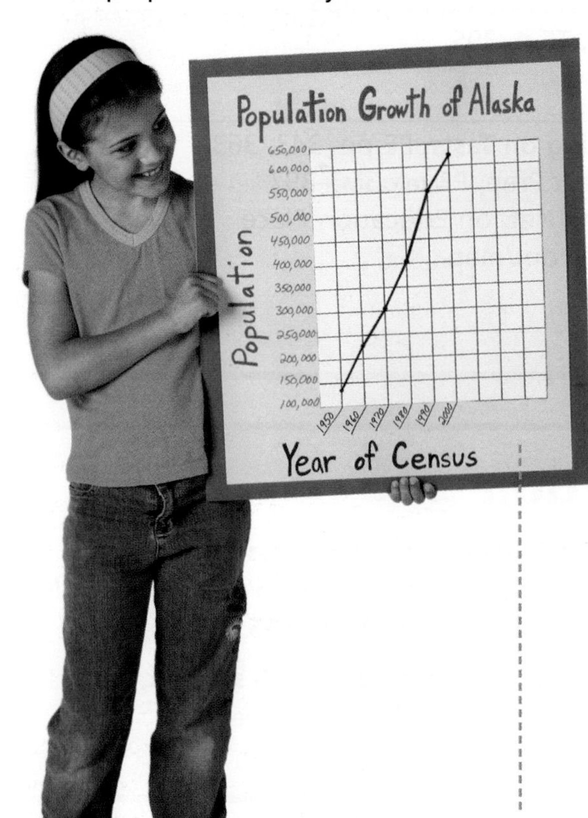

Spiral Review

Pairs	20 minutes
Objective	Determine elapsed time.
Materials	2 number cubes (1–6)
Visual, Tactual	

Elapsed Time Game

Students play in pairs. To begin, students write *12:00* on their paper. Each student rolls both number cubes and adds the numbers. Then they add that number of minutes to 12:00 and record it. For example, 5 + 6 = 11, 12:00 + 11 minutes = 12:11. Students take turns adding sums and tracing times until the first student reaches 2:00.

Vocabulary Activity

Small Groups	20 minutes
Objective	Reinforce unit vocabulary.
Materials	Bingo board with 25 blank squares, counters
Visual, Auditory, Tactual	

Measurement and Graphing Terms

List the Unit 5 vocabulary words on the board. Students make their own bingo boards by filling squares using 24 of the words listed. Have them leave one FREE space. Call out the definitions. Students put a counter on the square with the matching vocabulary word. Play continues until the first student has five in a row.

Take-Home Game

Small Groups	30 minutes
Objective	Find mode.
Materials	3 number cubes (1–6)
Tactual	

Predict the Mode

Make a tally chart with one column labeled *sums*. List numbers 3–18 in this column. Each player then predicts which sums will appear the most when the three number cubes are rolled and added together. Keep a tally of sums in the second column of the tally chart. After 20 turns, check whether any predictions were correct.

Repeatable Unit Game

Small Groups	30 minutes
Objective	Compare customary and metric units of length, capacity, and weight/mass.
Materials	30 index cards
Visual	

Measurement Match

- Write 15 measurements on one set of cards and 15 equivalent measurements on another set, such as 1 pound, 16 ounces, 4 cups, 1 quart.
- Shuffle cards and arrange them in rows facedown. The first player turns over two cards. If there is no match, the cards are turned back over. The next player takes a turn. Play continues until all cards are matched.

Math Expressions

Small Groups	30 minutes
Objective	Estimate and measure length and weight; collect and display data in circle graphs.
Materials	Books, inch or centimeter ruler, scale, several objects of different weights, clock, Workmat 8, straightedge
Visual, Tactual	

Estimate and Measure

This activity uses instructional practices from *Math Expressions* with the content of this unit.

Students choose from the following:

- **How Thick Is a Page?** Students estimate the thickness of a page in different books by measuring the thickness of a number of pages. After measuring a group of pages, students should divide by the number of pages in the group to compare the thickness.
- **Weighing In** Students select an object and make a new unit and name it, such as stapler = 1 "squib-ble". Students estimate the weight of several objects using the new unit. They use a scale to measure and check their estimates.
- **Jump to It** Students estimate how long it will take them to do 100 jumping jacks. They measure how long using a clock with a second hand and check their estimates.
- **Attribute Circle Graph** Students select an attribute to track in 12 classmates, such as type of shoe closure: lace, slip-on, Velcro. They make a circle graph to display results.

Starting Unit 5

Reading Mathematics

Use the Reading Mathematics pages to be sure that students have adequate understanding and fluency with the unit vocabulary. This provides the key foundation for developing the unit concepts and skills.

Reviewing Vocabulary

Read through this section with students. Notice that two of the terms are "units" and two of the terms are "amounts." Explain the difference between mass and weight. *Mass*, one of the base quantities in the metric system, is the amount of matter in an object. *Weight* is a force. It is the pull of gravity on a mass. Ask students if they remember other measurement words, and discuss them.

Reading Words and Symbols

To help students remember all the measurement vocabulary words in this chapter, make a chart like the one below showing the two systems of measurement, the categories, and units in each category.

	Customary	Metric
Length	in., ft, yd, mi	mm, cm, dm, m, km
Capacity	c, pt, qt, gal	mL, L
Weight/Mass	oz, lb, T	g, kg
Temperature	°F	°C

The abbreviated words for measurement units are called *symbols*. Except for the inch unit, all the other symbols have no period after them.

When completing **Questions 1 and 2** and other measurement questions, remind students to get in the habit of using labeled answers consisting of a number and a unit.

Reading Mathematics

Reviewing Vocabulary

Here are some math vocabulary words that you should know.

capacity	the amount that a container can hold
centimeter (cm)	a metric unit used to measure length
mass	the amount of matter in an object
ounce (oz)	a customary unit used to measure weight

Reading Words and Symbols

You can describe the capacity of an object by using customary units or metric units.

Customary Units

Read: The pitcher holds about one quart.

Write, using symbols: The pitcher holds about 1 qt.

Metric Units

Read: The pitcher holds about one liter.

Write, using symbols: The pitcher holds about 1 L.

Use words and symbols to answer the questions.

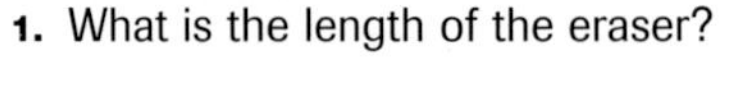

1. What is the length of the eraser?

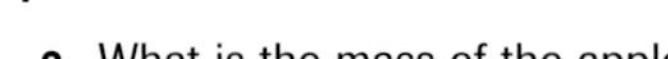

2. What is the mass of the apple?

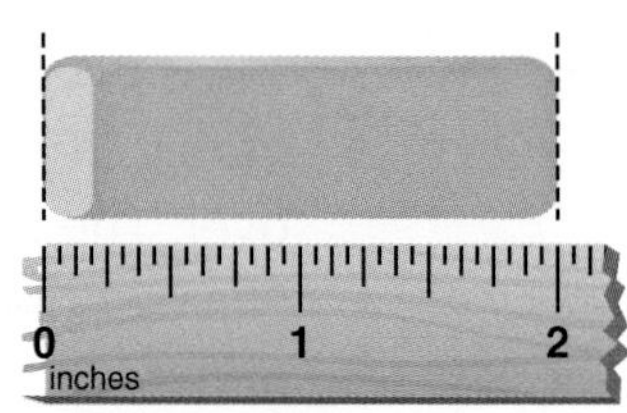

two inches; 2 in.

three hundred grams; 300 g

Reading Test Questions

Choose the correct answer for each.

3. What is the approximate weight of the apples?

   a. 1 pound c. 3 pounds

   (b.) 2 pounds d. 4 pounds

Approximate means "close to" or "about."

4. What unit of measure would you use to determine the height of a tree that is 100 years old?

   a. cups (c.) feet

   b. degrees d. seconds

Determine means "find out" or "decide."

5. Which word completes this sentence?

   Use a ____ to measure temperature.

   a. balance c. ruler

   b. bar graph (d.) thermometer

Completes means "finishes" or "fills in."

Learning Vocabulary

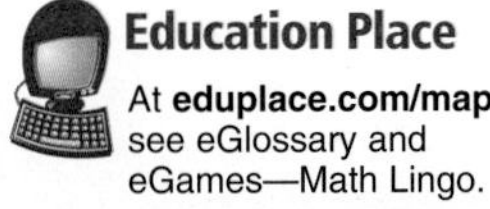

Watch for these words in this unit. Write their definitions in your journal.

- century
- decade
- milliliter (mL)
- degrees Celsius (°C)
- degrees Fahrenheit (°F)
- interval
- outlier

Literature Connection

Read "Lengths of Time" on Page 650. Then work with a partner to answer the questions about the story.

Education Place

At **eduplace.com/map** see eGlossary and eGames—Math Lingo.

Literature Connection

Student Book List Selection

You may use the ***Literature Connection*** (Student Edition page 650, Teacher's Edition page T53) at any time during this unit.

Other Literature Connections

What a Load of Trash!
by Steve Skidmore

Measuring
by Sally Hewitt

Measuring Penny
by Loreen Leedy

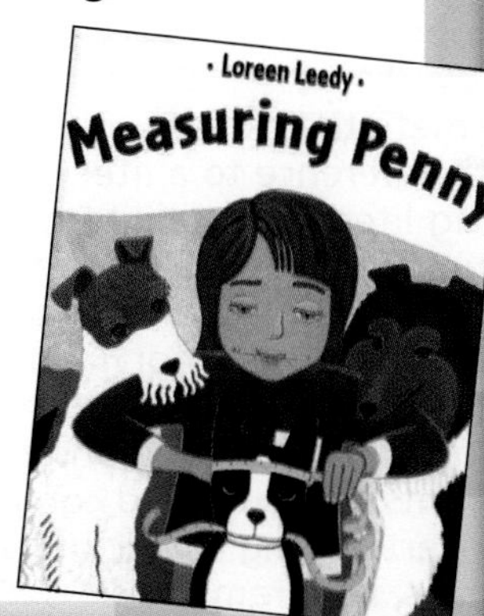

Reading Test Questions

Tell students to read each problem carefully. Suggest rereading the problem, this time with the choices in mind. Remind students that they may find the word *mass* in a question that involves metric units.

When answering multiple-choice items, try to eliminate unreasonable choices. For **Item 4**, remind students that *height* is in the same category as *length*. Other words, such as *width* or *thickness*, are also in the same category.

Learning Vocabulary

Go over the list of new words with the class. Help students to pronounce the words correctly, and explain that they will learn about these words as they work on this unit. If students are keeping Math Journals, be sure they enter the words and their definitions as they find them in the unit.

The *Building Vocabulary Kit* includes vocabulary cards and additional teaching strategies for unit vocabulary.

Writing in Mathematics

Writing helps students learn and remember. Throughout the unit, students have opportunities to write for different purposes:

- explaining their thinking or solution strategies
- creating new problems
- recording what they have learned
- listing questions they still have

Look for *Explain Your Thinking* questions in the student text and *Math Journal Prompts* in this Teacher's Edition.

CHAPTER 12

Planning Guide

Customary and Metric Measurement

Lesson	Overview	Objective/Vocabulary
1 Explore Customary Units of Length p. 306A	▸ Using customary units, estimate and measure lengths. ▸ Measure objects with inch rulers to the nearest inch, half inch, and quarter inch.	▸ Estimate and measure lengths using an inch ruler. inch (in) quarter inch half inch eighth inch
2 Inch, Foot, Yard, Mile p. 308A	▸ Convert among customary units of length (inches, feet, yards, miles).	▸ Change units of length. foot (ft) mile (mi) yard (yd)
3 Customary Units of Capacity p. 310A	▸ Convert among customary units of capacity, using cups, pints, quarts, and gallons. ▸ Choose the appropriate measure of capacity.	▸ Change units of capacity. gallon cup quart capacity pint
4 Hands On: Customary Units of Weight p. 312A	▸ Using a balance scale, estimate and measure with customary units of weight. ▸ Convert among customary units of weight (ounces, pounds, tons).	▸ Estimate and measure using customary units of weight. ton (t)
5 Problem-Solving Decision: Too Much or Too Little p. 316A	▸ Decide whether there is enough information to solve a problem. ▸ If so, practice previously learned operational skills to solve the problem.	▸ Find the information you need to solve a problem.
6 Hands On: Explore Metric Units of Length p. 318A	▸ Using metric units, estimate and measure lengths. ▸ Measure objects to the nearest centimeter and millimeter with centimeter rulers.	▸ Estimate and measure lengths using a centimeter ruler. millimeter (mm)
7 Metric Units of Length p. 320A	▸ Convert among metric units of length (millimeters, centimeters, decimeters, meters, kilometers). ▸ Choose the best estimate of length for an object.	▸ Change metric units of length. millimeter (mm) centimeter (cm) decimeter (dm) meter (m) kilometer (km)
8 Hands On: Metric Units of Capacity p. 322A	▸ Estimate the capacity of a container with reference to a liter. ▸ Using liters and milliliters, convert among metric units of capacity. ▸ Estimate lengths with benchmarks such as "finger width" for 1 cm.	▸ Change metric units of capacity. liter (L) milliliter (mL)
9 Hands On: Metric Units of Mass p. 326A	▸ Using a balance scale and metric weights, measure and compare mass. ▸ Convert among metric units of mass (grams, kilograms). ▸ Choose the best estimate of an object's weight.	▸ Change metric units of mass. gram (g) kilogram (kg)

Skills Trace: Customary and Metric Measurement		
Grade 3	**Grade 4**	**Grade 5**
• Estimate, measure, compare, and convert customary units of length, capacity, and weight (ch. 13) • Estimate, measure, compare, and convert metric units of length, capacity, and mass (ch. 14)	• Estimate, measure, compare, and convert customary units of length, capacity, and weight • Estimate, measure, compare, and convert metric units of length, capacity, and mass • Choose the most appropriate unit of measure of an object	• Convert among customary units of length, capacity, and weight (ch. 6) • Convert among metric units of length, capacity, and mass (ch. 6) • Add and subtract measurements (ch. 6)

Differentiated Instruction	Materials	NCTM Standards
▶ Differentiated Instruction activities, p. 306B ▶ *Chapter Challenges,* p. 67 *Ways to Success* CD-ROM: 12.1 ▶ *Ways to Success* Skillsheet 103	Rulers II Transparency, cutouts from Measurement Transparency, blank transparency, color markers, inch rulers	**Measurement:** Understand measurable attributes of objects and the units, systems, and processes of measurement. **Communication:** Use the language of mathematics to express mathematical ideas.
▶ Differentiated Instruction activities, p. 308B *Ways to Success* CD-ROM 12.2 ▶ *Ways to Success* Skillsheet 107 Audio Tutor: **2**/1 Listen and Understand	Tape measure, ruler, yardstick	**Measurement:** Carry out simple conversions, such as from centimeters to meters, within a system of measurement.
▶ Differentiated Instruction activities, p. 310B ▶ *Chapter Challenges,* p. 69 *Ways to Success* CD-ROM: 12.3 ▶ *Ways to Success* Skillsheet 109	Cup, quart, and gallon containers, blank transparency	**Measurement:** Understand the need for measuring with standard units and became familiar with standard units in the customary and metric systems.
▶ Differentiated Instruction activities, p. 312B *Ways to Success* CD-ROM: 12.4 ▶ *Ways to Success* Skillsheet 110	Calculator Transparency, blank transparency, calculators	**Measurement:** Understand the need for measuring with standard units and became familiar with standard units in the customary and metric systems.
▶ Differentiated Instruction activities, p. 316B ▶ *Chapter Challenges,* p. 71 *Ways to Success* CD-ROM: 12.5 ▶ *Ways to Success* Skillsheet 113 Audio Tutor: **2**/2 Listen and Understand	Index cards	**Problem Solving:** Solve problems that arise in mathematics and in other contexts. **Connections:** Recognize and use connections among mathematical ideas.
▶ Differentiated Instruction activities, p. 318B *Ways to Success* CD-ROM: 12.6 ▶ *Ways to Success* Skillsheet 104	Metric rulers	**Measurement:** Understand measurable attributes of objects and the units, systems, and processes of measurement. **Connections:** Recognize and use connections among mathematical ideas.
▶ Differentiated Instruction activities, p. 320B *Ways to Success* CD-ROM: 12.7 ▶ *Ways to Success* Skillsheet 108 Audio Tutor: **2**/3 Listen and Understand	Meterstick	**Measurement:** Carry out simple conversions, such as from centimeters to meters, such as from centimeters to meters, within a system of measurement.
▶ Differentiated Instruction activities, p. 322B *Ways to Success* CD-ROM: 12.8 ▶ *Ways to Success* Skillsheet 111	Blank transparency, containers of various sizes, liter measures marked in mL, water, centimeter or inch rulers, yard stick or meter stick	**Measurement:** Understand the need for measuring with standard units and become familiar with standard units in the customary and metric systems. **Connections:** Recognize and use connections among mathematical ideas.
▶ Differentiated Instruction activities, p. 326B *Ways to Success* CD-ROM: 12.9 ▶ *Ways to Success* Skillsheet 112	1 kg bag of rice, 1 kg mass, balance, metric masses, calculators	**Measurement:** Understand the need for measuring with standard units and become familiar with standard units in the customary and metric systems. **Connections:** Recognize and use connections among mathematical ideas.

Math Notes

Chapter Objectives

12A Measure length, using customary and metric units.

12B Convert among units of capacity and weight (mass).

12C Choose the most appropriate unit of measurement for customary and metric units of capacity and weight (mass).

12D Solve problems, using skills and strategies.

Mathematical Background

Customary and Metric Measurement

The **Customary system of measurement** is primarily used in the United States. Here are some equivalencies students should know.

Length	Capacity
12 inches (in.) = 1 foot (ft) 3 feet = 1 yard (yd) 1 yard = 36 inches 5,280 feet = 1 mile (mi)	2 cups (c) = 1 pint (pt) 2 pints = 1 quart (qt) 4 quarts = 1 gallon (gal) **Weight** 16 ounces (oz) = 1 pound (lb) 2,000 pounds = 1 ton (T)

The **Metric system of measurement** is based on powers of 10. To change from one unit to another, multiply or divide by a power of 10. **Kilograms** and **grams** are units of mass. Mass measures the amount of matter in an object. Weight measures the gravitational pull on an object. At earth's surface, a certain mass always corresponds to a certain weight. For example, 1 kilogram corresponds to approximately 2.2 pounds. In everyday life, grams and kilograms are commonly used to indicate weight.

Here are some equivalencies students should know.

Length	Mass
1,000 millimeters (mm) = 1 meter (m) 100 centimeters (cm) = 1 meter 10 decimeters (dm) = 1 meter 1,000 meters = 1 kilometer (km)	1,000 grams (g) = 1 kilogram (kg) **Capacity** 1,000 milliliters (mL) = 1 liter (L)

Research-Based Teaching

As Monroe and Nelson (2000) point out, the United States is one of the few nations not to use the metric system. The National Council of Teachers of Mathematics (NCTM, 2000) advises that "students should learn both the customary and metric systems and should know some rough equivalences between the metric and customary systems." See *Professional Resources Handbook, Grade 4,* Unit 5.

For more ideas relating to Unit 5, see the Teacher Support Handbook at the back of this Teacher's Edition.

Language Intervention

In East Asian countries, children learn that just as numbers can be composed and decomposed as sets and subsets, units of measurement can be composed and decomposed as well. For further explanation, see *Mathematical Language and Measurement* in the *Professional Resources Handbook, Grade 4.*

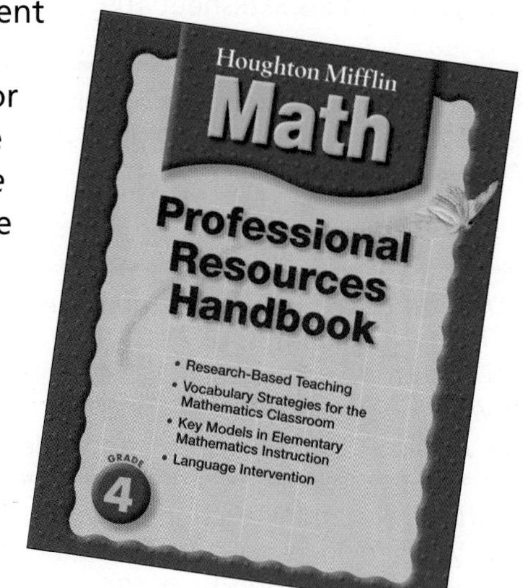

Chapter Activities

Connecting to the Unit Project

Individuals	15–20 minutes
Objective	Collect and organize data.
Materials	None
Visual, tactual	

Organize Measurement Data

- Have students organize the data they found involving measurements in their state.
- Encourage students to make illustrations of rivers, mountains, bridges, and so on, and label them with measurements (for example, Black Mountain, 11,340 ft high).

Named Peaks in Texas Above 8,000 Feet

Guadalupe Peak – 8,749
Shumard Peak – 8,615
Bartlett Peak – 8,508
Mount Livermore – 8,378
Hunter Peak – 8,368
El Capitan – 8,085

Assessing Prior Knowledge

Small Groups	30–45 minutes
Objective	Reinforce knowledge of customary and metric systems of measurement.
Materials	12 index cards
Visual, Auditory	

Units of Measurement

- Make two sets of cards labeled *Length, Capacity,* and *Weight or Mass* (one term per card). Then place all six cards in a pile facedown.
- Make three sets of cards labeled *Metric* and *Customary* (one term per card). Then place all six cards in a pile facedown.
- Divide the class into six groups. Have one student from each group pick a card from each pile (for example, *Customary* and *Capacity*).
- Ask each group to brainstorm all they know about the combination they chose. List units, measurement tools, and objects measured in terms of these units.
- After 15 minutes, have each group write their ideas on the board for the whole class to share. Encourage other students to add to the list.

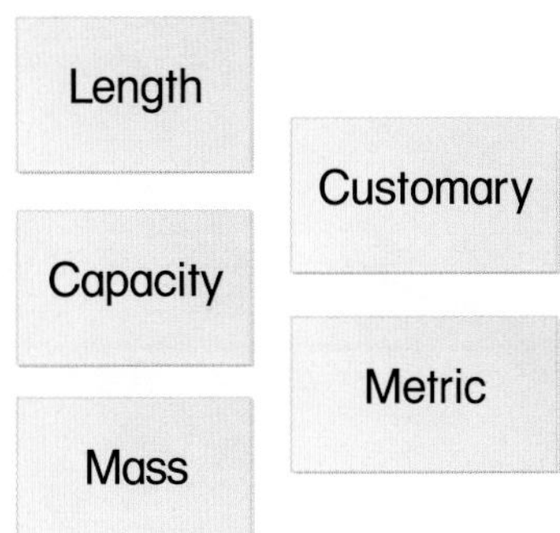

Math Expressions

Small Groups	25 minutes
Objective	Identify the structure of metric measurement units as base-ten.
Materials	Meter stick, yard stick
Tactual	

Metric Units of Measurement

This activity uses instructional practices from *Math Expressions* with the content from this unit.

- Have students tell what they know about metric units of measurement. Introduce the term meter and describe it as a length unit in the metric system of measurement. Display a meter stick. Help students see that a meter is about the same length as a yard.
- Explain to students that smaller units than a meter in the metric system include decimeters, centimeters, and millimeters. There are 10 decimeters in 1 meter, 100 centimeters in 1 meter, and 1,000 millimeters in 1 meter. Tell students that each unit is 10 times smaller than the next unit.
- Continue similarly with metric units for capacity and for mass.

Starting Chapter 12

Investigation

Using Data

Have students work in small groups to answer the question posed on page 304.

To extend the investigation, have students do the following activity.

- Research the record height for a sunflower. Write the height using customary and metric units.

For more information about projects and investigations,

Visit **Education Place**®
www.eduplace.com/mat

CHAPTER 12

Customary and Metric Measurement

INVESTIGATION

Using Data

Sunflowers can grow as high as 3 meters! The table shows how tall one sunflower grew in four weeks. How tall do you think the sunflower would be after 6 weeks? How can you use the information in the chart to make your estimate?

180 cm; I can use the chart to see that I need to multiply the number of weeks by 30.

Growth of a Sunflower

Number of Weeks	Height in Centimeters
1	30
2	60
3	90
4	120

304

Chapter 12 Prerequisite Skills Pretest

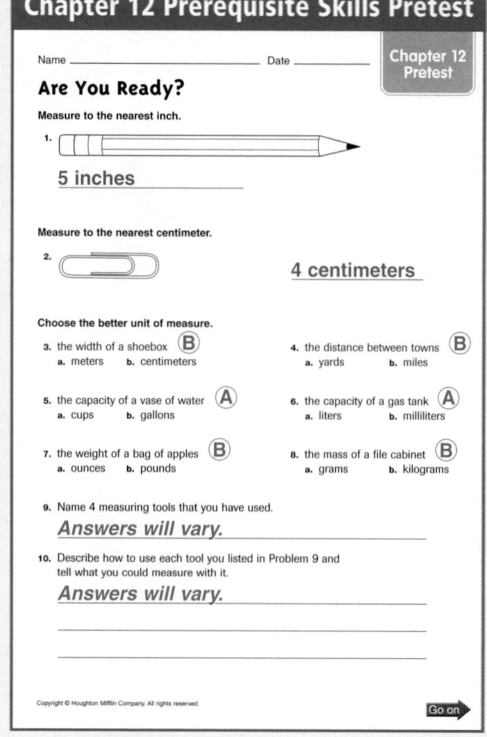

Name ______________ Date ________

Chapter 12 Pretest

Are You Ready?

Measure to the nearest inch.

1. 5 inches

Measure to the nearest centimeter.

2. 4 centimeters

Choose the better unit of measure.

3. the width of a shoebox (B)
   a. meters b. centimeters
4. the distance between towns (B)
   a. yards b. miles
5. the capacity of a vase of water (A)
   a. cups b. gallons
6. the capacity of a gas tank (A)
   a. liters b. milliliters
7. the weight of a bag of apples (B)
   a. ounces b. pounds
8. the mass of a file cabinet (B)
   a. grams b. kilograms
9. Name 4 measuring tools that you have used.
   Answers will vary.
10. Describe how to use each tool you listed in Problem 9 and tell what you could measure with it.
   Answers will vary.

Go on

Use What You Know

Use this page to review and remember what you need to know for this chapter.

VOCABULARY

Choose the best word to complete each sentence.

Vocabulary
quart
ounce
pound
gallons

1. A pencil weighs about one _____. **ounce**
2. A grocer sells potatoes by the _____. **pound**
3. The amount of water in a swimming pool would best be measured in _____. **gallons**

CONCEPTS AND SKILLS

Measure to the nearest inch.

4. 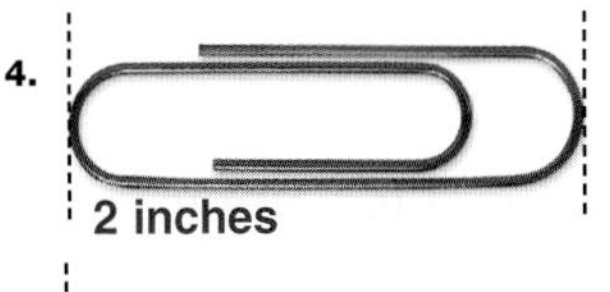
2 inches

5. **5 inches**

Choose the better unit of measure.

6. the width of a book
 a. meters (b.) centimeters
7. the length of a car
 (a.) meters b. kilometers
8. the length of an eraser
 (a.) inches b. feet
9. the distance between towns
 a. yards (b.) miles

10. Name 4 measuring tools that you have used. Describe how to use them and tell what you could measure with them.
See above.

Write About It *Possible answers:* yardstick, ruler, scale, cup. You could measure the length of a room with the yardstick. You could measure tables with your ruler. You could weigh fruit with the scale. You could measure water with the cup.

Facts Practice, See page 670.

Use What You Know

Use this page for informal assessment and review of prerequisite skills.

- Items 1–3: Use math vocabulary
- Items 4–5: Measure to the nearest inch
- Items 6–9: Choose the appropriate unit
- Item 10: Name and describe measurement tools

Customize Your Instruction

Use the Chapter Pretest in the Unit Resource folder to help customize and pace instruction.

Objectives and Resources

Prerequisite Skills Pretest

- Item 1–2: Measure length.
- Items 3–8: Choose the more appropriate unit of measure.
- Items 9–10: Name and describe measurement tools.

New Content Pretest

- Items 1–2: Measure length.
- Items 3–6: Convert among units of capacity and weight (mass).
- Items 7–14, 15–18: Choose the appropriate unit of measure. Compare units of measure.
- Items 19–20: Solve problems using skills and strategies.

For Students Having Difficulty

- *Ways to Success* CD-ROM, 12A, 12D
- *Ways to Success* Skillsheet, 103–106

For Students Having Success

- Enrichment 12.1–12.9

For Mathematically Promising Students

Explore: Egyptian Measures, p. 67, after Lesson 1

Extend: Missing Units, p. 69, after Lesson 3

Connect: Estimating Measurements, p. 71, after Lesson 5

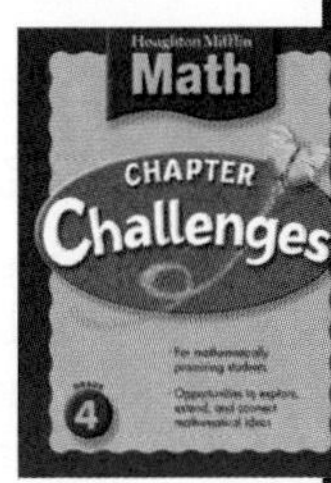

Chapter 12 New Content Pretest

Name _____ Date _____ Chapter 12 Pretest continued

Check What You Know

Measure to the nearest inch, half-inch, and quarter inch.

1. **2 inches; $2\frac{1}{2}$ inches; $2\frac{1}{4}$ inches**

Measure the length to the nearest centimeter and nearest millimeter.

2. **5 centimeters; 52 millimeters**

Find each missing number.

3. 2 T = **4,000** lb
4. 16,000 mL = **16** L
5. 2 kg = **2,000** g
6. **4** gal = 32 pt

Choose the better estimate of weight or mass.

7. a dog (B) a. 25 g b. 25 kg
8. a whale (A) a. 13 T b. 13 lb

Choose the better estimate of length.

9. a thumbtack (A) a. 1 cm b. 1 m
10. a fire truck (A) a. 30 ft b. 10 mi

Go on

Chapter 12 New Content Pretest

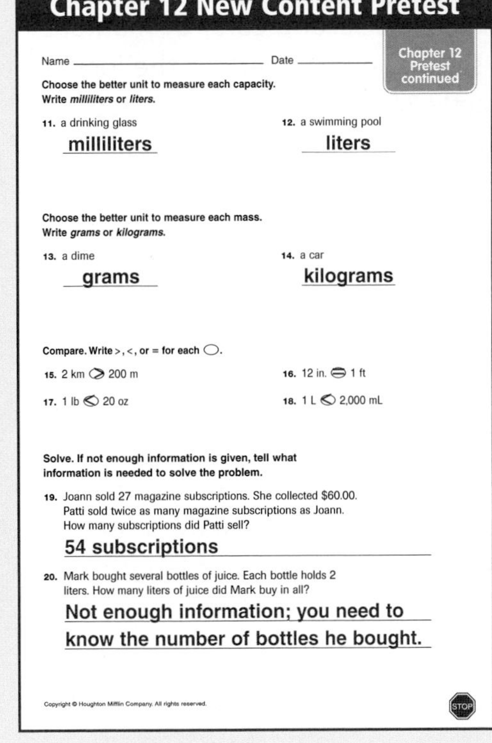

Name _____ Date _____ Chapter 12 Pretest continued

Choose the better unit to measure each capacity. Write *milliliters* or *liters*.

11. a drinking glass **milliliters**
12. a swimming pool **liters**

Choose the better unit to measure each mass. Write *grams* or *kilograms*.

13. a dime **grams**
14. a car **kilograms**

Compare. Write >, <, or = for each ◯.

15. 2 km > 200 m
16. 12 in. = 1 ft
17. 1 lb < 20 oz
18. 1 L < 2,000 mL

Solve. If not enough information is given, tell what information is needed to solve the problem.

19. Joann sold 27 magazine subscriptions. She collected $60.00. Patti sold twice as many magazine subscriptions as Joann. How many subscriptions did Patti sell? **54 subscriptions**
20. Mark bought several bottles of juice. Each bottle holds 2 liters. How many liters of juice did Mark buy in all? **Not enough information; you need to know the number of bottles he bought.**

STOP

Hands On Lesson 12.1

Explore Customary Units of Length

Planning

Lesson Objective Estimate and measure lengths, using an inch ruler.

Math Background

An inch was originally defined in England as the width of a man's thumb at the base of the nail. Almost every culture has used the human foot as a unit of measurement, which is related to the foot used today.

Technology Resources

- *Ways to Success* CD-ROM 12.1
- Education Place: Extra Practice, eGames www.eduplace.com/map

Lesson 12.1 Transparency

Problem of the Day

1 foot = 12 inches. How long is your *real* foot? Is it greater than or less than a foot long? Estimate, then measure to find out. (Answers will vary.)

Spiral Review

Write each fraction.

1. one half ($\frac{1}{2}$) **2.** one fourth ($\frac{1}{4}$)

3. three fourths ($\frac{3}{4}$) **4.** five eighths ($\frac{5}{8}$)

5. seven eighths ($\frac{7}{8}$)

Lesson Quiz

Measure to the nearest inch, half inch, and quarter inch.

1. ______________________
(3 in., $2\frac{1}{2}$ in., $2\frac{2}{4}$ in.)

2. ________________
(1 in., 1 in., $1\frac{1}{4}$ in.)

3. _________
(1 in., $\frac{1}{2}$ in., $\frac{3}{4}$ in.)

NCTM Standards

Measurement: Understand measurable attributes of objects and the units, systems, and processes of measurement.
Communication: Use the language of mathematics to express mathematical ideas precisely.

Getting Started

Building Math Vocabulary

You may wish to review these words with students.

inch (in.) a customary unit of length; 12 inches = 1 foot

half inch a customary unit of length; a half inch is $\frac{1}{2}$ the length of an inch

quarter inch a customary unit of length; a quarter inch is $\frac{1}{4}$ the length of an inch

eighth inch a customary unit of length; an eighth inch is $\frac{1}{8}$ the length of an inch

Measuring Length

Whole Class	15 minutes
Objective	Measure lengths using a ruler.
Materials	Rulers II Transparency, cutouts from Measurement Transparency, blank transparency, color markers
Auditory, Tactual	

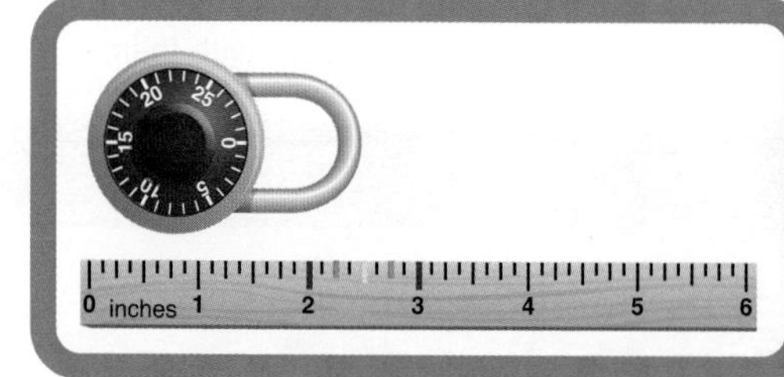

- Display the cutout lock and the inch ruler on the blank transparency. **About how long is the lock?** (2–3 in.) Have a volunteer use one color of marker to show those marks. **Is it closer to 2 or 3 inches?** (2 in.) Use a second color of marker to show the inch mark. Is the lock exactly $2\frac{1}{2}$ inches long? (no) Let's get a more exact measure.
- Use the third color of marker to highlight the quarter-inch mark. **Let's summarize. To the nearest inch, the lock is 2 inches long. To the nearest quarter inch, the lock is $2\frac{2}{4}$ inches long, which is the same as $2\frac{1}{2}$ inches.**
- Tell students that the lesson provides additional information on using customary units of length.

Differentiated Instruction

English Learners

Small Groups	10 minutes
Objective	Estimate and measure lengths using a ruler.
Materials	Inch ruler
Auditory, Visual	

Early Production

- Students may need more help identifying the different markings on an inch ruler.
- Show students how to identify an eighth inch, quarter inch, half inch, and inch on a ruler.
- Say: **Show me a half (quarter, one eighth) inch.**

Intermediate/Advanced

- English Learner Resource 12.1
- English Learner Handbook

Intervention

Small Groups	5–10 minutes
Objective	Measure lengths using a ruler.
Materials	Paper rulers calibrated to eighths, colored markers
Visual, Tactual	

- Some students have trouble naming a fraction of an inch when they encounter equivalent fractions such as $\frac{2}{4} = \frac{1}{2}$.
- Prepare paper rulers marked off by eighth inches. Guide students to color-code the ruler by highlighting all half-inch marks in red, all quarter-inch marks in blue, and all eighth-inch marks in yellow. This can help to clarify the equivalent fractions.
- Have students use the rulers to measure objects to the nearest quarter and eighth inch.

Other Resources

- *Ways to Success* CD-ROM 12.1

Early Finishers

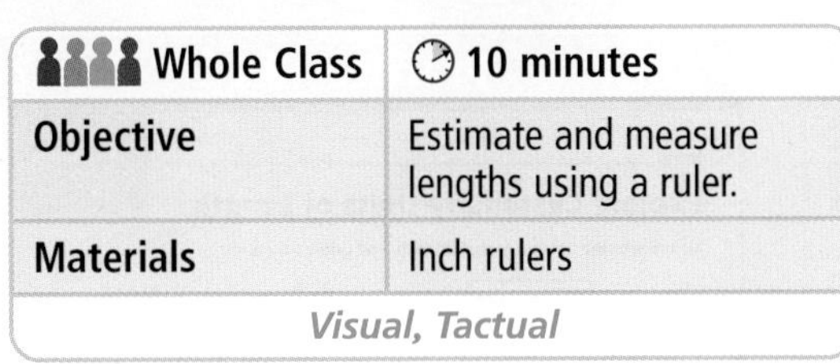

Whole Class	10 minutes
Objective	Estimate and measure lengths using a ruler.
Materials	Inch rulers
Visual, Tactual	

- Have students go on a mini scavenger hunt in which they seek different classroom objects that are between 1 and 6 inches long.
- Have them list their findings and measure them to within an eighth of an inch. Students can share and compare their lists.

Alternate Teaching Strategy

Ask students to come up with an everyday object that they could use to describe the following lengths: $\frac{1}{2}$ inch, $\frac{1}{4}$ inch, 1 inch, and 1 foot. Students should share their ideas with the class.

❶ Introduce

Read the objective with students and tell them that in this lesson they will estimate and measure lengths using customary units. Explain that inch rulers are used to measure objects to the nearest inch, half inch, and quarter inch.

❷ Teach

Work Together

- **What must we line up to measure an object?** (the end of the object with the zero mark of the ruler) **How many measurements will be in your chart?** (4)
- Work through **Steps 1–5** with students. Guide them to read the ruler and record each measurement as accurately as possible. As needed, help students identify intermediate marks. **Why do some rulers have more marks between inches than others?** (Rulers with more marks give more exact measurements.)

Explore Customary Units of Length

Objective Estimate and measure lengths, using an inch ruler.

Work Together

Work with a partner to estimate length and then measure, using an inch ruler.

STEP 1 Estimate the length of the pea pod above. Record your estimate in a table like the one at the right.
Estimates may vary.

Estimate:
Nearest inch:
Nearest half inch:
Nearest quarter inch:

STEP 2 Use an inch ruler to measure the pea pod to the nearest inch. Use a half-inch mark to decide which inch mark is closer to the end of the pea pod. Record the length. **3 inches**

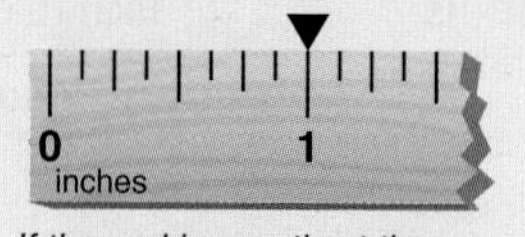

If the end is exactly at the half–inch mark, round to the next inch.

STEP 3 Now measure the pea pod to the nearest half inch. Use a quarter-inch mark to decide which half-inch mark is closer to the end. Record the length. **$3\frac{1}{2}$ inches**

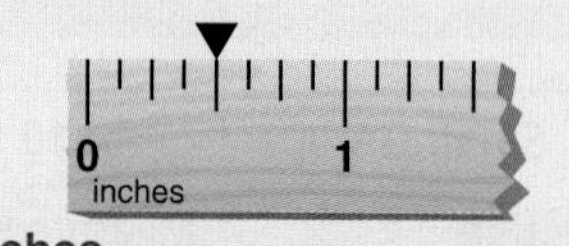

STEP 4 Measure the pea pod to the nearest quarter inch. Use an eighth-inch mark to decide which quarter-inch mark is closer to the end. **$3\frac{1}{4}$ inches**

The more marks your ruler has, the more accurately you will be able to measure.

Compare your estimate and the three measurements of the pea pod. Which is closest to the actual length of the pea pod? **the nearest quarter inch; $3\frac{1}{4}$ inches**

306

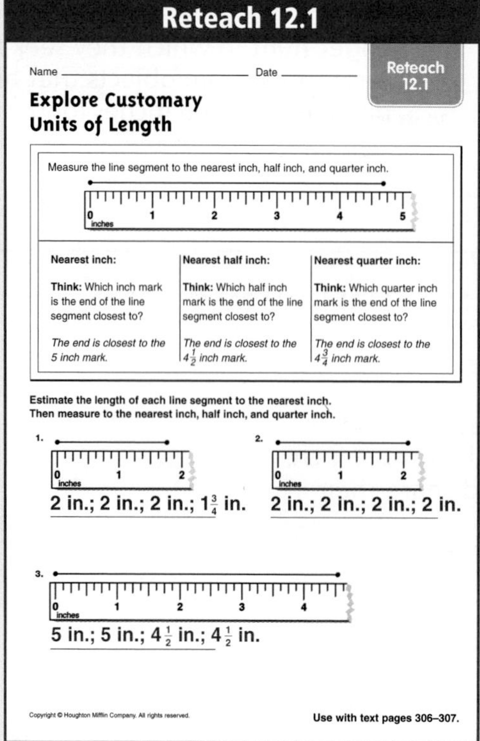

Reteach 12.1

Name ____________ Date ________ Reteach 12.1

Explore Customary Units of Length

Measure the line segment to the nearest inch, half inch, and quarter inch.

Nearest inch:	Nearest half inch:	Nearest quarter inch:
Think: Which inch mark is the end of the line segment closest to?	**Think:** Which half inch mark is the end of the line segment closest to?	**Think:** Which quarter inch mark is the end of the line segment closest to?
The end is closest to the 5 inch mark.	*The end is closest to the $4\frac{1}{2}$ inch mark.*	*The end is closest to the $4\frac{3}{4}$ inch mark.*

Estimate the length of each line segment to the nearest inch. Then measure to the nearest inch, half inch, and quarter inch.

1. 2 in.; 2 in.; 2 in.; $1\frac{3}{4}$ in.
2. 2 in.; 2 in.; 2 in.; 2 in.
3. 5 in.; 5 in.; $4\frac{1}{2}$ in.; $4\frac{1}{2}$ in.

Use with text pages 306–307.

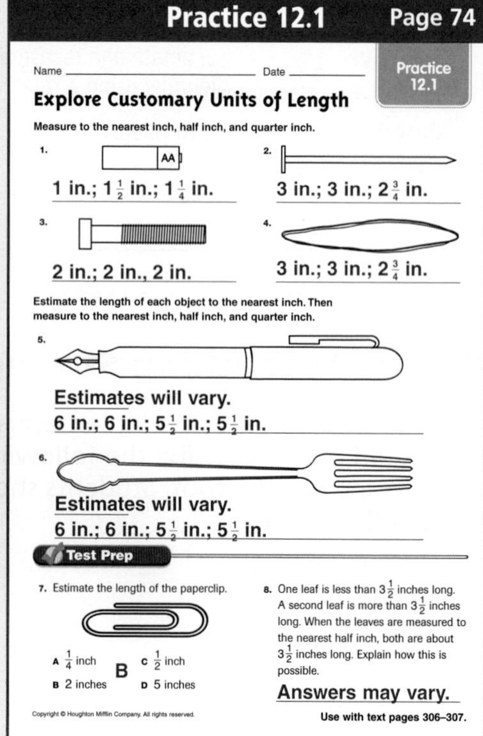

Practice 12.1 Page 74

Name ____________ Date ________ Practice 12.1

Explore Customary Units of Length

Measure to the nearest inch, half inch, and quarter inch.

1. 1 in.; $1\frac{1}{2}$ in.; $1\frac{1}{4}$ in.
2. 3 in.; 3 in.; $2\frac{3}{4}$ in.
3. 2 in.; 2 in., 2 in.
4. 3 in.; 3 in.; $2\frac{3}{4}$ in.

Estimate the length of each object to the nearest inch. Then measure to the nearest inch, half inch, and quarter inch.

5. Estimates will vary.
6 in.; 6 in.; $5\frac{1}{2}$ in.; $5\frac{1}{2}$ in.
6. Estimates will vary.
6 in.; 6 in.; $5\frac{1}{2}$ in.; $5\frac{1}{2}$ in.

Test Prep

7. Estimate the length of the paperclip.
A $\frac{1}{4}$ inch
B 2 inches
C $\frac{1}{2}$ inch
D 5 inches
B

8. One leaf is less than $3\frac{1}{2}$ inches long. A second leaf is more than $3\frac{1}{2}$ inches long. When the leaves are measured to the nearest half inch, both are about $3\frac{1}{2}$ inches long. Explain how this is possible.
Answers may vary.

Use with text pages 306–307.

Find five objects to measure. Estimate the length of each object to the nearest inch. Then measure each object to the nearest inch, half inch, and quarter inch. Record your work.
Check students' measurements.

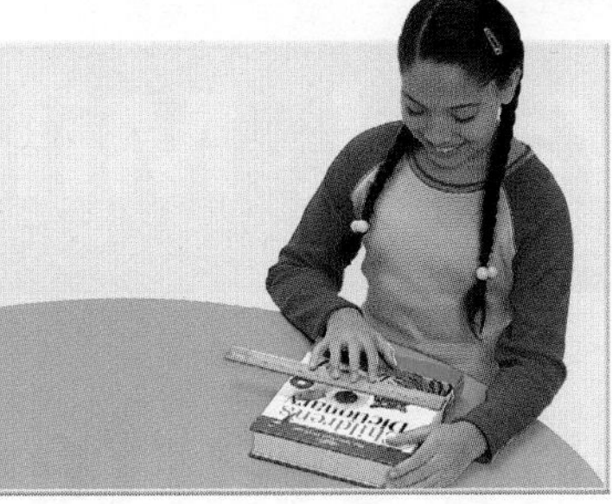

On Your Own

Measure to the nearest inch, half inch, and quarter inch.

1. 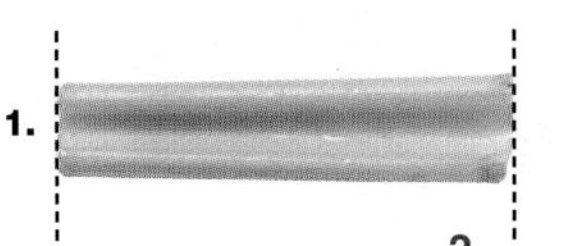

2 inches; 2 inches; $1\frac{3}{4}$ inches

2. 2 inches; $2\frac{1}{2}$ inches; $2\frac{1}{2}$ inches

Estimate the length of each object to the nearest inch. Then measure to the nearest inch, half inch, and quarter inch. *Estimates may vary.*

3. 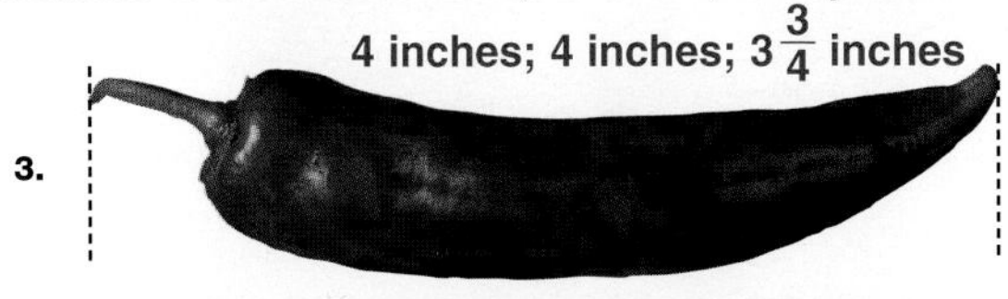

4 inches; 4 inches; $3\frac{3}{4}$ inches

4. 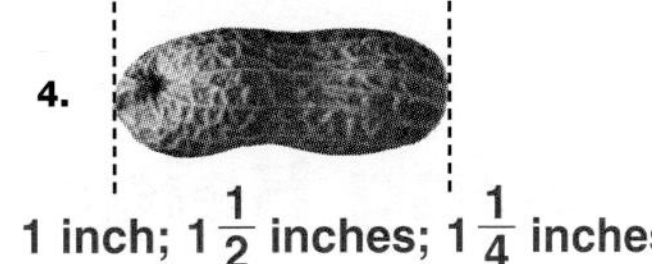

1 inch; $1\frac{1}{2}$ inches; $1\frac{1}{4}$ inches

Talk About It • Write About It

You have learned to measure to the nearest inch, half inch, and quarter inch.

5. One green bean is less than 5 inches long, and another is more than 5 inches long. When they are measured to the nearest inch, both are about 5 inches long. Explain how this is possible.
See Additional Answers.
6. What is the length of this green bean to the nearest quarter inch? $3\frac{3}{4}$ inches

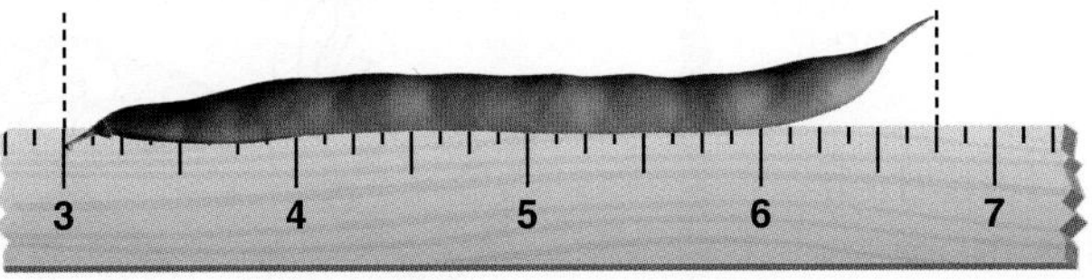

3 Practice

On Your Own

Select from **Exercises 1–6** as independent work.

How is the task different for Exercises 1–2 than for Exercises 3–4? (For Exercises 3–4, you estimate first and then find exact measurements.)

4 Assess & Close

Math Talk in Action

Refer to the ***Talk About It • Write About It*** problems to conclude the lesson.

- **What is unusual about how the green bean is measured in Exercise 6?** (It is placed along the middle of the ruler.)
- **How is using a ruler like rounding numbers?** (In both, you look for a halfway mark to help you decide the closer measure or number.)

Math Journal Prompt

Have students write about a real experience they have had using a ruler to measure length.

Lesson Quiz

Use the quiz on Lesson Transparency 12.1.

Lesson 12.1 Transparency

Test Prep & Spiral Review

Use Test Prep Transparency 12.1.

Test Prep 12.1 Transparency

Enrichment 12.1

Name ______ Date ______ Enrichment 12.1

What Are Your Measurements?

0 1 2 3 4 5 6 inches

Trace the ruler on a piece of paper. Use your paper to measure objects in the room. Find at least 3 objects that are the same length or shorter than your traced ruler and 5 objects that are larger than your traced ruler. Measure each object to the nearest inch, half inch, and quarter inch. Record your measurements in the table below.

Object	Nearest Inch	Nearest Half Inch	Nearest Quarter Inch

Write About It How did you use your traced ruler to measure objects larger than 6 inches?
Answers will vary.
Check students' measurements.

 Use with text pages 306–307.

Problem Solving 12.1

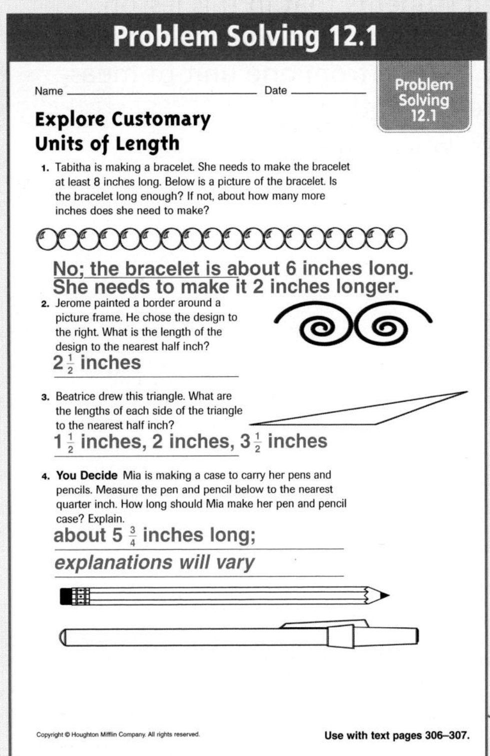

Name ______ Date ______ Problem Solving 12.1

Explore Customary Units of Length

1. Tabitha is making a bracelet. She needs to make the bracelet at least 8 inches long. Below is a picture of the bracelet. Is the bracelet long enough? If not, about how many more inches does she need to make?
No; the bracelet is about 6 inches long. She needs to make it 2 inches longer.
2. Jerome painted a border around a picture frame. He chose the design to the right. What is the length of the design to the nearest half inch?
$2\frac{1}{2}$ inches
3. Beatrice drew this triangle. What are the lengths of each side of the triangle to the nearest half inch?
$1\frac{1}{2}$ inches, 2 inches, $3\frac{1}{2}$ inches
4. **You Decide** Mia is making a case to carry her pens and pencils. Measure the pen and pencil below to the nearest quarter inch. How long should Mia make her pen and pencil case? Explain.
about $5\frac{3}{4}$ inches long;
explanations will vary

 Use with text pages 306–307.

Homework 12.1 Page 74

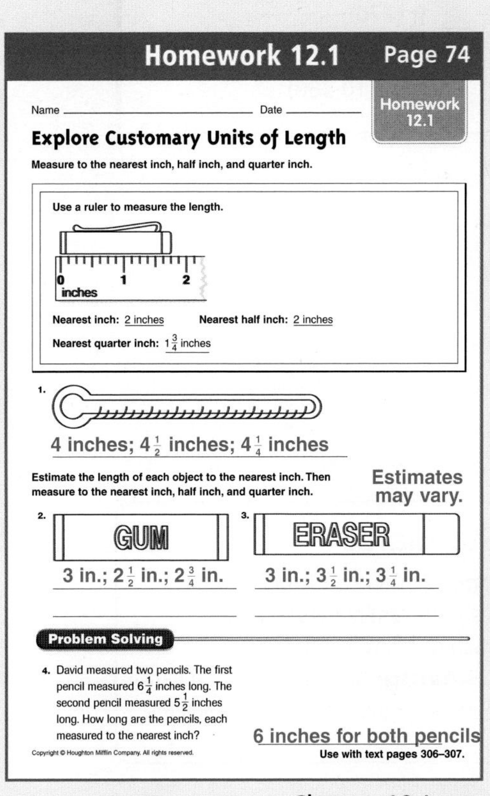

Name ______ Date ______ Homework 12.1

Explore Customary Units of Length

Measure to the nearest inch, half inch, and quarter inch.

Use a ruler to measure the length.

0 1 2 inches

Nearest inch: 2 inches Nearest half inch: 2 inches
Nearest quarter inch: $1\frac{3}{4}$ inches

1. 4 inches; $4\frac{1}{2}$ inches; $4\frac{1}{4}$ inches

Estimate the length of each object to the nearest inch. Then measure to the nearest inch, half inch, and quarter inch. Estimates may vary.

2. GUM
3 in.; $2\frac{1}{2}$ in.; $2\frac{3}{4}$ in.
3. ERASER
3 in.; $3\frac{1}{2}$ in.; $3\frac{1}{4}$ in.

Problem Solving

4. David measured two pencils. The first pencil measured $6\frac{1}{4}$ inches long. The second pencil measured $5\frac{1}{2}$ inches long. How long are the pencils, each measured to the nearest inch?
6 inches for both pencils

 Use with text pages 306–307.

Lesson 12.2

Inch, Foot, Yard, Mile

Planning

Lesson Objective Change units of length.

Technology Resources

- Audio Tutor **2**/1 Listen and Understand
- *Ways to Success* CD-ROM 12.2
- Education Place: Extra Practice, eGames www.eduplace.com/map

Lesson 12.2 Transparency

Problem of the Day

Kyle has a 2-foot-long fruit roll. He wants to divide it equally among himself and 2 friends. How long should each piece be? (8 in.)

Spiral Review

Estimate, then measure, the length of each item to the nearest inch, half inch, and quarter inch. (Answers will vary.)

1. pencil
2. paper clip
3. drinking straw
4. crayon
5. stapler

Lesson Quiz

Find each missing number.

1. 6 ft = ___ in. (72)
2. 42 ft = ___ yd (14)
3. 90 yd = ___ ft (270)
4. 3 yd = ___ in. (108)
5. 2 mi = ______ ft (10,560)

NCTM Standards

Measurement: Carry out simple conversions, such as from centimeters to meters, within a system of measurement.
Problem Solving: Apply and adapt a variety of appropriate strategies to solve problems.

Getting Started

Building Math Vocabulary

You may wish to review these words with students.

foot (ft) a customary unit of length; 12 inches = 1 foot
yard (yd) a customary unit of length; 1 yard = 3 feet
mile (mi) a customary unit of length; 1 mile = 5,280 feet

Measuring Height

Whole Class	5 minutes
Objective	Change units of length.
Materials	Tape measure, ruler, yardstick
Visual, Kinesthetic	

- **How tall are you?** Invite students who know their heights to share this data. Write the heights on the board.
- Invite some volunteers to find their heights in inches. **Which is more: 4 feet or 48 inches?** (the same) **How can they be the same?** (same length described using different units)
- Tell students that in this lesson, they will learn to multiply or divide to change from one unit of measure to another.

Differentiated Instruction

English Learners

Small Groups	10 minutes
Objective	Change units of length.
Materials	Student page 308, index cards
Auditory, Visual	

Early Production

- Students may need additional practice with units of length.
- Have students copy the customary units of length from Student page 308 on an index card and practice saying them.
- Have students measure items in the room in yards, feet, or inches and convert each measurement into the other units.

Intermediate/Advanced

- English Learner Resource 12.2
- English Learner Handbook

Intervention

Small Groups	5–10 minutes
Objective	Change units of length.
Materials	Rulers, yardsticks, tape measures
Tactual, Kinesthetic	

- Students can benefit from more hands-on measuring experience to have a better understanding of unit conversions.
- Have students find classroom and schoolyard lengths to the nearest yard. Then have them change those measurements into feet, and then into inches.
- Then have them reverse the process, finding measures in inches and changing them to feet and/or yards.

Other Resources

- *Ways to Success* CD-ROM 12.2

Gifted & Talented

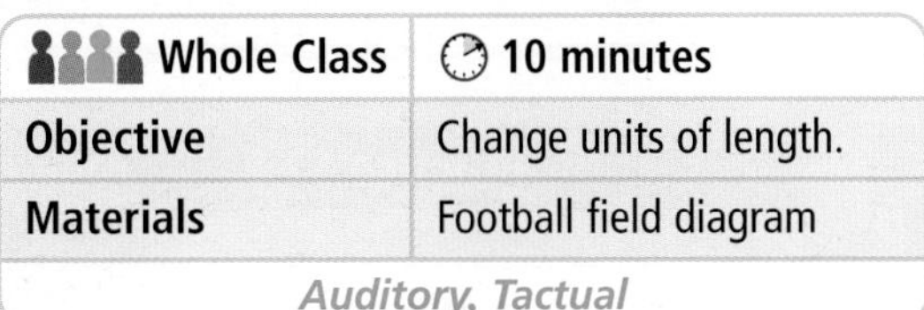

Whole Class	10 minutes
Objective	Change units of length.
Materials	Football field diagram
Auditory, Tactual	

- Tell students that an official NFL football field is 120 yd long. The main field is 100 yd, with a 10-yd end zone at each end. It is 160 ft wide.
- Have students convert each measure into inches and into feet or yards. (120 yd = 360 ft or 4,320 in.; 160 ft = 53 yd 1 ft or 1,920 in.)

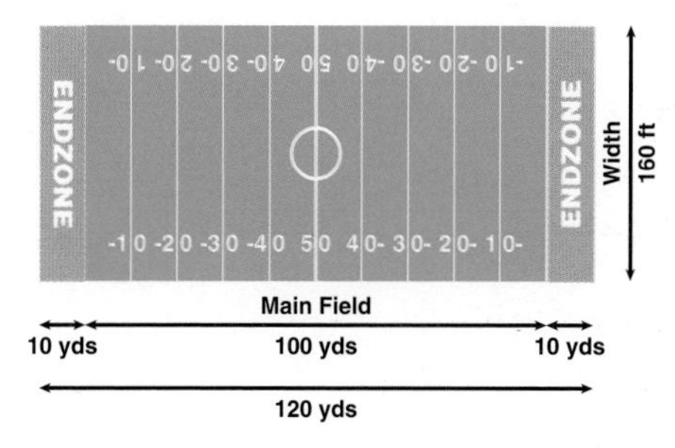

Literature Connection

Materials: *The Biggest, Smallest, Fastest, Tallest Things You've Ever Heard Of* by Robert Lopshire

- Read all or part of Robert Lopshire's book about things of amazing sizes.
- Have students choose some of the given measurements and change them to related units using the skills they learned in this lesson.

❶ Introduce

Read the objective, *change units of length*, to the students and tell them that in this lesson they will convert among customary units of length (inches, feet, yards, miles).

❷ Teach

Learn About It

- Have students read the opening problem. **What unit is given?** (feet) **What must we change to?** (inches, yards)
- **Why is going from feet to inches a change of larger units to smaller ones?** (Feet are made up of inches.) **What operation do we use?** (multiplication) **What do we multiply?** (9×12) **Now let's change from feet to yards. Why is this a change from smaller units to larger ones?** (Feet make up yards.) **What operation is used?** (division) **What do we divide?** ($9 \div 3$)

Guided Practice

Have students complete **Exercises 1–4** as you observe. Remind them to use the *Ask Yourself* questions to help. Give students the opportunity to talk about the question in *Explain Your Thinking*.

Common Error

- **Using the wrong operation** The hardest part of converting units of measure is deciding whether to multiply or divide.
- **Intervention:** Have students compare the given units from left to right. Have them draw an inequality symbol to show whether they go from smaller to larger (<) or larger to smaller (>). Once students decide this, they will know whether to multiply (>) or divide (<). Guide them to consult the equivalency chart to determine what number to multiply or divide by.

Lesson 2

Audio Tutor 2/1 Listen and Understand

Inch, Foot, Yard, Mile

Objective Change units of length.

Learn About It

The fourth grade planted flowers in the school courtyard. The length of the flower bed is 9 feet. What is the length in inches? in yards?

Inch, foot, yard, and mile are customary units of measure.

Change Feet to Inches

When you change from larger units to smaller units, the number of units increases. So multiply.

Multiply by the number of inches in 1 foot.

$$9 \times 12 = 108$$

9	×	12	=	108
number of feet		inches in foot		inches in 9 feet

Customary Units of Length

1 foot (ft)	=	12 inches (in.)
1 yard (yd)	=	3 feet
1 yard (yd)	=	36 inches
1 mile (mi)	=	1,760 yards
1 mile (mi)	=	5,280 feet

Change Feet to Yards

When you change from smaller units to larger units, the number of units decreases. So divide.

Divide by the number of feet in 1 yard.

$$9 \div 3 = 3$$

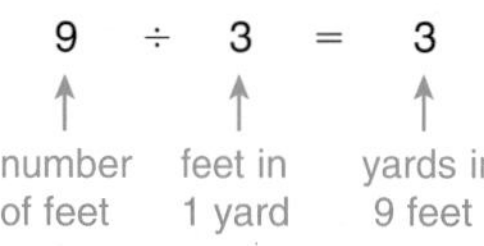

9	÷	3	=	3
number of feet		feet in 1 yard		yards in 9 feet

Solution: The length of the flower bed is 108 inches, or 3 yards.

Other Examples

A. Miles to Yards

2 miles = ____ yards

$2 \times 1,760 = 3,520$

2 miles = 3,520 yards.

Think: Miles are larger than yards, so multiply.

B. Feet to Yards

144 feet = ____ yards

$144 \div 3 = 48$

144 feet = 48 yards.

Think: Feet are smaller than yards, so divide.

308

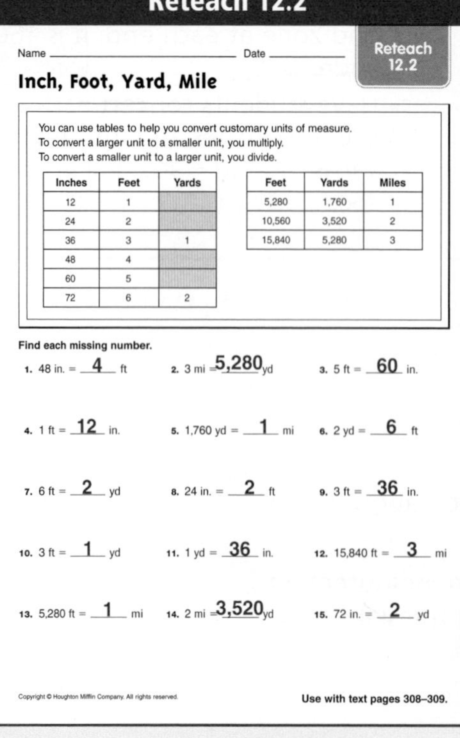

Reteach 12.2

Name ____________ Date ________ Reteach 12.2

Inch, Foot, Yard, Mile

You can use tables to help you convert customary units of measure.
To convert a larger unit to a smaller unit, you multiply.
To convert a smaller unit to a larger unit, you divide.

Inches	Feet	Yards
12	1	
24	2	
36	3	1
48	4	
60	5	
72	6	2

Feet	Yards	Miles
5,280	1,760	1
10,560	3,520	2
15,840	5,280	3

Find each missing number.

1. 48 in. = 4 ft
2. 3 mi = 5,280 yd
3. 5 ft = 60 in.
4. 1 ft = 12 in.
5. 1,760 yd = 1 mi
6. 2 yd = 6 ft
7. 6 ft = 2 yd
8. 24 in. = 2 ft
9. 3 ft = 36 in.
10. 3 ft = 1 yd
11. 1 yd = 36 in.
12. 15,840 ft = 3 mi
13. 5,280 ft = 1 mi
14. 2 mi = 3,520 yd
15. 72 in. = 2 yd

Use with text pages 308–309.

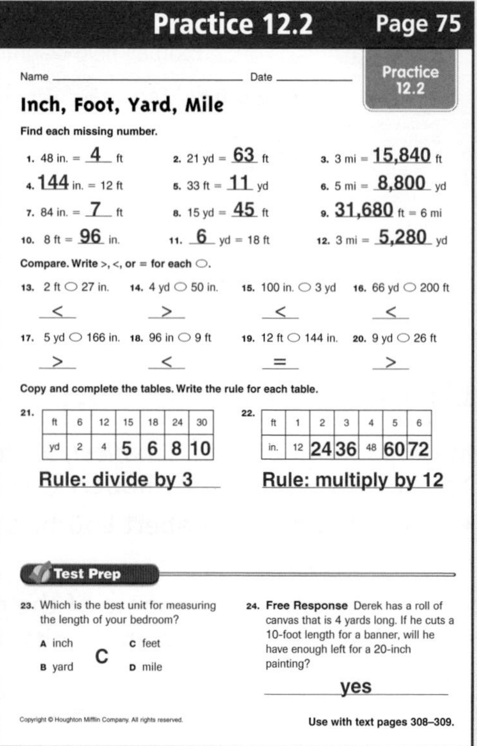

Practice 12.2 Page 75

Name ____________ Date ________ Practice 12.2

Inch, Foot, Yard, Mile

Find each missing number.

1. 48 in. = 4 ft
2. 21 yd = 63 ft
3. 3 mi = 15,840 ft
4. 144 in. = 12 ft
5. 33 ft = 11 yd
6. 5 mi = 8,800 yd
7. 84 in. = 7 ft
8. 15 yd = 45 ft
9. 31,680 ft = 6 mi
10. 8 ft = 96 in.
11. 6 yd = 18 ft
12. 3 mi = 5,280 yd

Compare. Write >, <, or = for each ◯.

13. 2 ft ◯ 27 in. <
14. 4 yd ◯ 50 in. >
15. 100 in. ◯ 3 yd <
16. 66 yd ◯ 200 ft <
17. 5 yd ◯ 166 in. >
18. 96 in ◯ 9 ft <
19. 12 ft ◯ 144 in. =
20. 9 yd ◯ 26 ft >

Copy and complete the tables. Write the rule for each table.

21.

ft	6	12	15	18	24	30
yd	2	4	5	6	8	10

Rule: divide by 3

22.

ft	1	2	3	4	5	6
in.	12	24	36	48	60	72

Rule: multiply by 12

Test Prep

23. Which is the best unit for measuring the length of your bedroom?
   A inch
   B yard
   C feet
   D mile

   C

24. **Free Response** Derek has a roll of canvas that is 4 yards long. If he cuts a 10-foot length for a banner, will he have enough left for a 20-inch painting?

   yes

Use with text pages 308–309.

Guided Practice

Find each missing number.

1. 72 ft = 24 yd
2. 72 in. = 6 ft
3. 2 mi = 10,560 ft
4. 4 yd = 144 in.

Ask Yourself

- Am I converting to a larger or smaller unit?
- Should I multiply or divide?

Explain Your Thinking ▶ What unit of measure would you use to measure the length of your classroom?
Possible answers: yards or feet

Practice and Problem Solving

Find each missing number.

5. 72 yd = ____ ft 216
6. 5 ft = ____ in. 60
7. 10 yd = ____ ft 30
8. 4 mi = ____ ft 21,120
9. ____ yd = 3 mi 5,280
10. 21 ft = ____ yd 7

Compare. Write >, <, or = for each ⬭.

11. 3 ft ⬭ 36 in. =
12. 2 yd ⬭ 60 in. >
13. 5,280 yd ⬭ 2 mi >
14. 4 yd ⬭ 108 in. >
15. 5 ft ⬭ 60 in. =
16. 7 yd ⬭ 28 ft <

Copy and complete the tables. Write the rule for each table.

17. multiply by 12

ft	2	3	5	8	9	12
in.	24	36	■ 60	■ 96	■ 108	■ 144

18. divide by 3

ft	3	6	9	12	15	30
yd	1	■ 2	3	■ 4	■ 5	■ 10

Solve.

19. Alicia has a board that is 2 yards long. She cuts a 4-foot length for a fence. How long is the remaining piece? 2 ft

20. Seth estimates the length of his garden to be 20 feet. Sarah estimates it to be 7 yards. If the actual length is 19 feet, which is the better estimate? *See above.*

20. *Possible answer:* Seth's estimate. 7 yds = 21 ft; 20 ft is closer than 21 ft to 19 ft; so Seth's estimate is better.

Mixed Review and Test Prep

Open Response

Solve. (Ch. 4, Lesson 5)

21. 35 ÷ 7 5
22. 8 × 9 72
23. 56 ÷ 8 7
24. 90 ÷ 10 9
25. 6 × 7 42
26. 9 × 5 45
27. 54 ÷ 9 6
28. 8 × 7 56
29. 64 ÷ 8 8

Multiple Choice

30. Which is the best unit for measuring the distance from New York to Chicago?
(Ch. 12, Lesson 2)
A inch
B foot
C yard
(D) mile

Extra Practice See page 331, Set A.

3 Practice

Practice and Problem Solving

Select from **Exercises 5–30** as independent work.

Problem Solving for Problem 19 Before students try to solve this problem, have them identify the two units of measure they must consider. (yards and feet)

4 Assess & Close

123 Math Talk in Action

Review **Exercises 5–16** to conclude the lesson.

- **How do you know whether to multiply or divide to change between units?** (Multiply to change from a larger unit to a smaller one; divide to change from a smaller unit to a larger one.)
- **What else must you know to make the change?** (how many inches in a foot, feet in a mile, etc.)

Math Journal Prompt

Have students restate the customary measurement relationships of this lesson and suggest a way to remember each one.

Lesson Quiz

Use the quiz on Lesson Transparency 12.2.

Lesson 12.2 Transparency

Test Prep & Spiral Review

Use Test Prep Transparency 12.2.

Test Prep 12.2 Transparency

Enrichment 12.2

Name ____________ Date ________ Enrichment 12.2

What's My Measurement?

You have been hired by the Measurement Department of Detective Math Industries. Your job is to find the measurements of each of the items below. For some of the items, you may have to use a measuring device like a ruler, a yard stick, or a tape measure. For others you may need to do a little research. Look through books or search the Web for the information. Make sure you record the measurement in all the four different units if possible. Then continue the list by choosing two other items.

Item	Inches	Feet	Yards	Miles
the width of your hand	Answers may vary.			
your height	Answers may vary.			
the length of your foot	Answers may vary.			
the width of the room	Answers may vary.			
the average depth of the Atlantic Ocean	140,760	11,730	3,910	about 2 miles
the height of the Statue of Liberty	1,812	151	about 50	less than 1
the length of the Amazon River	over 252 million inches	over 21 million	about 7 million	about 4,000
the height of Mount Everest	348,420	29,035	about 9,678	about 5 miles

Use with text pages 308–309.

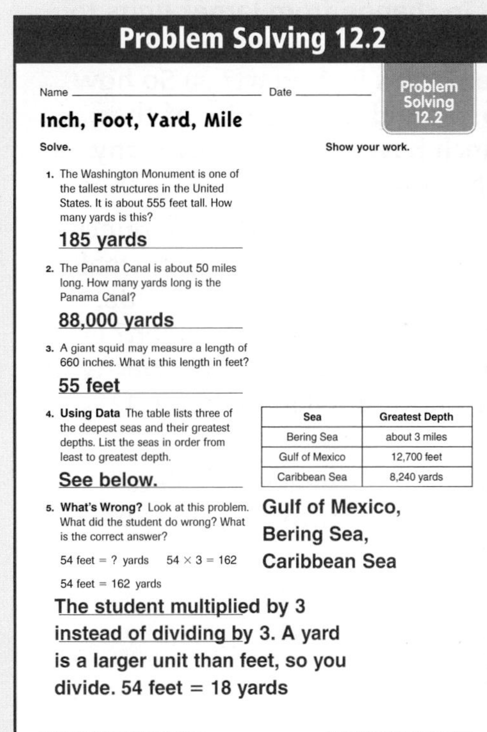

Problem Solving 12.2

Name ____________ Date ________ Problem Solving 12.2

Inch, Foot, Yard, Mile

Solve. Show your work.

1. The Washington Monument is one of the tallest structures in the United States. It is about 555 feet tall. How many yards is this? 185 yards
2. The Panama Canal is about 50 miles long. How many yards long is the Panama Canal? 88,000 yards
3. A giant squid may measure a length of 660 inches. What is this length in feet? 55 feet
4. **Using Data** The table lists three of the deepest seas and their greatest depths. List the seas in order from least to greatest depth. See below.

Sea	Greatest Depth
Bering Sea	about 3 miles
Gulf of Mexico	12,700 feet
Caribbean Sea	8,240 yards

Gulf of Mexico, Bering Sea, Caribbean Sea

5. **What's Wrong?** Look at this problem. What did the student do wrong? What is the correct answer?
54 feet = ? yards   54 × 3 = 162
54 feet = 162 yards
The student multiplied by 3 instead of dividing by 3. A yard is a larger unit than feet, so you divide. 54 feet = 18 yards

Use with text pages 308–309.

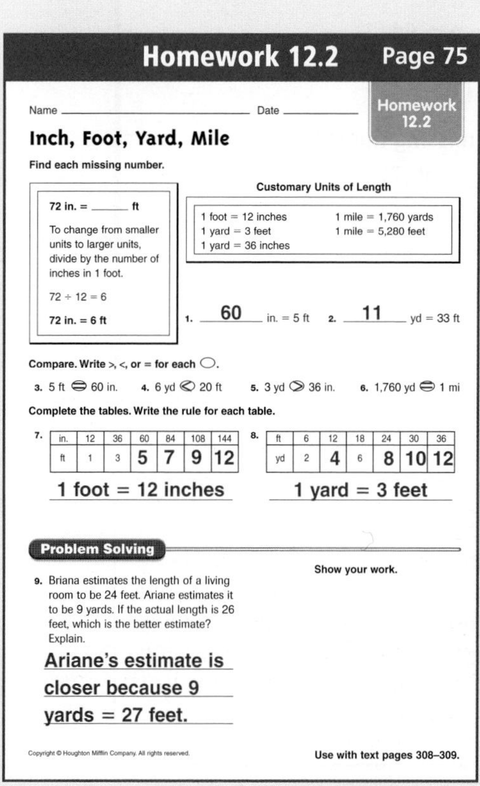

Homework 12.2 Page 75

Name ____________ Date ________ Homework 12.2

Inch, Foot, Yard, Mile

Find each missing number.

72 in. = ____ ft
To change from smaller units to larger units, divide by the number of inches in 1 foot.
72 ÷ 12 = 6
72 in. = 6 ft

Customary Units of Length

1 foot = 12 inches
1 yard = 3 feet
1 yard = 36 inches
1 mile = 1,760 yards
1 mile = 5,280 feet

1. 60 in. = 5 ft
2. 11 yd = 33 ft

Compare. Write >, <, or = for each ◯.

3. 5 ft = 60 in.
4. 6 yd < 20 ft
5. 3 yd > 36 in.
6. 1,760 yd = 1 mi

Complete the tables. Write the rule for each table.

7.

in.	12	36	60	84	108	144
ft	1	3	5	7	9	12

1 foot = 12 inches

8.

ft	6	12	18	24	30	36
yd	2	4	6	8	10	12

1 yard = 3 feet

Problem Solving

Show your work.

9. Briana estimates the length of a living room to be 24 feet. Ariane estimates it to be 9 yards. If the actual length is 26 feet, which is the better estimate? Explain.
Ariane's estimate is closer because 9 yards = 27 feet.

Use with text pages 308–309.

Lesson 12.3

Customary Units of Capacity

Planning

Lesson Objective Change units of capacity.

Math Background

The gallon was a traditional unit of liquid volume, derived from the Roman *galeta*, which meant "a pail-full". Gallons have been used since Roman times.

Technology Resources

- *Ways to Success* CD-ROM 12.3
- Education Place: Extra Practice, eGames www.eduplace.com/map

Lesson 12.3 Transparency

Problem of the Day

Amy is draining a 30-gallon fish tank so she can clean it. If the water drains at a rate of 1 pint per second, how long will it take to empty the tank?
(240 seconds, or 4 minutes)

Spiral Review

Solve for *n*.

1. $48 \div 4 = n$ (12)
2. $5 \times n = 80$ (16)
3. $320 \div 8 = n$ (40)
4. $n \div 6 = 8$ (48)
5. $8 \times 4 \times n = 64$ (2)

Lesson Quiz

Find each missing number.

1. 28 c = ___ qt (7)
2. ___ c = 7 pt (14)
3. 24 qt = ___ gal (6)
4. ___ gal = 40 qt (10)
5. 18 pt = ___ qt (9)

NCTM Standards

Measurement: Understand measurable attributes of objects and the units, systems, and processes of measurement; understand the need for measuring with standard units and become familiar with standard units in the customary and metric systems.

Getting Started

Building Math Vocabulary

You may wish to review these words with students.

gallon	customary unit of capacity: 1 gallon = 4 quarts
quart	customary unit of capacity: 1 quart = 2 pints
pint	customary unit of capacity: 1 pint = 2 cups
cup	customary unit of capacity: 2 cups = 1 pint
capacity	the amount a container can hold

Measuring Capacity

Whole Class	**10 minutes**
Objective	Change units of capacity.
Materials	Cup, quart, and gallon containers, blank transparency
	Visual, Auditory

- Write 1 quart = 4 cups and 1 gallon = 4 quarts on the transparency. Say: **Capacity is how much a container can hold. A punch bowl holds 12 quarts. Let's find out how many cups of punch this is.**
- **Which is larger, 1 quart or 1 cup?** (1 qt) **To change from larger units to smaller units, we multiply. How many cups in 1 quart?** (4) **So how do we find the capacity of the punch bowl?** (12 × 4) **How many cups of punch is this?** (48 cups)
- **How many gallons can the punch bowl hold? To change from smaller units to larger units, we divide. How many quarts in 1 gallon?** (4) **So how can we find the capacity of the punch bowl in gallons?** (12 quarts ÷ 4 = 3 gallons)
- Explain that the lesson will tell more about customary units of capacity.

Punch bowl holds 12 quarts or 48 cups

Differentiated Instruction

English Learners

Small Groups	10 minutes
Objective	Change units of capacity.
Materials	Student page 310, index cards
Auditory, Visual	

Early Production

- Provide additional practice with units of capacity.
- Have students copy the Customary Units of Capacity from the chart on Student page 310 on an index card and practice saying them.

Write three amounts on the board and ask students to find the measurements in cups, pints, and quarts.

Intermediate/Advanced

- English Learner Resource 12.3
- English Learner Handbook

Intervention

Small Groups	5–10 minutes
Objective	Change units of capacity.
Materials	Containers with labels
Visual, Tactual	

- One way to help students recall relationships among units of capacity is to relate them to a smaller unit common to them all: the *fluid ounce (oz)*. The lesson doesn't include the fluid ounce, but it appears on many labels students see.
- Have students examine container labels to find the equivalent measure in fluid ounces for cups, pints, quarts, and gallons. (8, 16, 32, 128)

Other Resources

- *Ways to Success* CD-ROM 12.3

Special Needs

Small Groups	10 minutes
Objective	Change units of capacity.
Materials	Containers (1c, 1 pt, 1 qt, 1 gal), tape, sand
Visual, Tactual	

- Have students label each container by writing each unit of measure on tape.
- Have students use one container to fill another with sand, counting and recording what they do.
- Let students use the containers to help them solve the problems on page 311.

Science Connection

Materials: 1 clear gallon jar, measuring cup, water, red food coloring, spoon

Make a solution and then dilute it with water.

- Pour 1 cup of water into the gallon jar. Add 2 drops of red food coloring. Stir. The water will look pink.
- Now add clean water, 1 cup at a time, to the gallon jar. Describe what happens to the color of the solution after each cup of water is added.

Facts Practice

Give students a recipe for making punch for their birthday party. Ask students to rewrite the recipe in terms of pints, cups, quarts, and gallons.

1 Introduce

Read ... units of capacity, to the class and tell them that in this lesson they will convert among customary units of capacity using cups, pints, quarts, and gallons. They will also learn to choose the appropriate measure of capacity.

2 Teach

Learn About It

- Have students read the opening problem. **Why is going from quarts to cups a change from larger units to smaller ones?** (1 qt = 4 c) **What operation do we use?** (multiplication) **What do we multiply?** (8 × 4) **Now let's change from quarts to gallons. Why is this a change from smaller units to larger?** (4 qt = 1 gal) **What operation is used?** (division) **What do we divide?** (8 ÷ 4)
- **Look at the *Other Examples* from left to right. How do cups and pints compare?** (c < pt) **How do gallons and pints compare?** (gal > pt)

Guided Practice

Have students complete **Exercises 1–4** as you observe. Remind them to use the ***Ask Yourself*** questions to help. Give students the opportunity to talk about the question in ***Explain Your Thinking***.

Common Error

- **Using the wrong operation** Students may be unsure whether to multiply or divide.
- **Intervention:** Have them compare the given units from left to right, writing an inequality symbol to show whether they go from smaller to larger (<) or from larger to smaller (>). After determining this, students can consult the equivalency chart to check what number to multiply by (>) or divide by (<).

Lesson 3

Customary Units of Capacity

Objective Change units of capacity.

Learn About It

Angela's watering can holds 8 quarts of water. How many cups is that? how many gallons?

Gallons, quarts, pints, and cups all measure capacity, the amount a container can hold.

Change Quarts to Cups

When you change from larger units to smaller units, the number of units increases. So multiply.

Multiply by the number of cups in 1 quart.

8 × 4 = 32

↑ number of quarts ↑ cups in 1 quart ↑ cups in 8 quarts

Customary Units of Capacity		
1 pint (pt)	=	2 cups (c)
1 quart (qt)	=	2 pints
1 quart (qt)	=	4 cups
1 gallon (gal)	=	4 quarts
1 gallon (gal)	=	8 pints
1 gallon (gal)	=	16 cups

Change Quarts to Gallons

When you change from smaller units to larger units, the number of units decreases. So divide.

Divide by the number of quarts in 1 gallon.

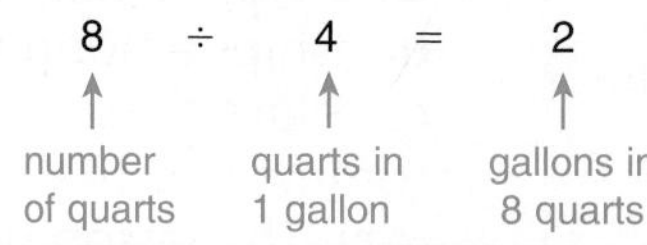

Solution: The watering can holds 32 cups, or 2 gallons, of water.

Other Examples

A. Cups to Pints

10 cups = ____ pints

10 ÷ 2 = 5

10 cups = 5 pints

Think: Cups are smaller than pints, so divide.

B. Gallons to Pints

3 gallons = ____ pints

3 × 8 = 24

3 gallons = 24 pints

Think: Gallons are larger than pints, so multiply.

Reteach 12.3

Name ____________ Date ________ Reteach 12.3

Customary Units of Capacity

Find the missing number.

8 qt = ______ pt

Think: When changing from larger units to smaller units, the number of units increases. So multiply.

8 × 2 = 16

↑ 2 pints = 1 quart

The missing number is 16.
8 quarts = 16 pints.

Find the missing number.

12 quarts = ______ gallons

Think: When changing from smaller units to larger units, the number of units decreases. So divide.

12 ÷ 4 = 3

↑ 4 quarts = 1 gallon

The missing number is 3.
12 quarts = 3 gallons.

Find each missing number.

1. 2 qt = 8 c
2. 4 gal = 16 qt
3. 2 gal = 16 pt
4. 48 c = 3 gal
5. 7 gal = 56 pt
6. 4 gal = 32 pt
7. 3 qt = 12 c
8. 2 gal = 8 qt
9. 12 c = 3 qt
10. 5 gal = 20 qt
11. 10 qt = 20 pt
12. 16 c = 4 qt
13. 15 pt = 30 c
14. 10 gal = 40 qt
15. 18 pt = 9 qt

Use with text pages 310–311.

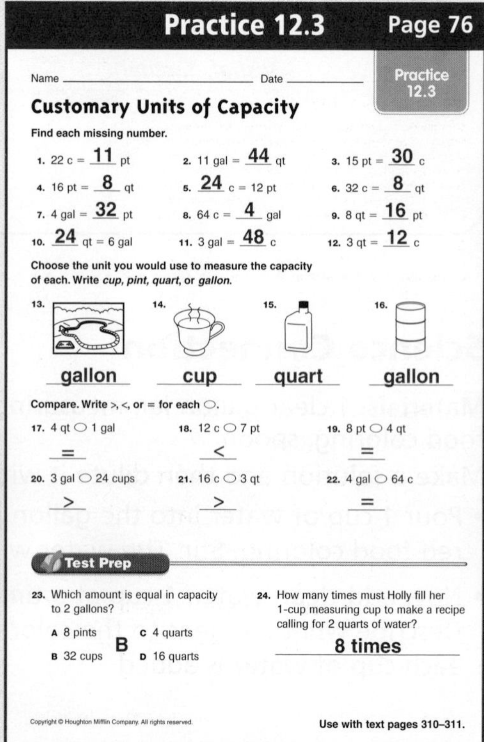

Practice 12.3 Page 76

Name ____________ Date ________ Practice 12.3

Customary Units of Capacity

Find each missing number.

1. 22 c = 11 pt
2. 11 gal = 44 qt
3. 15 pt = 30 c
4. 16 pt = 8 qt
5. 24 c = 12 pt
6. 32 c = 8 qt
7. 4 gal = 32 pt
8. 64 c = 4 gal
9. 8 qt = 16 pt
10. 24 qt = 6 gal
11. 3 gal = 48 c
12. 3 qt = 12 c

Choose the unit you would use to measure the capacity of each. Write *cup, pint, quart,* or *gallon.*

13. gallon
14. cup
15. quart
16. gallon

Compare. Write >, <, or = for each ○.

17. 4 qt ○ 1 gal =
18. 12 c ○ 7 pt <
19. 8 pt ○ 4 qt =
20. 3 gal ○ 24 cups >
21. 16 c ○ 3 qt >
22. 4 gal ○ 64 c =

Test Prep

23. Which amount is equal in capacity to 2 gallons?
A 8 pints
B 32 cups
C 4 quarts
D 16 quarts
B

24. How many times must Holly fill her 1-cup measuring cup to make a recipe calling for 2 quarts of water?
8 times

Use with text pages 310–311.

Guided Practice

Find each missing number.

1. 8 c = __4__ pt
2. __20__ qt = 5 gal
3. 16 pt = __8__ qt
4. 2 qt = __8__ c

Ask Yourself

- Am I converting to a larger or smaller unit?
- Should I multiply or divide?

Explain Your Thinking ▶ Describe how you found the missing number in Exercise 2. ***Possible answer:*** **To change from a larger unit to a smaller unit, multiply. There are 4 qt in 1 gal. In 5 gal there are 5 × 4, or 20 qt.**

Practice and Problem Solving

Find each missing number.

5. 14 c = __7__ pt
6. 8 gal = __32__ qt
7. 9 pt = __18__ c
8. __5__ qt = 10 pt
9. 4 pt = __2__ qt
10. 16 c = __4__ qt

Choose the unit you would use to measure the capacity of each item. Write *cup, pint, quart,* or *gallon.*

11.  **cup or pint**

12.  **gallon**

13.  **quart**

14.  **gallon**

Compare. Write >, <, or = for each ●.

15. 4 pt ● 6 c **>**
16. 8 gal ● 30 qt **>**
17. 13 pt ● 8 qt **<**
18. 16 c ● 8 qt **<**
19. 16 pt ● 4 gal **<**
20. 2 qt ● 4 c **>**

21. **Explain** Which is the better buy, 4 quarts of plant food for $5.00 or one half gallon for $3.00? Explain how you got your answer. **4 quarts for $5; *See Additional Answers.***

22. Jane has 5 cups of water. Al has 3 pints and Bert has 1 quart of water. List amounts in order from least to greatest. **1 quart < 5 cups < 3 pints**

Mixed Review and Test Prep

Open Response

Round each number to the nearest hundred. Then estimate. (Ch. 3, Lesson 3)

23. 5,321 − 2,192 **3,100**
24. 2,896 + 1,419 **4,300**
25. 7,099 − 3,299 **3,800**
26. 4,650 + 4,506 **9,200**

27. How many times must Taylor fill his 1-pint measuring cup to make a recipe calling for $\frac{1}{2}$ gallon of water? Explain how you got your answer. (Ch. 12, Lesson 3) **4 times; *See Additional Answers.***

Extra Practice See page 331, Set B.

3 Practice

Practice and Problem Solving

Select from **Exercises 5–27** as independent work.

Problem Solving for Problem 21 As needed, explain that "better buy" means the item with the lower price for the same quantity and quality.

4 Assess & Close

Math Talk in Action

Have students share answers to **Exercises 5–22** to conclude the lesson.

- **How do you know whether to multiply or divide to change units?** (Multiply to change from a larger unit to a smaller one; divide to change from a smaller unit to a larger one.)
- **What else must you know to make the change?** (how many cups in a quart, pints in a gallon, etc.)

Math Journal Prompt

Have students restate the customary capacity measures given in this lesson and suggest a way to remember each one.

Lesson Quiz

Use the quiz on Lesson Transparency 12.3.

Test Prep & Spiral Review

Use Test Prep Transparency 12.3.

Enrichment 12.3

Name ______ Date ______ Enrichment 12.3

Matching Capacity

Copy the game cards below and cut them out. Mix the cards and place them face down. Choose two cards and turn them over. Decide if the two cards show the same capacity. If they do, set the pair to the side. If the values do not match, turn the cards face down again. The game continues until all cards are matched. If there are two or more players, the winner is the player with the most matching pairs. ***Check student's matches.***

1 gallon	4 quarts	1 pint	2 cups
1 quart	2 pints	3 pints	6 cups
5 quarts	10 pints	2 quarts	8 cups
2 gallons	16 pints	3 gallons	48 cups
6 pints	3 quarts	5 pints	10 cups
1 quart	4 cups	1 gallon	8 pints

Use with text pages 310–311.

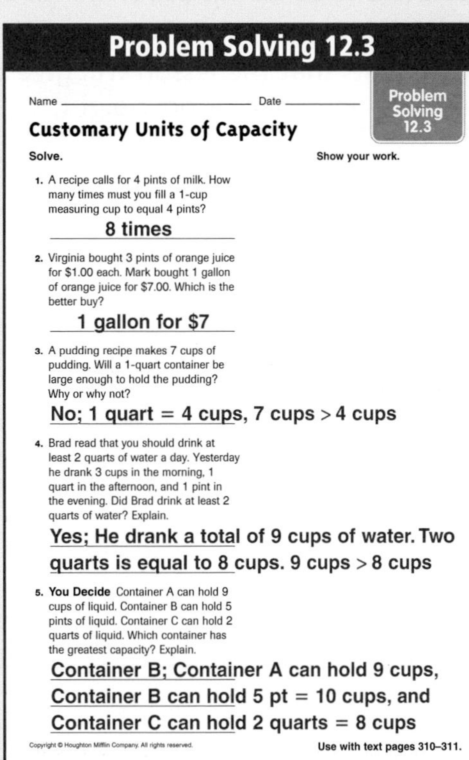

Problem Solving 12.3

Name ______ Date ______ Problem Solving 12.3

Customary Units of Capacity

Solve. Show your work.

1. A recipe calls for 4 pints of milk. How many times must you fill a 1-cup measuring cup to equal 4 pints? **8 times**
2. Virginia bought 3 pints of orange juice for $1.00 each. Mark bought 1 gallon of orange juice for $7.00. Which is the better buy? **1 gallon for $7**
3. A pudding recipe makes 7 cups of pudding. Will a 1-quart container be large enough to hold the pudding? Why or why not? **No; 1 quart = 4 cups, 7 cups > 4 cups**
4. Brad read that you should drink at least 2 quarts of water a day. Yesterday he drank 3 cups in the morning, 1 quart in the afternoon, and 1 pint in the evening. Did Brad drink at least 2 quarts of water? Explain. **Yes; He drank a total of 9 cups of water. Two quarts is equal to 8 cups. 9 cups > 8 cups**
5. **You Decide** Container A can hold 9 cups of liquid. Container B can hold 5 pints of liquid. Container C can hold 2 quarts of liquid. Which container has the greatest capacity? Explain. **Container B; Container A can hold 9 cups, Container B can hold 5 pt = 10 cups, and Container C can hold 2 quarts = 8 cups**

Use with text pages 310–311.

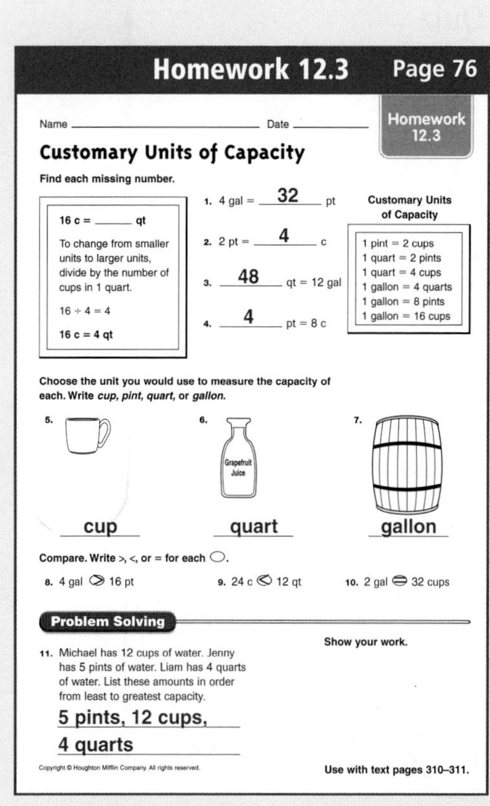

Homework 12.3 Page 76

Name ______ Date ______ Homework 12.3

Customary Units of Capacity

Find each missing number.

16 c = ___ qt

To change from smaller units to larger units, divide by the number of cups in 1 quart.

16 ÷ 4 = 4

16 c = 4 qt

1. 4 gal = __32__ pt
2. 2 pt = __4__ c
3. __48__ qt = 12 gal
4. __4__ pt = 8 c

Customary Units of Capacity

1 pint = 2 cups
1 quart = 2 pints
1 quart = 4 cups
1 gallon = 4 quarts
1 gallon = 8 pints
1 gallon = 16 cups

Choose the unit you would use to measure the capacity of each item. Write *cup, pint, quart,* or *gallon.*

5. **cup**
6. **quart**
7. **gallon**

Compare. Write >, <, or = for each ◯.

8. 4 gal ⊘ 16 pt **>**
9. 24 c ⊘ 12 qt **<**
10. 2 gal ⊜ 32 cups **=**

Problem Solving

Show your work.

11. Michael has 12 cups of water. Jenny has 5 pints of water. Liam has 4 quarts of water. List these amounts in order from least to greatest capacity. **5 pints, 12 cups, 4 quarts**

Use with text pages 310–311.

Hands On Lesson 12.4

Customary Units of Weight

Planning

Lesson Objective Estimate and measure, using customary units of weight.

Technology Resources

- *Ways to Success* CD-ROM 12.4
- Education Place: Extra Practice, eGlossary, eGames, Brain Teasers www.eduplace.com/map

Lesson 12.4 Transparency

Problem of the Day

Saffron is the world's most costly spice. A chef wants to buy a pound of saffron for her restaurant. One dealer sells it at $39 per ounce. Another dealer sells it at $650 per pound. Which is the better buy? Explain. ($39 per ounce; 16 x 39 = $624 is cheaper than $650 for the same quantity)

Spiral Review

Find each missing number.

1. 60 in = ___ ft (5)
2. 2 gal = ___ qt (8)
3. 3 mi = ___ yd (5,280)
4. 24 pt = ___ gal (3)
5. ___ yd = 1 mi (1,760)

Lesson Quiz

Compare. Write >, <, or = for each □.

1. 48 oz □ 3 lb (=)
2. 5 T □ 15,000 lb (<)
3. 64 oz □ 8 lb (<)
4. 1,234 lb □ $\frac{1}{2}$ t (>)
5. 10 lb □ 160 oz (=)

NCTM Standards

Measurement: Understand measurable attributes of objects and the units, systems and processes of measurement; understand the need for measuring with standard units and become familiar with standard units in the customary and metric systems.
Connections: Recognize and use connections among mathematical ideas.

Getting Started

Building Math Vocabulary

ton (T) customary unit of weight: 1 ton = 2,000 pounds

- List customary units of weight and their abbreviations: ounce (oz), pound (lb), ton (T). Ask students where they have seen, heard, or used these units.

Measuring Weight

Whole Class	5 minutes
Objective	Compare customary units of weight.
Materials	Calculator Transparency, blank transparency, calculators for students
Visual, Tactual	

- Write 1 lb = 16 oz and 1 T = 2,000 lb on the transparency. **Which weight is greater, a pound or a ton? A pound or an ounce?** (ton; pound)
- **Suppose a truck weighs 8,000 pounds. Do we multiply or divide to find how many tons this is?** (divide) **By what number?** (2,000) Have students use their calculators to solve this problem. Model and record the solution. (4 T)
- **Suppose a squash weighs 2 lb and we wonder how many ounces this is. What do we do: multiply or divide?** (multiply) **By what number?** (16) Have students use their calculators to solve this problem. Model and record the answer. (32 oz)
- Tell students that the lesson will give them more practice estimating and measuring weight.

Differentiated Instruction

English Learners

Small Groups	10 minutes
Objective	Change units of weight.
Materials	Student page 313, index cards
Auditory, Visual	

Early Production

- Before ***Guided Practice,*** have students practice converting units of weight.
- Ask students to write numbers 1–5 on a piece of paper, with *pound or pounds* next to each number.
- Have students change the measurements to ounces and read each equation aloud.
- Repeat changing tons to pounds.

Intermediate/Advanced

- English Learner Resource 12.4
- English Learner Handbook

Intervention

Whole Class	5 minutes
Objective	Estimate using customary units of weight.
Materials	1-lb box of pasta or rice
Visual, Tactual	

- Ask a volunteer to read the label on the box to find its weight. **How much does the box weigh?** (1 lb) Pass it around to familiarize students with the feel of 1 pound. **What other things are sold by the pound?** (Accept all reasonable answers.)
- **Do you know the smaller unit that makes up a pound?** (ounce) **Do you know the unit we use for very heavy things?** (ton)

Other Resources

- *Ways to Success* CD-ROM 12.4

Inclusion

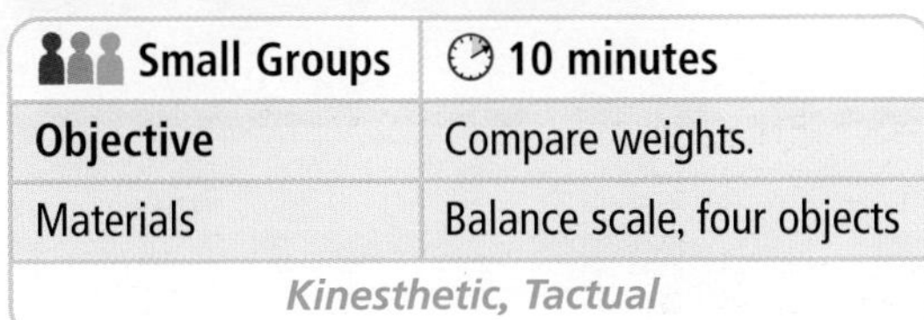

Small Groups	10 minutes
Objective	Compare weights.
Materials	Balance scale, four objects
Kinesthetic, Tactual	

- Give students more practice using a balance scale to explore weight.
- Provide four objects of different weights. Have students pick any two and use the scale to see which is lighter or heavier. Have them repeat for other pairs of objects.

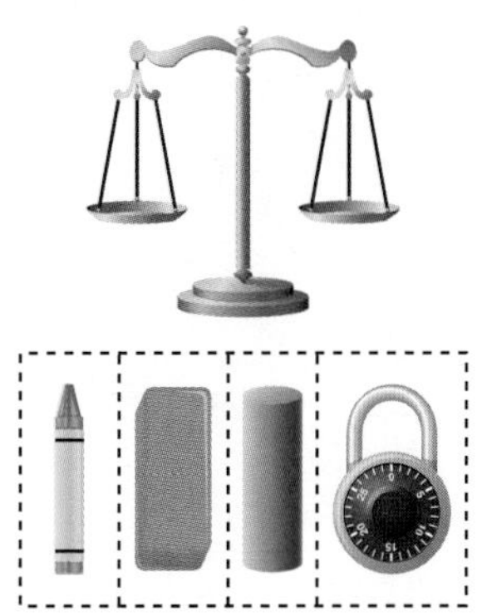

Art Connection

Materials: Modeling clay, balance scale, weights

- Form pairs. Give each student a lump of clay. Have partners decide how to form their clay into a lump that weighs as close to 1 pound as possible.
- Allow pairs to use a scale and weights *after* they make their best guess. Then they can adjust.

❶ Introduce

Read the objective, *estimate and measure using customary units of weight*, to the students and tell them that in this lesson they will use a balance scale to estimate and measure customary units of weight and will convert among customary units of weight (ounces, pounds, tons).

❷ Teach

Learn About It

- **Name the three customary units of weight from lightest to heaviest.** (oz, lb, T)
- Display the balance scale and weights. Let students feel the 1-lb weight. **Look at Step 1. Think about the feel of 1 pound. Now look around for three objects that might weigh about a pound each.** Have students collect and feel objects.
- **Look at Step 2. How do we use the balance scale to check the weight?** (Put an object in one pan and a 1-lb weight in the other pan. If pans balance, the object weighs 1 lb.) **What will the scale look like if the object is heavier than 1 pound?** (The pan holding the object will be lower.) **Do Step 3 on your own.**
- **Look at Step 4. Let's repeat the process, but now look for objects that weigh about 1 ounce.**

Common Error

- **Conversion errors**
- **Intervention:** Demonstrate how multiplication or repeated addition can be used to change a larger or greater unit to a smaller or lesser unit. Then demonstrate how division or repeated subtraction can be used to change a smaller or lesser unit to a larger or greater unit.

Customary Units of Weight

Objective Estimate and measure, using customary units of weight.

Vocabulary
tons

Materials
balance scale
1-pound weight
1-ounce weight

Learn About It

Ounces, pounds, and **tons** are units of weight. They are used to show how heavy an object is.

A strawberry weighs about one ounce.

A bunch of grapes weighs about one pound.

A tractor weighs about one ton.

Try this activity to measure and compare weight.

STEP 1 Find three objects in the classroom that you estimate weigh about one pound.

STEP 2 Weigh each object and record the weight. List the three objects from heaviest to lightest. Which object weighs closest to one pound? ***Answers for steps 2–4 will vary depending on students' choice of objects.***

STEP 3 Use the object closest to one pound to predict what other things in the classroom weigh. Make a list of four things that weigh more than, less than, and about one pound.

STEP 4 Repeat Step 1 and Step 2, looking for four objects in the classroom that weigh about 1 ounce. Which object weighs closest to one ounce?

312

Reteach 12.4

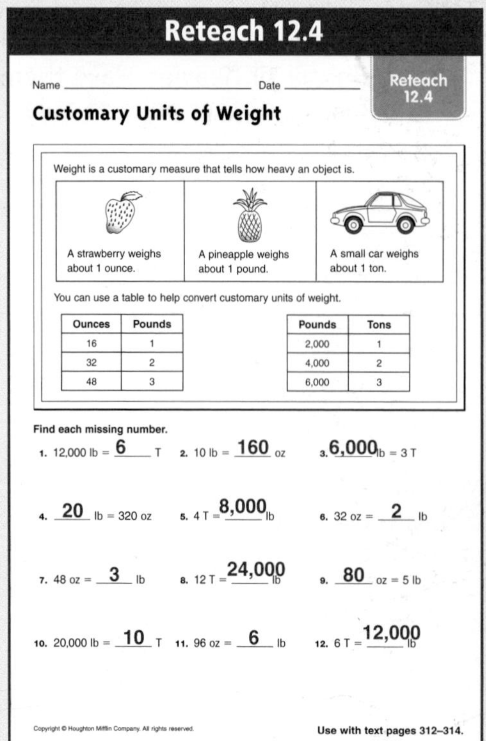

Name ____________ Date ________ Reteach 12.4

Customary Units of Weight

Weight is a customary measure that tells how heavy an object is.

A strawberry weighs about 1 ounce.	A pineapple weighs about 1 pound.	A small car weighs about 1 ton.

You can use a table to help convert customary units of weight.

Ounces	Pounds
16	1
32	2
48	3

Pounds	Tons
2,000	1
4,000	2
6,000	3

Find each missing number.

1. 12,000 lb = **6** T
2. 10 lb = **160** oz
3. **6,000** lb = 3 T
4. **20** lb = 320 oz
5. 4 T = **8,000** lb
6. 32 oz = **2** lb
7. 48 oz = **3** lb
8. 12 T = **24,000** lb
9. **80** oz = 5 lb
10. 20,000 lb = **10** T
11. 96 oz = **6** lb
12. 6 T = **12,000** lb

Use with text pages 312–314.

Practice 12.4 Page 77

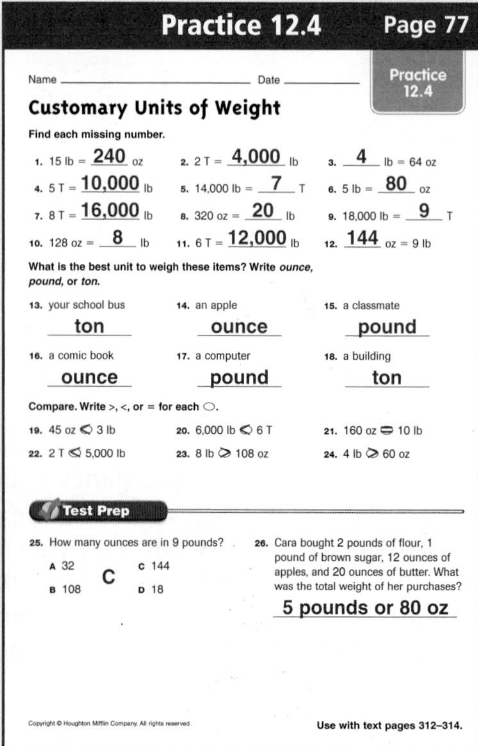

Name ____________ Date ________ Practice 12.4

Customary Units of Weight

Find each missing number.

1. 15 lb = **240** oz
2. 2 T = **4,000** lb
3. **4** lb = 64 oz
4. 5 T = **10,000** lb
5. 14,000 lb = **7** T
6. 5 lb = **80** oz
7. 8 T = **16,000** lb
8. 320 oz = **20** lb
9. 18,000 lb = **9** T
10. 128 oz = **8** lb
11. 6 T = **12,000** lb
12. **144** oz = 9 lb

What is the best unit to weigh these items? Write *ounce*, *pound*, or *ton*.

13. your school bus **ton**
14. an apple **ounce**
15. a classmate **pound**
16. a comic book **ounce**
17. a computer **pound**
18. a building **ton**

Compare. Write >, <, or = for each ○.

19. 45 oz < 3 lb
20. 6,000 lb < 6 T
21. 160 oz = 10 lb
22. 2 T < 5,000 lb
23. 8 lb > 108 oz
24. 4 lb > 60 oz

Test Prep

25. How many ounces are in 9 pounds? **C**
A 32
B 108
C 144
D 18

26. Cara bought 2 pounds of flour, 1 pound of brown sugar, 12 ounces of apples, and 20 ounces of butter. What was the total weight of her purchases? **5 pounds or 80 oz**

Use with text pages 312–314.

▶ Look at the truck. How many tons of watermelons are on it?

Change Pounds to Tons

When you change from smaller units to larger units, the number of units decreases. So divide.

Divide by the number of pounds in 1 ton.

4,000	÷	2,000	=	2
↑ number of pounds		↑ pounds in 1 ton		↑ tons in 4,000 pounds

Customary Units of Weight

1 pound (lb) = 16 ounces (oz)
1 ton (T) = 2,000 pounds

Solution: The truck carries 2 tons of watermelons.

▶ If one watermelon weighs 10 pounds, how many ounces does it weigh?

Change Pounds to Ounces

When you change from larger units to smaller units, the number of units increases. So multiply.

Multiply by the number of ounces in 1 pound.

10	×	16	=	160
↑ number of pounds		↑ ounces in 1 pound		↑ ounces in 10 pounds

Solution: The watermelon weighs 160 ounces.

Guided Practice

Find each missing number.

1. 8,000 lb = __4__ T
2. 5 lb = __80__ oz
3. 112 oz = __7__ lb
4. __6,000__ lb = 3 T

Ask Yourself

- Am I converting to a larger or smaller unit?
- Should I multiply or divide?

Explain Your Thinking ▶ Do small objects always weigh less than large ones? Give examples to support your answer.
No; *Possible example:* A small rock could weigh more than a pillow.

- **What do we know about the total weight of the watermelons?** (The sign says the truck holds 4,000 pounds.) **Is that more or less than 1 ton?** (more) **Why do we divide?** (to find how many groups of 2,000 in 4,000) **What numbers do we use?** (4,000 ÷ 2,000) **How can we use mental math to find the quotient?** (Use the basic fact 4 ÷ 2 = 2.)
- **What does the second problem ask us to find?** (how many ounces in 10 pounds) **How do we find this?** (multiply) **What numbers do we use? Explain.** (10 pounds for a watermelon × 16 ounces in each pound = 160 oz)

Guided Practice

Have students complete **Exercises 1–4** as you observe. Remind them to use the ***Ask Yourself*** questions to help. Give students the opportunity to talk about the question in ***Explain Your Thinking***.

Enrichment 12.4

Name ______ Date ______ Enrichment 12.4

Measure and Move

Start at 64. Solve each of the problems below. Each time you find an answer, move to the space in the circle below that has that answer. Always move in a clockwise direction. Keep track of how many times you go around the circle.

1. Find the number of pounds in 32 ounces. __2__
2. Find the number of pounds in 3 tons. __6,000__
3. Find the number of inches in 1 foot. __12__
4. Find the number of cups in 5 quarts. __20__
5. Find the number of ounces in 4 pounds. __64__
6. Find the number of ounces in 1 pound. __16__
7. Find the number of pints in 3 gallons. __24__
8. Find the number of pounds in 6 tons. __12,000__
9. Find the number of ounces in 1 ton. __32,000__
10. Find the number of ounces in 3 pounds. __48__
11. Find the number of miles in 10,560 feet. __2__
12. How many times did you go around the circle? __4 times__

64, 2, 12,000, 16, 6,000, 12, 48, 24, 20, 32,000

Use with text pages 312–314.

Problem Solving 12.4

Name ______ Date ______ Problem Solving 12.4

Customary Units of Weight

Use what you know about ounces, pounds, and tons to answer each question.

Show your work.

1. The largest monster truck is named "Bigfoot 5" and weighs 19 tons. How many pounds does this truck weigh?
38,000 lb
2. The smallest jet is the Silver Bullet. It was built in 1976 and weighs 437 pounds. How many ounces is this?
6,992 ounces
3. The largest ice cream sundae weighed more than 27 tons and used about 45,000 pounds of ice cream. About how many pounds of syrup and toppings were used on the sundae?
9,000 pounds
4. **Multistep** The most potatoes peeled by five people in 45 minutes was 1,064 pounds 6 ounces. How many total ounces of potatoes is this?
17,030 ounces
5. **What's Wrong?** Jessica found the number of ounces in 80 pounds. What did she do wrong? Give the correct answer. 80 pounds ÷ 16 = 5 ounces
An ounce is a smaller unit so you need to multiply. The student divided instead of multiplied. The correct answer is 80 × 16 = 1,280 ounces.

Use with text pages 312–314.

3 Practice

Practice and Problem Solving

Select from **Exercises 5–32** as independent work.

- For **Exercises 11–16**, point out that students need not measure the actual objects. Rather, they should use their number sense to pick the most likely unit to use.
- ***Problem 24*** Encourage students to read the problem closely to notice the different units used to describe what Darlene bought.

4 Assess & Close

Math Talk in Action

Refer to **Exercises 17–22** to conclude the lesson.

- **What is the largest customary unit of weight that you have learned?** (ton) **How many pounds equal 1 ton?** (2,000) **What is the smallest customary unit of weight that you have learned?** (ounce) **How many ounces equal 1 pound?** (16)
- **Suppose we wondered how many ounces there are in a ton. How could we find out?** (Multiply: 16 oz by 2,000 lb = 32,000 oz)

Math Journal Prompt

Have students give their weight (or an estimate of it) in pounds, and then explain how to express the same weight in ounces.

Lesson Quiz

Use the quiz on Lesson Transparency 12.4.

Test Prep & Spiral Review

Use Test Prep Transparency 12.4.

Practice and Problem Solving

Find each missing number.

5. 32,000 lb = 16 T
6. 48 oz = 3 lb
7. 32 oz = 2 lb
8. 144 oz = 9 lb
9. 8,000 lb = 4 T
10. 10 lb = 160 oz

What is the best unit to weigh these items? Write *ounce, pound,* or *ton.*

11. a bunch of bananas **pound**
12. a paper clip **ounce**
13. a car **ton**
14. an elephant **ton**
15. a handful of blueberries **ounce**
16. a table **pound**

Compare. Write >, <, or = for each ●.

17. 38 oz ● 2 lb **>**
18. 3,000 lb ● 3T **<**
19. 5 lb ● 80 oz **=**
20. 2 lb ● 40 oz **<**
21. 90 oz ● 6 lb **<**
22. 2 T ● 3,000 lb **>**

23. Shonte bought a 9-pound watermelon that cost $0.50 per pound. How much did she pay? **$4.50**
24. Darlene bought 3 pounds of peaches, 6 ounces of cherries and 14 ounces of plums. What was the total weight of her purchases? **4 pounds 4 ounces**
25. Mario bought 3 pounds of fruit. He bought strawberries, cherries, grapes, and blueberries. How much did each type of fruit weigh if they weighed the same? **12 ounces**

Mixed Review and Test Prep

Open Response

Round each number to the nearest hundred. Then estimate. (Ch. 3, Lesson 3)

26. 7,091 + 2,802 **9,900**
27. 3,399 − 1,239 **2,200**
28. 4,511 + 5,499 **10,000**
29. 1,887 − 1,102 **800**
30. 3,271 + 4,010 **7,300**
31. 6,487 − 2,296 **4,200**

Multiple Choice

32. How many ounces are in 5 pounds? (Ch. 12, Lesson 4)

A 16 ounces
(C) 80 ounces
B 20 ounces
D 2,000 ounces

314

Extra Practice See page 331, Set C.

Homework 12.4 Page 77

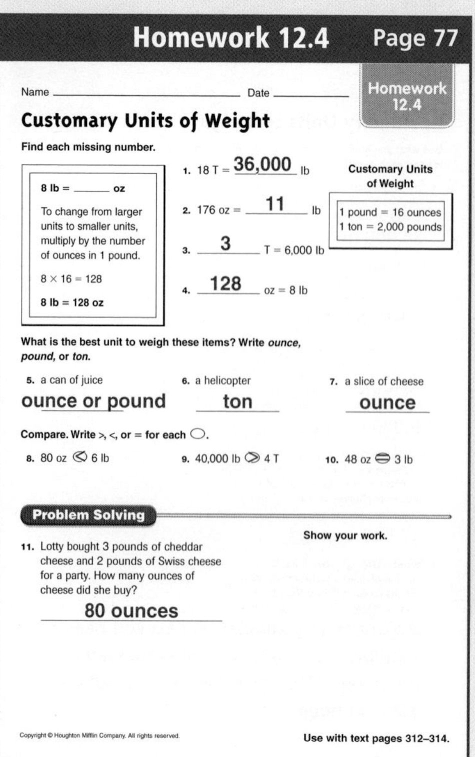

Name ________ Date ________

Homework 12.4

Customary Units of Weight

Find each missing number.

8 lb = ____ oz

To change from larger units to smaller units, multiply by the number of ounces in 1 pound.

8 × 16 = 128

8 lb = 128 oz

1. 18 T = 36,000 lb
2. 176 oz = 11 lb
3. 3 T = 6,000 lb
4. 128 oz = 8 lb

Customary Units of Weight

1 pound = 16 ounces
1 ton = 2,000 pounds

What is the best unit to weigh these items? Write *ounce, pound, or ton.*

5. a can of juice **ounce or pound**
6. a helicopter **ton**
7. a slice of cheese **ounce**

Compare. Write >, <, or = for each ○.

8. 80 oz < 6 lb
9. 40,000 lb > 4 T
10. 48 oz = 3 lb

Problem Solving

Show your work.

11. Lotty bought 3 pounds of cheddar cheese and 2 pounds of Swiss cheese for a party. How many ounces of cheese did she buy? **80 ounces**

Use with text pages 312–314.

Visual Thinking

Balancing Act

Which containers should you move so that each group has the same amount of juice? **Move one pint container from Group A to Group B.**

Group A

Science Connection

A Lot of Elephant!

An African elephant can weigh 12 tons. How many pounds is that? **24,000 pounds**

An elephant can drink as much as 40 gallons of water a day. How many quarts is that? **160 quarts**

An elephant's tusk can be as long as 8 feet. How many inches is that? **96 inches**

Brain Teaser

A snail is climbing a15-foot fence. Every day it climbs 3 feet, but slides back 1 foot every night. How long does it take the snail to climb to the top of the fence? **7 days**

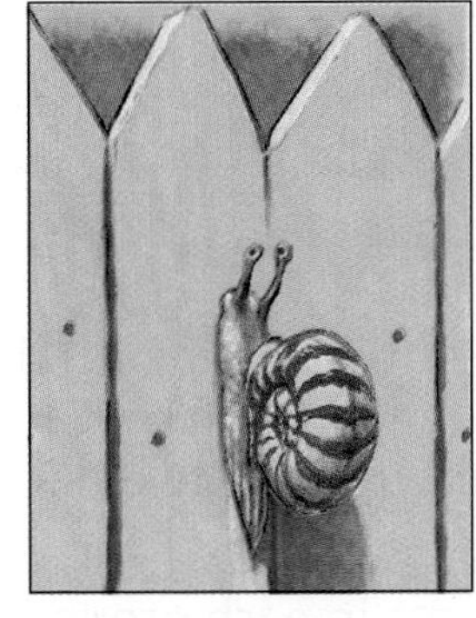

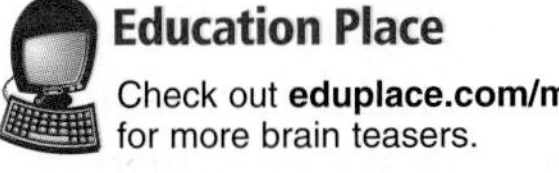

Education Place
Check out eduplace.com/map
for more brain teasers.

Visual Thinking

Balancing Act

Ask: What kinds of units are shown? (units of capacity) Have students name the capacity of the containers in each picture. (left: 1 qt, 2 pt; right: 1 pt, 2 c) **What do you know about how these units relate?** (1 qt = 2 pt; 1 pt = 2 c) Invite discussion about how to move just one container from one group into the other group so that both groups have equal capacity.

Science Connection

A Lot of Elephant

Have students work in pairs. Partners can discuss each statement and decide how to change the units of measure in each case.

In this section, students change units of weight, capacity, and length. Help students classify each kind of unit in the statement where it appears. If needed, let them refer to previous lessons where each type of unit was presented.

Brain Teaser

Suggest that students act out the snail problem, model it on a number line, or draw a picture of the situation. Any of these approaches will enable them to recognize the solution.

Lesson 12.5

Problem-Solving Decision: Too Much or Too Little Information

Planning

Lesson Objective Find the information you need to solve a problem.

Technology Resources

- Audio Tutor **2**/12 Listen and Understand
- *Ways to Success* CD-ROM 12.5
- Education Place: Extra Practice, Extra Help, www.eduplace.com/map
- *Ways to Assess* CD-ROM

Lesson 12.5 Transparency

Problem of the Day

Kara works for a hockey team. Tickets for hockey games cost $15 each, but she got some free. Kara got enough free tickets to give a pair to each of 7 friends. How many free tickets did Kara get? (14)

Spiral Review

Solve.

1. $9.45 ÷ 3 ($3.15)
2. 1,296 − 897 (399)
3. $2.55 × 34 ($86.70)
4. 77,613 + 402 + 9,014 (87,029)
5. 706 ÷ 16 (44 R2)

Lesson Quiz

Solve. If not enough information is given, tell what information is needed to solve the problem.

1. Small postcards cost 35¢ each. LeVon bought 8 small postcards and 3 large ones. How much did he spend? (Not enough information; you need the price of large postcards.)

NCTM Standards

Problem Solving: Solve problems that arise in mathematics and in other contexts; apply and adapt a variety of appropriate strategies to solve problems.
Connections: Recognize and use connections among mathematical ideas.

Getting Started

Building Math Vocabulary

Students should be familiar with the mathematical vocabulary in this lesson.

Write the word **information** on the board. Ask students to describe what it means (things we know; data, facts). Relate this word to the verb *to inform*, which means to tell what is known.

Getting the Right Information

Small Groups	10 minutes
Objective	Solve problems using skills and strategies.
Materials	Index cards
Visual	

- Split students into group of 4. Tell students that they want to get information about favorite dinner foods.
- Ask two students in each group to create a list of directed questions that will elicit only the information they want out of the responding people.
- Have the other two students in the group create a list of information that may relate to the questions but provides too much or too little information.
- Have groups write their questions and answers on index cards and then share these with the class to decide which are the best questions to ask.
- Tell the class that the lesson focuses on ways of identifying relevant information to solve math problems.

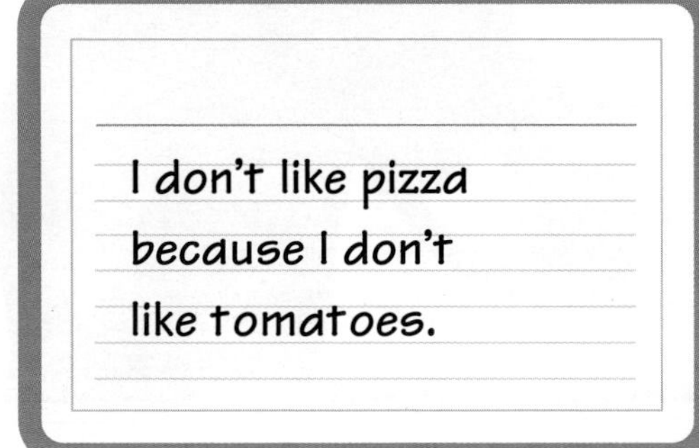

I don't like pizza
because I don't
like tomatoes.

Differentiated Instruction

English Learners

Small Groups	10 minutes
Objective	Solve problems using skills and strategies.
Materials	Student page 316
Auditory, Visual	

Early Production

- Pair students for ***Try These*** problems.
- Have one student the read the problem aloud, while the other student writes and reads responses to ***Ask Yourself*** questions. Then partners solve the problem together.
- Have students alternate roles for the remaining problems.

Intermediate/Advanced

- English Learner Resource 12.5
- English Learner Handbook

Intervention

Whole Class	5 minutes
Objective	Solve problems using skills and strategies.
Materials	None
Visual, Auditory	

- Ask students to guess your age. List their guesses on the board.
- **Suppose I tell you my birthday. Will that be enough information for you to figure out my age? Explain.** (No; they need the year you were born.) **I'm older than my sister. How does this fact help?** (It doesn't unless they know your sister's age; otherwise, it's an extra fact.)

Other Resources

- *Ways to Success* CD-ROM 12.5

Special Needs

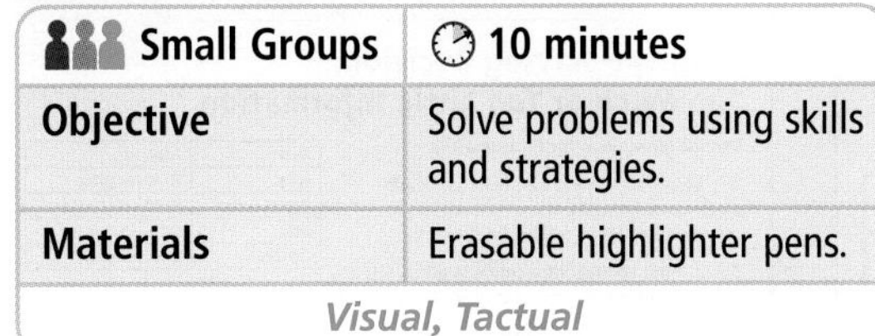

Small Groups	10 minutes
Objective	Solve problems using skills and strategies.
Materials	Erasable highlighter pens.
Visual, Tactual	

- Provide erasable highlighter pens students can use to mark key data.
- Have students highlight facts they must have to solve the problem, but not any extra information. If there is too little information highlighted, it will become clear when the student cannot solve the problem.

Alternate Teaching Strategy

Split students into pairs. Ask one student in each pair to read the problem aloud to their partner. The partner should copy down only the relevant information from the word problem. This will allow students to identify the relevant information.

1 Introduce

Read the objective, *find the information you need to solve a problem*, to the students and tell them that in this lesson they will decide whether there is enough information to solve a problem. If there is enough information, students practice operational skills learned in previous lessons to solve the problem.

2 Teach

- Ask a volunteer to read the opening problem. **Let's examine the *Ask Yourself* chart that can help us solve the problem. What does the first part show ?** (the question to solve) **What does the second part show?** (what is needed) **The third part?** (what is known)
- **Does this problem have too much or too little information?** (too much) **What is extra?** (Sam collected $19.00)

3 Practice

Try These

Select from the ***Try These*** problems as independent work. Clarify that students should find the solution only if there is enough information to do so. If there is not enough information, they should state what is missing.

4 Assess & Close

Math Talk in Action

Refer to **Problems 1–4** to conclude the lesson. Ask students to summarize how they would go about deciding whether they have enough information to solve a problem.

Math Journal Prompt

Have students explain how they can decide whether a problem has too much or too little information.

Lesson Quiz

Use the quiz on Lesson Transparency 12.5.

Test Prep & Spiral Review

Use Test Prep Transparency 12.5.

Test Prep
12.5
Transparency

Lesson 5

Audio Tutor 2/12 Listen and Understand

Problem-Solving Decision

Too Much or Too Little Information

Objective Find the information you need to solve a problem.

Problem Sam sold 38 seed packets. He collected $19.00. April sold four times as many seed packets as Sam. How many seed packets did April sell?

Ask Yourself

What is the question?	What do I need to know?	What do I know?
• How many seed packets did April sell?	• How many packets did Sam sell?	• Sam sold 38 packets. • April sold 4 times as many packets as Sam.

Solve the problem.

38	← number of packets Sam sold
× 4	← 4 times as many as Sam
152	← number of packets April sold

Solution: April sold 152 seed packets.

Try These **1. Not enough information. You would need to know how many vegetable or flower seed packets were sold.**

Solve. If not enough information is given, tell what information is needed to solve the problem.

1. Rebecca's club sold 343 flower and vegetable seed packets altogether. They collected $171.50. Were more flower or vegetable seeds sold? ***See above.***
2. Nate bought 8 one-pound packages of crocus bulbs for $1.50 a pound and a box of fertilizer for $4.00. How much did he spend on bulbs? **$12.00**
3. Ann planted 16 tulips and 12 lilies. She planted twice as many daffodils as tulips. How many daffodils did she plant? **32**
4. Lee planted marigold seeds in pots. Each pot held 20 ounces of soil. What was the weight of all the soil used? **Not enough information; you need to know the number of pots.**

316

Extra Help at eduplace.com/map

Reteach 12.5

Name ______________ Date ________ Reteach 12.5

Problem-Solving Decision: Too Much or Too Little Information

Read It Look for information.

The Golden Gate Bridge has 2 towers that rise 746 feet above the sea. The length of the bridge is 1.7 miles. The roadway is 220 feet above the sea. What is the distance from the roadway of the bridge to the top of the tower?

Picture It Here is a table of the information in the problem.

	Measurement	Needed Fact?
Height of Towers from Sea Level	746 feet	yes
Length of Bridge	1.7 miles	no
Height of Roadway from Sea Level	220 feet	yes

Solve It Use the table to solve the problem.

1. Subtract to find the distance from the roadway to the top of the tower.

   746 ft − 220 ft = **526** ft

2. The distance from the roadway to the top of the tower is **526** feet.

Try These! If not enough information is given, tell what information is needed to solve the problem.

3. The suspension cables of the Golden Gate Bridge are each 7,650 feet long. How much cable is used altogether in the bridge? **Not enough info; the number of cables**
4. Chicago's Sears Tower is 1,450 feet tall with 110 stories. The Petronas Twin Towers are 1,480 feet tall with 88 stories. How much taller are the Petronas Twin Towers than Chicago's Sears Tower? **30 ft**

Use with text page 316.

Practice 12.5 Page 78

Name ______________ Date ________ Practice 12.5

Problem-Solving Decision: Too Much or Too Little Information

Use the table below for Problems 1–3.

Mrs. Winter is planning a party for her fourth-grade class. The table at the right shows the cost of various items needed for the party.

Item	Cost
Juice	$2.50 per gallon
Peanut Butter	$3.50 per 16 oz jar
Jelly	$2.00 per 8 oz jar
Cookies	$4.00 per batch

Solve. If not enough information is given, tell what information is needed to solve the problem.

Show your work.

1. Mrs. Winter has 20 students. If she sets aside $10 for juice, will the students have enough to drink? **not enough information; need to know how much each student will drink**
2. One jar of peanut butter and 2 jars of jelly can make 10 sandwiches. Each sandwich is made with 2 pieces of bread. How many jars of peanut butter and how many jars of jelly will she need to make sure that each student will have 2 sandwiches? **4 jars of peanut butter and 8 jars of jelly**
3. Mrs. Winter buys 5 gallons of juice. She bought 3 gallons of grape juice and 2 gallons of apple juice. Will she have enough juice for each student to have 2 pints of juice to drink? **yes**

Use with text page 316.

Art Connection
Mobile Math

Hanging sculptures like the one in the photo are called mobiles. The artist needs to carefully balance the construction.

Calder might have used an equation like this to balance his mobile.

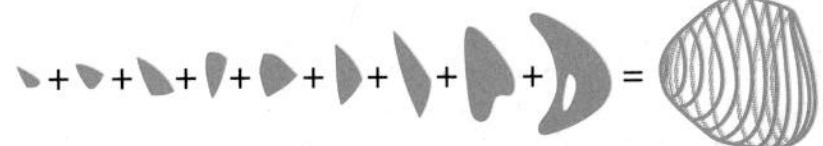

Use some of the shapes below to construct an imaginary mobile. Draw a picture equation to show how it will balance.

           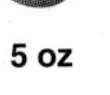 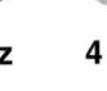     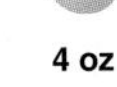      

3 oz 5 oz 4 oz 4 oz 1 lb 8 oz 2 oz

"Lobster Trap and Fish Tail" by Alexander Calder (1939)

See Additional Answers.

WEEKLY WR READER eduplace.com/map

Problem Solving

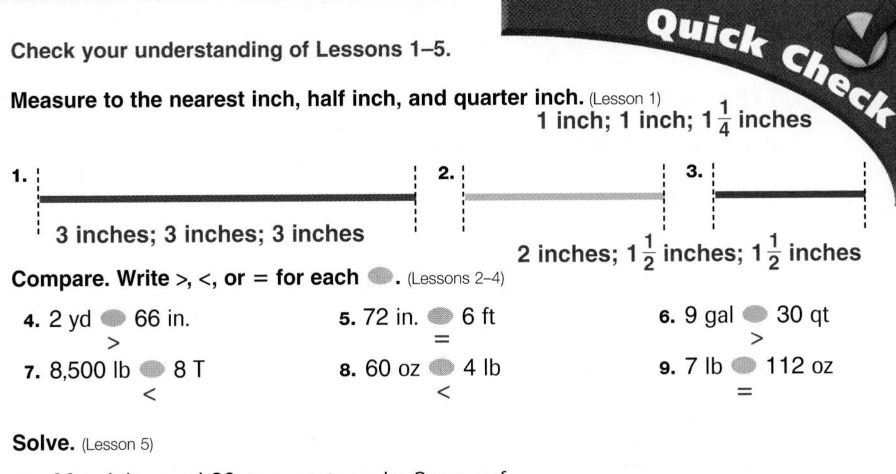

Quick Check

Check your understanding of Lessons 1–5.

Measure to the nearest inch, half inch, and quarter inch. (Lesson 1)

1 inch; 1 inch; $1\frac{1}{4}$ inches

1. **3 inches; 3 inches; 3 inches**

2.

3. **2 inches; $1\frac{1}{2}$ inches; $1\frac{1}{2}$ inches**

Compare. Write >, <, or = for each ●. (Lessons 2–4)

4. 2 yd ● 66 in. **>**

5. 72 in. ● 6 ft **=**

6. 9 gal ● 30 qt **>**

7. 8,500 lb ● 8 T **<**

8. 60 oz ● 4 lb **<**

9. 7 lb ● 112 oz **=**

Solve. (Lesson 5)

10. Mrs. Juba used 20 oranges to make 8 cups of juice. How many quarts of juice did she make? **2 quarts**

Extra Practice at **eduplace.com/map**

Art Connection
Mobile Math

Alexander (Sandy) Calder was born in Pennsylvania in 1898 to a family of artists. He lived until 1976. He invented mobiles, which were given that name because they are sculptures that are constantly in motion. Some of Calder's mobiles are motor-driven. Others are so delicately balanced that air currents move them.

✔Quick Check

The ***Quick Check*** allows you to assess the students' understanding of the concepts presented in Lessons 1–5.

Item	Objectives Tested	Pages	Intervention
1–3	Estimate and measure lengths, using an inch ruler.	306–307	Reteach Resources 12.1 *Ways to Success* CD-ROM 12.1
4–9	Change units of length. Change units of capacity. Estimate and measure, using customary units of weight.	308–314	Reteach Resources 12.2, 12.3, 12.4 *Ways to Success* CD-ROM 12.2, 12.3, 12.4
10	Find the information you need to solve a problem.	316	Reteach Resources 12.5 *Ways to Success* CD-ROM 12.5

Enrichment 12.5

Name ______ Date ______ Enrichment 12.5

Problem-Solving Decision: Too Much or Too Little Information

Read the statements below and look at the table. Choose a strategy to answer each question. If not enough information is given, tell what information is needed to solve the problem.

- Mt. Whitney is the highest point in California and Death Valley is the lowest point.
- The average flow of water over Niagara Falls is 212,200 cubic feet per second.
- The deepest point of Lake Huron is 750 feet.
- Lake Superior is 410 feet deeper than Lake Michigan. Lake Michigan is 173 feet deeper than Lake Huron.
- The average flow of water over Victoria Falls is 35,400 cubic feet per second.

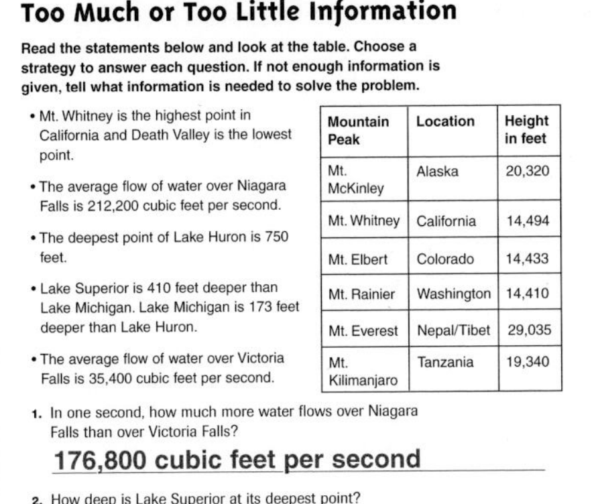

Mountain Peak	Location	Height in feet
Mt. McKinley	Alaska	20,320
Mt. Whitney	California	14,494
Mt. Elbert	Colorado	14,433
Mt. Rainier	Washington	14,410
Mt. Everest	Nepal/Tibet	29,035
Mt. Kilimanjaro	Tanzania	19,340

1. In one second, how much more water flows over Niagara Falls than over Victoria Falls? **176,800 cubic feet per second**
2. How deep is Lake Superior at its deepest point? **1,333 feet**
3. What is the difference between the highest and lowest points in California? **Not enough information; you need to know the elevation of Death Valley.**
4. Which mountain in the United States is higher than Mt. Kilimanjaro? How much higher is it? **Mt. McKinley; 980 ft higher**
5. How much higher is Mt. McKinley than Mt. Lhotse? **Not enough information; you need to know the height of Mt. Lhotse.**

Use with text page 316.

Problem Solving 12.5

Name ______ Date ______ Problem Solving 12.5

Problem-Solving Decision: Too Much or Too Little Information

Problem Beverly sold tickets to the school play. She sold 28 tickets and collected $140. Jeff sold twice as many tickets as Beverly. What was the price of each ticket?

UNDERSTAND

1. What information do you need to solve the problem? **How many tickets someone sold and how much money that person collected.**

PLAN

2. How will you solve the problem? **Divide the amount of money Beverly collected by the number of tickets she sold.**

SOLVE

3. Do you have enough information to solve the problem? If so, solve and explain your steps. If not, what information do you need? **Yes; divide: 140 ÷ 28 = 5. Each ticket cost $5.**

LOOK BACK

4. **Write About It** How can you tell if you have too much or too little information? **Look at the question and decide what information you need to answer the question. Then look at the information given to decide if you have all the information you need.**

Use with text page 316.

Homework 12.5 Page 78

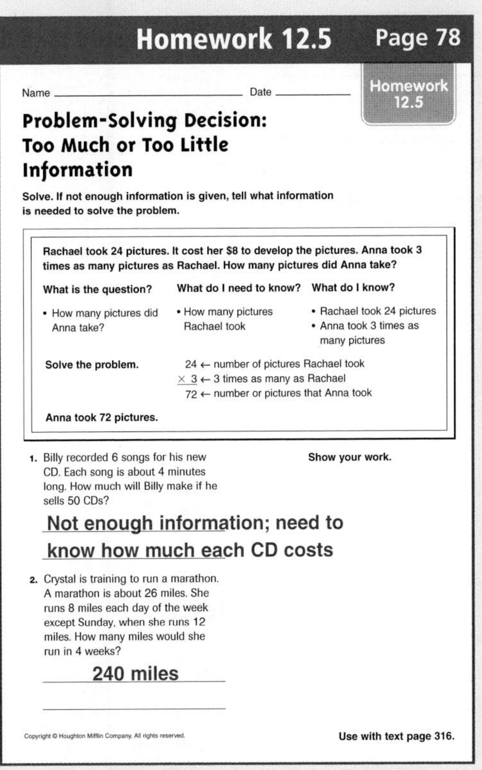

Name ______ Date ______ Homework 12.5

Problem-Solving Decision: Too Much or Too Little Information

Solve. If not enough information is given, tell what information is needed to solve the problem.

Rachael took 24 pictures. It cost her $8 to develop the pictures. Anna took 3 times as many pictures as Rachael. How many pictures did Anna take?

What is the question?	What do I need to know?	What do I know?
• How many pictures did Anna take?	• How many pictures Rachael took	• Rachael took 24 pictures • Anna took 3 times as many pictures

Solve the problem.

24 ← number of pictures Rachael took
× 3 ← 3 times as many as Rachael
72 ← number of pictures that Anna took

Anna took 72 pictures.

Show your work.

1. Billy recorded 6 songs for his new CD. Each song is about 4 minutes long. How much will Billy make if he sells 50 CDs? **Not enough information; need to know how much each CD costs**
2. Crystal is training to run a marathon. A marathon is about 26 miles. She runs 8 miles each day of the week except Sunday, when she runs 12 miles. How many miles would she run in 4 weeks? **240 miles**

Use with text page 316.

Hands On Lesson 12.6

Explore Metric Units of Length

Planning

Lesson Objective Estimate and measure lengths using a centimeter ruler.

Technology Resources

- *Ways to Success* CD-ROM 12.6
- Education Place: Extra Practice, eGlossary, eGames www.eduplace.com/map

Lesson 12.6 Transparency

Problem of the Day

Kai lives 3 blocks from school, so he walks. There are 12 houses on each block. 2 houses are blue, 5 are gray, 4 are yellow, and 1 is brick. How many houses does Kai pass on his way to school? (36)

Spiral Review

Solve for *n*.

1. $44 \times 10 = n$ (440)
2. $100 \times 53 = n$ (5,300)
3. $670 \div 10 = n$ (67)
4. $54{,}000 \div 60 = n$ (900)
5. $100 \times 1{,}000 = n$ (100,000)

Lesson Quiz

Measure the length to the nearest centimeter and millimeter.

1. ____________
(4 cm; 37mm)

2. ____________________
(6 cm; 62 mm)

3. ________________
(5 cm; 45 mm)

NCTM Standards

Measurement: Understand measurable attributes of objects and the units, systems, and processes of measurement.
Communication: Recognize and use connections among mathematical ideas.

Getting Started

Building Math Vocabulary

millimeter (mm) a metric unit of length: 10 millimeters = 1 centimeter

Write the term **metric** on the board. Tell students that the metric system, also known as *Systeme International,* uses a different group of units to measure length, capacity, and weight. Then display the vocabulary cards for **centimeter (cm)** and **millimeter (mm).** Discuss the examples with students.

Measure Length

Small Groups	10 minutes
Objective	Estimate and measure length using a centimeter ruler.
Materials	Metric rulers
Visual, Tactual	

- Distribute metric rulers to each student. Have them work in groups.
- Challenge them to find one common classroom object that is about a millimeter in length, a centimeter in length, and a meter in length.
- Bring the class back together and share these estimates and objects with the class. These common items can help students visualize the metric units as they continue with this lesson.

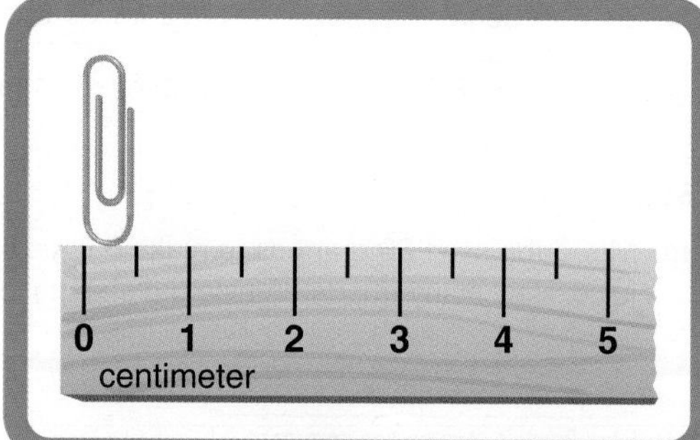

Differentiated Instruction

English Learners

Small Groups	10 minutes
Objective	Estimate lengths using metric units of measurement.
Materials	Student page 319
Auditory, Visual	

Early Production

- For the ***On Your Own*** exercises, ask students to say and write their answers in complete sentences using the exercise number to identify the object. For example: *Object one is thirty-seven millimeters long. I think object three is six centimeters long.*

Intermediate/Advanced

- English Learner Resource 12.6
- English Learner Handbook

Intervention

Small Groups	5–10 minutes
Objective	Measure lengths using a centimeter ruler.
Materials	Metric rulers
Visual, Tactual	

- Most students have no trouble measuring to the nearest centimeter, but may be unsure how to record lengths to the nearest millimeter.
- **Let's skip count by tens to 200.** Listen as students count. **Think of the centimeter ruler as a number line. To measure to the nearest millimeter, count by tens to the centimeter just shorter than the object. Then count by ones for the added millimeters.** Model this by measuring a classroom object.
- **How can multiples of 10 speed the task?** (Use mental math to multiply the number of centimeters by 10, such as 14 cm = 14 × 10, or 140 mm.)

Other Resources

- *Ways to Success* CD-ROM 12.6

Inclusion

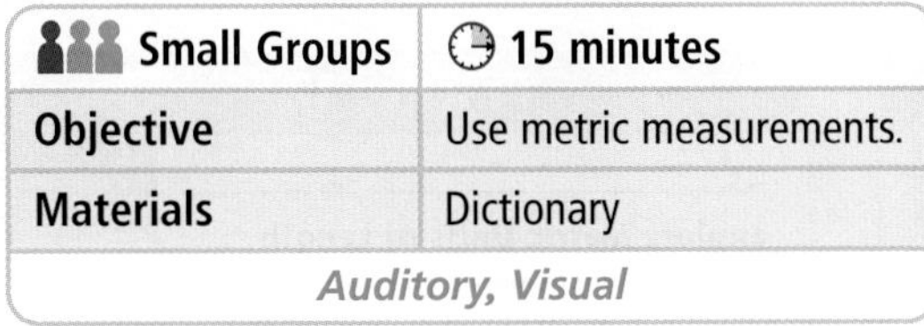

Small Groups	15 minutes
Objective	Use metric measurements.
Materials	Dictionary
Auditory, Visual	

- Point out to students the prefixes *centi-* and *milli-* on the metric measurements.
- Explain that *centi-* means 100 and *milli-* means 1,000.
- Challenge students to come up with a list of other words that use the same prefixes and to provide definitions for these words.

Social Studies Connection

Help students learn about the International System of Units (SI) (the modern metric system). Tell them that a decimal-based system of measures was proposed more than 400 years ago. Help them learn why scientists prefer the metric system to the customary system.

Facts Practice

Provide students with a series of three measurements. One should be in millimeters, one in centimeters, and one in meters. Challenge students to convert each measurement to two other metric units.

❶ Introduce

Read the objective to students and tell them that in this lesson they will use a centimeter ruler to measure objects to the nearest centimeter and millimeter.

❷ Teach

Work Together

- **Read Steps 1–3. What will you determine about the cattail?** (its estimated length, its length to the nearest cm, then to the nearest mm) **How do you write a length in millimeters?** (1 cm = 10 mm; count by 10s, add on extra millimeters)
- **Look at Step 4. Try to find objects whose lengths are different from each other to sharpen your estimating skills.**

❸ Practice

On Your Own

- Select from **Exercises 1–7** as independent work. Then have students complete the ***Talk About It •Write About It*** problems.
- Circulate as students work. Ask them to explain their measuring techniques. Check that students record each measure as a number followed by the correct abbreviation for the unit used.

Hands On Lesson 6

Explore Metric Units of Length

Vocabulary
millimeter (mm)

Objective Estimate and measure lengths using a centimeter ruler.

Work Together

Work with a partner to estimate lengths. Then use a centimeter ruler to measure lengths.

STEP 1 Estimate the length of the cattail above. Record your estimate in a table like the one shown.

Object	Estimate	Nearest Centimeter	Nearest Millimeter
cattail			

STEP 2 Use a centimeter ruler to measure the length of the cattail to the nearest centimeter. Use a half-centimeter mark to decide which centimeter mark is closer to the end of the cattail. Record the length in your table.
10 centimeters

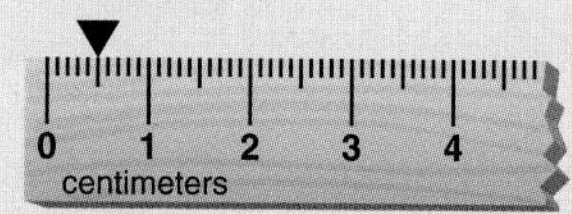

If the end is exactly halfway between centimeters, round to the next centimeter.

STEP 3 Now measure the cattail to the nearest **millimeter**. Decide which millimeter mark is closer to the end of the cattail. Record the length in millimeters in your table. **95 millimeters**

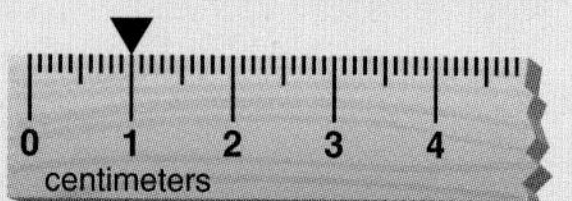

There are 10 millimeters in 1 centimeter.

318

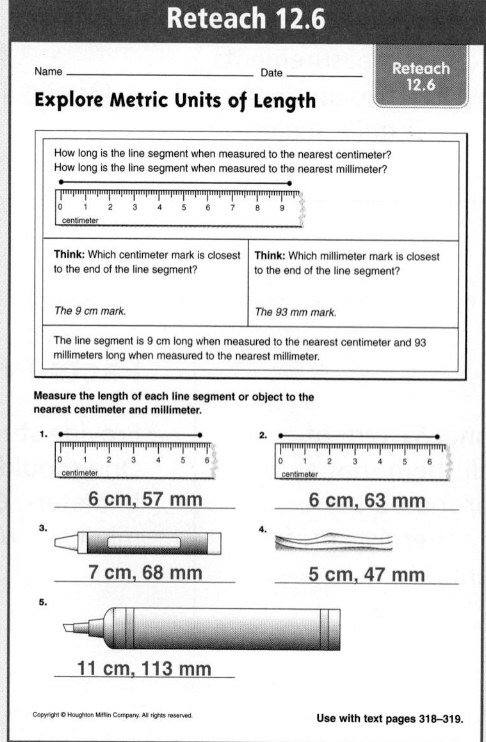

Reteach 12.6

Name ______________ Date ________

Reteach 12.6

Explore Metric Units of Length

How long is the line segment when measured to the nearest centimeter?
How long is the line segment when measured to the nearest millimeter?

Think: Which centimeter mark is closest to the end of the line segment?	**Think:** Which millimeter mark is closest to the end of the line segment?
The 9 cm mark.	*The 93 mm mark.*

The line segment is 9 cm long when measured to the nearest centimeter and 93 millimeters long when measured to the nearest millimeter.

Measure the length of each line segment or object to the nearest centimeter and millimeter.

1. 6 cm, 57 mm
2. 6 cm, 63 mm
3. 7 cm, 68 mm
4. 5 cm, 47 mm
5. 11 cm, 113 mm

Use with text pages 318–319.

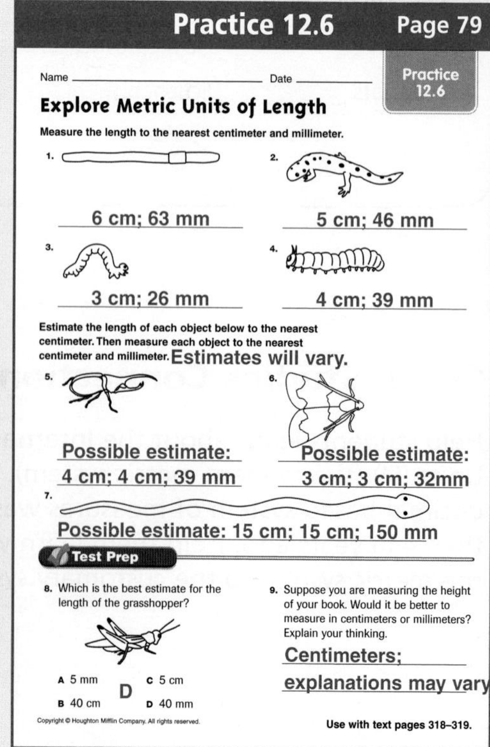

Practice 12.6 **Page 79**

Name ______________ Date ________

Practice 12.6

Explore Metric Units of Length

Measure the length to the nearest centimeter and millimeter.

1. 6 cm; 63 mm
2. 5 cm; 46 mm
3. 3 cm; 26 mm
4. 4 cm; 39 mm

Estimate the length of each object below to the nearest centimeter. Then measure each object to the nearest centimeter and millimeter. Estimates will vary.

5. Possible estimate: 4 cm; 4 cm; 39 mm
6. Possible estimate: 3 cm; 3 cm; 32mm
7. Possible estimate: 15 cm; 15 cm; 150 mm

Test Prep

8. Which is the best estimate for the length of the grasshopper?
   A 5 mm
   B 40 cm
   C 5 cm
   D 40 mm
   D

9. Suppose you are measuring the height of your book. Would it be better to measure in centimeters or millimeters? Explain your thinking.
   Centimeters; explanations may vary

Use with text pages 318–319.

Find 5 objects to measure. Estimate the length of each object to the nearest centimeter. Then measure each object to the nearest centimeter. Record your work in your table.

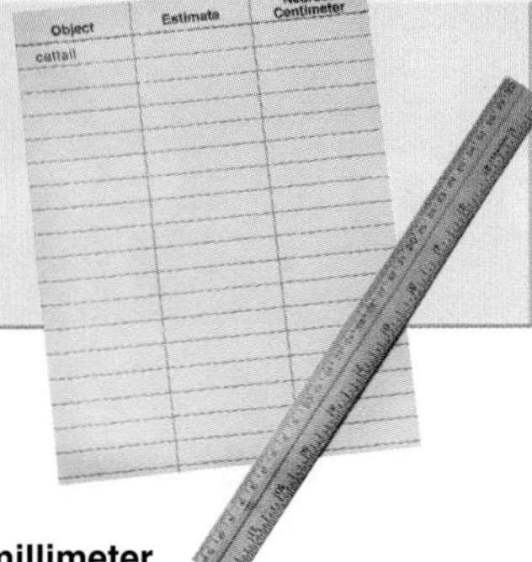

On Your Own

Measure the length to the nearest centimeter and millimeter.

1.  **4 cm 37 mm**
2.  **5 cm 52 mm**

Estimate the length. Then measure each object to the nearest centimeter and millimeter. ***Estimates may vary.***

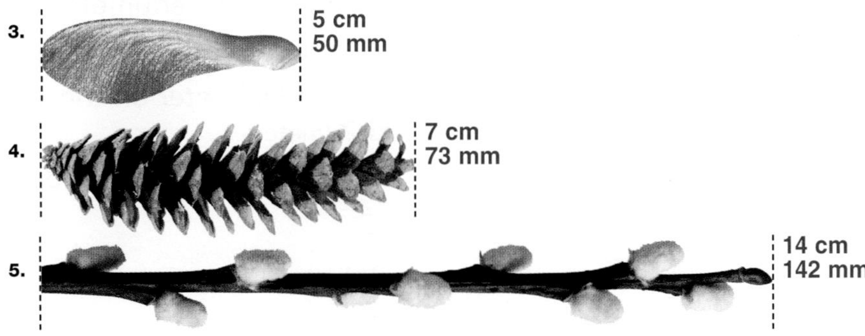

3. **5 cm 50 mm**
4. **7 cm 73 mm**
5. **14 cm 142 mm**

Talk About It • Write About It

You have learned to measure lengths in centimeters and millimeters.

6. Suppose you know how tall a plant is in centimeters. Explain how you can tell how tall it is in millimeters.

6. There are 10 millimeters in 1 centimeter, so you can multiply the number of centimeters by 10 to find the number of millimeters.

7. Suppose you are measuring a piece of wood for a birdhouse. Would it be better to measure in centimeters or in millimeters? Explain your thinking.

7. *Possible answer:* millimeters; Since millimeters are smaller, they provide a more precise measurement than centimeters.

4 Assess & Close

123 Math Talk in Action

- Invite students to share their responses to the ***Talk About It* • *Write About It*** problems. Encourage discussion of alternate viewpoints.
- **How are centimeters and millimeters related?** (1 cm = 10 mm) **If a crayon is 83 mm long, what is its length to the nearest centimeter?** (8 cm)

Math Journal Prompt

Have students write a description that compares and contrasts measuring to the nearest inch and half inch with measuring to the nearest centimeter and millimeter.

Lesson Quiz

Use the quiz on Lesson Transparency 12.6.

Test Prep & Spiral Review

Use Test Prep Transparency 12.6.

Enrichment 12.6

Name ______________ Date ______

Enrichment 12.6

Metric Measurements

0 1 2 3 4 5 6 7 8 9 10 centimeters

Trace the ruler on a piece of paper. Use your paper to measure objects in the room. Find at least 3 objects that are the same length or shorter than your traced ruler and 5 objects that are longer than your traced ruler. Measure each object to the nearest centimeter and the nearest millimeter.

Object	Nearest Centimeter	Nearest Millimeter

Write About It Measure an object with an inch ruler and with the centimeter ruler. What relationship do you see between inches and centimeters?

Answers will vary. Check students' measurements. 1 inch is about $2\frac{1}{2}$ centimeters.

Use with text pages 318–319.

Problem Solving 12.6

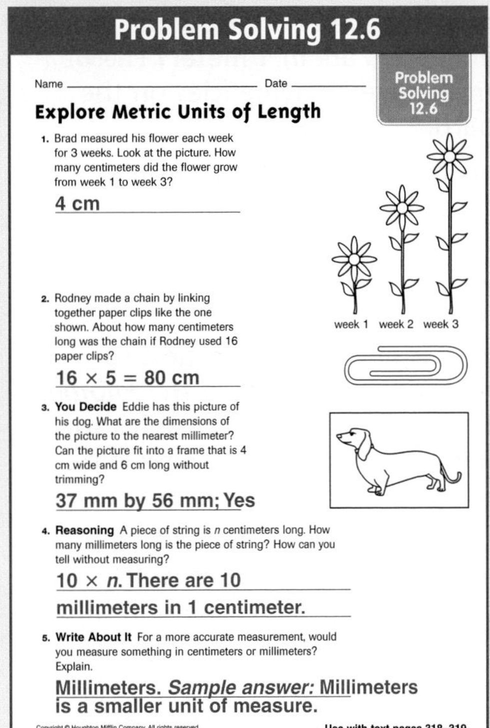

Name ______________ Date ______

Problem Solving 12.6

Explore Metric Units of Length

1. Brad measured his flower each week for 3 weeks. Look at the picture. How many centimeters did the flower grow from week 1 to week 3?
   4 cm

week 1 week 2 week 3

2. Rodney made a chain by linking together paper clips like the one shown. About how many centimeters long was the chain if Rodney used 16 paper clips?
   $16 \times 5 = 80$ cm
3. **You Decide** Eddie has this picture of his dog. What are the dimensions of the picture to the nearest millimeter? Can the picture fit into a frame that is 4 cm wide and 6 cm long without trimming?
   37 mm by 56 mm; Yes
4. **Reasoning** A piece of string is *n* centimeters long. How many millimeters long is the piece of string? How can you tell without measuring?
   $10 \times n$. There are 10 millimeters in 1 centimeter.
5. **Write About It** For a more accurate measurement, would you measure something in centimeters or millimeters? Explain.
   Millimeters. *Sample answer:* Millimeters is a smaller unit of measure.

Use with text pages 318–319.

Homework 12.6 Page 79

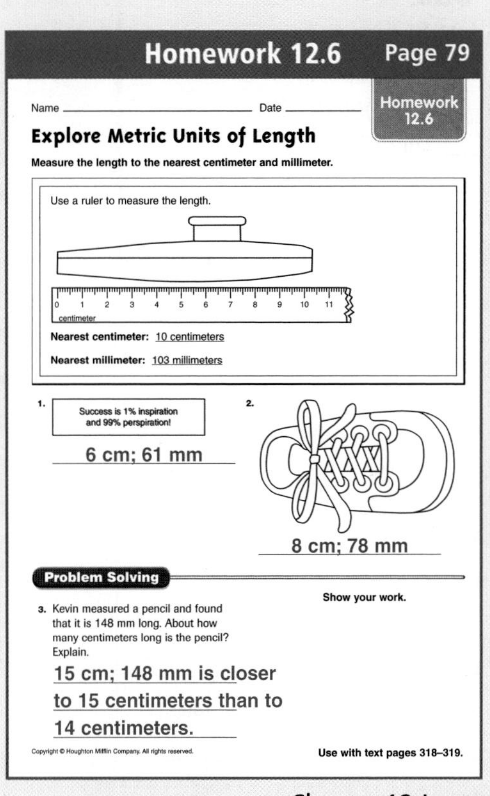

Name ______________ Date ______

Homework 12.6

Explore Metric Units of Length

Measure the length to the nearest centimeter and millimeter.

Use a ruler to measure the length.

0 1 2 3 4 5 6 7 8 9 10 11 centimeter

Nearest centimeter: 10 centimeters

Nearest millimeter: 103 millimeters

1. Success is 1% inspiration and 99% perspiration!
   6 cm; 61 mm
2. 8 cm; 78 mm

Problem Solving

Show your work.

3. Kevin measured a pencil and found that it is 148 mm long. About how many centimeters long is the pencil? Explain.
   15 cm; 148 mm is closer to 15 centimeters than to 14 centimeters.

Use with text pages 318–319.

Lesson 12.7

Metric Units of Length

Planning

Lesson Objective Change metric units of length.

Technology Resources

- Audio Tutor **2**/3 Listen and Understand
- *Ways to Success* CD-ROM 12.7
- Education Place: Extra Practice, eGlossary, eGames
  www.eduplace.com/map

Lesson 12.7 Transparency

Problem of the Day

A piece of lace is 70 cm long. Its design begins and ends with tiny rosebuds. A rosebud appears every 5 cm along the length of the piece of lace. How many rosebuds are on this piece of lace (15)

Spiral Review

Estimate, then measure the length of each item to the nearest cm and mm. (Answers will vary.)

1. a piece of chalk
2. a marker
3. your smallest finger
4. the height of your math book

Lesson Quiz

Find each missing number.

1. 60 cm = ___ mm (600)
2. 8 km = ___ m (8,000)
3. 5 dm = ___ cm (50)
4. 6 m = ___ cm (600)
5. 300 mm = ___ cm (30)

NCTM Standards

Measurement: Carry out simple conversions, such as from centimeters to meters, within a system of measurement.
Problem Solving: Apply and adapt a variety of appropriate strategies to solve problems.

Getting Started

Building Math Vocabulary

millimeter (mm) a metric unit of length; 10 millimeters = 1 centimeter
centimeter (cm) a metric unit of length; 100 centimeters = 1 meter
decimeter (dm) a metric unit of length; 1 decimeter = 10 centimeters
meter (m) a metric unit of length; 1 meter = 100 centimeters
kilometer (km) a metric unit of length; 1 kilometer = 1,000 meters

- Write ***meter, centimeter, millimeter, decimeter,*** and ***kilometer*** on the board. **What word do you see in each of these words?** (meter)
- Write the abbreviations on the board: **mm, cm, dm, m, km.** Have students match each abbreviation with its measure.

Measuring Length Using Metric Units

Whole Class	15 minutes
Objective	Change metric units of length.
Materials	Meterstick
Auditory, Tactual	

- Display the meterstick. **This is 1 meter long. The meter is the main unit of metric length.**
- Ask a volunteer to examine the meterstick. **How many centimeters are in 1 meter?** (100) **How many millimeters are in 1 meter?** (1,000) Write these equivalencies on the board.
- **This ruler includes another unit called the *decimeter.* There are 10 dm in 1 m.** Ask a student to point out the decimeter marks on the meterstick.
- **There is another metric unit for greater distances called the *kilometer.* I can't show it because it's too long to fit in our room. One kilometer is 1,000 meters long.**
- Explain that the lesson will explore metric units of length as well as how to change from one unit into another.

1 meter

1 yard

Differentiated Instruction

English Learners

Small Groups	10 minutes
Objective	Change metric units of length.
Materials	Student pages 320–321
Auditory, Visual	

Early Production

- Before ***Guided Practice***, do the ***Intervention*** activity below to help familiarize students with metric units of length.
- Have them copy the chart into their Math Journals spelling and saying the name of each unit under the abbreviation.

Suggest they use the chart for ***Guided Practice*** and read each expression aloud.

Intermediate/Advanced

- English Learner Resource 12.7
- English Learner Handbook

Intervention

Pairs	10 minutes
Objective	Change metric units of length.
Materials	Metric chart
Visual, Kinesthetic	

- Prepare a simple chart like the one shown.
- Tell students that the metric chart is like a place-value chart. Each column stands for a metric place. The unlabeled columns between *km* and *m* account for 1 km = 1,000 m.
- To change 5 m to cm, have students write a *5* in the m place. They should then write zeros to get to the cm place. (500)
- To change 600 mm to dm, students write *600* in the mm place. They then drop one zero for each place they move to the left. Point out that 600 mm equals 60 cm or 6 dm.

Other Resources

- *Ways to Success* CD-ROM 12.7

km			m	dm	cm	mm

Early Finishers

Small Groups	10 minutes
Objective	Change metric units of length.
Materials	Almanac
Visual, Auditory	

- Have students use an almanac to find the lengths, in meters, of six World Track and Field running events.
- Have them change each chosen distance of less than 1,000 m into dm, cm, and mm.
- Have them change each chosen distance of 1,000 m or more into km.

Language Arts Connection

Materials: Colored chalk

- Write the length measures on the board, using the same color for the word *meter* in each unit name.
- With another color, circle *milli-*, *centi-*, *deci-*, and *kilo-*. Tell Students that these prefixes repeat in the metric system.
- Work together to chart the meaning of the prefixes: *milli-* = $\frac{1}{1,000}$; *centi-* = $\frac{1}{100}$; *deci-* = $\frac{1}{10}$; *kilo-* = 1,000.

❶ Introduce

Read the objective to students and tell them that in this lesson they will convert among metric units of length (millimeters, centimeters, decimeters, meters, kilometers). They will also decide on the best estimate of length for an object.

❷ Teach

Learn About It

- **Look at the first example in the box. What units do we change?** (m to dm) **How many dm in 1 m?** (10) **Why do we multiply?** (The number of units (dm) must increase.) **Look at the second example in the box. What units do we change?** (m to km) **Which unit is greater?** (km) **Why do we divide?** (The number of units (km) must decrease.)
- **Look at *Other Example A*.** What fact must we know to change m to cm? (1 m = 100 cm) **Look at *Example B*. What fact must we know?** (1 cm = 10 mm)

Guided Practice

Have students complete **Exercises 1–4** as you observe. Remind them to use the ***Ask Yourself*** questions to help. Give students the opportunity to talk about he question in ***Explain Your Thinking.***

Common Error

- **Using the wrong equivalence** Some students may use the wrong factor to multiply or divide by when they begin using metric units.
- **Intervention** Students may need more time to learn the relationships among metric units of length. Allow them to refer to the table on page 320 as an aid until they know the relationships by heart. It can also help them to look at metric rulers as they work.

Lesson 7

Audio Tutor 2/3 Listen and Understand

Metric Units of Length

Objective Change metric units of length.

Vocabulary
millimeter (mm)
centimeter (cm)
decimeter (dm)
meter (m)
kilometer (km)

Learn About It

Millimeters, **centimeters**, **decimeters**, **meters**, and **kilometers** are metric units used to measure length.

A corn kernel is about 1 centimeter long.

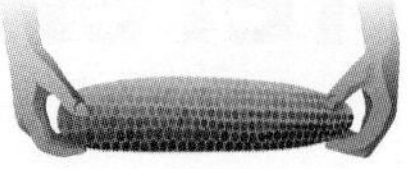

An ear of corn is about 2 decimeters long.

A young corn plant is about 1 meter tall.

A road can be about 1 kilometer long.

Change Meters to Decimeters

When you change from larger units to smaller units, the number of units increases. So multiply.

Multiply by the number of decimeters in 1 meter.

4,000	×	10	=	40,000
↑ number of meters		↑ decimeters in 1 meter		↑ decimeters in 4,000 meters

4,000 meters = 40,000 decimeters

Metric Units of Length		
1 centimeter (cm)	=	10 millimeters (mm)
1 decimeter (dm)	=	10 centimeters
1 meter (m)	=	10 decimeters
1 kilometer (km)	=	1,000 meters

Change Meters to Kilometers

When you change from smaller units to larger units, the number of units decreases. So divide.

Divide by the number of meters in 1 kilometer.

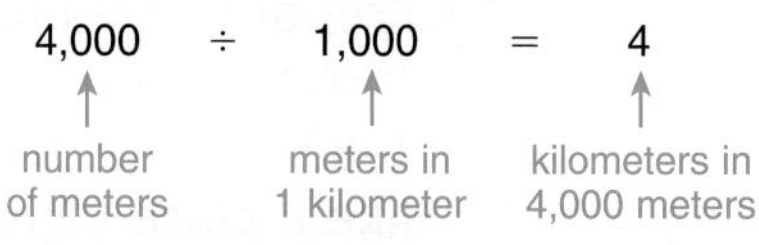

4,000	÷	1,000	=	4
↑ number of meters		↑ meters in 1 kilometer		↑ kilometers in 4,000 meters

4,000 meters = 4 kilometers

Other Examples

A. Meters to Centimeters

5 meters = ____ centimeters

$5 \times 100 = 500$

5 meters = 500 centimeters

B. Millimeters to Centimeters

80 millimeters = ____ centimeters

$80 \div 10 = 8$

80 millimeters = 8 centimeters

Reteach 12.7

Name ____________ Date ________ Reteach 12.7

Metric Units of Length

Metric Units
1 centimer (cm) = 10 millimeters (mm)
1 decimeter (dm) = 10 centimeters (cm)
1 meter (m) = 10 decimeters (dm) or 100 centimeters
1 kilometer (km) = 1,000 meters (m)

Remember:

Think: 1 cm = 10 mm
So, a centimeter is larger than a millimeter

To convert a larger unit to a smaller unit, multiply.

5 cm = ? mm

$5 \times 10 = 50$

5 cm = 50 mm

Think: 100 cm = 1m
So, a centimeter is smaller than a meter

To convert a smaller unit to a larger unit, divide.

300 cm = ? m

$300 \div 100 = 3$

300 cm = 3 m

Find each missing number.

1. 4 cm = **40** mm
2. **50** dm = 5 m
3. **800** mm = 80 cm
4. 3 km = **3,000** m
5. 6 dm = **60** cm
6. 500 dm = **50** m
7. 2 dm = **20** cm
8. **50** mm = 5 cm
9. **8,000** m = 8 km
10. 5,000 m = **5** km
11. **60** mm = 6 cm
12. **2,000** m = 2 km
13. 40 dm = **4** m
14. 3 dm = **30** cm
15. 70 mm = **7** cm

Use with text pages 320–321.

Practice 12.7 Page 80

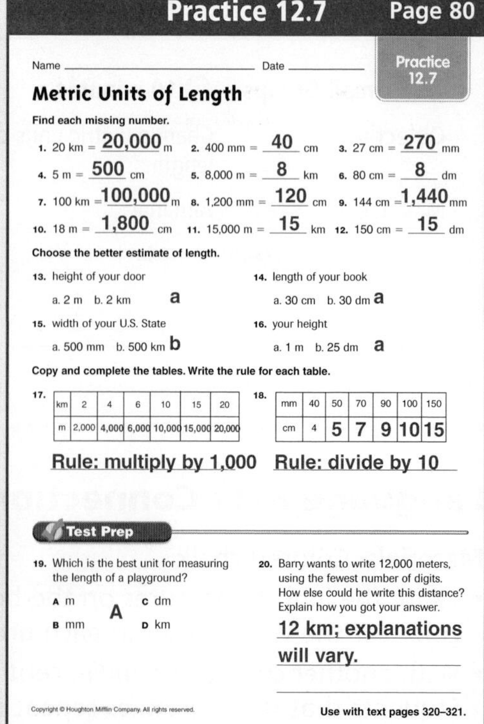

Name ____________ Date ________ Practice 12.7

Metric Units of Length

Find each missing number.

1. 20 km = **20,000** m
2. 400 mm = **40** cm
3. 27 cm = **270** mm
4. 5 m = **500** cm
5. 8,000 m = **8** km
6. 80 cm = **8** dm
7. 100 km = **100,000** m
8. 1,200 mm = **120** cm
9. 144 cm = **1,440** mm
10. 18 m = **1,800** cm
11. 15,000 m = **15** km
12. 150 cm = **15** dm

Choose the better estimate of length.

13. height of your door
a. 2 m b. 2 km **a**
14. length of your book
a. 30 cm b. 30 dm **a**
15. width of your U.S. State
a. 500 mm b. 500 km **b**
16. your height
a. 1 m b. 25 dm **a**

Copy and complete the tables. Write the rule for each table.

17.

km	2	4	6	10	15	20
m	2,000	4,000	6,000	10,000	15,000	20,000

Rule: multiply by 1,000

18.

mm	40	50	70	90	100	150
cm	4	**5**	**7**	**9**	**10**	**15**

Rule: divide by 10

Test Prep

19. Which is the best unit for measuring the length of a playground?
A m C dm
B mm D km
A

20. Barry wants to write 12,000 meters, using the fewest number of digits. How else could he write this distance? Explain how you got your answer.
12 km; explanations will vary.

Use with text pages 320–321.

Guided Practice

Ask Yourself

- Am I converting to a larger or smaller unit?
- Should I multiply or divide?

Find each missing number.

1. 40 cm = 400 mm
2. 200 cm = 2 m
3. 3 km = 3,000 m
4. 50 cm = 5 dm

Explain Your Thinking ▶ What is the best unit to use when measuring the distance between two cities? ***Possible answer:*** **The best unit is kilometers. The number would be very large if you used smaller units.**

Practice and Problem Solving

Find each missing number.

5. 50 km = 50,000 m
6. 600 mm = 60 cm
7. 90 mm = 9 cm
8. 3 m = 300 cm
9. 5,000 m = 5 km
10. 4 dm = 40 cm

Choose the better estimate of length.

11. length of a garden row
    (a.) 10 m   b. 10 mm
12. width of your fingertip
    a. 1 dm   (b.) 1 cm
13. the length of a street
    (a.) 3 km   b. 3 dm
14. the height of a window
    (a.) 1 m   b. 10 mm

Copy and complete the tables. Write the rule for each table.

15. Multiply by 1,000

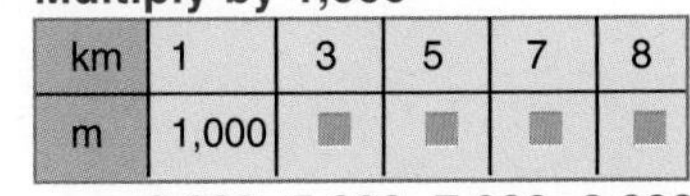

km	1	3	5	7	8
m	1,000	■	■	■	■

3,000; 5,000; 7,000; 8,000

16. Divide by 10

mm	10	20	30	60	80
cm	1	■	■	■	■

2 3 6 8

17. **Estimate** Sue estimates that there are 9 dm between plants. Lee estimates 1 m. The actual distance is 97 cm. Who made the closer estimate? **Lee**
18. Maxine has a piece of string that is 2 m long. If she cuts off a piece that is 105 cm long, will she have at least 35 cm left? ***See above.***

18. **Yes, 2 meters is 200 centimeters. 200 cm − 105 cm = 95 cm; 95 cm > 35 cm**

Mixed Review and Test Prep

Open Response

Solve. (Ch. 4, Lesson 5)

19. 72 ÷ 9 **8**
20. 36 ÷ 6 **6**
21. 56 ÷ 7 **8**
22. 49 ÷ 7 **7**
23. 27 ÷ 9 **3**
24. 72 ÷ 8 **9**

Multiple Choice

25. Which length is closest to 1 kilometer? (Ch. 12, Lesson 7)
    A 10 dm   C 1,000 cm
    B 900 m   (D) 999 m

Extra Practice See page 331, Set D.

3 Practice

Practice and Problem Solving

Select from **Exercises 5–25** as independent work.

Problem 17 Invite students to share their responses. Point out that while Lee's estimate was indeed closer to the actual distance, Sue's estimate was pretty good, too.

4 Assess & Close

Math Talk in Action

Refer to **Exercises 15–16** to conclude the lesson.

- **Which metric unit do we use to measure long distances?** (km) **for the smallest lengths?** (mm)
- **How do we know whether to multiply or divide to change units?** (Multiply to change to smaller units; divide to change to greater units.)

Math Journal Prompt

Have students find and describe useful benchmarks they can use to help them visualize 1 m, 1 dm, and 1 cm.

Lesson Quiz

Use the quiz on Lesson Transparency 12.7.

Test Prep & Spiral Review

Use Test Prep Transparency 12.7.

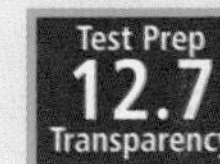

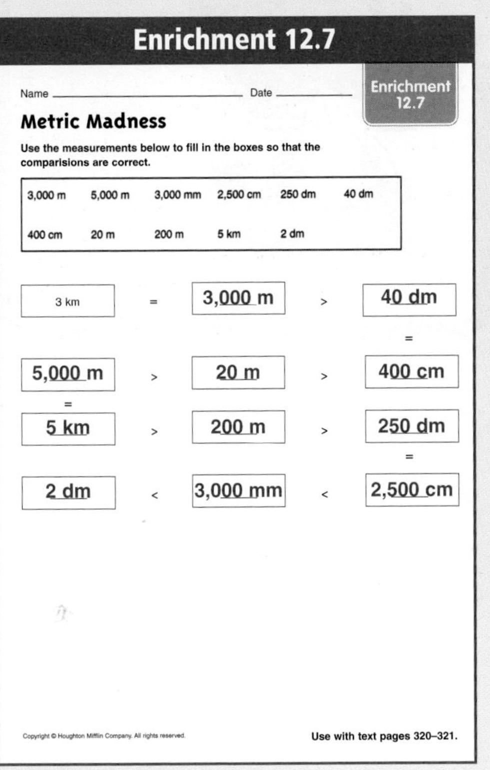

Enrichment 12.7

Name ______ Date ______ Enrichment 12.7

Metric Madness

Use the measurements below to fill in the boxes so that the comparisions are correct.

3,000 m   5,000 m   3,000 mm   2,500 cm   250 dm   40 dm
400 cm   20 m   200 m   5 km   2 dm

3 km = 3,000 m > 40 dm
(40 dm = 400 cm)
5,000 m > 20 m > 400 cm
(5,000 m = 5 km)
5 km > 200 m > 250 dm
(250 dm = 2,500 cm)
2 dm < 3,000 mm < 2,500 cm

Use with text pages 320–321.

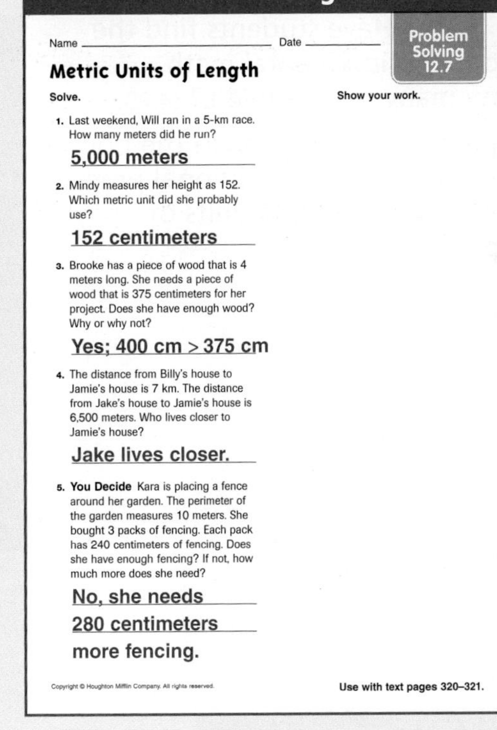

Problem Solving 12.7

Name ______ Date ______ Problem Solving 12.7

Metric Units of Length

Solve. **Show your work.**

1. Last weekend, Will ran in a 5-km race. How many meters did he run? **5,000 meters**
2. Mindy measures her height as 152. Which metric unit did she probably use? **152 centimeters**
3. Brooke has a piece of wood that is 4 meters long. She needs a piece of wood that is 375 centimeters for her project. Does she have enough wood? Why or why not? **Yes; 400 cm > 375 cm**
4. The distance from Billy's house to Jamie's house is 7 km. The distance from Jake's house to Jamie's house is 6,500 meters. Who lives closer to Jamie's house? **Jake lives closer.**
5. **You Decide** Kara is placing a fence around her garden. The perimeter of the garden measures 10 meters. She bought 3 packs of fencing. Each pack has 240 centimeters of fencing. Does she have enough fencing? If not, how much more does she need? **No, she needs 280 centimeters more fencing.**

Use with text pages 320–321.

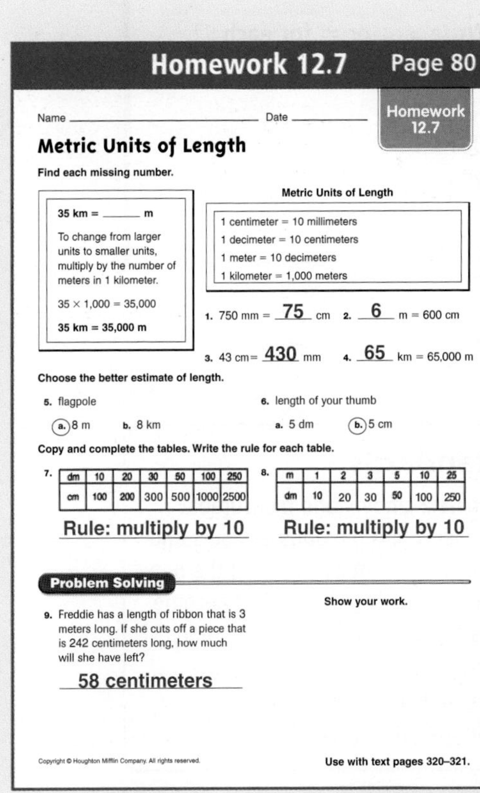

Homework 12.7 Page 80

Name ______ Date ______ Homework 12.7

Metric Units of Length

Find each missing number.

35 km = ______ m

To change from larger units to smaller units, multiply by the number of meters in 1 kilometer.

35 × 1,000 = 35,000

35 km = 35,000 m

Metric Units of Length

1 centimeter = 10 millimeters
1 decimeter = 10 centimeters
1 meter = 10 decimeters
1 kilometer = 1,000 meters

1. 750 mm = **75** cm
2. **6** m = 600 cm
3. 43 cm = **430** mm
4. **65** km = 65,000 m

Choose the better estimate of length.

5. flagpole
   (a.) 8 m   b. 8 km
6. length of your thumb
   a. 5 dm   (b.) 5 cm

Copy and complete the tables. Write the rule for each table.

7.

dm	10	20	30	50	100	250
cm	100	200	300	500	1000	2500

Rule: multiply by 10

8.

m	1	2	3	5	10	25
dm	10	20	30	50	100	250

Rule: multiply by 10

Problem Solving

Show your work.

9. Freddie has a length of ribbon that is 3 meters long. If she cuts off a piece that is 242 centimeters long, how much will she have left? **58 centimeters**

Use with text pages 320–321.

Hands On Lesson 12.8

Metric Units of Capacity

Planning

Lesson Objective Change metric units of capacity.

Technology Resources

- *Ways to Success* CD-ROM 12.8
- Education Place: Extra Practice, eGlossary, eGames www.eduplace.com/map

Lesson 12.8 Transparency

Problem of the Day

Omar bought a 250 mL carton of freshly squeezed orange juice for $1.49. Asa bought a half-liter carton of the same juice for $2.98. Which is the better buy? (1/2 L = 500 mL; Asa got twice as much juice for exactly twice as much money, so neither is a better buy; the prices are equivalent.)

Spiral Review

Use mental math to multiply or divide.

1. 6,000 ÷ 6 (1,000)
2. 25 × 100 (2,500)
3. 700 ÷ 70 (10)
4. 41 × 1,000 (41,000)
5. 9,000 ÷ 90 (100)

Lesson Quiz

Compare. Write >, <, or = for each □.

1. 9 mL □ 9,000 L (<)
2. 32 L □ 3,200 mL (>)
3. 4 L □ 4,000 mL (=)
4. 6 L □ 5,789 mL (>)
5. 875 mL □ 1 L (<)

NCTM Standards

Measurement: Understand measurable attributes of objects and the units, systems and processes of measurement; understand the need for measuring with standard units and become familiar with standard units in the customary and metric systems.
Connections: Recognize and use connections among mathematical ideas.

Getting Started

Building Math Vocabulary

liter (L) a metric unit of capacity; 1 liter = 1,000 milliliters
milliliter (mL) a metric unit of capacity; 1,000 milliliters = 1 liter

- Review the meaning of ***capacity*** as how much a container can hold. Ask students what customary units of capacity they know. (gal, qt, pt, c)
- Display the vocabulary cards for ***liter*** (L) and ***milliliter*** (mL). Discuss the meaning of each unit.

Metric Capacity

Whole Class	5 minutes
Objective	Change metric units of capacity.
Materials	Blank transparency
Visual, Tactual	

- Write *1 liter = 1,000 milliliters* on the blank transparency. **Suppose a container holds 4 L of milk. How many mL of milk is this? Let's find out.**
- **Which is greater, 1 L or 1 mL?** (1 L) **To change from a larger unit to smaller units, we multiply. What numbers will we multiply?** (4 × 1,000) Have students find the product using mental math. **How many mL are in 4 L?** (4,000)
- Explain that the lesson in the book will give students additional practice changing metric units of capacity.

1st period
5/13

Differentiated Instruction

English Learners

Pairs	10 minutes
Objective	Change metric units of capacity.
Materials	Student page 324
Auditory, Visual	

Early Production

- Have students practice using the words *liter* and *milliliter* and understanding their relationship by explaining how they found their answers to **Problems 36–40.**
- One student in a pair reads the problem and the other explains the answer.
- Partners alternate roles for the remaining problems.

Intermediate/Advanced

- English Learner Resource 12.8
- English Learner Handbook

Intervention

Whole Class	5 minutes
Objective	Review metric units of capacity.
Materials	1L and 2L bottles
Visual, Tactual	

- Display the bottles. **What usually comes in containers like these?** (soft drinks)
- **What does capacity mean?** (how much a container holds) **What is the capacity of these containers?** (1L, 2L)
- Write the metric basic unit of capacity on the board: *liter (L)*. Pronounce the term for students.

Other Resources

- *Ways to Success* CD-ROM 12.8

Gifted & Talented

Small Groups	10 minutes
Objective	Solve problems using skills and strategies.
Materials	None
Visual, Auditory	

Give this problem to students to solve.

Suppose you have a 3L jar, a 4L jug, and a big bucket. You want to pour 5 liters of water into the bucket. How can you do this? (One solution: Fill the 4-L jug with water, pour it into the bucket. Refill the 4L jug, pour 3 L of it into the jar, pour the other liter of water into the bucket.)

Science Connection

Materials: Assorted medicine droppers, test tubes

Tell students that by custom, doctors prescribe many medicines in metric dosages such as 10 mL.

- Display medicine droppers, test tubes and other tools marked in L or mL. Invite them to share their observations.
- If possible, invite a doctor, nurse, or pharmacist to talk to the class about how they use metric units in medicine.

❶ Introduce

Read the objective to students and tell them that in this lesson they will estimate the capacity of a container with reference to a liter, convert among metric units of capacity using liters and milliliters, and use benchmarks, such as a finger width for 1 cm, to estimate lengths.

❷ Teach

Learn About It

- **Look at Step 1. What will you do to begin this activity?** (Choose 3 containers that might hold about 1 L of water.) **How can we find out whether a container holds 1 L, more than 1 L, or less than 1 L?** (Fill it with water from a L measure.)
- **Look at Steps 2 and 3. How will you know if a container holds less than 1 liter?** (You won't be able to fit 1 L of water into it.) **More than 1 L?** (The container will have room for more than 1 L.)
- **Look at the *Other Examples* on page 323. In *Example A,* why does it make sense to multiply to change liters to milliliters?** (1 L = 1,000 mL; multiply to change a larger unit to a smaller one.) **In *Example B,* why do we divide to change from milliliters to liters?** (1,000 mL = 1 L; divide to change a smaller unit to a larger unit.)

Common Error

- **Incorrect operation** Some students may select the wrong operation when making conversions within a measurement system.
- **Intervention** Demonstrate how multiplication or repeated addition can be used to change a larger unit to a smaller unit, and how division or repeated subtraction can be used to change a smaller unit to a larger unit.

Hands On Lesson 8

Metric Units of Capacity

Objective Change metric units of capacity.

Vocabulary
liter (L)
milliliter (mL)

Learn About It

Materials
containers of various sizes
liter measure marked in mL
water

Liter and **milliliter** are units used to measure capacity in the metric system.

This bottle holds 1 liter.

This eyedropper holds 1 milliliter.

Metric Units of Capacity
1 liter (L) = 1,000 milliters (mL)

Try this activity to measure metric capacity.

STEP 1 Find three containers that you estimate will each hold about a liter of water.

STEP 2 Fill the liter measure with water. Pour it into each of the containers you selected.

STEP 3 Decide if the capacity of each container is greater than, less than, or equal to a liter.

Container Estimated	More or Less Than 1 Liter
Container 1	
Container 2	
Container 3	

- Which container has a capacity closest to one liter? Explain how you know. ***Answers will vary depending on students' choice of containers.***

322

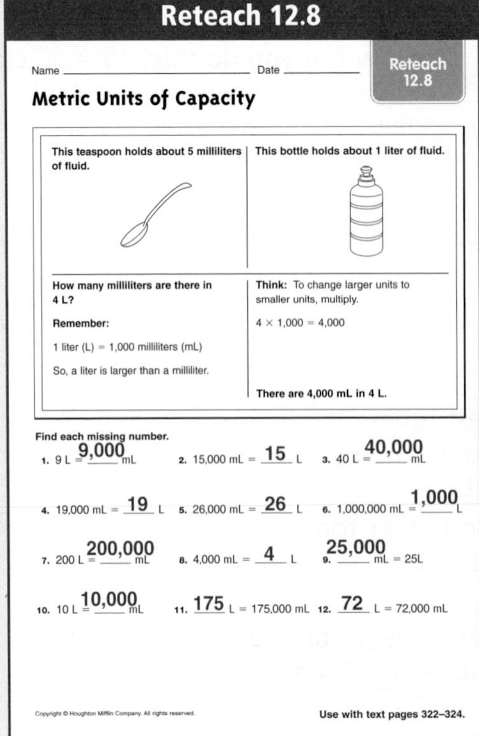

Reteach 12.8

Name ________ Date ________ Reteach 12.8

Metric Units of Capacity

This teaspoon holds about 5 milliliters of fluid.	This bottle holds about 1 liter of fluid.
How many milliliters are there in 4 L? **Remember:** 1 liter (L) = 1,000 milliliters (mL) So, a liter is larger than a milliliter.	**Think:** To change larger units to smaller units, multiply. 4 × 1,000 = 4,000 **There are 4,000 mL in 4 L.**

Find each missing number.

1. 9 L = **9,000** mL
2. 15,000 mL = **15** L
3. 40 L = **40,000** mL
4. 19,000 mL = **19** L
5. 26,000 mL = **26** L
6. 1,000,000 mL = **1,000** L
7. 200 L = **200,000** mL
8. 4,000 mL = **4** L
9. **25,000** mL = 25L
10. 10 L = **10,000** mL
11. **175** L = 175,000 mL
12. **72** L = 72,000 mL

Use with text pages 322–324.

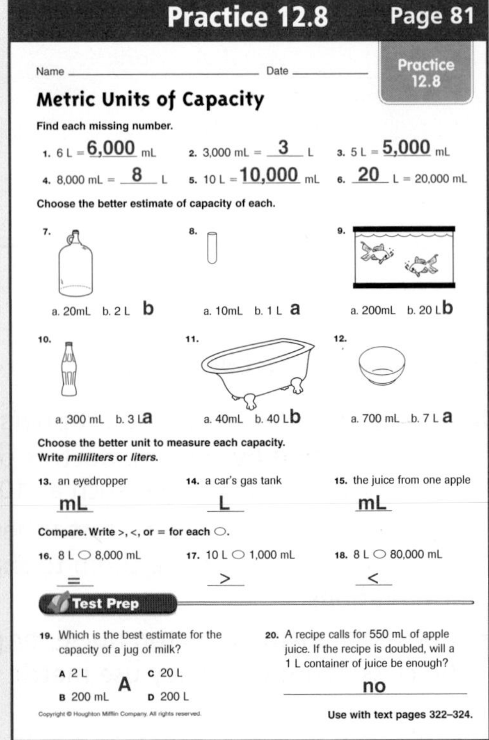

Practice 12.8 Page 81

Name ________ Date ________ Practice 12.8

Metric Units of Capacity

Find each missing number.

1. 6 L = **6,000** mL
2. 3,000 mL = **3** L
3. 5 L = **5,000** mL
4. 8,000 mL = **8** L
5. 10 L = **10,000** mL
6. **20** L = 20,000 mL

Choose the better estimate of capacity of each.

7. a. 20mL b. 2 L **b**
8. a. 10mL b. 1 L **a**
9. a. 200mL b. 20 L **b**
10. a. 300 mL b. 3 L **a**
11. a. 40mL b. 40 L **b**
12. a. 700 mL b. 7 L **a**

Choose the better unit to measure each capacity. Write *milliliters* or *liters*.

13. an eyedropper **mL**
14. a car's gas tank **L**
15. the juice from one apple **mL**

Compare. Write >, <, or = for each ○.

16. 8 L ○ 8,000 mL **=**
17. 10 L ○ 1,000 mL **>**
18. 8 L ○ 80,000 mL **<**

Test Prep

19. Which is the best estimate for the capacity of a jug of milk?
A 2 L
B 200 mL
C 20 L
D 200 L
A

20. A recipe calls for 550 mL of apple juice. If the recipe is doubled, will a 1 L container of juice be enough? **no**

Use with text pages 322–324.

Other Examples

A. Liters to Milliliters

4 liters = ____ milliliters

4 × 1,000 = 4,000

4 liters = 4,000 milliliters

B. Milliliters to Liters

2,000 milliliters = ____ liters

2,000 ÷ 1,000 = 2

2,000 milliliters = 2 liters

Guided Practice

Find each missing number.

1. 9 L = 9,000 mL
2. 5 L = 5,000 mL
3. 3,000 mL = 3 L
4. 4,000 mL = 4 L

Ask Yourself

- Am I converting to a larger or smaller unit?
- Should I multiply or divide?

Explain Your Thinking ▶ Why is it useful to measure capacity by using milliliters and liters instead of by using a small container and a large container?

Possible answer: **If you don't have a standard of measure, then you aren't sure that you will have the same amount if you measure it another time or another way.**

Practice and Problem Solving

Find each missing number.

5. 3,000 mL = 3 L
6. 2 L = 2,000 mL
7. 6,000 mL = 6 L
8. 10,000 mL = 10 L
9. 4,000 mL = 4 L
10. 25 L = 25,000 mL

Choose the better estimate of capacity for each item.

11.  

a. 20 mL (b.) 20 L

12.  

(a.) 400 mL b. 400 L

13. 

(a.) 250 mL b. 25 L

14. 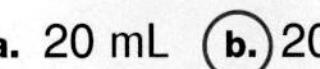

a. 8 mL (b.) 8 L

15.  

(a.) 215 mL b. 215 L

16. 

(a.) 280 mL b. 28 L

Go On

Guided Practice

Have students complete **Exercises 1–4** as you observe. Remind them to use the ***Ask Yourself*** questions to help. Give students the opportunity to talk about the question in ***Explain Your Thinking.***

❸ Practice

Practice and Problem Solving

Select from **Exercises 5–43** as independent work.

Enrichment 12.8

Name ____________ Date ______ Enrichment 12.8

More Liquid, Please!

Find the difference between the measurement of capacity on the left and the measurement of capacity on the right. Write the difference on the line between them. Then add up the differences from problems 4, 5, and 6 and subtract this from the sum of the differences from problems 1, 2, and 3. The result will be the answer to this question:

How many milliliters are in 1 gallon?

10,000 ml	1. 1,000 mL	9 L
17 L	2. 2,200 mL	14,800 ml
28,800 ml	3. 3,800 mL	25 L
600 ml	4. 400 mL	1 L
2,185 ml	5. 815 mL	3 L
66,000 ml	6. 2,000 mL	64 L

7. Sum of problems 1, 2, and 3: 7,000 mL
8. Sum of problems 4, 5, and 6: 3,215 mL
9. Difference: 3,785 mL
10. How many milliliters are in 1 gallon? 3,785 mL

Use with text pages 322–324.

Problem Solving 12.8

Name ____________ Date ______ Problem Solving 12.8

Metric Units of Capacity

1. Morgan had a 1-liter container of water. She drank half of the water in the container. How many milliliters of water does Morgan have left?

500 mL

2. Yesterday, Kathy drank 2 liters of water. Holly drank 2,500 milliliters of water. Who drank more? Explain.

Holly; 2L = 2,000 mL 2,500 mL > 2,000 L

3. **Multistep** Mr. Murphy has a 2-liter container of grape juice. He pours three glasses of grape juice for his children. Each glass holds 225 mL. How much grape juice does he have left?

1,325 mL

4. **Reasoning** For a chemistry experiment, Tom needs to measure 750 mL of hydrogen peroxide. Tom only has a 1-liter container and a 250-mL container. How can he accurately measure 750 mL?

Q#4. He can fill the 1-liter container, and then fill the 250 mL container from the 1-liter container. 1L = 1,000 mL and 750 mL & 250 mL = 1,000 mL.

5. **Use Data** Look at the recipe to the right. Darla's Smoothie Store sells a 350-mL serving of Banana Berry Smoothie for $2.00. How many servings does the recipe make? How much will the store make if it sells the entire amount the recipe makes?

11 servings; $22

Banana Berry Smoothie Recipe
2 L milk
750 mL crushed strawberries
525 mL crushed blueberries
575 mL crushed bananas

Use with text pages 322–324.

- ***Problems 23–35*** Remind students to refer to the table on page 322 to remember the relationship between liters and milliliters.
- ***Data*** After students complete this lesson, you might work together to prepare this recipe. Invite students to help you measure and mix the ingredients. Be sure everyone gets a taste.

4 Assess & Close

Math Talk in Action

- **For what sorts of measurement do we use liters and milliliters?** (capacity)
- **What is the relationship between liters and milliliters?** (1 L = 1,000 mL)
- **Which unit would you probably use to describe the amount of liquid in a baby bottle?** (mL)

Math Journal Prompt

Have students explain how to change 5,000 mL to liters and 12 L to milliliters.

Lesson Quiz

Use the quiz on Lesson Transparency 12.8.

Test Prep & Spiral Review

Use Test Prep Transparency 12.8.

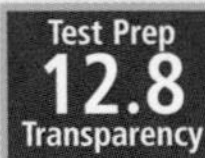

Choose the better unit to measure each capacity. Write *milliliters* or *liters.*

17. a glass of milk **milliliters**
18. a kitchen sink **liters**
19. the juice from one lemon **milliliters**
20. a bathtub **liters**
21. a spoon **milliliters**
22. a swimming pool **liters**

Compare. Write >, <, or = for each ●.

23. 6 mL ● 6,000 L **<**
24. 8 L ● 8,000 mL **=**
25. 30 L ● 300 mL **>**
26. 4,500 mL ● 45 L **<**
27. 4 L ● 350 mL **>**
28. 2,000 mL ● 2 L **=**
29. 7 L ● 7,000 mL **=**
30. 550 mL ● 5 L **<**
31. 60 L ● 60,000 mL **=**

Solve.

32. Carla has 4 bottles of water. Each bottle has a capacity of 500 mL. How many liters of water can the bottles hold altogether? **2 L**
33. It takes 12 average-size oranges to make 1 liter of orange juice. How many mL of juice can be expected from 18 oranges? **1,500 mL**
34. **Estimate** A recipe calls for 250 mL of apple juice. If the recipe is tripled, will a 1 L container of apple juice be enough? **yes**
35. A large cooler can hold 20 L and a small cooler can hold 5 L. How many more milliliters can a large cooler hold than a small cooler? **15,000 mL more**

Data Use the recipe for Problems 36–40.

36. How many liters will Sonya's punch recipe make? **4**
37. How many 250 mL servings are in this recipe? **16**
38. If each serving is 250 mL, how many liters of punch will be needed for 40 servings? **10**
39. How many more milliliters of lemon-lime soda are in this recipe than orange juice? **1,250**
40. **Money** How much will each 250 mL serving cost if the ingredients in the recipe cost a total of $5.60? **$0.35**

Sonya's Citrus Punch
750 mL orange juice
250 mL grapefruit juice
600 mL lemonade
400 mL limeade
2 L lemon lime soda

324

Extra Practice See page 331, Set E.

Homework 12.8 **Page 81**

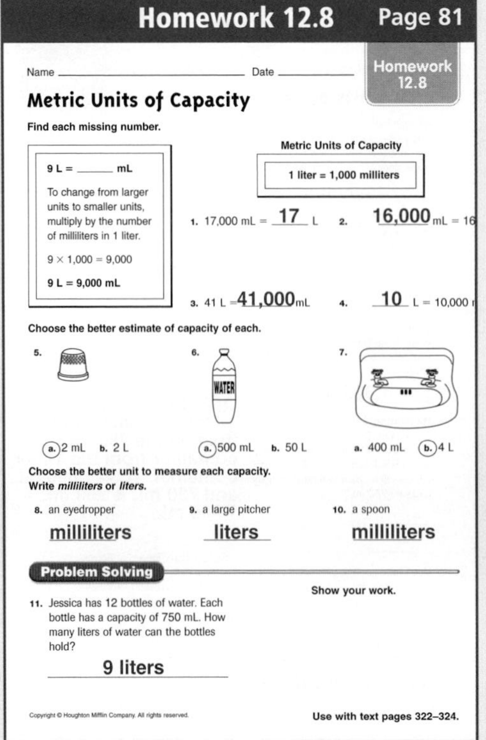

Name ______ Date ______

Homework 12.8

Metric Units of Capacity

Find each missing number.

9 L = ____ mL

To change from larger units to smaller units, multiply by the number of milliliters in 1 liter.

9 × 1,000 = 9,000

9 L = 9,000 mL

Metric Units of Capacity

1 liter = 1,000 milliliters

1. 17,000 mL = **17** L
2. **16,000** mL = 16
3. 41 L = **41,000** mL
4. **10** L = 10,000

Choose the better estimate of capacity of each.

5. (a.) 2 mL b. 2 L
6. (a.) 500 mL b. 50 L
7. a. 400 mL (b.) 4 L

Choose the better unit to measure each capacity. Write *milliliters* or *liters*.

8. an eyedropper **milliliters**
9. a large pitcher **liters**
10. a spoon **milliliters**

Problem Solving

Show your work.

11. Jessica has 12 bottles of water. Each bottle has a capacity of 750 mL. How many liters of water can the bottles hold? **9 liters**

Use with text pages 322–324.

41. *Possible answer:* 7:10; ten minutes after seven

Mixed Review and Test Prep

Open Response

Write the time in two ways. (Grade 3)

41. 

See above.

42. 

See below.

43. Anna wants to write 7,000 milliliters, using the fewest digits. How else could she write this capacity? (Chapter 12, Lesson 8)

Explain how you got your answer. **7 liters; There are 1,000 milliliters in 1 liter**

42. *Possible answer:* 10:45; quarter to eleven

Math Reasoning

Using Benchmarks

Activity

Materials: centimeter or inch ruler
yardstick or meter stick

Here are some useful ways to estimate length.

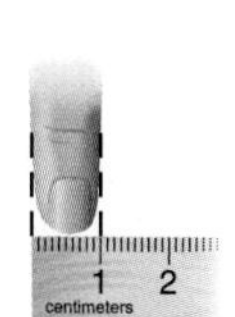

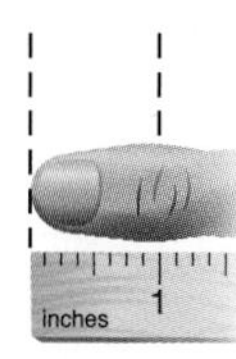

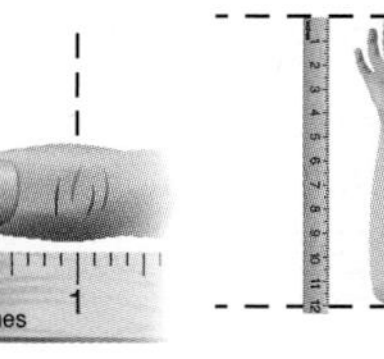

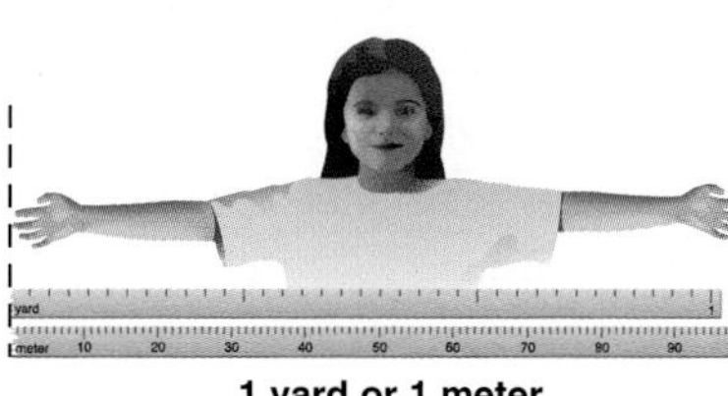

1 centimeter | 1 inch | 1 foot | 1 yard or 1 meter

Work with a partner.

STEP 1 Check the measurements shown above to find your personal benchmarks for length. ***Check students' work.***

- Is your finger about 1 centimeter wide?
- Is the first joint in your thumb about 1 inch long?
- Does your arm from elbow to hand measure about 1 foot?
- Does your arm span measure about 1 yard? 1 meter?

STEP 2 Use your personal benchmarks to estimate the length of 5 objects in the classroom. Order and record your estimates. Then measure the objects using metric or customary units. Order and record your measurements.

How close were your estimates? ***Answers will vary depending on objects measured.***

Math Reasoning

Using Benchmarks

Materials: cm or inch ruler, yardstick or meterstick

Background Explain that surveyors who would mark a known height on something permanent, such as a prominent rock, and then use it as a reference point to determine other measures originally used the term *benchmark*.

Tips Encourage students to make a handy chart of the personal benchmarks they have found. They can always refer to this chart whenever they want to estimate lengths in metric and customary units.

ACHIEVING Mathematical Proficiency

Helping Students Become Learners

One goal in teaching math proficiency is to **help students become independent learners**. Homework is often given for that purpose. Before homework is given, however, students should understand a skill well enough that they do not practice it incorrectly on their own. There are other **settings in which students can begin to learn on their own**. Students can work individually, in pairs, or in groups within the classroom. One scenario involves students learning about measurement. As students estimate measurements, particularly less-familiar metric values, they can **question each other, argue a point of view, and explain** what they are doing. Students become **better learners when they talk with each other about mathematical ideas** in addition to practicing math skills independently.

Hands On Lesson 12.9

Metric Units of Mass

Planning

Lesson Objective Change metric units of mass.

Technology Resources

- *Ways to Success* CD-ROM 12.9
- Education Place: Extra Practice, eGlossary, eGames www.eduplace.com/map

Lesson 12.9 Transparency

Problem of the Day

Ed's rabbit had a litter of 7 bunnies. The mass of the biggest was 80 g. Two were 75 g each, 3 were 70 g each, and the mass of the tiniest was 60 g. After a week, all the bunnies had doubled their mass. What was the total mass of the bunnies after 1 week? (1 kg)

Spiral Review

Divide.

1. 10,000 ÷ 2,000 (5)
2. 810 ÷ 90 (9)
3. 3,600 ÷ 40 (90)
4. 42,000 ÷ 6,000 (7)
5. 20,000 ÷ 500 (40)

Lesson Quiz

Find each missing number.

1. 6 kg = ___ g (6,000)
2. ___ g = 3 kg (3,000)
3. 12 kg = ___ g (12,000)
4. ___ g = 5 kg (5,000)
5. 10,000 g = ___ kg (10)

NCTM Standards

Measurement: Understand measurable attributes of objects and the units, systems and processes of measurement; understand the need for measuring with standard units and become familiar with standard units in the customary and metric systems.
Connections: Recognize and use connections among mathematical ideas.

Getting Started

Building Math Vocabulary

gram (g) a metric unit of mass; 1,000 grams = 1 kilogram

kilogram (kg) a metric unit of mass; 1 kilogram = 1,000 grams

- Display the vocabulary cards for ***gram (g)*** and ***kilogram (kg)*** and discuss the meaning of each unit. Tell students that we use these metric units to measure mass. Discuss the meaning of the prefix *kilo-* and help students recall its use in other metric units.

Measuring Mass in Metric Units

Whole Class	5 minutes
Objective	Change metric units of mass.
Materials	1 kg bag of rice, 1 kg mass
	Visual, Tactual

- Ask a student to read the label on the bag to find its mass. **What is the mass of the bag?** (1 kg) Pass it and the metric mass around so students can compare the two. **What else might be sold in kilograms?** (Accept all reasonable answers.)
- **Think of what you already know about metric measures. What does *kilo-* mean?** (1,000) **What is the name of the smaller unit that makes up a kilogram?** (gram)
- Tell students that in this lesson, they will explore metric units of mass.

Differentiated Instruction

English Learners

Small Groups	10 minutes
Objective	Change metric units of mass.
Materials	Student page 326
Auditory, Visual	

Early Production

- After ***Introduce*** and ***Teach,*** provide additional practice using *kilogram, gram,* and their abbreviations.
- Ask students to write numbers 1–10 on a piece of paper with the abbreviation *km* next to each number.
- Students write the corresponding numbers of grams and read their answers aloud.

Intermediate/Advanced

- English Learner Resource 12.9
- English Learner Handbook

Intervention

Small Groups	5-10 minutes
Objective	Change metric units of mass.
Materials	None
Visual, Auditory	

- Relate the relative sizes of g to kg and m to km, since both relationships involve a factor of 1,000.
- Highlight the prefix *kilo-* in *kilo*meter and *kilo*gram. Remind students that *kilo-* always means 1,000 times the base unit. Point out that a km is a great length, yet a kg is a moderate mass because of the relative size of grams vs. meters.
- Have students make their own mass chart to which they can refer as they work.

Other Resources

- *Ways to Success* CD-ROM, Lesson 12.9

Special Needs

Small Groups	10 minutes
Objective	Compare masses using metric units.
Materials	Balance scale, four objects, metric masses
Tactile, Visual	

- Provide 4 objects of different masses. Have students pick any two and use the scale to see which has the greater mass.
- Have them repeat for other pairs of items so they can order all four objects from least to greatest mass.

Science Connection

Materials: reference materials, graph paper

- Zoologists know that each type of animal baby has a usual weight at birth.
- Have students work in pairs to find the weight at birth of five animals of their choice. They can use encyclopedias, science books, or the Internet.
- Help students organize their data into a group chart that orders the animals according to weight.

❶ Introduce

Read the objective to students and tell them that in this lesson they will measure and compare mass using a balance scale and metric masses, convert among metric units of mass (grams, kilograms), and choose the best estimate of the mass of an object.

❷ Teach

Learn About It

- **What is the relationship between grams and kilograms?** (1 kg = 1,000 g)
- **Look at Step 1. Order the masses of the three objects from least to greatest.** (1g, 100 g, 500 g) **Which mass is the same as $\frac{1}{2}$ kg?** (500 g)
- **Look at Step 2. How will you find the actual masses of the objects you select?** (with the balance and metric masses)
- **Look at Step 3. How can you use what you already know to predict the mass of other objects?** (Lift an object, feel its mass compared to one you know.)
- **Look at *Other Examples A* and *B*. In *Example A*, do we change from larger to smaller units or from smaller to larger units?** (larger to smaller) ***In Example B?*** (smaller to larger)

Common Error

- **Confusing units of mass**
- **Intervention** Students who choose the incorrect unit of mass may need more hands-on experience measuring with grams and kilograms. They may also need familiar benchmarks to grasp the relative mass of these units. Tell students that the mass of a large paper clip is about 1 g, and the mass of a full-size wooden baseball bat is about 1 kg.

Metric Units of Mass

Objective Change metric units of mass.

Vocabulary
gram (g)
kilogram (kg)

Materials
balance
metric masses

Learn About It

These four pumpkin seeds have a mass of 1 gram. The pumpkin has a mass of 45 kilograms.

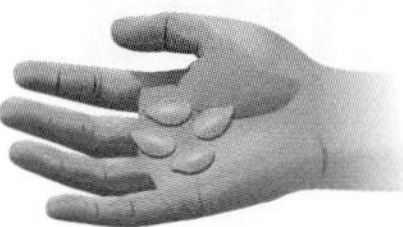

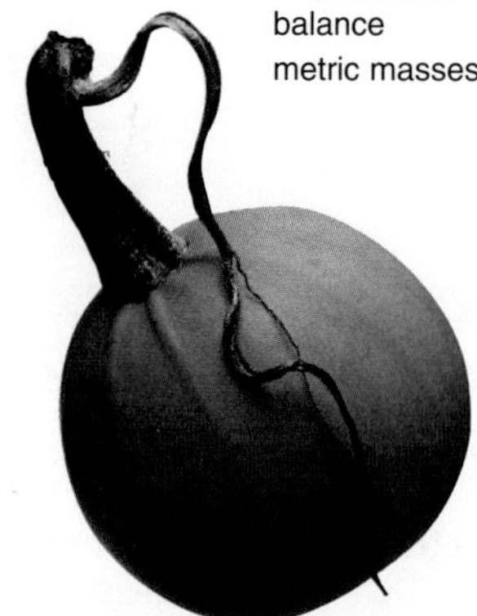

Gram and **kilogram** are metric units of mass.

Try this activity to measure and compare mass.

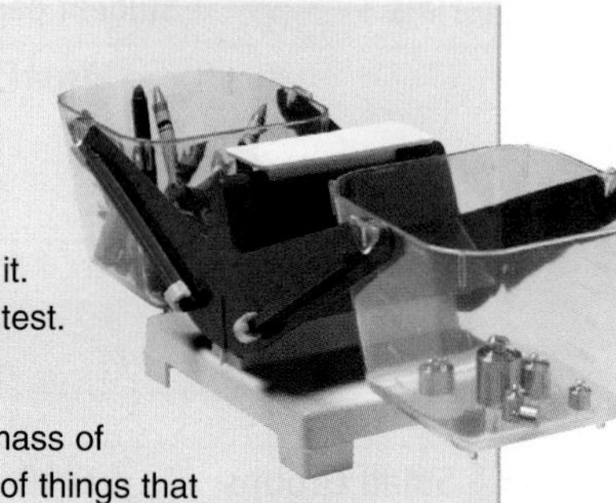

STEP 1 Find three objects in the classroom that you estimate will have a mass of 500 grams, 1 gram, and 100 grams.

STEP 2 Determine each object's mass and record it. List the three objects from heaviest to lightest.

STEP 3 Use the objects you found to predict the mass of other things in the classroom. Make a list of things that have a mass of about 1 gram, about 100 grams, and about 500 grams.

Metric Units of Mass
1 kilogram (kg) = 1,000 grams (g)

Other Examples

A. Kilograms to Grams

3 kilograms = ____ grams
$3 \times 1{,}000 = 3{,}000$
3 kilograms = 3,000 grams

B. Grams to Kilograms

2,000 grams = ____ kilograms
$2{,}000 \div 1{,}000 = 2$
2,000 grams = 2 kilograms

326

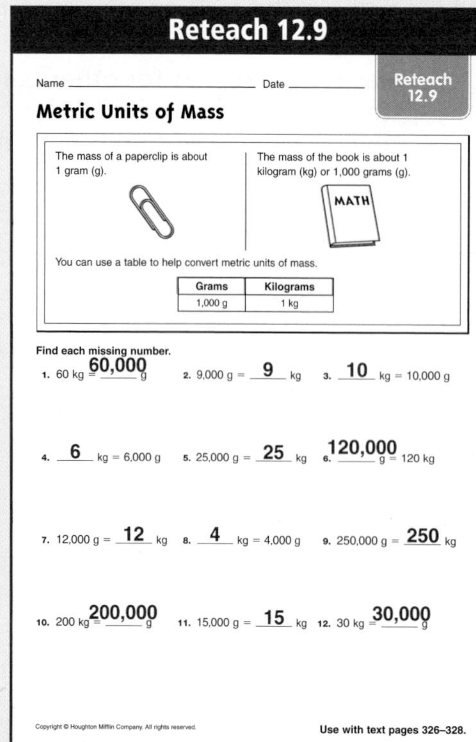

Reteach 12.9

Name ____________ Date ________

Reteach 12.9

Metric Units of Mass

The mass of a paperclip is about 1 gram (g).

The mass of the book is about 1 kilogram (kg) or 1,000 grams (g).

MATH

You can use a table to help convert metric units of mass.

Grams	Kilograms
1,000 g	1 kg

Find each missing number.

1. 60 kg = 60,000 g
2. 9,000 g = 9 kg
3. 10 kg = 10,000 g
4. 6 kg = 6,000 g
5. 25,000 g = 25 kg
6. 120,000 g = 120 kg
7. 12,000 g = 12 kg
8. 4 kg = 4,000 g
9. 250,000 g = 250 kg
10. 200 kg = 200,000 g
11. 15,000 g = 15 kg
12. 30 kg = 30,000 g

Use with text pages 326–328.

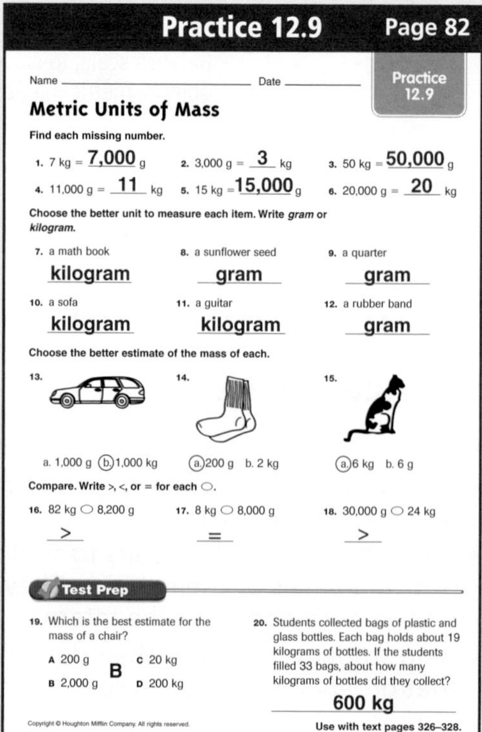

Practice 12.9 Page 82

Name ____________ Date ________

Practice 12.9

Metric Units of Mass

Find each missing number.

1. 7 kg = 7,000 g
2. 3,000 g = 3 kg
3. 50 kg = 50,000 g
4. 11,000 g = 11 kg
5. 15 kg = 15,000 g
6. 20,000 g = 20 kg

Choose the better unit to measure each item. Write *gram* or *kilogram*.

7. a math book kilogram
8. a sunflower seed gram
9. a quarter gram
10. a sofa kilogram
11. a guitar kilogram
12. a rubber band gram

Choose the better estimate of the mass of each.

13. a. 1,000 g (b.) 1,000 kg
14. (a.) 200 g b. 2 kg
15. (a.) 6 kg b. 6 g

Compare. Write >, <, or = for each ○.

16. 82 kg ○ 8,200 g >
17. 8 kg ○ 8,000 g =
18. 30,000 g ○ 24 kg >

Test Prep

19. Which is the best estimate for the mass of a chair?
A 200 g
B 2,000 g
C 20 kg
D 200 kg
B

20. Students collected bags of plastic and glass bottles. Each bag holds about 19 kilograms of bottles. If the students filled 33 bags, about how many kilograms of bottles did they collect?
600 kg

Use with text pages 326–328.

Guided Practice

Find each missing number.

1. 8 kg = **8,000** g
2. **9** kg = 9,000 g
3. **5** kg = 5,000 g
4. 7 kg = **7,000** g

Explain Your Thinking ▶ Why is mental math useful in converting kilograms to grams? **There are 1,000 milligrams in a gram, so you can multiply the kilograms by 1,000 to get grams.**

Practice and Problem Solving

Find each missing number.

5. 5 kg = **5,000** g
6. **3** kg = 3,000 g
7. **8,000** g = 8 kg
8. 10 kg = **10,000** g
9. **4,000** g = 4 kg
10. 6 kg = **6,000** g

Choose the better unit to measure each. Write *gram* or *kilogram*.

11. a paper clip **gram**
12. a stapler **gram**
13. a desk **kilogram**
14. a dictionary **kilogram**
15. a pencil **gram**
16. a cherry **gram**

Choose the better estimate of the weight of each.

17. 

a. 40 g (b.) 4 kg

18. 

(a.) 450 g b. 45 kg

19. 

(a.) 60g b. 6 kg

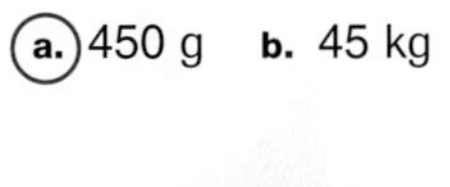

20. 

a. 8 g (b.) 8 kg

21. 

(a.) 100 g b. 10 kg

22. 

a. 300 g (b.) 300 kg

Guided Practice

Have students complete **Exercises 1–4** as you observe. Remind them to use the ***Ask Yourself*** questions to help. Give students the opportunity to talk about the question in ***Explain Your Thinking.***

❸ Practice

Practice and Problem Solving

Select from **Exercises 5–41** as independent work.

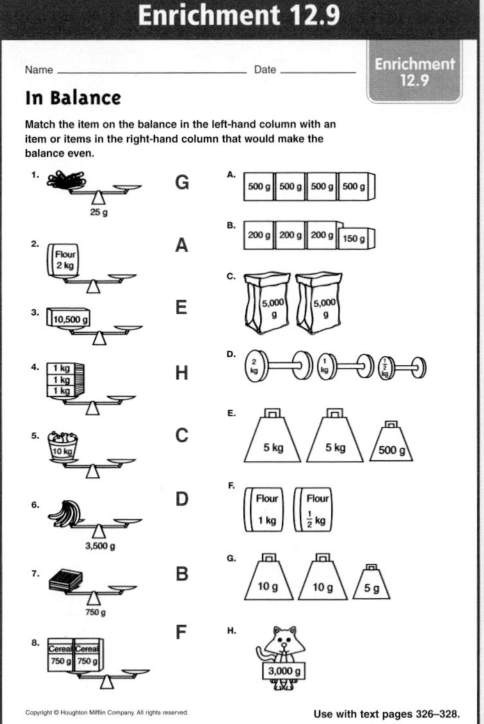

Enrichment 12.9

Name ______________ Date ______ Enrichment 12.9

In Balance

Match the item on the balance in the left-hand column with an item or items in the right-hand column that would make the balance even.

1. 25 g **G**
2. Flour 2 kg **A**
3. 10,500 g **E**
4. 1 kg 1 kg 1 kg **H**
5. 10 kg **C**
6. 3,500 g **D**
7. 750 g **B**
8. Cereal 750 g Cereal 750 g **F**

A. 500 g 500 g 500 g 500 g
B. 200 g 200 g 200 g 150 g
C. 5,000 g 5,000 g
D. 2 kg 1 kg $\frac{1}{2}$ kg
E. 5 kg 5 kg 500 g
F. Flour 1 kg Flour $\frac{1}{2}$ kg
G. 10 g 10 g 5 g
H. 3,000 g

Use with text pages 326–328.

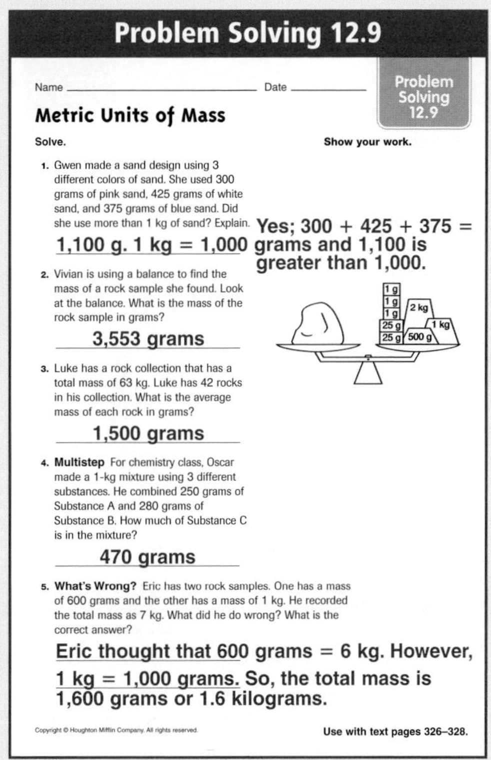

Problem Solving 12.9

Name ______________ Date ______ Problem Solving 12.9

Metric Units of Mass

Solve. Show your work.

1. Gwen made a sand design using 3 different colors of sand. She used 300 grams of pink sand, 425 grams of white sand, and 375 grams of blue sand. Did she use more than 1 kg of sand? Explain. **Yes; 300 + 425 + 375 = 1,100 g. 1 kg = 1,000 grams and 1,100 is greater than 1,000.**
2. Vivian is using a balance to find the mass of a rock sample she found. Look at the balance. What is the mass of the rock sample in grams? **3,553 grams**
3. Luke has a rock collection that has a total mass of 63 kg. Luke has 42 rocks in his collection. What is the average mass of each rock in grams? **1,500 grams**
4. **Multistep** For chemistry class, Oscar made a 1-kg mixture using 3 different substances. He combined 250 grams of Substance A and 280 grams of Substance B. How much of Substance C is in the mixture? **470 grams**
5. **What's Wrong?** Eric has two rock samples. One has a mass of 600 grams and the other has a mass of 1 kg. He recorded the total mass as 7 kg. What did he do wrong? What is the correct answer? **Eric thought that 600 grams = 6 kg. However, 1 kg = 1,000 grams. So, the total mass is 1,600 grams or 1.6 kilograms.**

Use with text pages 326–328.

- ***Problem 32*** **What operation will you use to estimate the answer?** (multiplication)
- ***Problem 35*** If necessary, review the method for finding averages.

4 Assess & Close

Math Talk in Action

- **What metric units do we use to express mass?** (g, kg)
- **What is the relationship between the gram and the kilogram?** (1,000 g = 1 kg)

Math Journal Prompt

Have students compare and contrast changing between customary units of measure and between metric units. Have them give examples to support their positions.

Lesson Quiz

Use the quiz on Lesson Transparency 12.9.

Test Prep & Spiral Review

Use Test Prep Transparency 12.9.

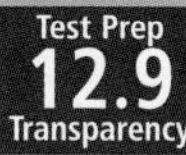

Compare. Write >, <, or = for each ⬬.

23. 95 kg ⬬ 950 g >	**24.** 3 kg ⬬ 3,000 g =	**25.** 1,000 g ⬬ 2 kg <
26. 5 g ⬬ 5,000 kg <	**27.** 25 kg ⬬ 2,500 g >	**28.** 700 g ⬬ 7 kg <
29. 3 kg ⬬ 6,000 g <	**30.** 125 kg ⬬ 4,000 g >	**31.** 1,990 g ⬬ 19 kg <

Solve.

32. **Estimate** Workers put apples in baskets that hold about 12 kg each. The workers filled 17 baskets. About how many kg of apples did they put in baskets? **about 200 kg**

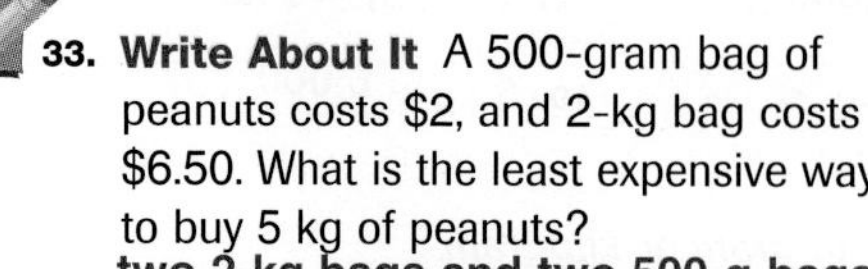

33. **Write About It** A 500-gram bag of peanuts costs $2, and 2-kg bag costs $6.50. What is the least expensive way to buy 5 kg of peanuts? **two 2-kg bags and two 500-g bags**

34. Paul sold 3-kg bags of apples for $3.90 each. He sold pears for $1.20 per kg. He found that he had sold 15 kg of apples and 7 kg of pears. How much money did he collect? **$27.90**

35. Delroy weighed the pumpkins shown below. What is the average mass of the pumpkins? **2,750 g**

36. Delroy decided to sell the pumpkins for 1 cent per gram. How much money will he collect if he sells all the pumpkins? **$192.50**

Extra Practice See page 331, Set F.

Homework 12.9 **Page 82**

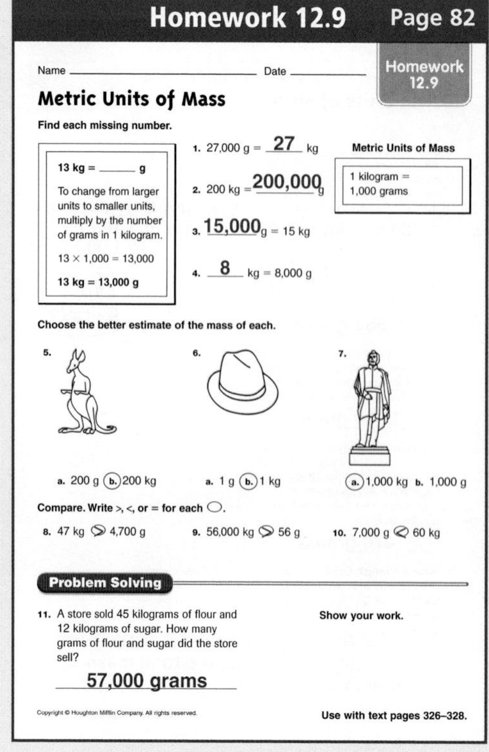

Name ____________ Date ________ Homework 12.9

Metric Units of Mass

Find each missing number.

13 kg = ____ g
To change from larger units to smaller units, multiply by the number of grams in 1 kilogram.
13 × 1,000 = 13,000
13 kg = 13,000 g

1. 27,000 g = **27** kg
2. 200 kg = **200,000** g
3. **15,000** g = 15 kg
4. **8** kg = 8,000 g

Metric Units of Mass
1 kilogram = 1,000 grams

Choose the better estimate of the mass of each.

5. a. 200 g (b.) 200 kg
6. a. 1 g (b.) 1 kg
7. (a.) 1,000 kg b. 1,000 g

Compare. Write >, <, or = for each ◯.

8. 47 kg > 4,700 g
9. 56,000 kg > 56 g
10. 7,000 g < 60 kg

Problem Solving

11. A store sold 45 kilograms of flour and 12 kilograms of sugar. How many grams of flour and sugar did the store sell? **57,000 grams**

Show your work.

Use with text pages 326–328.

Mixed Review and Test Prep 

Open Response

Estimate. Then Divide. (Ch. 11, Lesson 6)

37. 16)339 21 R3

38. 22)628 28 R12

39. 893 ÷ 47 19

40. 990 ÷ 38 26 R2

41. The local market sells cornmeal in 2,000-gram bags. Kristen needs 5 kilograms of cornmeal to make cornbread for the town fair. How many bags of cornmeal should she buy? Will she have any cornmeal left over? (Chapter 12, Lesson 9)
She should buy 3 bags; Yes, she will have 1 kg left over.

Problem Solving

Calculator Connection
Crafty Conversions

Use your calculator to estimate conversions between metric and customary units.

1. 5 yd is about 4.5 m
2. 12 oz is about 336 g
3. 36 lb is about 18 kg
4. 5 mi is about 8 km
5. 10 cm is about 4 in.
6. 6 qt is about 5.4 L
7. 3 m is about 9 ft
8. 4 ft is about 120 cm

Estimated Equivalents
Length
1 in. is about 2.5 cm
1 yd is about 0.9 m
1 mi is about 1.6 km
Weight/Mass
1 oz is about 28 g
1lb is about 0.5 kg
Capacity
1 qt is about 0.9 L

Visual Thinking

Crafty Conversions

There are precise formulas that can be used to convert between customary and metric units of length, weight/mass, capacity, and other forms of measure. However, the estimates given in this activity are accurate enough for everyday use.

Explain to students that the statement "1 oz is about 28 g" means that on Earth, a mass of 28 grams weighs about 1 oz. Similarly, a mass of 0.5 kg weighs about 1 lb.

Reaching All Learners

Measurement Sense

Changing Metric Units Remind students that the metric system of measures is based on 10 and multiples of 10. Changing from one metric unit to another involves multiplying or dividing by a multiple of 10. Remind students that they multiply to change from larger units to smaller units. They divide to change from smaller units to larger units.

Have students complete the following exercises.

1. 100 m = ___ dm (1,000)
2. 5,000 g = ___ kg (5)
3. 2,000 dm = ___ cm (20,000)
4. 20,000 mL = ___ L (20)
5. 200 L = ___ mL (200,000)
6. 10,000 mm = ___ m (10)
7. 500 dm = ___ mm (50,000)
8. 600 cm = ___ m (6)

Differentiated Assignments		
At Risk	**Average**	**Advanced**
Exercises 1–4	Exercises 1–6	Exercises 3–8

Monitoring Student Progress

Chapter Review/Test

Chapter Review/Test Items 1–20

To assign a numerical grade for this Chapter Review/Test, use 5 points for each item.

Check Understanding

You can use the ***Write About It*** question to assess student understanding of a key chapter concept.

Customize Your Instruction

The Chapter Review/Test is a formal evaluation of chapter objectives. For students who have not yet mastered these objectives, you can use the Reteaching Resources listed in the chart below.

Additional Assessment Resources

Alternate Chapter Test A Chapter Test is also provided in the Unit Resource folder. You might use the Review/Test in the student book as review and the test in the Unit Resource folder as a summary test for the chapter.

***Ways to Assess* CD-ROM** allows you to create your own lesson, chapter, or unit tests or practice and review worksheets.

Adequate Yearly Progress Guide helps familiarize your students with the format of standardized tests.

Chapter Review/Test

VOCABULARY

Choose the best word to complete each sentence.

Vocabulary
mile
liter
gram
weight

1. A unit used to describe mass is a **gram**
2. A unit used to describe length is a **mile**
3. A unit used to describe liquid measure is a **liter**

CONCEPTS AND SKILLS

Measure this ribbon. (Lessons 1 and 6, pp. 306–307, pp. 318–319)

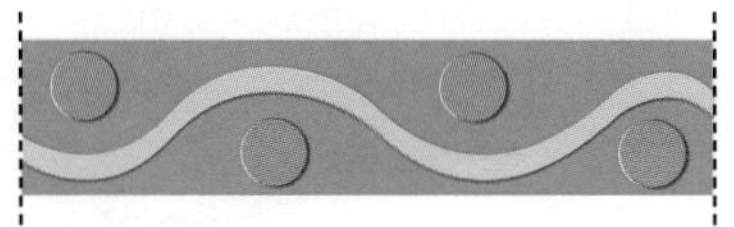

4. to the nearest inch **3 in.**
5. to the nearest quarter inch $2\frac{3}{4}$ **in.**
6. to the nearest centimeter **7 cm**
7. to the nearest millimeter **68 mm**

Find each missing number. (Lessons 2–4, pp. 308–314)

8. 4 yd = **144** in.
9. 60 ft = **20** yd
10. 2 mi = **10,560** ft
11. 5 gal = **20** qt
12. 12 c = **6** pt
13. 2 gal = **32** c
14. 4 lb = **64** oz
15. 2 T = **4,000** lb
16. 32 oz = **2** lb

Choose the metric unit you would use to describe each. (Lessons 7–9, pp. 320–328)

17. the length of a flea **millimeters**
18. the capacity of a sink **liters**
19. the mass of a pencil **grams**

PROBLEM SOLVING

Solve. (Lesson 5, p. 316)

20. Maria is 3 feet 9 inches tall. Naeem is 47 inches tall. Paula is 5 feet tall. What is the difference in inches between Paula's height and Naeem's height? **13 inches**

Write About It

Show You Understand

Tony has a 22 gallon aquarium. Ian said that it holds 90 quarts of water. Is Ian correct? **No, 22 gal is 88 qt.** Explain why or why not.

There are 4 qt in 1 gal. 4 × 22 = 88

Chapter Review/Test Items	Objectives	Covered On Teacher's Edition Pages	Use These Reteaching Resources
2, 4–7	**12A** Measure length, using customary and metric units.	306A–307, 318A–319	Reteach Resources 12.1, 12.6; *Ways to Success* CD-ROM 12.1, 12.6 Skillsheets 103, 104
1, 3, 8–16	**12B** Convert among units of capacity and weight (mass).	308A–314	Reteach Resources 12.2, 12.3, 12.4 *Ways to Success* CD-ROM 12.2, 12.3, 12.4 Skillsheets 107, 109, 110
17–19	**12C** Choose the most appropriate unit of measure for customary and metric units.	320A–328	Reteach Resources 12.7, 12.8, 12.9 *Ways to Success* CD-ROM 12.7, 12.8, 12.9 Skillsheets 108, 111, 112
20	**12D** Solve problems using skills and strategies.	316A–316	Reteach Resources 12.5 *Ways to Success* CD-ROM 12.5 Skillsheet 113

Extra Practice

Set A (Lesson 2, pp. 308–309)

Find each missing number.

1. 3 yd = **108** in.
2. 24 in. = **2** ft
3. **72** in. = 6 ft
4. **5,280** ft = 1 mi
5. 4 yd = **12** ft
6. 3 mi = **5,280** yd

Set B (Lesson 3, pp. 310–311)

Find each missing number.

1. 16 c = **8** pt
2. 4 gal = **64** c
3. 8 pt = **1** gal
4. **3** gal = 12 qt
5. 11 pt = **22** c
6. **12** pt = 6 qt

Set C (Lesson 4, pp. 312–314)

Compare. Write >, <, or = for each ⬬.

1. 3,000 lb **<** 3 T
2. 6 lb **>** 80 oz
3. 36 oz **>** 2 lb

Set D (Lesson 7, pp. 320–321)

Find each missing number.

1. 3 dm = **30** cm
2. 5 cm = **50** mm
3. 200 cm = **2** m
4. **5** km = 5,000 m
5. 30 cm = **3** dm
6. 700 mm = **70** cm

Set E (Lesson 8, pp. 322–324)

Find each missing number.

1. 2 L = **2,000** mL
2. **6** L = 6,000 mL
3. **10,000** mL = 10 L
4. 4000 mL = **4** L
5. **8,000** mL = 8 L
6. 5 L = **5,000** mL

Set F (Lesson 9, pp. 326–328)

Compare. Write >, <, or = for each ⬬.

1. 2 kg **<** 2,500 g
2. 17 kg **=** 17,000 g
3. 850 g **<** 85 kg

Extra Practice at **eduplace.com/map**

CHAPTER 12 TEST

Name ______ Date ______ Chapter 12 Test

Measure to the nearest inch, half-inch, and quarter inch.

1. 3 inches; $3\frac{1}{2}$ inches; $3\frac{1}{2}$ inches

Measure the length to the nearest centimeter and nearest millimeter.

2. 4 centimeters; 37 millimeters

Find each missing number.

3. 5,000 mL = **5** L
4. 8 T = **16,000** lb
5. **16** kg = 16,000 g
6. 4 gal = **16** qt

Choose the better estimate of weight or mass.

7. a child **(B)** a. 20 g b. 20 kg
8. a basket of apples **(B)** a. 3 oz b. 3 lb

Choose the better estimate of length.

9. a pencil **(B)** a. 7 ft b. 7 in.
10. a bee **(A)** a. 30 mm b. 30 cm

CHAPTER 12 TEST

Name ______ Date ______ Chapter 12 Test continued

Choose the better unit to measure each capacity. Write *milliliters* or *liters*.

11. a soup can **milliliters**
12. a goldfish tank **liters**

Choose the better unit to measure each weight. Write *ounces, pounds,* or *tons.*

13. a penny **ounces**
14. a hippopotamus **tons**

Compare. Write >, <, or = for each ○.

15. 2 ft **>** 20 in.
16. 13 pt **<** 8 qt
17. 5 lb **=** 80 oz
18. 8 L **=** 8,000 mL

Solve. If not enough information is given, tell what information is needed to solve the problem.

19. Jane, Leah, and Amanda played in a soccer game. Jane made 4 goals and Leah made 2 goals. Amanda made twice as many goals as Leah. How many goals did Amanda make?
4 goals

20. To make the roof for a birdhouse, Will cut 9 inches off each end of a plank of wood. How long is the plank now?
Not enough information; you need to know the length of the original plank.

CHAPTER 13

Planning Guide

Time and Temperature

Lesson	Overview	Objective/Vocabulary
1 Calendar p. 334A	▶ Convert among calendar units, including day, week, month, year, decade, and century time units. ▶ Use calendars and a schedule to find elapsed times.	▶ Use a calendar to find elapsed time. decade century
2 Elapsed Time p. 336A	▶ Convert among clock time units from hours to weeks and vice versa. ▶ Find elapsed clock time and tell time to the second on analog clock faces. ▶ Decide whether an estimated or exact time is needed in a real-life situation.	▶ Find elapsed times. elapsed time A.M. P.M.
3 Problem-Solving Strategy: Guess and Check p. 340A	▶ Solve problems using the Guess and Check strategy. ▶ Follow a step-by-step example to see how solving a problem may take several guesses. ▶ Practice problem-solving strategies learned earlier.	▶ Use the Guess and Check strategy to solve a problem.
4 Temperature and Negative Numbers p. 344A	▶ Read, write, and compare temperatures in degrees Fahrenheit and Celsius. ▶ Familiarize students with benchmark temperatures—for example, room temperature is about 20°C—and help them associate appropriate temperatures with different situations. ▶ Indicate temperatures above and below zero with positive and negative numbers. ▶ Count up or down on a thermometer to find the difference between temperatures.	▶ Use a thermometer to read temperatures above and below zero. positive numbers negative numbers degrees Fahrenheit (°F) degrees Celsius (°C)
5 Problem-Solving Application: Use Temperature p. 348A	▶ Solve word problems involving temperature. ▶ Choose a computation method to solve a problem. ▶ Determine which years are leap years.	▶ Solve problems about temperature.

Skills Trace: Time and Temperature		
Grade 3	**Grade 4**	**Grade 5**
• Read and write time to the minute (ch. 12) • Determine elapsed time using calendars and clocks (ch. 12) • Read, write, and compare temperature in degrees Fahrenheit and Celsius (ch. 12)	• Read and write time to the second • Determine elapsed time using calendars and clocks • Read, write, and compare temperatures in degrees Fahrenheit and Celsius • Use positive and negative numbers to indicate temperatures above and below zero	• Understand, compare, and order integers (ch. 22) • Add and subtract integers (ch. 22) • Analyze and solve problems using integers (ch. 22)

Differentiated Instruction	Materials	NCTM Standards
▶ Differentiated Instruction activities, p. 334B ▶ *Chapter Challenges,* p. 73 *Ways to Success* CD-ROM 13.1 ▶ *Ways to Success* Skillsheet 115	Calendars	**Measurement:** Select and apply appropriate standard units and tools to measure length, area, volume, weight, time, temperature, and the size of angles. **Problem Solving:** Solve problems that arise in mathematics and other contexts. **Representation:** Create and use representations to organize, record, and communicate mathematical ideas.
▶ Differentiated Instruction activities, p. 336B *Ways to Success* CD-ROM 13.2 ▶ *Ways to Success* Skillsheet 118 Audio Tutor **2**/4 Listen and Understand	Analog clock, blank clock faces (Learning Tool 16)	**Measurement:** Understand measurable attributes of objects and the units, systems, and processes of measurement. **Problem Solving:** Solve problems that arise in mathematics and in other contexts.
▶ Differentiated Instruction activities, p. 340B ▶ *Chapter Challenges,* p. 75 *Ways to Success* CD-ROM 13.3 ▶ *Ways to Success* Skillsheet 120		**Problem Solving:** Solve problems that arise in mathematics and in other contexts; apply and adapt a variety of appropriate strategies to solve problems. **Number and Operations:** Compute fluently and make reasonable estimates.
▶ Differentiated Instruction activities, p. 344B *Ways to Success* CD-ROM 13.4 ▶ *Ways to Success* Skillsheet 119 Audio Tutor **2**/5 Listen and Understand	Fahrenheit and Celsius Thermometer Transparencies, thermometers	**Measurement:** Select and apply appropriate standard units and tools to measure length, area, volume, weight, time, temperature, and the size of angles. **Connections:** Recognize and use connections among mathematical ideas.
▶ Differentiated Instruction activities, p. 348B ▶ *Chapter Challenges,* p. 77 *Ways to Success* CD-ROM 13.5	Fahrenheit and Celsius Thermometer Transparencies, tap water, Fahrenheit thermometers	**Measurement:** Select and apply appropriate standard units and tools to measure length, area, volume, weight, time, temperature, and the size of angles. **Connections:** Recognize and use connections among mathematical ideas.

Math Notes

Chapter Objectives

13A Determine elapsed time using clocks and calendars.

13B Measure temperature above and below zero using degrees Fahrenheit and degrees Celsius.

13C Solve problems using skills and strategies.

Mathematical Background

Time and Temperature

When learning about time, it is important for students to remember that there are 24 hours in a day, 60 minutes in an hour, and 60 seconds in a minute. When finding elapsed time, it is also important to notice whether the times are A.M. or P.M.

In this chapter, students will read temperatures both above and below 0° using customary units, degrees *Fahrenheit (F°),* and metric units, degrees *Celsius (C°).* To read temperatures below zero, negative numbers are used.

Integers are the counting numbers 1, 2, 3 . . . and their opposites ⁻1, ⁻2, ⁻3 . . . and 0. The number line can be used to represent integers. A thermometer is like a vertical number line.

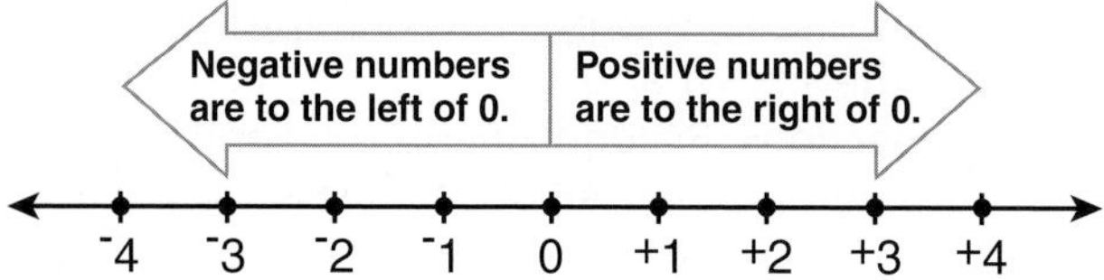

Here are some important temperatures students should know.

Water Boils	Water Freezes	Normal Body Temperature
212°F	32°F	98.6°F
100°C	0°C	37°C

Research-Based Teaching

Research by Shaw and Puckett Cliatt (1989) in the area of measurement has led to the term *measurement sense* to describe what students should know as a result of instruction. Measurement sense involves a knowledge of strategies for estimating lengths, temperature, volume, mass, and time. Good estimators know several strategies and choose the one that is applicable to the situation. See *Professional Resources Handbook, Grade 4,* Unit 5.

For more ideas relating to Unit 5, see the Teacher Support Handbook at the back of this Teacher's Edition.

Language Intervention

In East Asian countries, children learn that just as numbers can be composed and decomposed as sets and subsets, units of measurement can be composed and decomposed as well. For further explanation, see "Mathematical Language and Measurement" in the *Professional Resources Handbook, Grade 4.*

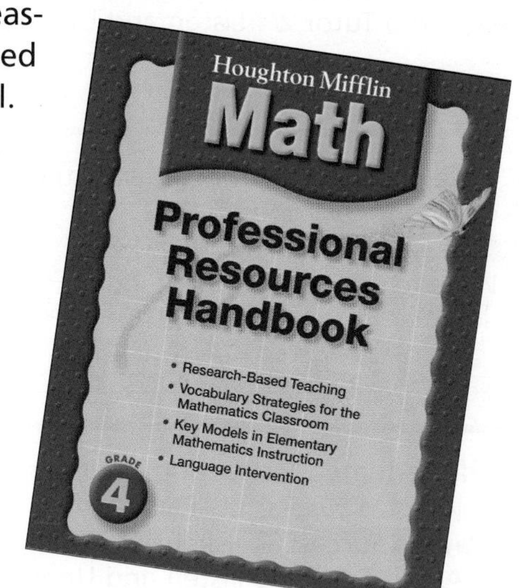

Chapter Activities

Connecting to the Unit Project

Whole Class	30 minutes
Objective	Collect, organize, and analyze data.
Materials	Chart paper, yarn, markers, index cards, or other art materials
Visual, Kinesthetic	

Make a State Time Line

- Have students organize all of the historical dates and information that they have found about their states.
- Ask them to make a time line using all of the dates. Students may refer to the Enrichment lesson on page 394 to learn about a time line.
- Encourage students to write elapsed-time story problems about the historical dates they found.

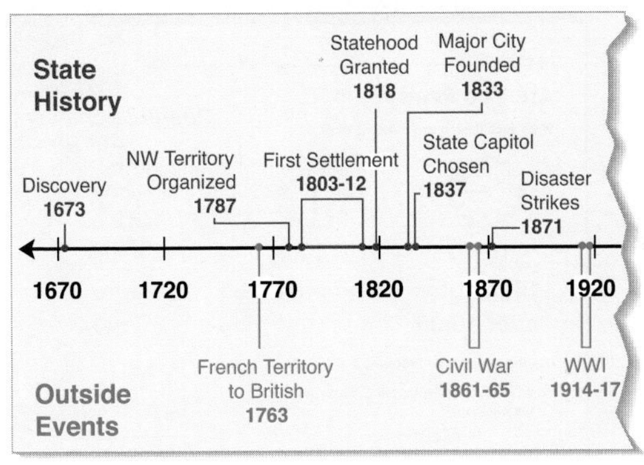

Ongoing Skill Activity

Individuals	10 minutes
Objective	Determine elapsed time using calendars and measure temperature in °Fahrenheit or °Celsius.
Materials	Calendars, news media
Visual, Kinesthetic	

Date and Temperature Data

- Assign students alphabetically or some other way to be responsible for presenting the date and temperature range for the following day.
- At the beginning of each day or of each mathematics class, have the designated student write the date (month, day, year) and the temperature range for the day. Encourage students to listen to the radio, watch television, or check the Internet for this information before they come to school. The student may also draw a sun, clouds, or raindrops to indicate the weather that goes along with the temperature.
- Students should get into the habit of knowing the date and temperature at the beginning of each day to prepare for the day ahead.

Math Expressions

Pairs	15 minutes
Objective	Use clocks to find elapsed time.
Materials	Clock Times Copymaster
Visual	

Elapsed Time

This activity uses instructional practices from Math Expressions with the content of this unit.

- Distribute 3 copies of the Clock Times Copymaster to pairs of students. Have students tell what they see on the page. two clock faces
- Display the problems listed below. Have students draw clock hands to show the start time and end time in each problem. To find the difference in time (in hours and minutes) between the two times, show students how to count by ones for hours and by 5s for minutes for each numeral on the clock.

1. Etta arrives at the concert at 6:20. The concert begins at 8:05. How long does she have to wait for the concert to begin?
2. Alberto finished his science project at 3:45. He started the project at 1:30. How much time did he spend on his project?
3. Lauren's dance class ended at 12:15. The class started at 10:35. How long did the dance class last?

Starting Chapter 13

Investigation

Using Data

Have students work in small groups to answer the question posed on page 332.

To extend the investigation, have students do the following activity.

- Find similar data about another interesting bird, such as the ostrich or kiwi. Does it take longer for flamingo eggs to hatch than this bird's eggs? If so, how much longer? Do flamingos have a longer or shorter lifespan than this type of bird?

For more information about projects and investigations,

Visit **Education Place®**
www.eduplace.com/mat

CHAPTER 13

Time and Temperature

INVESTIGATION

Using Data

Flamingos are beautiful pink birds that live in tropical climates. Look at the list of facts about flamingos. About how many weeks does it take a flamingo egg to hatch? What information do you need to write each of the Flamingos facts in terms of weeks? **about 4 weeks; Check students' answers.**

Flamingos

- It takes between 26 and 31 days for a flamingo egg to hatch.
- It takes between 1 and 3 years for the gray flamingo chick to turn pink.
- A flamingo can live up to 50 years.

332

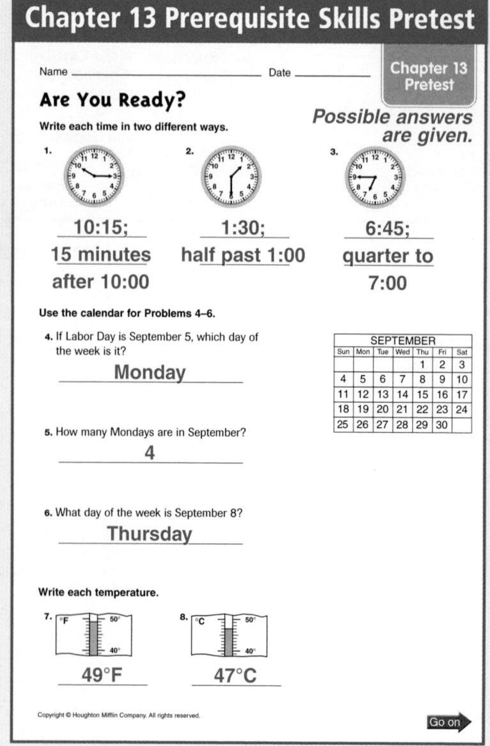
Chapter 13 Prerequisite Skills Pretest

Name ________ Date ________

Chapter 13 Pretest

Are You Ready?

Possible answers are given.

Write each time in two different ways.

1. 10:15; 15 minutes after 10:00
2. 1:30; half past 1:00
3. 6:45; quarter to 7:00

Use the calendar for Problems 4–6.

SEPTEMBER						
Sun	Mon	Tue	Wed	Thu	Fri	Sat
				1	2	3
4	5	6	7	8	9	10
11	12	13	14	15	16	17
18	19	20	21	22	23	24
25	26	27	28	29	30	

4. If Labor Day is September 5, which day of the week is it? Monday
5. How many Mondays are in September? 4
6. What day of the week is September 8? Thursday

Write each temperature.

7. 49°F
8. 47°C

Go on

✓ Use What You Know

Use this page to review and remember what you need to know for this chapter.

VOCABULARY

Choose the best term to complete each sentence.

Vocabulary
year
calendar
thermometer
degrees Fahrenheit

1. The tool for measuring temperature is a ____. **thermometer**
2. Temperature can be measured in ____. **degrees Fahrenheit**
3. A ____ shows the days, weeks, and months in a year. **calendar**

CONCEPTS AND SKILLS

Write each time in two different ways. ***Possible answers given at right.***

4. 9:15; 45 minutes before 10
5. 6:25; 35 minutes before 7
6. 2:33; 27 minutes before 3

4. 

5. 

6. 

Use the calendar for Questions 7–9.

7. The first Monday of September is Labor Day. What is the date? **September 5**
8. What is the date of the third Wednesday? **September 21**
9. How many Fridays are there in the month shown? **5**

September						
Sun.	Mon.	Tue.	Wed.	Thu.	Fri.	Sat.
				1	2	3
4	5	6	7	8	9	10
11	12	13	14	15	16	17
18	19	20	21	22	23	24
25	26	27	28	29	30	

10. ***Possible answer:*** **There are 60 minutes in an hour, so half of the minutes between 7:00 and 8:00 have passed.**

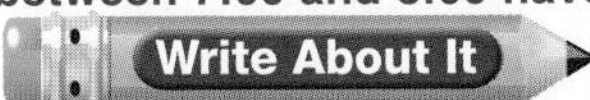

10. Why is 7:30 sometimes called half past seven? Use words or pictures to explain your thinking. ***See above.***

Facts Practice, See page 671.

Chapter 13 New Content Pretest

Chapter 13 Pretest continued

Name ____________ Date ________

Check What You Know

Look at each pair of times. Write how much time has passed.

1. Start: 2:10 P.M. End: 4:25 P.M. **2 h 15 min**
2. Start: 5:30 A.M. End: 7:15 A.M. **1 h 45 min**
3. Start: 11:40 A.M. End: 2:15 P.M. **2 h 35 min**

Tell what time it will be. Use the Clock A for Problems 4–5. Use the second Clock B for Problems 6–7.

4. in 2 hours. **3:25**
5. in 15 minutes. **1:40**
6. in 10 minutes. **12:05**
7. in 3 hours. **2:55**

A B

Use the calendar for Problems 8–11.

8. How many Fridays are in February? **4**
9. What is the date of the third Thursday in February? **February 21**
10. What day of the week is February 1st? **Friday**
11. What is the date of the second Wednesday in February? **February 13**

FEBRUARY						
Sun	Mon	Tue	Wed	Thu	Fri	Sat
					1	2
3	4	5	6	7	8	9
10	11	12	13	14	15	16
17	18	19	20	21	22	23
24	25	26	27	28		

Go on

Chapter 13 New Content Pretest

Chapter 13 Pretest continued

Name ____________ Date ________

Write each temperature.

12. °C 30° 20° **25°C**
13. °F 100° 90° **96°F**
14. °F 0° −10° **−8°F**

Find the difference between the temperatures.

15. 98°F and 115°F **17°F**
16. 26°C and 11°C **15°C**
17. −8°C and 16°C **24°C**

Use Guess and Check to solve each problem.

18. There are 8 more boys than there are girls in the fourth grade. Altogether there are 56 fourth-graders. How many boys and how many girls are there in the fourth grade? **32 boys and 24 girls**
19. The product of two numbers is 16. The difference between the numbers is 6. What are the numbers? **8 and 2**
20. Jared collects $90 for a fundraiser. He collects only $5 bills and $10 bills. He collects 15 bills in all. How many of each kind of bill does Jared collect? **twelve $5 bills and three $10 bills**

STOP

Use What You Know

Use this page for informal assessment and review of prerequisite skills.

- Items 1–3: Use math vocabulary
- Items 4–6, 10: Tell time two ways
- Items 7–9: Tell time using a calendar
- Item 10: Explain two different names for a time.

Customize Your Instruction

Use the Chapter Pretest in the Unit Resource folder to help customize and pace instruction.

Objectives and Resources

▶ Prerequisite Skills Pretest

- Items 1–3: Tell time to the nearest quarter hour.
- Items 4–6: Tell time using a calendar.
- Items 7–8: Read and write temperatures in degrees Fahrenheit and Celsius.

▶ New Content Pretest

- Items 1–11: Determine elapsed time using clocks and calendars.
- Items 12–17: Measure temperature above and below zero, using degrees Fahrenheit and degrees Celsius.
- Items 18–20: Solve problems using skills and strategies.

▶ For Students Having Difficulty

- Ways to Success CD-ROM 13A–B, D

▶ For Students Having Success

- Enrichment 13.1-13.5

▶ For Mathematically Promising Students

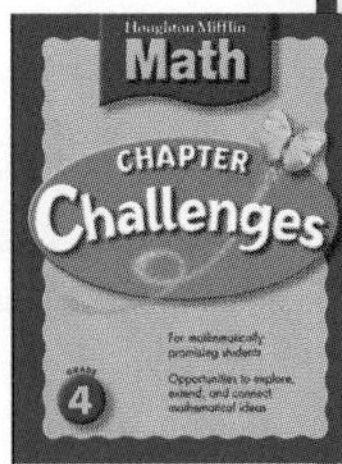

Explore: Calendar Conversions, p. 73, after Lesson 1

Extend: Time Zones, p. 75, after Lesson 3

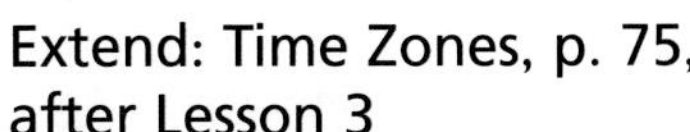

Connect: A Temperature Experiment, p. 77, after Lesson 5

Lesson 13.1

Calendar

Planning

Lesson Objective Use a calendar to find elapsed time.

Technology Resources

- *Ways to Success* CD-ROM 13.1
- Education Place: Extra Practice, eGlossary, eGames
  www.eduplace.com/map

Lesson 13.1 Transparency

Problem of the Day

Yolanda is making a calendar for the month of May. She is using individual stickers with the digits 0–9 to show all the dates. How many stickers with the digit 1 will she need? The digit 2? The digit 3? (14; 13; 5)

Spiral Review

Find each missing number.

1. 5 m = __ cm (500)
2. 80 dm = __ m (8)
3. 600 cm = __ m (6)
4. 2 kg = ___ g (2,000)

Lesson Quiz

Find each missing number.

1. 3 weeks = ___ days (21)
2. 7 decades = ___ years (70)
3. 2 leap years = ___ days (732)
4. 4 centuries, 3 decades = ____ years (430)
5. ___ centuries = 900 years (9)

NCTM Standards

Measurement: Select and apply appropriate standard units and tools to measure length, area, volume, weight, time, temperature, and the size of angles.
Problem Solving: Solve problems that arise in mathematics and other contexts.
Representation: Create and use representations to organize, record, and communicate mathematical ideas.

Getting Started

Building Math Vocabulary

decade a unit of time; 1 decade = 10 years

century a unit of time; 1 century = 100 years

Use the vocabulary cards for ***century*** and ***decade*** to relate each term to other words students know with the same prefix, such as *centi*meter (100 cm = 1 m; 1 century = 100 yr) and *deci*meter (10 dm = 1 m; 1 decade = 10 yr).

Using a Calendar to Tell Time

Whole Class	20 minutes
Objective	Determine elapsed time using calendars.
Materials	Calendar
Visual	

- Display the calendar for the current month for students to examine. **How many days are in this month? Which days of the week appear most often this month? Why are there empty spaces before the first (or after the last) day of this month? What date is one week from today? What date was one week ago?**
- **How many ways can we write today's date?** (Accept all reasonable answers, such as MM/DD/YY, as well as full names and abbreviations.)
- Tell students that in this lesson, they will be using various units of calendar time, including some that are less commonly used, but important to know.

Sun.	Mon.	Tues.	Wed.	Thur.	Fri.	Sat.
			1	2	3	4
5	6	7	8	9	10	11
12	13	14	15	16	17	18
19	20	21	22	23	24	25
26	27	28	29	30	31	

Differentiated Instruction

English Learners

Pairs	15 minutes
Objective	Determine elapsed time using calendars.
Materials	Student page 335, index cards
Auditory, Visual	

Early Production

- Before ***Practice and Problem Solving,*** pair up students to do the following activity.
- Have partners use index cards to make a set of study aids for calendar measures. Have them write one relationship per card for *week, year* (in months, weeks, and days), *leap year* (in days), *decade,* and *century.*
- As students work through **Exercises 11–18,** have them describe the relationship written on the card, then compare it to the problem. Ask them to verbalize the unit relationship and identify the numbers they would multiply to determine the equivalent measure. For example: *One week equals 7 days, so 2 weeks times 7 equals 14 days.*

Intermediate/Advanced

- English Learner Resource 13.1
- English Learner Handbook

Intervention

Small Groups	10 minutes
Objective	Discuss calendars.
Materials	Variety of different calendars
Auditory, Visual	

- Show students a variety of calendars in different formats. Have them compare and contrast the different calendars, such as the standard-array model, one-day-at-a-time calendars, datebooks, online digital calendars, calendars in VCRs, and so on. Have them consider which formats are most useful for different purposes.
- Have students brainstorm and list all of the calendar words they may know, such as *day, week, month, year, decade, and century.* Write their equivalents in terms of days or years.

Other Resources

- *Ways to Success* CD-ROM 13.1

Gifted & Talented

Pairs	15 minutes
Objective	Determine elapsed time using calendars.
Materials	Calendars, calculators
Auditory, Visual	

- Challenge students to find the number of days since their last birthday and until their next birthday. Allow them to use calculators to do the computation, but have them record their methods.
- When appropriate, remind students to include any calculations needed to keep the answer in line with leap years. Ask students why this might be necessary. (Every four years, we add an extra day to account for the extra quarter day in the standard year.)

Social Studies Connection

Materials: *Calendar Art: 13 Days, Weeks, Months, Years from Around the World* by Leonard Everett Fisher

- Read parts of Fisher's book to students. Clarify the various calendar systems presented.
- Form small groups. Have each group make a poster that explains a different calendar system. Display the posters in the room.

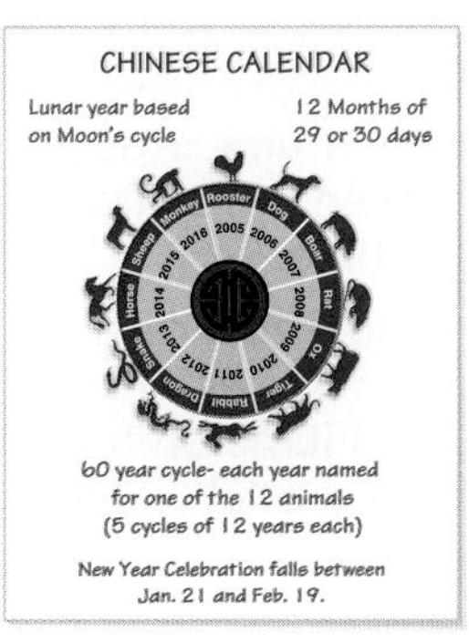

CHINESE CALENDAR
Lunar year based on Moon's cycle
12 Months of 29 or 30 days
60 year cycle- each year named for one of the 12 animals (5 cycles of 12 years each)
New Year Celebration falls between Jan. 21 and Feb. 19.

❶ Introduce

Brainstorm with students a list of the ways they typically use calendars in their everyday life. (Possible answers: to check their daily schedule, to scan a list of special events at a museum, to figure out when library books are due, to find out when a birthday or a national holiday falls, to sequence recent events, to make a time line of historical events, or to find out when an invention or discovery took place.) Tell students that the lesson will explain how to use calendars to find out how much time has passed between events.

❷ Teach

Learn About It

- Have a volunteer read the opening problem. **What is the difference between a day and a date?** (A day is a name, such as *Friday*; a date is a number in a month, such as *April 25*.) **How do you decide where to start counting?** (Find April 25; count the next date as *1*, and so on, until you reach the 13th day after.) **Why are there calendars for April and May?** (13 days takes us into May.)
- **Look at *Other Examples.* Which units are compared?** (years, centuries; years, decades) **Which operation is used?** (multiplication) **Which calculation method is easiest?** (mental math)

Guided Practice

Have students complete **Exercises 1–4** as you observe. Remind them to use the ***Ask Yourself*** questions to help. Give students the opportunity to talk about the question in ***Explain Your Thinking.***

Common Error

- **Miscounting elapsed calendar time** Students may, in error, count the given day as Day 1 when they figure elapsed time.
- **Intervention** Help them visualize a calendar as a number line divided into rows. From one day to the next is like a jump on the number line. Have students model "jumps" as they go.

Lesson 1

Calendar

Objective Use a calendar to find elapsed time.

Vocabulary
decade
century

Learn About It

A cardinal laid eggs on Monday, April 25. They hatched 13 days later. On what day and date did the eggs hatch?

You can use a calendar to find elapsed time by counting the number of days.

Find April 25. Start counting forward from the next day. Count 13 days.

APRIL

S	M	T	W	T	F	S
					1	2
3	4	5	6	7	8	9
10	11	12	13	14	15	16
17	18	19	20	21	22	23
24	25	26	27	28	29	30

MAY

S	M	T	W	T	F	S
1	2	3	4	5	6	7
8	9	10	11	12	13	14
15	16	17	18	19	20	21
22	23	24	25	26	27	28
29	30	31				

Solution: The eggs hatched on Sunday, May 8.

Units of Time
1 week = 7 days
1 year = 12 months
1 year = 52 weeks
1 year = 365 days
1 leap year = 366 days

Other Examples

A. A **decade** is equal to 10 years. How many years equal 5 decades?

Think
1 decade = 10 years
So 5 decades = 5×10, or 50 years

5 decades = 50 years

B. A **century** is equal to 100 years. How many years equal 5 centuries?

Think
1 century = 100 years
So 5 centuries = 5×100 or 500 years

5 centuries = 500 years

Guided Practice

Use the calendars above for Questions 1–4.

1. Write the day and date 10 days after May 3. **Friday, May 13**
2. Write the day and date 5 days after April 29. **Wednesday, May 4**
3. Write the day and date 2 weeks before May 4. **Wednesday, April 20**
4. Write the day and date 3 weeks after May 10. **Tuesday, May 31**

Ask Yourself
- On what day do I begin counting?
- Should I count forward or backward?
- How many days do I count?

Explain Your Thinking ▶ What multiplication fact could you use to find how many years are in 8 decades? 4 centuries?
$8 \times 10 = 80$; $4 \times 100 = 400$

334

Reteach 13.1

Name ______ Date ______

Reteach 13.1

Calendar

What is the date 4 days after April 3?

Step 1. Place your finger on April 3.

Step 2. Begin counting on the day after April 3.

APRIL

S	M	T	W	T	F	S
					1	2
3	4	5	6	7	8	9
10	11	12	13	14	15	16
17	18	19	20	21	22	23
24	25	26	27	28	29	30

April 7th is 4 days after April 3rd.

Solution: Thursday, April 7 is 4 days after April 3.

Use the calendars on page 334 for Questions 1-6.

1. Write the day and date 5 days after May 5. **Tuesday, May 10**
2. Write the day and date 3 weeks before April 28. **Thursday, April 7**
3. Write the day and date 8 days after May 16. **Tuesday, May 24**
4. Write the day and date 2 days before April 10. **Friday, April 8**
5. Write the day and date for the first Monday after May 5. **Monday, May 9**
6. Write the day and date 6 weeks after April 1. **Friday, May 13**

Use with text pages 334–335.

Practice 13.1 Page 83

Name ______ Date ______

Practice 13.1

Calendar

Use the calendars on page 334. Write the day and the date.

1. 2 days before April 13 **Monday, April 11**
2. 5 days after April 19 **Sunday, April 24**
3. 8 days before May 20 **Thursday, May 12**
4. 3 days after May 6 **Monday, May 9**
5. 1 week before April 9 **Saturday, April 2**
6. 3 weeks after April 3 **Sunday, April 24**
7. 1 week after May 13 **Friday, May 20**
8. 2 weeks before May 25 **Wednesday, May 11**

Find each missing number.

9. 3 weeks = **21** days
10. 4 decades = **40** years
11. 3 years = **156** weeks
12. 4 centuries = **400** years
13. 1 year 6 weeks = **58** weeks
14. 3 years, 5 months = **41** months

Test Prep

15. Jim started a 10-day soccer camp on Monday, May 16. What will be the date of his last day of camp?
    A May 27 B May 17 C May 25 D May 15 **C**
16. Maureen is three weeks older than her friend Audrey. Maureen's birthday is April 6. When is Audrey's birthday? Explain how you found your answer. **April 27; explanations may vary.**

Use with text pages 334–335.

Practice and Problem Solving

Use the calendars on Page 334. Write the day and date.

5. 2 days before May 4 **Monday, May 2**
6. 6 days after May 22 **Saturday, May 28**
7. 9 days before April 27 **Monday, April 18**
8. 1 week after May 10 **Tuesday, May 17**
9. 1 week after April 24 **Sunday, May 1**
10. 2 weeks before May 9 **Monday, April 25**

Find each missing number.

11. 2 weeks = **14** days
12. 3 decades = **30** years
13. 2 years = **104** weeks
14. 5 centuries = **500** years
15. 1 year 2 weeks = **54** weeks
16. 2 years 3 months = **27** months
17. 4 decades 3 years = **43** years
18. 6 centuries = **60** decades
19. How many days is it from February 23 to March 15 in a leap year when February has 29 days? **21 days**
20. Look at this pattern of leap years.
    2004 2008 2012 2016
    When is the next leap year? **2020**

Use the calendars on Page 334 and the schedule on the right for Problems 21–23.

21. How many meetings are planned for Bird Watching? **25 meetings**
22. Jed plans to attend the series on *Habits of Chipmunks* and *Trees and Bushes.* How many meetings will that be? **25 meetings**
23. Mark wants to attend the series Animals of the Night and one other series. What other series can he attend? **Habits of Chipmunks**

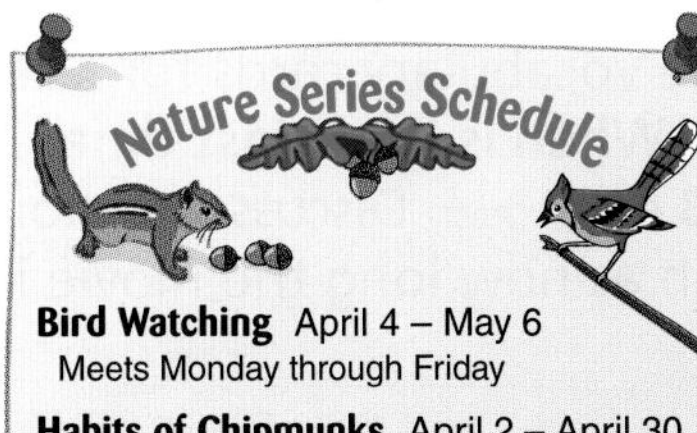

Bird Watching April 4 – May 6
Meets Monday through Friday

Habits of Chipmunks April 2 – April 30
Meets Tuesdays and Saturdays

Trees and Bushes April 4 – May 25
Meets Mondays and Wednesdays

Animals of the Night April 6 – May 27
Meets Wednesdays and Fridays

Mixed Review and Test Prep

Open Response

Write each number in word form.
(Ch. 1, Lesson 2)

See Additional Answers.

24. 406
25. 758
26. 10,002
27. 4,250
28. 9,345
29. 16,400
30. 20,250
31. 900,050
32. 607,844

Multiple Choice

33. On April 7, Edmundo is looking forward to the school trip, which is in 5 days. What is the date of the school trip?
(Ch. 13, Lesson 1)
A April 2
(C) April 12
B April 7
D April 13

Extra Practice See page 353, Set A.

3 Practice

Practice and Problem Solving

Select from **Exercises 5–33** as independent work.

- ***Problem 19*** Tell students that a leap year is an adjustment we make to the calendar once every four years.
- ***Problem 21*** Remind students that the bird watchers meet Monday through Friday, but for more than one week.

4 Assess & Close

Math Talk in Action

- **How does your age compare to a decade? Explain.** (Accept all reasonable answers.) **How much longer is a century than a decade?** (90 years, or 10 times longer)
- **What pattern do you see in the leap years given in Problem 20?** (The last two digits are all multiples of four.)

Math Journal Prompt

Have students copy the calendar measurement equivalences into their journal. Have them identify the one they find most useful and explain.

Lesson Quiz

Use the quiz on Lesson Transparency 13.1.

Test Prep & Spiral Review

Use Test Prep Transparency 13.1.

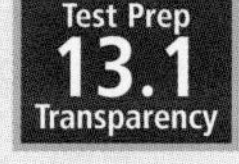

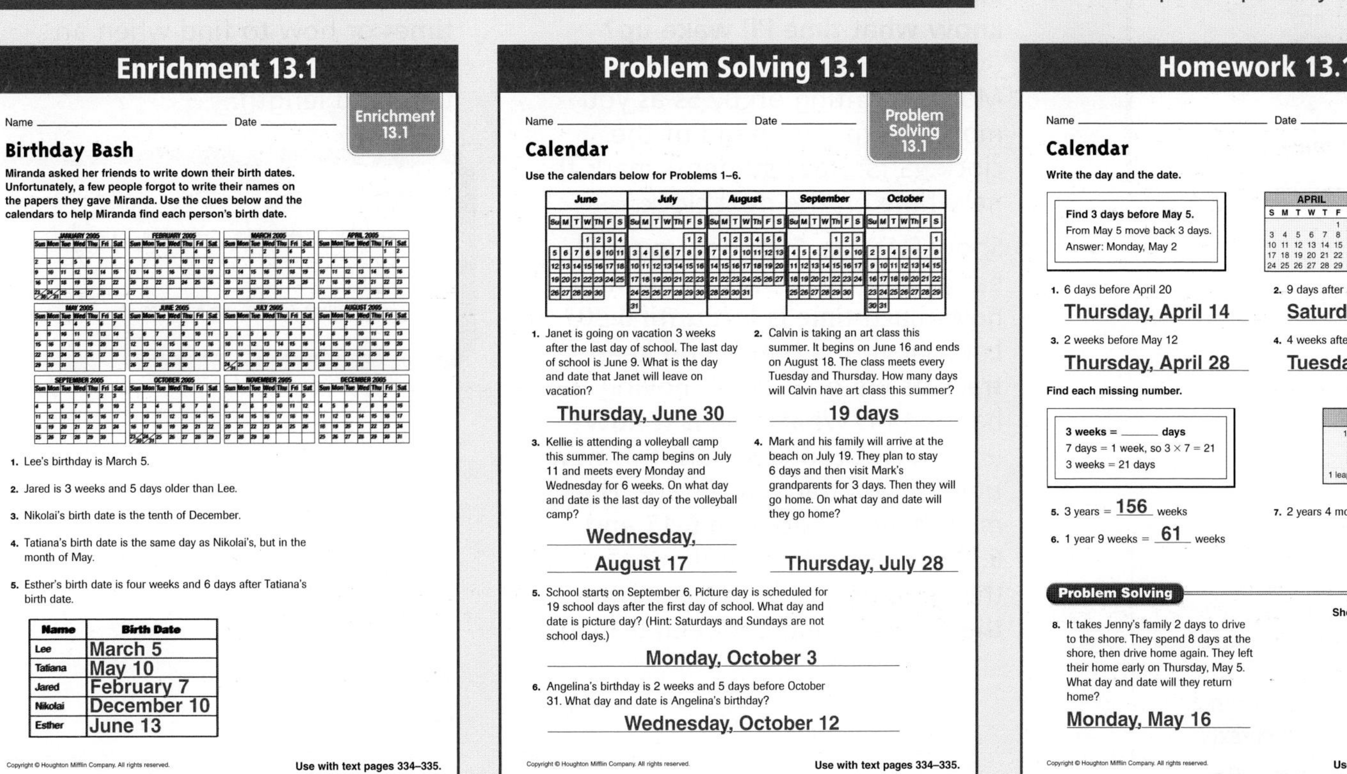

Enrichment 13.1
Birthday Bash
Miranda asked her friends to write down their birth dates. Unfortunately, a few people forgot to write their names on the papers they gave Miranda. Use the clues below and the calendars to help Miranda find each person's birth date.
1. Lee's birthday is March 5.
2. Jared is 3 weeks and 5 days older than Lee.
3. Nikolai's birth date is the tenth of December.
4. Tatiana's birth date is the same day as Nikolai's, but in the month of May.
5. Esther's birth date is four weeks and 6 days after Tatiana's birth date.
Lee March 5
Tatiana May 10
Jared February 7
Nikolai December 10
Esther June 13
Use with text pages 334–335.
Problem Solving 13.1
Calendar
Use the calendars below for Problems 1–6.
1. Janet is going on vacation 3 weeks after the last day of school. The last day of school is June 9. What is the day and date that Janet will leave on vacation?
Thursday, June 30
2. Calvin is taking an art class this summer. It begins on June 16 and ends on August 18. The class meets every Tuesday and Thursday. How many days will Calvin have art class this summer?
19 days
3. Kellie is attending a volleyball camp this summer. The camp begins on July 11 and meets every Monday and Wednesday for 6 weeks. On what day and date is the last day of the volleyball camp?
Wednesday, August 17
4. Mark and his family will arrive at the beach on July 19. They plan to stay 6 days and then visit Mark's grandparents for 3 days. Then they will go home. On what day and date will they go home?
Thursday, July 28
5. School starts on September 6. Picture day is scheduled for 19 school days after the first day of school. What day and date is picture day? (Hint: Saturdays and Sundays are not school days.)
Monday, October 3
6. Angelina's birthday is 2 weeks and 5 days before October 31. What day and date is Angelina's birthday?
Wednesday, October 12
Use with text pages 334–335.

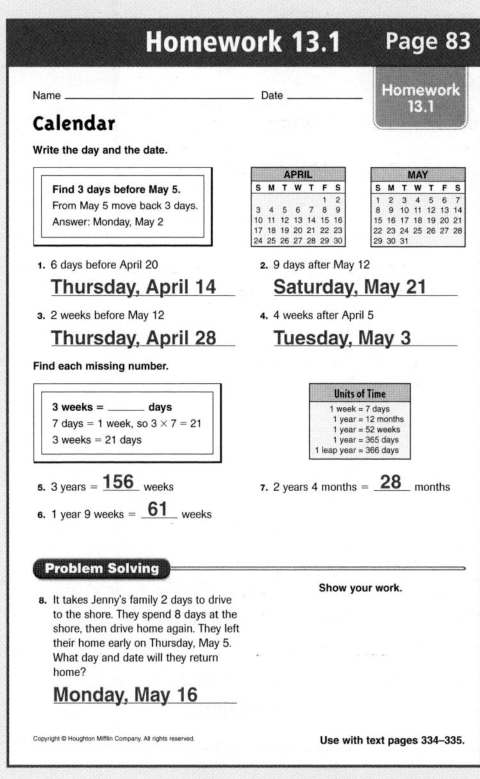

Homework 13.1 Page 83
Calendar
Write the day and the date.
Find 3 days before May 5.
From May 5 move back 3 days.
Answer: Monday, May 2
1. 6 days before April 20 Thursday, April 14
2. 9 days after May 12 Saturday, May 21
3. 2 weeks before May 12 Thursday, April 28
4. 4 weeks after April 5 Tuesday, May 3
Find each missing number.
3 weeks = ___ days
7 days = 1 week, so 3 × 7 = 21
3 weeks = 21 days
Units of Time
1 week = 7 days
1 year = 12 months
1 year = 52 weeks
1 year = 365 days
1 leap year = 366 days
5. 3 years = 156 weeks
6. 1 year 9 weeks = 61 weeks
7. 2 years 4 months = 28 months
Problem Solving
Show your work.
8. It takes Jenny's family 2 days to drive to the shore. They spend 8 days at the shore, then drive home again. They left their home early on Thursday, May 5. What day and date will they return home?
Monday, May 16
Use with text pages 334–335.

Lesson 13.2

Elapsed Time

Planning

Lesson Objective Find elapsed time.

Technology Resources

- Audio Tutor **2**/4 Listen and Understand
- *Ways to Success* CD-ROM 13.2
- Education Place: Extra Practice, eGlossary, Extra Help, eGames www.eduplace.com/map

Lesson 13.2 Transparency

Problem of the Day

An electrical storm caused power outages to all of the homes on Jared's block. His clock stopped at 7:55 A.M. Crews finally restored the power 5 hours 55 minutes later. What time should Jared set his clock to read? (1:50 P.M.)

Spiral Review

Rename.

1. 3 hundreds 12 tens (4 hundreds 2 tens)

2. 5 feet, 16 inches (6 ft 4 in.)

Lesson Quiz

Look at each pair of times. Write how much time has elapsed.

1. Start: 2:20 A.M.
End: 7:45 A.M. (5 h 25 min)

2. Start: 10:10 A.M.
End: 1:54 P.M. (3 h 44 min)

3. Start: 9:40 P.M.
End: 11:08 P.M. (1 h 28 min)

NCTM Standards

Measurement: Understand measurable attributes of objects and the units, systems, and processes of measurement.
Problem Solving: Solve problems that arise in mathematics and in other contexts.

Getting Started

Building Math Vocabulary

elapsed time	the time that passes between the beginning and the end of an activity
A.M.	the time between 12:00 midnight and 12:00 noon
P.M.	the time between 12:00 noon and 12:00 midnight

Display the vocabulary cards for *A.M.* and *P.M.* Review these terms by posing questions. **When is breakfast time: 7 A.M. or P.M.?** (A.M.) **When does school end: 3 A.M. or 3 P.M.?** (P.M.) Discuss occasions when people want to know **elapsed times,** such as how long the movie lasts or how long until the May Flower Show.

Finding Elapsed Time

Whole Class	20 minutes
Objective	Determine elapsed time using clocks.
Materials	Analog clock, Learning Tool 16
Visual, Tactual	

- Distribute copies of Learning Tool 16. Show 4:30 on the analog clock. Have students mark this time on the first clock face.
- **Suppose I nap for 45 minutes, starting at this time. How can we know what time I'll wake up?** (Accept all reasonable responses.) Model counting on by 5s as you move the minute hand of the clock. (5:15) Have students mark the new time on the next clock.
- Show 5:15 P.M. **Suppose you will eat at 6:30 P.M. How can we find how much time is left until 6:30? Let's move the hands and keep track as we go.** Model moving the hands 1 hr. **What time is it now?** (6:15) Have students mark this new time on the third clock face. **How much time is between 6:15 and 6:30?** (15 min) Have students show this time on the next face. **What is the elapsed time between 5:15 P.M. and dinner?** (1 h 15 min) **What is the total elapsed time from the start of the nap until dinner?** (2 h)
- Tell students that the lesson explains how to find how much time passes between two known times or how to find when an event ends if we know its start time and length.

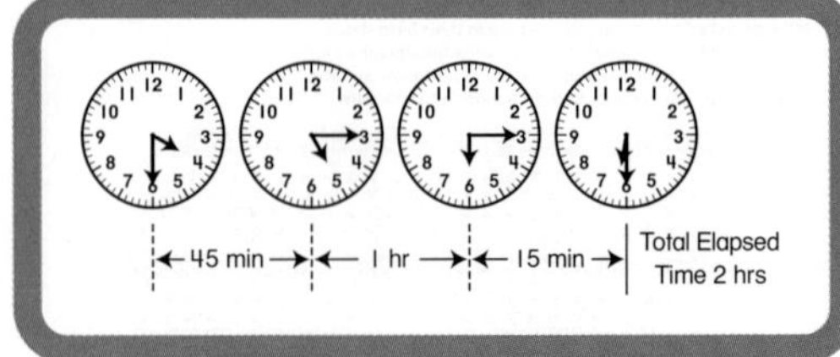

Differentiated Instruction

English Learners

Whole Class	15 minutes
Objective	Determine elapsed time using clocks.
Materials	Student page 337
Auditory	

Early Production

- Show students how to use the words *elapsed* and *passed* when talking about time.
- After completing ***Guided Practice***, have students practice saying the times and telling how much time elapsed in between.
- Model **Exercise 1: Three hours elapsed between nine-thirty and twelve-thirty.**

Intermediate/Advanced

- English Learner Resource 13.2
- English Learner Handbook

Intervention

Whole Class	10 minutes
Objective	Discuss lesson vocabulary.
Materials	None
Auditory	

- Explain that *meridiem* means *noon.* **It marks the time when the sun is highest in the sky. *Ante* means *before* and *post* means *after.* What do A.M. and P.M. mean?** (before noon, after noon) **This divides the day into two blocks of time of 12 hours each.**
- **When are the two dividing times between A.M. and P.M.?** (noon, midnight)
- **Why must we include A.M. and P.M. when we write times?** (Because the numbers repeat, you need those letters to indicate *which* 9 o'clock you mean.)

Other Resources

- *Ways to Success* CD-ROM 13.2

Special Needs

Pairs	15 minutes
Objective	Determine elapsed time using clocks.
Materials	Analog clocks (or watches)
Tactual, Visual	

- Review counting by 5's. Begin at any multiple of 5 from 0 to 55.
- Have students move the hands on analog timepieces to find elapsed times.
- If students work in pairs, one student can move the hands and the other can keep track of each time the hour hand moves a full hour.

Alternate Teaching Strategy

Materials: Chart with time relationships

- If students become confused when regrouping time measurements, display in chart form relationships such as 60 min = 1 hr, 30 min = half hour, and 15 min = quarter hour.
- Review general concepts of regrouping. Then point out that to regroup times, they must use these time relationships, not the usual base-ten groupings.
- Have students work in pairs to remind each other of the quantities to use and to check each other's work.

Facts Practice

- Review multiplication facts of 5–12 with students. Have students work with partners to say their multiples of these numbers. Once students believe they have mastered these fact patterns, have them test orally with the teacher. Then have students work on counting these multiple patterns backwards (i.e., 60, 55, 50...5, 0).

❶ Introduce

Explain that a day is twenty-four hours because this is the amount of time it takes Earth to spin once on its axis. Tell students that the system we use to divide up time comes from the ancient Near East. The Babylonians used a base-60 number system, which the Romans adopted, so hours and minutes are divided into 60 equal parts. Explain that the lesson will describe how to use clocks to find elapsed time.

❷ Teach

Learn About It

- Read and discuss the opening problem. **When does the next tour begin?** (1:45 P.M.) **Is that a night or a day time?** (day) **How do you know?** (1:45 P.M. is after noon but before midnight.)
- **Let's see how long Mariah must wait. Look at the box. Why do we begin with 11:00 A.M.?** (That is when she starts to wait.) Use an analog clock to model how to count the hours and then the minutes to find how much time passes between 11:00 A.M. and 1:45 P.M. (2 h 45 min)

Common Error

- **Omitting A.M. and P.M.** Some students may forget this key piece of information.
- **Intervention** Remind students that they must label a time as A.M. or P.M. so others will know which part of the day they mean.

Lesson 2

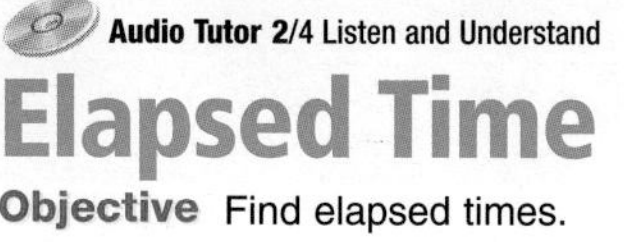

Elapsed Time

Objective Find elapsed times.

Vocabulary
- elapsed time
- A.M.
- P.M.

Learn About It

Mariah finds that a tour of the Raptor Center is full when she arrives at 11:00 A.M. How long will she have to wait for the next tour?

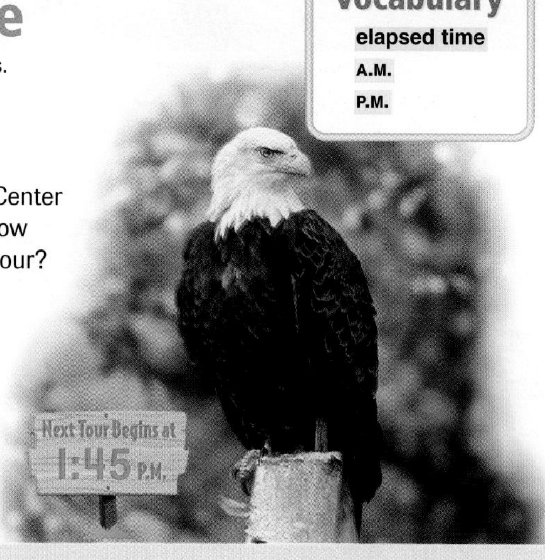

Elapsed time is the time that passes between one time and another.

A.M. is used for the hours between 12 midnight and 12 noon.

P.M. is used for the hours between 12 noon and 12 midnight.

▶ **You can use a clock to find how long it will be until the next tour.**

Start at 11:00.

Count the hours.
11:00 to 1:00 is 2 hours.

Then count the minutes.
1:00 to 1:45 is 45 minutes.

Solution: Mariah will have to wait 2 hours and 45 minutes.

▶ **If the tour starts at 1:45 P.M. and lasts 50 minutes, at what time does the tour end?**

If you know when the tour starts and how long it lasts, you can find when the tour ends.

Start at 1:45.

Count ahead 50 minutes to 2:35.

Solution: The tour ends at 2:35 P.M.

336

Extra Help at eduplace.com/map

Reteach 13.2

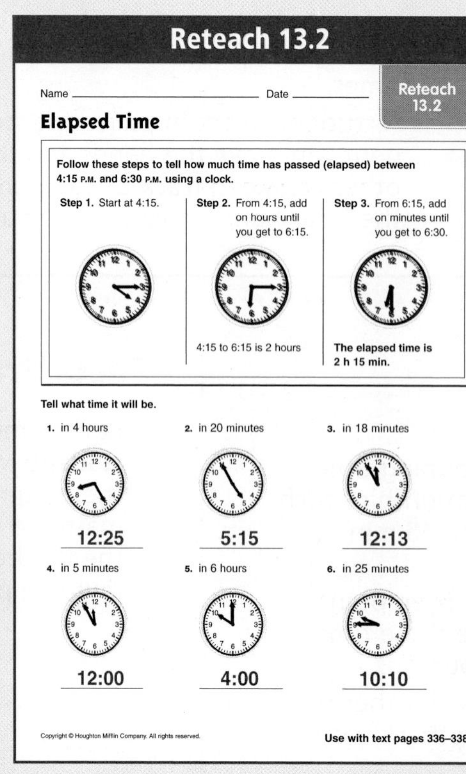

Name ______ Date ______

Reteach 13.2

Elapsed Time

Follow these steps to tell how much time has passed (elapsed) between 4:15 P.M. and 6:30 P.M. using a clock.

Step 1. Start at 4:15.

Step 2. From 4:15, add on hours until you get to 6:15.

4:15 to 6:15 is 2 hours

Step 3. From 6:15, add on minutes until you get to 6:30.

The elapsed time is 2 h 15 min.

Tell what time it will be.

1. in 4 hours — 12:25
2. in 20 minutes — 5:15
3. in 18 minutes — 12:13
4. in 5 minutes — 12:00
5. in 6 hours — 4:00
6. in 25 minutes — 10:10

Use with text pages 336–338.

Practice 13.2 Page 84

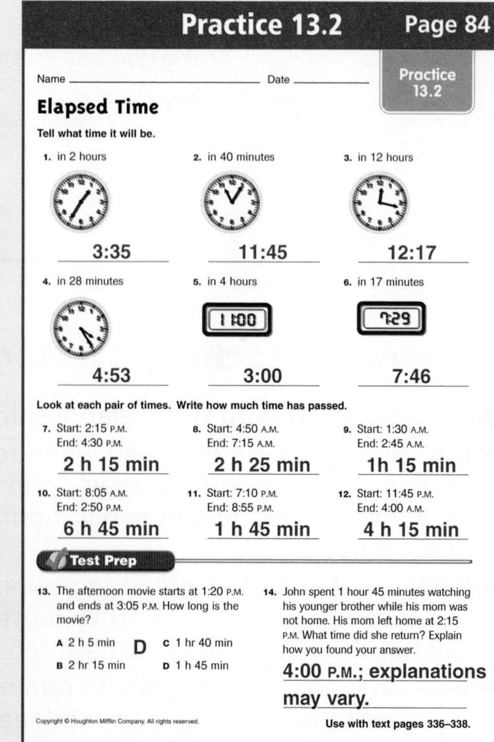

Name ______ Date ______

Practice 13.2

Elapsed Time

Tell what time it will be.

1. in 2 hours — 3:35
2. in 40 minutes — 11:45
3. in 12 hours — 12:17
4. in 28 minutes — 4:53
5. in 4 hours — 3:00
6. in 17 minutes — 7:46

Look at each pair of times. Write how much time has passed.

7. Start: 2:15 P.M. End: 4:30 P.M. — 2 h 15 min
8. Start: 4:50 A.M. End: 7:15 A.M. — 2 h 25 min
9. Start: 1:30 A.M. End: 2:45 A.M. — 1h 15 min
10. Start: 8:05 A.M. End: 2:50 P.M. — 6 h 45 min
11. Start: 7:10 P.M. End: 8:55 P.M. — 1 h 45 min
12. Start: 11:45 P.M. End: 4:00 A.M. — 4 h 15 min

Test Prep

13. The afternoon movie starts at 1:20 P.M. and ends at 3:05 P.M. How long is the movie?
    A 2 h 5 min
    B 2 hr 15 min
    C 1 hr 40 min
    D 1 h 45 min
    Answer: D

14. John spent 1 hour 45 minutes watching his younger brother while his mom was not home. His mom left home at 2:15 P.M. What time did she return? Explain how you found your answer.
    4:00 P.M.; explanations may vary.

Use with text pages 336–338.

You also can add or subtract to find elapsed time.

Units of Time
60 second(s) = 1 minute (min)
60 minutes = 1 hour (h)
24 hours = 1 day (d)
7 days = 1 week (wk)

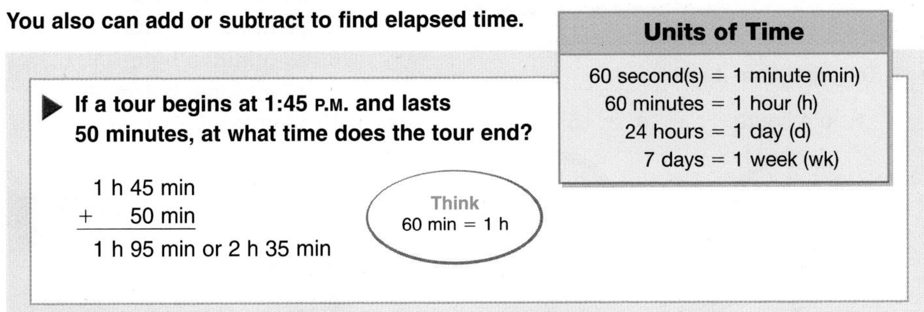

▶ **If a tour begins at 1:45 P.M. and lasts 50 minutes, at what time does the tour end?**

1 h 45 min
+ 50 min
1 h 95 min or 2 h 35 min

Think: 60 min = 1 h

Solution: The tour ends at 2:35 P.M.

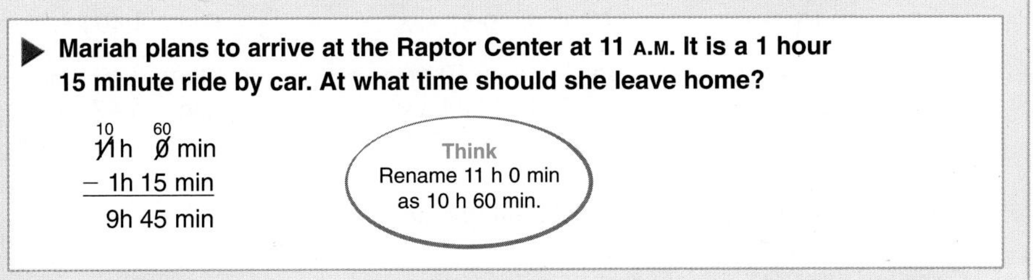

▶ **Mariah plans to arrive at the Raptor Center at 11 A.M. It is a 1 hour 15 minute ride by car. At what time should she leave home?**

11 h 0 min (renamed as 10 h 60 min)
− 1h 15 min
9h 45 min

Think: Rename 11 h 0 min as 10 h 60 min.

Solution: Mariah should leave home at 9:45 A.M.

Another Example

Reading Time to the Second

Read or Write 6:23:15
six twenty-three and fifteen seconds, or
twenty-three minutes fifteen seconds after six.

Guided Practice

Tell what time it will be.

1. in 3 hours
2. in 20 minutes
3. in 5 minutes

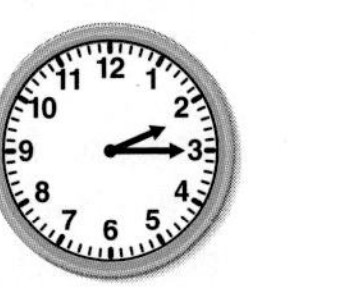

12:30 | 2:35 | 5:12:20

Ask Yourself
- At what time do I start counting?
- Do I need to count hours?
- Do I need to count minutes?

Explain Your Thinking ▶ How much time will elapse between 3:20 A.M. and 9:45 P.M.? How did you find the elapsed time?

18 h 25 min; *Possible explanation:* Count to find the amount of time between 3:20 A.M. and noon: add 9:45 to that time.

- **Look at the example at the top of the page. Why do we rename 95 minutes?** (95 min > 1 h)
- **Look at the second problem. Why do we subtract?** (to find when Mariah should leave her house to arrive by 11:00 A.M.) **Explain the renaming.** (Trade 1 h of the 11 h for 60 min to have enough minutes to subtract.)
- Discuss *Another Example*.

Guided Practice

Have students complete Exercises 1–3 as you observe. Remind them to use the *Ask Yourself* questions to help. Give students the opportunity to discuss the questions in *Explain Your Thinking*.

Enrichment 13.2

Name ______ Date ______ Enrichment 13.2

Time Zoning

The length of a day (24 hours) is based on the time it takes for Earth to rotate one time on its axis. Because the earth is round, and different areas face the sun at different times, Earth is divided into 24 time zones. The line passing through Greenwich, England is the starting point or Prime Meridian. If you travel west from this line, you subtract an hour for every 15 degrees of longitude. If you travel east from this line, you add an hour for every 15 degrees of longitude. Look at the map of time zones below.

The time in Greenwich England is 3:00 P.M. Find the time in each city.

1. New York **10:00 A.M.**
2. Beijing **11:00 P.M.**
3. When it is 8:00 A.M in New York, what time is it in Los Angeles? **5:00 A.M.**
4. A plane leaves Memphis at 1:20 P.M. for Denver. The flight takes 2 hours and 45 minutes. What time does it arrive? **3:05 P.M.**

Use with text pages 336–338.

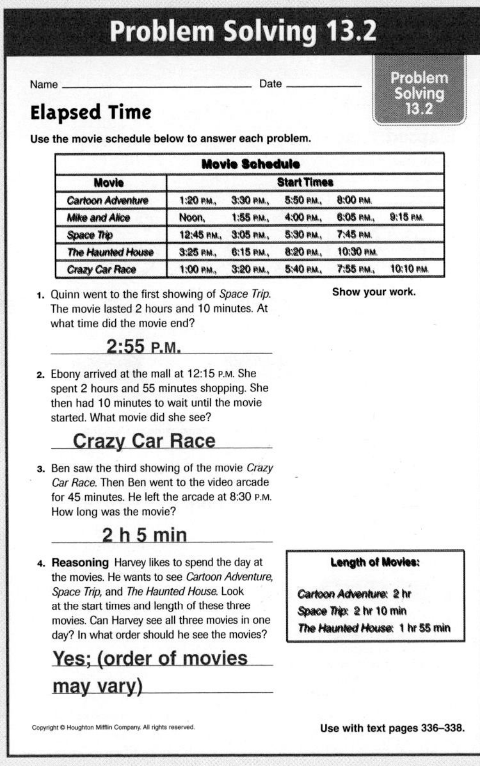

Problem Solving 13.2

Name ______ Date ______ Problem Solving 13.2

Elapsed Time

Use the movie schedule below to answer each problem.

Movie	Start Times				
Cartoon Adventure	1:20 P.M.,	3:30 P.M.,	5:50 P.M.,	8:00 P.M.	
Mike and Alice	Noon,	1:55 P.M.,	4:00 P.M.,	6:05 P.M.,	9:15 P.M.
Space Trip	12:45 P.M.,	3:05 P.M.,	5:30 P.M.,	7:45 P.M.	
The Haunted House	3:25 P.M.,	6:15 P.M.,	8:20 P.M.,	10:30 P.M.	
Crazy Car Race	1:00 P.M.,	3:20 P.M.,	5:40 P.M.,	7:55 P.M.,	10:10 P.M.

Show your work.

1. Quinn went to the first showing of *Space Trip*. The movie lasted 2 hours and 10 minutes. At what time did the movie end? **2:55 P.M.**
2. Ebony arrived at the mall at 12:15 P.M. She spent 2 hours and 55 minutes shopping. She then had 10 minutes to wait until the movie started. What movie did she see? **Crazy Car Race**
3. Ben saw the third showing of the movie *Crazy Car Race*. Then Ben went to the video arcade for 45 minutes. He left the arcade at 8:30 P.M. How long was the movie? **2 h 5 min**
4. **Reasoning** Harvey likes to spend the day at the movies. He wants to see *Cartoon Adventure, Space Trip,* and *The Haunted House*. Look at the start times and length of these three movies. Can Harvey see all three movies in one day? In what order should he see the movies? **Yes; (order of movies may vary)**

Length of Movies:
Cartoon Adventure: 2 hr
Space Trip: 2 hr 10 min
The Haunted House: 1 hr 55 min

Use with text pages 336–338.

❸ Practice

Practice and Problem Solving

Select from **Exercises 4–32** as independent work.

- ***Problem 24*** **Greg's arrival time does not say A.M. or P.M. How can we tell which it is?** (11:40 in the morning is A.M.) **Why is this important?** (to correctly give the time Greg left)

❹ Assess & Close

Math Talk in Action

- **What is elapsed time?** (how much time goes by between two known times)
- **When might it be helpful to know about elapsed times?** (possible answers: to determine how long a special event will last, to find out when you need to leave for an activity, and to stay on schedule throughout the day)

Math Journal Prompt

Have students write about how to find the elapsed time between 10:45 P.M. and 1:00 A.M. Then have them write about how to find when a movie ends if it starts at 2:20 P.M. and lasts 1 hour 35 minutes.

Lesson Quiz

Use the quiz on Lesson Transparency 13.2.

Test Prep & Spiral Review

Use Test Prep Transparency 13.2.

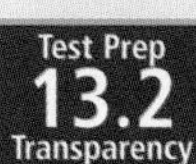

Practice and Problem Solving

Tell what time it will be.

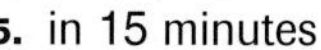

4. in 4 hours

6:32

5. in 15 minutes

5:05

6. in 13 minutes

8:13:10

7. in 10 hours

8:47

Look at each pair of times. Write how much time has passed.

8. Start: 1:05 P.M. End: 6:15 P.M. **5 h 10 min**
9. Start: 6:50 A.M. End: 9:57 A.M. **3 h 7 min**
10. Start: 8:35 A.M. End: 1:40 P.M. **5 h 5 min**
11. Start: 11:45 A.M. End: 3:20 P.M. **3 h 35 min**
12. Start: 9:10 P.M. End: 12:34 A.M. **3 h 24 min**
13. Start: 7:40 A.M. End: 11:47 P.M. **16 h 7 min**

Write the time shown on the clock before the hour and then after the hour.
Possible answers above.

14. 
15.  
16. 
17. 

14. 22 minutes before 9; 8:38
15. 38 minutes before 11; 10:22
16. 25 minutes before 6; 5:35
17. 55 minutes before 4; 3:05

Find each missing number.

18. 2 hours = **120** minutes
19. 3 minutes = **180** seconds
20. 90 minutes = 1 hour **30** minutes
21. 1 hour 25 minutes = **85** minutes
22. 4 minutes = **240** seconds
23. 95 minutes = 1 hour **35** minutes
24. Greg spent 2 hours 45 minutes visiting the Raptor Center. He arrived at 11:40 in the morning. What time did he leave? **2:25 P.M.**
25. Rita went to the Raptor Center at half-past four in the afternoon. How long was she there if she left at 8:25 P.M.? **3 h 55 min**
26. **What's Wrong?** Bird-watching videos are shown every 20 minutes. The last video was at 2:25 P.M. Ann says that the next videos will be at 2:45 P.M. and 2:65 P.M. What did Ann do wrong? **Ann added 20 minutes to 2:45, but since there are 60 minutes in an hour, she should have said 3:05 instead of 2:65.**
27. **Analyze** Mr. Motts started working at the Raptor Center at 2:40 P.M. He led a tour for 2 hours 10 minutes. Then he worked in the office for 90 minutes. Was he finished before 7 P.M.? **yes**

338

Extra Practice See page 353, Set B.

Homework 13.2 **Page 84**

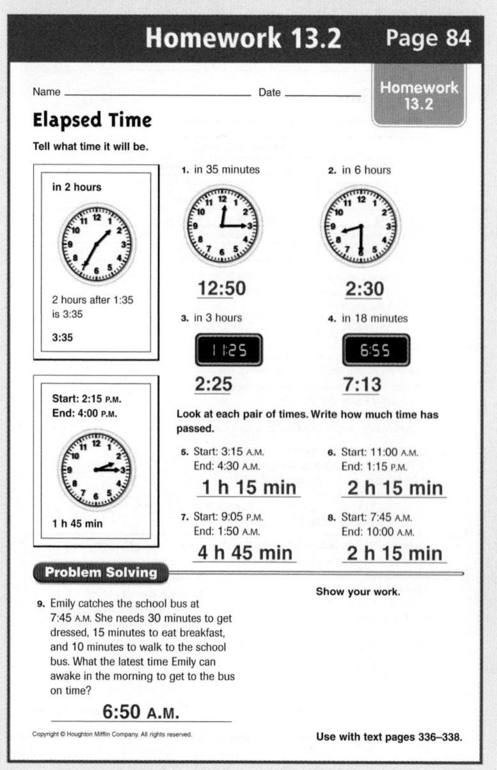

Name ____________ Date ________ Homework 13.2

Elapsed Time

Tell what time it will be.

in 2 hours
2 hours after 1:35 is 3:35
3:35

1. in 35 minutes **12:50**
2. in 6 hours **2:30**
3. in 3 hours **2:25**
4. in 18 minutes **7:13**

Start: 2:15 P.M.
End: 4:00 P.M.
1 h 45 min

Look at each pair of times. Write how much time has passed.

5. Start: 3:15 A.M. End: 4:30 A.M. **1 h 15 min**
6. Start: 11:00 A.M. End: 1:15 P.M. **2 h 15 min**
7. Start: 9:05 P.M. End: 1:50 A.M. **4 h 45 min**
8. Start: 7:45 A.M. End: 10:00 A.M. **2 h 15 min**

Problem Solving Show your work.

9. Emily catches the school bus at 7:45 A.M. She needs 30 minutes to get dressed, 15 minutes to eat breakfast, and 10 minutes to walk to the school bus. What the latest time Emily can awake in the morning to get to the bus on time? **6:50 A.M.**

Use with text pages 336–338.

Mixed Review and Test Prep

Open Response

Round each number to the nearest ten cents. Then estimate. (Ch. 3, Lesson 3)

28. \$0.57 + \$0.81
about \$1.40

29. \$0.49 − \$0.22
about \$0.30

30. \$4.65 + \$8.32
about \$13.00

31. \$9.44 − \$0.11
about \$9.30

Multiple Choice

32. A yard sale starts at 8:30 A.M. and ends at 1:00 P.M. How long is the yard sale? (Ch. 13, Lesson 2)

A 3 h 30 min
B 4 h
(C) 4 h 30 min
D 7 h 30 min

Problem Solving

Math Reasoning

Estimating Time

You don't always need to know the exact time. Sometimes you can use an estimate.

Use the clocks for Problems 1–2.

▶ **You can estimate time to the nearest quarter hour.**

1. Suppose it takes 15 minutes to walk to the library. To the nearest quarter hour, at what time would you arrive? **12:45**

▶ **You can estimate time to the nearest 5 minutes.**

2. Suppose a friend stops to ask what time it is. If you round to the nearest 5 minutes, what time will you tell your friend? **9:35**

▶ **You can estimate elapsed time.**
See Additional Answers.

3. The sign at the right lists the movies that are showing at the Raptor Center. How long will each movie last
   a. to the nearest quarter hour?
   b. to the nearest 5 minutes?

MOVIE TIMES AT THE RAPTOR CENTER

Movie	Time
The Eagle Soars	11:00 A.M.–11:22 A.M.
Owls of the Night	1:15 P.M.–2:43 P.M.
Hawks on High	2:10 P.M.–3:24 P.M.

Math Reasoning

Estimating Time

Compare situations in which an exact time is important with situations in which an estimate is adequate. For instance, students might estimate an arrival time to account for an unknown amount of traffic. But they would give an exact time to describe an airplane departure.

Tell students that when they estimate times, they may round to the nearest minute, 5 minutes, quarter hour (15 min), half hour (30 min), or hour, depending on the degree of accuracy that fits the situation.

ACHIEVING Mathematical Proficiency

Helping Students Become Learners

An important factor that helps students become learners is **convincing them that what they are learning is useful and relevant to their lives.** Having students find elapsed time is an activity that helps students understand different lengths of time. Students use analog clocks and skip counting as well as addition and subtraction to find elapsed time.

It is helpful to point out that nearly everything students use in their daily lives relates to time. **As students go through their daily activities, they come to appreciate the relevance of time to their own lives.**

Reaching All Learners

Measurement Sense

Elapsed Time Remind students that A.M. is used for times before noon and P.M. for times after noon. Discuss with students what their typical school day looks like. At what time do they get up, eat breakfast, leave for school, and so on?

1. Have students make a list of their activities during a typical school day. Have them write the time of each activity, using A.M. or P.M.
2. Have students complete **Exercise 1.** Then have them pick the morning or afternoon and find the elapsed time between activities.
3. Have students complete **Exercise 1.** Then have them draw a time line of their day and find the elapsed time between activities.

(Check student responses for reasonableness.)

Differentiated Assignments		
At Risk	**Average**	**Advanced**
Exercise 1	Exercise 2	Exercise 3

Lesson 13.3

Problem-Solving Strategy: Guess and Check

Planning

Lesson Objective Use the Guess and Check strategy to solve a problem.

Technology Resources

- *Ways to Success* CD-ROM 13.3
- Education Place: Extra Practice www.eduplace.com/map

Lesson 13.3 Transparency

Problem of the Day

Darla's dad is 4 times older than Darla. Darla's mom is 3 times older than Darla. The sum of all their ages is 88. Find the age of each person. (Darla is 11; dad is 44; mom is 33.)

Spiral Review

Find the missing number.

1. 5 weeks = ___ days (35)
2. 8 decades = ___ years (80)
3. 5 centuries = ___ years (500)

Lesson Quiz

Use Guess and Check to solve each problem.

1. The product of two whole numbers is 36. The difference between the numbers is 5. What are the numbers? (9, 4)

2. During his first day working at a ferry dock, Reggie collected $225 in $5 and $10 bills. He got half as many of one kind of bill than the other. How many of each kind of bill did Reggie collect? (nine $5s and eighteen $10s)

NCTM Standards

Problem Solving: Solve problems that arise in mathematics and in other contexts; apply and adapt a variety of appropriate strategies to solve problems.
Number and Operations: Compute fluently and make reasonable estimates.

Getting Started

Building Math Vocabulary

Students should be familiar with the mathematical vocabulary in this lesson.

Twenty Questions

Whole Class	15 minutes
Objective	Solve problems using skills and strategies.
Materials	None
Auditory	

- Play a game of "Twenty Questions" with the class. Point out that the best players use responses, including no, to ask the next questions, leading at last to the answer.
- **How can a wrong answer help?** (It lets you eliminate certain possibilities.)
- **What's the difference between wild guesses and educated guesses?** (Educated guesses account for previous details; wild guesses are unconnected.)
- Tell students that in this lesson they'll use a problem-solving strategy that involves guessing and adjusting to find answers.

Differentiated Instruction

English Learners

Pairs	15 minutes
Objective	Solve problems using skills and strategies.
Materials	Student page 342
Auditory, Visual	

Early Production

- Have students practice showing their work and explaining their answers to other students.
- Pair students and have them choose one problem from ***Mixed Problem Solving*** to share with their partners. Encourage students to say what strategy they used and show how they used it to find the answer.

Intermediate/Advanced

- English Learner Resource 13.3
- English Learner Handbook

Intervention

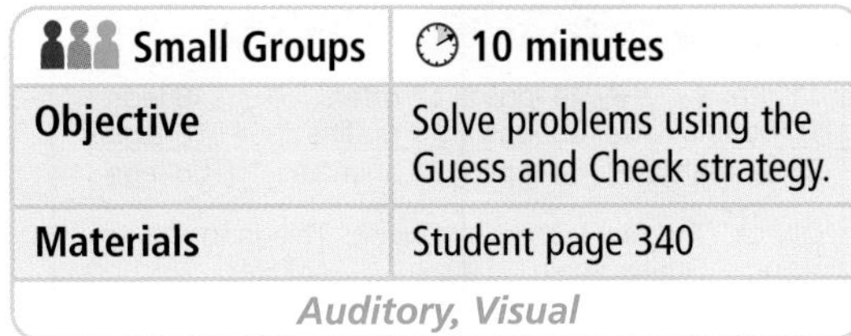

Small Groups	10 minutes
Objective	Solve problems using the Guess and Check strategy.
Materials	Student page 340
Auditory, Visual	

- Help students see that to best use this strategy, we turn errors into hints.
- Revisit page 340. **What about the first guess works?** (animal total) **What doesn't work?** (That mix has too many legs.)
- **Why does the second guess make sense?** (It adjusts the number of each animal, but now there are too few legs.) **How can you use this to make a good third guess?** (Choose a number of each animal between the first two guesses.)
- **Will this strategy always give an answer by the third guess?** (No) **So what do you do?** (Keep guessing and adjusting.)

Other Resources

- *Ways to Success* CD-ROM 13.3

Gifted & Talented

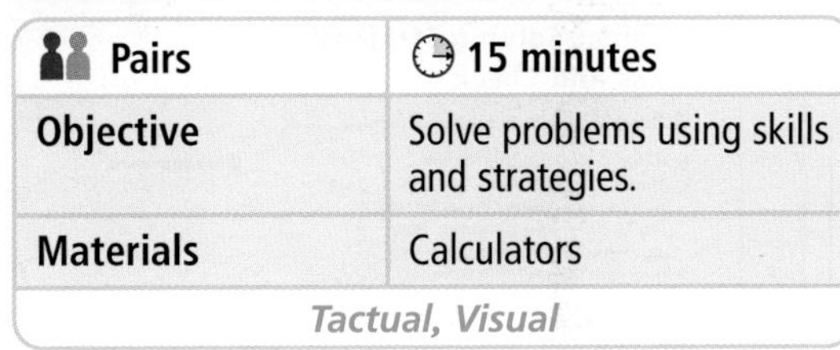

Pairs	15 minutes
Objective	Solve problems using skills and strategies.
Materials	Calculators
Tactual, Visual	

- **Consecutive numbers are numbers given in counting order.**
- **Find 3 consecutive numbers whose sum is 282.** (93, 94, 95)
- **Find 4 consecutive numbers whose sum is 158.** (38, 39, 40, 41)
- **Find 3 consecutive numbers whose product is 336.** (6, 7, 8)

Science Connection

Materials: Index cards, drawing paper or poster board, markers or colored pencils

- Have students gather data on puffins and share the data in poster form.
- Have students use the puffin data to write word problems. They can write the problems on colored index cards and post them for classmates to solve.

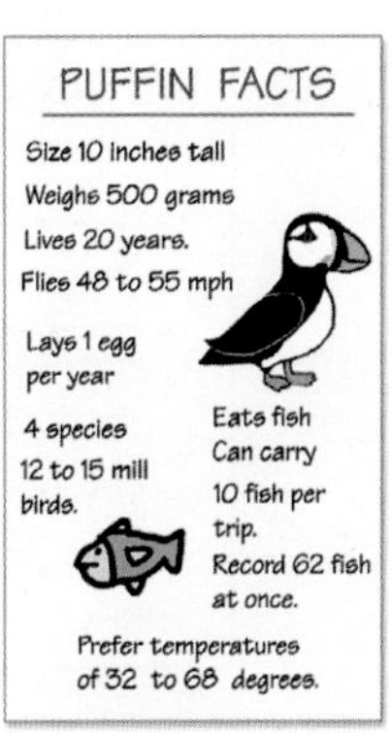

PUFFIN FACTS
Size 10 inches tall
Weighs 500 grams
Lives 20 years.
Flies 48 to 55 mph
Lays 1 egg per year
4 species
12 to 15 mill birds.
Eats fish
Can carry 10 fish per trip.
Record 62 fish at once.
Prefer temperatures of 32 to 68 degrees.

❶ Introduce

Invite students to define the word *strategy*. (an organized plan used to solve a problem) Point out that people use strategies to solve math problems or any kind of problem that they encounter in the real world, such as how to get something that is just out of reach. Tell them that the lesson in the book will describe a strategy that suggests that you guess an answer, test the guess against facts, and then adjust your guess based on the results.

❷ Teach

Guess and Check

- Have a volunteer read the opening problem aloud. **How many kinds of animals are named?** (2) **What can you learn about the animals from the pictures?** (how many legs each has)
- **Look at the Understand step. Why do we note what we know as our first step?** (to organize facts) **What do we need to find?** (Find some number of puffins and otters that totals 21, with 66 legs in all.)
- **Look at the Plan step. How do you know where to begin guessing?** (Find 2 numbers that add up to 21.) **Look at the Solve step. What does the first guess show?** (right number of animals, too many legs) **How should this fact affect the second guess?** (Find a combination with fewer legs.) **What can we learn from the second guess?** (We are nearer to the solution.)
- **Look at the Look Back step. How do we use our guesses to reach the answer?** (Adjust as needed to get closer and closer to numbers that work.)

Lesson 3

Problem-Solving Strategy

Guess and Check

Objective Use the Guess and Check strategy to solve a problem.

Sometimes a good way to solve a problem is to guess and check.

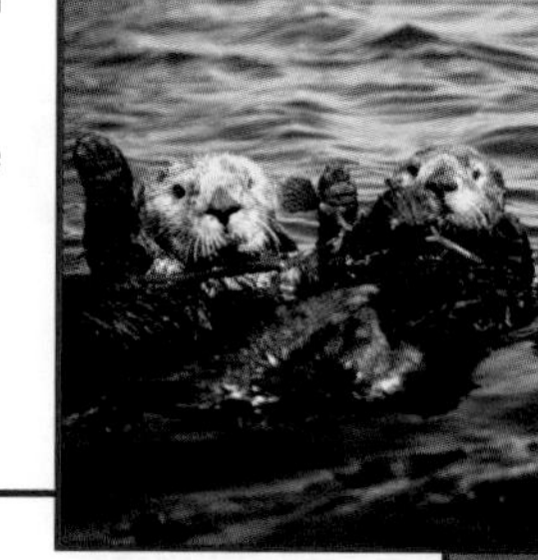

Problem A nature photographer took some pictures of puffins and otters. She photographed 21 animals with 66 legs altogether. How many puffins and otters did she photograph?

UNDERSTAND

This is what you know.

- The 21 animals have 66 legs altogether.
- Puffins have 2 legs and otters have 4 legs.

PLAN

Use the Guess and Check strategy.

Guess two numbers. Then check to see if they are correct. If not, use your result to improve your next guess.

SOLVE

Use your result to make your next guess.

1st Guess	2nd Guess	3rd Guess
14 otters → 56 legs 7 puffins → 14 legs 21 animals 70 legs	11 otters → 44 legs 10 puffins → 20 legs 21 animals 64 legs	12 otters → 48 legs 9 puffins → 18 legs 21 animals 66 legs
Check: Too many legs. Guess again.	Check: Too few legs. Guess again.	Check: This is the answer.

Solution: She photographed 9 puffins and 12 otters.

LOOK BACK

Reread the problem.

Does the solution fit the facts of the problem?
Yes, there are 21 animals with 66 legs.

340

Reteach 13.3

Name ________ Date ________

Reteach 13.3

Problem-Solving Strategy: Guess and Check

Read It Look for information.

There are 68 third-graders and fourth-graders in Mason School. There are 8 more fourth-graders than third-graders. How many fourth-graders are there?

Picture It Use a table to record your guesses.

68 Students	
Third Graders	Fourth Graders
____	____ + 8

Solve It Guess and check to solve the problem.

1. To reach a sum of 68, try 25 + 33 = **58**.
   That guess was too low. Try 35 + 43 = **78**.
   That guess was too high. Try 30 + 38 = **68**.
   The number of students in fourth grade is **38**.

Try These! Use the Guess and Check strategy to solve. **Show your work.**

2. Brandi has 6 pets, all either cats or birds. Her pets have a total of 22 legs. How many cats and birds does Brandi have?
   5 cats, 1 bird
3. The product of two numbers is 56. The difference between the numbers is 1. What are the numbers?
   7, 8

Use with text pages 340–342.

Practice 13.3 Page 85

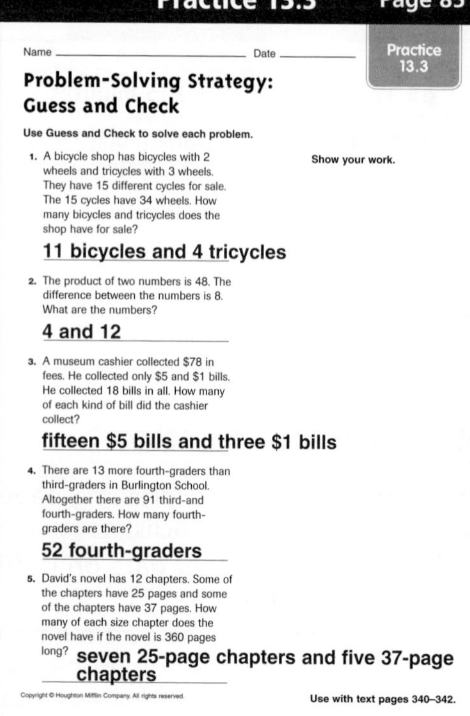

Name ________ Date ________

Practice 13.3

Problem-Solving Strategy: Guess and Check

Use Guess and Check to solve each problem. **Show your work.**

1. A bicycle shop has bicycles with 2 wheels and tricycles with 3 wheels. They have 15 different cycles for sale. The 15 cycles have 34 wheels. How many bicycles and tricycles does the shop have for sale?
   11 bicycles and 4 tricycles
2. The product of two numbers is 48. The difference between the numbers is 8. What are the numbers?
   4 and 12
3. A museum cashier collected $78 in fees. He collected only $5 and $1 bills. He collected 18 bills in all. How many of each kind of bill did the cashier collect?
   fifteen $5 bills and three $1 bills
4. There are 13 more fourth-graders than third-graders in Burlington School. Altogether there are 91 third-and fourth-graders. How many fourth-graders are there?
   52 fourth-graders
5. David's novel has 12 chapters. Some of the chapters have 25 pages and some of the chapters have 37 pages. How many of each size chapter does the novel have if the novel is 360 pages long? **seven 25-page chapters and five 37-page chapters**

Use with text pages 340–342.

Guided Practice

Use the Ask Yourself questions to help you solve each problem.

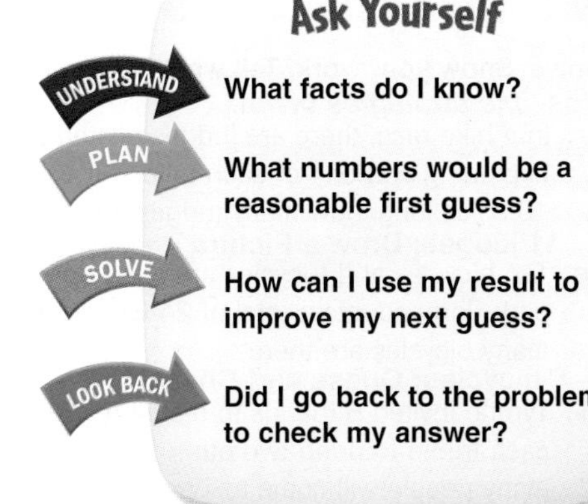

Ask Yourself
UNDERSTAND
What facts do I know?
PLAN
What numbers would be a reasonable first guess?
SOLVE
How can I use my result to improve my next guess?
LOOK BACK
Did I go back to the problem to check my answer?

1. Altogether, there are 10 birds and bees in Ali's garden. If the birds and bees have 48 legs in all, how many birds and bees are there? **3 birds; 7 bees**

   Hint A bee has 6 legs.

2. Tim and Jared collect trading cards of rare birds. Tim has 8 more cards than Jared. Together they have 104 cards. How many cards does each boy have?
   Tim has 56 cards. Jared has 48 cards.

Independent Practice

Use Guess and Check to solve each problem.

3. A photographer said that the only animals he saw on an island were lizards and parrots. He saw 8 animals with 22 legs altogether on that island. How many lizards and parrots did he see?
   3 lizards and 5 parrots

4. **Money** On a nature tour the guide collects $260 in fares. He collects only $10 bills and $20 bills. He collects 22 bills in all. How many of each kind of bill does the guide collect?
   eighteen $10 bills; four $20 bills

5. Carol has 8 booklets about birds. Some of the booklets have 26 pages and the others have 41 pages. How many of each size booklet does she have if the pages total 253?
   five 26-page booklets; three 41-page booklets

6. The product of two numbers is 24. The difference between the numbers is 10. What are the numbers? **12; 2**

Go On

Guided Practice

Have students complete **Problems 1–2** as you observe. Remind them to use the ***Ask Yourself*** questions to help.

3 Practice

Independent Practice

Select from **Problems 3–14** as independent work.

- ***Problem 3*** **What about the animals must you know to solve this problem?** (how many legs on a parrot and on a lizard)

Enrichment 13.3

Name ______________ Date ________ Enrichment 13.3

Problem-Solving Strategy: Guess and Check

Mr. Rodriguez has a garden in his backyard. Mr. Rodriguez visits Flower Depot and buys new flowers to plant.

Help Mr. Rodriguez decide which flowers to buy and how to plant them.

1. Mr. Rodriguez decides he wants to buy 24 flowers. What is the least and greatest amount that he could spend on 24 flowers? Explain.
   Least amount: $48; Greatest amount: $168

Flower Depot Flower Sale	
Type of Flower	Cost
Mums	$2.00 each
Roses	$7.00 each
Violets	$3.00 each

2. If Mr. Rodriguez has $100 to spend and he wants to buy the same number of each type of flower, what is the maximum number of each type of flower he can buy? How many total flowers would this be? Explain how you found your answer.
   8 of each type: (8 × $7) + (8 × $3) + (8 × $2) = $96; 24 total; *Answers may vary.*

3. If Mr. Rodriguez spends $86 on 24 flowers, how many of each type of flower did he buy?
   He bought 6 roses, 10 mums, and 8 violets.

4. Mr. Rodriguez has a rectangular garden. How many different ways can he arrange the 24 flowers in his garden if he wants to plant them in equal rows with at least six flowers in each row? Make a drawing of each possible arrangement.
   There are 4 possible arrangements: 24 flowers in 1 row; 12 flowers in 2 rows; 8 flowers in 3 rows; 6 flowers in 4 rows; *check students' drawings.*

Use with text pages 340–342.

Problem Solving 13.3

Name ______________ Date ________ Problem Solving 13.3

Problem-Solving Strategy: Guess and Check

The movie theatre charges $4.00 for each child's ticket and $7.00 for each adult's ticket. The art club purchased a total of 20 tickets and spent $101. How many of each type of ticket did the club buy?

UNDERSTAND

1. What operations will you need to use?
   Addition and multiplication

PLAN

2. How will you check your guesses?
   Compare the sum of the number of tickets to 20 and the total cost to $101.

SOLVE

3. Use the table to make guesses and check your guesses. If you need more workspace, use a separate sheet of paper. **Check students' tables.**

	1st Guess		2nd Guess		3rd Guess	
	Number of tickets	Cost	Number of tickets	Cost	Number of tickets	Cost
Child's					13	$52
Adult's					7	$49
Total					20	$101

LOOK BACK

4. **Write About It** How did you use your first guess to help make the next guess?
   Answers will vary.

Use with text pages 340–342.

Mixed Problem Solving

Problems 7–10 Tell students that they may use any of the strategies in the table, or a combination of strategies, to solve the problems. Remind them to look back at their work to be sure they have answered the question that was asked.

Have students review their answers to make sure they have done the following:

- expressed the solution clearly
- used appropriate mathematical notation and terms
- explained their choice of strategy
- determined the reasonableness of their answer.

Mixed Problem Solving

Solve. Show your work. Tell what strategy you used.
Possible strategies given.

7. In a bike race, there are judges posted at the beginning and end of each mile. If the race is 10 miles long, how many judges are needed?
11 judges; Draw a Picture

8. Ten bicycles and tricycles are lined up at the park. Jerry counts a total of 24 wheels. How many bicycles are there?
6 bicycles; Guess and Check

9. Tyrone invited 8 friends to his party. He asked each friend to bring two other friends. How many people will come to Tyrone's party?
24 people; Write an Equation

10. Five friends stood in line. Jamie was fourth in line. Jose stood right behind Ned. Lee was not third or last. Alice was also in line. In what order did the friends stand?
Lee, Ned, Jose, Jamie, Alice; Use Logical Reasoning

You Choose

Strategy
- Act It Out
- Draw a Picture
- Guess and Check
- Use Logical Reasoning
- Write an Equation

Computation Method
- Mental Math
- Estimation
- Paper and Pencil
- Calculator

Data Use the graph to solve Problems 11–13.

Students at Whitney School planted trees on Arbor Day. The graph at the right shows the number of trees planted by Grades 3–6.

11. How many trees were planted altogether?
56 trees

12. Suppose it takes 15 minutes to plant each tree. How long will it take the fourth grade to plant all their trees?
4 hours

13. Altogether, how many more trees did the fifth and sixth graders plant than the fourth graders?
13 more trees

14. You Decide Meg has $200 to buy trees. She can choose 2 kinds of trees. Pine trees cost $10, elm trees cost $8, and oak trees cost $12 each. How many of each type of tree can Meg buy?
Check that answers total $200.
***Possible answer:* 10 elm trees and 10 oaks.**

Arbor Day Planting

Number of Trees: 0, 2, 4, 6, 8, 10, 12, 14, 16
Grade Level: 3, 4, 5, 6

342

Homework 13.3 **Page 85**

Name ________________ Date ________ Homework 13.3

Problem-Solving Strategy: Guess and Check

Use Guess and Check to solve each problem.

A waiter at a restaurant collected $59 in tips. He collected only five- and one-dollar bills. He collected 15 bills in all. How many of each kind of bill did the waiter collect?

You can use Guess and Check to solve the problem.
Try two numbers. If they are not correct, use your result to improve your next guess.

Number of one-dollar bills	Number of five-dollar bills	Total	Check
5	10	$5 \times 1 = 5$ $10 \times 5 = 50$ $5 + 50 = 55$	Too low
3	12	$3 \times 1 = 3$ $12 \times 5 = 60$ $3 + 60 = 63$	Too high
4	11	$4 \times 1 = 4$ $11 \times 5 = 55$ $4 + 55 = 59$	Correct

The waiter collected 4 one-dollar bills and 11 five-dollar bills.

1. Bernadette's math test has 14 sections. Each section has either 8 or 12 problems. How many sections are there of each size if the test is 132 problems long? **9 sections with 8 problems and 5 sections with 12 problems**

2. A moving truck rental company has a total of 24 trucks in its lot. The trucks are either 4-wheelers or 18-wheelers. How many of each kind of truck does the company have if the total number of wheels is 138?
21 4-wheelers and 3 18-wheelers

Use with text pages 340–342.

Problem Solving on Tests

Multiple Choice

Choose the letter of the correct answer. If a correct answer is not here, choose NH.

1. The length of a pencil is 16 centimeters. How many millimeters are equal to 16 centimeters?

   A 16,000   Ⓒ 160

   B 1,600   **D** NH

   (Chapter 12, Lesson 7)

2. About how much water can this sink hold?

   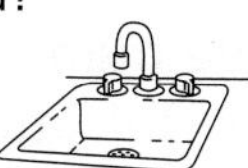

   F 160 gallons   **H** 10 quarts

   Ⓖ 10 gallons   **J** 600 quarts

   (Chapter 12, Lesson 3)

Open Response

Solve each problem.

3. Sixty-seven students are taking part in a game. Teams can have no fewer than 3 and no more than 8 members. What is the smallest number of teams possible? Draw a diagram or write an equation to explain your answer.

   $67 \div 8 \rightarrow 8$ R3. (Chapter 8, Lesson 3)

4. A soccer team begins practice at quarter after 3 and ends practice at quarter to 5. How many minutes does the team practice? Explain how you found your answer. (Chapter 13, Lesson 2)

See Additional Answers.

Extended Response

5. You and your friend are going to the County Fair. You each have \$15.00 to spend on rides. Use the table below to solve this problem.

County Fair Rides	
High Jumper	4 tickets
Crazy Cups	3 tickets
Scrambler	6 tickets
Hidden River	5 tickets
Carousel	2 tickets

   a. You can buy tickets individually for \$1.00 each or in blocks of 10 tickets for \$7.00. How many tickets can you afford to buy? Will you have any money left over?

   b. What rides could you go on with tickets bought with \$15.00?

   c. Suppose you have 21 tickets. Plan your rides so that you don't have any tickets left. You can take the same ride more than one time. Tell how you will use the 21 tickets.

   d. If you could go on a hot-air balloon ride for \$12.00, how would you spend your \$15.00? Explain why you made your decision.

See Additional Answers. (Chapter 11, Lesson 7)

Education Place

See **eduplace.com/map** for more Test-Taking Tips.

Problem-Solving on Tests

Problem-Solving on Tests provides an opportunity for students to apply previously learned skills in the types of problem contexts typically encountered in standardized tests.

Problem-Solving on Tests includes practice in a variety of formats: multiple choice, extended response, and open response.

Students will gain experience in writing about mathematics and using various representations to solve problems. Discuss students' solutions. Have several students explain the thinking behind their work.

More test practice is available on Houghton Mifflin's Web site, **Education Place.** Go to **www.eduplace.com/map.**

4 Assess & Close

Math Talk in Action

- **What does it mean to guess and check as a way to solve a problem?** (See what you know, make an educated guess based on the data, adjust your guess if it doesn't work, and keep guessing and adjusting until your answer fits the facts.)
- **How are errors helpful in this strategy?** (They help you make your next guess.)

Math Journal Prompt

Have students describe how they used the Guess and Check problem-solving strategy to solve **Problem 6.**

Lesson Quiz

Use the quiz on Lesson Transparency 13.3.

Test Prep & Spiral Review

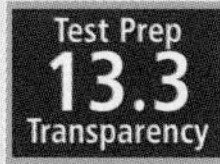

Use Test Prep Transparency 13.3.

ACHIEVING Mathematical Proficiency

What Is Mathematical Proficiency?

Part of being successful in mathematics is **viewing mathematics as sensible and useful and applying it** to solve real-world problems. These two aspects of mathematical proficiency are related to and closely interwoven with understanding, computing, and reasoning.

To make sense of problems, students need to identify the elements of a problem—what they know, what they need to find—and **to represent the problem in a way that can be solved mathematically.** The time and temperature lessons in this chapter allow students to see how math applies to their daily world.

Students see that **the steps they take to solve time and temperature problems** are worthwhile, and that **the math is useful in a broader context** outside of school.

Lesson 13.4

Temperature and Negative Numbers

Planning

Lesson Objective Use a thermometer to read temperatures above and below zero.

Technology Resources

- Audio Tutor **2**/5 Listen and understand
- *Ways to Success* CD-ROM 13.4
- *Ways to Assess* CD-ROM
- Education Place: Extra Practice, eGlossary, eGames, Weekly Reader www.eduplace.com/map

Problem of the Day

Rajiv looks outside one day to see icicles on the trees. His thermometer says 15°, but he's not sure if that's degrees Celsius or Fahrenheit. How can you tell Rajiv which scale it is? (Fahrenheit; 15°C is above freezing, so there wouldn't be icicles; but 15°F is below freezing.)

Spiral Review

Compute.

1. 4,307 + 1,296 (5,603)
2. 8,703 − 986 (7,717)
3. 314 × 27 (8,478)
4. 7,032 ÷ 9 (781 R3)
5. 17)5,432 (319 R9)

Lesson Quiz

Find the difference between the temperatures.

1. 80°F and 12°F (68°F)
2. ⁻4°C and 13°C (17°C)
3. 77°F and 106°F (29°F)
4. ⁻24°F and ⁻3°F (21°F)
5. 11°C and ⁻38°C (49°C)

NCTM Standards

Measurement: Select and apply appropriate standard units and tools to measure length, area, volume, weight, time, temperature, and the size of angles.
Connections: Recognize and use connections among mathematical ideas.

Getting Started

Building Math Vocabulary

positive numbers	numbers that are greater than zero
negative numbers	numbers that are less than zero
degrees Fahrenheit (°F)	the customary temperature scale
degrees Celsius (°C)	the metric temperature scale

Write *negative* on the board. Tell students that a **negative number** has a value less than zero. **What is the opposite of negative?** (positive) Tell students that a **positive number** has a value greater than zero. Point to a number line and ask students to supply examples of each kind of number. (⁺2, ⁺3 ⁺8; ⁻7 ⁻6 ⁻5)

Identify **degrees Fahrenheit (°F)** and **degrees Celsius (°C)** as units of measurement for temperature; Fahrenheit is a customary measurement, Celsius is metric.

Finding Temperatures

Whole Class	10 minutes
Objective	Read temperature using degrees Fahrenheit and degrees Celsius.
Materials	Fahrenheit and Celsius Thermometer Transparencies
Auditory, Visual	

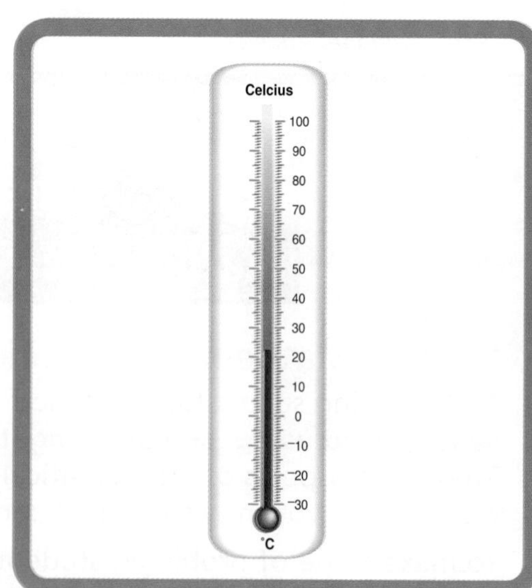

- Conduct a discussion about temperatures. **What is the outside temperature today?** Record student responses with the degree symbol (°). Discuss whether to call this a cold, cool, warm, or hot day.
- **When do we use temperature data?** (Accept all reasonable responses.) **How do we measure temperatures?** (with a thermometer) Invite volunteers to describe types of thermometers they have seen and used.
- Display the thermometer transparencies and explain that in this lesson they will use these two temperature scales.

Differentiated Instruction

English Learners

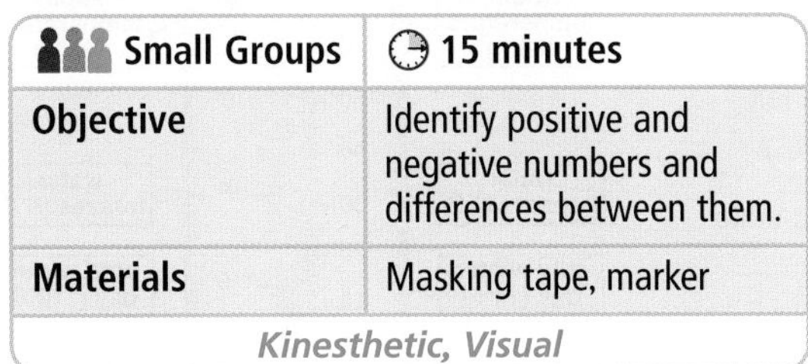

Pairs	15 minutes
Objective	Read temperature using degrees Fahrenheit and degrees Celsius.
Materials	Student page 345
Auditory	

Early Production

- Give students practice using the vocabulary they learned about temperature and positive and negative numbers.
- After completing ***Guided Practice,*** have students read their answers aloud, using the correct terms.
- Model the first three problems, asking students to repeat what you say. Have them say their answers to a partner.

Intermediate/Advanced

- English Learner Resource 13.4
- English Learner Handbook

Intervention

Small Groups	15 minutes
Objective	Identify positive and negative numbers and differences between them.
Materials	Masking tape, marker
Kinesthetic, Visual	

- Make a number line calibrated from $^-10$ to $^+10$ by writing the numbers on a piece of masking tape attached to the floor.
- Have students stand on numbers that you name, such as "negative 8" or "positive 5."
- To grasp the difference between numbers like this, have a volunteer walk and count off steps between numbers.
- Extend the number line in both directions. Repeat as needed.

Other Resources

- *Ways to Success* CD-ROM 13.4

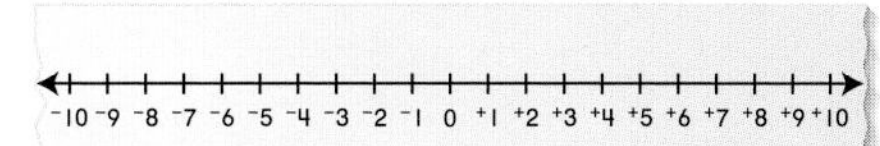

Early Finishers

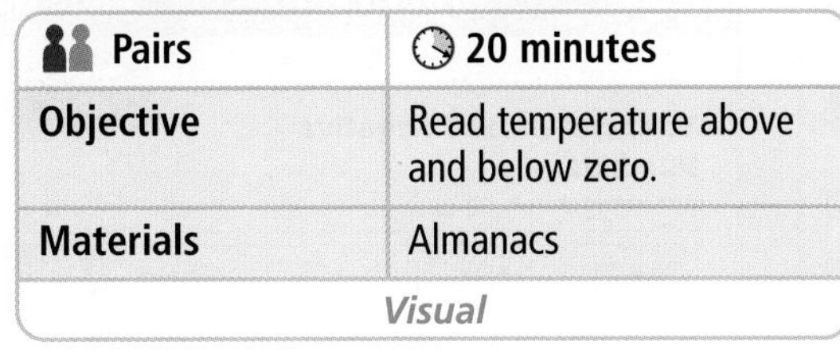

Pairs	20 minutes
Objective	Read temperature above and below zero.
Materials	Almanacs
Visual	

- Help students find in an almanac of the United States. Record high and low temperatures.
- Have them make a table of the extreme temperatures logged in any 5 states that start with M.
- Have them find the difference between the highest and lowest recorded temperatures.
- Display the tables in the math corner of your classroom or on a bulletin board.

Alternate Teaching Strategy

Materials: Clear cups, thermometers

- Help your students connect math to the real world and read the temperature of water.
- Have students fill 4 different cups with hot water, warm water, cool water, and cold water.
- Have them put the thermometers in each cup to get both the Celsius and Fahrenheit temperatures.
- Have them record the temperatures in a table and compare the differences between pairs of temperature readings.

❶ Introduce

Display the thermometer transparencies. Explain that a thermometer uses both positive and negative numbers to measure how hot or cold something is. **What measurement unit does a thermometer use?** (degrees) **What do the *F* and *C* on the thermometers stand for?** (*F* stands for *Fahrenheit* and *C* stands for *Celsius,* two different temperature scales.) Tell students that the lesson will explain how to read and compare temperatures.

❷ Teach

Learn About It

- **In what ways is a thermometer like a number line?** (Accept all reasonable answers.) Discuss the marks between each multiple of 10 and explain that they represent single degrees.
- **Find some key temperatures on both scales. At what temperatures does water freeze?** (0°C; 32°F) **At what temperatures does water boil?** (100°C; 212°F) **Another name for the Celsius scale is *Centigrade.* Using what you know about metric prefixes, what do you think Centigrade means?** (The scale is based on 100 degrees.)

Common Error

- **Confusion computing with negative numbers** Some students may make errors because they are unfamiliar with adding and subtracting negative numbers.
- **Intervention** When students must find a difference between a negative and a positive number, have them first count from the negative number to 0 and record that difference. Then have them find the difference between 0 and the positive number, and combine the two quantities for the total difference.

Lesson 4

Audio Tutor 2/5 Listen and Understand

Temperature and Negative Numbers

Objective Use a thermometer to read temperatures above and below zero.

Vocabulary
positive numbers
negative numbers
degrees Fahrenheit (°F)
degrees Celsius (°C)

Learn About It

A thermometer can be used to measure temperature in degrees Fahrenheit or degrees Celsius.

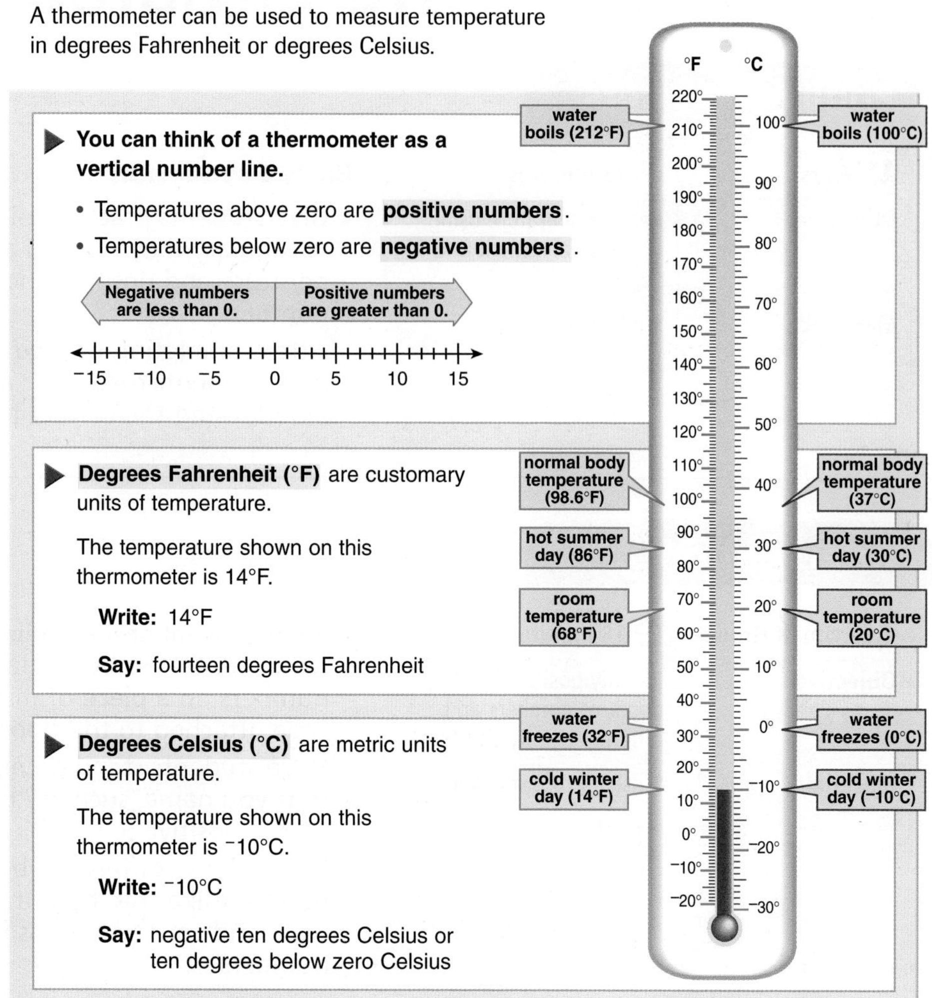

▶ **You can think of a thermometer as a vertical number line.**

- Temperatures above zero are **positive numbers**.
- Temperatures below zero are **negative numbers**.

▶ **Degrees Fahrenheit (°F)** are customary units of temperature.

The temperature shown on this thermometer is 14°F.

Write: 14°F

Say: fourteen degrees Fahrenheit

▶ **Degrees Celsius (°C)** are metric units of temperature.

The temperature shown on this thermometer is ⁻10°C.

Write: ⁻10°C

Say: negative ten degrees Celsius or ten degrees below zero Celsius

344

Reteach 13.4

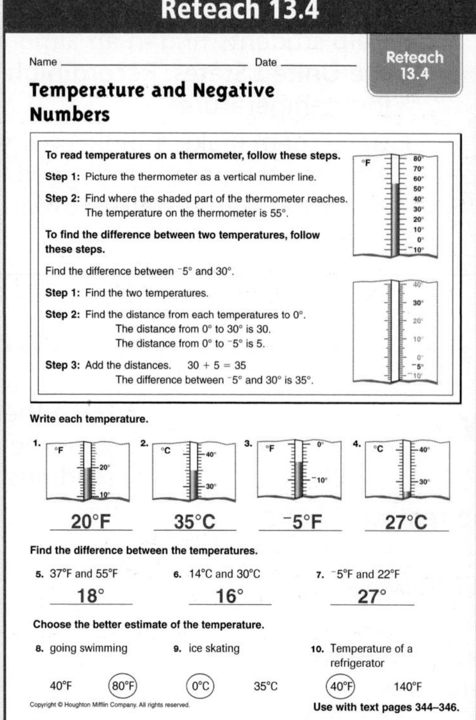

Name ______ Date ______ Reteach 13.4

Temperature and Negative Numbers

To read temperatures on a thermometer, follow these steps.

Step 1: Picture the thermometer as a vertical number line.

Step 2: Find where the shaded part of the thermometer reaches. The temperature on the thermometer is 55°.

To find the difference between two temperatures, follow these steps.

Find the difference between ⁻5° and 30°.

Step 1: Find the two temperatures.

Step 2: Find the distance from each temperatures to 0°. The distance from 0° to 30° is 30. The distance from 0° to ⁻5° is 5.

Step 3: Add the distances. 30 + 5 = 35 The difference between ⁻5° and 30° is 35°.

Write each temperature.

1. 20°F 2. 35°C 3. ⁻5°F 4. 27°C

Find the difference between the temperatures.

5. 37°F and 55°F 18°
6. 14°C and 30°C 16°
7. ⁻5°F and 22°F 27°

Choose the better estimate of the temperature.

8. going swimming 40°F (80°F)
9. ice skating (0°C) 35°C
10. Temperature of a refrigerator (40°F) 140°F

Use with text pages 344–346.

Practice 13.4 Page 86

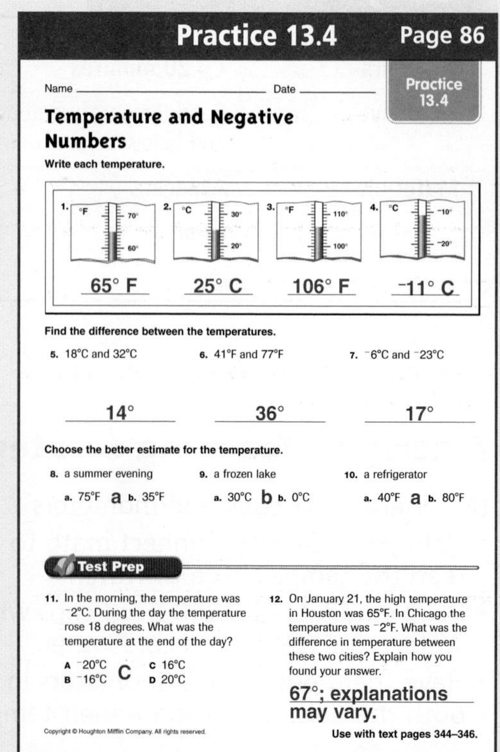

Name ______ Date ______ Practice 13.4

Temperature and Negative Numbers

Write each temperature.

1. 65° F 2. 25° C 3. 106° F 4. ⁻11° C

Find the difference between the temperatures.

5. 18°C and 32°C 14°
6. 41°F and 77°F 36°
7. ⁻6°C and ⁻23°C 17°

Choose the better estimate for the temperature.

8. a summer evening a. 75°F b. 35°F **a**
9. a frozen lake a. 30°C b. 0°C **b**
10. a refrigerator a. 40°F b. 80°F **a**

Test Prep

11. In the morning, the temperature was ⁻2°C. During the day the temperature rose 18 degrees. What was the temperature at the end of the day?
A ⁻20°C B ⁻16°C C 16°C D 20°C **C**

12. On January 21, the high temperature in Houston was 65°F. In Chicago the temperature was ⁻2°F. What was the difference in temperature between these two cities? Explain how you found your answer.
67°; explanations may vary.

Use with text pages 344–346.

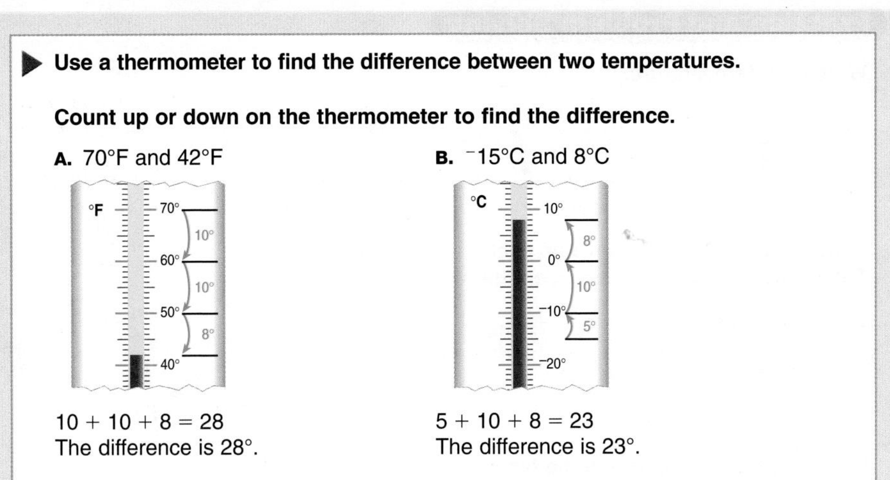

▶ **Use a thermometer to find the difference between two temperatures.**

Count up or down on the thermometer to find the difference.

A. 70°F and 42°F

10 + 10 + 8 = 28
The difference is 28°.

B. ⁻15°C and 8°C

5 + 10 + 8 = 23
The difference is 23°.

- **Look at Example A. How can you use the thermometer to compare two temperatures?** (Count back, or subtract, as if it were a number line.) **Look at Example B. What is different in this case?** (One temperature is a negative number; the other is a positive number.) **How do we figure the difference?** (Count up.)

Guided Practice

Have students complete **Exercises 1–12** as you observe. Remind them to use the *Ask Yourself* questions to help. Give students the opportunity to talk about the questions in *Explain Your Thinking.*

Guided Practice

Write each temperature.

1. 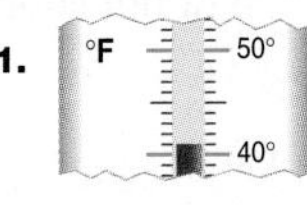 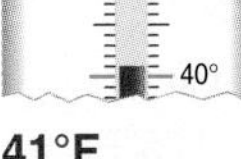 41°F

2. 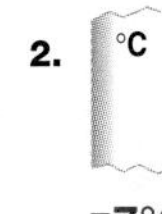 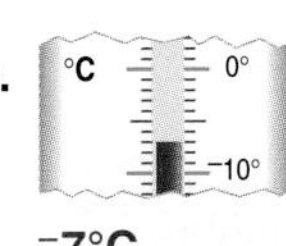 ⁻7°C

3. 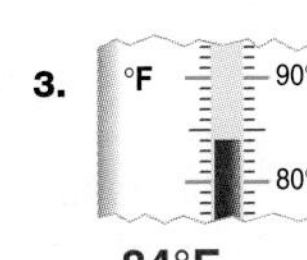 84°F

Ask Yourself

- What numbers is the temperature between?
- Is the temperature positive or negative?
- Is the temperature in degrees Fahrenheit or degrees Celsius?

Find the difference between the temperatures.

4. 2°C and 4°C 2°
5. ⁻3°F and 2°F 5°
6. 27°F and 45°F 18°
7. ⁻8°F and 15°F 23°
8. ⁻12°C and ⁻26°C 14°
9. 13°C and ⁻2°C 15°

Choose the better estimate of the temperature.

10. a cold day
(**a.**) ⁻10°C **b.** 30°C

11. a hot day
(**a.**) 90°F **b.** 37°F

12. room temperature
a. 20°F (**b.**) 70°F

Explain Your Thinking ▶ Which is lower, 5°C or ⁻15°C? How do you know? **⁻15°C; it is lower on the thermometer.**

Enrichment 13.4

Name ______________ Date ________ Enrichment 13.4

Boiling Over?

The thermometers below show the temperature at the freezing point. The thermometer on the right is in degrees Celsius and the one on the left is in degrees Fahrenheit.

Answer each question. Add your answer to the temperatures shown on the thermometer, and mark the new temperature. Add each new answer to the last temperature you marked and make a new mark. For help, see the thermometer on page 344.

1. What is 72° below boiling on the Celsius scale? **28°C**

2. What is 9° below room temperature on the Fahrenheit scale? **59°F**

3. What is the number of degrees between ⁻3° and 21°? Add this answer to both thermometers. **24°**

4. What is 12° below room temperature on the Celsius scale? **8°C**

5. What is 4°C above the freezing point increased by 3°C? **7°C**

6. What is normal body temperature for humans in °F and in °C? **98.6°F; 37°C**

7. Did you reach the boiling point on either scale? Explain. **I reached the boiling point on both scales. (213.6°F and the boiling point is 212°F) (104°C and the boiling point is 100°C)**

 Use with text pages 344–346.

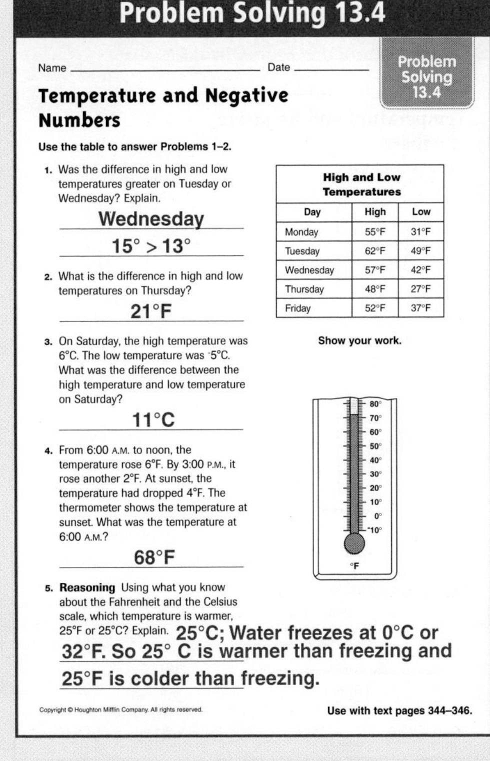

Problem Solving 13.4

Name ______________ Date ________ Problem Solving 13.4

Temperature and Negative Numbers

Use the table to answer Problems 1–2.

High and Low Temperatures		
Day	**High**	**Low**
Monday	55°F	31°F
Tuesday	62°F	49°F
Wednesday	57°F	42°F
Thursday	48°F	27°F
Friday	52°F	37°F

1. Was the difference in high and low temperatures greater on Tuesday or Wednesday? Explain. **Wednesday 15° > 13°**

2. What is the difference in high and low temperatures on Thursday? **21°F**

Show your work.

3. On Saturday, the high temperature was 6°C. The low temperature was ⁻5°C. What was the difference between the high temperature and low temperature on Saturday? **11°C**

4. From 6:00 A.M. to noon, the temperature rose 6°F. By 3:00 P.M., it rose another 2°F. At sunset, the temperature had dropped 4°F. The thermometer shows the temperature at sunset. What was the temperature at 6:00 A.M.? **68°F**

5. Reasoning Using what you know about the Fahrenheit and the Celsius scale, which temperature is warmer, 25°F or 25°C? Explain. **25°C; Water freezes at 0°C or 32°F. So 25° C is warmer than freezing and 25°F is colder than freezing.**

 Use with text pages 344–346.

3 Practice

Practice and Problem-Solving

Select from **Exercises 13–33** as independent work.

- For **Exercises 19–24,** refer students to the thermometer on page 344 to count on.
- ***Data*** You may want to discuss the trend the data show—temperatures are generally higher at midday (noon) than in the morning and evening.
- ***Problem 33*** Suggest that students draw a picture to fit the data or work backward from the known information to solve.

4 Assess & Close

Math Talk in Action

- **Suppose the temperature outside is 25°. How would it feel? Explain.** (If it's 25°C, it would feel warm and pleasant; if it's 25°F, it would feel very cold because it's below freezing.)
- **What is the difference in temperature between 35°C and ⁻5°C? Explain.** (40°; 35° to 0°, then 5° more to ⁻5°, for a total of 40° as the difference)

Math Journal Prompt

Have students write an explanation of how to find the difference between 21°F and ⁻8°F.

Lesson Quiz

Use the quiz on Lesson Transparency 13.4.

Lesson 13.4 Transparency

Test Prep & Spiral Review

Use Test Prep Transparency 13.4.

Test Prep 13.4 Transparency

Practice and Problem Solving

Write each temperature.

13. 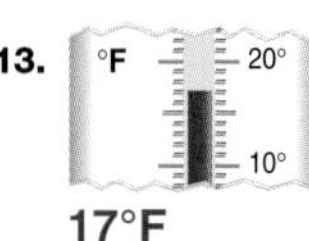 17°F

14. 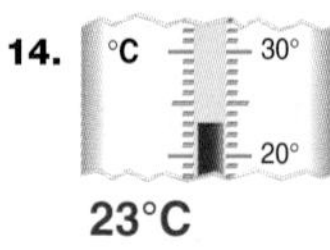 23°C

15. 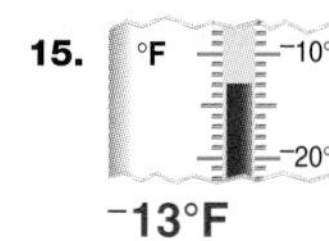 ⁻13°F

16. 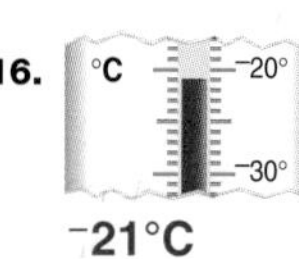 ⁻21°C

Write the temperature shown on each thermometer. Then write the difference between the two temperatures.

17. 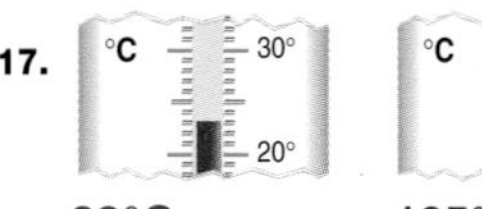 23°C 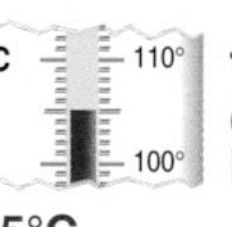 105°C The difference is 82°.

18. 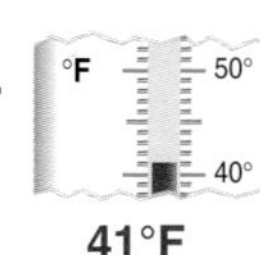 41°F 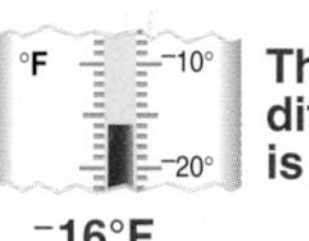 ⁻16°F The difference is 57°.

Find the difference between the temperatures.

19. 88°F and 110°F 22°

20. ⁻5°C and 10°C 15°

21. ⁻3°F and ⁻10°F 7°

22. 27°C and 13°C 14°

23. 71°F and 39°F 32°

24. ⁻26°C and ⁻8°C 18°

Choose the better estimate of the temperature.

25. room temperature (**a.**) 22°C **b.** 39°C

26. swim at the beach **a.** 32°F (**b.**) 85°F

27. cup of hot soup (**a.**) 73°C **b.** 14°C

28. build a snowman **a.** 10°C (**b.**) ⁻10°C

29. rake leaves **a.** 20°F (**b.**) 60°F

30. play baseball (**a.**) 75°F **b.** 17°F

Data Use the table for Problems 31–32.

Temperatures on July 27	
Time	Temperature
6:00 A.M.	64°F
9:00 A.M.	70°F
Noon	87°F
3:00 P.M.	78°F
6:00 P.M.	71°F

31. Was the difference in temperature greater between 6:00 A.M. and noon or between noon and 6:00 P.M.?
between 6:00 A.M. and noon

32. Reasoning Do you think the temperature at 7:00 A.M. was greater than or less than 70°F? Explain.
less than 70°F; *See below.*

33. Analyze After the sun rose one morning, the temperature rose 5°. In the afternoon, the temperature fell 3°. If the temperature was 24°C then, what was the temperature when the sun rose? **22°C**

32. *Possible explanation:* The temperature probably increased gradually from 6:00 A.M. to 9:00 A.M., so it was not likely to be 70°F at both 7:00 A.M. and 9:00 A.M.

346

Extra Practice See page 353, Set C

Homework 13.4 Page 86

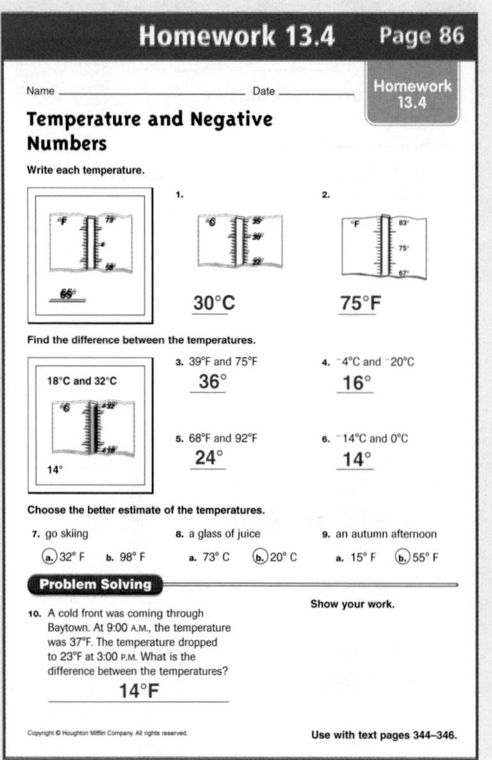

Name ______ Date ______ Homework 13.4

Temperature and Negative Numbers

Write each temperature.

Example: 66°F

1. 30°C
2. 75°F

Find the difference between the temperatures.

Example: 18°C and 32°C — 14°

3. 39°F and 75°F 36°
4. ⁻4°C and ⁻20°C 16°
5. 68°F and 92°F 24°
6. ⁻14°C and 0°C 14°

Choose the better estimate of the temperatures.

7. go skiing (a.) 32° F b. 98° F
8. a glass of juice a. 73° C (b.) 20° C
9. an autumn afternoon a. 15° F (b.) 55° F

Problem Solving

Show your work.

10. A cold front was coming through Baytown. At 9:00 A.M., the temperature was 37°F. The temperature dropped to 23°F at 3:00 P.M. What is the difference between the temperatures? 14°F

Use with text pages 344–346.

Problem Solving

Real World Connection
Why Do We Leap?

Earth takes a little more than 365 days to orbit the sun, but our calendars usually have only 365 days. After several hundred years, the extra time would build up, and our seasons would be turned around.

Long ago, people came up with a solution–leap year. Every fourth year, an extra day is added to February.

In leap years, February has 29 days.

- You can use division to find out which years are leap years. Pick any five years from 1904 to 2005. If you can divide the year evenly by 4, it is a leap year.
- How many leap years did you pick? *Answers may vary.*

WEEKLY WR READER

eduplace.com/map

Quick Check

Check your understanding of Lessons 1–4.

Find each missing number. (Lesson 1)

1. 2 years = 104 weeks
2. 3 weeks = 21 days

Look at each pair of times. Write how much time has passed. (Lesson 2)

3. Start: 2:20 P.M. End: 3:05 P.M. **45 min**
4. Start: 10:35 A.M. End: 12:15 P.M. **1 h 40 min**
5. Start: 9:03 A.M. End: 10:10 P.M. **13 h 7 min**

Find the difference between the temperatures. (Lesson 4)

6. 15°C and 23°C **8°**
7. $^-$4°F and 12°F **16°**
8. 7°C and $^-$7°C **14°**

Solve. (Lessons 3 and 4)

9. There are 3 more dogs than cats in a pet store. There are 21 cats and dogs altogether. How many cats are there? **9 cats**
10. At 9 A.M. the temperature was $^-$3°F. At 3 P.M. the temperature was 15° warmer. What was the temperature at 3 P.M.? **12°F**

Real World Connection

Why Do We Leap?

In 46 B.C.E., Julius Caesar instituted the Julian calendar. A year had 365 days, and one day was added every 4th or "leap" year. In 1582 Pope Gregory XIII made an exception to the rule of leap years—to years ending in 00—and we still follow that exception today. Most century years are *not* leap years—only those divisible by 400. So 1900 was not a leap year, but 2000 was.

Quick Check

The *Quick Check* allows you to assess students' understanding of the concepts presented in Lessons 1–4.

Items	Objectives Tested	Pages	Intervention
1–2	Use a calendar to find elapsed time.	334–335	Reteach Resource 13.1, *Ways to Success* CD-ROM 13.1
3–5	Find elapsed time.	336–339	Reteach Resource 13.2, *Ways to Success* CD-ROM 13.2
6–8	Use a thermometer to read temperatures above and below zero.	344–347	Reteach Resource 13.4, *Ways to Success* CD-ROM 13.4
9–10	Use the Guess and Check strategy to solve a problem.	340–343	Reteach Resource 12.3, *Ways to Success* CD-ROM 13.3

Reaching All Learners

Number Sense

Counting With Negative Numbers

Have students look at a thermometer that shows temperatures below zero. Ask students to start at $^-$8° and count by twos to $^+$8°. Have students complete the following exercises, writing down the numbers as they count.

1. Count by ones from $^-$12° to zero.
2. Count by tens from $^+$20° to $^-$20°.
3. Count by twos from $^-$4° to $^+$14°.
4. Count by twos from $^-$13° to $^+$13°.
5. Count by twos from $^+$19° to $^-$19°.
6. Count by fives from $^+$15° to $^-$15°.

Answers:

Check students' responses.

Differentiated Assignments		
At Risk	Average	Advanced
Exercise 1–3	Exercise 3–5	Exercise 4–6

Lesson 13.5

Problem-Solving Application: Use Temperature

Planning

Lesson Objective Solve problems about temperature.

Technology Resources

- *Ways to Success* CD-ROM 13.5
- Education Place: Extra Practice www.eduplace.com/map

Lesson 13.5 Transparency

Problem of the Day

Rémi is playing a game on a number line. He starts at 0. He moves forward 6 spaces, back 8 spaces, forward 7 spaces, back 2, forward 3, and back 7. Where is Rémi now? (⁻1)

Spiral Review

Choose the better estimate of the temperature.

1. ski slope 27°F or 55°F (27°F)
2. hot cocoa 75°C or 32°C (75°C)
3. snowball 30°C or 30°F (30°F)

Lesson Quiz

Solve each problem.

1. Suppose it is 24°C inside and ⁻7°C outside. How much warmer it is inside than outside? (31°C)
2. Eve's outdoor thermometer reads 11°F. The weather report says that because of strong winds, it will feel like ⁻5°F. What is the difference? (16°F)

NCTM Standards

Measurement: Select and apply appropriate standard units and tools to measure length, area, volume, weight, time, temperature, and the size of angles.

Connections: Recognize and use connections among mathematical ideas.

Getting Started

Building Math Vocabulary

Students should be familiar with the mathematical vocabulary in this lesson.

Using Thermometers to Compare Temperature

Whole Class	10 minutes
Objective	Read, write, and compare temperatures in degrees Fahrenheit and degrees Celsius.
Materials	Fahrenheit and Celsius Thermometer Transparencies
Visual	

- Display the thermometer transparencies. **What is the freezing point of water on each scale?** (32°F; 0°C) Have a volunteer label these points on the thermometers.
- **What is the boiling point of water on each scale?** (212°F; 100°C) Have a volunteer label these points on the thermometer transparencies.
- **How many degrees are between ⁻8°F and 15°F?** (23°F) **Between 15°C and ⁻8°C?** (23°C) Have a volunteer demonstrate how to count up or down on the transparencies to find the difference between the two temperatures.
- Tell students that the lesson will explain how to use what they have learned about temperature to solve problems.

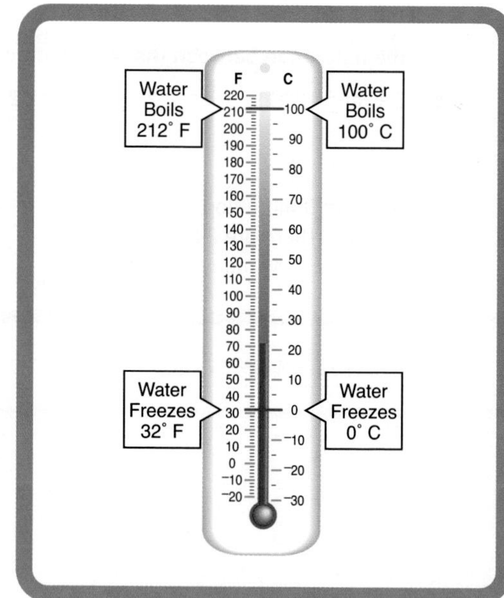

Differentiated Instruction

English Learners

Pairs	15 minutes
Objective	Solve problems about temperature.
Materials	Student page 349
Auditory, Visual	

Early Production

- For ***Guided Practice and Independent Practice,*** ask students to show their work by drawing pictures to count up or down as shown in the Solve step on Student page 348.
- After completing both sections, pair students to compare their work and answers. Have students say their answers aloud.

Intermediate/Advanced

- English Learner Resource 13.5
- English Learner Handbook

Intervention

Whole Class	15 minutes
Objective	Read, write, and compare temperatures.
Materials	Celsius and Fahrenheit Thermometer Transparencies
Tactual, Visual	

- Some students may benefit from modeling temperature problems on a thermometer
- Display the thermometer transparencies. Guide students to model the movement of temperatures up and down according to the facts given in each problem.
- Use the first ***Independent Practice*** problem as an example 1.
- As they model each part of the problem, ask students to read the temperature as they go. This will provide additional practice reading a thermometer.

Other Resources

- *Ways to Success* CD-ROM 13.5

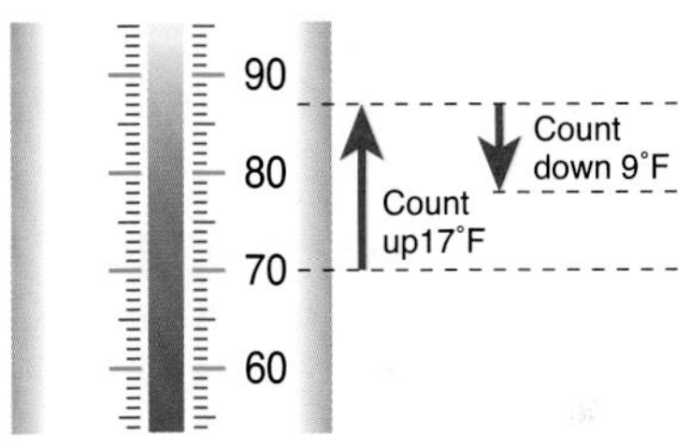

Inclusion

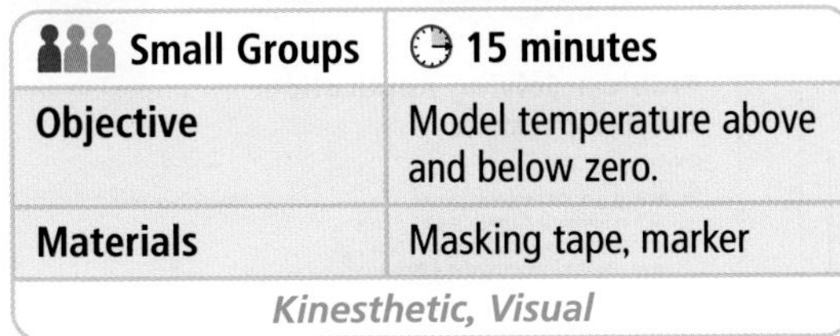

Small Groups	15 minutes
Objective	Model temperature above and below zero.
Materials	Masking tape, marker
Kinesthetic, Visual	

- To help students work with negative numbers, make a vertical walk-on number line out of masking tape. Label it from $^{-}10$ to $^{+}20$, far enough apart so students can step on the numbers.
- Help students walk *up* the line for rising temperatures and *down* the line for falling temperatures.

Science Connection

Materials: Reference books

- Tell students that the names of the two temperature scales honor scientists from the past: Daniel Fahrenheit (1686–1736) and Anders Celsius (1701–1744).
- Have students read about the two scientists and then write a short biography on each. Students should focus on each man's work on temperature scales.

Counting Practice

Have students practice counting aloud between negative and positive numbers. This will help students become more familiar with using temperature scales as well as other negative numbers. Students may need to use a number line in the beginning. Example: Begin students with a number such as −20 and have them count up by 2's (increase difficulty as success occurs) until they reach 20. (i.e., −20, −18, −16...18, 20)

❶ Introduce

Ask students to compare and contrast a thermometer scale with a number line. (Both give the numbers in counting order and use negative and positive numbers. The number line is usually horizontal from side to side, but the thermometer scale is turned vertically so that temperature is read up and down.) Tell students that the lesson in the book will describe how to solve real-world temperature problems.

❷ Teach

Use Temperature

- Read and discuss the opening problem.
- **Look at the Understand step. Why isn't the fact about Antarctica being the coldest continent in the box?** (It's not needed to solve the problem.)
- **Look at the Plan step. Why is a thermometer a good tool to use to solve this problem?** (because you can model the temperature changes and figure out how cold it is by 8:00 P.M.)
- **Look at the Solve step. How do you know that the first picture shows $^{-}6$°F?** (between $^{-}0$°F and $^{-}10$°F; count by ones up from 10.) **After the temperature rises 4°, what does the thermometer say?** ($^{-}2$°F)
- **Look at the Look Back step. How can we decide if the answer makes sense?** (Reread the problem, using the numbers you found to check its reasonableness.)

Common Error

- **Misreading scales** Some students may make errors reading the temperature because of confusion with reading the scale.
- **Intervention** Tell students to find the greatest multiple of 10 covered by the mercury, and then count by ones from that number to the mark that is level with the top of the mercury column.

Lesson 5

Problem-Solving Application

Use Temperature

Objective Solve problems about temperature.

You can use what you know about finding temperature to solve problems.

Problem Antarctica is the coldest continent on Earth. The temperature at noon one day is $^{-}6$°F. The temperature rises 4 degrees over the next two hours. Then by 8:00 P.M. the temperature falls 7 degrees. What is the temperature at 8:00 P.M.?

UNDERSTAND

This is what you know.

- The temperature is $^{-}6$°F at noon.
- The temperature rises 4 degrees and then falls 7 degrees by 8:00 P.M.

PLAN

You can use a thermometer to count up and down.

SOLVE

Count up or count down.

- Start at $^{-}6$°F.
- Count up 4 degrees.
- Count down 7 degrees.

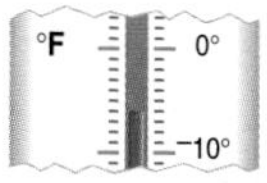

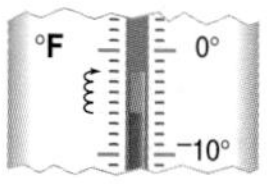

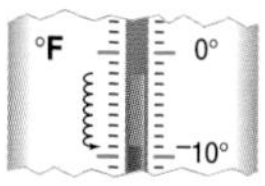

Solution: The temperature is $^{-}9$°F at 8:00 P.M.

LOOK BACK

Check your answer to see if it's reasonable. Since the temperature fell more than it rose, the answer should be less than $^{-}6$°F. $^{-}9$°F is less than $^{-}6$°F, so the answer is reasonable.

348

Reteach 13.5

Name ______ Date ______ Reteach 13.5

Problem-Solving Application: Use Temperature

Read It Look for information.

The temperature in the morning was 13°F. During the day, the temperature rose 5 degrees. The temperature then fell 8 degrees in the evening. What was the temperature in the evening?

Picture It Here is a model of the information.

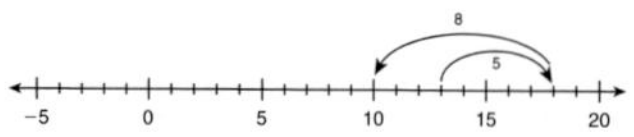

Count up when the temperature rises, count down when the temperature falls.

Solve It Use the model to solve the problem.

1. Start with the morning temperature, add the number of degrees the temperature rose, then subtract the number of degrees the temperature fell.
   13 + 5 − 8 = 10

Try These! Show your work.

2. In January, the average daily temperature for Matinsburg is 8°C. In February, the average daily temperature is 2 degrees lower than in January. In March, the average daily temperature is 4 degrees higher than in February. What is the average daily temperature in March? **10°C**
3. At 7 A.M. the temperature was 22°F. The temperature rose 2 degrees each hour. What was the temperature at 3 P.M.? **38°F**

Use with text pages 348–350.

Practice 13.5 Page 87

Name ______ Date ______ Practice 13.5

Problem-Solving Application: Use Temperature

Solve. Show your work.

1. At 9:00 A.M. the temperature was $^{-}9$°F in Montreal, Canada. If the temperature rose 3 degrees every hour, what was the temperature at 4:00 P.M.? **12°F**
2. Suppose the temperature decreases 2 degrees Celsius for every 500 meters you climb. If your thermometer showed 6°C before you started climbing and now it shows $^{-}2$°C, how many meters have you climbed? **2,000 meters**
3. A thermometer shows 22°F. The wind makes the air feel 25 degrees colder. How cold does it feel? **$^{-}3$°F**
4. The temperature was 63°F in the morning. It rose 24 degrees during the day and then dropped 11 degrees by 8:00 P.M. What was the temperature at 8:00 P.M.? **76°F**
5. On Tuesday, the low temperature was $^{-}5$°F and the high temperature was 28°F. On Wednesday, the low temperature was 3°F and the high temperature was 34°F. Which day had the greatest difference in temperature? **Tuesday**

Use with text pages 348–350.

Guided Practice

Use the Ask Yourself questions to help you solve each problem.

1. If it is 68°F inside and 24°F outside, how many degrees lower is the temperature outside than inside? **44°**

2. Mina recorded the temperature at noon. It then fell 6 degrees. Later it rose 4 degrees. If the last temperature was 17°C, what was it at noon? **19°C**

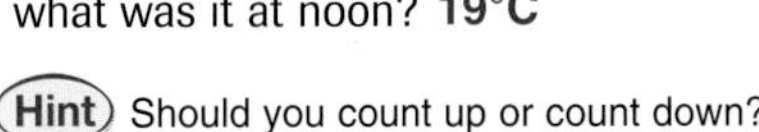

Hint Should you count up or count down?

Ask Yourself

UNDERSTAND — **What do I know?**

PLAN — **Can I use a thermometer?**

SOLVE — **Did I count up or count down the correct number of degrees?**

LOOK BACK — **Does my answer make sense?**

Independent Practice

3. The temperature was 70°F in the morning. It rose 17 degrees during the day and then dropped 9 degrees by 6 P.M. What was the temperature at 6 P.M.? **78°F**

4. At 10 A.M. the temperature was ⁻14°F at a bird research station in Antarctica. If the temperature rose 2 degrees every hour, what was the temperature at 3 P.M.? **⁻4°F**

5. Suppose the temperature falls 1 degree Celsius for every 100 meters you climb. If your thermometer shows 2°C now, what will it show after you climb 400 meters? **⁻2°C**

6. A thermometer shows 16°F. The wind makes the air feel 20 degrees colder. How cold does it feel? **⁻4°F**

7. On Monday the low temperature was ⁻37°C and the high temperature was ⁻12°C. On Tuesday the low temperature was ⁻23°C and the high was 4°C. Which day had the greatest difference in temperature? **Tuesday**

Go On

Guided Practice

Have students complete **Problems 1–2** as you observe. Remind them to use the ***Ask Yourself*** questions to help.

③ Practice

Independent Practice

Select from **Problems 3–13** as independent work.

Enrichment 13.5

Name ______ Date ______ Enrichment 13.5

Problem-Solving Application: Use Temperature

As part of a project on weather for her science class, Ann is researching the average high and low temperatures of several cities in the United States for the month of December.

Use the clues below to fill in the temperature chart.

1. In December, the low temperature in New York is equal to the freezing point of water and the low temperature in Denver is half this temperature.
2. If New York's low temperature rises 12 degrees and then drops 7 degrees, it will be the same temperature as Chicago's high temperature.
3. If Chicago's high temperature drops 10 degrees, rises 2 degrees, and then drops another 5 degrees, it will be at its low temperature.
4. Take Chicago's low temperature and double it. This is the low temperature in Los Angeles. If this temperature drops 4 degrees, it will equal New York's high temperature.
5. The high temperature for New York is the same as the high temperature for Denver.
6. If Los Angeles's low temperature rises 22 degrees and then rises another 10 degrees, it will equal Miami's high temperature. Miami's high temperature is 9 degrees higher than Los Angeles's high temperature.
7. At noon, Miami is at its average high temperature. The temperature rises 4 degrees by 2:00 P.M. and then decreases 4 degrees an hour. By 7:00 P.M. it is at its average low temperature.

Average High and Low Temperatures in December

City	New York	Los Angeles	Miami	Denver	Chicago
Avg. High Temp (°F)	44	71	80	44	37
Avg. Low Temp (°F)	32	48	64	16	24

 Use with text pages 348–350.

Problem Solving 13.5

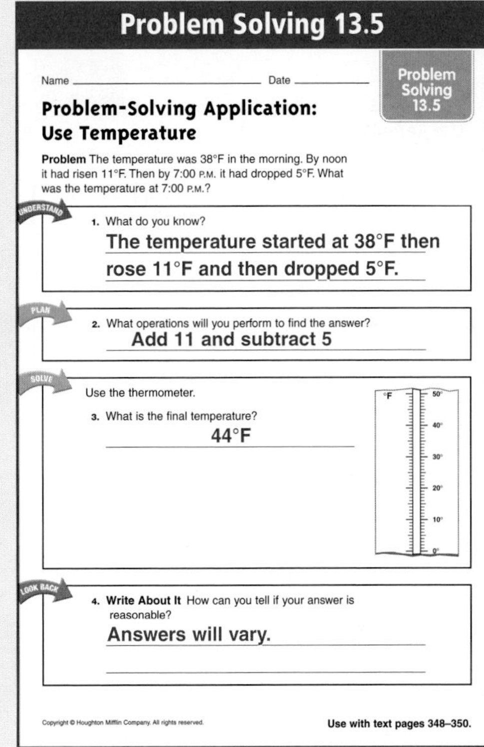

Name ______ Date ______ Problem Solving 13.5

Problem-Solving Application: Use Temperature

Problem The temperature was 38°F in the morning. By noon it had risen 11°F. Then by 7:00 P.M. it had dropped 5°F. What was the temperature at 7:00 P.M.?

UNDERSTAND
1. What do you know?
The temperature started at 38°F then rose 11°F and then dropped 5°F.

PLAN
2. What operations will you perform to find the answer?
Add 11 and subtract 5

SOLVE
Use the thermometer.
3. What is the final temperature?
44°F

LOOK BACK
4. **Write About It** How can you tell if your answer is reasonable?
Answers will vary.

 Use with text pages 348–350.

Mixed Problem-Solving

- For **Problems 8–10,** tell students that they may use any of the strategies listed, or a combination of strategies, as they wish. Remind them to look back at their work to be sure they have answered the question that was asked.

Have students review their answers to make sure they have done the following:

- expressed the solution clearly
- used appropriate mathematical notation and terms
- explained their choice of strategy
- determined the reasonableness of their answer.

4 Assess & Close

Math Talk in Action

- **When we solve problems with a thermometer, does the scale affect our solution plan? Explain.** (You follow the same counting-on method to work with either Fahrenheit or Celsius scales.)
- **How could you use a calculator to compute rising and falling temperatures?** (Add when temperatures rise, subtract when temperatures fall.)

Math Journal Prompt

Have students write an original problem about rising and falling temperatures and explain how to solve it.

Lesson Quiz

Use the quiz on Lesson Transparency 13.5.

Test Prep & Spiral Review

Use Test Prep Transparency 13.5.

Mixed Problem Solving

Solve. Show your work. Tell what strategy you used.
Possible strategies given.

You Choose

Strategy
- Find a Pattern
- Guess and Check
- Work Backward
- Write an Equation

Computation Method
- Mental Math
- Estimation
- Paper and Pencil
- Calculator

8. Mr. Ordono's class collected a total of 172 cans for a food drive. Jacob collected 16 cans and Lakia collected 9 cans. How many cans did the rest of the class collect?
147 cans; Write an Equation
9. **Money** Ben and Norman earned $63 together last weekend. Norman earned $9 more than Ben. How much did Ben earn? **$27; Guess and Check**
10. Ashley swam 2 laps on Monday, 4 laps on Tuesday, 7 laps on Wednesday, and 11 laps on Thursday. If she continues at the same rate, how many laps is she likely to swim on Friday?
Ashley will likely swim 16 laps on Friday; Find a Pattern

Solve. Tell which method you used.
Possible methods given.

11. Arctic terns migrate about 10,000 miles. This is about the same distance as two round trips from New York to Los Angeles. About how many miles apart are New York and Los Angeles?
about 2,500 miles; Mental Math
12. Look at the caption at the right. About how long was it between the time Albert Crary arrived at the North Pole and at the South Pole?
about 10 years; Estimation
13. **Explain** Marsha plans to cut a piece of string 97 inches long to show the wingspan of the American White Pelican. She has 7 feet of string. Is that enough? How do you know?
no; 7 feet of string is only 84 inches long; Paper and Pencil

Albert Paddock Crary was the first person to reach both the North Pole and the South Pole. He arrived at the North Pole in 1952, and the South Pole in 1961.

350

Homework 13.5 **Page 87**

Name ______________ Date ______________

Homework 13.5

Problem-Solving Application: Use Temperature

Solve.

The temperature was 43°F in the morning. It rose 26 degrees during the day and then dropped 17 degrees by 10:00 P.M. What was the temperature at 10:00 P.M.?

Step 1: Start at 43° F.

Step 2: Add 26.

$43 + 26 = 69$

Step 3: Subtract 17.

$69 - 17 = 52$

At 10:00 P.M. the temperature was 52°F.

Show your work.

1. On Thursday, the high temperature was 23°C and the low temperature was 14°C. On Sunday, the high temperature was 18°C and the low temperature was 10°C. What is the difference in Thursday's temperatures? What is the difference in Sunday's temperatures? Which day had the greatest difference in temperatures?
9°C; 8°C; Thursday
2. A thermometer shows 35°F. The wind makes the air feel 17 degrees colder. How cold does it feel?
18°F

Use with text pages 348–350.

Math Reasoning
In Hot Water!

Activity

Materials:
1 glass of hot water from the tap
1 glass of cold water from the tap
2 Fahrenheit thermometers

Have you ever left a cold drink outside on a hot day? When you try to drink it later, it's as hot as the air around it.

Try this activity to see how a liquid's temperature changes over time.

1. Make a table like the one at the right.
2. Measure the room temperature and record it.
3. Measure the temperature of each glass of water and record it.
   - What is the difference between each water temperature and the room temperature at the beginning of the experiment?
   - Predict which glass will reach room temperature first.
4. Repeat the water measurements every half hour and record them.
   - At what time did both glasses of water reach the same temperature?

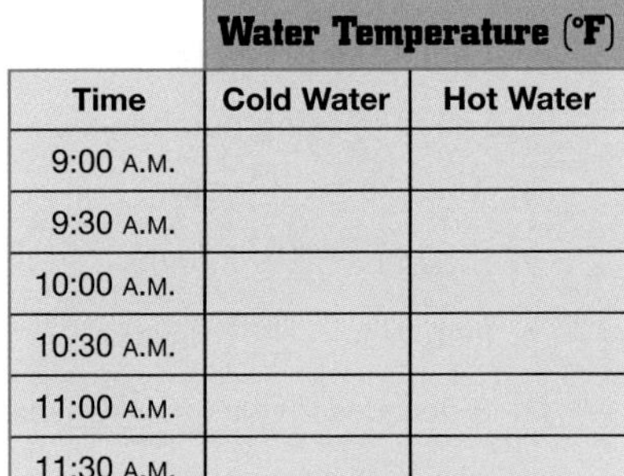

	Water Temperature (°F)	
Time	Cold Water	Hot Water
9:00 A.M.		
9:30 A.M.		
10:00 A.M.		
10:30 A.M.		
11:00 A.M.		
11:30 A.M.		

Room Temperature ____ °F

Check students' work.

Math Reasoning

In Hot Water!

Materials: 1 glass hot water, 1 glass cold water, 2 Fahrenheit thermometers

You may wish to repeat the activity using Celsius thermometers. If so, be sure to measure the room temperature in Celsius as well.

You might vary the activity by using different types of containers (for example, foam or paper) or adding ice to the cold water.

Chapter Review/Test

Chapter Review/Test Items 1–20

To assign a numerical grade to this Chapter Review/Test, use 5 points for each item.

Check Understanding

You can use the ***Write About It*** question to assess student understanding of a key chapter concept.

Customize Your Instruction

The Chapter Review/Test is a formal evaluation of chapter objectives. For students who have not yet mastered these objectives, you can use the *Reteaching Resources* listed in the chart below.

Additional Assessment Resources

Alternate Chapter Test A Chapter Test is also provided in the Unit Resource folder. You might use the Review/Test in the student book as review and the test in the Unit Resource folder as a summary test for the chapter.

***Ways to Assess* CD-ROM** allows you to create your own lesson, chapter, or unit tests or practice and review worksheets.

Adequate Yearly Progress Guide helps familiarize students with the format of standardized tests.

Chapter Review/Test

VOCABULARY

Choose the best term to complete each sentence.

Vocabulary
decade
century
positive number
negative number
elapsed time

1. The time that passes between one time and another is ____. **elapsed time**
2. A number that is less than 0 is a ____. **negative number**
3. There are 10 years in a ____. **decade**
4. There are 100 years in a ____. **century**

CONCEPTS AND SKILLS

Find each missing number. (Lesson 1, pp. 334–335)

5. 4 weeks = **28** days
6. 1 year = **365** days
7. 5 years = **60** months
8. 21 days = **3** weeks
9. leap year = **366** days
10. **52** weeks = 1 year
11. 3 decades 2 years = **32** years
12. 2 centuries 3 decades = **230** years

Look at each pair of times. Write how much time has passed. (Lesson 2, pp. 336–338)

13. Start: 9:00 A.M. End: 6:45 P.M. **9 hours 45 minutes**
14. Start: 4:10 P.M. End: 5:53 P.M. **1 hour 43 minutes**
15. Start: 8:17 A.M. End: 11:00 A.M. **2 hours 43 minutes**

Find the difference between the temperatures. (Lesson 4, pp. 344–347)

16. 25°F and 7°F **18°**
17. 12°C and $^{-}5$°C **17°**
18. $^{-}8$°F and $^{-}6$°F **2°**

PROBLEM SOLVING

Solve. (Lessons 3, 5, pp. 340–342, 348–350)

19. There are 13 children and dogs in the park. Altogether there are 34 legs. How many children and how many dogs are there? **9 children and 4 dogs**
20. Kelly read the temperature at noon. It rose 10 degrees by 3 P.M. then fell 5 degrees by 6 P.M. If the temperature was 3°F at 6 P.M., what was it at noon? **$^{-}2$°F**

Write About It

Show You Understand

Frank says that when it's 30°C, it is time to wear a warm coat. Is he correct? Explain why or why not.

***Possible answer:* No. He is not correct because 30°C is hot.**

Chapter Review/Test Items	Objectives	Covered On Teacher's Edition Pages	Use These Reteaching Resources
1, 3, 4, 5–15	**13A** Determine elapsed time using clocks and calendars.	334A–338	Reteach Resources 13.1, 13.2 *Ways to Success* CD-ROM 13.1, 13.2 *Ways to Success* Skillsheets 115, 118
2, 16–18	**13B** Measure temperature above and below zero using degrees Fahrenheit and degrees Celsius.	344A–346	Reteach Resources 13.4 *Ways to Success* CD-ROM 13.4 *Ways to Success* Skillsheet 119
19–20	**13C** Solve problems using skills and strategies.	340A–342, 348A–350	Reteach Resources 13.3, 13.5 *Ways to Success* CD-ROM 13.3, 13.5 *Ways to Success* Skillsheet 120

Extra Practice

Set A (Lesson 1, pp. 334–335)

Use the calendar.

January						
Sun.	Mon.	Tue.	Wed.	Thu.	Fri.	Sat.
						1
2	3	4	5	6	7	8
9	10	11	12	13	14	15
16	17	18	19	20	21	22
23	24	25	26	27	28	29
30	31					

1. Write the day and date 3 days before January 26. **Sunday, January 23**
2. Write the day and date 5 days after January 8. **Thursday, January 13**
3. Write the day and date 2 weeks after January 1. **Saturday, January 15**
4. Write the day and date 1 week before January 11. **Tuesday, January 4**

Find each missing number.

5. 3 weeks = **21** days
6. 1 year = **365** days
7. 2 decades = **20** years
8. 52 weeks = **1** year
9. 1 year 6 months = **18** months
10. 3 centuries = **300** years

Set B (Lesson 2, pp. 336–339)

Tell what time it will be.

1. in 3 hours **5:18**
2. in 20 minutes **10:01**
3. in 17 minutes **11:09**

Set C (Lesson 4, pp. 344–347)

Write the temperature shown on each thermometer.
Then write the difference between the two temperatures.

1. 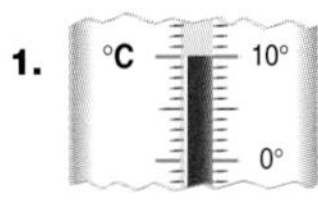
10°C **⁻4°C**
The difference is 14°.

2. 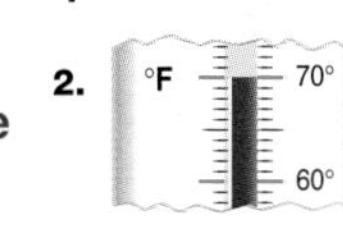 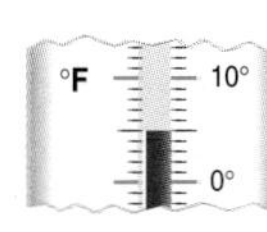
70°F **5°F**
The difference is 65°.

Find the difference between the temperatures.

3. 5°C and 12°C **7°**
4. ⁻3°F and 10°F **13°**
5. ⁻9°C and ⁻4°C **5°**

Extra Practice at **eduplace.com/map**

Chapter 13 Extra Practice 353

CHAPTER 13 TEST

Chapter 13 Test

Name ______________ Date ________

Look at each pair of times. Write how much time has passed.

1. Start: 8:15 A.M. End: 11:35 A.M. **3 h 20 min**
2. Start: 6:35 P.M. End: 11:50 P.M. **5 h 15 min**
3. Start: 10:30 A.M. End: 1:55 P.M. **3 h 25 min**

Tell what time it will be. Use the first Clock A for Problems 4–5. Use the second Clock B for Problems 6–7.

4. in 30 minutes. **2:46**
5. in 6 hours. **8:16**
6. in 35 minutes. **11:05**
7. in 4 hours. **2:30**

2:16

A B

Use the calendar for Problems 8–11.

JULY						
Sun	Mon	Tue	Wed	Thu	Fri	Sat
1	2	3	4	5	6	7
8	9	10	11	12	13	14
15	16	17	18	19	20	21
22	23	24	25	26	27	28
29	30	31				

8. How many Mondays are in July? **5**
9. What day of the week is July 12th? **Thursday**
10. What is the date of the fifth Tuesday in July? **July 31**
11. What is the date of the third Saturday in July? **July 21**

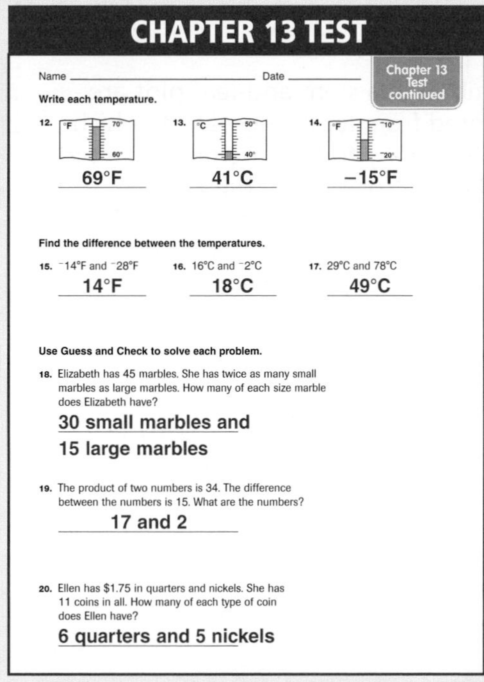

CHAPTER 13 TEST

Chapter 13 Test continued

Name ______________ Date ________

Write each temperature.

12. **69°F**
13. **41°C**
14. **−15°F**

Find the difference between the temperatures.

15. ⁻14°F and ⁻28°F **14°F**
16. 16°C and ⁻2°C **18°C**
17. 29°C and 78°C **49°C**

Use Guess and Check to solve each problem.

18. Elizabeth has 45 marbles. She has twice as many small marbles as large marbles. How many of each size marble does Elizabeth have?
30 small marbles and 15 large marbles

19. The product of two numbers is 34. The difference between the numbers is 15. What are the numbers?
17 and 2

20. Ellen has $1.75 in quarters and nickels. She has 11 coins in all. How many of each type of coin does Ellen have?
6 quarters and 5 nickels

CHAPTER 14

Planning Guide

Collect and Analyze Data

Lesson	Overview	Objective/Vocabulary
1 **Hands On: Collect and Analyze Data** p. 356A	► Students conduct a survey to collect data. ► To organize data, students use tally charts.	► Conduct a survey and organize information survey data
2 **Problem-Solving Strategy: Make a Table** p. 360A	► Students organize data in a table to solve a problem. ► Students practice problem-solving strategies learned earlier.	► Organize data in a table to solve a problem.
3 **Hands On: Mean, Median, Mode, and Range** p. 364A	► Students find the mean, median, mode, and range of a set of data. ► Students calculate the mean by finding the sum of all the numbers and then dividing it by the number of addends. ► To find the mean of a set of data quicker, students use calculators to perform the operations.	► Find the mean, median, mode, and range of a set of data. mean median mode range
4 **Line-Plots** p. 366A	► Students represent data on a line plot using X's. ► Numbers in a line plot are ordered from least to greatest, making it easy to find the median, mode, and range for a set of data.	► Make a line plot to represent data. line plot range median mode
5 **Stem-and Leaf Plots** p. 370A	► Students organize data into stem-and-leaf plots. ► Numbers in a stem-and-leaf plot are ordered from least to greatest, which makes it easy to find the median, mode, and range for a set of data. ► The *Math Reasoning* section of this lesson gives examples of finding modes of data that are not numerical.	► Read and make stem-and-leaf plots. stem-and-leaf plot outlier

Skills Trace: Collect and Analyze Data		
Grade 3	**Grade 4**	**Grade 5**
• Collect, organize, and analyze data (ch. 6) • Organize data in a table to solve a problem (ch. 6) • Explore mean, median, mode, and range of a set of data (ch. 6) • Make, read, and interpret line plots, pictographs, and bar graphs (ch. 6)	• Collect, organize, and analyze data • Organize data in a table to solve a problem • Find mean, median, mode, and range for a set of data • Make, read, and interpret line plots and stem-and-leaf plots	• Collect, organize, and analyze data in tables, plots, and graphs (ch. 8) • Organize data in a table to solve a problem (ch. 8) • Find mean, median, mode, and range for a set of data (ch. 8) • Draw conclusions and make predictions from data displays (ch. 8)

Differentiated Instruction	Materials	NCTM Standards
▶ Differentiated Instruction activities, p. 356B *Ways to Success* CD-ROM: 14.1 ▶ *Chapter Challenges*, p. 79 ▶ *Ways to Success* Skillsheets 122, 124	Table II Transparency, tally charts (Learning Tool 17), pennies, Igba-Ita scoring sheets (Learning Tool 18)	**Data Analysis and Probability:** Select and use appropriate statistical methods to analyze data.
▶ Differentiated Instruction activities, p. 360B *Ways to Success* CD-ROM: 14.2 ▶ *Ways to Success* Skillsheet 128		**Problem Solving:** Apply and adapt a variety of appropriate strategies to solve problems.
▶ Differentiated Instruction activities, p. 364B *Ways to Success* CD-ROM: 14.3 ▶ *Chapter Challenges*, p. 81 ▶ *Ways to Success* Skillsheet p. 125	Calculators	**Data Analysis and Probability:** Select and use appropriate statistical methods to analyze data.
▶ Differentiated Instruction activities, p. 366B *Ways to Success* CD-ROM: 14.4 Audio Tutor: **2**/6 Listen and Understand ▶ *Ways to Success* Skillsheet p. 126	Number Lines Transparency, blank transparency, erasable marker	**Data Analysis and Probability:** Select and use appropriate statistical methods to analyze data.
▶ Differentiated Instruction activities, p. 370B Audio Tutor: **2**/7 Listen and Understand *Ways to Success* CD-ROM: 14.5 ▶ Chapter Challenges, p. 83 ▶ *Ways to Success* Skillsheet p. 127	Blank transparency, erasable marker	**Data Analysis and Probability:** Select and use appropriate statistical methods to analyze data.

Math Notes

Chapter Objectives

14A Conduct surveys to collect data; use data to solve problems.

14B Find mean, median, mode, and range of numerical data.

14C Make, read, and interpret line plots and stem-and-leaf plots.

14D Solve problems using skills and strategies.

Mathematical Background

Mean, Median, and Mode

When analyzing data, there are three useful measures of central tendency: mean, median, and mode. Although each describes data in a different way, they all provide a numerical value that can be described as typical of the data.

Look at this data set: 2, 3, 2, 2, 4, 4, 13, 4, 2

The mean, or average, is the sum of the numbers divided by the number of addends.

$(2 + 3 + 2 + 2 + 4 + 4 + 13 + 4 + 2) \div 9 = 4$

The mean of the data set is 4. The number 4 is typical of this data because if every number in the list was 4, the sum would be the same.

The median is the number in the middle when the numbers are arranged in increasing order.

2 2 2 2 **3** 4 4 4 13

The median is 3. The number 3 is typical because there are 4 numbers less than 3 and 4 numbers greater than 3.

The mode is the number that appears most often. The mode of the data set above is 2. The number 2 is typical because there are more 2s than any other number.

Research-Based Teaching

Russell and Friel (1989) write that, in order for data collection problems to be meaningful to students, they need to be based on real problems. They define real problems as ones that begin with students either collecting the data themselves or getting the data from real-world sources. See *Professional Resources Handbook, Grade 4,* Unit 5.

For more ideas relating to Unit 5, see the Teacher Support Handbook at the back of this Teacher's Edition

Language Intervention

When new vocabulary words (for example, *mean, median, mode,* and *range*) are introduced in a lesson, have students write their own definitions. Use the students' definitions to help you identify misconceptions students may have.

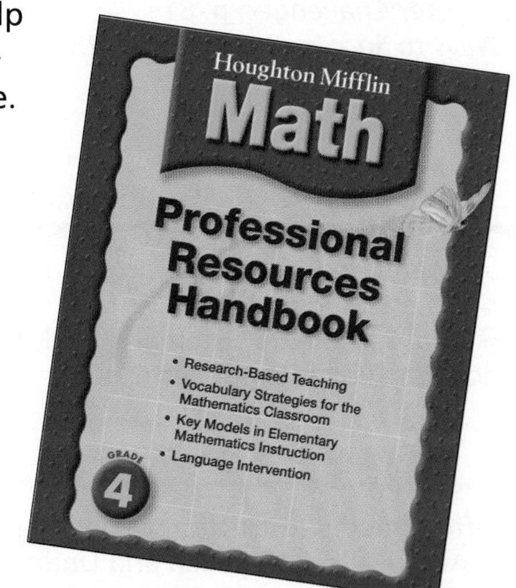

Chapter Activities

Connecting to the Unit Project

Whole Class	20 minutes
Objective	Conduct surveys to collect data.
Materials	None
Auditory, Tactual	

Conduct a Survey

- Have students survey their classmates about their favorite place in the state.
- Ask them to think of a survey question that could be recorded using a tally chart, line plot, or a stem-and-leaf plot.
- After the survey is completed, students analyze the data and write a summary paragraph about it. You may also wish to have them give oral reports summarizing their data.

Ongoing Skill Activity

Individuals	10 minutes
Objective	Find mean, median, mode, and range of numerical data.
Materials	None
Visual	

Mean, Median, Mode, and Range

- Have students keep track of their daily mathematics homework scores or weekly spelling scores.
- After a certain period of time, have students figure out the range and mean for that class.
- Students may want to find the median and mode of a set of scores if there are several of them.

Our Spelling Scores
April

May Ann	100	100	100
Terry	100	90	100
Freddy	90	90	95
Matt	95	85	100
Trisha	85	95	95

Math Expressions

Whole Class	25 minutes
Objective	Determine the best measure of central tendency to summarize data.
Materials	None
Auditory	

Measure of Central Tendency

- Explain that either mean, median, or mode could be the best measure to use to summarize data, depending on the situation. For example, if one of the numbers in a set is much greater than the other numbers, the median might be the best measure to use; the much-larger number does not change the number in the middle.
- Present the situations below. Have students decide which measure is best to use to summarize the data. Discuss student's answers and reasoning.

At his store, Mr. Garcia sells cereal in boxes that weigh 16, 20, and 24 ounces. One week, he sold boxes that weighed 16, 20, 16, 24, 16, 16, and 20 ounces. (mode)

Kimo found that it rained 11 cm in January, 12 cm in February, 14 cm in March, 16 cm in April, 13 cm in May, and 12 cm in June. (mean)

Janice bowled five games. Her 1st game score was 76. Her 2nd score was 85. Her 3rd game score was 82. Her 4th game score was 61. Her 5th game score was 79. (median)

Starting Chapter 14

Investigation

Using Data

Have students work in small groups to do the activity on page 354.

To extend the investigation, have students do the following activity.

- Conduct the survey from page 354 with the members of your class. Record your data in a tally chart. How were the results of your survey the same as the one on page 354? How were they different?

For more information about projects and investigations,

Visit **Education Place**®
www.eduplace.com/mat

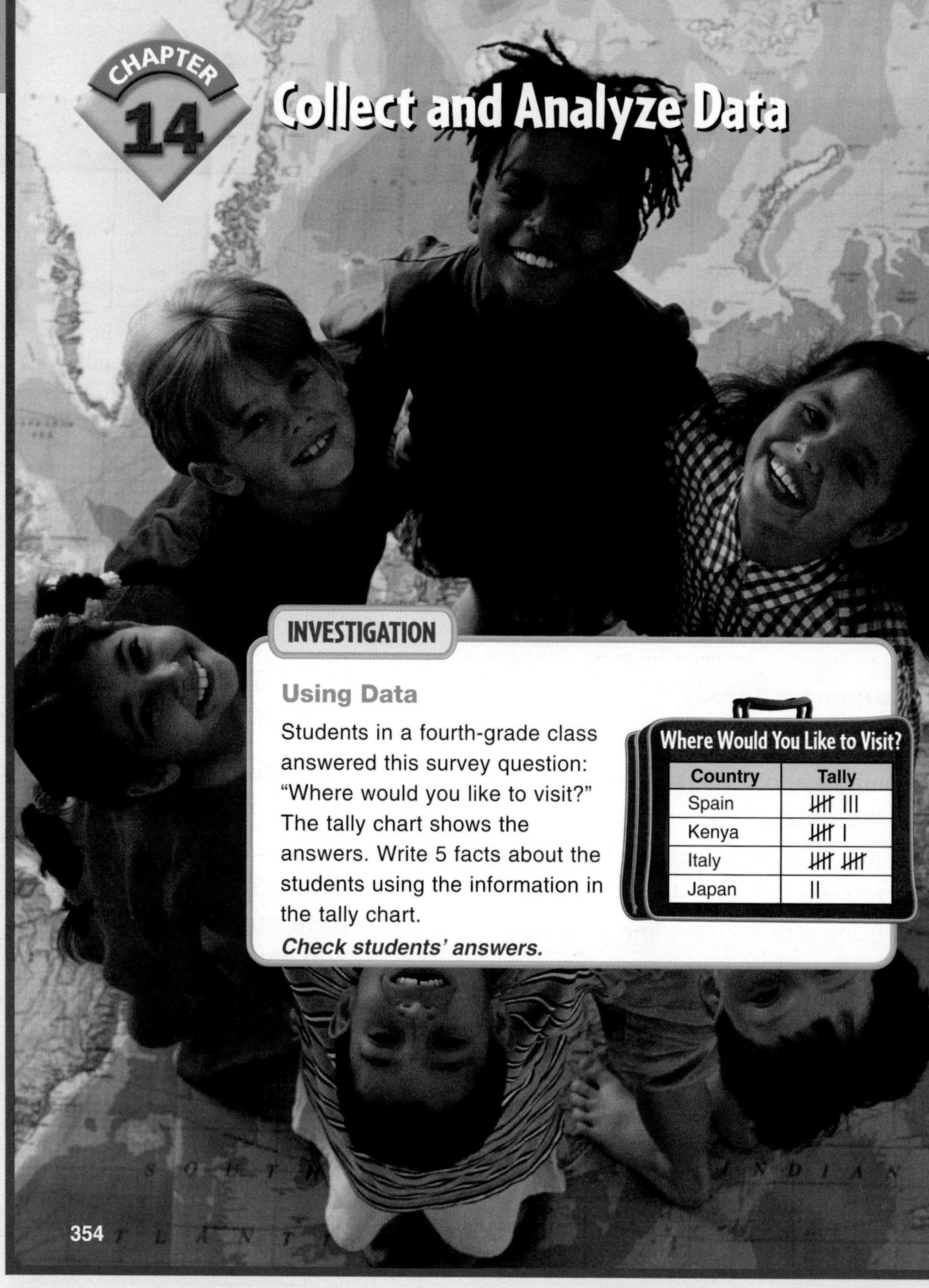

CHAPTER 14
Collect and Analyze Data
INVESTIGATION
Using Data
Students in a fourth-grade class answered this survey question: "Where would you like to visit?" The tally chart shows the answers. Write 5 facts about the students using the information in the tally chart.
Check students' answers.
Where Would You Like to Visit?
Country | Tally
Spain | 𝍸 III
Kenya | 𝍸 I
Italy | 𝍸 𝍸
Japan | II
354

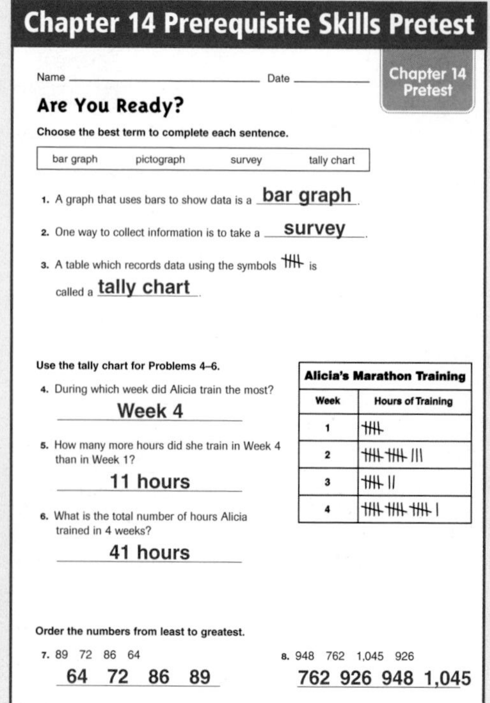

Chapter 14 Prerequisite Skills Pretest

Name ______ Date ______ Chapter 14 Pretest

Are You Ready?

Choose the best term to complete each sentence.

bar graph   pictograph   survey   tally chart

1. A graph that uses bars to show data is a **bar graph**.
2. One way to collect information is to take a **survey**.
3. A table which records data using the symbols 𝍸 is called a **tally chart**.

Use the tally chart for Problems 4–6.

4. During which week did Alicia train the most? **Week 4**
5. How many more hours did she train in Week 4 than in Week 1? **11 hours**
6. What is the total number of hours Alicia trained in 4 weeks? **41 hours**

Alicia's Marathon Training

Week	Hours of Training
1	𝍸
2	𝍸 𝍸 III
3	𝍸 II
4	𝍸 𝍸 𝍸 I

Order the numbers from least to greatest.

7. 89 72 86 64 — **64 72 86 89**
8. 948 762 1,045 926 — **762 926 948 1,045**

Go on

Use this page to review and remember what you need to know for this chapter.

VOCABULARY

Choose the best term to complete each sentence.

Vocabulary
survey
bar graph
pictograph
tally marks

1. A graph that uses pictures to show data is a ____. **pictograph**
2. One way to collect information is to take a ____. **survey**
3. The symbols 𝍸 are called ____. **tally marks**

CONCEPTS AND SKILLS

The tally chart at the right shows the number of hours Alicia trained for a marathon. Use the tally chart for Problems 4–6.

Alicia's Marathon Training	
Week	Hours of Training
1	𝍸
2	𝍸 𝍸 III
3	𝍸 II
4	𝍸 𝍸 𝍸 I

4. In which week did Alicia train the most? **Week 4**
5. How many more hours did she train in Week 4 than in Week 1? **11 more hours**
6. What is the total number of hours Alicia trained in 4 weeks? **41 hours**

Order the numbers from least to greatest.

7. 89 72 86 64
   64 72 86 89
8. 163 314 145 278
   145 163 278 314
9. 948 762 1,045 926
   762 926 948 1,045

10. What would be a good interval on a bar graph for the following data? Explain your reasoning. ***See above.***
    15 16 20 22 25 28

10. *Possible answer:* An interval of 2 would be good because all the bars would end on a line or halfway between lines.

Facts Practice, See page 664.

Use What You Know

Use this page for informal assessment and review of prerequisite skills.

- 1–3 Use math vocabulary
- 4–6 Use a tally chart to solve problems
- 7–9 Order numbers from least to greatest
- 10 Make a bar graph to display data

Customize Your Instruction

Use the Chapter Pretest in the Unit Resource Folder to help customize and pace instruction.

Objectives and Resources

Prerequisite Skills Pretest

- Items 1–3: Identify graphs and plots and their parts.
- Items 4–6: Use a tally chart to solve problems.
- Items 7–8: Order numbers from least to greatest.

New Content Pretest

- Items 1–5: Conduct surveys to collect data; use data to solve problems.
- Items 6–9: Find mean, median, mode, and range of *numerical* data.
- Items 10–17: Make, read, and interpret line plots and stem-and-leaf plots.
- Item 18: Solve problems using skills and strategies.

For Students Having Difficulty

- *Ways to Success* CD-ROM 14.2B

For Students Having Success

- Enrichment 14.1–14.5
- *Chapter Challenges*, Chapter 14

For Mathematically Promising Students

Explore: Number Cube Patterns, page 79, after Lesson 1

Extend: Data Challenge, page 81, after Lesson 3

Connect: Math and Architecture, page 83, after Lesson 5

Chapter 14 New Content Pretest

Name ____________ Date ________ Chapter 14 Pretest continued

Check What You Know

Use the tally chart for Problems 1–5.

What Is Your Favorite Winter Activity?		
Activity	Tally	Number
Skiing	𝍸 𝍸	10
Ice Skating	𝍸 I	6
Hockey	𝍸	5
Snowboarding	𝍸 𝍸 𝍸 I	16
Snowman Making	II	2

1. How many people answered the question? **39 people**
2. What is the survey question? **What is your favorite winter activity?**
3. Which answer was given most often? **snowboarding**
4. Which answer was given least often? **snowman making**
5. List the activities from most popular to least popular. **snowboarding, skiing, ice skating, hockey, snowman making**

Use the data in the box for Problems 6–9.

3	5	3	9

6. What is the range of the data? **6**
7. What is the mode of the data? **3**
8. What is the median of the data? **4**
9. What is the mean of the data? **5**

Go on

Chapter 14 New Content Pretest

Name ____________ Date ________ Chapter 14 Pretest continued

Use the line plot for Problems 10–12.

Number of Hockey Goals	0	1	2	3	4	5	6
	x x x	x x x x x x	x		x x x x		x

10. How many players had exactly 4 goals? **4 players**
11. How many players had 0 goals? **3 players**
12. What is the range of the data? **6**

Use the stem-and-leaf plot for Problems 13–16.

Books Read By Students	
Stem	Leaves
1	1 5 5 8
2	0 4 4 8 9
3	0 2

13. How many leaves are in the stem-and-leaf plot? **11 leaves**
14. How many students read more than 28 books? **3 students**
15. What is the least number of books read? **11 books**
16. What is the greatest number of books read? **32 books**

Make a table to solve each problem.

17. Don is 20 years old. Steve is 44 years old. How old will they both be when Steve is twice as old as Don? **Steve: 48; Don: 24**
18. The concert begins at 8:30 A.M. Maria is the first clarinet soloist, playing after 7 flute soloists. Each solo takes 5 minutes. When will Maria play? **9:05 A.M.**

STOP

Hands On Lesson 14.1

Collect and Organize Data

Planning

Lesson Objective Conduct a survey and organize information.

Technology Resources

- *Ways to Success* CD-ROM 14.1
- Education Place: Extra Practice, eGlossary, eGames www.eduplace.com/map

Lesson 14.1 Transparency

Problem of the Day

Four boys are waiting in line to buy tickets. Mike is between Jorge and Dan. Dan is between Mike and Kim. Jorge is at the end of the line. Which boy is first in line? (Kim)

Spiral Review

1. 7 + 4 + 3 + 6 = (20)
2. 13 + 0 + 8 + 7 = (28)
3. 5 + 6 + 9 + 4 + 1 = (25)

Lesson Quiz

How Many Children Are In Your Family?

Answer	Tally	Number
1	||	2
2	~~||||~~ ~~||||~~ |||	13
3	~~||||~~ |||	8
4	||	2
More than 4		0

1. What is the survey question? (How many children are in your family?)
2. Which answer was given most often? least often? (2 children; more than 4 children)

NCTM Standards

Data Analysis and Probability: Select and use appropriate statistical methods to analyze data.

Getting Started

Building Math Vocabulary

survey one method of collecting information

data a set of information

Talk with students about what it means to ***survey*** people to find out the most popular pets. (to collect information by asking questions) Explain that the information gathered is called ***data.*** Another term for data is "raw information."

Discuss Collecting and Organizing Data

Whole Class	5 minutes
Objective	Conduct a survey and organize data.
Materials	Table II Transparency
Visual, Auditory	

- Use the Table II Transparency to show students how to conduct a survey and organize data. Label the second column *Tally* and the third column *Number.* Fill in the rest of the chart as you complete the activity.
- With students, conduct a survey to find out the class's favorite color—red, yellow, green, or blue.
- **What should the survey question be?** (Which is your favorite color: red, green, yellow, or blue?) **What title should we give our chart?** (Favorite Color)
- Use tally marks to record students' responses to the survey question in the chart. As you work, be sure to clarify the standard way to make and read tally marks. Have volunteers count the tally marks for each color and record the numbers in the chart.
- Tell students they will now use page 356 of their books to begin a new survey.

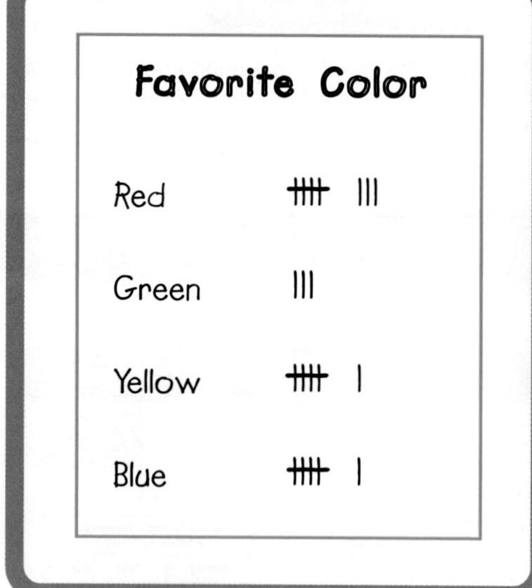

Differentiated Instruction

English Learners

Individuals	10 minutes
Objective	Practice writing tallies.
Materials	None
Visual	

Early Production

- Before ***On Your Own***, have students practice writing tallies.
- Write five to ten numbers under 20 on the board.
- Ask students to make the appropriate tally marks under each number.

After all of the tallies are completed, have students assess the work, explaining if each tally was done correctly or incorrectly.

Intermediate/Advanced

- English Learner Resource 14.1
- English Learner Handbook

Intervention

Whole Class	15 minutes
Objective	Conduct a survey and organize data.
Materials	None
Visual, Tactual	

- Have each student demonstrate how to make and read tally marks.
- Have the group conduct a survey to find out how many members are in each student's family.
- Use tally marks to record each student's response onto a chart.

Other Resources

- *Ways to Success* CD-ROM 14.1

Early Finishers

Individuals	15 minutes
Objective	Make a tally chart to show data.
Materials	None
Visual, Kinesthetic	

- Write the following passage on the board: **A survey was taken of fifty fourth-graders in California. The data showed that more students wanted to be firefighters than doctors.**
- Have students make a tally chart according to the number of letters in each word, such as how many five-letter words are there, how many six-letter words, etc.
- Have students make a tally chart to show the data.

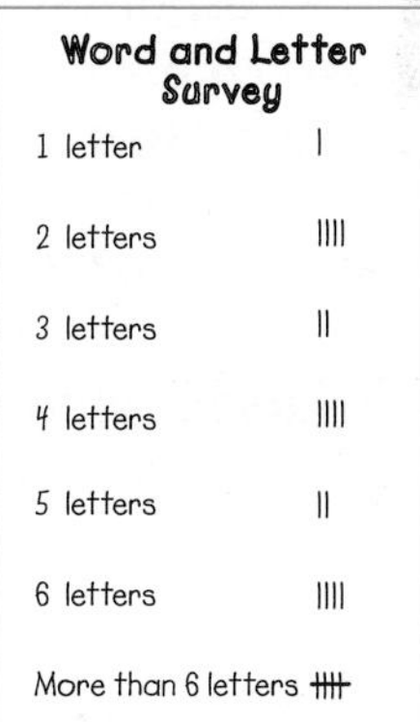

Word and Letter Survey

1 letter	I
2 letters	IIII
3 letters	II
4 letters	IIII
5 letters	II
6 letters	IIII
More than 6 letters	~~IIII~~

Music Connection

- Have students list 4–6 different musical instruments. Help them formulate a question about those instruments, such as, "Which of these instruments would you most like to be able to play?"
- To gather data about the question students decide to ask, have them survey one another. Have students make a tally chart for the data as they collect it, and write a summary.

❶ Introduce

Ask students if they have ever wondered how many of their classmates have cats, dogs, or hamsters. Tell them they can find out this information by conducting a survey and recording their findings, or data, onto a chart.

❷ Teach

Work Together

- **Why does the survey need to have a title?** (to tell what the data shows) **How are the tally marks organized?** (in groups of five, four crossed by a fifth) **Why do you think tally marks are organized this way?** (to make them easier to count) **Which was the least favorite type of food?** (salad) **Which foods were the top two favorites?** (chicken nuggets and corn) **Which food had only a few votes?** (tuna)
- As students work with partners to conduct their own surveys, ask questions such as these: **What topic did you choose for your survey? What question will you ask? How will you show it on your table? How will you organize your chart? What choices will you give as possible answers? How many answers will you allow each person to give? How will you keep track of the number of people you survey?** (Answers will vary.)
- Once partners have conducted their surveys and recorded the responses, ask questions such as these: **Which answer had the most votes? Which answer had the fewest votes?** (Answers will vary.) **How can you check that you surveyed 20 people?** (Count up the tally marks or votes, which should total 20.) **Were the results of your survey what you expected? Why or why not?** (Answers will vary.)

Common Error

- **Mismarking tallies** Some students record tallies improperly, thus misrepresenting the data they gather when they take a survey.
- **Intervention** Remind students that the purpose of making tallies in groups of five is for easy counting. Model the standard practice of making groups of five tallies by crossing every four lines with the fifth one, drawn at a diagonal.

Hands On Lesson 1

Collect and Organize Data

Objective Conduct a survey and organize information.

Vocabulary
data
survey

Materials
Tally Charts
(Learning Tool 17)

Work Together

A survey is one way to collect information, or **data**. When you conduct a **survey**, you ask a question and record the answers.

The question for a class survey was, "What do you like to eat?"

- Thirty students answered the question.
- The answer choices were *chicken nuggets, corn, French fries, salad,* and *tuna sandwich.*
- The answer *chicken nuggets* was given most often. Thirteen students liked chicken nuggets best.

What Do You Like to Eat?

Answer	Tally	Number
Chicken nuggets	卌 卌 III	13
Corn	卌 II	7
French fries	卌 I	6
Salad		0
Tuna sandwich	IIII	4

Work with a partner. Conduct a survey and organize your data.

STEP 1 Write a question that has 3 or 4 possible answers. List the possible answers in a tally chart like the one shown.

Question:________

Answer	Tally	Number

STEP 2 Survey 20 people. Allow each person to give only one answer. Make a tally mark for each answer. Then add the tally marks for each answer.

STEP 3 Analyze your data.

- How would you describe the results of your survey? ***Answers may vary.***

356

Reteach 14.1

Name ________ Date ______

Reteach 14.1

Collect and Organize Data

A tally chart is a way to show the information, or data, you have collected.

Survey Question ↓

What is your favorite fruit?

Fruit	Tally	Number
Apple	卌 I	6
Orange	卌 卌 I	11
Banana	IIII	4
Pear	卌 III	8

↑ Answers Given — ↑ Tally Marks (1 for each answer) — ↑ Total Number of Tally Marks for each answer

Use the tally chart to the right for Problems 1–6.

What is your favorite drink?

Drink	Tally	Number
Water	卌 II	7
Sports drink	IIII	4
Fruit juice	卌 卌 I	11
Hot cocoa	卌	5
Tea	III	3

1. What is the survey question? **What is your favorite drink?**
2. Which answer was given most often? **fruit juice**
3. Which answer was given least often? **tea**
4. How many students answered the survey question? **30**
5. List the drinks in order from most popular to least popular. **fruit juice, water, hot cocoa, sports drink, tea**
6. How many students chose fruit juice or water? **18**

Use with text pages 356–358.

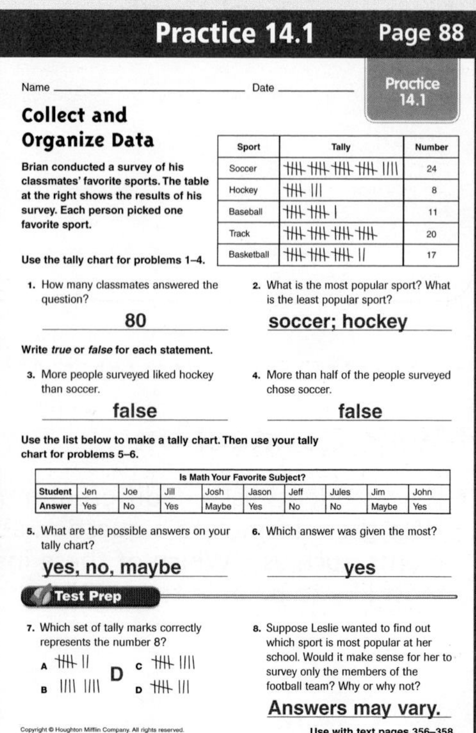

Practice 14.1 Page 88

Name ________ Date ______

Practice 14.1

Collect and Organize Data

Brian conducted a survey of his classmates' favorite sports. The table at the right shows the results of his survey. Each person picked one favorite sport.

Sport	Tally	Number
Soccer	卌 卌 卌 卌 IIII	24
Hockey	卌 III	8
Baseball	卌 卌 I	11
Track	卌 卌 卌 卌	20
Basketball	卌 卌 卌 II	17

Use the tally chart for problems 1–4.

1. How many classmates answered the question? **80**
2. What is the most popular sport? What is the least popular sport? **soccer; hockey**

Write *true* or *false* for each statement.

3. More people surveyed liked hockey than soccer. **false**
4. More than half of the people surveyed chose soccer. **false**

Use the list below to make a tally chart. Then use your tally chart for problems 5–6.

Is Math Your Favorite Subject?									
Student	Jen	Joe	Jill	Josh	Jason	Jeff	Jules	Jim	John
Answer	Yes	No	Yes	Maybe	Yes	No	No	Maybe	Yes

5. What are the possible answers on your tally chart? **yes, no, maybe**
6. Which answer was given the most? **yes**

Test Prep

7. Which set of tally marks correctly represents the number 8? **D**
   A 卌 II
   B IIII IIII
   C 卌 IIII
   D 卌 III
8. Suppose Leslie wanted to find out which sport is most popular at her school. Would it make sense for her to survey only the members of the football team? Why or why not? **Answers may vary.**

Use with text pages 356–358.

On Your Own

Use the tally chart for Problems 1–6.

1. What is the survey question?
What is your favorite summer activity?
2. Which answer was given most often? least often? most often: swimming; least often: going to camp
3. How many students answered the survey question?
41 students
4. How many students named the two most popular activities?
28 students
5. What is the order of activities from most to least popular?
See above.
6. **What's Wrong?** Dora says that more than half the class likes swimming or visiting grandparents best. Explain why that is not true. *See at right.*

5. swimming, bicycling, playing video games, visiting grandparents, going to camp

What Is Your Favorite Summer Activity?		
Activity	**Tally**	**Number**
Bicycling	卌 卌 ||	12
Going to camp	|||	3
Playing video games	卌 |	6
Swimming	卌 卌 卌 |	16
Visiting grandparents	||||	4

6. *Possible explanation:* There were 41 students surveyed. Twenty students like swimming or visiting grandparents. Twenty is less than half of 41.

Use the list at the right to make a tally chart. Then solve Problems 7–10.
See Additional Answers.

7. What are the possible answers on your tally chart?
always, sometimes, never
8. How many students never bring their lunch to school?
1 student
9. How many students sometimes bring their lunch to school?
5 students
10. How many students sometimes or always bring their lunch to school?
8 students

How Often Do You Bring Your Lunch to School?
Sandy always
Gina sometimes
Wilson never
Paco sometimes
Joy sometimes
Rosalie always
Bob sometimes
Joanna sometimes
Will always

Go On

❸ Practice

On Your Own

Select from **Exercises 1–21** as independent work.

- For **Exercise 6,** invite volunteers to explain their responses and how they arrived at the responses.
- For **Exercises 7–10,** elicit from students that the responses given in the list are raw, untallied data. Explain that they must first convert the data into a tally chart, which they will use to answer the questions.

Enrichment 14.1

Enrichment 14.1

Name ______________ Date ________

Favorite Music

Jan and Amber conducted a survey to find out about their classmates' favorite type of music. Jan recorded her data on a tally chart. Amber surveyed different students than Jan did, and she wrote her data as a list. Combine Jan's and Amber's data into one tally chart. Then answer the questions that follow.

Jan's Chart

What is your favorite type of music?		
Type of Music	**Tally**	**Total**
Country	卌 卌	10
Dance/Pop	卌 卌 ||	12
Rock	卌 ||||	9
Jazz/Classical	卌	5

Amber's List

Tyler - Dance
Pam - Country
Todd - Jazz
Ron - Dance
Zach - Rock
Kayla - Jazz
Joe - Dance
Pete - Dance
Cassie - Rock

1. What is the most popular type of music? What is the least popular?
Dance/pop; jazz/classical
2. How many more people like the most popular type of music than the least popular type of music?
7 people
3. This survey was taken among fourth grade classmates. Do you think that if Jan and Amber had surveyed a group of adults, a different type of music would have been most popular? Explain your reasoning.
Explanations will vary.

Use with text pages 356–358.

Problem Solving 14.1

Problem Solving 14.1

Name ______________ Date ________

Collect and Organize Data

Stephie conducted a survey to decide which color T-shirts she should sell at her store. She recorded her results in a tally chart.

Use the chart for Problems 1–3.

What is Your Favorite Color?		
Color	**Tally**	**Number**
Red	卌 卌 卌 |||	18
Yellow	卌 卌 ||	12
Blue	卌 卌 卌 卌 |	21
Green	卌 卌 卌 ||	17
Purple	卌 卌 ||	12

Show your work.

1. How many people did Stephie survey?
80 people
2. How many more people chose red than chose green?
1 more person
3. **Predict** Using the results of the survey, which color T-shirt is Stephie most likely to sell?
blue T-shirts
4. What survey question would you ask if you wanted to find out the average time fourth-graders spend doing homework? What might be your answer choices?
Questions and answer choices will vary.
5. **Write About It** Conduct your own survey and record your results in a tally chart. Then write a report about the data that you collected.
Answers may vary; check students' surveys and results.

Use with text pages 356–358.

- For **Exercise 13,** invite volunteers to give their report on the surveys they conducted.
- For **Exercises 14–18,** ask students to justify their true or false responses.

Talk About It • Write About It For **Exercises 20–21,** let students share and discuss their responses.

4 Assess & Close

Math Talk in Action

What is the purpose of a survey? (to gather information on a particular question)

What are the advantages of using tally marks as you collect data? (They are easy to use and count.)

In a tally chart, what two columns should show the same information? Explain. (The *Tally* and *Number* columns; one shows the votes as sets of marks, the other shows their total as a numeral.)

Why is it important to plan your questions in advance when you conduct a survey? (You need to limit the number of possible answer choices.)

Math Journal Prompt

Have students write two different questions they might want answered by conducting a survey. Have them write sets of likely responses for each question.

Lesson Quiz

Use the quiz on Lesson Transparency 14.1.

Test Prep & Spiral Review

Use Test Prep Transparency 14.1.

Conduct your own survey. Use the survey question "What do you like to eat?" or "What is your favorite summer activity?" Use the survey for Problems 11–13. ***Check students' work.***

11. How many students did you survey?
12. Compare your survey results to the survey results on pages 356 or 357. Are the results similar or different? Explain.

13. **Write About It** Write a report about the data you collected in your survey and present it to your class.

Use the tally chart for Problems 14–19. Write *true* or *false* for each statement.

What Items Do You Recycle?		
Answer	Tally	Number
Cans	𝍸 III	8
Cardboard	I	1
Glass	𝍸 I	6
Newspapers	𝍸 𝍸 II	12
Plastic	II	2

14. The greatest number of people in the survey recycle newspapers. **true**
15. More people recycle glass than cans. **false**
16. There were a total of 28 answers to the survey question. **false**
17. From least to greatest, the order of recycled items is cardboard, plastic, glass, cans, newspapers. **true**
18. More people recycle newspapers than plastic and cans combined. **true**
19. **Create and Solve** Use the tally chart to write a word problem. Then solve the problem. ***Check students' work.***

Talk About It • Write About It

You learned to conduct a survey and collect data.

20. Suppose a principal wants to know what color people prefer for the walls of a cafeteria. Does it make sense for the principal to survey only fourth-graders? Why or why not? ***Possible answer:*** **Probably not; teachers and students in other grades might have different opinions.**
21. Can a survey tell you anything about the opinions of people who did not take part in the survey? Explain your answer. ***Possible answers:*** **No; a survey is a collection of data only from people who take part in the survey. Yes; the people surveyed may represent others with the same opinion.**

358

Homework 14.1 Page 88

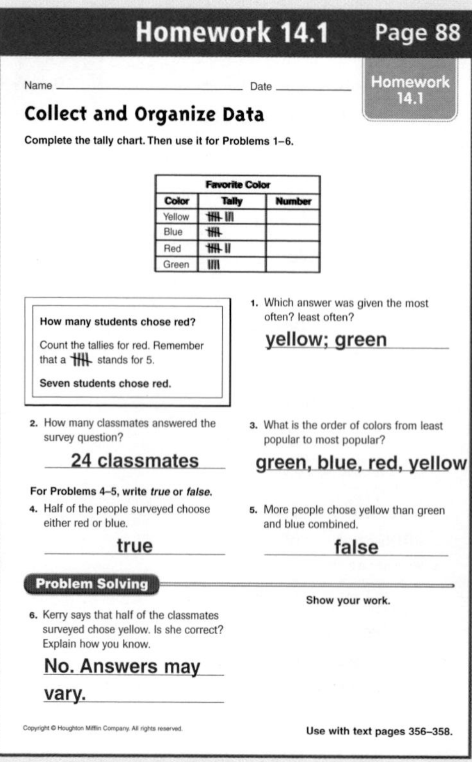

Name ______________ Date ________

Homework 14.1

Collect and Organize Data

Complete the tally chart. Then use it for Problems 1–6.

Favorite Color		
Color	Tally	Number
Yellow	𝍸 IIII	
Blue	𝍸	
Red	𝍸 II	
Green	IIII	

How many students chose red?

Count the tallies for red. Remember that a 𝍸 stands for 5.

Seven students chose red.

1. Which answer was given the most often? least often? **yellow; green**
2. How many classmates answered the survey question? **24 classmates**
3. What is the order of colors from least popular to most popular? **green, blue, red, yellow**

For Problems 4–5, write *true* or *false*.

4. Half of the people surveyed choose either red or blue. **true**
5. More people chose yellow than green and blue combined. **false**

Problem Solving

Show your work.

6. Kerry says that half of the classmates surveyed chose yellow. Is she correct? Explain how you know. **No. Answers may vary.**

Use with text pages 356–358.

Game

Igba-ita

In parts of Africa, people use small shells called cowries to play *Igba-ita*. You and a partner can play a similar game with pennies instead of cowries.

2 Players

What You'll Need
- 20 pennies for each player
- *Igba-Ita* Scoring sheets (Learning Tool 18)

How to Play

1. Look at the picture to see all the different ways four pennies tossed at the same time can land.
2. Make a scoring sheet. Write the numbers 0–4 in a column down the left side of your paper.
3. Take turns tossing four pennies. After each round, count the number of heads you and your partner tossed. The player with the greater number of heads tossed takes all eight pennies. Toss again if both players toss the same number of heads. Mark the scoring sheet with the number of heads each player tossed.
4. Keep playing until one player has all the pennies.

Game

Igba-Ita

Materials: 20 pennies, Learning Tool 18 or tally chart

Before students play, discuss all the possible ways that four indistinguishable pennies can land when tossed. (There are five ways: HHHH, HHHT, HHTT, HTTT, TTTT. This is if you exclude permutations. You may wish to tell students that for the purpose of this game, HHHT is the same as HHTH, HTHH, and THHH, and so on.) Guide them to match the possible outcome of a toss with its point value. You might want to play several demonstration rounds with the class to ensure that students grasp the rules of play and of keeping score.

Extending the Game Challenge students to create their own variation of Igba-Ita. For example, they might use a different number of coins, a different scoring system, or different rules of play. Invite students to demonstrate their new games. Two-color counters can also be used for this game in place of the pennies.

Lesson 14.2

Problem-Solving Strategy: Make a Table

Planning

Lesson Objective Organize data in a table to solve a problem.

Technology Resources

- *Ways to Success* CD-ROM 14.2
- Education Place: Extra Practice www.eduplace.com/map

Lesson 14.2 Transparency

Problem of the Day

Together, Herman's age and his sister's age equal 27. Herman's sister's age is twice Herman's age.
How old is Herman? How old is his sister? (9; 18)

Spiral Review

Find the next number in the pattern.

1. 5, 10, 15, 20, ___ (25)
2. 45, 46, 48, 51 ___ (55)
3. 86, 84, 80, 74, 66, ___ (56)

Lesson Quiz

Make a table to solve each problem.

1. Anna's puppy is on a special diet. It will eat 800 calories today, Monday. Each day after that it will eat 25 calories less than it ate the day before. On what day will the puppy eat 675 calories? (Saturday)

NCTM Standards

Problem Solving: Apply and adapt a variety of appropriate strategies to solve problems.

Getting Started

Building Math Vocabulary

Students should be familiar with the mathematical vocabulary in the lesson.

Making a Table

Whole Class	15 minutes
Objective	Make a table to find out information.
Materials	None
Visual, Auditory	

- Present this problem: Erin was 10 when her parents bought her a 1-year-old dog named Corky. They said that when Erin's age was twice Corky's age, she could get another dog. How old will Erin be when she is twice Corky's age? (18)
- **Let's make a table to find out.** Make a 2-column table. List Corky's age year by year in one column and Erin's age year by year in the other column. With students' help, fill in the ages.
- **Let's look at the table: What does it show us?** (Each year, Corky and Erin get 1 year older.) **How old will Erin be when Corky is 2?** (11) **When Corky is 3?** (12) Read down the table. **How old will Erin be when she is twice as old as Corky?** (18)
- Tell students that the lesson will present the strategy of making a table to solve a problem.

Corky's Age	Erin's Age
1	10
2	11
3	12
4	13
5	14
6	15
7	16
8	17
9	18

Differentiated Instruction

English Learners

Individuals	10 minutes
Objective	Practice making tables.
Materials	Student page 361

Auditory, Visual

Early Production

- Students may need help making a table to find the answers for the ***Guided Practice***.
- Ask questions to guide students in describing how to make the first table. Draw the table on the board.
- Let the students try making the table for the second problem independently.

Intermediate/Advanced

- English Learner Resource 14.2
- English Learner Handbook

Intervention

Small Groups	5 minutes
Objective	Read a table.
Materials	Movie timetable; 2-row table of ticket or food prices—for 1 item and for 2–6 of the same item

Visual, Auditory

- Hand out copies of the movie timetable to groups of students. Have them talk about whether that table does or does not show a pattern. (No; movies usually have different lengths; they start and end at different times.)
- Then hand out the table of prices that does have a pattern. Ask students to describe the pattern they see. (Students can see that if an item costs n dollars, then two cost $2n$ dollars, three cost $3n$ dollars, and so on.)

Other Resources

- *Ways to Success* CD-ROM 14.2

Daily News

Wahoo! Theater
Movies and Showtimes:
Super Action Team 11:35, 1:50, 4:35, 6:20
Flowers of Remembrance 11:55, 2:25, 4:55
Dragon Riders vs. Dracula 1:10, 4:10, 7:10
Flying Tigers 1:20, 4:25, 7:05, 10:20
Beyond Saturn's Moon 11:40, 2:20, 5:05

THIN CRUST PIZZA

	10" small	12" medium	14" large
Serves	1	1–2	3–4
Cheese	7.75	9.00	10.50
Special	10.75	12.75	15.00
Deluxe	12.75	15.25	18.00
Extra Toppings	1.00	1.25	1.50

Special Needs

Individuals	15 minutes
Objective	Make a table.
Materials	Nickels, dimes, quarters

Visual, Tactual

Provide students with several coins. Ask students to model ways to make $.30. Ask: **How many different ways are there?** Have students record their work in a 3-column table with headings *Quarter, Dime,* and *Nickel.* Ask students to describe any patterns they notice in their tables.

Science Connection

Materials: Science texts

- Have students work in pairs. Ask partners to work together to look through their science books to find five tables of information.
- Have pairs study each table to determine whether a pattern exists in the data shown.
- If students find a pattern in a table, ask them to write a brief description of what the data show and an explanation of the pattern they found.

Counting Practice

Problems 3–5 require students to skip count to fill a table. Before tackling these problems, suggest the students use a number line or hundreds table to help them count by twos, threes, fours, and sixes as needed.

1 Introduce

Ask students if they have seen information organized in a table before. Invite students to discuss the kinds of information they might see in a table. (Possible answers: products and their prices, survey results) Explain that in this lesson students will use tables to organize information from problems to help them solve the problems.

2 Teach

Make a Table

Guide students through the four steps of the problem-solving process.

Read the problem. What question does it ask? (How old will Jake and his dad be when Jake's dad is twice as old as he is?)

Read the ***Plan*** step aloud as students read along. **How can making a table help you to solve the problem about Jake and his dad?** (It can show how their ages compare year by year, and how old each will be when Jake's dad is twice as old as Jake.)

Work through the ***Solve*** step together. **What data appears in the first column of the table?** (Jake's age, year by year) **In the second column?** (Jake's dad's age) **How does the last column of the table use the data from the first two columns?** (It shows Jake's dad's age divided by Jake's age.)

Why does the table stop when Jake is 23 and his dad is 46? (Since 46 ÷ 23 = 2, Jake's dad will be twice as old as Jake will be at that time.)

Does the solution answer the question? (Yes, 46 ÷ 23 = 2; 46 is exactly twice 23.)

Common Error

- **Incorrectly setting up the table** Students may have difficulty right from the start when they try to set up their tables and insert data where it belongs.
- **Intervention** As a first step, guide students to look for ways to classify the data into categories. For Problem 5, for example, elicit from them that the categories are *books read* and *weeks*.

Lesson 2

Problem-Solving Strategy

Make a Table

Objective Organize data in a table to solve a problem.

Problem Jake is 18 years old. Jake's dad is 41 years old. How old will they both be when Jake's dad is twice as old as Jake?

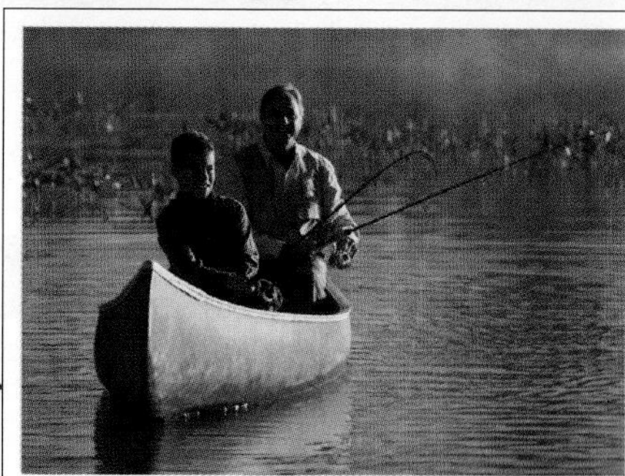

This is what you know.

- Jake is 18 years old now.
- Jake's dad is 41 years old now.

PLAN

You can make a table to help you solve the problem.

Divide Dad's age by Jake's age. When the quotient is 2, Dad's age will be twice Jake's age.

SOLVE

Make a table.

- Divide Dad's age by Jake's age. Write the quotient in the table.
- Keep adding one year to each person's age.
- Divide until you find an exact quotient of 2.

Think: $2 \times 23 = 46$

Solution: When Jake is 23, his dad will be 46.

Jake's Age	Dad's Age	Dad's Age ÷ Jake's Age
18	41	41 ÷ 18 → 2 R5
19	42	42 ÷ 19 → 2 R4
20	43	43 ÷ 20 → 2 R3
21	44	44 ÷ 21 → 2 R2
22	45	45 ÷ 22 → 2 R1
23	46	46 ÷ 23 = 2

LOOK BACK

Look back at the problem.

Does the solution answer the question?
Does the answer make sense?

360

Reteach 14.2

Name ______________ Date ________ Reteach 14.2

Problem-Solving Strategy: Make a Table

Read It Look for information.

Mike has 4 baseball cards. Each week he gets 2 more cards. Fredrico has 3 baseball cards and gets 1 more card each week. How many baseball cards will each have when they have a total of 19 baseball cards?

Picture It Here is a table of the information in the problem.

	Mike's Cards	Fredrico's Cards	Total Cards
Week 1	4	3	7
Week 2	6	4	10
Week 3	8	5	13
Week 4	10	6	16
Week 5	12	7	19

Solve It Use the table to solve the problem.

1. Complete the chart. Use it to find out how many cards each boy had when the total cards is 19.
So, Mike had 12 cards and Fredrico had 7 cards.

Try These! Make a table to solve each problem. **Show your work.**

2. Plant A is 9 inches tall, Plant B is 2 inches tall. If each plant grows 1 inch each week, how tall will each plant be when Plant A is twice as tall as Plant B?
Plant A-14 inches, Plant B-7 inches

3. Gina is 14 years old. Her uncle is 31 years old. How old will Gina and her uncle be when Gina's uncle is twice as old as she is?
17 years old, 34 years old

Use with text pages 360–362.

Practice 14.2 Page 89

Name ______________ Date ________ Practice 14.2

Problem-Solving Strategy: Make a Table

Make a table to solve each problem. **Show your work.**

1. Judy has made seven T-shirts. Each day she makes another four T-shirts. Harry has made eleven T-shirts and makes another three T-shirts every day. How many total T-shirts will Judy and Harry have made after six days?
60 T-shirts

2. Matt starts out with $640. If he were to cut this amount in half one time he would have $320. If he were to cut this amount in half two times he would have $160. How many times would he have to cut $640 in half before he reached $10?
6 times

3. A runner starts a race at the starting line. A second runner starts at 12 yards. If the first runner moves 5 yards each second and the second runner moves 3 yards each second, at what distance will the first runner catch the second runner?
30 yards

4. Martha's father puts some money (in dollars) aside for Martha every year on her birthday. The amount he puts aside is equal to three times how old she is. How much more money does he put aside when Martha is ten than when she was five?
$15

Use with text pages 360–362.

Guided Practice

Use the Ask Yourself questions to help you solve each problem.

1. Scott is 9 years old, and his sister is 2 years old. How old will each be when Scott is twice his sister's age?
Scott: 14 years old; sister: 7 years old

2. Ellen's aunt is 34 years old. Ellen is 15 years old. At what age will Ellen be exactly half her aunt's age? How old will Ellen's aunt be then?

(Hint) Ellen's aunt will be twice Ellen's age.

2. Ellen: 19 years old; aunt: 38 years old

Ask Yourself

UNDERSTAND **What do I know?**

PLAN **Can I make a table?**

SOLVE
- **Did I start with the correct numbers?**
- **Did I choose the correct operation?**

LOOK BACK **Does my solution answer the question?**

Check students' tables.

Independent Practice

Make a table to solve each problem.

3. Six people are in Steve's family. Each person is 8 inches taller than the next person. The tallest person is 70 inches tall. How tall is the shortest person?
30 inches tall
4. Steve has \$12. His sister Emily has \$7. Steve earns \$3 a week, and Emily earns \$2 a week doing chores. How much money will each have when Steve has exactly \$10 more than Emily?
Steve: \$27, Emily: \$17
5. Steve has read 5 books. Each week he reads 3 more books. Emily has read 6 books. Each week she reads 2 more. How many books will each have read when they have read a total of 41 books?
Steve, 23 books; Emily, 18 books
6. A fast-growing weed doubles its height every week. It is now 3 centimeters tall. How tall will it be at the end of 5 weeks?
96 centimeters

Look back at the table. What pattern do you notice in how the two ages compare, year by year? (With each succeeding year, Jake's dad's age gets closer and closer to exactly twice Jake's age.) **In future years, will the father be *more* or *less* than twice as old as the son?** (less than twice as old, according to the pattern the table shows)

Guided Practice

Have students complete **Problems 1–2** as you observe. Remind them to use the ***Ask Yourself*** questions for help.

3 Practice

Independent Practice

Select from **Problems 3–14** as independent work.

- For **Problems 3–6,** have students explain how they organized their tables of data to solve the problems.
- Students may need help setting up their tables for **Problem 6.** To help them, ask: **How tall will the weed be at the end of 1 week?** (6 cm) **At the end of 2 weeks?** (12 cm)

Enrichment 14.2

Name ______________ Date ________ Enrichment 14.2

Problem-Solving Strategy: Make a Table

Read each problem and make a table of the information. Use the table to answer each question. **Show your work.**

Problem Dan, Bruce, and Jim are brothers. Bruce is twice as old as Jim and Dan is 5 years younger than Jim. Jim is 9 years old.

1. How old is each brother now? **Dan is 4 years old. Jim is 9 years old. Bruce is 18 years old.**
2. How old will each brother be when Jim is twice as old as Dan? **Dan will be 5, Jim will be 10, and Bruce will be 19.**

Problem Both Sabrina and Rex are saving up to buy a new video game. Sabrina has \$15. Rex has \$9. Sabrina saves \$2 each week. Rex saves \$4 each week.

3. How many weeks will it be until Sabrina and Rex have the same amount of money saved? How much money will each person have then? **3 weeks; \$21 saved.**
4. The video game they want to buy costs \$35. How many weeks will it take each person to save enough money for the game? **It will take Rex 7 weeks to save \$35. It will take Sabrina 10 weeks to save \$35.**

 Use with text pages 360–362.

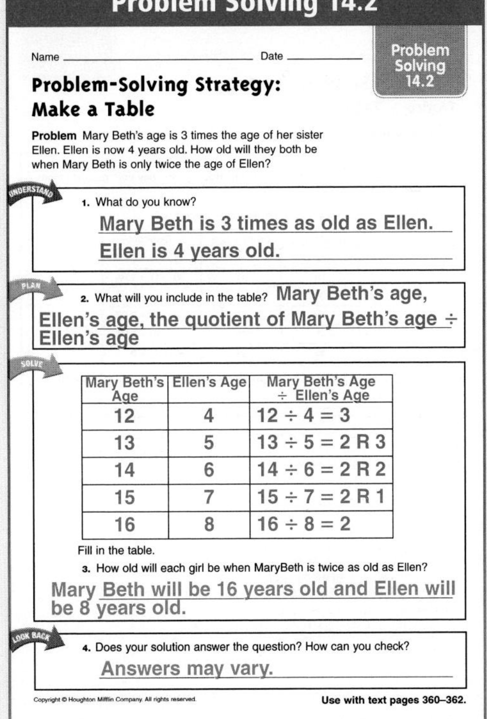

Problem Solving 14.2

Name ______________ Date ________ Problem Solving 14.2

Problem-Solving Strategy: Make a Table

Problem Mary Beth's age is 3 times the age of her sister Ellen. Ellen is now 4 years old. How old will they both be when Mary Beth is only twice the age of Ellen?

UNDERSTAND
1. What do you know? **Mary Beth is 3 times as old as Ellen. Ellen is 4 years old.**

PLAN
2. What will you include in the table? **Mary Beth's age, Ellen's age, the quotient of Mary Beth's age ÷ Ellen's age**

SOLVE

Mary Beth's Age	Ellen's Age	Mary Beth's Age ÷ Ellen's Age
12	4	12 ÷ 4 = 3
13	5	13 ÷ 5 = 2 R 3
14	6	14 ÷ 6 = 2 R 2
15	7	15 ÷ 7 = 2 R 1
16	8	16 ÷ 8 = 2

Fill in the table.

3. How old will each girl be when MaryBeth is twice as old as Ellen? **Mary Beth will be 16 years old and Ellen will be 8 years old.**

LOOK BACK
4. Does your solution answer the question? How can you check? **Answers may vary.**

 Use with text pages 360–362.

Mixed Problem Solving

- Remind students that for **Problems 7–10,** they can choose a strategy from the list at the right. Encourage students to discuss the strategies they use.
- ***Data*** Discuss how to read the value of bars that do not line up with the intervals on the graph.

Mixed Problem Solving

Solve. Show your work. Tell what strategy you used. ***Possible strategies given.***

You Choose

Strategy
- Find a Pattern
- Make a Table
- Use Logical Reasoning
- Work Backward
- Write an Equation

Computation Method
- Mental Math
- Estimation
- Paper and Pencil
- Calculator

7. Dalia, Jen, and Brad are wearing jackets that are either red, blue, or gray. Each is wearing a different color. Brad's jacket is not red. Jen's jacket is not red or blue. What color is each person's jacket? ***See below.***

8. Susan is 9 years old. Her uncle is 24 years old. At what age will Susan be half her uncle's age? How old will her uncle be then? ***See below.***

9. **Measurement** What is Martha's height in feet and inches if she is 10 inches less than five feet? **4 ft 2 in.; Write an Equation**

10. Copy the table below. Fill in the missing numbers so that the sum of the numbers in each row and column is equal. **Find a Pattern** ***See answers in table.***

6	13	3
12	8	2
4	1	17

7. Dalia: red; Jen: gray; Brad: blue; Use Logical Reasoning

8. Susan: 15 years old; uncle: 30 years old; Make a Table

Data **Use the graph about class birthdays for Problems 11–14.**

11. Which season has the greatest number of birthdays? **spring**

12. How many birthdays are in autumn and winter? **10 birthdays**

13. How many fewer birthdays are in summer than in the rest of the year? **17 fewer birthdays**

14. How many people were surveyed? **23 people**

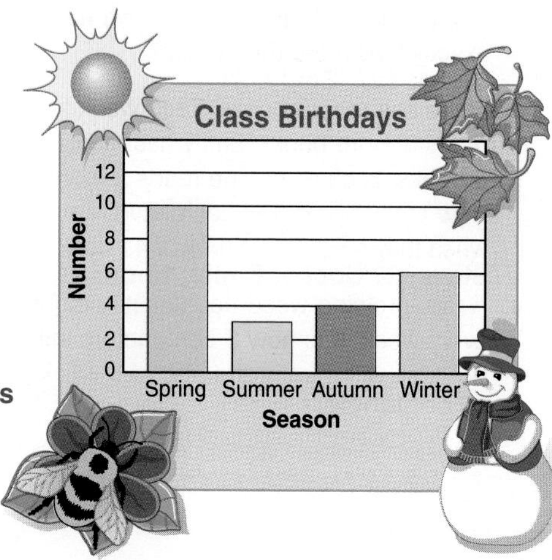

362

Homework 14.2 **Page 89**

Name ______________ Date ________

Homework 14.2

Problem-Solving Strategy: Make a Table

Make a table to solve each problem.

Daisy is 16 years old. Mom is 37 years old. How old will they both be when Mom is twice as old as Daisy?

Divide Mom's age by Daisy's age until you get a quotient of 2.

Mom's Age	Daisy's Age	Quotient
37	16	37 ÷ 16 = 2 R5
38	17	38 ÷ 17 = 2 R4
39	18	39 ÷ 18 = 2 R3
40	19	40 ÷ 19 = 2 R2
41	20	41 ÷ 20 = 2 R1
42	21	42 ÷ 21 = 2

Mom will be twice as old as Daisy when Mom is 42 years old and Daisy is 21 years old.

1. Kate is 15 years old, and her sister, Margaret, is 6 years old. How old will each be when Kate is twice her sister's age?

Show your work. **Check students' tables.**

Kate - 18; Margaret - 9

2. Sally's Aunt is 28 years old. Sally is 12 years old. How old will they both be when Sally's Aunt is twice as old as Sally?

Sally - 16; Sally's Aunt - 32

Use with text pages 360–362.

Problem Solving on Tests

Choose the letter of the correct answer.

Multiple Choice

1. The temperature at 3:00 P.M. was 2 degrees higher than the temperature at 2:00 P.M. If it was 6°C at 2:00 P.M., what was the temperature at 3:00 P.M.?

   A $^{-}2$°C **B** 2°C **C** 4°C **(D)** 8°C

   (Chapter 13, Lesson 4)

2. Marlena can pack 28 books into one box. How many boxes does she need in order to pack 224 books?

   F 7 **(G)** 8 **H** 78 **J** 196

   (Chapter 11, Lesson 4)

Open Response

Solve each problem.

3. Al uses 8 pins to hang 3 drawings.

   If Al hangs a total of 6 drawings the same way, how many pins will he use?
   14 pins (Chapter 10, Lesson 3)

4. Students estimated a doorway's height.

Name	Estimate
Andrew	2 yd
Sarah	75 in.
Christy	6 ft 1 in.
Mike	2 yd 1 ft

   The actual height is 6 ft 8 in. Whose estimate is closest to the actual height?
   See Additional Answers. (Chapter 12, Lesson 2)

Extended Response

5. Use the ad to solve the problems.

Georgia Peaches 3-pound bag $2.19
Delicious Apples 4-pound bag $1.48
Florida Oranges 5-pound bag $2.60
McIntosh Apples 5-pound bag $3.55
New York Pears 3-pound bag $1.95
Yellow Bananas 2 pounds $0.98

   a. Shoppers often estimate prices. Estimate the cost of 1 pound of each kind of fruit.

   b. Find the exact price of 1 pound of each fruit.

   c. Find the differences between your estimates and the actual prices. If your estimates were not close to the actual prices, check your division.

   See Additional Answers. (Chapters 8, 9)

Education Place

See **eduplace.com/map** for more Test-Taking Tips.

Problem Solving on Tests

Problem Solving on Tests provides an opportunity for students to apply previously learned skills in the types of problem contexts typically encountered in standardized tests.

Problem Solving on Tests includes practice in a variety of formats: multiple choice, extended response, and open response.

Students will gain experience in writing about mathematics and using various representations to solve problems. Discuss students' solutions. Have several students explain the thinking behind their work.

More test prep practice is available on Houghton Mifflin's Web site, **Education Place**. Go to **www.eduplace.com/map**.

4 Assess & Close

Math Talk in Action

To summarize the problem-solving strategy of organizing data into tables, ask these questions:

Why is it helpful to make a table in order to solve a problem? (Possible answer: because sometimes it is hard to determine number relationships from the information presented)

How can you use a table to help you spot a pattern? (Possible answer: list the numbers in one column or row and then use an operation or set of operations to find the corresponding numbers for the other column or row. Look for a pattern in the second column or row.)

Math Journal Prompt

Have students write about the value of making and using tables in problem solving. Encourage students to include an example from the lesson to support their conclusions.

Lesson Quiz

Use the quiz on Lesson Transparency 14.2.

Test Prep & Spiral Review

Use Test Prep Transparency 14.2.

Hands On Lesson 14.3

Mean, Median, Mode, and Range

Planning

Lesson Objective Find the mean, median, mode, and range of a set of data.

Math Background

- Students will apply previously learned operation skills to data to find the mean (average), median (middle number) and mode (most frequent number) of a set of numbers. These findings will help students to organize data into meaningful findings.

Technology Resources

- *Ways to Success* CD-ROM 14.3
- Education Place: Extra Practice, eGlossary, eGames www.eduplace.com/map

Lesson 14.3 Transparency

Problem of the Day

Turkey dogs come in packages of 8. Buns come in packages of 12. What is the fewest number of packages of each you could buy to have the same number of turkey dogs as buns? (3 packages of turkey dogs, 2 of buns)

Spiral Review

1. 35 − 19 = (16)
2. 134 + 128 + 156 + 130 = (548)
3. 548 ÷ 4 = (137)

Lesson Quiz

Use the data to answer the questions.

1. What is the range of ages in the Lattif family? (39 − 5 = 34)
2. What is the family's mean age? (21)

The Lattif Family

Name	Age
Mom	38
Dad	39
Jessie	14
Linda	9
Jon	5

NCTM Standards

Data Analysis and Probability: Select and use appropriate statistical methods to analyze data.

Getting Started

Building Math Vocabulary

You may wish to review these terms with students.

mean the number found by dividing a sum of a group of numbers by the number of addends; also called the *average*

median the middle number when a set of numbers is arranged from least to greatest

mode the number or numbers that occur most often in a set of data

range the difference between the least and greatest in a set of data

Help students make connections between the conventional meanings words have and the meanings they have in mathematics. Ask questions such as:

- Where is the **median** of a highway located? (in the middle of the highway)
- What does the **range** in temperature mean? (difference between high and low temperatures)

Then review the mathematical meaning of these four terms: ***mean***, ***median***, ***mode***, and ***range*** in relation to a set of data.

Finding the Mean (Average)

Whole Class	10–15 minutes
Objective	Find the mean, or average, of a set of numbers.
Materials	None
Visual, Auditory	

- Display the following test scores: 94, 86, 80, 92, 88, 80, 89
- Ask: **How can we find the mean of these test scores?** (Find the sum and divide that by the number of addends.)
- Work through the problem with students. (94 + 86 + 80 + 92 + 88 + 80 + 89 = 609 ÷ 7 = 87) Remind students that *mean* is another word for *average*.
- Tell students that the mean is one way to describe the data. Ask: **What other ways can we describe the data?** (Find the median (88), the mode (80), and the range (14)).
- Explain that the lesson will describe these different ways of analyzing sets of data.

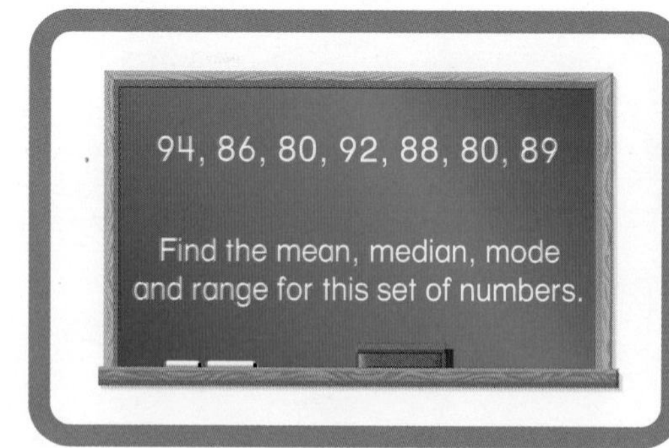
94, 86, 80, 92, 88, 80, 89
Find the mean, median, mode and range for this set of numbers.

Differentiated Instruction

English Learners

Individuals	10 minutes
Objective	Review math terms.
Materials	Student page 365, index cards
Visual	

Early Production

- Have students make flash cards for the math vocabulary in this lesson. They write the word on the front and the definition and example on the back.
- For ***On Your Own***, encourage students to decide what term to use, read the definition on the card, and then solve.

Intermediate/Advanced

- English Learner Resource 14.3
- English Learner Handbook

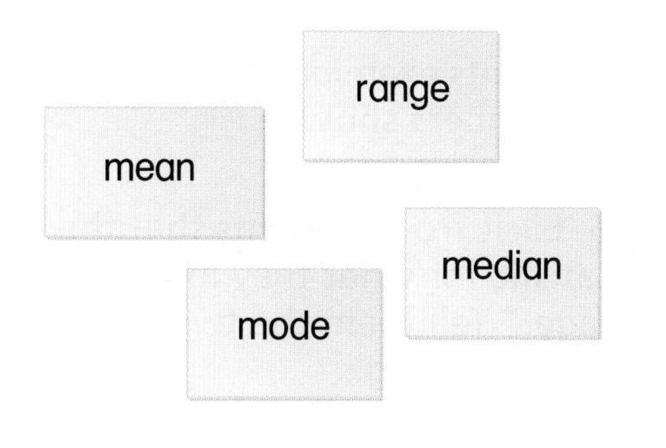

Intervention

Small Groups	15 minutes
Objective	Organize data.
Materials	None
Visual, Auditory	

- Tell students that these are math test scores for one fifth-grader: 89, 78, 85, 88, 92, 83, and 78.
- Ask: **How might we organize these scores?** (one way: from least to greatest)
- **If we put the scores in order from least to greatest, how could we find the difference between the lowest and highest score?** (subtract; 92 – 78 = 14) **What is the middle score?** (85) **Can you think of another way to describe these test scores? Explain.** (Students might suggest finding the "average" score; others may suggest indicating that one score occurred twice.)

Other Resources

- *Ways to Success* CD-ROM 14.3

Inclusion

Individuals	15 minutes
Objective	Find the mode, mean, and range of a set of numbers.
Materials	Connecting cubes
Visual, Tactual	

- Have students use connecting cubes to make five "trains" of the following lengths: 7, 14, 10, 5, and 14.
- Find the mode by identifying the two trains that are the same length. (14)
- Place the trains in size order to find the train with the median length. (10)
- Find the mean by forming five trains of equal length. (10)
- Find the range by aligning the longest and shortest trains, then finding the difference. (9)

Social Studies Connection

Materials: Almanac or other source

- Have pairs of students use an almanac to find the ages at inauguration (first term) of (the last) ten American Presidents.
- Then have students find the mean, median, mode, and range for the last ten Presidents' ages at inauguration.

❶ Introduce

Ask students to think about the math grade they received on their last report card. Tell them the report card grade was a result of the mean grade of their test scores.

❷ Teach

Work Together

- Have students examine the table. Ask: **What do the numbers show?** (heights in cm of a set of students)
- **Step 1** Elicit from students that the *mean* is the statistic for what they may think of as "average." Tell them the two words have the same meaning.
- **Step 2** Ask: **Why do we list the heights in size order to find the median? Why didn't we have to do so to find the mean?** (To find the middle one; to find the mean, add the numbers, in any order, and then divide by the number of addends.)
- **Steps 3 and 4** Ask: **Can the median and the mode be the same number? Give an example.** (Yes; Example should show middle numbers that are also the numbers that occur most often.) **What operation do we use to find the range?** (subtraction)

❸ Practice

On Your Own

Select from **Exercises 1–7** for independent work.

- For **Exercise 2,** ask students to give a strategy they can use to check Sandra's answer. (One way: arrange heights from least to greatest; see where hers fits.)

Common Error

- **Confusing the mode and median**
- **Intervention** Some students may find it helpful to think of "most often" for mode. They can think of a highway median to remind them that as it is in the middle of a road, the median of a set of numbers is the number in the middle.

Mean, Median, Mode, and Range

Objective Find the mean, median, mode, and range of a set of data.

Vocabulary
mean
median
mode
range

Work Together

Look at the data in the list. Then work with a partner to describe the data in different ways.

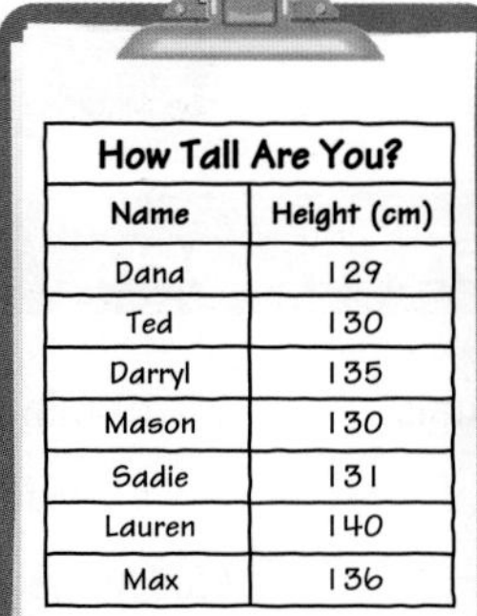

How Tall Are You?	
Name	Height (cm)
Dana	129
Ted	130
Darryl	135
Mason	130
Sadie	131
Lauren	140
Max	136

STEP 1 Find the **mean** of the data.
First, find the sum of the numbers: 931.
Divide the sum by the number of addends: 931 ÷ 7.

- What is the mean height of the students? **133 cm**

STEP 2 Find the **median** of the data.
When a set of numbers is ordered from least to greatest, the middle number is called the median.

- What is the median height of the students? **131 cm**

When there are two middle numbers in a data set, the median is the mean of those two numbers. Look at the data.
12, 12, 13, 15, 15, 15
13 + 15 = 28
28 ÷ 2 = 14
The median is 14.

STEP 3 Find the **mode** of the data.
The number that occurs most often in a data set is called the mode.

- What is the height that occurs most often? **130 cm**

STEP 4 Find the **range** of the data.
The difference between the greatest number and the least number is the range.

- What is the range of the students' heights? **11 cm**

364

Reteach 14.3

Name ______________ Date ________ Reteach 14.3

Mean, Median, Mode, and Range

Sue rode her bike each afternoon after school. One week she recorded the number of miles she rode her bike each day. The number of miles were 7, 4, 6, 5, 7, 5, and 8.
Find the mean, median, mode, and range.

Write the numbers in order from least to greatest:
4, 5, 5, 6, 7, 7, 8

What do you need to find?	How can you find it?	What do you do?
Range is the difference between the greatest and least number.	Subtract the least number from the greatest number.	8 − 4 = 4 The range is 4.
Mode is the number that occurs most often.	Find the number or numbers with the greatest frequency.	5 and 7 occur two times. The modes are 5 miles and 7 miles.
Median is the middle number.	Order the numbers from least to greatest. Then find the number in the center of the list.	4, 5, 5, **6**, 7, 7, 8 6 is in the middle. The median is 6 miles.
Mean is the sum of the numbers divided by the number of addends.	Add the numbers in the list. Then divide by the number of items in the set.	4+5+5+6+7+7+8=42 42 ÷ 7 = 6 The mean is 6 miles.

Use the data table to answer Problems 1–4.

Shots on Goal							
Name	Mark	Dylan	Hannah	Gina	Hank	Kendra	Simon
Number of Shots	6	3	9	2	2	5	8

1. What is the range of the data? 7
2. What is the median of the data? 5
3. What is the mode of the data? 2
4. What is the mean of the data? 5

Use with text pages 364–365.

Practice 14.3 Page 90

Name ______________ Date ________ Practice 14.3

Mean, Median, Mode, and Range

Mrs. Iko asked for 7 volunteers to help teach mean, median, mode, and range. The volunteers measured their heights in centimeters. The table at the right shows the results.

Mrs. Iko's Class	
Name	Height (cm)
Bell	116
Dale	124
Lucy	121
Mike	128
Gina	124
Georgia	119
Jay	122

Use the data in the table to answer problems 1–4.

1. Use a calculator to find the mean height of Mrs. Iko's students. 122 cm
2. What is the range of the data? 12 cm
3. Mrs. Iko added her own height to the table. She is 170 centimeters tall. How will this information change the mean, median, mode, and range? mean is 128 cm, median is 123 cm, mode is 124 cm, range is 54 cm
4. Mrs. Iko removed her height and Bell's height from the table. How did this change the mean, median, mode, and range? mean is 123, median is 123 cm, mode is 124 cm, range is 9 cm

Test Prep

5. Which number shows the mode of the data below?
   13, 14, 9, 17, 14, 8, 18, 10, 6
   A 14 B 11 C 12 D 13 — A
6. Jessica collected 87 glass bottles on Monday, 58 on Tuesday, 92 on Wednesday, 72 on Thursday, and 61 on Friday. What is the mean number of bottles she collected in a day? 74 bottles

Use with text pages 364–365.

Use the results of your work to describe the heights of the fourth-graders surveyed.

- Do you think your description would also describe your class? Explain. *Check students' answers.*

2. No; the median is 137 cm, Sandra's height, so an equal number of teammates are taller and shorter than she is.

On Your Own

Use the data in the table to answer Problems 1–5.

Sandra and her friends play basketball for the Star Hoopsters. Every year, their coach records the heights of the players. The table shows the data for this year.

Star Hoopsters

Name	Height (cm)
Lee	133
Elise	128
Maya	141
Sandra	137
Vince	141

1. Use a calculator to find the mean height of the players. **136 cm**
2. Sandra says that most of her teammates are taller than she is. Is she correct? Explain how you know. *See above.*
3. What is the mode of the data? **141 cm**
4. You do not have to be tall to play for the Star Hoopsters. Use the range to tell why that statement is true. *See below.*

5. **Analyze** Mr. Jordan, the basketball coach, played with the team on Tuesday. Suppose his height was added to the table. He is 184 cm tall. How will this information change the mean, median, mode, and range? **Mean is 144 cm; median is 139 cm; mode stays the same; range is 56 cm.**

Talk About It • Write About It

You learned to find the mean, median, mode, and range of a set of data.

6. Explain why it is helpful to put the data in order from least to greatest before you find the median, mode, and range. *See Additional Answers.*
7. Does the mode or the median give a better description of the Star Hoopsters? Explain your thinking. **The median; it tells the middle height of the team.**

4. The range is 13 cm. If everyone was tall and about the same height, the range would be less.

- For **Exercise 5,** point out that sometimes a set of numbers includes numbers that are distant from most of the others. **Which measures would be most affected if you include a much greater or much lesser number in the set?** (range and mean) Have students justify their answers.

4 Assess & Close

Math Talk in Action

Tell students that the following data shows how many students in six schools entered a contest: 14, 37, 50, 23, 37, 19. **What is the median number of students entered from these schools? How did you find it?** (30; order numbers; identify the two middle numbers and their mean: (23 + 37) ÷ 2.)

Math Journal Prompt

Have students come up with a set of numbers about something of interest to them, such as number of wins of various sports teams. Have them list their data and then find the mean, median, mode, and range for it.

Lesson Quiz

Use the quiz on Lesson Transparency 14.3.

Lesson 14.3 Transparency

Test Prep & Spiral Review

Use Test Prep Transparency 14.3.

Test Prep 14.3 Transparency

Enrichment 14.3

Name ______ Date ______ Enrichment 14.3

Data Descriptions

Each set of data in the left-hand column is described by one of the statements in the right hand column. In the space provided, write the letter of the statement next to the data set it describes.

1. 2 5 7 3 2 6 __c__ a. mean = 6
2. 4 4 3 6 8 9 __a__ b. range = 7
3. 5 3 6 10 16 __h__ c. mode = 2
4. 2 8 9 7 10 __d__ d. median = 8
5. 12 13 9 19 15 __f__ e. median = 12
6. 10 5 10 3 8 10 __b__ f. range = 10
7. 17 8 9 15 12 __e__ g. mode = 3
8. 3 9 6 5 3 __g__ h. mean = 8

Use with text pages 364–365.

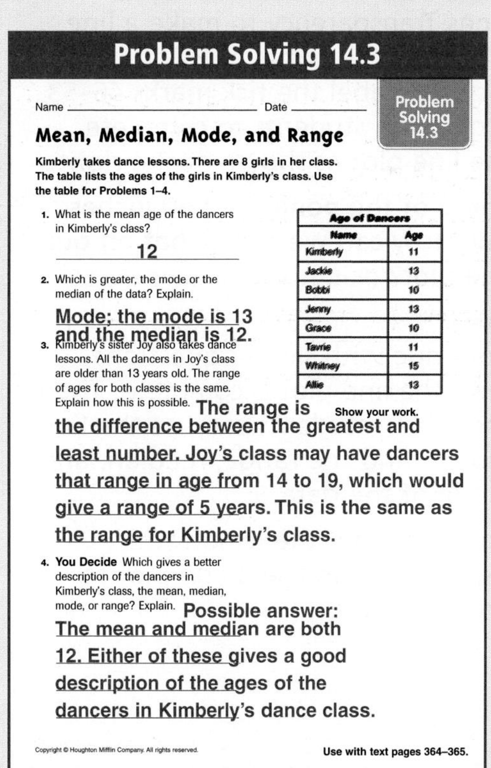

Problem Solving 14.3

Name ______ Date ______ Problem Solving 14.3

Mean, Median, Mode, and Range

Kimberly takes dance lessons. There are 8 girls in her class. The table lists the ages of the girls in Kimberly's class. Use the table for Problems 1–4.

Age of Dancers

Name	Age
Kimberly	11
Jackie	13
Bobbi	10
Jenny	13
Grace	10
Tavrie	11
Whitney	15
Allie	13

1. What is the mean age of the dancers in Kimberly's class? **12**
2. Which is greater, the mode or the median of the data? Explain. **Mode; the mode is 13 and the median is 12.**
3. Kimberly's sister Joy also takes dance lessons. All the dancers in Joy's class are older than 13 years old. The range of ages for both classes is the same. Explain how this is possible. **The range is the difference between the greatest and least number. Joy's class may have dancers that range in age from 14 to 19, which would give a range of 5 years. This is the same as the range for Kimberly's class.**

Show your work.

4. **You Decide** Which gives a better description of the dancers in Kimberly's class, the mean, median, mode, or range? Explain. **Possible answer: The mean and median are both 12. Either of these gives a good description of the ages of the dancers in Kimberly's dance class.**

Use with text pages 364–365.

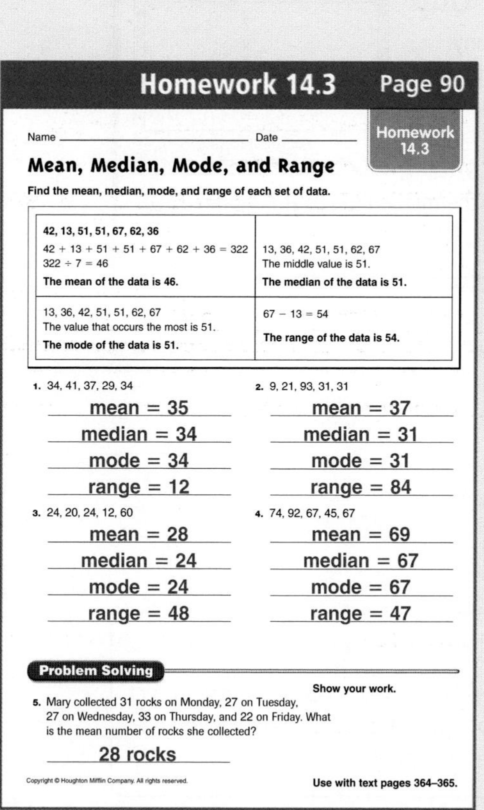

Homework 14.3 Page 90

Name ______ Date ______ Homework 14.3

Mean, Median, Mode, and Range

Find the mean, median, mode, and range of each set of data.

42, 13, 51, 51, 67, 62, 36 42 + 13 + 51 + 51 + 67 + 62 + 36 = 322 322 ÷ 7 = 46 **The mean of the data is 46.**	13, 36, 42, 51, 51, 62, 67 The middle value is 51. **The median of the data is 51.**
13, 36, 42, 51, 51, 62, 67 The value that occurs the most is 51. **The mode of the data is 51.**	67 − 13 = 54 **The range of the data is 54.**

1. 34, 41, 37, 29, 34 — **mean = 35; median = 34; mode = 34; range = 12**
2. 9, 21, 93, 31, 31 — **mean = 37; median = 31; mode = 31; range = 84**
3. 24, 20, 24, 12, 60 — **mean = 28; median = 24; mode = 24; range = 48**
4. 74, 92, 67, 45, 67 — **mean = 69; median = 67; mode = 67; range = 47**

Problem Solving

Show your work.

5. Mary collected 31 rocks on Monday, 27 on Tuesday, 27 on Wednesday, 33 on Thursday, and 22 on Friday. What is the mean number of rocks she collected? **28 rocks**

Use with text pages 364–365.

Lesson 14.4

Line Plots

Planning

Lesson Objective Make a line plot to represent data.

Technology Resources

- Audio Tutor **2**/6 Listen and Understand
- *Ways to Success* CD-ROM 14.4
- *Ways to Assess* CD-ROM
- Education Place: Extra Practice, eGlossary, eGames www.eduplace.com/map

Lesson 14.4 Transparency

Problem of the Day

On five tests, Maya got the following scores: 74, 84, 80, 84, and 68. Which measure is greater—her mean score or her median score? Explain. (median; 80 > 78)

Spiral Review

1. What is the range of the set of numbers? {14, 62, 38, 40} (48)
2. What is the median of the set of numbers? {40, 38, 54, 59} (47)
3. What is the mode of the set of numbers? {83, 107, 83, 59, 59, 83, 87} (83)

Lesson Quiz

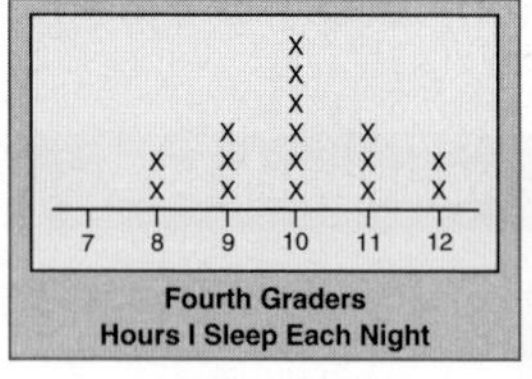

1. How many fourth-graders sleep for 10 hours each night? (6)
2. What is the median? (10) The mode? (10)

NCTM Standards

Data Analysis and Probability: Select and use appropriate statistical methods to analyze data.

Getting Started

Building Math Vocabulary

line plot	a diagram that organizes data using a number line
range	the difference between the least and greatest in a set of data
median	the middle number when a set of numbers is arranged from least to greatest
mode	the number or numbers that occur most often in a set of data

- Hold up the vocabulary card for ***line plot***. Give the definition and show the picture. Ask students to explain how a line plot is like a bar graph and how it is different from a bar graph.
- Guide students to see that in a line plot, data is organized along a number line.

Making a Line Plot

Whole Class	15 minutes
Objective	Practice representing data on a line plot.
Materials	Number Lines Transparency, blank transparency, erasable marker
Visual, Auditory	

- Use Number Line 2 on the Number Lines Transparency to make a line plot titled "Heights of 9 Ponies in Inches." Label the tick marks 46–53. Work with students to complete the line plot as shown at the right.
- **Three of the ponies are 50 inches tall. How can we show that on our line plot?** (Put three X's above the 50 tick mark.)
- Continue with similar questions until the line plot is complete. Then show how students can use the line plot to find the range, median, and mode of the data.
- Point out that the lesson will explain how to use a line plot to organize data.

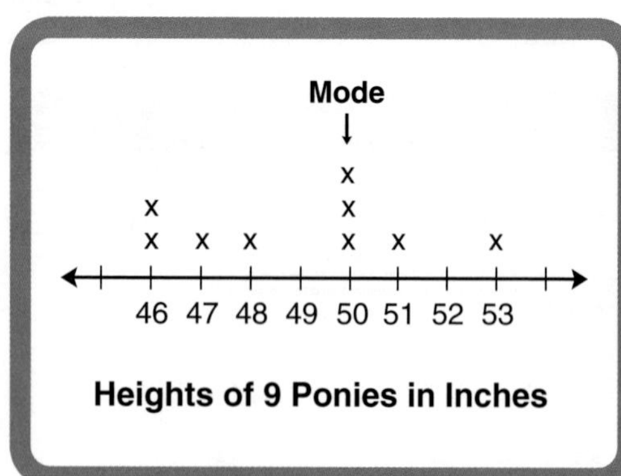

Differentiated Instruction

English Learners

Individuals	20 minutes
Objective	Practice math vocabulary.
Materials	Student page 367
Auditory, Visual	

Early Production

- Give students additional practice using and understanding new vocabulary words.
- After completing ***Guided Practice***, have students copy the line plot on a piece of paper. Ask them to label the parts of the diagram: line plot, range, median, and mode, and then use the labels to explain the line plot to a partner.

Intermediate/Advanced

- English Learner Resource 14.4
- English Learner Handbook

Intervention

Small Groups	20 minutes
Objective	Make a line plot.
Materials	Number Line Transparency
Auditory	

- Have each student tell in their own words the meanings of mode, median, and range.
- Have the group decide on a topic question for which they can make a line plot of the results, such as the number of students who saw a certain movie or read a certain book.
- Have them find the mode, median, and range of the data.

Other Resources

- *Ways to Success* CD-ROM 14.4

Gifted & Talented

Individuals	20 minutes
Objective	Make a line plot.
Materials	Blank transparency
Visual, Tactual	

- Have pairs of students survey classmates to find out how many hours of television they watch on a typical Tuesday night.
- Next, have students make a line plot to show the data. Ask them to find the mean, median, mode, and range of their data.
- Then have students write a summary of their findings.

TV Watching on Tuesday Night

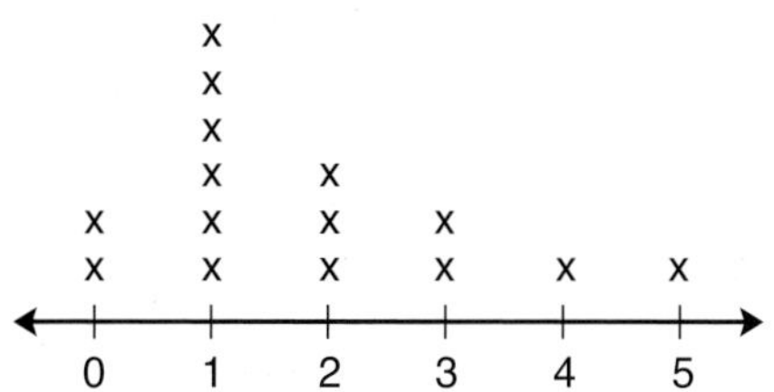

Literature Connection

- Brainstorm a list of authors whose books students have read. List the authors on the board.
- Survey students to find out which of these authors is their favorite. Have a student tally the responses on the board.
- Next, have students make a line plot to display the results of the tally.
- Have students find the mean, median, mode, and range of their data.

❶ Introduce

Tell students that line plots are another way to record and represent data.

❷ Teach

Learn About It

Talk about how the line plot shows the same information that is in the tally chart. Ask:

What do the numbers along the number line of the line plot show? (number of pets a student might have)

What does each X in the line plot show? (a student who has the number of pets listed directly below it) **How many students said that they have 2 pets?** (2) **3 pets?** (2)

How are X's related to tally marks? (Each X = one tally mark.)

Common Error

- **Placing X's in the wrong column** Students may not correctly align the X's in columns when they record data on the line plot, thereby misrepresenting the data.
- **Intervention** Suggest that they use graph paper or lined paper turned 90° to have one fixed column per number on the number line.

Lesson 4

Audio Tutor 2/6 Listen and Understand

Line Plots

Objective Make a line plot to represent data.

Vocabulary
line plot
range
median
mode

Learn About It

Cindy and Pete surveyed their classmates about family pets and made a tally chart. Then they made a line plot like the one below to show the data they collected.

How many pets do you have?

Number	Tally
0	||||
1	𝍸 |
2	||
3	||
4	
5	|

A **line plot** is a way to represent data using X's. You can use a line plot to find the median, mode, and range of a data set.

▶ To find the **range**, look at the number line on the line plot. Subtract the least value from the greatest value.

5 − 0 = 5 The range is 5.

▶ When a set of numbers is ordered from least to greatest, the middle number is called the **median**.

0 0 0 0 1 1 1 1 1 1 2 2 3 3 5

The median, or middle, of the data set is 1.

0	1	2	3	4	5
X X X X	X X X X X X	X X	X X		X

Number of Pets

▶ To find the **mode**, look for the number that has the most X's. Some data sets do not have a mode. Others have one or more modes.

The mode is 1.

366

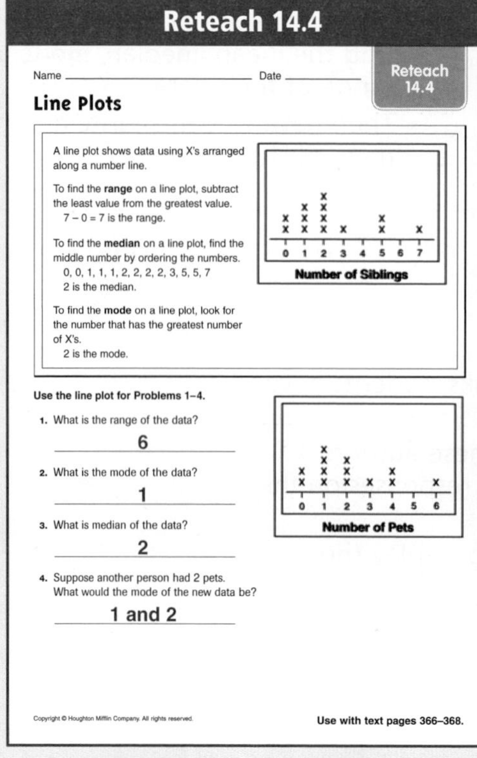

Reteach 14.4

Name ______ Date ______

Reteach 14.4

Line Plots

A line plot shows data using X's arranged along a number line.

To find the **range** on a line plot, subtract the least value from the greatest value.
7 − 0 = 7 is the range.

To find the **median** on a line plot, find the middle number by ordering the numbers.
0, 0, 1, 1, 1, 2, 2, 2, 2, 3, 5, 5, 7
2 is the median.

To find the **mode** on a line plot, look for the number that has the greatest number of X's.
2 is the mode.

0	1	2	3	4	5	6	7
X X	X X X	X X X X	X		X X		X

Number of Siblings

Use the line plot for Problems 1–4.

0	1	2	3	4	5	6
X X	X X X X	X X X	X	X X		X

Number of Pets

1. What is the range of the data? 6
2. What is the mode of the data? 1
3. What is median of the data? 2
4. Suppose another person had 2 pets. What would the mode of the new data be? 1 and 2

Use with text pages 366–368.

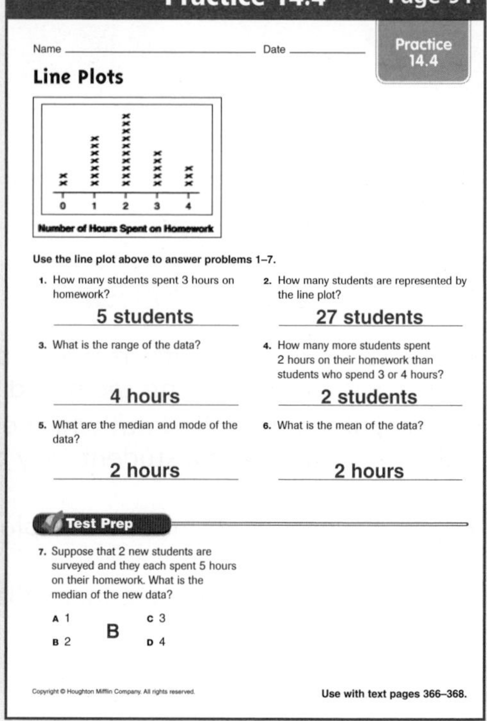

Practice 14.4 Page 91

Name ______ Date ______

Practice 14.4

Line Plots

0	1	2	3	4
X X	X X X X X X X	X X X X X X X X X X	X X X X X	X X X

Number of Hours Spent on Homework

Use the line plot above to answer problems 1–7.

1. How many students spent 3 hours on homework? 5 students
2. How many students are represented by the line plot? 27 students
3. What is the range of the data? 4 hours
4. How many more students spent 2 hours on their homework than students who spend 3 or 4 hours? 2 students
5. What are the median and mode of the data? 2 hours
6. What is the mean of the data? 2 hours

Test Prep

7. Suppose that 2 new students are surveyed and they each spent 5 hours on their homework. What is the median of the new data?

A 1 B 2 C 3 D 4

B

Use with text pages 366–368.

Guided Practice

Seven students weighed their dogs. The line plot shows the data. Use it for Problems 1–3.

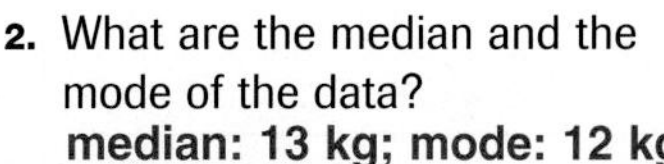

1. What is the range of the data? **7 kg**
2. What are the median and the mode of the data? **median: 13 kg; mode: 12 kg**
3. Suppose there was another dog weighing 15 kg. What would the median and mode be then? **median: 14 kg; modes: 12 and 15**

Line plot: 12 – XXX; 13 – X; 14 – none; 15 – XX; 16 – none; 17 – none; 18 – none; 19 – X

Weights of Dogs (kg)

Ask Yourself

- What do the X's represent?
- What does the number line represent?

Explain Your Thinking ▶ What is the mean of the data in the line plot above? How did you find it? **14 kg; Add the numbers to find the sum (98). Divide 98 by the number of addends: 98 ÷ 7 = 14.**

Practice and Problem Solving

Use the line plot at the right for Problems 4–6.

4. How many hours of TV did most fourth-graders watch on Tuesday? **2 hours**
5. What is the range of the data? **4 hours**
6. What are the mean, median, and mode of the data? **median: 2 hours; mean: 2 hours; mode: 2 hours**

Line plot: 0 – X; 1 – XX; 2 – XXXX; 3 – XX; 4 – X

Hours of TV Watched by Fourth-Graders on Tuesday

This line plot shows the hours students spent reading each week. Use the line plot to answer Problems 7–10.

7. How many students read for 2 hours each week? **1 student**
8. How many students answered the survey? Explain your answer. **17; There are 17 X's on the line plot.**
9. Did more students read for 3 hours or for 5 hours? **5 hours**

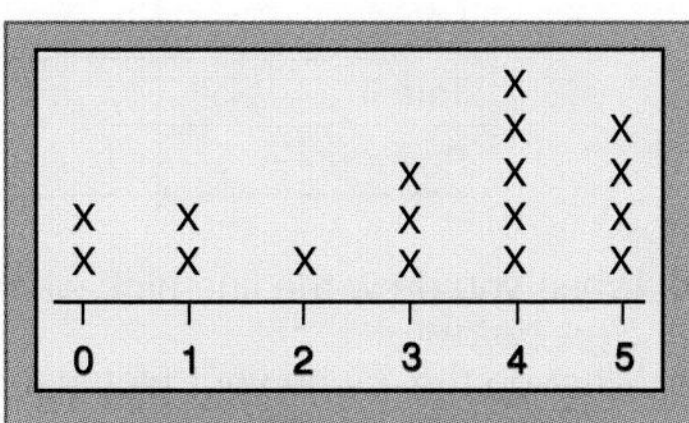

Hours Spent Reading

10. Describe how to find the median number of hours spent reading for the data in this plot. **List the numbers in order: 0, 0, 1, 1, 2, 3, 3, 3, 4, 4, 4, 4, 4, 5, 5, 5, 5 The middle number is the median, so 4 is the median.**

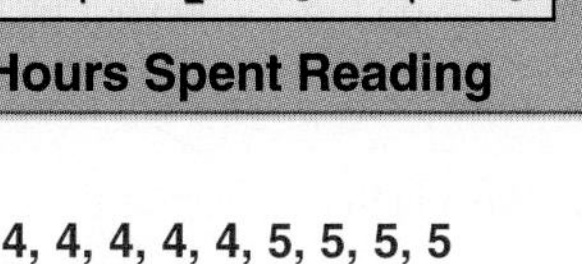

Go On

Guided Practice

Have students complete **Exercises 1–3** as you observe. Remind them to use the ***Ask Yourself*** questions for help. Give students the opportunity to talk about the questions in ***Explain Your Thinking***.

❸ Practice

Practice and Problem Solving

Select from **Exercises 4–21** for independent work.

- For **Exercise 4,** ask: **How many fourth-graders were surveyed? How do you know?** (10; count the X's.)
- For **Exercise 6,** ask: **Which of the statistics is easiest to spot? Why?** (Mode; simply look for the column with the most X's.)

Enrichment 14.4

Name ________ Date ________ Enrichment 14.4

Line Up!

Dimitri recorded the ages of the players on his baseball team. He recorded the ages in a table.

1. Use Dimitri's table to make a line plot of the players' ages.

Name	Age (Years)
Joseph	12
Theo	11
Nick	13
Fred	14
Missy	11
Cleo	14
Harvey	11

Name	Age (Years)
Tia	11
Peter	13
Lynn	13
Jerome	10
Billy	9
Martina	14
Tracy	12

Line plot: 9 – X; 10 – X; 11 – XXXX; 12 – XX; 13 – XXX; 14 – XXX

Ages of Players

Use your line plot to answer each question.

2. How many players are at least 12 years old? **8 players**
3. What are the mean and median of the data? **Mean: 12; median: 12**
4. What are the mode and range of the data? **Mode: 11; range: 5**

Use with text pages 366–368.

Problem Solving 14.4

Name ________ Date ________ Problem Solving 14.4

Line Plots

At the veterinarian's office, each animal is weighed before it visits the doctor. The line plot shows the weights of the cats that visited the veterinarian yesterday. Use the line plot for Problems 1–4.

1. How many cats visited the veterinarian yesterday? **15 cats**
2. Find the median, mode, and range of the data. **median: 8 lb mode: 8 lb range: 7**
3. What is the mean of the data in the line plot? Explain how you found the mean. **Mean = 8 lb; I listed the values that each *x* represents. I then added the values and divided by the number of *x*'s. 120 ÷ 15 = 8**
4. Jamie took his two cats to the vet. Mystic weighed 14 lbs and Timber weighed 12 lbs. Explain how these values would be shown on the line plot? **Possible answer: The line plot would have to be extended to include 13 and 14 lbs. One *x* would be placed above 14 to show Mystic's weight and another *x* would be placed above 12 to show Timber's weight.**

Line plot: 5 – XXXX; 6 – X; 7 – none; 8 – XXXXX; 9 – none; 10 – XXX; 11 – none; 12 – XX

Weight of Cats (lbs)

Show your work.

Use with text pages 366–368.

Exercises 11–16 all refer to the line plot and should be assigned together.

- For **Exercise 16,** students may need help thinking of a survey question. Guide them by suggesting questions involving sports, time spent exercising, or the number of siblings.

Before students answer **Exercises 17–21,** they must make a line plot of the data.

4 Assess & Close

Math Talk in Action

You are making a line plot to show the number of CDs fourth-graders own. What will each X you write above a number of CDs represent? (a student who has that many CDs)

Math Journal Prompt

Have students write a description of what a line plot is and what kinds of information it shows. Have them explain how a line plot and a tally table are alike and how they are different.

Lesson Quiz

Use the quiz on Lesson Transparency 14.4.

Test Prep & Spiral Review

Use Test Prep Transparency 14.4.

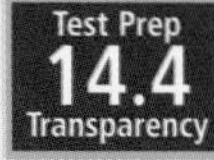

Ari asked the players on his soccer team how many goals they scored last season. This line plot shows the results. Use the line plot to answer Problems 11–15.

		X			
		X			
		X			
	X	X			
	X	X	X		
X	X	X	X	X	X
X	X	X	X	X	X
0	1	2	3	4	5

Goals Scored Last Season

11. How many players scored exactly 4 goals? **2**
12. How many players scored at least 2 goals? **14**
13. How many players did Ari survey altogether? **20**
14. What is the range of the data? **5**
15. Describe how to find the mode of the data in this plot. **The mode is the number with the most X's, or 2.**
16. Decide on a survey question for which the answers are numbers. There should be three or four possible answers. Conduct the survey and record your answers on a line plot. **Check students' surveys.**

The table below shows the number of penalty kicks that 5 players made during last season. Use the data to make a line plot. Then answer Questions 17–21. **Check students' line plots.**

Penalty Kicks Last Season

Name of Player	Number of Penalty Kicks
Josh	4
Kristen	5
Louis	8
Terrell	5
Sean	3

17. When you drew the line plot, what numbers did you use? ***See below.***
18. What do the X's on your plot stand for? **players**
19. How many players got more than 1 kick? **5**
20. What is the median of the data? **5**
21. What is the mode of the data? **5**

17. *Possible answer:* I used the number of penalty kicks, 3 through 8.

368

Extra Practice, See page 373, Set A.

Homework 14.4 **Page 91**

Name ______ Date ______ Homework 14.4

Line Plots

Use the line plot to answer each question.

What is the median of the data?

Order the data from least to greatest and find the middle value.

0, 1, 1, 1, 1, 1, 2, 2, 2, **2**, 2, 2, 2, 3, 3, 3, 3, 3, 4

The median of the data is 2.

Hours of Video Game Playing by Fourth Grade Students on Saturday

1. According to the line plot, how many students were surveyed? **19 students**
2. What is the range of the data? **4**
3. What is the mean of the data? **2**
4. What is the mode of the data? **2**

Problem Solving

Show your work.

5. Suppose that 5 more students had played 2 hours of video games on Saturday. What would the mean of the data set be then? Explain how you found your answer. **2; explanations may vary.**

Use with text pages 366–368.

Problem Solving

Math Reasoning

Mode of a Set

Mode can describe data sets that are not numerical. These dog tags are grouped by size. The mode for size is medium.

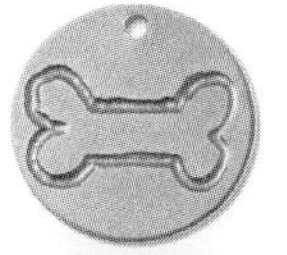
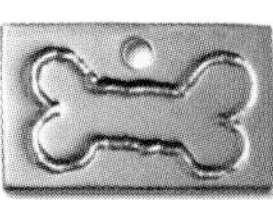

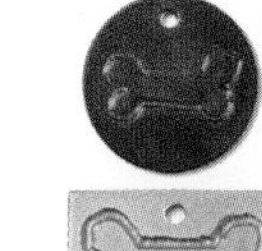

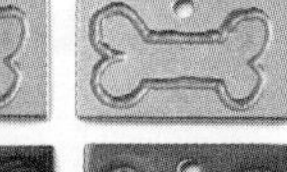
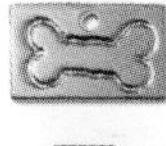

1. What is the mode for dog-tag shape: octagon, rectangle, or circle? **rectangle**
2. What is the mode for dog-tag color: red, blue, silver, gold, or green? **red**

Quick Check

Check your understanding of Lessons 1–4.

Use the tally chart. (Lesson 1)

What Is Your Favorite Color?

Color	Tally
Blue	𝍸 |||
Green	||||

1. How many people chose blue? **8 people**
2. How many people were surveyed? **12 people**

Use the line plot. (Lessons 3–4)

Size of Litters for Eight Animals

3. What is the range of the data set? **4**
4. What is the mean? **3**

Solve. (Lesson 2)

5. Lee saves $3 in Week 1. Each week, he doubles the amount he saves. What is the amount he saves in Week 5? **$48**

Extra Practice at **eduplace.com/map**

Math Reasoning

Mode of a Set

- Discuss with students that the mode of a data set is the item that occurs most often. Ask them to explain why mode is useful for describing sets that are not numerical, while median, mean, and range are not.
- Point out that there are several ways of grouping the dog tags in the picture. They are shown grouped by size. But they could also be grouped by shape or color.
- Guide students to recognize that this means there is a mode for each way of grouping: a mode for size, and different modes for shape or color.
- Ask students to think of other ways the tags could be grouped (material, weight, etc.)

Quick Check

The *Quick Check* allows you to assess the students' understanding of the concepts presented in Lessons 1–4.

Item	Objectives Tested	Pages	Intervention
1–2	Conduct a survey and organize information.	356–358	Reteach Resource 14.1 *Ways to Success* CD-ROM 14.1
3–4	Find the mean, median, mode, and range of a set of data. Make a line plot to represent data.	364–367	Reteach Resources 14.3, 14.4 *Ways to Success* CD-ROM 14.3, 14.4
5	Organize data in a table to solve a problem.	360–362	Reteach Resource 14.2, *Ways to Success* CD-ROM 14.2

Lesson 14.5

Stem-and-Leaf Plots

Planning

Lesson Objective Read and make stem-and-leaf plots.

Technology Resources

- Audio Tutor **2**/7 Listen and Understand
- *Ways to Success* CD-ROM 14.5
- Education Place: Extra Practice, eGlossary, Extra Help, eGames www.eduplace.com/map

Lesson 14.5 Transparency

Problem of the Day

Miguel sorted the numbers 37, 54, 38, 51, 31, 55, and 36 into two groups. What are two ways to do this? Show the numbers grouped both ways. (by even and odd numbers: 31, 37, 51, 55, and 36, 38, 54; by number of tens: 31, 36, 37, 38, and 51, 54, 55)

Spiral Review

Write each number in standard form.

1. thirty-two ones (32)
2. forty ones (40)
3. seven tens, three ones (71)

Lesson Quiz

Eight fourth-graders have collected cans for a food drive. These eight have collected 35, 22, 28, 29, 31, 34, 30, and 35 cans.

Make a stem-and-leaf plot to show the data.

2 | 2 8 9
3 | 0 1 4 55

NCTM Standards

Data Analysis and Probability: Select and use appropriate statistical methods to analyze data.

Getting Started

Building Math Vocabulary

stem-and-leaf plot a table that organizes information by place value

outlier a number or numbers that are at one or the other end of a set of data, arranged in order, where there is a gap between the end numbers and the rest of the data.

Make a connection between stems and leaves on a tree and two-digit numbers on a **stem-and-leaf plot.** Discuss that in a tree, the leaves extend from the branches, which are the stems. Guide students to see that the ones digits in a stem-and-leaf plot are the leaves that extend from the tens digits, the stems.

Making a Stem and Leaf Plot

Whole Class	15 minutes
Objective	Make a stem-and-leaf plot to represent data.
Materials	Blank transparency, erasable marker
	Visual, Auditory

- Write the following temperatures on the board: **60, 40, 58, 62, 69, 55, 72, 41, 67**
- Ask the students to make four columns on their paper: **40s, 50s, 60s, and 70s**. Model this on the overhead.
- Have students organize the temperatures into these columns placing the numbers in the correct column depending on their 10s digit from least to greatest.
- Have the students volunteer to give the mean, median, mode, and range for the set of numbers.
- Draw a stem-and-leaf plot on the overhead and ask students to copy this on their own papers. Label *Stems* and *Leaves*.
- Under the Stems column, list 4, 5, 6, and 7. Have students copy these numbers on their plot. Ask students where they think the ones digit for each temperature will go. (leaves)
- Begin placing the ones digit in the correct column, and ask for students to come up to the board to put the remaining numbers in the correct place.
- Tell students that this lesson will explain how to organize data with a stem-and-leaf plot.

Low Temperatures

Stem	Leaves
4	0 1
5	5 8
6	0 2 7 9
7	2

Differentiated Instruction

English Learners

Individuals	20 minutes
Objective	Read a stem-and-leaf plot.
Materials	Student page 370
Auditory, Visual	

Early Production

- Give students additional practice reading data from a stem-and-leaf plot.
- Before ***Guided Practice***, ask them what each row in the Mia's Earnings plot shows and the numbers each row represents. Then ask:

  How much money did Mia make altogether?

Intermediate/Advanced

- English Learner Resource 14.5
- English Learner Handbook

Intervention

Pairs	15 minutes
Objective	Make a stem-and-leaf plot.
Materials	None
Auditory, Visual	

- Draw a stem-and-leaf plot on the board that incorporates the following data: 60, 60, 62, 75, 76, 79, 88, 90, 91, 92, 100.
- Tell students that the stem-and-leaf plot represents test scores for a math test.
- Have students write the scores on their paper from least to greatest.
- **What is the range for the set of numbers?** (40) **Mean?** (79.36) **Median?** (79) **Mode?** (60)
- Have students pair up with a partner and each create a group of numbers for their partner to make into a stem-and-leaf plot.

Other Resources

- *Ways to Success* CD-ROM 14.5

Early Finishers

Individuals	20 minutes
Objective	Make a stem-and-leaf plot.
Materials	Blank Workmat
Visual, Tactual	

- Have students collect data from 10 classmates about how many minutes it takes them to get to school each morning. Ask them to do the following with the data:
- Arrange it from least to greatest.
- Display the data in a stem-and-leaf plot.
- Write a summary to describe the data.

Time Traveled to School (min.)

Stem	Leaves
1	0 1 2 3 5
2	2 3 6
3	4 5 6 8 9
4	1 2 4 5 5
5	
6	1

Science Connection

Materials: calendar

- Ask students to use the calendar to list in order from least to greatest the number of days in each month.
- Have them make a stem-and-leaf plot to display the data. But before they do, ask: **How many stems will there be in the stems column?** (2) **How many leaves will appear in the leaves column?** (12) **How do you know?** (The tens digits will be either 2 or 3; there are 12 months in a year.)

❶ Introduce

Students will look at sets of data and create stem-and-leaf plots as well as read stem-and-leaf plots to determine different findings of the data.

❷ Teach

Learn About It

Direct students' attention to the table at the right. **How is the information in the table organized?** (names listed in left column, minutes in right column; minutes not in counting order)

Guide students to see that in the stem-and-leaf plot the minutes are now listed in order from least to greatest. Discuss what an outlier is, then ask: **Why is 77 an outlier?** (It is much greater than the greatest of the other numbers.)

Why are there two 5s among the leaves for the 3 stem? (Two students spent 35 minutes on chores.)

Point out the key at the bottom of the plot. Ask: **How would you show 50 minutes? Explain.** (5 | 0; show 5 tens as the stem and 0 ones as the leaf.)

Next, have students look at the shape formed by the leaves on the stem-and-leaf plot. Ask: **What does this tell you about the data?** (Possible answer: The first set of leaves is the longest. This shows that among the sets of time periods, more students spent between 30 and 39 minutes on chores than between 40 and 49 minutes, or any other range of minutes shown.)

Guided Practice

Have students complete **Exercises 1–3** as you observe. Remind them to use the *Ask Yourself* questions to help.

Common Error

- **Not recording every piece of data in the plot** Students may neglect to include every ones digit, especially those that repeat, in the leaf column of their plot.
- **Intervention** Suggest to students that they work on scrap paper to first list all the data in order from least to greatest, for each group of tens. When they make their stem-and-leaf plots, they can cross out each number on the list as they represent it with a stem and a leaf. Guide students to write all the stems first.

Lesson 5

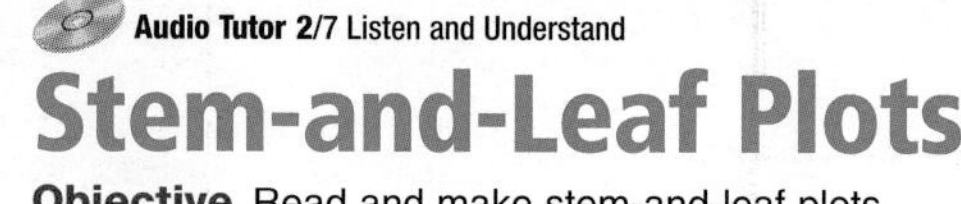

Audio Tutor 2/7 Listen and Understand

Stem-and-Leaf Plots

Objective Read and make stem-and-leaf plots.

Vocabulary
stem-and-leaf plot
outlier

Learn About It

Another way to organize data is with a **stem-and-leaf plot**. A stem-and-leaf plot shows information arranged by place value.

The table at the right shows how many minutes nine students spent doing chores. You can make a stem-and-leaf plot of the data.

Minutes Spent Doing Chores

Name	Minutes
Akio	77
Bonnie	30
Daniel	38
Ella	45
Julie	40
Miguel	35
Payat	55
Sarah	50
Tanya	35

- First, order the data from least to greatest.

30 35 35 38 40 45 50 55 77

- Then make a stem-and-leaf plot with digits in order from least to greatest.

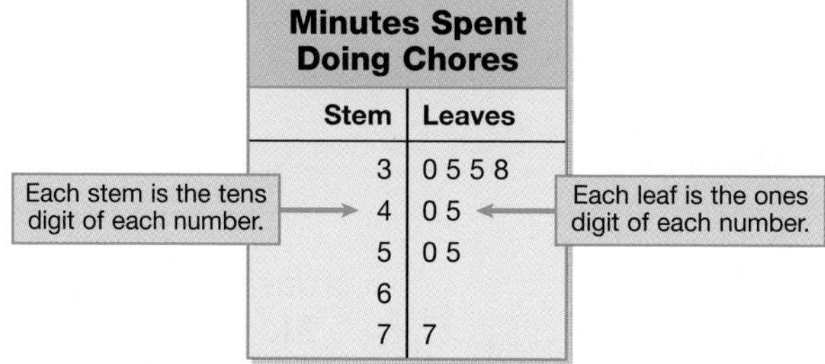

Minutes Spent Doing Chores

Stem	Leaves
3	0 5 5 8
4	0 5
5	0 5
6	
7	7

Each stem is the tens digit of each number.
Each leaf is the ones digit of each number.

3 | 0 = 30 minutes

The stem 7 and the leaf 7 tell you that one student spent 77 minutes doing chores. The number 77 is called an **outlier** because it is far from the other numbers.

You can use a stem-and-leaf plot to find the mean, median, mode, and range of the data set.

- What are these measures? **mean: 45; median: 40; mode: 35; range: 47**

Extra Help at **eduplace.com/map**

Reteach 14.5

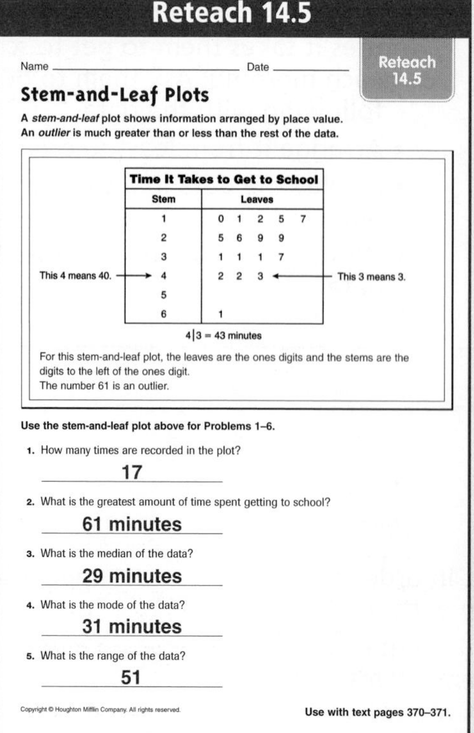

Name ____________ Date ________ Reteach 14.5

Stem-and-Leaf Plots

A *stem-and-leaf* plot shows information arranged by place value. An *outlier* is much greater than or less than the rest of the data.

Time It Takes to Get to School

Stem	Leaves
1	0 1 2 5 7
2	5 6 9 9
3	1 1 1 7
4	2 2 3
5	
6	1

This 4 means 40. This 3 means 3.

4|3 = 43 minutes

For this stem-and-leaf plot, the leaves are the ones digits and the stems are the digits to the left of the ones digit.
The number 61 is an outlier.

Use the stem-and-leaf plot above for Problems 1–6.

1. How many times are recorded in the plot? **17**
2. What is the greatest amount of time spent getting to school? **61 minutes**
3. What is the median of the data? **29 minutes**
4. What is the mode of the data? **31 minutes**
5. What is the range of the data? **51**

Use with text pages 370–371.

Practice 14.5 Page 92

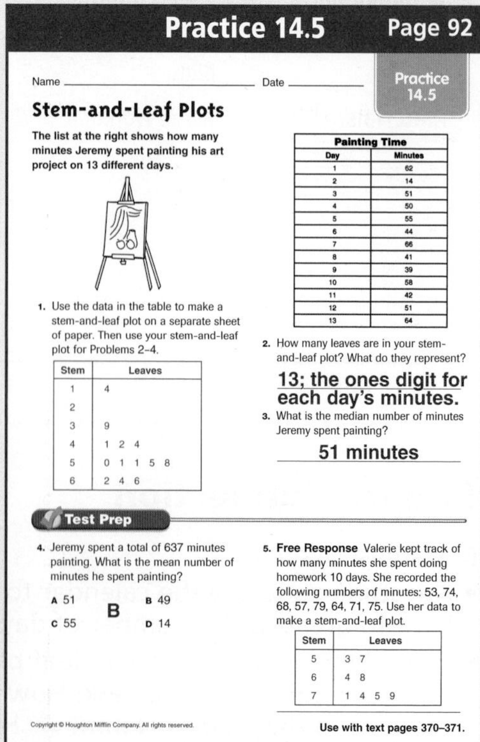

Name ____________ Date ________ Practice 14.5

Stem-and-Leaf Plots

The list at the right shows how many minutes Jeremy spent painting his art project on 13 different days.

Painting Time

Day	Minutes
1	62
2	14
3	51
4	50
5	55
6	44
7	66
8	41
9	39
10	58
11	42
12	51
13	64

1. Use the data in the table to make a stem-and-leaf plot on a separate sheet of paper. Then use your stem-and-leaf plot for Problems 2–4.

Stem	Leaves
1	4
2	
3	9
4	1 2 4
5	0 1 1 5 8
6	2 4 6

2. How many leaves are in your stem-and-leaf plot? What do they represent? **13; the ones digit for each day's minutes.**
3. What is the median number of minutes Jeremy spent painting? **51 minutes**

Test Prep

4. Jeremy spent a total of 637 minutes painting. What is the mean number of minutes he spent painting?
   A 51 B 49 C 55 D 14 **B**
5. **Free Response** Valerie kept track of how many minutes she spent doing homework 10 days. She recorded the following numbers of minutes: 53, 74, 68, 57, 79, 64, 71, 75. Use her data to make a stem-and-leaf plot.

Stem	Leaves
5	3 7
6	4 8
7	1 4 5 9

Use with text pages 370–371.

Guided Practice

The stem-and-leaf plot shows the amount of money Mia earned baby-sitting. Use the plot for Problems 1–3.

> **Ask Yourself**
> - What place do the stems represent?
> - What place do the leaves represent?

Mia's Earnings

Stem	Leaves
1	0 2 3 7 8 8
2	0 0 2 5
3	4

1 | 0 = $10

1. What is the median of the data? **median: 18**
2. What is the mode of the data? **modes: 18 and 20**
3. Is there an outlier? What does that tell you about the data? ***See below.***

Explain Your Thinking ▶ How are the stems and the leaves different in a stem-and-leaf plot? **They represent different place values.**

3. outlier: $34; It is a rare occurrence because most of the time she earns between $10 and $25.

Practice and Problem Solving

The list on the right shows how many minutes Lionel practiced the piano on eleven different days. Use the list for Problems 4–8.

Lionel's Piano Practice (minutes)	
60	55
50	30
65	46
48	63
60	57
60	

4. Use the data to make a stem-and-leaf plot. Then use your stem-and-leaf plot for Problems 5–8. ***See Additional Answers.***
5. How many leaves are in your stem-and-leaf plot? What do they represent? **11 leaves; ones**
6. What was the least number of minutes Lionel practiced? **30 minutes**
7. What is the median number of minutes Lionel spent practicing? **57 minutes**
8. **Analyze** Is the range a good way to describe Lionel's practice time? Why? **No; the range is 35 minutes; most of the time Lionel practices about one hour; the mode describes his practice time better.**

Mixed Review and Test Prep

Open Response

Find each missing number. (Ch. 12, Lesson 3)

9. 3 pints = __6__ cups
10. 1 gallon = __4__ quarts
11. 8 cups = __2__ quarts
12. Make a stem-and-leaf plot for the data. (Ch. 14, Lesson 5)

My Miniature Golf Scores
35, 40, 39, 45, 41, 32, 38, 44, 57

See Additional Answers.

Extra Practice, See page 373, Set B.

❸ Practice

Practice and Problem Solving

Select from **Exercises 4–12** for independent work.

- For **Exercise 4,** ask: **How many stems will your stem-and-leaf plot have? Why?** (4; the tens are 3, 4, 5 and 6.)
- For **Exercise 8,** elicit from students that the range is not a useful measure because of the outlier, 30. Ask: **What measure gives a better description of the data?** (either mode or median)

❹ Assess & Close

Math Talk in Action

Have students make a stem-and-leaf plot with the following data: 14, 36, 32, 25, 19, 40, 68, and 22.

What is the range of the data? How did you find it? (54; subtract 14 from 68.)

Is there a mode for this data? Explain. (No; none of the digits in the leaf column repeat.)

Math Journal Prompt

Have students write an explanation of how to make and read a stem-and-leaf plot.

Lesson Quiz

Use the quiz on Lesson Transparency 14.5.

Test Prep & Spiral Review

Use Test Prep Transparency 14.5.

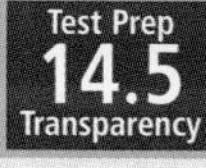

Enrichment 14.5

Name ____________ Date ________ Enrichment 14.5

How Tall Are You?

Colleen measured her height and the heights of her friends and family members. She recorded the heights in inches. She organized the data in a stem-and-leaf plot. Use the clues below to match the leaves to the correct stems. Write the leaves on the stem-and-leaf plot. Then use the stem-and-leaf plot to answer the question.

1. The shortest person is 39 inches tall.
2. The range of the data is 25 inches.
3. Three people are 60 inches tall.
4. Marc and Jess are both 48 inches tall.
5. The median of the data is 52 inches.
6. Yvette is one inch shorter than the tallest person.
7. Joey is 50 inches tall.
8. All of the four heights that are in the 40s are even numbers.

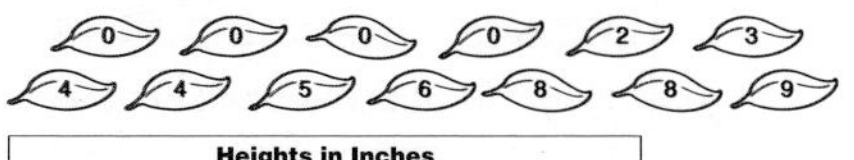

Heights in Inches	
Stem	Leaves
3	9
4	4 6 8 8
5	0 2 5
6	0 0 0 3 4

9. Colleen's height is equal to the mode of the data. How tall is Colleen? **60 inches**

Use with text pages 370–371.

Problem Solving 14.5

Name ____________ Date ________ Problem Solving 14.5

Stem-and-Leaf Plots

Solve.

Math Test Scores	
Stem	Leaves
6	4 8 8
7	2 2 2 6
8	0 0 0 4 4 8 8
9	2 2 6 6 6

1. Mrs. Gurecki recorded in a stem-and-leaf plot her class's scores on the last math test. How many test scores are shown? What is the median score? **19 scores; 80 is the median score**
2. In gym class, students recorded the number of pushups and sit-ups they completed in 1 minute. Make two stem-and-leaf plots of the data. Use your stem-and-leaf plots for Problems 3-6. **Check students' plots**

Number of Sit-ups and Pushups Completed in One Minute												
Sit-ups	42	45	46	38	26	50	35	36	46	44	48	38
Pushups	22	18	18	25	27	32	15	18	20	31	19	26

Show your work.

3. What was the least number of pushups completed in 1 minute? **15 pushups**
4. What is the median number of sit-ups completed in 1 minute? **43 sit-ups**
5. What are the mode and range of each set of data? **Push-ups: mode = 18, range = 17 sit-ups: mode = 38, 46, range = 24**
6. **Reasoning** Which is greater, the mean number of pushups in 1 minute or the mean number of sit-ups in 1 minute? How can you quickly tell without calculating? **Possible answer: The number of sit-ups. Most of the data values for the sit-ups are greater than the data values for pushups.**

Use with text pages 370–371.

Homework 14.5 Page 92

Name ____________ Date ________ Homework 14.5

Stem-and-Leaf Plots

What is the median of the data?

Find the middle value on the plot.

The median of the data is 37.

Stem	Leaves
1	2 5 8
2	3 3
3	6 7
4	0
5	1 2 3 3 5

The table shows how much Michael made each week by mowing lawns.

Week	Amount Earned
1	$37
2	$58
3	$55
4	$61
5	$58
6	$64
7	$67
8	$61
9	$58

1. Make a stem-and-leaf plot of the amount earned. **Check students' plots.**
2. How many leaves are in the stem-and-leaf plot? What do they represent? **9 leaves; the ones digits for each value in the data set.**
3. What was the greatest amount of money that Mark earned in one week? the least? **$67; $37**
4. What is the median weekly amount? **$58**
5. What weekly amount did Mark earn most often? **$58**

Use with text pages 370–371.

Monitoring Student Progress

Chapter Review/Test

Chapter Review/Test Items 1–10

To assign a numerical grade for this Chapter Review/Test, use 10 points for each test item.

Check Understanding

You can use the ***Write About It*** question to assess student understanding of a key chapter concept.

Customize Your Instruction

The Chapter Review/Test is a formal evaluation of chapter objectives. For students who have not yet mastered these objectives, you can use the Reteaching Resources listed in the chart below.

Additional Assessment Resources

Alternate Chapter Test A Chapter Test is also provided in the Unit Resource folder. You might use the Review/Test in the student book as review and the test in the Unit Resource folder as a summary test for the chapter.

***Ways to Assess* CD-ROM** allows you to create your own lesson, chapter, or unit tests or practice and review worksheets.

Adequate Yearly Progress Guide helps familiarize your students with the format of standardized tests.

Chapter Review/Test

VOCABULARY

Choose the best term to complete each sentence.

Vocabulary
mean
range
median
stem-and-leaf plot

1. The difference between the greatest number and the least number in a set of data is the ____. **range**
2. A way of displaying data as tens and ones is a ____. **stem-and-leaf plot**
3. When a set of numbers is arranged in order, the middle number is the ____. **median**

CONCEPTS AND SKILLS

Use the line plot for Problems 4–6. (Lessons 3, 4, pp. 364–368)

0	1	2	3	4	5
	X	XXX	XXXX	X	XX

Number of Runs in 11 Games

4. What is the median of the data? **3**
5. What is the range of the data? **4**
6. What is the mode of the data? **3**

Use the stem-and-leaf plot for Problems 7 and 8. (Lesson 5, pp. 370–371)

Test Scores

Stem	Leaves
5	0
6	
7	2 4 8
8	3 6 7 7

5 | 0 = 50

7. How many scores are there? **8 scores**
8. Is there an outlier? If so, which score is it? **yes; 50**

PROBLEM SOLVING

Make tables to solve Problems 9 and 10. (Lesson 2, pp. 360–362)

9. Jamal is 19 years old. Billy is 3 years old. How old will each one be when Jamal is three times as old as Billy? **Jamal: 24 years old; Billy: 8 years old**
10. A blue bus leaves every 3 minutes. A red bus leaves every 5 minutes. Both leave at 6:00 P.M. When is the next time a blue bus and a red bus will leave at the same time? **6:15 P.M.**

Write About It

Show You Understand

Do you think that a survey of 100 people will give more reliable information than a survey of 10 people? Explain your thinking. ***See above.***

Possible answer: **Yes; the greater the number of people surveyed, the more accurate the data most likely will be.**

Chapter Review/Test Items	Objectives	Covered on Teacher's Edition Pages	Use These Reteaching Resources
4–8	**14A** Conduct surveys to collect data; use data to solve problems.	356A–358, 366A–370	Reteach Resources 14.1, 14.4, 14.5 *Ways to Success* CD-ROM 14.1, 14.4, 14.5 *Ways to Success* Skillsheets 122, 124, 126
1, 3–6	**14B** Find the mean, median, mode, and range of numerical data.	364A–365	Reteach Resource 14.3 *Ways to Success* CD-ROM 14.3 *Ways to Success* Skillsheet 125
2, 4–8	**14C** Make, read, and interpret line plots and stem-and-leaf plots.	366A–371	Reteach Resources 14.4, 14.5 *Ways to Success* CD-ROM 14.4, 14.5 *Ways to Success* Skillsheets 126, 127
9–10	**14D** Solve problems using skills and strategies.	360A–362	Reteach Resource 14.2 *Ways to Success* CD-ROM 14.2 *Ways to Success* Skillsheet 128

Extra Practice

Set A (Lesson 4, pp. 366–368)

Use the line plot for Problems 1–6.

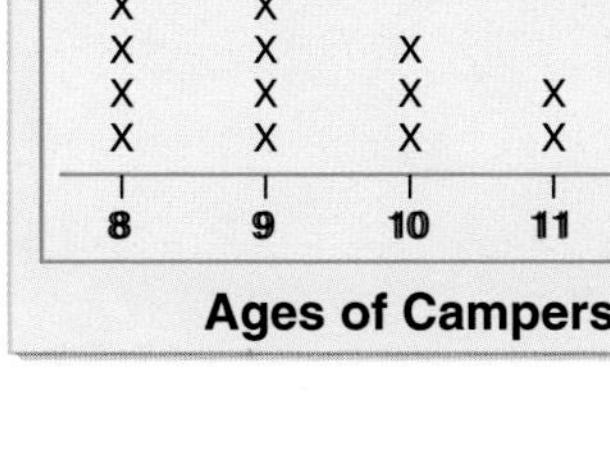

1. How many campers are there? **15 campers**
2. Are any of the campers younger than 8 years old? **no**
3. What is the age of the oldest camper? **12 years old**
4. What is the range of the data? **4 years**
5. What is the mode? **9 years**
6. What is the median? **9 years**

Set B (Lesson 5, pp. 370–371)

Use the stem-and-leaf plot at the right for Problems 1–5.

Daily High Temperatures in September (°F)

Stem	Leaves
4	9
5	
6	6 8 9 9
7	0 0 0 1 2 2 3 5 7 9

4 | 9 = 49

1. How many days are recorded? **15 days**
2. Which temperature is an outlier? **49°F**
3. What is the range? **30°**
4. What is the median? **70°F**
5. What is the mode? **70°F**

Use the stem-and-leaf plot at the right for Problems 6–10.

Basketball Scores

Stem	Leaves
6	8 9
7	1 5 6 6
8	4 7 8 8 8
9	0

6 | 8 = 68

6. Which measure—the mean, median, mode, or range—helps you understand the difference between the team's best and worst games? **range**
7. What was the highest score? **90 points**
8. What is the mean of the scores between 80 and 89? **87**
9. What is the median score? **80**
10. Is there an outlier? Explain your reasoning. **No; the highest and lowest scores are within 2 points of the next highest and lowest scores.**

Extra Practice at **eduplace.com/map**

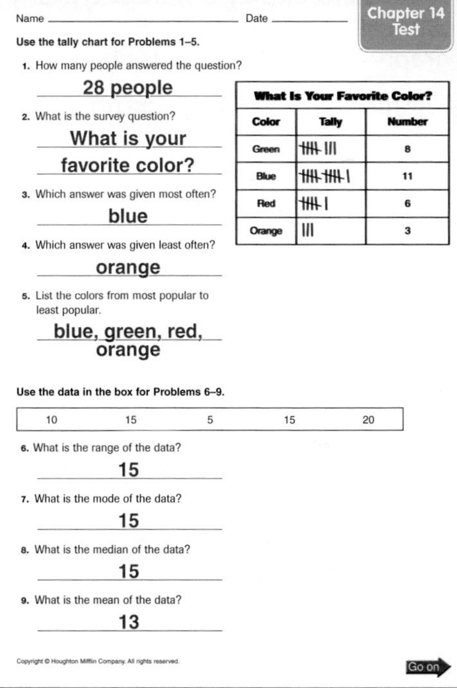

CHAPTER 14 TEST

Chapter 14 Test

Name ____________ Date ________

Use the tally chart for Problems 1–5.

What Is Your Favorite Color?

Color	Tally	Number
Green	~~||||~~ |||	8
Blue	~~||||~~ ~~||||~~		11
Red	~~||||~~		6
Orange	|||	3

1. How many people answered the question? **28 people**
2. What is the survey question? **What is your favorite color?**
3. Which answer was given most often? **blue**
4. Which answer was given least often? **orange**
5. List the colors from most popular to least popular. **blue, green, red, orange**

Use the data in the box for Problems 6–9.

10	15	5	15	20

6. What is the range of the data? **15**
7. What is the mode of the data? **15**
8. What is the median of the data? **15**
9. What is the mean of the data? **13**

Go on

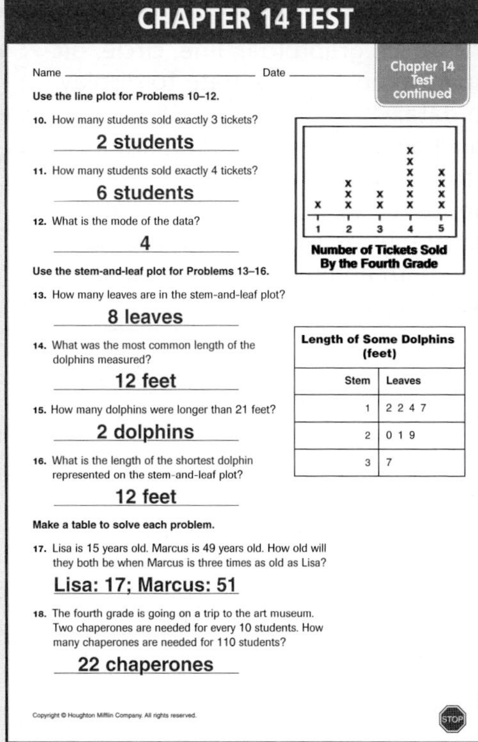

CHAPTER 14 TEST

Chapter 14 Test continued

Name ____________ Date ________

Use the line plot for Problems 10–12.

10. How many students sold exactly 3 tickets? **2 students**
11. How many students sold exactly 4 tickets? **6 students**
12. What is the mode of the data? **4**

Use the stem-and-leaf plot for Problems 13–16.

Length of Some Dolphins (feet)

Stem	Leaves
1	2 2 4 7
2	0 1 9
3	7

13. How many leaves are in the stem-and-leaf plot? **8 leaves**
14. What was the most common length of the dolphins measured? **12 feet**
15. How many dolphins were longer than 21 feet? **2 dolphins**
16. What is the length of the shortest dolphin represented on the stem-and-leaf plot? **12 feet**

Make a table to solve each problem.

17. Lisa is 15 years old. Marcus is 49 years old. How old will they both be when Marcus is three times as old as Lisa? **Lisa: 17; Marcus: 51**
18. The fourth grade is going on a trip to the art museum. Two chaperones are needed for every 10 students. How many chaperones are needed for 110 students? **22 chaperones**

STOP

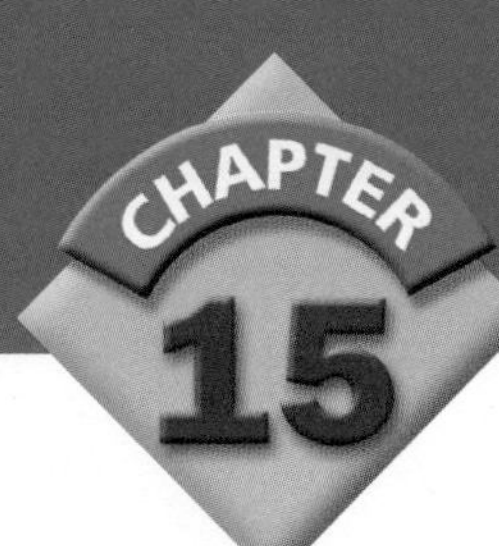

Planning Guide

Graph Data

Lesson	Overview	Objective/Vocabulary
1 Double Bar Graphs p. 376A	► Following a step-by-step procedure; make a double bar graph displaying two sets of data. ► Decide on the title, labels, key, and intervals for the graph.	► Make a double bar graph to compare two sets of data. double bar graph key interval
2 Circle Graphs p. 378A	► Learn that a circle graph, also known as a "pie chart," shows that parts make up a whole. ► Use fraction circle models to explore one-halves, one-fourths, and one-eighths of a circle graph.	► Use a circle graph to solve problems. circle graph
3 Problem-Solving Application: Interpret a Line Graph p. 380A	► Interpret line graphs to solve problems. ► Learn that a line graph shows the relationship between time and another quantity.	► Get information from a graph even if it does not give exact information. line graph
4 Hands On: Read and Make Line Graphs p. 382A	► Read, interpret, and make line graphs, following a step-by-step procedure. ► Identify the two axes needed to make a line graph and decide on the title, labels, and intervals.	► Read and make a line graph. line graph
5 Hands On: Analyze Graphs p. 384A	► Decide which graph (bar, line, circle, pictograph) is most appropriate to display given data. ► Conduct a survey, gather data, and display them appropriately. ► Introduce histograms, which are similar to bar graphs except that each bar is labeled with an interval indicating a numerical range.	► Use graphs to display different types of data. line graph bar graph circle graph pictograph

Skills Trace: Graph Data		
Grade 3	**Grade 4**	**Grade 5**
• Make, read, and interpret bar graphs (ch. 6) • Make, read, and interpret pictographs (ch. 6)	• Make, read, and interpret double bar graphs • Read and interpret circle graphs • Make, read, and interpret line graphs • Compare and analyze data in different types of graphs	• Make, read, and interpret double bar graphs and histograms (ch. 7) • Make, read, and interpret single and double line graphs (ch. 7) • Choose most appropriate graph to display data (ch. 7) • Identify and analyze misleading graphs (ch. 7) • Use a spreadsheet to make a graph (ch. 7)

Differentiated Instruction	Materials	NCTM Standards
▶ Differentiated Instruction activities, p. 376B ▶ *Chapter Challenges,* p. 85 *Ways to Success* CD-ROM 15.1 ▶ *Ways to Success* Skillsheet 133	Bar-Graph Grid Transparency, grid paper (Learning Tool 19), colored pencils	**Data Analysis and Probability:** Represent data using tables and graphs such as line plots, bar graphs, and line graphs.
▶ Differentiated Instruction activities, p. 378B *Ways to Success* CD-ROM 15.2 ▶ *Ways to Success* Skillsheet 134 Audio Tutor **2**/8 Listen and Understand	Fraction circle Models	**Data Analysis and Probability:** Represent data using tables and graphs such as line plots, bar graphs, and line graphs.
▶ Differentiated Instruction activities, p. 380B ▶ *Chapter Challenges,* p. 87 *Ways to Success* CD-ROM 15.3 ▶ *Ways to Success* Skillsheet 136	Line-Graph Grid Transparency (Learning Tool 21)	**Data Analysis and Probability:** Represent data using tables and graphs such as line plots, bar graphs, and line graphs.
▶ Differentiated Instruction activities, p. 382B *Ways to Success* CD-ROM 15.4 ▶ *Ways to Success* Skillsheet 135 Audio Tutor **2**/9 Listen and Understand	Line-Graph Grid Transparency (Learning Tool 21), grid paper	**Data Analysis and Probability:** Represent data using tables and graphs such as line plots, bar graphs, and line graphs.
▶ Differentiated Instruction activities, p. 384B ▶ *Chapter Challenges,* p. 89 *Ways to Success* CD-ROM 15.5 ▶ *Ways to Success* Skillsheet 132	Grid paper (Learning Tools 19, 20, and 21)	**Data Analysis and Probability:** Represent data using tables and graphs such as line plots, bar graphs, and line graphs; compare different representations of the same data and evaluate how well each representation shows important aspects of the data.

Math Notes

Chapter Objectives

15A Compare and analyze information from different types of graphs.

15B Make, read, and interpret a bar graph.

15C Make, read, and interpret a line graph.

15D Solve problems using skills and strategies.

Mathematical Background

Different Types of Graphs

Once a data set has been collected, there are many different ways it can be displayed in order to be read and interpreted more readily. Tables and graphs convey numerical data in a visual way.

A **bar graph** uses bars and a numerical scale to represent data. A **double bar graph** compares two sets of data. Bar graphs are useful in displaying data that can be counted.

A **line graph** uses a line and numerical scale to represent data that are continuous. Line graphs are often used to show changes over time.

A **circle graph** is a graph in which data are represented by parts of a circle. Circle graphs are useful in comparing parts of a whole. The circle graph below shows that half of the viewers chose *Comedy* and that the number that chose *Comedy* was twice the number that chose *Sports*.

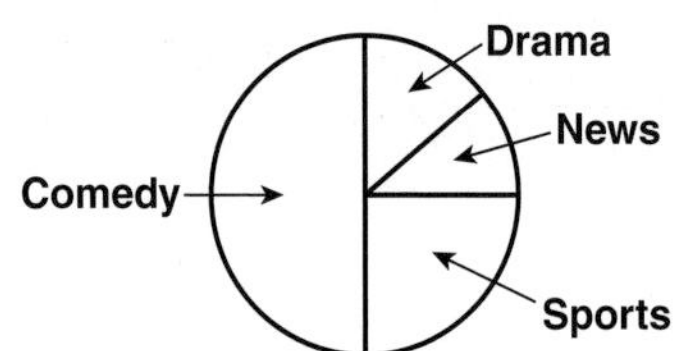

Research-Based Teaching

Once data are collected, they should be "examined, interpreted, and analyzed using multiple representations" (Russell and Friel, 1989), moving back and forth between tables and graphs, among different types of graphs, and so on. Data that have been collected and organized should be used to generate new questions, not just to obtain answers. See *Professional Resources Handbook, Grade 4,* Unit 5.

Language Intervention

When students are asked to explain their thinking, have students share their responses. This will help students improve their communication skills and their mathematics vocabulary.

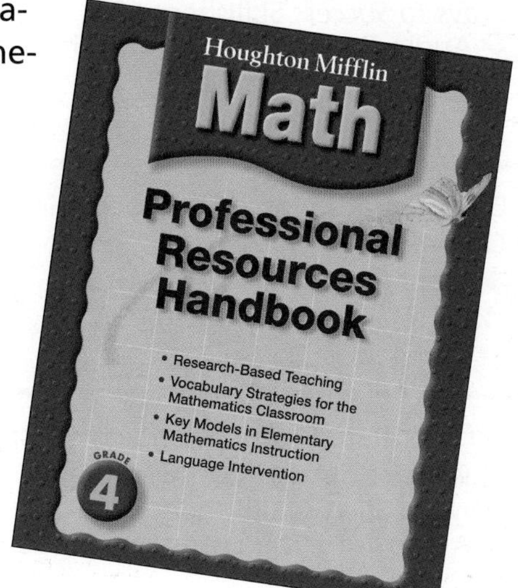

Chapter Activities

Connecting to the Unit Project

Individuals	20 minutes
Objective	Make graphs.
Materials	None
Tactual, Visual	

Graph Data

- Have students copy or draw graphs of data they find about their state during their research.
- Ask students to write a summary paragraph about the graphs.

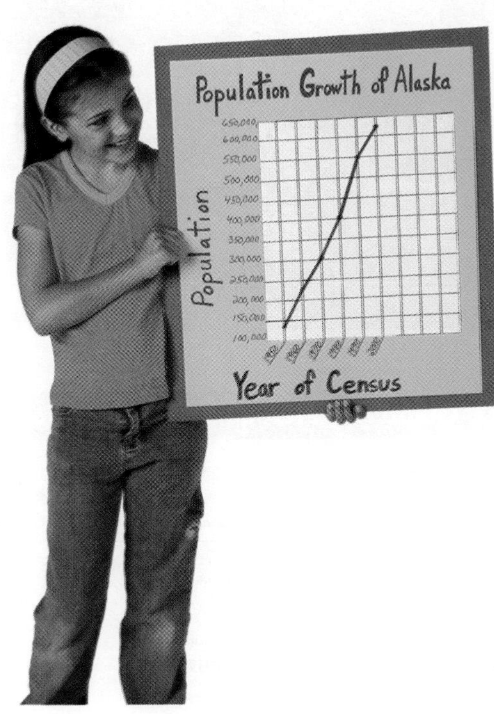

Ongoing Skill Activity

Whole Class	30 minutes
Objective	Find and interpret graphs.
Materials	Newspapers or weekly news magazines
Tactual, Visual	

Interpret Graphs

- Have students look through a newspaper or weekly news magazine for different types of graphs.
- Ask each student to read and interpret at least one of the graphs.
- Then ask them how the graph helped clarify the information in the article.

Assessing Prior Knowledge

Whole Class	15 minutes
Objective	Identify and interpret graphs.
Materials	Social studies textbooks
Visual, Auditory	

Interpret Graphs

- Ask students to find different types of graphs in their social studies textbook.
- Have them name the types of graphs, if they can.
- Then have them tell what the graphs are about.
- Ask students how the graphs are the same and how they are different from each other.

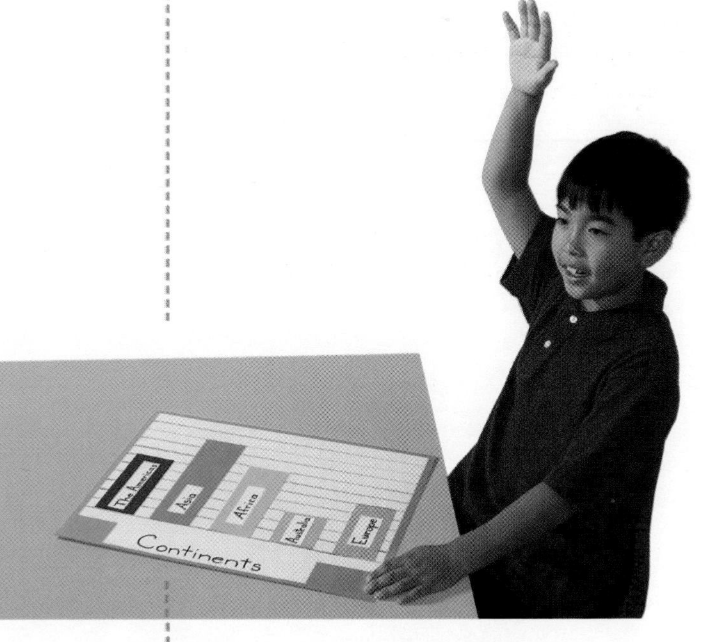

Starting Chapter 15

Investigation

Using Data

Have students work in small groups to answer the questions posed on page 374.

To extend the investigation, have students do the following activity.

- Look in newspapers to find data displayed in different types of graphs. Write an explanation of the data that each graph shows. Display the graphs and the explanations on a bulletin board.

For more information about projects and investigations,

Visit **Education Place**®
www.eduplace.com/mat

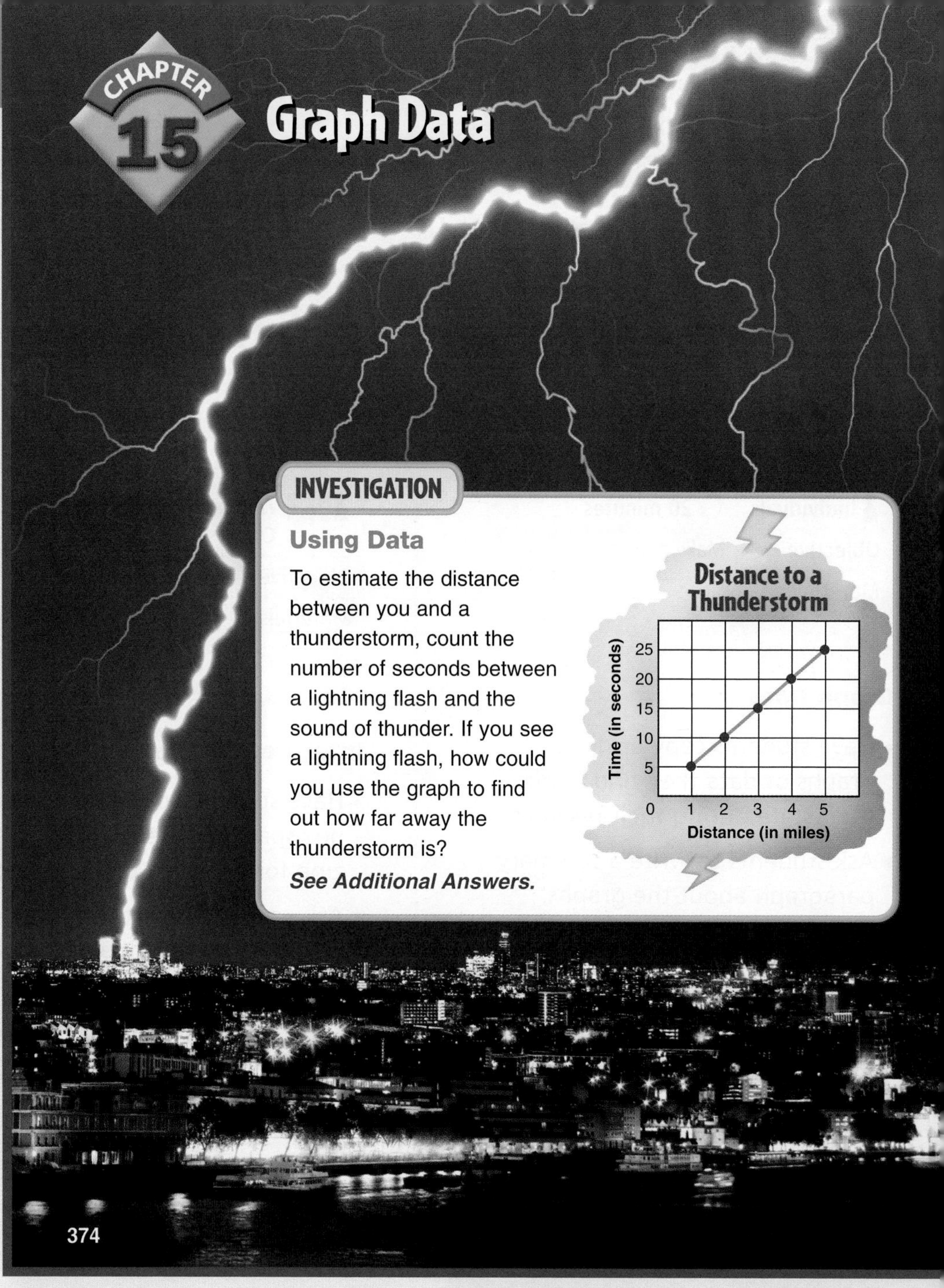

CHAPTER 15

Graph Data

INVESTIGATION

Using Data

To estimate the distance between you and a thunderstorm, count the number of seconds between a lightning flash and the sound of thunder. If you see a lightning flash, how could you use the graph to find out how far away the thunderstorm is?

See Additional Answers.

Distance to a Thunderstorm

Time (in seconds): 0, 5, 10, 15, 20, 25

Distance (in miles): 0, 1, 2, 3, 4, 5

374

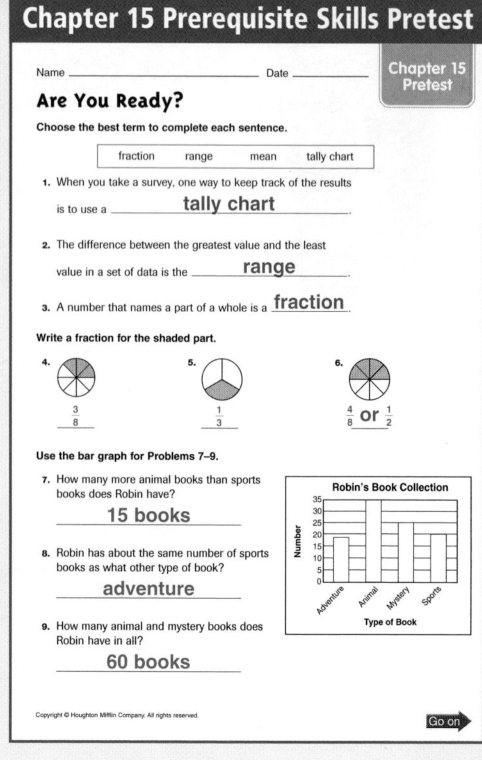

Chapter 15 Prerequisite Skills Pretest

Name ______ Date ______

Chapter 15 Pretest

Are You Ready?

Choose the best term to complete each sentence.

fraction	range	mean	tally chart

1. When you take a survey, one way to keep track of the results is to use a tally chart.
2. The difference between the greatest value and the least value in a set of data is the range.
3. A number that names a part of a whole is a fraction.

Write a fraction for the shaded part.

4. $\frac{3}{8}$
5. $\frac{1}{3}$
6. $\frac{4}{8}$ or $\frac{1}{2}$

Use the bar graph for Problems 7–9.

7. How many more animal books than sports books does Robin have? 15 books
8. Robin has about the same number of sports books as what other type of book? adventure
9. How many animal and mystery books does Robin have in all? 60 books

Robin's Book Collection

Number: 0, 5, 10, 15, 20, 25, 30, 35

Type of Book: Adventure, Animal, Mystery, Sports

Go on

Use this page to review and remember what you need to know for this chapter.

VOCABULARY

Choose the best term to complete each sentence.

Vocabulary
mean
range
fraction
tally chart

1. When you ask people questions, one way to keep track of the answers is to use a ____. **tally chart**
2. The difference between the greatest number and the least number in a set of data is the ____. **range**
3. A number that names a part of a whole is a ____. **fraction**

CONCEPTS AND SKILLS

Write a fraction for the shaded part.

4. 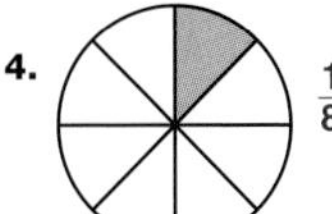 $\frac{1}{8}$

5. 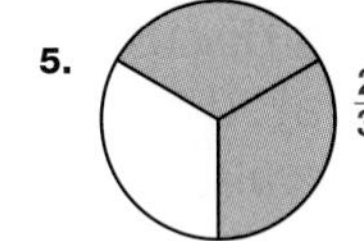 $\frac{2}{3}$

6. 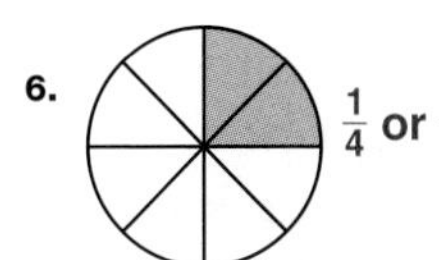 $\frac{1}{4}$ or $\frac{2}{8}$

Use the bar graph for Problems 7–9.

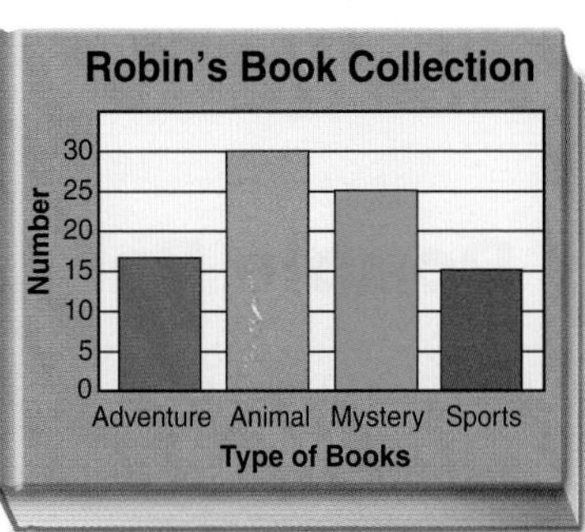

7. How many more animal books than sports books does Robin have? **15 more**
8. Robin has about the same number of sports books as what other type of book? **Adventure books**
9. How many animal and mystery books does Robin have altogether? **55 books**

Write About It

10. Think about what you know about pictographs and bar graphs. Explain how a bar graph is different from a pictograph. ***See Additional Answers.***

Facts Practice, See page 665.

Use What You Know

Use this page for informal assessment and review of prerequisite skills.

- Items 1–3: Use math vocabulary
- Items 4–6: Name fractional parts of a circle
- Items 7–9: Read and interpret a bar graph
- Item 10: Describe how a bar graph is different from a pictograph

Customize Your Instruction

Use the Chapter Pretest in the Unit Resource folder to help customize and pace instruction.

Objectives and Resources

▶ Prerequisite Skills Pretest

- Items 1–3: Use mathematical vocabulary.
- Items 4–6: Write fractions.
- Items 7–9: Read and interpret a bar graph.

▶ New Content Pretest

- Items 1–4: Read and interpret double bar graphs.
- Items 5–8: Read and interpret circle graphs.
- Items 9–12: Read and interpret line graphs.
- Items 13–16: Choose the appropriate graph.

▶ For Students Having Difficulty

- *Ways to Success* CD-ROM
- *Ways to Success* Skillsheet 129–131

▶ For Students Having Success

- Enrichment 15.1–15.5

▶ For Mathematically Promising Students

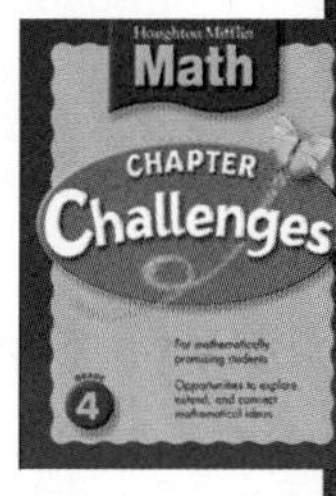

Explore: Averages and Bar Graphs, page 85, after Lesson 1

Extend: Changing the Scale, page 87, after Lesson 3

Connect: Graphing a Report, page 89, after Lesson 5

Chapter 15 New Content Pretest

Name ____ Date ____ Chapter 15 Pretest continued

Check What You Know

Use the double bar graph for Problems 1–4.

Ben and Carol's Vegetable Garden (Number of Plants; Lettuce, Carrots, Peas, Beans; Ben, Carol; Type of Bird)

1. How many carrot plants does Ben have in his garden? **15 plants**
2. Who has more pea plants, Ben or Carol? **Ben**
3. How many bean plants do Ben and Carol have altogether? **30 plants**
4. How many plants does Carol have in her garden altogether, if all her plants are shown on the graph? **60 plants**

Use the circle graph for Problems 5–8.

Favorite Subjects (Math, Social Studies, Reading, Science)

5. What fraction of the circle graph does reading represent? **$\frac{1}{2}$**
6. Which subjects are represented about equally in the graph? **math and social studies**
7. What fraction of the circle graph does science represent? **$\frac{1}{4}$**
8. Did more students choose science or math? **science**

Go on

Chapter 15 New Content Pretest

Name ____ Date ____ Chapter 15 Pretest continued

Use the line graph for Questions 9–12.

Growth of Nancy's Rose Bush (Height (cm); Time (days))

9. How much did Nancy's rose bush grow between Day 2 and Day 3? **3 centimeters**
10. Between which two consecutive days did the rose bush grow the fastest? **Day 1 and Day 2**
11. By Day 10, how tall was Nancy's rose bush? **21 centimeters**
12. How many days did it take for the rose bush to grow from 12 centimeters to 18 centimeters? **4 days**

Choose a graph to display the data for Problems 13–16. Write *bar graph, circle graph, line graph,* or *pictograph.* Explain your choice.

Answers may vary for Problems 13–16. Explanations should indicate an understanding of the appropriateness of different graphs.

13. compare the heights of two people **bar graph or pictograph**
14. the parts of a day spent doing different activities **circle graph**
15. the growth of a child **line graph**
16. the ways students get to school **pictograph or bar graph**

STOP

Hands On Lesson 15.1

Double Bar Graphs

Planning

Lesson Objective Make a double bar graph to compare two sets of data.

Math Background

One way students can display data is with a bar graph. Both bar graphs and double bar graphs work well for data that can be counted. A double bar graph is used to compare two sets of data.

Technology Resources

- *Ways to Success* CD-ROM 15.1
- Education Place: Extra Practice, eGlossary, eGames www.eduplace.com/map

Lesson 15.1 Transparency

Problem of the Day

A student polled 30 classmates to find out their favorite after-school activity. The following choices were offered: ride a bicycle, read a book, play a computer game, and play a sport. Half chose playing a computer game. Seven chose reading. There were 3 times as many votes for playing a sport than for bicycle riding. How many students chose bicycle riding as their favorite? (2)

Spiral Review

Round to the nearest 10.

1. 77 (80)
2. 133 (130)
3. 821 (820)

Lesson Quiz

You want to compare sales of Japanese cars and German cars in the United States during each of the past 5 years. Would you make a single bar graph or a double bar graph? Explain your choice. (double bar graph; comparing two sets of data)

NCTM Standards

Data Analysis and Probability:
Represent data using tables and graphs such as line plots, bar graphs, and line graphs.

Getting Started

Building Math Vocabulary

double bar graph	a graph in which data is compared by means of pairs of rectangular bars drawn next to each other
key	a part of a map, graph, or chart that explains what symbols mean
interval	the difference between two numbers on a scale

Use the vocabulary cards to introduce and discuss the meanings of ***key*** and ***interval.*** Talk about how each word is related to other meanings. Compare a graph key with a map key. Compare intervals on a graph with intervals in music. Then draw a double bar graph on the board and have students talk about why it is used to compare two sets of data.

Discuss Double Bar Graphs

Whole Class	10 minutes
Objective	Make, read, and interpret a bar graph.
Materials	Bar-Graph Grid Transparency
	Visual

- Tell students that a double bar graph compares two sets of data. Place one on the overhead that compares the kinds of music teens and adults prefer. Make up categories: Country, Classical, Jazz, and Rock. Label the horizontal axis *Type of Music* and the vertical axis *Number.* Use intervals of 2, from 0 to 18. Give the graph the title *Favorite Type of Music.* Provide a 2-color key.
- Guide students to identify all the features of the graph, including what the key shows.
- Tell students that the lesson in their books shows how to create double bar graphs to compare two sets of data.

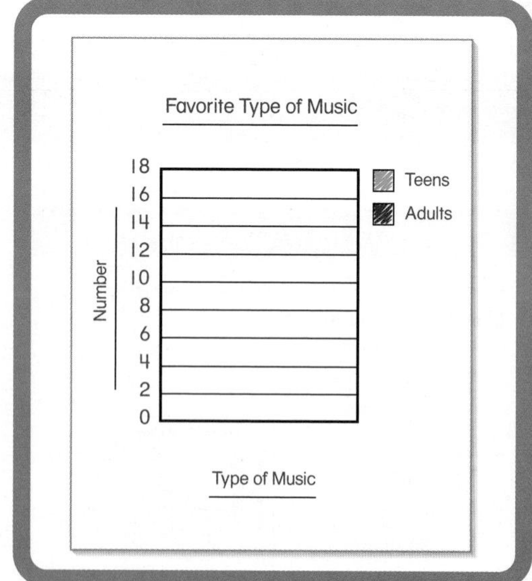

Differentiated Instruction

English Learners

Pairs	15 minutes
Objective	Make and read a bar graph.
Materials	Student page 377
Visual	

Early Production

- Give students additional practice using the lesson vocabulary.
- After students make a double bar graph for ***On Your Own,*** ask them to label the different parts of their graph. Then put students in pairs to explain what they labeled to a partner.

Intermediate/Advanced

- English Learner Resource 15.1
- English Learner Handbook

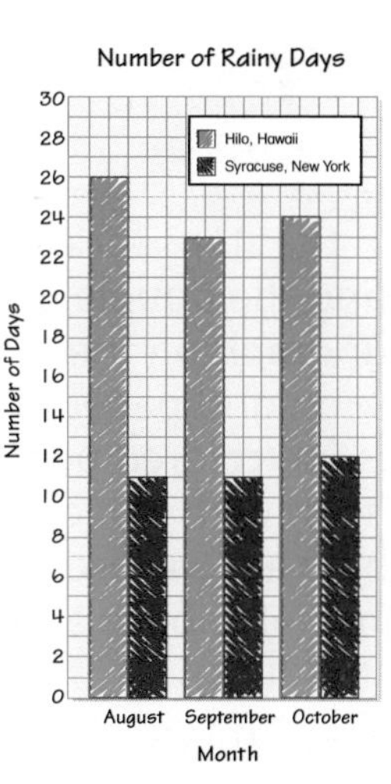

Intervention

Whole Class	20 minutes
Objective	Read and interpret a bar graph.
Materials	Newspapers or magazines
Auditory	

- Initiate a class discussion about bar graphs.
- **Where have you seen bar graphs?** (Answers will vary.) **What do they show?** (Answers will vary.) **How do they differ from line graphs?** (Answers will vary.) **When have you ever used a bar graph?** (Answers will vary.)
- Provide age-appropriate examples of single bar graphs from a newspaper, magazine, or textbook. Ask them a few questions to see how well they are able to read the graphs.

Other Resources

- *Ways to Success* CD-ROM 15.1

Inclusion

Small Groups	20 minutes
Objective	Make, read, and interpret a bar graph.
Materials	Workmat 6 or grid paper, colored pencils
Tactual, Visual	

- Have a group of three students work together to construct a triple bar graph to show the number of hours of reading they did over a two-day period. Guide them to make a key—one color per student—and to choose sensible intervals for book reading times.
- Ask students to summarize the information that their graph shows.

Real-World Connection

- Which do students prefer: reading or watching television? Have students poll 12 students per grade from grades 3–6. Have them use the results to make a double bar graph. Students need to make a key, choose labels and intervals, and give their graphs a title. Hint: Try four sets of double bars, one set per grade.
- When the graphs are completed, have students discuss what they show.

❶ Introduce

Have a student volunteer read the lesson objective aloud. Ask students to define "data" in their own words, and suggest examples of a "set of data."

Tell students that the lesson will explain how to use a bar graph to compare data.

❷ Teach

Work Together

- Work through the steps for making and interpreting the double bar graph. Construct your graph on the overhead as students work on grid paper at their seats. Have students use colored pencils to draw their bars. Discuss with students the basic relationship between vertical scale interval and bar height. Talk about all of the graph's features and the function of each feature.
- For Step 1, guide students to understand that the data determines a reasonable interval to use. Discuss other intervals that could have been used.
- For Step 3, ask students additional questions about the weather data to check students' understanding.
- You may wish to have students work in pairs on the ***On Your Own*** activity.

Double Bar Graphs

Objective Make a double bar graph to compare two sets of data.

Vocabulary
double bar graph
key
interval

Materials
Grid Paper
(Learning Tool 19)
colored pencils

Work Together

A **double bar graph** can be used to compare two sets of data.

The table on the right shows the number of rainy days during May, June, and July in Cleveland, Ohio, and Raleigh, North Carolina.

Work with a partner to make a double bar graph to compare the data.

Number of Rainy Days			
	May	June	July
Cleveland, OH	13	11	10
Raleigh, NC	10	9	11

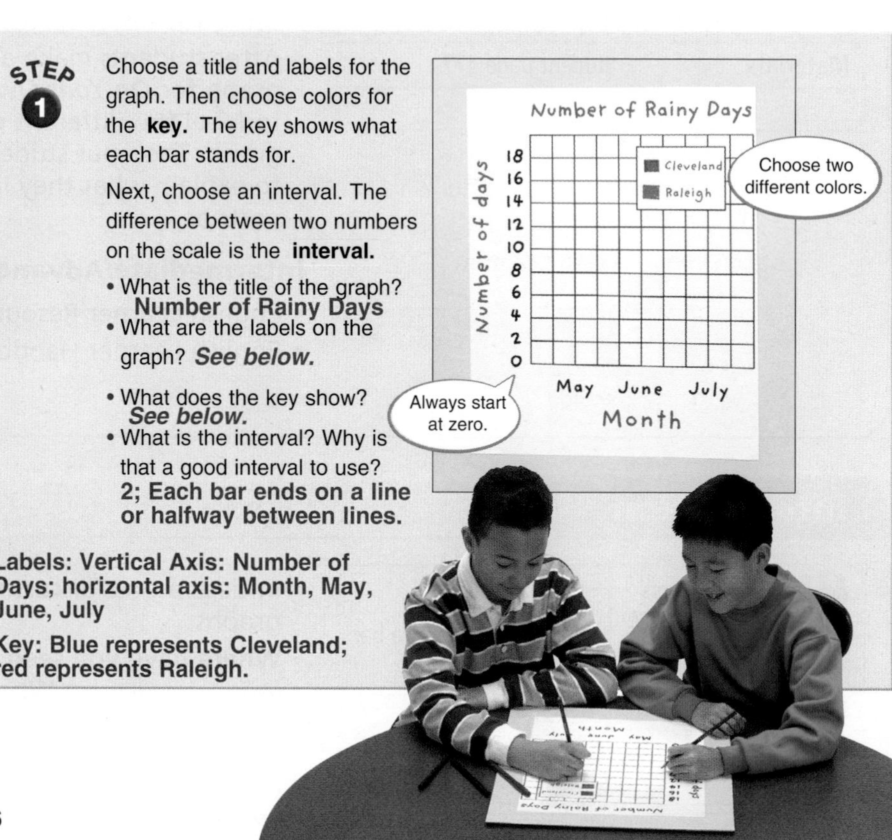

STEP 1 Choose a title and labels for the graph. Then choose colors for the **key.** The key shows what each bar stands for.

Next, choose an interval. The difference between two numbers on the scale is the **interval.**

- What is the title of the graph? **Number of Rainy Days**
- What are the labels on the graph? ***See below.***
- What does the key show? ***See below.***
- What is the interval? Why is that a good interval to use? **2; Each bar ends on a line or halfway between lines.**

Labels: Vertical Axis: Number of Days; horizontal axis: Month, May, June, July

Key: Blue represents Cleveland; red represents Raleigh.

376

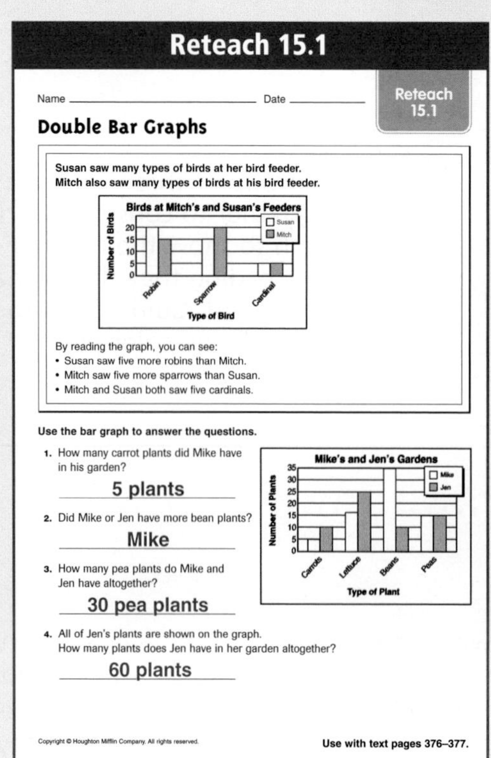

Reteach 15.1

Name ______________ Date ________ Reteach 15.1

Double Bar Graphs

Susan saw many types of birds at her bird feeder.
Mitch also saw many types of birds at his bird feeder.

By reading the graph, you can see:
- Susan saw five more robins than Mitch.
- Mitch saw five more sparrows than Susan.
- Mitch and Susan both saw five cardinals.

Use the bar graph to answer the questions.

1. How many carrot plants did Mike have in his garden? **5 plants**
2. Did Mike or Jen have more bean plants? **Mike**
3. How many pea plants do Mike and Jen have altogether? **30 pea plants**
4. All of Jen's plants are shown on the graph. How many plants does Jen have in her garden altogether? **60 plants**

Use with text pages 376–377.

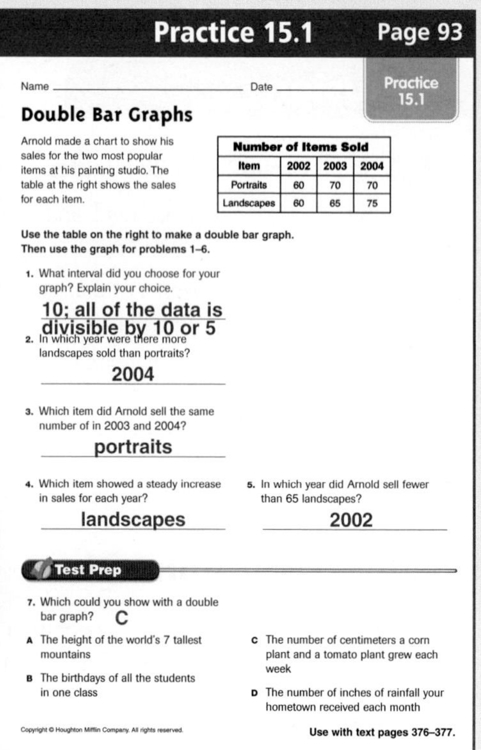

Practice 15.1 Page 93

Name ______________ Date ________ Practice 15.1

Double Bar Graphs

Arnold made a chart to show his sales for the two most popular items at his painting studio. The table at the right shows the sales for each item.

Number of Items Sold			
Item	2002	2003	2004
Portraits	60	70	70
Landscapes	60	65	75

Use the table on the right to make a double bar graph. Then use the graph for problems 1–6.

1. What interval did you choose for your graph? Explain your choice. **10; all of the data is divisible by 10 or 5**
2. In which year were there more landscapes sold than portraits? **2004**
3. Which item did Arnold sell the same number of in 2003 and 2004? **portraits**
4. Which item showed a steady increase in sales for each year? **landscapes**
5. In which year did Arnold sell fewer than 65 landscapes? **2002**

Test Prep

7. Which could you show with a double bar graph? **C**

A The height of the world's 7 tallest mountains
B The birthdays of all the students in one class
C The number of centimeters a corn plant and a tomato plant grew each week
D The number of inches of rainfall your hometown received each month

Use with text pages 376–377.

STEP 2 Use the data from the table to make the graph.

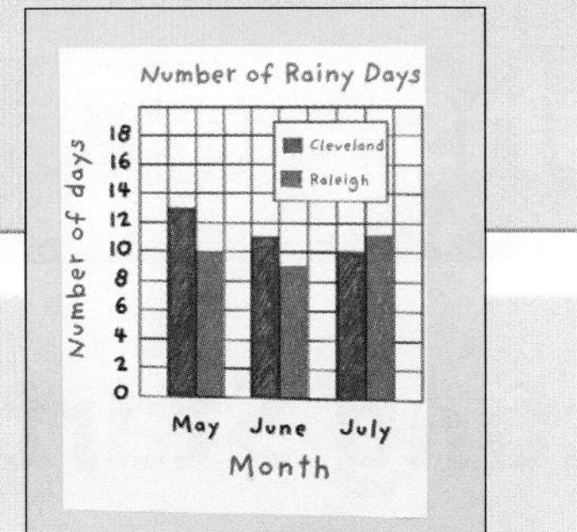

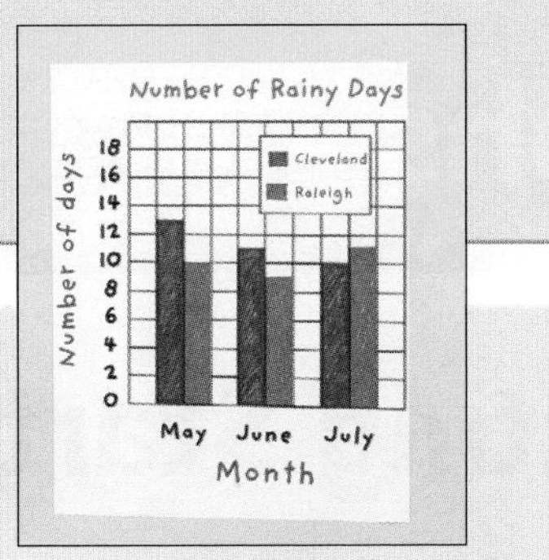

STEP 3 Use the completed graph to compare the data.

- In May, were there more rainy days in Cleveland or in Raleigh? **Cleveland**

On Your Own

Use the table below to make a double bar graph. Then use the graph for Problems 1–3.
See Additional Answers.

Number of Rainy Days			
	August	September	October
Hilo, Hawaii	26	23	24
Syracuse, New York	11	11	12

1. What interval did you choose for your graph? Explain your choice.
Check intervals and explanations.
2. In which month were there twice as many rainy days in Hilo as in Syracuse?
October
3. In which city was the number of rainy days the same in August and in September?
Syracuse
4. Choose four rainy-day activities. Ask the girls and boys in your class which activity they like best. Record the data in a table. Use the table to make a double bar graph. ***Check graphs.***

Talk About It • Write About It

You learned that you can make a double bar graph to compare two sets of data.

5. For the same graph, how would the length of the bars change if the interval were changed from 2 to 4?
The bars would be half as long as they were with an interval of 2.
6. Is a double bar graph a good way to show how much a puppy grew from birth to age 6? Why or why not?
No; a double bar graph compares two sets of countable data.

3 Practice

On Your Own

- Select from **Problems 1–6** as independent work. Tell students to include a title, appropriate labels, sensible intervals, and a key.

4 Assess & Close

Math Talk in Action

Discuss the ***Talk About It • Write About It*** section. Point out that doubling the scale interval decreases the height of the bars by half and that halving the interval doubles bar heights. For **Problem 6,** elicit that changes over time could be shown on a single bar graph but are better shown on a line graph.

Math Journal Prompt

Have students write an explanation of what a double bar graph does and how it differs from a single bar graph.

Lesson Quiz

Use the quiz on Lesson Transparency 15.1.

Lesson 15.1 Transparency

Test Prep & Spiral Review

Use Test Prep Transparency 15.1.

Test Prep 15.1 Transparency

Enrichment 15.1

Name ______________________ Date __________ Enrichment 15.1

Getting to School

Tim surveyed the students in the fourth and fifth grades to see how the students travel to school. The clues below give information about the data Tim collected. Use the clues to complete the double bar graph.

Title of Graph: How Students Get to School

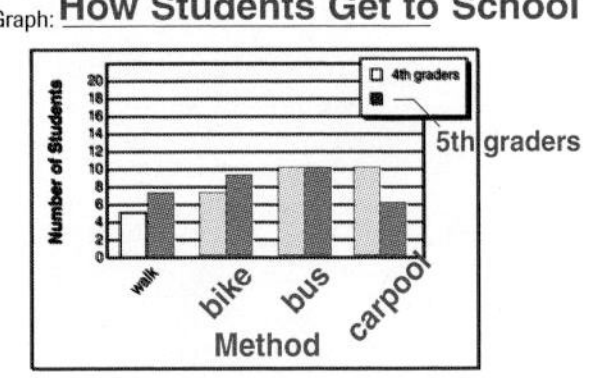

- The same number of fourth-graders ride a bus to school as carpool to school. This number is twice the number of fourth-graders who walk to school.
- Twelve students walk to school.
- The same number of fifth-graders and fourth-graders ride a bus to school.
- The number of fifth-graders that bike to school is 2 more than the number of fifth-graders that walk to school.
- Sixteen students carpool to school.
- The number of fourth-graders that bike to school is the same as the number of fifth-graders that walk to school.

Use the completed graph to answer each question.

1. How many students are in each grade?
There are 32 students in each grade.
2. How do most of the students get to school?
Most of the students ride a bus to school.

Use with text pages 376–377.

Problem Solving 15.1

Name ______________________ Date __________ Problem Solving 15.1

Double Bar Graphs

The table below lists four of the clubs at Mathville Middle School and the number of members in each club. Use the table for Problems 1–4.

1. Make two double bar graphs of the data in the table. Use an interval of 10 for one graph and an interval of 2 for the other graph.

Clubs at Mathville Middle School (Number of Members 0–40; Boys, Girls; Art, Science, Music, Sports; Club)

Clubs at Mathville Middle School (Number of Members 0–38; Boys, Girls; Art, Science, Music, Sports; Club)

2. How do the graphs look different when the interval is different?
When the interval is smaller, the bars on the graph are longer.
3. Which clubs have more girl members than boy members?
Science and sports
4. In which club are there 5 more boys than girls?
music club
5. **You Decide** Would a double bar graph be a good way to show how many fourth- and fifth-graders are in each club? Why or why not?
Yes; A double bar graph is used to compare two sets of data. You could have one bar represent fourth-graders and the other bar represent fifth-graders.

Clubs at Mathville Middle School		
Club	Number of Boys	Number of Girls
Art	25	21
Science	15	18
Music	37	32
Sports	28	30

Use with text pages 376–377.

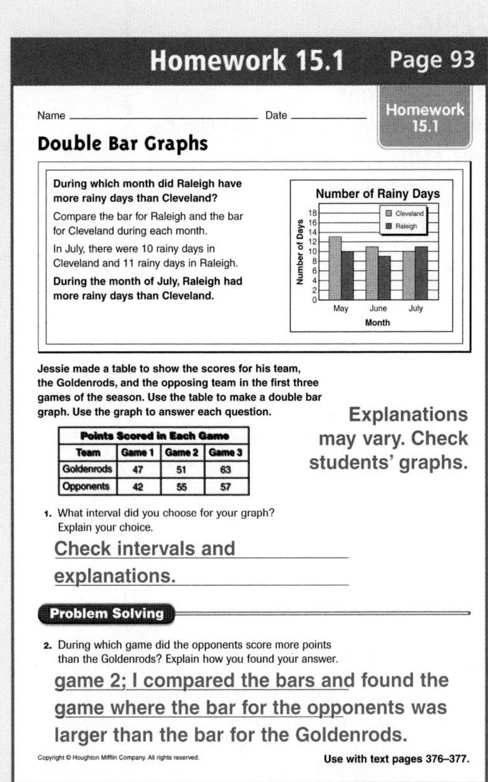

Homework 15.1 Page 93

Name ______________________ Date __________ Homework 15.1

Double Bar Graphs

During which month did Raleigh have more rainy days than Cleveland?

Compare the bar for Raleigh and the bar for Cleveland during each month.

In July, there were 10 rainy days in Cleveland and 11 rainy days in Raleigh.

During the month of July, Raleigh had more rainy days than Cleveland.

Number of Rainy Days (Number of Days 0–18; Cleveland, Raleigh; May, June, July; Month)

Jessie made a table to show the scores for his team, the Goldenrods, and the opposing team in the first three games of the season. Use the table to make a double bar graph. Use the graph to answer each question.

Explanations may vary. Check students' graphs.

Points Scored in Each Game			
Team	Game 1	Game 2	Game 3
Goldenrods	47	51	63
Opponents	42	55	57

1. What interval did you choose for your graph? Explain your choice.
Check intervals and explanations.

Problem Solving

2. During which game did the opponents score more points than the Goldenrods? Explain how you found your answer.
game 2; I compared the bars and found the game where the bar for the opponents was larger than the bar for the Goldenrods.

Use with text pages 376–377.

Lesson
15.2 Circle Graphs

Planning

Lesson Objective Use a circle graph to solve problems.

Technology Resources

- Audio Tutor 2/8 Listen and Understand
- *Ways to Success* CD-ROM 15.2
- Education Place: Extra Practice, eGlossary, Extra Help, eManipulatives, eGames www.eduplace.com/map

Lesson 15.2 Transparency

Problem of the Day

Suppose you had to choose between two plans for being paid for an 8-hour job. In Plan 1, you would be paid \$20 an hour. In Plan 2, you would be paid \$1 for the first hour, \$2 for the second hour, \$4 for the third, \$8 for the fourth, and so on. Which plan would you take? Why? (the doubling plan; $\$255 > \$160$)

Spiral Review

Solve. Write $>$, $<$, or $=$.

1. $\frac{1}{4}$ ● $\frac{1}{2}$ $(<)$

2. $\frac{1}{3}$ ● $\frac{1}{4}$ $(>)$

3. 3×20 ● $6 \times 5 \times 2$ $(=)$

4. 14 ● $\frac{1}{2}$ of 30 $(<)$

Lesson Quiz

Use the clouds circle graph on page 379 to answer the questions.

1. About how many days had cumulus clouds in February? (14)

2. About what fraction of the days had one kind of cloud or another? $(\frac{7}{8})$

NCTM Standards

Data Analysis and Probability:
Represent data using tables and graphs such as line plots, bar graphs, and line graphs.

Getting Started

Building Math Vocabulary

circle graph a graph that represents data as part of a circle

Use the vocabulary cards for ***circle graph.*** Talk about why a circle graph is called a *graph* sometimes and other times it is called a *pie chart*. Then ask them to tell where they have seen circle graphs used outside of the classroom.

Reviewing Fractions

Whole Class	10 minutes
Objective	Analyze information from graphs.
Materials	Fraction Circle Models
Visual, Tactual	

- Use fraction models (that use a circle as 1 whole) to review students' prior knowledge of fractions. Help students use the models to compare the common fractions: $\frac{1}{8}$, $\frac{1}{6}$, $\frac{1}{4}$, $\frac{1}{3}$, and $\frac{1}{2}$ to one another and to 1 whole. Guide them, for example, to model how many eighths, sixths, and fourths are equivalent to one half.
- Tell students that in this lesson they are going to explore how circle graphs show how parts of a whole compare to that whole and to one another.

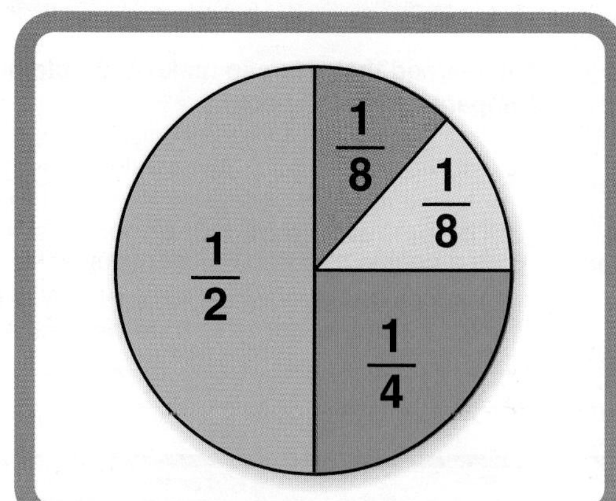

Differentiated Instruction

English Learners

Small Groups	10 minutes
Objective	Review fractions.
Materials	Student page 378, fraction tiles
Tactual, Visual	

Early Production

- Before ***Guided Practice,*** do the ***Intervention*** activity on this page to help students understand fraction vocabulary.
- Give students fraction tiles to help them solve the ***Guided Practice*** problems. Have them show the answer with the tiles and on paper.

Intermediate/Advanced

- English Learner Resource 15.2
- English Learner Handbook

Intervention

Small Groups	15 minutes
Objective	Model fractions.
Materials	None
Auditory, Visual	

- Guide students to understand the mathematical meaning of some common uses of fractions. For example, explain that to find half of a quantity means to divide that quantity by 2. **What is half of 10?** (5) **How many hours are in half a day?** (12)
- Ask similar questions to help students explore what it means to find a fourth of something (divide by 4), a third of something (divide by 3), and so on. **How many months are in a fourth of a year?** (3) Invite students to work with fraction models to demonstrate these computations.

Other Resources

- *Ways to Success* CD-ROM 15.2

Gifted & Talented

Individuals	20 minutes
Objective	Make a graph.
Materials	Compass, straightedge, crayons
Tactual, Visual	

- Challenge students to make a circle graph to show how a pet might spend its day.
- Suggest that they divide the pet's day into 5 or fewer activities, including sleep, which can take up half the day or more. Tell them to think of the day as having 24 hours.

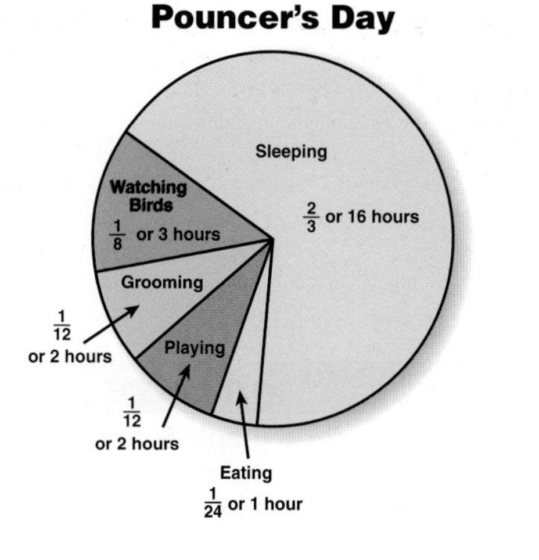

Literature Connection

Materials: *The Doorbell Rang* by Pat Hutchins

Two children are called upon to share cookies among an increasing number of people. By reading this tale, students explore the relationships among fractions like $\frac{1}{8}$, $\frac{1}{4}$, and $\frac{1}{2}$. They also investigate the idea of equivalency of fractions. Students can use fraction models to help them appreciate the concepts presented in this popular book.

❶ Introduce

Read the lesson objective aloud. Draw a sample circle graph on the chalk board. Ask students what kinds of food the graph makes them think of (pieces of pie, pizza, cheese, etc.).

❷ Teach

Learn About It

- Discuss the functionality of circle graphs. Point out how well they give a clear picture of parts of a whole.
- Focus students' attention on the *November Weather* graph. Guide them to understand that the graph represents all days in November.
- **If there are 30 days in November, about how many days were sunny?** (15) **How do you know?** (The sunny part is half the graph; $30 \div 2 = 15$.) **About how many were not sunny?** (15) **What fraction of the days in November had rain?** ($\frac{1}{4}$) **About how many days were rainy?** (7 or 8)

Guided Practice

Have students complete **Exercises 1–3** as you observe. Remind them to use the ***Ask Yourself*** questions to help. Give students the opportunity to talk about the question in ***Explain Your Thinking.***

Common Error

- **Misreading the circle graph** Some students may misinterpret the relative sizes of the parts that make up a circle graph.
- **Intervention** Emphasize that in a circle graph, whether it shows numbers or not, all the parts always add up to one whole. Point out that interpreting circle graphs involves visual estimation. Guide students to look first for the part easiest to understand visually, such as $\frac{1}{2}$, to figure out the sizes of the other parts. Provide students with practice comparing the sizes of common related fractions, such as $\frac{1}{8}$, $\frac{1}{4}$, and $\frac{1}{2}$.

Lesson 2

Audio Tutor 2/8 Listen and Understand

Circle Graphs

Objective Use a circle graph to solve problems.

Vocabulary
circle graph

Learn About It

Michael's class collected weather data for the month of November. The class made a circle graph to show their data. What fraction of November was sunny?

▶ A **circle graph** shows the parts that make up a whole. The circle on the right represents the whole month of November.

Each section of the circle represents the part of the month that was sunny, rainy, cloudy, or foggy. You can use a fraction to represent each part.

Find the section of the graph labeled *Sunny*. You can see that half the circle represents the part of November that was sunny.

Solution: In November, half the month was sunny.

Guided Practice

Use the circle graph above for Problems 1–3.

1. About what fraction of November was rainy? $\frac{1}{4}$
2. Were there more rainy days than foggy days during November? Explain how you know.
   Yes; the part of the circle for *Rainy* is greater than the part of the circle for *Foggy*.
3. Which types of weather are represented about equally in the graph? **foggy and cloudy**

Ask Yourself
- What does the circle represent?
- What do the circle's sections represent?

Explain Your Thinking ▶ If r represents the number of rainy days, what expression represents the number of sunny days?
The expression $2r$ represents the sunny days; the part of the circle graph representing *Sunny* is twice as great as the part representing *Rainy*.

Extra Help at **eduplace.com/map**

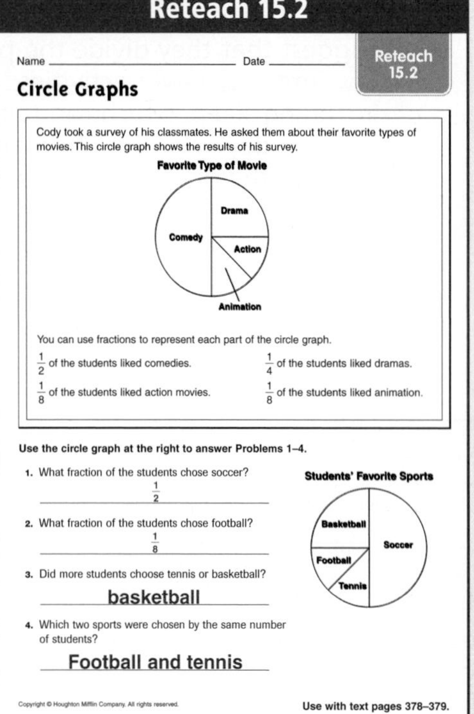

Reteach 15.2

Name ______ Date ______ Reteach 15.2

Circle Graphs

Cody took a survey of his classmates. He asked them about their favorite types of movies. This circle graph shows the results of his survey.

You can use fractions to represent each part of the circle graph.

$\frac{1}{2}$ of the students liked comedies. $\frac{1}{4}$ of the students liked dramas.

$\frac{1}{8}$ of the students liked action movies. $\frac{1}{8}$ of the students liked animation.

Use the circle graph at the right to answer Problems 1–4.

1. What fraction of the students chose soccer? $\frac{1}{2}$
2. What fraction of the students chose football? $\frac{1}{8}$
3. Did more students choose tennis or basketball? **basketball**
4. Which two sports were chosen by the same number of students? **Football and tennis**

Use with text pages 378–379.

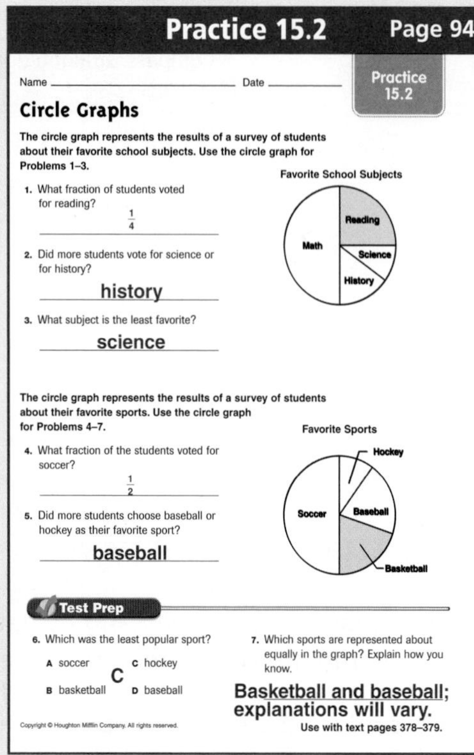

Practice 15.2 Page 94

Name ______ Date ______ Practice 15.2

Circle Graphs

The circle graph represents the results of a survey of students about their favorite school subjects. Use the circle graph for Problems 1–3.

1. What fraction of students voted for reading? $\frac{1}{4}$
2. Did more students vote for science or for history? **history**
3. What subject is the least favorite? **science**

The circle graph represents the results of a survey of students about their favorite sports. Use the circle graph for Problems 4–7.

4. What fraction of the students voted for soccer? $\frac{1}{2}$
5. Did more students choose baseball or hockey as their favorite sport? **baseball**

Test Prep

6. Which was the least popular sport?
   A soccer
   B basketball
   C hockey
   D baseball
   C
7. Which sports are represented about equally in the graph? Explain how you know.
   Basketball and baseball; explanations will vary.

Use with text pages 378–379.

Practice and Problem Solving

The circle graph represents the types of clouds Dianne saw in the sky each day in February. Use the circle graph for Problems 4–6.

4. What fraction of the days had cirrus clouds? $\frac{1}{4}$
5. Did Dianne see stratus clouds or cirrus clouds on more days during February? **cirrus**
6. What was the fraction of the month that the sky was clear of clouds? $\frac{1}{8}$
7. For a hike on a sunny day, Al packs 4 eight-packs and 3 six-packs of water. If 10 people go on the hike, how many bottles of water are there for each person? **5 bottles**
8. **Explain** Kate buys 5 books about the sky and stars. She pays a mean cost of \$10 per book. Trina buys 3 books with a mean cost of \$20. Does Kate or Trina spend more? **Trina**
9. **Create and Solve** Conduct a survey of 8 students. Record the answers in a circle graph. Write two questions that can be answered by using the graph. Have a classmate answer the questions. ***Check graphs and questions.***

Mixed Review and Test Prep

Open Response

Write the temperature that is 4° below the temperature shown. (Ch. 13, Lesson 4)

10. 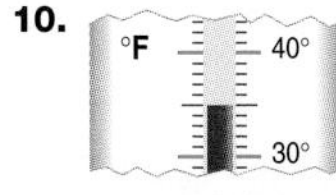

31°F

11. 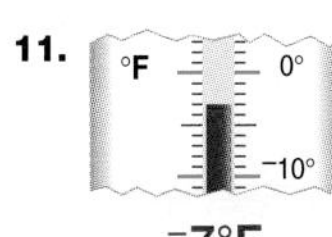

−7°F

12. 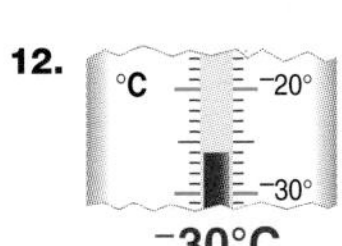

−30°C

13. 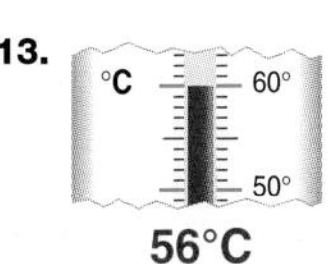

56°C

Multiple Choice

14. Which color is the favorite of $\frac{1}{4}$ of the class? (Ch. 15, Lesson 2)

Favorite Colors

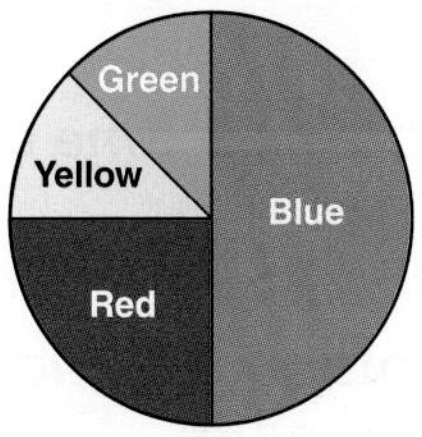

Green, Yellow, Blue, Red

(A) red **C** blue
B yellow **D** green

Extra Practice See page 389, Set A.

❸ Practice

Practice and Problem Solving

Select from **Problems 4–14** as independent work.

For **Problems 4–6,** have students use the circle graph of cloud cover provided. Suggest that students might like to observe the sky in your area for a week and make a similar graph. They can write word problems and exchange them with a classmate.

❹ Assess & Close

Math Talk in Action

Have students interpret data from circle graphs and explain their thinking.

Suppose someone constructed a circle graph containing this information: $\frac{1}{2}$ class likes math best; $\frac{1}{4}$ class likes reading best; $\frac{1}{2}$ class likes science best. **Why must this data be incorrect?** (Total is greater than 1 whole.)

Math Journal Prompt

Have students write an explanation of how a circle graph differs from a bar graph.

Lesson Quiz

Use the quiz on Lesson Transparency 15.2.

Test Prep & Spiral Review

Use Test Prep Transparency 15.2.

Test Prep 15.2 Transparency

Enrichment 15.2

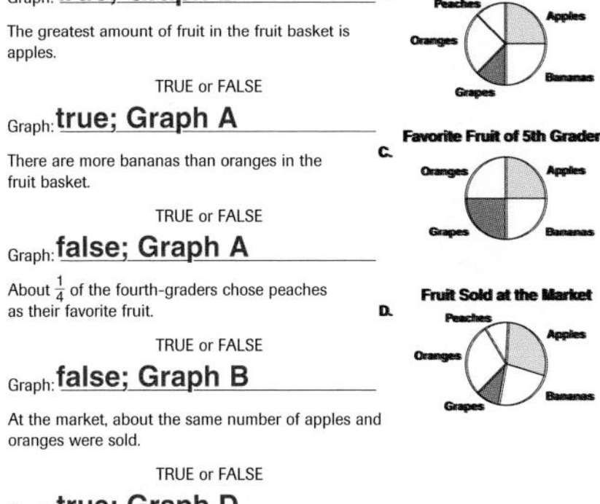

Name ______ Date ______ Enrichment 15.2

All in the Circles

Below are eight statements. Decide if the statement is true or false by looking at the circle graphs. Circle true or false. Write the letter of the circle graph that supports your answer.

1. The favorite fruit of fourth-graders is apples.
TRUE or FALSE
Graph: **false; Graph B**
2. The market sold more oranges than peaches.
TRUE or FALSE
Graph: **true; Graph D**
3. The greatest amount of fruit in the fruit basket is apples.
TRUE or FALSE
Graph: **true; Graph A**
4. There are more bananas than oranges in the fruit basket.
TRUE or FALSE
Graph: **false; Graph A**
5. About $\frac{1}{4}$ of the fourth-graders chose peaches as their favorite fruit.
TRUE or FALSE
Graph: **false; Graph B**
6. At the market, about the same number of apples and oranges were sold.
TRUE or FALSE
Graph: **true; Graph D**

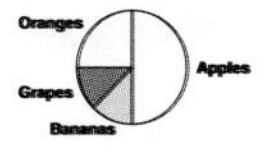

Use with text pages 378–379.

Problem Solving 15.2

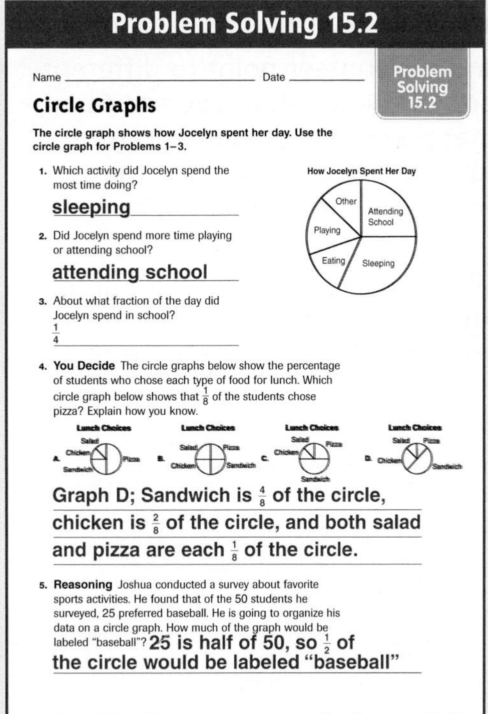

Name ______ Date ______ Problem Solving 15.2

Circle Graphs

The circle graph shows how Jocelyn spent her day. Use the circle graph for Problems 1–3.

1. Which activity did Jocelyn spend the most time doing? **sleeping**
2. Did Jocelyn spend more time playing or attending school? **attending school**
3. About what fraction of the day did Jocelyn spend in school? $\frac{1}{4}$
4. **You Decide** The circle graphs below show the percentage of students who chose each type of food for lunch. Which circle graph below shows that $\frac{1}{8}$ of the students chose pizza? Explain how you know.

Graph D; Sandwich is $\frac{4}{8}$ of the circle, chicken is $\frac{2}{8}$ of the circle, and both salad and pizza are each $\frac{1}{8}$ of the circle.

5. **Reasoning** Joshua conducted a survey about favorite sports activities. He found that of the 50 students he surveyed, 25 preferred baseball. He is going to organize his data on a circle graph. How much of the graph would be labeled "baseball"? **25 is half of 50, so $\frac{1}{2}$ of the circle would be labeled "baseball"**

Use with text pages 378–379.

Homework 15.2 Page 94

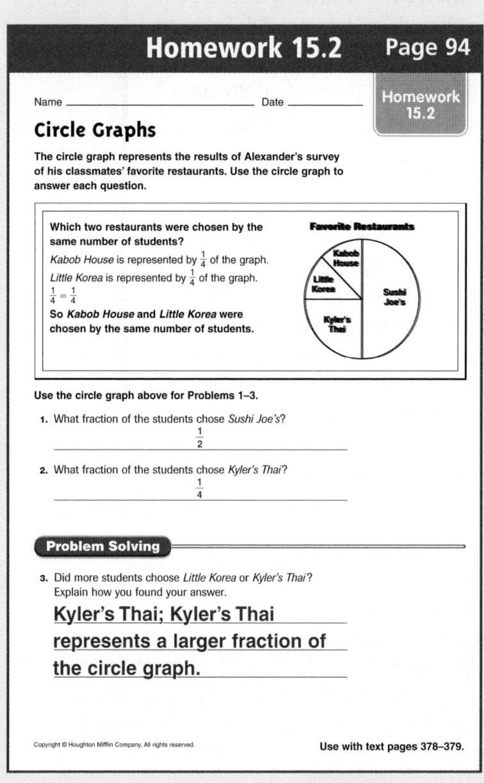

Name ______ Date ______ Homework 15.2

Circle Graphs

The circle graph represents the results of Alexander's survey of his classmates' favorite restaurants. Use the circle graph to answer each question.

Which two restaurants were chosen by the same number of students?

Kabob House is represented by $\frac{1}{4}$ of the graph.

Little Korea is represented by $\frac{1}{4}$ of the graph.

$\frac{1}{4} = \frac{1}{4}$

So *Kabob House* and *Little Korea* were chosen by the same number of students.

Use the circle graph above for Problems 1–3.

1. What fraction of the students chose *Sushi Joe's*? $\frac{1}{2}$
2. What fraction of the students chose *Kyler's Thai*? $\frac{1}{4}$

Problem Solving

3. Did more students choose *Little Korea* or *Kyler's Thai*? Explain how you found your answer. **Kyler's Thai; Kyler's Thai represents a larger fraction of the circle graph.**

Use with text pages 378–379.

Lesson 15.3

Problem-Solving Application: Interpret a Line Graph

Planning

Lesson Objective Get information from a graph even if it does not give exact information.

Math Background

A line graph is used to display continuous data and to show how data change over time. For example, the shape of a line graph can show how temperature increases and decreases during the day.

Technology Resources

- *Ways to Success* CD-ROM 15.3
- Education Place: Extra Practice, eGlossary, eGames
  www.eduplace.com/map

Lesson 15.3 Transparency

Problem of the Day

There was a parade of bicycles and tricycles. The crowd was so thick that Jackie could see only the wheels going by. At one point, she counted 23 wheels. Her taller friend was able to count the bicycles and tricycles. He counted a total of 10. How many were bicycles? How many were tricycles? (7; 3)

Spiral Review

A bar graph shows the following data about numbers of sunny days: January, 24; February, 16; March, 20; April, 22; and May, 28.

1. What is the mean number of sunny days for the months on the graph? (22)

Lesson Quiz

Use the graph on page 380.

1. Which point has the highest temperature? (E) the lowest temperature? (A and I)
2. What information would you need to find the average temperature for the hike? (the temperature at each point)

NCTM Standards

Data Analysis and Probability:
Represent data using tables and graphs such as line plots, bar graphs, and line graphs.

Getting Started

Building Math Vocabulary

line graph a graph that uses a line to show changes in data

Review the terms associated with a line graph: *vertical axis, horizontal axis, point, line,* and *interval.* Make a sketch on the board or overhead to help clarify the meanings of the terms by showing examples of each.

Parts of a Line Graph

Whole Class	15 minutes
Objective	Read and interpret a line graph.
Materials	Line-Graph Grid Transparency
Visual, Auditory	

- Label the horizontal axis *Time of Day* and the vertical axis *Temperature (°F).*
- Draw several points on the grid so that the temperature first increases, then decreases.
- Have a student volunteer connect the points in the graph.
- Explain that a line graph shows changes in data over time. Ask, **What does this graph show a change in over time?** (temperature)
- Have a volunteer point to different parts of the graph as you ask **At what point was the temperature highest? Lowest? Where is the temperature increasing? Where is it decreasing?**
- Tell students that the line graph on page 380 shows how the temperature changed over the course of a hike.

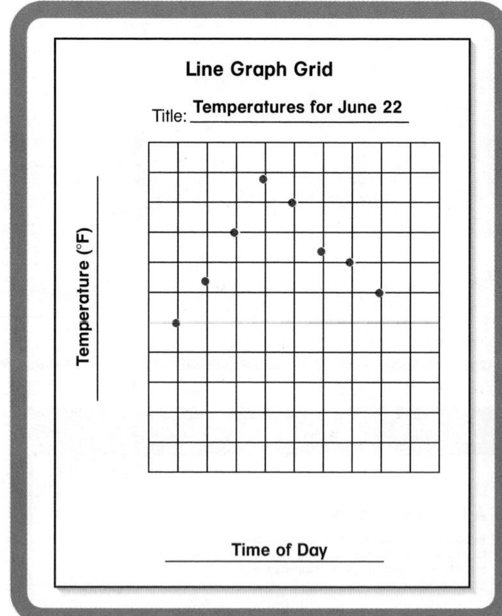

Differentiated Instruction

English Learners

Whole Class	15 minutes
Objective	Read and interpret a line graph.
Materials	Student page 381
Auditory, Visual	

Early Production

- For *Guided Practice*, give students additional *Ask Yourself* questions to help them understand the graph. **What does it mean when the line is going up? What does it mean when the line is going down? What do the letters on the line mean?**

Intermediate/Advanced

- English Learner Resource 15.3
- English Learner Handbook

Intervention

Whole Class	15 minutes
Objective	Read and interpret a line graph.
Materials	Student page 380
Auditory, Visual	

- Help students distinguish vertical lines from horizontal lines by helping them identify examples of each in the classroom.
- Then discuss questions about the graph on page 380, such as: **What do the horizontal lines show?** (temperature) **What do the vertical lines show?** (time)

Other Resources

- *Ways to Success* CD-ROM, Lesson 15.3

Early Finishers

Whole Class	15 minutes
Objective	Read and interpret a line graph.
Materials	Line-Graph Grid Transparency
Visual	

- On the transparency, show a line that rises at about a 45° angle from the origin, then goes flat and drops at an even steeper angle until it reaches the horizontal axis.
- Challenge students to write explanations for what this graph might be showing and tell why they think so. (Possible answer: a bathtub filling, being used and then emptying)

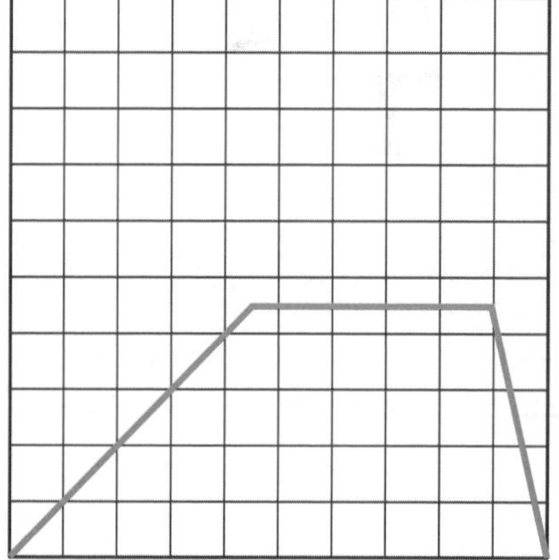

Social Studies Connection

Materials: Almanac

- Have students flip through an almanac to find data that shows change over time, such as population data, sports data, or weather data. Ask them to select data to use to draw a line graph. Have them provide a title but no numbers for their graph.
- Have students exchange graphs with a partner. Ask each to write a description of the changes in the data that the graph shows. Then ask partners to compare their descriptions.

Pattern Practice

Have each student draw a series of pictures that show amounts from least to greatest. For example, a circle that shows $\frac{1}{4}$, $\frac{1}{3}$, $\frac{1}{2}$, and $\frac{3}{4}$ shaded or baskets of apples that contain 2, 5, 7, and 10, apples. Have students separate the items in their pattern using scissors. Then, invite students to trade with others and put the pictures in the correct order.

❶ Introduce

Have a student volunteer read the lesson objective aloud. Write two sentences on the board: “It was 71 degrees at 6:30 A.M.” and “It was cool in the morning but hot by noon.” Ask students which one gives exact information about the temperature, and briefly discuss the differences between the statements.

❷ Teach

Interpret a Line Graph

- Discuss how the graph shows the temperatures at different times during the hike. **What does the graph *not* show about that information?** (exact times and temperatures)
- **Suppose you were to put in reasonable times and temperatures along each axis. What intervals might you use for time? for temperature?** (Possible answers: 1-hour time increments; 1 or 2-degree increments)
- **How would you summarize what the graph shows about temperatures during the hike?** (Possible answer: They rise fairly steeply, then stay about the same for a while, and then drop sharply.)

Guided Practice

Have students complete **Problems 1–2** as you observe. Remind them to use the *Ask Yourself* questions to help.

Common Error

- **Misreading intervals**
- **Intervention** Guide students to see that all horizontal lines are parallel to one another, as are all vertical lines. Show with a ruler that the distance between lines is always the same. Help them understand, therefore, that the difference in temperature from one line to the next is the same and that the difference in time between pairs of lines is the same as well.

Lesson 3

Problem-Solving Application

Interpret a Line Graph

Objective Get information from a graph even if it does not give exact information.

Vocabulary
line graph

Sometimes you can get information from a graph even though it does not have numbers or labels.

Jeff hiked on a trail in Great Smoky Mountains National Park with his dad. The **line graph** shows changes in temperature during the hike.

▶ **Use the line graph to understand how data change over time.**

The graph shows the temperature at different times during the hike.

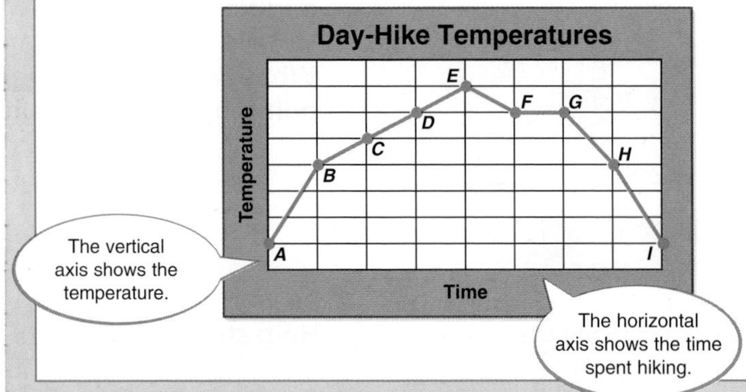

▶ **Use the line graph to compare data.**

- The line is flat between points *F* and *G*, which means the temperature did not go up or down. Time is passing, but the temperature is not changing.
- On the *Time* axis, there are more intervals between points *D* and *H* than between points *A* and *C*, so more time elapsed between points *D* and *H*.

Look Back Explain why the graph lines can't go straight up or down.
***Possible explanation:* A vertical line would represent different temperatures at exactly the same time, which is not possible.**

380

Reteach 15.3

Name ______________ Date ________

Reteach 15.3

Problem-Solving Application: Interpret a Line Graph

Read It Look for information.
Mr. O'Malley kept a record of the number of sandwiches sold one day at his shop. The line graph shows changes in the number of sandwiches sold.

Picture It Here is a line graph of Mr. O'Malley's data.

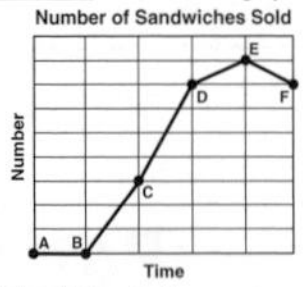

Look at each segment from left to right.
If it goes uphill, the quantity is increasing.
If it goes downhill, the quantity is decreasing.
If it is flat, the quantity is not changing.

Solve It Use the line graph.

1. What happened between points *A* and *B*? **There was no change in the number of sandwiches sold.**

Try These! Solve.

2. Explain what happened between points *B* and *E*.
Between points *B* and *E*, the number of sandwiches sold kept increasing. I can tell because the line graph is moving upwards.
3. Between which times were the most sandwiches sold? Explain how you know. ***C* and *D*; because the line increases the most between these points.**
4. Did more time pass between points *A* and *C* or between points *B* and *C*?
A* and *C

Use with text pages 380–381.

Practice 15.3 Page 95

Name ______________ Date ________

Practice 15.3

Problem-Solving Application: Interpret a Line Graph

The line graph represents the change in Dylan's savings during one year. Use the line graph for problems 1–4.

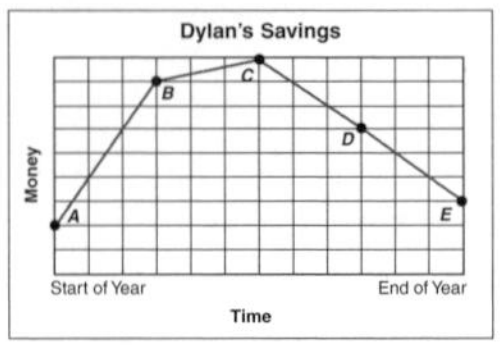

Show your work.

1. Did Dylan have more money saved at the start of the year or at the end of the year?
end of the year
2. Between which two consecutive points did the greatest change occur?
points *A* and *B*
3. Between which three points did the Dylan's savings decrease at a steady rate?
points *C, D,* and *E*
4. Was Dylan adding to his savings or spending his savings between points *D* and *E*? Tell how you know. **Dylan was spending his savings. Possible answer: Between D and E, the line is going down; therefore, Dylan's savings were getting smaller.**

Use with text pages 380–381.

Guided Practice

Ask Yourself
- How can I tell when the temperature is going up?
- How can I tell when time is passing?

Use the graph on Page 380 and the Ask Yourself questions to help you solve each problem.

1. Explain what happened between Point *A* and Point *B*. Tell how you know. ***See at right.***

   Hint: How are temperature and time related?

   1. The temperature was rising faster here than during the rest of the day because the graph indicates a greater increase in temperature between Point *A* and Point *B* than during any other similar time period.

2. Between which two points did the temperature drop the most? What explanation could there be?

   Between Point *H* and Point *I*. *Possible explanation:* The temperature usually goes down at the end of the day as the sun sets.

Independent Practice

Use the graph at the right for Problems 3–5.

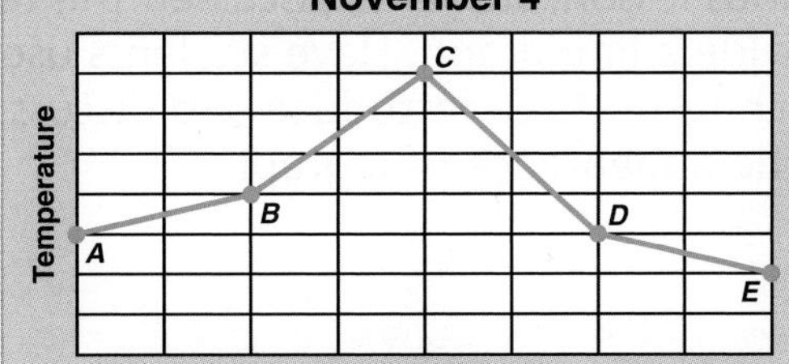

3. Was it colder at the start of the day or at the end of the day? **at the end of the day**
4. Between which two consecutive points did the greatest change occur? Can you tell how much the temperature changed during that time? Explain. **Between Points *C* and *D*; no; there is no scale on the vertical axis.**
5. Did more time pass between Point *A* and Point *B* or between Point *C* and Point *E*? **Between *C* and *E*; there are more intervals between those points.**

Use the graph at the right for Problems 6 and 7.

Climbing a Mountain

Height / Time — A, B, C, D, E, F, G, H, I

6. The graph shows the change in height during a climb and the time spent climbing. Which points show when the climbers probably stopped for lunch? **Points *C* and *D***
7. Explain what happened between Point *A* and Point *B*. Tell how you know. ***See Additional Answers.***
8. **Represent** Make a line graph without numbers. Show that the distance around a tree increases as the tree grows taller. **Check graphs; the line should increase from left to right.**

③ Practice

Independent Practice

Select from **Problems 3–8** as independent work.

- ***Problems 6–7*** Remind students that when the line moves upward from left to right, it shows an increase. When the line moves downward from left to right, it shows a decrease.

④ Assess & Close

Math Talk in Action

Have students interpret data from line graphs and explain their thinking.

Suppose you were making a line graph to show changes in a car's speed. How would your graph show the car braking?
(The line moves downward from left to right.)

Math Journal Prompt

Have students write an explanation of how a line graph shows various changes in data over time. Have them include a sketch of a line graph to demonstrate how the changes appear.

Lesson Quiz

Use the quiz on Lesson Transparency 15.3.

Lesson 15.3 Transparency

Test Prep & Spiral Review

Use Test Prep Transparency 15.3.

Test Prep 15.3 Transparency

Enrichment 15.3

Name ______ Date ______ Enrichment 15.3

Problem-Solving Application: Interpret a Line Graph

Mr. Tenalio works for a computer company. He tracked the sales of computers and recorded the data in this line graph. Use the graph to answer the questions.

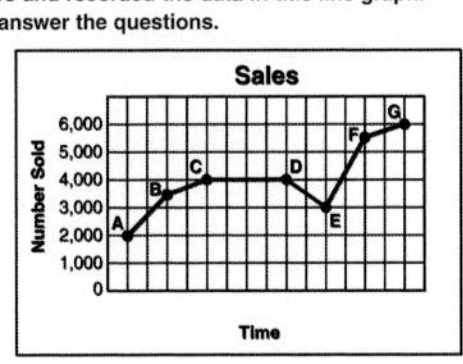

1. What is the graph comparing? Explain how you know. **sales and time; the axes are labeled "Time" and "Number Sold."**
2. At what point on the graph are sales the highest? The lowest? Explain how you know. **Highest: G; Lowest: A; the highest sales are at the highest point on the vertical axis.**
3. Were there any points at which the sales did not change? Explain. **Yes; between points C and D; this is shown by a flat line connecting the points.**
4. Write a statement summarizing how sales changed over time. Give possible reasons for the changing sales. ***Explanations may vary.*** **Sales increased, then leveled off. Sales decreased from point D to E, then increased again.**

 Use with text pages 380–381.

Problem Solving 15.3

Name ______ Date ______ Problem Solving 15.3

Problem-Solving Application: Interpret a Line Graph

Problem In Mrs. Gregory's science class, the students recorded the temperature throughout the day on Monday. The line graph shows the temperatures they recorded. Was it colder at the start of the day or at the end of the day?

Temperatures on Monday (Temperature / Time; A, B, C, D, E, F, G)

UNDERSTAND
1. What does the graph show you? **It shows the temperature at different times of the day.**

PLAN
2. How can you use the line graph to get the information you need? **Look for Point A and Point G on the line and decide which point has a lower temperature.**

SOLVE
3. Which temperature is lower, Point A or Point G? **Point A is lower.**
4. Was it colder at the start of the day or at the end of the day? **at the start of the day**

LOOK BACK
5. How can you be sure your answer is reasonable? ***Answers may vary.***

 Use with text pages 380–381.

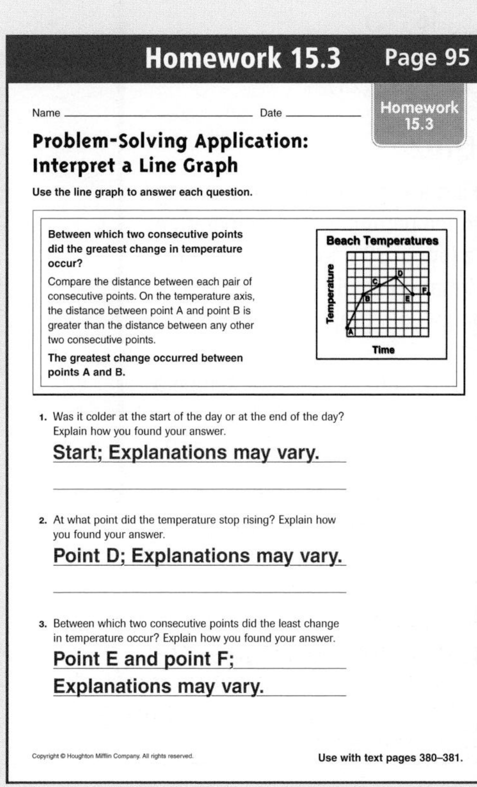

Homework 15.3 Page 95

Name ______ Date ______ Homework 15.3

Problem-Solving Application: Interpret a Line Graph

Use the line graph to answer each question.

Between which two consecutive points did the greatest change in temperature occur?
Compare the distance between each pair of consecutive points. On the temperature axis, the distance between point A and point B is greater than the distance between any other two consecutive points.
The greatest change occurred between points A and B.

1. Was it colder at the start of the day or at the end of the day? Explain how you found your answer. **Start; Explanations may vary.**
2. At what point did the temperature stop rising? Explain how you found your answer. **Point D; Explanations may vary.**
3. Between which two consecutive points did the least change in temperature occur? Explain how you found your answer. **Point E and point F; Explanations may vary.**

 Use with text pages 380–381.

Hands On Lesson 15.4

Read and Make Line Graphs

Planning

Lesson Objective Read and make a line graph.

Math Background

To make a line graph, students will label the horizontal and vertical axes and choose a numeric scale. They then use a data set to plot points on the grid. Last, they draw lines between the points.

Technology Resources

- Audio Tutor 2/9 Listen and Understand
- *Ways to Success* CD-ROM 15.4
- *Ways to Assess* CD-ROM

Lesson 15.4 Transparency

Problem of the Day

How many squares can you find in the figure? (13)

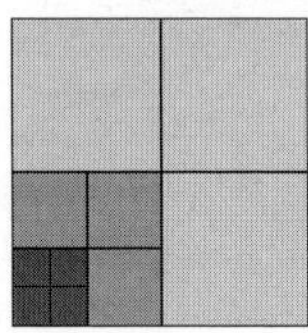

Spiral Review

Complete the pattern.

1. 3, 6, 9, ___, 15 (12)
2. 0, 4, 8, ___, 16 (12)
3. 2, 5, 9, 14, ___, 27 (20)
4. 1, 3, 7, 13, ___, 31 (21)

Lesson Quiz

You are making a line graph to show average monthly high temperatures. The temperatures range from a low of 30°F to a high of 75°F.

1. What information would you show along the bottom of your graph? (months of the year)

2. What intervals would you use for temperatures along the vertical scale? (Possible answer: 10-degree intervals from 0 to 80)

NCTM Standards

Data Analysis and Probability:
Represent data using tables and graphs such as line plots, bar graphs, and line graphs.

Getting Started

Building Math Vocabulary

line graph a graph that uses a line to show changes in data

In the previous lesson, students discussed the terms associated with line graphs. Provide a line graph. Have students use the graph to identify and describe each term. Then introduce and discuss what a scale is and how scales can affect the appearance of a graph.

Read a Line Graph

Whole Class	10 minutes
Objective	Read a line graph.
Materials	Line-Graph Grid Transparency (Learning Tool 21)
Visual, Auditory	

- On the overhead, draw a line graph showing the daily number of class absences over a 1-week period. Give it a title, label the axes, make a scale, and show the days of the week along the horizontal axis.
- Guide students to notice all the graph's features. Elicit why each is important. Then demonstrate how to read the graph by finding the day of the week and then moving up to find the line of the graph.
- Ask questions to check students' understanding of what the graph shows. For example: **How many pieces of data does the graph show?** (5) **How many students were absent on Wednesday?**
- Explain to students that their lesson discusses how line graphs can show changes in data over time.

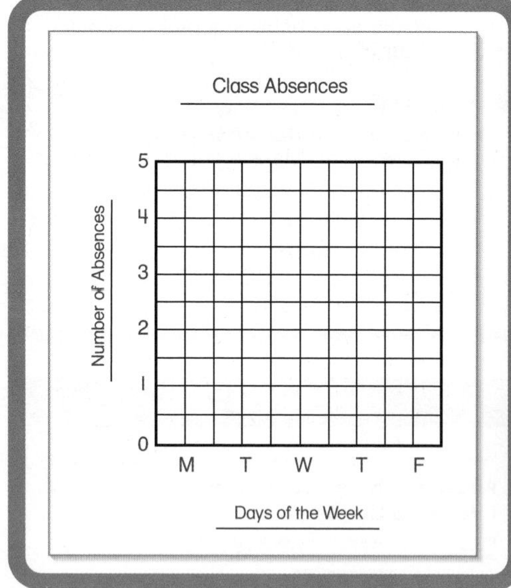

Differentiated Instruction

English Learners

Whole Class	10 minutes
Objective	Read a line graph.
Materials	Student page 382
Auditory, Visual	

Early Production

- Give students additional practice with vocabulary and reading a graph.
- Using the table on Student page 382, make a line graph with errors.

Ask students to tell what the errors are, where they are (e.g., vertical axis, title), and how to correct them.

Intermediate/Advanced

- English Learner Resource 15.4
- English Learner Handbook

Intervention

Whole Class	20 minutes
Objective	Make a line graph.
Materials	Line-Graph Grid Transparency, Workmat 6 or grid paper, straightedge
Auditory, Visual	

- On the overhead, sketch a line graph without numbers. Have students follow along on their workmats or graph paper. Plot points on the graph to show the line of the graph rising gradually from left to right.
- Ask students to explain what the graph shows. (rising values over time) Ask them to suggest data that might have a graph with this shape. Discuss their responses. Then ask them to suggest data for which the graph would have a different shape. Talk about those responses as well.

Other Resources

- *Ways to Success* CD-ROM 15.4

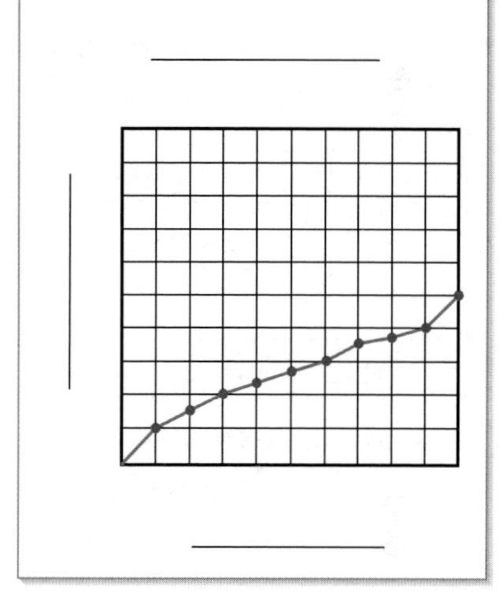

Early Finishers

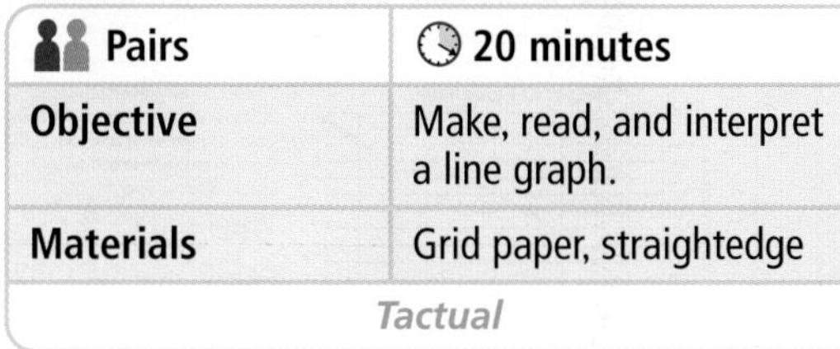

Pairs	20 minutes
Objective	Make, read, and interpret a line graph.
Materials	Grid paper, straightedge
Tactual	

- Invite students to create a table of data that changes with time.
- Have students swap tables with a partner.
- Using the tables, have students create line graphs.
- Have students talk about some of the decisions they made when creating their graphs, such as what intervals to use for the scale.
- Have students interpret their graphs, explaining any pattern or trends shown.

Science Connection

- Show how to find the pulse rate by counting the number of heart beats in 15 seconds and multiplying that number by 4 to get beats per minute.
- Have students investigate how exercise affects pulse rate. Have them pick an exercise that increases pulse rate, such as jumping jacks.
- Have students record their pulse at rest, do the exercise, and then record their pulse rate for different times after exercise. Help students graph their results. Discuss the graphs.

❶ Introduce

Invite a student volunteer to read the lesson objective aloud. Review with students the meanings of "horizontal" and "vertical".

❷ Teach

Learn About It

- **What pattern does the graph about snow depth show?** (Depth increases 2 inches per hour.) **What would it mean if the graph leveled and went in a horizontal direction after 4 hours?** (Possible answer: The snow stopped falling.)

Then focus on the 3-step process for making a line graph using data from a table. Have students construct their graphs on graph paper and use a straightedge to make the segments that connect the points on the graph.

Guided Practice

Have students complete **Problems 1–3** as you observe. Remind them to use the *Ask Yourself* question to help. Give students the opportunity to talk about the questions in *Explain Your Thinking*.

❸ Practice

Practice and Problem Solving

Select from **Problems 4–7** as independent work.

- For **Problem 4,** guide students to start the intervals on the vertical scale at 0.
- ***Problem 6*** Students are likely to suggest that the temperature will be lower because temperatures have been dropping since Thursday, but weather patterns change. (Accept reasonable answers.)

Common Error

- **Choosing incorrect intervals**
- **Intervention** Guide students to choose an interval for their scale that makes sense based on the numbers in the table. Have them consider the range of the numbers in the data to make that decision. Remind them to start the scale at 0.

Audio Tutor 2/9 Listen and Understand

Read and Make Line Graphs

Objective Read and make a line graph.

Vocabulary
line graph

Materials
Grid Paper
(Learning Tool 21)

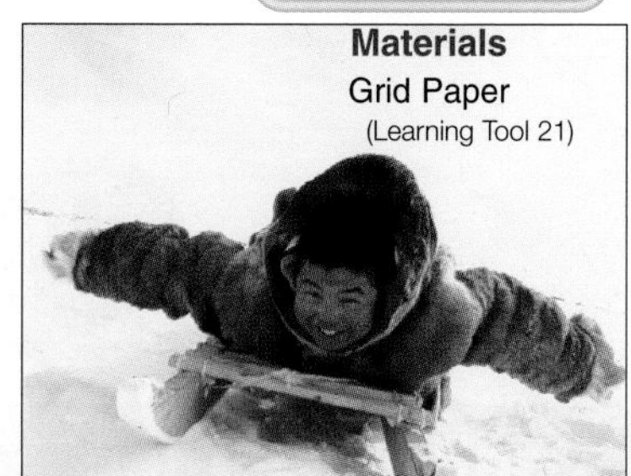

Learn About It

You can use a **line graph** to show how data change over time. This line graph shows how much snow fell in 4 hours. How deep was the snow after 2 hours?

To find the depth of the snow after 2 hours,

- Find 2 on the axis labeled *Hours*.
- Move up to the line of the graph.
- Move left to the axis labeled *Depth*. Read the depth in inches.

Depth of Snow

Depth (inches): 0, 1, 2, 3, 4, 5, 6, 7, 8, 9, 10

Hours: 1, 2, 3, 4

The vertical axis represents depth in inches.

The horizontal axis represents time in hours.

Solution: After 2 hours, the snow was 4 inches deep.

Try this activity to make a line graph.

STEP 1 Use the table to make a line graph. Write a title and labels. Then choose a scale to show the icicle lengths.
See Additional Answers.

STEP 2 Show 24 inches for Monday.
- Locate Monday on the horizontal axis.
- Move up to 24 inches on the vertical axis.
- Place a point where both lines meet.

STEP 3 Continue placing points, then connect them.

Icicle Lengths

Day	Length
Monday	24 inches
Tuesday	20 inches
Wednesday	12 inches
Thursday	16 inches
Friday	20 inches

382

Extra Practice, See page 389, Set B.

Reteach 15.4

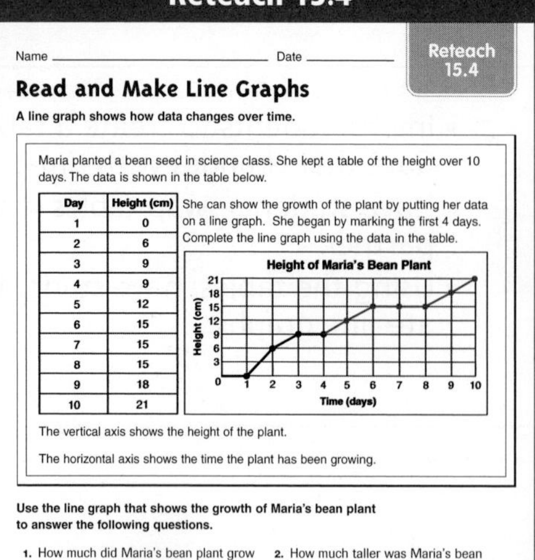

Name ____________ Date ________ Reteach 15.4

Read and Make Line Graphs

A line graph shows how data changes over time.

Maria planted a bean seed in science class. She kept a table of the height over 10 days. The data is shown in the table below.

Day	Height (cm)
1	0
2	6
3	9
4	9
5	12
6	15
7	15
8	15
9	18
10	21

She can show the growth of the plant by putting her data on a line graph. She began by marking the first 4 days. Complete the line graph using the data in the table.

The vertical axis shows the height of the plant.

The horizontal axis shows the time the plant has been growing.

Use the line graph that shows the growth of Maria's bean plant to answer the following questions.

1. How much did Maria's bean plant grow between day 2 and day 3? 3 cm
2. How much taller was Maria's bean plant on day 7 than on day 6? 0 cm
3. Between what two days did the bean plant grow the most quickly? Day 1 and Day 2
4. How much did the bean plant grow between day 8 and day 10? 6 cm
5. By day 5, how tall was Maria's bean plant? 12 cm
6. How many days did it take for the bean plant to grow from 12 cm to 18 cm? 4 days

Use with text pages 382–383.

Practice 15.4 Page 96

Name ____________ Date ________ Practice 15.4

Read and Make Line Graphs

The graph below shows the height of a ficus tree. Use the graph to answer Problem 1.

Height of Ficus Tree

Height (inches): 0, 16, 18, 20, 22, 24, 26, 28, 30, 32, 34, 36, 38, 40

Time (weeks): 0, 1, 2, 3, 4, 5, 6, 7, 8, 9, 10

1. The ficus tree grew more slowly for 2 weeks when it didn't receive any water. During what 2 weeks did the tree not receive any water? Explain your answer. Weeks 6 to 8; explanations may vary.

2. The table at the right shows how many people rented videos from Popcorn Video for each day of the week. Use the table to make a line graph on a separate sheet of paper. Check students' line graphs

Popcorn Video

Day	Videos Rented
Monday	128
Tuesday	102
Wednesday	155
Thursday	128
Friday	180
Saturday	195
Sunday	148

Use your line graph to answer Problems 3–5.

3. What happened to the number of videos rented from Thursday to Saturday? increased each day

Test Prep

4. On which two days did Popcorn Video rent the same number of videos? D
   - A Monday and Sunday
   - B Tuesday and Friday
   - C Wednesday and Saturday
   - D Thursday and Monday
5. How many more videos did Popcorn Video rent on its busiest day than on its slowest day? 93

Use with text pages 382–383.

Guided Practice

Use the *Depth of Snow* graph on Page 382 for Problems 1–3.

1. What was the depth of snow after 3 hours?
   6 inches
2. About what is the depth of snow after $2\frac{1}{2}$ hours?
   about 5 inches
3. The graph line goes up from left to right. Could the direction of the line ever change? Explain. **Yes; *Possible explanation:* The snow stops falling, or the snow starts melting.**

> **Ask Yourself**
> - What do the numbers on the side and bottom of the graph represent?

Explain Your Thinking ▶ What is the pattern on the Depth of Snow graph? If the pattern continues, what will the depth of the snow be after 5 hours? ***Possible answer:* Since the snow is accumulating 2 inches per hour, there are likely to be 10 inches after 5 hours.**

Practice and Problem Solving

4. Use the table at the right to make a line graph. Then use your line graph for Problems 5–7.
   See Additional Answers.
5. What happened to the temperatures from Thursday through Sunday?
   They decreased 15°.
6. **Predict** Would you expect the high temperature on the day after Sunday to be 20°F, 60°F, or 90°F? Explain your answer.
   See Additional Answers.
7. What is the range of the temperatures on your graph? **20°**

Daily High Temperatures

Day	Temperature
Monday	40°F
Tuesday	45°F
Wednesday	30°F
Thursday	40°F
Friday	35°F
Saturday	30°F
Sunday	25°F

Quick Check

Check your understanding for Lessons 1–4.

Use the graphs for Problems 1 and 2. (Lessons 1, 3, 4)

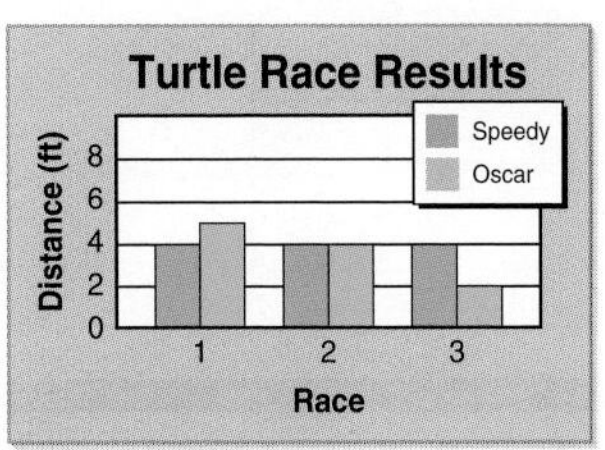

1. How far did Oscar travel in the race he won? **5 ft**

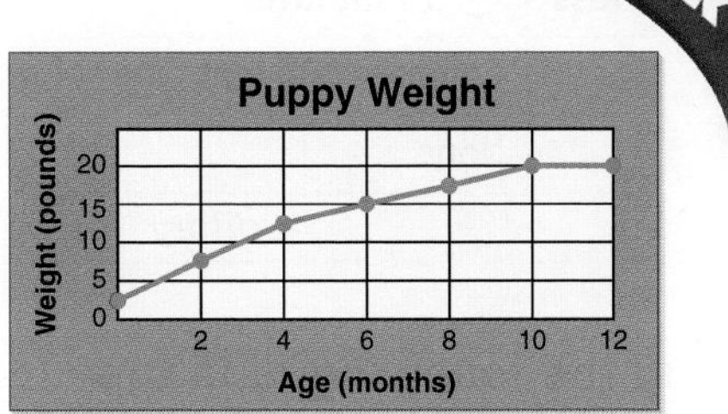

2. How much weight did the puppy gain between 6 months and 1 year?
   5 pounds

Extra Practice at **eduplace.com/map**

4 Assess & Close

Math Talk in Action

Have students discuss the different ways line graphs can be interpreted:

- What can you tell about a line graph without looking at the exact information? Give examples. (Accept all reasonable answers)

Math Journal Prompt

Have students explain how a line graph can help interpret data from a table.

Lesson Quiz

Use the quiz on Lesson Transparency 15.4.

Test Prep & Spiral Review

Use Test Prep Transparency 15.4.

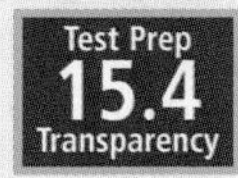

Quick Check

Have students complete the *Quick Check* independently to assess their understanding of skills taught in Lessons 1–4.

Items	Objectives Tested	Pages	Intervention
1–2	Read line graphs and double bar graphs.	376–377, 380–383	Reteach Resources 15.1, 15.3, 15.4 *Ways to Success* CD-ROM 15.1, 15.3, 15.4

Enrichment 15.4

Name ______________ Date ________

Enrichment 15.4

Leaks and Lines

Miss Doherty's classroom sink leaks. The students decided to graph the amount of water leaking from the faucets. Miguel graphed the amount of water leaking from the hot water faucet. Kara graphed the amount of water leaking from the cold water faucet. Use the line graphs to answer the questions.

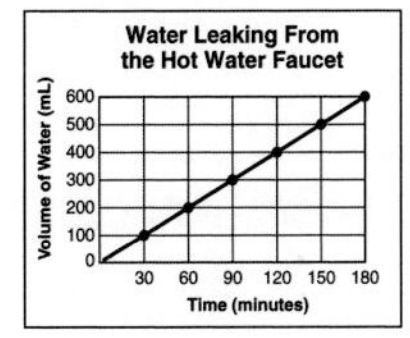

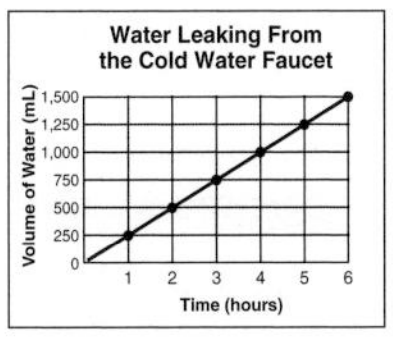

Water Leaking From the Hot Water Faucet — Volume of Water (mL): 0, 100, 200, 300, 400, 500, 600; Time (minutes): 30, 60, 90, 120, 150, 180

Water Leaking From the Cold Water Faucet — Volume of Water (mL): 0, 250, 500, 750, 1,000, 1,250, 1,500; Time (hours): 1, 2, 3, 4, 5, 6

1. What are the similarities and differences in the graphs that Kara and Miguel made?
   Both show the amount of water that leaked over time. Miguel graphed mL of water in minutes. Kara graphed mL of water in hours.
2. Which faucet is leaking more quickly? Explain how you found your answer.
   The cold water faucet; it is leaking 250 mL per hour. The hot water faucet is leaking 200 mL per hour.
3. **Predict** At this rate, how much water will have leaked from both faucets in 24 hours?
   The water is leaking at a rate of 450 mL per hour. So, in a day, 450 × 24 = 10,800 mL of water will have leaked out.

Use with text pages 382–383.

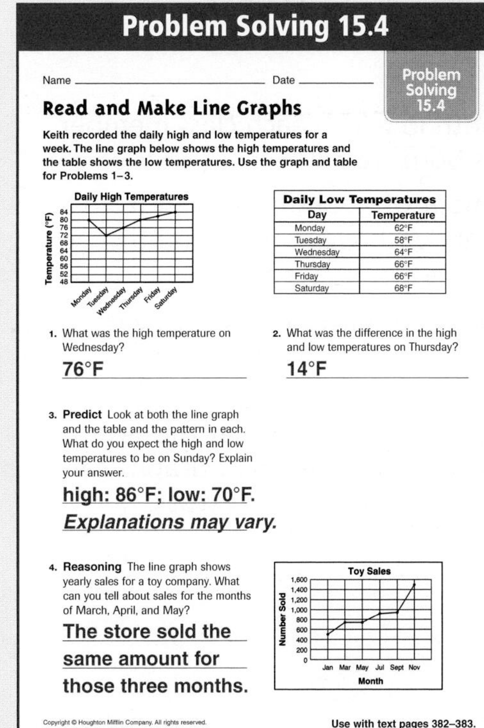

Problem Solving 15.4

Name ______________ Date ________

Problem Solving 15.4

Read and Make Line Graphs

Keith recorded the daily high and low temperatures for a week. The line graph below shows the high temperatures and the table shows the low temperatures. Use the graph and table for Problems 1–3.

Daily High Temperatures — Temperature (°F): 48, 52, 56, 60, 64, 68, 72, 76, 80, 84; Monday, Tuesday, Wednesday, Thursday, Friday, Saturday

Daily Low Temperatures

Day	Temperature
Monday	62°F
Tuesday	58°F
Wednesday	64°F
Thursday	66°F
Friday	66°F
Saturday	68°F

1. What was the high temperature on Wednesday?
   76°F
2. What was the difference in the high and low temperatures on Thursday?
   14°F
3. **Predict** Look at both the line graph and the table and the pattern in each. What do you expect the high and low temperatures to be on Sunday? Explain your answer.
   high: 86°F; low: 70°F. *Explanations may vary.*
4. **Reasoning** The line graph shows yearly sales for a toy company. What can you tell about sales for the months of March, April, and May?
   The store sold the same amount for those three months.

Toy Sales — Number Sold: 0, 200, 400, 600, 800, 1,000, 1,200, 1,400, 1,600; Month: Jan, Mar, May, Jul, Sept, Nov

Use with text pages 382–383.

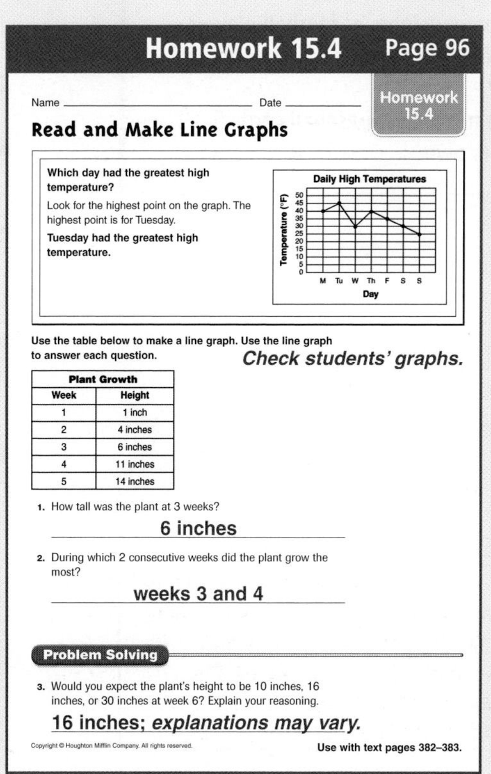

Homework 15.4 Page 96

Name ______________ Date ________

Homework 15.4

Read and Make Line Graphs

Which day had the greatest high temperature?

Look for the highest point on the graph. The highest point is for Tuesday.

Tuesday had the greatest high temperature.

Daily High Temperatures — Temperature (°F): 0, 5, 10, 15, 20, 25, 30, 35, 40, 45, 50; Day: M, Tu, W, Th, F, S, S

Use the table below to make a line graph. Use the line graph to answer each question. ***Check students' graphs.***

Plant Growth

Week	Height
1	1 inch
2	4 inches
3	6 inches
4	11 inches
5	14 inches

1. How tall was the plant at 3 weeks?
   6 inches
2. During which 2 consecutive weeks did the plant grow the most?
   weeks 3 and 4

Problem Solving

3. Would you expect the plant's height to be 10 inches, 16 inches, or 30 inches at week 6? Explain your reasoning.
   16 inches; *explanations may vary.*

Use with text pages 382–383.

Hands On Lesson 15.5

Analyze Graphs

Planning

Lesson Objective Use graphs to display different types of data.

Technology Resources

- *Ways to Success* CD-ROM 15.5
- Education Place: Extra Practice, eGames www.eduplace.com/map

Lesson 15.5 Transparency

Problem of the Day

An egg dropped 6 feet and did not break. How could that be? Give as many reasonable explanations as you can. (Possible answers: The egg was dropped into water, or the egg was hard-boiled.)

Spiral Review

Add or subtract. Use mental math.

1. 98 + 66 (164)
2. 83 + 45 + 17 (145)
3. 101 − 37 (64)
4. 135 − 39 + 4 (100)

Lesson Quiz

Choose a graph to display the data. Write *bar graph, circle graph, line graph, or pictograph.* (Answers will vary. Have students explain their choices.)

1. to show snowfall for a week
2. to compare weights of football players
3. to show how a school spends its yearly budget
4. to show how many baseball cards 5 collectors own

NCTM Standards

Data Analysis and Probability:
Represent data using tables and graphs such as line plots, bar graphs, and line graphs; compare different representations of the same data and evaluate how well each representation shows important aspects of the data.

Getting Started

Building Math Vocabulary

You may wish to review these words with students.

line graph a graph that uses a line to show changes in data

bar graph a graph in which information is shown by means of rectangular bars

circle graph a graph that represents data as part of a circle

pictograph a graph in which information is shown by means of pictures or symbols

Choosing an Appropriate Graph

Whole Class	15 minutes
Objective	Compare different types of graphs.
Materials	None
Auditory	

- Read aloud the following data topics to students. Ask them to choose the graph they would use to display each. Then discuss students' answers.
- temperature each hour for a day (Possible answer: line graph)
- number of each kind of pet in a store (Possible answers: bar graph or pictograph)
- month in which each class member was born (Possible answer: circle graph)
- number of books borrowed from a library each week for a month (Possible answer: bar graph)
- number of girls vs. boys in your class who play checkers (Possible answer: bar graph)
- Explain to students that this lesson discusses how different graphs can show data in different ways.

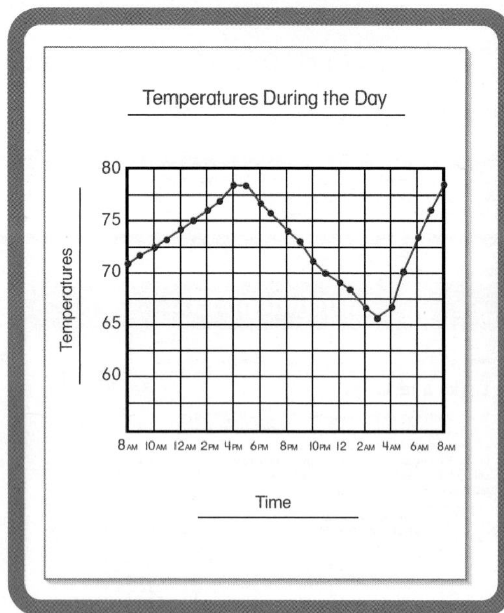

Differentiated Instruction

English Learners

Pairs	15 minutes
Objective	Compare different types of graphs.
Materials	Student pages 384 and 385, index cards
Auditory, Visual	

Early Production

- Provide practice identifying different graphs and their uses.
- Write situations on index cards that can be grap hed. Give pairs of students a card, and ask them to discuss the type of graph they would make and why.
- Rotate the cards among pairs.

Intermediate/Advanced

- English Learner Resource 15.5
- English Learner Handbook

Intervention

Small Groups	10 minutes
Objective	Analyze information from graphs.
Materials	None
Auditory, Visual	

- Help students understand the distinction between a scale for a bar graph or line graph and a key for a pictograph.
- Guide students to understand that the key is a picture of the symbol used in the graph and that it shows the value of one of those symbols. Compare keys for a pictograph with keys for a map—both show what the symbols that are used mean.
- **If a key shows that a circle represents $2, what would 3 circles on the pictograph mean?** ($6) **What would a half-circle mean?** ($1)

Other Resources

- *Ways to Success* CD-ROM 15.5

Cost of Fair Rides

Ferris Wheel	● ● ● ◖
Swings	● ◖
House of Mirrors	◖
Carousel	● ● ●

Each ● = $2 ticket

Early Finishers

Whole Class	20 minutes
Objective	Compare and analyze different types of graphs.
Materials	Newspapers and magazines
Visual, Auditory	

- Show students a variety of bar graphs, line graphs, circle graphs, and pictographs from newspapers and magazines.
- Ask them to identify and describe each one. Then provide the magazines to the group.
- Have students find and describe other examples of these four kinds of graphs.

Alternate Teaching Strategy

- Have students work in small groups of 3 to 4.
- Have each group write a short story based on the situations in the ***Practice and Problem Solving*** section of their book.
- Make sure the stories include specific, numeric information.
- Have groups trade stories. Then, have each group create a graph that displays the information in the story.
- Have each group present their graph to the class while a volunteer reads the story. Have the groups discuss what type of graph they used and why.

1 Introduce

Invite a student to read the lesson objective aloud. Have students recall the types of data they graphed so far in this chapter, and the types of graphs used to display the data. Make a list of these on the board.

2 Teach

Learn About It

Emphasize the importance of carefully reading titles and labels when interpreting graphs.

- For the line graph, guide students to appreciate that every point has meaning and that points are connected by line segments. Review and discuss the meaning of changes in the slope of a line. **What is the hottest time of the day in Death Valley?** (3:00 P.M.)
- For the bar graph, point out that bars can be either horizontal or vertical and that the height or length of a bar is determined by the data it represents. Discuss the location of the scale, relating it to the direction of the bars. **What is the difference in length between the longest and shortest hikes?** ($5\frac{1}{2}$ miles)

Common Error

- **Choosing the wrong graph** Some students may select the wrong type of graph to display the data.
- **Intervention** Have students work in pairs or small groups to review and discuss the different strengths of the four graphs. Provide additional examples of each in which its effectiveness for showing the data can be readily appreciated.

Hands On Lesson 5

Analyze Graphs

Objective Use graphs to display different types of data.

Materials
Grid Paper
(Learning Tools 19, 20, and 21)

Learn About It

Brian is doing a report on Death Valley, one of the hottest places in the world. These graphs show data about Death Valley in different ways.

On July 10, 1913, a high temperature of 134°F was recorded at Greenland Ranch in California's Death Valley.

▶ A **line graph** is a good way to show change over time.

- About how hot is it at 9:00 A.M.? How do you know? **about 90°**
- Between which two times does the temperature increase about 20°? **between 12:00 noon and 3:00 P.M.**

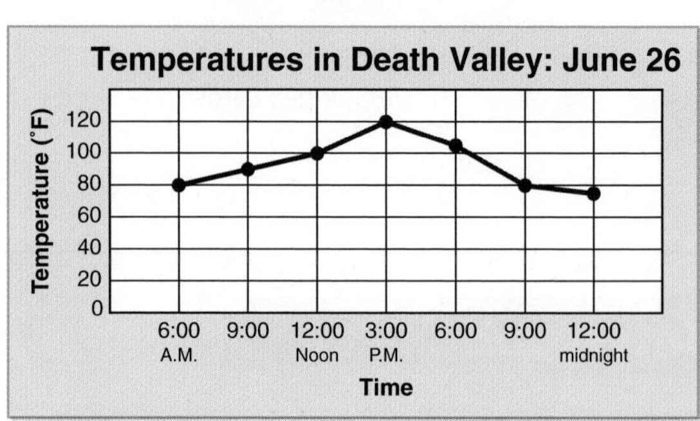

▶ A **bar graph** lets you compare data.

- Which hiking area is about $5\frac{1}{2}$ miles one way? **Badwater Salt Flat**
- Which area is about 3 miles longer than Dante's Ridge? **Telescope Peak**

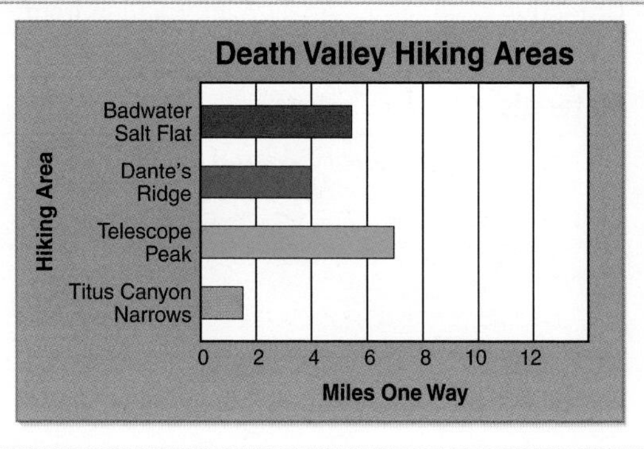

384

Reteach 15.5

Name ______________ Date ________ Reteach 15.5

Analyze Graphs

Different graphs work well to display different types of data.

Type of Graph	Bar Graph	Circle Graph	Line Graph	Pictograph
Example	Favorite Color (Number of Votes; Red, Blue, Green; Color)	Favorite Lunches (Peanut Butter, Hot Dog, Pizza, Grilled Cheese)	Plant Growth (Height (cm); Time (days))	After School Sports (Soccer, Baseball, Swimming, Tennis; ☺ = 4 People)
What it shows	This bar graph shows the number of votes for a favorite color so you can compare quantities.	This circle graph shows votes for favorite lunch so you can see what part of all the votes each choice received.	This line graph shows a plant's growth over 8 days so you can see how the plant grew from day to day.	This pictograph shows the people who participate in after school sports so you can compare quantities.
Uses	Good choice to compare data; uses a scale.	Good choice for comparing parts of a whole.	Good choice to show a change over time.	Good choice to compare data; uses pictures.

Choose a graph to display the data. Write *bar graph, circle graph, line graph,* or *pictograph.* Explain your choice. **Explanations may vary.**

1. rainfall for the month **line graph**
2. number of books read by students each month **bar or pictograph**
3. compare the height of three plants **bar or pictograph**
4. show how time during a school day is spent **circle graph**
5. compare the costs of renting bikes for a day **bar or pictograph**
6. growth of one plant for a week **line graph**

Use with text pages 384–386.

Practice 15.5 Page 97

Name ______________ Date ________ Practice 15.5

Analyze Graphs

Choose a graph to display the data for Problems 1-10. Write *bar graph, circle graph, line graph,* or *pictograph.* **Answers may vary.**

1. the results of a survey of students' favorite activities **circle graph**
2. the number of people who visit the park each month **line graph**
3. a comparison of the finish times of two different runners **bar graph**
4. the number of miles bicycled during the summer by 5 different cyclists **bar graph**
5. the parts of the school day spent in class, studying, eating lunch, and doing homework **circle graph**
6. the results of a survey about how students travel to school **circle graph**
7. the number of school days for each month of the year **bar graph**
8. snowfall for a week **line graph**
9. a poll of townspeople's favorite seasons **circle graph**
10. the number of CDs each member of your family owns **bar graph**

Test Prep

11. Which type of graph would be best to display the results of a survey of students that were asked if they had any pets? **B**
    A bar graph
    B circle graph
    C line graph
    D pictograph
12. Which type of graph would be best to display the change in weight of a growing baby during its first 12 months? Explain. **Line graph; explanations will vary.**

Use with text pages 384–386.

A **circle graph** shows the parts of a whole. It is a good choice for showing a budget.

- Which item will use about half the vacation budget? **Food and Water**
- Which budget item will cost about the same amount as a car rental? **Other**

Vacation Budget

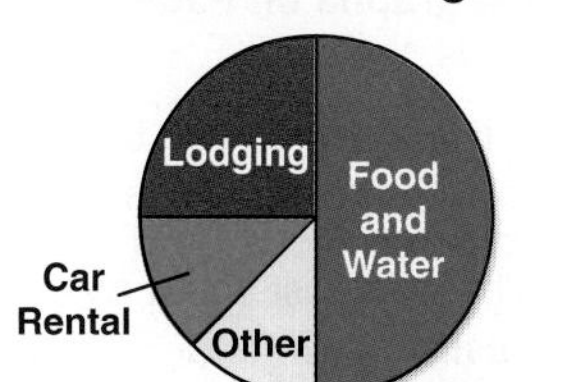

A **pictograph** uses a key instead of a scale. The pictograph shows the results of a survey that asked students to vote on the best month to visit Death Valley.

- Which month got the most votes? **April**
- What does the symbol ☀ stand for? **1 vote**

Best Month to Visit Death Valley	
March	☀ ☀
April	☀ ☀ ☀ ☀ ☀
May	☀ ☀ ½☀
June	☀ ☀
July	☀

Each ☀ = 2 votes.

Make a graph to analyze the results of a survey.

STEP 1 Choose a survey question like the one shown on the right. Then conduct a survey and record the data.

- How many students did you survey? ***Answers may vary.***

STEP 2 Make a graph to display the data you collected.

- Why did you choose the type of graph you did? ***See below.***

STEP 3 Write two questions about the data that can be answered using your graph. ***Questions may vary.***

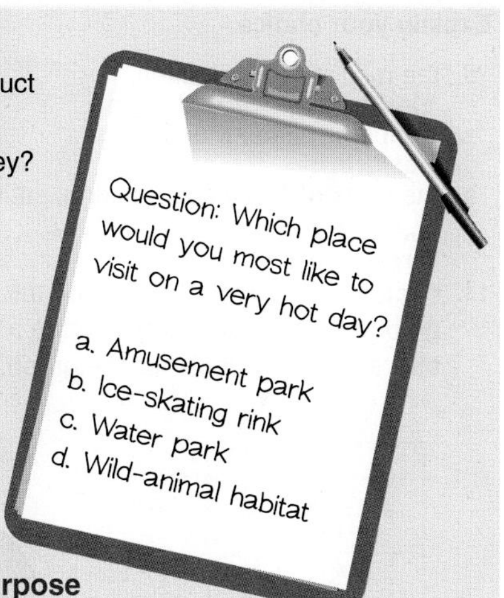

Question: Which place would you most like to visit on a very hot day?
a. Amusement park
b. Ice-skating rink
c. Water park
d. Wild-animal habitat

Step 2: Explanations may include the purpose of the graph and the ease of making the graph.

- For the circle graph, guide students to see that the interior is divided into regions that show parts of the whole—the larger the region, the greater the part. **Which item makes up about a fourth of the family's trip budget?** (lodging)
- For the pictograph, focus on the importance of the key. Guide students to first look for the key to see what the symbol represents. **Which two months got the same number of votes?** (March and June)

Enrichment 15.5

Name ______________ Date __________

Enrichment 15.5

Toy Meeting

You are an employee of *Toys, Toys, and More Toys.* You have a big meeting coming up and your boss has asked you to gather together all the information about toy sales this past year and present it to your coworkers. You have decided to show the information in graphs. Below are some statements about the data. Make a graph on a separate sheet of paper to support each statement.

1. Toy sales decreased from January until March. Then sales increased until July, when they leveled off. In October, sales increased again.
2. Dolls were sold the most this year. This is different from last year.
3. More board games were sold this year than last year.
4. The company has 4 stores. About half of the total toy sales for the company were made by Store B.
5. The average cost of a teddy bear is $12.
6. More people bought toys in October than in January.
7. More stuffed animals were sold last year than this year. Both years, more stuffed animals were sold than board games.
8. Store A sold more items than Store C and Store D.

Graphs may vary. Check students' graphs.

Use with text pages 384–386.

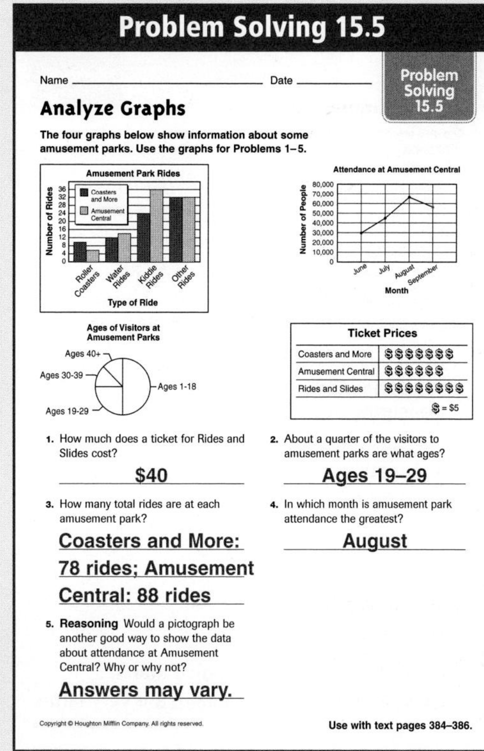

Problem Solving 15.5

Name ______________ Date __________

Problem Solving 15.5

Analyze Graphs

The four graphs below show information about some amusement parks. Use the graphs for Problems 1–5.

Ticket Prices	
Coasters and More	$$$$$$$
Amusement Central	$$$$$$
Rides and Slides	$$$$$$$$

$ = $5

1. How much does a ticket for Rides and Slides cost? **$40**
2. About a quarter of the visitors to amusement parks are what ages? **Ages 19–29**
3. How many total rides are at each amusement park? **Coasters and More: 78 rides; Amusement Central: 88 rides**
4. In which month is amusement park attendance the greatest? **August**
5. **Reasoning** Would a pictograph be another good way to show the data about attendance at Amusement Central? Why or why not? **Answers may vary.**

Use with text pages 384–386.

Guided Practice

Have students complete **Problems 1–4** as you observe. Remind them to use the *Ask Yourself* questions to help. Give students the opportunity to talk about the questions in *Explain Your Thinking.*

3 Practice

Practice and Problem Solving

Select from **Problems 5–11** as independent work.

- **Problems 5–11** Review and discuss students' answers. Explain that more than one type of graph might be effective for the data described. Encourage all reasonable answers that students can justify.

4 Assess & Close

Math Talk in Action

Have students revisit **Problems 5–11** to conclude the lesson.

- **Which graph would *not* work well as a way to show the data for Problem 5?** (line graph) **Why wouldn't a line graph work well?** (Possible answer: The data does not change over time.)

Math Journal Prompt

Have students write an explanation of why it is important to be able to choose the right graph to display a given set of data.

Lesson Quiz

Use the quiz on Lesson Transparency 15.5.

Lesson 15.5 Transparency

Test Prep & Spiral Review

Use Test Prep Transparency 15.5.

Test Prep 15.5 Transparency

Guided Practice

Use the graphs on Pages 384 and 385 for Problems 1–4.

Ask Yourself
- What is the purpose of the graph?
- Did I read the data on the graph correctly?

1. Between which two times on June 26 does the temperature increase the most? **between Noon and 3 P.M.**
2. What will cost about twice as much as a car rental? **lodging**
3. If Brian's family wants to hike a total of about 3 miles out and back, to which hiking area should they go? **Titus Canyon Narrows**
4. How many votes were recorded on the pictograph? **25 votes**

Explain Your Thinking ▶ Would a pictograph have been another good way to represent the data about Death Valley hiking areas? Why or why not? ***Possible answer:*** **No; it would not be easy to make a key with these data.**

Practice and Problem Solving

Choose a graph to display the data for Exercises 5–10. Write *bar graph*, *circle graph*, *line graph*, or *pictograph*. Explain your choice.

Answers may vary for Problems 5–10. **Explanations should indicate an understanding of the appropriateness of different graphs.**

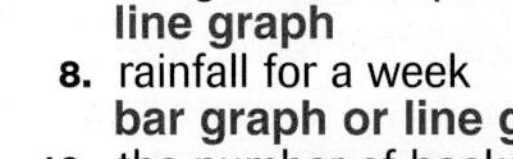

5. the results of an election **circle graph or bar graph**
6. the growth of a plant **line graph**
7. compare the heights of cacti **bar graph**
8. rainfall for a week **bar graph or line graph**
9. the parts of a day spent hiking, eating, and sleeping **circle graph**
10. the number of books read during the summer by 5 students **pictograph or bar graph**
11. **Create and Solve** What could the graph below be showing? Create a title, scale, and labels for the graph.

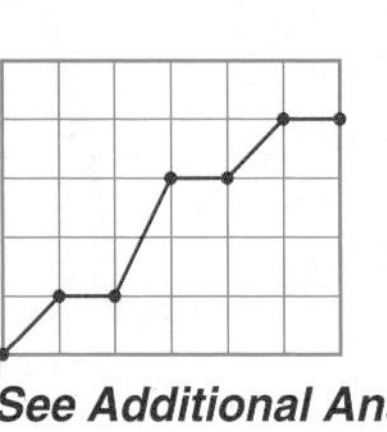

See Additional Answers.

Extra Practice See page 389, Set C.

Homework 15.5 — Page 97

Name ______________ Date ______ Homework 15.5

Analyze Graphs

Choose a graph to display each set of data. Write *bar graph, circle graph, line graph,* or *pictograph*. Explain your choice.

Explanations may vary. Samples are given.

> **the high temperatures in Burlington, Vermont from Monday to Sunday**
> A **line graph** is a good choice to show change over time, such as temperature.

1. the results of a survey of students' favorite snacks
   circle graph; they are good for surveys showing parts of a whole
2. how much money a business earned over time
   line graph; they are good for measuring over time
3. a comparison of the heights of different students
   bar graph or pictograph; they are good for comparing

Problem Solving

4. When is a bar graph a better choice than a pictograph? Explain your reasoning.
   A bar graph is a better choice than a pictograph when the numbers are very large.

Use with text pages 384–386.

Mixed Review and Test Prep

Open Response

Find the mean, median, mode, and range for each set of data. (Ch. 14, Lesson 3)
See Additional Answers.

12. 14, 3, 8, 1, 14

13. 5, 3, 11, 5

14. 13, 1, 13, 6, 2

15. 30, 40, 20, 30

16. 9, 6, 12, 9, 9

17. 15, 23, 17, 25

18. A line graph that shows the distance a bicyclist rode on a 1-hour trip levels off between two points in the middle of the graph. (Ch. 15, Lesson 5)

How could you explain this?
See Additional Answers.

Problem Solving

Math Reasoning
Histograms

A histogram shows how often data occur within equal intervals. This histogram shows the heights of 15 roadside animal statues.

1. Which interval shows the heights of the greatest number of statues? **10–19**

Remember
An interval is the amount of space between 2 things.

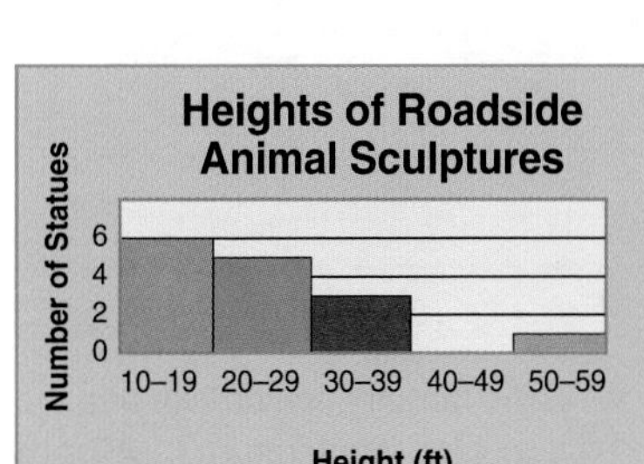

2. How many statues are less than 30 feet? **11 statues**

3. How many statues are between 30 and 39 feet high? **3 statues**

Math Reasoning
Histograms

- Discuss with students that a histogram is a special kind of graph that shows frequencies of data in intervals. Guide students to see the similarities and differences between bar graphs and histograms.
- Point out that histograms are useful for showing ranges of information, such as numbers of people shopping in a mall from noon to 2:00 or from 7:00 to 9:00, or numbers of people in different age groups, such as 10–19 or 40–49. Ask students to suggest other uses for histograms. (Possible answers: price ranges or shirt sizes)
- Guide students to notice that unlike bar graphs, histograms show no spaces between bars.

Monitoring Student Progress

Chapter Review/Test

Chapter Review/Test Items 1–10

To assign a numerical grade for this Chapter Review/Test, use 10 points for each item.

Check Understanding

You can use the *Write About It* question to assess student understanding of a key chapter concept.

Customize Your Instruction

The Chapter Review/Test is a formal evaluation of chapter objectives. For students who have not yet mastered these objectives, you can use the Reteaching Resources listed in the chart below.

Additional Assessment Resources

Alternate Chapter Test A Chapter Test is also provided in the Unit Resource folder. You might use the Review/Test in the student book as review and the test in the Unit Resource folder as a summary test for the chapter.

***Ways to Assess* CD-ROM** allows you to create your own lesson, chapter, or unit tests or practice and review worksheets.

Adequate Yearly Progress Guide helps familiarize your students with the format of standardized tests.

Chapter Review/Test

VOCABULARY

Choose the best term to complete each sentence.

Vocabulary
key
interval
line graph
circle graph
double bar graph

1. A ____ uses bars to compare two sets of data. **double bar graph**
2. The difference between two numbers on a scale is the ____. **interval**
3. A ____ shows the parts that make up a whole. **circle graph**

Write About It: ***Possible answer:*** **A line graph is a good choice for graphing changes over time.**

CONCEPTS AND SKILLS

Use the graphs to answer Problems 4–9. (Lessons 1, 2, 5, pp. 376–379, 384–386)

Normal Temperatures
Temperature (°F): 0, 10, 20, 30, 40, 50
Albany
Cleveland
Jan. Feb. Mar.
Month

Jamie's Spending

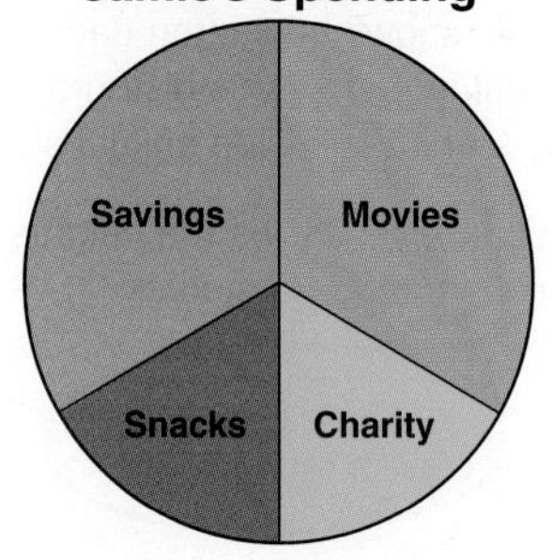

4. In January, which city has the colder temperature? **Albany**
5. In March, is it warmer in Albany or in Cleveland? **Cleveland**
6. Why is a double bar graph a good choice for these data? **A double bar graph compares two sets of data.**
7. What fraction of Jamie's money does she save? $\frac{1}{3}$
8. Does Jamie spend more on movies or on snacks? **movies**
9. Why is a circle graph a good choice for these data? **A circle graph shows parts of a whole.**

PROBLEM SOLVING

Solve. (Lessons 3, 4, pp. 380–383)

10. Draw a line graph to show the total distance hikers walked in a day. ***Check students' work.***

Write About It

Show You Understand

What kind of graph would best display changes in the high temperature outside a school during one week? Why? ***See above.***

388 **Chapter 15** Chapter Review/Test

Chapter Review/Test Items	Objectives	Covered On Teacher's Edition Pages	Use These Reteaching Resources
3, 4–9	**15A** Compare and analyze information from different types of graphs.	376A–379, 384A–386	Reteach Resources, 15.1, 15.2, 15.5 *Ways to Success* CD-ROM 15.1, 15.2, 15.5 *Ways to Success* Skillsheets 132, 133, 134
1, 2, 4–6	**15B** Make, read, and interpret a bar graph.	376A–377	Reteach Resource 15.1 *Ways to Success* CD-ROM 15.1 *Ways to Success* Skillsheet 133
10	**15C** Make, read, and interpret a line graph.	382A–383	Reteach Resource 15.4 *Ways to Success* CD-ROM 15.4 *Ways to Success* Skillsheet 135
10	**15D** Solve problems using skills and strategies.	380A–381	Reteach Resource 15.3 *Ways to Success* CD-ROM 15.3 *Ways to Success* Skillsheet 136

Extra Practice

Set A (Lesson 2, pp. 378–379)

Use the circle graph for Problems 1–3.

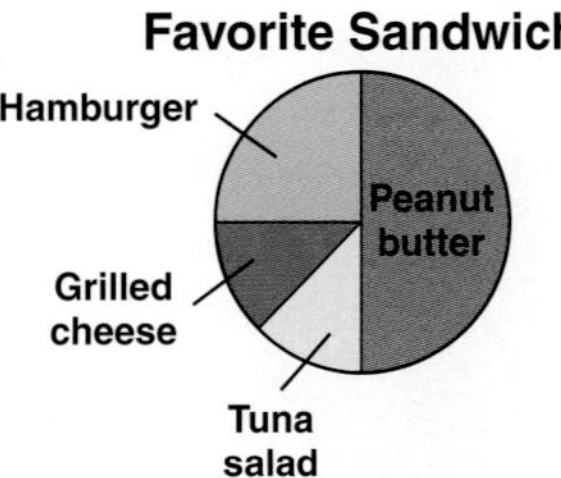

1. What fraction of people chose peanut butter? $\frac{1}{2}$
2. Did more people choose hamburger or tuna salad as their favorite sandwich? **hamburger**
3. Which choice shows about twice as many votes as grilled cheese? **hamburger**

Set B (Lesson 4, pp. 382–383)

Use the line graph for Problems 1–3.

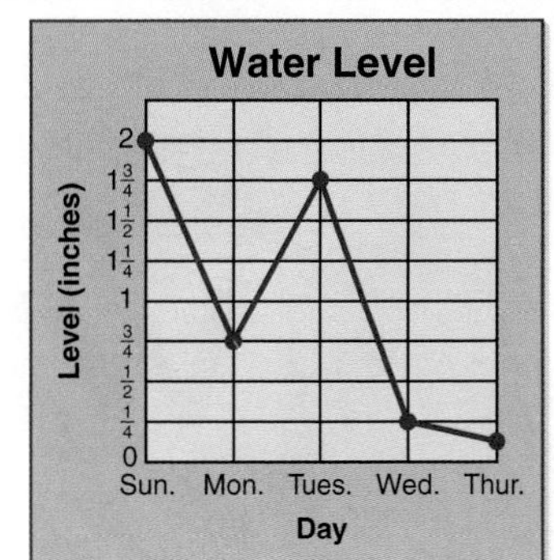

1. On which day was the water level the greatest? **Sunday**
2. On which days was the water level less than 1 inch? **Monday, Wednesday, and Thursday**
3. Between which two days did the water level decrease the most? **between Tuesday and Wednesday**

Set C (Lesson 5, pp. 384–386)

Write the letter of the graph that shows the information given in each problem.

A.

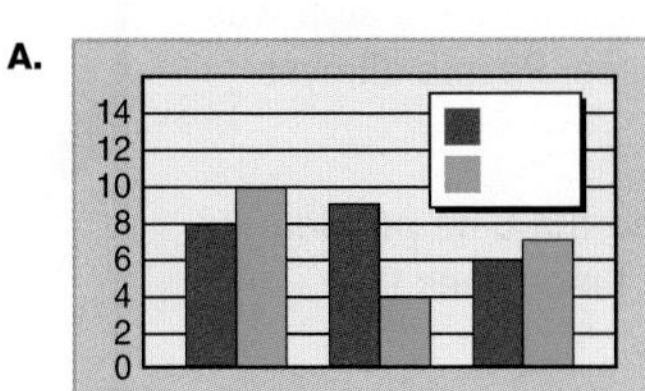

B.

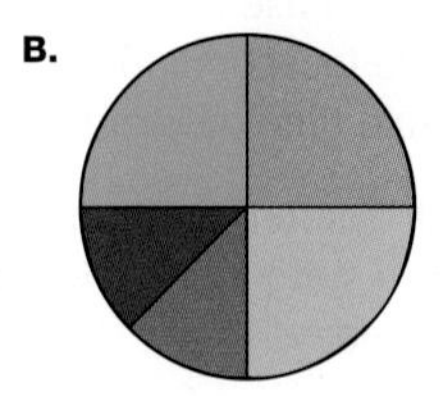

C.

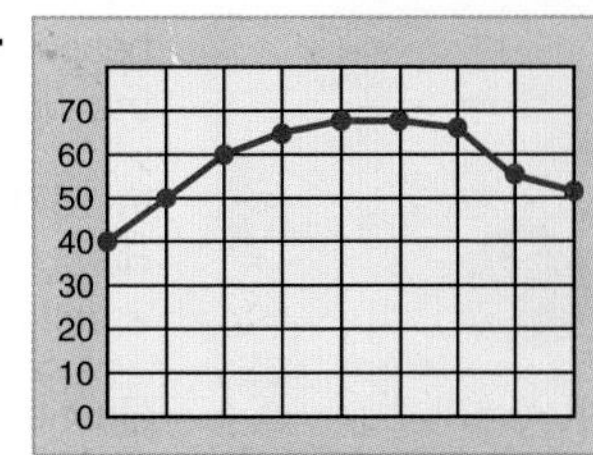

1. the amount spent on party supplies **B**
2. changes in temperature during a day **C**
3. a comparison of scores by two teams in three games **A**

Extra Practice at **eduplace.com/map**

CHAPTER 15 TEST

Name ______________________ Date __________

Chapter 15 Test

Use the double bar graph for Problems 1–4.

School Projects

Amount of Money Raised: $80, $70, $60, $50, $40, $30, $20, $10, 0

1st Grade / 2nd Grade

Project: Bake Sale, Candy Sale, Penny Collection

1. How much did the first grade raise during the bake sale? **$40**
2. During which school project did the first and second grades raise the same amount of money? **candy sale**
3. During which school project did the second grade earn $10 more than the first grade? **penny collection**
4. During which two school projects did the second grade earn a total of $130? **bake sale and candy sale**

Use the circle graph for Problems 5–8.

Jacob's Garden Plants

Peas, Beans, Corn, Tomatoes

5. Which plants are represented about equally in the graph? **peas and beans**
6. Does Jacob have more pea plants or more tomato plants in his garden? **tomato plants**
7. What fraction of the circle graph represents corn plants? $\frac{1}{2}$
8. What fraction of the circle graph represents tomato plants? $\frac{1}{4}$

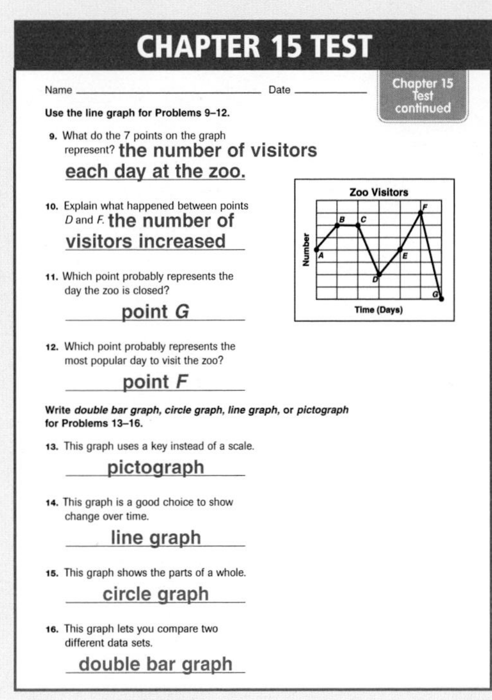

CHAPTER 15 TEST

Name ______________________ Date __________

Chapter 15 Test continued

Use the line graph for Problems 9–12.

Zoo Visitors

Number; Time (Days); A, B, C, D, E, F, G

9. What do the 7 points on the graph represent? **the number of visitors each day at the zoo.**
10. Explain what happened between points *D* and *F*. **the number of visitors increased**
11. Which point probably represents the day the zoo is closed? **point *G***
12. Which point probably represents the most popular day to visit the zoo? **point *F***

Write *double bar graph, circle graph, line graph,* or *pictograph* for Problems 13–16.

13. This graph uses a key instead of a scale. **pictograph**
14. This graph is a good choice to show change over time. **line graph**
15. This graph shows the parts of a whole. **circle graph**
16. This graph lets you compare two different data sets. **double bar graph**

Social Studies Connection

PURPOSE

Students tell time and find elapsed time using time zones in the United States.

- Ask students to think of a relative or a friend in another time zone. If they made a telephone call to that person right now, what time would it be in the other person's time zone?
- Have students list the states in each of the four time zones shown on this map. Notice that some states have more than one time zone.
- **There are two states not shown on this U. S. map. Which states are they?** (Alaska and Hawaii) Have students use a reference book to find out which time zones these two states are in. Then figure out the time it is right now in those two time zones.

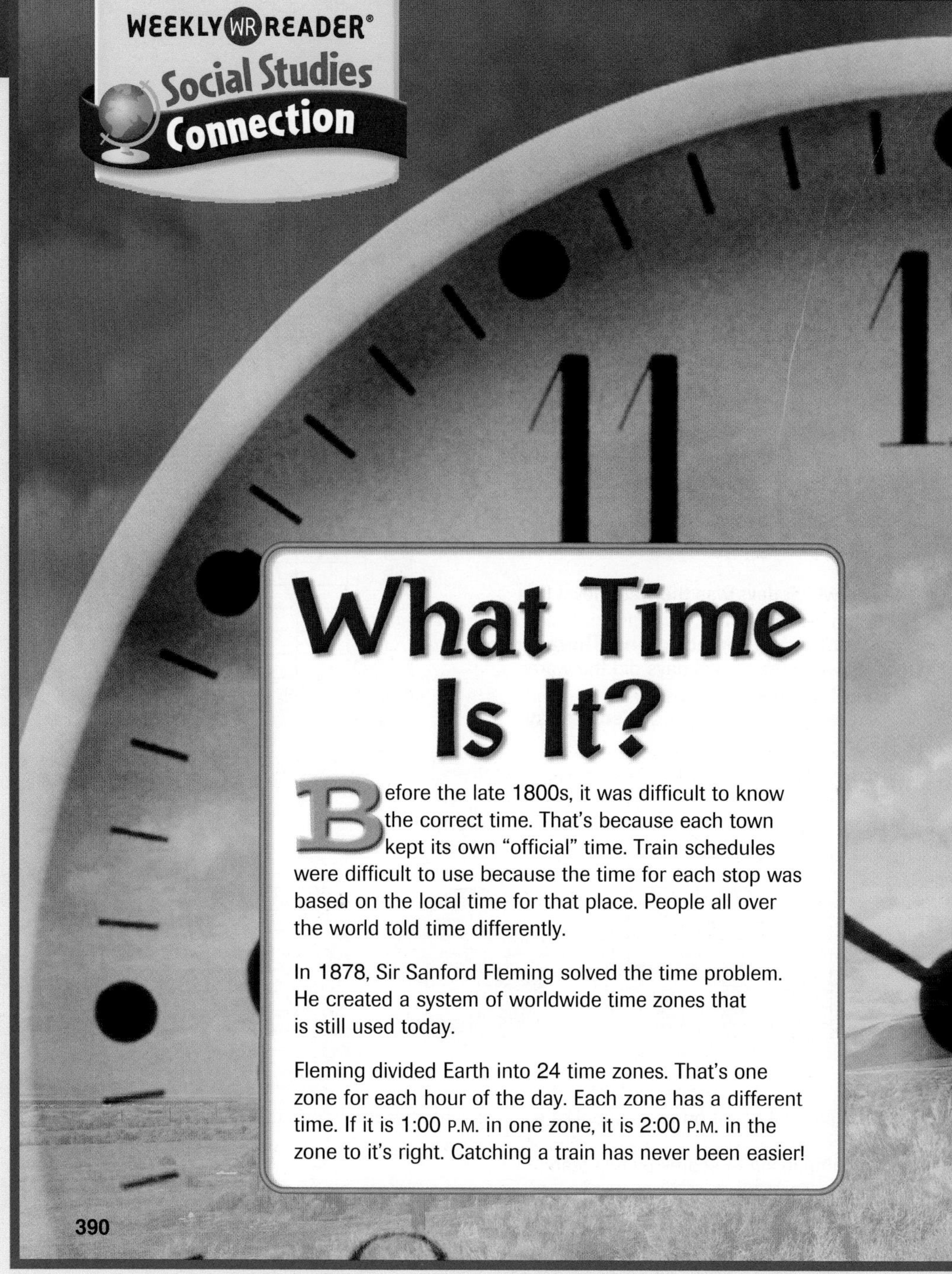

What Time Is It?

Before the late 1800s, it was difficult to know the correct time. That's because each town kept its own "official" time. Train schedules were difficult to use because the time for each stop was based on the local time for that place. People all over the world told time differently.

In 1878, Sir Sanford Fleming solved the time problem. He created a system of worldwide time zones that is still used today.

Fleming divided Earth into 24 time zones. That's one zone for each hour of the day. Each zone has a different time. If it is 1:00 P.M. in one zone, it is 2:00 P.M. in the zone to it's right. Catching a train has never been easier!

390

Problem Solving

The map shows time zones in the United States. The time in each zone is one hour later than the time in the zone to its left.

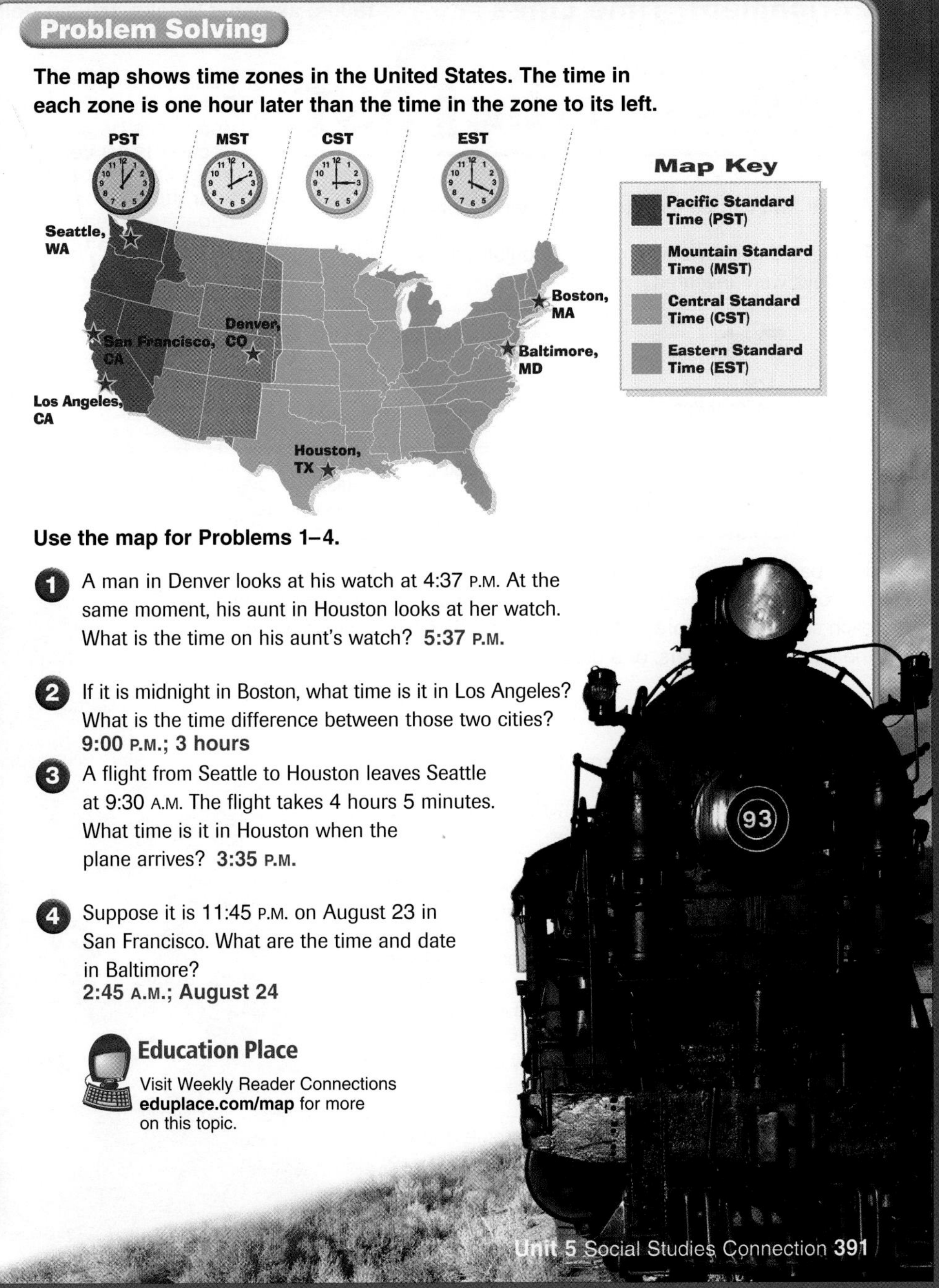

Use the map for Problems 1–4.

1. A man in Denver looks at his watch at 4:37 P.M. At the same moment, his aunt in Houston looks at her watch. What is the time on his aunt's watch? **5:37 P.M.**

2. If it is midnight in Boston, what time is it in Los Angeles? What is the time difference between those two cities? **9:00 P.M.; 3 hours**

3. A flight from Seattle to Houston leaves Seattle at 9:30 A.M. The flight takes 4 hours 5 minutes. What time is it in Houston when the plane arrives? **3:35 P.M.**

4. Suppose it is 11:45 P.M. on August 23 in San Francisco. What are the time and date in Baltimore? **2:45 A.M.; August 24**

Education Place
Visit Weekly Reader Connections **eduplace.com/map** for more on this topic.

Enrichment

PURPOSE

This page provides an opportunity for students to become acquainted with a time line.

This lesson utilizes the skills learned in Chapter 13 and applies them to a time line. As you work through the page, ask the students the following questions:

- **How is a time line similar to a number line?**
- **Why do you think the inventions are above and below the time line?**
- **Near which mark on the time line is the date for the invention of the teddy bear?** (1900) **jigsaw puzzle?** (1770)
- **How many years before the yo-yo were roller skates invented?** (170 years)

Enrichment: Time Lines

1. 1700s: roller skates, jigsaw puzzle; 1800s: alphabet blocks, talking doll

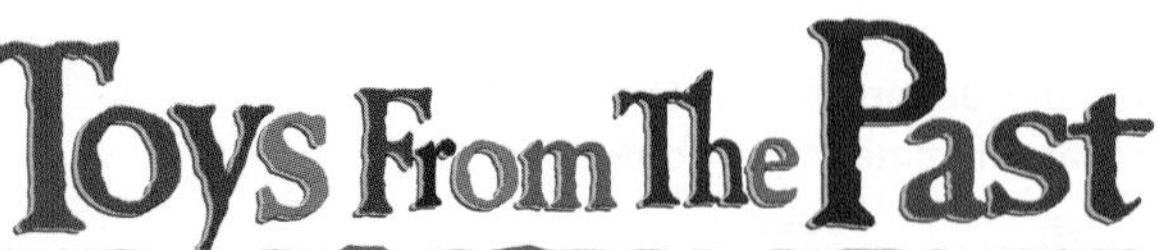

5. ***Possible answer:*** **For the past decade, use years because a decade is 10 years long. For the past year, use months because a year is 12 months long.**

A **time line** can be used to show when events happened.

This time line shows when some popular games and toys were invented.

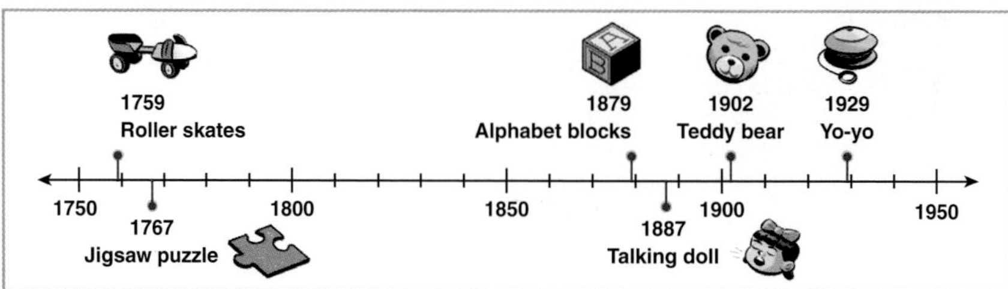

The space between the marks for 1750 and 1850 represents 100 years, or a century. It is divided into 10 smaller spaces. The amount of time each small space represents is called an interval. On this time line the interval is 10 years, or a decade.

Try These!

Use the time line for Problems 1–5.

1. What games or toys were invented in the 1700s? in the 1800s? ***See above.***
2. How many decades are between the invention of the jigsaw puzzle and the invention of the talking doll? **12 decades**
3. Was there more or less than a century between the invention of alphabet blocks and the yo-yo? Explain. **less; from 1879 to 1929 is 50 years**
4. There were 2 decades 3 years between the invention of alphabet blocks and the teddy bear. How many years was that? **23 years**
5. What interval would you use to create a time line of inventions of the past decade? the past year? How did you choose your interval? ***See above.***

Watch 'em Grow!

Mrs. Spinelli's class is growing vegetables in the school garden. The table on the right shows the growth of one of their tomato plants over 5 weeks.

Tomato Plant Growth

Week	Height
1	2 inches
2	3 inches
3	6 inches
4	6 inches
5	8 inches

You can use a graphing program to make a line graph of the data.

1. Fill out the cells of a graphing program as shown to track the tomato plant growth.
2. Highlight the column of numbers under **Height** by clicking and dragging your mouse over them.
3. Use graph or chart function in your graphing program to make a line graph. Name the graph **Tomato Plant Growth**.

	A	B	C	D
1	Week	Height		
2	1	2		
3	2	3		
4	3	6		
5	4	6		
6	5	8		
7				
8				
9				
10				
11				
12				
13				
14				

Use the line graph you created for Problems 1–4.

1. How tall was the tomato plant at the end of Week 4? **6 inches**
2. How many inches did the tomato plant grow between Week 1 and Week 3? **4 in.**
3. Between which two weeks did the growth of the tomato plant show the greatest increase? **Between Weeks 2 and 3.**
4. What are the mean, median, mode, and range of the heights? How did you find the mean? **mean: 5; median: 6; mode: 6; range: 6; I added the height of the plant at the end of each week and divided by the number of weeks.**

Watch 'em Grow!

PURPOSE

To use a graphing program to make a line graph.

- If students work in pairs, one of them could hand-draw the line graph to see how it compares to their partner's computer-generated line graph.
- After students have made the line graph with the computer program, ask them how using the program is the same and different from drawing the graph by hand.
- For **Exercise 3,** ask students what kind of slant the line needs to have to show the greatest increase.
- For **Exercise 4,** ask students how they found the mean, median, mode, and range of the heights.

Monitoring Student Progress

Unit 5 Test

Unit Test Items 1–25

PURPOSE

This test provides an informal assessment of the Unit 5 objectives.

To assign a numerical grade for this Unit Test, use 4 points for each test item.

Customize Your Instruction

For students who have not yet mastered these objectives, you can use the **Reteaching Resources** listed in the chart below. *Ways to Success* is Houghton Mifflin's Intervention program, available in CD-ROM and blackline master formats.

Assessment Options

Formal tests for this unit are also provided in the Unit Resources Folder.

Unit 5 Test

VOCABULARY Open Response

Choose the correct word to complete each sentence.

Vocabulary
- mode
- median
- interval
- capacity

1. The amount that a container can hold is its ____. **capacity**
2. The middle number in a set of numbers ordered from least to greatest is the ____. **median**
3. The difference between two numbers on the scale of a bar graph is the ____. **interval**

CONCEPTS AND SKILLS Open Response

Find each missing number. (Chapter 12)

4. __ pt = 32 c **16**
5. 6 L = __ mL **6,000**
6. __ lb = 48 oz **3**
7. 2 dm = __ cm **20**
8. __ g = 7 kg **7,000**
9. 60 yd = __ ft **180**

Look at each pair of times. Write how much time has elapsed. (Chapter 13)

10. Start: 3:42 A.M. End: 7:07 A.M. **3 hours 25 minutes**
11. Start: 8:15 A.M. End: 1:05 P.M. **4 hours 50 minutes**
12. Start: 10:20 P.M. End: 2:35 A.M. **4 hours 15 minutes**

Write each temperature. (Chapter 13)

13. °F 70° 60° **65°F**
14. °C 20° 10° **12°C**
15. °F 0° −10° **⁻5°F**
16. °C 100° 90° **98°C**

Use the line graph for Problems 17–19. (Chapter 15)

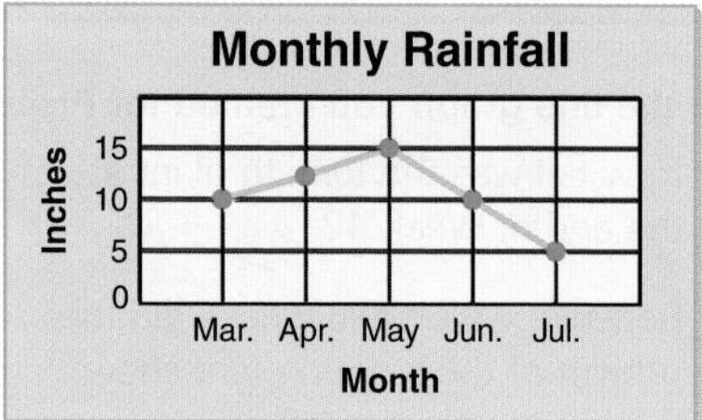

17. Which months had the same amount of rainfall? **March, June**
18. How much rain fell in the wettest month? Which month was it? **15 inches, May**
19. About how much rain fell between the beginning of May and the end of July? **about 30 inches**

394

Reteaching Support

Unit Test Item	Unit Objectives Tested	Covered on Teacher's Edition Pages	Use These Reteaching Resources
1, 4–9	5A Estimate, measure, compare, and convert customary and metric units of length, capacity, weight/mass.	306A–314, 320A–324, 326A–328	Reteach Resources and *Ways to Success,* 12.1–12.4, 12.7–12.9
10–12	5B Determine elapsed time using clocks and calendars.	334A–338	Reteach Resources and *Ways to Success,* 13.1, 13.2
13–16	5C Read, write, and compare temperatures.	344A–346	Reteach Resources and *Ways to Success,* 13.4
2, 21	5D Collect, organize, and analyze data; find mean, median, mode, and range.	364A–365	Reteach Resources and *Ways to Success,* 14.3
3, 17–19, 20	5E Make, read, and interpret line plots, stem-and-leaf plots, bar graphs, circle graphs, and line graphs.	366A–371, 380A–383	Reteach Resources and *Ways to Success,* 14.5, 15.3, 15.4
22–25	5F Solve problems using skills and strategies.	316A–316, 340A–342, 348A–350, 360A–362	Reteach Resources and *Ways to Success,* 12.5, 13.3, 13.5, 14.2

Use the data in the table for Problems 20 and 21. (Chapter 14)

Minutes Jacob Played in His Soccer Games				
1	25	13	13	20
13	14	25	20	

20. Use the data to make a stem-and-leaf plot. *See Additional Answers.*

21. Find the mean, median, and mode of the data. **mean: 16, median: 14; mode: 13**

PROBLEM SOLVING Open Response

22. A comic book doubled in price every 10 years. It cost $20 in 1950. How much did it cost 5 decades later? **$640**

23. Jim bought 4 muffins for $2.50 each and 2 snack bars for $1.25 each. How much did he spend on muffins? **$10.00**

24. In a park, there are 25 people and dogs with a total of 70 legs. How many people are there? **15 people**

25. It is 17°F at 8 P.M. If it gets 4° colder each hour for 3 hours, what will the temperature be then? **5°F**

Performance Assessment

Extended Response

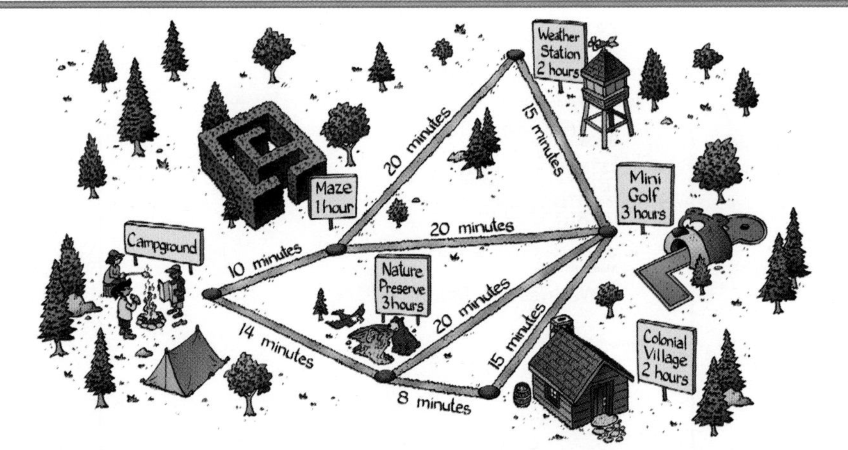

Task A club is planning what activities to do on a two-day camping trip.

Use the map and the information at the right to decide which activities the club should do in the two days. Make a schedule, including the times the club arrives and departs from each activity.

Information You Need

- The club wants to do at least four activities during the two-day trip.
- Club members want to leave the campground at 9 A.M. and be back by 4 P.M. each day.
- The time it takes to travel from activity to activity and the length of each activity are shown the map.

See Additional Answers.

Unit 5 Test 395

UNIT TEST – FORM A

Name ______ Date ______ Unit 5 Test Form A

Find each missing number.

1. 4 mi = 7,040 yd
2. 30 dm = 3 m
3. 16 qt = 4 gal
4. 6 lb = 96 oz

Compare. Write >, <, or = in each ○.

5. 24 ft = 8 yd
6. 3,000 g > 1 kg
7. 3 pt = 6 c
8. 1,900 m < 2 km

Choose the better unit to measure each.

9. the capacity of a paint bucket (C) a. cups b. pints c. gallons
10. the length of a football field (B) a. centimeters b. meters c. kilometers

Go on

UNIT TEST – FORM B

Name ______ Date ______ Unit 5 Test Form B

Choose the letter of the correct answer.
Find each missing number.

1. 2 L = (D) mL A 2 B 20 C 200 D 2,000
2. (H) lb = 6 T F 2,000 G 6,000 H 12,000 J 18,000
3. 8,000 g = (C) kg A 1 B 40 C 8 D 80
4. 16 pt = (G) gal F 1 G 2 H 4 J 8

Compare. Choose the correct symbol for each ○.

5. 25 in. ○ 1 yd A > B < C = D + (B)
6. 6 c ○ 2 pt F > G < H = J + (F)
7. 30 cm ○ 3 m A > B < C = D + (B)
8. 6 L ○ 60,000 mL F > G < H = J + (G)

Choose the better unit to measure each.

9. the weight of a whale A pounds B tons C ounces D liters (B)
10. the mass of a truck F grams G pints H quarts J kilograms (J)

Go on

Performance Assessment & Scoring Rubric

4 EXEMPLARY

Fully completes each task, shows an understanding of how to determine elapsed time using clocks and calendars. Provides an entertaining schedule of activities that accurately accounts for arrival and departure times, travel times between activities and the length of the individual activities within the time frame of the camping trip.

3 PROFICIENT

Shows an understanding of how to determine elapsed time using clocks and calendars but needs help drawing up a reasonable schedule of activities to account for arrival, departure, travel times, and the times of the planned activities.

2 ACCEPTABLE

Completes the task but makes some computational errors that may affect the accuracy of the activity schedule or members' enjoyment of the camping trip as a result of time conflicts with either the travel times overlapping the start of activities or their length.

1 LIMITED

Is unable to complete the tasks, makes computational errors, fails to represent the calculations in the form of an activity schedule that takes into account arrival and departure times, travel times, and their length even with assistance.

Unit 5 Test Answers: Form A

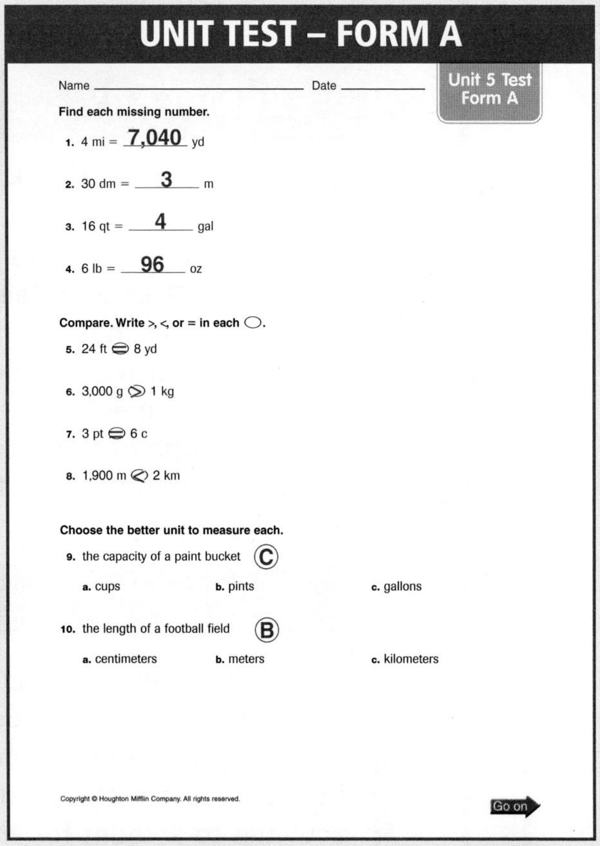

UNIT TEST – FORM A

Name ______________ Date ________ **Unit 5 Test Form A**

Find each missing number.

1. 4 mi = **7,040** yd
2. 30 dm = **3** m
3. 16 qt = **4** gal
4. 6 lb = **96** oz

Compare. Write >, <, or = in each ◯.

5. 24 ft **=** 8 yd
6. 3,000 g **>** 1 kg
7. 3 pt **=** 6 c
8. 1,900 m **<** 2 km

Choose the better unit to measure each.

9. the capacity of a paint bucket **(C)**
   a. cups b. pints c. gallons
10. the length of a football field **(B)**
   a. centimeters b. meters c. kilometers

Go on

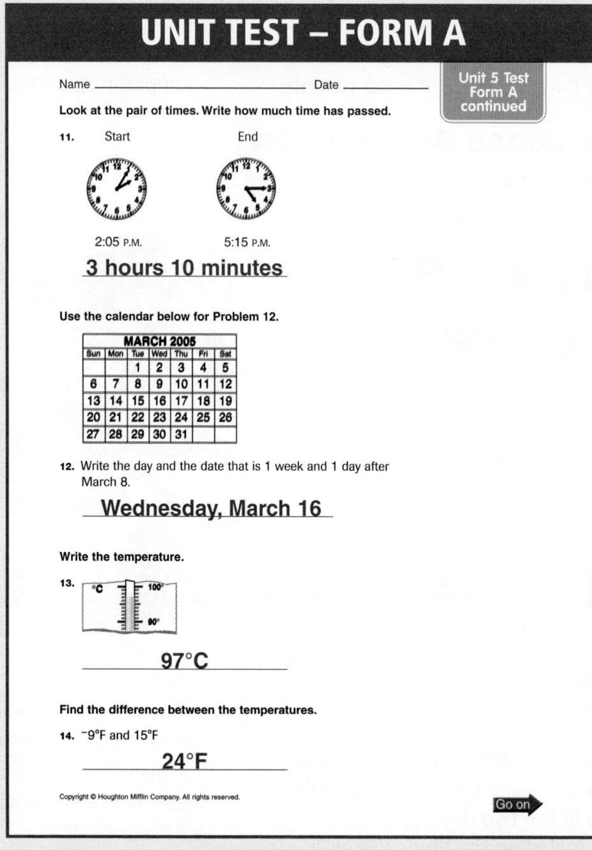

UNIT TEST – FORM A

Name ______________ Date ________ **Unit 5 Test Form A continued**

Look at the pair of times. Write how much time has passed.

11. Start 2:05 P.M. End 5:15 P.M.
3 hours 10 minutes

Use the calendar below for Problem 12.

MARCH 2005						
Sun	Mon	Tue	Wed	Thu	Fri	Sat
		1	2	3	4	5
6	7	8	9	10	11	12
13	14	15	16	17	18	19
20	21	22	23	24	25	26
27	28	29	30	31		

12. Write the day and the date that is 1 week and 1 day after March 8.
Wednesday, March 16

Write the temperature.

13. °C 100° 90°
97°C

Find the difference between the temperatures.

14. −9°F and 15°F
24°F

Go on

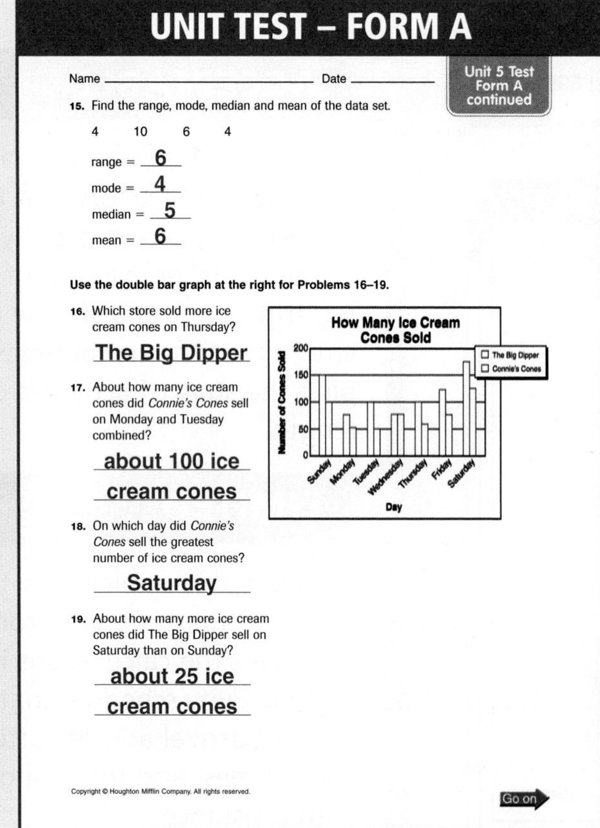

UNIT TEST – FORM A

Name ______________ Date ________ **Unit 5 Test Form A continued**

15. Find the range, mode, median and mean of the data set.
4 10 6 4
range = **6**
mode = **4**
median = **5**
mean = **6**

Use the double bar graph at the right for Problems 16–19.

How Many Ice Cream Cones Sold
(Number of Cones Sold: 0, 50, 100, 150, 200; Day: Sunday, Monday, Tuesday, Wednesday, Thursday, Friday, Saturday; ☐ The Big Dipper ☐ Connie's Cones)

16. Which store sold more ice cream cones on Thursday?
The Big Dipper
17. About how many ice cream cones did *Connie's Cones* sell on Monday and Tuesday combined?
about 100 ice cream cones
18. On which day did *Connie's Cones* sell the greatest number of ice cream cones?
Saturday
19. About how many more ice cream cones did The Big Dipper sell on Saturday than on Sunday?
about 25 ice cream cones

Go on

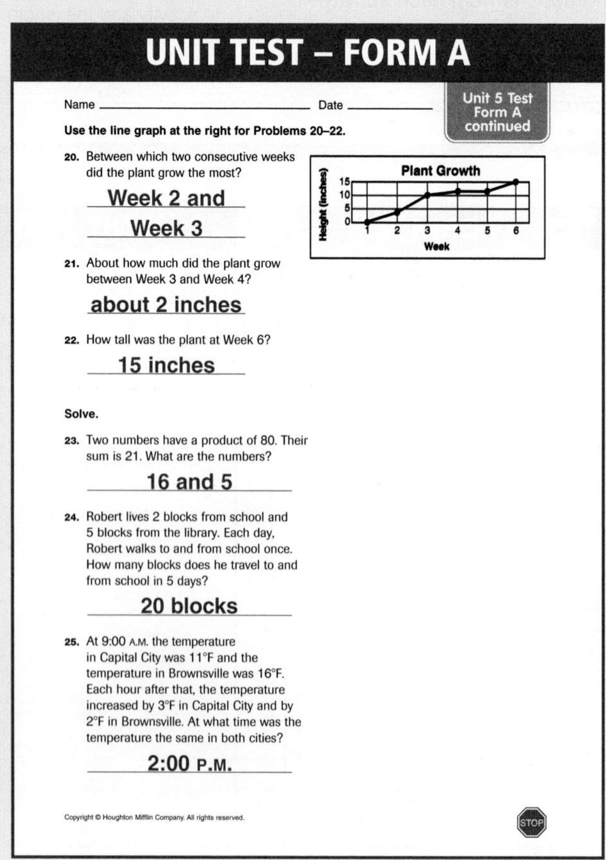

UNIT TEST – FORM A

Name ______________ Date ________ **Unit 5 Test Form A continued**

Use the line graph at the right for Problems 20–22.

Plant Growth
(Height (inches): 0, 5, 10, 15; Week: 1, 2, 3, 4, 5, 6)

20. Between which two consecutive weeks did the plant grow the most?
Week 2 and Week 3
21. About how much did the plant grow between Week 3 and Week 4?
about 2 inches
22. How tall was the plant at Week 6?
15 inches

Solve.

23. Two numbers have a product of 80. Their sum is 21. What are the numbers?
16 and 5
24. Robert lives 2 blocks from school and 5 blocks from the library. Each day, Robert walks to and from school once. How many blocks does he travel to and from school in 5 days?
20 blocks
25. At 9:00 A.M. the temperature in Capital City was 11°F and the temperature in Brownsville was 16°F. Each hour after that, the temperature increased by 3°F in Capital City and by 2°F in Brownsville. At what time was the temperature the same in both cities?
2:00 P.M.

STOP

Unit 5 Test Answers: Form B

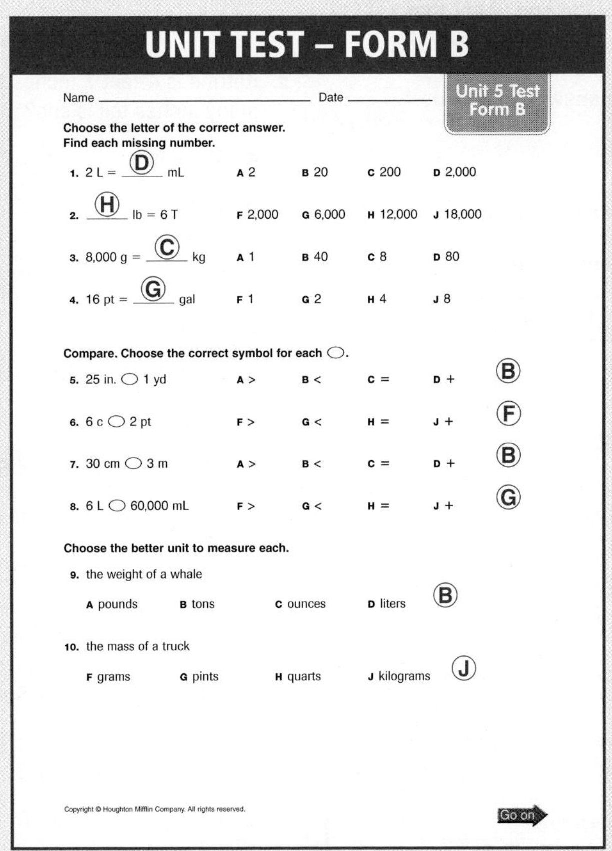

UNIT TEST – FORM B

Unit 5 Test Form B

Name ______________ Date ______________

Choose the letter of the correct answer. Find each missing number.

1. 2 L = (D) mL — A 2 B 20 C 200 D 2,000
2. (H) lb = 6 T — F 2,000 G 6,000 H 12,000 J 18,000
3. 8,000 g = (C) kg — A 1 B 40 C 8 D 80
4. 16 pt = (G) gal — F 1 G 2 H 4 J 8

Compare. Choose the correct symbol for each ◯.

5. 25 in. ◯ 1 yd — A > B < C = D + (B)
6. 6 c ◯ 2 pt — F > G < H = J + (F)
7. 30 cm ◯ 3 m — A > B < C = D + (B)
8. 6 L ◯ 60,000 mL — F > G < H = J + (G)

Choose the better unit to measure each.

9. the weight of a whale — A pounds B tons C ounces D liters (B)
10. the mass of a truck — F grams G pints H quarts J kilograms (J)

Go on

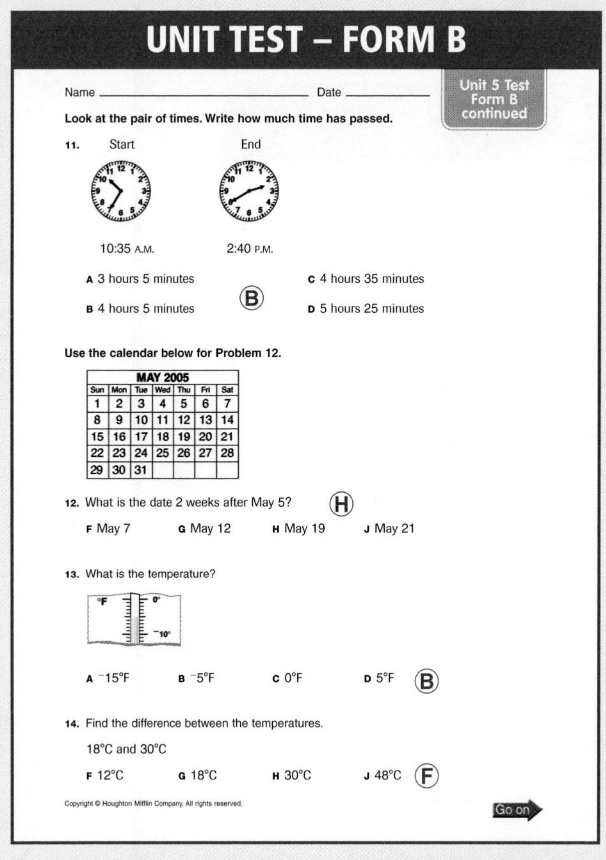

UNIT TEST – FORM B

Unit 5 Test Form B continued

Name ______________ Date ______________

Look at the pair of times. Write how much time has passed.

11. Start: 10:35 A.M. End: 2:40 P.M.

A 3 hours 5 minutes C 4 hours 35 minutes
B 4 hours 5 minutes D 5 hours 25 minutes (B)

Use the calendar below for Problem 12.

MAY 2005						
Sun	Mon	Tue	Wed	Thu	Fri	Sat
1	2	3	4	5	6	7
8	9	10	11	12	13	14
15	16	17	18	19	20	21
22	23	24	25	26	27	28
29	30	31				

12. What is the date 2 weeks after May 5? (H)

F May 7 G May 12 H May 19 J May 21

13. What is the temperature?

A ⁻15°F B ⁻5°F C 0°F D 5°F (B)

14. Find the difference between the temperatures.

18°C and 30°C

F 12°C G 18°C H 30°C J 48°C (F)

Go on

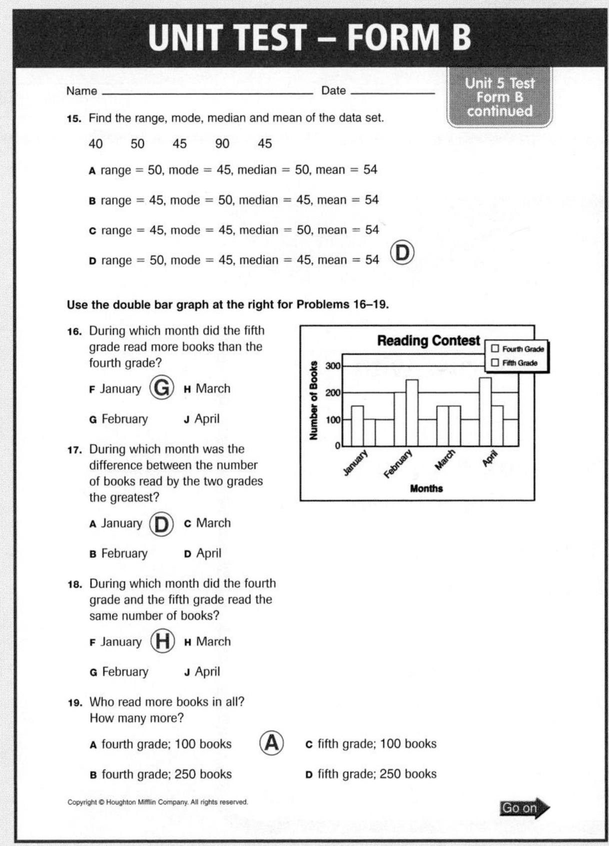

UNIT TEST – FORM B

Unit 5 Test Form B continued

Name ______________ Date ______________

15. Find the range, mode, median and mean of the data set.

40 50 45 90 45

A range = 50, mode = 45, median = 50, mean = 54
B range = 45, mode = 50, median = 45, mean = 54
C range = 45, mode = 45, median = 50, mean = 54
D range = 50, mode = 45, median = 45, mean = 54 (D)

Use the double bar graph at the right for Problems 16–19.

16. During which month did the fifth grade read more books than the fourth grade?

F January (G) H March
G February J April

17. During which month was the difference between the number of books read by the two grades the greatest?

A January (D) C March
B February D April

18. During which month did the fourth grade and the fifth grade read the same number of books?

F January (H) H March
G February J April

19. Who read more books in all? How many more?

A fourth grade; 100 books (A) C fifth grade; 100 books
B fourth grade; 250 books D fifth grade; 250 books

Go on

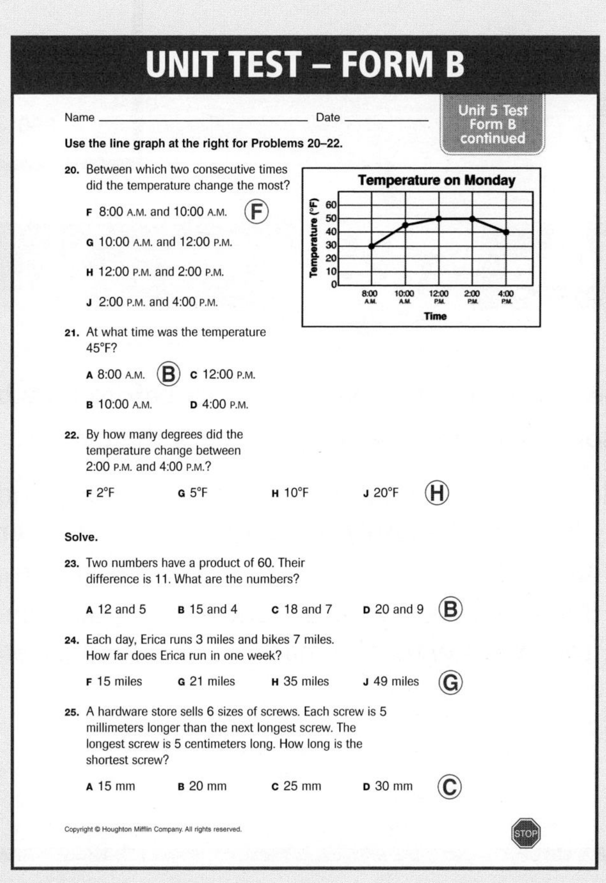

UNIT TEST – FORM B

Unit 5 Test Form B continued

Name ______________ Date ______________

Use the line graph at the right for Problems 20–22.

20. Between which two consecutive times did the temperature change the most?

F 8:00 A.M. and 10:00 A.M. (F)
G 10:00 A.M. and 12:00 P.M.
H 12:00 P.M. and 2:00 P.M.
J 2:00 P.M. and 4:00 P.M.

21. At what time was the temperature 45°F?

A 8:00 A.M. (B) C 12:00 P.M.
B 10:00 A.M. D 4:00 P.M.

22. By how many degrees did the temperature change between 2:00 P.M. and 4:00 P.M.?

F 2°F G 5°F H 10°F J 20°F (H)

Solve.

23. Two numbers have a product of 60. Their difference is 11. What are the numbers?

A 12 and 5 B 15 and 4 C 18 and 7 D 20 and 9 (B)

24. Each day, Erica runs 3 miles and bikes 7 miles. How far does Erica run in one week?

F 15 miles G 21 miles H 35 miles J 49 miles (G)

25. A hardware store sells 6 sizes of screws. Each screw is 5 millimeters longer than the next longest screw. The longest screw is 5 centimeters long. How long is the shortest screw?

A 15 mm B 20 mm C 25 mm D 30 mm (C)

STOP

Monitoring Student Progress

Cumulative Test Prep

PURPOSE

This page will familiarize students with the multiple-choice and open-response formats of many standardized state tests.

Cumulative Test Prep

Solve Problems 1–10.

Test-Taking Tip

A question may ask you to choose the statement that is true. All parts of the statement must be true for the answer to be true.

Look at the example below.

Which statement is true for these data?

14	18	11	14	14	15	12

A The mean is 13, and the mode is 14.

B The range is 10, and the median is 14.

C The mean is 3 more than the median.

(D) The mean, the median, and the mode are 14.

THINK

A is **not true** because the mean is not 13.
B is **not true** because the range is not 10.
C is **not true** because the mean and the median are both 14.
D is **true** because the mean, the median, and the mode are all 14.
So choose **D.**

Multiple Choice

1. Which is the product of 9 × 5,300?

   A 4,770 **(C)** 47,700
   B 45,900 **D** 50,000

   (Chapter 6, Lesson 7)

2. Katrina is 4 feet 7 inches tall. How many inches tall is she?

   F 45 inches **H** 52 inches
   G 47 inches **(J)** 55 inches

   (Chapter 12, Lesson 2)

3. Which statement is true of the numbers 3, 5, and 12?

   A They are all factors of 35.
   B They are all prime numbers.
   (C) They are all factors of 60.
   D They are all composite numbers.

   (Chapter 10, Lesson 2)

4. An orbit is the time it takes for a planet to go around the Sun. Mercury's orbit lasts 88 Earth days. How many times does Mercury orbit the Sun in 440 Earth days?

   F 3 **(H)** 5
   G 4 **J** 6

   (Chapter 11, Lesson 4)

396

For Test-Taking Tips, See page 658.

Test-Taking TIPS

Review the test-taking tips with students before they begin the test. Discuss with students some of the ways they can check their work.

- Tell students they can look back to be sure they have marked only one answer for each question.
- Remind them that if they have made a mistake, they must erase the mark completely.
- Remind students to look back to see if their answer fits what the problem asks.
- Tell students as they are checking their answer to ask themselves: Does my answer make sense?

Open Response

5. Khai has $12. Each week for 5 weeks, he saves $4. How much money does Khai have at the end of 5 weeks? **$32**

(Chapter 4, Lesson 4)

6. Copy and complete the function table.

Rule: ________	
x	*y*
1	6
3	18
10	60
12	**72**

Multiply by 6, or $6x = y$.

(Chapter 5, Lesson 6)

7. It took Teresa 16 minutes to walk from her house to school. She arrived at school at 9:05 A.M. At what time did Teresa leave her house? **8:49 A.M.**

(Chapter 13, Lesson 2)

8. Use the table.

Game	1	2	3	4	5	6
Runs	2	1	12	3	4	3

What are the mode and the range of the number of runs?
mode: 3; range: 11

(Chapter 14, Lesson 3)

9. A carton holds 12 eggs. If Jon has 11 cartons of eggs, how many eggs does he have? **132 eggs**

(Chapter 4, Lesson 6)

Extended Response

10. Matt has $5.00 and must buy lunch for himself and his sister Gina.

Lunch Menu	
Item	Price
Milk	$0.40
Orange Juice	$0.60
Pizza Slice	$1.15
Apple	$0.25
Combo (pizza slice, apple, and milk)	$1.65

A Matt wants 1 combo meal for himself, and 1 slice of pizza and 1 orange juice for his sister. How much will this cost? **$3.40**

B If Matt gives the cashier $5.00, how much change will he get? **$1.60**

C Whose lunch costs more, Matt's or Gina's? Tell how much more. **Gina's lunch; $0.10**

D How much money is Matt saving by buying the combo meal instead of buying each item in the combo meal separately? **$0.15**

(Chapter 2, Lesson 4)

Education Place
Look for Cumulative Test Prep at **eduplace.com/map** for more practice.

Test-Taking Vocabulary

- Read through the example with the students. Sometimes the word *not* can be confusing in true/false questions. For example, what if choice D was "The mean is not 13, and the mode and median are 14"? The statement is then true.
- Remind students that some test items contain multiple-step problems, such as parts C and D for Problem 10.

National and state tests might use these words in statements that students must identify as true or false:

- sometimes
- always
- never
- all
- none
- a few

Vocabulary Wrap-Up

PURPOSE

Use this page to encourage students to use math vocabulary to talk about the important concepts they have learned in this unit.

Big Ideas and Key Vocabulary

Review and discuss with students the Big Ideas of this unit using the Key Vocabulary terms *data, elapsed time, graph, mean, median,* and *mode.*

Math Conversations

Have students work together in small groups to discuss **Exercises 1–3.** Check to see whether individual students understand the key concepts and are able to use the math vocabulary correctly. Clear up any misunderstandings students may have. After students have discussed the exercises in small groups, continue the conversation as a whole class. Have volunteers from each group share what their group talked about.

Write About It Ask for volunteers to share their bar graphs with the class. Then ask students to explain how they found the median, mode, and range of their data.

Vocabulary Wrap-Up for Unit 5

Look back at the big ideas and vocabulary in this unit.

Big Ideas

You can use multiplication and division to convert from one unit of measure to another.

You can measure elapsed time on a calendar or a clock.

You can display data in a graph.

You can find the mean, median, and mode of a data set.

Key Vocabulary

data
elapsed time
mean
median
mode

Math Conversations

Use your new vocabulary to discuss these big ideas.

1. Explain how you can find the number of inches in 6 feet. ***See Additional Answers.***
2. Explain the difference between the mean, median, and mode of a data set. ***See Additional Answers.***
3. Explain how bar graphs and line graphs are alike and different. ***See Additional Answers.***

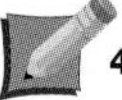

4. **Write About It** Measure the height of different textbooks to the nearest half inch. Make a bar graph to display the data. Find the median, mode, and range of the data. ***Check students' work.***

I recorded the temperature each day this week.
You could use a line graph to display your data.

398 Unit 5 Vocabulary Wrap-Up

Wrap Up the Unit Project

- Encourage students to peer edit each other's reports, checking for spelling, grammar, and mathematical errors especially relating to measurement and graphing.
- Some students may wish to generate state-related graphics, charts, and graphs on the computer to make a more professional presentation.
- Allow time and space for students to present their data about the state to the class orally and then display it on the bulletin board.
- Encourage students to use this information to relate this research to other classes, such as social studies, science, or reading.

UNIT 6

Geometry and Measurement

Standards

Unit 6 Objectives	Lessons	NCTM Standards	Your State's Standards
6A Identify, classify, and describe plane figures.	**16.1, 16.2, 16.3, 16.4, 16.5, 16.7**	**Geometry:** Analyze two- and three-dimensional shapes. Classify two- and three-dimensional shapes.	
6B Identify congruent figures and figures with line and rotational symmetry.	**17.1, 17.4**	**Geometry:** Analyze characteristics of two- and three-dimensional geometric shapes. Use visualization, spatial reasoning, and geometric modeling. Explore congruence and symmetry. **Communication:** Express mathematical idea precisely.	
6C Identify, perform, and predict the results of rotations, reflections, and translations.	**17.2**	**Geometry:** Apply transformations and use symmetry. Use visualization, spatial reasoning, and geometric modeling. **Communication:** Express mathematical idea precisely.	
6D Estimate and find perimeter, area, and volume.	**18.1, 18.2, 18.3, 18.4, 18.6**	**Measurement:** Apply standard units and tools to measure. Use formulas to find area and volume. **Algebra:** Represent the idea of a variable as an unknown quantity using a letter or a symbol.	
6E Identify, classify, and describe solid geometric figures.	**18.5**	**Geometry:** Identify and build a three-dimensional object from two-dimensional representations of that object.	
6F Solve problems using skills and strategies.	**16.6, 17.3, 17.5, 18.7**	**Problem Solving:** Apply and adapt strategies to solve problems. **Geometry:** Use visualization, spatial reasoning, and geometric modeling. **Measurement:** Use formulas to find the area of rectangles and related triangles and parallelograms.	

NCTM Process Standards	Sample Lessons or Features	Your State's Standards
Reasoning and Proof: Use various levels and types of reasoning, including formulating proofs, patterns, conjectures, and rules.	Reasoning, Problem Solving, and Algebra Readiness features. For example, see **Lessons 16.4, 16.6, 17.1, 17.2, 17.3, 17.5, 18.2, 18.3, 18.4, 18.6, 18.7.**	
Communication: Understand vocabulary, organization of processes, and how to communicate and comprehend mathematical concepts and justifications with accuracy.	Hands-On and Problem-Solving lessons, Explain Your Thinking questions, games, and Reading Mathematics and Create and Solve features. For example, see **Lessons 16.1, 16.3, 16.7, 17.1, 17.4, 18.1, 18.5.**	
Connections: Relate mathematics to real life and other subjects and make connections from one mathematical idea to another.	Connections features, skills lessons, and Problem-Solving lessons and features. For example, see **Lessons 16.6, 16.7, 17.3, 17.5, 18.4, 18.7.**	
Representation: Represent mathematical ideas using concrete objects, pictures, and symbols.	Occurs throughout as students use manipulatives, workmats, drawings, tables, symbols, and equations to model or explain. For example, see **Lessons 16.2, 16.4, 16.5, 17.2, 18.1, 18.3, 18.6.**	

For content corresponding to this *Houghton Mifflin Math* unit, see lessons in *Math Expressions*

- Unit A: Quadrilaterals
- Unit B: Lines, Angles, and Triangles
- Unit D: Polygons and Circles
- Unit E: Three-Dimensional Figures

Standards

Assessment System

Monitoring Student Progress

Unit Objectives

6A	Identify, classify, and describe plane figures.
6B	Identify congruent figures and figures with line and rotational symmetry.
6C	Identify, perform, and predict the results of rotations, reflections, and translations.
6D	Estimate and find perimeter, area, and volume.
6E	Identify, classify, and describe solid geometric figures.
6F	Solve problems using skills and strategies.

Classroom-Based Assessment

Prior Knowledge

Use What You Know, PE pp. 403, 429, 451
Chapters 16, 17, and 18 Pretests, Unit Resources
Unit 6 Reading Mathematics, PE pp. 400–401

Ongoing Assessment

Student Self-Assessment

Explain Your Thinking, PE pp. 405, 409, 414, 416, 423, 431, 435, 441, 455, 457, 461, 466, 469
Mixed Review & Test Prep, PE pp. 406, 409, 417, 425, 432, 435, 447, 455, 462, 467, 469
Quick Check, PE pp. 415, 443, 459
Vocabulary Wrap-Up, PE p. 484

Informal Assessment by Teachers

Problem of the Day, First page of every TE lesson
Spiral Review, First page of every TE lesson
Common Error/Intervention, TE pp. 404, 408, 412, 416, 430, 434, 440, 444, 454, 456, 460, 464, 468
Lesson Quiz, First page of every TE lesson

Diagnostic/Intervention

Quick Check, PE pp. 415, 443, 459
Common Error/Intervention, TE pp. 404, 408, 412, 416, 430, 434, 440, 444, 454, 456, 460, 464, 468
Chapter Review/Test, PE pp. 426, 448, 474
Unit 6 Test, PE pp. 480–481

Formal Evaluation

Chapter & Unit Assessment

Chapter Review/Test, PE pp. 426, 448, 474
Chapters 16–18 Tests, Unit Resources
***Unit Test, Form A and Form B,** Unit Resources
Unit 6 Test, PE pp. 480–481

Performance Assessment & Rubric

Performance Assessment, PE p. 481
Scoring Rubric, TE p. 481

Test Prep

***Problem-Solving on Tests,** PE pp. 421, 439
***Cumulative Test Prep,** PE pp. 482–483
Test Prep on the Net, on Education Place
www.eduplace.com/map

(Starred tests use standardized test formats.)

Test Generator

The ***Ways to Assess*** **CD-ROM** allows you to create and score customized tests or review pages. You can select items that assess your state's standards, NCTM standards, or lesson objectives of your choosing. The CD-ROM also includes program, chapter, and unit tests for online administration and scoring or for printing.

Intervention

Ways to Success **CD-ROM** Reteach the lesson objective, provide extra practice, or reteach a key prerequisite skill. **Lessons** 16.1–16.7, 17.1–17.5, 18.1–18.7

Audio Tutor For students who need extra support, who were absent, or who have reading difficulties. **Lessons** 16.4, 16.6, 16.7, 17.1, 17.2, 18.2, 18.3, 18.6

Unit Activities

Unit Project

Individuals	15 minutes
Objective	Identify, classify, and describe plane and geometric figures.
Materials	Construction paper, tangram and pattern block cutouts, toothpicks, string
Visual, Tactual	

Geometric Figures in Art

- Tell students that they are going to construct a creative piece of art for a Math Art Fair. They must use geometric figures and may include geometric concepts such as congruence and symmetry.
- Students may use a variety of materials, such as construction paper, tangram and pattern block cutouts, toothpicks, wire, string, wallpaper, thread, cloth, yarn, and tiles. Set up a schedule to include deadlines for submitting project ideas, check-up times, and the final due date.
- Use the activity found on page 484 to wrap up the Unit Project.

Spiral Review

Pairs	20 minutes
Objective	Identify, classify, and describe plane and geometric figures.
Materials	Notepads, pencils
Auditory, Tactual, Kinesthetic	

Geometric Figures in the Classroom

- Have pairs of students take a walk around the classroom and list as many examples of plane and solid shapes as they can.
- Have students write on their list the name of each object and the shape it shows. Then have students compare and share their lists. The pair with the most objects labeled correctly wins.

Vocabulary Activity

Individuals	30 minutes
Objective	Identify, classify, and describe plane and geometric figures.
Materials	2 sets of number cards 0–8; index cards labeled *hexagon, octagon, pentagon, rectangle, square, rhombus, trapezoid*
Tactual, Visual	

Names of Shapes

- Spread out the number cards facedown. Each student picks a shape card, then picks one or two number cards to match the number of sides.
- Students can pick one or two cards and add the numbers. If their number matches the number of sides of the shape, the student keeps that shape card. If not, the number cards are replaced. Play continues until all shape cards are used.

Take-Home Game

Pairs	15 minutes
Objective	Identify, classify, and describe solid geometric figures.
Materials	Household foods and dry goods items
Visual, Tactual	

Identify Shapes

- Have students describe food products to a family member. Have them give clues about the shape of the container, the shape of one face of the container, and something about the product.
- If the family member guesses the product, he or she gets 1 point. If not, the student gets 1 point. The game ends when one player gets 5 points.

Repeatable Unit Game

Pairs	15 minutes
Objective	Identify objects by geometric attribute.
Materials	Number cube, grid paper
Auditory, Visual	

Perimeter

- Students play in pairs. The object of the game is to draw the figure with the greatest perimeter. Players start by rolling a number cube twice to make a two-digit number.
- Next, players draw a figure on their grid paper that has an area in square units equal to the number rolled. Then they each find the perimeter. The player with the greater perimeter wins.

Math Expressions

Pairs	20 minutes
Objective	Draw shapes to explore their attributes.
Materials	Drawing Figures Copymaster
Tactual, Visual	

Drawing Shapes

This activity uses instructional practices from *Math Expressions* with the content of this unit.

- Have students describe what they know about these different shapes: quadrilaterals (rectangle, square, trapezoid, parallelogram, rhombus), other polygons (pentagon, hexagon, octagon), and triangles (equilateral, isosceles, scalene, right, obtuse, acute). Distribute copies of the Drawing Figures Copymaster to pairs.
- Tell students they can use the grid to help them make sure that the particular shapes they will be drawing have the correct side lengths, number of sides, or kind of angle.
- Have one partner choose a shape for the other partner to draw. The other partner uses the Drawing Figures grid to draw the shape. The partner checks the shape to see if it has the correct attributes. For example, square: sides of equal length and corners are right angles.
- Students can practice using the Drawing Figures Copymaster for drawing congruent and symmetrical shapes.

Starting Unit 6

Reading Mathematics

Use the *Reading Mathematics* pages to be sure that students have adequate understanding and fluency with the unit vocabulary. This provides the key foundation for developing the unit concepts and skills.

Reviewing Vocabulary

- Write the vocabulary words and their meanings on the board. Underline parts of the definition to help students understand the concept. This will also help them visualize the idea in their minds.
- Draw a picture for each vocabulary word.

Reading Words and Symbols

- Many geometric figures can be described by sides and angles as shown in the examples. Some can also be described in terms of other geometric figures.
- Below, see ways a square can be described. This may help students answer Problem 2.

  A square is . . .

  a rectangle with all sides of the same length.

  a rhombus with all right angles.

  a parallelogram with all right angles and all sides of the same length.

Reading Mathematics

Reviewing Vocabulary

Here are some math vocabulary words that you should know.

angle	two rays with a common endpoint	
line	a straight path of points that goes on without end in both directions	
line segment	a part of a line with two endpoints	
triangle	a polygon with 3 sides	

Reading Words and Symbols

There are many different geometric figures.

Look at the names of these polygons.

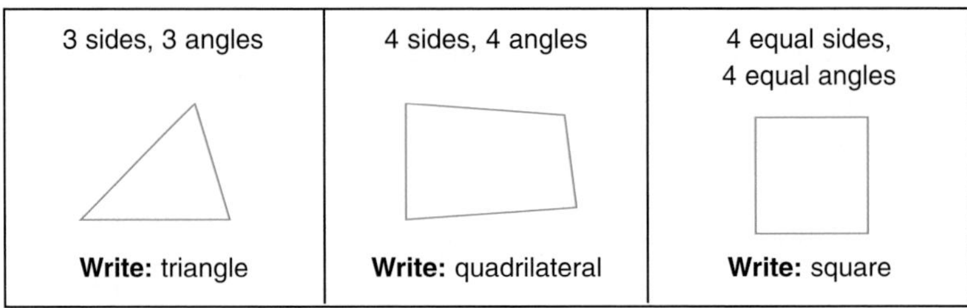

3 sides, 3 angles	4 sides, 4 angles	4 equal sides, 4 equal angles
Write: triangle	**Write:** quadrilateral	**Write:** square

Use the figure at the right for Problems 1–2.
Possible answers given.

1. What figure is shown at the right?
   square; quadrilateral, rectangle, rhombus
2. Are there other names you could give the figure? Explain your thinking.
   See Additional Answers.

Reading Test Questions

Choose the correct answer for each.

3. Which figure is a circle?

a. 

c. 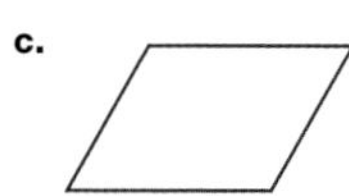

(b.) 

d. 

Figure means "shape."

4. Which pair of figures appears to be the same size and shape?

a. 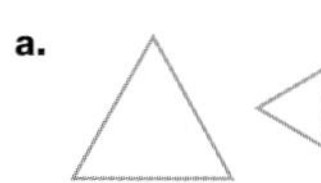

(c.) 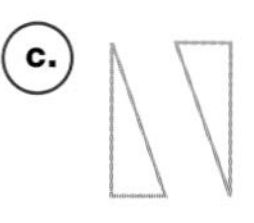

b. 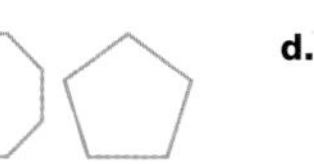

d. 

Pair means "group of two."

5. How many stars are inside the rectangular figure at the right?

a. 9 c. 18

b. 12 (d.) 24

Rectangular means "shaped like a rectangle."

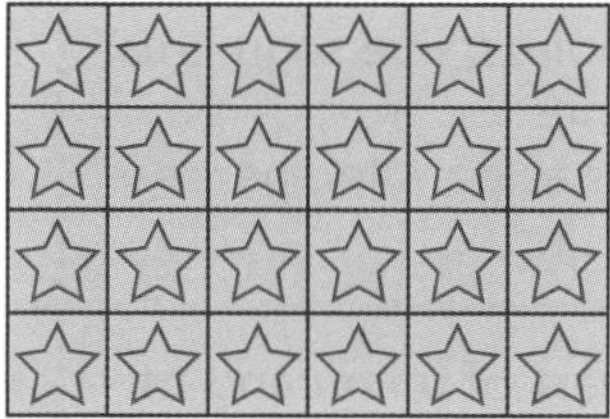

Learning Vocabulary

Watch for these words in this unit. Write their definitions in your journal.

- radius
- net
- acute angle
- reflection

Education Place

At **eduplace.com/map** see eGlossary and eGames—Math Lingo.

Literature Connection

Read "Dividing the Cheese" on Page 651. Then work with a partner to answer the questions about the story.

Literature Connection

Student Book List Selection

You may use the ***Literature Connection*** (Student Book page 651, Teacher's Edition Page T53) at any time during this unit.

Other Literature Connections

Counting on Frank
by Rod Clement

Polygons
by David L. Stienecker

Build It with Boxes
by Joan Irvine

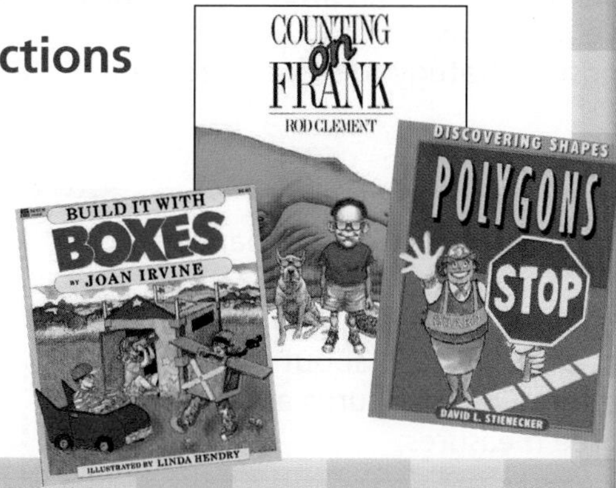

Reading Test Questions

- Tell students to focus on what the problem is asking. For **Item 3**, look for a round figure among the four figures shown to eliminate other choices. The question also might be asked: Which figure does not have any line segments?
- For **Item 4**, the word *congruent* may be used instead of "the same size and shape" to ask the same question. Remind students to think of the different transformational moves to help them find the answer.

Learning Vocabulary

- Go over the list of new words with the class. Help students pronounce the words correctly and explain that they will learn about these words as they work on this unit. If students are keeping Math Journals, be sure that they enter the words and their definitions as they find them in the unit.
- The *Building Vocabulary Kit* includes vocabulary cards and additional teaching strategies for unit vocabulary.

Writing in Mathematics

Writing helps students learn and remember. Throughout the unit, students have opportunities to write for different purposes:

- explaining their thinking or solution strategies
- creating new problems
- recording what they have learned
- listing questions they still have

Look for *Explain Your Thinking* questions in the student text and *Math Journal Prompts* in this Teacher's Edition.

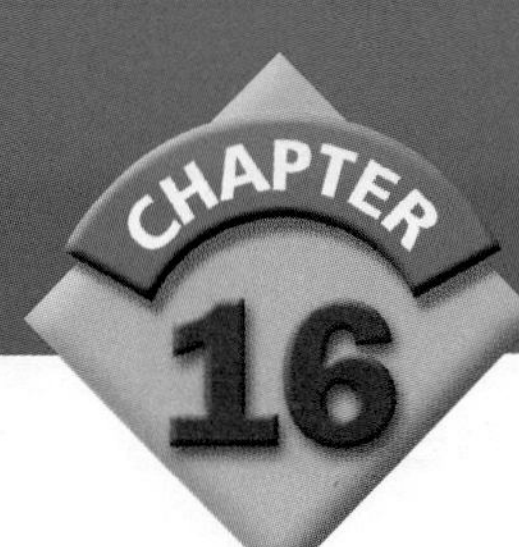

Planning Guide

Plane Figures

Lesson	Overview	Objective/Vocabulary
1 Points, Lines, and Line Segments p. 404A	▶ Using words, symbols, and letters, describe and label points, line segments, lines, and pairs of lines. ▶ Classify pairs of lines as parallel, perpendicular, and intersecting.	▶ Identify geometric figures. line segment, intersecting lines, parallel lines, perpendicular lines, endpoints, right angle
2 Rays and Angles p. 408A	▶ Learn that a ray is part of a line and of an angle. Words, letters, and symbols are used to label and name a ray. ▶ Given three points, label an angle three ways. ▶ Classify angles by the size of their openings between the rays: acute, right, obtuse, or straight.	▶ Name and describe rays and angles. ray, angle, sides, vertex, obtuse angle, acute angle, straight angle
3 Hands On: Measure Angles p. 410A	▶ Following step-by-step procedures, students learn to draw and measure angles with a protractor. ▶ Based on knowledge of types of angles, decide which scale on a protractor to use to draw or measure an angle.	▶ Use a protractor to measure angles. degrees, protractor
4 Quadrilaterals and Other Polygons p. 412A	▶ Learn about quadrilaterals with special names. ▶ Learn about regular or irregular polygons, such as triangles, pentagons, and octagons.	▶ Classify and identify polygons. polygons, rhombus, sides, trapezoid
5 Classify Triangles p. 416A	▶ Classify triangles by their side lengths or angle measurement. ▶ Draw or identify triangles, using these two triangle classifications methods.	▶ Identify and classify triangles. equilateral, isosceles, scalene, right, obtuse, acute
6 Problem-Solving Strategy: Find a Pattern p. 418A	▶ Find and describe geometric patterns to solve problems. ▶ Choose a strategy to solve a problem.	▶ Find patterns to solve problems.
7 Circles p. 422A	▶ Learn, describe, and label parts of a circle. ▶ Since a full circle has a full turn, or rotation, of 360°, learn about quarter, half, and three-quarter turns associated with degree measures.	▶ Identify parts of a circle. circle, center, radius (radii), diameter, chord

Skills Trace: Plane Figures		
Grade 3	**Grade 4**	**Grade 5**
• Identify lines, line segments, rays, and angles (ch. 15) • Classify plane figures, triangles, and quadrilaterals (ch. 15) • Solve problems by finding and completing patterns (ch. 15)	• Identify points, lines, line segments, and rays • Classify and measure angles • Classify triangles and quadrilaterals • Identify parts of a circle • Find patterns to solve problems	• Identify points, lines, and rays (ch. 15) • Classify, measure, and draw angles (ch. 15) • Classify triangles and quadrilaterals (ch. 15) • Find the circumference of a circle (ch. 16) • Use a pattern to solve a problem (ch. 16)

Differentiated Instruction	Materials	NCTM Standards
▶ Differentiated Instruction activities, p. 404B ▶ *Chapter Challenges,* p. 91 *Ways to Success* CD-ROM 16.1 ▶ *Ways to Success* Skillsheet 137	Blank transparency, Learning Tool 22	**Geometry:** Analyze attributes of two- and three-dimensional shapes and develop vocabulary to describe the attributes.
▶ Differentiated Instruction activities, p. 408B *Ways to Success* CD-ROM 16.2 ▶ *Ways to Success* Skillsheet 140	Protractor Transparency	**Geometry:** Analyze attributes of two- and three-dimensional shapes and develop vocabulary to describe the attributes.
▶ Differentiated Instruction activities, p. 410B ▶ *Chapter Challenges,* p. 93 *Ways to Success* CD-ROM 16.3 ▶ *Ways to Success* Skillsheet 140	Protractor, Protractor Transparency	**Geometry:** Classify two- and three-dimensional shapes according to their properties and develop definitions of classes of shapes.
▶ Differentiated Instruction activities, p. 412B *Ways to Success* CD-ROM 16.4 ▶ *Ways to Success* Skillsheet 138 Audio Tutor **2**/10 Listen and Understand	Construction paper, scissors	**Geometry:** Classify two- and three-dimensional shapes according to their properties and develop definitions of classes of shapes.
▶ Differentiated Instruction activities, p. 416B ▶ *Chapter Challenges,* p. 95 *Ways to Success* CD-ROM 16.5 ▶ *Ways to Success* Skillsheet 142	Triangles Transparency, Half-Centimeter Grid Transparency	**Geometry:** Classify two- and three-dimensional shapes according to their properties and develop definitions of classes of shapes.
▶ Differentiated Instruction activities, p. 418B *Ways to Success* CD-ROM 16.6 ▶ *Ways to Success* Skillsheet 144 Audio Tutor **2**/11 Listen and Understand		**Problem Solving:** Build new mathematical knowledge through problem solving; apply and adapt a variety of appropriate strategies to solve problems.
▶ Differentiated Instruction activities, p. 422B *Ways to Success* CD-ROM 16.7 ▶ *Ways to Success* Skillsheet 143 Audio Tutor **2**/12 Listen and Understand	Chalkboard compass	**Geometry:** Analyze attributes of two- and three-dimensional shapes and develop vocabulary to describe the attributes; classify two- and three-dimensional shapes according to their properties and develop definitions of classes of shapes.

Math Notes

Chapter Objectives

16A Name and describe characteristics of points, lines, line segments, rays, and angles.

16B Identify, classify, and describe plane geometric figures.

16C Solve problems using skills and strategies.

Mathematical Background

Polygons

A *polygon* is a simple, closed figure formed by three or more line segments that meet only at their endpoints. Polygons can be classified by the properties of their sides and the measures of their angles. At this grade level, students are expected to know the following polygons: triangle (3 sides), quadrilateral (4 sides), pentagon (5 sides), hexagon (6 sides), and octagon (8 sides).

Triangles are classified by the lengths of their sides and the measures of their angles.

acute equilateral	right isosceles	obtuse scalene

Quadrilaterals are classified by the properties of their sides and the measures of their angles.

quadrilateral, parallelogram, rectangle, rhombus, square	quadrilateral, parallelogram	quadrilateral, trapezoid

Research-Based Teaching

Dutch educators Pierre van Hiele and Dina van Hiele-Geldof (1959–1985) suggested that there were five levels of geometric thinking. Recent research confirms this and takes the idea one step further by asserting that these levels may be fluid. For example, students may regress from the analysis level to the visualization level when confronted with new geometric topics. See *Professional Resources Handbook, Grade 4,* Unit 6.

For more ideas relating to Unit 6, see the Teacher Support Handbook at the back of this Teacher's Edition.

Language Intervention

Visualization and geometry are considered important parts of East Asian mathematics, particularly elementary mathematics. For further explanation, see "Mathematical Language and Geometry" in the *Professional Resources Handbook, Grade 4.*

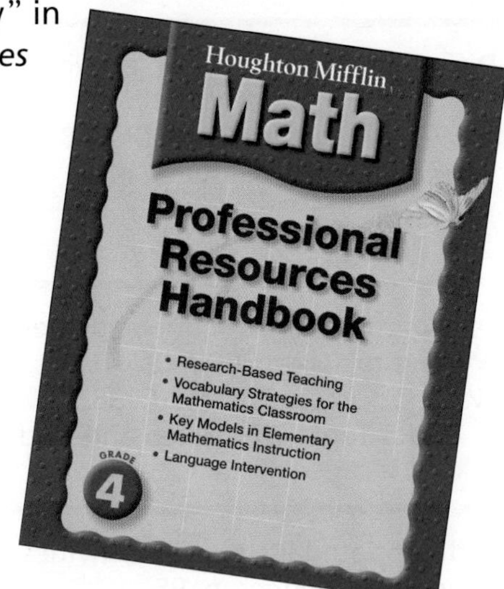

Chapter Activities

Connecting to the Unit Project

Pairs	25 minutes
Objective	Identify and draw geometric figures.
Materials	Research materials, art supplies
Visual, Tactual	

Create Geometric Art

- Tell students that they are going to create an artistic piece for a Math Art Fair.
- Have students research the paintings of artists such as Pablo Picasso, Piet Mondrian, Fernand Léger, and Juan Gris.
- Have students use these paintings as inspiration, or create their own ideas to create art that contains plane geometric figures.
- Have students present their pieces to the class.

Assessing Prior Knowledge

Whole Class	25 minutes
Objective	Identify geometric figures.
Materials	None
Visual, Tactual	

Names of Geometric Figures

- Write the words *point, line segment, angle, triangle,* and *quadrilateral* on the board in a column and have students copy the list.
- Tell students to look around the classroom to locate a particular geometric figure and say, for example, "I spy an angle."
- Then have students write the name of the object next to the word called out.
- Continue the game until all the words on the board are used. Have students share their responses.

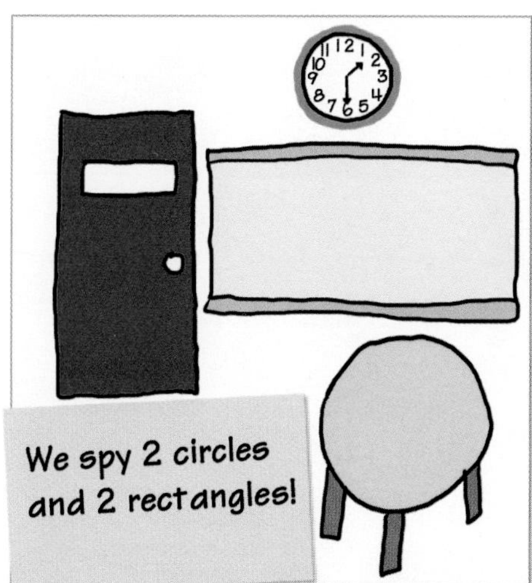
We spy 2 circles
and 2 rectangles!

Ongoing Skill Activity

Whole Class	10 minutes
Objective	Identify geometric figures.
Materials	Newspapers, magazines, advertisements
Visual, Tactual	

Real-World Geometric Figures

- Tell students to write the names of all the polygons mentioned in the lessons in this chapter.
- Students can bring newspapers, magazines, and advertisements to class to make a common resource area for them. Have students look for different types of polygons in the pictures.
- Have students share their findings with the whole class.

Starting Chapter 16

Investigation

Using Data

Have students work in small groups to answer the question posed on page 402.

To extend the investigation, have students do the following activity.

- From magazines, cut out pictures to show geometric figures. Use a colored marker to outline the figures. Name each figure according to the number of sides.

For more information about projects and investigations,

Visit **Education Place**®
www.eduplace.com/mat

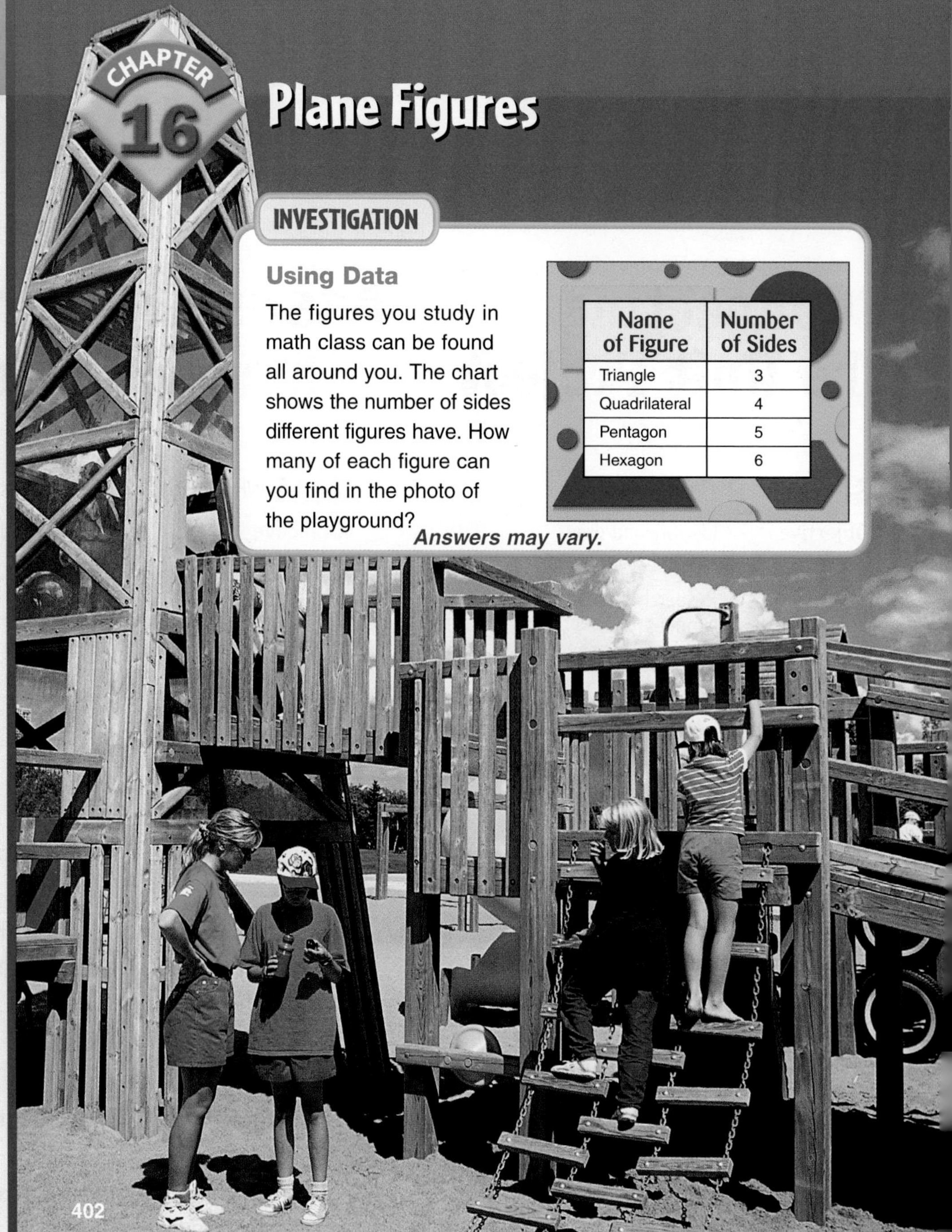

CHAPTER 16
Plane Figures
INVESTIGATION
Using Data
The figures you study in math class can be found all around you. The chart shows the number of sides different figures have. How many of each figure can you find in the photo of the playground?
Answers may vary.
402

Name of Figure	Number of Sides
Triangle	3
Quadrilateral	4
Pentagon	5
Hexagon	6

Chapter 16 Prerequisite Skills Pretest

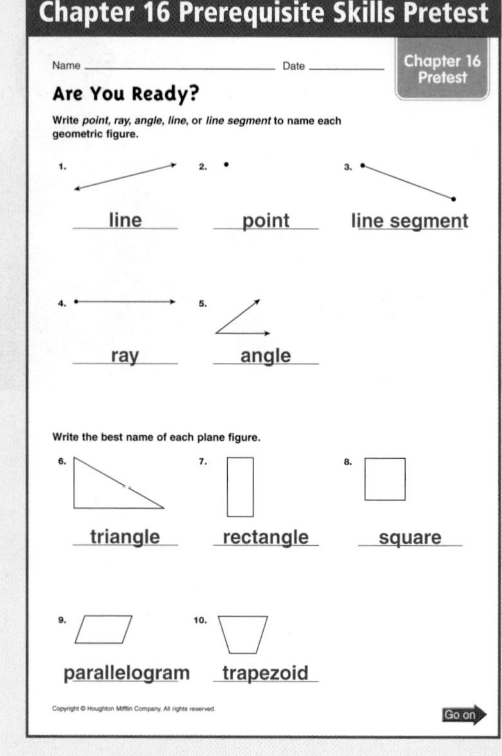

Name ______ Date ______ Chapter 16 Pretest

Are You Ready?

Write *point, ray, angle, line,* or *line segment* to name each geometric figure.

1. line
2. point
3. line segment
4. ray
5. angle

Write the best name of each plane figure.

6. triangle
7. rectangle
8. square
9. parallelogram
10. trapezoid

Go on

Use this page to review and remember what you need to know for this chapter.

VOCABULARY

Vocabulary
line
circle
triangle
rectangle

Choose the best word to complete each sentence.

1. A straight path of points that goes on without end in both directions is a ____. **line**
2. A polygon with exactly three sides is a ____. **triangle**
3. A ____ is a polygon with opposite sides parallel and four right angles. **rectangle**

CONCEPTS AND SKILLS

Tell whether each figure is a line, a line segment, or an angle.

4. **line segment**

5. 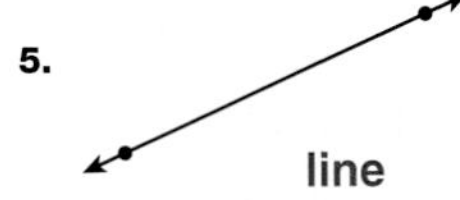 **line**

6. 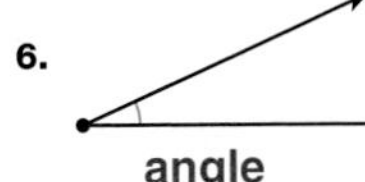 **angle**

Draw a polygon for each description. Name the polygon you drew. ***Possible figures given.***

7. a figure with four equal sides **square; *Check students' drawings.***
8. a figure with five sides **pentagon; *Check students' drawings.***
9. a figure with two pairs of parallel sides **parallelogram; *Check students' drawings.***

Possible answers: **4 equal sides, 4 right angles, square, rectangle, quadrilateral, parallelogram. Explanations should show an understanding of the definition of each word.**

10. Use as many different words as you can to describe this figure. Tell why those words are good descriptions. 

Facts Practice, See Page 667.

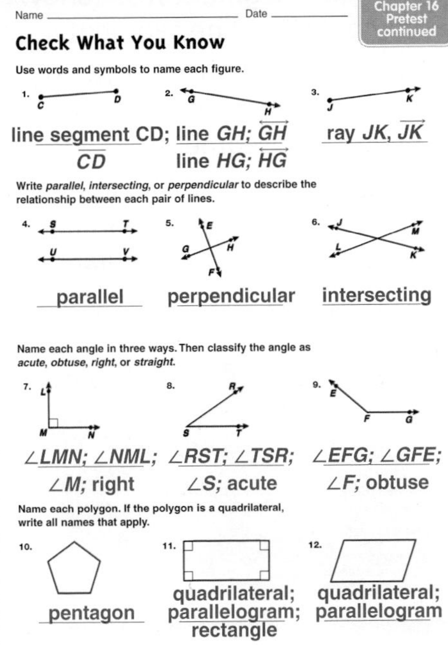

Chapter 16 New Content Pretest

Name ________ Date ________ Chapter 16 Pretest continued

Check What You Know

Use words and symbols to name each figure.

1. **line segment CD; $\overline{CD}$**
2. **line GH; $\overleftrightarrow{GH}$ line HG; $\overleftrightarrow{HG}$**
3. **ray JK, $\overrightarrow{JK}$**

Write *parallel*, *intersecting*, or *perpendicular* to describe the relationship between each pair of lines.

4. **parallel**
5. **perpendicular**
6. **intersecting**

Name each angle in three ways. Then classify the angle as *acute*, *obtuse*, *right*, or *straight*.

7. **∠LMN; ∠NML; ∠M; right**
8. **∠RST; ∠TSR; ∠S; acute**
9. **∠EFG; ∠GFE; ∠F; obtuse**

Name each polygon. If the polygon is a quadrilateral, write all names that apply.

10. **pentagon**
11. **quadrilateral; parallelogram; rectangle**
12. **quadrilateral; parallelogram**

Go on

Chapter 16 New Content Pretest

Name ________ Date ________ Chapter 16 Pretest continued

Classify each triangle as *equilateral*, *isosceles*, or *scalene* and as *right*, *obtuse*, or *acute*.

13. **equilateral acute**
14. **scalene right**
15. **scalene obtuse**

Name the part of each circle that is shown with a dotted line. Write *center*, *radius*, *diameter*, or *chord*.

16. **chord**
17. **diameter**
18. **radius**

Find the pattern to solve each problem.

19. A pattern has a repeating design that shows only a star, a rectangle, and a circle in a row. The circle is just before the star. The rectangle is first. Draw the first 8 figures in the pattern.
Check students' drawings; rectangle, circle, star, rectangle, circle, star, rectangle, circle

20. Jessica made a design in which 4 out of every 5 squares were red. Jessica's design contained 50 squares. How many squares were red?
40 squares

STOP

Use What You Know

Use this page for informal assessment and review of prerequisite skills.

- Items 1–3: Use math vocabulary
- Items 4–6: Identify lines, line segments, and angles
- Items 7–9: Draw and identify quadrilaterals and other polygons
- Item 10: Describe a square

Customize Your Instruction

Use the Chapter Pretest in the Unit Resource folder to help customize and pace instruction.

Objectives and Resources

▶ Prerequisite Skills Pretest

- Items 1–5: Identify points, lines, line segments, rays, and angles.
- Items 6–10: Identify triangles and quadrilaterals.

▶ New Content Pretest

- Items 1–9: Name and describe characteristics of points, lines, line segments, rays, and angles.
- Items 10–18: Identify, classify, and describe plane geometric figures.
- Items 19–20: Solve problems using skills and strategies.

▶ For Students Having Difficulty

- *Ways to Success* CD: 16A, 16B
- *Ways to Success* Skillsheet: 137–138

▶ For Students Having Success

- Enrichment 16.1–16.7

▶ For Mathematically Promising Students

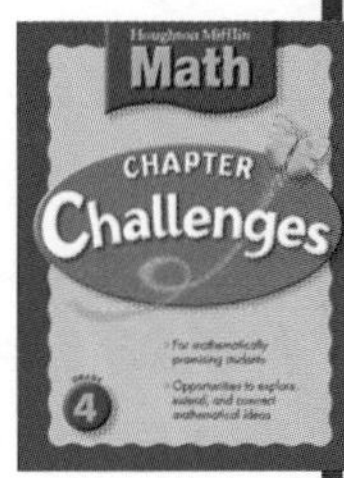

Explore: Lines and Strings, page 91, after Lesson 1

Extend: Circles and Compasses, page 93, after Lesson 3

Connect: Shapes of States, page 95, after Lesson 5

Lesson 16.1

Points, Lines, and Line Segments

Planning

Lesson Objective Identify geometric figures.

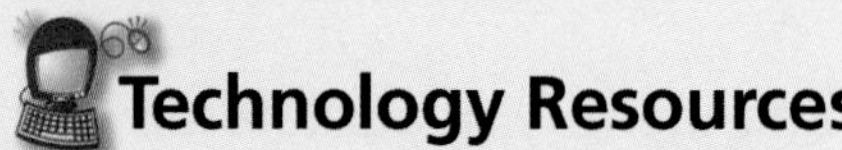

Technology Resources

- *Ways to Success* CD-ROM 16.1
- Education Place: Extra Practice, eGlossary, eGames
  www.eduplace.com/map

Lesson 16.1 Transparency

Problem of the Day

In how many different ways can Lucia, Kate, Mario, and Sharice stand in line if Kate is always first? (6 ways)

Spiral Review

Solve. Use the following set of numbers: {2, 3, 7, 3, 12, 5, 8, 1, 4}

1. What is the range of the numbers? (11)
2. What is the mode of the numbers? (3)
3. What is the mean of the numbers? (5)
4. What is the median of the numbers? (4)

Lesson Quiz

Write *true* or *false* for each sentence.

1. If two lines are parallel, they meet. (false)
2. Perpendicular lines intersect at right angles. (true)
3. A line segment has one endpoint. (false)
4. All intersecting lines are perpendicular. (false)

NCTM Standards

Geometry: Analyze attributes of two- and three-dimensional shapes and develop vocabulary to describe the attributes; classify two- and three-dimensional shapes according to their properties and develop definitions of classes and shapes.

Getting Started

Building Math Vocabulary

line segment	a part of a line that has two endpoints
endpoints	the points at either end of a line segment or the beginning point of a ray
parallel	lines that lie in the same plane and do not intersect are parallel; they are always the same distance apart
intersecting	lines that meet or cross at a common point are intersecting
perpendicular	two lines or line segments that cross or meet to form right angles are perpendicular
right angle	an angle made when two line segments meet to form a square corner; it measures 90°

Help students distinguish between lines and line segments. Guide them to understand that a line segment is a subset of a line and has two endpoints. Have students identify line segments in the classroom. Classify pairs of lines as parallel (those that never cross), intersecting (those that cross each other), and perpendicular (those that form right angles).

Points, Lines, and Line Segments

Whole Class	15 minutes
Objective	Name and describe points, lines, and line segments.
Materials	Blank transparency
Visual	

- Remind students that examples of points and lines are all around them. Explain that the period at the end of a sentence is a point, and that the top edge of the chalkboard represents a line segment.
- On a blank transparency, draw point *B* with line *CD* next to it. Next to that, draw line segment *QR*.
- Point to point *B*. **A point is a location in space. We say "point *B*" and write *B*.**
- Point to line *CD*. **A line goes on without end in two directions. We say "line *CD*" or "line *DC*."** Show the symbol for line.
- Then point to line segment *QR*. **A line segment is a part of a line. It has two endpoints.** Point to the endpoints. **We say "line segment *QR*" or "line segment *RQ*."** Show the symbol for a line segment.
- Invite one volunteer to draw two other lines, and another to draw two more line segments.
- Tell students that the lesson will identify pairs of lines as parallel, intersecting, or perpendicular.

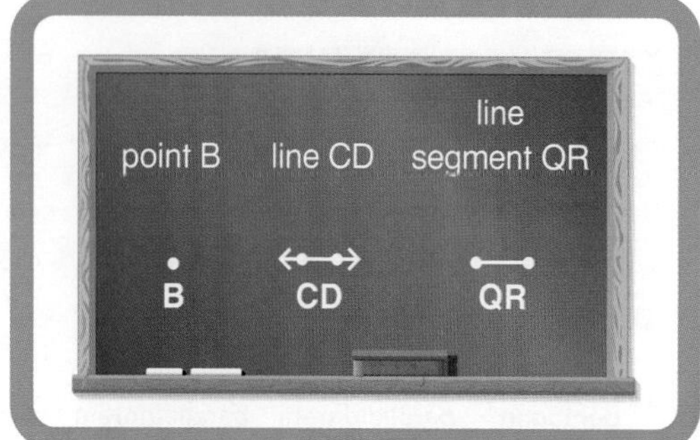

Differentiated Instruction

English Learners

Whole Class	10 minutes
Objective	Name points, lines, and line segments.
Materials	Student page 405
Visual, Auditory	

Early Production

- Students may need additional practice using new vocabulary.
- After completing ***Guided Practice,*** students can go back and label and say every part of each figure using words in the vocabulary box.
- After completing **Problems 8–16,** pair students and have them repeat every part of each figure.

Intermediate/Advanced

- English Learner Resource 16.1
- English Learner Handbook

Intervention

Small Groups	15 minutes
Objective	Name and describe points, lines, and line segments.
Materials	None
Auditory, Visual	

- Have students work in small groups. Before formally introducing the figures in the lesson, invite students to work together to come up with their own definitions of points and lines.
- For example, ask groups to discuss the following questions: **How would you describe a point? What words would you use to describe a line? How is a point different from a line?**
- Have groups briefly share and discuss their answers.

Other Resources

- *Ways to Success* CD-ROM 16.1

Special Needs

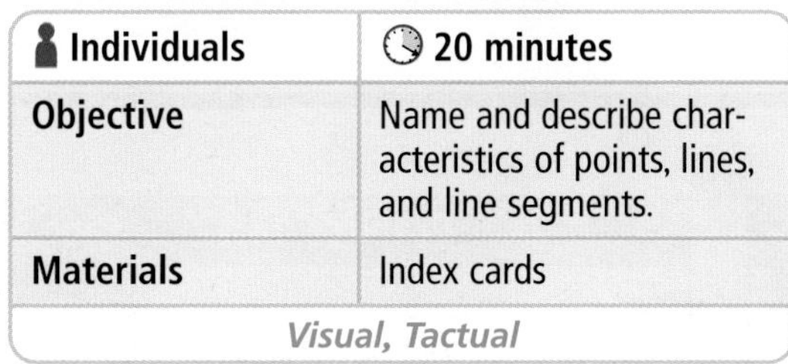

Individuals	20 minutes
Objective	Name and describe characteristics of points, lines, and line segments.
Materials	Index cards
Visual, Tactual	

- Guide students to make a labeled diagram for each figure shown on page 404, one per card.
- Check that students' diagrams are correct. Then have students use the cards to help them learn the differences and similarities among the figures, including the symbols used to identify each.

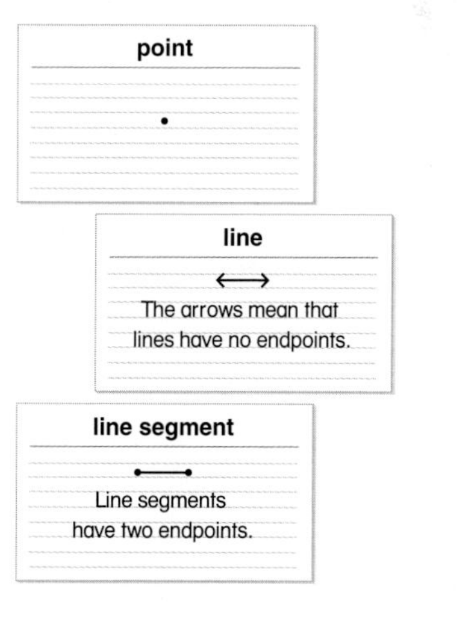

point
line
The arrows mean that lines have no endpoints.
line segment
Line segments have two endpoints.

Language Arts Connection

Materials: straightedge

- Write the capital letters *K* and *H* on the board, using only line segments. Point out the three segments for K. For H, discuss how the two vertical segments are parallel to each other and perpendicular to the horizontal segment.
- Have students write all the capital letters that are made of only line segments (A, E, F, H, I, K, L, M, N, T, V, W, X, Y, Z). Have them identify the parallel and perpendicular line segments in the letters.

❶ Introduce

Tell students that they will use words, symbols, and letters to describe and label points, lines, line segments, and pairs of lines. They will also classify pairs of lines as parallel, perpendicular, and intersecting.

❷ Teach

Learn About It

- Emphasize that we name a point with a dot and a capital letter. Explain that the place where two lines meet, or intersect, is a point.
- Discuss the difference between lines and line segments. **Why does the word segment make sense for describing part of a line?** (It means "piece.")
- Discuss parallel lines and the symbol for "is parallel to." **Why must railroad tracks be parallel lines?** (because a train's wheels are the same distance apart)
- **How are parallel lines different from intersecting lines?** (The distance between parallel lines is the same; the distance between intersecting lines is not.)
- **How many right angles are formed at the intersection of two perpendicular lines?** (4)

Common Error

- Confusing lines and line segments.
- **Intervention** Emphasize the importance of the endpoints and the arrows on each type of figure. Stress that lines have no endpoints, which is shown by the arrows pointing in either direction. Discuss that when we say *line* in everyday speech, we usually only mean line segment.

Lesson 1

Points, Lines, and Line Segments

Objective Identify geometric figures.

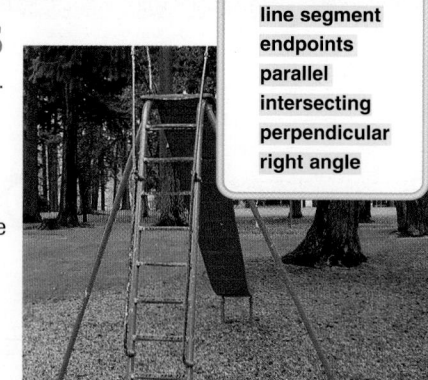

Vocabulary
line segment
endpoints
parallel
intersecting
perpendicular
right angle

Learn About It

Many everyday things can model geometric figures. The period at the end of this sentence is a model of a point. A solid painted stripe in the middle of a straight road is a model of a line. The rungs on a metal ladder are models of parallel line segments.

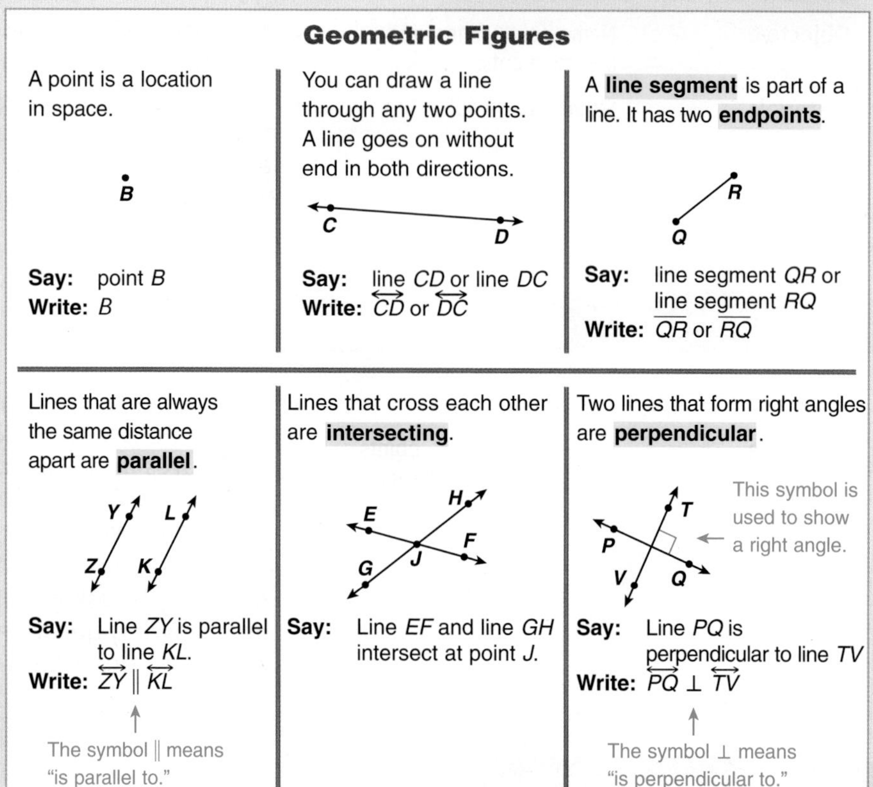

Geometric Figures

A point is a location in space. Say: point *B* Write: *B*	You can draw a line through any two points. A line goes on without end in both directions. Say: line *CD* or line *DC* Write: $\overleftrightarrow{CD}$ or $\overleftrightarrow{DC}$	A **line segment** is part of a line. It has two **endpoints**. Say: line segment *QR* or line segment *RQ* Write: $\overline{QR}$ or $\overline{RQ}$
Lines that are always the same distance apart are **parallel**. Say: Line *ZY* is parallel to line *KL*. Write: $\overleftrightarrow{ZY} \parallel \overleftrightarrow{KL}$ The symbol ∥ means "is parallel to."	Lines that cross each other are **intersecting**. Say: Line *EF* and line *GH* intersect at point *J*.	Two lines that form right angles are **perpendicular**. This symbol is used to show a right angle. Say: Line *PQ* is perpendicular to line *TV* Write: $\overleftrightarrow{PQ} \perp \overleftrightarrow{TV}$ The symbol ⊥ means "is perpendicular to."

Reteach 16.1

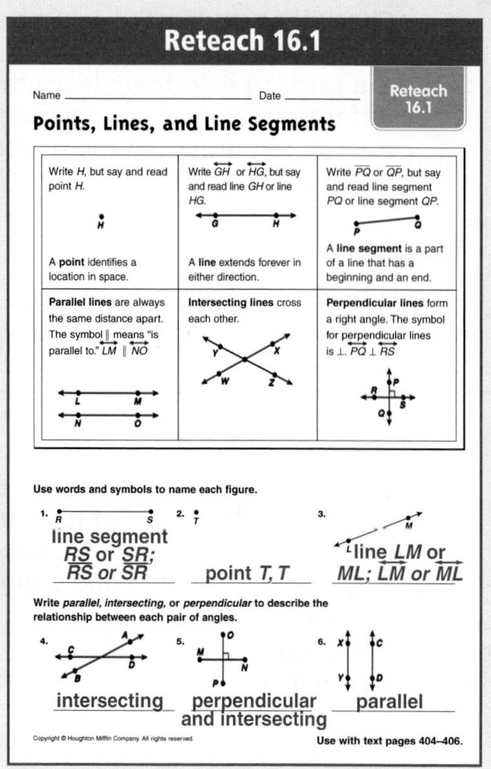

Name ______ Date ______ Reteach 16.1

Points, Lines, and Line Segments

Write *H*, but say and read point *H*. A **point** identifies a location in space.	Write $\overleftrightarrow{GH}$ or $\overleftrightarrow{HG}$, but say and read line *GH* or line *HG*. A **line** extends forever in either direction.	Write $\overline{PQ}$ or $\overline{QP}$, but say and read line segment *PQ* or line segment *QP*. A **line segment** is a part of a line that has a beginning and an end.
Parallel lines are always the same distance apart. The symbol ∥ means "is parallel to." $\overleftrightarrow{LM} \parallel \overleftrightarrow{NO}$	**Intersecting lines** cross each other.	**Perpendicular lines** form a right angle. The symbol for perpendicular lines is ⊥. $\overleftrightarrow{PQ} \perp \overleftrightarrow{RS}$

Use words and symbols to name each figure.

1. line segment $\overline{RS}$ or $\overline{SR}$; *RS* or *SR*
2. point *T*, *T*
3. line *LM* or *ML*; $\overleftrightarrow{LM}$ or $\overleftrightarrow{ML}$

Write *parallel*, *intersecting*, or *perpendicular* to describe the relationship between each pair of angles.

4. intersecting
5. perpendicular and intersecting
6. parallel

Use with text pages 404–406.

Practice 16.1 Page 98

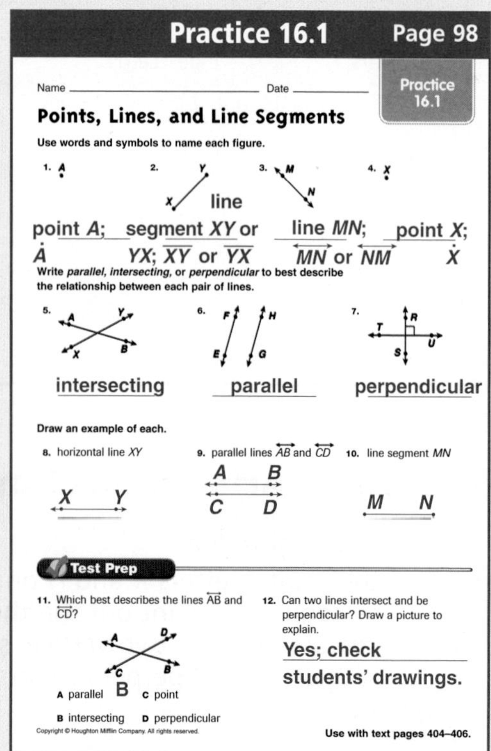

Name ______ Date ______ Practice 16.1

Points, Lines, and Line Segments

Use words and symbols to name each figure.

1. point *A*; *A*
2. line segment *XY* or *YX*; $\overline{XY}$ or $\overline{YX}$
3. line *MN*; $\overleftrightarrow{MN}$ or $\overleftrightarrow{NM}$
4. point *X*; *X*

Write *parallel*, *intersecting*, or *perpendicular* to best describe the relationship between each pair of lines.

5. intersecting
6. parallel
7. perpendicular

Draw an example of each.

8. horizontal line *XY*
9. parallel lines $\overleftrightarrow{AB}$ and $\overleftrightarrow{CD}$
10. line segment *MN*

Test Prep

11. Which best describes the lines $\overleftrightarrow{AB}$ and $\overleftrightarrow{CD}$?
A parallel B intersecting C point D perpendicular
Answer: B

12. Can two lines intersect and be perpendicular? Draw a picture to explain.
Yes; check students' drawings.

Use with text pages 404–406.

▶ In the picture at the right, the horizontal line is perpendicular to the vertical line. At their intersection, they form right angles.

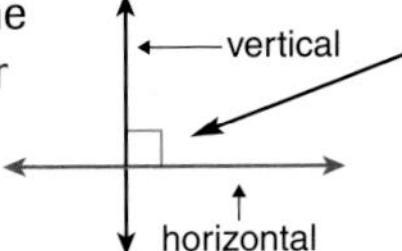

The angle makes a square corner, which is called a **right angle**.

1. line segment *JB* or line segment *BJ*; $\overline{JB}$ or $\overline{BJ}$

Guided Practice

Use words and symbols to name each figure.

1. 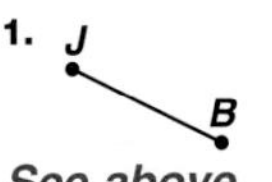 *See above.*
2. • *S* point *S*; *S*
3. line *RW* or line *WR*; $\overleftrightarrow{RW}$ or $\overleftrightarrow{WR}$

Ask Yourself

- Which point will I write first to name the figure?
- What symbol stands for the figure?

Write *parallel, intersecting,* or *perpendicular* to describe the relationship between each pair of lines.

4. 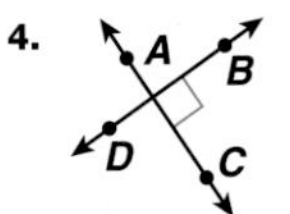 perpendicular, intersecting
5. intersecting
6. 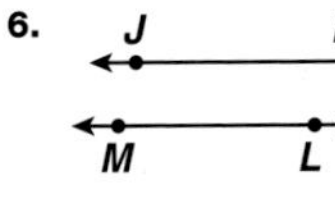 parallel
7. intersecting

Explain Your Thinking ▶ Can two lines be both intersecting and perpendicular? Can two lines be both intersecting and parallel? Explain your thinking. **Two lines can be intersecting and perpendicular because perpendicular lines intersect; Two lines cannot be intersecting and parallel because parallel lines never meet.**

Practice and Problem Solving

Use words and symbols to name each figure.

8. 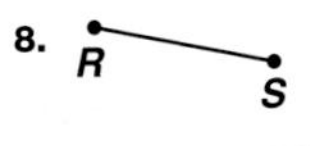 line segment *RS* or line segment *SR*; $\overline{RS}$ or $\overline{SR}$
9. 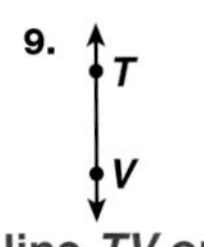 line *TV* or line *VT*; $\overleftrightarrow{TV}$ or $\overleftrightarrow{VT}$
10. line *WZ* or line *ZW*; $\overleftrightarrow{WZ}$ or $\overleftrightarrow{ZW}$
11. • *Q* point *Q*; *Q*
12. 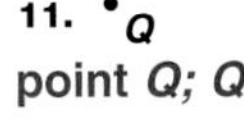 line segment *FP* or line segment *PF*; $\overline{FP}$ or $\overline{PF}$

Write *parallel, intersecting,* or *perpendicular* to describe the relationship between each pair of lines.

13. 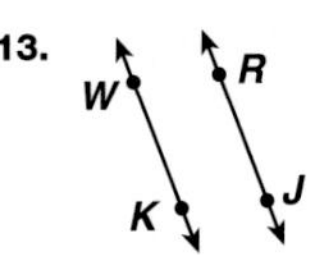 parallel
14. perpendicular
15. 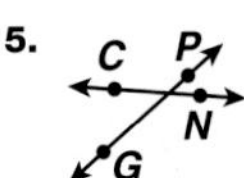 intersecting
16. 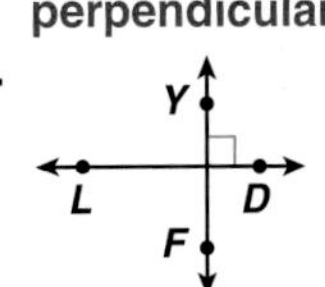 perpendicular

Go On

Guided Practice

Have students complete **Exercises 1–7** as you observe. Remind them to use the ***Ask Yourself*** questions to help. Give students the opportunity to talk about the question in ***Explain Your Thinking***.

❸ Practice

Practice and Problem Solving

Select from **Exercises 8–39** as independent work.

Enrichment 16.1

Name ______ Date ______ Enrichment 16.1

Lines in the Alphabet Soup

In the bowl of soup are some letters of the alphabet. Follow the steps below to group the letters.

1. Circle all the letters that contain perpendicular line segments.
2. Place a rectangle around all the letters that contain parallel line segments.
3. Place a triangle around all the letters that contain non-perpendicular intersecting lines.

O Z H X A P K S C T B L R I D N Y U F V E W M Q

4. Which letters, if any, have both parallel and perpendicular lines? E, F, H, I
5. Which letters have no intersecting lines? B, C, D, O, P, Q, R, S, U

 Use with text pages 404–406.

Problem Solving 16.1

Name ______ Date ______ Problem Solving 16.1

Points, Lines, and Line Segments

Use the map for Problems 1–4.

Main St., 1st St., 2nd St., 3rd St., Calder Way, Lower Ave.

1. Name two pairs of roads that are parallel. Possible answers: Main St. and Lower Ave.; 1st St. and 2nd St.
2. Name two pairs of roads that are perpendicular. Possible answer: Main St. and 1st St.; Lower Ave. and 2nd St.
3. Name two roads that intersect but are not perpendicular. Possible answer: Calder Way and Lower Ave.
4. **Reasoning** Nickel St. is located above Main St. and runs parallel to Main St. Which streets are parallel to and which streets are perpendicular to Nickel St? Possible answer: Nickel St. is parallel to both Main St. and Lower Ave. Therefore, it is also perpendicular to 1st, 2nd, and 3rd St.
5. **You Decide** Which of the first 10 letters of the alphabet contain parallel lines? Which contain perpendicular lines? E, F, H, and I contain parallel lines. E, F, H, I, and J contain perpendicular lines.

 Use with text pages 404–406.

- For **Exercises 17–25**, have students use a ruler when drawing lines and line segments. Also, remind students that a line segment has endpoints.
- For **Exercises 26–33**, ask: **Are all perpendicular lines intersecting lines? Explain.** (Yes; all pairs of perpendicular lines cross each other.)

4 Assess & Close

Math Talk in Action

Have students refer to **Problem 34** to conclude the lesson. Ask questions about real-life examples of the geometric figures from the lesson. For example:

- **What is a real-life example of a point?** (sample answer: the period at the end of a sentence)
- **Where might we find real-life examples of parallel line segments?** (sample answer: the rungs of a chair's back.)

Math Journal Prompt

Have students write a description of each of the geometric figures introduced in the lesson. Ask them to provide a correctly labeled example of each to accompany its description.

Lesson Quiz

Use the quiz on Lesson Transparency 16.1.

Test Prep & Spiral Review

Use Test Prep Transparency 16.1.

Draw an example of each. ***See Additional Answers.***

17. line segment JK **18.** line MN **19.** horizontal line segment WY

20. $\overleftrightarrow{EF} \parallel \overleftrightarrow{GH}$ **21.** $\overleftrightarrow{AB} \perp \overleftrightarrow{CD}$ **22.** horizontal $\overline{PQ}$ and vertical $\overline{PR}$

23. $\overleftrightarrow{CD}$ intersecting $\overleftrightarrow{ST}$ **24.** $\overline{VW} \parallel \overline{XY}$ **25.** $\overline{AB} \perp \overline{QR}$

Write *true* or *false* for each sentence. You can draw a picture to help find the answer.

26. If two lines are parallel, they never meet. **true**

27. If a line is horizontal, it is parallel to a vertical line. **false**

28. If two lines intersect, they are always perpendicular. **false**

29. If two lines are perpendicular, they are also parallel. **false**

Use the drawing at the right for Problems 30–33.

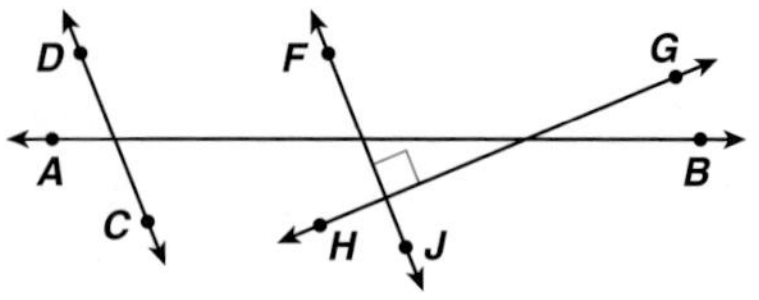

30. Name a line. ***Possible answer:* line *AB***

31. Name a pair of perpendicular lines. **line *FJ* and line *GH***

32. Name a pair of parallel lines. **line *DC* and line *FJ***

33. Explain Is $\overleftrightarrow{AB}$ is perpendicular to $\overleftrightarrow{FJ}$? Explain your answer. **No; *Possible explanation:* Line *AB* and line *FJ* intersect, but not at a right angle, so they are not perpendicular.**

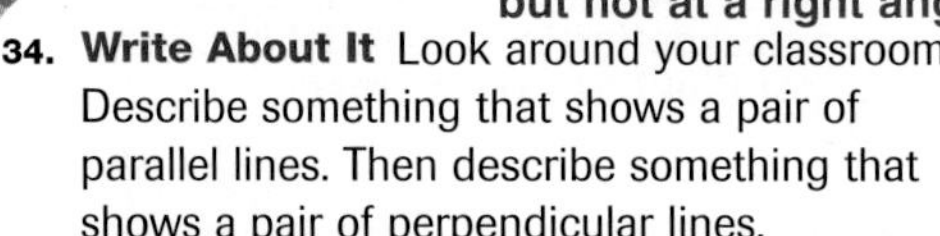

34. Write About It Look around your classroom. Describe something that shows a pair of parallel lines. Then describe something that shows a pair of perpendicular lines. ***Check answers.***

Mixed Review and Test Prep

Open Response

What letter is likely to come next in each pattern? (Grade 3)

35. t u u v v v w w w w x x x x **x**

36. a b a b c a b c d a b c d **e**

37. m n m n o m n o p m n o p **q**

38. a c a c e a c e g a c e g **i**

39. Which lines in the diagram below appear to be perpendicular? Explain your answer. (Ch. 16, Lesson 1) ***See below.***

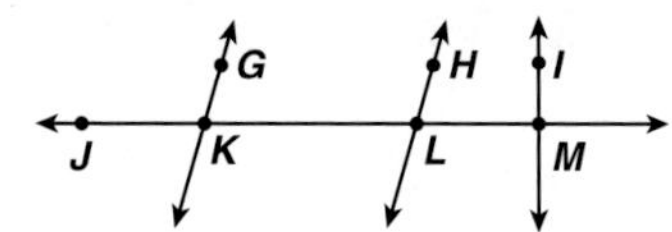

39. line *JM* and line *IM*. *Possible explanation:* Line *JM* and line *IM* intersect at what looks like a right angle.

406

Extra Practice See page 427, Set A.

Homework 16.1 Page 98

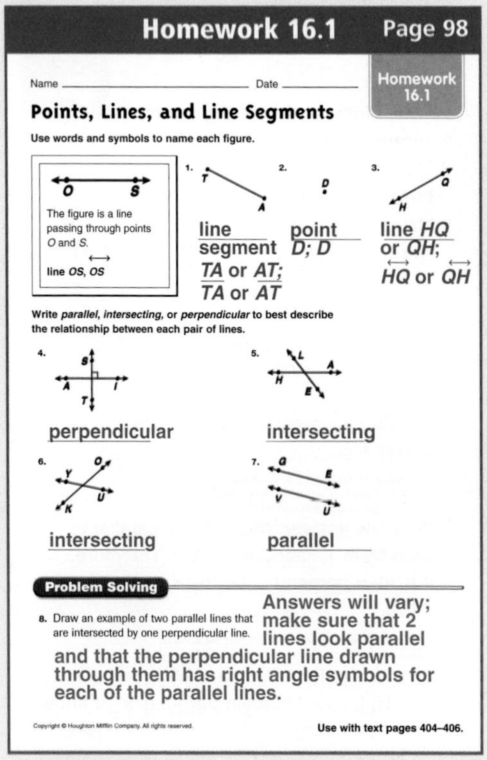

Name ______ Date ______ Homework 16.1

Points, Lines, and Line Segments

Use words and symbols to name each figure.

The figure is a line passing through points O and S. line $\overleftrightarrow{OS}$, $\overleftrightarrow{OS}$

1. **line segment $\overline{TA}$ or $\overline{AT}$; $\overline{TA}$ or $\overline{AT}$**
2. **point D; D**
3. **line HQ or QH; $\overleftrightarrow{HQ}$ or $\overleftrightarrow{QH}$**

Write *parallel*, *intersecting*, or *perpendicular* to best describe the relationship between each pair of lines.

4. **perpendicular**
5. **intersecting**
6. **intersecting**
7. **parallel**

Problem Solving

8. Draw an example of two parallel lines that are intersected by one perpendicular line. **Answers will vary; make sure that 2 lines look parallel and that the perpendicular line drawn through them has right angle symbols for each of the parallel lines.**

Use with text pages 404–406.

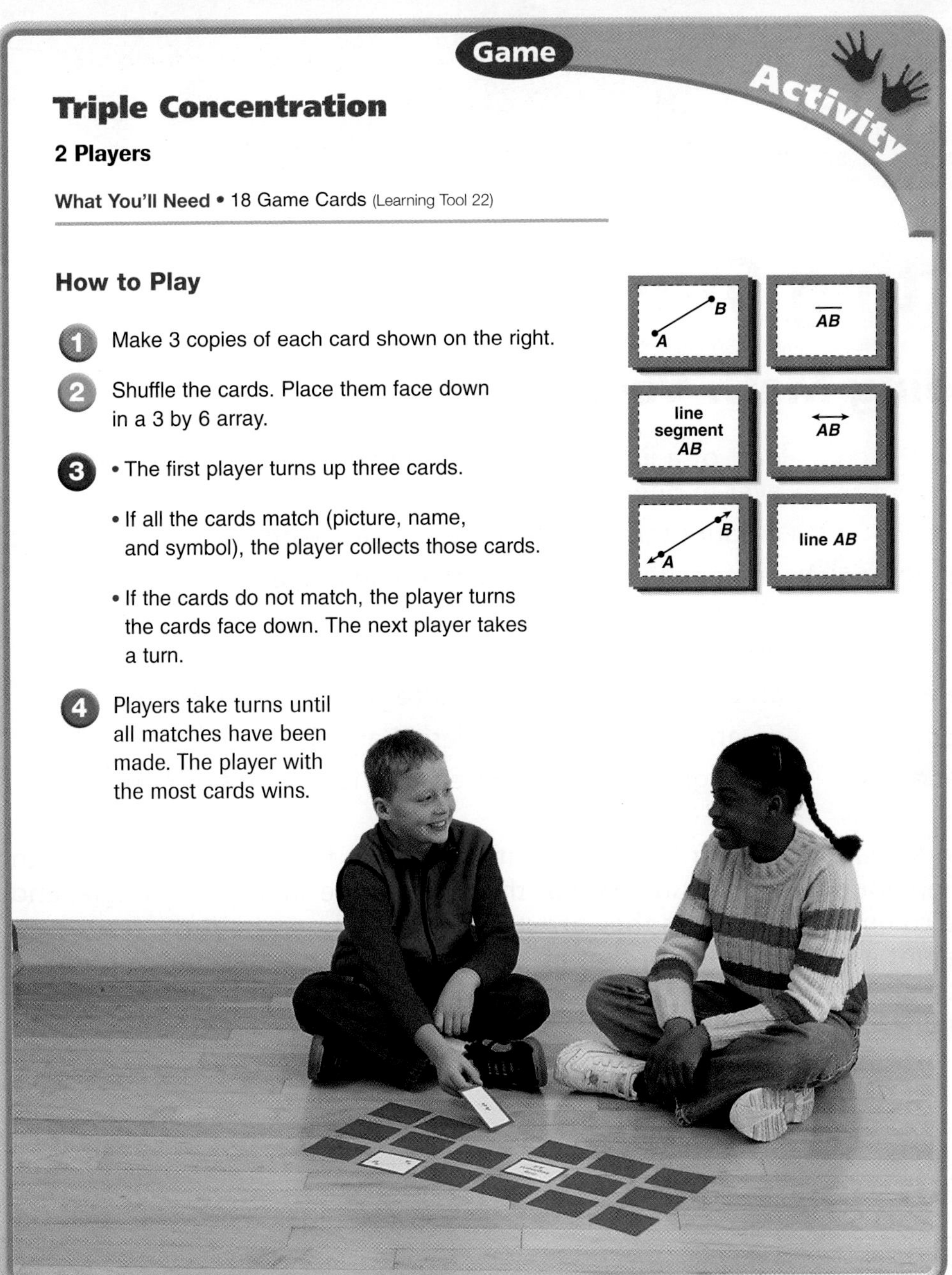
Game

Activity

Triple Concentration

2 Players

What You'll Need • 18 Game Cards (Learning Tool 22)

How to Play

1. Make 3 copies of each card shown on the right.
2. Shuffle the cards. Place them face down in a 3 by 6 array.
3. • The first player turns up three cards.
   • If all the cards match (picture, name, and symbol), the player collects those cards.
   • If the cards do not match, the player turns the cards face down. The next player takes a turn.
4. Players take turns until all matches have been made. The player with the most cards wins.

Game

Triple Concentration

- Review the rules for Concentration with students. Emphasize that unmatched cards need to be placed facedown exactly in their same position.
- Guide interested students to revise the game by adding sets of cards to increase the size of the array.
- Add sets of cards to the game yourself as your students learn about other geometric figures.

Lesson 16.2 Rays and Angles

Planning

Lesson Objective Name and describe rays and angles.

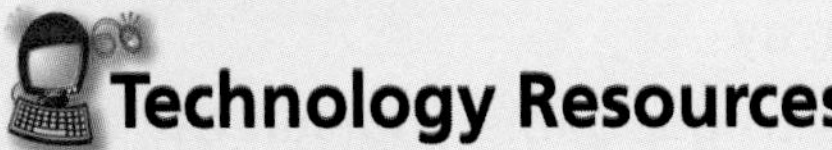

Technology Resources

- *Ways to Success* CD-ROM 16.2
- Education Place: Extra Practice, eGlossary, eGames
www.eduplace.com/map

Lesson 16.2 Transparency

Problem of the Day

Lines *MN*, *PQ*, and *RS* are on the same flat surface. Line *MN* is perpendicular to line *PQ*. Line *PQ* is perpendicular to line *RS*. How are lines *RS* and *MN* related? Hint: Draw a sketch to show your answer. (They are parallel.)

Spiral Review

Use the drawings.

1. Name each point. (*A*, *B*, *C*, *D*)
2. Name the parallel lines. ($\overleftrightarrow{AB}$ and $\overleftrightarrow{CD}$)
3. Name a pair of intersecting line segments. ($\overline{BD}$ and $\overline{AC}$)

Lesson Quiz

Use the drawing.

1. What is the name of this angle? ($\angle F$ or $\angle EFG$ or $\angle GFE$)
2. What kind of angle is it? (obtuse)
3. What is its vertex? (*F*)
4. What are its sides? ($\overrightarrow{FE}$ and $\overrightarrow{FG}$)

NCTM Standards

Geometry: Analyze attributes of two- and three-dimensional shapes and develop vocabulary to describe the attributes; classify two- and three-dimensional shapes according to their properties and develop definitions of classes of shapes.

Getting Started

Building Math Vocabulary

ray	part of a line that starts at an endpoint and goes on forever in one direction
angle	a figure that is formed by two rays with the same endpoint
side (of an angle)	one of the rays that make up an angle
vertex	points common to the sides of an angle or two sides of a polygon
obtuse angle	an angle that measures more than 90° and less than 180°
acute angle	an angle that measures less than 90°
straight angle	an angle that measures exactly 180°; a straight angle forms a straight line

Draw an angle on the board. Explain that an angle is formed by two rays with a common endpoint. Tell students that the rays are the sides of the angle, and that the common endpoint is the vertex. Distinguish among obtuse, acute, and straight angles, explaining that an obtuse angle is greater than a right angle, an acute angle is less than a right angle, and a straight angle forms a straight line.

Classifying Rays and Angles

Whole Class	15 minutes
Objective	Name and describe characteristics of rays and angles.
Materials	Protractor Transparency
Visual, Tactual	

- Students have learned that lines and line segments are geometric figures. Explain that rays and angles are also geometric figures.
- Use the overhead and Sheet 2 of the Protractor Transparency to introduce rays and angles, as well as naming conventions for both figures. Label the vertex *P*. Show the three different ways to name $\angle P$. Introduce the symbol $\angle$ for *angle*.
- Discuss what a vertex is. **What is always true about the middle letter in the name of an angle?** (It is the vertex of the angle.)
- Demonstrate how two rays form an angle and how to classify angles by the size of the opening formed by the intersection of the rays, or sides. **How do we classify angles?** (by the size of the measure of the opening between the rays of an angle)
- Invite volunteers to come to the board and draw right angles, acute angles, and obtuse angles.
- Tell students that the lesson in their book introduces the symbols used to identify different angles.

Differentiated Instruction

English Learners

Whole Class	10 minutes
Objective	Name angles.
Materials	None
Auditory, Visual	

Early Production

- Draw two or three different examples of each type of angle on the board. Point to any angle or part of an angle and have students call out its name. Go through all examples multiple times to help reinforce recognition, pronunciation, and correct naming of each angle and its parts.

Intermediate/Advanced

- English Learner Resource 16.2
- English Learner Handbook

Intervention

Small Groups	15 minutes
Objective	Name and describe angles.
Materials	None
Tactual, Visual	

- Help students understand that the width of an angle's opening, *not* the length of its sides, determines its size.
- Have students put their hands together and open them like an alligator's mouth, hinged at the wrists. Point out that in doing so, they have formed an angle. Have them open their hands wider. Emphasize that their angle increases in size as they open their hands wider. Tell students that the lengths of their fingers have nothing to do with the size of their angles.
- Draw several pairs of angles to show this concept.

Other Resources

- *Ways to Success* CD-ROM, Lesson 16.2

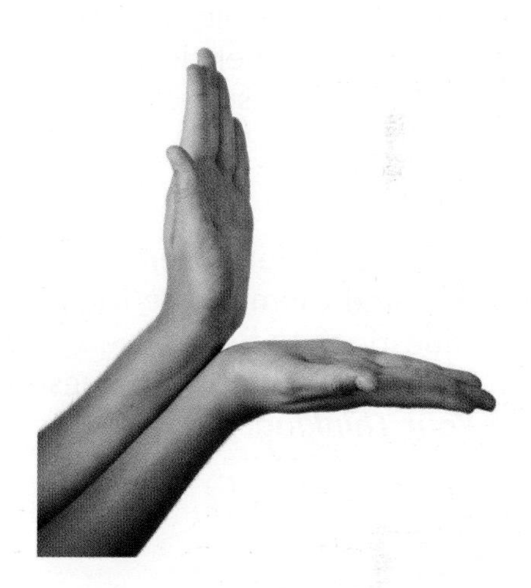

Inclusion

Whole Class	5 minutes
Objective	Describe rays.
Materials	Flashlight or other light source
Visual	

- Help students distinguish rays from lines and line segments by comparing them to rays of light that come from a flashlight. They can see that rays of light have only one endpoint—their source.

Alternate Teaching Strategy

Give each student two toothpicks and a ball of modeling clay. Tell students the clay represents the vertex and the toothpicks represent the sides of an angle. Demonstrate how to model a right angle with the materials. Then have students work in pairs. One partner moves the toothpicks to form acute, obtuse, or right angles while the other partner identifies the type of angle. Partners switch roles and continue the activity.

❶ Introduce

Explain to students that a ray is both a part of a line and a part of an angle. Tell students that the lesson in their book discusses four types of angles: acute, right, obtuse, and straight.

❷ Teach

Learn About It

- Have students describe ray *BA*. (endpoint is B; extends through point A, continues without end) **What are the rays in ∠*BCD*?** ($\overrightarrow{CB}$ and $\overrightarrow{CD}$)
- Explain that a right angle forms a square corner. **Which type of angle has a measure that is less than a right angle? greater?** (acute; obtuse) **Which type has a measure that is twice the measure of a right angle?** (straight angle) Ask a volunteer to demonstrate, using rulers, pencils, or cards, that a straight angle is the size of two right angles.

Guided Practice

Have students complete **Exercises 1–3** as you observe. Remind them to use the ***Ask Yourself*** questions to help. Give students the opportunity to talk about the question in ***Explain Your Thinking.***

❸ Practice

Practice and Problem Solving

Select from **Exercises 4–14** as independent work. Check that students have classified and named the angles correctly.

Common Error

- **Misnaming angles** Some students may struggle with naming angles.
- **Intervention** To help them, draw two identical angles. Label them ∠*ABC* and ∠*ACB*. Have students identify each vertex, and point out that the same letters are used to represent two different angles.

Lesson 2

Rays and Angles

Objective Name and describe rays and angles.

Vocabulary
ray
angle
sides
vertex
obtuse angle
acute angle
straight angle

Learn About It

You have learned about lines and line segments.

Rays and angles are also geometric figures.

▶ A **ray** is a part of a line. It has one endpoint and goes on without end in one direction.

Say: ray *BA*
Write: $\overrightarrow{BA}$

▶ An **angle** is formed by two rays with a common endpoint. The rays are the **sides** of the angle. The common endpoint is the **vertex** of the angle.

Say	Write
angle *C*	∠*C*
angle *BCD*	∠*BCD*
angle *DCB*	∠*DCB*

← Each of the angle names in the chart can be used to name the angle on the right.

← When naming an angle, the vertex is the middle letter.

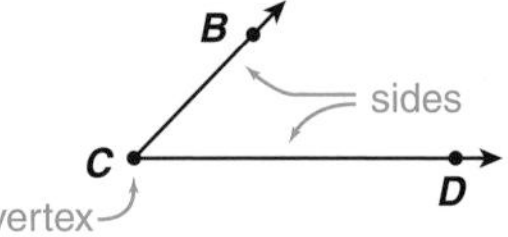

Angles are classified by the size of the opening between the sides.

This angle forms a square corner.

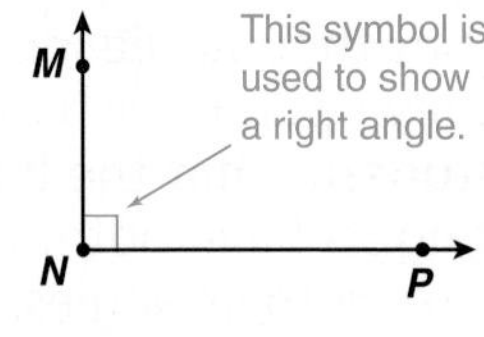

M
This symbol is used to show a right angle.
N
P

∠*MNP* is a right angle.

This angle is greater than a right angle.

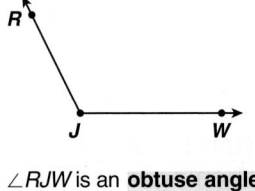

∠*RJW* is an **obtuse angle**.

This angle is less than a right angle.

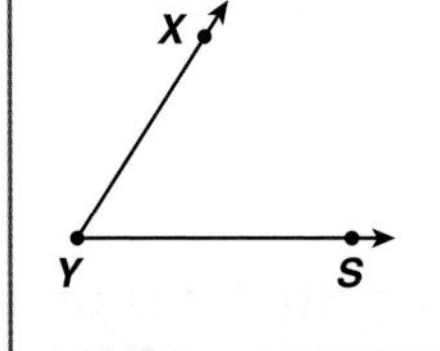

∠*XYS* is an **acute angle**.

This angle forms a straight line.

∠*FGH* is a **straight angle**.

408

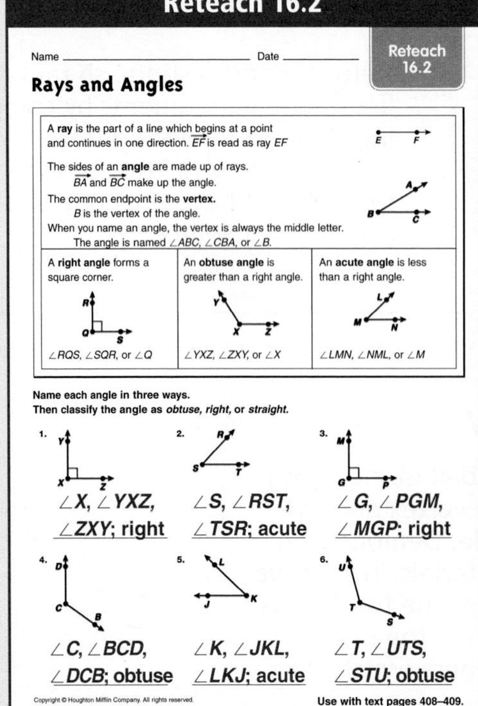

Reteach 16.2

Name ______ Date ______ Reteach 16.2

Rays and Angles

A **ray** is the part of a line which begins at a point and continues in one direction. $\overrightarrow{EF}$ is read as ray *EF*

The sides of an **angle** are made up of rays.
$\overrightarrow{BA}$ and $\overrightarrow{BC}$ make up the angle.
The common endpoint is the **vertex.**
B is the vertex of the angle.
When you name an angle, the vertex is always the middle letter.
The angle is named ∠*ABC*, ∠*CBA*, or ∠*B*.

A **right angle** forms a square corner.	An **obtuse angle** is greater than a right angle.	An **acute angle** is less than a right angle.
∠*RQS*, ∠*SQR*, or ∠*Q*	∠*YXZ*, ∠*ZXY*, or ∠*X*	∠*LMN*, ∠*NML*, or ∠*M*

Name each angle in three ways.
Then classify the angle as *obtuse, right,* or *straight.*

1. ∠X, ∠YXZ, ∠ZXY; right
2. ∠S, ∠RST, ∠TSR; acute
3. ∠G, ∠PGM, ∠MGP; right
4. ∠C, ∠BCD, ∠DCB; obtuse
5. ∠K, ∠JKL, ∠LKJ; acute
6. ∠T, ∠UTS, ∠STU; obtuse

Use with text pages 408–409.

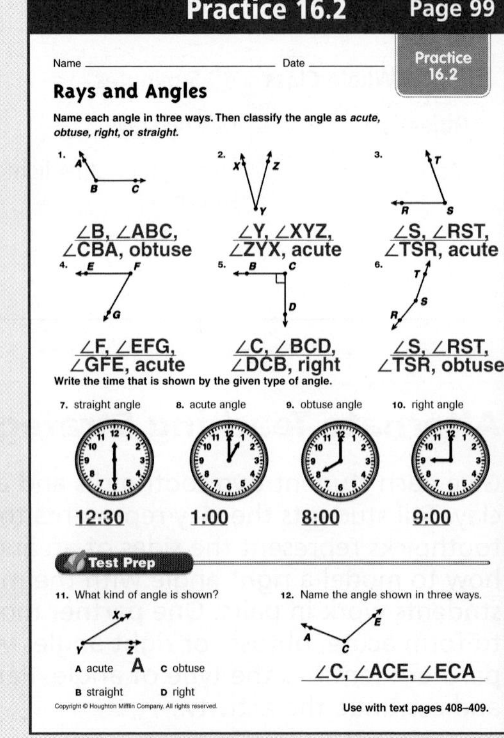

Practice 16.2 Page 99

Name ______ Date ______ Practice 16.2

Rays and Angles

Name each angle in three ways. Then classify the angle as *acute, obtuse, right,* or *straight.*

1. ∠B, ∠ABC, ∠CBA, obtuse
2. ∠Y, ∠XYZ, ∠ZYX, acute
3. ∠S, ∠RST, ∠TSR, acute
4. ∠F, ∠EFG, ∠GFE, acute
5. ∠C, ∠BCD, ∠DCB, right
6. ∠S, ∠RST, ∠TSR, obtuse

Write the time that is shown by the given type of angle.

7. straight angle 12:30
8. acute angle 1:00
9. obtuse angle 8:00
10. right angle 9:00

Test Prep

11. What kind of angle is shown?
A acute C obtuse
B straight D right
Answer: A

12. Name the angle shown in three ways.
∠C, ∠ACE, ∠ECA

Use with text pages 408–409.

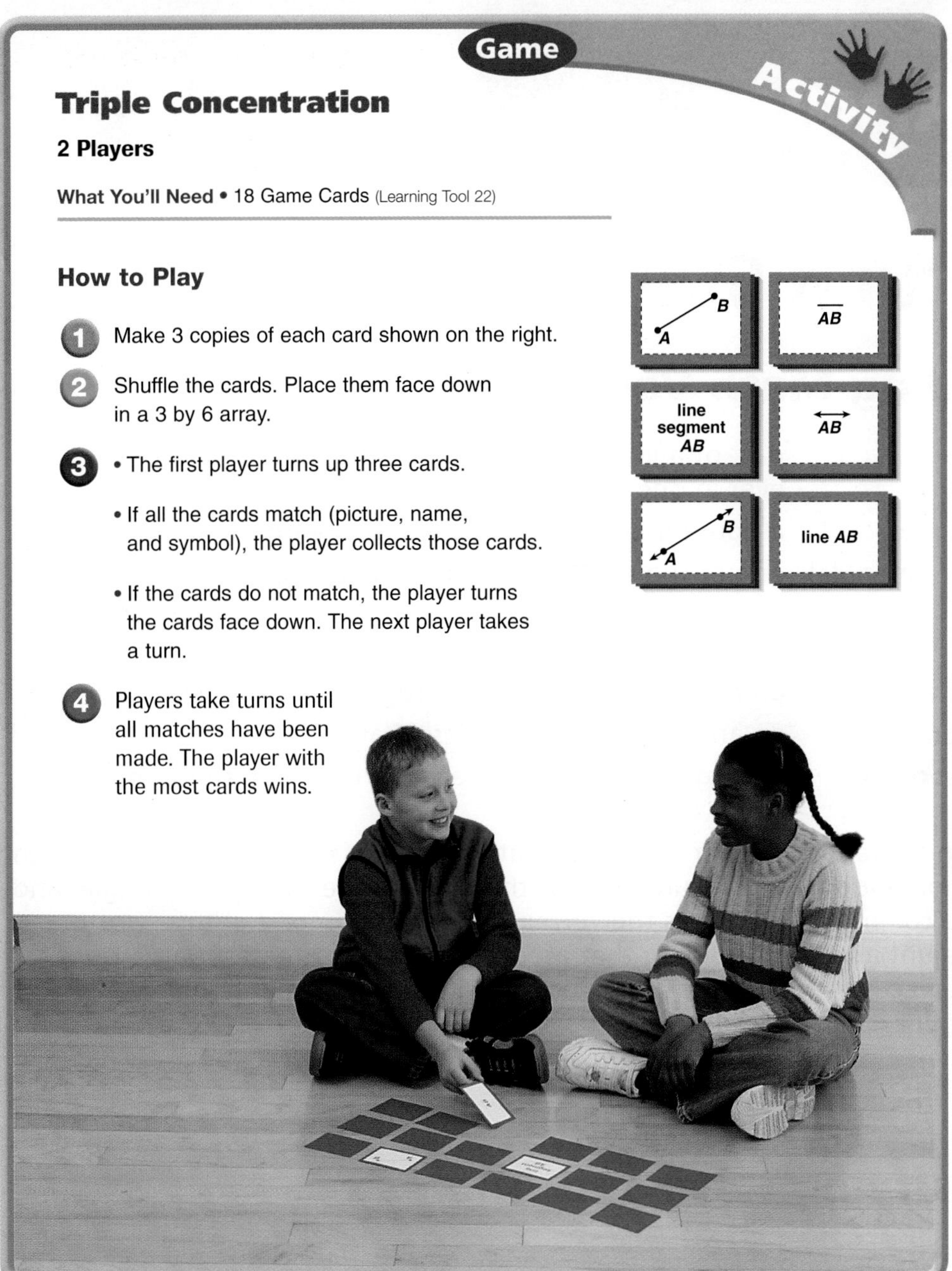
Game
Activity
Triple Concentration
2 Players
What You'll Need • 18 Game Cards (Learning Tool 22)
How to Play
1 Make 3 copies of each card shown on the right.
2 Shuffle the cards. Place them face down in a 3 by 6 array.
3 • The first player turns up three cards.
• If all the cards match (picture, name, and symbol), the player collects those cards.
• If the cards do not match, the player turns the cards face down. The next player takes a turn.
4 Players take turns until all matches have been made. The player with the most cards wins.
A
B
AB
line segment AB
AB
line AB

Game

Triple Concentration

- Review the rules for Concentration with students. Emphasize that unmatched cards need to be placed facedown exactly in their same position.
- Guide interested students to revise the game by adding sets of cards to increase the size of the array.
- Add sets of cards to the game yourself as your students learn about other geometric figures.

Lesson 16.2

Rays and Angles

Planning

Lesson Objective Name and describe rays and angles.

Technology Resources

- *Ways to Success* CD-ROM 16.2
- Education Place: Extra Practice, eGlossary, eGames www.eduplace.com/map

Lesson 16.2 Transparency

Problem of the Day

Lines *MN*, *PQ*, and *RS* are on the same flat surface. Line *MN* is perpendicular to line *PQ*. Line *PQ* is perpendicular to line *RS*. How are lines *RS* and *MN* related? Hint: Draw a sketch to show your answer. (They are parallel.)

Spiral Review

Use the drawings.

1. Name each point. (*A*, *B*, *C*, *D*)
2. Name the parallel lines. ($\overleftrightarrow{AB}$ and $\overleftrightarrow{CD}$)
3. Name a pair of intersecting line segments. ($\overline{BD}$ and $\overline{AC}$)

Lesson Quiz

Use the drawing.

1. What is the name of this angle? ($\angle F$ or $\angle EFG$ or $\angle GFE$)
2. What kind of angle is it? (obtuse)
3. What is its vertex? (*F*)
4. What are its sides? ($\overrightarrow{FE}$ and $\overrightarrow{FG}$)

NCTM Standards

Geometry: Analyze attributes of two- and three-dimensional shapes and develop vocabulary to describe the attributes; classify two- and three-dimensional shapes according to their properties and develop definitions of classes of shapes.

Getting Started

Building Math Vocabulary

ray	part of a line that starts at an endpoint and goes on forever in one direction
angle	a figure that is formed by two rays with the same endpoint
side (of an angle)	one of the rays that make up an angle
vertex	points common to the sides of an angle or two sides of a polygon
obtuse angle	an angle that measures more than 90° and less than 180°
acute angle	an angle that measures less than 90°
straight angle	an angle that measures exactly 180°; a straight angle forms a straight line

Draw an angle on the board. Explain that an angle is formed by two rays with a common endpoint. Tell students that the rays are the sides of the angle, and that the common endpoint is the vertex. Distinguish among obtuse, acute, and straight angles, explaining that an obtuse angle is greater than a right angle, an acute angle is less than a right angle, and a straight angle forms a straight line.

Classifying Rays and Angles

Whole Class	15 minutes
Objective	Name and describe characteristics of rays and angles.
Materials	Protractor Transparency
Visual, Tactual	

- Students have learned that lines and line segments are geometric figures. Explain that rays and angles are also geometric figures.
- Use the overhead and Sheet 2 of the Protractor Transparency to introduce rays and angles, as well as naming conventions for both figures. Label the vertex *P*. Show the three different ways to name $\angle P$. Introduce the symbol $\angle$ for *angle*.
- Discuss what a vertex is. **What is always true about the middle letter in the name of an angle?** (It is the vertex of the angle.)
- Demonstrate how two rays form an angle and how to classify angles by the size of the opening formed by the intersection of the rays, or sides. **How do we classify angles?** (by the size of the measure of the opening between the rays of an angle)
- Invite volunteers to come to the board and draw right angles, acute angles, and obtuse angles.
- Tell students that the lesson in their book introduces the symbols used to identify different angles.

14. *Labeling may vary.* For an angle labeled ∠*ABC*: ∠*B*, ∠*CBA*; acute

Guided Practice

Name each angle in three ways. Then classify the angle as *acute*, *obtuse*, *right*, or *straight*.

1. 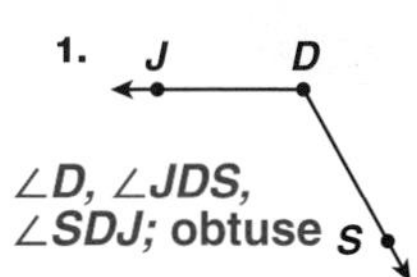
∠*D*, ∠*JDS*, ∠*SDJ*; obtuse

2. 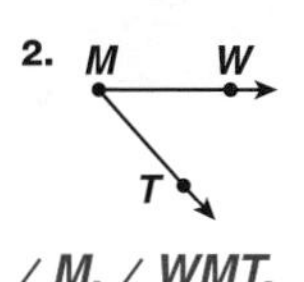
∠*M*, ∠*WMT*, ∠*TMW*; acute

3. 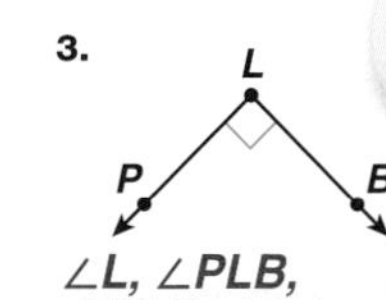
∠*L*, ∠*PLB*, ∠*BLP*; right

Ask Yourself

- What point will be the middle letter in the name of the angle?
- How does the size of the angle compare to the size of a right angle?

Explain Your Thinking ▶ Can ∠*PQR* also be named ∠*PRQ*? Why or why not? **No. *Possible explanation:* The center letter in an angle name must identify the vertex. An angle only has one vertex, so *Q* and *R* cannot both be the vertex.**

Practice and Problem Solving

Name each angle in three ways. Then classify the angle as *acute*, *obtuse*, *right*, or *straight*.

4. 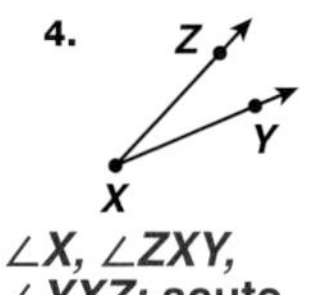
∠*X*, ∠*ZXY*, ∠*YXZ*; acute

5. 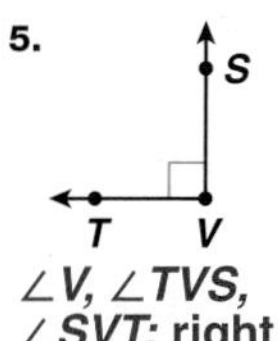
∠*V*, ∠*TVS*, ∠*SVT*; right

6. 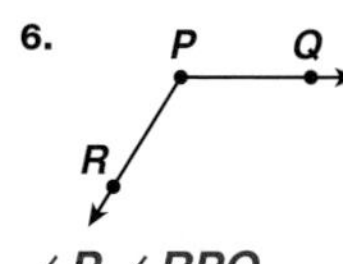
∠*P*, ∠*RPQ*, ∠*QPR*; obtuse

7. 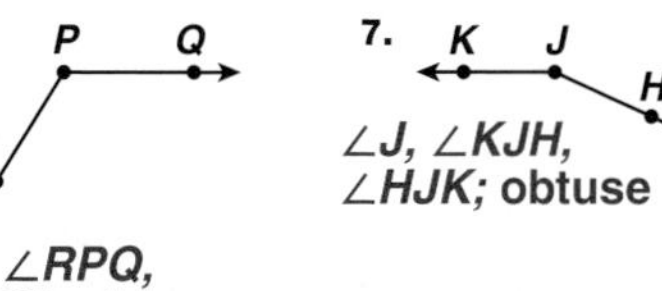
∠*J*, ∠*KJH*, ∠*HJK*; obtuse

Solve.

8. What is the time on the clock with hands that show
   a. a right angle? **3:00** **b.** an obtuse angle? **5:00**
   c. an acute angle? **2:00** **d.** a straight angle? **6:00**

9. **Write About It** Draw two angles. Label them ∠*MHP* and ∠*TWZ*. Write a sentence to describe each angle. Use the words *vertex* and *sides*. Then classify your angles.
Check angles and descriptions.

Mixed Review and Test Prep

Open Response

Add or subtract. (Ch. 3, Lesson 8)

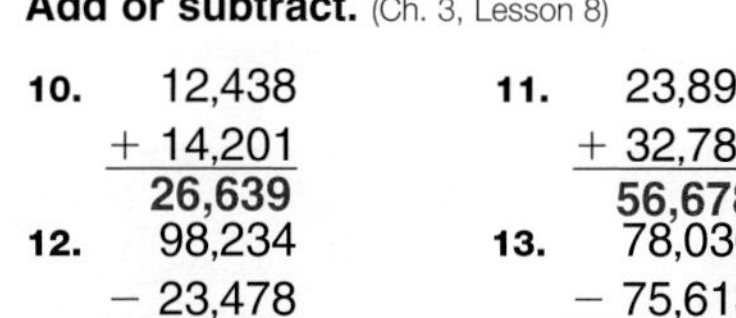

10. 12,438 + 14,201 = **26,639**

11. 23,894 + 32,784 = **56,678**

12. 98,234 − 23,478 = **74,756**

13. 78,036 − 75,613 = **2,423**

14. Copy the angle below. Label the angle. Then describe it in as many ways as you can. ***See above.*** (Ch. 16, Lesson 2)

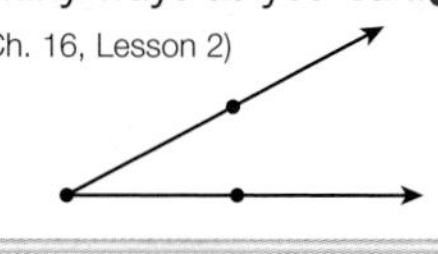

Extra Practice See page 427, Set B.

- ***Exercise 8*** Challenge students to name other times that the hands of the clock would make each of the four kinds of angles. Invite them to use a clock to demonstrate their answers.

4 Assess & Close

Math Talk in Action

Have students refer to **Exercise 9** to conclude the lesson. Ask questions such as the following:

- **How can you describe the sides of ∠*MHP*?**
- **How would you classify ∠*MHP*?**

Math Journal Prompt

Have students write a summary of what they learned about angles in this lesson. Then have them draw a diagram of intersecting lines that form different kinds of angles. Have students label the figures in their diagram and describe and classify the angles formed.

Lesson Quiz

Use the quiz on Lesson Transparency 16.2.

Test Prep & Spiral Review

Use Test Prep Transparency 16.2.

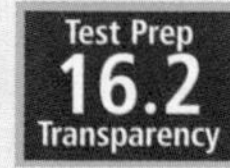

Enrichment 16.2

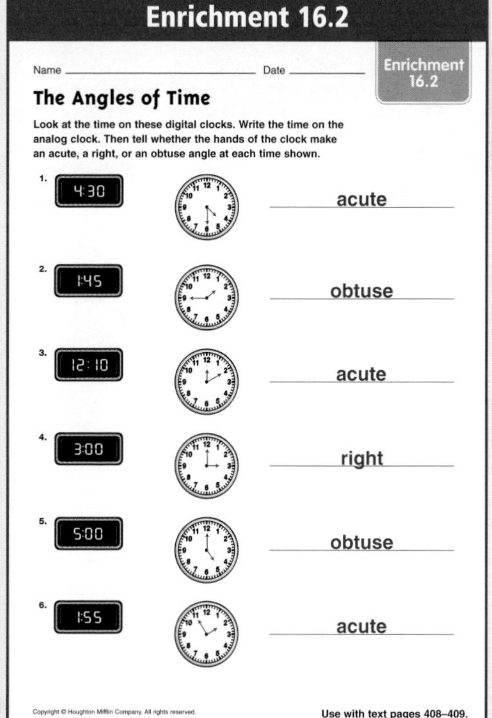

Name ______ Date ______ Enrichment 16.2

The Angles of Time

Look at the time on these digital clocks. Write the time on the analog clock. Then tell whether the hands of the clock make an acute, a right, or an obtuse angle at each time shown.

1. 4:30 — acute
2. 1:45 — obtuse
3. 12:10 — acute
4. 3:00 — right
5. 5:00 — obtuse
6. 1:55 — acute

Use with text pages 408–409.

Problem Solving 16.2

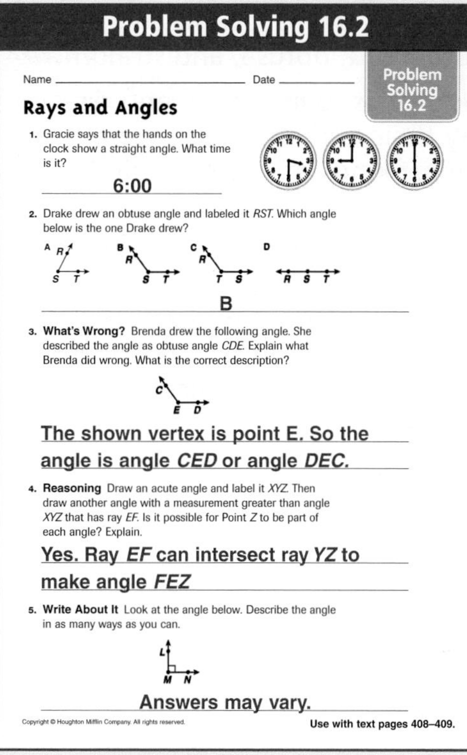

Name ______ Date ______ Problem Solving 16.2

Rays and Angles

1. Gracie says that the hands on the clock show a straight angle. What time is it?
6:00
2. Drake drew an obtuse angle and labeled it *RST*. Which angle below is the one Drake drew?
B
3. **What's Wrong?** Brenda drew the following angle. She described the angle as obtuse angle *CDE*. Explain what Brenda did wrong. What is the correct description?
The shown vertex is point E. So the angle is angle *CED* or angle *DEC*.
4. **Reasoning** Draw an acute angle and label it *XYZ*. Then draw another angle with a measurement greater than angle *XYZ* that has ray *EF*. Is it possible for Point *Z* to be part of each angle? Explain.
Yes. Ray *EF* can intersect ray *YZ* to make angle *FEZ*
5. **Write About It** Look at the angle below. Describe the angle in as many ways as you can.
Answers may vary.

Use with text pages 408–409.

Homework 16.2 Page 99

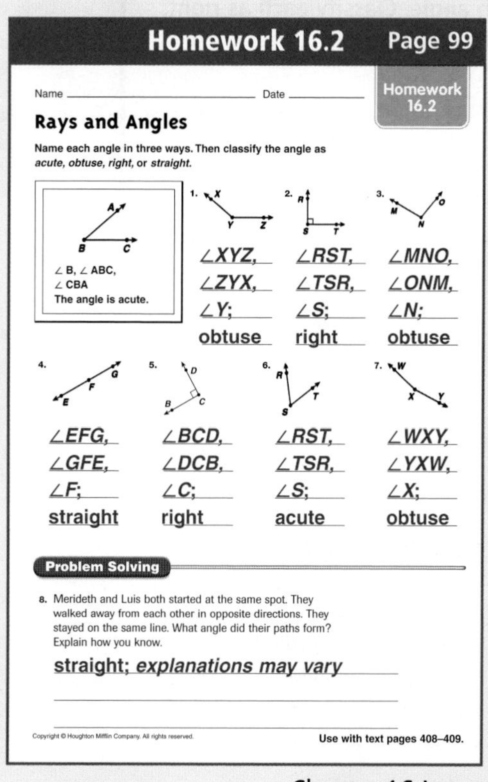

Name ______ Date ______ Homework 16.2

Rays and Angles

Name each angle in three ways. Then classify the angle as *acute, obtuse, right,* or *straight*.

Example: ∠B, ∠ABC, ∠CBA. The angle is acute.

1. ∠*XYZ*, ∠*ZYX*, ∠*Y*; obtuse
2. ∠*RST*, ∠*TSR*, ∠*S*; right
3. ∠*MNO*, ∠*ONM*, ∠*N*; obtuse
4. ∠*EFG*, ∠*GFE*, ∠*F*; straight
5. ∠*BCD*, ∠*DCB*, ∠*C*; right
6. ∠*RST*, ∠*TSR*, ∠*S*; acute
7. ∠*WXY*, ∠*YXW*, ∠*X*; obtuse

Problem Solving

8. Merideth and Luis both started at the same spot. They walked away from each other in opposite directions. They stayed on the same line. What angle did their paths form? Explain how you know.
straight; *explanations may vary*

Use with text pages 408–409.

Hands On Lesson 16.3

Measure Angles

Planning

Lesson Objective Use a protractor to measure angles.

Technology Resources

- *Ways to Success* CD-ROM 16.3
- Education Place: Extra Practice, eGlossary, eGames www.eduplace.com/map

Lesson 16.3 Transparency

Problem of the Day

Albert walks 8 blocks east, then 5 blocks south. He walks 2 more blocks south and then turns west. He walks 12 blocks. Then he turns north and walks 7 blocks and stops. How far and in what direction must Albert walk to reach his starting point? (4 blocks east)

Spiral Review

Draw and label each of the following. (Check students' drawings.)

1. Ray *RS*
2. Line segment *MN*
3. Obtuse angle *DEF*
4. Straight angle *JKL*

Lesson Quiz

Draw each angle. Classify each as right, acute, obtuse, or straight. (Check students' drawings.)

1. 60° (acute)
2. 120° (obtuse)
3. 90° (right)
4. 20° (acute)

NCTM Standards

Geometry: Analyze attributes of two- and three-dimensional shapes and develop vocabulary to describe the attributes; classify two- and three-dimensional shapes according to their properties and develop definitions of classes and shapes.

Getting Started

Building Math Vocabulary

degrees units for measuring angles or temperature

protractor a device used to measure and draw angles

Display and discuss the vocabulary card for *degrees*. Contrast meanings that students know from real life, such as temperatures in degrees, with the geometric meaning: units for measuring the sizes of angles. Guide students to see that the greater the degree measure, the larger the angle. Tell students that they will use a protractor to draw and measure angles.

Angles in Classroom Objects

Whole Class	10 minutes
Objective	Name and describe angles.
Materials	None
Visual	

- Students have learned to classify angles by the size of their openings. Now they will learn to draw and measure angles with a protractor.
- Hold a brief scavenger hunt in the classroom.
- Divide students into groups. Have each group find several examples of each of the following angles: acute, right, obtuse, and straight.
- Ask groups to introduce and display their findings. **What were the hardest kinds of angles to find? Which kind was the easiest to find?** Have students discuss their views.
- Tell students that the lesson will discuss which scale on a protractor to use to measure particular angles.

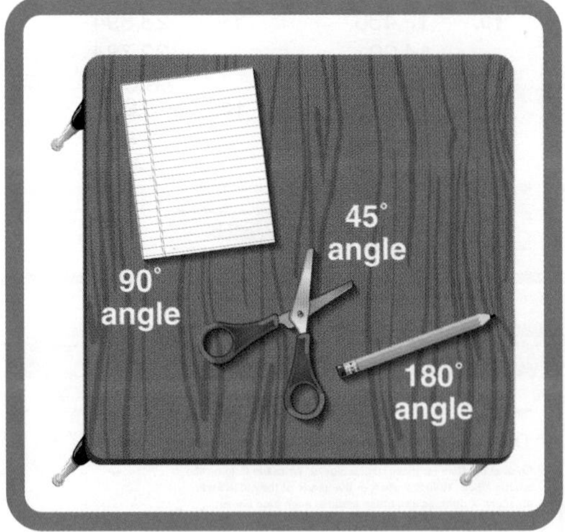

Differentiated Instruction

English Learners

Whole Class	10 minutes
Objective	Name and describe angles.
Materials	Student page 411
Auditory, Visual	

Early Production

- After completing ***On Your Own,*** have students go back and say the degree and classification of each angle. For example, *Angle number 1 is a right angle that measures 90°.*

A right angle measures exactly 90°

Intermediate/Advanced

- English Learner Resource 16.3
- English Learner Handbook

Intervention

Small Groups	15 minutes
Objective	Describe characteristics of angles.
Materials	None
Visual, Tactual	

- Demonstrate how to make a 90° angle using your arm. Explain that the elbow is the vertex of the angle and the forearm and upper arm are its sides.
- Have students observe as you extend your arm out from your side and form a right angle at your elbow. Then move your forearm upward toward your shoulder and stop. **Is this angle greater or less than 90°?** (less) Then extend your forearm down toward your side and stop. **Is this angle greater or less than 90°?** (greater) Guide students to estimate both measurements.
- Have a volunteer draw some angles on the board. Direct students to use their arms as models to estimate the measure of the angles.

Other Resources

- *Ways to Success* CD-ROM, Lesson 16.3

Early Finishers

Pairs	20 minutes
Objective	Name and describe angles.
Materials	Protractor, straightedge
Visual, Tactual	

- Have students work with partners. One draws an angle. The other student estimates and then measures it with a protractor, classifying it as acute, right, obtuse, or straight. Have students swap roles repeatedly.

Real-World Connection

- Arrange students into groups. Have them brainstorm the many ways angles are used in real-life activities. Groups can focus on one broad topic (such as sports) or on unlimited topics.
- Provide examples to get groups started. These might include angles used in archery, on ski slopes, in airplane take-offs, or in highway exits and entrances.
- Give groups 10 minutes to come up with their ideas, then discuss students' ideas as a class.

Facts Practice

Write the number 12 on the board. Have students suggest as many ways as possible to rename 12 using known facts. Some possible answers include $11 + 1$, $14 - 2$, 4×3, or $24 \div 2$.

❶ Introduce

Explain to students that by following step-by-step instructions, they will learn to draw and measure angles using a protractor.

❷ Teach

Work Together

Have students read the information about angle measures at the top of the page. Point out that these degrees are not the same as the degrees with which temperatures are measured. Draw additional examples of angles with their degree measures. Ask students to tell in which category each belongs.

- Demonstrate, step by step, the process of using the protractor to measure an angle. Emphasize the importance of being able to distinguish obtuse and acute angles in order to use the correct scale.
- Provide students with additional practice measuring angles. Point out that they may need to extend the sides of angles to measure them.
- Work through the steps for making an angle of a given size. Again, provide additional practice.

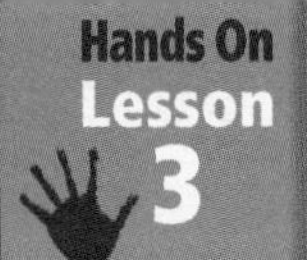

Hands On Lesson 3

Measure Angles

Objective Use a protractor to measure angles.

Vocabulary
degrees
protractor

Materials
protractor

Work Together

An angle can be measured in units called **degrees** (written as °). You will measure angles between 0° and 180°.

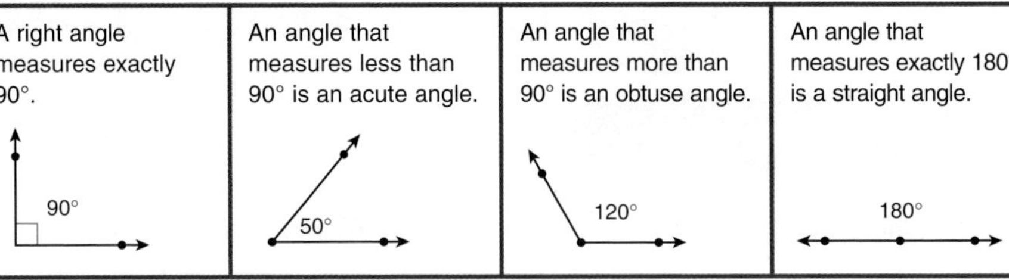

A right angle measures exactly 90°.	An angle that measures less than 90° is an acute angle.	An angle that measures more than 90° is an obtuse angle.	An angle that measures exactly 180° is a straight angle.
90°	50°	120°	180°

Work with a partner to use a **protractor** to measure angles.

Find the number of degrees in ∠*TRU* and ∠*QRT.*

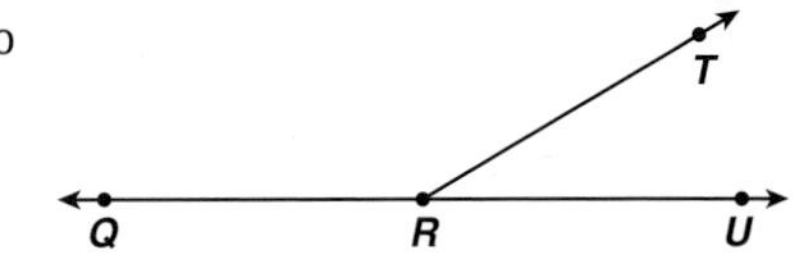

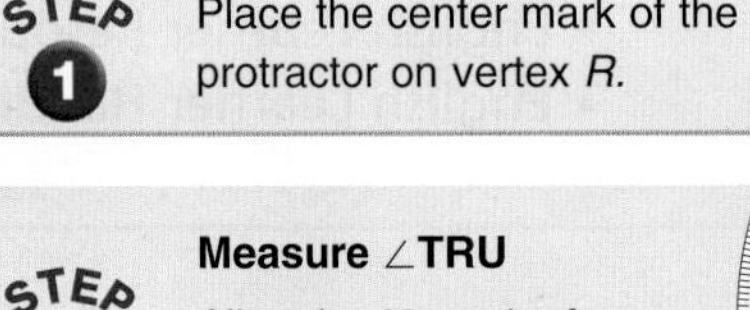

STEP 1 Place the center mark of the protractor on vertex *R*.

For an acute angle, read the scale that shows less than 90°.

STEP 2 **Measure ∠TRU**

Align the 0° mark of one of the protractor scales with one ray of the angle to be measured.

The measure of ∠*TRU* is 30°.

STEP 3 **Measure ∠QRT**

Find where the other ray passes through the same scale. Read the measure of the angle on that scale.

- What is the measure of ∠*QRT*? 150°

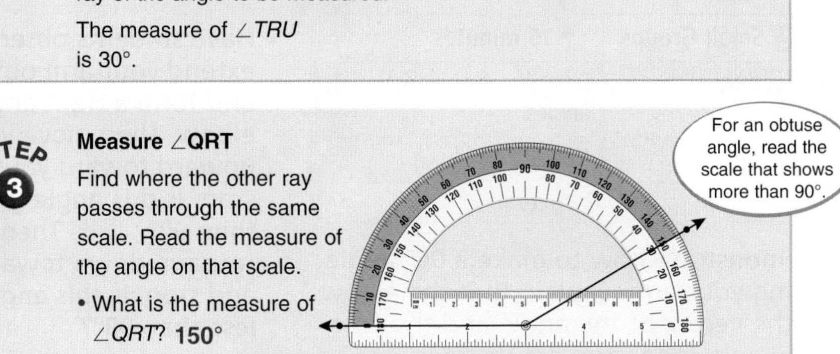

For an obtuse angle, read the scale that shows more than 90°.

410

Reteach 16.3

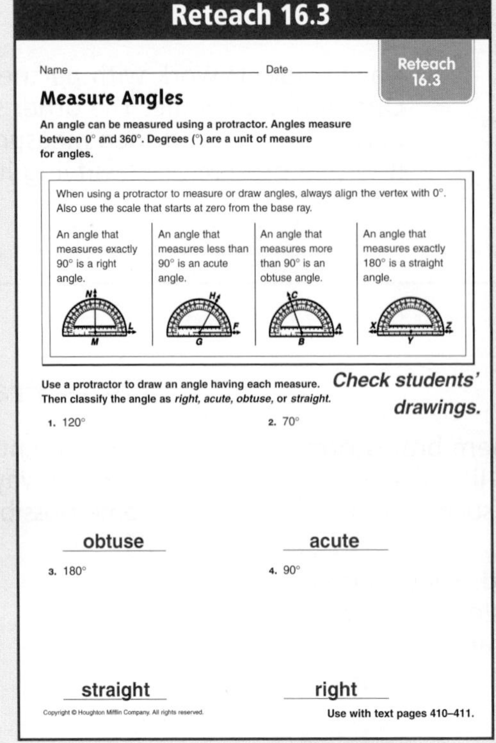

Name ______ Date ______ Reteach 16.3

Measure Angles

An angle can be measured using a protractor. Angles measure between 0° and 360°. Degrees (°) are a unit of measure for angles.

When using a protractor to measure or draw angles, always align the vertex with 0°. Also use the scale that starts at zero from the base ray.

An angle that measures exactly 90° is a right angle.	An angle that measures less than 90° is an acute angle.	An angle that measures more than 90° is an obtuse angle.	An angle that measures exactly 180° is a straight angle.

Use a protractor to draw an angle having each measure. Then classify the angle as *right, acute, obtuse,* or *straight.* Check students' drawings.

1. 120° obtuse
2. 70° acute
3. 180° straight
4. 90° right

Use with text pages 410–411.

Practice 16.3 Page 100

Name ______ Date ______ Practice 16.3

Measure Angles

Use a protractor to draw an angle having each measure. Then classify the angle as *right, acute, obtuse,* or *straight.*

1. 60° acute
2. 120° obtuse
3. 30° acute
4. 90° right
5. 80° acute
6. 100° obtuse
7. 150° obtuse
8. 180° straight

Test Prep

9. Use a protractor to find the measure of the angle shown.
   A 130° B 50° C 40° D 90° — **B**

10. Look at your angles for Exercises 1–8. How can you quickly tell which one is 90°? Exercise 4; 90 degrees is a right angle.

Use with text pages 410–411.

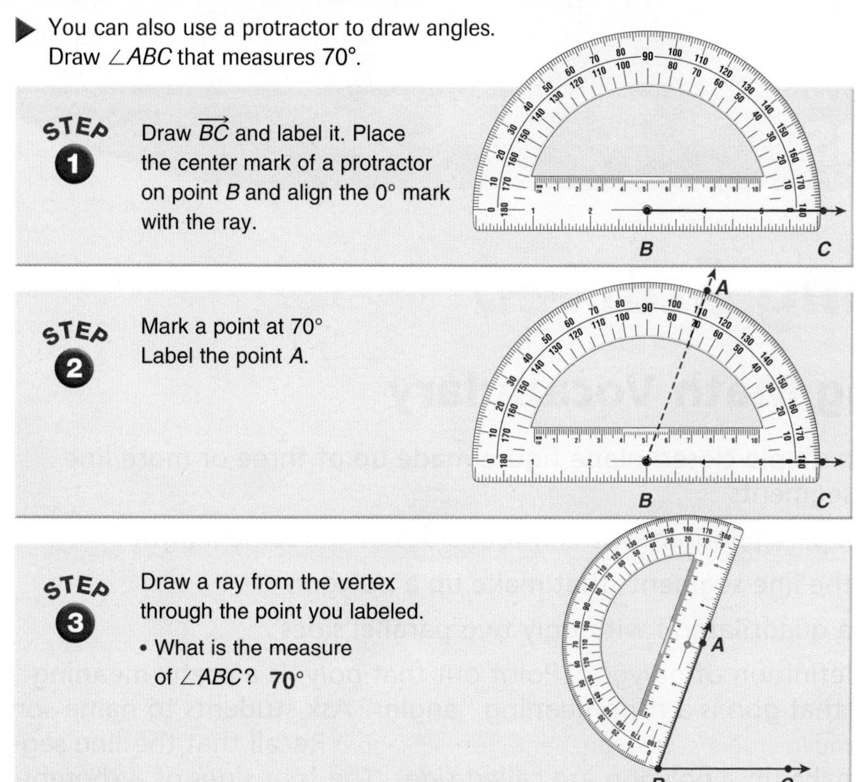

You can also use a protractor to draw angles.
Draw ∠ABC that measures 70°.
STEP 1
Draw $\overrightarrow{BC}$ and label it. Place the center mark of a protractor on point B and align the 0° mark with the ray.
B
C
STEP 2
Mark a point at 70°
Label the point A.
A
B
C
STEP 3
Draw a ray from the vertex through the point you labeled.
• What is the measure of ∠ABC? 70°
A
B
C

Use a protractor to draw an angle having each measure. Then classify the angle as *right, acute, obtuse,* or *straight.* *See Additional Answers.*

1. 90° right
2. 40° acute
3. 180° straight
4. 130° obtuse
5. 110° obtuse

Talk About It • Write About It

You learned to measure and draw angles.

6. Look at your angles for Exercises 1–5. How can you tell quickly which one is 40°? **The angle for Exercise 2 is the only one that is less than 90°.**
7. **Analyze** A protractor has two scales. How do you decide which scale to use to measure an angle?

Use the greater scale for angles greater than 90° and the lesser scale for angles less than 90°.

❸ Practice

On Your Own

- Select from **Exercises 1–5** as independent work. Circulate as students make their measurements. Help them place the protractor correctly and to read the right sale.
- Anticipate that students may find using a protractor a challenge. You may want to pair students who are having success with those who are struggling.

❹ Assess & Close

Math Talk in Action

Have students refer to ***Talk About It • Write About It*** to conclude the lesson. Ask the following question:

- **How do you decide which scale on a protractor to use to measure an angle?** (Use the greater number for angles greater than 90° and the lesser number for angles less than 90°.)

Math Journal Prompt

Have students write an explanation of how to use a protractor to measure an acute angle. Have them describe how to use one to draw an angle of 120°.

Lesson Quiz

Use the quiz on Lesson Transparency 16.3.

Test Prep & Spiral Review

Use Test Prep Transparency 16.3.

Enrichment 16.3

Name ______ Date ______ Enrichment 16.3

Angle Scavenger Hunt

On this scavenger hunt you are searching for angles. Look at the list below. The list has different angle measures, or objects that have angles. What you need to do is find an object that has the given angle measure, or measure the angle of the given object. You may wish to trace some of the objects to make it easier to measure the angle. Good luck!

Answers will vary. Check students' chart entries.

Angle Scavenger Hunt		
Object	**Type of Angle**	**Angle Measure**
your desk		
	obtuse	
		45°
stapler	acute	
		135°
map	obtuse	
		60°
	right	

 Use with text pages 410–411.

Problem Solving 16.3

Name ______ Date ______ Problem Solving 16.3

Measure Angles

Use a protractor for Problems 1–4.

1. Gwen drew angle *ABC*. The angle measured 80°. Draw Gwen's angle and classify it as right, acute, obtuse, or straight. **acute**
2. Mr. Hornet has three trees in his yard. Connect trees *T, U,* and *V* to make an angle. What is the approximate measure of the angle? Classify the angle as right, acute, obtuse, or straight. **100°, obtuse**
3. **Predict** Vin said that the hands on the clock were at a 120° angle. The minute hand was at 12. Where was the hour hand? What time could it be? **Possible answers: 4:00 or 8:00**
4. What is the least measurement of an obtuse angle? What is the greatest measurement of an obtuse angle? Draw each. **The least measurement of an obtuse angle is 91° and the greatest measurement is 179°. Check students' drawings.**

 Use with text pages 410–411.

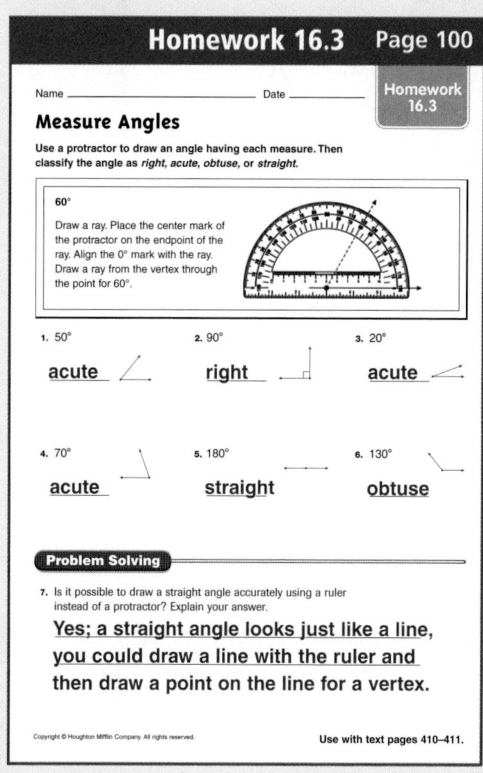

Homework 16.3 Page 100

Name ______ Date ______ Homework 16.3

Measure Angles

Use a protractor to draw an angle having each measure. Then classify the angle as *right, acute, obtuse,* or *straight.*

60°
Draw a ray. Place the center mark of the protractor on the endpoint of the ray. Align the 0° mark with the ray. Draw a ray from the vertex through the point for 60°.

1. 50° **acute**
2. 90° **right**
3. 20° **acute**
4. 70° **acute**
5. 180° **straight**
6. 130° **obtuse**

Problem Solving

7. Is it possible to draw a straight angle accurately using a ruler instead of a protractor? Explain your answer. **Yes; a straight angle looks just like a line, you could draw a line with the ruler and then draw a point on the line for a vertex.**

 Use with text pages 410–411.

Lesson 16.4

Quadrilaterals and Other Polygons

Planning

Lesson Objective Classify and identify polygons.

Technology Resources

- Audio Tutor **2**/10 Listen and Understand
- *Ways to Success* CD-ROM 16.4
- *Ways to Assess* CD-ROM
- Education Place: Extra Practice, eGlossary, Extra Help www.eduplace.com/map

Lesson 16.4 Transparency

Problem of the Day

The sum of the measure of three angles is 180°. One angle measures 40°. Of the two remaining angles, the measure of one is 20° more than the measure of the other. What are the degree measures of the three angles? (40°, 60°, 80°)

Spiral Review

1. Draw an acute angle.
2. Draw an obtuse angle.
3. Draw an angle of 75°.
4. Draw a right angle.
(Check students' drawings.)

Lesson Quiz

Name each figure.

1. (rectangle)

2. (triangle)

3. (hexagon)

4. 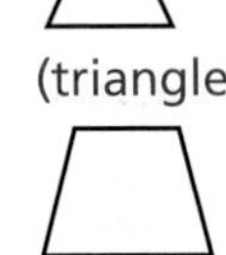 (trapezoid)

NCTM Standards

Geometry: Analyze attributes of two- and three-dimensional shapes and develop vocabulary to describe the attributes; classify two- and three-dimensional shapes according to their properties and develop definitions of classes and shapes.

Getting Started

Building Math Vocabulary

polygon a simple closed plane figure made up of three or more line segments

rhombus a parallelogram with all four sides of the same length

sides the line segments that make up a polygon

trapezoid a quadrilateral with only two parallel sides

Discuss the definition of *polygon*. Point out that *poly-* is a prefix meaning "many" and that *gon* is a root meaning "angle." Ask students to name some polygons. (Sample answers: triangle, pentagon, hexagon) Recall that the line segments that make up a polygon are called *sides*. The four sides of a rhombus are all the same length, while the opposite sides of a parallelogram are the same length. A trapezoid is a quadrilateral with just two parallel sides.

Construct and Classify Polygons

Pairs	15 minutes
Objective	Identify, classify, and describe plane geometric figures.
Materials	Construction paper, scissors
Visual, Tactual	

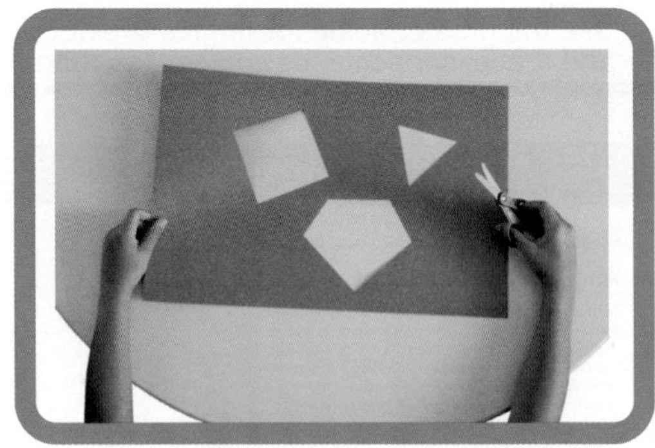

- Students have learned that line segments, or sides, make up the closed plane figure called a *polygon*. Now they will construct different polygons and classify them according to the number or length of their sides.
- Have students cut out four different shapes from construction paper. Each shape should have sides that are line segments.
- Have pairs look at their shapes. **How can you describe the shape you have cut out?**
- Have pairs share their descriptions. Guide students to appreciate that the shapes can be described in several ways: by their size, their color, the number or length of their sides, or the number or size of their angles.
- Tell students that the lesson in their book will show them how to differentiate between regular and irregular polygons.

Differentiated Instruction

English Learners

Whole Class	20 minutes
Objective	Identify and describe plane geometric figures.
Materials	Student pages 412 and 413, index cards
Auditory, Visual	

Early Production

- Students will need to practice recognizing and saying shape names and definitions.
- Have them make flash cards for highlighted words on pages 412 and 413, writing the name on the front and the definition on the back.
- Students practice reading both names and definitions aloud.

Intermediate/Advanced

- English Learner Resource 16.4
- English Learner Handbook

Intervention

Small Groups	15 minutes
Objective	Classify plane geometric figures.
Materials	None
Visual	

- Draw several open and closed plane figures on the board, clustered in one large group. Have students figure out a way to sort the figures into two groups. Guide them to do so by a key characteristic: open or closed.
- You may wish to do a similar activity, this time with all closed shapes. Some shapes should be formed by line segments only, while others should have one or more curves forming their outlines.

Other Resources

- *Ways to Success* CD-ROM, Lesson 16.4

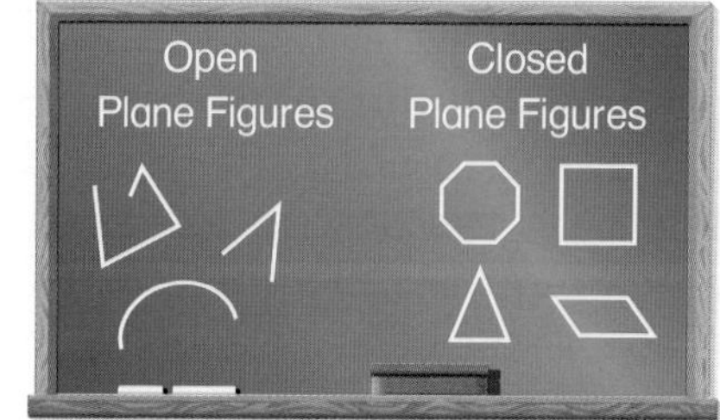

Gifted & Talented

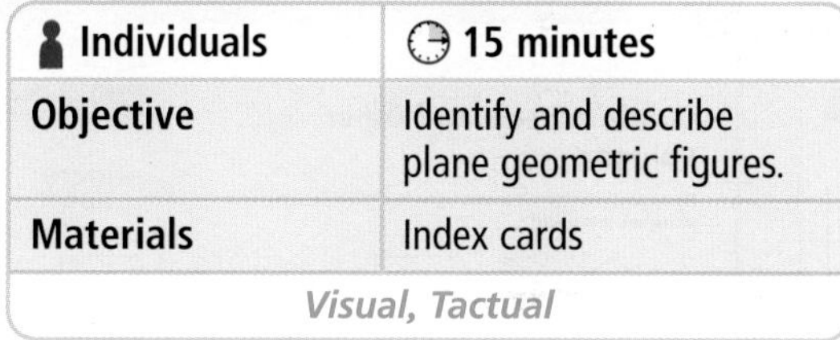

Individuals	15 minutes
Objective	Identify and describe plane geometric figures.
Materials	Index cards
Visual, Tactual	

- Have students create a matching activity.
- On one card, students write the name of a polygon. On the other, they write its definition. Have them make 5 sets of cards.
- Students mix up cards and swap with classmates, who must match each word with its meaning.

Art Connection

Materials: construction and wrapping paper, wallpaper samples, magazines, straightedge, scissors, glue

- Invite students to make a creative multitexture design featuring quadrilaterals and other polygons.
- Guide students to place the shapes in different combinations and positions before pasting them into place for the final design. Use students' designs to make a bulletin board display.

❶ Introduce

Read the objective statement with students and remind them that quadrilaterals are four-sided closed figures whose sides are line segments. Use the Quadrilaterals Transparency to introduce different types of polygons.

❷ Teach

Learn About It

- Have a volunteer read aloud the definition of *polygon*. Tell students that the figures they examined on the overhead transparency were all polygons.
- Have students examine the five polygons on page 412. **What determines the name of a polygon?** (number of sides or angles) **Why aren't there any two-sided polygons?** (Two line segments can't form a closed figure.)
- **Quadrilaterals are polygons with four sides. Every quadrilateral is a polygon. Is every polygon a quadrilateral?** (no)
- **Is a stop sign a polygon?** (yes) **How many sides does a stop sign have?** (8) **What kind of polygon is it?** (octagon)
- Focus students on the regular and irregular polygons at the top of page 413. Have a volunteer read the description of each. **Is a stop sign a regular polygon?** (Yes; its sides and angles have the same measure.)

Common Error

- **Confusing classifications.**
- **Intervention** To help students understand ideas such as *Every square is a rectangle, but not every rectangle is a square,* use analogous real-world situations. For example, guide students to see that although everyone in the Lopez family has brown eyes, not everyone with brown eyes is a member of the Lopez family.

Lesson 4

Audio Tutor 2/10 Listen and Understand

Quadrilaterals and Other Polygons

Objective Classify and identify polygons.

Vocabulary
polygon
rhombus
sides
trapezoid

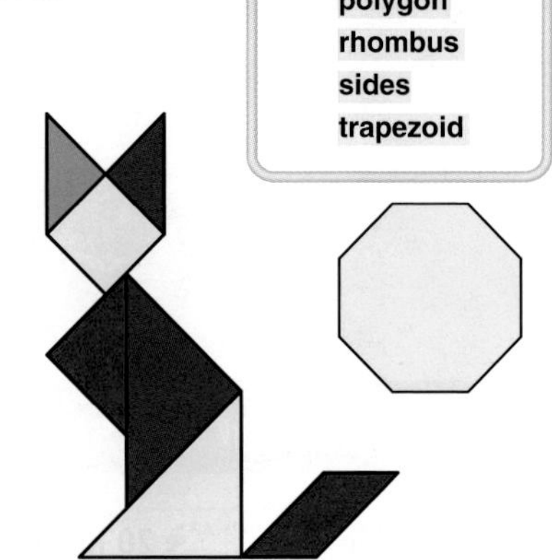

Learn About It

Look at the shapes in the picture at the right. How would you describe those shapes?
Answers may vary.

A **polygon** is a flat, closed plane figure made up of three or more line segments called **sides**. The sides meet only at their endpoints.

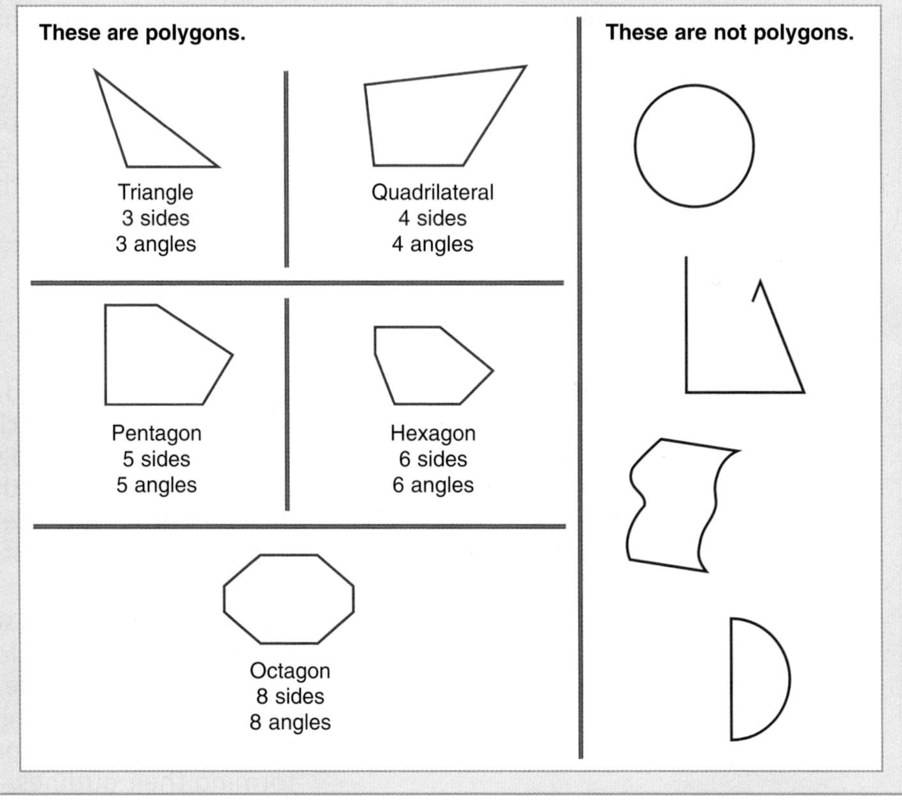

Extra Help at eduplace.com/map

Reteach 16.4

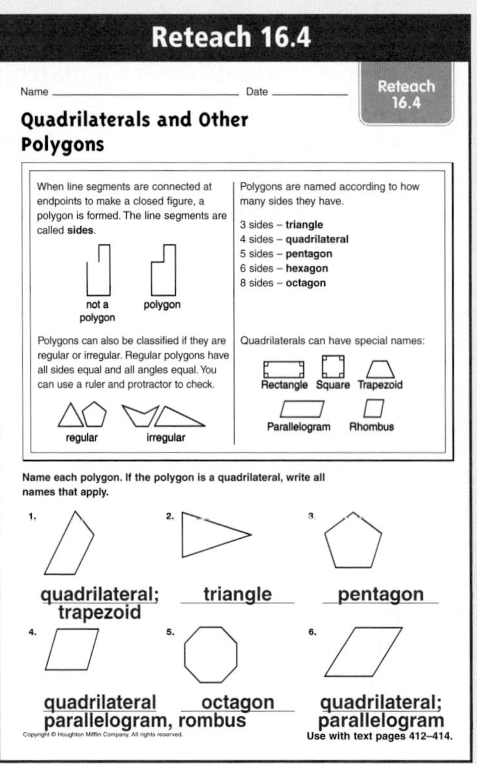

Name ________ Date ________ Reteach 16.4

Quadrilaterals and Other Polygons

When line segments are connected at endpoints to make a closed figure, a polygon is formed. The line segments are called **sides**.

not a polygon — polygon

Polygons are named according to how many sides they have.
3 sides – **triangle**
4 sides – **quadrilateral**
5 sides – **pentagon**
6 sides – **hexagon**
8 sides – **octagon**

Polygons can also be classified if they are regular or irregular. Regular polygons have all sides equal and all angles equal. You can use a ruler and protractor to check.

regular — irregular

Quadrilaterals can have special names:
Rectangle Square Trapezoid
Parallelogram Rhombus

Name each polygon. If the polygon is a quadrilateral, write all names that apply.

1. quadrilateral; trapezoid
2. triangle
3. pentagon
4. quadrilateral parallelogram, rombus
5. octagon
6. quadrilateral; parallelogram

Use with text pages 412–414.

Practice 16.4 Page 101

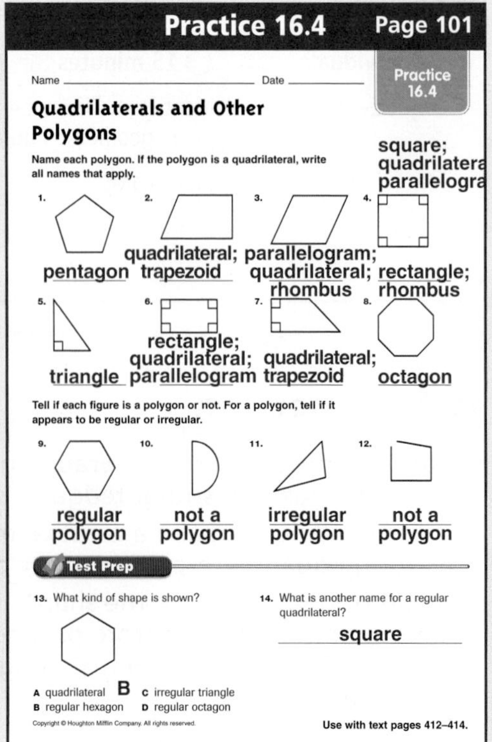

Name ________ Date ________ Practice 16.4

Quadrilaterals and Other Polygons

Name each polygon. If the polygon is a quadrilateral, write all names that apply.

1. pentagon
2. quadrilateral; trapezoid
3. parallelogram; quadrilateral; rhombus
4. square; quadrilateral; parallelogram; rectangle; rhombus
5. triangle
6. rectangle; quadrilateral; parallelogram
7. quadrilateral; trapezoid
8. octagon

Tell if each figure is a polygon or not. For a polygon, tell if it appears to be regular or irregular.

9. regular polygon
10. not a polygon
11. irregular polygon
12. not a polygon

Test Prep

13. What kind of shape is shown?
A quadrilateral B regular hexagon C irregular triangle D regular octagon — **B**

14. What is another name for a regular quadrilateral? square

Use with text pages 412–414.

▶ **Some polygons are regular. Some are irregular.**

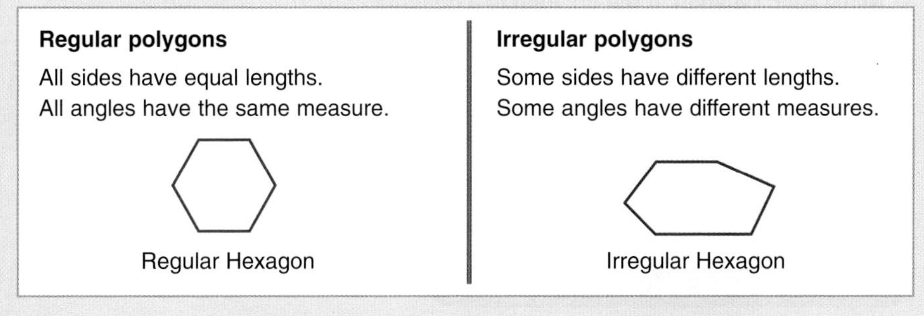

All sides have equal lengths.

Some angles have different measures.

▶ **Some quadrilaterals have special names.**

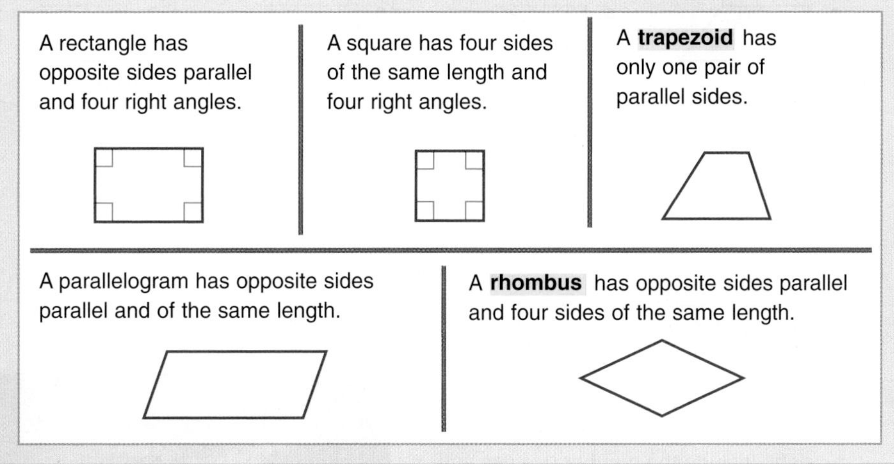

▶ **Polygons with more than 3 sides have diagonals.**

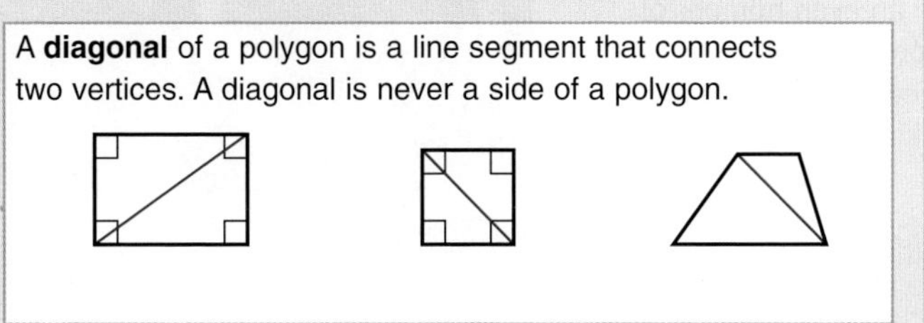

A diagonal of a polygon is a line segment that connects two vertices. A diagonal is never a side of a polygon.

Go On

- Discuss special quadrilaterals. **Why is every square, rectangle, and rhombus also a parallelogram?** (Opposite sides are parallel and of the same length.)
- **Is every square a rectangle? Why?** (Yes; every square has four right angles and opposite sides that are the same length.)
- **How are parallelograms and trapezoids alike? In what way are they different?** (Both are quadrilaterals; parallelograms have two pairs of parallel sides, while trapezoids have one pair.)

Enrichment 16.4

Name ______________ Date ______________

Enrichment 16.4

Shape Definitions

On the lines provided, write the letter of the shape that each definition describes.

f	1. a four-sided polygon with opposite sides parallel and all sides the same length	a. pentagon
g	2. a four-sided polygon with all sides the same length and four right angles	b. trapezoid
h	3. a polygon with three sides	c. quadrilateral
e	4. a polygon with six sides	d. parallelogram
j	5. a polygon with eight sides	e. hexagon
c	6. a polygon with four sides	f. rhombus
d	7. a four-sided polygon with opposite sides parallel	g. square
b	8. a four-sided polygon with only one pair of parallel sides	h. triangle
i	9. a four-sided polygon with opposite sides parallel and four right angles	i. rectangle
a	10. a polygon with five sides.	j. octagon

Circle True or False for each statement.

11. All squares are rectangles.	(TRUE)	FALSE
12. All rectangles are parallelograms.	(TRUE)	FALSE
13. All trapezoids are rhombuses.	TRUE	(FALSE)
14. All quadrilaterals are parallelograms.	TRUE	(FALSE)

Use with text pages 412–414.

Problem Solving 16.4

Name ______________ Date ______________

Problem Solving 16.4

Quadrilaterals and Other Polygons

1. In art class, Shalia drew this picture. Describe the three different types of polygons that are in Shalia's drawing.
 a triangle, a rectangle, and a hexagon

2. Kim drew a four-sided figure. Two of the sides were parallel and the other two sides were not. What type of polygon did Kim draw?
 a trapezoid

3. Rick drew a figure with six sides. Four of the sides were 4 cm long and two of the sides were 6 cm long. What type of polygon did Rick draw?
 an irregular hexagon

4. **What's Wrong?** Charlize said the figure below is an irregular hexagon. What did she do wrong?
 All hexagons are polygons. The figure shown is not a polygon because it has a curved line.

5. **Reasoning** Are both statements true? Why or why not? All rhombuses are squares. All squares are rhombuses.
 No. *Explanations may vary.*

Use with text pages 412–414.

Guided Practice

Have students complete **Exercises 1–3** as you observe. Remind them to use the ***Ask Yourself*** questions to help. Give students the opportunity to talk about the question in ***Explain Your Thinking***.

❸ Practice

Practice and Problem Solving

Select from **Exercises 4–13** as independent work.

- For **Exercise 4**, ask: **Why isn't this quadrilateral a square?** (Its angles are not right angles, and its sides are not the same length.)
- Guide students to use the terms *line segments, sides*, and *angles* as they explain their answers to **Exercises 8–11**.

❹ Assess & Close

Math Talk in Action

Draw figures on the board. Include a parallelogram, an open figure, and some line segments. Ask questions about the figures, such as:

- **How do you know if this polygon is or is not a parallelogram?**
- **Why isn't this figure a polygon?**

Discuss students' answers.

Math Journal Prompt

Have students draw four different polygons, including quadrilaterals, that are not parallelograms. Ask them to explain why each polygon is not a parallelogram.

Lesson Quiz

Use the quiz on Lesson Transparency 16.4.

Test Prep & Spiral Review

Use Test Prep Transparency 16.4.

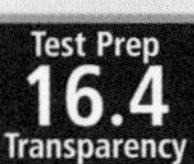

Guided Practice

3. square; quadrilateral; rhombus; rectangle; parallelogram

Ask Yourself

- How many sides does the polygon have?
- If there are 4 sides, are there any parallel sides or right angles?

Name each polygon. If the polygon is a quadrilateral, write all names that apply.

1. pentagon
2. regular hexagon
3. *See above.*

Explain Your Thinking ▶ Why is a circle not a polygon? **A circle does not have three or more sides.**

Practice and Problem Solving

Name each polygon. If the polygon is a quadrilateral, write all names that apply.

4.  parallelogram; quadrilateral
5. 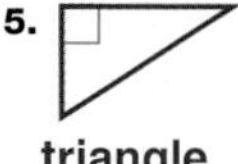 triangle
6. 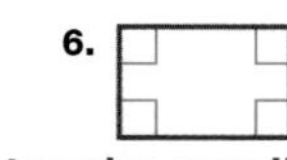 rectangle; parallelogram; quadrilateral
7.  trapezoid; quadrilateral

Tell if each figure is a polygon or not. For a polygon, tell if it appears to be regular or irregular.

8. 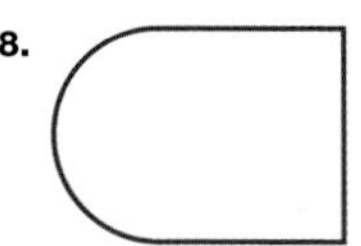 not a polygon
9. 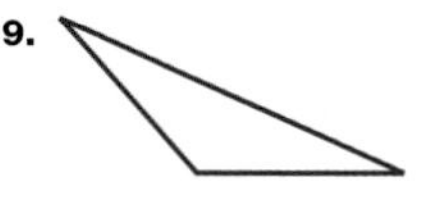 polygon; irregular
10. 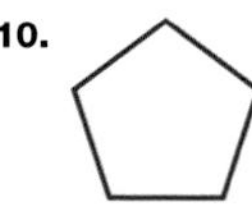 polygon; regular
11.  not a polygon

Solve.

12. **Write About It** Describe three different figures you see in the swing set on the right. Include the number of sides and angles. ***See below.***

13. **Analyze** I have an even number of sides. I have more sides than a pentagon, but fewer sides than an octagon. What kind of polygon am I? **hexagon**

12. ***Possible answer:*** **I see triangles that have 3 sides and 3 acute angles. The sections of the rope ladder appear to be squares with 4 equal sides and 4 right angles. The sections of the wood ladder form rectangles that have 4 right angles and 4 sides.**

414

Extra Practice See page 427, Set C.

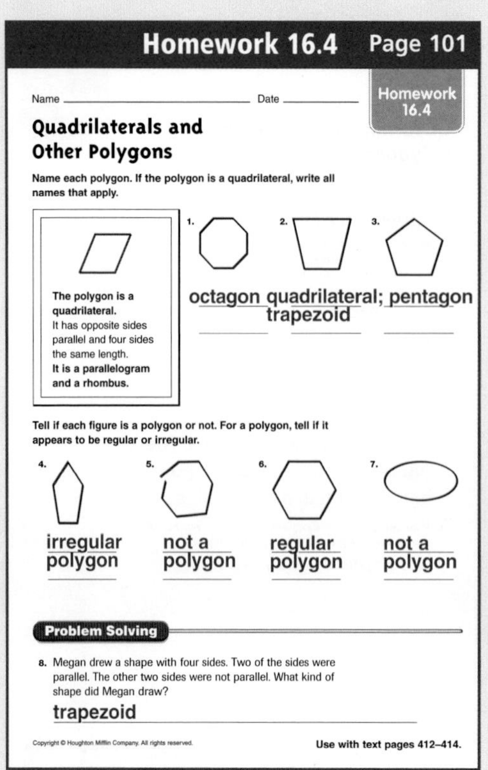

Homework 16.4 Page 101

Name ______________ Date ______________

Homework 16.4

Quadrilaterals and Other Polygons

Name each polygon. If the polygon is a quadrilateral, write all names that apply.

The polygon is a quadrilateral. It has opposite sides parallel and four sides the same length. **It is a parallelogram and a rhombus.**

1. octagon
2. quadrilateral; trapezoid
3. pentagon

Tell if each figure is a polygon or not. For a polygon, tell if it appears to be regular or irregular.

4. irregular polygon
5. not a polygon
6. regular polygon
7. not a polygon

Problem Solving

8. Megan drew a shape with four sides. Two of the sides were parallel. The other two sides were not parallel. What kind of shape did Megan draw? trapezoid

Use with text pages 412–414.

Math Reasoning

Midpoint

The midpoint of a line segment lies halfway between the endpoints.

Look at the diagram. The midpoint of $\overline{XY}$ is Z because it is the same distance from both X and Y.

Identify which points in the diagram below are midpoints. Explain your thinking.

1. Is point D the midpoint of $\overleftrightarrow{AG}$? **1. Yes; *D* looks like it is halfway between *A* and *G*.**
2. Is point E the midpoint of $\overleftrightarrow{BH}$? **2. No; *E* looks closer to *B* than to *H*.**
3. Is point E the midpoint of $\overleftrightarrow{CF}$? **3. Yes. *E* looks like it is halfway between *C* and *F*.**

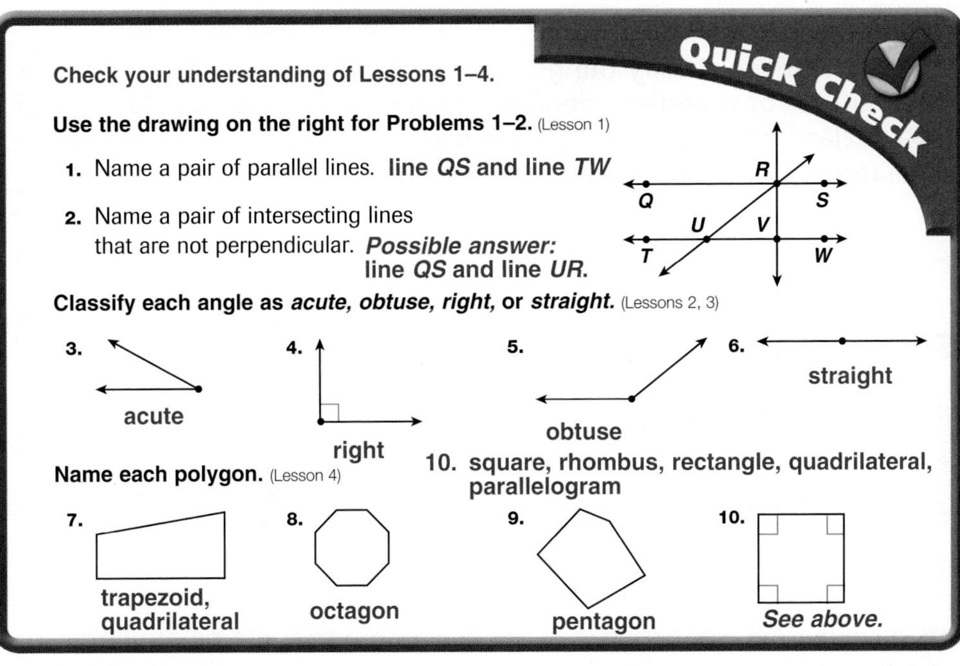

Check your understanding of Lessons 1–4.

Use the drawing on the right for Problems 1–2. (Lesson 1)

1. Name a pair of parallel lines. **line *QS* and line *TW***
2. Name a pair of intersecting lines that are not perpendicular. ***Possible answer:* line *QS* and line *UR*.**

Classify each angle as *acute, obtuse, right,* or *straight*. (Lessons 2, 3)

3. **acute**
4. **right**
5. **obtuse**
6. **straight**

Name each polygon. (Lesson 4)

7. **trapezoid, quadrilateral**
8. **octagon**
9. **pentagon**
10. ***See above.*** **10. square, rhombus, rectangle, quadrilateral, parallelogram**

Extra Practice at **eduplace.com/map**

Math Reasoning

Midpoint

- You can use the idea of midpoint to have students play a game in which they practice their skill at estimating lengths.
- Have students work in pairs. One uses a straightedge to draw a line segment of any length. The other uses visual estimation to mark the midpoint of the segment. Students use a ruler to check the estimate.
- Have partners swap roles and play this estimation game several times. Ask them to note whether they are improving in their ability to judge where the midpoint of a line segment is. Have students share their results and any discoveries with classmates.

Quick Check

The ***Quick Check*** allows you to assess students' understanding of the concepts presented in Lessons 1–4.

Items	Objectives Tested	Pages	Intervention
1–2	Identify geometric figures.	404–406	Reteach Resource 16.1 *Ways to Success* CD-ROM 16.1
3–6	Name and describe rays and angles.	408–409	Reteach Resource 16.2 *Ways to Success* CD-ROM 16.2
7–10	Classify and identify polygons.	412–414	Reteach Resource 16.4 *Ways to Success* CD-ROM 16.4

Lesson 16.5

Classify Triangles

Planning

Lesson Objective Identify and classify triangles.

Technology Resources

- *Ways to Success* CD-ROM 16.5
- Education Place: Extra Practice, eGlossary, eGames
  www.eduplace.com/map

Problem of the Day

A snail is walking along the sides of a rectangle. The rectangle is 20 inches long and 12 inches wide. It takes the snail 2 minutes to move 1 inch. How long does it take the snail to walk all the way around the rectangle?
(128 minutes, or 2 h, 8 min)

Spiral Review

Write *true* or *false*.

1. Every parallelogram is a polygon. (true)
2. Regular pentagons have 5 sides of equal length. (true)
3. Every rhombus is a square. (false)
4. Some polygons are open figures. (false)

Lesson Quiz

Draw each of the following.

1. a right scalene triangle
2. an equilateral triangle
3. an obtuse triangle
4. an acute triangle

(Check students' drawings.)

NCTM Standards

Geometry: Analyze attributes of two- and three-dimensional shapes and develop vocabulary to describe the attributes; classify two- and three-dimensional shapes according to their properties and develop definitions of classes and shapes.

Getting Started

Building Math Vocabulary

equilateral triangle a triangle that has three congruent sides
isosceles triangle a triangle that has two congruent sides
scalene triangle a triangle with all sides of different lengths
right triangle a triangle in which one of the angles measures 90°
obtuse triangle a triangle that has one obtuse angle
acute triangle a triangle in which each of the three angles is acute

Discuss what it means to classify things. (arrange them into groups) Elicit that we can use the features of triangles—degree measures of their angles, lengths of their sides—to classify them. Introduce and discuss the names of different triangles: *equilateral, isosceles, scalene, right, obtuse,* and *acute*.

Classify Triangles

Whole Class	20 minutes
Objective	Identify, classify, and describe plane geometric figures.
Materials	Triangles Transparency, Half-Centimeter Grid Transparency
Visual	

- Students have learned that triangles are a type of polygon. Now they will learn to classify different types of triangles.
- Place the equilateral triangle (Triangle B) on the Half-Centimeter Grid Transparency. **This is an equilateral triangle. All sides are the same length.**
- Turn the triangle on the grid to show the lengths of its sides. Then label it *Equilateral*. Repeat for the isosceles (E) and scalene (F) triangles. Define each kind of triangle.
- Place the right triangle (D) on the grid. **This is a right triangle. It has one right angle.** Use the grid lines to show the 90° angle. Label the triangle. Repeat for acute (C) and obtuse (K) triangles. Define each one.
- Ask: **Can a triangle be equilateral and isosceles?** (yes) **Can it be both isosceles and scalene?** (no) Discuss students' answers.
- Tell students that the lesson shows two ways to classify triangles: by their side lengths and by angle measurements.

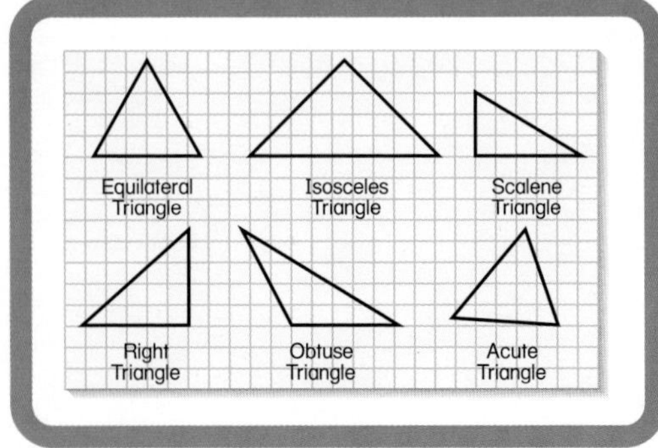

Differentiated Instruction

English Learners

Whole Class	15 minutes
Objective	Identify plane geometric figures.
Materials	Student page 416
Auditory, Visual	

Early Production

- Students may need to practice saying and recognizing different types of triangles.
- Call out definitions or draw pictures of different triangles and ask students to tell you the name.
- While doing ***Guided Practice,*** ask students to repeat each answer three times: *This is an equilateral, acute triangle.*

Intermediate/Advanced

- English Learner Resource 16.5
- English Learner Handbook

Intervention

Small Groups	15 minutes
Objective	Identify, classify, and describe plane geometric figures.
Materials	Blank transparency
Visual	

- On a blank transparency, draw the following triangles: isosceles, equilateral, and scalene.
- Point to the scalene triangle. **Which triangle is this? How do you know?** (scalene; its sides have different lengths)
- Point to the equilateral triangle. **Which triangle is this? How do you know?** (equilateral; its sides are the same length)
- Point to the isosceles triangle. **Which triangle is this? How do you know?** (isosceles; it has just two sides of the same length)
- Repeat the exercise with acute, right, and obtuse triangles.

Other Resources

- *Ways to Success* CD-ROM 16.5

Special Needs

Individuals	20 minutes
Objective	Identify, classify, and describe plane geometric figures.
Materials	Workmat 1
Visual, Tactual	

- On their workmats, students can make a three-column table to help them distinguish among the different types of triangles.
- Have them label the columns *Name, Length of Sides,* and *Examples.*
- Guide them to draw two examples of each kind to help them see that triangles can look different but still have the same name.

Name	Length of Sides	Example
Equilateral	equal	△
Isosceles	2 sides are equal	△
Scalene	all sides are different	△

Alternate Teaching Strategy

Some students have difficulty visually classifying triangles. Provide students with an index card and a centimeter ruler. Using **Exercises 1–3** on page 416, show students how to use the square corner of the index card to determine if the triangle's angles are acute or obtuse. Then, demonstrate for students how to use the centimeter ruler to measure the sides of each triangle. Guide students to understand how they can use this information to correctly classify triangles.

❶ Introduce

Explain to students that there are two ways to classify triangles: by the length of their sides and by their angle measurements. They will be able to identify different types of triangles using these two methods.

❷ Teach

Learn About It

- **What kind of angles are in an equilateral triangle?** (acute) **How many right angles are in a right triangle?** (1) **Can an obtuse triangle be isosceles?** (yes) **What kind of triangle has sides that measure 20 cm, 20 cm, and 25 cm?** (isosceles) Guide students to see that a triangle can be named both by the lengths of its sides and the measures of its angles.
- **What would we call a triangle with an obtuse angle and sides of different lengths?** (obtuse scalene)

Guided Practice

Have students complete **Exercises 1–3.** Remind them to use the *Ask Yourself* questions to help. Give students the opportunity to talk about the question in *Explain Your Thinking.*

Common Error

- **Classifying triangles incorrectly.**
- **Intervention** Encourage students to make vocabulary cards for each kind of triangle. Each card should include a name, definition, and a picture. Students can work with partners to use the cards to recall the kinds of triangles. In addition, students can use a corner of an index card to help them determine whether an angle in a triangle is a right angle.

Lesson 5

Classify Triangles

Objective Identify and classify triangles.

Vocabulary
- equilateral triangle
- isosceles triangle
- scalene triangle
- right triangle
- obtuse triangle
- acute triangle

Learn About It

Triangles are used to build many things, even jungle gyms! Triangles help make structures rigid and strong.

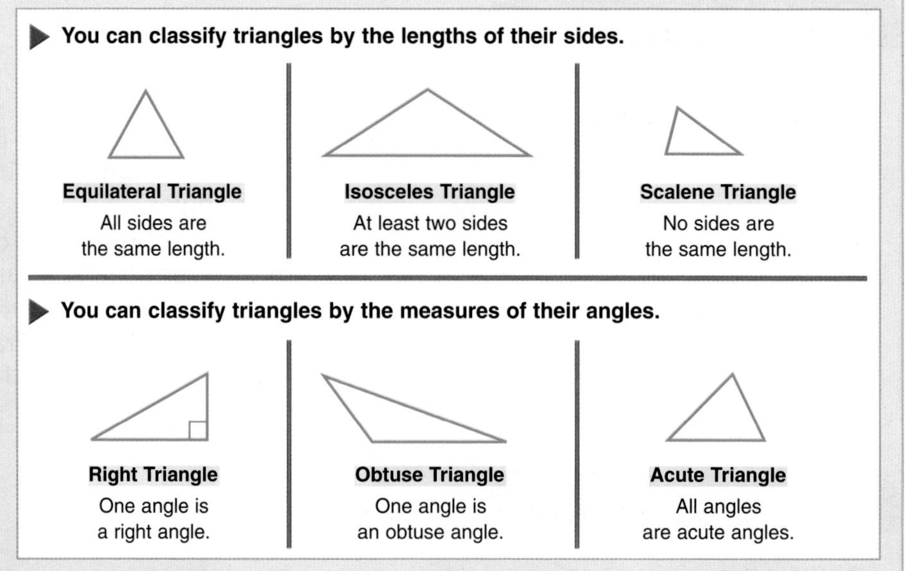

You can classify triangles by the lengths of their sides.
Equilateral Triangle
All sides are the same length.
Isosceles Triangle
At least two sides are the same length.
Scalene Triangle
No sides are the same length.
You can classify triangles by the measures of their angles.
Right Triangle
One angle is a right angle.
Obtuse Triangle
One angle is an obtuse angle.
Acute Triangle
All angles are acute angles.

Guided Practice

Classify each triangle as *equilateral, isosceles,* or *scalene* and as *right, obtuse,* or *acute.*

Ask Yourself
- Are any sides the same length?
- What kinds of angles does the triangle have?

1. equilateral; acute
2. isosceles; right
3. scalene; obtuse

Explain Your Thinking ▶ Can a triangle be both isosceles and obtuse? Explain why or why not.
Possible answer: **Yes; if it has two sides of the same length and one angle greater than a right angle.**

416

Reteach 16.5

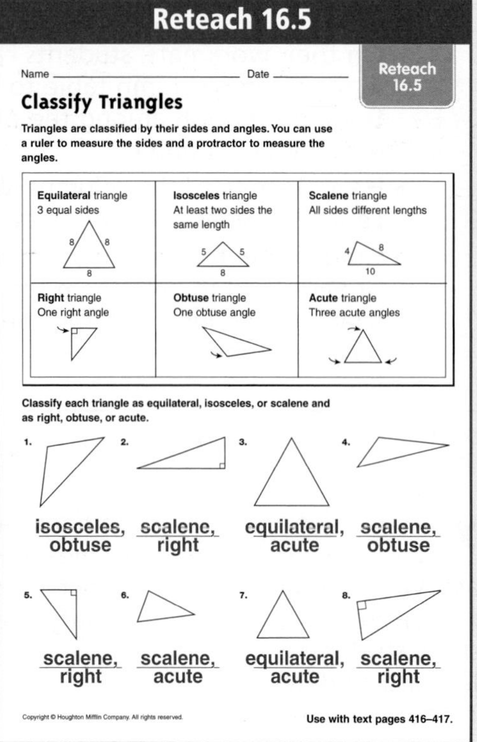

Name ______ Date ______

Reteach 16.5

Classify Triangles

Triangles are classified by their sides and angles. You can use a ruler to measure the sides and a protractor to measure the angles.

Equilateral triangle 3 equal sides	Isosceles triangle At least two sides the same length	Scalene triangle All sides different lengths
Right triangle One right angle	Obtuse triangle One obtuse angle	Acute triangle Three acute angles

Classify each triangle as equilateral, isosceles, or scalene and as right, obtuse, or acute.

1. isosceles, obtuse
2. scalene, right
3. equilateral, acute
4. scalene, obtuse
5. scalene, right
6. scalene, acute
7. equilateral, acute
8. scalene, right

Use with text pages 416–417.

Practice 16.5 **Page 102**

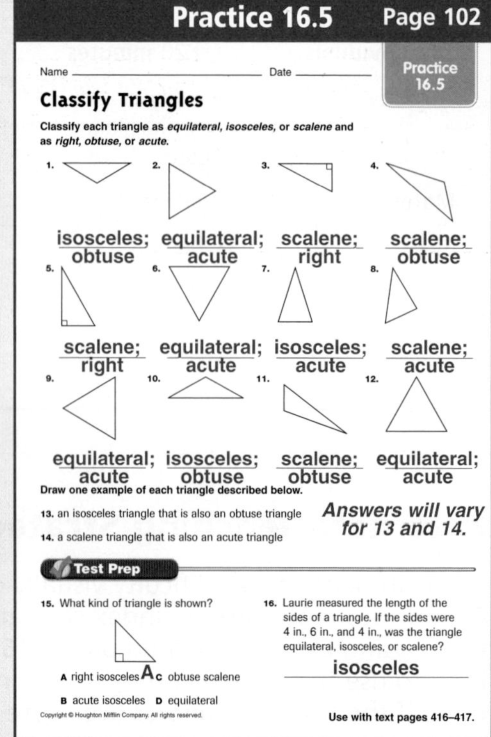

Name ______ Date ______

Practice 16.5

Classify Triangles

Classify each triangle as *equilateral, isosceles,* or *scalene* and as *right, obtuse,* or *acute.*

1. isosceles; obtuse
2. equilateral; acute
3. scalene; right
4. scalene; obtuse
5. scalene; right
6. equilateral; acute
7. isosceles; acute
8. scalene; acute
9. equilateral; acute
10. isosceles; obtuse
11. scalene; obtuse
12. equilateral; acute

Draw one example of each triangle described below.

13. an isosceles triangle that is also an obtuse triangle
14. a scalene triangle that is also an acute triangle

Answers will vary for 13 and 14.

Test Prep

15. What kind of triangle is shown?
A right isosceles **C** obtuse scalene
B acute isosceles D equilateral

16. Laurie measured the length of the sides of a triangle. If the sides were 4 in., 6 in., and 4 in., was the triangle equilateral, isosceles, or scalene? isosceles

Use with text pages 416–417.

Practice and Problem Solving

Classify each triangle as *equilateral, isosceles,* or *scalene* and as *right, obtuse,* or *acute.*

4. 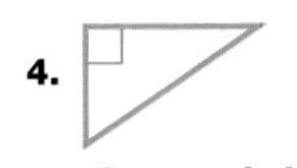 scalene; right
5. 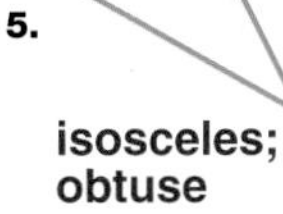 isosceles; obtuse
6.  equilateral; acute
7. scalene; acute
8. isosceles; acute
9. scalene; right
10. scalene; obtuse
11.  equilateral; acute

Draw one example of each triangle described below. ***See Additional Answers.***

12. an equilateral triangle that is also an acute triangle
13. an isosceles triangle that is also a right triangle
14. a scalene triangle that is also an obtuse triangle

Solve.

15. **Analyze** A triangle measures 3 cm on one side. The other two sides are twice as long as the first side. Is the triangle equilateral, isosceles, or scalene? Explain your reasoning. **isosceles**
16. Look at the picture of the jungle gym at the right. Draw the triangles you see. Classify each triangle as *acute, obtuse,* or *right.* ***Check drawings.***

Mixed Review and Test Prep

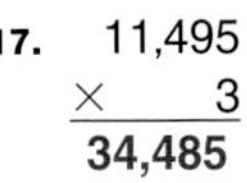

Open Response

Find the product. (Ch. 6, Lesson 7)

17. $11,495 \times 3$ = **34,485**
18. $24,459 \times 3$ = **73,377**
19. $45,395 \times 8$ = **363,160**
20. $78,231 \times 6$ = **469,386**

Multiple Choice

21. Which is **not** an acute triangle? (Ch. 16, Lesson 5)

A 

C

(B) 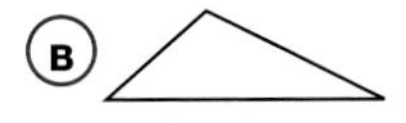

D 

Extra Practice See page 427, Set D.

3 Practice

Practice and Problem Solving

Select from **Exercises 4–21** as independent work.

For **Exercises 12–14**, have students try to draw the following kinds of triangles and describe their results:

- an equilateral triangle with a right angle
- a right triangle with an obtuse angle
- an obtuse triangle with two obtuse angles (None can be drawn.)

4 Assess & Close

Math Talk in Action

Have students work with a partner. Have them review and discuss their answers to **Exercises 4–11.** Ask: **Which of the triangles are acute?** (6, 7, 8, 11) **Which triangles are equilateral?** (6, 11) Ask students to draw another example of each of these triangles.

Math Journal Prompt

Have students write an explanation of how to identify triangles. Ask them to describe any differences they notice between naming triangles and naming other kinds of polygons.

Lesson Quiz

Lesson 16.5 Transparency

Use the quiz on Lesson Transparency 16.5.

Test Prep & Spiral Review

Test Prep 16.5 Transparency

Use Test Prep Transparency 16.5.

Enrichment 16.5

Name ______ Date ______ Enrichment 16.5

Triangle Designs

Copy and cut out the cards below. In one bag, place the cards that classify a triangle by its sides, and in another bag, place the cards that classify a triangle by its angles. Choose a card from each bag. Draw the type of triangle you picked. If it is not possible to draw that type of triangle, write *not possible* in the last column. If you need more space, use a separate sheet of paper.

SCALENE	ISOSCELES	EQUILATERAL
ACUTE	OBTUSE	RIGHT

Sides	Angle	Design

Check students' work. Not possible triangles: obtuse equilateral, right equilateral

Use with text pages 416–417.

Problem Solving 16.5

Name ______ Date ______ Problem Solving 16.5

Classify Triangles

Solve. Show your work.

1. Martin drew a triangle with two sides of length 5 cm. One of the angles measured 90°. What type of triangle did Martin draw? **isosceles right triangle**
2. Jeffrey drew a triangle that had sides that measured 3 cm, 4 cm, and 7 cm. One of the angles measured 135°. What type of triangle did Jeffrey draw? **scalene obtuse**
3. Mrs. Peterson made a triangular garden. All three sides measured 4 feet. What type of triangle is Mrs. Peterson's garden? **equilateral**
4. A triangle has one angle that measures 40°, one angle that measures 80°, and one angle that measures 60°. None of the sides have the same measure. What type of triangle is it? **scalene acute**
5. **Reasoning** Can a triangle be an obtuse triangle and an equilateral triangle? Explain. Draw a picture to show your answer. **No; all equilateral triangles are acute triangles.**

Use with text pages 416–417.

Homework 16.5 Page 102

Name ______ Date ______ Homework 16.5

Classify Triangles

Classify each triangle as *equilateral, isosceles,* or *scalene* and as *right, obtuse,* or *acute.*

The triangle has 3 sides of unequal length. **It is scalene.** The triangle has 1 obtuse angle. **It is obtuse.**

1. **isosceles; right**
2. **equilateral; acute**
3. **isosceles acute**

Draw one example of each triangle described below.

4. an isosceles triangle that is also a right triangle **Drawings may vary.**
5. an equilateral triangle that is also an acute triangle **Drawings may vary.**
6. a scalene triangle that is also an obtuse triangle **Drawings may vary.**

Problem Solving

7. Misty drew a triangle. One angle is about 112°. Two of the sides measure 5 cm and 7 cm in length. The sum of the lengths of all three sides is 22 cm. What kind of triangle did Misty draw? **scalene, obtuse**

Use with text pages 416–417.

Lesson 16.6

Problem-Solving Strategy: Find a Pattern

Planning

Lesson Objective Find patterns to solve problems.

Technology Resources

- Audio Tutor **2**/11 Listen and Understand
- *Ways to Success* CD-ROM 16.6
- Education Place: Extra Practice www.eduplace.com/map

Problem of the Day

How many triangles are in the drawing? *Hint:* There are three different sizes of triangles in the figure. Find how many of each size. (9)

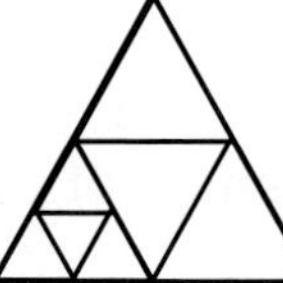

Spiral Review

Name the figure.

1. 6-sided polygon (hexagon)
2. triangle with 3 sides the same length (equilateral triangle)
3. parallelogram with 4 sides the same length and no right angles (rhombus)
4. triangle with an obtuse angle and 2 sides the same length (obtuse isosceles triangle)

Lesson Quiz

Complete each pattern.

1. ∩ ∪ Δ ∩ ∩ _ _ Δ Δ (∪ ∪)
2. 1, 2, 3, 5, 8, _, _, 34 (13, 21)

NCTM Standards

Problem Solving: Build new mathematical knowledge through problem solving; apply and adapt a variety of appropriate strategies to solve problems.

Getting Started

Building Math Vocabulary

Students should be familiar with the mathematical vocabulary in this lesson.

Using Patterns to Solve Problems

Whole Class	15 minutes
Objective	Find patterns to solve problems.
Materials	None
Visual, Tactual	

- Students have learned that patterns can involve shapes, colors, and sizes. Once they recognize a pattern, they can use the information to solve a problem.
- On the board, draw a triangle with 6-in. sides. Label the lengths. **What is the distance around the triangle?** (18 in.)
- Next, draw and label a triangle with 12-in. sides. **What is the distance around this triangle?** (36 in.)
- Then draw and label a triangle with 18 in. sides. **What is the distance around this triangle?** (54 in.)
- Have students make a table to show the data.
- **How can we use the pattern the table shows to find the distance around a triangle with 30-inch sides?** (Discuss students' answers.)

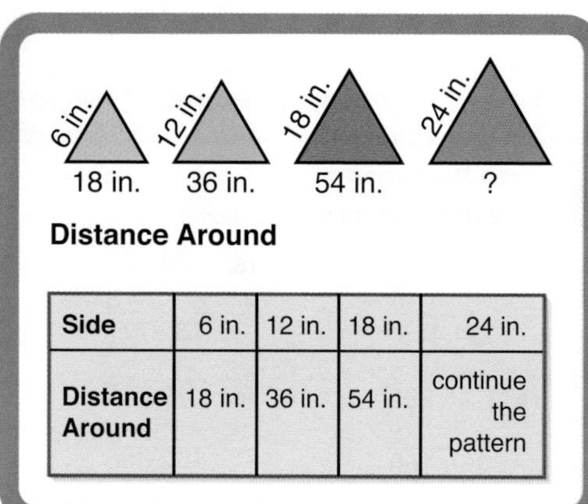

Side	6 in.	12 in.	18 in.	24 in.
Distance Around	18 in.	36 in.	54 in.	continue the pattern

Differentiated Instruction

English Learners

Small Groups	15 minutes
Objective	Find patterns to solve problems.
Materials	Student page 419, pattern blocks
Auditory, Visual	

Early Production

- Do the ***Intervention*** activity below to help students practice making and recognizing patterns.
- After students make their own patterns, have them make a pattern with blocks missing. Another student fills in the missing blocks and verbalizes the pattern.

Intermediate/Advanced

- English Learner Resource 16.6
- English Learner Handbook

Intervention

Small Groups	20 minutes
Objective	Find patterns to solve problems.
Materials	Pattern blocks
Visual, Tactual	

- Provide groups of students with pattern blocks. Have them work together to use the blocks to model and continue the following pattern: red square, red trapezoid; red square, red trapezoid; red square, red trapezoid; and so on. Have students verbalize the pattern they see.
- Repeat with simple (but increasingly complex) patterns. Invite students to use the blocks to create their own patterns.

Other Resources

- *Ways to Success* CD-ROM 16.6

Continue the Pattern

Inclusion

Individuals	15 minutes
Objective	Find patterns to solve problems.
Materials	Workmat 6
Visual, Tactual	

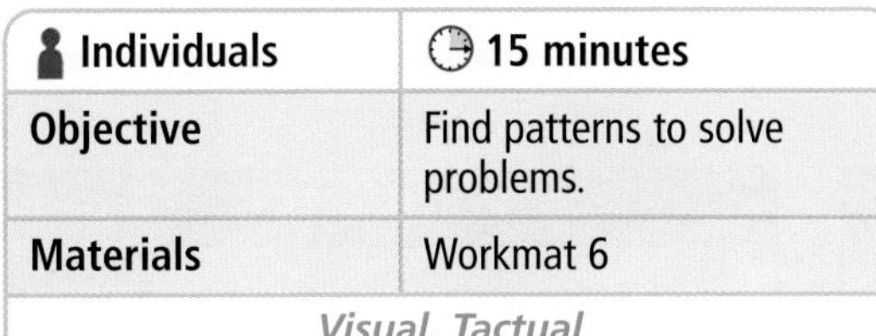

- Have students work together on their workmats to model the pattern below:

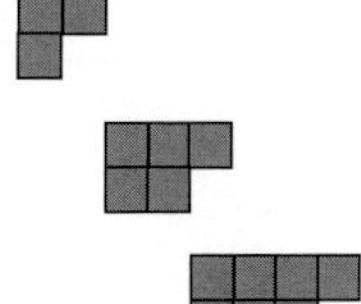

- Have students describe and continue the pattern.

Art Connection

Materials: Art books

- Show students examples of the geometric patterns that play a large part in the art and design of different cultures. Show, for instance, examples of Islamic tile work, Oriental carpets, and Native American rugs or sand paintings. Have students discuss patterns they see.
- Invite students to create their own rug or wallpaper designs made from cutout geometric shapes.

Facts Practice

Have students work with a partner. Each student shows a factor from 0 to 10 using their fingers. Partners multiply the two factors and name the product. The first partner to name the product earns one point. Partners play until one reaches five points.

❶ Introduce

Discuss with students that patterns can be seen in everyday life—from patterns in wallpaper to patterns in behavior. Tell them that the lesson in their book shows how to recognize patterns in order to solve problems.

❷ Teach

Find a Pattern

Guide students through the four parts of the problem-solving plan. You might want to use the four-part problem solving transparency.

- Begin by having a volunteer read the opening problem.
- For *Understand,* discuss with students what they know about the shapes in John's mural. (regular hexagon)
- For *Plan,* elicit from students that any pattern involves a relationship between a number or a figure and the number or figure that comes next. **What about the tiles changes in each row, column, or diagonal?** (their color)
- For *Solve,* make sure all students understand the distinction between rows, columns, and diagonals.
- For *Look Back,* have a volunteer explain why choice **c** is correct.

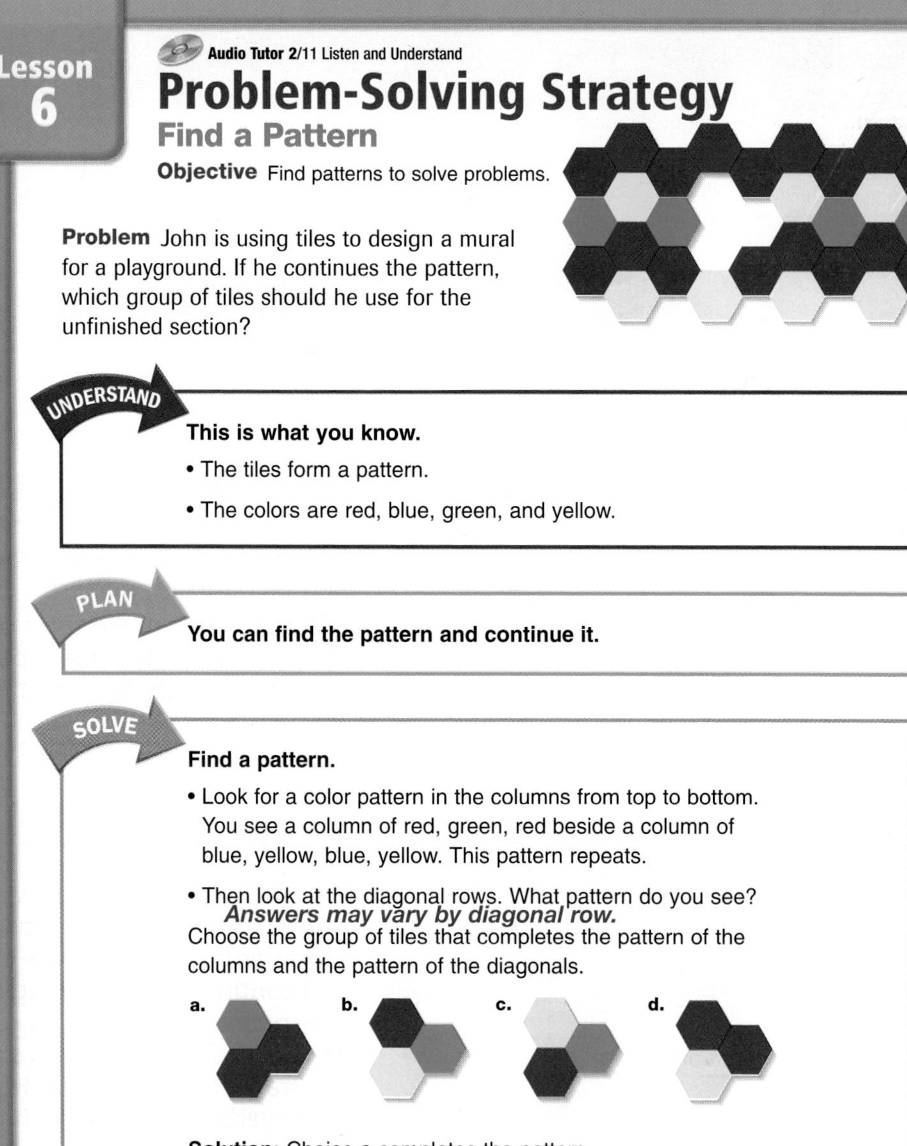

Lesson 6

Audio Tutor 2/11 Listen and Understand

Problem-Solving Strategy

Find a Pattern

Objective Find patterns to solve problems.

Problem John is using tiles to design a mural for a playground. If he continues the pattern, which group of tiles should he use for the unfinished section?

UNDERSTAND

This is what you know.

- The tiles form a pattern.
- The colors are red, blue, green, and yellow.

PLAN

You can find the pattern and continue it.

SOLVE

Find a pattern.

- Look for a color pattern in the columns from top to bottom. You see a column of red, green, red beside a column of blue, yellow, blue, yellow. This pattern repeats.
- Then look at the diagonal rows. What pattern do you see? ***Answers may vary by diagonal row.***

Choose the group of tiles that completes the pattern of the columns and the pattern of the diagonals.

a. **b.** **c.** **d.**

Solution: Choice **c** completes the pattern.

LOOK BACK

Why would the other choices not complete the pattern?
Possible answer: **The pattern for the columns does not match.**

418

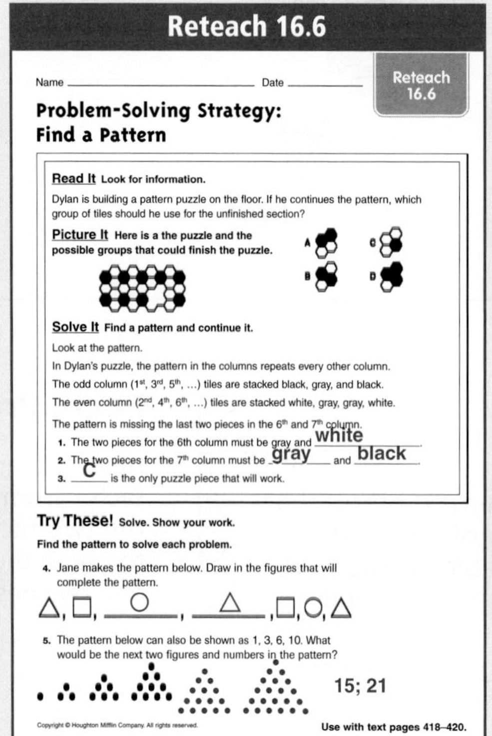

Reteach 16.6

Name ______ Date ______ Reteach 16.6

Problem-Solving Strategy: Find a Pattern

Read It Look for information.

Dylan is building a pattern puzzle on the floor. If he continues the pattern, which group of tiles should he use for the unfinished section?

Picture It Here is a the puzzle and the possible groups that could finish the puzzle.

A B C D

Solve It Find a pattern and continue it.

Look at the pattern.

In Dylan's puzzle, the pattern in the columns repeats every other column.

The odd column (1st, 3rd, 5th, ...) tiles are stacked black, gray, and black.

The even column (2nd, 4th, 6th, ...) tiles are stacked white, gray, gray, white.

The pattern is missing the last two pieces in the 6th and 7th column.

1. The two pieces for the 6th column must be gray and **white**.
2. The two pieces for the 7th column must be **gray** and **black**.
3. **C** is the only puzzle piece that will work.

Try These! Solve. Show your work.

Find the pattern to solve each problem.

4. Jane makes the pattern below. Draw in the figures that will complete the pattern.
△, □, **○**, **△**, □, ○, △
5. The pattern below can also be shown as 1, 3, 6, 10. What would be the next two figures and numbers in the pattern? **15; 21**

Use with text pages 418–420.

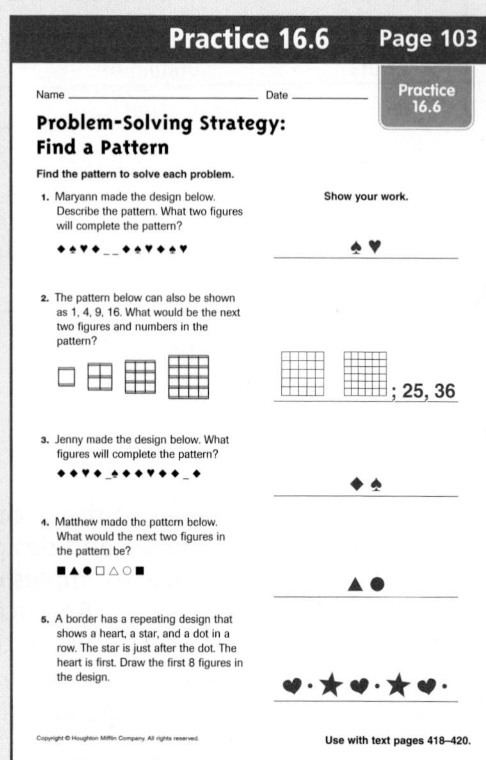

Practice 16.6 Page 103

Name ______ Date ______ Practice 16.6

Problem-Solving Strategy: Find a Pattern

Find the pattern to solve each problem. Show your work.

1. Maryann made the design below. Describe the pattern. What two figures will complete the pattern?
◆♠♥◆_ _◆♠♥◆♠♥ **♠ ♥**
2. The pattern below can also be shown as 1, 4, 9, 16. What would be the next two figures and numbers in the pattern? **; 25, 36**
3. Jenny made the design below. What figures will complete the pattern?
◆◆♥◆_♠◆◆♥◆◆_◆ **◆ ♠**
4. Matthew made the pattern below. What would the next two figures in the pattern be?
■▲●□△○■ **▲ ●**
5. A border has a repeating design that shows a heart, a star, and a dot in a row. The star is just after the dot. The heart is first. Draw the first 8 figures in the design. **♥ · ★ ♥ · ★ ♥ ·**

Use with text pages 418–420.

Guided Practice

Use the Ask Yourself questions to help you solve each problem.

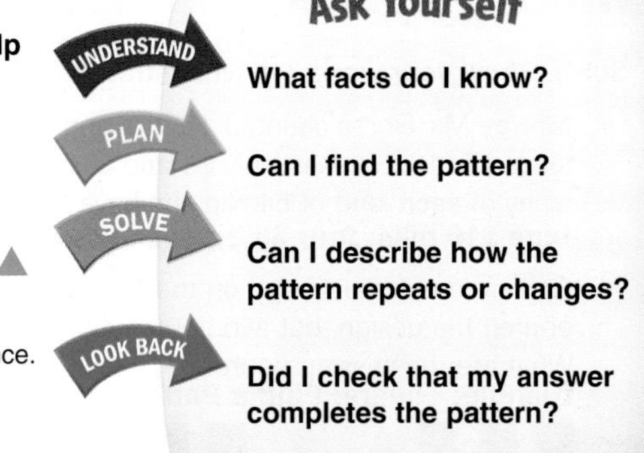

Ask Yourself

What facts do I know?

Can I find the pattern?

Can I describe how the pattern repeats or changes?

Did I check that my answer completes the pattern?

1. Describe the pattern. What figures will complete the pattern?
   dark blue square, blue triangle

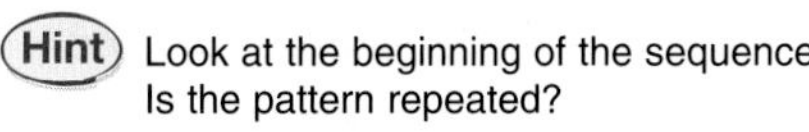

Hint Look at the beginning of the sequence. Is the pattern repeated?

2. Which piece completes the pattern?

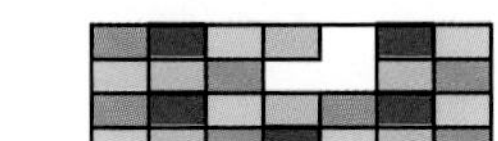

a.  b.  (c.)  d. 

Independent Practice

Find the pattern to solve each problem.

3. Nia makes the design on the right. Describe the pattern. What figures will complete the pattern? **The pattern is heart, triangle, square; the missing figures are: square, heart.**

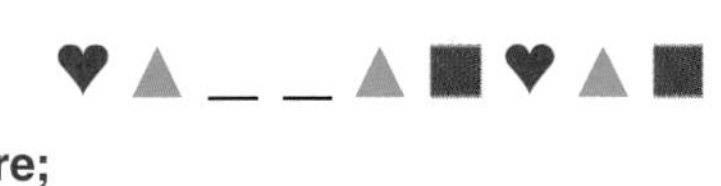

4. **Represent** A border has a repeating design that shows a triangle, a circle, and a pentagon in a row. The triangle is just before the pentagon. The circle is first. Draw the first eight figures in the design.
   circle, triangle, pentagon, circle, triangle, pentagon, circle, triangle
5. The pattern on the right can also be shown as 1, 3, 6, 10. What would be the next two figures and numbers in the pattern?
   See at right.

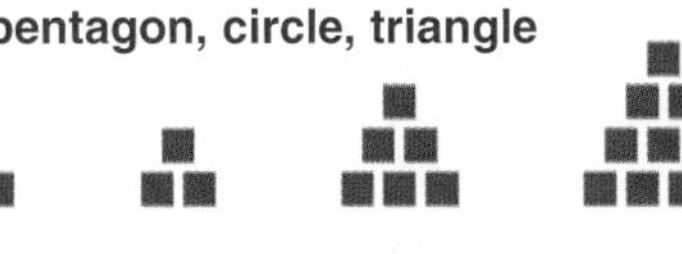

6. **Analyze** Vincent made a design in which 3 out of every 7 quadrilaterals were green. Vincent colored 56 quadrilaterals. How many quadrilaterals did Vincent color green?
   24 quadrilaterals

5.

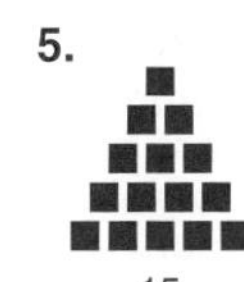
15

21

Guided Practice

Have students complete **Exercises 1–2** as you observe. Remind them to use the ***Ask Yourself*** questions to help.

❸ Practice

Independent Practice

Select from **Exercises 3–14** as independent work. Pair up students who would benefit by working with a partner.

- For **Problems 3–6**, point out to students that they may need to examine the whole pattern shown and then work backward to understand and extend it.
- ***Problem 3*** In this problem, for example, students can look ahead in the pattern of shapes to see that a square follows a triangle.
- ***Problem 5*** This pattern involves triangular numbers. Students may have success here by drawing the next two figures.

Enrichment 16.6

Name ______________________ Date __________

Enrichment 16.6

Problem-Solving Strategy: Find a Pattern

Problem Jennifer painted a border around her room. Part of the border is pictured below.

1. What pattern did she use to make the border?
   moon, star, star, moon, star
2. Continue the pattern to show the next four figures.
3. Jennifer also used a pattern of colors. The pattern was purple, yellow, white. Draw the pattern and label the colors of each shape. In the original problem, what color will the next figure in the pattern be?
   check students' drawings; yellow

Problem George described a pattern of polygons using numbers. He said the pattern was 3, 4, 5, 4, 6, 4...

4. Draw a geometric pattern that could be represented with these numbers. **possible answer: triangle, quadrilateral, pentagon, quadrilateral, hexagon, quadrilateral**
5. If the pattern continues, what will be the next two figures and numbers in the pattern? Draw them. **possible answer: 7-sided figure, quadrilateral; 7, 4**

 Use with text pages 418–420.

Problem Solving 16.6

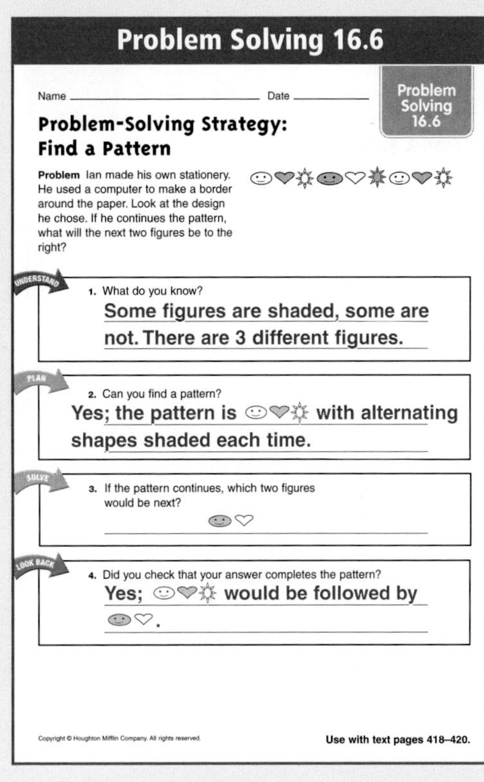

Name ______________________ Date __________

Problem Solving 16.6

Problem-Solving Strategy: Find a Pattern

Problem Ian made his own stationery. He used a computer to make a border around the paper. Look at the design he chose. If he continues the pattern, what will the next two figures be to the right?

UNDERSTAND
1. What do you know?
   Some figures are shaded, some are not. There are 3 different figures.

PLAN
2. Can you find a pattern?
   Yes; the pattern is ☺♡☼ with alternating shapes shaded each time.

SOLVE
3. If the pattern continues, which two figures would be next?

LOOK BACK
4. Did you check that your answer completes the pattern?
   Yes; ☺♡☼ would be followed by

 Use with text pages 418–420.

Mixed Problem Solving

- Remind students that they can choose any strategy and any computation method to solve **Problems 7–9**.
- For **Problems 10–14,** be sure students understand that Evan's results are shown in gold and Ariana's results are shown in green.

Mixed Problem Solving

Possible strategies given.

Solve. Show your work. Tell what strategy you used.

You Choose

Strategy
- Find a Pattern
- Guess and Check
- Make an Organized List
- Write an Equation

Computation Method
- Mental Math
- Estimation
- Paper and Pencil
- Calculator

7. **Money** Ms. Flores counted 13 bills and found they totaled $110. She had only $5 and $10 bills. How many of each kind of bill did she have?
   nine $10 bills; four $5 bills; Guess and Check
8. Antoine created a design on the computer. He printed the design, but two figures did not print. What are the missing figures?
   triangle; square; Find a Pattern

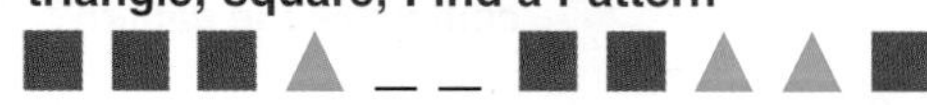

9. A fruit stand sells different sizes of fruit baskets. Each piece of fruit costs $3, and the basket costs $11. What is the price of a fruit basket with 6 pieces of fruit?
   $29; Write an Equation

Data **Evan and Ariana used shapes to make puppets. Use the double bar graph for Problems 10–14.**

10. How many shapes did Evan use?
    85 shapes
11. Who used more shapes, Evan or Ariana? **Evan**
12. How many more triangles would Evan have to use in order to use the same number as Ariana?
    5 more triangles
13. Ariana used equal numbers of which two shapes? **triangles, circles**
14. **Explain** Since all squares are rectangles, can you use the graph to find how many squares Evan used? Explain your thinking.
    No; *Sample explanation:* Not all rectangles are squares, and the graph does not tell how many of the rectangles were squares.

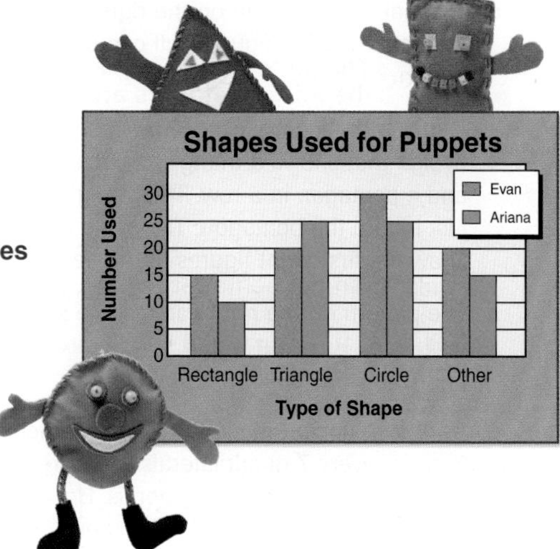

Homework 16.6 **Page 103**

Name ______________ Date ________

Homework 16.6

Problem-Solving Strategy: Find a Pattern

Find the pattern to solve each problem.

A border has a repeating design that shows a star, a circle, and a square in a row. The circle is just after the star. The square is first. Which figure is eighth in the pattern?

Use the clues to make the pattern.

Think: The square is first. The circle comes after the star, so the star must be second.

Draw the pattern. Repeat the pattern.

□☆○□☆○□☆○

Find the eighth figure.

The star is eighth in the pattern.

1. Matthew made the pattern below. Describe the pattern. What would the next two letters in the pattern be?
   ◇○△○◇○△○ ____ ____
   The pattern is ◇○△○; ◇○
2. Judith made the design below. Describe the pattern. What figures will complete the pattern?
   ♦♠♠♥♦ ____ ♠♥ ____ ♠♠♥
   The pattern is diamond, spade, spade, heart; ♠, ♦

Use with text pages 418–420.

Problem Solving on Tests

Choose the letter of the correct answer.

Multiple Choice

1. A library has 42 shelves of books with about 25 books on each shelf. About how many books are there?

   A about 100 ⓒ about 1,000
   B about 200 **D** about 2,000

   (Chapter 7, Lesson 5)

2. The fourth-grade classes at Hilltop School have 23, 26, 29, and 22 students. What is the average number of students in a fourth-grade?

   F 20 **G** 24 Ⓗ 25 **J** 29

   (Chapter 10, Lesson 5)

Open Response

3–4. *See Additional Answers.*

Solve each problem.

3. This stem-and-leaf plot shows the ages of people at a picnic. How many people are at the picnic? Explain.

Ages of People at a Picnic

Stem	Leaves
3	0 1 4 5
4	2 4 6 7 9
5	0 2
6	0 1

(Chapter 14, Lesson 5)

4. Dale's family took a trip. They spent the following amounts on T-shirts.

   $10, $14, $10, $16, $50

   Explain Which best describes the cost of a T-shirt: the mean, the median, the mode, or the range? Why?

   (Chapter 14, Lesson 3)

Extended Response

5. The line graph shows the total distance the Dunn family drove during four hours Saturday going to their summer cabin.

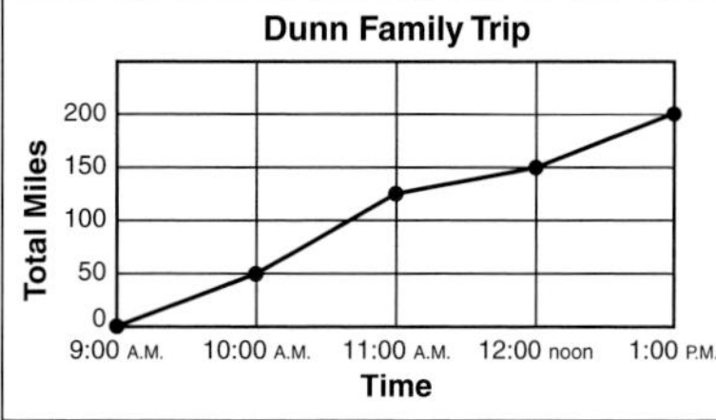

   a. Between what hours did the Dunn family travel the greatest distance? About how far did they travel? How do you know?

   b. The Dunn family stopped at a scenic overlook to take pictures once during their trip. About what time might they have stopped? Explain your reason for selecting that time.

   c. Mr. Dunn thought it cost about $0.05 a mile for gasoline for the trip. About how much did it cost for gasoline to drive to the cabin and back home? Show how you know.

   (Chapter 15, Lesson 4)

5. *See Additional Answers.*

Education Place
See **eduplace.com/map** for more Test-Taking Tips.

Problem Solving on Tests

Problem Solving on Tests provides an opportunity for students to apply previously learned skills in the types of problem contexts typically encountered in standardized tests. ***Problem Solving on Tests*** includes practice in a variety of formats: multiple choice, extended response, and open response.

Students will gain experience in writing about mathematics and using various representations to solve problems. Discuss students' solutions. Have several students explain the thinking behind their work.

More test prep practice is available on Houghton Mifflin's Web site, **Education Place.** Go to www.eduplace.com/map.

4 Assess & Close

Math Talk in Action

Have students refer to the pattern below to conclude the lesson.

- **How many circles will be in the figure that has 6 triangles?** (12)

Math Journal Prompt

Have students draw or describe a pattern. Have them include a problem to solve about that pattern. Ask them to solve that problem and record their answer.

Lesson Quiz

Use the quiz on Lesson Transparency 16.6.

Test Prep & Spiral Review

Use Test Prep Transparency 16.6.

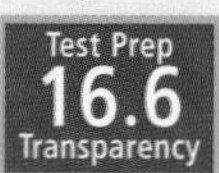

Lesson
16.7 Circles

Planning

Lesson Objective Identify parts of a circle.

Technology Resources

- Audio Tutor **2**/12 Listen and Understand
- *Ways to Success* CD-ROM 16.7
- Education Place: Extra Practice, eGlossary, eGames
  www.eduplace.com/map

Lesson 16.7 Transparency

Problem of the Day

Juan does sit-ups every day. Each time, he does 3 more sit-ups than he did the time before. Today, Tuesday, Juan did 27 sit-ups. If he sticks to his plan, how many will he do next Tuesday, one week from today? (48)

Spiral Review

Name each figure.

1. 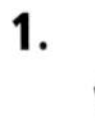 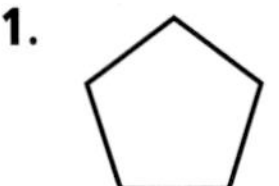 

(pentagon)

2. 

(obtuse angle)

Lesson Quiz

1. Draw a circle by tracing around a circular object. Name it *P*.
2. Draw radius *PQ*.
3. Draw chord *MN* that is not a diameter.
4. Draw chord *ST* that is a diameter.

(Check students' drawings.)

NCTM Standards

Geometry: Analyze attributes of two- and three-dimensional shapes and develop vocabulary to describe the attributes; classify two- and three-dimensional shapes according to their properties and develop definitions of classes of shapes.

Getting Started

Building Math Vocabulary

circle	a closed figure in which every point is the same distance from a given point called the center of the circle
center	a point inside a circle; every point on a circle is the same distance from this point
radius (radii)	a segment that connects the center of a circle to any point on the circle
diameter	a line segment that connects two points on the circle and passes through the center
chord	a line segment that connects two points on a circle

Display and discuss the vocabulary cards for **circle** and its parts: **center, radius, diameter,** and **chord.** Draw a large circle on the board. Point out and label each of its parts.

Angles as Part of a Circle

Whole Class	15 minutes
Objective	Examine angles as part of a circle.
Materials	Chalkboard compass
	Visual

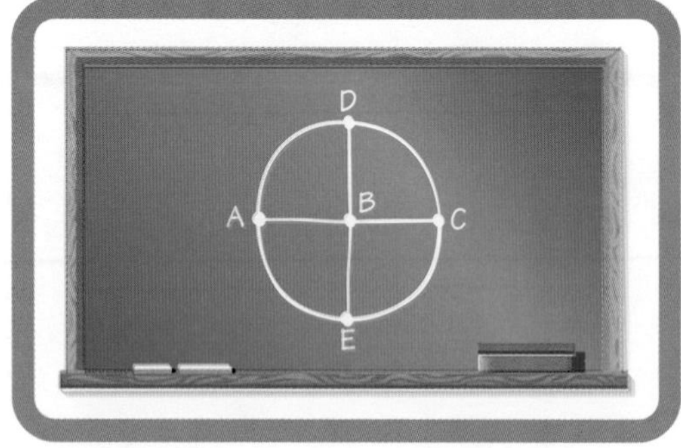

- Students have learned how to use a protractor to determine the degree measures of straight and right angles.
- Draw a right angle and a straight angle on the board. Elicit that there are 90° in a right angle and 180° in a straight angle. Then draw a large circle on the board. Draw diameter $\overline{AC}$. Label the center of the circle point *B*.
- **What kind of angle is ∠*ABC*?** (straight angle) Then draw diameter $\overline{DE}$ perpendicular to $\overline{AC}$. **What kind of angles have we formed?** (right angles) **What is the total degree measure of the angles?** (360°)
- Tell students that they are now going to examine the circle and its parts.

Differentiated Instruction

English Learners

Whole Class	10 minutes
Objective	Identify parts of a circle.
Materials	English Learner Resource 16.7, Student page 423
Auditory, Visual	

Early Production

- Give students additional help practicing new vocabulary and definitions.
- While doing ***Guided Practice,*** ask students to verbalize their answers and the definitions in their own words. If they are not sure how to define the term, have them read the definition from Learning Resource 16.7.

Intermediate/Advanced

- English Learner Resource 16.7
- English Learner Handbook

Intervention

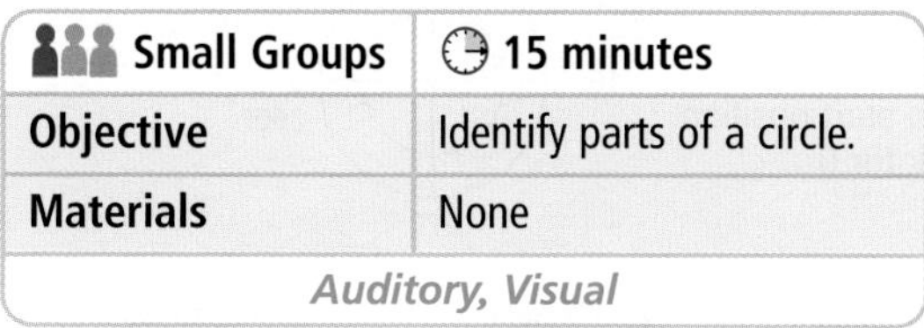

Small Groups	15 minutes
Objective	Identify parts of a circle.
Materials	None
Auditory, Visual	

- Use students' real-life experiences to introduce the idea of circles. For instance, discuss what a "360" is in snowboarding or skating. (making a full turn with one's body)
- Discuss real-life examples of circles, such as plates, the lid of a jar, or a traffic circle. Discuss also how circles differ from spheres.
- Then elicit from students the ways that circles are similar to and different from the other plane figures they have been studying.

Other Resources

- *Ways to Success* CD-ROM 16.7

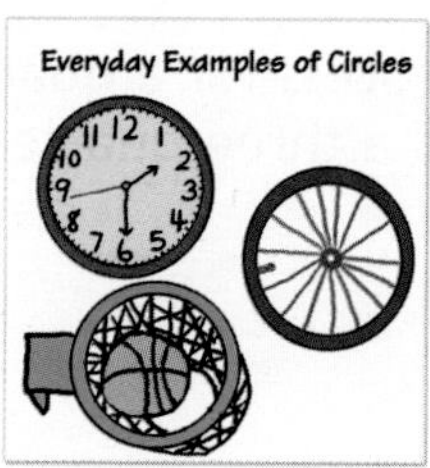

Special Needs

Individuals	10 minutes
Objective	Model and identify parts of a circle.
Materials	Scissors, paper
Visual, Tactual	

- Have students trace a circle, cut it out, and fold it in half. Discuss that the fold is the diameter.
- Have students fold the circle in half again. The point where the line segments cross is the center. Point out that the line segments going from the center of the circle to a point on the circle are radii.

Literature Connection

Materials: *Sir Cumference and the Dragon of Pi* by Cindy Neuschwander

- This book, fancifully illustrated by Wayne Geehan, introduces the concept of pi (the ratio of the length of the distance around a circle, its circumference, to the length of its diameter) in a way that students will enjoy. The setting is a medieval fairy tale.
- Encourage interested students to create their own tale in which the main character uses knowledge of geometry to save someone or something, or to achieve something.

❶ Introduce

Discuss with students that circular shapes are one of the most recognized geometric figures. Explain that the lesson explores the different parts of a circle and that students will learn about quarter, half, and three-quarter turns and the degree measures associated with each turn.

❷ Teach

Learn About It

Have a volunteer read aloud the paragraph at the top of the page. Then discuss radii.

- Why can radius $\overline{DE}$ also be written as $\overline{ED}$? (Line segments have two endpoints; $\overline{DE}$ and $\overline{ED}$ name the same segment.)
- Discuss chords with students. **When is a chord a diameter?** (if it passes through the center of a circle)
- Then have students focus on the degree measures of a circle. Have a volunteer model a 360° turn. **(Name) has just turned 360°, or a full circle. Every circle has 360°.** Repeat the process for a quarter turn, a half turn, and a three-quarter turn.

Lesson 7

Audio Tutor 2/12 Listen and Understand

Circles

Objective Identify parts of a circle.

Vocabulary
circle
center
radius (radii)
diameter
chord

Learn About It

A **circle** is made up of all points in a plane that are the same distance from a given point in that plane, called the center. Point *D* is the **center** of the circle below.

Circles

A **radius** is any line segment that joins a point on the circle to the center of the circle.

$\overline{DE}$ or $\overline{ED}$ is a radius of this circle.
$\overline{DG}$ and $\overline{DF}$ are also radii of this circle.

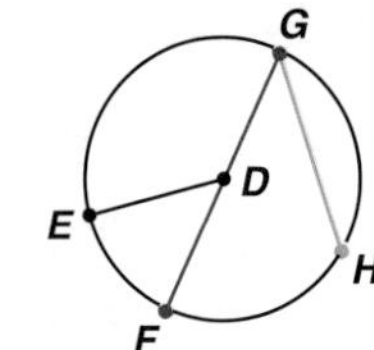

A **diameter** is any line segment that passes through the center of a circle and has its endpoints on the circle.

$\overline{GF}$ or $\overline{FG}$ is a diameter of this circle.

A **chord** is any line segment that has its endpoints on the circle. It does not need to pass through the center.

$\overline{GH}$ or $\overline{HG}$ is a chord of this circle.
The diameter, $\overline{GF}$, is also a chord.

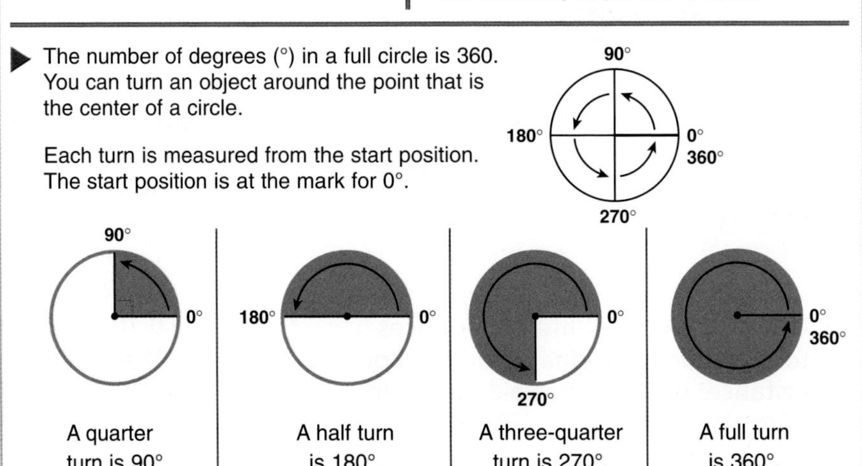

▶ The number of degrees (°) in a full circle is 360. You can turn an object around the point that is the center of a circle.

Each turn is measured from the start position. The start position is at the mark for 0°.

A quarter turn is 90°.

A half turn is 180°.

A three-quarter turn is 270°.

A full turn is 360°.

422

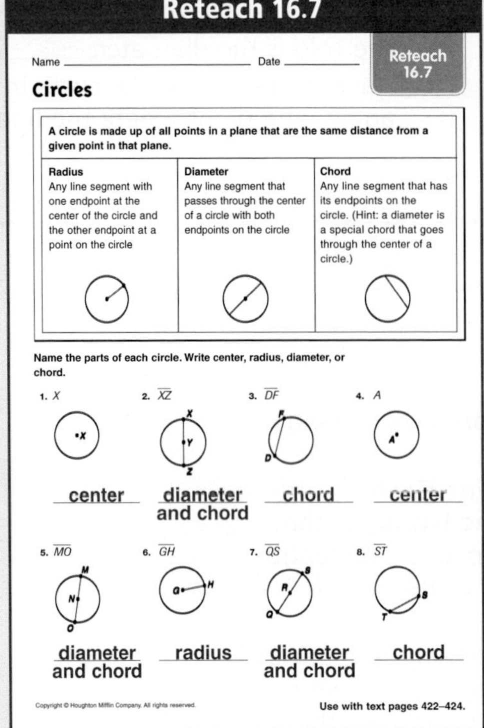

Reteach 16.7

Name ________ Date ________ Reteach 16.7

Circles

A circle is made up of all points in a plane that are the same distance from a given point in that plane.

Radius	Diameter	Chord
Any line segment with one endpoint at the center of the circle and the other endpoint at a point on the circle	Any line segment that passes through the center of a circle with both endpoints on the circle	Any line segment that has its endpoints on the circle. (Hint: a diameter is a special chord that goes through the center of a circle.)

Name the parts of each circle. Write center, radius, diameter, or chord.

1. *X* — center
2. $\overline{XZ}$ — diameter and chord
3. $\overline{DF}$ — chord
4. *A* — center
5. $\overline{MO}$ — diameter and chord
6. $\overline{GH}$ — radius
7. $\overline{QS}$ — diameter and chord
8. $\overline{ST}$ — chord

Use with text pages 422–424.

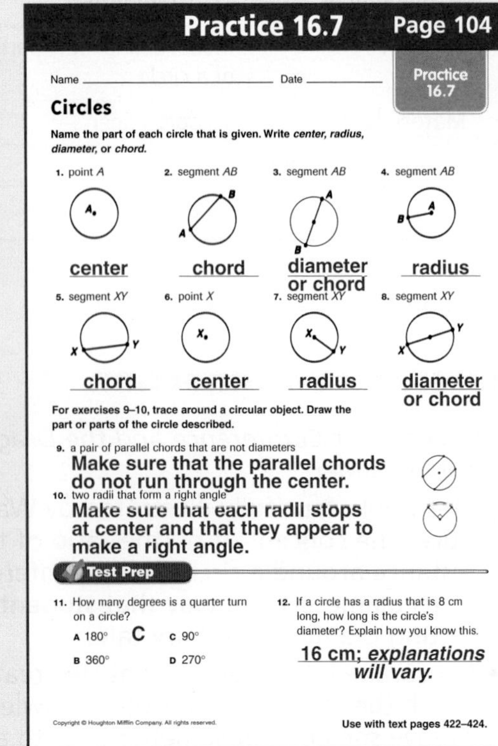

Practice 16.7 Page 104

Name ________ Date ________ Practice 16.7

Circles

Name the part of each circle that is given. Write *center, radius, diameter,* or *chord.*

1. point *A* — center
2. segment *AB* — chord
3. segment *AB* — diameter or chord
4. segment *AB* — radius
5. segment *XY* — chord
6. point *X* — center
7. segment *XY* — radius
8. segment *XY* — diameter or chord

For exercises 9–10, trace around a circular object. Draw the part or parts of the circle described.

9. a pair of parallel chords that are not diameters
Make sure that the parallel chords do not run through the center.
10. two radii that form a right angle
Make sure that each radii stops at center and that they appear to make a right angle.

Test Prep

11. How many degrees is a quarter turn on a circle?
A 180° B 360° C 90° D 270°
C

12. If a circle has a radius that is 8 cm long, how long is the circle's diameter? Explain how you know this.
16 cm; *explanations will vary.*

Use with text pages 422–424.

Guided Practice

Name the parts of the circle. Write *center, radius, diameter,* or *chord.*

1. *G* center
2. $\overline{FH}$ diameter or chord
3. $\overline{DE}$ chord
4. $\overline{FG}$ radius

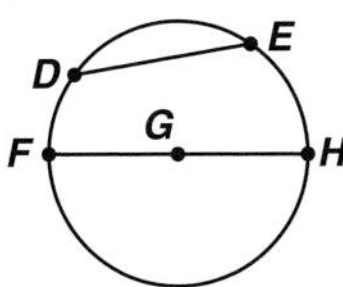

Ask Yourself

- Does the line segment connect a point on the circle to the center?
- Does the line segment pass through the center of the circle?

Explain Your Thinking ▶ How does the length of a diameter of a circle compare to the length of its radius? **A diameter of a circle is twice as long as a radius of that circle.**

Practice and Problem Solving

Name the part of each circle that is shown in red. Write *center, radius, diameter,* or *chord.*

5. 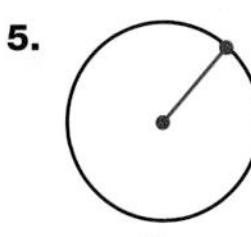 **radius**
6.  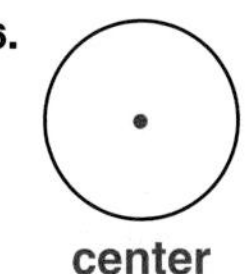 **center**
7. 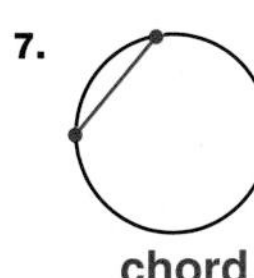 **chord**
8. 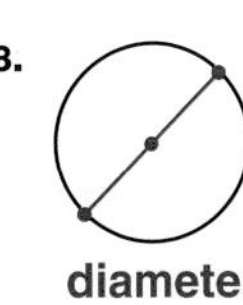 **diameter or chord**

Solve.

9. Look at the circles below. Describe the pattern. Then draw the missing figures in the pattern. **a 90° clockwise rotation**

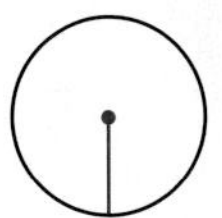 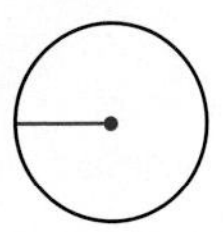 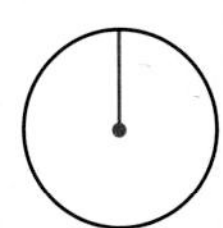 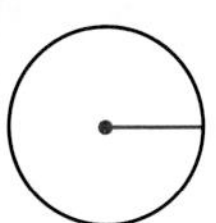 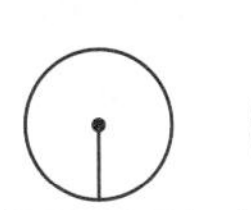 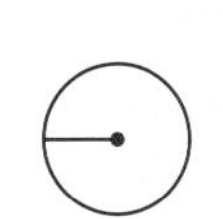 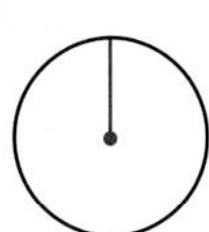

10. One radius of a circle is 4 meters long. How long would a different radius of the same circle be? Why? **4 meters; all radii of the same circle are the same length.**
11. If the minute hand of this clock moves from 12 to 6, will it have made a quarter turn, a half turn, or a three-quarter turn? What time will it be when the minute hand has made a full turn? **half turn; 4:00**

Guided Practice

Have students complete **Exercises 1–4** as you observe. Remind them to use the ***Ask Yourself*** question to help. Give students the opportunity to talk about the question in ***Explain Your Thinking***.

3 Practice

Practice and Problem Solving

Select from **Exercises 5–26** as independent work.

Enrichment 16.7

Name ______________ Date ______________ Enrichment 16.7

Circle Designs

Follow the directions for the circle, then answer the question that follows.

1. Name the center *F*.
2. Draw diameter *BC* through point *F*.
3. Place point *A* 90° from point *B*.
4. Place point *D* 45° from point *B* and 135° from point *A*.
5. Place point *E* 45° from point *C* and 90° from point *D*.
6. Draw the following chords: *AB, BD, DE, CE,* and *AC*.
7. There are 3 polygons inside the circle. What are they?

   Hint: Do not include the outside of the circle in any of the polygons.

   quadrilateral, triangle, pentagon

Use with text pages 422–424.

Problem Solving 16.7

Name ______________ Date ______________ Problem Solving 16.7

Circles

Solve. **Show your work.**

1. How far apart are the star and the square – half turn, quarter turn, or three-quarter turn?

   quarter turn
2. **Reasoning** Circle *R* has a radius *RT*. *RT* is 5 inches long. *RL* is also a radius of Circle *R*. How long is *RL*? Explain how you know.

   5 inches; all radii of a circle are the same length.
3. **You Decide** The diameter of a circle measures 12 inches. *XY* is a chord of the circle. Is *XY* longer or shorter than 12 inches? Explain your thinking.

   Possible answer: Shorter than 12 inches. The diameter is the longest line connecting two points on a circle and passes through the center. So, any chord that is not a diameter will be shorter.
4. **Write About It** Line segment *PQ* forms a diameter of Circle *A*. Draw Circle *A* and diameter *PQ*. What is the measure of ∠*PAQ*? How do you know? Name a radius of Circle *A*.

   The measure of ∠*PAQ* is 180°. A radius of circle *A* is segment *AQ* or segment *AP*.

Use with text pages 422–424.

- For **Problem 12**, students can use a watch to check their answers.
- ***Data*** Refer students to the circle graph. **Why is a circle graph an appropriate choice to use for this set of data?** (It shows how a whole—a group of fourth graders—is divided into parts.)

4 Assess & Close

Math Talk in Action

Have students refer to the circle graph on page 424 to conclude the lesson.

- **What do we call the line segment that separates *jungle gym* and *batting* from all the other activities?** (diameter or chord)
- **What do we call the line segment that separates *hopscotch* from *running*?** (radius)

Math Journal Prompt

Have students trace a circle. Have them draw and label its center, a radius, a chord, and a diameter.

Lesson Quiz

Use the quiz on Lesson Transparency 16.7.

Test Prep & Spiral Review

Use Test Prep Transparency 16.7.

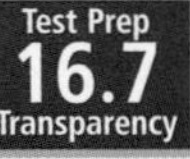

Marvin and Lisa are riding the wheel on the right. Use the picture for Problems 12–14.

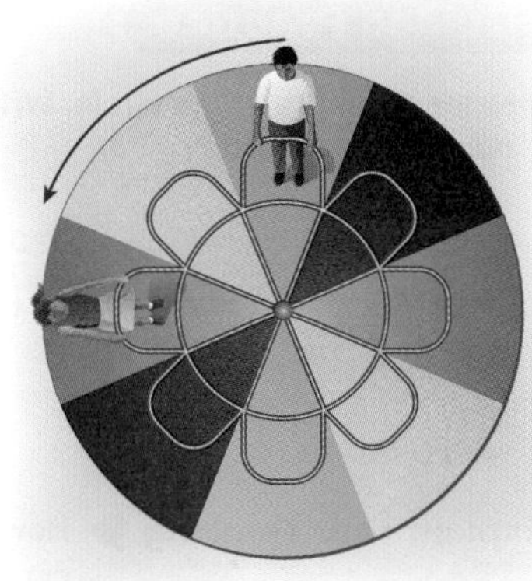

12. The arrow shows the direction the wheel is turning. Which best describes the turn needed to move Marvin to Lisa's location–half turn, quarter turn, or full turn? **quarter turn**

13. From the starting position, which best describes the turn needed to move Lisa to Marvin's position–quarter turn, half turn, or three-quarter turn? **three-quarter turn**

14. How many degrees has the wheel turned each time Lisa arrives back in the same place she started? **360°**

For Exercises 15–17, trace around a circular object. Draw the part or parts of the circle described. ***Drawings may vary. See at right.***

15. two radii that do not form a diameter

16. a chord that is not a diameter

17. a horizontal diameter and a vertical diameter

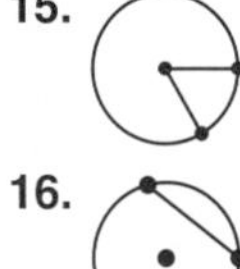

Data **Use the circle graph for Problems 18–22.**

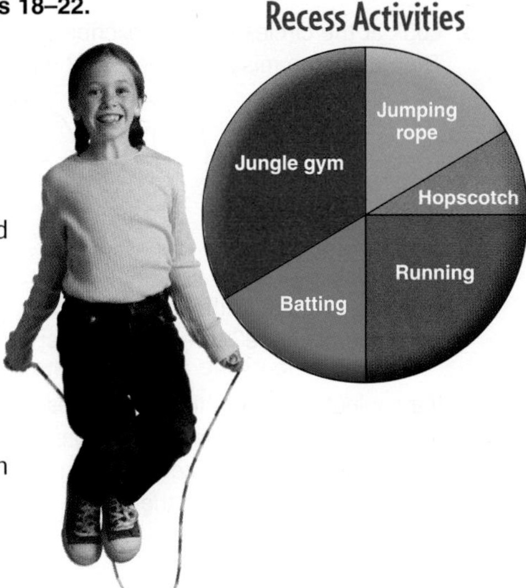

18. In which activity did the greatest number of students participate? **Jungle gym**

19. Which activity did about $\frac{1}{4}$ of the students do? **Running**

20. **Mental Math** If 50 fourth-graders had recess, about how many of them did either jungle gym or jumping rope? **about 25 students**

21. **Analyze** Which two activities had about the same number of students participating? **Jumping rope and Batting**

22. **Create and Solve** Make a circle graph and write two questions about it. Give your questions to a classmate to solve. ***Check graphs and questions.***

424

Extra Practice See page 427, Set E.

Homework 16.7 **Page 104**

Name ______________ Date ______________

Homework 16.7

Circles

Name the part of each circle that is shown with a point or a point and a dashed line. Write *center, radius, diameter,* or *chord.*

The line segment has its endpoints on the circle. **It is a chord.**

1. **center**
2. **radius**
3. **diameter**

For Problems 4–5, trace around a circular object. Draw the part or parts of the circle described.

4. a set of two diameters that are perpendicular to each other
Drawings may vary.

5. three chords which form a triangle
Drawings may vary.

Problem Solving

6. The hour hand on a clock starts on 12:00 noon. George checks the clock later in the day. The hour hand has made a three-quarter turn around the clock. What time is it?
9:00 P.M.

Use with text pages 422–424.

Mixed Review and Test Prep 

Open Response

Choose a graph to display the data. Write *bar graph*, *circle graph*, *line graph*, or *pictograph*. Explain your choice.

(Ch. 15, Lesson 5)

23. wind speeds during a storm

24. the number of goals scored by 4 hockey players during one month

25. the results of a survey that asked students to choose their favorite pet ***23–25: Answers may vary; Check students' explanations.***

26. A circle has a diameter labeled $\overline{FG}$. Could F be the center of the circle? Explain your thinking.

(Ch. 16, Lesson 7) **No; Possible explanation: The diameter runs though the center of the circle, so *F* is somewhere on the circle.**

Art Connection

Be an Artist

Activity

Geometry often inspires artists. Painters such as Pablo Picasso, Piet Mondrian, Fernand Léger, and Juan Gris used geometric figures in their paintings.

1. Look at the painting. What geometric figures do you see? ***See below.***
2. **Challenge** Use at least three geometric figures and colored pencils to create a work of art.

1. *Possible answers:* square, rectangle, hexagon, quadrilateral, circle, pentagon.

Composition, 1924, by Fernand Léger

WEEKLY WR READER eduplace.com/map

Art Connection

Be an Artist

- Challenge students to create their works of art by cutting and pasting colored construction paper. Or invite them to make their designs using only one kind of geometric shape. Post students' work on the bulletin board.
- Encourage interested students to find other examples of geometry in art, such as in architecture or in furniture design. Have them share what they discover.

Monitoring Student Progress

Chapter Review/Test

Chapter Review/Test Items 1–20

To assign a numerical grade for this Chapter Review/Test, use 5 points for each test item.

Check Understanding

You can use the ***Write About It*** question to assess student understanding of a key chapter concept.

Customize Your Instruction

The Chapter Review/Test is a formal evaluation of chapter objectives. For students who have not yet mastered these objectives, you can use the Reteaching Resources listed in the chart below.

Additional Assessment Resources

Alternate Chapter Test A Chapter Test is also provided in the Unit Resource folder. You might use the Review/Test in the student book as review and the test in the Unit Resource folder as a summary test for the chapter.

***Ways to Assess* CD-ROM** allows you to create your own lesson, chapter, or unit tests or practice and review worksheets.

Adequate Yearly Progress Guide helps familiarize your students with the format of standardized tests.

Chapter Review/Test

VOCABULARY

Choose the best word to complete each sentence.

Vocabulary
radius
triangle
trapezoid
perpendicular

1. A line segment that joins a point on a circle to the center of the circle is a ____. **radius**
2. Two lines that intersect to form right angles are ____. **perpendicular**
3. A quadrilateral that has only one pair of parallel sides is a ____. **trapezoid**

CONCEPTS AND SKILLS

Use words and symbols to name each figure. (Lessons 1–2, pp. 404–409)

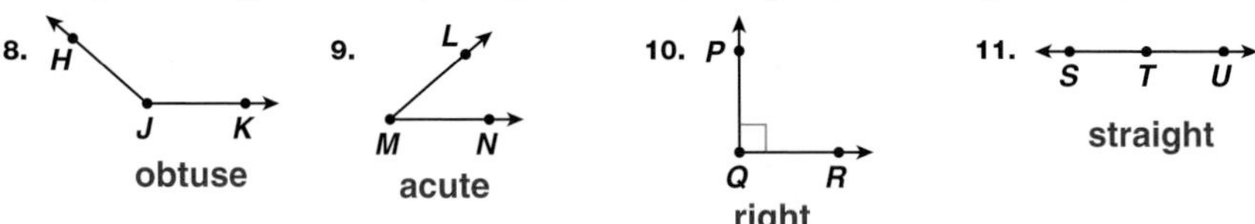

Classify each angle as *acute, straight, obtuse,* or *right.* (Lessons 2–3, pp. 408–411)

8. H J K — **obtuse**
9. L M N — **acute**
10. P Q R — **right**
11. S T U — **straight**

Name each polygon. Write all the names that apply. (Lessons 4–5, pp. 412–417)

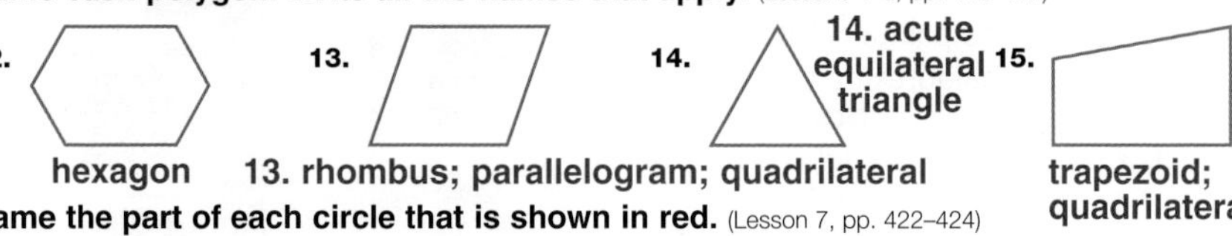

Name the part of each circle that is shown in red. (Lesson 7, pp. 422–424)

16. **diameter or chord**
17. **chord**
18. **center**
19. **radius**

PROBLEM SOLVING

Solve. (Lesson 6, pp. 418–420)

20. Look at the design. If the pattern continues, what kind of polygon should the fifteenth figure be?

triangle

Show You Understand

How are an equilateral triangle and an isosceles triangle alike? How are they different?

See Additional Answers.

426 **Chapter 16** Chapter Review/Test

Chapter Review/Test Items	Objectives	Covered On Teacher's Edition Pages	Use These Reteaching Resources
2, 4–11	**16A** Name and describe characteristics of points, lines, line segments, rays, and angles.	404A–406, 408A–411	Reteach Resources 16.1, 16.2, 16.3 *Ways to Success* CD-ROM 16.1, 16.2, 16.3 *Ways to Success* Skillsheet 137
1, 3, 12–19	**16B** Identify, classify, and describe plane geometric figures.	412A–414, 416A–417, 422A–424	Reteach Resources 16.4, 16.5, 16.7 *Ways to Success* CD-ROM 16.4, 16.5, 16.7 *Ways to Success* Skillsheets 138, 142, 143
20	**16C** Solve problems using skills and strategies.	418A–420	Reteach Resources 16.6 *Ways to Success* CD-ROM 16.6; *Ways to Success* Skillsheet 144

Extra Practice

Set C: 1. quadrilateral, rectangle, parallelogram
2. quadrilateral, trapezoid

Set A (Lesson 1, pp. 404–406)

Use words and symbols to name each figure.

1. K F — line segment KF; $\overline{KF}$
2. •M — point M; M
3. 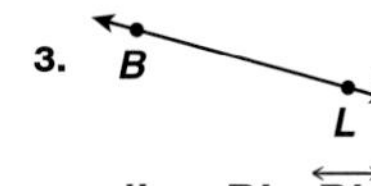 B L — line BL; $\overleftrightarrow{BL}$
4. X Y — line segment XY; $\overline{XY}$

Write *parallel, intersecting,* or *perpendicular.*

5. perpendicular, intersecting
6. intersecting
7. parallel
8. perpendicular, intersecting

Set B (Lesson 2, pp. 408–409)

Classify each angle as *acute, obtuse, right,* or *straight.*

1. straight
2. 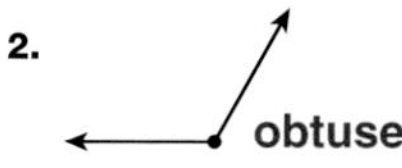 obtuse
3. 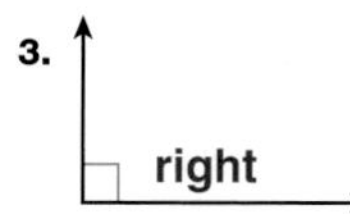 right
4.  acute

Set C (Lesson 4, pp. 412–414)

Name each polygon. Write all names that apply.

1. 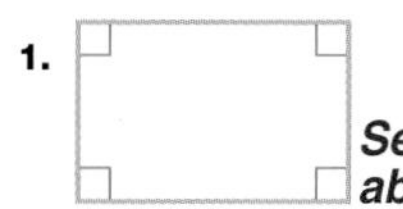 See above.
2.  See above.
3. 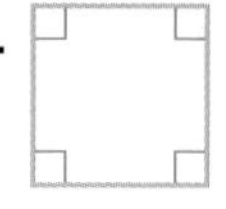 quadrilateral, parallelogram, rectangle, rhombus, square
4.  regular octagon

Set D (Lesson 5, pp. 416–417)

Classify each triangle as *equilateral, isosceles,* or *scalene.*

1. 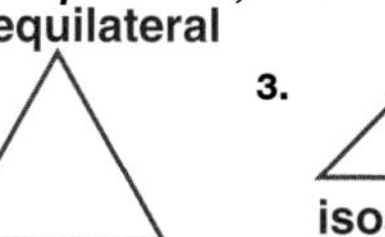 scalene
2. 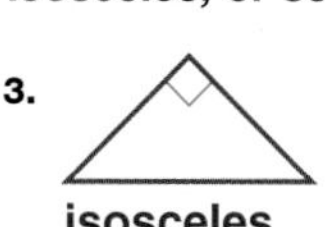 equilateral
3. 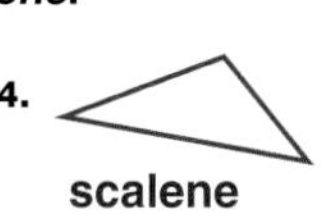 isosceles
4.  scalene
5.  isosceles

Set E (Lesson 7, pp. 422–424)

Name the part of each circle that is shown in red.

1. 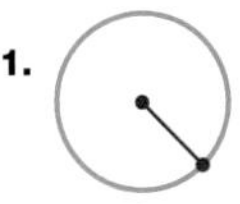 radius
2. 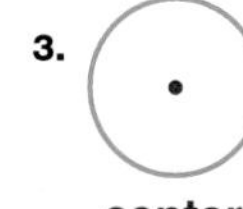 diameter
3. 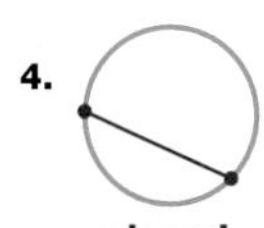 center
4. 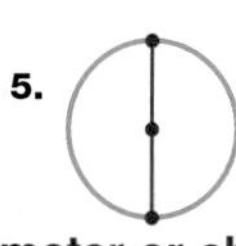 chord
5. diameter or chord

Extra Practice at **eduplace.com/map**

CHAPTER 16 TEST

Chapter 16 Test

Name ______ Date ______

Use words and symbols to name each figure.

1. ray BC, $\overrightarrow{BC}$
2. line segment FG or GF; $\overline{FG}$ or $\overline{GF}$
3. line OP or PO; $\overleftrightarrow{OP}$ or $\overleftrightarrow{PO}$

Write *parallel, intersecting,* or *perpendicular* to describe the relationship between each pair of lines.

4. intersecting
5. parallel
6. perpendicular

Name each angle in three ways. Then classify the angle as *acute, obtuse, right,* or *straight.*

7. ∠JKL; ∠LKJ; ∠K; right
8. ∠XYZ; ∠ZYX; ∠Y; obtuse
9. ∠RST; ∠TSR; ∠S; straight

Name each polygon. If the polygon is a quadrilateral, write all names that apply.

10. octagon
11. quadrilateral; parallelogram; rectangle; rhombus; square
12. hexagon

CHAPTER 16 TEST

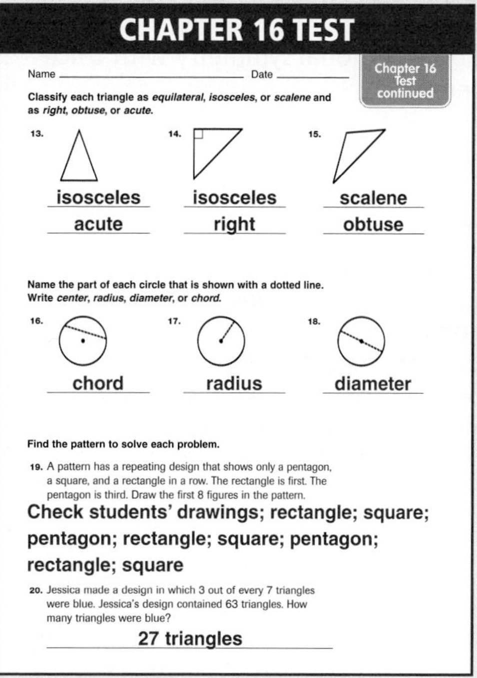
Chapter 16 Test continued

Name ______ Date ______

Classify each triangle as *equilateral, isosceles,* or *scalene* and as *right, obtuse,* or *acute.*

13. isosceles, acute
14. isosceles, right
15. scalene, obtuse

Name the part of each circle that is shown with a dotted line. Write *center, radius, diameter,* or *chord.*

16. chord
17. radius
18. diameter

Find the pattern to solve each problem.

19. A pattern has a repeating design that shows only a pentagon, a square, and a rectangle in a row. The rectangle is first. The pentagon is third. Draw the first 8 figures in the pattern.
Check students' drawings; rectangle; square; pentagon; rectangle; square; pentagon; rectangle; square

20. Jessica made a design in which 3 out of every 7 triangles were blue. Jessica's design contained 63 triangles. How many triangles were blue?
27 triangles

Planning Guide

Congruence, Symmetry, and Transformations

Lesson	Overview	Objective/Vocabulary
1 Hands On: Congruent Figures p. 430A	▶ Explore congruence by placing cutouts of various figures on top of each other to see which have the same size and shape. ▶ Identify pairs of congruent figures and draw them on grid paper. ▶ Use a Venn diagram to show the relationship among different types of quadrilaterals.	▶ Learn about figures that have the same size and shape. congruent
2 Hands On: Rotations, Reflections, and Translations p. 434A	▶ Predict results of transformational moves on a figure, including *translations* (slides) along a straight line, *rotations* (turns) around a point, and *reflections* (flips) over a line. ▶ Transformational moves preserve the congruence of resulting figures to the original; all are the same size and shape but in different locations on the plane.	▶ Learn about rotations, reflections, and translations. rotation reflection translation transformations
3 Problem-Solving Strategy: Act It Out p. 436A	▶ Learn and practice the Act It Out strategy for solving problems. ▶ Model congruent figures with tangram pieces and toothpicks. ▶ Choose a strategy to solve problems.	▶ Learn how to solve a problem by using a model to act it out. congruent figures pentagon square triangle
4 Hands On: Symmetry p. 440A	▶ Find a line of symmetry by folding cutouts of geometric figures. ▶ Explore rotational symmetry with trace paper.	▶ Learn how to identify figures that can be folded into matching parts. line symmetry line of symmetry rotational symmetry
5 Problem-Solving Application: Visual Thinking p. 444A	▶ Solve problems with visual thinking. ▶ Visual thinking involves "seeing or moving objects in your mind" to find hidden figures or a resulting figure. ▶ Choose a problem-solving strategy and computation method.	▶ Solve problems using visual thinking. triangle right triangle

Skills Trace: Congruence, Symmetry, and Transformations		
Grade 3	**Grade 4**	**Grade 5**
• Identify congruent figures (Ch. 16) • Explore rotations, reflections, and translations (Ch. 16) • Identify figures with a line of symmetry (Ch. 16) • Solve a problem by using models (Ch. 19)	• Identify congruent figures • Identify and predict results of rotations, reflections, and translations • Identify figures with line and rotational symmetry • Learn how to solve a problem by using a model to act it out	• Identify congruent figures (Ch. 15) • Identify and predict results of rotations, reflections, and translations (Ch. 15) • Identify figures with line and rotational symmetry (Ch. 15) • Make models to solve tesselation problems (Ch. 15)

Differentiated Instruction	Materials	NCTM Standards
▶ Differentiated Instruction activities, p. 430B ▶ *Chapter Challenges,* p. 97 *Ways to Success* CD-ROM 17.1 ▶ *Ways to Success* Skillsheets 145, 146, 148 Audio Tutor **2**/13 Listen and Understand	Large Plane Figures and Small Plane Figures transparencies, blank transparency, grid paper, scissors	**Geometry:** Analyze characteristics and properties of two- and three-dimensional geometric shapes and develop mathematical arguments about geometric relationships; use visualization, spatial reasoning, and geometric modeling to solve problems.
▶ Differentiated Instruction activities, p. 434B *Ways to Success* CD-ROM 17.2 ▶ *Ways to Success* Skillsheet 150 Audio Tutor **2**/14 Listen and Understand	Large Plane Figures Transparency, Centimeter Grid Transparency, trapezoid pattern block or Learning Tool 25, grid paper	**Geometry:** Apply transformations and use symmetry to analyze mathematical situations; use visualization, spatial reasoning, and geometric modeling to solve problems. **Communication:** Use the language of mathematics to express mathematical ideas precisely.
▶ Differentiated Instruction activities, p. 436B ▶ *Chapter Challenges,* p. 99 *Ways to Success* CD-ROM 17.3	Tangram pieces (Learning Tool 24), scissors	**Problem Solving:** Apply and adapt a variety of appropriate strategies to solve problems. **Geometry:** Use visualization, spatial reasoning, and geometric modeling to solve problems.
▶ Differentiated Instruction activities, p. 440B *Ways to Success* CD-ROM 17.4 ▶ *Ways to Success* Skillsheets 147, 149	Small Plane Figures Transparency, Circle Transparency, Circle Spinner Transparency, grid paper	**Geometry:** Explore congruence and symmetry; identify and describe line and rotational symmetry in two- and three-dimensional shapes and designs. **Communication:** Use the language of mathematics to express mathematical ideas precisely.
▶ Differentiated Instruction activities, p. 444B ▶ *Chapter Challenges,* p. 101 *Ways to Success* CD-ROM 17.5 ▶ *Ways to Success* Skillsheet 151	Framed photograph	**Geometry:** Use visualization, spatial reasoning, and geometric modeling to solve problems. **Problem Solving:** Apply and adapt a variety of appropriate strategies to solve problems.

Math Notes

Chapter Objectives

17A Identify congruent figures and figures with line and rotational symmetry.

17 B Identify, perform, and predict the results of rotations, reflections, and translations.

17 C Solve problems using skills and strategies.

Mathematical Background

Congruence, Transformations, and Symmetry

Figures that are the same size and shape are **congruent.** Figures that have the same shape but not necessarily the same size are **similar.** If two figures are similar, either they are congruent or one is a reduction or enlargement of the other.

A transformation shows a change in position of a figure due to a **rotation, reflection,** or **translation.**

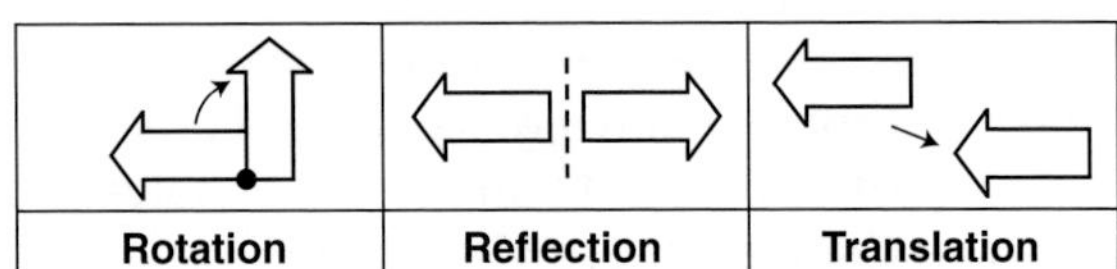

A figure has **rotational symmetry** if it can be rotated less than a full turn about a point and it looks the same as it did before the rotation. Look at the example below.

Figure A has rotational symmetry. Figure B does not.

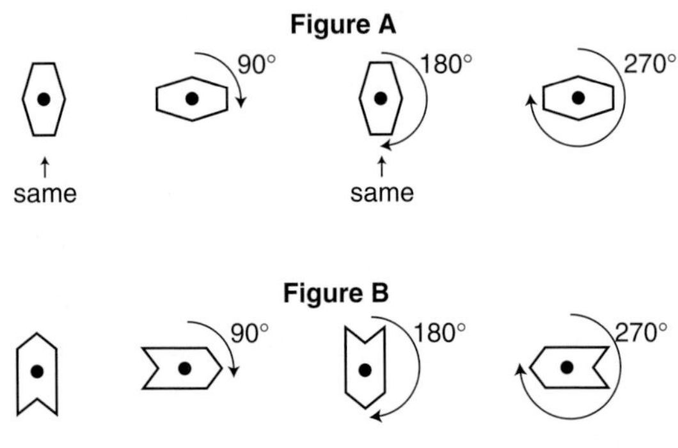

Research-Based Teaching

Many researchers believe that geometric understanding is integral to the development of number sense (Nickson, 2000; NCTM, 2000). Using geometry to provide opportunities for discovery and the use of technology and manipulatives in appropriate ways can help develop future mathematicians from your fourth-grade class. See *Professional Resources Handbook, Grade 4,* Unit 6.

For more ideas relating to Unit 6, see the Teacher Support Handbook at the back of this Teacher's Edition.

Language Intervention

Visualization and geometry are considered important parts of East Asian mathematics, particularly elementary mathematics. For further explanation, see "Mathematical Language and Geometry" in the *Professional Resources Handbook, Grade 4.*

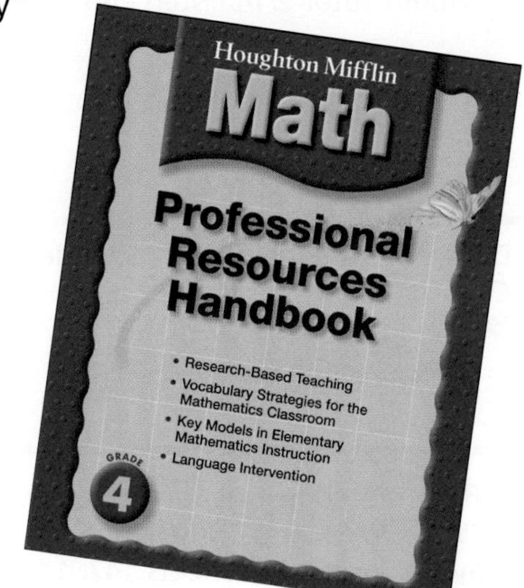

Chapter Activities

Connecting to the Unit Project

Individuals	20 minutes
Objective	Connect to the Unit Project.
Materials	None
Tactual	

Geometric Figures in Art

- Contact students to check on the progress they are making on their art projects for the Math Art Fair.
- Permit students to modify their creations to include geometric concepts studied in this chapter.

Ongoing Skill Activity

Whole Class	25 minutes
Objective	Identify congruent figures and figures with symmetry or transformations.
Materials	Library books
Visual	

Symmetry and Transformations

- Tell students to go to the media center or public library to find art books or books with geometric ideas that have photographs or illustrations that show congruence, symmetry, or transformations. Each student should check out a book and bring it to math class.
- As a quick opener or end-of-class activity, have each student show one or two pictures in the book and describe them. Identify the figures and tell if they are congruent or symmetric. Point out if the elements of the design resulted from a rotation, a reflection, or a translation.

Math Expressions

Whole Class	25 minutes
Objective	Explore symmetry and congruence by drawing the image of a quadrilateral across a line of reflection.
Materials	Paper squares, paper rectangles, scissors
Tactual	

Symmetry and Congruence

- Give each student a square dot grid. (These can be cut from regular dot paper.) Have students draw a quadrilateral on the paper.
- Have them fold the paper back along the diagonal, then hold the paper up to the light and trace the quadrilateral on the front side.
- Students unfold the square and compare the figures.
- Encourage discussion with questions.
- How are the two figures the same? (They are congruent to each other.)
- How are the two figures different? (One is flipped. It is like a mirror image of the other. You can't fit one on top of the other without flipping it.)
- The diagonal of the square is called the line of reflection. What do you notice about the distance of each point from the line of reflection? (Each point is the same distance from the line.)

Starting Chapter 17

Investigation

Using Data

Have students work in small groups to describe the pattern on page 428.

To extend the investigation, have students do the following activity.

- Find photos of animals that have patterns on their bodies. Are the patterns on one side of the animals' bodies always a reflection of the other side, like on the ladybug?

For more information about projects and investigations,

Visit **Education Place®**
www.eduplace.com/mat

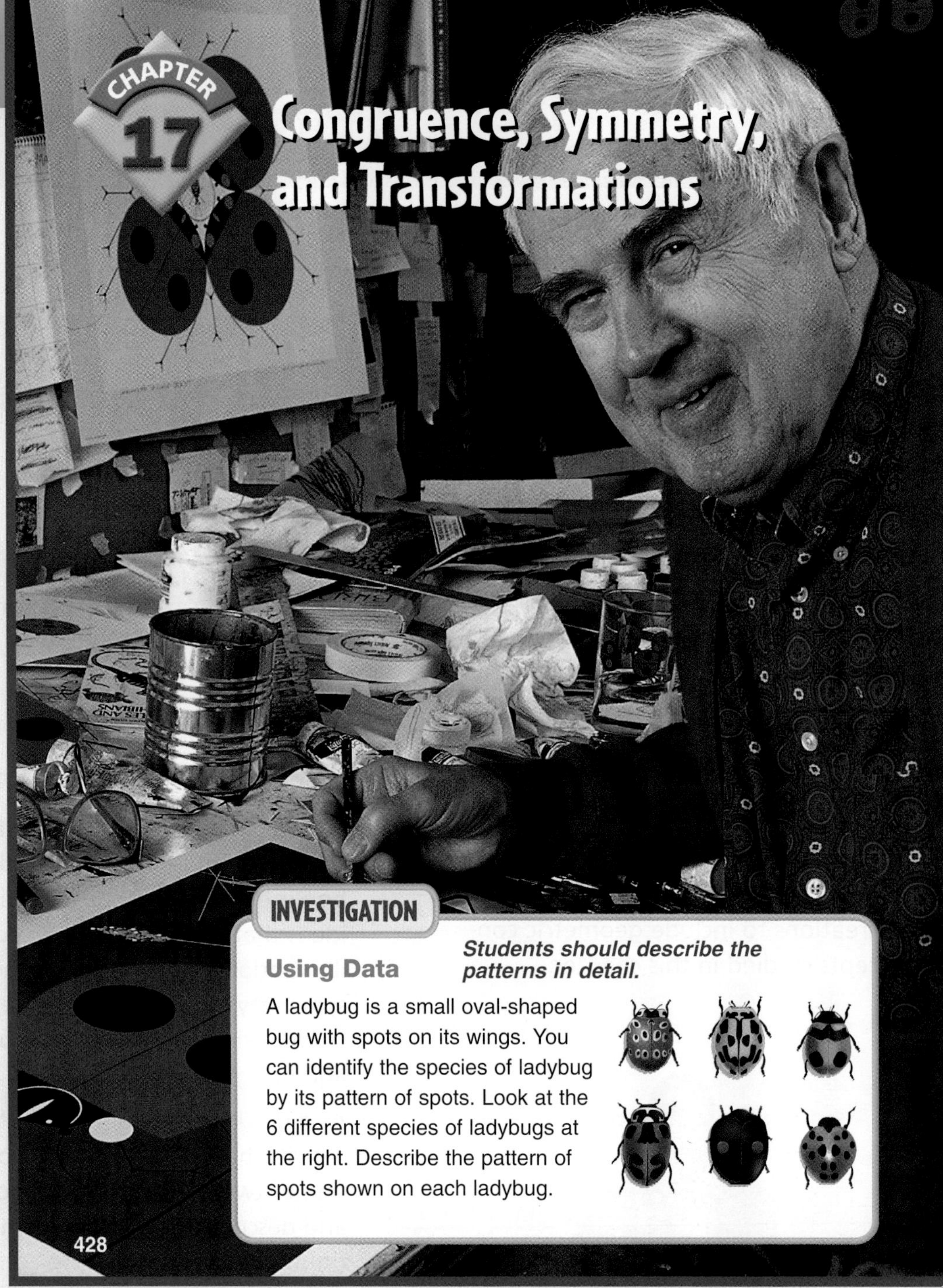

CHAPTER 17

Congruence, Symmetry, and Transformations

INVESTIGATION

Using Data *Students should describe the patterns in detail.*

A ladybug is a small oval-shaped bug with spots on its wings. You can identify the species of ladybug by its pattern of spots. Look at the 6 different species of ladybugs at the right. Describe the pattern of spots shown on each ladybug.

428

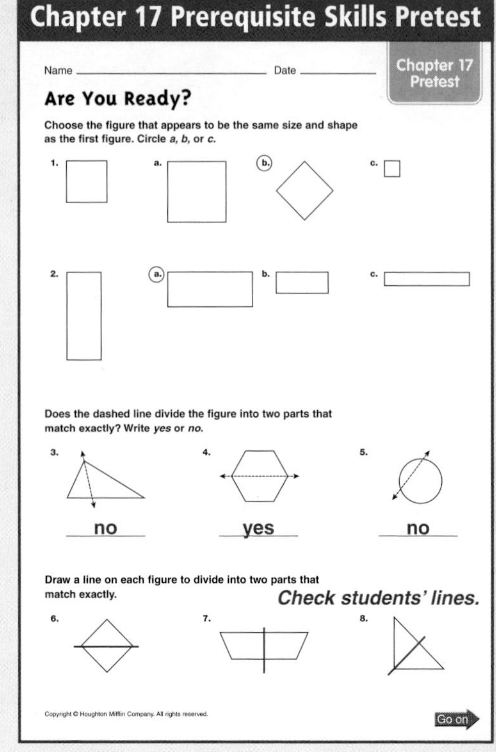

Chapter 17 Prerequisite Skills Pretest

Name ____________ Date ________ Chapter 17 Pretest

Are You Ready?

Choose the figure that appears to be the same size and shape as the first figure. Circle *a*, *b*, or *c*.

1. a. (b.) c.

2. (a.) b. c.

Does the dashed line divide the figure into two parts that match exactly? Write *yes* or *no*.

3. *no* 4. *yes* 5. *no*

Draw a line on each figure to divide into two parts that match exactly. *Check students' lines.*

6. 7. 8.

Go on

Use What You Know

Use this page to review and remember what you need to know for this chapter.

VOCABULARY

Choose the best term to complete each sentence.

Vocabulary
ray
line
point
rhombus
trapezoid

1. A location in space is called a ____. **point**
2. A ____ goes on without end in both directions. **line**
3. A ____ always has four sides of the same length. **rhombus**
4. A quadrilateral that has exactly one pair of parallel sides is a ____. **trapezoid**

CONCEPTS AND SKILLS

Choose the figure that appears to be the same size and shape as the first figure. Write *a*, *b*, or *c*.

5.  a. 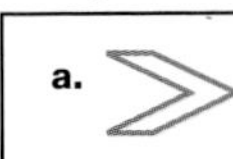 b.  (c.) 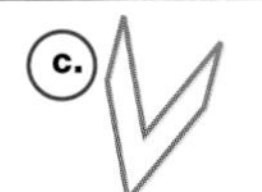

6.  a. 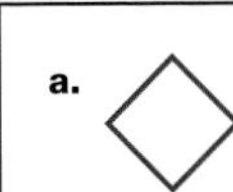 (b.) 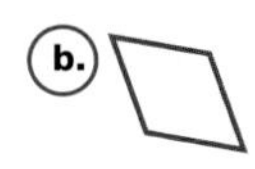 c. 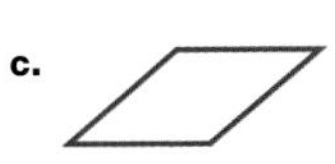

Does the dashed line divide the figure into two parts that match exactly? Write *yes* or *no*.

7. 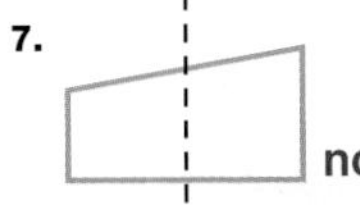 **no**

8. 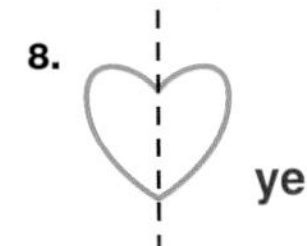 **yes**

9. 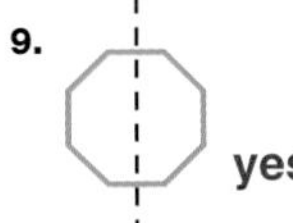 **yes**

Write About It

10. How are a square, rhombus, trapezoid, and parallelogram the same? How are they different?
See Additional Answers.

Facts Practice, See Page 666.

Chapter 17 New Content Pretest

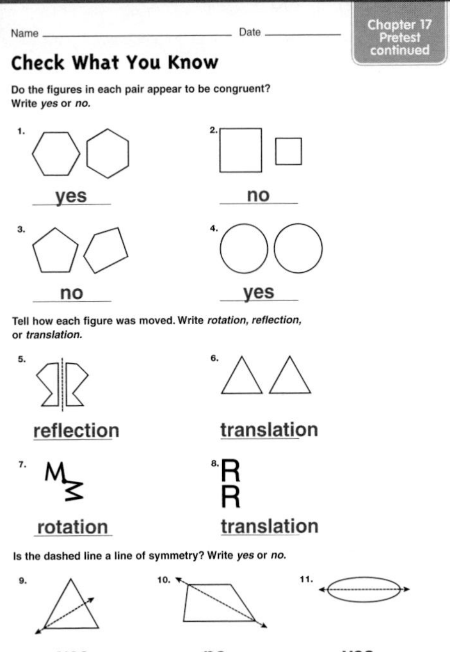

Name ____________ Date ________

Chapter 17 Pretest continued

Check What You Know

Do the figures in each pair appear to be congruent? Write *yes* or *no*.

1. yes
2. no
3. no
4. yes

Tell how each figure was moved. Write *rotation, reflection,* or *translation*.

5. reflection
6. translation
7. rotation
8. translation

Is the dashed line a line of symmetry? Write *yes* or *no*.

9. yes
10. no
11. yes

Go on

Chapter 17 New Content Pretest

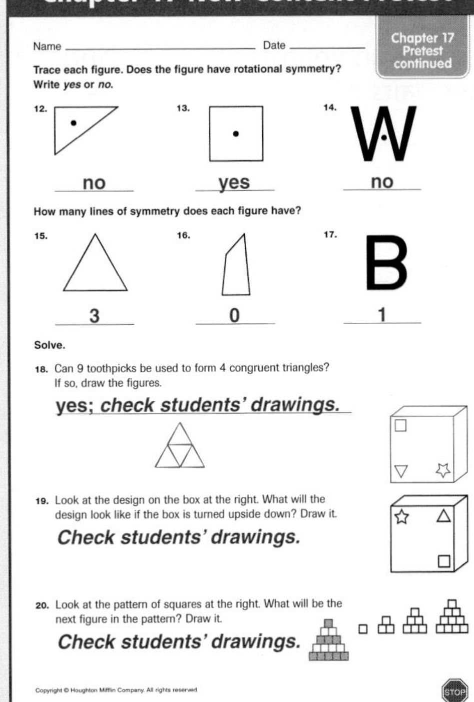

Name ____________ Date ________

Chapter 17 Pretest continued

Trace each figure. Does the figure have rotational symmetry? Write *yes* or *no*.

12. no
13. yes
14. no

How many lines of symmetry does each figure have?

15. 3
16. 0
17. 1

Solve.

18. Can 9 toothpicks be used to form 4 congruent triangles? If so, draw the figures.
yes; *check students' drawings.*
19. Look at the design on the box at the right. What will the design look like if the box is turned upside down? Draw it.
Check students' drawings.
20. Look at the pattern of squares at the right. What will be the next figure in the pattern? Draw it.
Check students' drawings.

STOP

Use What You Know

Use this page for informal assessment and review of prerequisite skills.

- Items 1–4: Use math vocabulary
- Items 5–6: Identify congruent figures
- Items 7–9: Identify symmetric figures
- Item 10: Describe the similarities and differences of different types of quadrilaterals

Customize Your Instruction

Use the Chapter Pretest in the Unit Resource folder to help customize and pace instruction.

Objectives and Resources

► Prerequisite Skills Pretest

- Items 1–2: Identify congruent figures.
- Items 3–5: Identify symmetric figures.
- Items 6–8: Find the line of symmetry in a figure.

► New Content Pretest

- Items 1–4, 9–17: Identify congruent figures and figures with line and rotational symmetry.
- Items 5–8: Identify, perform, and predict the results of rotations, reflections, and translations.
- Items 18–20: Solve problems using skills and strategies.

► For Students Having Difficulty

- *Ways to Success* CD: 17A, 17B
- *Ways to Success* Skillsheets: 145–147

► For Students Having Success

- Enrichment 17.1–17.5

► For Mathematically Promising Students

Explore: Congruent Triangles, page 97, after Lesson 1

Extend: Glide Reflections, page 99, after Lesson 3

Connect: Symmetry and Letters, page 101, after Lesson 5

Hands On
Lesson
17.1

Congruent Figures

Planning

Lesson Objective Learn about figures that have the same size and shape.

Technology Resources

- Audio Tutor **2**/13 Listen and Understand
- *Ways to Success* CD-ROM 17.1
- Education Place: Extra Practice, eGlossary, Extra Help, eGames www.eduplace.com/map

Lesson 17.1 Transparency

Problem of the Day

What is the smallest number of line segments you need in order to make 2 congruent triangles? Explain. (4; you could make an isosceles or equilateral triangle with 3 segments, and use a 4th segment to divide it into congruent halves.)

Spiral Review

Draw and label each figure. (Check students' drawings.)

1. line segment *ST*
2. a pentagon
3. acute angle *DEF*
4. a right triangle
5. a circle with radius *JK*

Lesson Quiz

1. Draw a figure congruent to the hexagon.

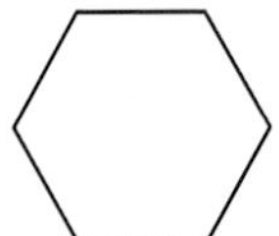

2. Draw a figure congruent to the polygon.

NCTM Standards

Geometry: Analyze characteristics and properties of two- and three-dimensional geometric shapes and develop mathematical arguments about geometric relationships; use visualization, spatial reasoning, and geometric modeling to solve problems.

Getting Started

Building Math Vocabulary

congruent figures have the same size and the same shape

Write the term ***congruent figures*** on the board. Tell students that figures are congruent when they have exactly the same size and shape. Display three sheets of paper, two of which are congruent and one that is not. Have students identify the congruent sheets of paper.

Recognizing Congruent Plane Figures

Whole Class	10 minutes
Objective	Explore figures that have the same size and shape.
Materials	Large Plane Figures and Small Plane Figures transparencies, blank transparency
Visual, Tactual	

- Display cutouts on the bottom $\frac{2}{3}$ of the blank transparency. Draw a horizontal line above the cutouts. **Polygons that have exactly the same shape and size are called congruent figures.** Ask a volunteer to place a set of congruent figures above the line.
- **How can we test that these figures are really congruent?** (Put one on top of the other and see if they fit exactly.) Model this.
- Repeat with volunteers displaying other pairs of congruent figures.
- Tell students that the cutout polygons that fit exactly on top of one another are congruent figures, which they will learn more about in the lesson in their book.

Differentiated Instruction

English Learners

Individuals	10 minutes
Objective	Identify congruent figures.
Materials	None
Auditory, Visual	

Early Production

- Students may need help recognizing congruence in objects with different orientations.
- Draw 4 to 5 pairs of congruent objects with different orientations on the board.
- Ask students to come up and outline the similarities in a pair until they see the congruence. Have them explain their work.

Intermediate/Advanced

- English Learner Resource 17.1
- English Learner Handbook

Intervention

Small Groups	10 minutes
Objective	Identify congruent figures.
Materials	Large Plane Figures and Small Plane Figures transparencies, blank transparency
Visual, Tactual	

- Focus on distinctions between congruent and similar figures to reinforce the concepts.
- Display cutouts on the bottom $\frac{2}{3}$ of the blank transparency. **Figures with the same shape, but not necessarily the same size, are called similar.**
- Have students match pairs of similar, but not congruent, figures.
- Guide students to see how similar and congruent figures are related. Emphasize that if figures are congruent, they are also similar, but similar figures are not always congruent.

Other Resources

- *Ways to Success* CD-ROM 17.1

Early Finishers

Individuals	15 minutes
Objective	Draw congruent figures.
Materials	Pattern blocks or color tiles, crayons
Visual, Tactual	

- Have students use manipulatives to form simple, small geometric figures or designs. Then have them make a congruent drawing of each figure they create, using the colors that match the manipulatives. Display the drawings.

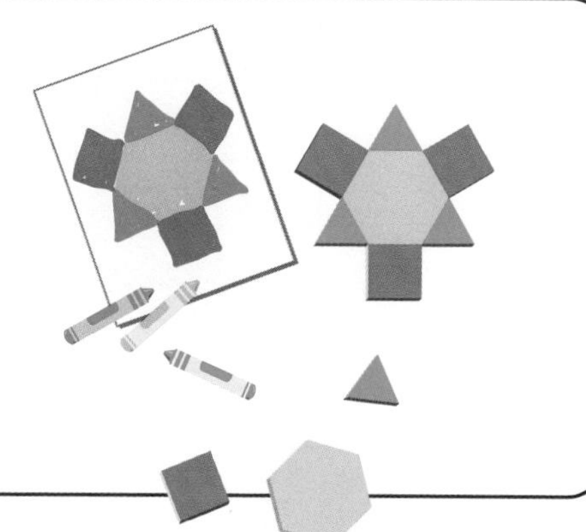

Alternate Teaching Strategy

Have students draw and cut out shapes that are congruent to one another and ones that are not congruent. Have groups mix all their shapes together. Students can work together or independently to match up the shapes that are congruent to one another. Have students look at the shapes that are similar but not congruent and decide what keeps them from being congruent.

❶ Introduce

Display the figures from the Large Plane Figures and Small Plane Figures Transparencies, and call on volunteers to identify each one. **Do any of the plane figures have exactly the same shape? Do any have the same shape *and* size?** Tell students that the lesson will explore a mathematical way to describe plane figures with the same size and shape.

❷ Teach

Learn About It

- **When you do a jigsaw puzzle, how do you know if you have the right piece?** (It fits exactly.)
- **Look at the pairs of figures in the box. What do you notice about the pair that is *not* congruent?** (same shape, different size) **How can you tell that the third pair is congruent?** (Flip one in your mind to see if it matches the other.)
- **Look at the activity. Be sure to label each figure before you cut it out.**
- Move around the room as students work. **What test do you use for congruence?** (See if two figures fit exactly on top of one another.)

Hands On Lesson 1

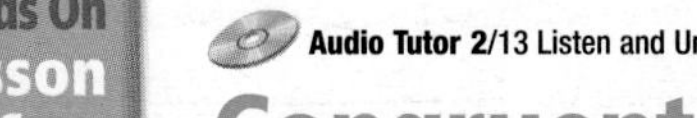

Audio Tutor 2/13 Listen and Understand

Congruent Figures

Objective Learn about figures that have the same size and shape.

Vocabulary
congruent

Materials
grid paper
scissors

Learn About It

Sari is designing a puzzle on her computer. Look at the puzzle and the puzzle piece. You can tell that the piece belongs in the puzzle because it is the same size and shape as the empty space.

Plane figures that have the same size and shape are **congruent** figures.

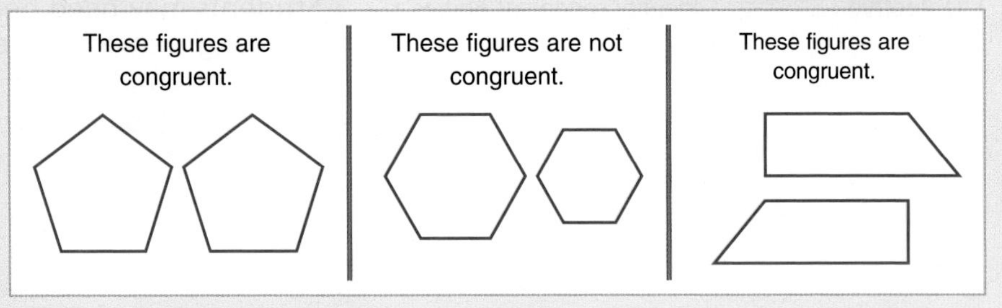

These figures are congruent.
These figures are not congruent.
These figures are congruent.

Try this activity to explore congruence.

STEP 1 Copy Figures A, B, C, and D on grid paper. Cut out Figures B, C, and D. Look at the figures. Which figures appear to be congruent? ***A and B***

STEP 2 Place each cut-out figure on top of Figure A, turning it to check for congruence. Which figure is congruent to A? How do you know? **Figure B; it is the same size and shape.**

STEP 3 Draw another figure on grid paper. Cut it out. Trace it. Are these two new figures congruent? Explain. ***Check students' drawings.*** **Yes; the figures are the same size and shape.**

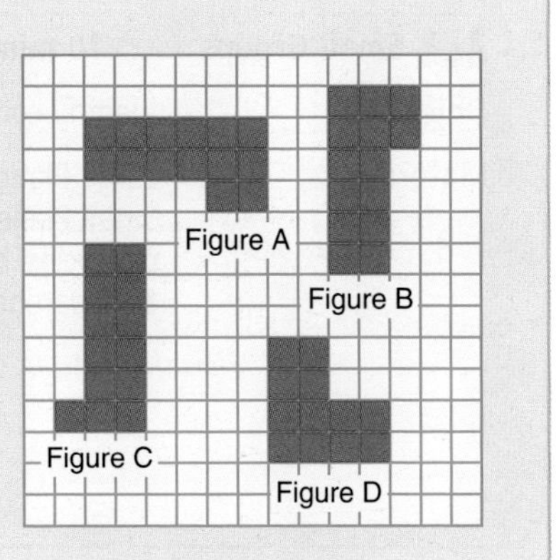

Figure A
Figure B
Figure C
Figure D

430

Extra Help at **eduplace.com/map**

Reteach 17.1

Name ______________ Date ________ Reteach 17.1

Congruent Figures

These figures have the same size and shape. The figures are **congruent.**

These figures are not the same size. The figures are **not congruent.**

These figures have the same size and shape. The figures are **congruent** even though they are not in the same position.

These figures are not the same shape. The figures are **not congruent.**

Do the figures in each pair appear to be congruent? Write *yes* or *no*.

1. no
2. no
3. yes
4. no
5. yes
6. no

Use with text pages 430–432.

Practice 17.1 Page 105

Name ______________ Date ________ Practice 17.1

Congruent Figures

Do the figures in each pair appear to be congruent? Write *yes* or *no*. Explain your answer. Explanations will vary.

1. No
2. Yes
3. No

Draw a figure congruent to each figure shown.

4. Check students' drawings.
5.

Use the figures at the right for Problem 6.

6. Isosceles triangles have two sides that are congruent. Use a centimeter ruler. Which of the figures at the right is made up of isosceles triangles? B

A. B.

Test Prep

7. Which figure appears to be congruent to this figure?

A C B D — A

8. When you draw a line from one corner of a quadrilateral to the opposite corner, you split the quadrilateral into two triangles. If you do this to a trapezoid, are the resulting triangles congruent? No

Use with text pages 430–432.

Common Error

- **Not recognizing congruence**
- **Intervention** Remind students that figures are congruent if they are the same size and shape. However, orientation doesn't matter. Have students use tracings to help them determine congruence. Encourage them to flip, turn, or slide a tracing however they wish to check its fit.

Guided Practice

Ask Yourself
- Are the figures the same size?
- Are the figures the same shape?

Do the figures in each pair appear to be congruent? Write *yes* or *no*.

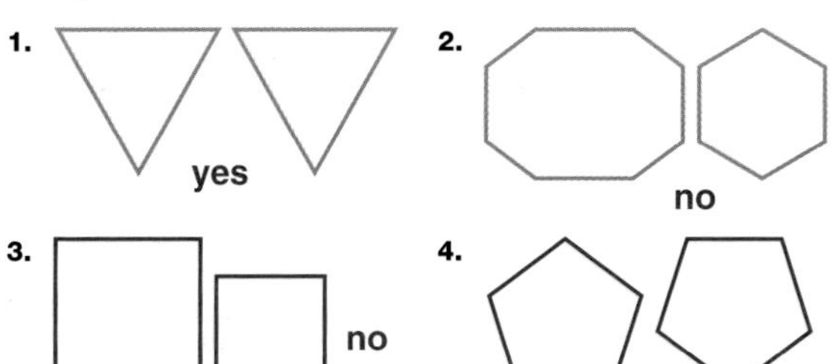

1. yes
2. no

3. no
4. yes
5. Draw a figure congruent to the figures in Exercise 4. Explain how you know it is congruent. ***Check students' drawings;* The figures are the same size and shape.**

Explain Your Thinking ▶ Are all circles with radii of 4 inches congruent? Why or why not?
Yes; all circles are the same shape, and if they have a radius of 4 inches, they will also be the same size.

Practice and Problem Solving

Do the figures in each pair appear to be congruent? Write *yes* or *no*. Explain your answer.

6. no

7. yes

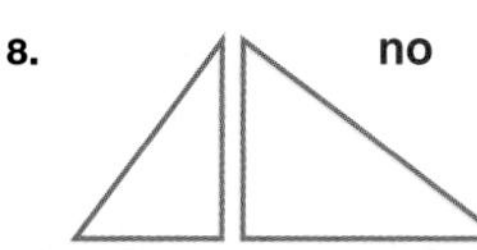

8. no

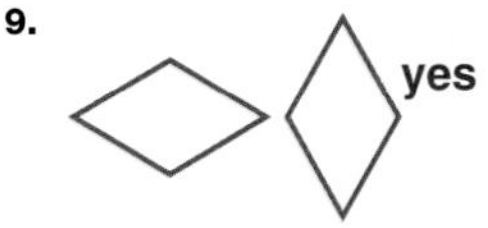

9. yes

10. yes

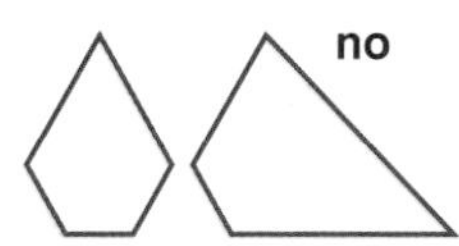

11. no

Draw a figure like each shape below. Then draw a figure congruent to the one you drew.

12. 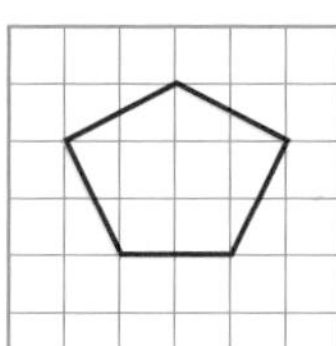
Check students' drawings.

13. 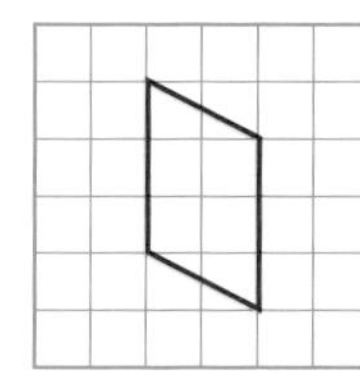
Check students' drawings.

Guided Practice

Have students complete **Exercises 1–5** as you observe. Remind them to use the ***Ask Yourself*** questions to help. Give students the opportunity to talk about the question, in ***Explain Your Thinking***.

❸ Practice

Practice and Problem Solving

Select from **Exercises 6–24** as independent work.

- Provide grid paper and rulers students can use to draw congruent figures for **Exercises 12 and 13**.

Enrichment 17.1

Name ____________ Date ________ Enrichment 17.1

Pair Them Up

Match each figure on the left with the figure on the right that is congruent.

1. D
2. C
3. G
4. F
5. A
6. E
7. B

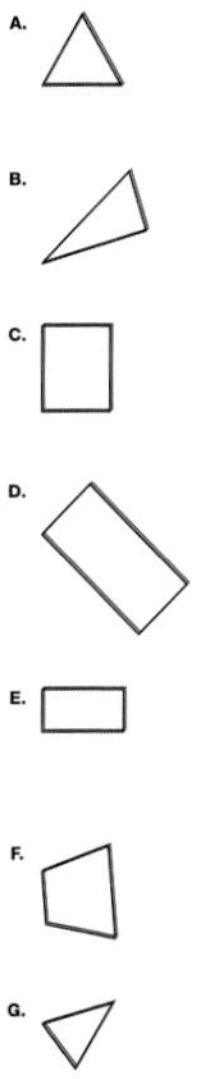

Use with text pages 430–432.

Problem Solving 17.1

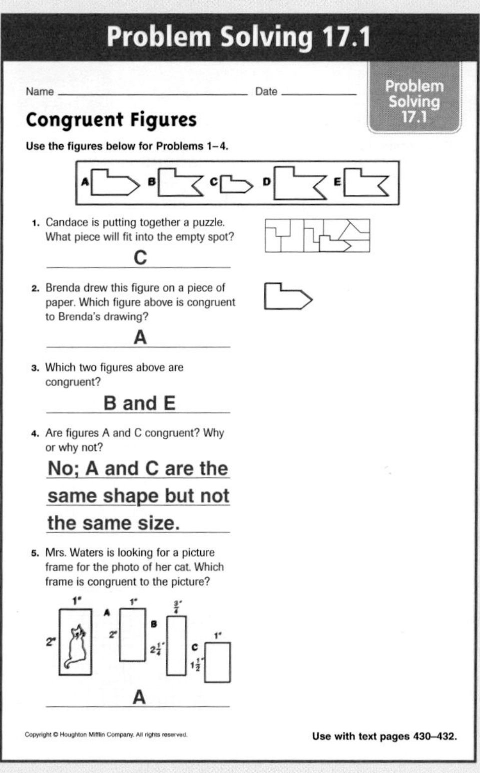

Name ____________ Date ________ Problem Solving 17.1

Congruent Figures

Use the figures below for Problems 1–4.

1. Candace is putting together a puzzle. What piece will fit into the empty spot?
C
2. Brenda drew this figure on a piece of paper. Which figure above is congruent to Brenda's drawing?
A
3. Which two figures above are congruent?
B and E
4. Are figures A and C congruent? Why or why not?
No; A and C are the same shape but not the same size.
5. Mrs. Waters is looking for a picture frame for the photo of her cat. Which frame is congruent to the picture?
A

Use with text pages 430–432.

- ***Problem 17*** If necessary, allow students to review quadrilaterals, as presented in Chapter 16, Lesson 4, pages 412–414.

4 Assess & Close

Math Talk in Action

What real-life situations can you think of in which we apply the idea of congruent figures? (Accept all reasonable responses, such as congruence in jigsaw puzzles, keys fitting locks, tiles in floor patterns, art, and design.)

Math Journal Prompt

Have students write a list of steps to follow to test whether two plane figures are congruent.

Lesson Quiz

Use the quiz on Lesson Transparency 17.1.

Test Prep & Spiral Review

Use Test Prep Transparency 17.1.

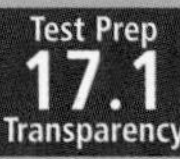

Use the figures at the right for Problems 14–16.

14. **Measurement** Parallelograms have 2 pairs of opposite sides that are congruent. Use a centimeter ruler. Which of the figures at the right are parallelograms?
    Figures A and D
15. Which figure has right angles? Is it a rectangle? a square? Explain your answer. ***See at right.***
16. **Analyze** Six congruent triangles form Figure D. What geometric figure is it? Draw a picture of another way to combine the triangles to make a different geometric figure. **parallelogram; *Check students' drawings.***

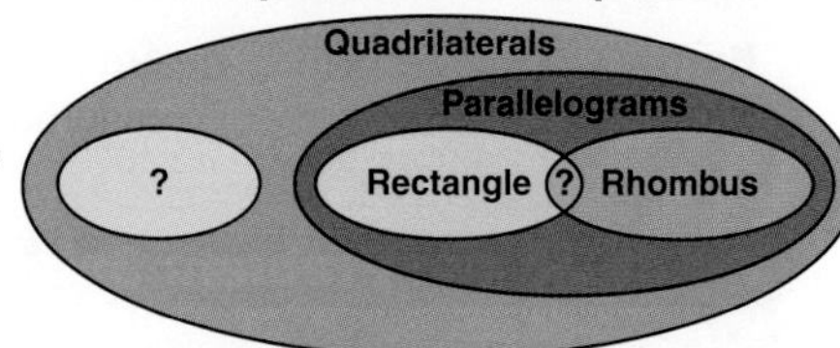

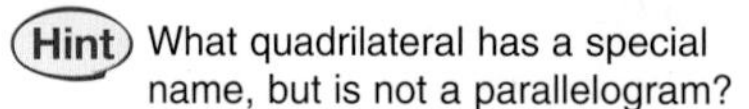

15. Figure B; no; no; not all angles are right angles, not all sides are the same length, and the bottom and top sides are not parallel.

17. **Reasoning** Copy the Venn Diagram at the right. *Trapezoid* and *Square* are the terms that are missing from the diagram. Which term should go in the green section? Which should go in the pink section? Explain how you decided. ***See below.***

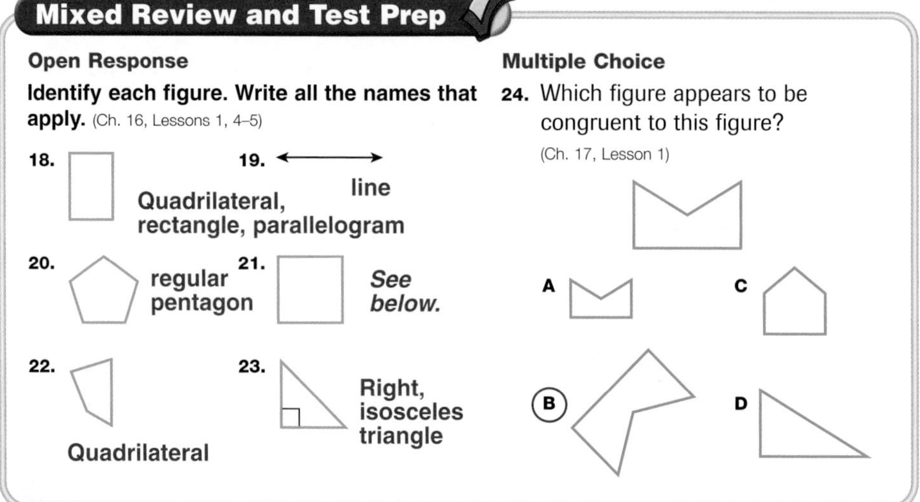

Hint: What quadrilateral has a special name, but is not a parallelogram?

Hint: What figure is both a rectangle and a rhombus?

17. *Square* should go in the green section because it is both a rectangle and a rhombus; *Trapezoid* should go in the pink section because it is quadrilateral, but not a parallelogram.

Mixed Review and Test Prep

Open Response

Identify each figure. Write all the names that apply. (Ch. 16, Lessons 1, 4–5)

18. **Quadrilateral, rectangle, parallelogram**
19. **line**
20. **regular pentagon**
21. ***See below.***
22. **Quadrilateral**
23. **Right, isosceles triangle**

Multiple Choice

24. Which figure appears to be congruent to this figure? (Ch. 17, Lesson 1)
    A
    (B)
    C
    D

21. Quadrilateral, rhombus, square, regular polygon, paralellogram, rectangle

Extra Practice See page 449, Set A.

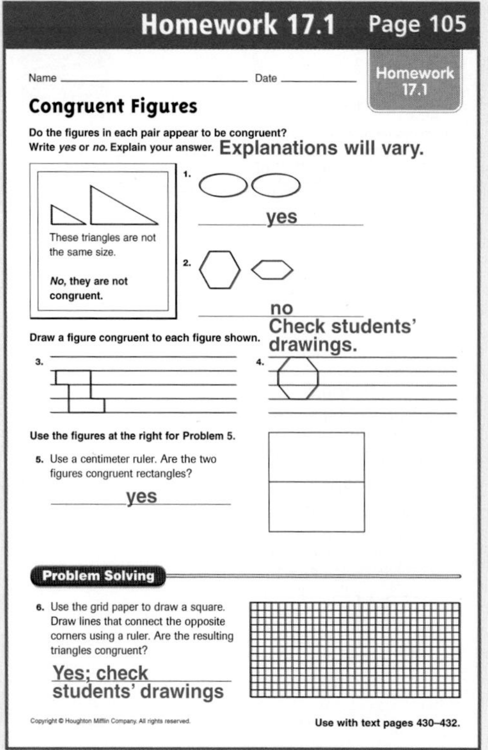
Homework 17.1 Page 105

Name ______ Date ______ Homework 17.1

Congruent Figures

Do the figures in each pair appear to be congruent? Write *yes* or *no*. Explain your answer. **Explanations will vary.**

These triangles are not the same size. *No*, they are not congruent.

1. **yes**
2. **no**

Draw a figure congruent to each figure shown. **Check students' drawings.**

3.
4.

Use the figures at the right for Problem 5.

5. Use a centimeter ruler. Are the two figures congruent rectangles? **yes**

Problem Solving

6. Use the grid paper to draw a square. Draw lines that connect the opposite corners using a ruler. Are the resulting triangles congruent? **Yes; check students' drawings**

Use with text pages 430–432.

Problem Solving

Math Reasoning

Similar Figures

You have learned that congruent figures are the same size and shape. **Similar** figures are the same shape, but not necessarily the same size.

Vocabulary
similar

Look at the figures below.

Same shape Not the same size	Not the same shape Not the same size	Same shape Same size
Similar Not Congruent	Not Similar Not Congruent	Similar Congruent

Tell if the figures in each pair are *congruent, similar,* or *neither.*

1. similar, congruent
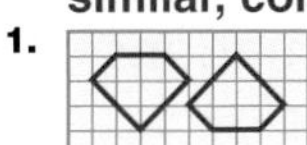

2. neither
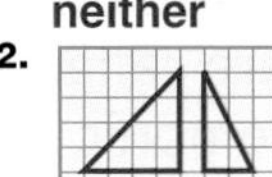

3. similar
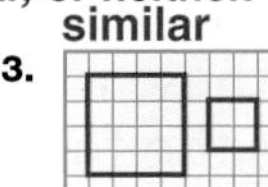

Write *true* or *false* for each sentence. Then draw an example to support your answer.
Check students' drawings.

4. All squares are similar.
true
5. If shapes are similar, they must be congruent.
false
6. All hexagons are similar.
false
7. If shapes are congruent, they must be similar.
true
8. All circles are similar.
true
9. If shapes are *not* congruent, they cannot be similar.
false

Math Reasoning

Similar Figures

Materials: Large Plane Figures and Small Plane Figures Transparencies cutouts

Display the cutouts on the overhead. Have students identify pairs of congruent figures and pairs of similar figures. Leave the figures on display to assist students as they do **Exercises 4–9.**

Discuss the term *similar* in its general, every-day sense. For example, brothers may have similar smiles, or songs may sound similar. Then focus on the mathematical meaning of similarity.

Hands On Lesson 17.2

Rotations, Reflections, and Translations

Planning

Lesson Objective Learn about rotations, reflections, and translations.

Technology Resources

- Audio Tutor **2**/14 Listen and Understand
- *Ways to Success* CD-ROM 17.2
- Education Place: Extra Practice, eGlossary, eGames
  www.eduplace.com/map

Lesson 17.2 Transparency

Problem of the Day

Dora has an 8" square pan and an 8" round pan. She bakes cakes in each pan. When the cakes are done, she wants to serve them in a heart shape. How can she do it? (Rotate the square cake to form a diamond; cut the round cake in half; place each $\frac{1}{2}$ along connecting sides of the square.)

Spiral Review

Draw each figure. (Check students' drawings.)

1. right angle *ABC*
2. acute angle *DEF*
3. obtuse angle *JKL*
4. straight angle *RST*
5. Parallel lines *RS* and *XY*

Lesson Quiz

Tell how each figure was moved. Write *rotation*, *reflection*, or *translation*.

1. 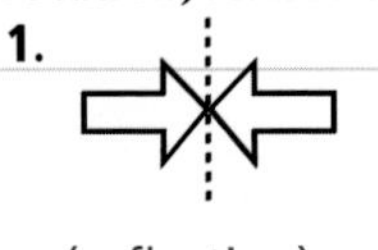 (reflection)

2. 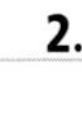  (rotation)

NCTM Standards

Geometry: Apply transformations and use symmetry to analyze mathematical situations; use visualization, spatial reasoning, and geometric modeling to solve problems.
Communication: Use the language of mathematics to express mathematical ideas precisely.

Getting Started

Building Math Vocabulary

rotation	a move that turns a figure around a point
reflection	to turn something over, front to back
translation	an action that slides a figure in a straight line
transformations	rotations, reflections, and translations; a transformation changes the position of a plane figure

Display the vocabulary cards for ***reflection, rotation,*** and ***transformations.*** Explain to students that these movements are called transformations. Share and discuss with students the following mnemonic "equations":

ro<u>t</u>ation = <u>t</u>urn   re<u>fl</u>ection = <u>fl</u>ip   tran<u>sl</u>ation = <u>sl</u>ide

Identifying Results of Transformations

Whole Class	15 minutes
Objective	Identify the results of rotations, reflections, and translations.
Materials	Large Plane Figures Transparency, Centimeter Grid Transparency
Visual	

- Display the pentagon so that one corner of the figure meets a point on the grid. **Watch as I move this figure. Notice what stays where it started out.** Rotate the figure around the point. Have students describe what they see.
- Now align one side of the pentagon along a grid line. **Watch again. Notice how the figure moves and what doesn't move.** Flip the figure over the line. Have students describe what they see.
- **Watch again and tell me how the figure moves and what doesn't move.** Slide the figure anywhere on the grid. Invite students to describe the movement.
- Tell students that the pentagon has been rotated, reflected, and translated, all of which they will learn more about in the lesson in their book.

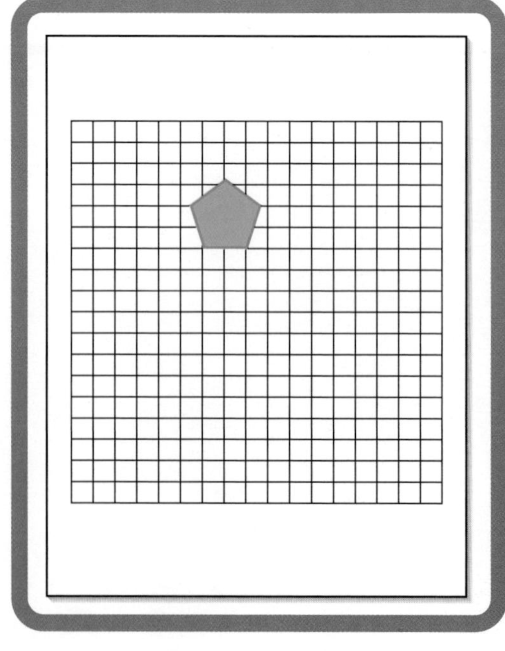

Differentiated Instruction

English Learners

Individuals	10 minutes
Objective	Identify and perform rotations, reflections, and translations.
Materials	Cutouts of plane figures
Visual, Tactual	

Early Production

- Before doing the ***Guided Practice,*** have students practice identifying and representing transformations with cutouts of plane figures.
- Call on students to give you names of different transformations. Use the cutouts to show the transformation.
- Call out a transformation, and have the students use the cutouts to show it.

Intermediate/Advanced

- English Learner Resource 17.2
- English Learner Handbook

Intervention

Small Groups	10 minutes
Objective	Identify congruent figures and the results of rotations, reflections, and translations.
Materials	Common classroom objects
Tactual, Kinesthetic	

- Use the movement of objects to highlight transformation and congruence.
- Display a pair of identical objects, such as two paper clips. Have students watch as you flip, turn, and slide one along a surface (plane), while the other remains where it started.
- Repeat, having students identify each type of movement you do. **Does the size or shape of the object change? What *does* change?** (no; where it is on the surface)

Other Resources

- *Ways to Success* CD-ROM 17.2

Gifted & Talented

Individuals	20 minutes
Objective	Identify rotations, reflections, and translations.
Materials	Native American patterns
Visual, Tactual	

- Provide examples of Native American patterns in pottery, beadwork, or weaving.
- Have students study a repeating pattern to analyze the use of translations, rotations, or reflections.
- Display patterns and students' written analyses.

Science Connection

Materials: Tumbling *E* chart

- The "Tumbling *E*" chart is used to test vision. It has capital *E*s facing four ways. The subject tells whether the *E* points up, down, left, or right.
- Make up a Tumbling *E* chart of two or three rows of block-letter, capital *E*s facing in four different directions. Have students analyze the chart to identify which *E*s are rotated, reflected, or translated.

Pattern Practice

Present several patterns of shapes to students on the chalkboard or overhead. Have students continue the patterns through another complete cycle at their table or call for volunteers. Make sure patterns test recent skills such as congruence, rotation, reflection, translation, and transformations.

❶ Introduce

Show the class two index cards and review the meaning of the term *congruent figures*. **How can we tell if the cards are congruent?** (Try to fit them on each other.) **Will a change in direction change the figure?** (no) Tell students that the lesson will explore movements that plane figures can make.

❷ Teach

Learn About It

- Have a student read the opening problem. **How many ways can a plane figure move?** (3) Talk about the three transformations with students.
- Have students try the activity. Circulate as students work, helping them make the movements accurately.

Guided Practice

Have students complete **Exercises 1–2** as you observe. Remind them to use the *Ask Yourself* questions to help. Give students the opportunity to talk about the questions in *Explain Your Thinking*.

Common Error

- **Confusing rotations and reflections**
- **Intervention** To help students grasp the difference between these two transformations, have them use their hands to do each movement kinesthetically on their desktop. In a reflection, the hand flips over (palm up vs. palm down). For a rotation, the same side of the hand is always face up.

Audio Tutor 2/14 Listen and Understand

Rotations, Reflections, and Translations

Objective Learn about rotations, reflections, and translations.

Vocabulary
rotation
reflection
translation
transformations

Materials
trapezoid pattern block or Learning Tool 25
grid paper

Learn About It

Vincent is a graphic artist. He is designing a logo for his company's product. He moves the figure shown in different ways to create the logo.

There are different ways to move a figure.

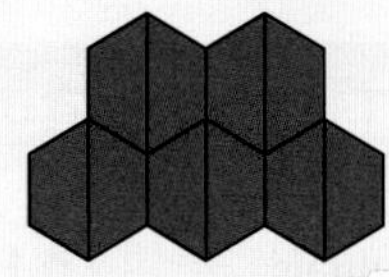

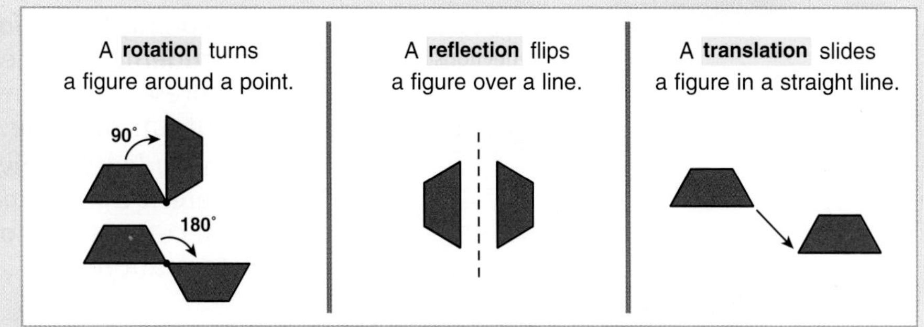

Rotations, reflections, and translations are called **transformations**.

Try this activity to show rotations, reflections, and translations. ***Check students' drawings.***

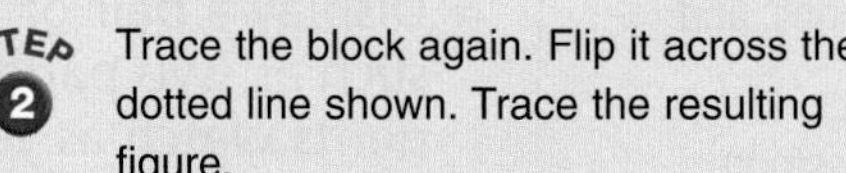

STEP 1 Trace the pattern block on grid paper. Rotate it around the point shown. Trace the resulting figure.

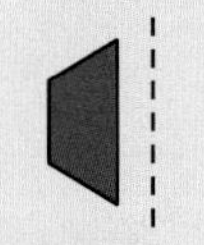

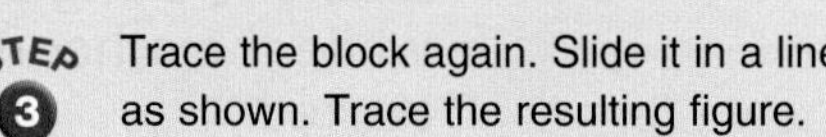

STEP 2 Trace the block again. Flip it across the dotted line shown. Trace the resulting figure.

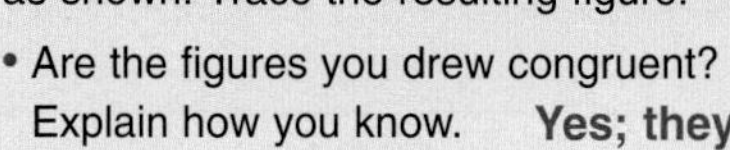

STEP 3 Trace the block again. Slide it in a line as shown. Trace the resulting figure.

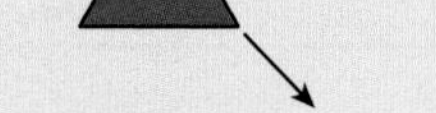

- Are the figures you drew congruent? Explain how you know. **Yes; they are all the same size and shape.**

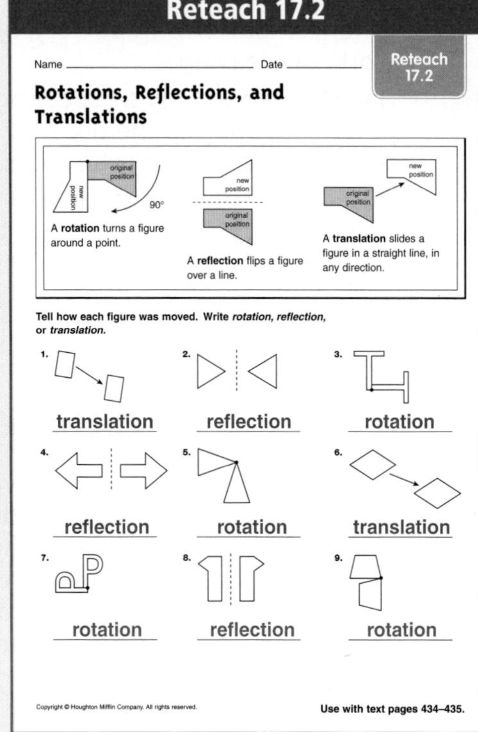

Reteach 17.2

Name ______ Date ______ Reteach 17.2

Rotations, Reflections, and Translations

A **rotation** turns a figure around a point. (original position, new position, 90°)
A **reflection** flips a figure over a line. (new position, original position)
A **translation** slides a figure in a straight line, in any direction. (original position, new position)

Tell how each figure was moved. Write *rotation, reflection,* or *translation*.

1. translation
2. reflection
3. rotation
4. reflection
5. rotation
6. translation
7. rotation
8. reflection
9. rotation

Use with text pages 434–435.

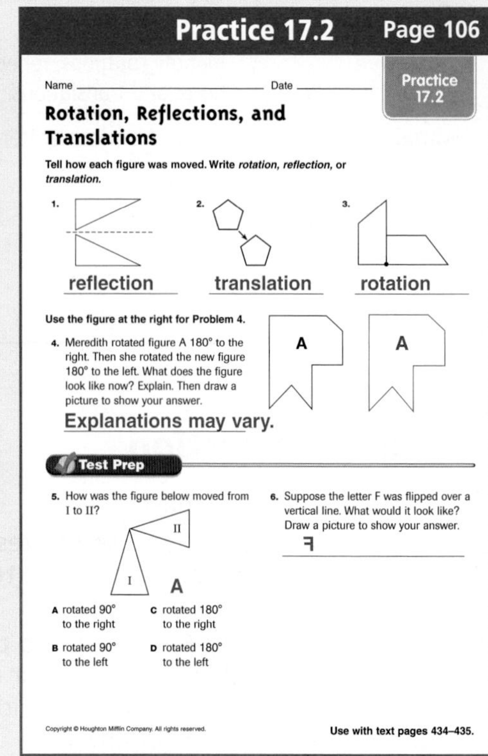

Practice 17.2 **Page 106**

Name ______ Date ______ Practice 17.2

Rotation, Reflections, and Translations

Tell how each figure was moved. Write *rotation, reflection,* or *translation*.

1. reflection
2. translation
3. rotation

Use the figure at the right for Problem 4.

4. Meredith rotated figure A 180° to the right. Then she rotated the new figure 180° to the left. What does the figure look like now? Explain. Then draw a picture to show your answer. Explanations may vary.

Test Prep

5. How was the figure below moved from I to II? **A**
A rotated 90° to the right
B rotated 90° to the left
C rotated 180° to the right
D rotated 180° to the left

6. Suppose the letter F was flipped over a vertical line. What would it look like? Draw a picture to show your answer. ꟻ

Use with text pages 434–435.

Guided Practice

Tell how each figure was moved. Write *rotation, reflection,* or *translation.*

1. 
reflection

2. 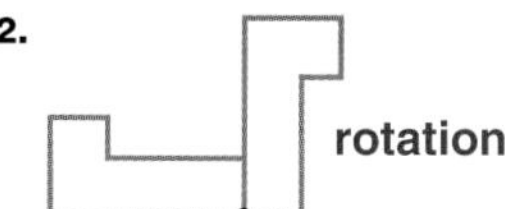
rotation

Ask Yourself

- Was the figure turned around a point?
- Was the figure flipped over a line?
- Was the figure slid along a straight line?

Explain Your Thinking ▶ Look at the figures in Exercise 2. Are they congruent? How can you use transformations to find out? **Yes. If you rotate one of the figures so it covers the other, you can see they are exactly the same size and shape.**

Practice and Problem Solving

Tell how each figure was moved. Write *rotation, reflection,* or *translation.*

3. 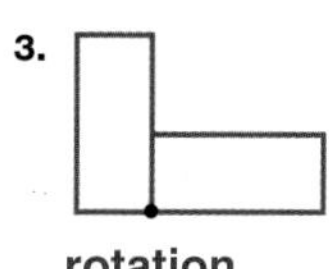
rotation

4. 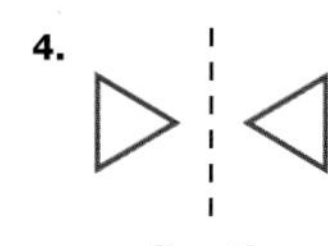
reflection

5. 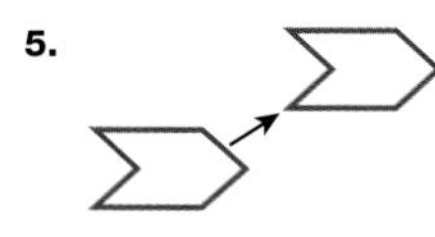
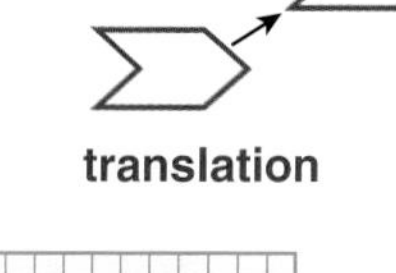
translation

Copy Figure A on grid paper and cut it out. Use the cut-out figure for Problems 6–7.

Figure A

6. **Represent** Vincent rotated Figure A 90° to the right. What does the figure look like now? Draw a picture to show your answer.
   See Additional Answers.
7. **Predict** If you flip Figure A, what will it look like? Draw the resulting figure. Is this the only answer? Explain.
   See Additional Answers.
8. Vincent is designing another logo. He started with Figure B. How did he move the figure to make Figure C? Explain your answer.
   He rotated it and reflected it.

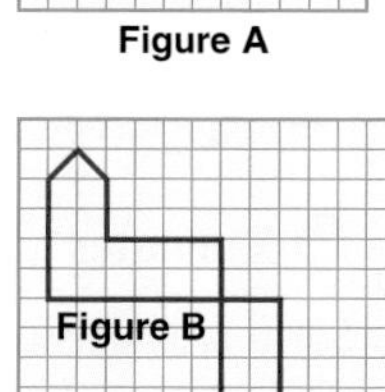
Figure B

Figure C

Mixed Review and Test Prep

Open Response

Solve each equation. (Ch. 5, Lesson 4)

9. $12 = n + 4$ **$n = 8$**
10. $16 - n = 9$ **$n = 7$**
11. $40n = 120$ **$n = 3$**
12. $n \div 5 = 27$ **$n = 135$**

13. Suppose the letter P was rotated 180° to the left. What would it look like? Draw a picture to show your answer. (Ch. 17, Lesson 2) **d**

Extra Practice See page 449, Set B.

3 Practice

Practice and Problem Solving

Select from **Exercises 3–13** as independent work.

- ***Problem 6*** Ask students to name the angle that measures 90°, or a quarter-turn. (right angle)
- ***Problem 7*** Allow students to move their tracing of Figure A, as the problem describes, to help them visualize the outcome.

4 Assess & Close

Math Talk in Action

What effect do transformations have on congruent figures? (The figures are still congruent but may be oriented differently.) Have students discuss how rotation, reflection, and translation of certain figures might change their orientation.

Math Journal Prompt

Have students list and define the three types of transformations and how to remember each type.

Lesson Quiz

Use the quiz on Lesson Transparency 17.2.

Test Prep & Spiral Review

Use Test Prep Transparency 17.2.

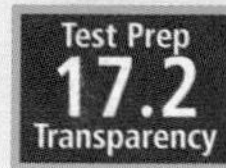

Enrichment 17.2

Name ______________ Date ________

Enrichment 17.2

Art Transformations

At the art gallery, Rudy Rabbit was bouncing around and transformed some of the art. Help him find the original way the art was displayed. Look at the pictures in the grid below. Use the clues to draw the figures in the their original places.

1. Figure A needs to be translated 4 units right.
2. Figure B needs to be rotated 180° and translated 3 units up.
3. Figure C needs to be reflected over line B and rotated 90° right.
4. Figure D needs to be rotated 90° and then rotated another 180°.
5. Figure E needs to be translated 2 units down and rotated a three-quarter turn left.
6. Figure F needs to be rotated 90° right and reflected over line 8.

Use with text pages 434–435.

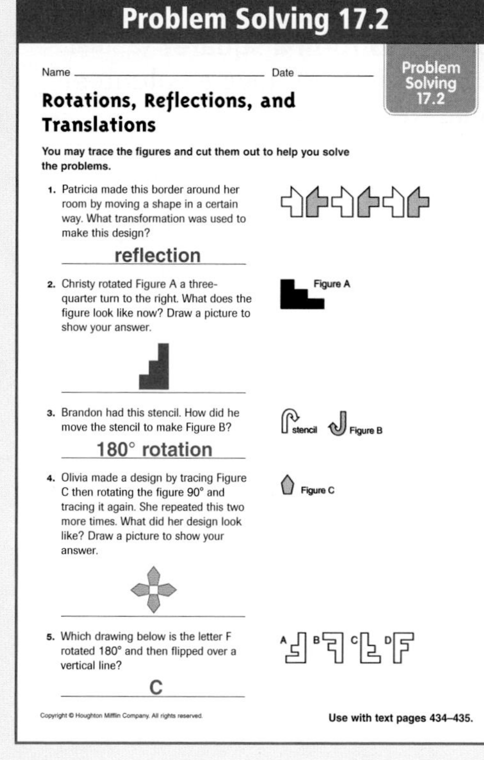

Problem Solving 17.2

Name ______________ Date ________

Problem Solving 17.2

Rotations, Reflections, and Translations

You may trace the figures and cut them out to help you solve the problems.

1. Patricia made this border around her room by moving a shape in a certain way. What transformation was used to make this design?
   reflection
2. Christy rotated Figure A a three-quarter turn to the right. What does the figure look like now? Draw a picture to show your answer.
   Figure A
3. Brandon had this stencil. How did he move the stencil to make Figure B?
   stencil Figure B
   180° rotation
4. Olivia made a design by tracing Figure C then rotating the figure 90° and tracing it again. She repeated this two more times. What did her design look like? Draw a picture to show your answer.
   Figure C
5. Which drawing below is the letter F rotated 180° and then flipped over a vertical line?
   A B C D
   C

Use with text pages 434–435.

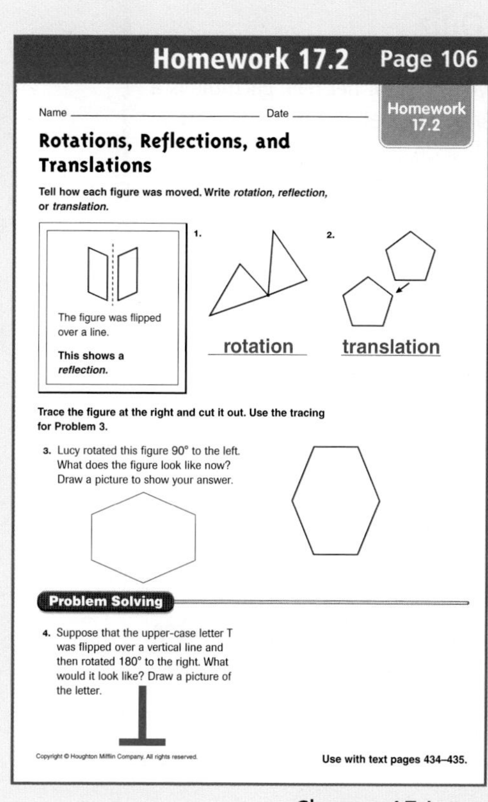

Homework 17.2 Page 106

Name ______________ Date ________

Homework 17.2

Rotations, Reflections, and Translations

Tell how each figure was moved. Write *rotation, reflection,* or *translation.*

The figure was flipped over a line.

This shows a *reflection.*

1. rotation
2. translation

Trace the figure at the right and cut it out. Use the tracing for Problem 3.

3. Lucy rotated this figure 90° to the left. What does the figure look like now? Draw a picture to show your answer.

Problem Solving

4. Suppose that the upper-case letter T was flipped over a vertical line and then rotated 180° to the right. What would it look like? Draw a picture of the letter.

Use with text pages 434–435.

Lesson 17.3

Problem-Solving Strategy: Act It Out

Planning

Lesson Objective Learn how to solve a problem by using a model to act it out.

Technology Resources

- *Ways to Success* CD-ROM 17.3
- Education Place: Extra Practice, eGames www.eduplace.com/map

Lesson 17.3 Transparency

Problem of the Day

A H X R E L

One of the letters does not belong with the others in the box. Identify that letter and tell why. (R; all other letters are formed only with straight lines, but R has curves.)

Spiral Review

Solve.

1. 4 gal = __ qt (16)
2. 2 mi = __ ft (10,560)
3. 8,000 lb = __ T (4)
4. 27 yd = __ ft (81)
5. 2 years = __ weeks (104)

Lesson Quiz

Kayla is buying tiles for her hall. Each tile is a 6-inch square. If her hall is a rectangle 6 ft long and 4 ft wide, how many tiles does she need to cover the space? (96)

NCTM Standards

Geometry: Use visualization, spatial reasoning, and geometric modeling to solve problems.
Problem Solving: Apply and adapt a variety of appropriate strategies to solve problems.

Getting Started

Building Math Vocabulary

You may wish to review these words with students.

congruent figures	figures that have the same size and the same shape
pentagon	a five-sided polygon
square	a polygon with four right angles and four congruent sides
triangle	a polygon with three sides and three vertices

Building a Square

Whole Class	5 minutes
Objective	Solve problems using skills and strategies.
Materials	Tangram Pieces (Learning Tool 24), scissors
Visual, Tactual	

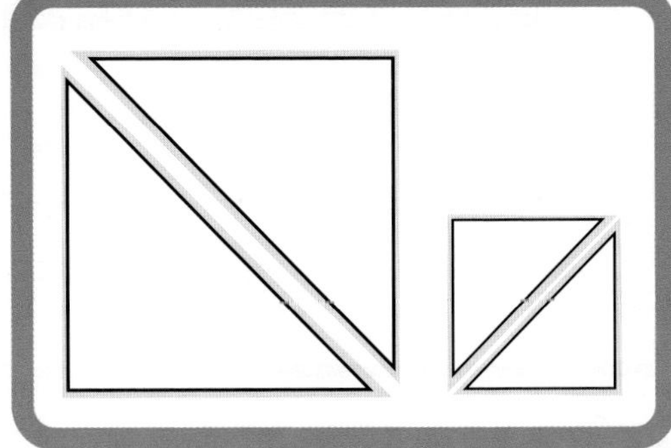

- Cut out and display the 7 pieces in a set of tangrams. Have students identify each piece by its geometric name. (2 small right triangles, 1 medium right triangle, 2 large right triangles, 1 square, 1 parallelogram)
- **Which, if any, of the tangrams are congruent?** (2 small and 2 large triangles)
- **Can you find 2 pieces we can put together to form a square?** (2 small or 2 large triangles) Have a volunteer model this solution.
- Tell students that they just acted out a solution using models. They will learn to solve more problems using the Act It Out strategy in the lesson in their books.

Differentiated Instruction

English Learners

Pairs	15 minutes
Objective	Solve a problem by using a model to act it out.
Materials	Student page 437
Visual, Auditory	

Early Production

- Pair students for ***Guided Practice***, and tell them to verbalize their thinking while working.
- Ask students to say the words *fits inside* and *overlapping*. Encourage them to show examples of these words while working.

Intermediate/Advanced

- English Learner Resource 17.3
- English Learner Handbook

Intervention

Small Groups	5 minutes
Objective	Solve a problem by using a model to act it out.
Materials	Tangrams
Tactual, Visual	

- Students may have more success solving the problems in this lesson if they use plastic or wooden tangrams rather than paper cutouts.
- You may want to provide students with outlines of each shape, like frames, within which to move the pieces.

Other Resources

- *Ways to Success* CD-ROM 17.3

Early Finishers

Individuals	20 minutes
Objective	Solve a problem by using a model to act it out.
Materials	Toothpicks
Visual, Tactual	

- Arrange 16 toothpicks as shown below. Move 2 toothpicks so there are just 4 squares.

- Arrange 9 toothpicks as shown below. Take away 2 toothpicks and move 1 toothpick so there are still 3 triangles.

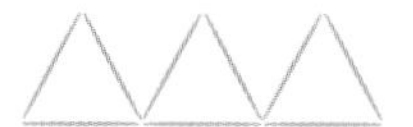

Literature Connection

Materials: Tangram pieces (Learning Tool 24), *Grandfather Tang's Story* by Ann Tompert, construction paper, markers

- Distribute the tangram pieces to students so they can make the figures as you read the story to them.
- Give students time to create their own tangram figures.
- Have them trace their best figures onto construction paper, name them, and display them in the room.

❶ Introduce

Display a square piece of paper. **What two congruent shapes are in this figure?** (possible answers: triangles, rectangles) Demonstrate by cutting a diagonal line from one corner to the opposite corner. Explain to students that the lesson shows how to use the Act It Out strategy to model a solution.

❷ Teach

Act It Out

- Have a volunteer read the opening problem. **Explain in your own words what you are trying to find out.** (Combine the pieces to form a congruent square.)
- ***Understand*** **If one shape was larger than the big square, could we solve this problem?** (No; the 5 shapes couldn't fit inside it.)
- ***Plan*** **How many of the small shapes must you use?** (all 5)
- ***Solve*** **If you arranged the 5 shapes into a square with a size different from that of the given square, would that be an acceptable solution?** (No; the problem calls for a congruent square.)
- ***Look Back*** **If you rotated the completed square to the right, would it still be congruent to the given square?** (yes)

Lesson 3

Problem-Solving Strategy

Act It Out

Objective Learn how to solve a problem by using a model to act it out.

Problem Can these five figures be arranged to form a figure that is congruent to the large square at the right?

UNDERSTAND

This is what you know.

Congruent figures have the same size and shape.

PLAN

You can make and use models to solve the problem.

SOLVE

Act it out.

- To make models, trace the five figures and the large square on grid paper. Cut out the five figures.
- Now, try to arrange the five figures so that they fit inside the large square without overlapping.

Solution: Yes, the five figures can be arranged to form a figure that is congruent to the large square.

LOOK BACK

Look back at the problem.

How can you be sure your answer is correct?

Possible answer: **You can place the square you made over the square in the book to be sure they are congruent.**

436

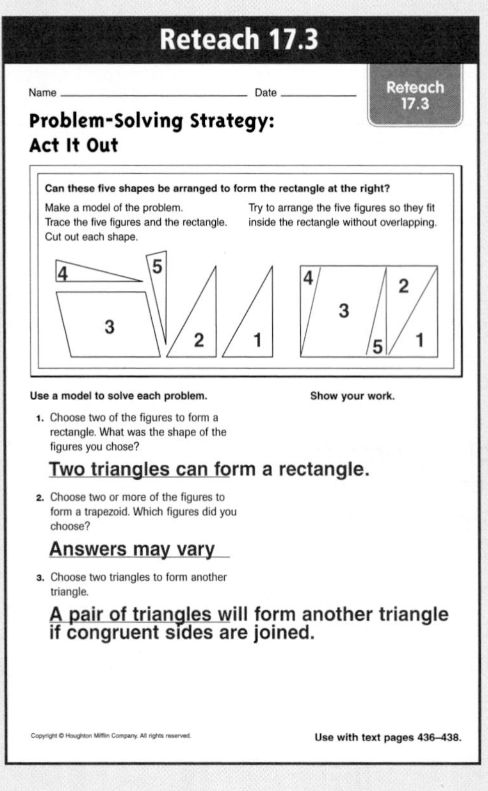

Reteach 17.3

Name ______ Date ______ Reteach 17.3

Problem-Solving Strategy: Act It Out

Can these five shapes be arranged to form the rectangle at the right?

Make a model of the problem. Trace the five figures and the rectangle. Cut out each shape.

Try to arrange the five figures so they fit inside the rectangle without overlapping.

Use a model to solve each problem. **Show your work.**

1. Choose two of the figures to form a rectangle. What was the shape of the figures you chose?
   Two triangles can form a rectangle.
2. Choose two or more of the figures to form a trapezoid. Which figures did you choose?
   Answers may vary
3. Choose two triangles to form another triangle.
   A pair of triangles will form another triangle if congruent sides are joined.

Use with text pages 436–438.

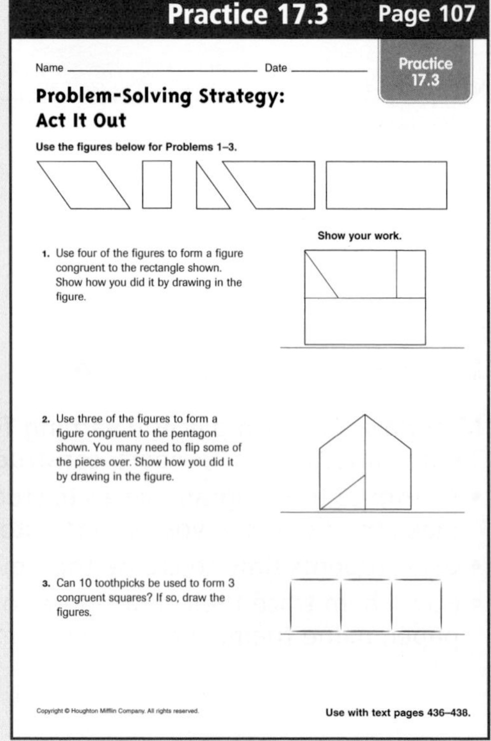

Practice 17.3 Page 107

Name ______ Date ______ Practice 17.3

Problem-Solving Strategy: Act It Out

Use the figures below for Problems 1–3.

Show your work.

1. Use four of the figures to form a figure congruent to the rectangle shown. Show how you did it by drawing in the figure.
2. Use three of the figures to form a figure congruent to the pentagon shown. You many need to flip some of the pieces over. Show how you did it by drawing in the figure.
3. Can 10 toothpicks be used to form 3 congruent squares? If so, draw the figures.

Use with text pages 436–438.

Guided Practice

Use the figures on Page 436 to solve each problem. Make a drawing to show your answer.
See Additional Answers.

1. Arrange all the figures except the largest triangle to form a figure congruent to the parallelogram below.

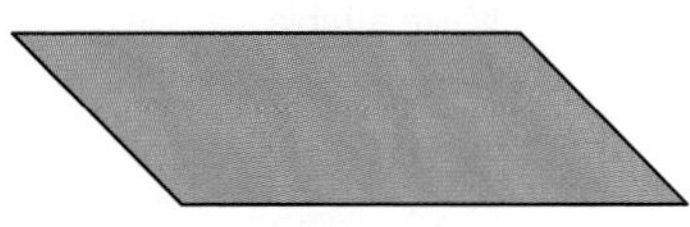

2. Arrange the largest triangle, the parallelogram, and one of the small triangles to form a figure congruent to the quadrilateral at the right.

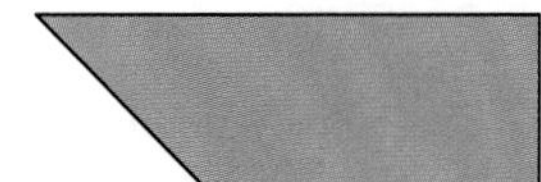

Hint: Where must right angles be?

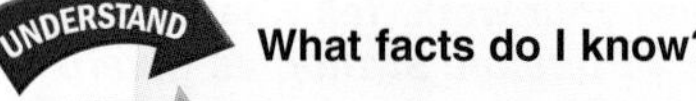
Ask Yourself

UNDERSTAND **What facts do I know?**

PLAN **Can I make a model?**

SOLVE
- **Did I make and use the correct models?**
- **Does the figure I made match the figure in the problem exactly?**

LOOK BACK **Did I check to see if my answer is correct?**

Independent Practice

Use the figures on Page 436 for Problems 3 and 4. Make a drawing to show your answer. *See Additional Answers.*

3. Use four of the figures to form a figure congruent to the pentagon shown below.

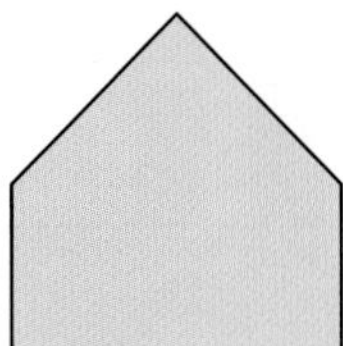

4. Use all five of the figures to form a figure congruent to the triangle shown below.

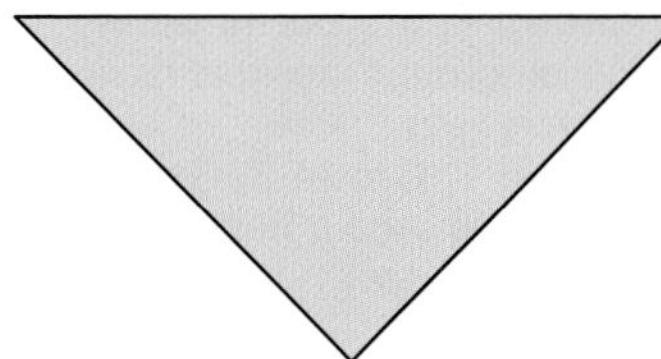

5. Can 12 toothpicks be used to form 4 congruent squares?

6. Can 9 toothpicks be used to form 4 congruent triangles?

Guided Practice

Have students complete **Exercises 1–2** as you observe. Remind them to use the ***Ask Yourself*** questions to help.

3 Practice

Independent Practice

Select from **Exercises 3–14** as independent work.

- ***Problems 5–6*** You may wish to provide toothpicks so students can model the solutions before they try to draw them.

Enrichment 17.3

Name ____________ Date ________ Enrichment 17.3

Problem-Solving Strategy: Act It Out

Problem Margo has a puzzle set. The pieces are different geometric figures. The puzzle came with a list of different shapes that can be made using some or all of the puzzle pieces. Trace and cut out each figure.

1. Use the pieces you cut out to make a rectangle that is congruent to the rectangle shown. You can do it at least two different ways. Each way uses 3 of the pieces. Draw two different arrangements in the figures below. **Possible answers:**

2. Use the pieces to make a square that is congruent to the square shown. You can do it at least two different ways. Each way uses 4 of the pieces. Draw two different arrangements in the figures below. **Possible answers:**

3. Can you make any other shapes using some or all of the shapes? Show some possible arrangements. **Answers may vary.**

 Use with text pages 436–438.

Problem Solving 17.3

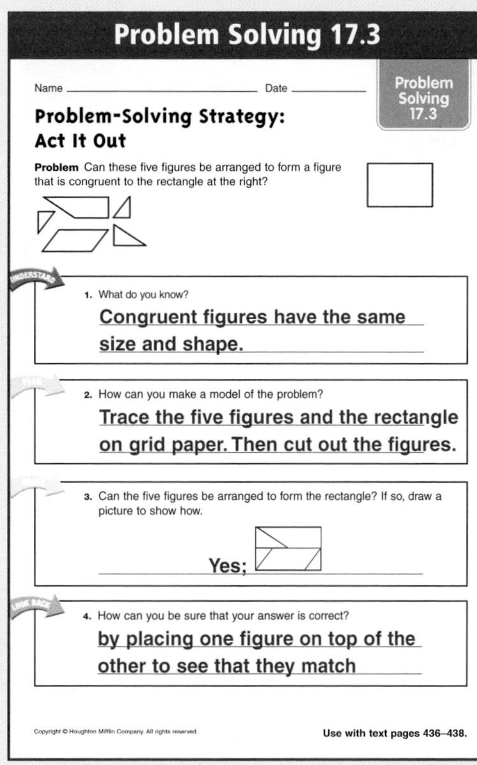
Name ____________ Date ________ Problem Solving 17.3

Problem-Solving Strategy: Act It Out

Problem Can these five figures be arranged to form a figure that is congruent to the rectangle at the right?

1. What do you know? Congruent figures have the same size and shape.
2. How can you make a model of the problem? Trace the five figures and the rectangle on grid paper. Then cut out the figures.
3. Can the five figures be arranged to form the rectangle? If so, draw a picture to show how. Yes;
4. How can you be sure that your answer is correct? by placing one figure on top of the other to see that they match

 Use with text pages 436–438.

Mixed Problem Solving

- Tell students that they may use any of the strategies in the table or a combination of strategies, as they wish. Remind them to look back at their work to be sure they have answered the question that was asked.
- ***Data*** If necessary, help students recall that the graph for **Problems 11–14** is a bar graph.

Have students review their answers to make sure they have done the following:

- expressed the solution clearly
- used appropriate mathematical notation and terms
- supported their solution with verbal and symbolic work
- determined the reasonableness of the solution in the context of the original problem.

Mixed Problem Solving

Solve. Show your work. Tell what strategy you used. ***Possible strategies given.***

You Choose

Strategy
- Act it Out
- Draw a picture
- Guess and Check
- Make a Table
- Write an Equation

Computation Method
- Mental Math
- Estimation
- Paper and Pencil
- Calculator

7. A salad costs $1.50 more than a sandwich. Together the salad and sandwich cost $10.50. How much does each cost?
salad - $6, sandwich - $4.50; Guess and Check
8. Guitar lessons start at 3:30 P.M. Each lesson is 45 minutes long. There are 6 lessons scheduled. At what time does the last lesson start?
7:15 P.M.; Make a Table
9. Lorenzo draws 20 circles in a row. Each circle has a diameter of 25 mm. Each circle touches the next circle at only one point. What is the length of the row of circles?
500 mm; Draw a Picture
10. Danny has two buckets. One holds 7 quarts and the other holds 4 quarts. How can Danny use the two buckets to measure 6 quarts? **Fill the 7-quart bucket. Use it to fill the 4-quart bucket. The remainder will be 3 quarts. Place the 3 quarts in a separate bucket, then repeat; Act it Out.**

Data **Groups of students are using blocks to make designs in art class. The graph shows the number of blocks in four groups' designs. Use the bar graph for Problems 11–14.**

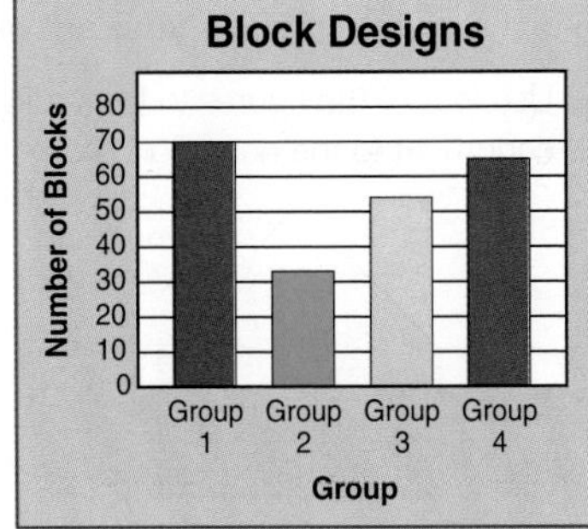

11. Which group used the greatest number of blocks? How many did they use?
Group 1; 70 blocks
12. **Explain** Did Group 3 or Group 4 use more blocks? Explain how you know.
Group 4, the bar is taller
13. Which groups' designs have more than 50 blocks?
Group 1, Group 3, Group 4
14. **Estimate** About how many blocks did Group 4 use? Explain how you made your estimate.
Estimates should be about 65. The bar stops half way between the 60 and 70, at about 65.

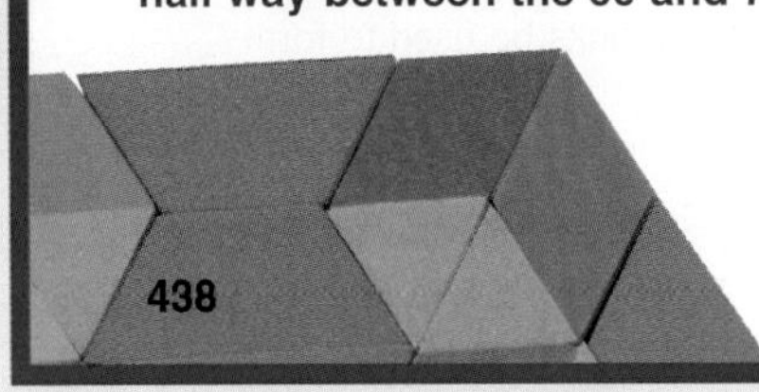

438

Homework 17.3 **Page 107**

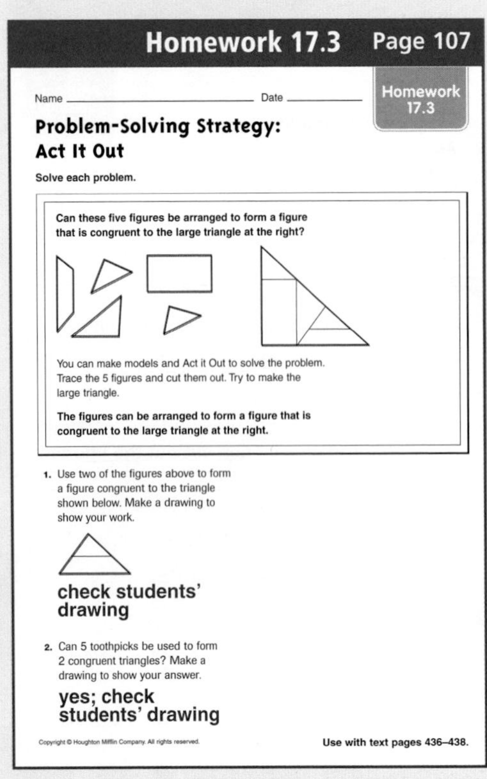

Name ______________________ Date __________

Homework 17.3

Problem-Solving Strategy: Act It Out

Solve each problem.

Can these five figures be arranged to form a figure that is congruent to the large triangle at the right?

You can make models and Act it Out to solve the problem. Trace the 5 figures and cut them out. Try to make the large triangle.

The figures can be arranged to form a figure that is congruent to the large triangle at the right.

1. Use two of the figures above to form a figure congruent to the triangle shown below. Make a drawing to show your work.
check students' drawing
2. Can 5 toothpicks be used to form 2 congruent triangles? Make a drawing to show your answer.
yes; check students' drawing

Use with text pages 436–438.

Problem Solving on Tests

Multiple Choice

Choose the letter of the correct answer.

1. Dan multiplied (5 × 2) × 3. Paul multiplied 5 × (2 × 3). What property says that they both got the same answer?

   A Zero Property

   B Commutative Property

   C Property of One

   (**D**) Associative Property

2. A glove costs $25.50. A bat costs $10.45. Jim buys 3 gloves and 4 bats for his club. What is the total cost?

   F $35.95   **H** $133.35

   (**G**) $118.30   **J** $147.45

Open Response 3–4. ***See Additional Answers.***

Solve each problem.

3. 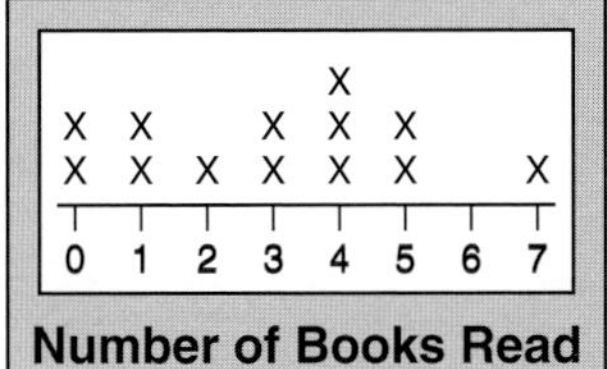

   Explain Which is greater, the median or the mean of the data? Explain.

4. At 10:00 A.M. the temperature was 3°C. By noon, it was 2 degrees higher. By 2:00 P.M., it was 3 degrees lower than it was at noon. What was the temperature at 2:00 P.M.?
   Represent Use a number line to solve the problem.

Constructed Response

5. Toby and Anna work for a florist. Potted flowers are on sale for $4.89 each. A sign reads, "Buy 2 plants and get one free." The pictograph below shows the assortment of plants.

Potted Summer Flowers	
Pansies	✿✿✿✿✿✿
Zinnias	✿✿✿✿✿✿✿✿✿✿✿
Daisies	✿✿✿✿✿✿✿✿
Petunias	✿✿✿✿
Snapdragons	✿✿✿✿✿✿✿

✿ = 5 plants

   a. Toby and Anna displayed the plants in rows. Decide how many rows of plants they might set up.

   b. Mr. Perez wanted 5 potted daisies and 4 potted pansies. How many plants did he pay for? How much will he spend? Show your work.

   c. At the end of the sale, Toby and Anna collected almost $420. Make a diagram to show about how many plants were given away free.
   See Additional Answers.

Education Place

Check out **eduplace.com/map** for more Test-Taking Tips.

Problem Solving on Tests

Problem Solving on Tests provides an opportunity for students to apply previously learned skills in the types of problem contexts typically encountered in standardized tests. ***Problem Solving on Tests*** includes practice in a variety of formats: multiple choice, constructed response, and open response.

Students will gain experience in writing about mathematics and using various representations to solve problems. Discuss students' solutions. Have several students explain the thinking behind their work.

More test prep practice is available on Houghton Mifflin's Web site, **Education Place**. Go to www.eduplace.com/map.

4 Assess & Close

Math Talk in Action

What are the characteristics of two figures that are congruent? (They have the same shape and size.) **What are the characteristics of similar figures?** (They have the same shape but not necessarily the same size.) **Are all similar figures congruent?** (no) **Are all congruent figures similar?** (yes)

Math Journal Prompt

Have students describe how they used the Act It Out strategy to solve a problem in this lesson.

Lesson Quiz

Use the quiz on Lesson Transparency 17.3.

Test Prep & Spiral Review

Use Test Prep Transparency 17.3.

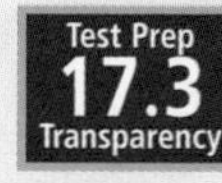

ACHIEVING Mathematical Proficiency

Students display understanding of congruence and symmetry when they are quite young. They typically construct their own ways to decide if figures are equal in size and shape. They can **identify symmetric figures** and seem to innately prefer them, but they **need practice identifying symmetry other than vertical symmetry** and multiple lines of symmetry.

Understanding transformations is more difficult. A slide (translation) is the easiest of geometric motions for students to model and understand. The flip (reflection) is easily modeled with a mirror, but the abstraction or mental image is more difficult to attain. Most difficult is the turn (rotation).

Modeling, including computer modeling of the geometric concepts of symmetry, congruence, and transformation, **should be an integral part of mathematical instruction**.

Hands On Lesson 17.4

Symmetry

Planning

Lesson Objective Learn how to identify figures that can be folded into matching parts.

Technology Resources

- *Ways to Success* CD-ROM 17.4
- *Ways to Assess* CD-ROM
- Education Place: Extra Practice, eGlossary, eGames
  www.eduplace.com/map

Lesson 17.4 Transparency

Problem of the Day

The great Spanish artist Pablo Picasso was born in a 19th-century year containing numerals with two lines of symmetry. Which year could it be: 1871, 1881, or 1801? (1881)

Spiral Review

Complete each sentence.

1. A ______ turns a figure around a point.
2. A ______ flips a figure over a line.
3. A ______ slides a figure in a straight line.
4. ______ figures have exactly the same size and the same shape.
5. Figures with the same shape but different sizes are ______. (1. rotation; 2. reflection; 3. translation; 4. congruent; 5. similar)

Lesson Quiz

How many lines of symmetry does each figure have? (1. 0; 2. 4; 3. 1)

1.

2.

3.

NCTM Standards

Geometry: Explore congruence and symmetry; identify and describe line and rotational symmetry in two- and three-dimensional shapes and designs.
Communication: Use the language of mathematics to express mathematical ideas precisely.

Getting Started

Building Math Vocabulary

line symmetry	describes whether a figure can be folded in half so that its two parts match exactly
line of symmetry	the line along which a figure can be folded so that the two halves match exactly
rotational symmetry	a figure has rotational symmetry if, after it is rotated about a point, the figure is the same as when in its original position

Display the vocabulary cards for ***line symmetry*** and ***line of symmetry.*** Draw an upper-case *A*. Show its line of symmetry as a dashed vertical line. Have students suggest another letter of the alphabet that has line symmetry. Draw and discuss students' suggested examples.

Rotating Hexagons

Whole Class	**15 minutes**
Objective	Identify figures with rotational symmetry.
Materials	Small Plane Figures, Circle, and Circle Spinner Transparencies
	Visual

- Prepare the circle as shown. Tape one regular hexagon at the 0° mark, another on the ray of the Circle Spinner. Align them both.

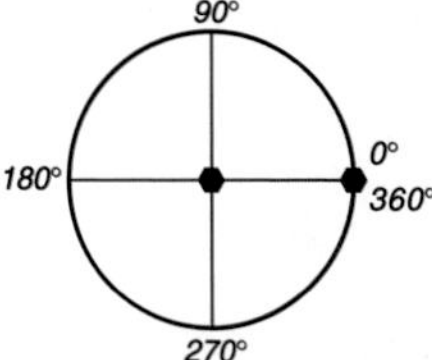

- **A figure has rotational symmetry if you can rotate it around a point less than a full turn and it still looks exactly the same.** Ask students to watch you rotate the hexagon on the Circle Spinner to 90°. **I rotated the hexagon a quarter turn. Does it look exactly as it did before?** (no; same shape, different orientation)
- **Watch as I rotate it more.** Rotate the Circle Spinner to 180°. **What do you see?** (The hexagon looks exactly like it did at first.)

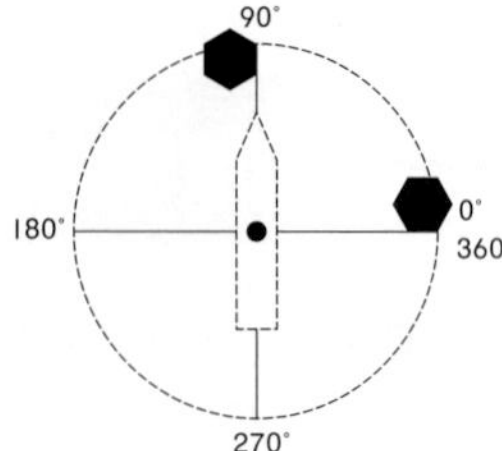

- Tell students that in this lesson they will learn to identify figures with line and rotational symmetry.

Differentiated Instruction

English Learners

Pairs	15 minutes
Objective	Identify figures with line and rotational symmetry.
Materials	Student pages 441 and 442, tracing paper, scissors
Visual, Tactual	

Early Production

- Students may need to use tangible objects to see symmetry. Have them trace and cut out shapes from Student pages 441 and 442. Students use the traced objects to check for line or rotational symmetry.
- Invite students to choose a shape and discuss their answer with a partner.

Intermediate/Advanced

- English Learner Resource 17.4
- English Learner Handbook

Intervention

Small Groups	5 minutes
Objective	Model congruence and symmetry.
Materials	Plain paper
Visual, Auditory	

- Draw pairs of congruent shapes on the board. **What makes figures congruent?** (same size and shape)
- Have students watch as you fold a sheet of paper in half and open it again. **Are the halves congruent?** (yes) **How can you be sure?** (Fold them back onto one another to see that they fit.)
- Tell students that in this lesson they will apply ideas about congruent figures to a geometric concept called symmetry.

Other Resources

- *Ways to Success* CD-ROM 17.4

Inclusion

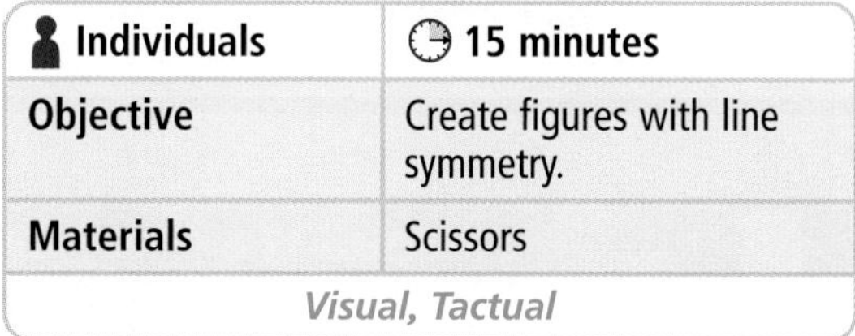

Individuals	15 minutes
Objective	Create figures with line symmetry.
Materials	Scissors
Visual, Tactual	

- Help students fold a piece of paper in half. Have them cut a figure around the fold, which becomes the line of symmetry.
- Then have students fold another piece of paper twice before they cut to create two lines of symmetry.
- Display the figures, sorted by number of lines of symmetry.

Social Studies Connection

Materials: origami paper

- Origami is the Japanese art of paper-folding. Find easy origami books, such as *Origami 1-2-3* by David Petty.
- At each step of the way, ask students to identify symmetry, congruence, and any of the other geometric concepts that emerge.

Pattern Practice

Write the following pattern on the chalkboard or overhead. Have students find the missing numbers.

0, 4, 3, 7, 6, 10, 9, __, __ (13, 12)

Present several patterns that challenge students with all operations. Have students record their answer at their desk or call for volunteers to complete the task.

❶ Introduce

Display a square piece of paper. **What is this figure?** (a square) Fold it in half, into a rectangle. **Are these two parts congruent?** (yes) Open the paper and show the folded line. Explain to students that the lesson will explore figures that can be folded into congruent parts.

❷ Teach

Learn About It

- Have a volunteer read the opening problem aloud. **Why does Amir fold the paper before cutting?** (to make the parts of his shape exactly alike, congruent)
- **Look at the figures with line symmetry. What do the dashed lines stand for?** (folds, or lines of symmetry)
- **A full rotation of a circle is 360°. How many degrees in a quarter-turn rotation?** (90°) **In a half-turn? Three-quarter turn?** (180°, 270°)

Common Error

- **Confusion with rotational symmetry**
- **Intervention** Have students trace and cut out the figures they want to test for rotational symmetry. Model how to use the point of a pencil to stand for the point around which a figure rotates.
- **Missing multiple lines of symmetry** Some students will find one line of symmetry but fail to notice additional ones.
- **Intervention** Model how to rotate the figure or look at it from different angles to try to locate other lines of symmetry.

Hands On Lesson 4

Symmetry

Objective Learn how to identify figures that can be folded into matching parts.

Vocabulary
line symmetry
line of symmetry
rotational symmetry

Materials
grid paper

Learn About It

Amir's art class made photo albums. Amir is decorating the front of his album with geometric shapes. He folds the paper in half before he cuts to be sure the two parts of his shape match exactly.

A figure has **line symmetry** if it can be folded in half so the two parts match exactly. The fold line is a **line of symmetry**.

▶ Figures can have one or more than one line of symmetry.

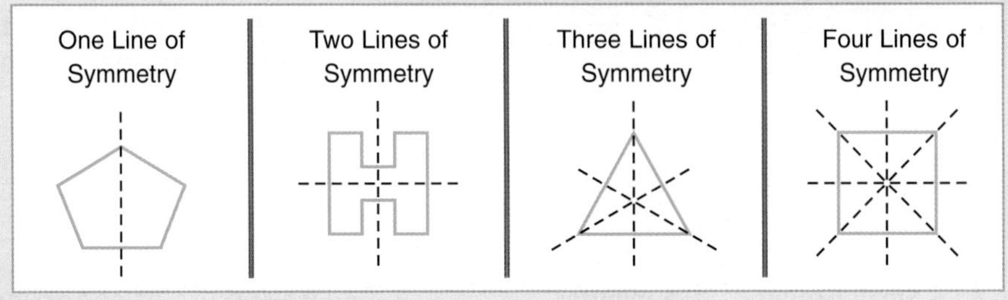

▶ Some figures have **rotational symmetry**.

A figure has rotational symmetry if you can rotate it less than a full turn (360°) around a point and it looks the same as it did before the turn.

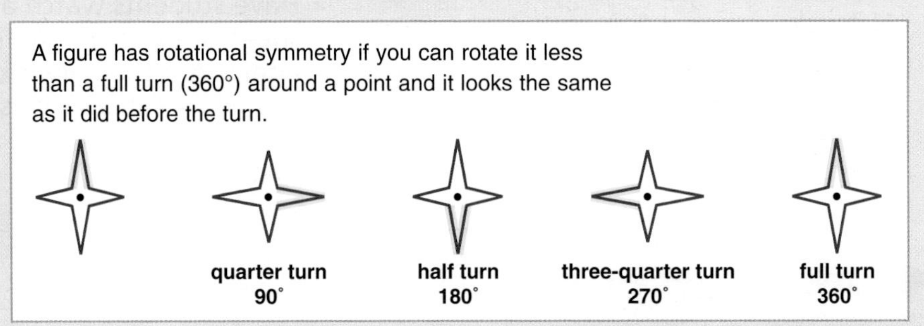

440

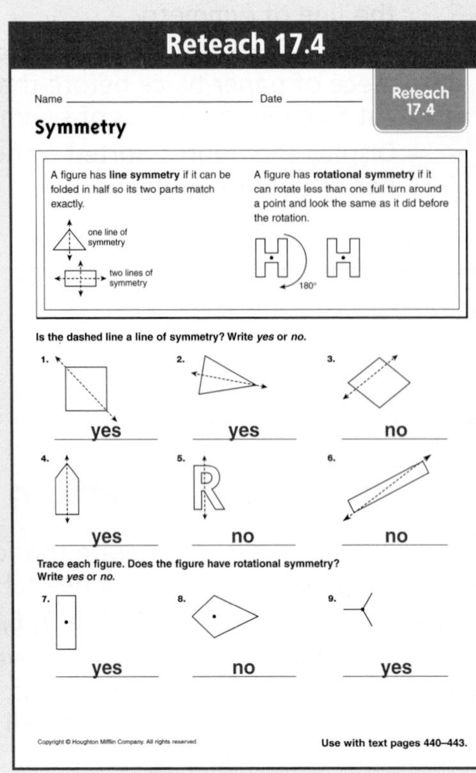

Reteach 17.4

Name ______ Date ______ Reteach 17.4

Symmetry

A figure has **line symmetry** if it can be folded in half so its two parts match exactly.

one line of symmetry
two lines of symmetry

A figure has **rotational symmetry** if it can rotate less than one full turn around a point and look the same as it did before the rotation.

180°

Is the dashed line a line of symmetry? Write *yes* or *no*.

1. yes
2. yes
3. no
4. yes
5. no
6. no

Trace each figure. Does the figure have rotational symmetry? Write *yes* or *no*.

7. yes
8. no
9. yes

Use with text pages 440–443.

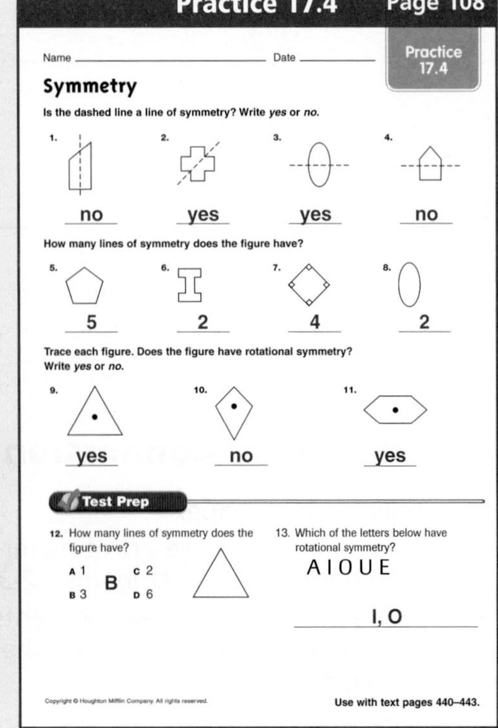

Practice 17.4 Page 108

Name ______ Date ______ Practice 17.4

Symmetry

Is the dashed line a line of symmetry? Write *yes* or *no*.

1. no
2. yes
3. yes
4. no

How many lines of symmetry does the figure have?

5. 5
6. 2
7. 4
8. 2

Trace each figure. Does the figure have rotational symmetry? Write *yes* or *no*.

9. yes
10. no
11. yes

Test Prep

12. How many lines of symmetry does the figure have?
A 1 B 3 C 2 D 6 — B

13. Which of the letters below have rotational symmetry?
A I O U E
I, O

Use with text pages 440–443.

Try this activity to explore symmetry.

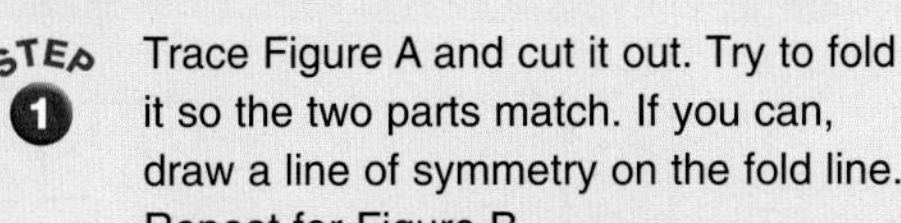

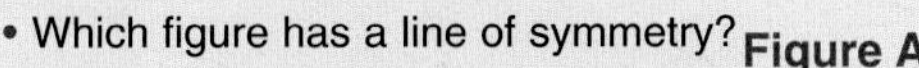

STEP 1 Trace Figure A and cut it out. Try to fold it so the two parts match. If you can, draw a line of symmetry on the fold line. Repeat for Figure B.

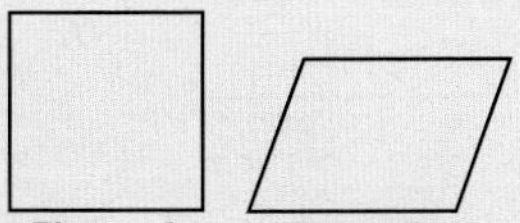

- Which figure has a line of symmetry? **Figure A**
- Does it have more than one? How can you tell? **Yes you can fold it along 4 lines and have both parts match exactly.**

Figure A | Figure B

STEP 2 On grid paper draw a dashed line of symmetry and the design shown at the right.

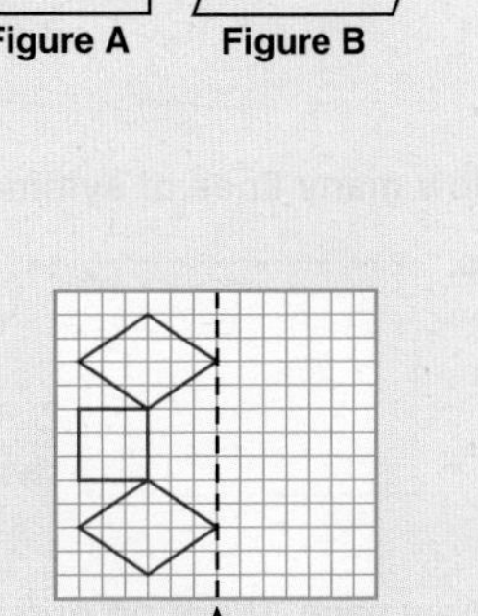

STEP 3 Draw a mirror image of the design on the right side of the line.

- How did you transform the figures on the left to get the figures on the right? Explain. ***See Additional Answers.***
- How do you know the dashed line is a line of symmetry? **If you fold the design along the dashed line, the 2 parts match exactly.**

Guided Practice

Is the dashed line a line of symmetry? Write *yes* or *no*.

Ask Yourself

- Do the two parts match exactly?
- How does the figure look when I turn it less than 360°?

1. 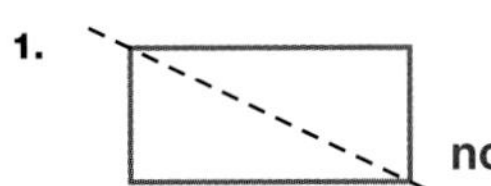 **no**

2. 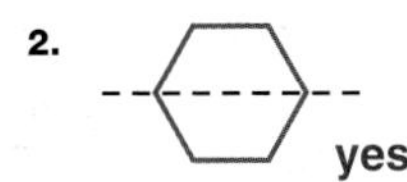 **yes**

Trace each figure. Does the figure have rotational symmetry? Write *yes* or *no*.

3.  **yes**

4. 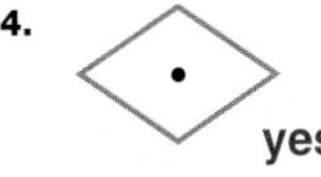 **yes**

5. 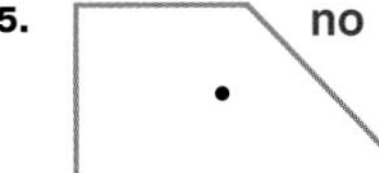 **no**

Explain Your Thinking ▶ How can you use a tracing of a figure to find out if it has rotational symmetry?

Put the tracing over the original figure and turn it. If at any time before a full turn, the figures are identical, it has rotational symmetry.

Go On

Guide students to the symmetry activity on page 441. Circulate as students work. Ask them to tell what they are doing, using the precise mathematical terms they have been learning.

- **What do you notice about Figure B?** (It does not have line symmetry.) **What about Figure A?** (It has more than one line of symmetry.)
- **In Step 3, what transformation do you use to make the design across the line of symmetry?** (flip)
- **How could you prove that the dashed line is a line of symmetry?** (Test whether both sides of the design match exactly by folding.)

Guided Practice

Have students complete **Exercises 1–5** as you observe. Remind them to use the ***Ask Yourself*** questions to help. Give students the opportunity to talk about the question in ***Explain Your Thinking***.

Enrichment 17.4

Name ______________ Date ______________ Enrichment 17.4

Design Me Some Symmetry

Symmetrical Shapes

1. Fold a square piece of paper in half.
2. Trace this design on one half of the paper.
3. Keep the paper folded and cut along the design.
4. Open up the cut-out design. What symmetrical shape did you make? **A Heart**

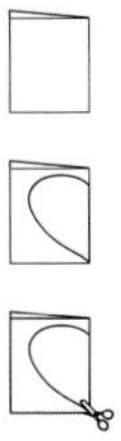

Symmetrical Drawings

5. Fold a piece of grid paper in half.
6. On one side of the paper make a drawing by coloring in squares or drawing lines or shapes.
7. Unfold the piece of paper and try to copy the drawing on the other side.

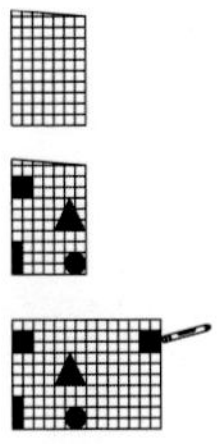

 Use with text pages 440–443.

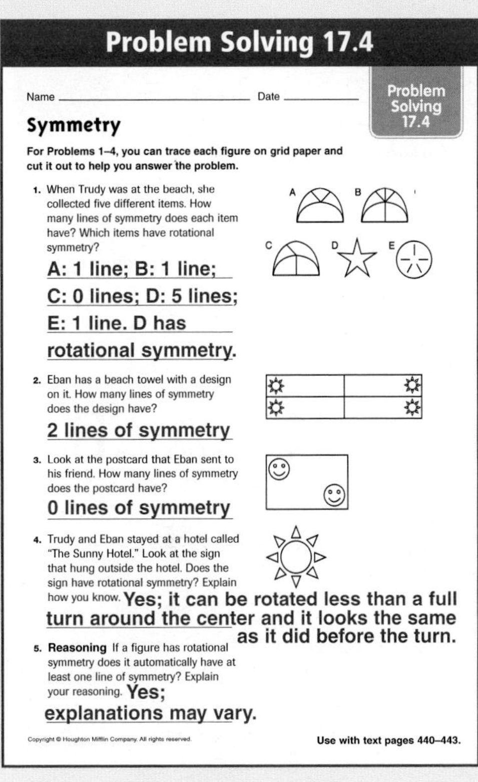

Problem Solving 17.4

Name ______________ Date ______________ Problem Solving 17.4

Symmetry

For Problems 1–4, you can trace each figure on grid paper and cut it out to help you answer the problem.

1. When Trudy was at the beach, she collected five different items. How many lines of symmetry does each item have? Which items have rotational symmetry? **A: 1 line; B: 1 line; C: 0 lines; D: 5 lines; E: 1 line. D has rotational symmetry.**
2. Eban has a beach towel with a design on it. How many lines of symmetry does the design have? **2 lines of symmetry**
3. Look at the postcard that Eban sent to his friend. How many lines of symmetry does the postcard have? **0 lines of symmetry**
4. Trudy and Eban stayed at a hotel called "The Sunny Hotel." Look at the sign that hung outside the hotel. Does the sign have rotational symmetry? Explain how you know. **Yes; it can be rotated less than a full turn around the center and it looks the same as it did before the turn.**
5. **Reasoning** If a figure has rotational symmetry does it automatically have at least one line of symmetry? Explain your reasoning. **Yes; explanations may vary.**

 Use with text pages 440–443.

3 Practice

Practice and Problem Solving

Select from **Exercises 6–30** as independent work. Guide students to read each direction line carefully so that they respond in the proper format. Encourage students to explain their reasoning as they work.

4 Assess & Close

Math Talk in Action

Compare and contrast rotational symmetry and line symmetry. (Both have congruent figures. Line symmetry is like reflection—the line of symmetry is the line across which a figure flips. Rotational symmetry is about turning a figure around a point, not a line.)

Math Journal Prompt

Have students write a word that has line symmetry, such as OHIO.

Lesson Quiz

Use the quiz on Lesson Transparency 17.4.

Test Prep & Spiral Review

Use Test Prep Transparency 17.4.

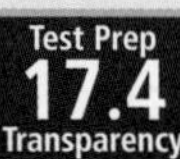

Practice and Problem Solving

Is the dashed line a line of symmetry? Write *yes* or *no*.

6.  yes
7. 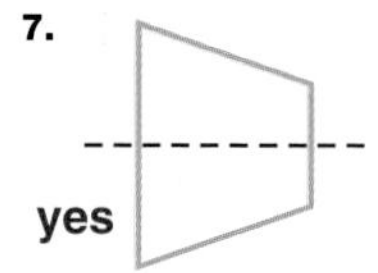 yes
8. 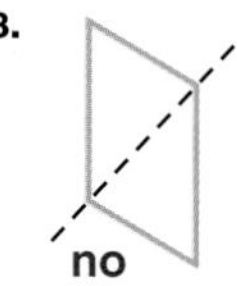 no
9. 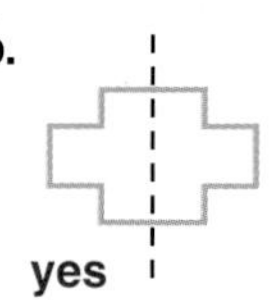 yes

How many lines of symmetry does the figure have?

10.  two
11. 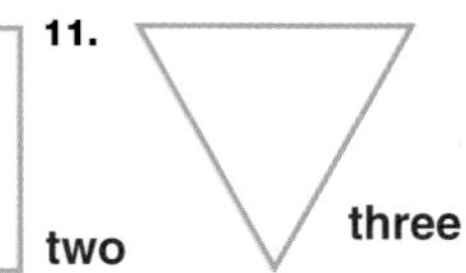 three
12. 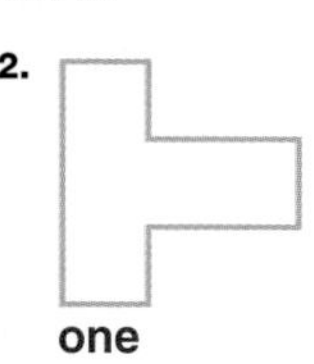 one
13. 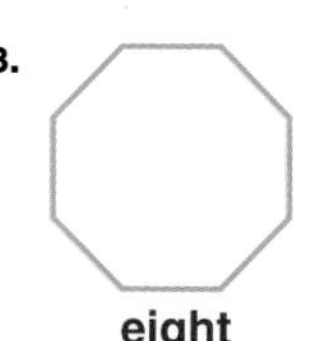 eight

Draw each figure on grid paper. Draw the line of symmetry. Complete the figure to show line symmetry.
See Additional Answers.

14. 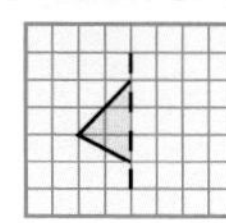
15. 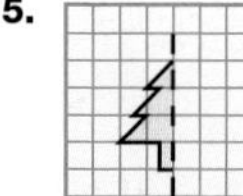
16. 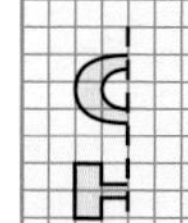
17. 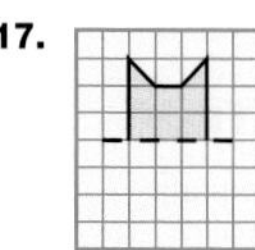
18. 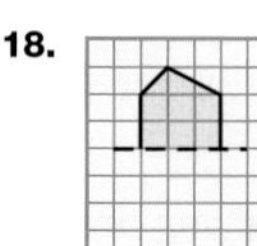
19. 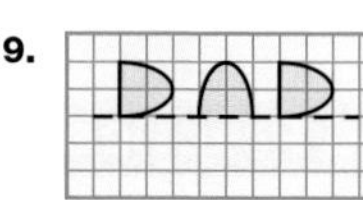

Trace each figure. Does the figure have rotational symmetry? Write *yes* or *no*.

20. 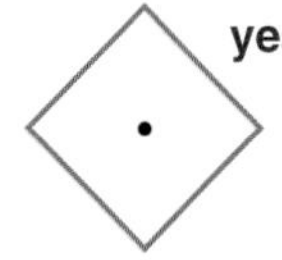 yes
21. 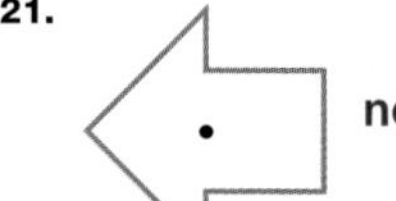 no
22. 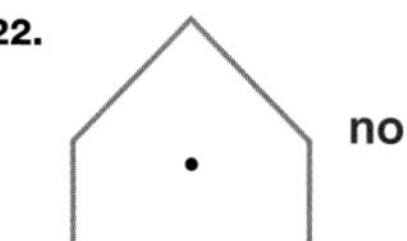 no
23. no 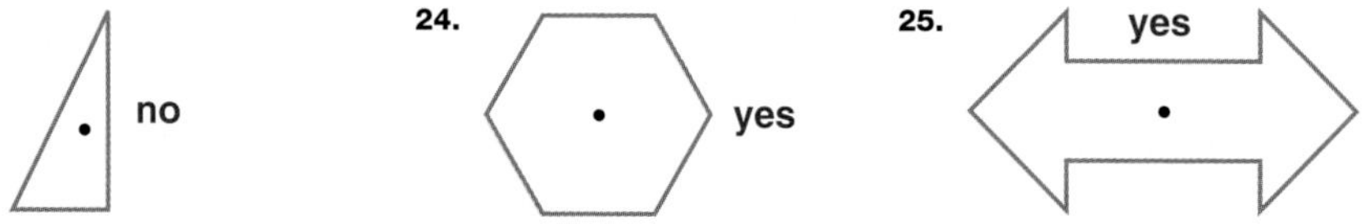
24. 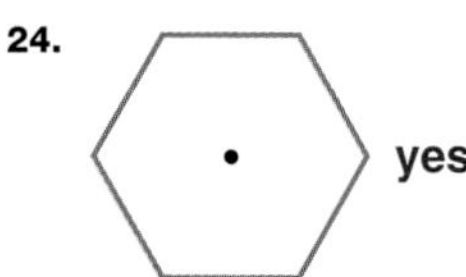 yes
25. 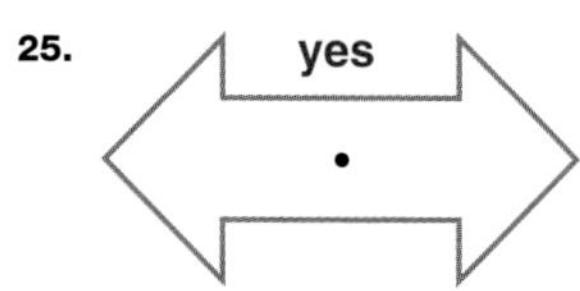 yes

442

Extra Practice, See page 449, Set C.

Homework 17.4 Page 108

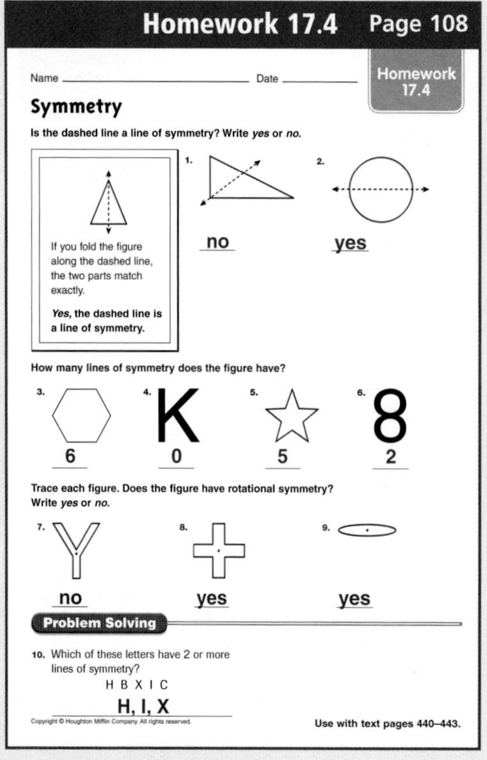

Name ______ Date ______ Homework 17.4

Symmetry

Is the dashed line a line of symmetry? Write *yes* or *no*.

If you fold the figure along the dashed line, the two parts match exactly.

***Yes,* the dashed line is a line of symmetry.**

1. no
2. yes

How many lines of symmetry does the figure have?

3. 6
4. K 0
5. 5
6. 8 2

Trace each figure. Does the figure have rotational symmetry? Write *yes* or *no*.

7. Y no
8. yes
9. yes

Problem Solving

10. Which of these letters have 2 or more lines of symmetry?
H B X I C
H, I, X

Use with text pages 440–443.

Solve.

26. Represent Suppose each of the letters below is rotated a half turn around the point. Draw a picture to show what each letter would look like.

a.  **W**

b.  **d**

c. 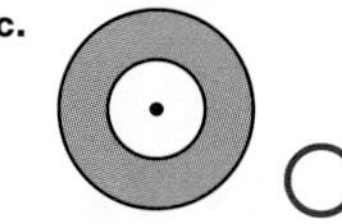 **O**

d. 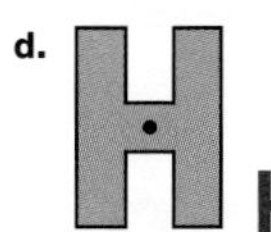 **H**

27. Which of the letters in Exercise 26 have rotational symmetry? How do you know?
See above.

28. Which of the letters in Exercise 26 have line symmetry? Use a drawing to help you explain. **M, O, H**
See Additional Answers.

29. Explain Amir made the figure below in art class. Trace the figure. Turn it. Does the figure have rotational symmetry around the point? Explain how you got your answer.
See above.

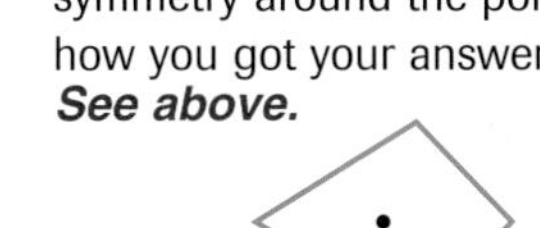

30. Trace the circle below. Cut it out. Fold it on line segment *NP*. What happens to points *M* and *O*? How many lines of symmetry does a circle have? Explain your thinking. ***See below.***

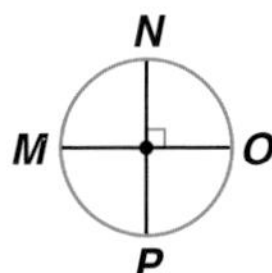

27. O, H; They look the same after being rotated less than a full turn.

29. No; the figure does not look the same after you rotate it.

30. Points *M* and *O* are at the same place; an infinite number. No matter how you fold it in half, the two parts match exactly.

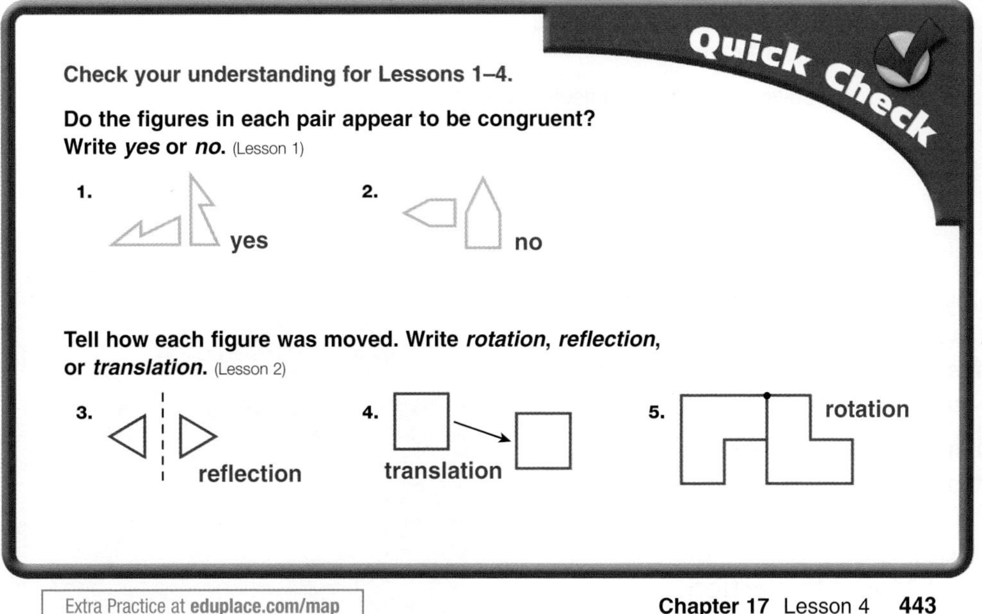

Quick Check

Check your understanding for Lessons 1–4.

Do the figures in each pair appear to be congruent? Write *yes* or *no*. (Lesson 1)

1. yes

2. no

Tell how each figure was moved. Write *rotation*, *reflection*, or *translation*. (Lesson 2)

3. reflection

4. translation

5. rotation

Quick Check

The ***Quick Check*** allows you to assess the students' understanding of the concepts presented in Lessons 1–4.

Items	Objectives Tested	Pages	Intervention
1–2	Learn about figures that have the same size and shape.	430–432	Reteach Resource 17.1, *Ways to Success* CD-ROM 17.1
3–5	Learn about rotations, reflections, and translations.	434–435	Reteach Resource 17.2, *Ways to Success* CD-ROM 17.2

Technology Connection

Briefly review the definition of symmetry. Have students offer examples of symmetrical objects. Then have them complete the activity below.

- Have students work in pairs and use the Internet to search for examples of symmetry in art, science, and nature.
- Tell students to print any examples of symmetry that they find. Using a word-processing program, have them record the Web address and any additional reference information for each example.
- In the space below each Web address, have students describe the examples of symmetry found on that site. Have them print their work and attach the pictures they printed earlier.

Lesson 17.5

Problem-Solving Application: Visual Thinking

Planning

Lesson Objective Solve problems using visual thinking.

Technology Resources

- *Ways to Success* CD-ROM 17.5
- Education Place: Extra Practice, eGlossary, eGames www.eduplace.com/map

Lesson 17.5 Transparency

Problem of the Day

Tan and red bricks form a border around a pool. The pattern is 2 red bricks for every tan brick. It took 327 bricks to make the border. How many bricks are red? (218)

Spiral Review

Is the dashed line a line of symmetry? Write *yes* or *no*.

1. 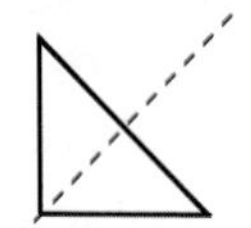
2. 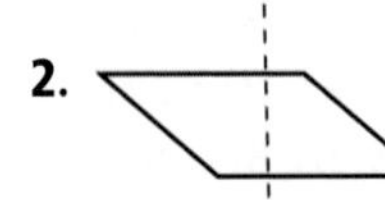
3. 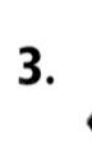 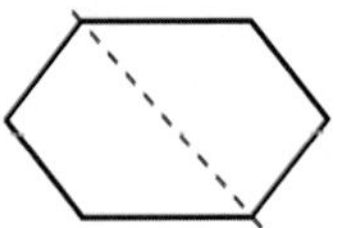
4. 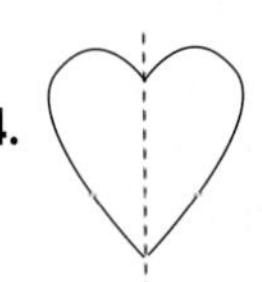

(1. yes; 2. no; 3. no; 4. yes)

Lesson Quiz

Pri made this solid block. She used 27 cubes snapped together. How many cubes are completely hidden? (1)

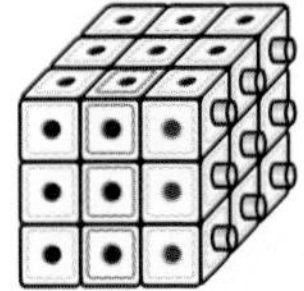

NCTM Standards

Geometry: Use visualization, spatial reasoning, and geometric modeling to solve problems.
Problem Solving: Apply and adapt a variety of appropriate strategies to solve problems.

Getting Started

Building Math Vocabulary

You may wish to review these words with students.

triangle	a polygon with three sides and three vertices
right triangle	a triangle in which one of the angles measures 90°

Picture This

Whole Class	10 minutes
Objective	Solve problems using geometric modeling and visual thinking.
Materials	Framed photograph
Visual	

- Display the framed photo. **Which way will the photo face if I rotate the frame a quarter turn?** (photo will rotate 90°) Model this action.
- Return the frame to the normal position. **Which way will the photo face if I reflect the frame around one side?** (photo will face the opposite direction) Model this action.
- Return the frame to the normal position. **What will happen to the photo if I rotate the frame 180° and reflect it over?** (photo will face the opposite direction and be upside down) Model this action.
- **How did you know how the photo would look before I moved the frame?** (Responses should suggest visualizing the action in the mind's eye.)
- Tell students that they used visual thinking to solve the problems and that they will learn more about this problem-solving strategy in the lesson in their book.

Differentiated Instruction

English Learners

Individuals	5 minutes
Objective	Solve problems using geometric models and visual thinking.
Materials	Student page 444, scissors
Visual, Tactual	

Early Production

- Have students practice rotating physical objects before doing ***Guided Practice***. Ask them to cut pieces of paper into creative shapes.
- Encourage students to try to visualize turning the shape. Then have them rotate the paper to see what happens.
- Invite students to explain what happened.

Intermediate/Advanced

- English Learner Resource 17.5
- English Learner Handbook

Intervention

Small Groups	10 minutes
Objective	Solve problems using geometric models.
Materials	Cubes, stickers, Student page 444
Visual, Tactual	

- Some students need to model the opening problem to strengthen their visual thinking skills. For these students, provide cubes and small stickers.
- Have students place a sticker on one face of the cube and draw on it an arrow like the picture of the box on page 444.
- Have students turn the cube upside down, noting how the position of the arrow changes.
- Have them repeat this kind of activity by moving the cube in other directions.

Other Resources

- *Ways to Success* CD-ROM 17.5

Early Finishers

Individuals	10 minutes
Objective	Solve problems using visual thinking and geometric models.
Materials	Colored paper, scissors
Visual, Tactual	

- Have students make visual-thinking problems classmates can solve.
- Students fold the paper in half, then in half again. Tell them to sketch a simple design to cut out around the fold. But before they cut, have them sketch how they think the design will look after they cut and unfold it.

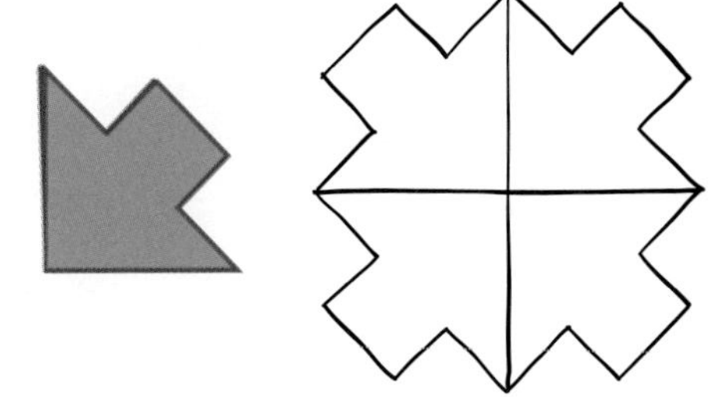

Science Connection

Materials: Small mirrors, assorted objects

- Have students strengthen their visual thinking by exploring mirror images.
- Provide small mirrors, including hinged mirrors. Have groups predict and then see how views of objects look and change when they tilt the mirror or use a pair of hinged mirrors. Have students examine two- and three-dimensional objects, as well as letters and numbers.

❶Introduce

Write on the board *evaluate the facts, think about relationships, think about real-life experiences*, and *examine the facts* to review logical ways of thinking to solve problems. Explain to students that the lesson shows how to use the way things look and what you know about geometry and spatial relationships to solve a problem.

❷Teach

Visual Thinking

Use the Four-Part Problem-Solving Transparency to guide students through the problem-solving plan.

- ***Understand*** **Why do we begin by listing what is known?** (to understand the details before trying to solve the problem) **Why must we notice the position and direction of the design?** (because the box will move, so the design may look different after the movement)
- ***Plan*** **How do we apply visual thinking?** (Try to picture in the mind's eye what will happen as the box is turned upside down.)
- ***Solve*** **Move your hand to show how the box will move.** (Watch as students act out turning the box upside down.)
- ***Look Back*** **How else might we have solved this problem?** (Make a model; act it out.)

Common Error

- **Difficulty visualizing spatial movement** Some students have trouble mentally manipulating objects in space.
- **Intervention** Provide these students with hands-on materials to help them solve the problems.

Lesson 5

Problem-Solving Application

Visual Thinking

Objective Solve problems using visual thinking.

Sometimes you can use visual thinking to solve problems.

Look at the arrow on the box at the right. What will the box look like when it is turned upside down?

UNDERSTAND

This is what you know.

- The arrow is in the lower right-hand corner of the box.
- The arrow is pointing up.
- The box is going to be turned upside down.

PLAN

You can use visual thinking to solve the problem.

SOLVE

Use visual thinking to move the box in your mind.

- The arrow will be in the upper left-hand corner of the box.
- The arrow will point down.

Then decide which of the choices below shows the box after it is turned.

a. **b.**  **c.** 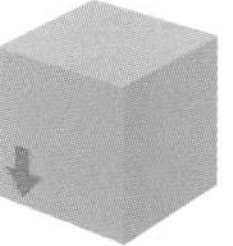

Solution: When the box is turned upside down, it will look like choice *b*.

LOOK BACK

Look back at the problem.

How else could you have solved this problem?

Possible answer: **You could make a model to solve the problem.**

444

Reteach 17.5

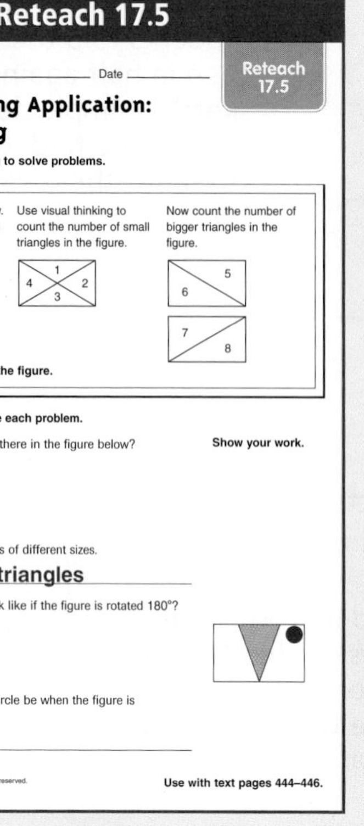
Name ______ Date ______ Reteach 17.5

Problem-Solving Application: Visual Thinking

You can use visual thinking to solve problems.

Kyle drew the figure below. How many triangles are in the figure? Use visual thinking to count the number of small triangles in the figure. Now count the number of bigger triangles in the figure.

There are 8 triangles in the figure.

Use visual thinking to solve each problem.

1. How many triangles are there in the figure below? **Show your work.**

   Think: Look for triangles of different sizes.

   6 triangles

2. What will the design look like if the figure is rotated 180°?

   Think: Where will the circle be when the figure is rotated 180°

Use with text pages 444–446.

Practice 17.5 Page 109

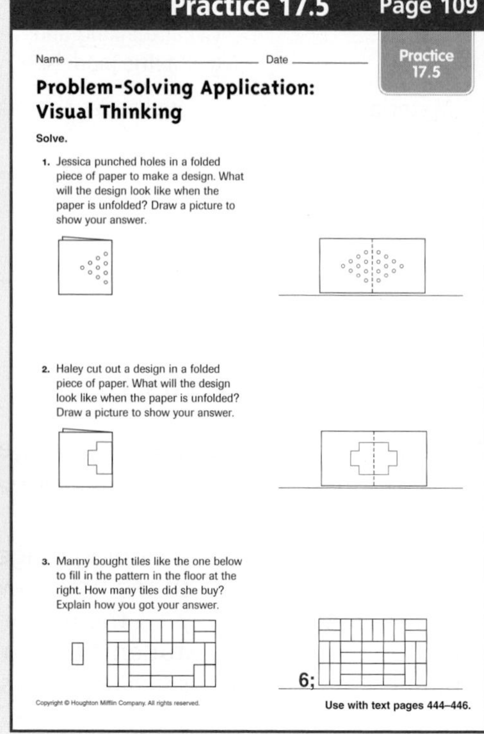
Name ______ Date ______ Practice 17.5

Problem-Solving Application: Visual Thinking

Solve.

1. Jessica punched holes in a folded piece of paper to make a design. What will the design look like when the paper is unfolded? Draw a picture to show your answer.
2. Haley cut out a design in a folded piece of paper. What will the design look like when the paper is unfolded? Draw a picture to show your answer.
3. Manny bought tiles like the one below to fill in the pattern in the floor at the right. How many tiles did she buy? Explain how you got your answer.

   6;

Use with text pages 444–446.

Guided Practice

Use the Ask Yourself questions to help you solve each problem.

1. What will be the next figure in this pattern? Choose *a, b,* or *c.*

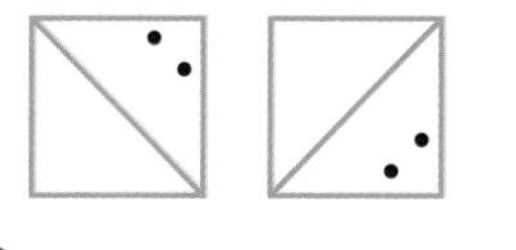

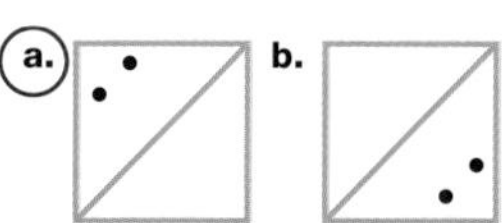

(a.) b. c.

2. Willis drew the figure at the right. How many right triangles are in the figure? Explain your solution. **44**

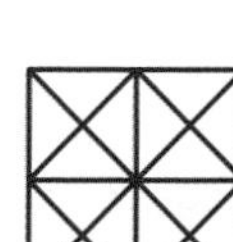

See Additional Answers.

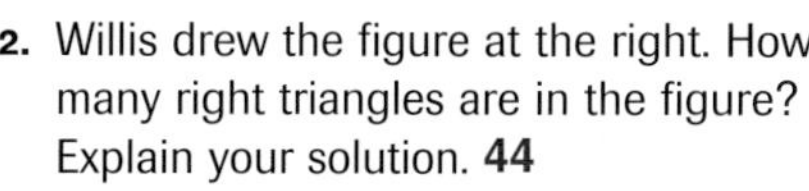

Hint: Look for 4 different sizes of triangles.

Ask Yourself

UNDERSTAND — **What facts do I know?**

PLAN — **Can I use visual thinking to solve the problem?**

SOLVE — **Did I move the objects correctly in my mind?**

LOOK BACK — **Did I check to be sure my answer is correct?**

Independent Practice

Solve.

3. Tammy punched holes in the folded piece of paper at the right. What will the paper look like when it is unfolded? Choose a, b, or c.

a. 

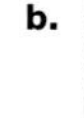

b. 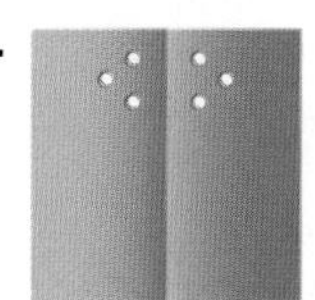

(c.) 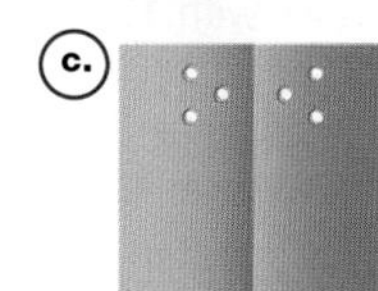

4. Sarah bought some tiles like the one below to fill in the pattern in the floor shown at the right. How many tiles did she buy? Explain your answer.

10 tiles;
Possible explanation:
1 tile is needed in the 2nd row,
5 tiles are needed in the 3rd row,
3 tiles are needed in the 4th row, and
1 tile is needed in the 5th row.

Guided Practice

Have students complete **Exercises 1–2** as you observe. Remind them to use the ***Ask Yourself*** questions to help.

3 Practice

Independent Practice

Select from **Exercises 3–16** as independent work.

- As students work, circulate to answer their questions, help them correctly interpret the given data, and help them focus on the key details required to solve the problems.

Enrichment 17.5

Name ______________ Date ______

Problem-Solving Application: Visual Thinking

Mandy made these five square designs.

A. B. C. D. E.

1. Draw what Square A would look like if it was rotated 180°.
2. Draw what Square D would look like if it was turned a quarter turn to the right.
3. Mandy turned one of the squares a three-quarter turn to the right. Below is a picture of the square after the turn. Which square did she turn?
   B
4. Which of the choices below shows Square E after it is turned a quarter turn to the right?
   C

A. B. C. D. E.

 Use with text pages 444–446.

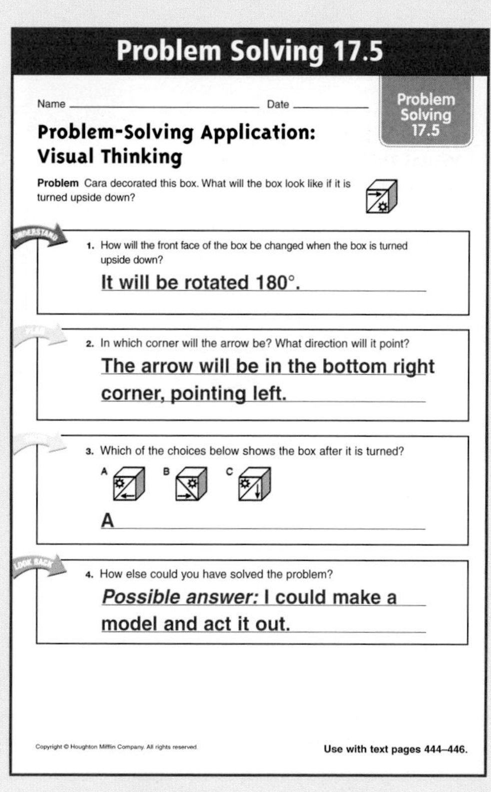

Problem Solving 17.5

Name ______________ Date ______

Problem-Solving Application: Visual Thinking

Problem Cara decorated this box. What will the box look like if it is turned upside down?

1. How will the front face of the box be changed when the box is turned upside down?
   It will be rotated 180°.
2. In which corner will the arrow be? What direction will it point?
   The arrow will be in the bottom right corner, pointing left.
3. Which of the choices below shows the box after it is turned?
   A B C
   A
4. How else could you have solved the problem?
   Possible answer: **I could make a model and act it out.**

 Use with text pages 444–446.

Mixed Problem Solving

Problem 7 Guide students to make an organized list or find a pattern.

Provide calculators for students who choose the calculator method.

4 Assess & Close

Math Talk in Action

Why would we want to strengthen our ability to solve problems using visual thinking?
(because we don't always have materials to model a problem) Have students discuss examples of real-life problems that could best be solved by using visual thinking.

Math Journal Prompt

Have students evaluate their own visual thinking skills. They can explain what they find easy and what is difficult for them.

Lesson Quiz

Use the quiz on Lesson Transparency 17.5.

Test Prep & Spiral Review

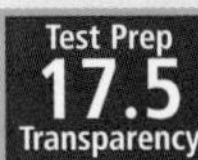

Use Test Prep Transparency 17.5.

Mixed Problem Solving

Solve. Show your work. Tell what strategy you used. *Possible strategies given.*

You Choose

Strategy
- Find a Pattern
- Guess and Check
- Solve a Simpler Problem
- Work Backward

Computation Method
- Mental Math
- Estimation
- Paper and Pencil
- Calculator

5. Sammy bought art supplies for $4.95. His mom gave him $5.00. Then he bought paper for $12.50. He had $6.50 left. How much money did Sammy have at the start? **$18.95; Work Backward**

6. At a craft store, 2 pieces of felt cost 75¢. Three pieces of felt cost 95¢, and four pieces of felt cost $1.15. If the prices follow a pattern, how much are seven pieces of felt likely to cost? **$1.75; Find a Pattern**

7. Five teams are competing in a tournament. Each team must compete against each of the other teams once. How many rounds of competition are needed? **10 rounds; Make an Organized List**

Solve. Show your work. Tell which method you used. *Possible methods are given.*

8. Matt is sponge-painting designs on shirts. He buys one shirt for $7.25 and 2 packages of sponges for $2.95 each. He pays with a $20 bill. About how much change does he receive? **about $7; Estimation**

9. One shirt has 10 rows with 12 shapes in each row. A second shirt has 13 rows with 10 shapes in each row. Which shirt has the most shapes? **the second shirt; Mental Math**

10. **Money** Supplies for another craft project cost $29.99. Matt has $15.50. How much more money does he need? **$14.49; Paper and Pencil**

11. A craft store sold 135,375 sponge stamps in January, 104,476 in February, and 85,904 in March. How many sponge stamps were sold in those 3 months? **325,755; Calculator**

446

Homework 17.5 Page 109

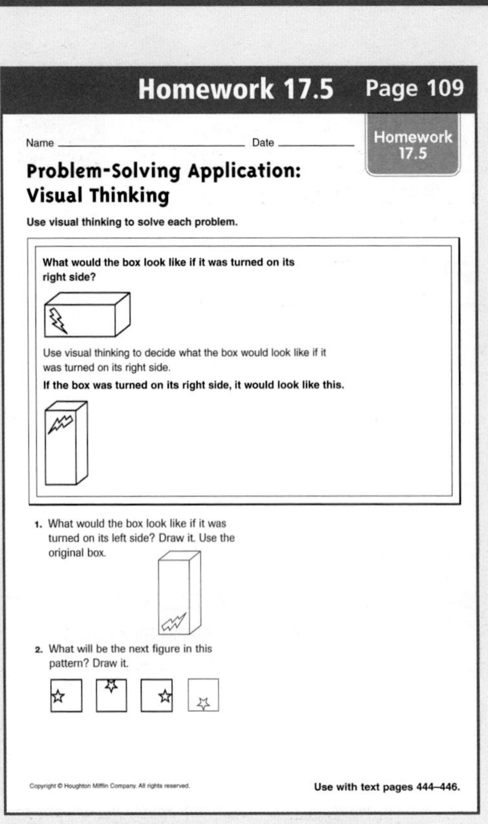

Name ________________ Date ________ Homework 17.5

Problem-Solving Application: Visual Thinking

Use visual thinking to solve each problem.

What would the box look like if it was turned on its right side?

Use visual thinking to decide what the box would look like if it was turned on its right side.

If the box was turned on its right side, it would look like this.

1. What would the box look like if it was turned on its left side? Draw it. Use the original box.

2. What will be the next figure in this pattern? Draw it.

Copyright © Houghton Mifflin Company. All rights reserved.

Use with text pages 444–446.

Mixed Review and Test Prep

Open Response

Name each polygon. (Ch. 16, Lesson 4)

12. hexagon

13. trapezoid, quadrilateral

14. parallelogram, quadrilateral

15. rhombus, parallelogram, or quadrilateral

16. Twelve toothpicks are arranged as shown. Can you remove 2 of the toothpicks so that only 2 squares remain? Draw a picture to show your answer. (Ch. 17, Lesson 5)

See Additional Answers.

Visual Thinking
Kuba Cloth Patterns

Activity

Many of the patterns Kuba weavers use today are the same patterns that have been used for hundreds of years!

You can make your own Kuba pattern.

- Trace pattern blocks or other small objects.
- Cut out the figures you traced.
- Turn, flip, or slide your figures to create a pattern.

Check students' drawings.

The Kuba people of central Africa use geometry to weave patterns into cloth.

Visual Thinking

Kuba Cloth Patterns

Kuba cloth begins as plain raffia squares woven by men. Women then decorate the squares, using detailed needlework and cutting individual tufts of cloth. It may take a month to complete one square.

Kuba cloth patterns inspired the work of artists such as Klee, Picasso, and Matisse, who had an extensive collection of Kuba cloth.

Chapter Review/Test

Chapter Test Items 1–10

To assign a numerical grade for this Chapter Review/Test, use 10 points for each item.

Check Understanding

You can use the ***Write About It*** question to assess student understanding of a key chapter concept.

Customize Your Instruction

The Chapter Review/Test is a formal evaluation of chapter objectives. For students who have not yet mastered these objectives, you can use the Reteaching Resources listed in the chart below.

Additional Assessment Resources

Alternate Chapter Test A Chapter Test is also provided in the Unit Resource folder. You might use the Review/Test in the student book as review and the test in the Unit Resource folder as a summary test for the chapter.

***Ways to Assess* CD-ROM** allows you to create your own lesson, chapter, or unit tests or practice and review worksheets.

Adequate Yearly Progress Guide helps familiarize your students with the format of standardized tests.

Chapter Review/Test

VOCABULARY

Choose the best term to complete each sentence.

Vocabulary
reflection
congruent
translation
line symmetry

1. If a figure can be folded along a line so that the two parts match exactly, it has ____. **line symmetry**
2. Figures that have the same size and shape are ____ figures. **congruent**
3. A change in position resulting from a slide is called a ____. **translation**

CONCEPTS AND SKILLS

Do the figures in each pair appear to be congruent? Write *yes* or *no*. (Lesson 1, pp. 430–433)

4. **no**

5. **yes**

Tell how each figure was moved. Write *rotation*, *reflection*, or *translation*. (Lesson 2, pp. 434–435)

6. 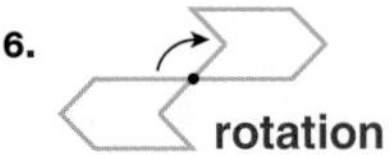 **rotation**

7. **reflection**

Which figures have both line symmetry and rotational symmetry? (Lesson 4, pp. 440–443) **figures b and d**

8. a. 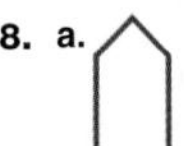 b. 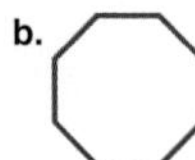 c. 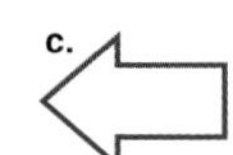 d.

Write About It: No. Circles are always the same shape, but they are not always the same size. Only circles that have the same radius and diameter are the same size.

PROBLEM SOLVING

Solve. Draw a picture to show your answer. (Lesson 3, 5, pp. 436–439, 444–447)

See Additional Answers.

9. How can you cut the letter X in half so that the two parts match exactly?
10. What will the letter Y look like if it is turned 90° to the left?

Write About It

Show You Understand

Consuela thinks that circles are always congruent. Is she correct? Explain why or why not. ***See above.***

Chapter Review/Test Items	Objectives	Covered On Teacher's Edition Pages	Use These Reteaching Resources
1–2, 4–5, 8	**17A** Identify congruent figures and figures with line and rotational symmetry.	430A–432, 440A–443	Reteach Resources 17.1, 17.4 *Ways to Success* CD-ROM 17.1, 17.4 *Ways to Success* Skillsheets 145–149
3, 6–7	**17B** Identify, perform, and predict the results of rotations, reflections, and translations.	434A–435	Reteach Resources 17.2 *Ways to Success* CD-ROM 17.2 *Ways to Success* Skillsheet 150
9–10	**17C** Solve problems using skills and strategies.	436A–438, 444A–446	Reteach Resources 17.3, 17.5 *Ways to Success* CD-ROM 17.3, 17.5 *Ways to Success* Skillsheet 151

Extra Practice

Set A (Lesson 1, pp. 430–433)

Do the figures in each pair appear to be congruent? Write *yes* or *no*.

1. yes
2. no
3. yes
4. no
5. yes
6. no

Set B (Lesson 2, pp. 434–435)

Tell how each figure was moved. Write *rotation*, *reflection*, or *translation*.

1. translation
2.  reflection
3. 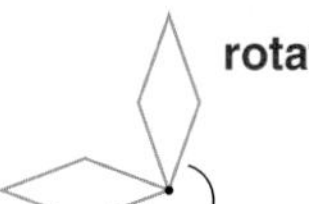 rotation
4. rotation
5. translation
6. reflection

Set C (Lesson 4, pp. 440–443)

Is the dashed line a line of symmetry? Write *yes* or *no*.

1. no
2.  yes
3. 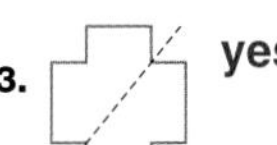 yes
4.  yes
5. 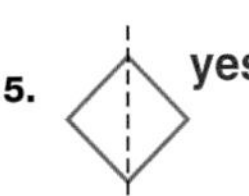 yes
6.  no

Does the figure have rotational symmetry? Write *yes* or *no*.

7. yes
8. 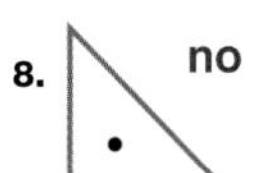 no
9.  yes
10.  no
11. 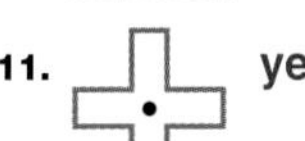 yes
12.  yes

Extra Practice at eduplace.com/map

CHAPTER 17 TEST

Chapter 17 Test

Name ________ Date ________

Do the figures in each pair appear to be congruent? Write *yes* or *no*. Explain your answer. Explanations will vary.

1. no
2. yes
3. no
4. yes

Tell how each figure was moved. Write *rotation*, *reflection*, or *translation*.

5. translation
6. reflection
7. rotation
8. reflection

Is the dashed line a line of symmetry? Write *yes* or *no*.

9. no
10. no
11. yes

Go on

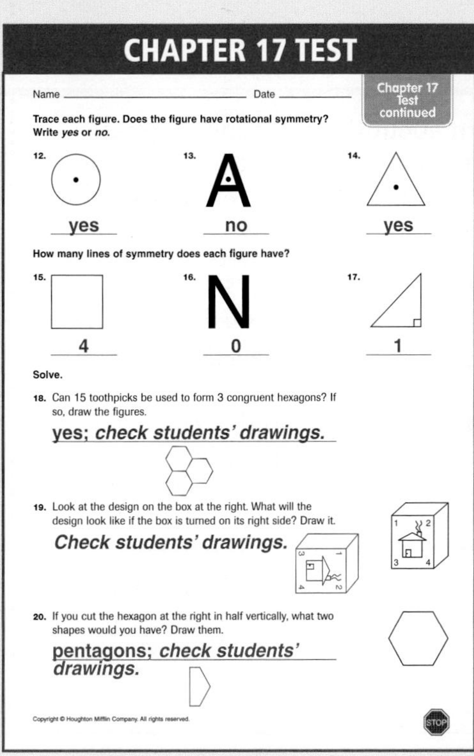

CHAPTER 17 TEST

Chapter 17 Test continued

Name ________ Date ________

Trace each figure. Does the figure have rotational symmetry? Write *yes* or *no*.

12. yes
13. no
14. yes

How many lines of symmetry does each figure have?

15. 4
16. 0
17. 1

Solve.

18. Can 15 toothpicks be used to form 3 congruent hexagons? If so, draw the figures.
yes; check students' drawings.

19. Look at the design on the box at the right. What will the design look like if the box is turned on its right side? Draw it.
Check students' drawings.

20. If you cut the hexagon at the right in half vertically, what two shapes would you have? Draw them.
pentagons; check students' drawings.

STOP

CHAPTER 18

Planning Guide

Perimeter, Area, and Volume

Lesson	Overview	Objective/Vocabulary
1 Hands On: Explore Perimeter and Area p. 452A	▶ Find the perimeter and area of squares and rectangles. ▶ Find the perimeter by counting the units around a grid paper cutout, and label its measure in units. ▶ Find the area by counting the squares inside the grid paper cutout, and label its measure in square units.	▶ Use models to explore perimeter and area. perimeter area
2 Hands On: Algebra: Perimeter p. 454A	▶ Estimate, then find, the actual perimeter of objects with rulers. ▶ Calculate the perimeter of a rectangle with the formula $P = (2 \times l) + (2 \times w)$.	▶ Find perimeters of polygons. perimeter
3 Hands On: Algebra: Area p. 456A	▶ Find the actual area of classroom objects with rulers and a formula. ▶ Find the area for a square and rectangle with the formulas $A = s \times s$ and $A = l \times w$. ▶ Find the areas of floor space of rooms shown on a floor plan.	▶ Find the area of a rectangle. area
4 Algebra: Perimeter and Area of Complex Figures p. 460A	▶ Subdivide a complex figure into squares and rectangles to find its perimeter and area.	▶ Find the perimeter and area of figures that are not rectangles.
5 Hands On: Solid Figures and Nets p. 464A	▶ Learn about the eight solid figures. ▶ Form a two-dimensional net of a three-dimensional figure with the faces of a solid figure. ▶ Identify solid figures, nets, and top, bottom, and side views of a solid.	▶ Identify and make solid shapes. faces vertex (vertices) edge net
6 Hands On: Algebra: Volume p. 468A	▶ Find the volume of a rectangular prism with cubes. ▶ Find volume, measured in cubic units, by calculation, using the formula $V = l \times w \times h$ when the length, width, and height are known.	▶ Find the volume of a rectangular prism. volume cubic centimeter cubic units
7 Problem-Solving Application: Use Formulas p. 470A	▶ Choose a formula to solve a problem.	▶ Decide which formula to use to solve a problem. perimeter area volume

Skills Trace: Perimeter, Area, and Volume		
Grade 3	**Grade 4**	**Grade 5**
• Estimate and find perimeter and area (ch. 17) • Identify solid geometric figures (ch. 15) • Estimate and find volume (ch. 17)	• Find perimeter and area • Use formulas to find perimeter and area of squares and rectangles • Identify solid geometric figures; use nets • Find the volume of a rectangular solid	• Find perimeter of polygons and complex figures (ch. 16) • Find area of parallelograms and triangles (ch. 16) • Identify, classify, and find two-dimensional views of solid figures (ch. 17) • Find volume and surface areas of solid figures (ch. 17)

Differentiated Instruction	Materials	NCTM Standards
▶ Differentiated Instruction activities, p. 452B ▶ *Chapter Challenges,* p. 103 *Ways to Success* CD-ROM: 18.1	Centimeter Grid Transparency, grid paper (Learning Tool 27)	**Geometry:** Identify, compare, and analyze attributes of two- and three- dimensional shapes and develop vocabulary to describe the attributes. **Measurement:** Select and apply appropriate standard units and tools to measure length, area, volume, weight, time, temperature, and the size of angles.
▶ Differentiated Instruction activities, p. 454B *Ways to Success* CD-ROM: 18.2 ▶ *Ways to Success* Skillsheet 152 Audio Tutor: **2**/15 Listen and Understand	CD jewel case, centimeter rulers	**Measurement:** Use standard units and tools to measure length, area, volume, weight, time, temperature, and angles. **Algebra:** Represent a variable as an unknown quantity using a letter or a symbol.
▶ Differentiated Instruction activities, p. 456B ▶ *Chapter Challenges,* p. 105 *Ways to Success* CD-ROM: 18.3 ▶ *Ways to Success* Skillsheet 153 Audio Tutor: **2**/16 Listen and Understand	Centimeter Grid Transparency, rulers	**Geometry:** Analyze characteristics and properties of two- and three- dimensional shapes. **Algebra:** Express mathematical relationship using equations. **Measurement:** Use formulas to find the area of rectangles and related triangles and parallelograms.
▶ Differentiated Instruction activities, p. 460B *Ways to Success* CD-ROM: 18.4 ▶ *Ways to Success* Skillsheet 157	Centimeter Grid Transparency	**Geometry:** Analyze characteristics and properties of two- and three- dimensional shapes. **Algebra:** Express mathematical relationship using equations.
▶ Differentiated Instruction activities, p. 464B ▶ *Chapter Challenges,* p. 107 *Ways to Success* CD-ROM: 18.5 ▶ *Ways to Success* Skillsheet 158	Solid cube, Nets I Transparency, paper cube nets, tape, Learning Tools 28–33, scissors	**Geometry:** Classify two- and three- dimensional shapes according to their properties and develop definitions of classes of shapes such as triangles and pyramids. Identify and build a three-dimensional object from two-dimensional representations of that object.
▶ Differentiated Instruction activities, p. 468B *Ways to Success* CD-ROM: 18.6 ▶ *Ways to Success* Skillsheet 159 Audio Tutor: **2**/17 Listen and Understand	Volume of Cubes Transparency, centimeter cubes, small box	**Geometry:** Use geometric models to solve problems in other areas of mathematics, such as number and measurement. **Measurement:** Develop strategies to determine the surface area and volumes of rectangular solids.
▶ Differentiated Instruction activities, p. 470B *Ways to Success* CD-ROM: 18.7 ▶ *Ways to Success* Skillsheet 160	Workmat 4	**Measurement:** Develop strategies to determine the surface areas and volumes of rectangular solids.

Math Notes

Chapter Objectives

18A Find perimeter and area.

18B Identify, classify, and describe solid geometric figures.

18C Determine the volume of solid figures.

18D Solve problems using skills and strategies.

Mathematical Background

Perimeter, Area, and Volume

Perimeter is the distance around a polygon. Because the opposite sides of a rectangle are congruent, the formula for its perimeter is $P = l + w + l + w$, or $P = 2l + 2w$, where l = length and w = width. Perimeter is a linear measurement, so it is measured in units of length.

Area is the number of square units it takes to cover an object without any overlap. The formula for the area of a rectangle is $A = l \times w$. Although length is often considered the longer dimension and the width the shorter one, when finding area, they are interchangeable. Area is a square measurement, so it is measured in square units.

For example, if the length of a rectangle is 3 inches and the width is 2 inches, then:

$P = 2(3) + 2(2) = 10$ in.

$A = 2 \times 3 = 6$ square inches (in.^{2})

2 in.

3 in.

Volume is the number of cubic units that fit inside a figure. A cubic unit is a cube that is 1 unit in length, 1 unit in width, and 1 unit in height. Only solid figures have volume. At this grade level, students will only find the volume of cubes and rectangular prisms. The formula for the volume of each is $V = l \times w \times h$. Volume is a cubic measurement, so it is measured in cubic units.

Research-Based Teaching

NCTM (2000) suggests that "by representing three-dimensional shapes in two dimensions and constructing three-dimensional shapes from two-dimensional representations, students learn about the characteristics of shapes." This can be done using nets. See *Professional Resources Handbook, Grade 4,* Unit 6.

For more ideas relating to Unit 6, see the Teacher Support Handbook at the back of this Teacher's Edition.

Language Intervention

In East Asian countries, children learn that just as numbers can be composed and decomposed as sets and subsets, geometric figures can be composed and decomposed as well. For further explanation, see "Mathematical Language and Measurement" in the *Professional Resources Handbook, Grade 4.*

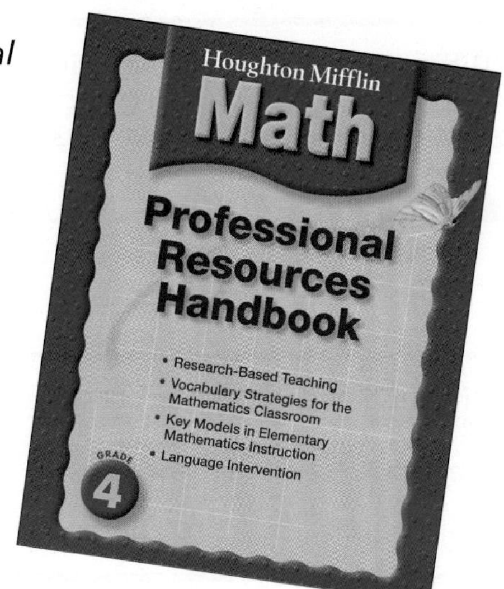

Chapter Activities

Connecting to the Unit Project

Whole Class	20 minutes
Objective	Estimate area.
Materials	None
Tactual, Visual	

Estimate Area

- To display the art projects for the Math Art Fair, students must find adequate floor, table, or bulletin board space in the classroom.
- Suggest that they allow 1 square foot of space per project. Based on the number of students in the class, figure out the total amount of space needed, and then decide how many tables to use or amount of space on the floor or bulletin board to mark off.
- If a bulletin board is used, have students figure out the amount of border material to trim. If tables are used, have students figure out how much ribbon or crepe paper might be used to decorate around each project.

Ongoing Skill Activity

Individuals	30 minutes
Objective	Find perimeter and area.
Materials	Tape measure, graph paper
Tactual, Visual	

Perimeter and Area

- Ask students to measure the length, width, and height of one of the rooms in their houses, and then have them draw the floor plan of the room.
- Tell them to calculate the area of the floor and the perimeter and volume of the room.
- Encourage students to share their findings with the whole class.

Math Expressions

Small Groups	25 minutes
Objective	Use units to find perimeter and area of shapes.
Materials	Units of Perimeter Area Copymaster
Tactual	

This activity uses instructional practices from *Math Expressions* with the content of this unit.

- Review perimeter as the distance around the outside of a shape. Explain that perimeter is measured in units of length, such as inches and centimeters. Distribute copies of the copymaster. Have students share ideas for how to find the perimeter of rectangle *X*.
- Direct students' attention to the lines along the edge of the sides of the rectangle. Tell them these lines mark off the units of length. Have students count the number of unit lengths around the outside of the rectangle. 14 Discuss quicker ways to find the total. Possible answer: Count only 2 adjacent sides, double each number. Relate these ideas to the formulas: $l + w + l + w = P$ and $(l \times 2) + (w \times 2) = P$.
- Have pairs of students find the perimeter of rectangles *Y* and *Z*.
- Repeat the process for area. Discuss the formula: $l \times w = A$.

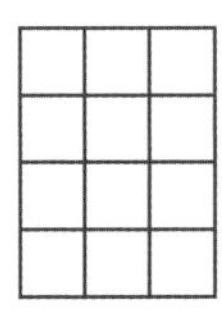

Starting Chapter 18

Investigation

Using Data

Have students work in small groups to answer the questions posed on page 450.

To extend the investigation, have students do the following activity.

- Make a blueprint of your classroom. Label the length and width of the room, windows, closets, and doorways. Use customary or metric units.

For more information about projects and investigations,

Visit **Education Place®**
www.eduplace.com/mat

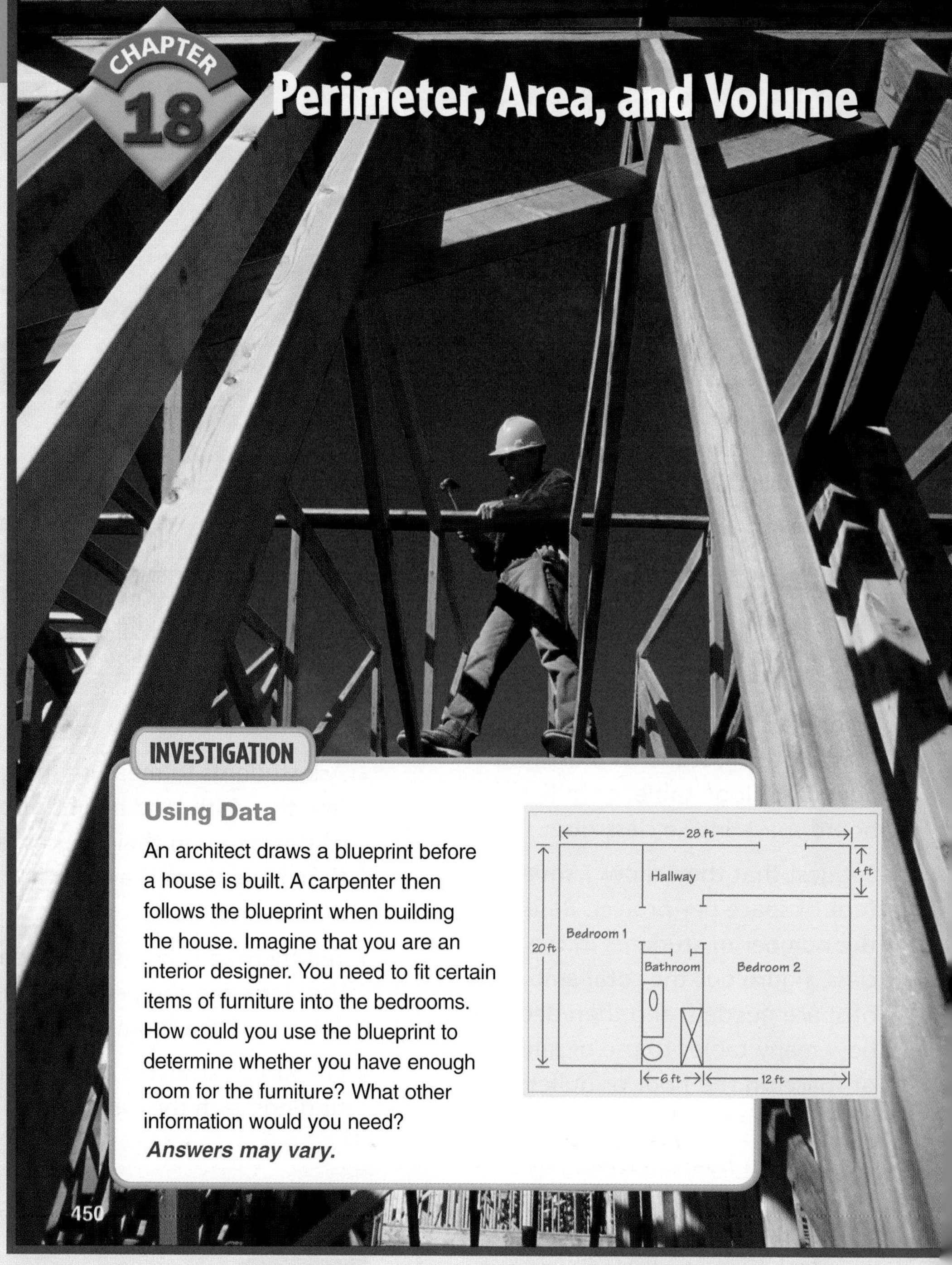

CHAPTER
18
Perimeter, Area, and Volume
INVESTIGATION
Using Data
An architect draws a blueprint before a house is built. A carpenter then follows the blueprint when building the house. Imagine that you are an interior designer. You need to fit certain items of furniture into the bedrooms. How could you use the blueprint to determine whether you have enough room for the furniture? What other information would you need?
Answers may vary.
28 ft
4 ft
Hallway
Bedroom 1
20 ft
Bathroom
Bedroom 2
6 ft
12 ft
450

Chapter 18 Prerequisite Skills Pretest

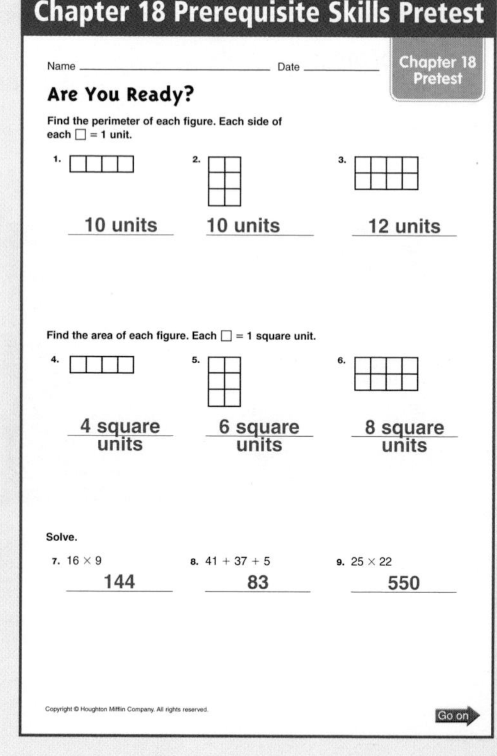

Name ____________ Date ____________

Chapter 18 Pretest

Are You Ready?

Find the perimeter of each figure. Each side of each □ = 1 unit.

1. 10 units
2. 10 units
3. 12 units

Find the area of each figure. Each □ = 1 square unit.

4. 4 square units
5. 6 square units
6. 8 square units

Solve.

7. 16×9 144
8. $41 + 37 + 5$ 83
9. 25×22 550

Go on

Use this page to review and remember what you need to know for this chapter.

VOCABULARY

Choose the best word to complete each statement.

Vocabulary
square
hexagon
octagon
pentagon
triangle

1. A polygon with five sides is a ____. **pentagon**
2. A polygon with eight sides is an ____. **octagon**
3. A polygon with four equal sides is a ____. **square**
4. A polygon with six sides is a ____. **hexagon**

CONCEPTS AND SKILLS

Solve.

5. 83 × 3 **249**
6. 45 × 7 **315**
7. 68 × 44 **2,992**
8. 75 + 24 + 5 **104**
9. 26 + 7 + 14 + 3 **50**
10. 32 + 19 + 23 **74**

Write *regular* or *irregular* for each figure.

11. 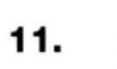  **irregular**
12.  **irregular**
13. 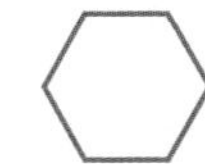 **regular**

Find each missing number.

14. 12 in. = **1** ft
15. **1** yd = 3 ft
16. 36 in. = **1** yd
17. 7 km = **7,000** m
18. 3 m = **300** cm
19. 500 cm = **5** m

Write About It

20. How are regular polygons and irregular polygons the same? How are they different? Explain your reasoning. ***See Additional Answers.***

Facts Practice, See Page 668.

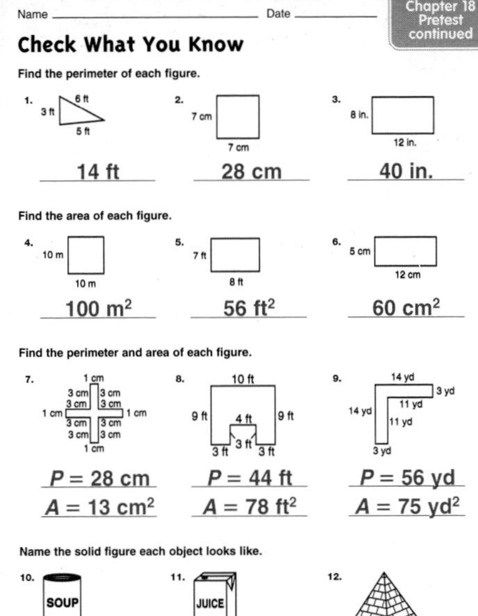

Chapter 18 New Content Pretest

Chapter 18 Pretest continued

Name ________ Date ________

Check What You Know

Find the perimeter of each figure.

1. (3 ft, 6 ft, 5 ft) **14 ft**
2. (7 cm, 7 cm) **28 cm**
3. (8 in., 12 in.) **40 in.**

Find the area of each figure.

4. (10 m, 10 m) **100 m²**
5. (7 ft, 8 ft) **56 ft²**
6. (5 cm, 12 cm) **60 cm²**

Find the perimeter and area of each figure.

7. **P = 28 cm**, **A = 13 cm²**
8. **P = 44 ft**, **A = 78 ft²**
9. **P = 56 yd**, **A = 75 yd²**

Name the solid figure each object looks like.

10. SOUP **cylinder**
11. JUICE **rectangular prism**
12. **square pyramid**

Go on

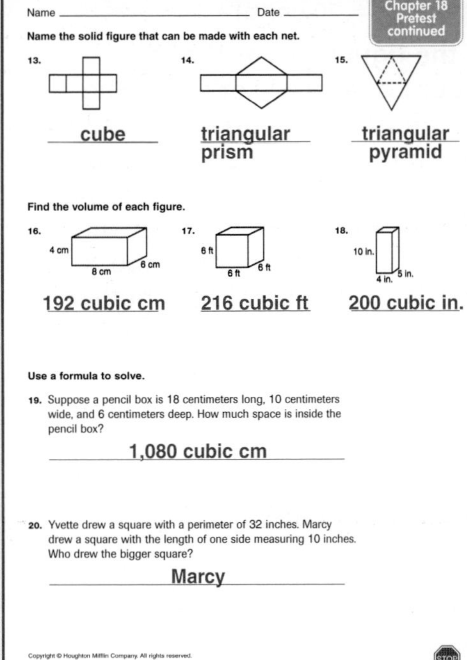

Chapter 18 New Content Pretest

Chapter 18 Pretest continued

Name ________ Date ________

Name the solid figure that can be made with each net.

13. **cube**
14. **triangular prism**
15. **triangular pyramid**

Find the volume of each figure.

16. (4 cm, 8 cm, 6 cm) **192 cubic cm**
17. (6 ft, 6 ft, 6 ft) **216 cubic ft**
18. (10 in., 4 in., 5 in.) **200 cubic in.**

Use a formula to solve.

19. Suppose a pencil box is 18 centimeters long, 10 centimeters wide, and 6 centimeters deep. How much space is inside the pencil box? **1,080 cubic cm**

20. Yvette drew a square with a perimeter of 32 inches. Marcy drew a square with the length of one side measuring 10 inches. Who drew the bigger square? **Marcy**

STOP

Use What You Know

Use this page for informal assessment and review of prerequisite skills.

- Items 1–4: Use math vocabulary
- Items 5–7: Multiply by one- or two-digit numbers
- Items 8–10: Add three or more addends
- Items 11–13, 20: Identify and describe regular and irregular figures
- Items 14–16: Convert among customary units of length
- Items 17–19: Convert among metric units of length

Customize Your Instruction

Use the Chapter Pretest in the Unit Resource folder to help customize and pace instruction.

Objectives and Resources

► Prerequisite Skills Pretest

- Items 1-3: Find perimeter of a figure
- Items 4-6: Find area of a figure
- Items 7-9: Multiply and add numbers.

► New Content Pretest

- Items 1–9: Find perimeter and area.
- Items 10–15: Identify, classify, and describe solid figures.
- Items 16–18: Determine volume of solid figures.
- Items 19–20: Solve problems.

► For Students Having Difficulty

- *Ways to Success* CD-ROM: 18A–18C
- *Ways to Success* Skillsheets 150–152

► For Students Having Success

- Enrichment 18.1–18.7

► For Mathematically Promising Students

Explore: Perimeter and Area, page 103, after Lesson 1

Extend: Mowing Lawn Areas, page 105, after Lesson 3

Connect: More Prisms, page 107, after Lesson 5

Hands On Lesson 18.1

Explore Perimeter and Area

Planning

Lesson Objective Use models to explore perimeter and area.

Technology Resources

- *Ways to Success* CD-ROM 18.1
- Education Place: Extra Practice, eGlossary, eGames www.eduplace.com/map

Lesson 18.1 Transparency

Problem of the Day

Xavier drew a square whose area and perimeter have the same number of units. What size is the square? (4 × 4)

Spiral Review

Solve.

1. 8 × 8 (64)
2. 12 × 12 (144)
3. 30 × 30 (900)
4. 700 × 700 (490,000)
5. 25 × 25 (625)

Lesson Quiz

Use grid paper to solve each problem.

1. Draw a rectangle with an area of 28 square units and a perimeter greater than 28 units. (1 × 28 or 2 × 14)
2. Draw a rectangle with an area of 30 square units and a perimeter less than 30 units. (5 × 6 or 10 × 3)

NCTM Standards

Geometry: Identify, compare, and analyze attributes of two- and three-dimensional shapes and develop vocabulary to describe the attributes.
Measurement: Select and apply appropriate standard units and tools to measure length, area, volume, weight, time, temperature, and the size of angles.

Getting Started

Building Math Vocabulary

perimeter the distance around a figure

area the number of square units in a region

Introduce the terms ***perimeter*** and ***area.*** Define perimeter as the distance around the outside of a figure. List synonyms for the general meaning of *area* as the number of square units that cover a figure.

Discuss Perimeter and Area Models of Rectangles

Whole Class	15 minutes
Objective	Model perimeter and area.
Materials	Centimeter Grid Transparency
Visual, Auditory	

- Draw a 5 × 5 figure *B*, 7 × 3 *C*, and 4 × 6 *D*.
- Display the transparency. **What shape is figure *B*?** (square) **What is the perimeter, or distance around, *B*?** (20 cm) Have a volunteer count the number of units around *B*. Write *P* = 20 units below *B*.
- Repeat for figures *C* and *D*. **What do you notice about the perimeters of figures *B, C,* and *D*?** (They are all the same, *P* = 20 units.)
- **Do the figures cover the same amount of space? Let's see. The number of square units needed to cover a figure is called the *area*. How many square units cover figure *B*?** Have a student count the number of square units inside *B*. Write *A* = *25 square units* below the square. Repeat for *C* and *D*. (*A* = 21 sq. units; *A* = 24 sq. units)
- Tell students that in this lesson they are going to explore rectangular arrays on grid paper to learn about perimeter and area.

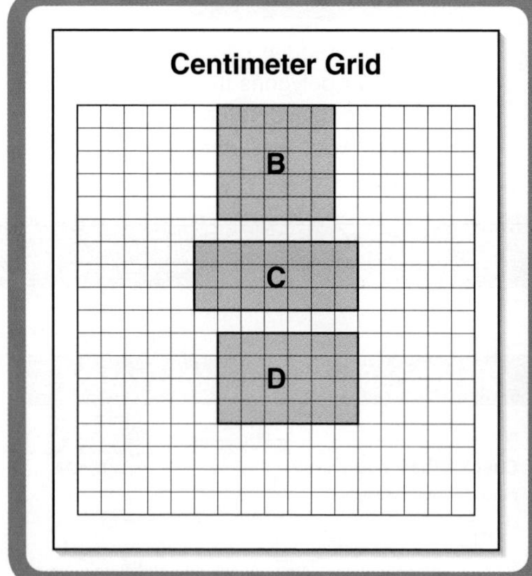

Differentiated Instruction

English Learners

Individuals	10 minutes
Objective	Differentiate between perimeter and area.
Materials	Student page 453, two colors of colored pencils
Tactual, Visual	

Early Production

- Students may need help differentiating between perimeter and area.
- For ***On Your Own,*** have students label the perimeters and areas of all objects. They should use one color to outline all perimeters and another color to shade in all areas.
- Have them verbalize while visualizing their answers.

Intermediate/Advanced

- English Learner Resource 18.1
- English Learner Handbook

Intervention

Whole Class	5 minutes
Objective	Discuss arrays.
Materials	3 × 5 grid paper rectangle
Visual, Auditory	

- Review the word *array* as a layout in equal columns and rows. Draw an array of 15 stars in 3 rows of 5 stars per row.
- Display the grid paper rectangle. **Is this an array? Explain.** (Yes, it has boxes or squares in equal columns and rows.)

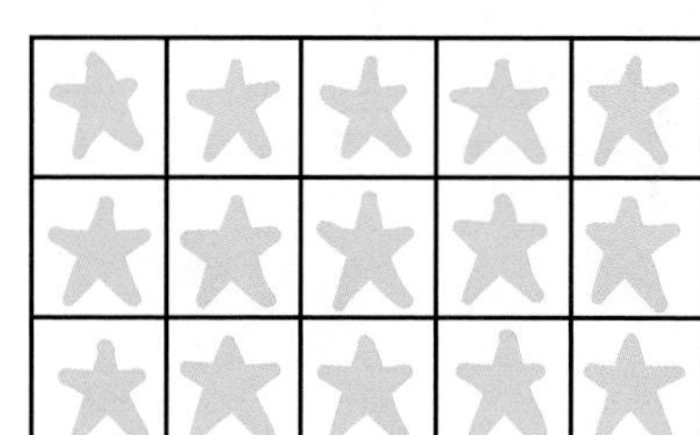

Other Resources

- *Ways to Success* CD-ROM 18.1

Inclusion

Individuals	10 minutes
Objective	Model perimeter and area.
Materials	Grid paper, poster-board rectangles, two colors of crayons
Tactual, Visual	

- Have students trace the rectangles onto grid paper, aligning sides along grid lines. With one color, have them mark off and count the units around the edge for the perimeter.
- With the other color, have them shade and count the squares inside for the area.

Alternate Teaching Strategy

- Have pairs of students cut one-centimeter squares from Learning Tool 27.
- Have one partner draw a square or rectangle on a piece of centimeter grid paper. Then have the other partner lay squares over it. Students work together to find the perimeter and area of the square or rectangle. Partners trade roles and repeat the activity.

❶ Introduce

On the board draw a square with a heavy outline. Trace your finger around the edge and explain that perimeter measures the border of a figure. Then lightly shade the inside of the square as you explain area measures the inside of a figure. Explain that the lesson will describe both ways of measuring geometric figures.

❷ Teach

Work Together

- **For Step 1, how do we get a perimeter of 12 units?** (Count the units of all of the sides.)
- **For Step 2, why is area described in square units?** (because square units will cover the surface and linear units won't)
- Discuss students' responses in **Step 3. What conclusion can you make about the relationship between perimeter and area?** (Figures with the same perimeter can be different shapes and have different areas.)

Explore Perimeter and Area

Objective Use models to explore perimeter and area.

Vocabulary
perimeter
area

Materials
grid paper
(Learning Tool 27)

Work Together

Does the **perimeter**, or distance around a figure, determine the number of square units needed to cover the figure?

Work with a partner to find out.

STEP 1 Look at the figures at the right. Find the perimeter of each figure by counting the number of units around the outside of the figure.

- Record your answers in a table like the one below.

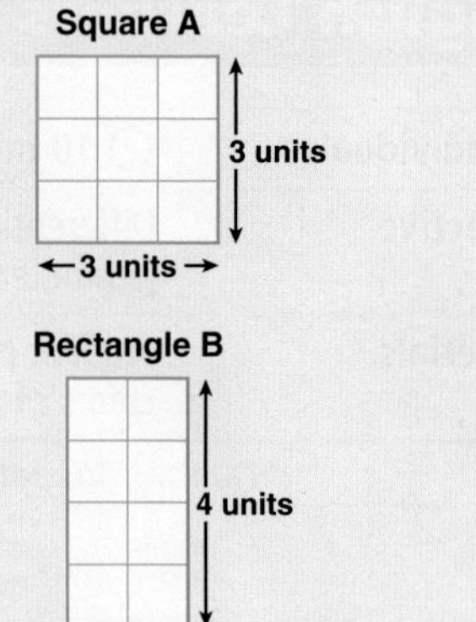

Figure	Perimeter	Area
Square A	12 units	■ square units 9
Rectangle B	■ units 12	■ square units 8

STEP 2 Now find the number of square units needed to cover each of the figures.

The number of square units needed to cover a figure is the **area** of the figure.

- Count to find the area of each figure.
- Record your answers in your table.

STEP 3 Look at your table.

- Can a square have the same perimeter as a rectangle? **yes**
- Can rectangles and squares with the same perimeter have different areas? **yes**

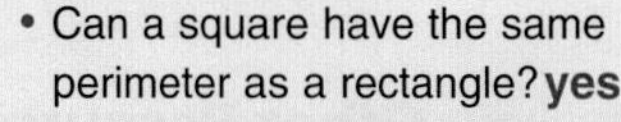

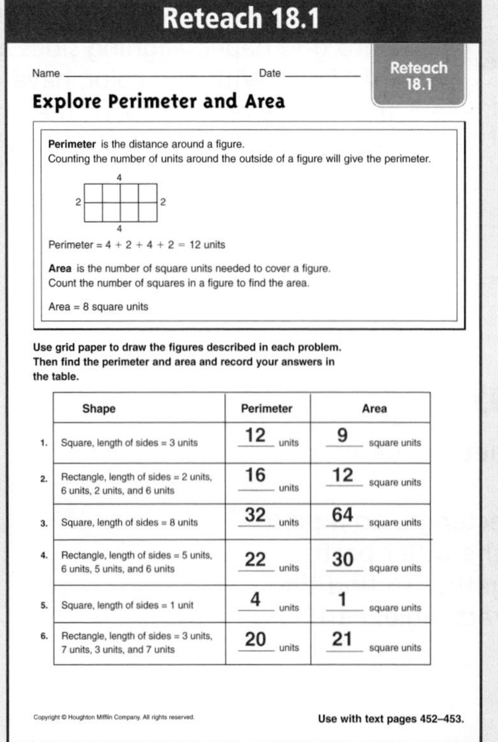

Reteach 18.1

Name ______________ Date ________

Reteach 18.1

Explore Perimeter and Area

Perimeter is the distance around a figure.
Counting the number of units around the outside of a figure will give the perimeter.

Perimeter = 4 + 2 + 4 + 2 = 12 units

Area is the number of square units needed to cover a figure.
Count the number of squares in a figure to find the area.

Area = 8 square units

Use grid paper to draw the figures described in each problem. Then find the perimeter and area and record your answers in the table.

	Shape	Perimeter	Area
1.	Square, length of sides = 3 units	12 units	9 square units
2.	Rectangle, length of sides = 2 units, 6 units, 2 units, and 6 units	16 units	12 square units
3.	Square, length of sides = 8 units	32 units	64 square units
4.	Rectangle, length of sides = 5 units, 6 units, 5 units, and 6 units	22 units	30 square units
5.	Square, length of sides = 1 unit	4 units	1 square units
6.	Rectangle, length of sides = 3 units, 7 units, 3 units, and 7 units	20 units	21 square units

Use with text pages 452–453.

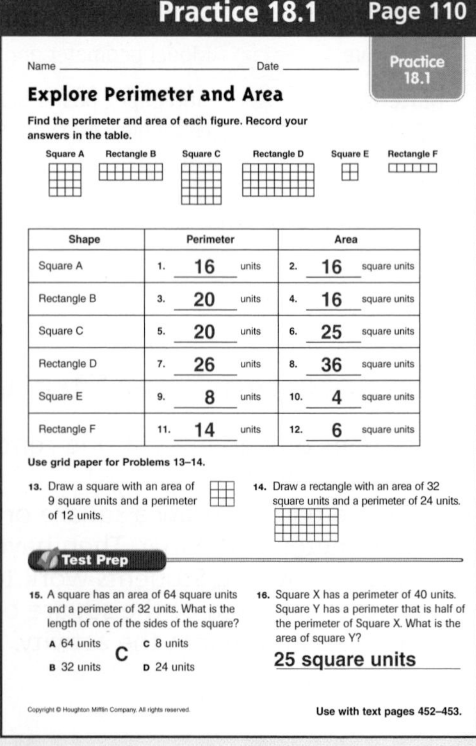

Practice 18.1 Page 110

Name ______________ Date ________

Practice 18.1

Explore Perimeter and Area

Find the perimeter and area of each figure. Record your answers in the table.

Square A Rectangle B Square C Rectangle D Square E Rectangle F

Shape	Perimeter	Area
Square A	1. 16 units	2. 16 square units
Rectangle B	3. 20 units	4. 16 square units
Square C	5. 20 units	6. 25 square units
Rectangle D	7. 26 units	8. 36 square units
Square E	9. 8 units	10. 4 square units
Rectangle F	11. 14 units	12. 6 square units

Use grid paper for Problems 13–14.

13. Draw a square with an area of 9 square units and a perimeter of 12 units.

14. Draw a rectangle with an area of 32 square units and a perimeter of 24 units.

Test Prep

15. A square has an area of 64 square units and a perimeter of 32 units. What is the length of one of the sides of the square?
   A 64 units B 32 units C 8 units D 24 units
   C

16. Square X has a perimeter of 40 units. Square Y has a perimeter that is half of the perimeter of Square X. What is the area of square Y?
   25 square units

Use with text pages 452–453.

On Your Own

Find the perimeter and area of each figure. Record your answers in a table like this:

	Figure	Perimeter	Area	
1.	Rectangle C	▒ units **20**	▒ square units	**16**
2.	Square D	▒ units **16**	▒ square units	**16**
3.	Rectangle E	▒ units **34**	▒ square units	**16**

Rectangle C

Square D

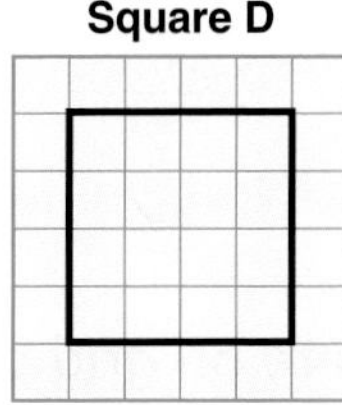

Rectangle E

Use your table to answer these questions.

4. Can a square have the same area as a rectangle? **yes**
5. Can rectangles and squares with the same area have different perimeters? **yes**

Use grid paper for Problems 6–8. ***Check students' drawings.***

6. Draw a rectangle with an area of 20 square units and a perimeter greater than 20 units. ***Possible answer:*** **2 by 10 rectangle**
7. Draw a rectangle with an area of 18 square units and a perimeter of 18 units. **3 by 6 rectangle**
8. **Analyze** If you double the length and width of a figure will its area double also? Double the length and width of figures C, D, and E above. What can you conclude? **Not necessarily; *Possible answer:* When you double the length and width, the area becomes 4 times larger.**

Talk About It • Write About It

You learned how perimeter and area can be measured.

9. How are perimeter and area different? **Perimeter is the distance around, area is the surface covered.**
10. Suppose two figures have different shapes. If one figure has a greater perimeter than the other, does it also have a greater area? Explain your thinking.

10. Not necessarily. *Possible answer:* Look at Rectangles C, D, and E above. Rectangles C and E have a greater perimeter than Rectangle D, but their areas are all equal.

3 Practice

On Your Own

Select from **Problems 1–10** as independent work.

- ***Problems 1–3*** You might have students include the data for figures *C-E* on the same table they began earlier in the lesson.
- ***Problem 8*** Have students test their conclusions using grid paper. Invite volunteers to share their work and the proof they found to support it.

4 Assess & Close

Math Talk in Action

- **What connection is there between perimeter and area?** (Both are measures of geometric figures.)
- **What are some real-life applications of area and perimeter?** (Accept all reasonable responses.)

Math Journal Prompt

Have students write about how to describe and find the area and perimeter of a 6 × 7 rectangle.

Lesson Quiz

Use the quiz on Lesson Transparency 18.1.

Test Prep & Spiral Review

Use Test Prep Transparency 18.1.

Enrichment 18.1

Name ______ Date ______ Enrichment 18.1

On the Farm

Farmer Mathman wants to redesign his farm. The table lists the number of each type of animal he has. He needs to build pens for each type of animal. Each animal gets one square unit in a pen. Farmer Mathman only likes rectangular pens. Help Farmer Mathman design pens for his farm. Use the table below to help guide you. Draw your answers on grid paper.

Animals on Farmer Mathman's Farm				
Animal	cows	horses	chickens	sheep
Number	12	8	24	16

1. How many ways can Farmer Mathman make a pen for the chickens? Draw all the possible rectangular pens on grid paper. **4 ways; 1 × 24, 2 × 12, 3 × 8, 4 × 6; Check students drawings.**
2. Farmer Mathman has 16 units of fencing to make a pen for the cows. Draw all the possible ways he can design the cow pen on grid paper, using all the fencing. **2 × 6**
3. Draw all the possible pens he can build for the horses on grid paper. Which pen would use the least amount of fencing? **1 × 8 and 2 × 4; The pen that is 2 feet wide and 4 feet long will use the least amount of fencing.**
4. Can he build a square pen for any of the animals? If so, which type of animal or animals? **Yes; he can build a square pen for the sheep with each side being 4 units long.**

Check students' drawings; size of pens should be the dimensions listed.

 Use with text pages 452–453.

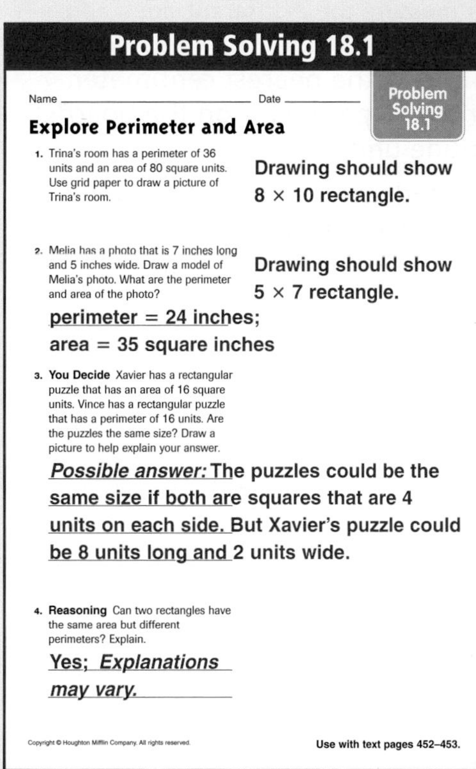

Problem Solving 18.1

Name ______ Date ______ Problem Solving 18.1

Explore Perimeter and Area

1. Trina's room has a perimeter of 36 units and an area of 80 square units. Use grid paper to draw a picture of Trina's room. **Drawing should show 8 × 10 rectangle.**
2. Melia has a photo that is 7 inches long and 5 inches wide. Draw a model of Melia's photo. What are the perimeter and area of the photo? **Drawing should show 5 × 7 rectangle. perimeter = 24 inches; area = 35 square inches**
3. **You Decide** Xavier has a rectangular puzzle that has an area of 16 square units. Vince has a rectangular puzzle that has a perimeter of 16 units. Are the puzzles the same size? Draw a picture to help explain your answer. ***Possible answer:*** **The puzzles could be the same size if both are squares that are 4 units on each side. But Xavier's puzzle could be 8 units long and 2 units wide.**
4. **Reasoning** Can two rectangles have the same area but different perimeters? Explain. **Yes; *Explanations may vary.***

 Use with text pages 452–453.

Homework 18.1 Page 110

Name ______ Date ______ Homework 18.1

Explore Perimeter and Area

Solve.

Do the rectangles have the same perimeter?
Do the rectangles have the same area?

5 units / 2 units — 4 units / 3 units

Find the perimeter and area of each rectangle.

Length	Width	Perimeter	Area
5 units	2 units	14 units	10 square units
4 units	3 units	14 units	12 square units

The rectangles have the same perimeter.
The rectangles do not have the same area.

1. Draw two rectangles with the same area but with different perimeters. **Check students' drawings.**
2. Draw two rectangles with different areas but the same perimeter. **Check students' drawings.**

Problem Solving

3. Draw a rectangle with an area of 24 square units and a perimeter greater than 24 units. **Check students' drawings.**

 Use with text pages 452–453.

Hands On Lesson 18.2

Algebra: Perimeter

Planning

Lesson Objective Find perimeters of polygons.

Technology Resources

- Audio Tutor **2**/15 Listen and Understand
- *Ways to Success* CD-ROM 18.2
- Education Place: Extra Practice, eGlossary, eGames
  www.eduplace.com/map

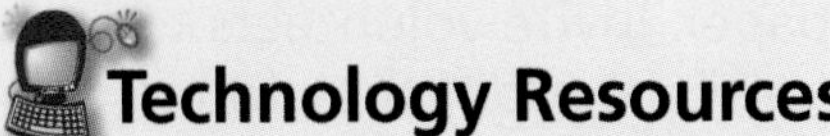

Lesson 18.2 Transparency

Problem of the Day

A rectangle is twice as long as it is wide. Its perimeter is 42 cm. Find the length and width of the rectangle. (l = 14 cm; w = 7 cm)

Spiral Review

Use grid paper to solve each problem.

1. Draw a rectangle with an area of 14 square units and a perimeter of 30 units. (1 × 14)
2. Draw a rectangle with an area of 26 square units and a perimeter of 30 units. (2 × 13)

Lesson Quiz

Write a formula to find each perimeter. Then solve.

1. regular octagon with sides 7 cm long ($P = 8 \times s$; $P = 56$ cm)
2. regular pentagon with sides 8 cm long ($P = 5 \times s$; $P = 40$ cm)
3. equilateral triangle with sides 9 in. long ($P = 3 \times s$; $P = 27$ in.)

NCTM Standards

Geometry: Identify, compare, and analyze attributes of two- and three-dimensional shapes and develop vocabulary to describe the attributes.
Measurement: Select and apply appropriate standard units and tools to measure length, area, volume, weight, time, temperature, and the size of angles.
Algebra: Represent the idea of a variable as an unknown quantity using a letter or a symbol.

Getting Started

Building Math Vocabulary

perimeter the distance around a figure

Review the meaning of ***perimeter*** by displaying a 6 × 6 square on grid paper.

- **What is the perimeter of this figure?** (24 units)
- **How do you find perimeter?** (Find the lengths of all sides of a figure.)

Find Perimeter

Whole Class	10 minutes
Objective	Find the perimeter of a CD jewel case
Materials	CD jewel case, centimeter ruler
Visual, Auditory	

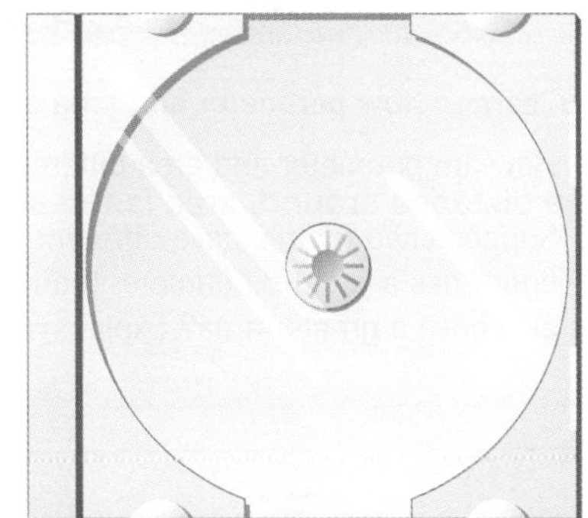

- Display the CD case. **This case has no grid lines on it, but it still has a perimeter. How could we find the perimeter?** (Students should suggest using a ruler to measure the length of the sides.)
- **What shape is the CD case?** (rectangle) **Do we have to measure all four sides to get the data we need to find the perimeter? Explain.** (No, just measure the 2 different sides, add, and double.) Model this method. Round to the nearest centimeter. Write the perimeter on the board; include units.
- Tell students that in this lesson they are going to explore different ways to find perimeter.

Differentiated Instruction

English Learners

Individuals	10 minutes
Objective	Find the perimeter of a polygon.
Materials	Student page 454
Tactual, Visual	

Early Production

- Give students additional support with the activity on Student page 454.
- Change or add the following steps: Have students use a ruler to measure the sides. Then have them draw a picture and label the length and width measurements. Students should find the perimeter using Way 1 and Way 2. Finally, have the students read their answers aloud.

Intermediate/Advanced

- English Learner Resource 18.2
- English Learner Handbook

Intervention

Whole Class	5 minutes
Objective	Find perimeters of rectangles.
Materials	Assorted grid-paper rectangles
Visual, Auditory	

- Display grid-paper rectangles. Ask students to explain how to find the perimeter of the figures. (Find the total length around the outside.)
- Have students find the perimeter of the rectangles you prepared. **How did you find the perimeter?** Invite volunteers to explain their methods. Encourage students to respect alternate strategies.

Other Resources

- *Ways to Success* CD-ROM 18.2

Early Finishers

Pairs	20 minutes
Objective	Find perimeter of a classroom
Materials	Rulers
Kinesthetic, Visual	

- Have pairs of students determine the perimeter of the classroom. They can measure in metric or customary units.
- Partners should first estimate the perimeter, and then measure. Have them record partial measures, as needed, and then find the total perimeter.

Real-World Connection

Materials: checkerboards

- Display several standard checkerboards of various sizes. Using the given square as the unit of measure, have students find their perimeters and areas (excluding borders). ($A = 64$ square units; $P = 32$ units)
- Discuss using non-standard units: all checkerboards have the same area and perimeter in square units, yet different sizes. Talk about alternative standard and non-standard units.

Facts Practice

- As students are lining up, have the first student say a one-digit number, have the second students say a one-digit number, and have the third student find the product of those two numbers. Repeat until all students are in line.

❶ Introduce

Show students a grid-paper rectangle. Ask students to explain how to find the perimeter around the figure using addition. Encourage students to identify both methods they are fimiliar with: adding the length of each side and using a formula to find the perimeter.

❷ Teach

Learn About It

- **How is Paul's border a perimeter?** (total length around the rectangular opening of the diorama)
- **Look at Way 1. What do the letters in the formula mean?** (length + width + length + width)
- **Look at Way 2. How is this formula different from the other one?** (It doubles the length and doubles the width.)
- Have students complete the activity. Invite them to share their findings.

Guided Practice

Have students complete **Exercises 1–4** as you observe. Remind them to use the ***Ask Yourself*** questions to help. Give students the opportunity to talk about ***Explain Your Thinking.***

❸ Practice

Practice and Problem Solving

Select from **Exercises 5–17** as independent work.

Common Error

- **Omitting labels** Some students may forget to include units with their measurements.
- **Intervention** Tell students that because a perimeter is a particular measurement, it must have both a number and a unit to be complete. Remind students to review their answers to check that each perimeter includes the unit they used.

Hands On Lesson 2

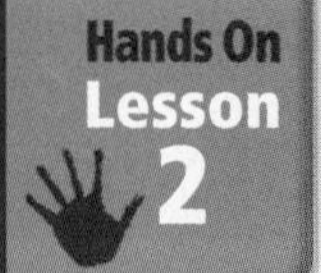

Audio Tutor 2/15 Listen and Understand

Algebra

Perimeter

Objective Find perimeters of polygons.

Vocabulary
perimeter

Materials
ruler

Learn About It

Paul is building a diorama. He plans to glue a strip of leather around the edge. The diorama is 12 inches long and 8 inches wide. How many inches of leather edging will he need?

To find the length of the edges, find the **perimeter** or distance around the diorama.

Different Ways to Find Perimeter

Way 1 You can add the lengths of the sides.

Perimeter $= l + w + l + w$

$P = 12 \text{ in.} + 8 \text{ in.} + 12 \text{ in.} + 8 \text{ in.}$

$P = 40 \text{ in.}$

Way 2 You can use the formula to find the perimeter of a rectangle.

Perimeter $= (2 \times l) + (2 \times w)$

$P = (2 \times 12 \text{ in.}) + (2 \times 8 \text{ in.})$

$P = 24 \text{ in.} + 16 \text{ in.}$

$P = 40 \text{ in.}$

Remember
Do what is in parentheses first.

Solution: Paul needs 40 inches of leather edging.

Estimate and then find the perimeter of objects.

STEP 1 Choose three objects in your classroom.

STEP 2 Estimate what the perimeter of each might be. Record your estimate.

STEP 3 Use your ruler to find the exact perimeter. Record the actual perimeter.

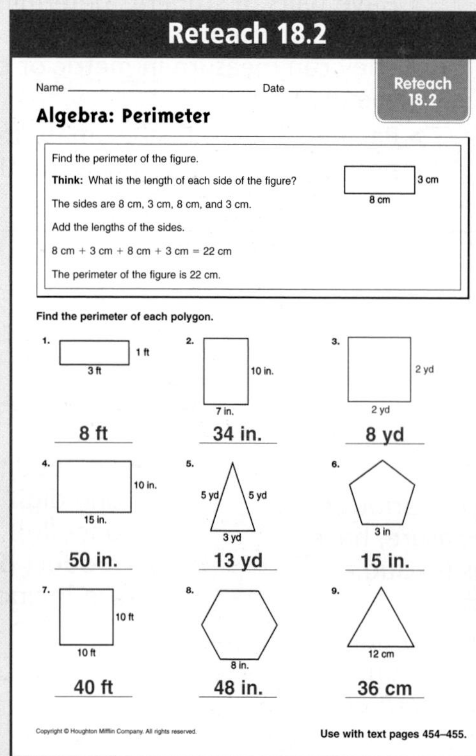

Reteach 18.2

Name ______ Date ______ Reteach 18.2

Algebra: Perimeter

Find the perimeter of the figure.

Think: What is the length of each side of the figure?

The sides are 8 cm, 3 cm, 8 cm, and 3 cm.

Add the lengths of the sides.

8 cm + 3 cm + 8 cm + 3 cm = 22 cm

The perimeter of the figure is 22 cm.

Find the perimeter of each polygon.

1. (3 ft, 1 ft) 8 ft
2. (7 in., 10 in.) 34 in.
3. (2 yd, 2 yd) 8 yd
4. (15 in., 10 in.) 50 in.
5. (5 yd, 5 yd, 3 yd) 13 yd
6. (3 in) 15 in.
7. (10 ft, 10 ft) 40 ft
8. (8 in.) 48 in.
9. (12 cm) 36 cm

Use with text pages 454–455.

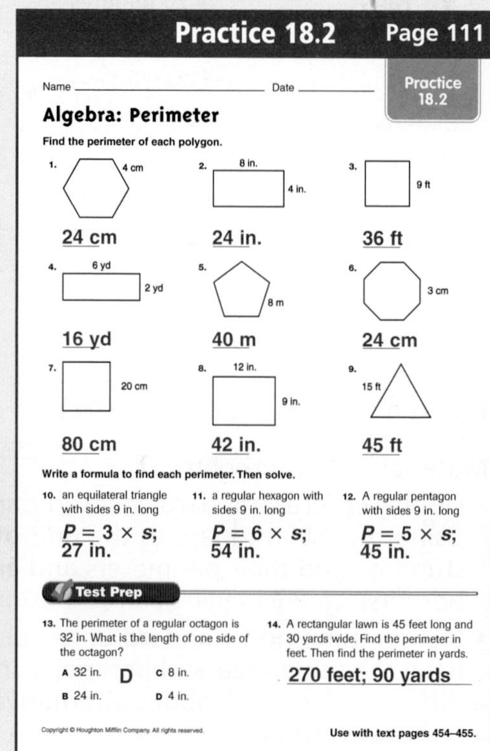

Practice 18.2 Page 111

Name ______ Date ______ Practice 18.2

Algebra: Perimeter

Find the perimeter of each polygon.

1. (4 cm) 24 cm
2. (8 in., 4 in.) 24 in.
3. (9 ft) 36 ft
4. (6 yd, 2 yd) 16 yd
5. (8 m) 40 m
6. (3 cm) 24 cm
7. (20 cm) 80 cm
8. (12 in., 9 in.) 42 in.
9. (15 ft) 45 ft

Write a formula to find each perimeter. Then solve.

10. an equilateral triangle with sides 9 in. long
$P = 3 \times s$; 27 in.
11. a regular hexagon with sides 9 in. long
$P = 6 \times s$; 54 in.
12. A regular pentagon with sides 9 in. long
$P = 5 \times s$; 45 in.

Test Prep

13. The perimeter of a regular octagon is 32 in. What is the length of one side of the octagon? D
A 32 in. B 24 in. C 8 in. D 4 in.
14. A rectangular lawn is 45 feet long and 30 yards wide. Find the perimeter in feet. Then find the perimeter in yards.
270 feet; 90 yards

Use with text pages 454–455.

Guided Practice

Find the perimeter of each polygon.

1. 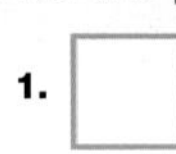 4 in. **16 in.**

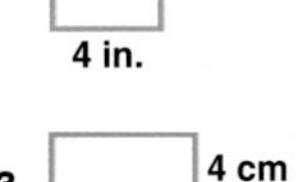

2. 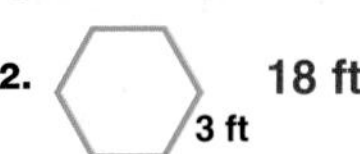 3 ft **18 ft**

3. 4 cm, 8 cm **24 cm**

4. 3 cm, 7 cm, 5 cm **15 cm**

> **Ask Yourself**
> - Is the figure a regular or irregular polygon?
> - Can I use a formula?

12. *Possible answer:* He can lay the piece of string on the outline and cut it where it meets. Then he can measure the string with the ruler.

Explain Your Thinking ▶ Write a formula for finding the perimeter of a square. $P = 4 \times s$

Practice and Problem Solving

Find the perimeter of each polygon.

5. 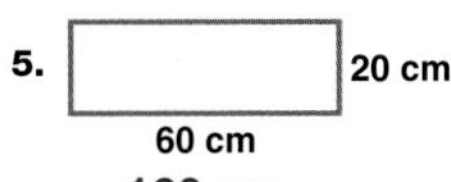 20 cm, 60 cm **160 cm**

6. 2 yd **10 yd**

7. 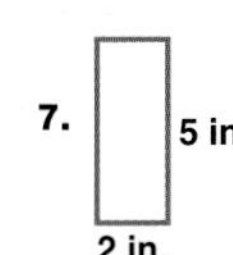 5 in., 2 in. **14 in.**

Write a formula to find each perimeter. Then solve.
Possible formulas given.

8. a regular pentagon with sides 8 cm long
9. a regular hexagon with sides 8 cm long
10. a regular octagon with sides 8 cm long

Solve. 8. $P = 5 \times s$, $P = 40$ cm 9. $P = 6 \times s$, $P = 48$ cm 10. $P = 8 \times s$, $P = 64$ cm

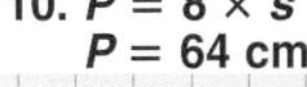

11. A rectangular room is 15 feet long and 7 yards wide. Find the perimeter in feet. Then find the perimeter in yards. **72 ft; 24 yd**

12. **Explain** Reggie is making sandals. He traced his foot on grid paper. How can he find its perimeter with a piece of string and a ruler? *See above.*

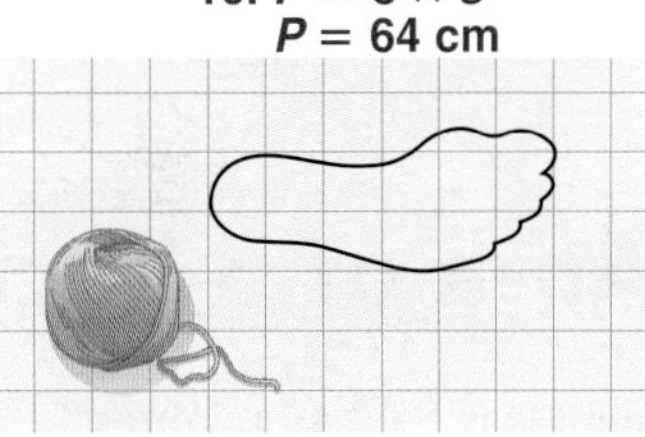

Mixed Review and Test Prep

Open Response

Write >, <, or = for each ●. (Ch. 3, Lesson 1)

13. 9 + 4 − 3 ● 7 + 8 **<**
14. 13 − 5 ● 2 + 6 **=**
15. 5 + 9 − 1 ● 4 + 8 **>**
16. 4 + 7 − 2 ● 5 + 8 − 3 **<**

Multiple Choice

17. The perimeter of a square is 36 cm. What is the length of one side of the square? (Ch. 18, Lesson 2)

A 4 cm **(C) 9 cm**
B 32 cm D 40 cm

Extra Practice See page 475, Set A.

- To help students write formulas to solve **Exercises 8–10,** review the meaning of *regular* and the number of sides of each polygon. Suggest that in their formulas they use the letter *s* to stand for the length of a side.
- ***Exercise 12*** You can have students do what Reggie did for their own feet.

4 Assess & Close

Math Talk in Action

- **What is a formula?** (a mathematical rule)
- **What must we include in all perimeter answers?** (a unit of measure)

Math Journal Prompt

Have students write a formula and apply it to find the perimeter of a square that measures 10 inches on each side. They can use the variable *s* to stand for *side*.

Lesson Quiz

Use the quiz on Lesson Transparency 18.2.

Test Prep & Spiral Review

Use Test Prep Transparency 18.2.

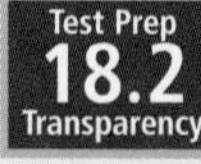

Enrichment 18.2

Name ______ Date ______ Enrichment 18.2

Plot My Perimeter

Draw each figure on the grid below and then answer each question. **Check students' drawings.**

1. I have a perimeter of 15. I am not a square. Each of my sides is 3 units long. What shape am I? **regular pentagon**
2. I am a rectangle with one side 4 units long and another side twice as long. What is my perimeter? **24 units**
3. I am a triangle with all my sides equal in length. My perimeter is less than 14 units but greater than 10 units. How long are my sides? **4 units**
4. I have a perimeter of 18 units. I am a rectangle. My length is 1 unit greater than my width. What are my dimensions? **5 units long, 4 units wide**
5. I am a regular hexagon with each side 4 units long. What is my perimeter? **24 units**
6. I have a perimeter of 20. What shape could I be? Give my dimensions. **Answers will vary.**
7. Draw as many shapes as you can with a perimeter of 24 units. **Drawings will vary.**
8. Draw as many shapes as you can with a perimeter of 16 units. **Drawings will vary.**

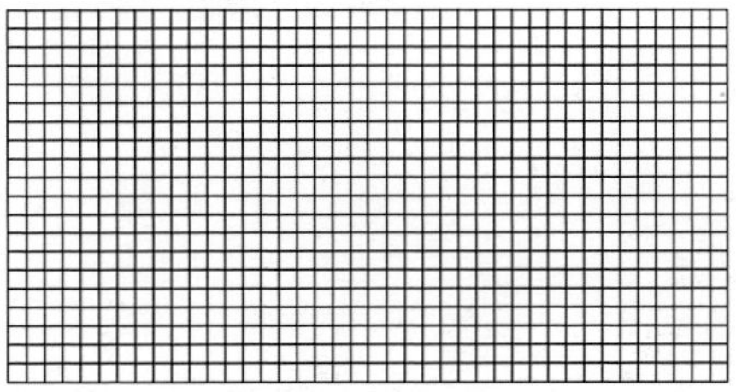

Use with text pages 454–455.

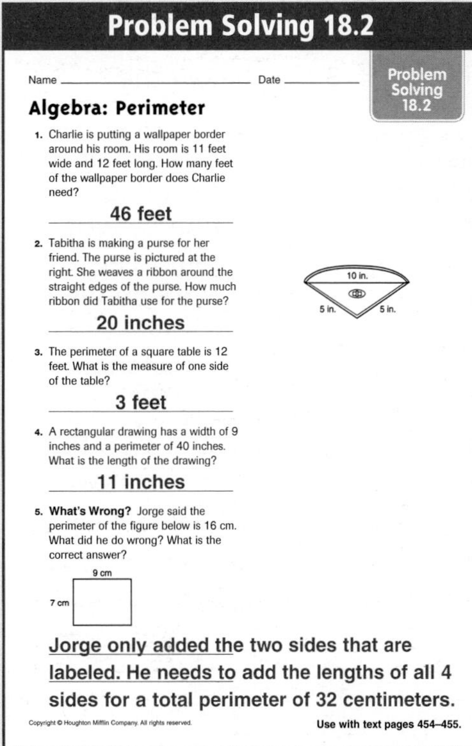

Problem Solving 18.2

Name ______ Date ______ Problem Solving 18.2

Algebra: Perimeter

1. Charlie is putting a wallpaper border around his room. His room is 11 feet wide and 12 feet long. How many feet of the wallpaper border does Charlie need? **46 feet**
2. Tabitha is making a purse for her friend. The purse is pictured at the right. She weaves a ribbon around the straight edges of the purse. How much ribbon did Tabitha use for the purse? **20 inches**
3. The perimeter of a square table is 12 feet. What is the measure of one side of the table? **3 feet**
4. A rectangular drawing has a width of 9 inches and a perimeter of 40 inches. What is the length of the drawing? **11 inches**
5. **What's Wrong?** Jorge said the perimeter of the figure below is 16 cm. What did he do wrong? What is the correct answer?

9 cm, 7 cm

Jorge only added the two sides that are labeled. He needs to add the lengths of all 4 sides for a total perimeter of 32 centimeters.

Use with text pages 454–455.

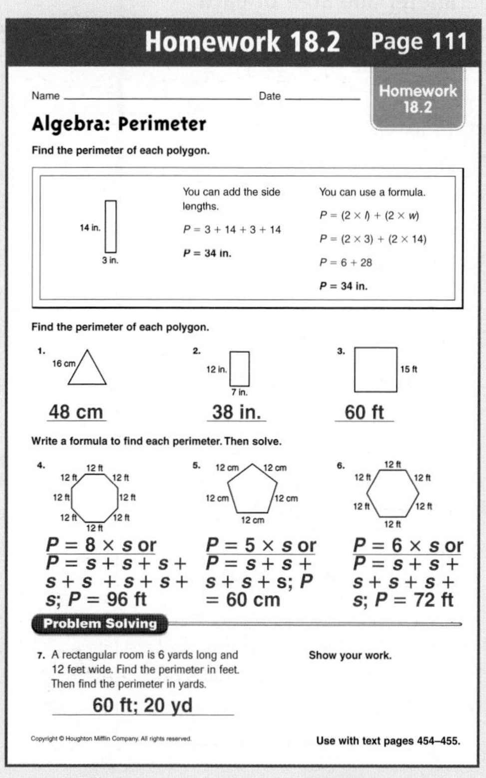

Homework 18.2 Page 111

Name ______ Date ______ Homework 18.2

Algebra: Perimeter

Find the perimeter of each polygon.

14 in., 3 in.

You can add the side lengths.
$P = 3 + 14 + 3 + 14$
$P = 34$ in.

You can use a formula.
$P = (2 \times l) + (2 \times w)$
$P = (2 \times 3) + (2 \times 14)$
$P = 6 + 28$
$P = 34$ in.

Find the perimeter of each polygon.

1. 16 cm **48 cm**
2. 12 in., 7 in. **38 in.**
3. 15 ft **60 ft**

Write a formula to find each perimeter. Then solve.

4. 12 ft **$P = 8 \times s$ or $P = s + s + s + s + s + s + s + s$; $P = 96$ ft**
5. 12 cm **$P = 5 \times s$ or $P = s + s + s + s + s$; $P = 60$ cm**
6. 12 ft **$P = 6 \times s$ or $P = s + s + s + s + s + s$; $P = 72$ ft**

Problem Solving

7. A rectangular room is 6 yards long and 12 feet wide. Find the perimeter in feet. Then find the perimeter in yards. Show your work. **60 ft; 20 yd**

Use with text pages 454–455.

Hands On Lesson 18.3

Algebra: Area

Planning

Lesson Objective Find the area of a rectangle.

Technology Resources

- Audio Tutor **2**/16 Listen and Understand
- *Ways to Success* CD-ROM 18.3
- *Ways to Assess* CD-ROM

Problem of the Day

Helen wants to cover her garden for the winter. To get the right amount of material, she must find the area of the space. Helen's garden is 12 feet long and 18 feet wide. What is its area? (216 square feet)

Spiral Review

Find each product.

1. 18 × 9 (162)
2. 11 × 25 (275)
3. 13 × 14 (182)
4. 24 × 36 (864)
5. 35 × 48 (1,680)

Lesson Quiz

Find the perimeter and area of each rectangle.

1. 12 yd long, 4 yd wide (P = 32 yd; A = 48 yd^2)
2. 6 in. long, 18 in. wide (P = 48 in.; A = 108 in.^{2})
3. 9 mm long, 22 mm wide (P = 62 mm; A = 198 mm^2)
4. 4 mi long, 19 mi wide (P = 46 mi; A = 76 mi^2)

NCTM Standards

Geometry: Analyze characteristics and properties of two- and three-dimensional shapes and develop mathematical arguments about geometric relationships.
Algebra: Express mathematical relationships using equations.
Measurement: Develop, understand, and use formulas to find the area of rectangles and related triangles and parallelograms.

Getting Started

Building Math Vocabulary

area the number of square units in a region

Explain that one way of finding the **area** of a geometric figure is to use a formula.

Review the meaning of a mathematical formula. Students may define it as an equation in which letters stand for certain values. To use the equation, students substitute numerical values for the letters and then perform the given operation(s).

Find Area of a Rectangle

Whole Class	10 minutes
Objective	Find the area of a rectangle.
Materials	Centimeter Grid Transparency
Visual, Auditory	

- Draw and label a rectangle 8 ft by 5 ft. **We can use a formula to find the area of a rectangle.** Write $A = l \times w$ below the rectangle. **What do you think the letters stand for?** (A = area; l = length; w = width)
- **What is the length of this rectangle?** (8 ft) Model how to substitute the number into the equation by writing $A = 8 \times w$ below the formula.
- **What is the width of this rectangle?** (5 ft) Substitute this number for the w in the equation by writing $A = 8 \times 5$. Ask a volunteer to find the product. (40) **How do we label the answer?** (in square feet) **So, what is the area of the rectangle?** (40 square feet) Write $A = 40\ ft^2$.
- Tell students that in this lesson they are going to explore different ways to find the area of a rectangle.

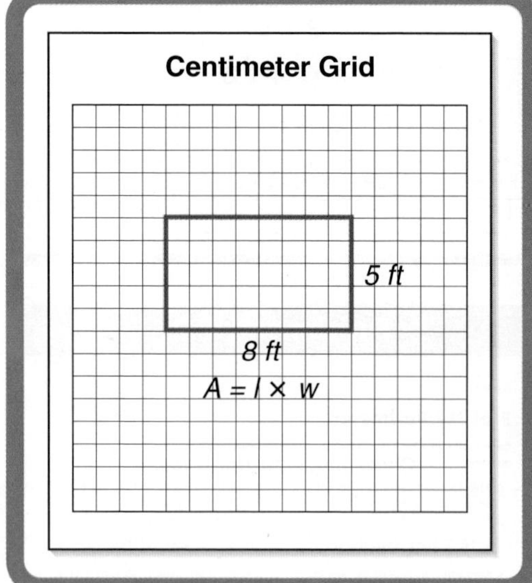

Differentiated Instruction

English Learners

Individuals	10 minutes
Objective	Find the area of a rectangle.
Materials	Student page 457
Auditory, Visual	

Early Production

- Model the first ***Guided Practice*** problem for students using Way 2. Then read the equation and answer aloud, putting emphasis on measurement units. For example: **3 *miles* times 2 *miles* equals *6 square miles.***
- Ask students to do the second problem independently in the same way.

Intermediate/Advanced

- English Learner Resource 18.3
- English Learner Handbook

Intervention

Whole Class	5 minutes
Objective	Find areas of rectangles.
Materials	Assorted grid paper rectangles
Visual, Auditory	

- Display grid-paper rectangles. Ask students to explain how to find the area of the figures. (Find the total number of squares the figure covers.)
- Have students find the area of the rectangles you prepared. **How did you find the area?** Invite volunteers to explain their methods. Encourage students to respect alternate strategies.

Other Resources

- *Ways to Success* CD-ROM 18.3

Gifted & Talented

Pairs	20 minutes
Objective	Find area of a classroom.
Materials	Rulers
Kinesthetic, Visual	

- Tell students that most house paint is sold by the gallon. Painters estimate 1 gallon of paint to cover about 400 square feet.
- Challenge students to estimate, then measure, to find the area of wall space in the classroom. Have them use this figure to decide how many gallons would be needed to paint the room.

Social Studies Connection

- A national park is land owned by the government. Some national parks are pieces of natural beauty, historic sites, or regions of special meaning.
- Tell students that land area is often given in acres. 640 acres = 1 square mile.
- Help students use an almanac to find the areas of national parks in your part of the country.

❶ Introduce

Draw a 4 × 4 square unit array on the board. Write the factors on each side. Ask students to identify how they use arrays to solve multiplication problems. Relate the square unit array to the formula for finding area.

❷ Teach

Learn About It

- Have a volunteer read the opening problem. **Why is this problem about area?** (Finding the amount of slate needed in square feet involves finding the area.)
- **Look at Way 1. What does the picture show?** (a diagram of the patio; each square stands for 1 ft²)
- **Look at Way 2. What data do we need to use the area formula.** (length, width) **Why do we multiply?** (to find the total of same-sized groups) **In what units is the area measured?** (square feet)
- **Look at *Another Example.* Why is there a different formula for the area of a square?** (Each side of a square is the same length.)

Common Error

- **Confusing operations** Students may perform the wrong operation when they find perimeter or area.
- **Intervention** Remind students of the array model of multiplication, which resembles a space covered by squares. This may help them remember to multiply when finding area.

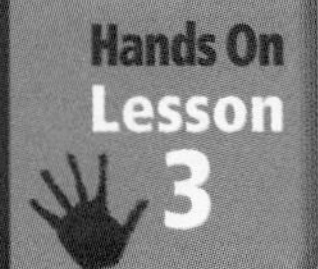

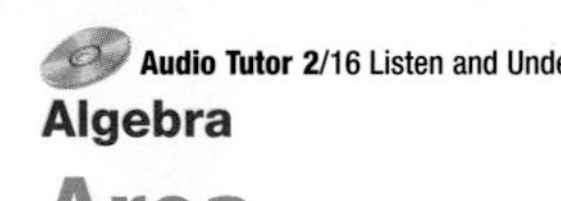

Audio Tutor 2/16 Listen and Understand

Algebra

Area

Objective Find the area of a rectangle.

Vocabulary
area

Materials
rulers

Learn About It

Jake's grandfather is building a patio. He wants to know how many square feet of slate he needs to order.

To find how much slate is needed, you need to find the **area** or square units within the patio. You can find area in two ways.

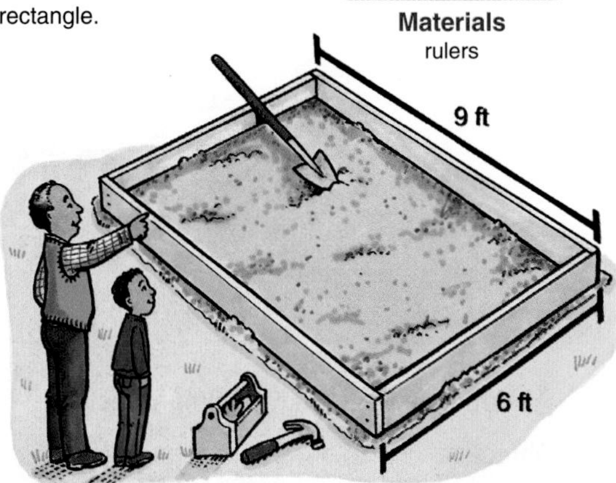

Different Ways to Find Area

Way ❶ You can draw a model and count the squares.

1	2	3	4	5	6	7	8	9
10	11	12	13	14	15	16	17	18
19	20	21	22	23	24	25	26	27
28	29	30	31	32	33	34	35	36
37	38	39	40	41	42	43	44	45
46	47	48	49	50	51	52	53	54

Each square is 1 square foot or 1 ft².

Way ❷ You can use the formula to find the area of a rectangle.

Area = length × width

Area = $l \times w$

$A = 9 \text{ ft} \times 6 \text{ ft}$

$A = 54 \text{ ft}^2$ or 54 square feet

Solution: The patio will be 54 square feet in area. So, he will need 54 square feet of slate.

Another Example

Area of a Square

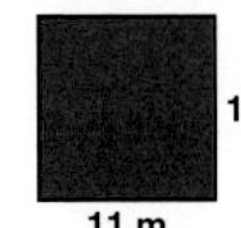

$A = s \times s$

$A = 11 \text{ m} \times 11 \text{ m}$

$A = 121 \text{ m}^2$

Remember
Each side of a square is the same length.

456

Reteach 18.3

Name ______ Date ______ Reteach 18.3

Algebra: Area

Find the area of the figure. (6 ft, 4 ft)

Think: What is the formula for the area of a rectangle?

Area = length × width
Area = $l \times w$
$A = 6 \text{ ft} \times 4 \text{ ft}$
$A = 24 \text{ ft}^2$

The area of the rectangle is 24 square feet.

Use a formula to find the area of each figure.

1. 2 cm, 4 cm — **8 cm²**
2. 6 ft, 8 ft — **48 ft²**
3. 4 cm, 4 cm — **16 cm²**
4. 7 ft, 3 ft — **21 ft²**
5. 9 m, 9 m — **81 m²**
6. 15 ft, 6 ft — **90 ft²**
7. 2 mm, 13 mm — **26 mm²**
8. 4 cm, 20 cm — **80 cm²**
9. 14 yd, 3 yd — **42 yd²**

 Use with text pages 456–458.

Practice 18.3 Page 112

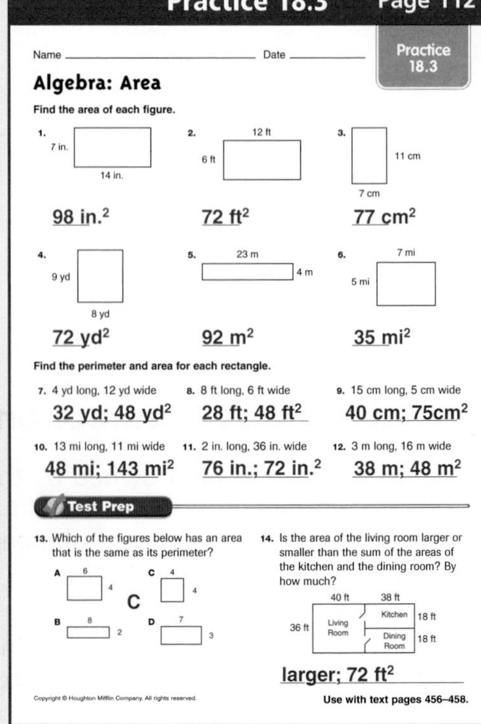

Name ______ Date ______ Practice 18.3

Algebra: Area

Find the area of each figure.

1. 7 in., 14 in. — **98 in.²**
2. 12 ft, 6 ft — **72 ft²**
3. 11 cm, 7 cm — **77 cm²**
4. 9 yd, 8 yd — **72 yd²**
5. 23 m, 4 m — **92 m²**
6. 7 mi, 5 mi — **35 mi²**

Find the perimeter and area for each rectangle.

7. 4 yd long, 12 yd wide — **32 yd; 48 yd²**
8. 8 ft long, 6 ft wide — **28 ft; 48 ft²**
9. 15 cm long, 5 cm wide — **40 cm; 75cm²**
10. 13 mi long, 11 mi wide — **48 mi; 143 mi²**
11. 2 in. long, 36 in. wide — **76 in.; 72 in.²**
12. 3 m long, 16 m wide — **38 m; 48 m²**

Test Prep

13. Which of the figures below has an area that is the same as its perimeter? A (6, 4) B (8, 2) C (4, 4) D (7, 3) — **C**
14. Is the area of the living room larger or smaller than the sum of the areas of the kitchen and the dining room? By how much? (40 ft, 38 ft, 36 ft, 18 ft, 18 ft; Living Room, Kitchen, Dining Room) — **larger; 72 ft²**

 Use with text pages 456–458.

Try this activity to estimate and find the area of objects.

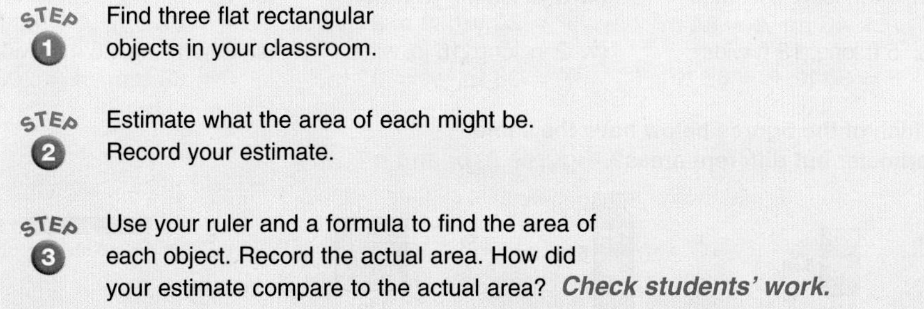

STEP 1 Find three flat rectangular objects in your classroom.

STEP 2 Estimate what the area of each might be. Record your estimate.

STEP 3 Use your ruler and a formula to find the area of each object. Record the actual area. How did your estimate compare to the actual area? *Check students' work.*

Guided Practice

Use a formula to find the area of each figure.

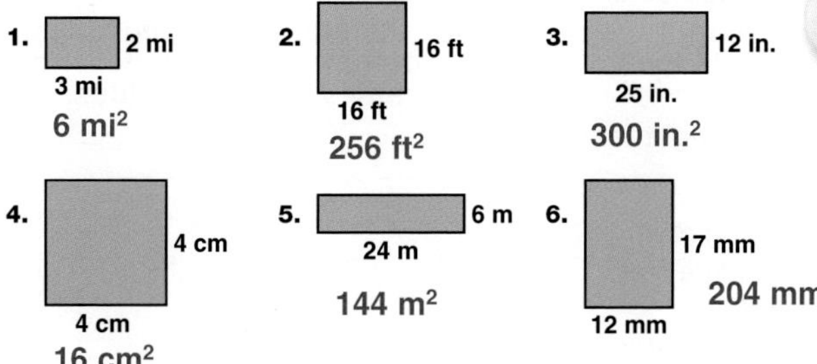

1. 2 mi, 3 mi — 6 mi²
2. 16 ft, 16 ft — 256 ft²
3. 12 in., 25 in. — 300 in.²
4. 4 cm, 4 cm — 16 cm²
5. 6 m, 24 m — 144 m²
6. 17 mm, 12 mm — 204 mm²

Ask Yourself

- What formula can I use?
- What unit do I need?

Explain Your Thinking ▶ How could you find the perimeter of a square that has an area of 25 square inches? **You know that 5 multiplied by itself is 25, so each side of the square is 5 inches. So, the perimeter is 4 x 5 = 20, or 20 inches.**

Practice and Problem Solving

Find the area of each figure.

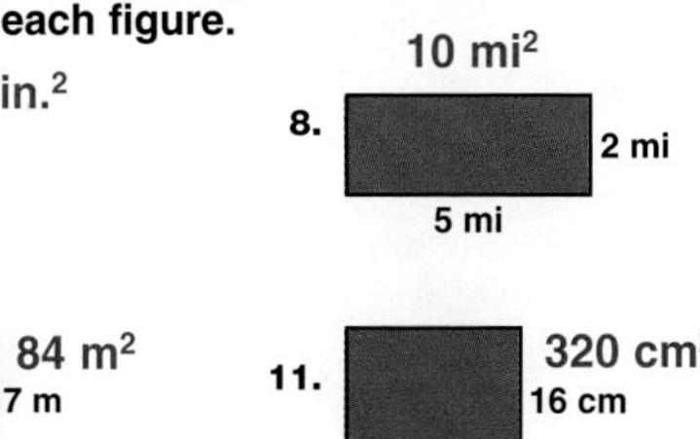

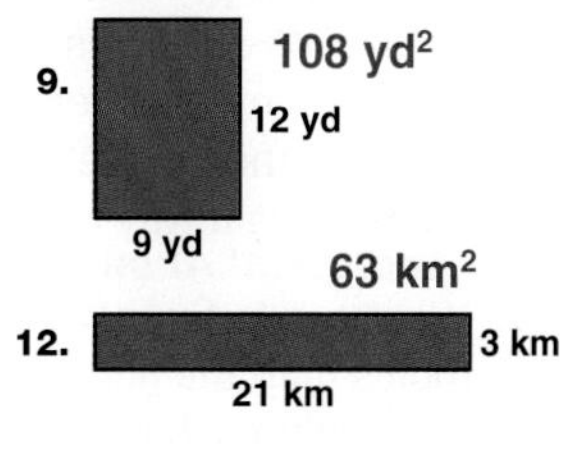

7. 14 in., 14 in. — 196 in.²
8. 2 mi, 5 mi — 10 mi²
9. 12 yd, 9 yd — 108 yd²
10. 7 m, 12 m — 84 m²
11. 16 cm, 20 cm — 320 cm²
12. 3 km, 21 km — 63 km²

- Have students try the activity on page 457. Have them record the information in a simple table that shows the length, width, and area of each object measured.

Guided Practice

Select from **Exercises 1–6** for students to complete as you observe. Remind them to use the *Ask Yourself* questions to help. Give students the opportunity to talk about the question in *Explain Your Thinking*.

3 Practice

Practice and Problem Solving

Select from **Exercises 7–26** as independent work.

- Remind students to label all solutions to area problems in square units.

Enrichment 18.3

Name ______________ Date ______ Enrichment 18.3

Greatest and Least Area

- Copy and cut out the cards below. Place the cards in a bag or face down on a table.
- Each player takes turns drawing a card from the bag. Record the measurement in one of the columns in the game card.
- Play continues until each player filled in all the columns for length and width. Find the area of each rectangle.
- Score 1 point if you have a rectangle with the greatest area, and score 1 point if you have a rectangle with the least area. Score 2 points for each square that you made.

1 ft	2 ft	3 ft	4 ft	5 ft
6 ft	7 ft	8 ft	9 ft	10 ft
11 ft	12 ft	13 ft	14 ft	15 ft

	Rectangle A	Rectangle B	Rectangle C
Length			
Width			
Area			

Check students' work.

Use with text pages 456–458.

Problem Solving 18.3

Name ______________ Date ______ Problem Solving 18.3

Algebra: Area

Use the gardens below for Problems 1–3.

A 5 ft × 6 ft; B 6 ft × 7 ft; C 4 ft × 8 ft; D 4 ft × 9 ft; E 8 ft × 7 ft; F 5 ft × 9 ft

Show your work.

1. Mr. Aldo has a garden with an area greater than 40 square feet but less than 45 square feet. Which garden is Mr. Aldo's?
   B
2. Lori says that her garden has the same area as Garden D, but her garden is a square. What is the length of one side of Lori's garden?
   6 feet
3. Monica's garden has a perimeter of 28 feet. Which garden is Monica's? What is the area of Monica's garden?
   F; 45 square feet
4. Kip's garden is a square with each side measuring 8 feet. A bag of topsoil covers 4 square feet. How many bags of topsoil will Kip need to cover his garden? If each bag of topsoil costs $2.35, how much will Kip spend on topsoil?
   16 bags of topsoil; $37.60
5. **You Decide** Mr. Torez's yard is 20 feet long and 18 feet wide. He wants to plant a garden that takes up no more than one-third of the area of his yard. What is the greatest area the garden can have? What could be the length and width of the garden?
   120 square feet; *possible answer:* 12 feet by 10 feet

Use with text pages 456–458.

- ***Problem 21*** Suggest that students model several examples of this situation to determine their response.
- ***Data*** Assist students in reading information from the floor plan, as needed. Point out, for example, the symbols for doorways. Help them determine the boundaries of the given dimensions.

4 Assess & Close

123 Math Talk in Action

- **What is the formula for finding the area of a rectangle?** ($A = l \times w$)
- **How do we always give area measures?** (in square units)
- **How is the area of a figure different from its perimeter?** (Area measures how many units cover a surface or region; perimeter measures the distance around that surface or region.)

Math Journal Prompt

Have students write about how to use a formula to find the area of a film screen that is 7 feet wide and 4 feet tall.

Lesson Quiz

Use the quiz on Lesson Transparency 18.3.

Test Prep & Spiral Review

Use Test Prep Transparency 18.3.

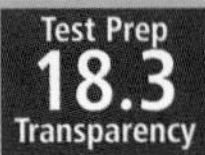

Find the perimeter and area for each rectangle.

13. 14 m long, 6 m wide **$P = 40$ m; $A = 84$ m^2**
14. 3 yd long, 7 yd wide **$P = 20$ yd; $A = 21$ yd^2**
15. 15 cm long, 4 cm wide **$P = 38$ cm; $A = 60$ cm^2**
16. 5 ft long, 13 ft wide **$P = 36$ ft; $A = 65$ ft^2**
17. 2 in. long, 16 in. wide **$P = 36$ in.; $A = 32$ in.^{2}**
18. 8 mm long, 26 mm wide **$P = 68$ mm; $A = 208$ mm^2**

Which of the figures below have the same perimeter but different areas? **Figures a, b, and c**

19.
a. 5 in. by 3 in.
b. 6 in. by 2 in.
c. 4 in. by 4 in.
d. 1 in. by 8 in.

Solve.

20. The area of Kahli's closet is 15 square feet. One side is 3 feet long. How long is the other side? What did you do to get your answer? **5 feet long; I divided 15 by 3.**
21. **Analyze** Does the area of a rectangle double when the length and width are doubled? How do you know? **no; The area will be multiplied by 4. You have changed the length of all 4 sides, not just 2 sides.**

Data **Use the floor plan at the right for Problems 22–26.**

22. Is the floor space of the living room greater or less than 200 square feet? How much greater or less? **less than 200 square ft; 29 square ft**
23. **Money** Anna wants to tile the kitchen floor. Each tile is 1 foot square and costs $1.75. How much will it cost for the tiles? **$126**
24. The rug in the living room is 10 feet by 8 feet. How much floor space is not covered by the rug? **91 square ft**
25. **What's Wrong?** Ben finds the total perimeter of the three rooms by doubling the perimeter of the living room. Explain why that is not correct. ***See Additional Answers.***
26. **You Decide** Suppose you added two rooms onto the floor plan shown. What size might each be? What would the total area of the five rooms become? ***Answers may vary.***

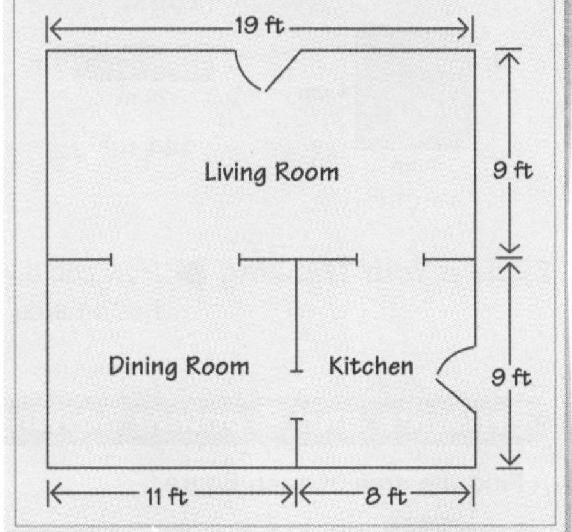

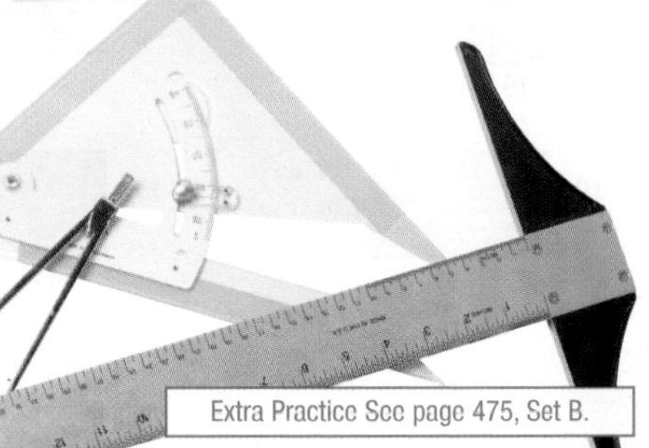

Extra Practice See page 475, Set B.

Homework 18.3 Page 112

Name ______________ Date ______________

Homework 18.3

Algebra: Area

Find the area of each figure.

	You can draw a model and count the squares.	You can use a formula.
3 in. by 5 in.	3 in. by 5 in. grid $A = 15$ square feet $A = 15$ ft^2	A = length × width $A = l \times w$ $A = 5 \times 3$ $A = 15$ square feet $A = 15$ ft^2

1. 13 in., 4 in. **52 in^2**
2. 15 ft, 7 ft **105 ft^2**
3. 20 cm, 8 cm **160 cm^2**

Find the perimeter and area for each rectangle.

4. 9 yd long, 11 yd wide **40 yd; 99 yd^2**
5. 14 ft long, 9 ft wide **46 ft; 126 ft^2**
6. 18 cm long, 6 cm wide **48 cm; 108 cm^2**

Problem Solving

7. Helen wants to carpet her bedroom. Her bedroom is 14 feet long and 12 feet wide. How many square feet of carpeting will Helen need to carpet the entire bedroom? **168 square feet**

Show your work.

Use with text pages 456–458.

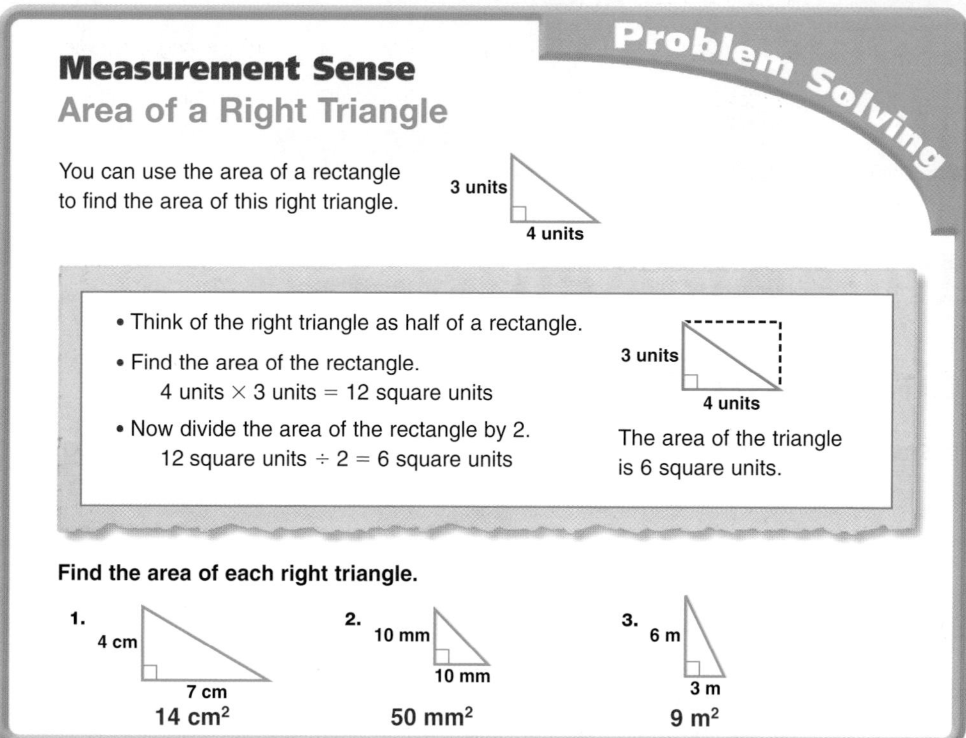
Problem Solving

Measurement Sense
Area of a Right Triangle

You can use the area of a rectangle to find the area of this right triangle.

- Think of the right triangle as half of a rectangle.
- Find the area of the rectangle.
  4 units × 3 units = 12 square units
- Now divide the area of the rectangle by 2.
  12 square units ÷ 2 = 6 square units

The area of the triangle is 6 square units.

Find the area of each right triangle.

1. 4 cm, 7 cm — 14 cm²
2. 10 mm, 10 mm — 50 mm²
3. 6 m, 3 m — 9 m²

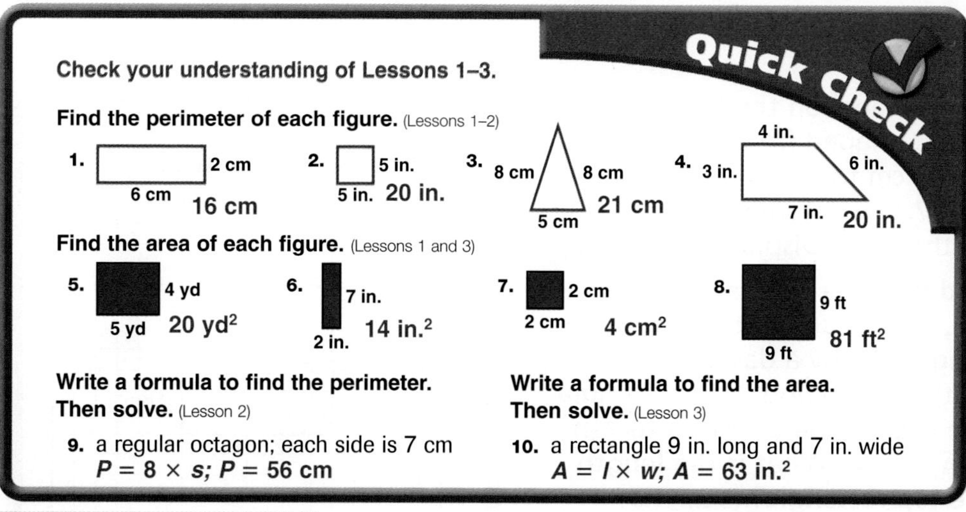
Quick Check

Check your understanding of Lessons 1–3.

Find the perimeter of each figure. (Lessons 1–2)

1. 2 cm, 6 cm — 16 cm
2. 5 in., 5 in. — 20 in.
3. 8 cm, 8 cm, 5 cm — 21 cm
4. 4 in., 3 in., 6 in., 7 in. — 20 in.

Find the area of each figure. (Lessons 1 and 3)

5. 4 yd, 5 yd — 20 yd²
6. 7 in., 2 in. — 14 in.²
7. 2 cm, 2 cm — 4 cm²
8. 9 ft, 9 ft — 81 ft²

Write a formula to find the perimeter. Then solve. (Lesson 2)

9. a regular octagon; each side is 7 cm
   $P = 8 \times s$; $P = 56$ cm

Write a formula to find the area. Then solve. (Lesson 3)

10. a rectangle 9 in. long and 7 in. wide
    $A = l \times w$; $A = 63$ in.²

Measurement Sense

Area of a Right Triangle

To demonstrate that the area of a right triangle is $\frac{1}{2}$ the area of a rectangle, have students draw a rectangle and its diagonal on dot paper or grid paper. Shade in one of the right triangles that are formed, and count the full and partial squares to find the area of both the rectangle and the triangle. Note that the length of the rectangle (l) is the same as the base of the triangle (b). Note also that the width of the rectangle (w) is the same as the height of the triangle (h). It is this relationship that leads to the area of a triangle formula: $A = \frac{1}{2} b \times h$.

Quick Check

Have students complete the ***Quick Check*** exercises independently to assess their understanding of concepts and skills taught in Lessons 1–3.

Items	Objectives Tested	Pages	Intervention
1–4, 9	Find perimeters of polygons.	452–455	Reteach Resource 18.1, 18.2 *Ways to Success* CD-ROM 18.1, 18.2
5–8, 10	Find the area of a rectangle.	452–453, 456–458	Reteach Resource 18.1, 18.3 *Ways to Success* CD-ROM 18.1, 18.3

Lesson 18.4 Algebra: Perimeter and Area of Complex Figures

Planning

Lesson Objective Find the perimeter and area of figures that are not rectangles.

Technology Resources

- *Ways to Success* CD-ROM 18.4

Problem of the Day

How can you form 2 equilateral triangles with sides 12 cm long using a single 60 cm length of wire? (Form 2 equilateral triangles that share a side.)

Spiral Review

Find the perimeter and area for each rectangle.

1. 25 ft long, 8 ft wide ($P = 66$ ft; $A = 200$ ft^2)
2. 16 cm long, 13 cm wide ($P = 58$ cm; $A = 208$ cm^2)
3. 3 km long, 14 km wide ($P = 34$ km; $A = 42$ km^2)
4. 46 in. long, 27 in. wide ($P = 146$ in.; $A = 1{,}242$ in^2)

Lesson Quiz

Find the perimeter and area of each figure.

1. ($P = 98$ cm; $A = 490$ cm^2)

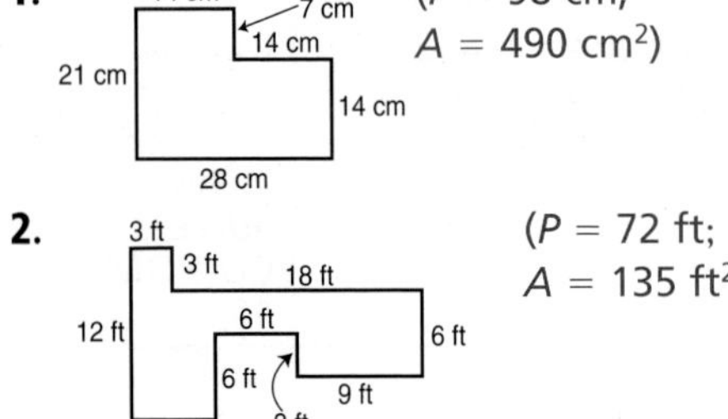

2. ($P = 72$ ft; $A = 135$ ft^2)

NCTM Standards

Geometry: Analyze characteristics and properties of two- and three-dimensional shapes and develop mathematical arguments about geometric relationships.
Algebra: Express mathematical relationships using equations.
Measurement: Develop, understand, and use formulas to find the area of rectangles and related triangles and parallelograms.

Getting Started

Building Math Vocabulary

Students should be familiar with the mathematical vocabulary in this lesson.

Find Area of a Complex Figure

Whole Class	10 minutes
Objective	Find the area of an L-shaped figure.
Materials	Centimeter Grid Transparency
Visual, Auditory	

- Draw and label on the transparency an L-shaped figure with a 5 cm × 2 cm top rectangle and a 2 cm × 7 cm bottom rectangle. Label the sides. Display it.
- **To find the area of this L-shaped figure, we can separate it into two rectangles.** Draw a dashed line to show the separation. **What formula do we use for the area of a rectangle?** ($A = l \times w$) **What is the length of the top rectangle?** (5 cm) **Its width?** (2 cm) **What is the area?** (10 cm^2)
- Repeat for the area of the other rectangle. (14 cm^2) **We have the area of both parts of the L-shaped figure, so how do we find its total area?** (add) **What is the area of the figure?** (24 cm^2)
- Tell students that in this lesson they will explore area of complex figures.

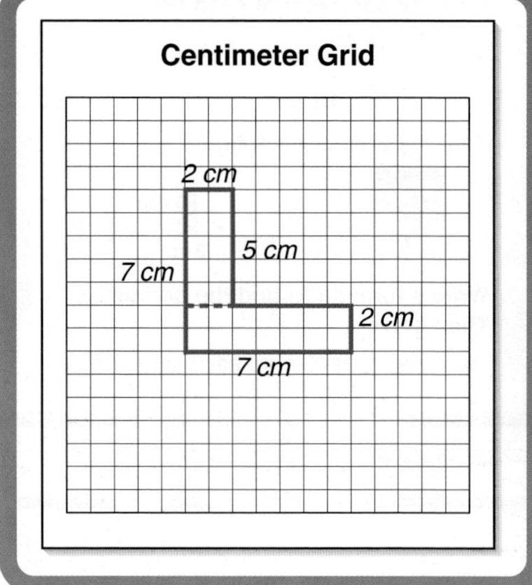

Differentiated Instruction

English Learners

Individuals	10 minutes
Objective	Discuss finding perimeter of a nonrectangular figure.
Materials	Student page 461
Auditory, Visual	

Early Production

- Students may separate the figure before finding the perimeter, adding an extra side to the answer.
- Model the first problem in ***Guided Practice*** by separating the figure, then incorrectly finding the perimeter. **Is the answer correct? What did I do wrong?**

Intermediate/Advanced

- English Learner Resource 18.4
- English Learner Handbook

Intervention

Individuals	15 minutes
Objective	Find the area of an L-shaped figure.
Materials	Grid paper, scissors
Visual, Tactual	

- Distribute grid paper. Have students trace or copy the garden figure from page 460 onto the grid paper.
- Have students cut the figure apart along grid lines to form a square and a rectangle. There are two possible ways to divide the L-shaped figure. Have groups of students divide the figure in different ways. Then compare the total areas obtained by each method.
- After students find the total area, have them reassemble the pieces to show that one method covers the same area as the other method.

Other Resources

- *Ways to Success* CD-ROM 18.4

Special Needs

Pairs	20 minutes
Objective	Find areas of complex figures.
Materials	Grid paper, colored pencils
Tactual, Visual	

- Have students trace a complex figure onto grid paper and divide the figure into as few rectangles as they can. Have them shade each region a distinct color.
- Then have students find separate areas and combine them for the figure's total area.

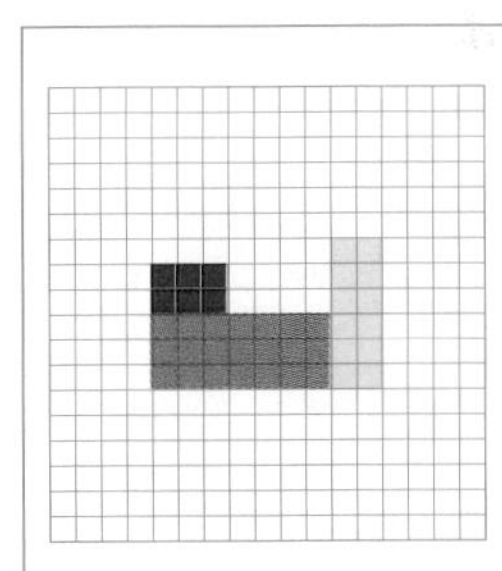

Language Arts Connection

Have students write a basic guide for finding the area of complex figures.

- Tell students that their audience is a classmate who was absent on the day this lesson was taught.
- They should give the instructions in step-by-step order. Sentences should be clear, complete, and concise.
- Have peer editors review each other's work to find ways to make it better.

1 Introduce

Draw a complex figure using a 3×3 square and a 4×5 rectangle. Shade the square blue and outline the perimeter with blue. Shade the rectangle yellow and outline the rectangle with yellow. Guide students to understand that they can find the area of the figure by adding the areas of the square and the rectangle, but they will need to calculate perimeter separately since the square and the rectangle share part of a side.

2 Teach

Learn About It

- Have students read aloud the opening problem.
- **Look at Step 1. Why do we divide it into a square and a rectangle?** (We can find the area of those shapes.) Discuss how the shapes fit Andy's garden.
- **After we form the two shapes, how do we know the correct dimensions to use?** (The opposite sides of a rectangle are the same length.)
- Go over Step 2. Be sure that students understand how each separate area was determined.
- **Look at Step 3. What do the addends represent?** (areas of the parts into which the figure was separated)

Common Error

- **Incorrect Number of addends or products** Remind students that when they add to find the perimeter of a complex figure, they must account for the length of every side.
- **Intervention** Suggest that students write down the lengths in a column and match the number of addends to the number of sides. Also, when they find separate areas, they must remember to add all the products to get the correct total area.

Lesson 4

Algebra

Perimeter and Area of Complex Figures

Objective Find the perimeter and area of figures that are not rectangles.

Learn About It

Andy wants to put a fence around his garden. The space he will use is shown at the right. How much fence should he buy? What is the area of his garden?

Find the perimeter.

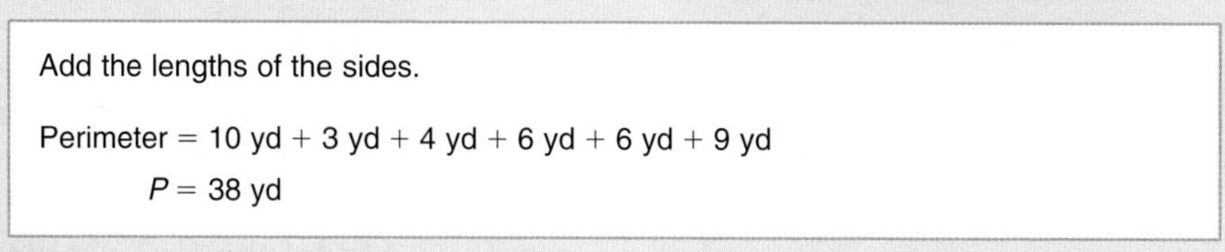

Add the lengths of the sides.

Perimeter = 10 yd + 3 yd + 4 yd + 6 yd + 6 yd + 9 yd

P = 38 yd

Solution: He should buy 38 yards of fence.

Find the area.

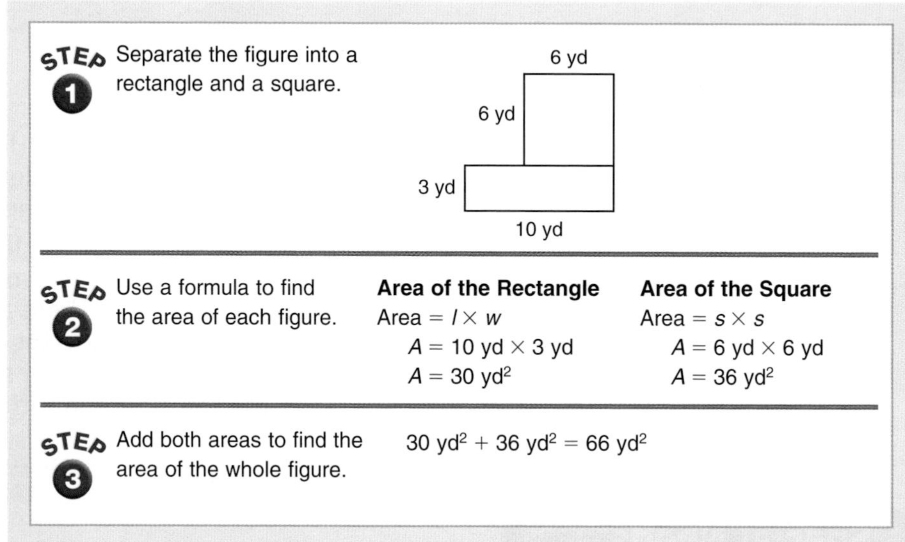

STEP 1 Separate the figure into a rectangle and a square.

STEP 2 Use a formula to find the area of each figure.

Area of the Rectangle
Area = $l \times w$
A = 10 yd × 3 yd
A = 30 yd²

Area of the Square
Area = $s \times s$
A = 6 yd × 6 yd
A = 36 yd²

STEP 3 Add both areas to find the area of the whole figure.

30 yd² + 36 yd² = 66 yd²

Solution: The area of the garden is 66 square yards.

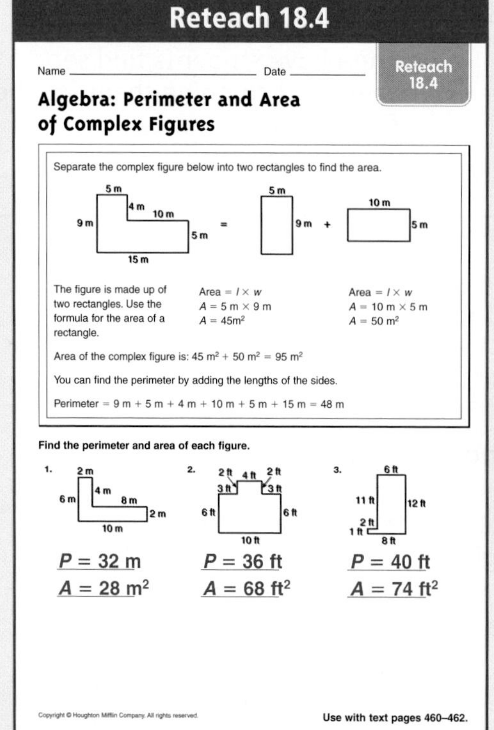

Reteach 18.4

Name ______ Date ______ Reteach 18.4

Algebra: Perimeter and Area of Complex Figures

Separate the complex figure below into two rectangles to find the area.

The figure is made up of two rectangles. Use the formula for the area of a rectangle.

Area = $l \times w$
A = 5 m × 9 m
A = 45m²

Area = $l \times w$
A = 10 m × 5 m
A = 50 m²

Area of the complex figure is: 45 m² + 50 m² = 95 m²

You can find the perimeter by adding the lengths of the sides.

Perimeter = 9 m + 5 m + 4 m + 10 m + 5 m + 15 m = 48 m

Find the perimeter and area of each figure.

1. P = 32 m, A = 28 m²
2. P = 36 ft, A = 68 ft²
3. P = 40 ft, A = 74 ft²

Use with text pages 460–462.

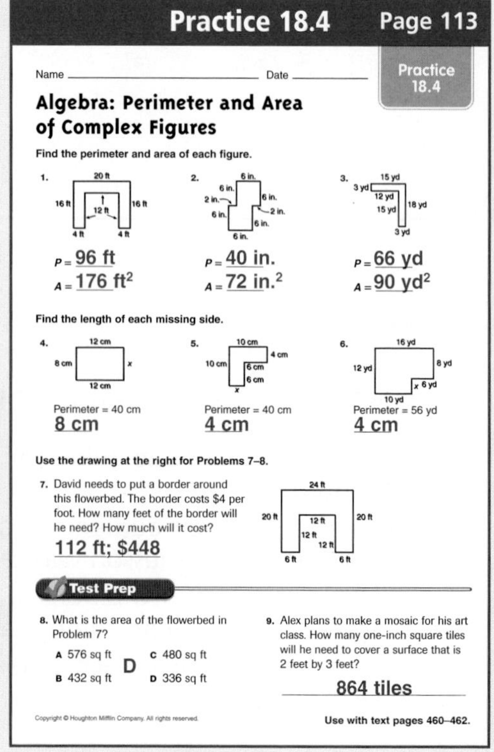

Practice 18.4 Page 113

Name ______ Date ______ Practice 18.4

Algebra: Perimeter and Area of Complex Figures

Find the perimeter and area of each figure.

1. P = 96 ft, A = 176 ft²
2. P = 40 in., A = 72 in.²
3. P = 66 yd, A = 90 yd²

Find the length of each missing side.

4. Perimeter = 40 cm — 8 cm
5. Perimeter = 40 cm — 4 cm
6. Perimeter = 56 yd — 4 cm

Use the drawing at the right for Problems 7–8.

7. David needs to put a border around this flowerbed. The border costs $4 per foot. How many feet of the border will he need? How much will it cost? 112 ft; $448

Test Prep

8. What is the area of the flowerbed in Problem 7?
   A 576 sq ft B 432 sq ft C 480 sq ft D 336 sq ft — D
9. Alex plans to make a mosaic for his art class. How many one-inch square tiles will he need to cover a surface that is 2 feet by 3 feet? 864 tiles

Use with text pages 460–462.

Guided Practice

Find the perimeter and area of each figure.

Ask Yourself

- How can I divide the figure into squares and rectangles?
- How should I label the answer?

1\. 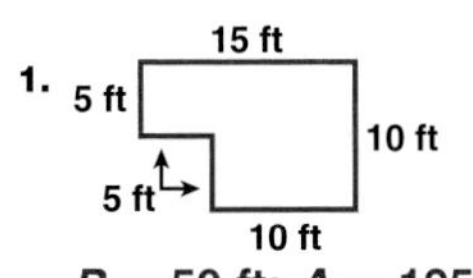

$P = 50$ ft; $A = 125$ ft^2

2\. 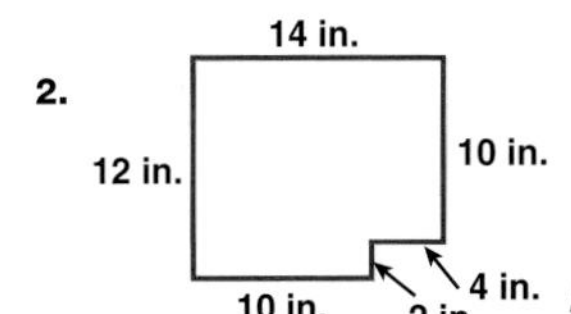

$P = 52$ in.; $A = 160$ in.^{2}

Explain Your Thinking ▶ How could you find the area of your classroom? What tools would you need? What formula would you use? ***Possible answer:*** **Multiply the length of the room by the width of the room. You will need a ruler or a yardstick. $A = l \times w$**

Practice and Problem Solving

Find the perimeter and area of each figure.

3\. 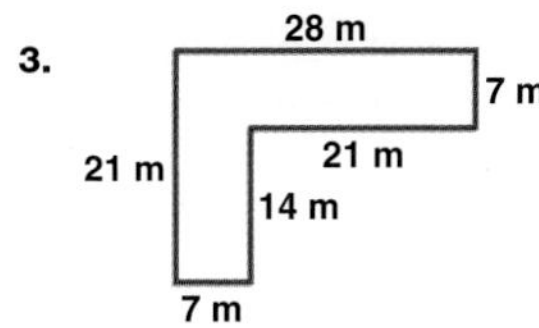

$P = 98$ m; $A = 294$ m^2

4\. 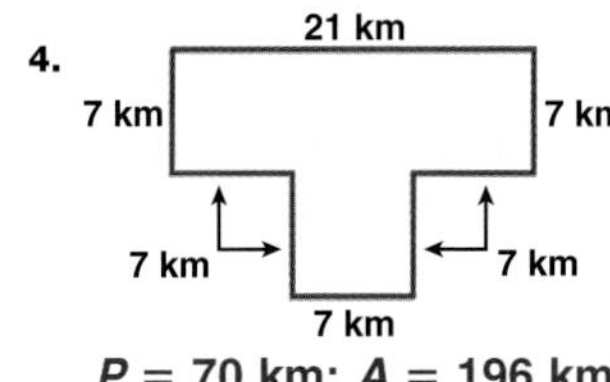

$P = 70$ km; $A = 196$ km^2

5\. 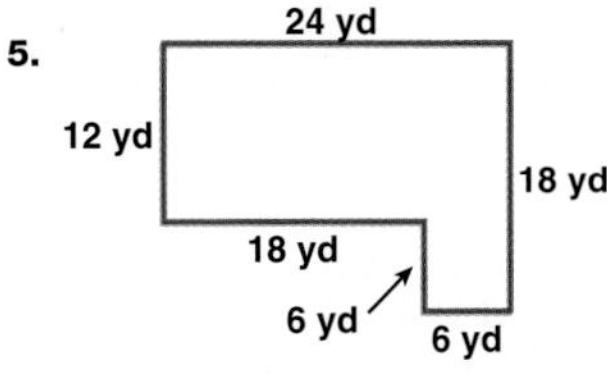

$P = 84$ yd; $A = 324$ yd^2

6\. 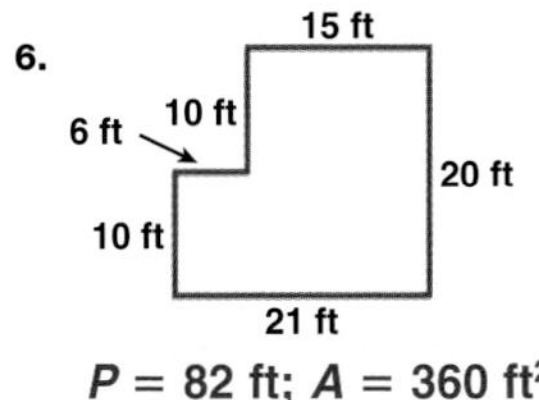

$P = 82$ ft; $A = 360$ ft^2

7\. 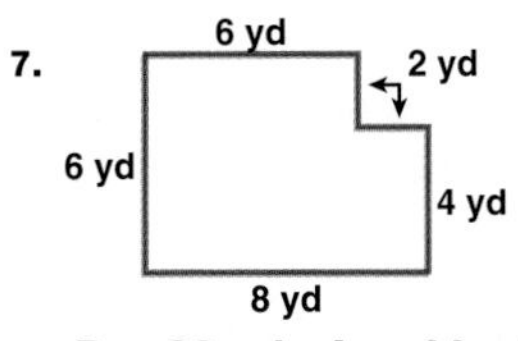

$P = 28$ yd; $A = 44$ yd^2

8\. 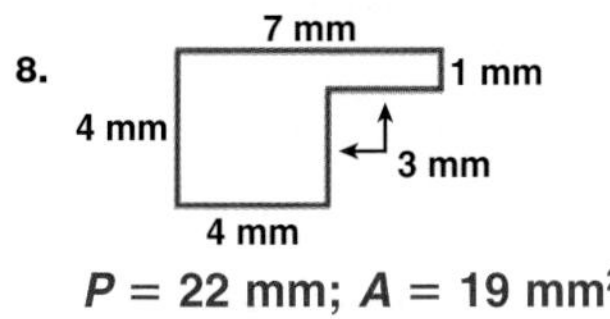

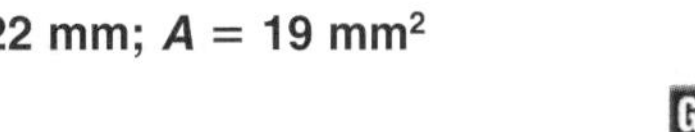

$P = 22$ mm; $A = 19$ mm^2

Go On

Guided Practice

Have students complete **Exercises 1–2** as you observe. Remind them to use the *Ask Yourself* questions to help. Give students the opportunity to talk about the questions in *Explain Your Thinking*.

❸ Practice

Practice and Problem Solving

Select from **Exercises 3–18** as independent work.

- Remind students to label each perimeter and area measure with the correct units. They can show the answers as equations, such as $A = 125$ m^2 and $P = 45$ m.

Enrichment 18.4

Name ____________ Date ________ Enrichment 18.4

My Dream Bedroom

Design your dream bedroom. Make a floor plan on the grid below or on a separate sheet of paper. Make sure you do the following:

- You must make the room a complex figure. It can not be a simple rectangle or square.
- Label all of the room's dimensions. You may want to measure your room at home to help you know how long and wide to make your dream bedroom.
- Find the area and perimeter of your dream bedroom.
- Add and label items you would want to have in your dream bedroom.

Check students' work.

Perimeter ____________

Area ____________

Use with text pages 460–462.

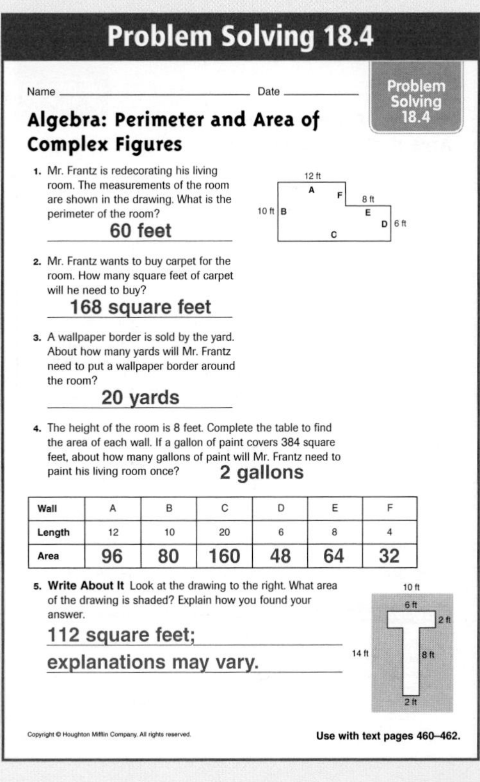

Problem Solving 18.4

Name ____________ Date ________ Problem Solving 18.4

Algebra: Perimeter and Area of Complex Figures

1. Mr. Frantz is redecorating his living room. The measurements of the room are shown in the drawing. What is the perimeter of the room? **60 feet**
2. Mr. Frantz wants to buy carpet for the room. How many square feet of carpet will he need to buy? **168 square feet**
3. A wallpaper border is sold by the yard. About how many yards will Mr. Frantz need to put a wallpaper border around the room? **20 yards**
4. The height of the room is 8 feet. Complete the table to find the area of each wall. If a gallon of paint covers 384 square feet, about how many gallons of paint will Mr. Frantz need to paint his living room once? **2 gallons**

Wall	A	B	C	D	E	F
Length	12	10	20	6	8	4
Area	96	80	160	48	64	32

5. **Write About It** Look at the drawing to the right. What area of the drawing is shaded? Explain how you found your answer. **112 square feet; explanations may vary.**

Use with text pages 460–462.

- *Data* **What operations must you use to answer the questions in Problem 12?** (Add to find perimeter; multiply to find the total cost.) **What strategy could you use to solve Problem 14?** (guess and check; work backward; solve a simpler problem)

4 Assess & Close

Math Talk in Action

- **Compare and contrast finding the perimeter of a square or rectangle with finding the perimeter of a complex figure.** (Both involve finding the sum of the lengths of all sides; they differ in the number of addends.)
- **Explain how to use the area formulas for squares and rectangles to find the area of a complex figure.** (Divide the figure into rectangles and/or squares; find the area of each separate region; combine areas for the total area.)

Math Journal Prompt

Have students draw an E-shaped figure on centimeter grid paper, label the lengths of its sides, and find its area and perimeter.

Lesson Quiz

Use the quiz on Lesson Transparency 18.4.

Test Prep & Spiral Review

Use Test Prep Transparency 18.4.

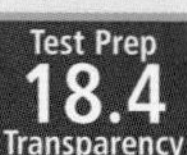

Find the length of each missing side.

9.

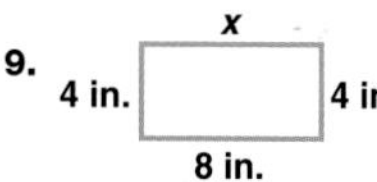

Perimeter = 24 inches
x = 8 in.

10.

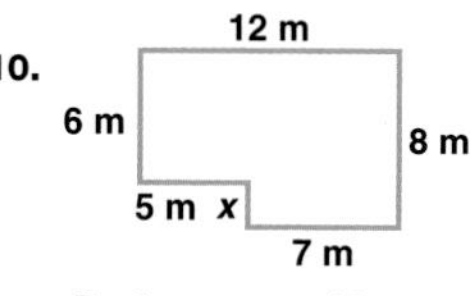

Perimeter = 40 meters
x = 2 m

11.

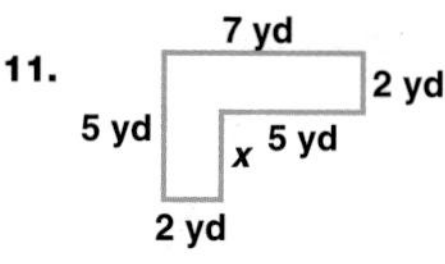

Perimeter = 24 yards
x = 3 yd

Data **Use the drawing of Dee's backyard below and the table at the right for Problems 12–15.**

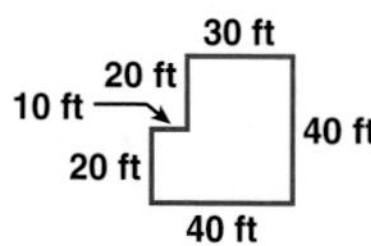

12. **Money** Dee needs to put a fence around this yard. Fencing costs $3 per foot. How many feet of fencing are needed? How much will it cost? **160 ft; $480**
13. **Analyze** Dee wants to put grass seed on the yard. How many pounds of grass seed will she need? **2 lb**
14. Joel purchased 3 pounds of grass seed. What might the length and width of his yard be? ***Possible answer:*** **40 ft by 50 ft**

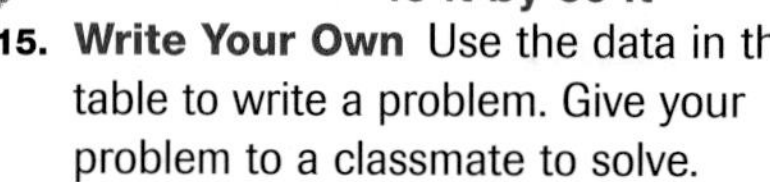

15. **Write Your Own** Use the data in the table to write a problem. Give your problem to a classmate to solve.

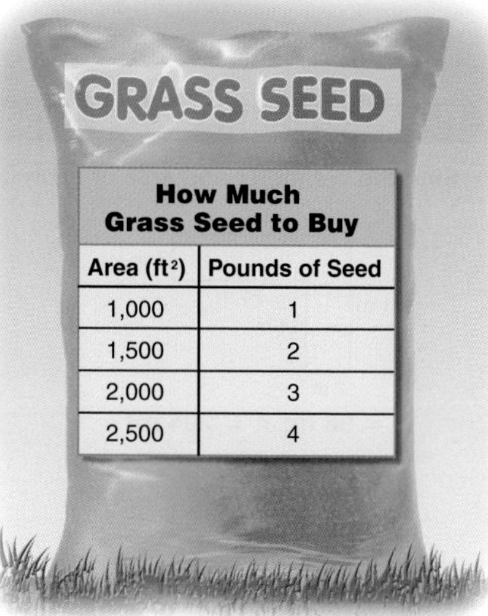

How Much Grass Seed to Buy

Area (ft²)	Pounds of Seed
1,000	1
1,500	2
2,000	3
2,500	4

18. 9 ft = 3 yd
12 ft = 4 yd
3 yd × 4 yd = 12 square yd

Mixed Review and Test Prep

Open Response

Is the dashed line a line of symmetry? Write *yes* or *no*. (Ch. 17, Lesson 4)

16. **17.**

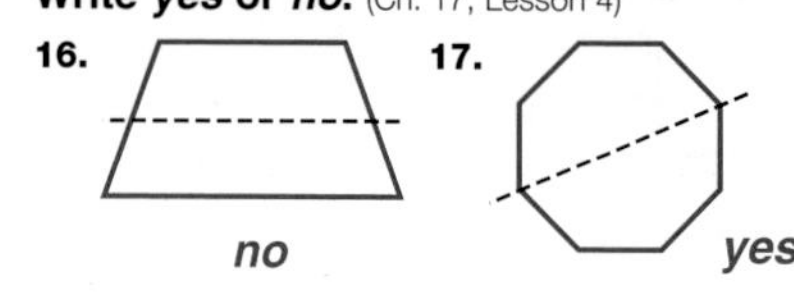

no ***yes***

18. Aldo plans to put new tiles on the kitchen floor. How many square yards of tile does he need if the kitchen measures 9 feet by 12 feet? (Ch. 18, Lesson 4) **12 square yards**
Explain your thinking. ***See above.***

462

Extra Practice See Page 475, Set C.

Homework 18.4 Page 113

Name ______________ Date ______________ Homework 18.4

Algebra: Perimeter and Area of Complex Figures

Find the area of the figure.

10 ft, 14 ft, 20 ft, 12 ft, 6 ft, 22 ft

Step 1: Separate the figure into 2 rectangles. (10 ft, 20 ft; 12 ft, 6 ft)

Step 2: Use a formula to find the area of each rectangle.
$A = l \times w$
$A = 20 \times 10$
$A = 200$
$A = l \times w$
$A = 12 \times 6$
$A = 72$

Step 3: Add both areas to find the area of the whole figure.
$A = 200 + 72$
$A = 272$
The area of the figure is 272 ft².

Find the perimeter and the area of each figure.

1. 10 in., 4 in., 10 in., 3 in., 6 in., 7 in. — 40 in.; 82 in.²
2. 3 ft, 3 ft, 6 ft, 6 ft, 18 ft, 18 ft, 18 ft, 24 ft — 100 ft; 288 ft²
3. 12 yd, 10 yd, 10 yd, 4 yd, 4 yd, 3 yd, 4 yd, 3 yd — 50 yd; 132 yd²

Problem Solving

4. Hugo wants to carpet the room at the right. If carpet costs $2 per square foot, how much will it cost to carpet the room? **$592**
Show your work.
16 ft, 14 ft, 18 ft, 2 ft, 4 ft, 18 ft

Use with text pages 460–462.

Visual Thinking
Estimating Area

Look at the shape below.

You can use grid paper to help you estimate the area of unusual shapes like this one by counting the square units within the shape.

- If the shape covers $\frac{1}{2}$ or more than $\frac{1}{2}$ of a square, count it as 1 square unit.
- If the shape covers less than $\frac{1}{2}$ of a square, don't count it.

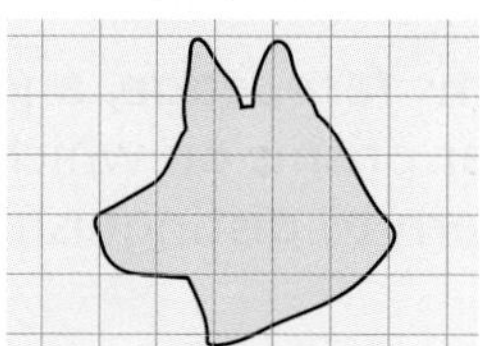

The area is about 15 square units.

Estimate the area of these shapes.
Possible estimates given.

1. 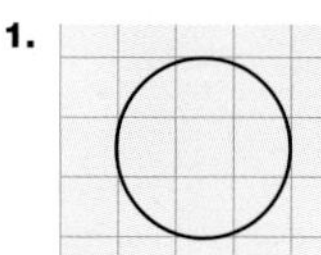 

about 9 square units

2. 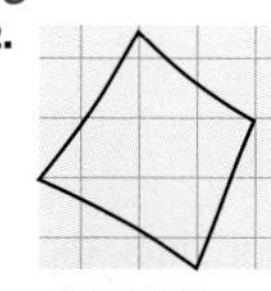

about 7 square units

3. 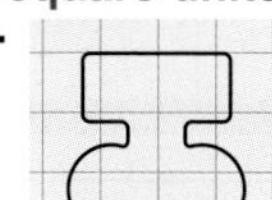

about 6 square units

Art Connection
Stencil Patterns

Vivian is stenciling a border on her bedroom wall. Which of the pieces below will complete the unfinished section? Explain how you know.

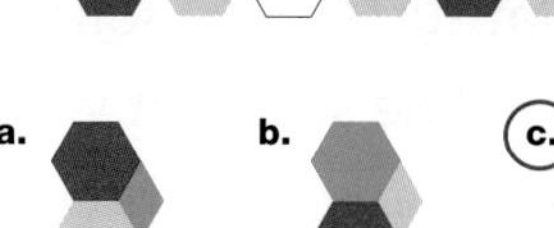

The colors repeat in this pattern.

Brain Teaser

Mr. Tanz is building a 48-foot fence along one side of his yard. He plans to put a post on each end. He wants to place the remaining posts every 8 feet.

How many posts does he need? 7 posts

Education Place
Check out **eduplace.com/map** for more brain teasers.

Visual Thinking

Estimating Area

Tell students that just as they can estimate to find sums, differences, products, and quotients, they can estimate to find approximate areas. This strategy is especially useful when they explore irregular shapes with curves, such as the head in the example.

To extend the activity, have students trace their feet on grid paper. They can apply the estimation strategy to find the area of the tracing.

Art Connection

Stencil Patterns

Provide pattern blocks students can use if they want to model the problem to test their solution.

Brain Teaser

Suggest that students draw a picture on grid paper to help them solve this problem. They can have each grid box equal 4 ft. Point out that a fence needs a post at either end for support.

Hands On Lesson 18.5

Solid Figures and Nets

Planning

Lesson Objective Identify and make solid shapes.

Technology Resources

- *Ways to Success* CD-ROM 18.5
- Education Place: Extra Practice, eGlossary, eGames
  www.eduplace.com/map

Lesson 18.5 Transparency

Problem of the Day

Jenny is having a snack. It's red, and it looks like a sphere. What could the snack be? (possible answer: apple)

Spiral Review

Name the polygon that has . . .

1. 6 sides (hexagon)
2. 8 sides (octagon)
3. 3 sides, 2 of which are the same length (isosceles triangle)
4. 5 sides of equal length (regular pentagon)
5. 4 sides of different lengths (quadrilateral)

Lesson Quiz

Answer the questions about solid figures.

1. How many faces are on a triangular prism? (5)
2. How many edges are on a rectangular prism? (12)
3. How many vertices are on a triangular pyramid? (4)

NCTM Standards

Geometry: Classify two- and three-dimensional shapes according to their properties and develop definitions of classes of shapes such as triangles and pyramids. Identify and build a three-dimensional object from two-dimensional representations of that object.

Getting Started

Building Math Vocabulary

faces	flat surfaces of solid figures
edge	the line segment where two faces of a solid figure meet
vertex (vertices)	a point where three or more edges of a solid figure meet
net	a flat pattern that can be folded to make a solid

Use the vocabulary cards to introduce the terms ***face, edge,*** and ***vertex*** (pl. ***vertices***). Display several cubes and rectangular prisms on which students can point out faces, edges, and vertices as they learn to distinguish among them.

Identify and Create Solid Shapes

Whole Class	10 minutes
Objective	Discuss 3-dimensional figures.
Materials	Solid cube, Nets 1 transparency, paper cube nets, tape
Visual, Auditory	

- Display the cube. **How many faces does a cube have?** (6) **What shape is each face?** (square)
- Display the Nets 1 Transparency and Nets A and B. **These patterns are called *nets.* Which net could be folded to make the cube?** (Net B) **Why?** (It has all square sections.)
- Have several volunteers try to fold the nets to form cubes and tape the figure together. **As some students fold the cube net, let's use our visual thinking skills to predict the figure we would get if we folded Net A into a solid figure.** (Possible answers: box, rectangular prism) **How did you make this prediction?** (rectangular faces)
- Tell students that in this lesson they will explore 3-dimensional figures, which are also known as solid figures.

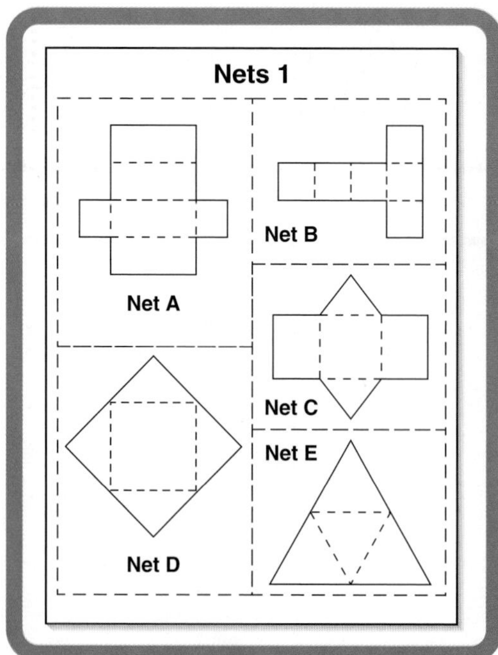

Differentiated Instruction

English Learners

Whole Class	10 minutes
Objective	Identify and discuss solid shapes.
Materials	Student page 466, geometric solids
Tactual, Visual	

Early Production

- Have students use geometric solids to do ***Guided Practice.*** Ask them to identify and say the names of the figures and shapes of the faces. Tell them to count the faces, edges, and vertices.
- Give students additional geometric solids, and have them follow the same directions.

Intermediate/Advanced

- English Learner Resource 18.5
- English Learner Handbook

Intervention

Small Groups	10 minutes
Objective	Discuss and make solid shapes.
Materials	Solid models of triangular pyramid, square pyramid, triangular prism; Nets I Transparency, paper net cutouts, tape
Visual, Tactual	

- Display the models of the triangular and square pyramids and triangular prism. Have students count the faces on each.
- Display those nets on the transparency. **How many faces does the triangular prism have?** (5) **How many of its faces are triangles?** (2) **Which net could be folded to make a triangular prism?** (Net C) Have students fold the paper cutout of Net C to make a triangular prism.
- Repeat for the other two solid figures.

Other Resources

- *Ways to Success* CD-ROM 18.5

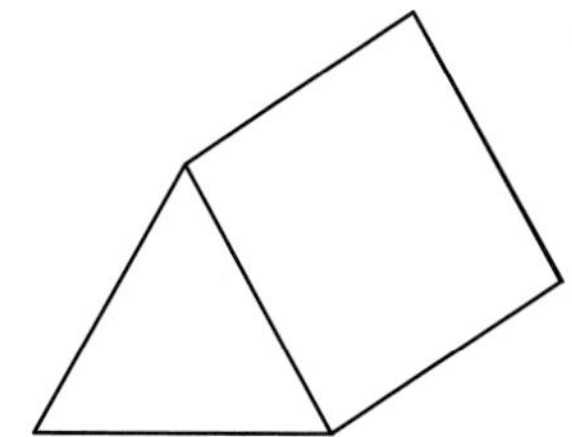

Gifted & Talented

Small Groups	15 minutes
Objective	Discuss solid figures.
Materials	Magazines and catalogs, poster paper, scissors, tape.
Auditory, Visual	

- Have students name some real-life examples of each solid figure shown on page 464.
- Have students present their examples as illustrated posters. Invite them to add sketches or photographs of as many of the items as possible.
- Display the posters around the classroom.

Alternate Teaching Strategy

- Give small groups a solid shape and sticky notes. Have students work together to make a net for their solid shape by tracing the faces onto paper. Students can place a sticky note on each face after tracing it to avoid repeating or forgetting to trace one face. Have groups share and compare their drawings.

❶ Introduce

Display common objects that are solid shapes, such as a classroom globe, number cubes, tissue boxes, or pencil holders. As a class, describe the faces of each figure and relate the number and shape of each face to the solid shape's net.

❷ Teach

Learn About It

- **How would you describe a solid figure in your own words?** (Accept all reasonable responses, including 3 dimensions, fills space, not flat.)
- **Let's add to what we already know about cubes. What do we call each flat side?** (face) **What do we call the corners?** (vertex, vertices) **What do we call the place where two faces meet?** (edge)
- **Look at the table of solid figures. What is true about all figures on the left?** (Faces are in the shape of polygons.) **Why don't the cylinder and cone belong with the other solid figures?** (They have curves.) **What makes the sphere unique?** (It has no faces at all.)

Common Error

- **Miscounting attributes** Some students have trouble counting faces, edges, and vertices without a physical model to manipulate.
- **Intervention** Allow these students extra time to handle solid models. They will also benefit from folding nets into solid figures. Also, have these students use self-stick dots to mark off faces, edges, and vertices as they count them.

Solid Figures and Nets

Objective Identify and make solid shapes.

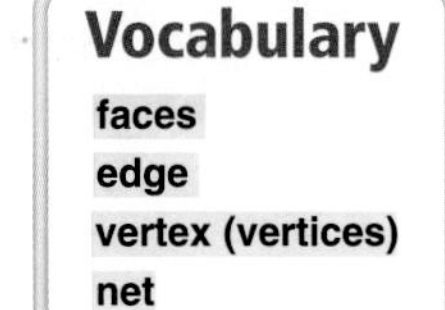

Materials
Learning Tools 28–33
scissors
tape

Learn About It

Sand castles are fun to make. You create solid figures when you build sand castles. Solid figures are objects that take up space.

This solid figure is called a cube.

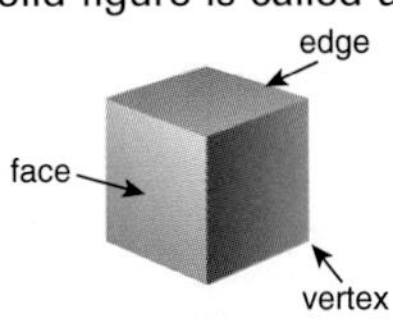

- A cube has 6 **faces**.
- Two faces meet to form an **edge**.
- The point where 3 edges meet is a **vertex**. A cube has 8 vertices.

Here are more solid figures.

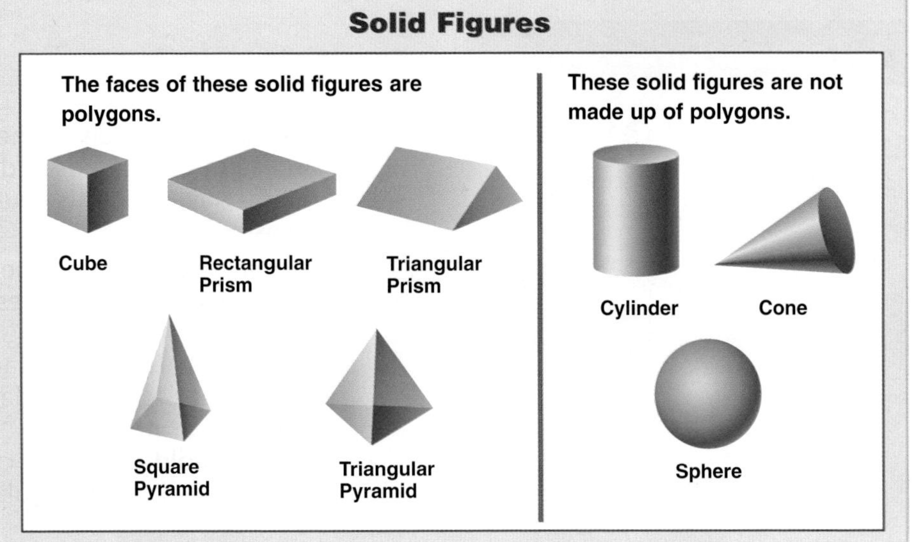

464

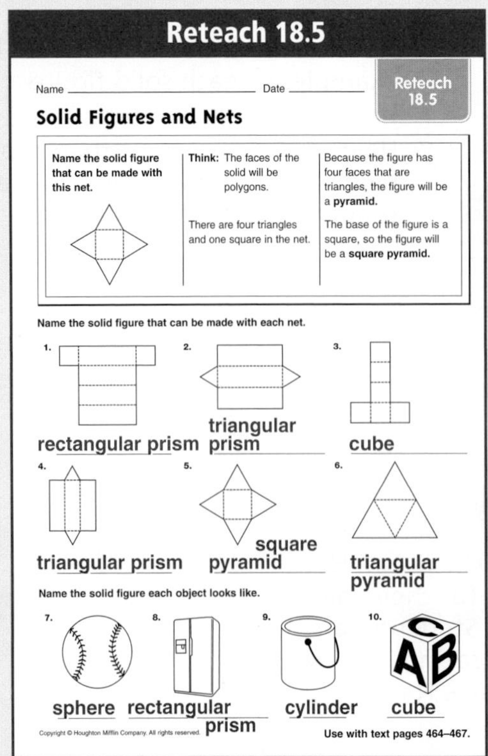

Reteach 18.5

Name __________ Date ______

Reteach 18.5

Solid Figures and Nets

Name the solid figure that can be made with this net.	Think: The faces of the solid will be polygons. There are four triangles and one square in the net.	Because the figure has four faces that are triangles, the figure will be a **pyramid.** The base of the figure is a square, so the figure will be a **square pyramid.**

Name the solid figure that can be made with each net.

1. rectangular prism
2. triangular prism
3. cube
4. triangular prism
5. square pyramid
6. triangular pyramid

Name the solid figure each object looks like.

7. sphere
8. rectangular prism
9. cylinder
10. cube

Use with text pages 464–467.

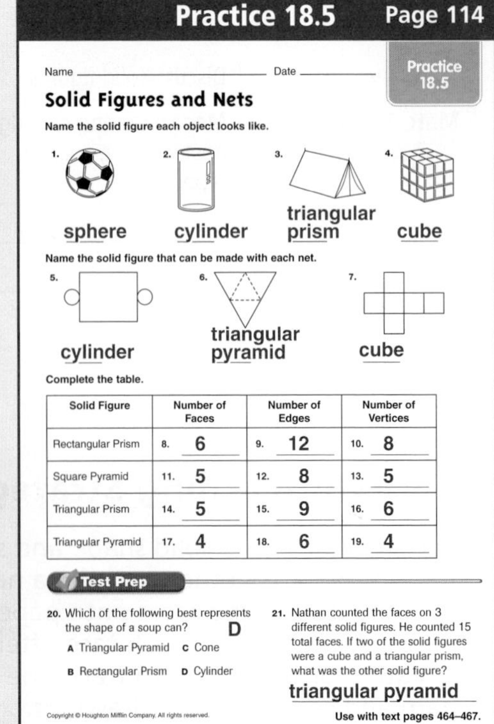

Practice 18.5 Page 114

Name __________ Date ______

Practice 18.5

Solid Figures and Nets

Name the solid figure each object looks like.

1. sphere
2. cylinder
3. triangular prism
4. cube

Name the solid figure that can be made with each net.

5. cylinder
6. triangular pyramid
7. cube

Complete the table.

Solid Figure	Number of Faces	Number of Edges	Number of Vertices
Rectangular Prism	8. 6	9. 12	10. 8
Square Pyramid	11. 5	12. 8	13. 5
Triangular Prism	14. 5	15. 9	16. 6
Triangular Pyramid	17. 4	18. 6	19. 4

Test Prep

20. Which of the following best represents the shape of a soup can? D
    - A Triangular Pyramid
    - B Rectangular Prism
    - C Cone
    - D Cylinder

21. Nathan counted the faces on 3 different solid figures. He counted 15 total faces. If two of the solid figures were a cube and a triangular prism, what was the other solid figure? triangular pyramid

Use with text pages 464–467.

These patterns are **nets**. If you cut out a net and fold it on the dotted lines, you can make a solid figure.

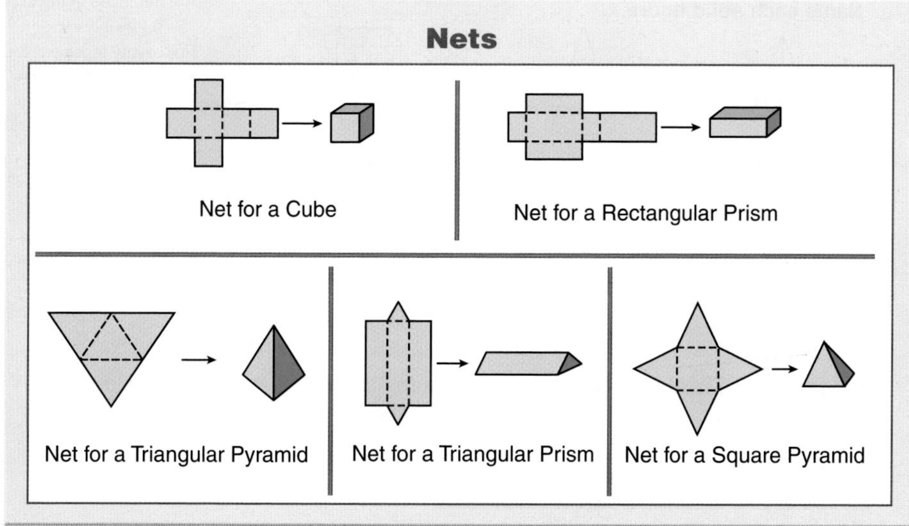

Try this activity to make solid figures.

STEP 1 Cut out three nets from Learning Tools 28–33.

STEP 2 Fold on the dotted lines and tape closed.

STEP 3 Make a table to record the name of each figure you constructed. Then write the number of faces, edges, and vertices of each figure. ***See Additional Answers.***

- Have students study the nets on page 465. **What is a net?** (pattern of the faces of a solid figure) **Why do the nets look different from one another?** (Each is a net for a different solid figure.)
- Have students complete the activity as you circulate to answer questions or offer help.

Enrichment 18.5

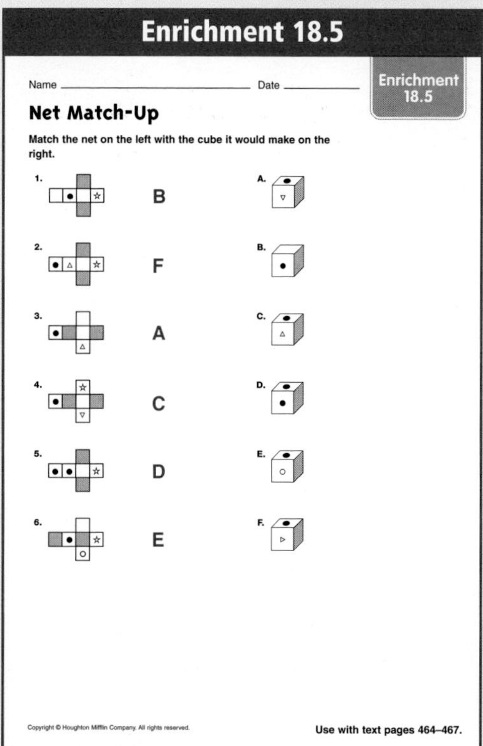

Name ____________ Date ________ Enrichment 18.5

Net Match-Up

Match the net on the left with the cube it would make on the right.

1. B
2. F
3. A
4. C
5. D
6. E

 Use with text pages 464–467.

Problem Solving 18.5

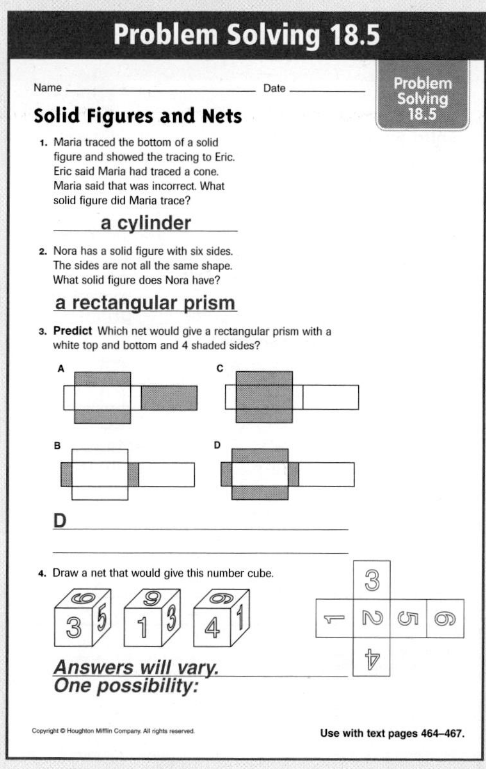

Name ____________ Date ________ Problem Solving 18.5

Solid Figures and Nets

1. Maria traced the bottom of a solid figure and showed the tracing to Eric. Eric said Maria had traced a cone. Maria said that was incorrect. What solid figure did Maria trace?
 a cylinder
2. Nora has a solid figure with six sides. The sides are not all the same shape. What solid figure does Nora have?
 a rectangular prism
3. **Predict** Which net would give a rectangular prism with a white top and bottom and 4 shaded sides?
 A C B D
 D
4. Draw a net that would give this number cube.
 Answers will vary. One possibility:

 Use with text pages 464–467.

Guided Practice

Have students complete **Exercises 1–4** as you observe. Remind them to use the ***Ask Yourself*** questions to help. Give students the opportunity to talk about the questions in ***Explain Your Thinking.***

❸ Practice

Practice and Problem Solving

Select from **Exercises 5–26** as independent work.

- To help students complete the table for **Exercises 12–15,** provide solid figure models.
- ***Problems 16–17*** You may need to help students visualize what these problems ask of them. You can do this by holding a solid figure so that students can look at the different views of it and see only one face at a time.

Guided Practice

Name each solid figure.

1. 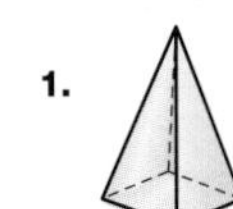
square pyramid

2. 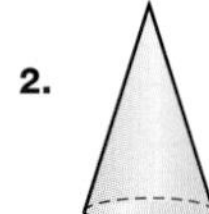
cone

3. 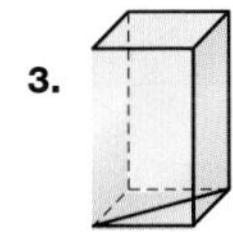 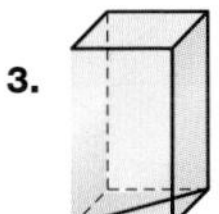
rectangular prism

4. Which net can be folded to make a cube?

a. 
b. 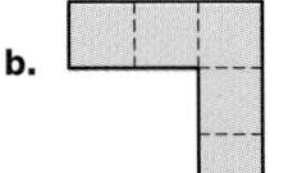
c. 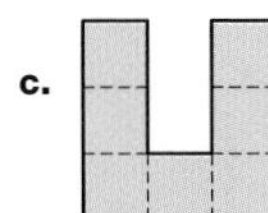
(d.) 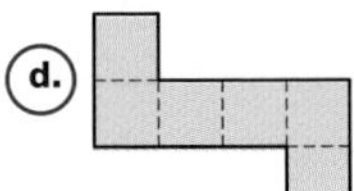

> **Ask Yourself**
> - Are the faces of the solid figure polygons or circles?
> - How many faces will the solid figure have when the net is folded?

Explain Your Thinking ▶ Which solid figure has faces that are all triangles?
triangular pyramid

Practice and Problem Solving

Name the solid figure each object looks like.

5. 

cylinder

6. 
sphere

7. 
rectangular prism

8. 
triangular prism

Name the solid figure that can be made with each net.

9. 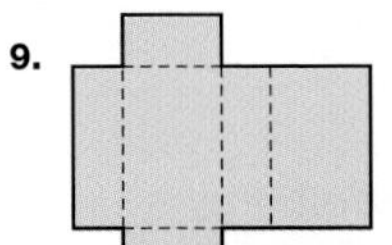
rectangular prism

10. **square pyramid**

11. 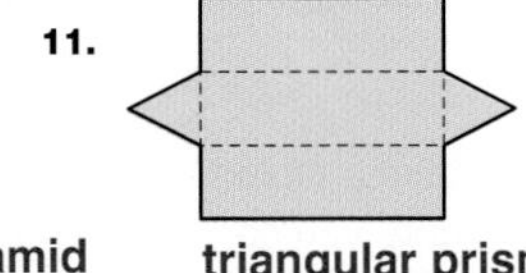
triangular prism

Copy and complete the table.

	Solid Figure	Number of Faces	Number of Edges	Number of Vertices
12.	Cylinder	2	0	0
13.	Triangular Prism	5	9	6
14.	Rectangular Prism	6	12	8
15.	Triangular Pyramid	4	6	4

466

Homework 18.5 Page 114

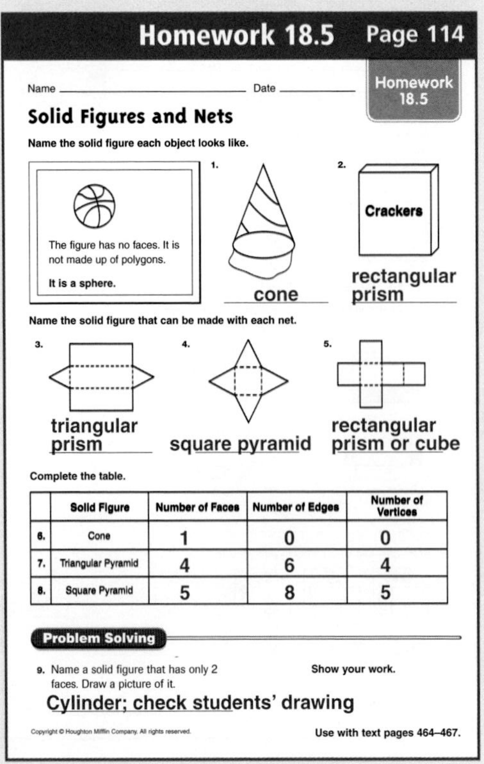
Name ______ Date ______ Homework 18.5

Solid Figures and Nets

Name the solid figure each object looks like.

The figure has no faces. It is not made up of polygons.
It is a sphere.

1. cone

2. Crackers — rectangular prism

Name the solid figure that can be made with each net.

3. triangular prism

4. square pyramid

5. rectangular prism or cube

Complete the table.

	Solid Figure	Number of Faces	Number of Edges	Number of Vertices
6.	Cone	1	0	0
7.	Triangular Pyramid	4	6	4
8.	Square Pyramid	5	8	5

Problem Solving

9. Name a solid figure that has only 2 faces. Draw a picture of it. Show your work.
Cylinder; check students' drawing

Copyright © Houghton Mifflin Company. All rights reserved. Use with text pages 464–467.

Name the solid figure with the following faces.

16. Top View | Bottom View | Side View

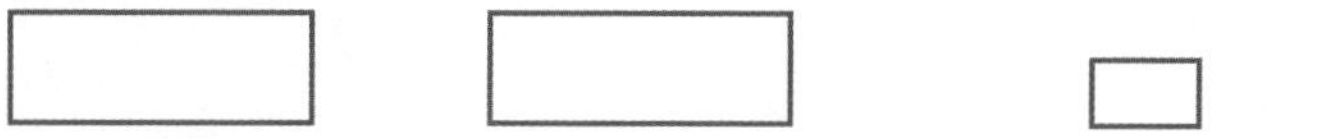

rectangular prism

17. Top View | Bottom View | Side View

cylinder

Solve.

18. Name 3 solid figures that have curved surfaces.
cone, cylinder, sphere

19. Name a solid figure that has only 4 faces. Draw a picture of it. **triangular pyramid**

20. Analyze Sarah built a pyramid out of sand. The bottom of the pyramid was a square. What shape were the other faces of the pyramid? How many other faces were there?
triangles; 4

21. Kari was thinking of a solid figure with 5 faces. Jo guessed it was a square pyramid. Kari said it was another figure that she was thinking of. What figure might it be?
triangular prism

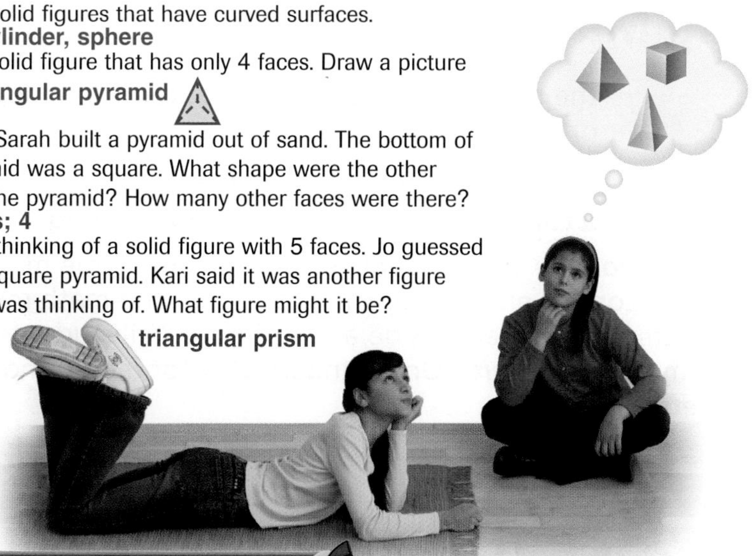

Mixed Review and Test Prep

Open Response

Does the figure have rotational symmetry? Write *yes* or *no*. (Ch. 17, Lesson 4)

22. 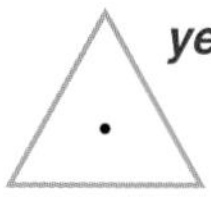 *yes*

23. 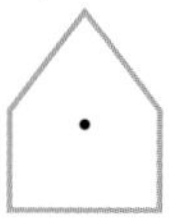 *no*

24. 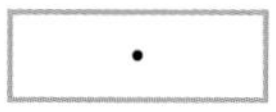 *yes*

25.  *yes*

Multiple Choice

26. If you tape 4 identical cubes in a row, what figure can be formed? (Ch. 18, Lesson 5)

A cylinder
(B) rectangular prism
C square pyramid
D large cube

Extra Practice Page 475, Set D.

4 Assess & Close

Math Talk in Action

Have students refer to their nets as you wrap up the lesson.

- **How does knowing the shapes of faces in a solid figure help you identify its net?** (Look for the net with a particular combination of shapes that match that solid figure.)
- **Describe the difference between an edge and a vertex.** (An edge is a line segment; a vertex is a point.)
- **What is the main difference between a prism and a pyramid?** (Prisms have two identical bases and a four-sided face for each side of a base. Pyramids have one base and a three-sided face for each side of the base.)

Math Journal Prompt

Have students list the eight solid figures they explored in this lesson along with an example of something in real life that has each shape.

Lesson Quiz

Use the quiz on Lesson Transparency 18.5.

Test Prep & Spiral Review

Use Test Prep Transparency 18.5.

Hands On Lesson 18.6

Algebra: Volume

Planning

Lesson Objective Find the volume of a rectangular prism.

Technology Resources

- Audio Tutor **2**/17 Listen and Understand
- *Ways to Success* CD-ROM 18.6
- Education Place: Extra Practice, eGlossary, Extra Help, eGames www.eduplace.com/map

Lesson 18.6 Transparency

Problem of the Day

A cube that measures 5 cm on a side holds a smaller cube inside it that measures 4 cm on a side. What is the volume of empty space inside the larger cube? (61 cm^3)

Spiral Review

Write how many.

1. vertices on a cube (8)

2. vertices on a sphere (0)

3. faces on a triangular pyramid (4)

4. edges on a triangular prism (9)

Lesson Quiz

Solve.

1. A box is 10 in. long, 8 in. high, and 6 in. wide. What is its volume? (480 $in.^3$)

2. A cube measures 7 cm on a side. What is the volume of the cube? (343 cm^3)

3. Shanti knows that the volume of a box is 100 ft^3. If the height is 10 ft and the width is 2 ft, what is the length? (5 ft)

NCTM Standards

Geometry: Use geometric models to solve problems in other areas of mathematics, such as number and measurement.

Measurement: Develop strategies to determine the surface area and volumes of rectangular solids.

Getting Started

Building Math Vocabulary

volume	the number of cubic units that can fit inside a container or a solid figure
cubic units	units used to measure volume
cubic centimeter	a cube with each edge 1 centimeter long

Present the term ***volume.*** Ask students what it means. Some may say loudness, as in the volume control on a radio. Emphasize that the math meaning of *volume* is the amount of space inside a solid figure. Tell students that we measure volume in ***cubic units.*** One standard unit for measuring volume is the ***cubic centimeter.***

Discuss Cubic Units

Whole Class	5 minutes
Objective	Find the volume of a rectangular prism.
Materials	Volume of Cubes Transparency cutouts
Visual, Auditory	

Place Figures *A, C,* and *D* on the overhead, with Figure *D* as the bottom layer of Figure *C*.

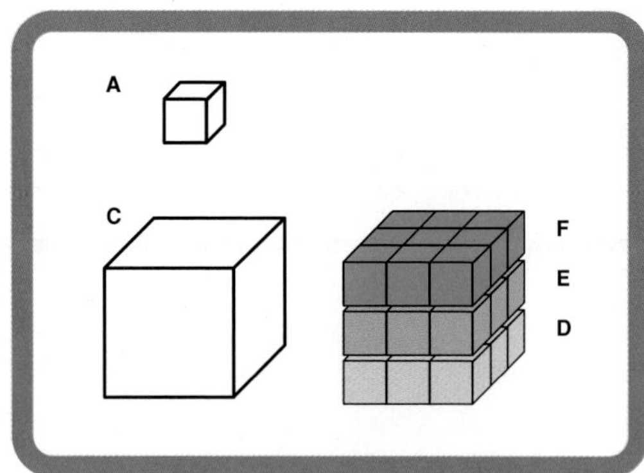

- **Volume is the number of cubic units that fill a solid figure.** Point to *A*. **This is a cubic unit. Let's count how many cubic units fill Figure *C*.**
- Have a volunteer count the cubic units in the bottom layer. (9) **Is the volume of Figure *C* 9 cubic units? Explain.** (No, it's not full yet.)
- Place Figure *E* on top of Figure *D* to form a second layer of cubes. **How many cubic units are in this layer?** (9) Have a volunteer place Figure *F* on top of *E* to fill *C*. **How many cubic units are in the top layer?** (9) **What is the volume of *C*?** (27 cubic units) **How do we get that number?** (3 layers of 9 cubes each)

Tell students that in this lesson they will explore ways to measure how much a box can hold.

Differentiated Instruction

English Learners

Whole Class	10 minutes
Objective	Reinforce steps for finding the volume of a rectangular prism.
Materials	Student page 469
Auditory, Tactual	

Early Production

- For ***Guided Practice,*** have students draw the figure and label the length, width, and height.
- Have students practice verbalizing and writing each step: 1. Volume equals length times width times height; 2. Volume equals 12 inches times 12 inches times 12 inches; and 3. Volume equals 1,728 cubic inches.

Intermediate/Advanced

- English Learner Resource 18.6
- English Learner Handbook

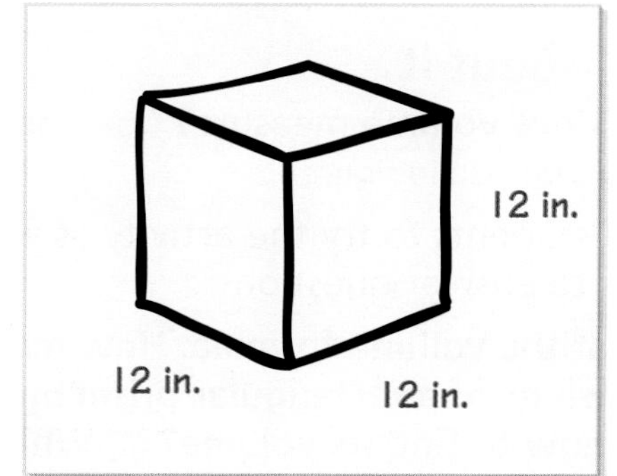

Intervention

Whole Class	10 minutes
Objective	Find the volume of rectangular solids.
Materials	Calculators
Visual, Auditory	

- Students who make multiplication errors may benefit from using a calculator.
- First have students record the factors they multiply in the form of an equation based on $V = l \times w \times h$.
- Have them enter the numbers to find the product.
- Remind students to record their answers in cubic units.

Other Resources

- *Ways to Success* CD-ROM 18.6

Early Finishers

Pairs	15 minutes
Objective	Model rectangular prisms
Materials	Connecting cubes, Student page 469
Visual, Tactual	

- Have students build rectangular prisms out of connecting cubes to reinforce the idea of volume as a 3-dimensional measure.
- Have students model the solid figures on page 469. They can count the cubes they use to verify their solutions.
- Have students build other rectangular solids and then find their volumes.

Science Connection

Many people enjoy the hobby of keeping a home aquarium.

- Invite students who have an aquarium at home to measure its three dimensions to find its volume. If there is an aquarium in your school, have students find its volume.
- Have students learn more about optimum conditions for a home aquarium, such as volume, temperature, water quality, and plants.

❶ Introduce

Ask a volunteer to read the lesson objective on page 468 aloud. Discuss with students why perimeter and area can be found for plane shapes, but volume can only be found for solid shapes.

❷ Teach

Learn About It

- **What does volume measure?** (the amount of space inside a solid figure)
- Guide students to try the activity as you circulate to answer questions.
- **Look at the volume formula. How many dimensions of a rectangular prism must you know to find its volume?** (3) **Which dimensions?** (length, width, height) **How are volume measures labeled?** (in cubic units)

Guided Practice

Have students complete **Exercises 1–2** as you observe. Remind them to use the ***Ask Yourself*** questions to help. Give students the opportunity to talk about the question in ***Explain Your Thinking.***

Common Error

- **Multiplying incorrectly** To find volume, students must find the product of three factors: length, width, and height.
- **Intervention** Remind students that the Commutative Property allows them to multiply factors in any order and still get the same product, but they must account for all three factors.

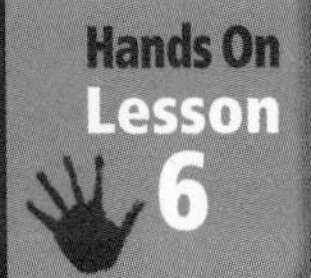

Audio Tutor 2/17 Listen and Understand

Algebra

Volume

Objective Find the volume of a rectangular prism.

Vocabulary
volume
cubic units
cubic centimeter

Materials
centimeter cubes
small box

Learn About It

Suppose you need to know how much a box can hold. You need to find the volume of the box.

Volume is the amount of space inside a solid figure. Volume is measured in **cubic units**.

One standard unit used for describing volume is a cube with each edge 1 centimeter long. This unit is called a **cubic centimeter**.

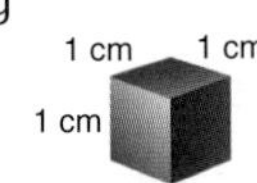

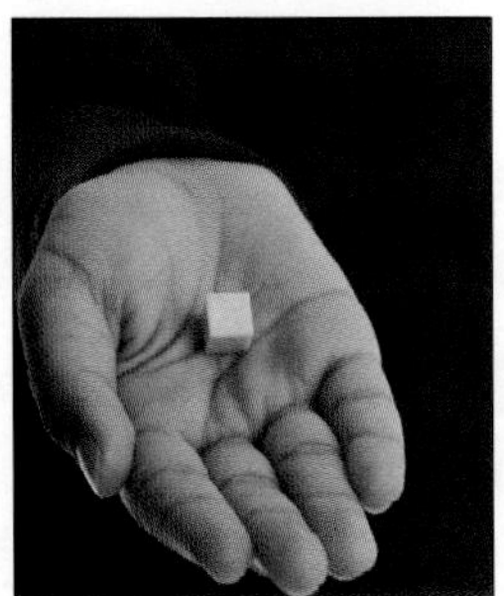

Try this activity to find the volume of a box.

STEP 1 Estimate how many cubes it will take to fill a small box. Record your estimate.

STEP 2 Fill the box with cubes. Count the cubes to find the volume of the box.

STEP 3 Record the number of cubes that fit in the box.

How did your estimate compare to the actual volume?
Answers may vary.

You can also use a formula to find the volume of a box.

A rectangular prism has three dimensions: length (l), width (w), and height (h). You can find its volume (V) by multiplying these dimensions.

The result is the same as counting the number of cubes that would fit in the box.

The volume of the box at the right is 24 cubic centimeters.

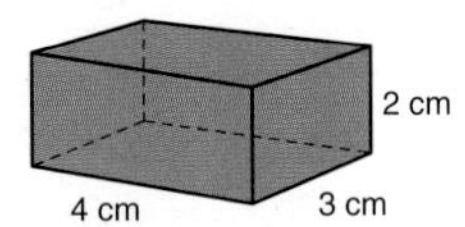

Volume = length × width × height

$V = l \times w \times h$
$V = 4 \text{ cm} \times 3 \text{ cm} \times 2 \text{ cm}$
$V = 24$ cubic centimeters or 24 cm^3

Extra Help at **eduplace.com/map**

Reteach 18.6

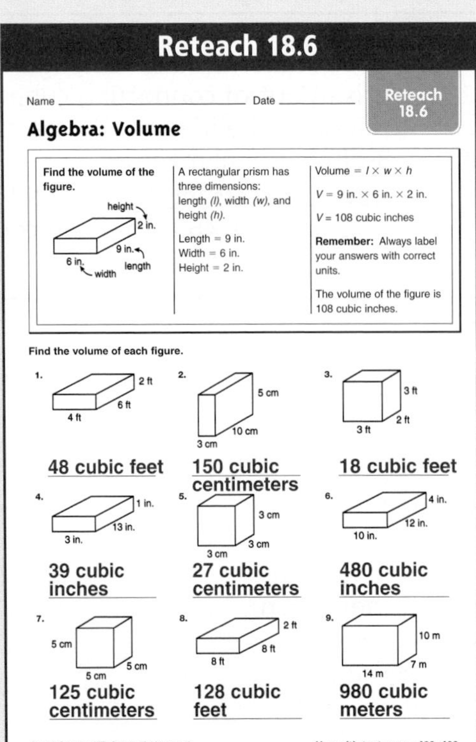

Name ______ Date ______ Reteach 18.6

Algebra: Volume

Find the volume of the figure. (height 2 in., length 9 in., width 6 in.)

A rectangular prism has three dimensions: length (l), width (w), and height (h).
Length = 9 in.
Width = 6 in.
Height = 2 in.

Volume = $l \times w \times h$
V = 9 in. × 6 in. × 2 in.
V = 108 cubic inches

Remember: Always label your answers with correct units.

The volume of the figure is 108 cubic inches.

Find the volume of each figure.

1. 4 ft, 6 ft, 2 ft — 48 cubic feet
2. 3 cm, 10 cm, 5 cm — 150 cubic centimeters
3. 3 ft, 2 ft, 3 ft — 18 cubic feet
4. 3 in., 13 in., 1 in. — 39 cubic inches
5. 3 cm, 3 cm, 3 cm — 27 cubic centimeters
6. 10 in., 12 in., 4 in. — 480 cubic inches
7. 5 cm, 5 cm, 5 cm — 125 cubic centimeters
8. 8 ft, 8 ft, 2 ft — 128 cubic feet
9. 14 m, 7 m, 10 m — 980 cubic meters

Use with text pages 468–469.

Practice 18.6 Page 115

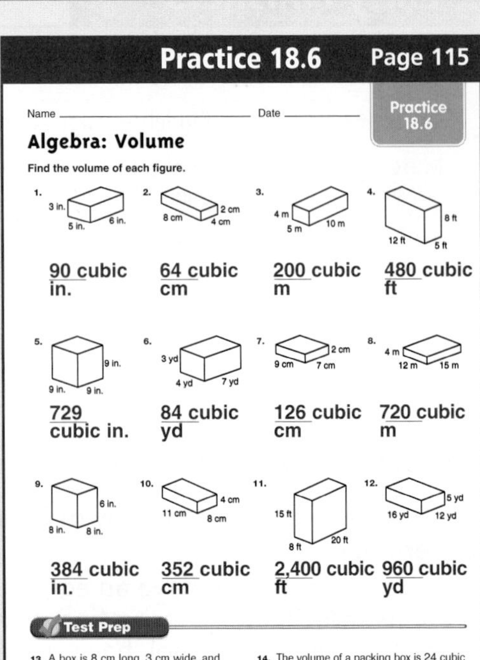

Name ______ Date ______ Practice 18.6

Algebra: Volume

Find the volume of each figure.

1. 5 in., 6 in., 3 in. — 90 cubic in.
2. 8 cm, 4 cm, 2 cm — 64 cubic cm
3. 5 m, 10 m, 4 m — 200 cubic m
4. 12 ft, 5 ft, 8 ft — 480 cubic ft
5. 9 in., 9 in., 9 in. — 729 cubic in.
6. 4 yd, 7 yd, 3 yd — 84 cubic yd
7. 9 cm, 7 cm, 2 cm — 126 cubic cm
8. 12 m, 15 m, 4 m — 720 cubic m
9. 8 in., 8 in., 6 in. — 384 cubic in.
10. 11 cm, 8 cm, 4 cm — 352 cubic cm
11. 8 ft, 20 ft, 15 ft — 2,400 cubic ft
12. 16 yd, 12 yd, 5 yd — 960 cubic yd

Test Prep

13. A box is 8 cm long, 3 cm wide, and 1 cm high. What is the volume of the box?
A 12 cm^3
B 24 cm^3
C 12 cm^2
D 24 cm^2
B

14. The volume of a packing box is 24 cubic feet. The height is 2 feet, and the width is 4 feet. What is the length of the box? Explain how you found the length.
3 feet; explanations will vary

Use with text pages 468–469.

Guided Practice

Find the volume of each figure.

1. 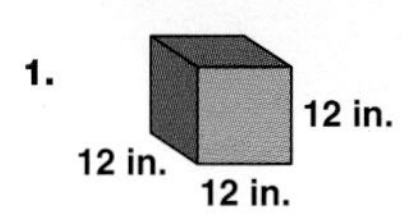

1,728 in.^{3}

2. 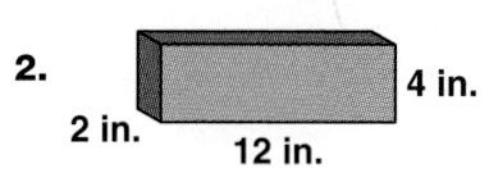

96 in.^{3}

Ask Yourself

- What formula can I use to find the volume?
- What units do I use to label the answer?

Explain Your Thinking ▶ Why is volume always written as cubic units?

***Possible answer:* Volume measures the amount of space, which is three-dimensional. One needs to multiply length × width × height.**

Practice and Problem Solving

Find the volume of each figure.

3. 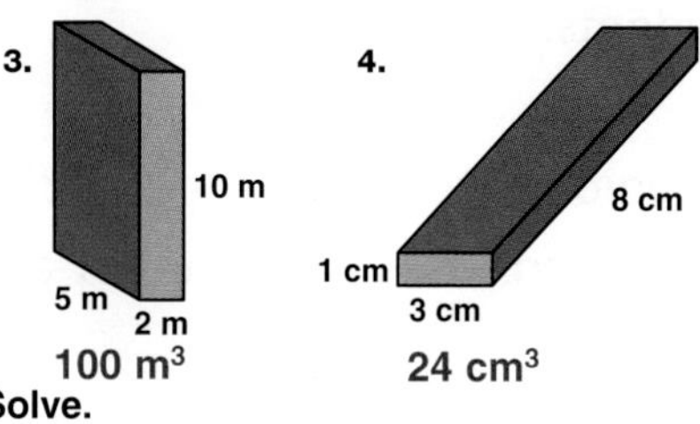

100 m^3

4. 8 cm, 1 cm, 3 cm

24 cm^3

5. 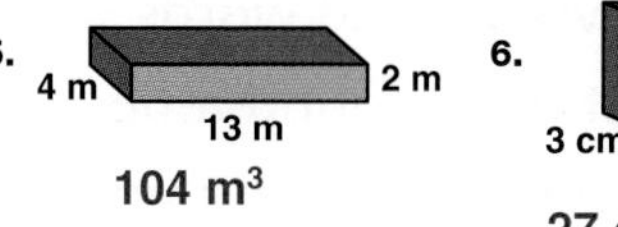

104 m^3

6. 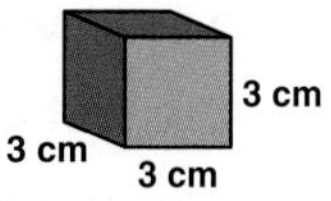 3 cm, 3 cm, 3 cm

27 cm^3

Solve.

7. A box is 27 cm long, 5 cm wide, and 5 cm high. What is the volume of the box? **675 cm^3**

8. **Explain** Does the volume of a box double if the dimensions are doubled? How do you know? ***See above.***

No, the volume of a box is multiplied by 8 when each dimension is doubled.

9. Matt's box measures 3 inches on each edge. Penny's box measures 6 inches on each edge. How much greater is the volume of Penny's box than Matt's box? **Penny's box is 8 times as big, or 189 cubic inches greater.**

10. Peli is putting soil in a terrarium. The space he needs to fill is 9 inches by 13 inches by 2 inches. How many cubic inches of soil will he need to put in the terrarium? **Peli will need 234 cubic inches of soil.**

Mixed Review and Test Prep

Open Response

Identify the parts of this circle.

(Ch. 16, Lesson 7)

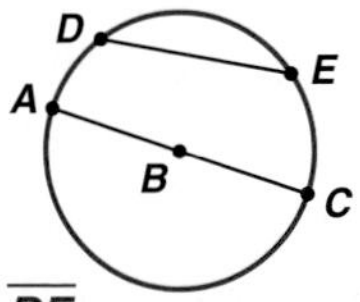

11. the center **point *B***

12. a radius **$\overline{AB}$ or $\overline{BC}$**

13. the diameter **$\overline{AC}$**

14. a chord **$\overline{AC}$ or $\overline{DE}$**

(Circle with points D, E, A, B, C)

15. The volume of a gift box is 36 cubic inches. The height is 3 inches, and the width is 2 inches. What is the length of the box?

(Ch. 18, Lesson 6)

6 inches

Explain how you found the length.

See Additional Answers.

Extra Practice See page 475, Set E.

3 Practice

Practice and Problem Solving

Select from **Exercises 3–15** as independent work.

- ***Problem 8*** Provide connecting cubes that students can use to explore and model this conjecture.
- ***Problem 9*** **What shape are Matt's and Penny's boxes?** (cubes) **How do you know?** (The edges of each box are all the same length.)

4 Assess & Close

Math Talk in Action

- **How do we find the volume of a rectangular prism?** (multiply length by height by width)
- **Some people call solid figures three-dimensional figures. Why is this?** (because solid figures can be measured in three directions: height, length, width)

Math Journal Prompt

Have students write an explanation of how to find the volume of a box that measures 5 ft in length, 4 ft in width, and 3 ft in height.

Lesson Quiz

Use the quiz on Lesson Transparency 18.6.

Lesson 18.6 Transparency

Test Prep & Spiral Review

Use Test Prep Transparency 18.6.

Enrichment 18.6

Name ______ Date ______ Enrichment 18.6

Order Up the Volume

Find the volume of each of the containers below. Then, answer the questions below.

A. 4 ft, 6 ft, 5 ft — **120 ft^3**

B. 4 ft, 1 ft, 8 ft — **32 ft^3**

C. 8 ft, 2 ft, 6 ft — **96 ft^3**

D. 3 ft, 3 ft, 6 ft — **54 ft^3**

E. 5 ft, 2 ft, 2 ft — **20 ft^3**

F. 3 ft, 3 ft, 3 ft — **27 ft^3**

G. 3 ft, 2 ft, 2 ft — **12 ft^3**

H. 6 ft, 4 ft, 6 ft — **144 ft^3**

1. List the containers in order from least volume to greatest volume.
G, E, F, B, D, C, A, H

2. This cone can fit into Box D. Estimate the volume of the cone.
Estimate may vary, but it should be less than 54 cubic feet.

3. This cylinder can fit into Box E. Estimate the volume of the cylinder.
Estimate may vary, but it should be less than 20 cubic feet.

4. Which box above would this sphere best fit into?
F

Use with text pages 468–469.

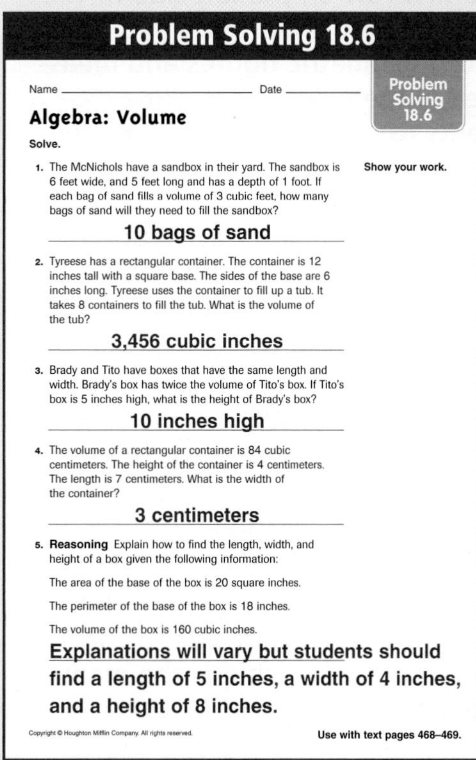

Problem Solving 18.6

Name ______ Date ______ Problem Solving 18.6

Algebra: Volume

Solve. Show your work.

1. The McNichols have a sandbox in their yard. The sandbox is 6 feet wide, and 5 feet long and has a depth of 1 foot. If each bag of sand fills a volume of 3 cubic feet, how many bags of sand will they need to fill the sandbox?
10 bags of sand

2. Tyreese has a rectangular container. The container is 12 inches tall with a square base. The sides of the base are 6 inches long. Tyreese uses the container to fill up a tub. It takes 8 containers to fill the tub. What is the volume of the tub?
3,456 cubic inches

3. Brady and Tito have boxes that have the same length and width. Brady's box has twice the volume of Tito's box. If Tito's box is 5 inches high, what is the height of Brady's box?
10 inches high

4. The volume of a rectangular container is 84 cubic centimeters. The height of the container is 4 centimeters. The length is 7 centimeters. What is the width of the container?
3 centimeters

5. **Reasoning** Explain how to find the length, width, and height of a box given the following information:
The area of the base of the box is 20 square inches.
The perimeter of the base of the box is 18 inches.
The volume of the box is 160 cubic inches.
Explanations will vary but students should find a length of 5 inches, a width of 4 inches, and a height of 8 inches.

Use with text pages 468–469.

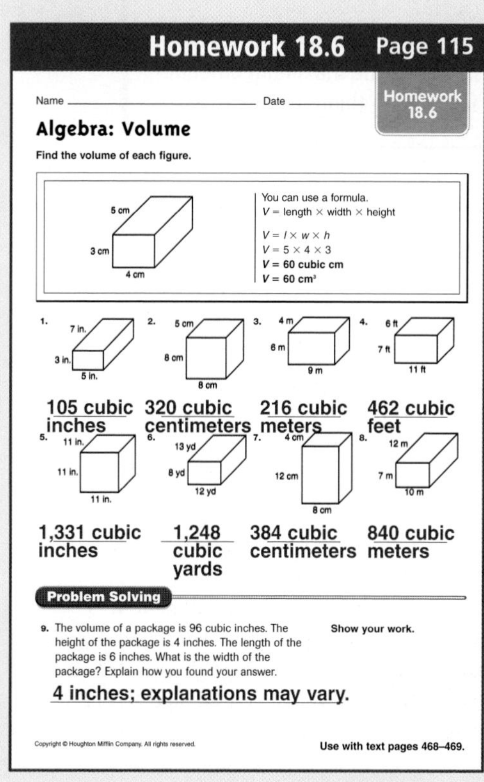

Homework 18.6 Page 115

Name ______ Date ______ Homework 18.6

Algebra: Volume

Find the volume of each figure.

You can use a formula.
V = length × width × height
$V = l \times w \times h$
$V = 5 \times 4 \times 3$
V = 60 cubic cm
V = 60 cm^3

(5 cm, 3 cm, 4 cm)

1. 7 in., 3 in., 5 in. — **105 cubic inches**
2. 5 cm, 8 cm, 8 cm — **320 cubic centimeters**
3. 4 m, 6 m, 9 m — **216 cubic meters**
4. 6 ft, 7 ft, 11 ft — **462 cubic feet**
5. 11 in., 11 in., 11 in. — **1,331 cubic inches**
6. 13 yd, 8 yd, 12 yd — **1,248 cubic yards**
7. 4 cm, 12 cm, 8 cm — **384 cubic centimeters**
8. 12 m, 7 m, 10 m — **840 cubic meters**

Problem Solving

9. The volume of a package is 96 cubic inches. The height of the package is 4 inches. The length of the package is 6 inches. What is the width of the package? Explain how you found your answer. Show your work.
4 inches; explanations may vary.

Use with text pages 468–469.

Lesson 18.7

Problem-Solving Application: Use Formulas

Planning

Lesson Objective Decide which formula to use to solve a problem.

Technology Resources

- *Ways to Success* CD-ROM 18.7
- Education Place: Extra Practice, eGames www.eduplace.com/map

Lesson 18.7 Transparency

Problem of the Day

Mark drew a square with a perimeter of 36 inches. Tia drew a square with a perimeter of 32 inches. Beth drew a square with an area of 64 square inches. Which two students drew congruent squares? (Tia and Beth)

Spiral Review

Simplify each expression.

1. (7 × 2) + (11 × 2) (36)
2. (2 × 5) + (2 × 8) + (2 × 6) (38)
3. (5 × 7) + (7 × 7) + (9 × 7) (147)
4. (11 + 22) × (13 + 10) (759)
5. (16 + 8) × (48 − 16) (768)

Lesson Quiz

Use a formula to solve.

1. A bin is 4 ft wide, 2 ft high, and 1 ft long. How much storage space is there inside the bin? (8 ft^3)
2. A bulletin board measures 48 inches by 20 inches. What is the maximum amount of space for posting things? (960 $in.^2$)

NCTM Standards

Geometry: Recognize geometric ideas and relationships and apply them to other disciplines and to problems that arise in the classroom or in everyday life.
Measurement: Develop, understand, and use formulas to find the area of rectangles and related triangles and parallelograms. Develop strategies to determine the surface areas and volumes of rectangular solids.
Problem Solving: Apply and adapt a variety of appropriate strategies to solve problems.

Getting Started

Building Math Vocabulary

You may wish to review these words with students.

perimeter the distance around a figure

area the number of square units in a region

volume the number of cubic units that can fit inside a container or a solid figure

Discuss Steps for Solving Problems

Whole Class	20 minutes
Objective	Discuss the four-part problem-solving method.
Materials	Workmat 4
Tactual, Auditory	

- Ask students to say, in order, the four steps of the general problem-solving method. Have them use their Workmats to fill in the answers to the following questions as they go. Have students label the top table on the Workmat: *Problem-Solving Method*.
- Have students write *Understand* in the first row on the left side of the Workmat table. **For problems about geometric figures and measures of them, what are some elements to clarify in the Understand step?** (shape of the figure, whether it is a flat or a solid figure, the meanings of given measures, units) Have students describe the Understand step in the right column of the table.
- Have students write *Plan* in the second row on the left side of the Workmat table. **What is the key decision in the Plan step?** (which formula to use for the needed measure) Have students describe the Plan step in the right column of the table.
- Have students write *Solve* in the third row on the left side of the Workmat table. **What is the main job in the Solve step?** (to use the right numbers and operation(s) to compute the answer) Have students describe the Solve step in the right column of the table.
- Have students write *Look Back* in the last row on the left side of the Workmat table. **What is the key role of the Look Back step?** (to see that your answer makes sense with the data given; to see that you have included the correct label, such as cubic feet or square yards) Have students describe the Look Back step in the right column of the table.
- Tell students that in this lesson they will explore how to figure out which formula to use to solve a problem.

Workmat 4

Problem-Solving Method	
Understand	What does the question ask me to find?
Plan	Which formula should I use?
Solve	Did I use the correct numbers and operations?
Look Back	Does my answer make sense?

Differentiated Instruction

English Learners

Pairs	20 minutes
Objective	Act out a problem.
Materials	Student page 471, grid paper, scissors
Auditory, Tactual	

Early Production

- For ***Guided Practice,*** have students work in pairs, using the act-it-out strategy.
- Tell them to read the problem aloud. Then use grid paper to draw and cut out the objects described in the problems.
- Ask students to verbalize and write the answers to the ***Ask Yourself*** questions as they work.

Intermediate/Advanced

- English Learner Resource 18.7
- English Learner Handbook

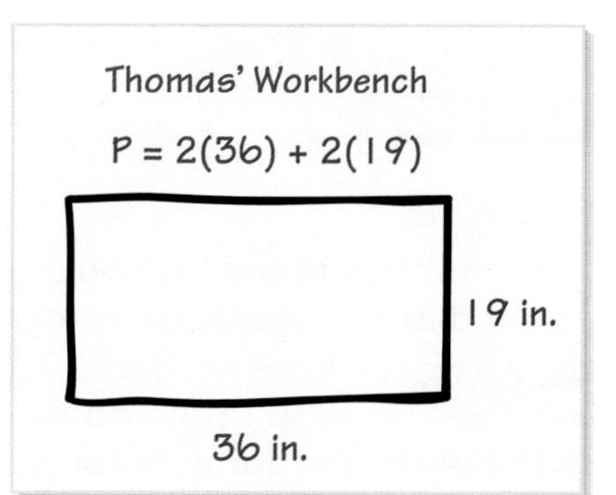

Intervention

Whole Class	10 minutes
Objective	Discuss which formulas to use to solve a problem.
Materials	Box
Visual, Auditory	

- Display the box. **We have learned some formulas to help us describe various measurements of geometric figures. Suppose we want to know the perimeter of one face of this box. What formula do we use?** ($P = 2l + 2w$)
- **What formula would we use to find the area of that same face?** ($A = l \times w$)
- **What formula do we use to find the volume of the box?** ($V = l \times w \times h$)

Other Resources

- *Ways to Success* CD-ROM 18.7

Special Needs

Individuals	15 minutes
Objective	Model volume, perimeter, and area.
Materials	Index cards
Visual, Tactual	

- Help students prepare three cue cards—one each with the formula for volume, perimeter, and area.
- Students should make a diagram to indicate the dimensions they need to use.
- Have students write units for each measurement.
- Help students add key phrases, such as *around the figure* for perimeter.

Alternate Teaching Strategy

- Label several boxes each with a different problem that requires students to find perimeter, area, or volume to solve the problem. Have students work in small groups, select a box, and use a formula to solve the problem.
- Students will need to work together to determine what they need to measure on each box in order to have the correct measurements for the formula. Allow time for groups to complete the activity for several different boxes.

Facts Practice

- Have students pair up and tell each other the number of their birthday month (i.e., September is 9). Students then multiply the two numbers to find the product.

❶ Introduce

Show students a rectangular box. Ask questions such as: **If I wanted to wrap a ribbon around this box, what would I need to know? How could I calculate that information?** Guide students to identify if you will need to find perimeter, area or volume and identify the formula for finding each measurement.

❷ Teach

Use Formulas

- **Read the problem in the first box. How do you know that it is about perimeter?** (It asks about a row of decals to go around the box; *around* suggest perimeter.) **How do we know to use the perimeter formula for a rectangle?** (The bottom face of the box is a rectangle.)
- **Read the problem in the second box. How do you know that it is about area?** (It asks about lining the bottom of the box with felt; area is about space covered.) **How do we know which numbers to use in the area formula?** (Use the given data for the length and width of the box.)
- **Read the problem in the third box. How do you know that it is about volume?** (It asks about the amount of space in the treasure box; *space inside* suggests volume.) **Why does the volume formula involve three factors?** (one for each of the three dimensions: length, width, height)

Lesson 7

Problem-Solving Application

Use Formulas

Objective Decide which formula to use to solve a problem.

You can use formulas for perimeter, area, and volume to solve word problems.

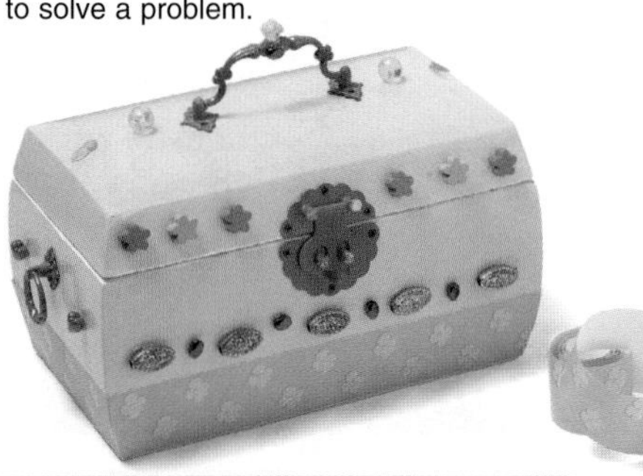

Thomas is decorating a treasure box for his sister Sarah. The box is 12 inches long, 8 inches wide, and 6 inches high.

He wants to buy the right amount of decorative materials for it.

▶ Sometimes you need to find perimeter.

A row of decals will go around the box along the bottom of the box. How long will the row of decals be?

$P = (2 \times l) + (2 \times w)$

$P = (2 \times 12 \text{ in.}) + (2 \times 8 \text{ in.})$
$P = 24 \text{ in.} + 16 \text{ in.}$
$P = 40 \text{ in.}$

Solution: The row will be 40 inches long.

▶ Sometimes you need to find area.

Thomas plans to line the bottom of the box with felt. How much felt should he buy?

$A = l \times w$

$A = 12 \text{ in.} \times 8 \text{ in.}$
$A = 96 \text{ in.}^2$

Solution: He should buy 96 square inches of felt.

▶ Sometimes you need to find volume.

How much space will Sarah have for her treasures?

$V = l \times w \times h$

$V = 12 \text{ in.} \times 8 \text{ in.} \times 6 \text{ in.}$
$V = 576 \text{ in.}^3$

Solution: Sarah will have 576 cubic inches of space.

Look Back What is the difference between inches, square inches, and cubic inches? **Inches are used to measure length. Square inches are used to measure area. Cubic inches are used to measure volume.**

470

Reteach 18.7

Name ____________ Date ________

Reteach 18.7

Problem-Solving Application: Use Formulas

The Alvin family is building a pool. The pool is 20 feet long, 12 feet wide, and 4 feet deep.

12 ft, 4 ft, 20 ft

Use the perimeter formula to find the distance around the edge of the pool.	Use the area formula to find the area of the bottom of the pool.	Use the volume formula to find the number of cubic feet in the pool.
$P = 2 \cdot l + 2 \cdot w$ $P = 2 \cdot 20 \text{ ft} + 2 \cdot 12 \text{ ft}$ $P = 40 \text{ ft} + 24 \text{ ft}$ $P = 64 \text{ ft}$	$A = l \cdot w$ $A = 20 \text{ ft} \cdot 12 \text{ ft}$ $A = 240$ square feet	$V = l \cdot w \cdot h$ $V = 20 \text{ ft} \cdot 12 \text{ ft} \cdot 4 \text{ ft}$ $V = 960$ cubic feet
The perimeter of the pool is 64 feet.	The area of the bottom of the pool is 240 square feet.	The volume of the pool is 960 cubic feet.

Use a formula to solve.

Show your work.

1. A pencil box is 12 inches long, 3 inches wide, and 2 inches deep. How much space is inside the box?
   72 cubic inches
2. Lucy wants to glue ribbon around a picture frame that is 8 inches wide and 10 inches long. How much ribbon will she need?
   36 inches
3. Marianne is painting a canvas. The canvas is 9 in. by 12 in. What is the area of the canvas?
   108 square inches

Use with text pages 470–472.

Practice 18.7 Page 116

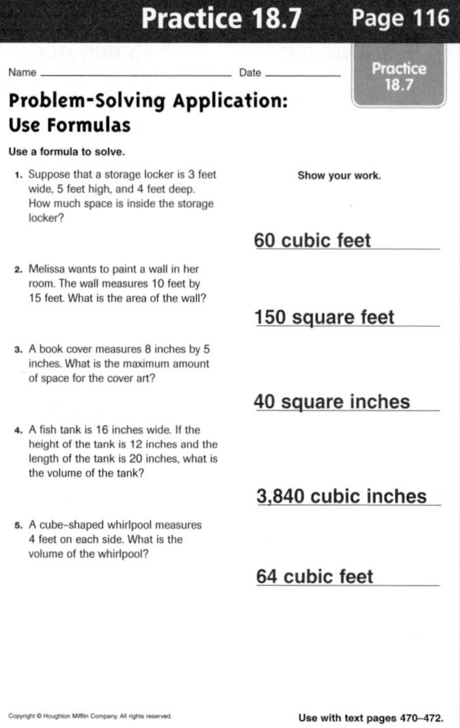

Name ____________ Date ________

Practice 18.7

Problem-Solving Application: Use Formulas

Use a formula to solve.

Show your work.

1. Suppose that a storage locker is 3 feet wide, 5 feet high, and 4 feet deep. How much space is inside the storage locker?
   60 cubic feet
2. Melissa wants to paint a wall in her room. The wall measures 10 feet by 15 feet. What is the area of the wall?
   150 square feet
3. A book cover measures 8 inches by 5 inches. What is the maximum amount of space for the cover art?
   40 square inches
4. A fish tank is 16 inches wide. If the height of the tank is 12 inches and the length of the tank is 20 inches, what is the volume of the tank?
   3,840 cubic inches
5. A cube-shaped whirlpool measures 4 feet on each side. What is the volume of the whirlpool?
   64 cubic feet

Use with text pages 470–472.

Guided Practice

Use the Ask Yourself questions to help you solve each problem.

1. Thomas's workbench measures 19 inches by 36 inches. What is the perimeter of his workbench? **110 inches**
2. Sarah will place the treasure box on her desk. The desk measures 24 inches by 30 inches. How much room will be left on the desk? **624 square inches**

Remember to subtract the area of the treasure box.

Ask Yourself

Does the question ask me to find perimeter, area, or volume?

What formula should I use?

SOLVE

Did I answer with the correct unit?

LOOK BACK

Did I need inches, square inches or cubic inches?

Independent Practice

Use a formula to solve.

3. Suppose a toolbox is 1 foot high, 20 inches long, and 9 inches wide. How much space is inside the toolbox? **2,160 cubic inches**
4. A workshop is 10 feet on each side. What area will be left for working if 6 square feet are used for a workbench? **94 square feet**
5. **Mental Math** A garage wall that measures 10 feet by 30 feet needs to be painted. How many square feet is that? **300 square feet**
6. **Analyze** You have 72 cm of wood to make a picture frame. How can you cut the wood to make a frame with the greatest area for a picture? What shape will it be? **The picture frame should be a square with sides of 18 cm. Then the area is 324 cm².**

Go On

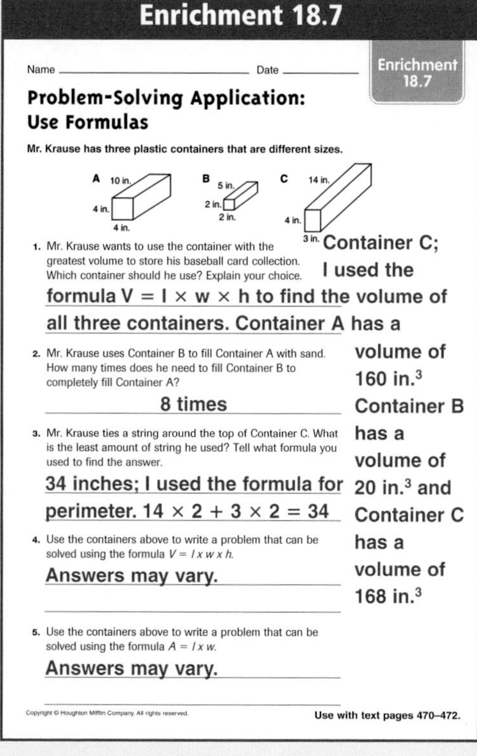

Enrichment 18.7

Name ______ Date ______

Enrichment 18.7

Problem-Solving Application: Use Formulas

Mr. Krause has three plastic containers that are different sizes.

A 10 in., 4 in., 4 in. B 5 in., 2 in., 2 in. C 14 in., 4 in., 3 in.

1. Mr. Krause wants to use the container with the greatest volume to store his baseball card collection. Which container should he use? Explain your choice. **Container C; I used the formula V = l × w × h to find the volume of all three containers. Container A has a volume of 160 in.³ Container B has a volume of 20 in.³ and Container C has a volume of 168 in.³**
2. Mr. Krause uses Container B to fill Container A with sand. How many times does he need to fill Container B to completely fill Container A? **8 times**
3. Mr. Krause ties a string around the top of Container C. What is the least amount of string he used? Tell what formula you used to find the answer. **34 inches; I used the formula for perimeter. 14 × 2 + 3 × 2 = 34**
4. Use the containers above to write a problem that can be solved using the formula $V = l \times w \times h$. **Answers may vary.**
5. Use the containers above to write a problem that can be solved using the formula $A = l \times w$. **Answers may vary.**

Use with text pages 470–472.

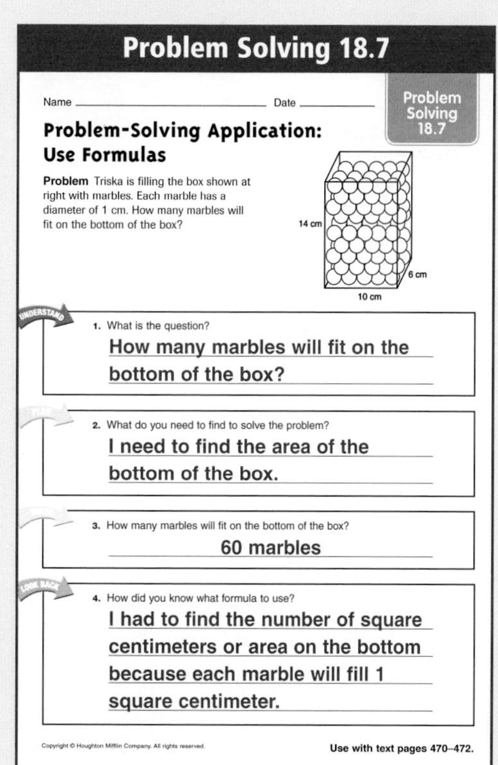

Problem Solving 18.7

Name ______ Date ______

Problem Solving 18.7

Problem-Solving Application: Use Formulas

Problem Triska is filling the box shown at right with marbles. Each marble has a diameter of 1 cm. How many marbles will fit on the bottom of the box?

14 cm, 10 cm, 6 cm

1. What is the question? **How many marbles will fit on the bottom of the box?**
2. What do you need to find to solve the problem? **I need to find the area of the bottom of the box.**
3. How many marbles will fit on the bottom of the box? **60 marbles**
4. How did you know what formula to use? **I had to find the number of square centimeters or area on the bottom because each marble will fill 1 square centimeter.**

Use with text pages 470–472.

Guided Practice

Have students complete **Exercises 1–2** as you observe. Remind them to use the ***Ask Yourself*** questions to help.

❸ Practice

Independent Practice

Select from **Problems 3–13** as independent work.

- For **Problems 3–6,** have students write the formula that applies and then show the work they do to find the solution.
- For **Problem 6,** students might need to make drawings on grid paper to help them solve this problem.

Have students review their answers to make sure they have:

- expressed the solution clearly
- used appropriate mathematical notation and terms
- supported their solution with verbal and symbolic work
- determined the reasonableness of the solution in the context of the original problem

Mixed Problem Solving

- ***Problems 7–9*** Remind students that they can use any of the strategies listed in the box or a combination of strategies to solve.
- ***Problems 10–13*** Remind students to indicate which computation method they use. Suggest that students use a second method to check the answer they found with the first-choice method.

4 Assess & Close

Math Talk in Action

Have students share their solutions to conclude the lesson.

- **Explain how to recognize whether a problem is about perimeter, area, or volume.** (Listen for responses that indicate an understanding of the distinctions among these three measures and the operations involved in applying them.)
- **Why is it important to include the correct unit with the answer in problems like these?** (The units differ for each kind of measure, so without the proper unit, the answer is incomplete.)

Math Journal Prompt

Have students write their own explanation of how to distinguish among perimeter, area, and volume.

Lesson Quiz

Use the quiz on Lesson Transparency 18.7.

Test Prep & Spiral Review

Use Test Prep Transparency 18.7.

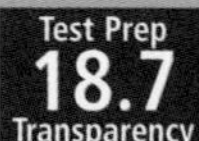

Mixed Problem Solving

Solve. Show your work. Tell what strategy you used. ***Possible strategies given.***

You Choose

Strategy
- Draw a Picture
- Solve a Simpler Problem
- Work Backward
- Write an Equation

Computation Method
- Mental Math
- Estimation
- Paper and Pencil
- Calculator

7. There are 8 teams competing in a soccer tournament. Each team plays every other team once. How many games are played? **28 games are played; Make an Organized List**
8. Mary planted flowers every 6 inches along a garden path. She planted them at the beginning, end, and along both sides of the 14-foot path. How many flowers did she plant? **58 flowers; Draw a Picture**
9. Steven is thinking of a number. If he multiplies the number by 6 and then adds 123, the result is 621. What number is he thinking of? **83; Work Backward**

Solve. Tell which method you chose. ***Possible methods given.***

10. **Money** Mr. Brown's class put 8 small plants and 5 large plants in a terrarium. The small plants cost \$2.19 each. The large plants cost \$3.86 each. About how much was spent on plants? **about \$36.00; Estimation**
11. Sheila is starting a train trip. Her watch indicates that it is now 12 noon. The trip will end 2 days later at 3 P.M. How many hours will she be traveling? **51 hours; Paper and Pencil**
12. Mike is framing a square picture that measures 20 inches on each side. What is the length of wood he will need for the frame? **80 inches; Mental Math**
13. A factory produces birdbaths. Workers can make 50 birdbaths in 30 minutes. How many birdbaths can be made in an 8-hour day? in a 40-hour week? **800 birdbaths in an 8-hour day; 4,000 birdbaths in a 40-hour week; Calculator**

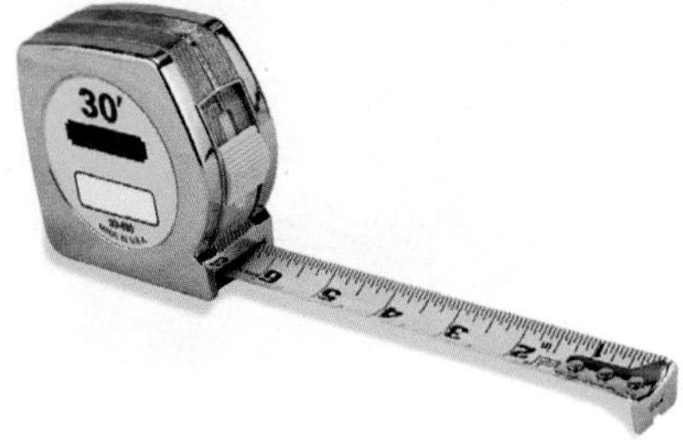

472

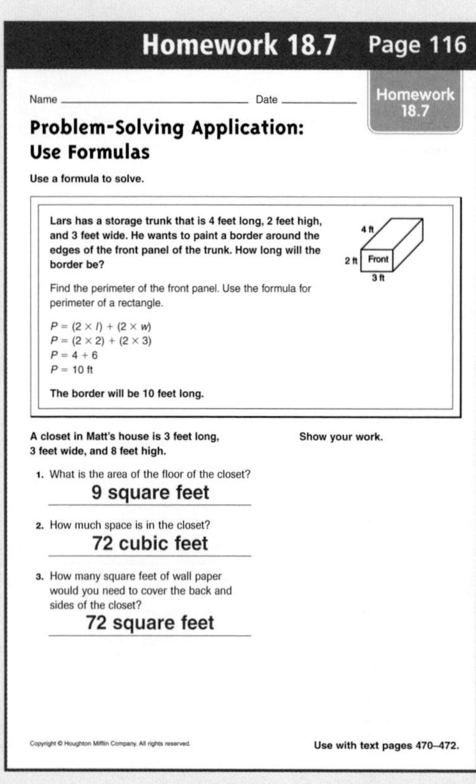

Homework 18.7 Page 116

Name ____________ Date ________

Homework 18.7

Problem-Solving Application: Use Formulas

Use a formula to solve.

Lars has a storage trunk that is 4 feet long, 2 feet high, and 3 feet wide. He wants to paint a border around the edges of the front panel of the trunk. How long will the border be?

4 ft, 2 ft, Front, 3 ft

Find the perimeter of the front panel. Use the formula for perimeter of a rectangle.

$P = (2 \times l) + (2 \times w)$
$P = (2 \times 2) + (2 \times 3)$
$P = 4 + 6$
$P = 10$ ft

The border will be 10 feet long.

A closet in Matt's house is 3 feet long, 3 feet wide, and 8 feet high.

Show your work.

1. What is the area of the floor of the closet? 9 square feet
2. How much space is in the closet? 72 cubic feet
3. How many square feet of wall paper would you need to cover the back and sides of the closet? 72 square feet

Use with text pages 470–472.

Visual Thinking
Graphing in a Different Way

Problem Solving

The coach drew this graph to show spring sports teams. She uses the graph to schedule games.

- Each dot or vertex stands for a different team: Kickball, Track, Lacrosse, and Soccer.
- Each line segment or edge that connects vertices stands for students who are members of both teams.

SOCCER
LACROSSE
KICKBALL
TRACK

Use the graph to solve.

1. Are there students who play soccer and lacrosse? Are there students who play soccer and kickball? How do you know?
2. Can the coach schedule a kickball game on the same day as a track meet? Why or why not?
3. How could you use a graph to show how many students in your class are involved in more than one after-school activity? What steps would you need to take to get the data? How might a graph be a useful tool?
   See Additional Answers.

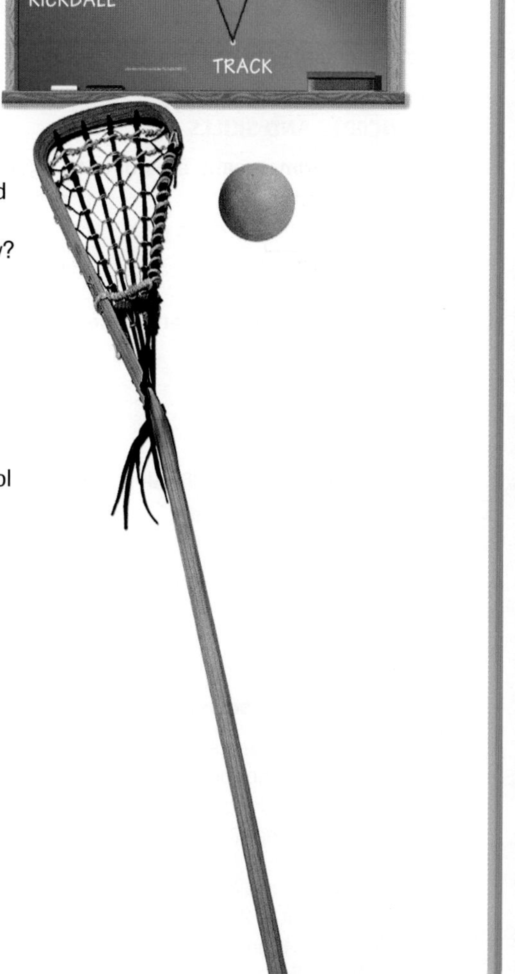

Visual Thinking
Graphing in a Different Way

Background Like a graph, a *glyph* is a visual display of information. The word glyph is related to the word *hieroglyphics*. A glyph uses pictures to convey meaning. But unlike a pictograph, which also uses pictures, a glyph allows for wider creativity and can convey more than numerical data.

Monitoring Student Progress

Chapter Review/Test

Chapter Review/Test Items 1–10

To assign a numerical grade for this Chapter Review/Test, use 10 points for each item.

Check Understanding

You can use the ***Write About It*** question to assess student understanding of a key chapter concept.

Customize Your Instruction

The Chapter Review/Test is a formal evaluation of chapter objectives. For students who have not yet mastered these objectives, you can use the Reteaching Resources listed in the chart below.

Additional Assessment Resources

Alternate Chapter Test A Chapter Test is also provided in the Unit Resource folder. You might use the Review/Test in the student book as review and the test in the Unit Resource folder as a summary test for the chapter.

***Ways to Assess* CD-ROM** allows you to create your own lesson, chapter, or unit tests or practice and review worksheets.

Adequate Yearly Progress Guide helps familiarize your students with the format of standardized tests.

Chapter Review/Test

VOCABULARY

Choose the best word to complete each sentence.

Vocabulary
- area
- vertex
- volume
- perimeter

1. The number of cubic units in a solid figure is the ____. **volume**
2. The point where 3 edges of a solid figure meet is a ____. **vertex**
3. The number of square units in a region is the ____. **area**

CONCEPTS AND SKILLS

Find the perimeter and area of each figure. (Lessons 1–4, pp. 452–462)

4. 3 ft, 5 ft — **$P = 16$ ft; $A = 15$ ft^2**
5. 14 mm, 14 mm — **$P = 56$ mm; $A = 196$ mm^2**

Name the solid figure that can be made with the net. (Lesson 5, pp. 464–467)

6. 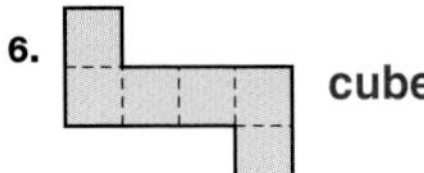 **cube**

Find the volume of each figure. (Lesson 6, pp. 468–469)

7. **150 cm^3**
8. **980 m^3**

PROBLEM SOLVING

Use a formula to solve. (Lesson 7, pp. 470–472)

9. Mrs. Cortez wants to buy wall-to-wall carpeting. The room is 10 feet wide and 12 feet long. How much carpeting does she need? **120 ft^2**
10. The volume of a box is 24 cubic inches. The height is 2 inches and the width is 3 inches. What is the length? **4 inches**

Write About It

Show You Understand

Kim has a rectangle with an area of 12 square inches. Mona says the length can only be 6 inches, and the width can only be 2 inches. Is she correct?

Explain your reasoning.

No; the dimensions can be 6 in. by 2 in., 12 in. by 1 in., or 4 in. by 3 in.

474 **Chapter 18** Chapter Review/Test

Chapter Review/Test Items	Objectives	Covered On Teacher's Edition Pages	Use These Reteaching Resources
3–5	**18A** Find perimeter and area.	452A–458, 460A–462	Reteach Resources 18.1–18.4 *Ways to Success* CD-ROM 18.1–18.4 *Ways to Success* Skillsheets 152, 153, 157
2, 6	**18B** Identify, classify, and describe solid geometric figures.	464A–467	Reteach Resources 18.5 *Ways to Success* CD-ROM 18.5 *Ways to Success* Skillsheet 158
1, 7–8	**18C** Determine the volume of solid figures.	468A–469	Reteach Resources 18.6 *Ways to Success* CD-ROM 18.6 *Ways to Success* Skillsheet 159
9–10	**18D** Solve problems using skills and strategies.	470A–472	Reteach Resources 18.7 *Ways to Success* CD-ROM 18.7 *Ways to Success* Skillsheet 160

Extra Practice

Set A (Lesson 2, pp. 454–455)

Write a formula to find each perimeter. Then solve.

1. a square with sides 7 centimeters long
   $P = 4 \times s$; $P = 28$ cm
2. a regular pentagon with sides 3 meters long
   $P = 5 \times s$; $P = 15$ m
3. a rectangle with sides 2 feet and 5 feet long
   $P = (2 \times l) + (2 \times w)$; $P = 14$ ft

Set B (Lesson 3 pp. 456–458)

Find the area of each figure.

1. a rectangle with sides 4 inches and 6 inches long
   24 in.^{2}
2. a square with sides 13 millimeters long
   169 mm^2
3. a rectangle with sides 5 feet and 9 feet long
   45 ft^2

Set C (Lesson 4, pp. 460–462)

Find the perimeter and area of each figure.

1. 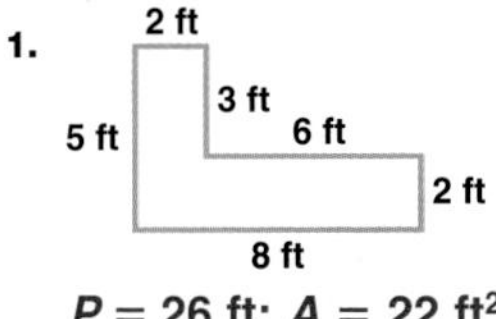

   $P = 26$ ft; $A = 22$ ft^2
2. 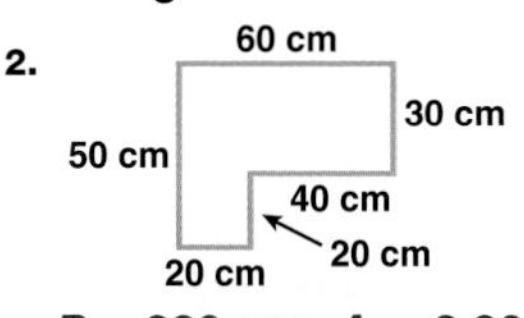

   $P = 220$ cm; $A = 2,200$ cm^2
3. 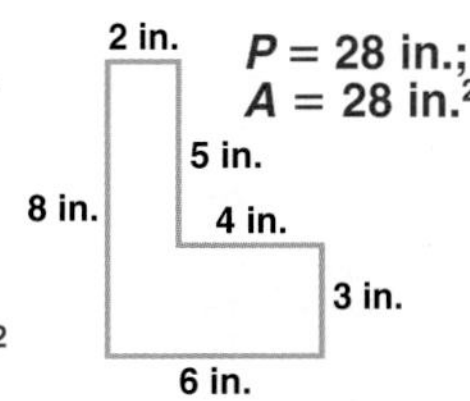

   $P = 28$ in.; $A = 28$ in.^{2}

Set D (Lesson 5, pp. 464–467)

Name the solid figure that can be made with each net.

1. 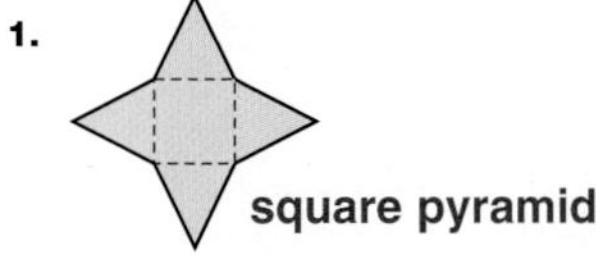
   square pyramid
2. 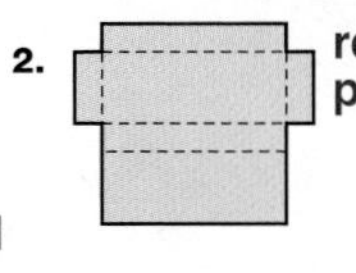
   rectangular prism
3. 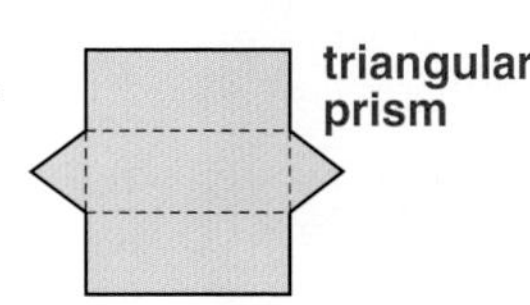
   triangular prism

Set E (Lesson 6, pp. 468–469)

Find the volume of each figure.

1. 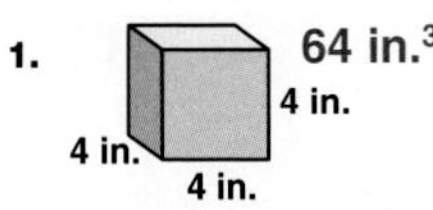

   64 in.^{3}
2. 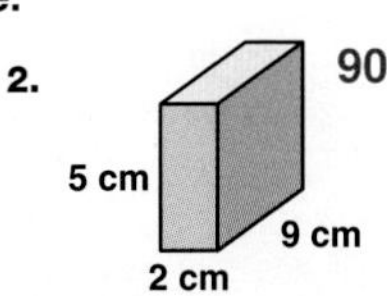

   90 cm^3
3. 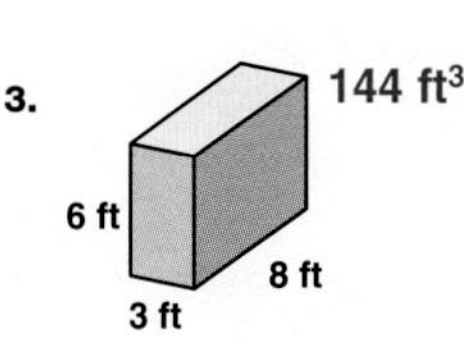

   144 ft^3

Extra Practice at eduplace.com/map

CHAPTER 18 TEST

Chapter 18 Test

Name ______ Date ______

Find the perimeter of each figure.

1. 8 ft, 14 ft — 44 ft
2. 15 cm, 15 cm, 15 cm — 45 cm
3. 11 in., 11 in. — 44 in.

Find the area of each figure.

4. 5 m, 12 m — 60 m^2
5. 8 ft, 8 ft — 64 ft^2
6. 9 cm, 10 cm — 90 cm^2

Find the perimeter and area of each figure.

7. $P = 36$ in., $A = 32$ in.^{2}
8. $P = 26$ ft, $A = 38$ ft^2
9. $P = 44$ yd, $A = 116$ yd^2

Name the solid figure each object looks like.

10. sphere
11. pyramid
12. rectangular prism

Go on

CHAPTER 18 TEST

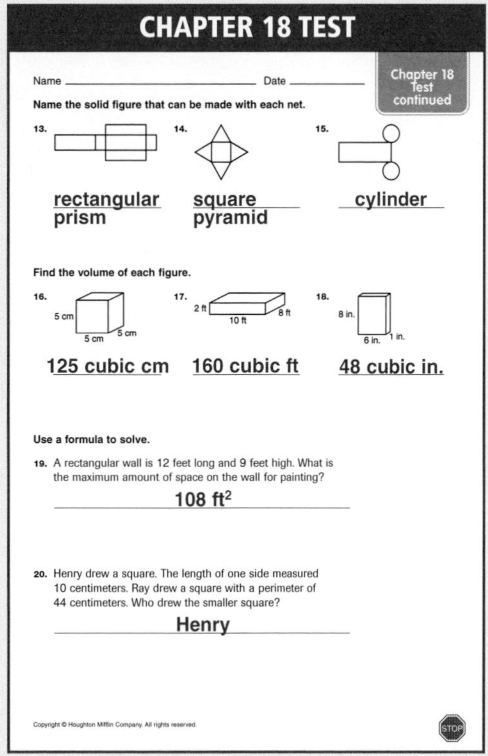

Chapter 18 Test continued

Name ______ Date ______

Name the solid figure that can be made with each net.

13. rectangular prism
14. square pyramid
15. cylinder

Find the volume of each figure.

16. 5 cm, 5 cm, 5 cm — 125 cubic cm
17. 2 ft, 10 ft, 8 ft — 160 cubic ft
18. 8 in., 6 in., 1 in. — 48 cubic in.

Use a formula to solve.

19. A rectangular wall is 12 feet long and 9 feet high. What is the maximum amount of space on the wall for painting?
    108 ft^2

20. Henry drew a square. The length of one side measured 10 centimeters. Ray drew a square with a perimeter of 44 centimeters. Who drew the smaller square?
    Henry

STOP

Art Connection

PURPOSE

Students identify geometric figures and relationships and describe and make a tessellation.

- Tell students that Dutch-born M. C. Escher (1898–1972) was not particularly interested in mathematics and science as a child. However, he was methodical in the way he completed his woodcarving projects.
- During the 1920s, Escher was influenced by geometric patterns that he saw in Spain. He then studied geometry to gain a greater understanding of symmetry and transformations.
- By using transformations on grids of equilateral triangles and certain regular polygons, he created tessellations, or tilings.
- To make a simple tessellation, have students trace around a regular hexagon cutout or the yellow pattern block piece to make the honeycomb in a beehive. Ask them if there are any gaps or overlaps.
- After students complete Exercises 4 and 5, display them on the bulletin board. Ask students to identify the geometric figures and transformational moves in their tessellations.
- For more information on how to create Escher-style tessellations, read *Introduction to Tessellations* by Dale Seymour and Jill Britton (1989).

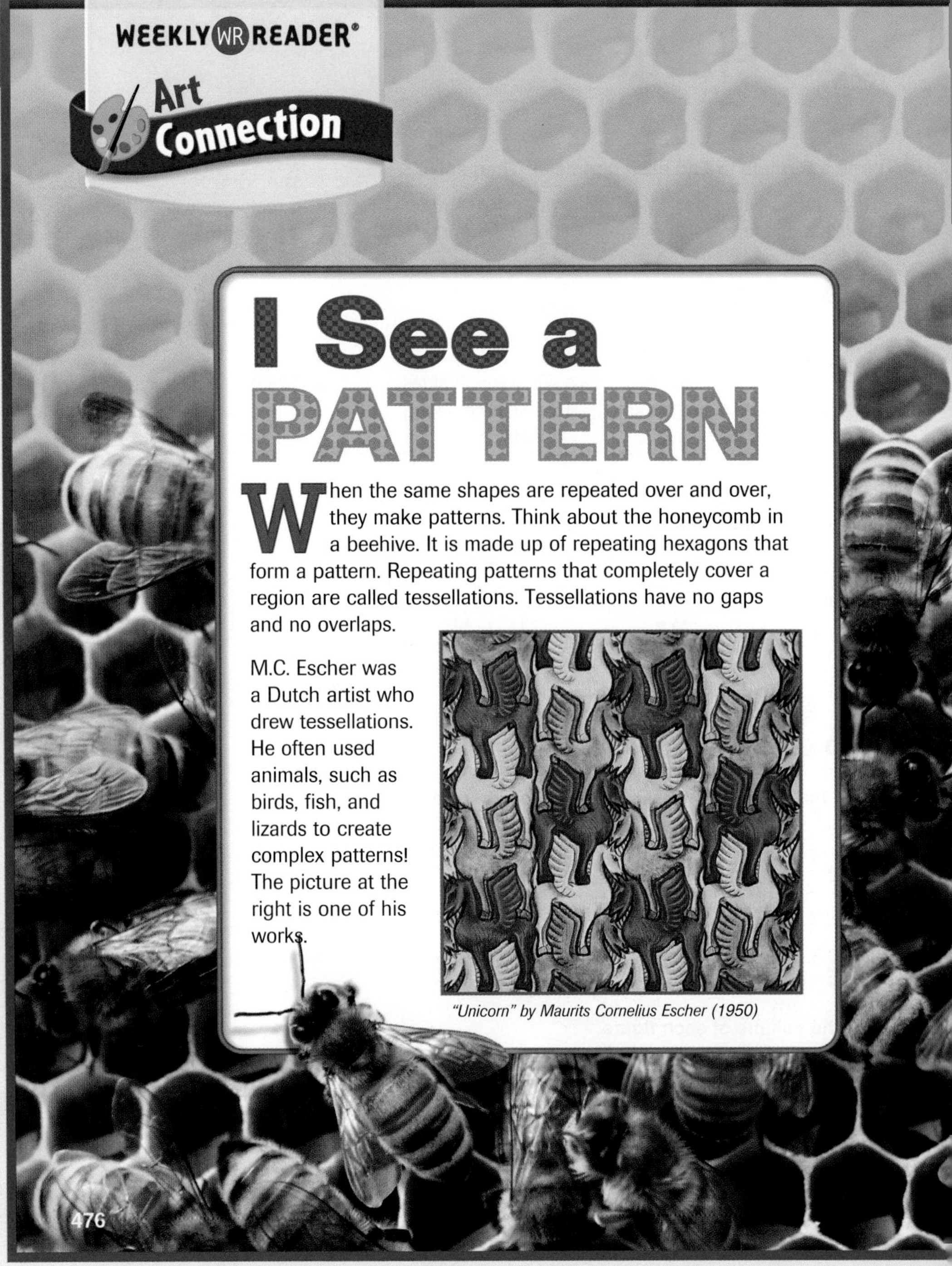

WEEKLY WR READER®

Art Connection

I See a PATTERN

When the same shapes are repeated over and over, they make patterns. Think about the honeycomb in a beehive. It is made up of repeating hexagons that form a pattern. Repeating patterns that completely cover a region are called tessellations. Tessellations have no gaps and no overlaps.

M.C. Escher was a Dutch artist who drew tessellations. He often used animals, such as birds, fish, and lizards to create complex patterns! The picture at the right is one of his works.

"Unicorn" by Maurits Cornelius Escher (1950)

476

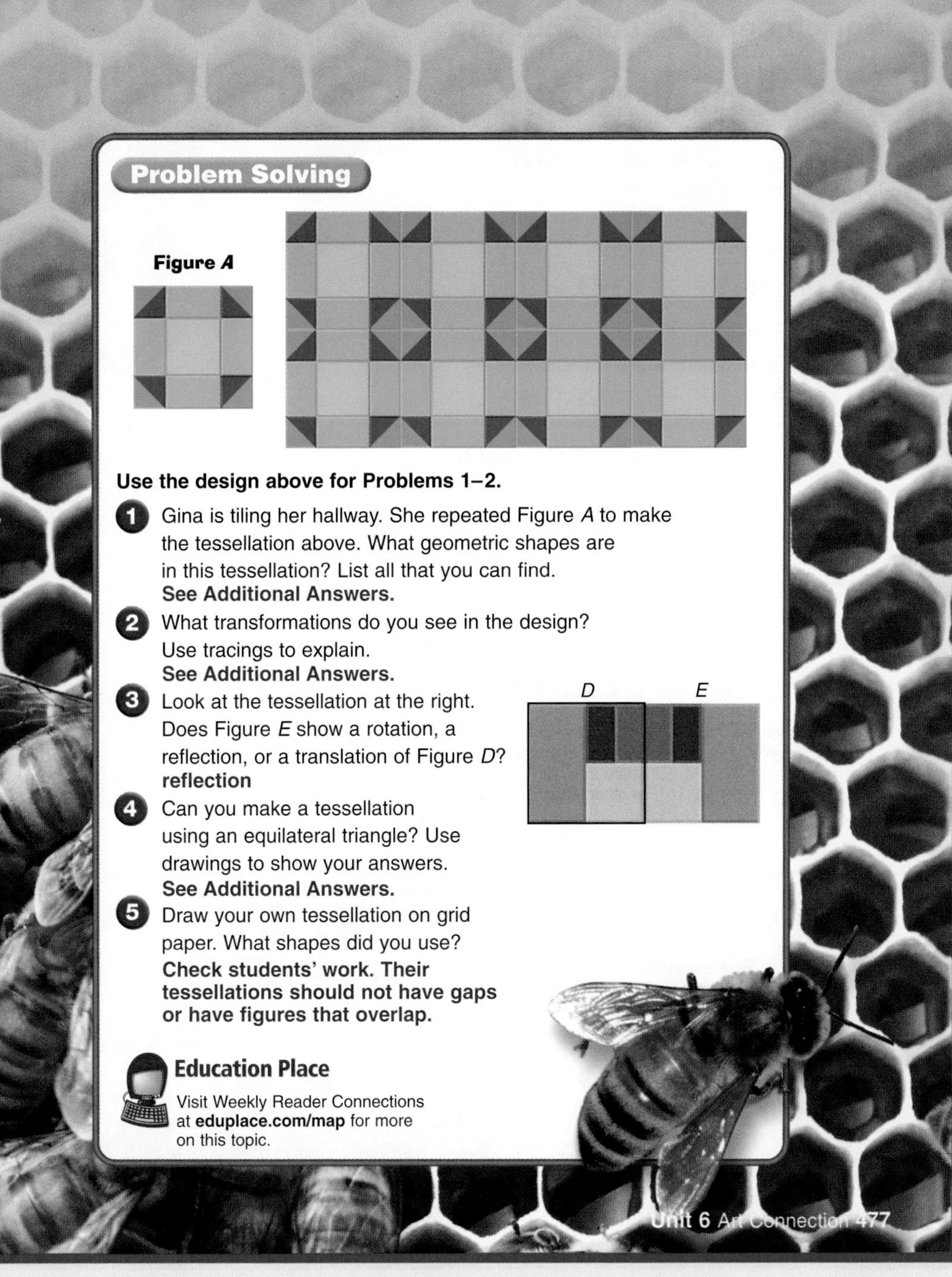

Problem Solving

Use the design above for Problems 1–2.

1. Gina is tiling her hallway. She repeated Figure *A* to make the tessellation above. What geometric shapes are in this tessellation? List all that you can find.
   See Additional Answers.
2. What transformations do you see in the design? Use tracings to explain.
   See Additional Answers.
3. Look at the tessellation at the right. Does Figure *E* show a rotation, a reflection, or a translation of Figure *D*?
   reflection

4. Can you make a tessellation using an equilateral triangle? Use drawings to show your answers.
   See Additional Answers.
5. Draw your own tessellation on grid paper. What shapes did you use?
   Check students' work. Their tessellations should not have gaps or have figures that overlap.

Education Place

Visit Weekly Reader Connections at **eduplace.com/map** for more on this topic.

Enrichment

PURPOSE

Students become familiar with pentominoes and apply visual thinking.

- This lesson utilizes the concepts learned in Chapters 16 and 17 and applies them to identifying and creating pentominoes.
- Provide students with cutouts of 5 congruent squares or grid paper to complete the exercises if they have difficulty visualizing pentominoes.
- As students work through the page, ask questions such as: **What is the perimeter (or area) of a pentomino? Does each of the different pentominoes have the same perimeter (or area)?** (Pentominoes can have different perimeters, but all have the same area, which is 5 square units.)
- Offer the students this challenge: **Put some or all of the pentominoes together to form a rectangle. What are the perimeter and area?** (Answers may vary.)

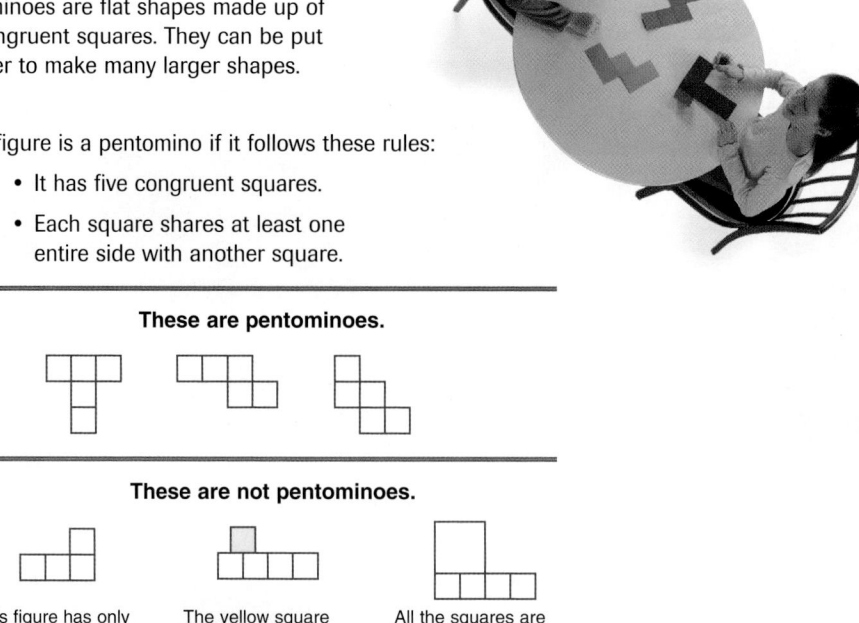

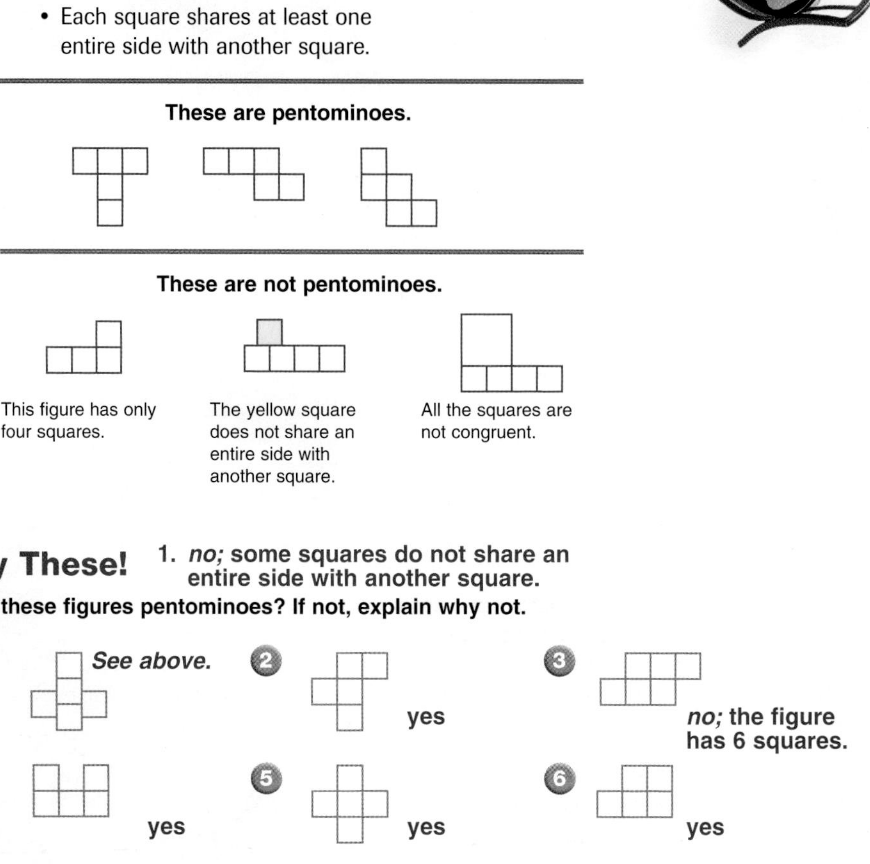

Enrichment: Visual Thinking

Pentominoes

Pentominoes are flat shapes made up of five congruent squares. They can be put together to make many larger shapes.

A figure is a pentomino if it follows these rules:

- It has five congruent squares.
- Each square shares at least one entire side with another square.

These are pentominoes.

These are not pentominoes.

This figure has only four squares.

The yellow square does not share an entire side with another square.

All the squares are not congruent.

Try These!

1. ***no;*** **some squares do not share an entire side with another square.**

Are these figures pentominoes? If not, explain why not.

1. ***See above.***
2. **yes**
3. ***no;*** **the figure has 6 squares.**
4. **yes**
5. **yes**
6. **yes**
7. **Challenge** There are only 12 possible pentominoes. Draw the five not shown on this page. ***See Additional Answers.***

Maximize the Size

Use your calculator to explore area and perimeter.

1. Find the area and perimeter of each of the figures below.
Figure A: area 5 ft^2, perimeter 12 ft; Figure B: area 8 ft^2, perimeter 12 ft; Figure C: area 9 ft^2, perimeter 12 ft

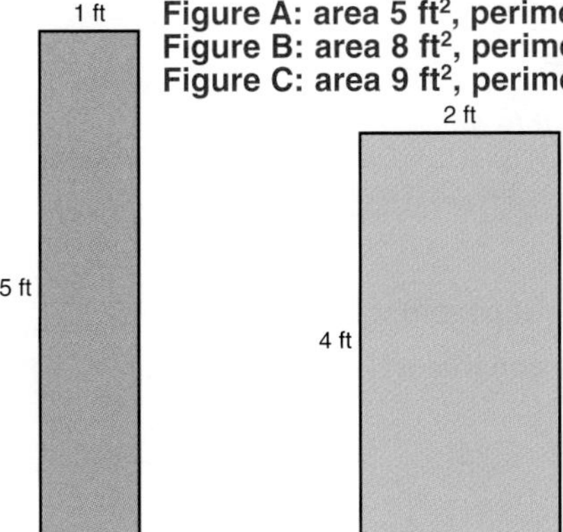

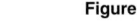

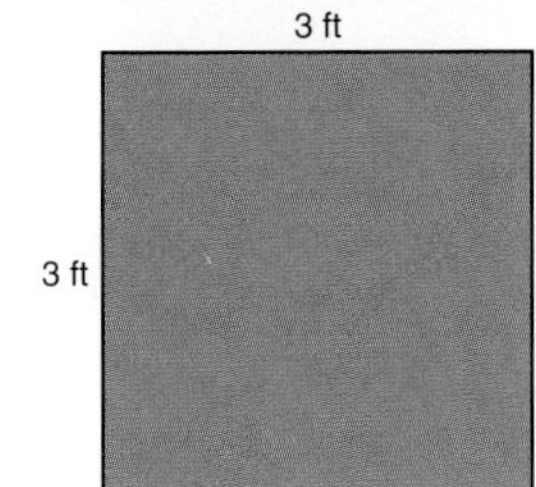

Figure A Figure B Figure C

2. What do you notice about the perimeters of the figures above?
All three have a perimeter of 12 ft.
3. Which figure has the greatest area?
Figure C.
4. Use graph paper to draw 5 different rectangles that each have a perimeter of 20 centimeters. Which rectangle has the greatest area? ***See below.***
5. Use your calculator to find 5 different rectangles that have a perimeter of 40 centimeters. Which has the greatest area?***See below.***
6. **Analyze** Look at your answers for Exercises 2–5. What rectangle always seems to have the greatest area for any perimeter?
The rectangle that is closest to a square.
7. **Challenge** Find the length and width of the rectangle with the greatest area that has a perimeter of 144 meters.
Each side is 36 meters.

4. **The rectangle in which all the sides are 5 cm.**

5. ***Possible answer:*** **The rectangle in which all the sides are 10 cm.**

Maximize the Size

PURPOSE

To use a calculator to find perimeter and area.

- Students can work in pairs to complete this page. They can take turns recording and calculating. One student can draw the rectangle while the other calculates the perimeter and area for it using a calculator.
- Besides finding out what size rectangle has the most area for a given perimeter, this page also provides practice calculating perimeter and area.
- For **Exercises 4–7,** suggest that students make an organized list to find all of the areas for all the different combinations of dimensions for rectangles with a given perimeter.
- Ask students how to begin to find at least one of the combinations of length and width for a rectangle. Remind them that the perimeter of a rectangle is twice the sum of its length and width. So, if $P = 2(l + w)$, then $\frac{1}{2}P = l + w$. If $P = 20$, then $\frac{1}{2}P = 10 = l + w$. Think of pairs of two whole numbers whose sum is 10, such as $9 + 1$ or $8 + 2$, for the length and width.
- After completing **Exercises 4 and 5,** ask students how the calculator helps them with this exploration activity.

Monitoring Student Progress

Unit 6 Test

PURPOSE

This test provides an informal assessment of the Unit 6 objectives.

Unit Test Items 1–25

To assign a numerical grade for this Unit Test, use 4 points for each test item.

Customize Your Instruction

For students who have not yet mastered these objectives, you can use the **Reteaching Resources** listed in the chart below. ***Ways to Success*** is Houghton Mifflin's Intervention program, available in CD-ROM and blackline master formats.

Assessment Options

Formal tests for this unit are also provided in the Unit Resource Folder.

- Unit 6 Open Response Test (Form A)
- Unit 6 Multiple Choice Test (Form B)

Unit 6 Test

VOCABULARY Open Response

Choose the best term to complete each sentence.

Vocabulary
ray
line
parallel
parallelogram
perpendicular
regular polygon

1. A figure that has only one endpoint and goes on without end in one direction is called a ____. **ray**
2. A figure whose sides are congruent and angles are congruent is called a ____. **regular polygon**
3. Two lines that form right angles are ____ to each other. **perpendicular**

CONCEPTS AND SKILLS Open Response

Name each plane figure. (Chapter 16) ***Possible answers given.***

4.  **pentagon**
5.  ***See above.***
6.  **trapezoid, quadrilateral**
7. 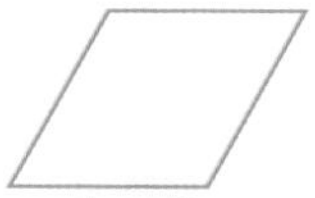  **rhombus, parallelogram, quadrilateral**

5. square, rhombus, rectangle, parallelogram, quadrilateral

Do the figures in each pair appear to be congruent? Write *yes* or *no*. (Chapter 17)

8. 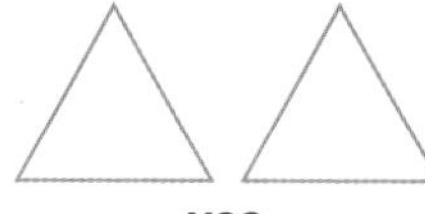 ***yes***
9. 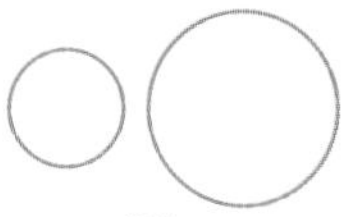 ***no***
10. 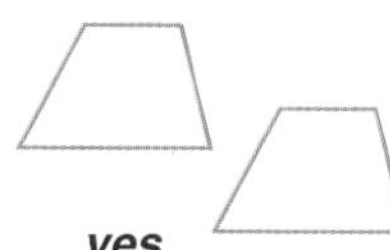 ***yes***

Tell how each figure was moved. Write *rotation*, *reflection*, or *translation*. (Chapter 17)

11. 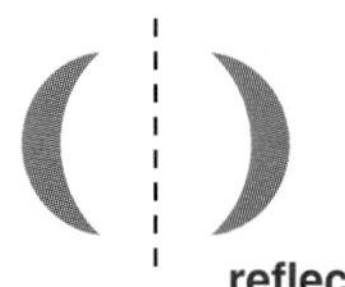 **reflection**
12. 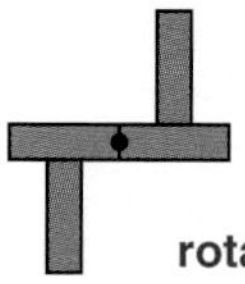 **rotation**
13. 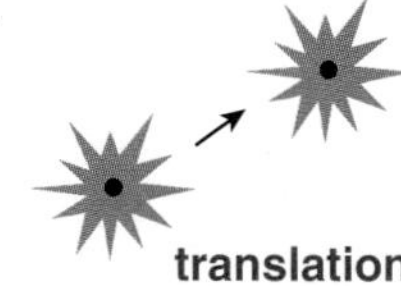 **translation**

How many lines of symmetry does the figure have? Does the figure have rotational symmetry? Write *yes* or *no*. (Chapter 17)

14. 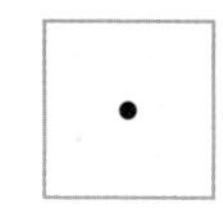 ***4; yes***
15. 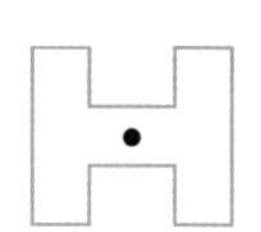 ***2; yes***
16. 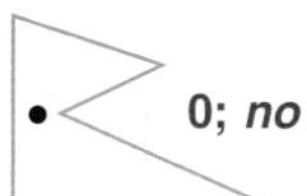 ***0; no***

480

Reteaching Support

Unit Test Items	Unit Objectives Tested	Covered On Teacher's Edition Pages	Use These Reteaching Resources
1–7	**6A** Identify, classify, and describe plane figures.	404A–406, 408A–409, 412A–414, 416A–417	Reteach Resources and *Ways to Success* CD-ROM, 16.1–16.2, 16.4–16.5
8–10, 14–16	**6B** Identify congruent figures and figures with line and rotational symmetry.	430A–432, 440A–443	Reteach Resources and *Ways to Success* CD-ROM, 17.1, 17.4
11–13	**6C** Identify, perform, and predict the results of rotations, reflections, and translations.	434A–435	Reteach Resources and *Ways to Success* CD-ROM, 17.2
17–19, 20–21	**6D** Estimate and find perimeter, area, and volume.	452A–458, 460A–462, 468A–469	Reteach Resources and *Ways to Success* CD-ROM, 18.1–18.4, 18.6
20–21	**6E** Identify, classify, and describe solid geometric figures.	464A–467	Reteach Resources and *Ways to Success* CD-ROM, 18.5
22–25	**6F** Solve problems using skills and strategies.	418A–420, 436A–438, 444A–446, 470A–472	Reteach Resources and *Ways to Success* CD-ROM, 16.6, 17.3, 17.5, 18.7

Find the perimeter and area of each figure. (Chapter 18)

17. 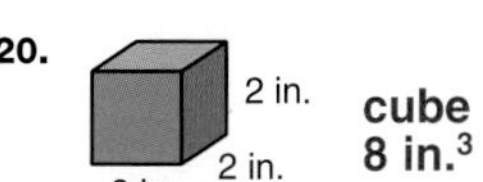

$P = 24$ cm
$A = 32$ cm^2

18. 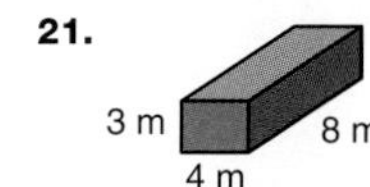

$P = 18$ in.
$A = 18$ in.^{2}

19. 7 ft, 7 ft
$P = 28$ ft
$A = 49$ ft^2

Name each solid figure. Then find the volume of each. (Chapter 18)

20. 2 in., 2 in., 2 in.
cube
8 in.^{3}

21. 3 m, 8 m, 4 m
rectangular prism
96 m^3

PROBLEM SOLVING Open Response *See Additional Answers.*

22. A repeating design has a circle after a hexagon. A square is first. What are the first 8 figures in the design?

23. Can an equilateral triangle, a parallelogram, and a trapezoid be used to make a hexagon? Use a drawing to explain.

24. A rectangular trunk is 5 ft long, 2 ft wide, and 2 ft high. What is the volume of the trunk? Explain. 20 ft^3

25. Can 17 toothpicks be used to form 6 congruent squares? If so, draw the figures.

Performance Assessment

Constructed Response

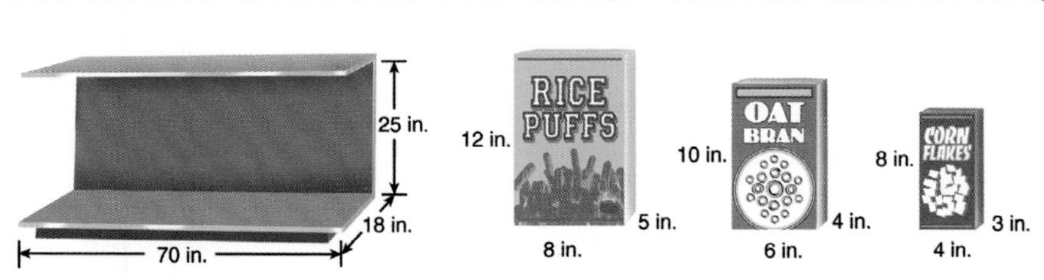

Task Mr. Alou needs to fill a supermarket shelf with the cereal boxes shown above. He needs to display some of each kind of cereal.

Use the information above and at the right to find a way Mr. Alou can display the cereal. How many of each kind of cereal are in your display? Explain your thinking. Use the words *across*, *deep*, and *high* to describe your display.

Information You Need

- All boxes must be upright and face forward.
- Only the same kinds of cereal are placed in front of one another.
- Only the same kinds of cereal are stacked on top of one another.

See Additional Answers.

Unit 6 Test **481**

Performance Assessment & Scoring Rubric

4 EXEMPLARY

Fully completes each task showing an understanding of how to estimate and find perimeter, area, and volume; identifies congruent figures and predicts the results of rotations, reflections, and translations using the information provided. Provides a complete and clear description of the resultant cereal box display and fully explains reasoning used to plan the display.

3 PROFICIENT

Shows an understanding of perimeter, area, volume and congruent figures and translations, but may need help in devising the display or in explaining the choices made.

2 ACCEPTABLE

Fully completes each task but makes some calculation errors resulting in a display which does not meet all of the criteria specified in the problem or fails to fully explain reasoning used.

1 LIMITED

Is unable to complete all the tasks, fails to estimate and find perimeter, area, and volume measurements or to successfully predict the results of translations needed to create a feasible box display. Is unable to explain the reasoning used or choices made even with assistance.

UNIT TEST – FORM A

Unit 6 Test Form A

Name ______ Date ______

Use words and symbols to name the figure.

1. F G — line segment *FG*; line segment *GF*; $\overline{FG}$; or $\overline{GF}$

Write *parallel*, *intersecting*, or *perpendicular* to describe the relationship between the pair of lines.

2. intersecting

Name the angle in three ways. Then classify the angle as *acute*, *obtuse*, *right*, or *straight*.

3. $\angle LMN$; $\angle NML$; $\angle M$; right

Name the polygon. If the polygon is a quadrilateral, write all names that apply.

4. quadrilateral; parallelogram; rectangle

Go on

UNIT TEST – FORM B

Unit 6 Test Form B

Name ______ Date ______

Choose the letter of the correct answer.

1. Use symbols to name the figure.
A $\overline{OP}$ C $\overleftrightarrow{PO}$
B $\overrightarrow{PO}$ D $\overrightarrow{OP}$
(D)

2. Describe the relationship between the pair of lines.
F intersecting H perpendicular
G parallel J none of these
(G)

3. Name and classify the angle.
A $\angle XZY$; acute C $\angle XZY$; obtuse
B $\angle ZXY$; obtuse D $\angle ZXY$; acute
(A)

4. Name the polygon.
F pentagon H quadrilateral
G hexagon J octagon
(F)

Go on

Unit 6 Test Answers: Form A

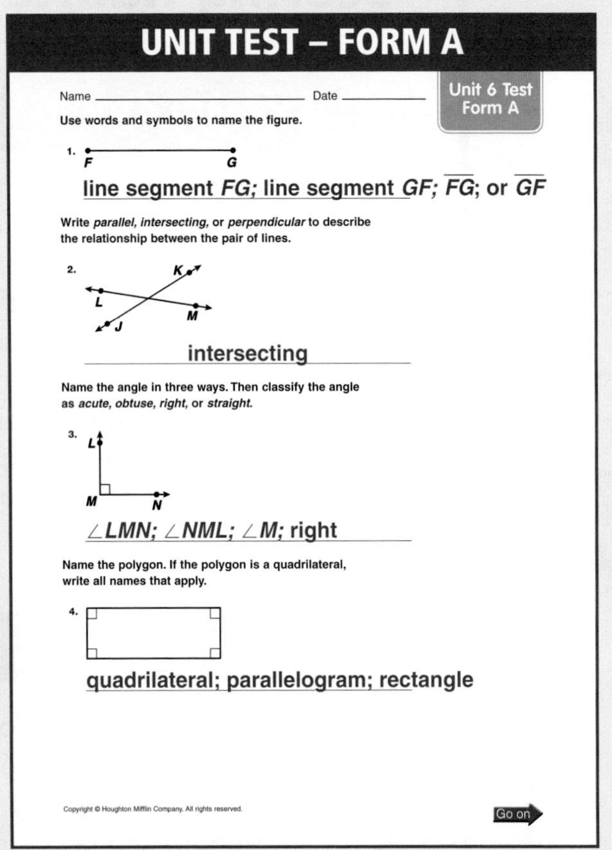

UNIT TEST – FORM A

Unit 6 Test Form A

Name ______ Date ______

Use words and symbols to name the figure.

1. line segment *FG*; line segment *GF*; $\overline{FG}$; or $\overline{GF}$

Write *parallel, intersecting,* or *perpendicular* to describe the relationship between the pair of lines.

2. intersecting

Name the angle in three ways. Then classify the angle as *acute, obtuse, right,* or *straight.*

3. ∠*LMN*; ∠*NML*; ∠*M*; right

Name the polygon. If the polygon is a quadrilateral, write all names that apply.

4. quadrilateral; parallelogram; rectangle

Go on

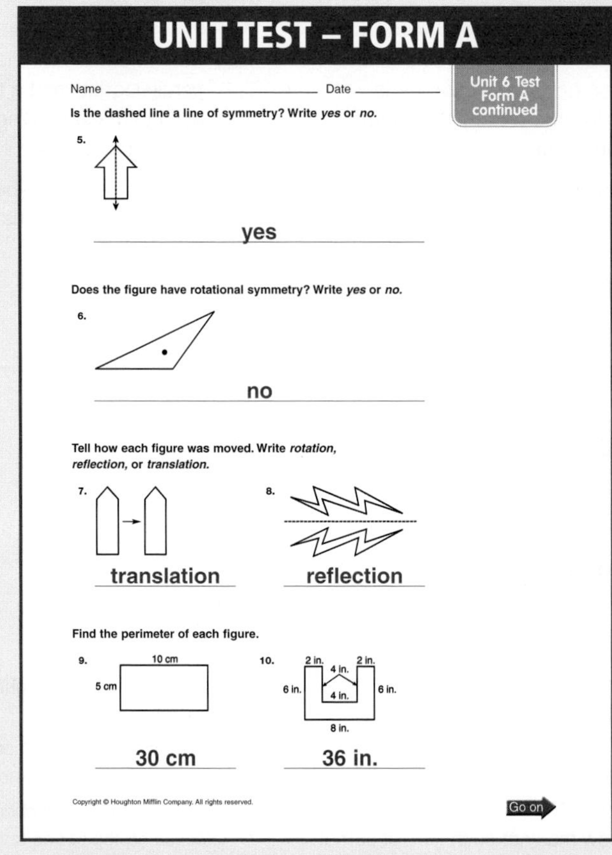

UNIT TEST – FORM A

Unit 6 Test Form A continued

Name ______ Date ______

Is the dashed line a line of symmetry? Write *yes* or *no.*

5. yes

Does the figure have rotational symmetry? Write *yes* or *no.*

6. no

Tell how each figure was moved. Write *rotation, reflection,* or *translation.*

7. translation

8. reflection

Find the perimeter of each figure.

9. 30 cm

10. 36 in.

Go on

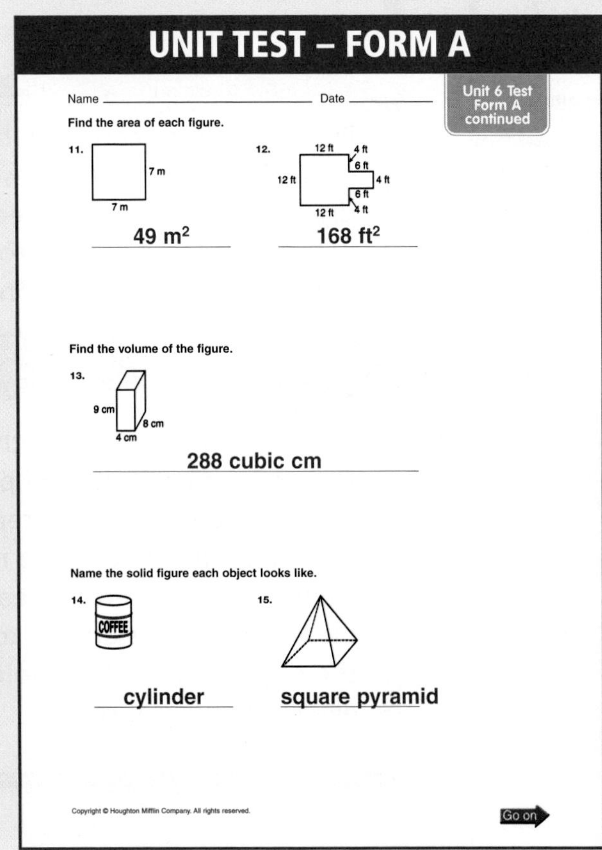

UNIT TEST – FORM A

Unit 6 Test Form A continued

Name ______ Date ______

Find the area of each figure.

11. 49 m^2

12. 168 ft^2

Find the volume of the figure.

13. 288 cubic cm

Name the solid figure each object looks like.

14. cylinder

15. square pyramid

Go on

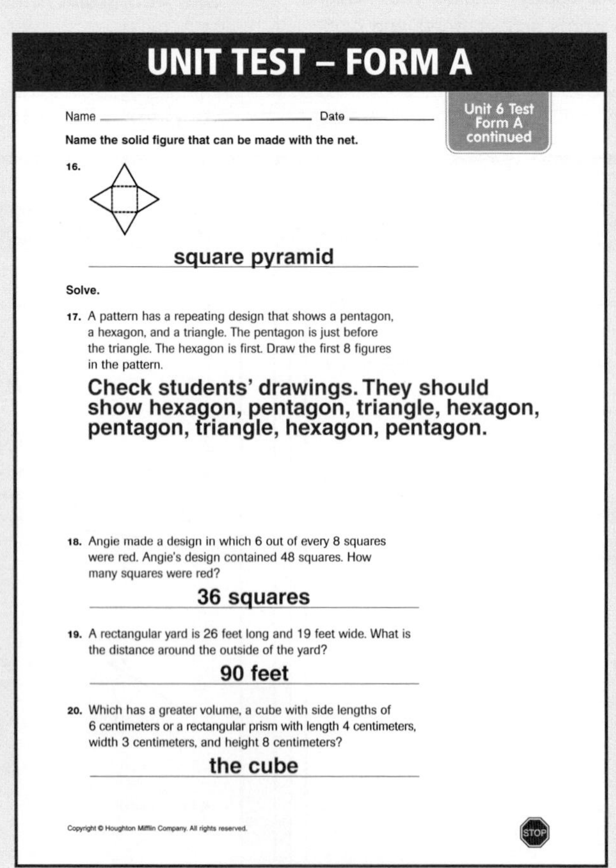

UNIT TEST – FORM A

Unit 6 Test Form A continued

Name ______ Date ______

Name the solid figure that can be made with the net.

16. square pyramid

Solve.

17. A pattern has a repeating design that shows a pentagon, a hexagon, and a triangle. The pentagon is just before the triangle. The hexagon is first. Draw the first 8 figures in the pattern.

Check students' drawings. They should show hexagon, pentagon, triangle, hexagon, pentagon, triangle, hexagon, pentagon.

18. Angie made a design in which 6 out of every 8 squares were red. Angie's design contained 48 squares. How many squares were red?

36 squares

19. A rectangular yard is 26 feet long and 19 feet wide. What is the distance around the outside of the yard?

90 feet

20. Which has a greater volume, a cube with side lengths of 6 centimeters or a rectangular prism with length 4 centimeters, width 3 centimeters, and height 8 centimeters?

the cube

STOP

Unit 6 Test Answers: Form B

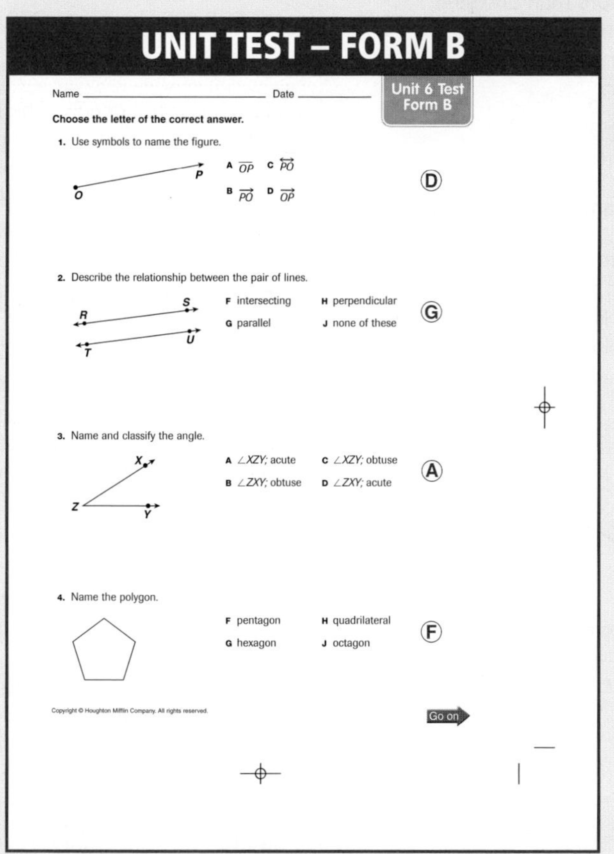

UNIT TEST – FORM B

Name ______________________ Date __________ Unit 6 Test Form B

Choose the letter of the correct answer.

1. Use symbols to name the figure. (D)

   A $\overline{OP}$ C $\overrightarrow{PO}$

   B $\overleftrightarrow{PO}$ D $\overrightarrow{OP}$

2. Describe the relationship between the pair of lines. (G)

   F intersecting H perpendicular

   G parallel J none of these

3. Name and classify the angle. (A)

   A ∠XZY; acute C ∠XZY; obtuse

   B ∠ZXY; obtuse D ∠ZXY; acute

4. Name the polygon. (F)

   F pentagon H quadrilateral

   G hexagon J octagon

Go on

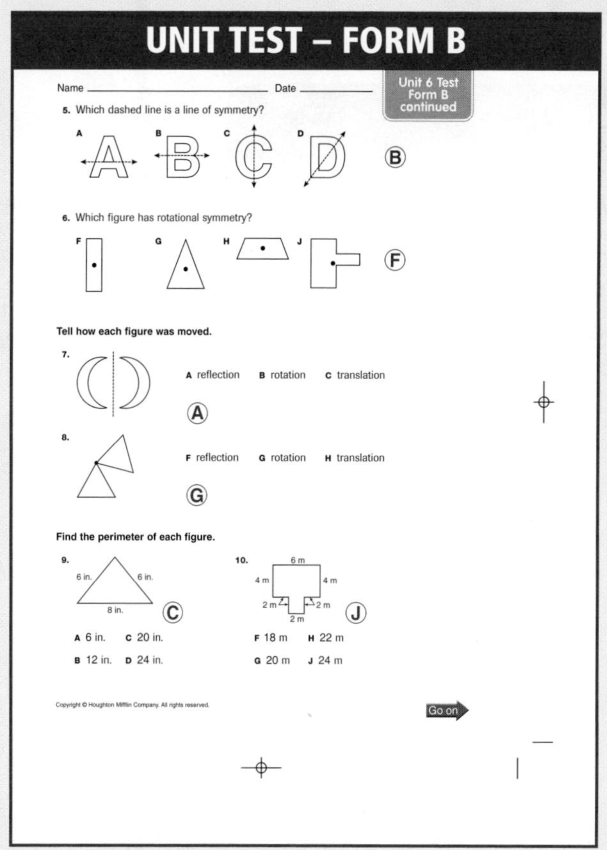

UNIT TEST – FORM B

Name ______________________ Date __________ Unit 6 Test Form B continued

5. Which dashed line is a line of symmetry? (B)

6. Which figure has rotational symmetry? (F)

Tell how each figure was moved.

7. A reflection B rotation C translation (A)

8. F reflection G rotation H translation (G)

Find the perimeter of each figure.

9. (C)

   A 6 in. C 20 in.

   B 12 in. D 24 in.

10. (J)

    F 18 m H 22 m

    G 20 m J 24 m

Go on

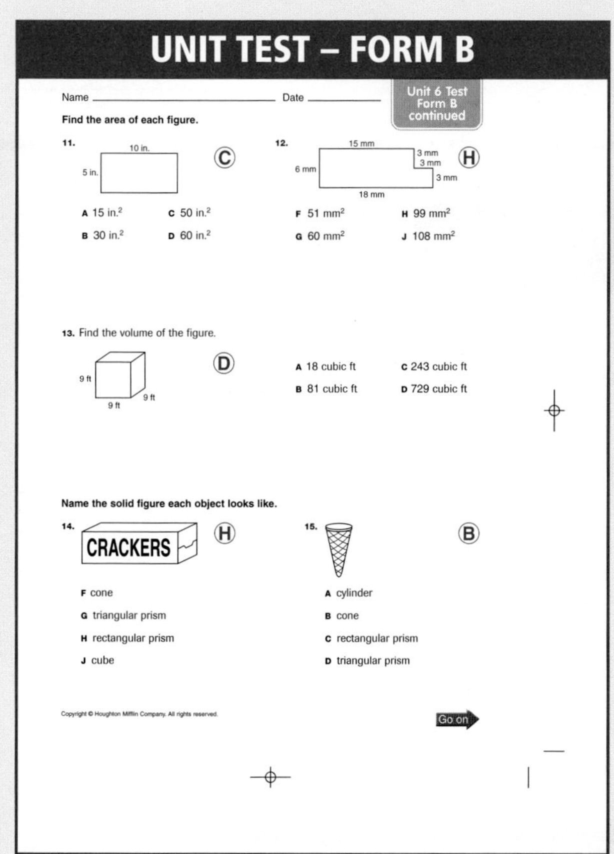

UNIT TEST – FORM B

Name ______________________ Date __________ Unit 6 Test Form B continued

Find the area of each figure.

11. (C)

    A 15 in.^{2} C 50 in.^{2}

    B 30 in.^{2} D 60 in.^{2}

12. (H)

    F 51 mm^2 H 99 mm^2

    G 60 mm^2 J 108 mm^2

13. Find the volume of the figure. (D)

    A 18 cubic ft C 243 cubic ft

    B 81 cubic ft D 729 cubic ft

Name the solid figure each object looks like.

14. (H)

    F cone

    G triangular prism

    H rectangular prism

    J cube

15. (B)

    A cylinder

    B cone

    C rectangular prism

    D triangular prism

Go on

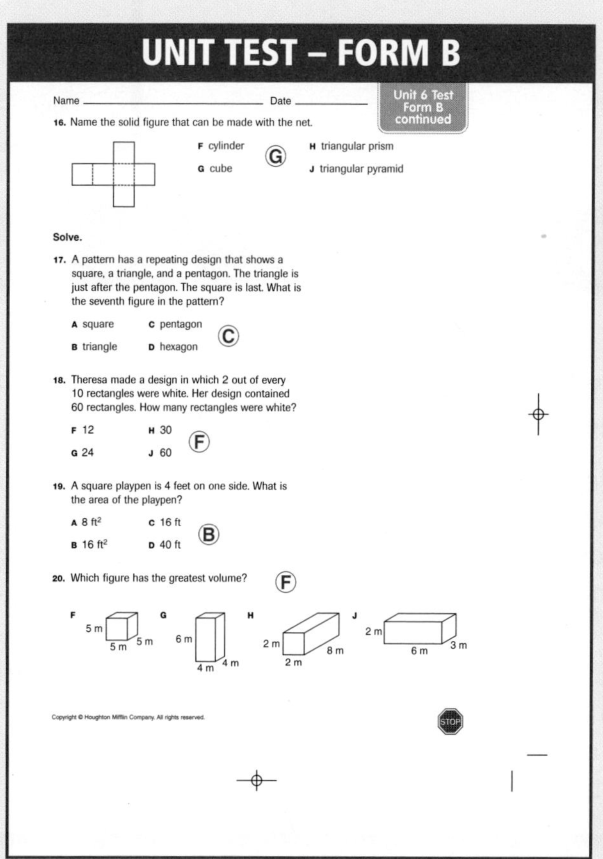

UNIT TEST – FORM B

Name ______________________ Date __________ Unit 6 Test Form B continued

16. Name the solid figure that can be made with the net. (G)

    F cylinder H triangular prism

    G cube J triangular pyramid

Solve.

17. A pattern has a repeating design that shows a square, a triangle, and a pentagon. The triangle is just after the pentagon. The square is last. What is the seventh figure in the pattern? (C)

    A square C pentagon

    B triangle D hexagon

18. Theresa made a design in which 2 out of every 10 rectangles were white. Her design contained 60 rectangles. How many rectangles were white? (F)

    F 12 H 30

    G 24 J 60

19. A square playpen is 4 feet on one side. What is the area of the playpen? (B)

    A 8 ft^2 C 16 ft

    B 16 ft^2 D 40 ft

20. Which figure has the greatest volume? (F)

STOP

Monitoring Student Progress

Cumulative Test Prep

PURPOSE

This page will familiarize students with the multiple-choice and open-response formats of many standardized state tests.

Cumulative Test Prep

Solve Problems 1–10.

Test-Taking Tip

To solve problems that have more than one step, break the problem into smaller steps.

Look at the example below.

Kasib's bedroom is 10 ft wide and 15 ft long. The rug in his bedroom is 9 ft wide and 12 ft long. How many square feet of the floor of Kasib's bedroom are **not** covered by the rug?

A 25 ft^2 C 96 ft^2

(B) 42 ft^2 D 138 ft^2

THINK

Area of room: 10 ft × 15 ft = 150 ft^2
Area of rug: 9 ft × 12 ft = 108 ft^2
Area of room minus area of rug:
150 ft^2 − 108 ft^2 = 42 ft^2
Choose **B**.

Multiple Choice

1. If 278,099 > ■, which number could be the value of ■?

A 279,067 C 278,099

B 278,136 (D) 278,081

(Chapter 2, Lesson 1)

2. Tani has 2 red pencils. She is given 10 blue, 10 yellow, and 10 green pencils. Which expression represents the number of pencils Tani has now?

F (2 + 10) × 3 H (10 − 2) × 3

(G) 2 + (10 × 3) J 10 + (2 × 3)

(Chapter 5, Lesson 2)

3. John is putting a fence around a rectangular dog pen. The pen is 25 feet long and 32 feet wide. John has 20 yards of fencing. How many more yards does he need?

A 8 yards C 32 yards

(B) 18 yards D 38 yards

(Chapter 18, Lesson 2)

4. Jeff has a block of wood. He cuts it in half. How many more faces are there now than before Jeff made the cut?

F 18 H 8

G 12 (J) 6

(Chapter 18, Lesson 5)

482

For Test-Taking Tips, See Page 658.

Test-Taking TIPS

Review the test-taking tips with students before they begin the test. Discuss with students some of the ways they can check their work.

- Tell students that they should read the problem slowly and think about what the words mean and how the words and numbers can be used to solve the problem.
- With multiple-choice questions, tell students to limit their choices by crossing out any choices that they are sure are incorrect.
- Encourage students to make notes or draw pictures to help them solve problems.
- Suggest that students look back to be sure they have marked only one answer for each question.

Open Response

5. Together Rodrigo and Marci earned \$86. How much money did they each earn if Marci earned \$4 more than Rodrigo? **Marci earned \$45, and Rodrigo earned \$41.**
(Chapter 9, Lesson 3)

6. It is 9° C. What would the temperature be if it were 11 degrees colder?
$^{-}2$°C (Chapter 13, Lesson 4)

7. Look at the figure.

Which angle in the figure is an acute angle?

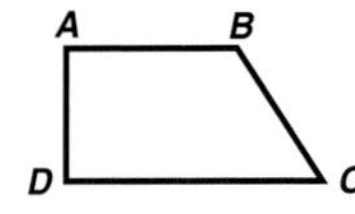

angle *C* (Chapter 16, Lesson 2)

8. What are the prime factors of 72?
2, 2, 2, 3, 3 (Chapter 10, Lesson 5)

9. The table shows how many miles the Vaughn family drove each day during their vacation.

Miles Driven Each Day	
Day	**Miles**
Monday	23
Tuesday	21
Wednesday	13
Thursday	31

What is the average number of miles the Vaughn family drove each day?
22 miles
(Chapter 10, Lesson 5)

Extended Response

10. The School Store is placing an order for balloons and mugs. A case of balloons costs \$4. A case of mugs costs \$22. The school needs to order more than 1 case of each.

Let *b* stand for the number of cases of balloons.

Let *m* stand for the number of cases of mugs.

Let *T* stand for the total.

a Write an equation to find the total cost of the balloons and mugs ordered. $T = 4b + 22m$

b Suppose the School Store ordered 3 cases of balloons and 2 cases of mugs. Use the equation you wrote to find the total cost of all the items.
\$56

c The School Store also needs to order erasers. A case of erasers costs \$5. Change the equation you wrote to include the cost of the erasers. Let *e* stand for the number of cases.
$T = 4b + 22m + 5e$ (Chapter 5, Lesson 5)

Education Place
Look for Cumulative Test Prep at **eduplace.com/map** for more practice.

Unit 6 Cumulative Test Prep **483**

Test-Taking Vocabulary

- In **Item 2,** tell students to pay attention to the quantities that are surrounded by parentheses because that's the operation that is calculated first in an expression.
- The dimensions of the dog pen are given in feet in **Item 3,** but the amount of fencing and the answer choices are given in yards. Caution students to convert the perimeter to yards before dealing with the fencing.
- The word *average* is used in the question in **Item 9.** Ask students which measure—mean, median, or mode—is most appropriate for this problem.

National and state tests might also use this word to indicate *subtraction:*

- now than before
- how many more
- how many less
- fewer

Vocabulary Wrap-Up

PURPOSE

Use this page to encourage students to use math vocabulary to talk about the important concepts they have learned in this unit.

Big Ideas and Key Vocabulary

Review and discuss with students the Big Ideas of this unit using the Key Vocabulary terms *rotate, reflect, translate, and formula*.

Math Conversations

Have students work together in small groups to discuss **Exercises 1–4.** Check to see whether individual students understand the key concepts and are able to use the math vocabulary correctly. Clear up any misunderstandings students may have. After students have discussed the exercises in small groups, continue the conversation as a whole class. Have volunteers from each group share what their group talked about.

Write About It Encourage students to include a sketch of each of the examples they found. Then have students share their examples with the class as you or a student record them on the board.

Vocabulary Wrap-Up for Unit 6

Look back at the big ideas and vocabulary in this unit.

Big Ideas

You can rotate, reflect, or translate plane figures.

You can use formulas to find perimeter, area, or volume.

Key Vocabulary

rotate
reflect
translate
formula

1. **Translation, rotation, and reflection; *Check students' drawings.***

Math Conversations

Use your new vocabulary to discuss these big ideas.

1. What are the 3 ways you can move figures? Use drawings to give examples of each way. ***See above.***
2. Use a rectangle and a rectangular prism to describe area, perimeter, and volume. Give a formula for each. ***See Additional Answers.***
3. Explain the difference between line symmetry and rotational symmetry. ***See Additional Answers.***
4. Explain how to determine if a pair of figures is congruent. ***See below.***
5. **Write About It** Search for examples of plane and solid figures near your home or school. Identify and describe what you find.

   Check students' work.

How can we find the perimeter of our classroom?
We can measure its length and width and then use the formula.

4. **A pair of figures is congruent if they are exactly the same size and shape.**

484 Unit 6 Vocabulary Wrap-Up

Wrap-Up the Unit Project

- Display each art project in a designated space in the classroom. Ask each student to give a brief description orally of his or her creation, emphasizing the geometric figures and relationships used to make the piece of art.
- Invite other classrooms to visit the **Math Art Fair.** Encourage students to volunteer to act as docents during these visitations.
- Invite parents to visit the **Math Art Fair** during parent-teacher conferences and PTA nights. Students should be available to point out the mathematical and geometric elements of their creations.
- Encourage students to enter their creations in art or mathematics contests.

UNIT 7

Fractions and Decimals

Standards

Unit 7 Objectives	Lessons	NCTM Standards	Your State's Standards
7A Identify parts of regions and groups; find fractional parts of a group; find equivalent fractions.	**19.1, 19.2, 19.3, 19.5**	**Number and Operations:** Develop understanding of fractions as parts of unit wholes, as parts of collections.	
7B Identify and write mixed numbers.	**19.7**	**Number and Operations:** Develop understanding of fractions as parts of unit wholes or collections.	
7C Compare and order fractions.	**19.4**	**Number and Operations:** Use models, benchmarks, and equivalent forms to judge the size of fractions.	
7D Add and subtract fractions and mixed numbers with like denominators; use models to add and subtract fractions with unlike denominators.	**20.1, 20.2, 20.4, 20.6, 20.7**	**Number and Operations:** Use visual models, benchmarks, and equivalent forms to add and subtract commonly used fractions. Develop and use strategies to estimate the results of computations involving fractions and decimals in situations relevant to students' experience.	
7E Write fractions and mixed numbers as decimals, and vice versa.	**21.1, 21.2, 21.3, 21.4**	**Number and Operations:** Recognize and generate equivalent forms of commonly used fractions, decimals, and percent.	
7F Identify, compare, order, and round decimals.	**21.6, 21.7, 22.1**	**Number and Operations:** Understand the place-value structure of the base-ten number system and be able to represent and compare decimals.	
7G Estimate, add, and subtract decimals to thousandths.	**22.2, 22.3, 22.4**	**Number and Operations:** Estimate the results of computations involving decimals. **Representations:** Select, apply, and translate among mathematical representations to solve problems.	
7H Solve problems using skills and strategies.	**19.6, 20.3, 20.5, 20.8, 21.5, 22.5**	**Problem Solving:** Apply and adapt a variety of appropriate strategies to solve problems. **Data Analysis and Probability:** Represent data using tables and graphs. **Algebra:** Describe, extend, and make generalizations about patterns.	

NCTM Process Standards	Sample Lessons or Features	Your State's Standards
Reasoning and Proof: Use various levels and types of reasoning, including formulating proofs, patterns, conjectures, and rules.	Reasoning, Problem Solving, and Algebra Readiness features. For example, see **Lessons 19.6, 20.1, 20.3, 20.5, 20.7, 20.8, 21.5, 21.6, 21.7, 22.5.**	
Communication: Understand vocabulary, organization of processes, and how to communicate and comprehend mathematical concepts and justifications with accuracy.	Hands-On and Problem-Solving lessons, Explain Your Thinking questions, games, and Reading Mathematics. For example, see **Lessons 19.2, 19.3, 20.1, 20.2, 20.3, 20.6, 20.7, 20.8, 21.1, 21.2, 22.2, 22.3, 22.4.**	
Connections: Relate mathematics to real life and other subject areas and make connections from one mathematical idea to another.	Connections features, skills lessons, and Problem-Solving lessons and features. For example, see **Lessons 19.1, 19.4, 19.6, 20.3, 20.5, 20.8, 21.3, 21.5. 21.7, 22.5.**	
Representation: Represent mathematical ideas using concrete objects, pictures, and symbols.	Occurs throughout as students use manipulatives, workmats, drawings, tables, symbols, and equations to model or explain. For example, see **Lessons 19.2, 19.3, 19.5, 19.6, 19.7, 20.4, 20.6, 20.7, 21.1, 21.2, 21.4, 22.1, 22.3.**	

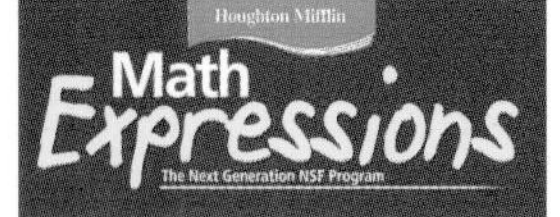

For content corresponding to this *Houghton Mifflin Math* unit, see in *Math Expressions*

- Unit 5: Fractions
- Unit 6: Decimal Numbers

Assessment System

Monitoring Student Progress

Unit Objectives

7A Identify parts of regions and groups; find fractional parts of a group; find equivalent fractions.

7B Identify and write mixed numbers.

7C Compare and order fractions.

7D Add and subtract fractions and mixed numbers with like denominators; use models to add and subtract fractions with unlike denominators.

7E Write fractions and mixed numbers as decimals, and vice versa.

7F Identify, compare, order, and round decimals.

7G Estimate, add, and subtract decimals to thousandths.

7H Solve problems using skills and strategies.

Classroom-Based Assessment

Prior Knowledge

Use What You Know, PE pp. 489, 515, 541, 567
Chapters 19, 20, 21, and 22 Pretests, Unit Resources
Unit 7 Reading Mathematics, PE pp. 486–487

Ongoing Assessment

Student Self-Assessment

Explain Your Thinking, PE pp. 490, 495, 499, 503, 509, 517, 520, 525, 545, 547, 551, 559, 561, 569, 571, 575
Mixed Review & Test Prep, PE pp. 491, 497, 503, 511, 519, 521, 525, 545, 552, 559, 563, 569, 571
Quick Check, PE pp. 501, 527, 549, 575
Vocabulary Wrap-Up, PE p. 590

Informal Assessment by Teachers

Problem of the Day, First page of every TE lesson
Spiral Review, First page of every TE lesson
Common Error/Intervention, TE pp. 490, 494, 498, 502, 508, 516, 520, 524, 534, 544, 546, 550, 554, 558, 560, 568, 570, 574, 576
Lesson Quiz, First page of every TE lesson

Diagnostic/Intervention

Quick Check, PE pp. 501, 527, 549, 575
Common Error/Intervention, TE pp. 490, 494, 498, 502, 508, 516, 520, 524, 534, 544, 546, 550, 554, 558, 560, 568, 570, 574, 576
Chapter Review/Test, PE pp. 512, 538, 564, 580
Unit Test, PE pp. 586–587

Formal Evaluation

Chapter & Unit Assessment

Chapter Review/Test, PE pp. 512, 538, 564, 580
Chapter 19 Test, Unit Resources
Chapter 20 Test, Unit Resources
Chapter 21 Test, Unit Resources
Chapter 22 Test, Unit Resources
***Unit Test, Form A and Form B,** Unit Resources
Unit 7 Test, PE pp. 586–587

Performance Assessment & Rubric

Performance Assessment, PE p. 587
Scoring Rubric, TE p. 587

Test Prep

***Problem-Solving on Tests,** PE pp. 507, 557
***Cumulative Test Prep,** PE pp. 588–589
Test Prep on the Net, on Education Place
www.eduplace.com/map

(Starred tests use standardized test formats.)

Test Generator 

The *Ways to Assess* CD-ROM allows you to create and score customized tests or review pages. You can select items that assess your state's standards, NCTM standards, or lesson objectives of your choosing. The CD-ROM also includes program, chapter, and unit tests for online administration and scoring or for printing.

Intervention 

***Ways to Success* CD-ROM** Reteach the lesson objective, provide extra practice, or reteach a key prerequisite skill. **Lessons** 19.1–19.7, 20.1–20.8, 21.1–21.7, 22.1–22.5

Audio Tutor For students who need extra support, who were absent, or who have reading difficulties. **Lessons** 19.2, 19.4, 19.6, 19.7, 20.1, 20.2, 21.2, 21.4, 21.7, 22.1, 22.4

Unit Activities

Unit Project

Whole Class	15 minutes
Objective	Compare and order fractions.
Materials	None
Visual, Tactual	

Compare and Order Fractions

- Ask students what they know about the Olympic Summer Games. Tell students that for this Unit Project, they are going to produce a mock television show about the events at the most recent Olympic Summer Games.
- Remind students to include fractions and decimals in their measurements and costs when they research, organize, display their data in charts or graphs, and write their scripts.
- Use the activity found on page 590 to wrap up the Unit Project.

Spiral Review

Pairs	20 minutes
Objective	Find fractional parts of a group.
Materials	None
Visual	

Fractional Parts of a Group

- Write the following on the board: ______ *of the* ______ *are* ______.
- Have both students fill in the first blank with a fraction and the next blank with a set of objects or people in the room that have something in common. For example, $\frac{12}{25}$ of the students in the room are ______. Partners exchange sentences and try to guess what belongs in the third blank, then check their answers. Repeat with new sets as time allows.

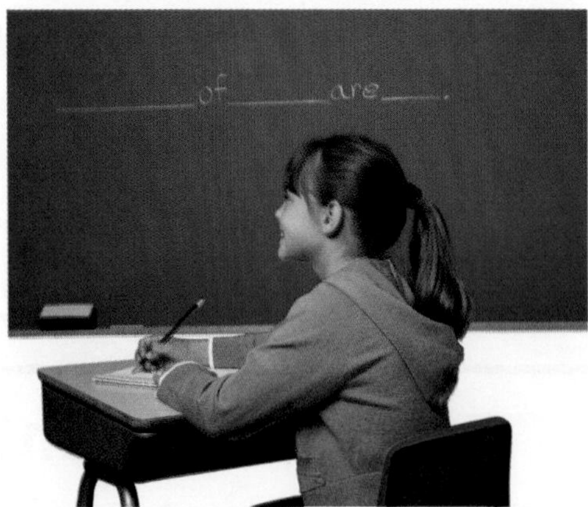

Vocabulary Activity

Pairs	30 minutes
Objective	Discuss vocabulary words.
Materials	Vocabulary cards for the words *decimal point, estimate, hundredth, round, tenth, equivalent, improper, mixed number,* and *simplest form*
Tactual, Visual	

Fraction and Decimal Terms

- One student picks a card, and then draws a picture to demonstrate the word without using the word or talking. The partner guesses the word.
- Both partners discuss if the answer is correct and tell why or why not. Then students switch roles and play again until all of the words have been used.

Take-Home Game

Pairs	15 minutes
Objective	Compare fractions and decimals.
Materials	Set of 20 fraction and decimal cards labeled: $\frac{1}{2}$, $\frac{1}{3}$, $\frac{1}{4}$, $\frac{1}{5}$, $\frac{2}{3}$, $\frac{2}{4}$, $\frac{3}{4}$, $\frac{2}{5}$, $\frac{3}{5}$, $\frac{4}{5}$, 0.2, 0.3, 0.4, 0.25, 0.5, 0.6, 0.7, 0.75, 0.8, 0.9
Visual, Tactual	

Compare Fractions and Decimals

- Distribute shuffled cards. Each player turns over one card and at the same time they compare the numbers.
- The player with the greater number keeps both cards. If the numbers are equivalent, both players turn over the next card. The player with the greater number keeps all four cards. The player with the most cards after all cards have been turned over wins.

Repeatable Unit Game

Pairs	15 minutes
Objective	Find fractional parts of a group.
Materials	Two blank number cubes
Auditory, Visual	

Find Fractional Parts

- Label each of the two cubes with the numbers 1, 2, 3, 4, 6, and 12.
- Each player rolls both cubes and uses the numbers to fill in the fraction part of the expression $\frac{\square}{\square}$ of 12. The greater number is the denominator in the fraction. Remind students that, if both numbers are equal, the fraction they form is equal to 1.
- The player who forms the expression with the greater value scores 1 point. A score of 5 wins.
- Repeat with other numbers and expressions, such as the following
  1, 2, 3, 6, 9, 18 $\frac{\square}{\square}$ of 18
  1, 2, 3, 4, 6, 8 $\frac{\square}{\square}$ of 24
  1, 2, 3, 5, 6, 10 $\frac{\square}{\square}$ of 30

Math Expressions

Small Groups	25 minutes
Objective	Explore fractions by folding a whole into parts.
Materials	Paper strips
Tactual, Visual	

Explore Fractions

- Give each student seven equal-length, pre-cut strips of paper to use. Have the students write 1 whole in the middle of one of their strips and set it aside on their desks.
- Have students fold a second strip in half. Have the students make a vertical mark on their strip at the fold and write $\frac{1}{2}$ in the center of each half. Have them place this strip below their 1 whole strip on their desks.

1 whole	
$\frac{1}{2}$	$\frac{1}{2}$

- Have students discuss how they can fold equal parts for thirds, fourths, sixths, eighths, and twelfths. As they discuss each new fractional part, have them mark and label a new strip of paper.
- Encourage students to look for relationships among different fractions as they fold. Students may discover that:
  - The more parts there are, the smaller each part is.
  - 12 is a bigger whole number than 2, but the fraction $\frac{1}{12}$ is a much smaller part of a whole than $\frac{1}{2}$.
  - $\frac{1}{2}$, $\frac{2}{4}$, $\frac{3}{6}$, and $\frac{6}{12}$ all make up the same total part of a whole.

Starting Unit 7

Reading Mathematics

Use the *Reading Mathematics* pages to be sure that students have adequate understanding and fluency with the unit vocabulary. This provides the key foundation for developing the unit concepts and skills.

Reviewing Vocabulary

Talk about the vocabulary words with students. Remind students that *numerator* and *denominator* are parts of a *fraction.* Use a graphic like the one below to show the relationship of parts to a whole.

numerator → $\frac{3}{10}$ ← number shaded
denominator → ← number in whole

Also remind students that a decimal can be used to show parts of a whole. For example, the fraction $\frac{3}{10}$ is equivalent to the decimal 0.3, and both forms are read as "three-tenths." A decimal has a decimal point to separate the ones and tenths places.

Review place value of decimal numbers by drawing a whole-number place-value chart on the board and then extending it through hundredths. Explain that hundreds, tens, and ones name whole numbers, while ten*th*s and hundred*th*s name parts of whole numbers.

Reading Words and Symbols

This section reinforces the different ways to represent a number using graphics and in word, decimal, and fraction forms. Remind students to read a fraction from top to bottom. The denominator of the fraction tells how many equal parts there are in the whole.

Reading Mathematics

Reviewing Vocabulary

Here are some math vocabulary words that you should know.

fraction	a number that names a part of a whole or part of a group
denominator	the number below the bar in a fraction that tells how many equal parts there are
numerator	the number above the bar in a fraction that tells how many equal parts have been counted
decimal	a number with one or more digits to the right of a decimal point
decimal point	a symbol (.) used to separate the ones and tenths places in a decimal

Reading Words and Symbols

Fractions and decimals both name parts of a whole.
Look at the rectangle on the right.

Read: Seven tenths of the rectangle is red.

Write as a fraction: $\frac{7}{10}$ of the rectangle is red.

Write as a decimal: 0.7 of the rectangle is red.

Use words and symbols to answer the questions.

1. In the fraction $\frac{7}{10}$, which number is the numerator? **7**
   What does that number mean? **Seven parts have been counted.**
2. What decimal names the part of the rectangle that is blue? **0.1**
   How would you write it as a fraction? $\frac{1}{10}$

Reading Test Questions

Choose the correct answer for each.

3. Which statement is false?

   a. $\frac{1}{8}$ of the circles are blue.

   b. $\frac{2}{8}$ of the circles are green.

   c. $\frac{1}{2}$ of the circles are red.

   (d.) $\frac{8}{8}$ of the circles are yellow.

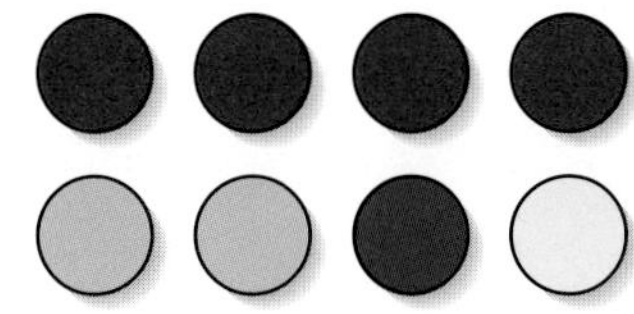

False means "not true" or "wrong."

4. Which fraction represents the green part of the rectangle?

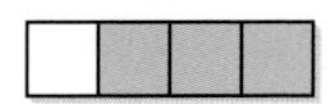

   a. $\frac{1}{4}$ c. $\frac{2}{3}$

   b. $\frac{1}{2}$ (d.) $\frac{3}{4}$

Represents means "stands for," or "shows," or "names."

5. Which decimal represents the shaded part of the rectangle?

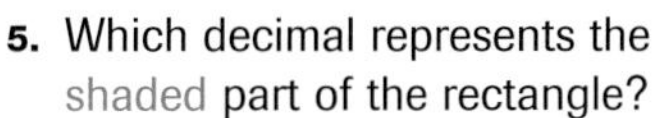

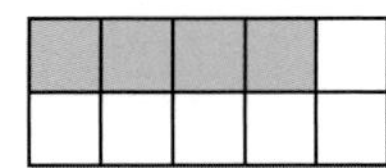

   a. 0.3 c. 0.5

   (b.) 0.4 d. 0.6

Shaded means "colored in."

Learning Vocabulary

Watch for these words in this unit. Write their definitions in your journal.

equivalent fractions
improper fraction
tenth
hundredth

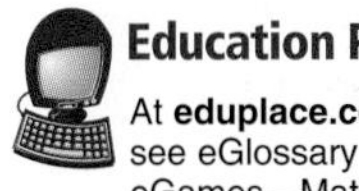

Education Place
At **eduplace.com/map** see eGlossary and eGames—Math Lingo.

Literature Connection

Read "Hold the Meat!" on Pages 652–653. Then work with a partner to answer the questions about the story.

Reading Test Questions

- Remind students to read the problem and the answer choices very carefully. When each answer choice refers to a graphic, suggest that students look at the graphic each time they read a different answer choice.
- Caution students that test problems like Item 5 may be asked about the part of the rectangle that is *not* shaded, in which case the answer would be choice D instead of choice B.

Learning Vocabulary

- Go over the list of new words with the class. Help students pronounce the words correctly and explain that they will learn about these words as they work on this unit. If students are keeping Math Journals, be sure that they enter the words and their definitions as they find them in the unit.
- The *Building Vocabulary Kit* includes vocabulary cards and additional teaching strategies for unit vocabulary.

Writing in Mathematics

Writing helps students learn and remember. Throughout the unit, students have opportunities to write for different purposes:

- explaining their thinking or solution strategies
- creating new problems
- recording what they have learned
- listing questions they still have

Look for ***Explain Your Thinking*** questions in the student text and ***Math Journal Prompts*** in this Teacher's Edition.

Literature Connection

Student Book List Selection

You may use the ***Literature Connection*** (Student Book pp. 652–653, Teacher's Edition p. T54) at any time during this unit.

Other Literature Connections

Mega-Fun Fractions
by Marcia Miller and Martin Lee

Gator Pie
by Louise Matthews

CHAPTER 19

Planning Guide

Understand Fractions

Lesson	Overview	Objective/Vocabulary
1 Represent Fractions p. 490A	▶ Learn basic information and terminology about fractions. ▶ To learn more about fractions, identify and draw pictures of fractional parts of regions or sets.	▶ Read, write, and identify fractions. fraction numerator denominator
2 Hands On: Explore Equivalent Fractions p. 492A	▶ Use fraction strips to find fractions equivalent to a given fraction. ▶ Identify equivalent fractions using number lines.	▶ Use models to identify equivalent fractions. equivalent fractions
3 Equivalent Fractions and Simplest Form p. 494A	▶ Find equivalent fractions with number lines, multiplication, or division. ▶ Express a fraction in simplest form by dividing the numerator and denominator until they can be divided only by 1.	▶ Find equivalent fractions and write fractions in simplest form. simplest form
4 Compare and Order Fractions p. 498A	▶ Compare fractions with either fraction strips or by finding equivalent fractions. ▶ Order fractions with two methods: using a number line and finding equivalent fractions.	▶ Compare and order fractions.
5 Find Part of a Number p. 502A	▶ Find a fractional part of a number using models and a two-step process involving division and multiplication.	▶ Find a fractional part of a number.
6 Problem-Solving Strategy: Draw a Picture p. 504A	▶ Draw a picture to solve a problem. ▶ Choose the best strategy to solve a problem.	▶ Draw a picture to solve a problem.
7 Mixed Numbers and Improper Fractions p. 508A	▶ Work with fractional numbers greater than 1—improper fractions and mixed numbers. ▶ Change from improper fractions to mixed numbers and vice versa. ▶ Round fractions to benchmarks 0, $\frac{1}{2}$, or 1.	▶ Write mixed numbers and improper fractions. mixed number improper fraction

Skills Trace: Understand Fractions		
Grade 3	**Grade 4**	**Grade 5**
• Read, write, and identify fractions and mixed numbers (ch. 18) • Find equivalent fractions (ch. 18) • Compare and order fractions (ch. 19) • Draw a picture to solve a problem (ch. 11)	• Read, write, and identify fractions and mixed numbers • Find equivalent fractions; write fractions in simplest form • Compare and order fractions • Find a fractional part of a number • Draw a picture to solve a problem	• Read, write, and identify fractions and mixed numbers (ch. 9) • Find equivalent fractions; write fractions in simplest form (ch. 9) • Relate and compare fractions, mixed numbers, and decimals (ch. 9) • Draw a diagram (ch. 10)

Differentiated Instruction	Materials	NCTM Standards
▶ Differentiated Instruction activities, p. 490B ▶ *Chapter Challenges,* p. 109 *Ways to Success* CD-ROM 19.1 ▶ *Ways to Success* Skillsheet 161		**Number and Operations:** Develop understanding of fractions as parts of unit wholes, as parts of collections; use models, benchmarks, and equivalent forms to judge the size of fractions.
▶ Differentiated Instruction activities, p. 492B *Ways to Success* CD-ROM 19.2 ▶ *Ways to Success* Skillsheets 162, 166 Audio Tutor **2**/18 Listen and Understand	Fraction Pieces Transparency, blank transparency, Fraction pieces (Learning Tool 34)	**Number and Operations:** Develop understanding of fractions as parts of unit wholes, as parts of collections; use models, benchmarks, and equivalent forms to judge the size of fractions.
▶ Differentiated Instruction activities, p. 494B ▶ *Chapter Challenges,* p. 111 *Ways to Success* CD-ROM 19.3 ▶ *Ways to Success* Skillsheet 165	Fraction Pieces Transparency, blank transparency, index cards (Learning Tool 37)	**Number and Operations:** Develop understanding of fractions as parts of unit wholes, as parts of collections; use models, benchmarks, and equivalent forms to judge the size of fractions.
▶ Differentiated Instruction activities, p. 498B *Ways to Success* CD-ROM 19.4 ▶ *Ways to Success* Skillsheet 166 Audio Tutor **2**/19 Listen and Understand		**Number and Operations:** Develop understanding of fractions as parts of unit wholes, as parts of collections; use models, benchmarks, and equivalent forms to judge the size of fractions.
▶ Differentiated Instruction activities, p. 502B ▶ *Chapter Challenges,* p. 113 *Ways to Success* CD-ROM 19.5 ▶ *Ways to Success* Skillsheets 163, 164	Blank transparency, overhead counters, two-color counters	**Number and Operations:** Develop understanding of fractions as parts of unit wholes, as parts of collections; use models, benchmarks, and equivalent forms to judge the size of fractions.
▶ Differentiated Instruction activities, p. 504B *Ways to Success* CD-ROM 19.6 ▶ *Ways to Success* Skillsheet 168 Audio Tutor **2**/20 Listen and Understand	Four-Part Problem-Solving Transparency, blank transparency	**Problem Solving:** Build new mathematical knowledge through problem solving; apply and adapt a variety of appropriate strategies to solve problems.
▶ Differentiated Instruction activities, p. 508B *Ways to Success* CD-ROM 19.7 ▶ *Ways to Success* Skillsheet 167 Audio Tutor **2**/21 Listen and Understand		**Number and Operations:** Develop understanding of fractions as parts of unit wholes, as parts of collections; use models, benchmarks, and equivalent forms to judge the size of fractions.

Math Notes

Chapter Objectives

19A Represent a fraction of a region, of a set, and of a number.

19B Find equivalent fractions.

19C Compare and order fractions.

19D Write mixed numbers.

19E Solve problems using skills and strategies.

Mathematical Background

Fractions

The fraction $\frac{3}{4}$ means "3 out of 4." This means 3 parts of a whole divided into 4 equal parts or 3 out of a group of 4. Fractions can also show division. When a and b are integers and $b \neq 0$, then the solution to the division problem $a \div b$ can be expressed as $\frac{a}{b}$.

A **proper fraction** has a numerator that is less than the denominator. An **improper fraction** has a numerator that is equal to, or greater than, the denominator. An improper fraction can be changed into a whole number or **mixed number,** for example $\frac{35}{7} = 5$ and $\frac{16}{5} = 3\frac{1}{5}$.

Two fractions $\frac{a}{b}$ and $\frac{c}{d}$ are called **equivalent fractions** if there is a non zero number m such that:

$$\frac{m \times a}{m \times b} = \frac{c}{d}$$

Equivalent fractions can be used to compare fractions with unlike denominators, but if fractions have the same denominator, the greater fraction has the greater numerator. If fractions have the same numerator, the greater fraction has the lesser denominator.

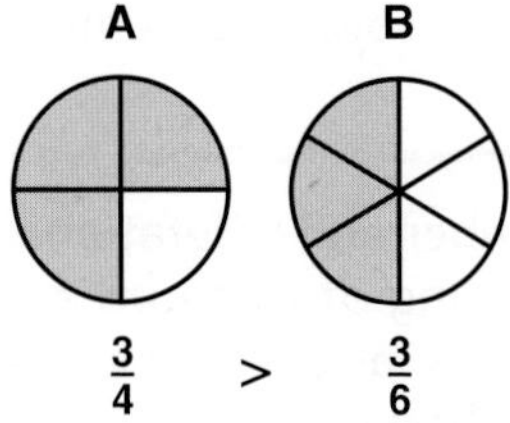

Research-Based Teaching

Nickson (2000) pointed out that care must be taken in choosing manipulatives to teach fraction concepts. If students are given a square, a rectangle, and a disc divided into halves, thirds, or fourths, they may lose the concept of a half. For example, if they try to put together half of a disc and half of a rectangle, they may think they have a whole of something. NCTM (2000) recommends using an area model in which part of a region is shaded. See *Professional Resources Handbook, Grade 4,* Unit 7.

For more ideas relating to Unit 7, see the Teacher Support Handbook at the back of this Teacher's Edition.

Language Intervention

In East Asian countries, children learn that just as numbers can be composed and decomposed as sets and subsets, fractions can be composed and decomposed as well. For further explanation, see "Mathematical Language and Fractions" in the *Professional Resources Handbook, Grade 4.*

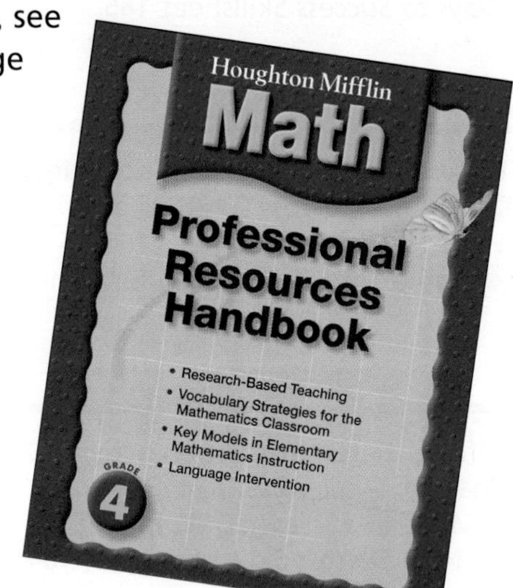

Chapter Activities

Assessing Prior Knowledge

Whole class	15 minutes
Objective	Relate time concepts to fractions.
Materials	None
Visual, Tactual	

Fractions on a Clock

- Draw clock faces for 6:00, 3:00, 9:00, 4:00, and 2:00 on the board.
- Review with students what hours are shown on a clock face and what a clockwise turn is.
- Ask students what part of a full clockwise turn is shown on each clock face if the hour hand went from 12 to the time shown. (6:00: $\frac{1}{2}$ turn)

Ongoing Skill Activity

Pairs	10 minutes
Objective	Make fractions.
Materials	None
Visual, Tactual	

Fractions of a Group

- Each day for about a week ask 3 to 8 students to stand in front of the room in a line.
- Ask various questions about the students in the line, such as *What fraction of the group is wearing glasses?*
- Encourage those students at their desks to ask more questions or make fraction statements about the group of students that is standing.

Math Expressions

Small Groups	20 minutes
Objective	Build fractions by combining unit fractions.
Materials	Paper for Class Fraction Cards
Tactual, Visual	

Fraction Cards

- Prepare Class Fraction Cards. A Class Fraction Card is a quarter-sheet of paper with a unit fraction written on one side of it. A class set of cards will include at least:
  - ten $\frac{1}{10}$ cards
  - nine $\frac{1}{9}$ cards
  - eight $\frac{1}{8}$ cards
  - seven $\frac{1}{7}$ cards
  - six $\frac{1}{6}$ cards
  - five $\frac{1}{5}$ cards
  - four $\frac{1}{4}$ cards
  - three $\frac{1}{3}$ cards
  - two $\frac{1}{2}$ cards
- Hand out the Class Fraction Cards randomly to students. (Each student will get at least one card; some students may get two cards.) Have six students with $\frac{1}{9}$ cards go to the front of the room, stand in a row, and hold up their cards. As each student points to his or her card, have the class say the addition of the units and then say the total.

  Class says:
  1 ninth plus 1 ninth plus
  1 ninth plus 1 ninth plus
  1 ninth plus 1 ninth
  equals 6 ninths.

  Repeat using other totals:
  5 sixths, 6 eighths, and so on.

Starting Chapter 19

Investigation

Using Data

Have students work in small groups to answer the question posed on page 488.

To extend the investigation, have students do the following activity.

- Survey 12 people to see if they like orange juice, grapefruit juice, or both. Make a Venn diagram to show the results of the survey. What fraction of the people surveyed said they liked both types of juice?

For more information about projects and investigations,

Visit **Education Place**®
www.eduplace.com/mat

CHAPTER 19

Understand Fractions

INVESTIGATION

Using Data $\frac{3}{10}$ **students**

The Venn diagram shows the pizza toppings that 10 students chose at lunch. What fraction of the students chose both mushrooms and pepperoni? How might the school lunch staff use this information when preparing pizzas?

Pizza Toppings

Mushrooms | Pepperoni

Both mushrooms and pepperoni

See Additional Answers.

488

Chapter 19 Prerequisite Skills Pretest

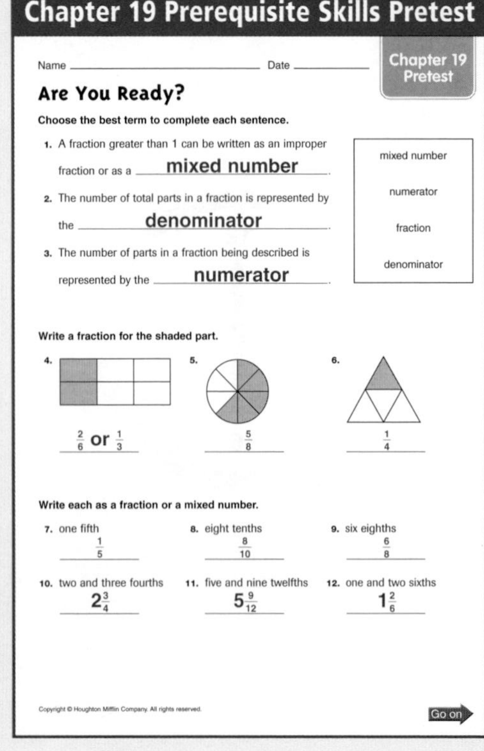
Name ____________ Date ______

Chapter 19 Pretest

Are You Ready?

Choose the best term to complete each sentence.

1. A fraction greater than 1 can be written as an improper fraction or as a **mixed number**.
2. The number of total parts in a fraction is represented by the **denominator**.
3. The number of parts in a fraction being described is represented by the **numerator**.

mixed number
numerator
fraction
denominator

Write a fraction for the shaded part.

4. $\frac{2}{6}$ or $\frac{1}{3}$
5. $\frac{5}{8}$
6. $\frac{1}{4}$

Write each as a fraction or a mixed number.

7. one fifth $\frac{1}{5}$
8. eight tenths $\frac{8}{10}$
9. six eighths $\frac{6}{8}$
10. two and three fourths $2\frac{3}{4}$
11. five and nine twelfths $5\frac{9}{12}$
12. one and two sixths $1\frac{2}{6}$

Go on

Use What You Know

Use this page to review and remember what you need to know for this chapter.

VOCABULARY

Choose the best term to complete each sentence.

Vocabulary
fraction
numerator
denominator
mixed number
whole number

1. The number below the bar in a fraction is the ____. **denominator**
2. A ____ names a part of a whole. **fraction or numerator**
3. A number that contains a whole number and a fraction is known as a ____. **mixed number**
4. The number above the bar in a fraction is the ____. **numerator**

CONCEPTS AND SKILLS

Write a fraction for the shaded part.

5. 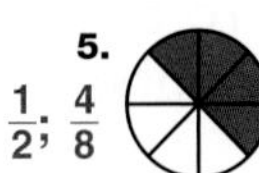 $\frac{1}{2}$; $\frac{4}{8}$

6. 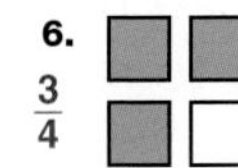 $\frac{3}{4}$

7. 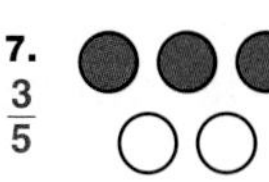 $\frac{3}{5}$

Write each as a fraction or mixed number.

8. two thirds $\frac{2}{3}$
9. one eighth $\frac{1}{8}$
10. two and one third $2\frac{1}{3}$
11. three fourths $\frac{3}{4}$
12. one fifth $\frac{1}{5}$
13. six and three tenths $6\frac{3}{10}$
14. six eighths $\frac{6}{8}$
15. seven tenths $\frac{7}{10}$
16. three and two fifths $3\frac{2}{5}$
17. five twelfths $\frac{5}{12}$
18. eight eighths $\frac{8}{8}$
19. one and nine tenths $1\frac{9}{10}$

Write About It

20. Can the fraction $\frac{2}{6}$ be used to represent the shaded part of this circle? Explain why or why not.
No; *Possible explanation:* The circle is not divided into equal parts.

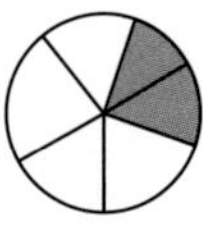

Facts Practice, See Page 667.

Use What You Know

Use this page for informal assessment and review of prerequisite skills.

- Items 1–4: Use math vocabulary
- Items 5–7, 20: Write a fraction for the shaded part of a model
- Items 8–19: Write a fraction or mixed number for each fraction phrase

Customize Your Instruction

Use the Chapter Pretest in the Unit Resource folder to help customize and pace instruction.

Objectives and Resources

Prerequisite Skills Pretest

- Items 1–3: Use vocabulary.
- Items 4–6: Write a fraction for the shaded part of a picture.
- Items 7–12: Write a fraction or mixed number for each phrase.

New Content Pretest

- Items 1–3, 13–15: Represent a fraction of a region, of a set, of a number.
- Items 4–9: Find equivalent fractions.
- Items 10–12: Compare and order fractions.
- Items 16–18: Write mixed numbers.
- Items 19–20: Solve problems using skills and strategies.

For Students Having Difficulty

- *Ways to Success* CD-ROM: 19A, 19F
- *Ways to Success* Skillsheets 161, 162, 163

For Students Having Success

- Enrichment 19.1, 19.5

For Mathematically Promising Students

Explore: Fractions Between Fractions, p. 109, after Lesson 1

Extend: Cross Products, p. 111, after Lesson 3

Connect: Simplify in One Step, p. 113, after Lesson 5

Chapter 19 New Content Pretest

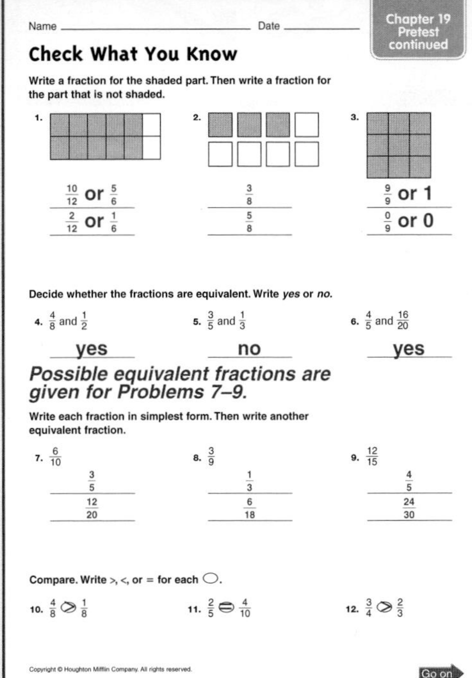

Name ____ Date ____ Chapter 19 Pretest continued

Check What You Know

Write a fraction for the shaded part. Then write a fraction for the part that is not shaded.

1. $\frac{10}{12}$ or $\frac{5}{6}$; $\frac{2}{12}$ or $\frac{1}{6}$
2. $\frac{3}{8}$; $\frac{5}{8}$
3. $\frac{9}{9}$ or 1; $\frac{0}{9}$ or 0

Decide whether the fractions are equivalent. Write *yes* or *no*.

4. $\frac{4}{8}$ and $\frac{1}{2}$ **yes**
5. $\frac{3}{5}$ and $\frac{1}{3}$ **no**
6. $\frac{4}{5}$ and $\frac{16}{20}$ **yes**

Possible equivalent fractions are given for Problems 7–9.

Write each fraction in simplest form. Then write another equivalent fraction.

7. $\frac{6}{10}$ $\frac{3}{5}$; $\frac{12}{20}$
8. $\frac{3}{9}$ $\frac{1}{3}$; $\frac{6}{18}$
9. $\frac{12}{15}$ $\frac{4}{5}$; $\frac{24}{30}$

Compare. Write $>$, $<$, or $=$ for each ○.

10. $\frac{4}{8} > \frac{1}{8}$
11. $\frac{2}{5} = \frac{4}{10}$
12. $\frac{3}{4} > \frac{2}{3}$

 Go on

Chapter 19 New Content Pretest

Name ____ Date ____ Chapter 19 Pretest continued

Find the fractional part of each number.

13. $\frac{1}{3}$ of 30 **10**
14. $\frac{3}{5}$ of 45 **27**
15. $\frac{4}{6}$ of 24 **16**

Write an improper fraction and a mixed number or whole number to describe the shaded parts.

16. $\frac{6}{4}$ or $\frac{3}{2}$; $1\frac{2}{4}$ or $1\frac{1}{2}$
17. $\frac{7}{3}$; $2\frac{1}{3}$
18. $\frac{7}{2}$; $3\frac{1}{2}$

Draw a picture to solve each problem.

19. Bobby has only pennies, dimes, and quarters. One half of Bobby's coins are pennies. One fourth of his coins are quarters. Three of his coins are dimes. How many coins does Bobby have?
12 coins; check students' drawings.

20. At the animal shelter, $\frac{1}{3}$ of the animals are dogs, $\frac{1}{6}$ are cats, and 19 are other animals. How many animals are at the shelter?
38 animals; check students' drawings.

 STOP

Lesson 19.1

Represent Fractions

Planning

Lesson Objective Read, write, and identify fractions.

Math Background

- At this grade level, students should learn to identify fractions with models that convey their properties. For example, proper fractions should be modeled in terms of a part of a whole.

Technology Resources

- *Ways to Success* CD-ROM 19.1
- Education Place: Extra Practice, eGlossary, eGames
  www.eduplace.com/map

Lesson 19.1 Transparency

Problem of the Day

Ray and Eva get equal shares of a pizza cut into 8 slices. Ray decides to split his share evenly with Carlos. How many slices of pizza does Carlos get? (2)

Spiral Review

Use the diagram.

1. Name a chord. ($\overline{AB}$)

2. What kind of angle is $\angle ADB$? (straight angle)

3. What is the measure of $\angle ADB$? (180°)

4. What is the measure of $\angle CDB$? (90°)

Lesson Quiz

Draw a picture to show each fraction.
(Check students' drawings.)

1. $\frac{1}{2}$

2. $\frac{1}{8}$

3. $\frac{2}{5}$

4. $\frac{2}{3}$

5. $\frac{7}{12}$

NCTM Standards

Number and Operations: Develop understanding of fractions as parts of unit wholes, as parts of collections; use models, benchmarks, and equivalent forms to judge the size of fractions.

Getting Started

Building Math Vocabulary

fraction a number that names a part of a whole, a part of a collection, or a part of a region

numerator the number above the bar in a fraction

denominator the number below the bar in a fraction

Discuss the vocabulary cards for *numerator* and *denominator.* Help students recall that the numerator of a ***fraction*** can be used to represent zero or more parts of a whole, while the denominator is used to represent the number of equal parts in the whole.

Everyday Fractions

Whole Class	5 minutes
Objective	Apply fractions to real life.
Materials	None
Visual, Auditory	

- Discuss with students times they have heard fractions used in their daily lives. Ask, for example, what a "half-day" at school means, how long three-quarters of an hour is, or how many slices are in a third of a 6-slice pizza.
- Have students brainstorm a list of other real-world uses of fractions. Have them suggest ways in which fractions come in handy in people's lives, such as when they are food shopping, cooking, sewing, or measuring things.
- Tell students that the lesson will explain how to read, write, and identify fractions.

Differentiated Instruction

English Learners

Whole Class	5–10 minutes
Objective	Practice reading and writing fractions.
Materials	Student page 491
Auditory, Visual	

Early Production

- Students will need to practice spelling and verbalizing fractions.
- For **Exercises 4–7,** ask students to say the answer and write it in word form.
- Remind students to say the correct form of the denominator: halves, thirds, fourths, and so on. Provide examples.

Intermediate/Advanced

- English Learner Resource 19.1
- English Learner Handbook

Intervention

Small Groups	5 minutes
Objective	Understand equal parts.
Materials	None
Auditory, Visual	

- On the board, draw the following figures:

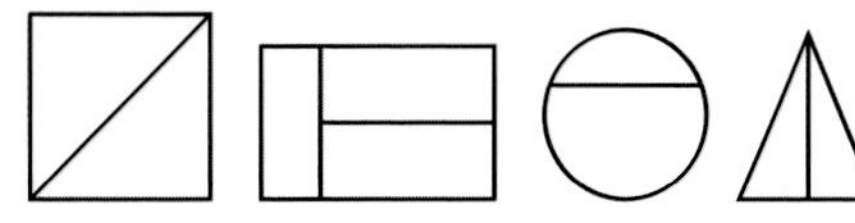

- Ask students to decide which of these figures show equal parts. (Square and triangle) Discuss their answers and explanations.
- Then guide them to figure out how to divide the rectangle and circle into two (or more) equal parts.

Other Resources

- *Ways to Success* CD-ROM 19.1

Inclusion

Small Groups	5 minutes
Objective	Understand a fraction as a division of a whole.
Materials	Grid paper
Auditory, Visual	

- Have students draw a 4 × 4 square on the grid paper. Tell them to divide the square into two equal parts.
- **How can you tell whether the parts are the same size?** (They cover the same amount of space.)
- Have students label each part as $\frac{1}{2}$.
- Repeat these steps to show $\frac{1}{4}$ and $\frac{1}{8}$.

Social Studies Connection

Materials: Almanac or encyclopedia

Have students list all the state capitals. Then have them answer these questions:

1. What fraction of the capitals begin with a vowel? A consonant?
2. What fraction have populations less than 1 million?
3. What fraction are the largest cities in their state?

Counting Practice

Draw a number line on the chalkboard that begins at 0 and ends at 2. Mark out fourths on the number line, and label 0, $\frac{1}{4}$, $\frac{1}{2}$, $\frac{3}{4}$, 1, $1\frac{1}{4}$, $1\frac{1}{2}$, $1\frac{3}{4}$, and 2. As you point to each whole number and fraction on the number line, have a student volunteer draw a picture that represents that fraction.

❶ Introduce

Explain to students that this lesson will describe what the top and bottom numbers of a fraction represent.

❷ Teach

Learn About It

- Discuss the idea that the denominator of a fraction names the number of parts in a whole. Ask: **How many parts are in the pizza?** (4) Explain that the numerator names the number of parts we are talking about. Emphasize that the numerator is written *above* the fraction bar, and that the denominator is always written *below* it.
- **Now look at the group of peppers. Suppose all of them were yellow peppers. What fraction could we write to name how many are green?** ($\frac{0}{4}$)

Guided Practice

Have students complete **Exercises 1–3** as you observe. Remind them to use the ***Ask Yourself*** question to help. Give students the opportunity to talk about the question in ***Explain Your Thinking.***

Lesson 1

Represent Fractions

Objective Read, write, and identify fractions.

Vocabulary
fraction
numerator
denominator

Learn About It

John helped his dad make a rectangular pizza for dinner. They used green and yellow peppers as toppings. You can use **fractions** to describe the pizza and the peppers.

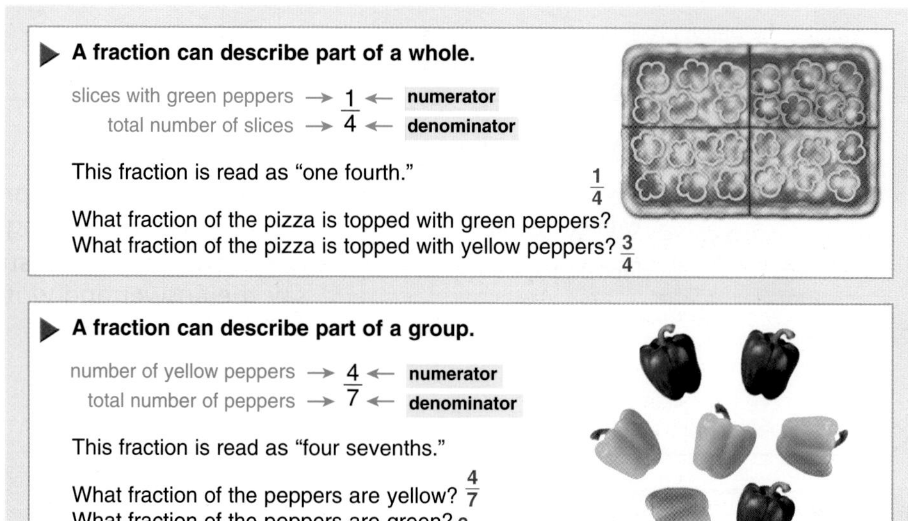

▶ A fraction can describe part of a whole.

slices with green peppers → 1 ← **numerator**
total number of slices → 4 ← **denominator**

This fraction is read as "one fourth."

What fraction of the pizza is topped with green peppers? $\frac{1}{4}$
What fraction of the pizza is topped with yellow peppers? $\frac{3}{4}$

▶ A fraction can describe part of a group.

number of yellow peppers → 4 ← **numerator**
total number of peppers → 7 ← **denominator**

This fraction is read as "four sevenths."

What fraction of the peppers are yellow? $\frac{4}{7}$
What fraction of the peppers are green? $\frac{3}{7}$

Guided Practice

Write a fraction for the shaded part. Then write a fraction for the part that is not shaded.

1. ○○○ $\frac{2}{3}$; $\frac{1}{3}$

2. 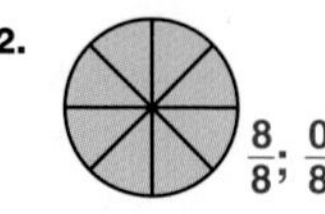 $\frac{8}{8}$; $\frac{0}{8}$

3. △△△ △△△ $\frac{4}{6}$; $\frac{2}{6}$

Ask Yourself
- How many equal parts are there?
- How many parts are shaded? not shaded?

Explain Your Thinking ▶ Look back at Exercise 2. What whole number could represent the shaded part of the circle? 1

490

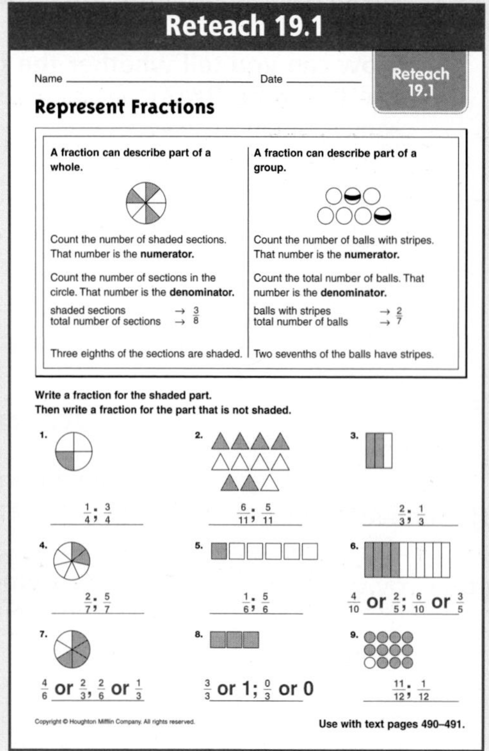

Reteach 19.1

Name ____________ Date ________

Reteach 19.1

Represent Fractions

A fraction can describe part of a whole.	**A fraction can describe part of a group.**
Count the number of shaded sections. That number is the **numerator.**	Count the number of balls with stripes. That number is the **numerator.**
Count the number of sections in the circle. That number is the **denominator.**	Count the total number of balls. That number is the **denominator.**
shaded sections → 3 total number of sections → 8	balls with stripes → 2 total number of balls → 7
Three eighths of the sections are shaded.	Two sevenths of the balls have stripes.

Write a fraction for the shaded part.
Then write a fraction for the part that is not shaded.

1. $\frac{1}{4}$; $\frac{3}{4}$
2. $\frac{6}{11}$; $\frac{5}{11}$
3. $\frac{2}{3}$; $\frac{1}{3}$
4. $\frac{2}{7}$; $\frac{5}{7}$
5. $\frac{1}{6}$; $\frac{5}{6}$
6. $\frac{4}{10}$ or $\frac{2}{5}$; $\frac{6}{10}$ or $\frac{3}{5}$
7. $\frac{4}{6}$ or $\frac{2}{3}$, $\frac{2}{6}$ or $\frac{1}{3}$
8. $\frac{3}{3}$ or 1; $\frac{0}{3}$ or 0
9. $\frac{11}{12}$; $\frac{1}{12}$

Use with text pages 490–491.

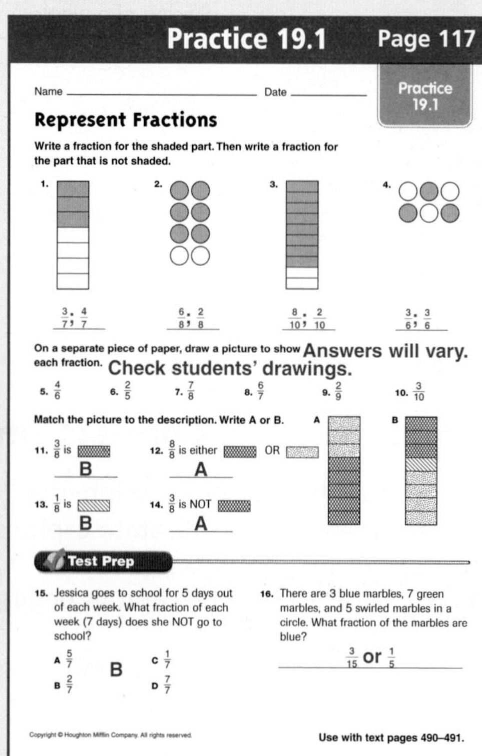

Practice 19.1 Page 117

Name ____________ Date ________

Practice 19.1

Represent Fractions

Write a fraction for the shaded part. Then write a fraction for the part that is not shaded.

1. $\frac{3}{7}$; $\frac{4}{7}$
2. $\frac{6}{8}$; $\frac{2}{8}$
3. $\frac{8}{10}$; $\frac{2}{10}$
4. $\frac{3}{6}$; $\frac{3}{6}$

On a separate piece of paper, draw a picture to show each fraction. Answers will vary. Check students' drawings.

5. $\frac{4}{6}$ 6. $\frac{2}{5}$ 7. $\frac{7}{8}$ 8. $\frac{6}{7}$ 9. $\frac{2}{9}$ 10. $\frac{3}{10}$

Match the picture to the description. Write A or B. A B

11. $\frac{3}{8}$ is ▒ B
12. $\frac{8}{8}$ is either ▒ OR ▒ A
13. $\frac{1}{8}$ is ▒ B
14. $\frac{3}{8}$ is NOT ▒ A

Test Prep

15. Jessica goes to school for 5 days out of each week. What fraction of each week (7 days) does she NOT go to school?
    A $\frac{5}{7}$ B $\frac{2}{7}$ C $\frac{1}{7}$ D $\frac{7}{7}$ — B

16. There are 3 blue marbles, 7 green marbles, and 5 swirled marbles in a circle. What fraction of the marbles are blue? $\frac{3}{15}$ or $\frac{1}{5}$

Use with text pages 490–491.

Common Error

- **Transposing terms in a fraction** Some students may transpose the terms in a fraction.
- **Intervention** For these students, emphasize that the denominator is always the total number of equal parts and that it is always written under the fraction bar.

Practice and Problem Solving

20. Smaller; Possible explanation: If an object is divided into more parts, each part must be smaller.

Write a fraction for the shaded part. Then write a fraction for the part that is not shaded.

4. 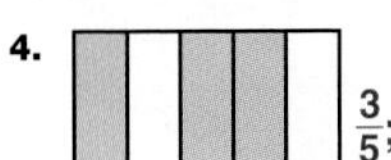 $\frac{3}{5}$; $\frac{2}{5}$

5. 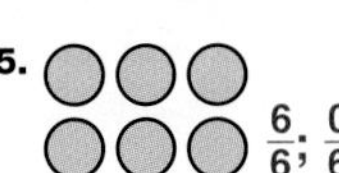 $\frac{6}{6}$; $\frac{0}{6}$

6. 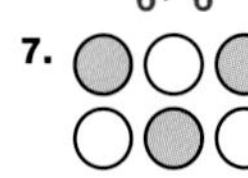 $\frac{6}{12}$; $\frac{6}{12}$

7. $\frac{3}{6}$; $\frac{3}{6}$

Draw a picture to show each fraction. Student drawings should match the fractions indicated.

8. $\frac{3}{4}$ 9. $\frac{1}{3}$ 10. $\frac{1}{2}$ 11. $\frac{3}{8}$ 12. $\frac{5}{8}$ 13. $\frac{2}{2}$ 14. $\frac{7}{10}$ 15. $\frac{4}{12}$

Match the picture to the description. Write *A* or *B*.

16. $\frac{2}{5}$ is orange. *A*

17. $\frac{3}{5}$ is NOT green. *B*

18. $\frac{1}{5}$ is yellow. *B*

19. $\frac{5}{5}$ is orange OR green. *A*

A 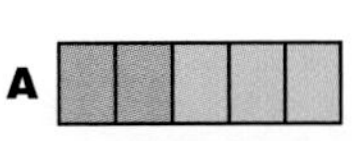

B

Solve.

20. Suppose the pizza on page 490 was divided into eighths. Would each slice be larger or smaller than when the pizza was divided into fourths? Explain. *See above.*

21. A pizza had 6 equal slices. Natalie ate 3 slices. Her brothers shared the remaining slices. What fraction of the pizza did her brothers eat? $\frac{3}{6}$

22. There are 5 yellow apples, 6 red apples, and 3 green apples in a bowl. What fraction of the apples are red? $\frac{6}{14}$

23. Suppose the number of red apples in Problem 22 is doubled. Then what fraction of the apples are red? $\frac{12}{20}$

24. **Represent** Jon and Meg buy a pie and cut it into 8 pieces. They eat 5 pieces. Draw a picture to show the fraction of the pie that is left. Drawing should show $\frac{3}{8}$.

25. At a flower shop, spring flowers cost \$2 each, and vases cost \$9 each. What is the total cost for a vase with 8 spring flowers? \$25

Mixed Review and Test Prep

Open Response

Solve. (Ch. 12, Lessons 2, 7)

26. 1 yd = ■ ft **3**

27. 4 ft = ■ in. **48**

28. ■ yd = 6 ft **2**

29. ■ in. = 2 yd **72**

30. 400 cm = ■ m **4**

31. ■ m = 2 km **2,000**

32. 96 in. = ■ ft **8**

33. ■ cm = 500 m **50,000**

Multiple Choice

34. Maria sleeps for 9 hours each night. What fraction of each day (24 hours) is she NOT sleeping? (Ch. 19, Lesson 1)

A $\frac{9}{24}$ **(C)** $\frac{15}{24}$

B $\frac{9}{15}$ D $\frac{3}{8}$

Extra Practice See page 513, Set A.

3 Practice

Practice and Problem Solving

Select from **Exercises 4–34** as independent work. Guide students to use grid paper or fraction models to help them draw the pictures of fractions for **Exercises 8–15**.

- ***Problem 20*** Students are likely to think of pizzas as being round. Elicit how to show a rectangular pizza divided into eighths. (One way: Divide into fourths, then divide each fourth in half.)

4 Assess & Close

Math Talk in Action

Draw on the board or overhead a "flag" that is divided into 5 equal columns. Shade 2 of the columns.

- **What fraction can we write to show the fraction of the flag that is shaded? The fraction that is not shaded?**

Math Journal Prompt

Have students write the following three fractions: a fraction equal to 1, a fraction with a numerator of 1, and a fraction with a denominator of 3.

Lesson Quiz

Use the quiz on Lesson Transparency 19.1.

Test Prep & Spiral Review

Use Test Prep Transparency 19.1.

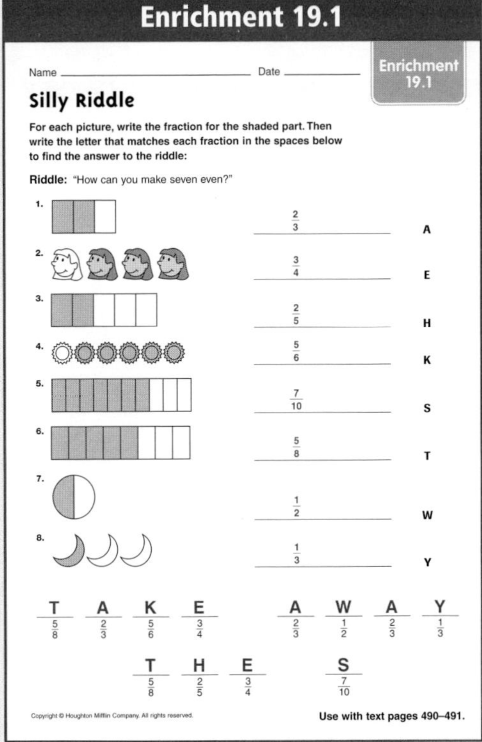
Enrichment 19.1

Silly Riddle

For each picture, write the fraction for the shaded part. Then write the letter that matches each fraction in the spaces below to find the answer to the riddle:

Riddle: "How can you make seven even?"

TAKE AWAY THE S

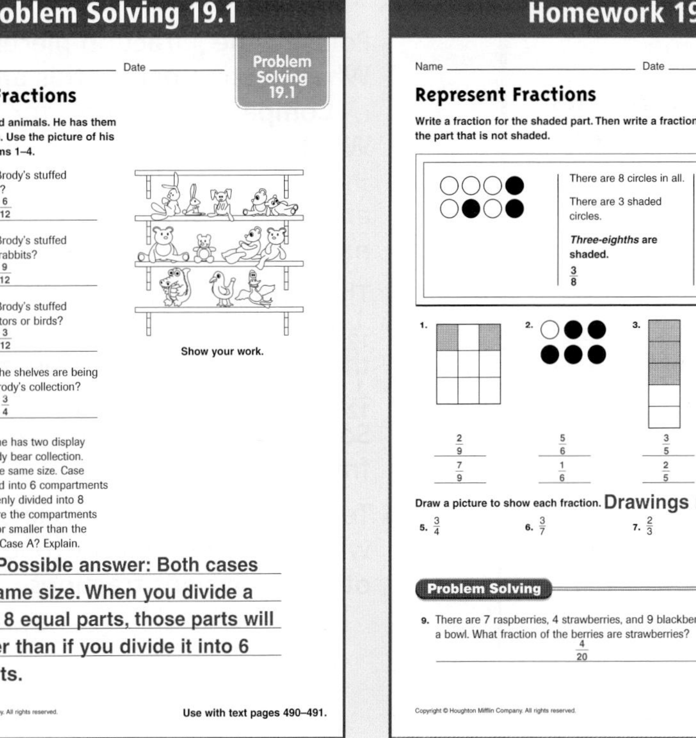
Problem Solving 19.1

Represent Fractions

Brody collects stuffed animals. He has them displayed on shelves. Use the picture of his collection for Problems 1–4.

1. What fraction of Brody's stuffed animals are bears? $\frac{6}{12}$
2. What fraction of Brody's stuffed animals are NOT rabbits? $\frac{9}{12}$
3. What fraction of Brody's stuffed animals are alligators or birds? $\frac{3}{12}$
4. What fraction of the shelves are being used to display Brody's collection? $\frac{3}{4}$
5. **You Decide** Anne has two display cases for her teddy bear collection. Both cases are the same size. Case A is evenly divided into 6 compartments and Case B is evenly divided into 8 compartments. Are the compartments in Case B larger or smaller than the compartments in Case A? Explain.

Smaller; Possible answer: Both cases are the same size. When you divide a case into 8 equal parts, those parts will be smaller than if you divide it into 6 equal parts.

Show your work.

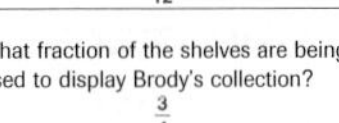

Homework 19.1 Page 117

Represent Fractions

Write a fraction for the shaded part. Then write a fraction for the part that is not shaded.

There are 8 circles in all. There are 3 shaded circles. *Three-eighths* are shaded. $\frac{3}{8}$

There are 8 circles in all. There are 5 circles that are not shaded. *Five-eighths* are not shaded. $\frac{5}{8}$

1. $\frac{2}{9}$; $\frac{7}{9}$ 2. $\frac{5}{6}$; $\frac{1}{6}$ 3. $\frac{3}{5}$; $\frac{2}{5}$ 4. $\frac{1}{7}$; $\frac{6}{7}$

Draw a picture to show each fraction. Drawings may vary.

5. $\frac{3}{4}$ 6. $\frac{3}{7}$ 7. $\frac{2}{3}$ 8. $\frac{8}{10}$

Problem Solving

9. There are 7 raspberries, 4 strawberries, and 9 blackberries in a bowl. What fraction of the berries are strawberries? $\frac{4}{20}$

Use with text pages 490–491.

Hands On Lesson 19.2

Explore Equivalent Fractions

Planning

Lesson Objective Use models to identify equivalent fractions.

Technology Resources

- Audio Tutor **2**/18 Listen and Understand
- *Ways to Success* CD-ROM 19.2
- Education Place: Extra Practice, eGlossary, eManipulatives, eGames www.eduplace.com/map

Lesson 19.2 Transparency

Problem of the Day

A school principal called 3 people to tell them about a meeting. Each person she called phoned 3 other people. Then each of them phoned 3 people. Including the principal, how many people heard about the meeting?
$(1 + 3 + 9 + 27 = 40)$

Spiral Review

Write a fraction for the shaded part.

1.  $(\frac{7}{8})$

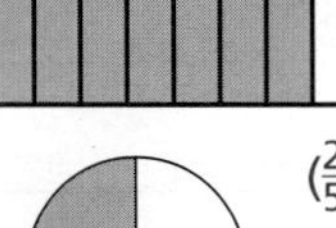

2. 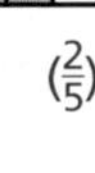 $(\frac{2}{5})$

Lesson Quiz

Are the fractions equivalent? Write *yes* or *no*. Use fraction pieces to help you.

1. $\frac{3}{4}$ and $\frac{5}{6}$ (no)
2. $\frac{4}{12}$ and $\frac{1}{3}$ (yes)
3. $\frac{1}{6}$ and $\frac{1}{12}$ (no)
4. $\frac{1}{10}$ and $\frac{2}{5}$ (no)

NCTM Standards

Number and Operations: Develop understanding of fractions as parts of unit wholes, as parts of collections; use models, benchmarks, and equivalent forms to judge the size of fractions.

Getting Started

Building Math Vocabulary

equivalent fractions fractions that name the same amount

Introduce the idea of equivalence to students with a kinesthetic example. Model and say: **nodding your head is equivalent to saying "yes."** Discuss the meaning of the word *equivalent* with students. Brainstorm other examples of equivalent behaviors of ideas. Then use the vocabulary card for ***equivalent fractions.***

Model Equivalent Fractions

Whole Class	5 minutes
Objective	Model equivalent fractions
Materials	Fraction Pieces Transparency, blank transparency
Visual, Auditory	

- Use the 1 fraction piece, $\frac{1}{2}$ fraction pieces, $\frac{1}{6}$ fraction pieces, and $\frac{1}{12}$ fraction pieces cut out from the Fraction Pieces Transparency.
- Place the 1 fraction piece at the top of a blank transparency. Place a $\frac{1}{2}$ fraction piece beneath it, aligned at the left. Then line up three $\frac{1}{6}$ fraction pieces to fit below the $\frac{1}{2}$ fraction piece.
- Point to the $\frac{1}{6}$ fraction pieces. Ask: **What fraction names this amount?** $(\frac{3}{6})$ **Compare the models for $\frac{3}{6}$ and $\frac{1}{2}$. What do you see?** (The models are the same length.) **We say that $\frac{1}{2}$ and $\frac{3}{6}$ are *equivalent fractions.* They name the same amount.**
- Then ask a volunteer to line up $\frac{1}{12}$ fraction pieces to fit beneath the $\frac{1}{6}$ fraction pieces. **How many $\frac{1}{12}$ fraction pieces did you use?** (6) **So $\frac{1}{2}$, $\frac{3}{6}$, and $\frac{6}{12}$ are equivalent fractions.**
- Tell students that in this lesson they will use fraction pieces to identify other equivalent fractions.

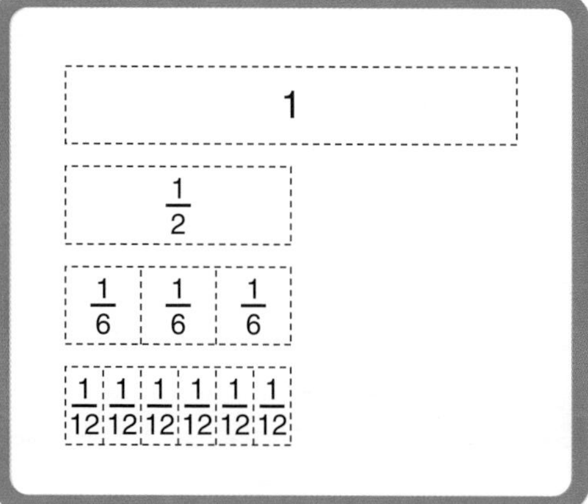

Differentiated Instruction

English Learners

Whole Class	10 minutes
Objective	Model equivalent fractions.
Materials	Fraction pieces (Learning Tool 34)
Auditory, Visual	

Early Production

- Before doing ***On Your Own,*** have students practice modeling equivalent fractions with fraction pieces. They put the fraction pieces on top of each other to determine which ones are equivalent and which are not.
- Students can practice vocabulary from the lesson such as: *These fractions are equal, equivalent, etc.*

Intermediate/Advanced

- English Learner Resource 19.2
- English Learner Handbook

Intervention

Whole Class	5 minutes
Objective	Understand equivalent fractions.
Materials	None
Auditory, Visual	

- Draw a rectangle divided into eighths on the board. **This is a picture of a delicious loaf of banana bread. You are hungry and you can have either $\frac{2}{8}$ of the loaf or $\frac{1}{4}$. Which will you choose?** (Discuss that the two choices are equivalent because they are the same size.)
- Tell students that today they are going to use fraction models to explore equivalent fractions. Ask students to suggest synonyms for *equivalent.* (of equal value or size, same amount)

Other Resources

- *Ways to Success* CD-ROM 19.2

Special Needs

Small Groups	5 minutes
Objective	Understand equivalent fractions.
Materials	Learning Tool 35 (Fraction Circles), scissors
Auditory, Visual	

- Have students fold a fraction circle in half and then cut it along the fold. With more circles, fold and cut to make fourths and eighths.
- Have students label them $\frac{1}{2}$, $\frac{1}{4}$, $\frac{1}{8}$.
- Then have students put smaller slices atop larger ones to create various equivalent fractions.

Alternate Teaching Strategy

Materials: Grid paper, colored pencils

Help students see how two different fractions can name the same part of a whole. Work at the board while students follow along using the grid paper and colored pencils at their seats.

- Draw a square. Shade half. **Shade your square in the same way I shaded mine.**
- **What fraction of the square is shaded?** ($\frac{1}{2}$)
- Then divide the square into fourths and have students do the same.
- **Has the amount of the shaded area changed?** (no)
- Repeat the process using a circle.

❶ Introduce

Tell students that equivalent fractions are fractions that are equal or express the same value.

❷ Teach

Work Together

- Distribute fraction pieces to students. Ask them to use the fraction pieces to model the equivalences shown on the overhead.
- Have volunteers come up and use the fraction pieces to find other fractions that are equivalent to $\frac{1}{2}$. ($\frac{3}{6}$, $\frac{5}{10}$, $\frac{6}{12}$) Ask students at their seats to do the same.
- Check students' equivalence tables. Then have them focus on the number lines. **What can you say about any fractions that have 0 as the numerator as long as 0 is not the denominator?** (They are equivalent.) **What can you say about any fractions that have the same numerator and denominator?** (also equivalent—all equal to 1) Guide students to use a straightedge to help them align the equivalent fractions on the number line.

Audio Tutor 2/18 Listen and Understand

Explore Equivalent Fractions

Objective Use models to identify equivalent fractions.

Vocabulary
equivalent fractions

Materials
Fraction Pieces
(Learning Tool 34)

Work Together

Fractions that name the same amount are **equivalent fractions**.

Work with a partner to find fractions that are equivalent to $\frac{1}{2}$.

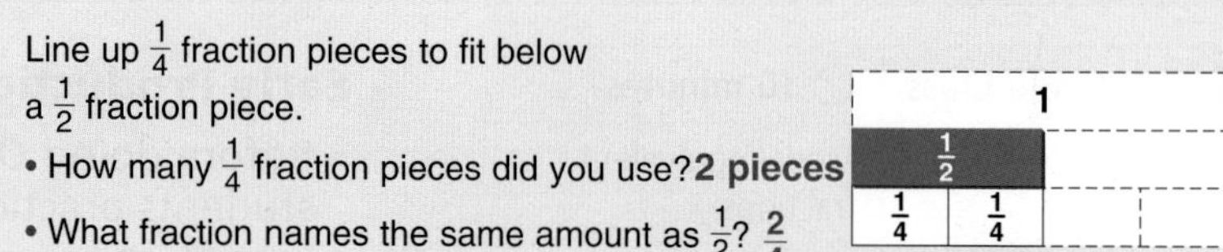

STEP 1 Line up $\frac{1}{4}$ fraction pieces to fit below a $\frac{1}{2}$ fraction piece.

- How many $\frac{1}{4}$ fraction pieces did you use? **2 pieces**
- What fraction names the same amount as $\frac{1}{2}$? $\frac{2}{4}$

STEP 2 Line up $\frac{1}{8}$ fraction pieces to fit below the $\frac{1}{4}$ fraction pieces.

- How many $\frac{1}{8}$ fraction pieces did you use? **4 pieces**
- What fraction names the same amount as $\frac{1}{2}$ and $\frac{2}{4}$? $\frac{4}{8}$

$\frac{1}{2}$, $\frac{2}{4}$, and $\frac{4}{8}$ are equivalent fractions.

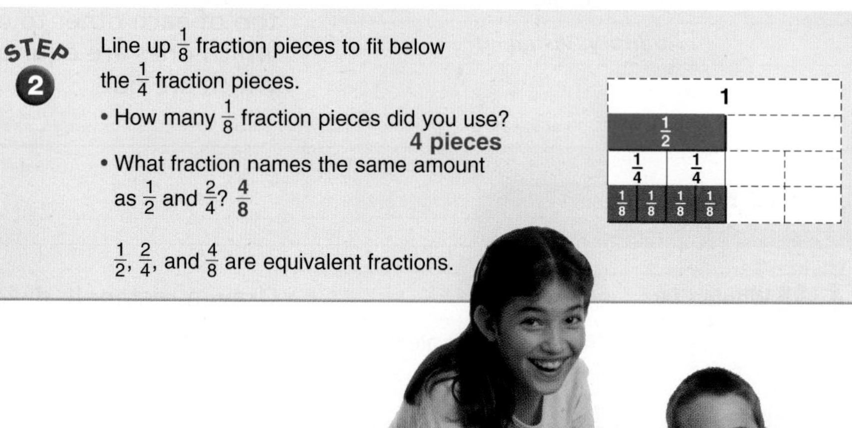

492

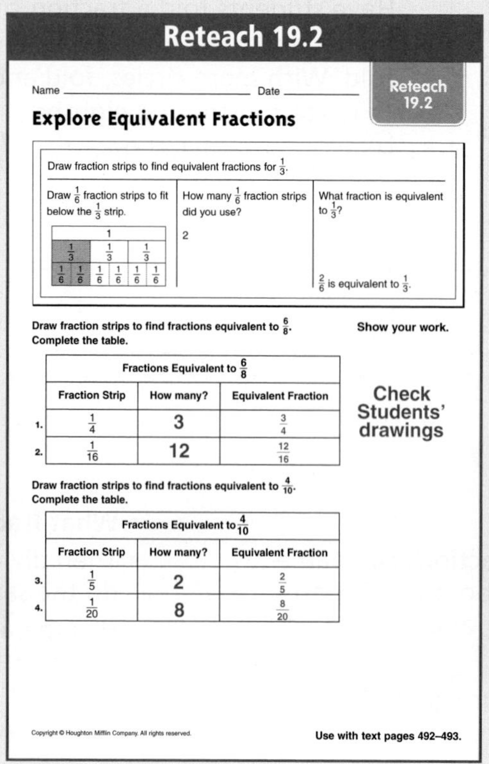

Reteach 19.2

Name ______ Date ______ Reteach 19.2

Explore Equivalent Fractions

Draw fraction strips to find equivalent fractions for $\frac{1}{3}$.

Draw $\frac{1}{6}$ fraction strips to fit below the $\frac{1}{3}$ strip.	How many $\frac{1}{6}$ fraction strips did you use?	What fraction is equivalent to $\frac{1}{3}$?
1; $\frac{1}{3}$ $\frac{1}{3}$ $\frac{1}{3}$; $\frac{1}{6}$ $\frac{1}{6}$ $\frac{1}{6}$ $\frac{1}{6}$ $\frac{1}{6}$ $\frac{1}{6}$	2	$\frac{2}{6}$ is equivalent to $\frac{1}{3}$.

Draw fraction strips to find fractions equivalent to $\frac{6}{8}$. Complete the table. **Show your work.**

Check Students' drawings

	Fractions Equivalent to $\frac{6}{8}$		
	Fraction Strip	How many?	Equivalent Fraction
1.	$\frac{1}{4}$	3	$\frac{3}{4}$
2.	$\frac{1}{16}$	12	$\frac{12}{16}$

Draw fraction strips to find fractions equivalent to $\frac{4}{10}$. Complete the table.

	Fractions Equivalent to $\frac{4}{10}$		
	Fraction Strip	How many?	Equivalent Fraction
3.	$\frac{1}{5}$	2	$\frac{2}{5}$
4.	$\frac{1}{20}$	8	$\frac{8}{20}$

Use with text pages 492–493.

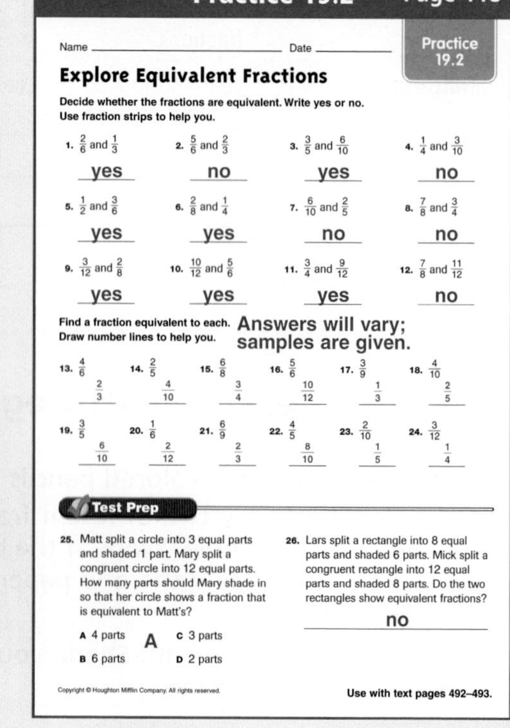

Practice 19.2 Page 118

Name ______ Date ______ Practice 19.2

Explore Equivalent Fractions

Decide whether the fractions are equivalent. Write yes or no. Use fraction strips to help you.

1. $\frac{2}{6}$ and $\frac{1}{3}$ yes
2. $\frac{5}{6}$ and $\frac{2}{3}$ no
3. $\frac{3}{5}$ and $\frac{6}{10}$ yes
4. $\frac{1}{4}$ and $\frac{3}{10}$ no
5. $\frac{1}{2}$ and $\frac{3}{6}$ yes
6. $\frac{2}{8}$ and $\frac{1}{4}$ yes
7. $\frac{6}{10}$ and $\frac{2}{5}$ no
8. $\frac{7}{8}$ and $\frac{3}{4}$ no
9. $\frac{3}{12}$ and $\frac{2}{8}$ yes
10. $\frac{10}{12}$ and $\frac{5}{6}$ yes
11. $\frac{3}{4}$ and $\frac{9}{12}$ yes
12. $\frac{7}{8}$ and $\frac{11}{12}$ no

Find a fraction equivalent to each. Draw number lines to help you. Answers will vary; samples are given.

13. $\frac{4}{6}$ $\frac{2}{3}$
14. $\frac{2}{5}$ $\frac{4}{10}$
15. $\frac{6}{8}$ $\frac{3}{4}$
16. $\frac{5}{6}$ $\frac{10}{12}$
17. $\frac{3}{9}$ $\frac{1}{3}$
18. $\frac{4}{10}$ $\frac{2}{5}$
19. $\frac{3}{5}$ $\frac{6}{10}$
20. $\frac{1}{6}$ $\frac{2}{12}$
21. $\frac{6}{9}$ $\frac{2}{3}$
22. $\frac{4}{5}$ $\frac{8}{10}$
23. $\frac{2}{10}$ $\frac{1}{5}$
24. $\frac{3}{12}$ $\frac{1}{4}$

Test Prep

25. Matt split a circle into 3 equal parts and shaded 1 part. Mary split a congruent circle into 12 equal parts. How many parts should Mary shade in so that her circle shows a fraction that is equivalent to Matt's?

    A 4 parts C 3 parts
    B 6 parts D 2 parts

    A

26. Lars split a rectangle into 8 equal parts and shaded 6 parts. Mick split a congruent rectangle into 12 equal parts and shaded 8 parts. Do the two rectangles show equivalent fractions? no

Use with text pages 492–493.

STEP 3 Use fraction pieces to find as many other fractions as you can that are equivalent to $\frac{1}{2}$. Make a table like the one shown at the right to record your work.

Fractions Equivalent to $\frac{1}{2}$

Fraction Piece	How many?	Equivalent fractions
$\frac{1}{4}$	2	$\frac{2}{4} = \frac{1}{2}$
$\frac{1}{6}$		$= \frac{1}{2}$
$\frac{1}{8}$		$= \frac{1}{2}$

STEP 4 Now look at the number lines at the right.

- Which fractions are equivalent to $\frac{1}{3}$? $\frac{2}{6}$; $\frac{3}{9}$
- Which fractions are equivalent to $\frac{2}{3}$? $\frac{4}{6}$; $\frac{6}{9}$

Use fraction pieces to check your answers.

0 to 1: $\frac{0}{3}$ $\frac{1}{3}$ $\frac{2}{3}$ $\frac{3}{3}$

0 to 1: $\frac{0}{6}$ $\frac{1}{6}$ $\frac{2}{6}$ $\frac{3}{6}$ $\frac{4}{6}$ $\frac{5}{6}$ $\frac{6}{6}$

0 to 1: $\frac{0}{9}$ $\frac{1}{9}$ $\frac{2}{9}$ $\frac{3}{9}$ $\frac{4}{9}$ $\frac{5}{9}$ $\frac{6}{9}$ $\frac{7}{9}$ $\frac{8}{9}$ $\frac{9}{9}$

On Your Own

Decide whether the fractions are equivalent. Write *yes* or *no*. Use fraction pieces to help you.

1. $\frac{3}{4}$ and $\frac{6}{8}$ *yes*
2. $\frac{7}{10}$ and $\frac{5}{6}$ *no*
3. $\frac{8}{12}$ and $\frac{4}{6}$ *yes*
4. $\frac{5}{6}$ and $\frac{10}{12}$ *yes*

Find a fraction equivalent to each. Draw number lines to help you. *Possible equivalent fractions given.*

5. $\frac{2}{10}$ $\frac{1}{5}$
6. $\frac{4}{4}$ $\frac{1}{1}$
7. $\frac{1}{6}$ $\frac{2}{12}$
8. $\frac{4}{12}$ $\frac{1}{3}$
9. $\frac{3}{4}$ $\frac{6}{8}$
10. $\frac{2}{3}$ $\frac{4}{6}$

Talk About It • Write About It

You learned that equivalent fractions name the same amount.

11. Describe the pattern you see in the equivalent fractions at the right. Then continue the pattern and find two more equivalent fractions. $\frac{4}{6} = \frac{6}{9} = \frac{8}{12} = \frac{10}{15}$ **The numerators increase by 2; the denominators increase by 3; $\frac{12}{18}$; $\frac{14}{21}$**
12. If you know that $\frac{4}{5} = \frac{8}{10}$ and $\frac{8}{10} = \frac{16}{20}$, what can you say about $\frac{4}{5}$ and $\frac{16}{20}$? Explain. **$\frac{4}{5}$ and $\frac{16}{20}$ are equivalent. They name the same amount.**

3 Practice

On Your Own

Select from **Exercises 1–12** as independent work.

- For **Exercises 1–4**, ask: **How can you tell by using the fraction pieces that two fractions are equivalent?** (The fraction pieces make up the same length.)
- ***Talk About It • Write About It*** Students should look for a pattern of numerators and a different pattern of denominators and use those patterns to write the additional equivalent fractions.

4 Assess & Close

Math Talk in Action

Have students refer to both the lesson and to the ***Talk About It • Write About It*** section. Ask them to describe in their own words different ways to find equivalent fractions.

Math Journal Prompt

Have students write an explanation that describes equivalent fractions. Have them provide examples other than those found in the lesson.

Lesson Quiz

Use the quiz on Lesson Transparency 19.2.

Test Prep & Spiral Review

Use Test Prep Transparency 19.2.

Enrichment 19.2

Name ______ Date ______ Enrichment 19.2

True or Not True?

In each problem only one of the number statements is true. Draw fraction strips to model each statement. Then circle the statement that is true.

Check students' drawings.

1. ($\frac{3}{4} = \frac{6}{8}$) or $\frac{9}{12} = \frac{3}{8}$
2. $\frac{9}{10} = \frac{16}{20}$ or ($\frac{1}{2} = \frac{5}{10}$)
3. ($\frac{1}{2} = \frac{6}{12}$) or $\frac{5}{15} = \frac{2}{3}$
4. ($\frac{8}{10} = \frac{4}{5}$) or $\frac{12}{20} = \frac{6}{12}$
5. $\frac{1}{3} = \frac{3}{12}$ or ($\frac{3}{5} = \frac{6}{10}$)

 Use with text pages 492–493.

Problem Solving 19.2

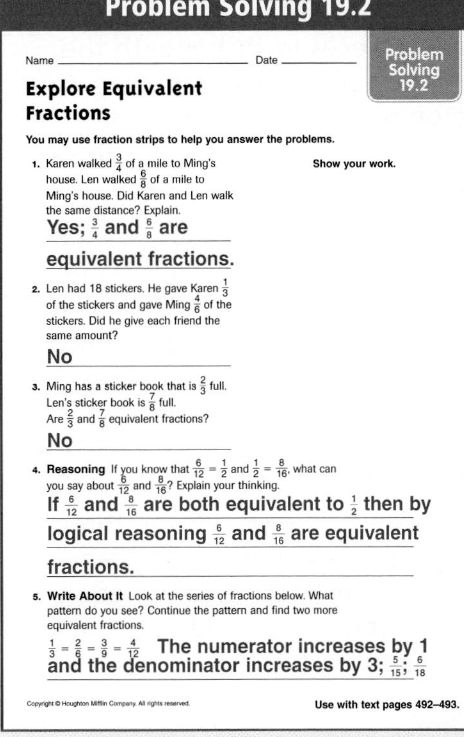
Name ______ Date ______ Problem Solving 19.2

Explore Equivalent Fractions

You may use fraction strips to help you answer the problems.

Show your work.

1. Karen walked $\frac{3}{4}$ of a mile to Ming's house. Len walked $\frac{6}{8}$ of a mile to Ming's house. Did Karen and Len walk the same distance? Explain. **Yes; $\frac{3}{4}$ and $\frac{6}{8}$ are equivalent fractions.**
2. Len had 18 stickers. He gave Karen $\frac{1}{3}$ of the stickers and gave Ming $\frac{4}{6}$ of the stickers. Did he give each friend the same amount? **No**
3. Ming has a sticker book that is $\frac{2}{3}$ full. Len's sticker book is $\frac{7}{8}$ full. Are $\frac{2}{3}$ and $\frac{7}{8}$ equivalent fractions? **No**
4. **Reasoning** If you know that $\frac{6}{12} = \frac{1}{2}$ and $\frac{1}{2} = \frac{8}{16}$, what can you say about $\frac{6}{12}$ and $\frac{8}{16}$? Explain your thinking. **If $\frac{6}{12}$ and $\frac{8}{16}$ are both equivalent to $\frac{1}{2}$ then by logical reasoning $\frac{6}{12}$ and $\frac{8}{16}$ are equivalent fractions.**
5. **Write About It** Look at the series of fractions below. What pattern do you see? Continue the pattern and find two more equivalent fractions. $\frac{1}{3} = \frac{2}{6} = \frac{3}{9} = \frac{4}{12}$ **The numerator increases by 1 and the denominator increases by 3; $\frac{5}{15}$; $\frac{6}{18}$**

 Use with text pages 492–493.

Homework 19.2 Page 118

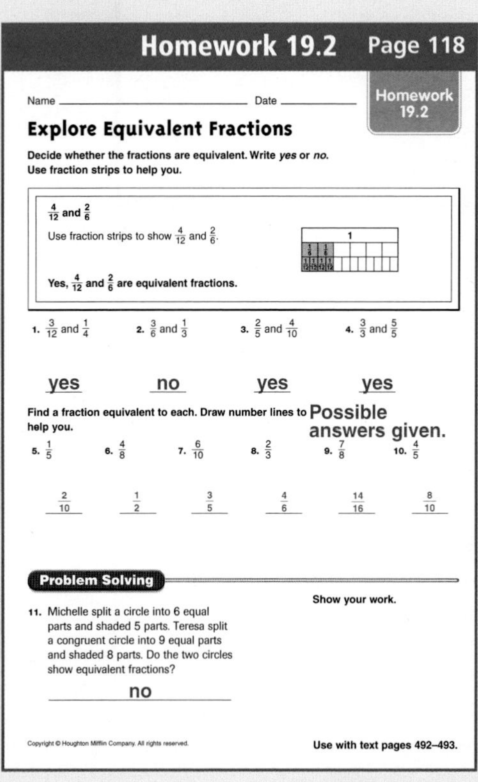
Name ______ Date ______ Homework 19.2

Explore Equivalent Fractions

Decide whether the fractions are equivalent. Write *yes* or *no*. Use fraction strips to help you.

$\frac{4}{12}$ and $\frac{2}{6}$

Use fraction strips to show $\frac{4}{12}$ and $\frac{2}{6}$.

Yes, $\frac{4}{12}$ and $\frac{2}{6}$ are equivalent fractions.

1. $\frac{3}{12}$ and $\frac{1}{4}$ **yes**
2. $\frac{3}{6}$ and $\frac{1}{3}$ **no**
3. $\frac{2}{5}$ and $\frac{4}{10}$ **yes**
4. $\frac{3}{3}$ and $\frac{5}{5}$ **yes**

Find a fraction equivalent to each. Draw number lines to help you. **Possible answers given.**

5. $\frac{1}{5}$ $\frac{2}{10}$
6. $\frac{4}{8}$ $\frac{1}{2}$
7. $\frac{6}{10}$ $\frac{3}{5}$
8. $\frac{2}{3}$ $\frac{4}{6}$
9. $\frac{7}{8}$ $\frac{14}{16}$
10. $\frac{4}{5}$ $\frac{8}{10}$

Problem Solving

Show your work.

11. Michelle split a circle into 6 equal parts and shaded 5 parts. Teresa split a congruent circle into 9 equal parts and shaded 8 parts. Do the two circles show equivalent fractions? **no**

 Use with text pages 492–493.

Lesson 19.3

Equivalent Fractions and Simplest Form

Planning

Lesson Objective Find equivalent fractions and write fractions in simplest form.

Technology Resources

- *Ways to Success* CD-ROM 19.3
- Education Place: Extra Practice, eGlossary, eManipulatives, eGames www.eduplace.com/map

Lesson 19.3 Transparency

Problem of the Day

Natalie's class held a raffle. There were 12 prizes in all. Natalie won 2 of the prizes. What fraction of the prizes did Natalie *not* win? ($\frac{10}{12}$)

Spiral Review

Find two fractions that are equivalent.

1. $\frac{2}{3}$ (sample answer: $\frac{4}{6}$, $\frac{6}{9}$)
2. $\frac{6}{8}$ (sample answer: $\frac{3}{4}$, $\frac{12}{16}$)
3. $\frac{7}{10}$ (sample answer: $\frac{14}{20}$, $\frac{21}{30}$)
4. $\frac{3}{12}$ (sample answer: $\frac{1}{4}$, $\frac{6}{24}$)

Lesson Quiz

Write each fraction in simplest form.

1. $\frac{10}{12}$ ($\frac{5}{6}$)
2. $\frac{12}{15}$ ($\frac{4}{5}$)
3. $\frac{6}{10}$ ($\frac{3}{5}$)
4. $\frac{7}{21}$ ($\frac{1}{3}$)
5. $\frac{10}{18}$ ($\frac{5}{9}$)
6. $\frac{5}{20}$ ($\frac{1}{4}$)

NCTM Standards

Number and Operations: Develop understanding of fractions as parts of unit wholes, as parts of collections; use models, benchmarks, and equivalent forms to judge the size of fractions.

Getting Started

Building Math Vocabulary

simplest form a fraction whose numerator and denominator have the number 1 as the only common factor

Discuss with students that we can get an idea across more effectively when we say it simply. Discuss an example that uses fractions. For instance: **Half of the 6,854 fans left the stadium early. Three thousand four hundred twenty-seven of the 6,854 fans left the stadium early.** Elicit that the first sentence is easier to understand because it uses a simpler number. Then show and discuss the vocabulary card for fractions in ***simplest form.***

Model Simplest Form

Whole Class	5 minutes
Objective	Model the simplest form of a fraction.
Materials	Fraction Pieces Transparency, blank transparency
Visual, Auditory	

- Use the 1 fraction piece, $\frac{1}{6}$ fraction pieces, $\frac{1}{3}$ fraction pieces, and $\frac{1}{12}$ fraction pieces cut out from the Fraction Pieces Transparency.
- Place the 1 fraction piece at the top of a blank transparency. Place eight $\frac{1}{12}$ fraction pieces beneath it, with the first one aligned at the left. Ask a volunteer to line up $\frac{1}{6}$ fraction pieces to fit beneath the $\frac{1}{12}$ fraction pieces. **How many $\frac{1}{6}$ fracton pieces did you use?** (4)
- Ask: **Is there another way to show the same amount?** (Yes, use two $\frac{1}{3}$ fraction pieces.) Line up two $\frac{1}{3}$ fraction pieces beneath the $\frac{1}{6}$ fraction pieces.
- Ask: **Is there another way to show the same amount?** (no) **So we found three ways to show the same amount. Which way uses the fewest pieces?** (two $\frac{1}{3}$ fraction pieces.)
- Elicit from students that the three fractions modeled were $\frac{8}{12}$, $\frac{4}{6}$, and $\frac{2}{3}$. Remind them that these are equivalent fractions. Tell students that $\frac{2}{3}$ is the *simplest form* of all these equivalent fractions. In this lesson they will use fraction pieces to identify equivalent fractions and find the simplest form.

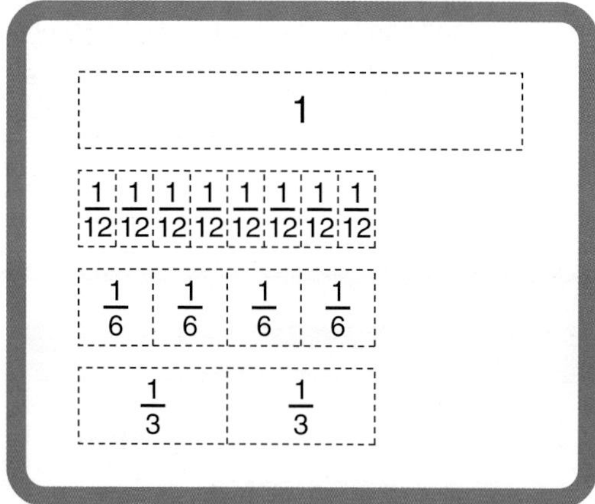

Differentiated Instruction

English Learners

Pairs	10 minutes
Objective	Model equivalent fractions.
Materials	Fraction pieces (Learning Tool 34)
Auditory, Visual	

Early Production

- After ***Introduce*** and ***Teach,*** have students practice finding and visualizing the simplest form with fraction pieces.
- Give each pair of students the fraction pieces. Ask them to model and write up to five fractions equivalent to $\frac{1}{2}$.
- Encourage them to discuss how to find the simplest form.

Intermediate/Advanced

- English Learner Resource 19.3
- English Learner Handbook

Intervention

Whole Class	5 minutes
Objective	Review multiplication and division facts.
Materials	None
Auditory, Visual	

- Provide a brief review of basic multiplication and division facts.

  $3 \times 8 = ■$ 24 $\quad 6 \times 9 = ■$ 54
  $4 \times 5 = ■$ 20

  $24 \div 8 = ■$ 3 $\quad 54 \div 9 = ■$ 6
  $20 \div 5 = ■$ 4
- Then ask questions such as the following: **If you start with 8 as a factor, how could you get 40 as a product?** (Multiply 8 by 5.) **If you start with 28 as the dividend, how could you get 4 as a quotient?** (Divide 28 by 7.)
- Then tell students that in this lesson they are going to continue their work with equivalent fractions. Point out that ***Way 2*** and ***Way 3*** use these basic multiplication and division facts.

Other Resources

- *Ways to Success* CD-ROM 19.3

Inclusion

Small Groups	5 minutes
Objective	Understand equivalent fractions.
Materials	Colored pencils
Auditory, Visual	

- Use a visual model to help students find equivalent fractions. For instance, for $\frac{2}{4} = \frac{4}{8}$, use red for the original fraction and blue for the equivalent fraction.

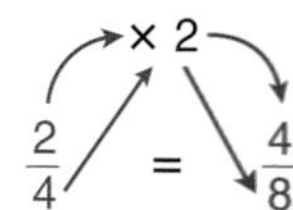

- Have students read aloud as you follow the arrows with your finger.

Literature Connection

Materials: *Gator Pie,* by Louise Mathews

- In this book, alligators get together to share a pie equally. As more and more come by, the pieces, which need to be the same size for each guest, get smaller and smaller.
- Reading this humorous book can help students to better understand equivalent fractions. It also will provide them with opportunities to write using appropriate math vocabulary.

Facts Practice

Give each student one index card with a fraction on it in simplest form. Also give each student a blank card. On the blank card, students should write a fraction that is equivalent to the first. Collect the cards and shuffle into a deck. Throughout the day, have students take turns matching the equivalent fractions, or have pairs of students play a memory game with the cards.

❶ Introduce

Explain to students that, when a fraction is in simplest form, the denominator and numerator are no longer divisible by the same number.

❷ Teach

Learn About It

Have a volunteer read aloud the opening problem.

- Focus students' attention on ***Way 1.*** Discuss how to use a number line to find equivalent fractions. Guide students to see that all fractions along the same vertical line are equivalent.
- Work through ***Way 2*** with students. **Why does multiplying the numerator and denominator of a fraction by the same number not change the value of the fraction?** (It is the same as multiplying the entire fraction by 1.)
- Work through ***Way 3*** with students. **Why does dividing the numerator and denominator of a fraction by the same number not change the value of the fraction?** (It is the same as dividing the entire fraction by 1.)

Common Error

- **Confusing simplest form**
- **Intervention** Guide students to consider each fraction they simplify to check whether any number other than 1 can divide both the numerator and denominator with no remainder. If there is no such number, then the fraction is in simplest form.

Lesson 3

Equivalent Fractions and Simplest Form

Vocabulary
simplest form

Objective Find equivalent fractions and write fractions in simplest form.

Learn About It

Reni is making fruit shakes. She needs $\frac{4}{8}$ cup of pineapple juice. Her measuring cup does not show eighths. What other fractions are equivalent to $\frac{4}{8}$?

Here are some different ways to find equivalent fractions.

Different Ways to Find Fractions Equivalent to $\frac{4}{8}$

Way ① You can use number lines.

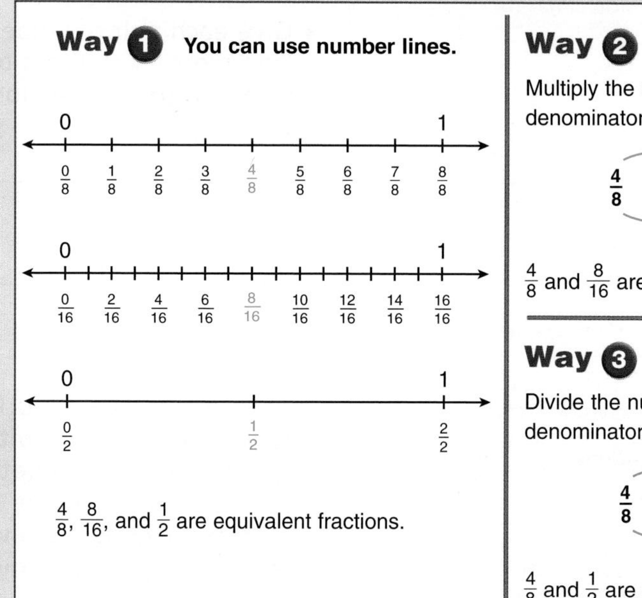

$\frac{4}{8}$, $\frac{8}{16}$, and $\frac{1}{2}$ are equivalent fractions.

Way ② You can multiply.

Multiply the numerator and denominator by the same number.

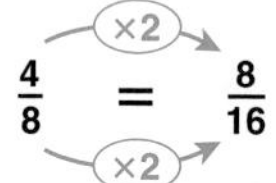

$\frac{4}{8}$ and $\frac{8}{16}$ are equivalent fractions.

Way ③ You can divide.

Divide the numerator and denominator by the same number.

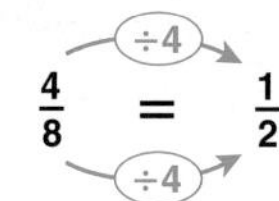

$\frac{4}{8}$ and $\frac{1}{2}$ are equivalent fractions.

Solution: $\frac{8}{16}$ and $\frac{1}{2}$ are both equivalent to $\frac{4}{8}$.

494

Reteach 19.3

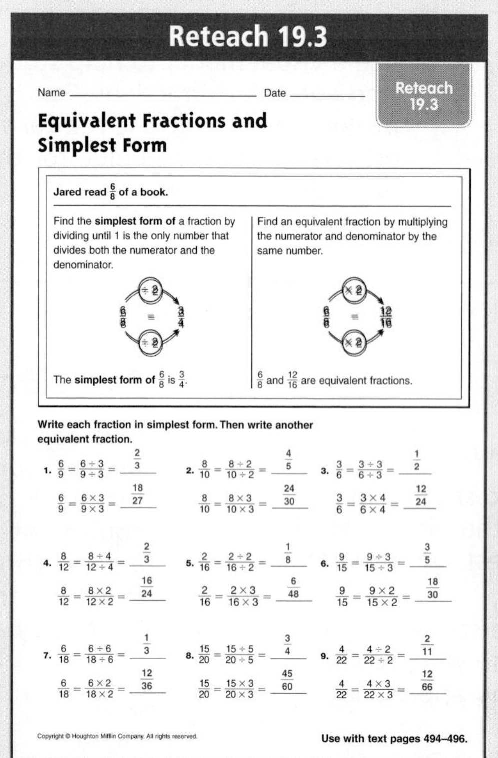

Name ______ Date ______

Reteach 19.3

Equivalent Fractions and Simplest Form

Jared read $\frac{6}{8}$ of a book.

Find the **simplest form of** a fraction by dividing until 1 is the only number that divides both the numerator and the denominator.

$\frac{6}{8} = \frac{3}{4}$ (÷2)

The **simplest form of** $\frac{6}{8}$ is $\frac{3}{4}$.

Find an equivalent fraction by multiplying the numerator and denominator by the same number.

$\frac{6}{8} = \frac{12}{16}$ (×2)

$\frac{6}{8}$ and $\frac{12}{16}$ are equivalent fractions.

Write each fraction in simplest form. Then write another equivalent fraction.

1. $\frac{6}{9} = \frac{6 \div 3}{9 \div 3} = \frac{2}{3}$; $\frac{6}{9} = \frac{6 \times 3}{9 \times 3} = \frac{18}{27}$
2. $\frac{8}{10} = \frac{8 \div 2}{10 \div 2} = \frac{4}{5}$; $\frac{8}{10} = \frac{8 \times 3}{10 \times 3} = \frac{24}{30}$
3. $\frac{3}{6} = \frac{3 \div 3}{6 \div 3} = \frac{1}{2}$; $\frac{3}{6} = \frac{3 \times 4}{6 \times 4} = \frac{12}{24}$
4. $\frac{8}{12} = \frac{8 \div 4}{12 \div 4} = \frac{2}{3}$; $\frac{8}{12} = \frac{8 \times 2}{12 \times 2} = \frac{16}{24}$
5. $\frac{2}{16} = \frac{2 \div 2}{16 \div 2} = \frac{1}{8}$; $\frac{2}{16} = \frac{2 \times 3}{16 \times 3} = \frac{6}{48}$
6. $\frac{9}{15} = \frac{9 \div 3}{15 \div 3} = \frac{3}{5}$; $\frac{9}{15} = \frac{9 \times 2}{15 \times 2} = \frac{18}{30}$
7. $\frac{6}{18} = \frac{6 \div 6}{18 \div 6} = \frac{1}{3}$; $\frac{6}{18} = \frac{6 \times 2}{18 \times 2} = \frac{12}{36}$
8. $\frac{15}{20} = \frac{15 \div 5}{20 \div 5} = \frac{3}{4}$; $\frac{15}{20} = \frac{15 \times 3}{20 \times 3} = \frac{45}{60}$
9. $\frac{4}{22} = \frac{4 \div 2}{22 \div 2} = \frac{2}{11}$; $\frac{4}{22} = \frac{4 \times 3}{22 \times 3} = \frac{12}{66}$

Use with text pages 494–496.

Practice 19.3 Page 119

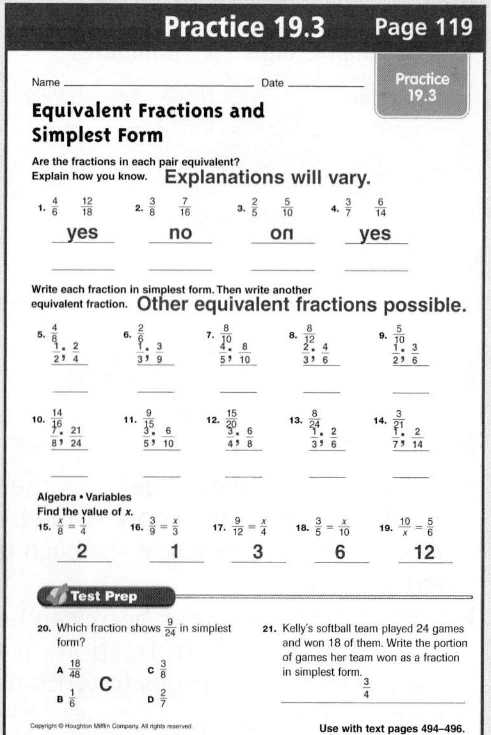

Name ______ Date ______

Practice 19.3

Equivalent Fractions and Simplest Form

Are the fractions in each pair equivalent? Explain how you know. Explanations will vary.

1. $\frac{4}{6}$ $\frac{12}{18}$ yes
2. $\frac{3}{8}$ $\frac{7}{16}$ no
3. $\frac{2}{5}$ $\frac{5}{10}$ on
4. $\frac{3}{7}$ $\frac{6}{14}$ yes

Write each fraction in simplest form. Then write another equivalent fraction. Other equivalent fractions possible.

5. $\frac{4}{8}$ $\frac{1}{2}$; $\frac{2}{4}$
6. $\frac{2}{6}$ $\frac{1}{3}$; $\frac{3}{9}$
7. $\frac{8}{10}$ $\frac{4}{5}$; $\frac{8}{10}$
8. $\frac{8}{12}$ $\frac{2}{3}$; $\frac{4}{6}$
9. $\frac{5}{10}$ $\frac{1}{2}$; $\frac{3}{6}$
10. $\frac{14}{16}$ $\frac{7}{8}$; $\frac{21}{24}$
11. $\frac{9}{15}$ $\frac{3}{5}$; $\frac{6}{10}$
12. $\frac{15}{20}$ $\frac{3}{4}$; $\frac{6}{8}$
13. $\frac{8}{24}$ $\frac{1}{3}$; $\frac{2}{6}$
14. $\frac{3}{21}$ $\frac{1}{7}$; $\frac{2}{14}$

Algebra • Variables
Find the value of *x*.

15. $\frac{x}{8} = \frac{1}{4}$ 2
16. $\frac{3}{9} = \frac{x}{3}$ 1
17. $\frac{9}{12} = \frac{x}{4}$ 3
18. $\frac{3}{5} = \frac{x}{10}$ 6
19. $\frac{10}{x} = \frac{5}{6}$ 12

Test Prep

20. Which fraction shows $\frac{9}{24}$ in simplest form? C
    A $\frac{18}{48}$
    B $\frac{1}{6}$
    C $\frac{3}{8}$
    D $\frac{2}{7}$
21. Kelly's softball team played 24 games and won 18 of them. Write the portion of games her team won as a fraction in simplest form. $\frac{3}{4}$

Use with text pages 494–496.

▶ A fraction is in **simplest form** when 1 is the only number that divides both the numerator and the denominator with no remainder.

These fractions are in simplest form.	These fractions are not in simplest form.
$\frac{1}{2}$ $\frac{2}{3}$ $\frac{3}{8}$ $\frac{2}{7}$ $\frac{5}{9}$	$\frac{2}{4}$ $\frac{4}{8}$ $\frac{3}{15}$ $\frac{6}{9}$ $\frac{8}{12}$

Juan and Brooke both used equivalent fractions to write $\frac{12}{18}$ in simplest form.

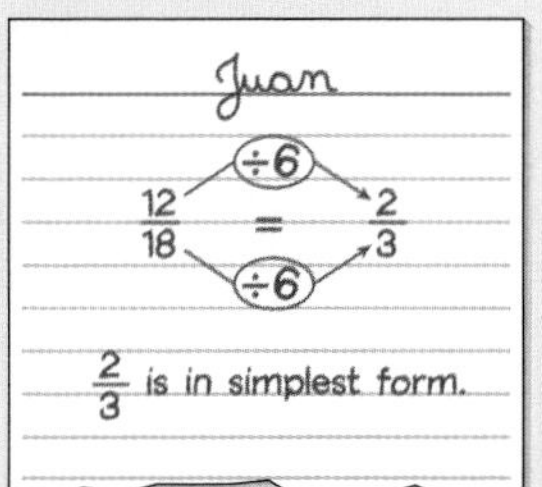

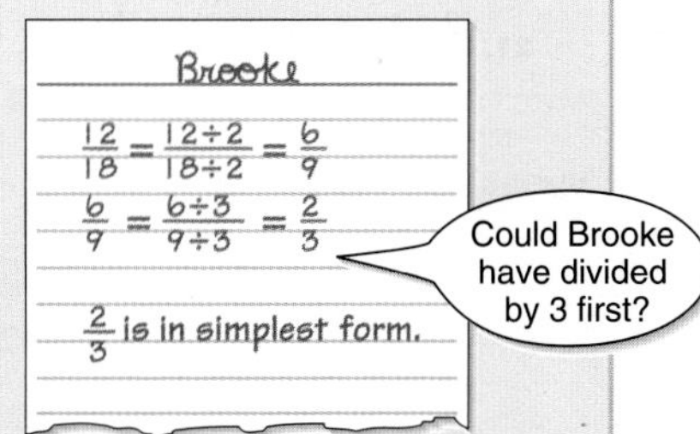

Brooke
$\frac{12}{18} = \frac{12 \div 2}{18 \div 2} = \frac{6}{9}$
$\frac{6}{9} = \frac{6 \div 3}{9 \div 3} = \frac{2}{3}$
$\frac{2}{3}$ is in simplest form.
Could Brooke have divided by 3 first?

$\frac{2}{3}$ is in simplest form because 1 is the only number that can divide both 2 and 3 with no remainder.

- How are Juan's work and Brooke's work alike?
- How are they different? **Both divided by common factors. Juan divided by the greatest common factor. Brooke divided by the least common factor.**

Guided Practice

Write each fraction in simplest form. Then write another equivalent fraction. ***Possible equivalent fractions given.***

1. $\frac{2}{6}$ **$\frac{1}{3}$; $\frac{4}{12}$**
2. $\frac{4}{10}$ **$\frac{2}{5}$; $\frac{8}{20}$**
3. $\frac{6}{12}$ **$\frac{1}{2}$; $\frac{3}{6}$**
4. $\frac{10}{16}$ **$\frac{5}{8}$; $\frac{20}{32}$**

Ask Yourself

- Did I multiply or divide the numerator and the denominator by the same number?

Complete the equivalent fraction. What number did you multiply or divide the numerator or denominator by?

5. $\frac{1}{2} = \frac{3}{■}$ **6** **multiply by 3**
6. $\frac{15}{20} = \frac{■}{4}$ **3** **divide by 5**
7. $\frac{4}{10} = \frac{■}{5}$ **2** **divide by 2**
8. $\frac{2}{3} = \frac{4}{■}$ **6** **multiply by 2**

Explain Your Thinking ▶ Can you always multiply or divide to find equivalent fractions? ***Possible explanation:*** **You can always multiply to find an equivalent fraction. You need to find a common factor to divide to find an equivalent fraction.**

- Read aloud the definition of a fraction in simplest form and have students study the examples. **Why isn't the fraction $\frac{6}{8}$ in simplest form?** (The numerator and denominator can each be divided by 2.)

Guided Practice

Have students complete **Exercises 1–8** as you observe. Remind them to use the ***Ask Yourself*** question to help. Give students the opportunity to talk about the question in ***Explain Your Thinking.***

Enrichment 19.3

Name ________ Date ________

Enrichment 19.3

Where's My Equivalent?

In each problem, make a list of all the fractions from the box that are equivalent to the given fraction. In each list, circle the fraction that is in simplest form.

$\frac{2}{14}$	$\frac{50}{100}$	$\frac{1}{8}$	$\frac{2}{3}$
$\frac{2}{10}$	$\frac{4}{6}$	$\frac{25}{30}$	$\frac{4}{28}$
$\frac{6}{12}$	$\frac{3}{24}$	$\frac{10}{12}$	$\frac{1}{5}$

1. $\frac{5}{40}$ **$\frac{1}{8}$, $\frac{3}{24}$, ($\frac{1}{8}$ circled)**
2. $\frac{5}{6}$ **$\frac{25}{30}$, $\frac{10}{12}$, ($\frac{5}{6}$ circled)**
3. $\frac{1}{7}$ **$\frac{2}{14}$, $\frac{4}{28}$, ($\frac{1}{7}$ circled)**
4. $\frac{9}{45}$ **$\frac{2}{10}$, $\frac{1}{5}$, ($\frac{1}{5}$ circled)**
5. $\frac{1}{2}$ **$\frac{50}{100}$, $\frac{6}{12}$, ($\frac{1}{2}$ circled)**
6. $\frac{20}{30}$ **$\frac{2}{3}$, $\frac{4}{6}$, ($\frac{2}{3}$ circled)**

Use with text pages 494–496.

Problem Solving 19.3

Name ________ Date ________

Problem Solving 19.3

Equivalent Fractions and Simplest Form

Ms. Billets bought several items at the craft store. The table shows how much of each item she bought. Use the table for Problems 1–3.

Item	Yarn	Ribbon	Fabric	String
Amount	6 feet	4 yards	$\frac{3}{4}$ yard	12 feet

Show your work.

1. Ms. Billets used 1 yard of ribbon to make a dress for a doll. Write two equivalent fractions to show what fraction of the ribbon that she bought was used for the dress.
   Possible answers: $\frac{1}{4}$, $\frac{2}{8}$
2. Ms. Billets used 2 feet of yarn to make an ornament. Write this length as a fraction of the total length of yarn she bought. Is this fraction in simplest form? Explain.
   $\frac{2}{6}$; No, this fraction in simplest form is $\frac{1}{3}$.
3. Ms. Billets used 8 feet of string to tie together newspapers to take to the recycling center. What fraction of the string that she bought does she have left? Write the fraction in simplest form.
   $\frac{4}{12} = \frac{1}{3}$
4. **What's Wrong?** Look at Heather's work below. She said that $\frac{6}{8}$ in simplest form is $\frac{1}{3}$. What did she do wrong? Give the correct answer.
   $\frac{6}{8} - \frac{5}{5} = \frac{1}{3}$
   $\frac{6}{8}$ in simplest form is $\frac{3}{4}$; explanations may vary.

Use with text pages 494–496.

3 Practice

Practice and Problem Solving

Select from **Exercises 9–45** as independent work.

- ***Algebra* • *Variables*** You may wish to demonstrate a strategy students can use to find the variable. For each equation, guide students to look across the numerators of both fractions or across both denominators to find a pair *without* a variable. Have them notice the relationship between the two numbers and then apply that relationship to find the missing number. For example, in **Exercise 25,** students can see that both denominators are given and that the 4 in the first fraction is *half* of the 8 in the second. So the x in the numerator of the first fraction must be *half* the 2, the numerator of the second fraction. Since 1 is half of 2, $x = 1$.

4 Assess & Close

Math Talk in Action

Have students refer to the following problem to conclude the lesson: **There are 18 players on Nico's team. Twelve players are older than Nico. What fraction, in simplest form, shows the number of players on the team that are older than Nico?** ($\frac{2}{3}$)

- **How did you figure out the answer?** (Accept reasonable explanations.)

Math Journal Prompt

Have students write an explanation that describes what a fraction in simplest form is. Ask them to also provide three equivalent fractions, one of which is expressed in simplest form.

Lesson Quiz

Use the quiz on Lesson Transparency 19.3.

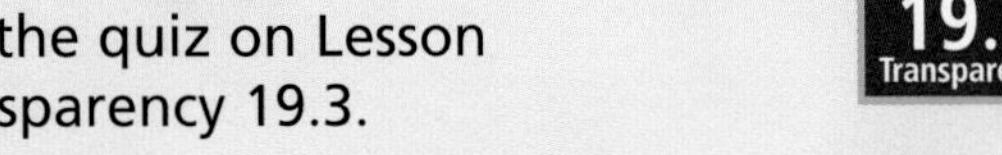

Lesson 19.3 Transparency

Test Prep & Spiral Review

Use Test Prep Transparency 19.3.

Test Prep 19.3 Transparency

Practice and Problem Solving *Explanations may vary.*

Are the fractions in each pair equivalent? Explain how you know.

9. $\frac{2}{8}$ $\frac{4}{16}$ **yes**
10. $\frac{2}{4}$ $\frac{5}{10}$ **yes**
11. $\frac{6}{9}$ $\frac{8}{12}$ **yes**
12. $\frac{5}{5}$ $\frac{8}{8}$ **yes**
13. $\frac{6}{15}$ $\frac{2}{5}$ **yes**
14. $\frac{14}{16}$ $\frac{7}{9}$ **no**

Write each fraction in simplest form. Then write another equivalent fraction. ***Possible equivalent fractions given.***

15. $\frac{3}{9}$ **$\frac{1}{3}$; $\frac{2}{6}$**
16. $\frac{6}{8}$ **$\frac{3}{4}$; $\frac{9}{12}$**
17. $\frac{9}{12}$ **$\frac{3}{4}$; $\frac{6}{8}$**
18. $\frac{6}{15}$ **$\frac{2}{5}$; $\frac{4}{10}$**
19. $\frac{15}{18}$ **$\frac{5}{6}$; $\frac{10}{12}$**
20. $\frac{4}{14}$ **$\frac{2}{7}$; $\frac{6}{21}$**
21. $\frac{2}{3}$ **$\frac{2}{3}$; $\frac{4}{6}$**
22. $\frac{20}{20}$ **1; $\frac{2}{2}$**
23. $\frac{9}{21}$ **$\frac{3}{7}$; $\frac{6}{14}$**
24. $\frac{18}{36}$ **$\frac{1}{2}$; $\frac{2}{4}$**

Algebra • Variables Find the value of x.

25. $\frac{x}{4} = \frac{2}{8}$ **1**
26. $\frac{9}{12} = \frac{x}{4}$ **3**
27. $\frac{x}{5} = \frac{15}{15}$ **5**
28. $\frac{10}{x} = \frac{2}{3}$ **15**
29. $\frac{18}{27} = \frac{2}{x}$ **3**
30. $\frac{x}{42} = \frac{1}{7}$ **6**

31. No; $\frac{1}{2}$ is equivalent to $\frac{2}{4}$, not $\frac{3}{4}$.

Use the recipe for Problems 31–33.

Reni's Fruit Shake

1 large banana	$\frac{3}{4}$ cup cranberry juice
1 cup strawberries	$\frac{1}{2}$ cup pineapple juice
1 mango, cubed	1 cup ice cubes

Put all ingredients in blender.
Blend until thick and smooth.
Makes 3 servings.

31. Are the amounts of cranberry juice and pineapple juice equivalent? Explain. ***See above.***
32. Reni made 12 servings of her fruit shake for her friends. How many bananas did she use? **4 bananas**
33. Lila will make one serving of Reni's recipe. How much cranberry juice does she need? Use fraction strips to solve the problem. **$\frac{1}{4}$ cup cranberry juice**

34. **Write About It** Justine says that $\frac{2}{3}$ and $\frac{16}{25}$ are equivalent fractions. Is she correct? Explain your thinking. **No; *Possible explanation:* multiplying the numerator and denominator of $\frac{2}{3}$ by 8 equals $\frac{16}{24}$, not $\frac{16}{25}$.**
35. **Reasoning** Can you add the same number to the numerator and denominator to find equivalent fractions? Why or why not? **No; *Possible explanation:* if you add 1 to the numerator and denominator of $\frac{1}{2}$ you get $\frac{2}{3}$, which is not equivalent to $\frac{1}{2}$ $\left(\frac{1}{2} = \frac{3}{6} \text{ and } \frac{2}{3} = \frac{4}{6}\right)$.**

496

Extra Practice See page 513, Set B.

Homework 19.3 Page 119

Name ______ Date ______ Homework 19.3

Equivalent Fractions and Simplest Form

Are the fractions in each pair equivalent? Explain how you know. **Explanations may vary.**

$\frac{2}{4}$ and $\frac{3}{6}$

You can use number lines. | You can multiply the numerator and denominator of a fraction by the same number. $\frac{2}{4} = \frac{(2 \times 3)}{(4 \times 3)} = \frac{6}{12}$; $\frac{3}{6} = \frac{(3 \times 2)}{(6 \times 2)} = \frac{6}{12}$ | You can divide the numerator and denominator of a fraction by the same number. $\frac{2}{4} = \frac{(2 \div 2)}{(4 \div 2)} = \frac{1}{2}$; $\frac{3}{6} = \frac{(3 \div 3)}{(6 \div 3)} = \frac{1}{2}$

Yes, $\frac{2}{4}$ and $\frac{3}{6}$ are equivalent fractions.

1. $\frac{4}{5}$ $\frac{8}{10}$ **yes**
2. $\frac{2}{8}$ $\frac{1}{6}$ **no**
3. $\frac{1}{3}$ $\frac{3}{9}$ **yes**
4. $\frac{10}{12}$ $\frac{6}{7}$ **no**

Write each fraction in simplest form. Then write another equivalent fraction. **Possible answers given.**

5. $\frac{6}{12}$ **$\frac{1}{2}$; $\frac{2}{4}$**
6. $\frac{10}{14}$ **$\frac{5}{7}$; $\frac{15}{21}$**
7. $\frac{8}{20}$ **$\frac{2}{5}$; $\frac{4}{10}$**
8. $\frac{9}{15}$ **$\frac{3}{5}$; $\frac{6}{10}$**
9. $\frac{10}{24}$ **$\frac{5}{12}$; $\frac{20}{48}$**

Algebra • Variables Find the value of x.

10. $\frac{x}{18} = \frac{6}{9}$ **12**
11. $\frac{2}{5} = \frac{4}{x}$ **10**
12. $\frac{4}{16} = \frac{x}{4}$ **1**
13. $\frac{1}{5} = \frac{x}{25}$ **5**
14. $\frac{15}{20} = \frac{x}{4}$ **3**

Problem Solving

15. If a recipe that calls for 2 cups of sugar makes servings for 10 people, how much sugar should you use if you want to make servings for 20 people? **4 cups**

Use with text pages 494–496.

Mixed Review and Test Prep

Open Response

Solve. (Ch. 6, Lesson 4; Ch. 8, Lesson 2)

36. $4\overline{)78}$ **19 R2**	**37.** $8\overline{)26}$ **3 R2**	**38.** 18×7 **126**
39. $6\overline{)45}$ **7 R3**	**40.** 86×3 **258**	**41.** 25×9 **225**
42. 31×4 **124**	**43.** $8\overline{)38}$ **4 R6**	**44.** $4\overline{)89}$ **22 R1**

45. Dora's team won 10 of 15 games. Pedro's team played 6 games and won the same fraction of their games as Dora's. How many games did Pedro's team win? Explain your thinking. (Ch. 19, Lesson 3) ***See below.***

Fraction Match-up

Game Activity

2 Players

What You'll Need • 16 index cards (Learning Tool 37)

How to Play

1. Use Learning Tool 37 or make 16 cards like the ones shown.
2. Shuffle the cards. Place them facedown in any order in a 4 × 4 array.
3. A player turns over any two cards. If the cards show two equivalent fractions, the player keeps both cards. If not, the player turns the cards over and places them in the same positions.
4. Players take turns repeating Step 3 until all 8 matches have been made. The player with the greater number of cards is the winner.

$\frac{3}{6}$	$\frac{1}{2}$	$\frac{4}{6}$	$\frac{2}{3}$
$\frac{15}{25}$	$\frac{3}{5}$	$\frac{14}{35}$	$\frac{2}{5}$
$\frac{9}{21}$	$\frac{3}{7}$	$\frac{3}{18}$	$\frac{1}{6}$
$\frac{12}{40}$	$\frac{3}{10}$	$\frac{15}{24}$	$\frac{5}{8}$

45. 4 games; *Possible explanation:* Dora's team won $\frac{10}{15}$ (which is equivalent to $\frac{2}{3}$) of their games. $\frac{2}{3}$ is equivalent to $\frac{4}{6}$ so Pedro's team won 4 out of 6 games.

Game

Fraction Match-Up

- Provide the materials needed and discuss the rules and goals of the game. Guide students to understand that this game is another one that uses the "concentration" format and rules of play.
- Vary the structure of the game to suit the needs of your students. For example, have them make a 5-by-5, a 6-by-6, or a 3-by-3 array of equivalent fractions.
- You may find it useful to have students watch a practice game played on the overhead by two volunteers.
- Challenge interested students to think of other games they could play with the cards to practice equivalent fractions.

Lesson 19.4

Compare and Order Fractions

Planning

Lesson Objective Compare and order fractions.

Technology Resources

- Audio Tutor 2/19 Listen and Understand
- *Ways to Success* CD-ROM 19.4
- *Ways to Assess* CD-ROM
- Education Place: Extra Practice, Extra Help, eManipulatives www.eduplace.com/map

Lesson 19.4 Transparency

Problem of the Day

The floor of a square room is covered by 6 rows of 6 large square tiles. Which is greater, the fraction of tiles that forms the edge of the room, or the fraction of inside tiles? Hint: Draw a diagram. (edge; $\frac{20}{36} > \frac{16}{36}$)

Spiral Review

Write each fraction in simplest form.

1. $\frac{10}{20}$ ($\frac{1}{2}$)
2. $\frac{12}{18}$ ($\frac{2}{3}$)
3. $\frac{6}{14}$ ($\frac{3}{7}$)
4. $\frac{9}{21}$ ($\frac{3}{7}$)
5. $\frac{10}{25}$ ($\frac{2}{5}$)
6. $\frac{4}{24}$ ($\frac{1}{6}$)

Lesson Quiz

Compare. Write >, <, or = for each ●

1. $\frac{1}{3}$ ● $\frac{1}{2}$ (<)
2. $\frac{3}{8}$ ● $\frac{7}{8}$ (<)
3. $\frac{2}{4}$ ● $\frac{3}{5}$ (<)
4. $\frac{5}{6}$ ● $\frac{4}{5}$ (>)
5. $\frac{6}{8}$ ● $\frac{8}{12}$ (>)
6. $\frac{2}{4}$ ● $\frac{8}{16}$ (=)

NCTM Standards

Number and Operations: Develop understanding of fractions as parts of unit wholes, as parts of a collection; use models, benchmarks, and equivalent forms to judge the size of fractions.

Getting Started

Building Math Vocabulary

Students should be familiar with the vocabulary in this lesson.

Using Equivalent Fractions and Fractions in Simplest Form

Whole Class	5 minutes
Objective	Understand correlation between equivalent fractions and simplest form.
Materials	None
Visual, Auditory	

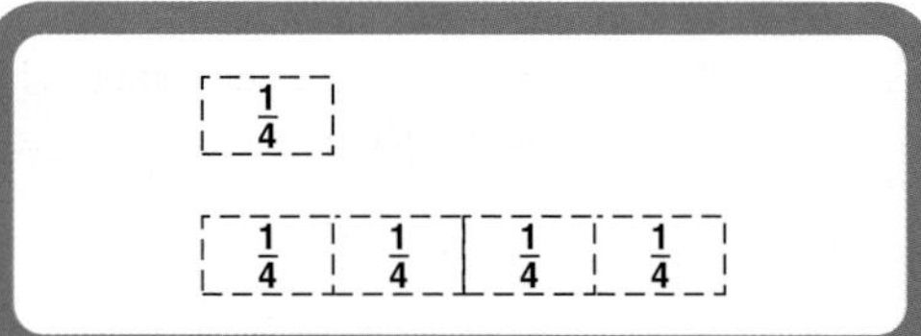

- Name a fraction. Ask students to name fractions equivalent to it. Repeat with other fractions. Then discuss the similarity between finding equivalent fractions and writing fractions in simplest form. Elicit from students that we need to perform the same operation on *both* the numerator and the denominator of a fraction.
- Next, write the fractions $\frac{1}{4}$ and $\frac{4}{4}$. **Which is greater? Why?** ($\frac{4}{4}$, it is equal to 1) Tell students that the lesson will introduce ways to compare fractions and to order them from least to greatest.

Differentiated Instruction

English Learners

Pairs	10 minutes
Objective	Compare and order fractions.
Materials	Fraction pieces, Student page 499
Auditory, Visual	

Early Production

- Encourage students to verbalize the ***Ask Yourself*** questions and answers while doing ***Guided Practice.***
- Model the first exercise using both ways suggested on Student page 498, then read the answer.
- Have the students do the next two exercises independently, in the same way.

Intermediate/Advanced

- English Learner Resource 19.4
- English Learner Handbook

Intervention

Pairs	5 minutes
Objective	Use a ruler to compare fractions.
Materials	Inch ruler
Auditory, Visual	

- Have students work in pairs, using an inch ruler to compare fractions. Guide them to use the 0–1 inch section of the ruler to compare halves, fourths, and eighths. For instance, you can have them compare $\frac{3}{8}$ of an inch with $\frac{3}{4}$ of an inch.
- Keep in mind that you may need to help students read the $\frac{1}{8}$ inch segments. You can extend this activity to include comparing sixteenths of an inch.

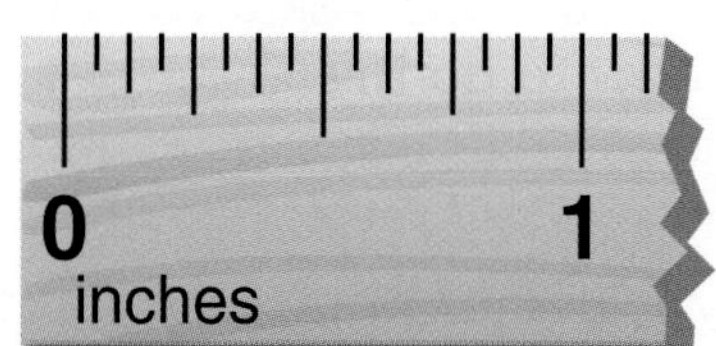

Other Resources

- *Ways to Success* CD-ROM 19.4

Special Needs

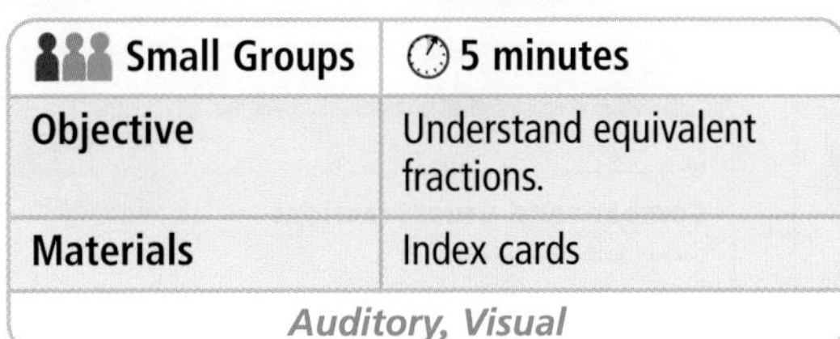

Small Groups	5 minutes
Objective	Understand equivalent fractions.
Materials	Index cards
Auditory, Visual	

- Write three fractions with unlike denominators. Have partners copy each fraction on an index card. Ask them to list equivalent fractions for each until they find a denominator that is common to all three fractions.
- Have the partners arrange the fractions with the like denominators in order from least to greatest.

Social Studies Connection

Tell the group that the students at Watson Elementary School voted on the issues listed below. Read the results. Ask students to record the data. Have them compare votes to list preferences from least preferred to most preferred.

- $\frac{2}{3}$ voted for longer recess. (3)
- $\frac{2}{5}$ voted for more homework. (2)
- $\frac{3}{10}$ voted for wearing school uniforms. (1)
- $\frac{5}{6}$ voted to allow pets in the classroom. (4)

① Introduce

Write the fractions $\frac{2}{6}$ and $\frac{1}{6}$ on the board. Ask students to compare the fractions. Guide students to see that comparing fractions means telling which is greater and which is lesser. Tell students that ordering fractions will also show which are greater and which are lesser. Explain that in this lesson, students will compare and order fractions with the same and different numerators and denominators.

② Teach

Learn About It

- Have a student read the opening problem aloud. Review that $\frac{2}{6} > \frac{1}{6}$ because $2 > 1$. Ask a volunteer to explain the rule for comparing fractions with common denominators.
- For ***Way 1,*** write $\frac{2}{6}$ ⬭ $\frac{1}{2}$ on the board. Have students use fraction pieces to compare these two fractions. Ask a volunteer to explain how to do this. (Align two $\frac{1}{6}$ fraction pieces and one $\frac{1}{2}$ fraction piece at the left; the longer model is the greater fraction.)
- For ***Way 2,*** demonstrate how to use equivalent fractions to compare $\frac{2}{6}$ and $\frac{1}{2}$. **What do we multiply a fraction by to find an equivalent fraction?** (a fraction equivalent to 1)

Common Error

- **Multiplying both fractions by the same number**
- **Intervention** Emphasize that the point of multiplying a fraction by a fraction equivalent to 1 is to get common denominators for the two fractions we are comparing. Point out with examples like $\frac{3}{4}$ ⬭ $\frac{2}{3}$ that sometimes we need to multiply *both* fractions, but *not* by the same number. In cases like this one, guide students to find the denominator of the first fraction and then find the second equivalent fraction with that same denominator.

Lesson 4

Audio Tutor 2/19 Listen and Understand

Compare and Order Fractions

Objective Compare and order fractions.

Learn About It

Clay used $\frac{2}{6}$ of his garden for pumpkins, $\frac{1}{2}$ for lettuce, and $\frac{1}{6}$ for tomatoes. Was more of his garden used for pumpkins or for tomatoes?

To compare fractions that have the same denominators, just compare the numerators.

Compare $\frac{2}{6}$ and $\frac{1}{6}$.

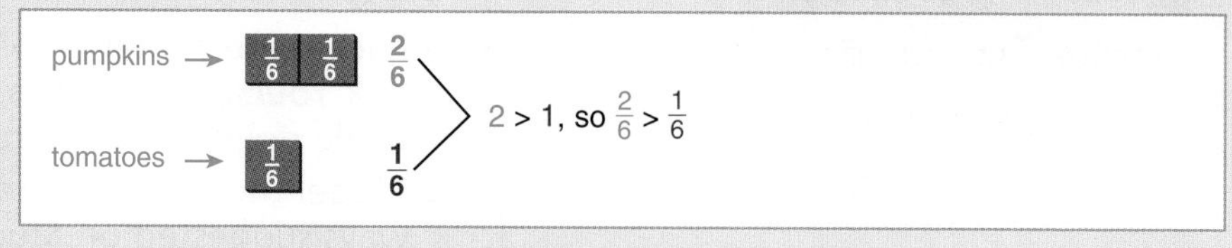

Solution: Clay used more of his garden for pumpkins than tomatoes.

▶ You can also compare fractions with different denominators.

Compare $\frac{2}{6}$ and $\frac{1}{2}$.

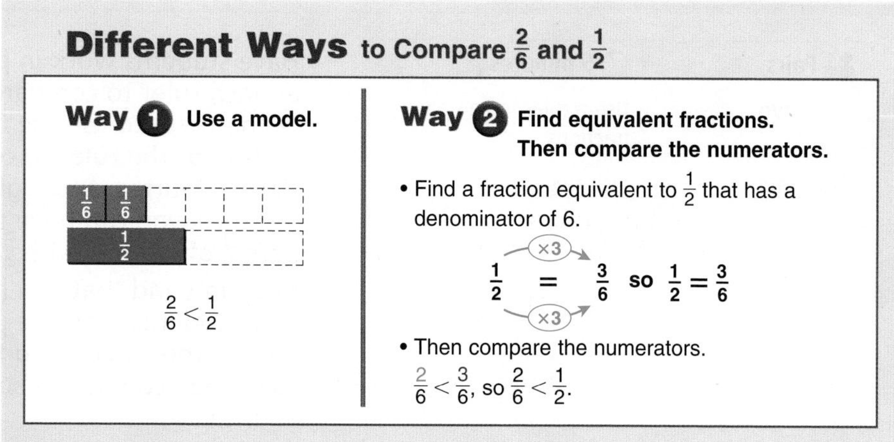

Solution: $\frac{2}{6}$ is less than $\frac{1}{2}$.

498

Extra Help at **eduplace.com/map**

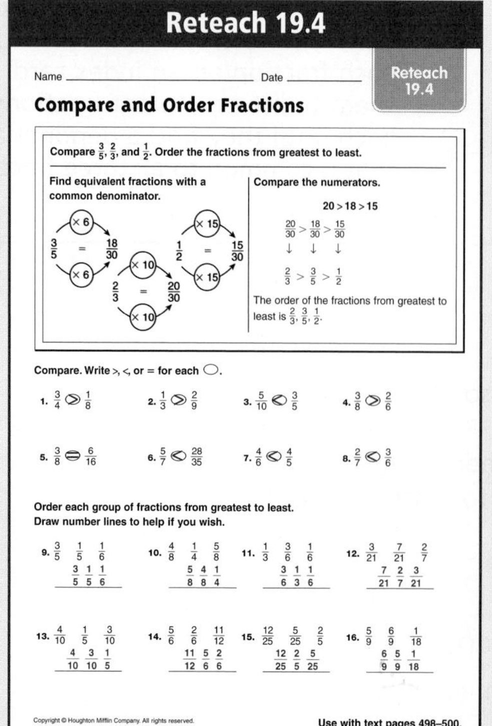

Reteach 19.4

Name ______ Date ______ Reteach 19.4

Compare and Order Fractions

Compare $\frac{3}{5}$, $\frac{2}{3}$, and $\frac{1}{2}$. Order the fractions from greatest to least.

Find equivalent fractions with a common denominator.

$\frac{3}{5} \xrightarrow{\times 6} \frac{18}{30}$ $\frac{2}{3} \xrightarrow{\times 10} \frac{20}{30}$ $\frac{1}{2} \xrightarrow{\times 15} \frac{15}{30}$

Compare the numerators.

20 > 18 > 15

$\frac{20}{30} > \frac{18}{30} > \frac{15}{30}$

↓ ↓ ↓

$\frac{2}{3} > \frac{3}{5} > \frac{1}{2}$

The order of the fractions from greatest to least is $\frac{2}{3}, \frac{3}{5}, \frac{1}{2}$.

Compare. Write >, <, or = for each ⬭.

1. $\frac{3}{4}$ (>) $\frac{1}{8}$ 2. $\frac{1}{3}$ (>) $\frac{2}{9}$ 3. $\frac{5}{10}$ (<) $\frac{3}{5}$ 4. $\frac{3}{8}$ (>) $\frac{2}{6}$
5. $\frac{3}{8}$ (=) $\frac{6}{16}$ 6. $\frac{5}{7}$ (<) $\frac{28}{35}$ 7. $\frac{4}{6}$ (<) $\frac{4}{5}$ 8. $\frac{2}{7}$ (<) $\frac{3}{6}$

Order each group of fractions from greatest to least. Draw number lines to help if you wish.

9. $\frac{3}{5}$ $\frac{1}{5}$ $\frac{1}{6}$ — $\frac{3}{5}$ $\frac{1}{5}$ $\frac{1}{6}$
10. $\frac{4}{8}$ $\frac{1}{4}$ $\frac{5}{8}$ — $\frac{5}{8}$ $\frac{4}{8}$ $\frac{1}{4}$
11. $\frac{1}{3}$ $\frac{3}{6}$ $\frac{1}{6}$ — $\frac{3}{6}$ $\frac{1}{3}$ $\frac{1}{6}$
12. $\frac{3}{21}$ $\frac{7}{21}$ $\frac{2}{7}$ — $\frac{7}{21}$ $\frac{2}{7}$ $\frac{3}{21}$
13. $\frac{4}{10}$ $\frac{1}{5}$ $\frac{3}{10}$ — $\frac{4}{10}$ $\frac{3}{10}$ $\frac{1}{5}$
14. $\frac{5}{6}$ $\frac{2}{6}$ $\frac{11}{12}$ — $\frac{11}{12}$ $\frac{5}{6}$ $\frac{2}{6}$
15. $\frac{12}{25}$ $\frac{5}{25}$ $\frac{2}{5}$ — $\frac{12}{25}$ $\frac{2}{5}$ $\frac{5}{25}$
16. $\frac{5}{9}$ $\frac{6}{9}$ $\frac{1}{18}$ — $\frac{6}{9}$ $\frac{5}{9}$ $\frac{1}{18}$

Use with text pages 498–500.

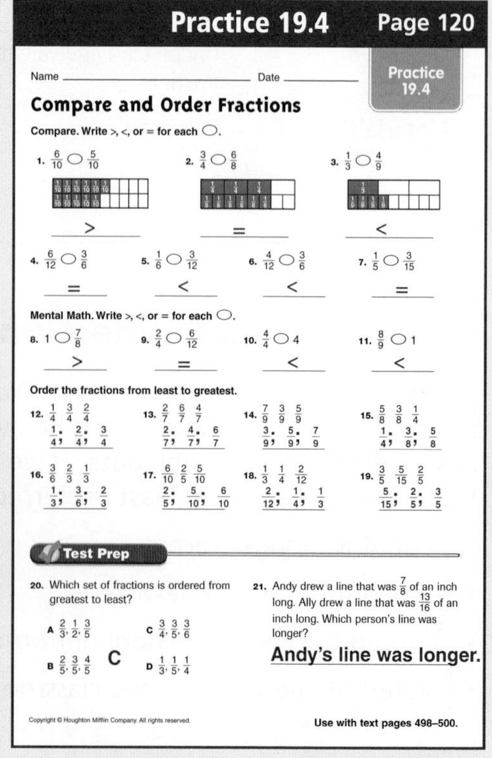

Practice 19.4 **Page 120**

Name ______ Date ______ Practice 19.4

Compare and Order Fractions

Compare. Write >, <, or = for each ⬭.

1. $\frac{6}{10}$ ⬭ $\frac{5}{10}$ — >
2. $\frac{3}{4}$ ⬭ $\frac{6}{8}$ — =
3. $\frac{1}{3}$ ⬭ $\frac{4}{9}$ — <
4. $\frac{6}{12}$ ⬭ $\frac{3}{6}$ — =
5. $\frac{1}{6}$ ⬭ $\frac{3}{12}$ — <
6. $\frac{4}{12}$ ⬭ $\frac{3}{6}$ — <
7. $\frac{1}{5}$ ⬭ $\frac{3}{15}$ — =

Mental Math. Write >, <, or = for each ⬭.

8. 1 ⬭ $\frac{7}{8}$ — >
9. $\frac{2}{4}$ ⬭ $\frac{6}{12}$ — =
10. $\frac{4}{4}$ ⬭ 4 — <
11. $\frac{8}{9}$ ⬭ 1 — <

Order the fractions from least to greatest.

12. $\frac{1}{4}$ $\frac{3}{4}$ $\frac{2}{4}$ — $\frac{1}{4}$, $\frac{2}{4}$, $\frac{3}{4}$
13. $\frac{2}{7}$ $\frac{6}{7}$ $\frac{4}{7}$ — $\frac{2}{7}$, $\frac{4}{7}$, $\frac{6}{7}$
14. $\frac{7}{9}$ $\frac{3}{9}$ $\frac{5}{9}$ — $\frac{3}{9}$, $\frac{5}{9}$, $\frac{7}{9}$
15. $\frac{5}{8}$ $\frac{3}{8}$ $\frac{1}{4}$ — $\frac{1}{4}$, $\frac{3}{8}$, $\frac{5}{8}$
16. $\frac{3}{6}$ $\frac{2}{3}$ $\frac{1}{3}$ — $\frac{1}{3}$, $\frac{3}{6}$, $\frac{2}{3}$
17. $\frac{6}{10}$ $\frac{2}{5}$ $\frac{5}{10}$ — $\frac{2}{5}$, $\frac{5}{10}$, $\frac{6}{10}$
18. $\frac{1}{3}$ $\frac{1}{4}$ $\frac{2}{12}$ — $\frac{2}{12}$, $\frac{1}{4}$, $\frac{1}{3}$
19. $\frac{3}{5}$ $\frac{5}{15}$ $\frac{2}{5}$ — $\frac{5}{15}$, $\frac{2}{5}$, $\frac{3}{5}$

Test Prep

20. Which set of fractions is ordered from greatest to least?
A $\frac{2}{3}, \frac{1}{2}, \frac{3}{5}$ C $\frac{3}{4}, \frac{3}{5}, \frac{3}{6}$
B $\frac{2}{5}, \frac{3}{5}, \frac{4}{5}$ D $\frac{1}{3}, \frac{1}{5}, \frac{1}{4}$
C

21. Andy drew a line that was $\frac{7}{8}$ of an inch long. Ally drew a line that was $\frac{13}{16}$ of an inch long. Which person's line was longer?
Andy's line was longer.

Use with text pages 498–500.

▶ You can use what you know about comparing fractions to order fractions.

Order $\frac{2}{6}$, $\frac{1}{2}$, and $\frac{1}{6}$ from least to greatest.

Different Ways to Order $\frac{2}{6}$, $\frac{1}{2}$, and $\frac{1}{6}$

Way 1 **Find equivalent fractions. Then compare the numerators.**

- Find a fraction equivalent to $\frac{1}{2}$ that has a denominator of 6.

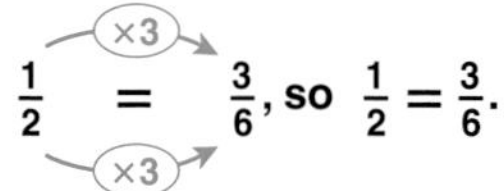

$\frac{1}{2} \overset{\times 3}{=} \frac{3}{6}$, so $\frac{1}{2} = \frac{3}{6}$.

- Then compare the numerators and order the fractions.

$1 < 2 < 3$, so $\frac{1}{6} < \frac{2}{6} < \frac{1}{2}$

Way 2 **Use a number line.**

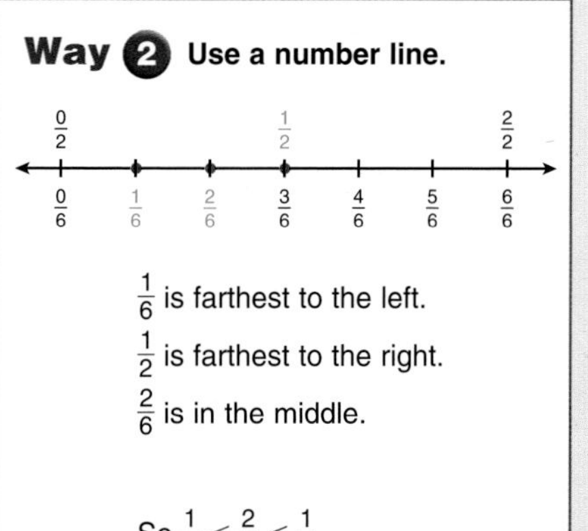

$\frac{1}{6}$ is farthest to the left.

$\frac{1}{2}$ is farthest to the right.

$\frac{2}{6}$ is in the middle.

So $\frac{1}{6} < \frac{2}{6} < \frac{1}{2}$

Solution: The order of the fractions from least to greatest is: $\frac{1}{6}$ $\frac{2}{6}$ $\frac{1}{2}$

Guided Practice

Compare. Write >, <, or = for each ●.

1. $\frac{3}{4}$ ● $\frac{5}{8}$ >

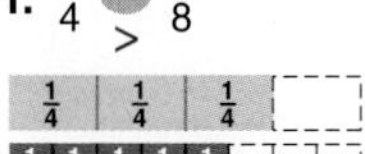

2. $\frac{2}{3}$ ● $\frac{5}{6}$ <

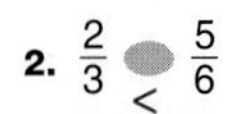

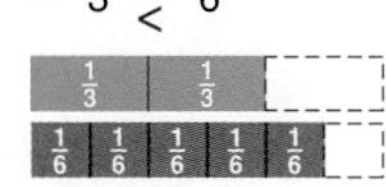

3. $\frac{4}{6}$ ● $\frac{2}{3}$ =

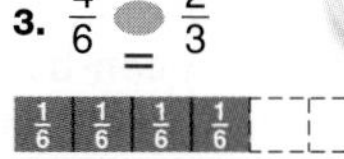

Ask Yourself

- Do the fractions have like denominators?
- If not, how can I find equivalent fractions?

Order the fractions from greatest to least. Draw number lines to help if you wish.

4. $\frac{2}{7}$ $\frac{6}{7}$ $\frac{4}{7}$ $\frac{6}{7}$ $\frac{4}{7}$ $\frac{2}{7}$

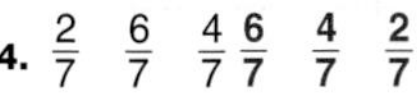

5. $\frac{3}{4}$ $\frac{7}{8}$ $\frac{5}{8}$ $\frac{7}{8}$ $\frac{3}{4}$ $\frac{5}{8}$

6. $\frac{1}{5}$ $\frac{1}{10}$ $\frac{4}{5}$ $\frac{4}{5}$ $\frac{1}{5}$ $\frac{1}{10}$

7. $\frac{6}{12}$ $\frac{1}{3}$ $\frac{3}{3}$ $\frac{3}{3}$ $\frac{6}{12}$ $\frac{1}{3}$

Explain Your Thinking ▶ Suppose you have to order $\frac{2}{3}$, $\frac{1}{4}$, and $\frac{1}{2}$. What is the smallest denominator you can use to write equivalent fractions for $\frac{2}{3}$, $\frac{1}{4}$, and $\frac{1}{2}$? 12

Enrichment 19.4

Name ____________ Date ______

Enrichment 19.4

Single File Fractions

Look at each series of fractions. Decide whether the fractions are in order from least value to greatest value or from greatest value to least value. Pick the fraction from the box at the bottom of the page that will fit in each blank.

1. $\frac{1}{3}$ $\frac{4}{9}$ $\frac{5}{9}$ __$\frac{2}{3}$__ $\frac{7}{9}$ $\frac{8}{9}$

2. $\frac{4}{20}$ $\frac{2}{5}$ __$\frac{6}{10}$__ $\frac{8}{10}$ $\frac{5}{5}$

3. $\frac{1}{4}$ __$\frac{12}{32}$__ $\frac{1}{2}$ $\frac{10}{16}$ __$\frac{3}{4}$__ $\frac{7}{8}$ $\frac{2}{2}$

4. $\frac{1}{10}$ __$\frac{1}{5}$__ $\frac{3}{10}$ __$\frac{8}{20}$__ $\frac{1}{2}$ $\frac{3}{5}$ $\frac{7}{10}$

5. $\frac{1}{7}$ __$\frac{8}{28}$__ $\frac{3}{7}$ $\frac{8}{14}$ $\frac{5}{7}$ __$\frac{36}{42}$__

$\frac{3}{4}$	$\frac{2}{3}$	$\frac{1}{5}$	$\frac{36}{42}$
$\frac{8}{28}$	$\frac{12}{32}$	$\frac{6}{10}$	$\frac{8}{20}$

Use with text pages 498–500.

Problem Solving 19.4

Name ____________ Date ______

Problem Solving 19.4

Compare and Order Fractions

Solve.

Show your work.

1. Andrea is on the track team. At practice on Monday, she ran $\frac{3}{4}$ mile. On Wednesday, she ran $\frac{7}{12}$ mile. On which day did she run farther?

   Monday

2. Coach Lutz ordered T-shirts for the baseball team. Of the shirts he ordered, $\frac{1}{4}$ were size small, $\frac{5}{12}$ were size medium, and $\frac{1}{3}$ were size large. Order the sizes from least to greatest amount ordered.

   small, large, medium

3. On Wednesday, $\frac{2}{5}$ of the fourth-grade class went to the basketball game. On Saturday, $\frac{7}{10}$ of the fourth-grade class went to the game. On Tuesday, $\frac{1}{2}$ of the fourth-graders went to the game. On which day did the most fourth-graders attend the game? The least?

   most: Saturday; least: Wednesday

4. **Reasoning** Lori says that $\frac{2}{3}$ of the baseball hats in her collection are red. Mark says that $\frac{2}{3}$ of the baseball hats in his collection are blue. The number of blue hats that Mark has is less than the number of red hats that Lori has. Who has more baseball hats? Explain your reasoning.

   Lori has more baseball hats; explanations may vary.

Use with text pages 498–500.

- Work through **Way 1** for ordering fractions. Work on the board as students work at their seats. Use colored chalk—one color for the numerators and another for the denominators—to show the multiplication. **Why did we multiply $\frac{1}{2}$ by $\frac{3}{3}$?** (to get a denominator of 6, the denominator of $\frac{3}{6}$)
- Focus on **Way 2:** Use a number line. **How can we use a number line to compare fractions with unlike denominators?** (One way: mark the location of each fraction; the one farthest to the right is the greatest and the one farthest to the left is the least.) Guide students to see the order of these fractions on the number line.

Guided Practice

Have students complete **Exercises 1–7** as you observe. Remind them to use the *Ask Yourself* questions to help. Give students the opportunity to talk about the question in *Explain Your Thinking.*

3 Practice

Practice and Problem Solving

Select from **Exercises 8–35** as independent work. Have students compare answers with a partner.

- ***Problem 32*** Elicit that if the numerators of two fractions are the same, then the fraction with the lesser denominator is the greater fraction.
- ***Data*** You may wish to extend this activity by adding additional bean lengths to the table.

4 Assess & Close

Math Talk in Action

Have students choose any one exercise from the lesson and write an explanation of how to compare the two fractions. Then have students share their explanations with the class and discuss them.

Math Journal Prompt

Have students write three fractions with at least two different denominators. Ask them to write an explanation of how to place the fractions in order from least to greatest.

Lesson Quiz

Use the quiz on Lesson Transparency 19.4.

Lesson 19.4 Transparency

Test Prep & Spiral Review

Use Test Prep Transparency 19.4.

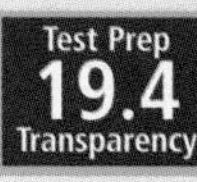

Test Prep 19.4 Transparency

Practice and Problem Solving

Compare. Write >, <, or = for each ●.

8. $\frac{2}{6}$ ● $\frac{4}{6}$ <
9. $\frac{1}{2}$ ● $\frac{2}{4}$ =
10. $\frac{1}{4}$ ● $\frac{3}{8}$ <

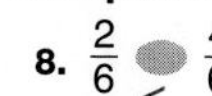

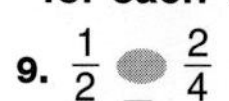

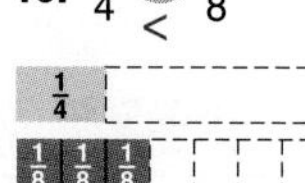

11. $\frac{6}{7}$ ● $\frac{5}{7}$ >
12. $\frac{4}{9}$ ● $\frac{1}{3}$ >
13. $\frac{3}{5}$ ● $\frac{2}{10}$ >
14. $\frac{2}{3}$ ● $\frac{1}{4}$ >

Mental Math Write >, <, or = for each ●.

15. 1 ● $\frac{5}{6}$ >
16. $\frac{2}{4}$ ● $\frac{2}{8}$ >
17. $\frac{3}{5}$ ● $\frac{3}{8}$ >
18. 2 ● $\frac{4}{8}$ >
19. $\frac{2}{5}$ ● $\frac{4}{5}$ <
20. $\frac{6}{7}$ ● 1 <
21. $\frac{2}{2}$ ● 2 <
22. $\frac{3}{3}$ ● $\frac{6}{6}$ =

Order the fractions from least to greatest.

23. $\frac{1}{5}$ $\frac{4}{5}$ $\frac{2}{5}$ — $\frac{1}{5}$ $\frac{2}{5}$ $\frac{4}{5}$
24. $\frac{5}{7}$ $\frac{2}{7}$ $\frac{6}{7}$ — $\frac{2}{7}$ $\frac{5}{7}$ $\frac{6}{7}$
25. $\frac{4}{8}$ $\frac{7}{8}$ $\frac{1}{8}$ — $\frac{1}{8}$ $\frac{4}{8}$ $\frac{7}{8}$
26. $\frac{7}{12}$ $\frac{10}{12}$ $\frac{3}{4}$ — $\frac{7}{12}$ $\frac{3}{4}$ $\frac{10}{12}$
27. $\frac{5}{8}$ $\frac{3}{4}$ $\frac{1}{4}$ — $\frac{1}{4}$ $\frac{5}{8}$ $\frac{3}{4}$
28. $\frac{2}{3}$ $\frac{2}{6}$ $\frac{3}{6}$ — $\frac{2}{6}$ $\frac{3}{6}$ $\frac{2}{3}$
29. $\frac{1}{2}$ $\frac{4}{6}$ $\frac{5}{12}$ — $\frac{5}{12}$ $\frac{1}{2}$ $\frac{4}{6}$
30. $\frac{3}{4}$ $\frac{1}{2}$ $\frac{1}{3}$ — $\frac{1}{3}$ $\frac{1}{2}$ $\frac{3}{4}$

Solve. *For Problems 31–32, See Additional Answers.*

31. **Write About It** Why is it easier to compare fractions with the same rather than different denominators?

32. **Analyze** Explain why you can compare $\frac{2}{12}$ and $\frac{2}{16}$ without finding equivalent fractions.

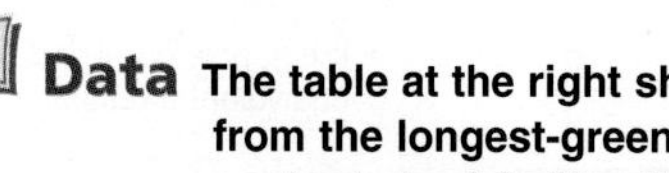

Data The table at the right shows results from the longest-green-bean contest at a fair. Use the table for Problems 33–35.

33. Who entered a longer green bean, Sara or Brian? **Sara**

34. List the lengths of the green beans in order from shortest to longest. $\frac{1}{2}$ $\frac{7}{12}$ $\frac{5}{6}$

35. Which people entered green beans that were less than $\frac{2}{3}$ yd long? **Tom, Brian**

Longest Green Beans at County Fair

Name	Length
Sara	$\frac{5}{6}$ yd
Tom	$\frac{1}{2}$ yd
Brian	$\frac{7}{12}$ yd

500

Extra Practice See page 513, Set C.

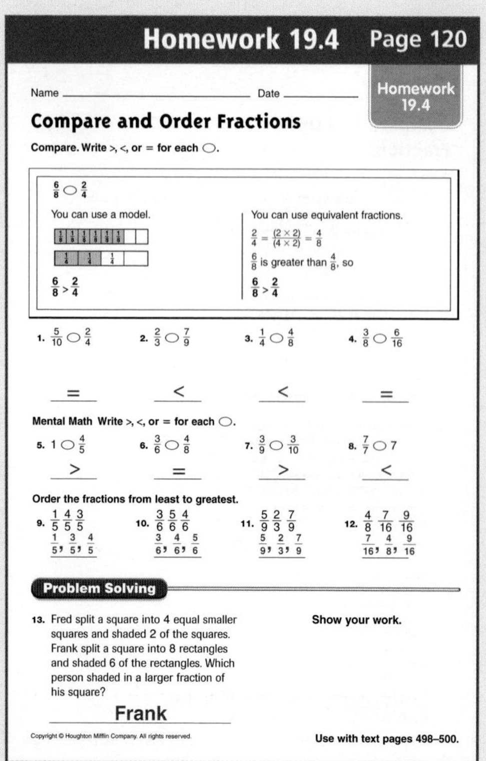

Homework 19.4 Page 120

Name ______ Date ______ Homework 19.4

Compare and Order Fractions

Compare. Write >, <, or = for each ○.

$\frac{6}{8}$ ○ $\frac{2}{4}$

You can use a model. $\frac{6}{8} > \frac{2}{4}$

You can use equivalent fractions. $\frac{2}{4} = \frac{(2 \times 2)}{(4 \times 2)} = \frac{4}{8}$; $\frac{6}{8}$ is greater than $\frac{4}{8}$, so $\frac{6}{8} > \frac{2}{4}$

1. $\frac{5}{10}$ ○ $\frac{2}{4}$ =
2. $\frac{2}{3}$ ○ $\frac{7}{9}$ <
3. $\frac{1}{4}$ ○ $\frac{4}{8}$ <
4. $\frac{3}{8}$ ○ $\frac{6}{16}$ =

Mental Math Write >, <, or = for each ○.

5. 1 ○ $\frac{4}{5}$ >
6. $\frac{3}{6}$ ○ $\frac{4}{8}$ =
7. $\frac{3}{9}$ ○ $\frac{3}{10}$ >
8. $\frac{7}{7}$ ○ 7 <

Order the fractions from least to greatest.

9. $\frac{1}{5}$ $\frac{4}{5}$ $\frac{3}{5}$ — $\frac{1}{5}$, $\frac{3}{5}$, $\frac{4}{5}$
10. $\frac{3}{6}$ $\frac{5}{6}$ $\frac{4}{6}$ — $\frac{3}{6}$, $\frac{4}{6}$, $\frac{5}{6}$
11. $\frac{5}{9}$ $\frac{2}{3}$ $\frac{7}{9}$ — $\frac{5}{9}$, $\frac{2}{3}$, $\frac{7}{9}$
12. $\frac{4}{8}$ $\frac{7}{16}$ $\frac{9}{16}$ — $\frac{7}{16}$, $\frac{4}{8}$, $\frac{9}{16}$

Problem Solving

13. Fred split a square into 4 equal smaller squares and shaded 2 of the squares. Frank split a square into 8 rectangles and shaded 6 of the rectangles. Which person shaded in a larger fraction of his square? Frank

Show your work.

Use with text pages 498–500.

Social Studies Connection

Flags of Africa

Problem Solving

Five students were studying African countries. They each drew and colored the flag of the country they were studying. From the clues, decide who colored each flag.

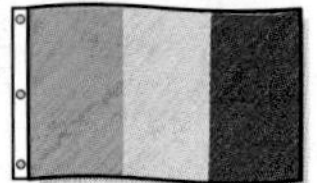
A
José

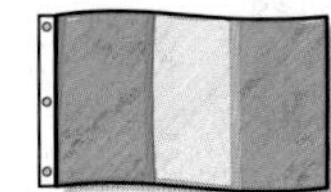
B
Maribeth

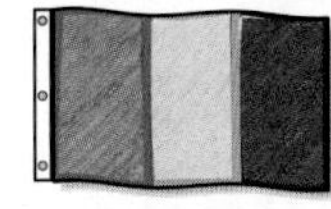
C
Inga

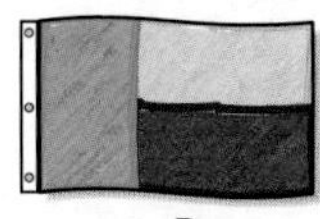
D
Ken

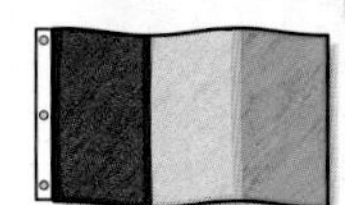
E
Heather

- José said, "Inga's flag and my flag are both $\frac{1}{3}$ red, with the red stripe on the right."
- Heather said, "My flag has the same colors as José's flag and Ken's flag."
- Ken said, "The thirds on my flag are not the same as the thirds on all the other flags."
- Maribeth said, "My flag is $\frac{2}{3}$ green."

Challenge Do research to find the name of each country being studied. **A. Mali; B. Nigeria; C. Chad; D. Benin; E. Guinea**

WEEKLY WR READER eduplace.com/map

Quick Check

Check your understanding of Lessons 1–4.

Write a fraction for the part that is shaded. Then write a fraction for the part that is not shaded. (Lesson 1)

1. 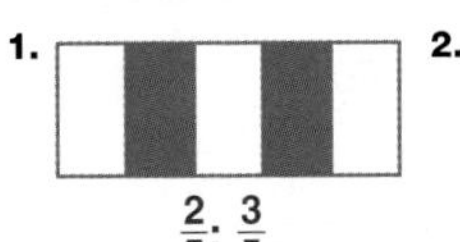
$\frac{2}{5}$; $\frac{3}{5}$

2. 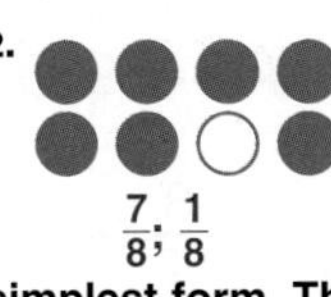
$\frac{7}{8}$; $\frac{1}{8}$

3. 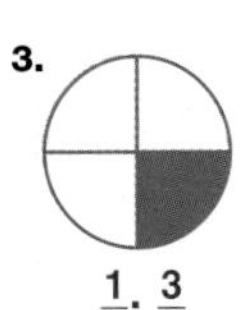
$\frac{1}{4}$; $\frac{3}{4}$

4. 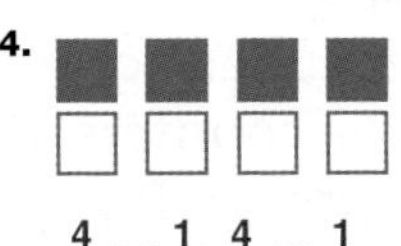
$\frac{4}{8}$ or $\frac{1}{2}$; $\frac{4}{8}$ or $\frac{1}{2}$

Write each fraction in simplest form. Then write another equivalent fraction. (Lessons 2–3) ***Possible equivalent fractions given.***

5. $\frac{4}{6}$ $\frac{2}{3}$; $\frac{6}{9}$
6. $\frac{9}{12}$ $\frac{3}{4}$; $\frac{6}{8}$
7. $\frac{10}{20}$ $\frac{1}{2}$; $\frac{2}{4}$
8. $\frac{8}{18}$ $\frac{4}{9}$; $\frac{12}{27}$

Order the fractions from greatest to least. (Lesson 4)

9. $\frac{3}{4}$ $\frac{7}{8}$ $\frac{5}{8}$ $\frac{7}{8}$ $\frac{3}{4}$ $\frac{5}{8}$
10. $\frac{2}{5}$ $\frac{3}{10}$ $\frac{7}{10}$ $\frac{7}{10}$ $\frac{2}{5}$ $\frac{3}{10}$

Extra Practice at eduplace.com/map

Social Studies Connection

Flags of Africa

- Have a volunteer read the introductory information. Inform students that many flags have recognizable fractional parts and that many are very similar in color and design. Invite students to look at a variety of flags in an almanac. Ask them to tell which ones they like the best. Ask them to describe their favorites using the language of fractions.
- Tell students that solving this problem involves using the clues provided and logical reasoning. Invite students to work in pairs. Guide them to carefully read all the clues. Provide the hint that problems like this may list clues out of order. Encourage students to use a table to help them keep track of their answers.

Quick Check

The *Quick Check* allows you to assess the students' understanding of the concepts presented in Lessons 1–4.

Items	Objectives Tested	Pages	Intervention
1–4	Read, write, and identify fractions.	490–493	Reteach Resources 19.1, 19.2 *Ways to Success* CD-ROM 19.1, 19.2
5–8	Find equivalent fractions and write fractions in simplest form.	494–497	Reteach Resources 19.3 *Ways to Success* CD-ROM 19.3
9–10	Compare and order fractions.	498–501	Reteach Resources 19.4 *Ways to Success* CD-ROM 19.4

Lesson 19.5

Find Part of a Number

Planning

Lesson Objective Find a fractional part of a number.

Math Background

- The word *of* is used to pose problems involving finding fractional parts of a number. The problem of finding $\frac{1}{3}$ of 6 can be modeled in terms of a group of 6 objects that has been separated into 3 smaller equal groups, each of which has 2 objects.

Technology Resources

- *Ways to Success* CD-ROM 19.5

Lesson 19.5 Transparency

Problem of the Day

Find fractions of numbers in our classroom. What fraction of the class is absent today? What fraction of the class is wearing sneakers? (Answers will vary.)

Spiral Review

Write each set of fractions in order from least to greatest.

1. $\frac{2}{3}, \frac{3}{9}, \frac{2}{6}$ $(\frac{2}{9}, \frac{2}{6}, \frac{2}{3})$
2. $\frac{4}{5}, \frac{3}{10}, \frac{1}{5}$ $(\frac{1}{5}, \frac{3}{10}, \frac{4}{5})$
3. $\frac{3}{8}, \frac{3}{4}, \frac{3}{6}$ $(\frac{3}{8}, \frac{3}{6}, \frac{3}{4})$
4. $\frac{1}{3}, \frac{5}{6}, \frac{4}{9}$ $(\frac{1}{3}, \frac{4}{9}, \frac{5}{6})$

Lesson Quiz

Find the fractional part of each number.

1. $\frac{1}{2}$ of 22 (11)
2. $\frac{3}{5}$ of 25 (15)
3. $\frac{7}{8}$ of 32 (28)
4. $\frac{7}{10}$ of 70 (49)
5. $\frac{1}{6}$ of 48 (8)
6. $\frac{3}{4}$ of 40 (30)

NCTM Standards

Number and Operations: Develop understanding of fractions as parts of unit wholes, as parts of a collection; use models, benchmarks, and equivalent forms to judge the size of fractions.

Getting Started

Building Math Vocabulary

Students should be familiar with the vocabulary in this lesson.

Parts of a Whole

Whole Class	10 minutes
Objective	Identify fractional parts of numbers.
Materials	Blank transparency, overhead counters, two-color counters
Visual, Auditory	

- Distribute two-color counters to groups. Have student groups manipulate the counters at their seats as you explain. Place a cluster of 12 counters on a blank transparency on the overhead.

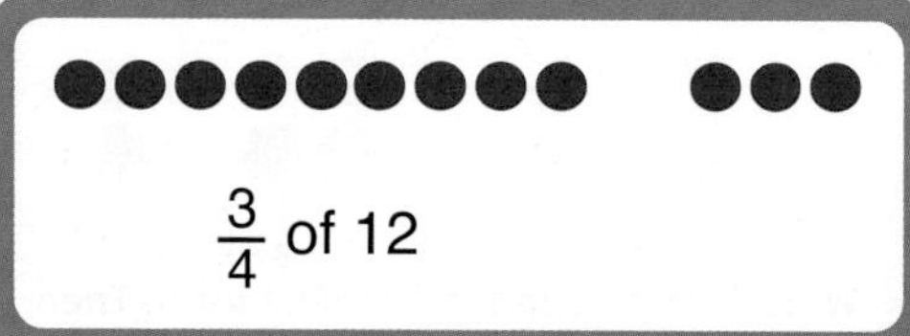

- **There are 12 counters. We want to find $\frac{3}{4}$ of 12.** Write *$\frac{3}{4}$ of 12 is ___.* **First we separate them into 4 equal groups.** Draw 4 ovals. Invite a volunteer to separate the counters into 4 equal groups. **Then we find the number of counters in 3 of the groups.** Ring 3 of the ovals. **How many counters are in 3 groups?** (9) **So $\frac{3}{4}$ of 12 is 9.** Write *9* to complete the equation.
- **We can also use division and multiplication to find $\frac{3}{4}$ of 12. First we divide 12 by 4 to find the number in each group.** ($\frac{12}{4} = 3$) **Then we multiply the number in each group by 3.** ($3 \times 3 = 9$) **$\frac{3}{4}$ of 12 is 9.**
- Tell students the lesson will describe several ways to find a fractional part of a number.

Differentiated Instruction

English Learners

Pairs	15 minutes
Objective	Model fractional parts
Materials	Counters, Student page 503
Auditory, Visual	

Early Production

- Students may need to use models to help visualize the problems.
- During the ***Guided Practice,*** students can use division and multiplication to find the answer, and then use counters to check their work.
- Ask students to verbalize the steps to find the answer while they work.

Intermediate/Advanced

- English Learner Resource 19.5
- English Learner Handbook

Intervention

Small Groups	15 minutes
Objective	Find a fracional part of a number.
Materials	Learning Tool 26, colored pencils
Auditory, Visual	

Have students work on grid paper to explore finding a fractional part of a number. Demonstrate how to find $\frac{3}{4}$ of 20.

- First mark around 20 squares on a 4×5 grid using a colored pencil.
- Divide the grid into 4 equal groups. Then shade 3 of those groups.
- Have students count shaded squares to see that $\frac{3}{4}$ of 20 is 15.
- Then help students use this approach to find $\frac{1}{4}$ of 16 and $\frac{3}{4}$ of 12.

Other Resources

- *Ways to Success* CD-ROM 19.5

Early Finishers

Small Groups	10 minutes
Objective	Find a fractional part of a number.
Materials	None
Auditory, Visual	

Have students write additional exercises like **Exercises 8–17**. Have them swap exercises with another student and solve. Provide this hint: **Choose numbers that are multiples of the denominator of the fraction.**

Alternate Teaching Strategy

Ask students how many hands everybody has. (2) **How many fingers make up each hand?** (5) Write the fractional parts on the board as students answer the following questions. Ask them to describe in fractional form how many of the fingers on one hand are not thumbs. ($\frac{4}{5}$) Then ask them to use a fraction to describe how many fingers that are not thumbs are found on both hands. ($\frac{8}{10}$) Ask: **How many of the fingers on one hand are thumbs?** ($\frac{1}{5}$) Finally, ask them to tell you in simplest form what fractional part of all their fingers are thumbs. ($\frac{2}{10}$ or $\frac{1}{5}$)

1 Introduce

Tell students that they are going to find fractional parts of a number and that they will draw upon their understanding of division and division facts to do so.

2 Teach

Learn About It

- **For Way 1,** help students to see that the denominator of the fraction indicates the number of equal groups. **Why do we separate the counters into 4 groups?** (denominator is 4) **Suppose we had to find $\frac{4}{5}$ of 20. How many equal groups would we make? Why?** (5; denominator is 5)
- **For Way 2,** help students see how to use multiplication and division to find part of a number. **By what number do we multiply when we know how many in each group?** (the numerator) **Suppose we want to find $\frac{5}{8}$ of 40. By what number do we divide? By what number do we multiply the quotient?** (8, 5)

Guided Practice

Have students complete **Exercises 1–7** as you observe. Remind them to use the *Ask Yourself* questions to help. Give students the opportunity to talk about the question in *Explain Your Thinking*.

Common Error

- **Forgetting to Multiply** Some students may forget to multiply after dividing to find part of a number.
- **Intervention** Remind students to multiply by the numerator after dividing to find the fractional part of a number.

Lesson 5

Find Part of a Number

Objective Find a fractional part of a number.

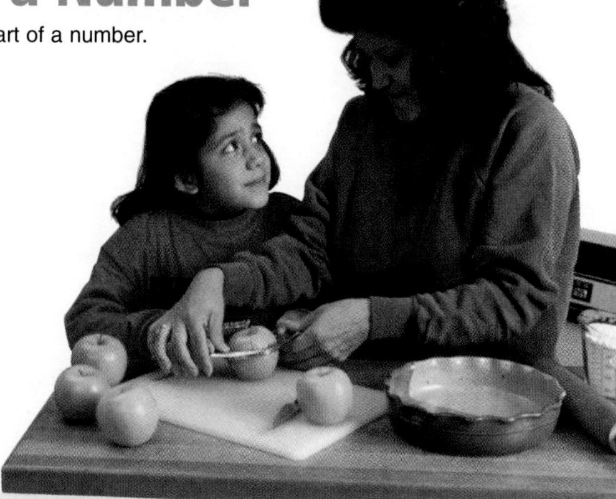

Learn About It

Maria and her mother use 20 apples to make apple pies. One fourth of the apples are green and three fourths are red. How many apples are red?

How can you find $\frac{3}{4}$ of 20?

Different Ways to Find $\frac{3}{4}$ of 20

Way 1 **You can use a model.**

STEP 1 The denominator, 4, tells you to separate the 20 counters into 4 equal groups.

STEP 2 The numerator, 3, tells you to count the number in 3 groups.

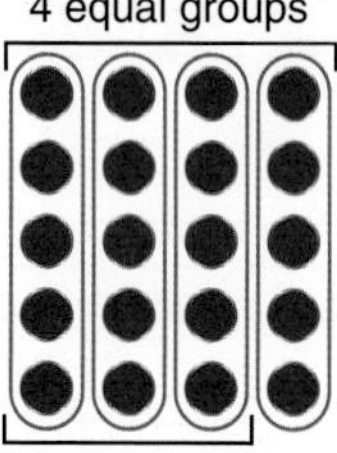

$\frac{3}{4}$ of 20 is 15.

Way 2 **You can use division and multiplication.**

STEP 1 Divide 20 by 4 to find the number in each group.

number of apples → 20; number of equal groups → 4

$20 \div 4 = 5$

number in each group → 5

STEP 2 Multiply the number in each group by 3.

$5 \times 3 = 15$

$\frac{3}{4}$ of 20 is 15.

Solution: 15 apples are red.

502

Reteach 19.5

Name ______ Date ______ Reteach 19.5

Find Part of a Number

Alicia had a basket with 15 cookies in it. Her friends ate $\frac{2}{3}$ of the cookies. How many cookies did her friends eat?

Find $\frac{2}{3}$ of 15.

Divide the total number by the denominator of the fraction.	Multiply the quotient by the numerator of the fraction.	$\frac{2}{3}$ of 15 is 10.
Total number: 15 ÷ Denominator of fraction: 3 = Quotient: 5	Numerator of fraction: 2 × Quotient: 5 = Fractional part of the number: 10	Alicia's friends ate 10 cookies.

Find the fractional part of each number.

1. $\frac{1}{2}$ of 14 **7**
2. $\frac{3}{4}$ of 12 **9**
3. $\frac{2}{5}$ of 10 **4**
4. $\frac{2}{3}$ of 9 **6**
5. $\frac{3}{5}$ of 20 **12**
6. $\frac{1}{6}$ of 18 **3**
7. $\frac{4}{4}$ of 12 **12**
8. $\frac{3}{7}$ of 14 **6**
9. $\frac{2}{9}$ of 18 **4**
10. $\frac{2}{3}$ of 21 **14**
11. $\frac{5}{9}$ of 27 **15**
12. $\frac{5}{6}$ of 30 **25**
13. $\frac{4}{5}$ of 25 **20**
14. $\frac{3}{7}$ of 21 **9**
15. $\frac{5}{8}$ of 24 **15**
16. $\frac{1}{3}$ of 30 **10**

Use with text pages 502–503.

Practice 19.5 Page 121

Name ______ Date ______ Practice 19.5

Find Part of a Number

Find the fractional part of each number.

1. $\frac{2}{3}$ of 9 **6**
2. $\frac{1}{6}$ of 12 **2**
3. $\frac{1}{3}$ of 15 **5**
4. $\frac{2}{3}$ of 18 **12**
5. $\frac{1}{10}$ of 30 **3**
6. $\frac{3}{4}$ of 8 **6**
7. $\frac{2}{7}$ of 21 **6**
8. $\frac{4}{5}$ of 25 **20**
9. $\frac{5}{12}$ of 24 **10**
10. $\frac{5}{7}$ of 14 **10**
11. $\frac{8}{9}$ of 18 **16**
12. $\frac{1}{3}$ of 6 **2**
13. $\frac{5}{8}$ of 16 **10**
14. $\frac{7}{10}$ of 30 **21**
15. $\frac{5}{6}$ of 24 **20**
16. $\frac{9}{10}$ of 50 **45**
17. $\frac{2}{5}$ of 15 **6**
18. $\frac{2}{3}$ of 12 **8**
19. $\frac{3}{4}$ of 16 **12**
20. $\frac{5}{6}$ of 36 **30**
21. $\frac{7}{8}$ of 80 **70**
22. $\frac{1}{3}$ of 27 **9**
23. $\frac{1}{4}$ of 32 **8**
24. $\frac{7}{9}$ of 45 **35**

Test Prep

25. Lucy is $\frac{1}{5}$ as old as her grandmother, Dorothy. If Dorothy is 60 years old, how old is Lucy? **D**
    A 6 C 5
    B 15 D 12
26. Jake has 28 trading cards. Three fourths of the cards are baseball cards. How many of the cards are baseball cards? **21**

Use with text pages 502–503.

Guided Practice

Ask Yourself
- How many equal parts are there?
- How many equal parts do I need to count?

Find the fractional part of each number.

1. ● ● ● ● / ● ● ● ●
   $\frac{1}{4}$ of 8
   2

2. ▲ ▲ ▲ ▲ ▲ / ▲ ▲ ▲ ▲ ▲
   $\frac{3}{5}$ of 10
   6

3. $\frac{2}{3}$ of 9 **6**
4. $\frac{1}{6}$ of 24 **4**
5. $\frac{2}{5}$ of 20 **8**
6. $\frac{3}{4}$ of 16 **12**
7. $\frac{4}{5}$ of 15 **12**

Explain Your Thinking ▶ How does knowing $\frac{1}{5}$ of 10 help you find $\frac{2}{5}$ of 10?
$\frac{2}{5} = \frac{1}{5} + \frac{1}{5}$ so $\frac{2}{5}$ of 10 would be $\frac{1}{5}$ of 10 + $\frac{1}{5}$ of 10.

Practice and Problem Solving

Find the fractional part of each number.

8. $\frac{1}{2}$ of 14 **7**
9. $\frac{2}{3}$ of 30 **20**
10. $\frac{1}{4}$ of 12 **3**
11. $\frac{3}{7}$ of 14 **6**
12. $\frac{2}{10}$ of 10 **2**
13. $\frac{3}{5}$ of 20 **12**
14. $\frac{7}{9}$ of 18 **14**
15. $\frac{3}{8}$ of 16 **6**
16. $\frac{5}{6}$ of 12 **10**
17. $\frac{3}{10}$ of 100 **30**

Solve.

18. Mina has 21 apples. Two thirds of the apples are green. How many of the apples are green? **14 apples**

19. Keisha's family eats $\frac{3}{4}$ of an 8-piece apple pie. How many pieces are not eaten? **2 pieces**

20. **Analyze** Mike's dad has 100 quarters. He tells Mike that he can have either $\frac{3}{4}$ or $\frac{6}{10}$ of them. Which should Mike choose? Explain.
$\frac{3}{4}$; $\frac{3}{4}$ of 100 is equal to 75 while $\frac{6}{10}$ of 100 is equal to 60.

21. **Represent** Show why $\frac{2}{3}$ of 9 and $\frac{1}{3}$ of 18 name the same number. Use counters or draw a picture to explain your reasoning. ***Check students' work.***

Mixed Review and Test Prep

Open Response

Solve. (Ch. 6, Lessons 4, 6; Ch. 9, Lessons 2, 3)

22. 67 × 8 **536**
23. 105 × 6 **630**
24. 504 ÷ 7 **72**
25. \$5.60 ÷ 5 **\$1.12**
26. 317 ÷ 9 **35 R2**
27. \$7.24 ÷ 4 **\$1.81**

Multiple Choice

28. Donya is $\frac{1}{4}$ as old as her sister, Amy. If Amy is 24, how old is Donya? (Ch. 19, Lesson 5)

A 4 **(B) 6** C 8 D 14

Extra Practice See page 513, Set D.

3 Practice

Practice and Problem Solving

Select from **Exercises 8–28** as independent work.

- ***Problem 20*** Guide students to see that they could also compare the fractions to answer the question.
- ***Problem Solving for Problem 21*** Some students may use their number sense to reason as follows: $\frac{2}{3}$ is twice as many as $\frac{1}{3}$ of 9. Invite students to provide other examples in support of their thinking.

4 Assess & Close

Math Talk in Action

Have students refer to **Exercise 10** to conclude the lesson.

- **How is finding $\frac{1}{4}$ of 12 like dividing 12 by 4?** (In both cases, we separate a group of 12 into 4 equal parts.)

Math Journal Prompt

Have students write an explanation of how to use counters to find $\frac{5}{8}$ of 24. Have them explain how to use division and multiplication to find the same part. Ask them to show their work.

Lesson Quiz

Use the quiz on Lesson Transparency 19.5.

Lesson 19.5 Transparency

Test Prep & Spiral Review

Use Test Prep Transparency 19.5.

Test Prep 19.5 Transparency

Enrichment 19.5

Name ______ Date ______ Enrichment 19.5

Batter Up!

Use the clues and the measurements of a professional ballpark to fill in the measurements of Slugger's Ballpark.

Professional Ball Park: 440 ft Center Field; 350 ft Left Field; 300 ft Right Field; 1st Base; 90 ft; Home Plate

Slugger's Ballpark: **200 ft** Left Field; **220 ft** Center Field; **180 ft** Right Field; 1st Base; **60 ft**; Home Plate

1. At Slugger's ballpark, the distance from home plate to first base is $\frac{2}{3}$ of the distance from home plate to first base in the professional ballpark. **60 ft**
2. The left field measurement at Slugger's Ballpark is $\frac{4}{7}$ of the professional field's left field measurement. **200 ft**
3. The center field measurement of Slugger's Ballpark is $\frac{1}{2}$ the measured distance of the center field at the professional ballpark. **220 ft**
4. The right field measurement of Slugger's Ballpark is $\frac{6}{10}$ of the measured distance of the right field at the professional ballpark. **180 ft**
5. The pitching rubber on the pitcher's mound is approximately $\frac{2}{3}$ of the distance from home plate to first base. About how far from home plate should the Sluggers place their pitching rubber? **about 40 ft**

Use with text pages 502–503.

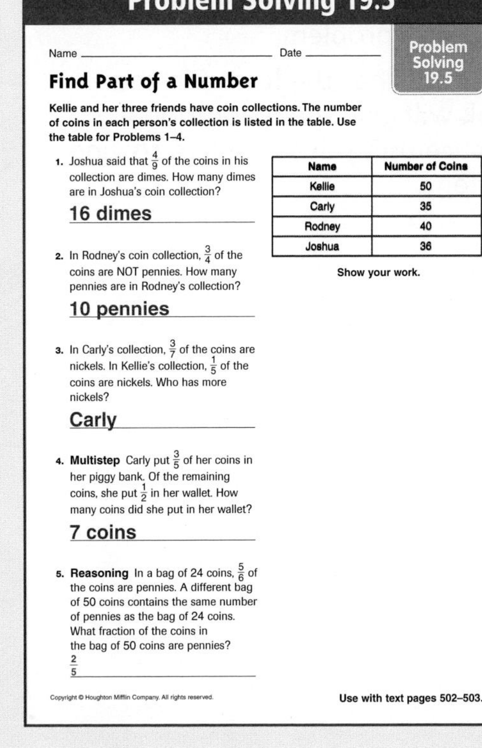

Problem Solving 19.5

Name ______ Date ______ Problem Solving 19.5

Find Part of a Number

Kellie and her three friends have coin collections. The number of coins in each person's collection is listed in the table. Use the table for Problems 1–4.

Name	Number of Coins
Kellie	50
Carly	35
Rodney	40
Joshua	36

Show your work.

1. Joshua said that $\frac{4}{9}$ of the coins in his collection are dimes. How many dimes are in Joshua's coin collection? **16 dimes**
2. In Rodney's coin collection, $\frac{3}{4}$ of the coins are NOT pennies. How many pennies are in Rodney's collection? **10 pennies**
3. In Carly's collection, $\frac{3}{7}$ of the coins are nickels. In Kellie's collection, $\frac{1}{5}$ of the coins are nickels. Who has more nickels? **Carly**
4. **Multistep** Carly put $\frac{3}{5}$ of her coins in her piggy bank. Of the remaining coins, she put $\frac{1}{2}$ in her wallet. How many coins did she put in her wallet? **7 coins**
5. **Reasoning** In a bag of 24 coins, $\frac{5}{6}$ of the coins are pennies. A different bag of 50 coins contains the same number of pennies as the bag of 24 coins. What fraction of the coins in the bag of 50 coins are pennies? **$\frac{2}{5}$**

Use with text pages 502–503.

Homework 19.5 Page 121

Name ______ Date ______ Homework 19.5

Find Part of a Number

Find the fractional part of each number.

> **$\frac{2}{3}$ of 12**
> Divide to find the number in each group.
> 12 ÷ 3 = 4
> Multiply by the number of groups.
> 4 × 2 = 8
> **$\frac{2}{3}$ of 12 = 8**

1. $\frac{2}{3}$ of 6 **4**
2. $\frac{3}{8}$ of 24 **9**
3. $\frac{2}{5}$ of 25 **10**
4. $\frac{3}{10}$ of 50 **15**
5. $\frac{4}{7}$ of 35 **20**
6. $\frac{3}{4}$ of 36 **27**
7. $\frac{1}{4}$ of 32 **8**
8. $\frac{2}{11}$ of 44 **8**
9. $\frac{3}{5}$ of 45 **27**
10. $\frac{5}{9}$ of 27 **15**
11. $\frac{5}{8}$ of 64 **40**
12. $\frac{7}{10}$ of 80 **56**
13. $\frac{11}{15}$ of 45 **33**
14. $\frac{3}{20}$ of 120 **18**
15. $\frac{2}{3}$ of 42 **28**
16. $\frac{1}{8}$ of 40 **5**

Problem Solving

Show your work.

17. Blake has 15 musical instruments. Guitars make up $\frac{2}{5}$ of the instruments Blake has. How many of the musical instruments are guitars? **6 musical instruments**

Use with text pages 502–503.

Lesson 19.6

Problem-Solving Strategy: Draw a Picture

Planning

Lesson Objective Draw a picture to solve a problem.

Technology Resources

- Audio Tutor **2**/20 Listen and Understand
- *Ways to Success* CD-ROM 19.6
- Education Place: Extra Practice www.eduplace.com/map

Lesson 19.6 Transparency

Problem of the Day

Rank the following money amounts from least to greatest: $\frac{1}{2}$ of a dime, $\frac{1}{4}$ of a dollar, $\frac{4}{5}$ of a quarter, and $\frac{4}{5}$ of a nickel. ($\frac{4}{5}$ nickel, $\frac{1}{2}$ dime, $\frac{4}{5}$ quarter, $\frac{1}{4}$ dollar)

Spiral Review

Find the fractional part of each number.

1. $\frac{1}{2}$ of 32 (16)

2. $\frac{2}{5}$ of 35 (14)

3. $\frac{5}{8}$ of 24 (15)

4. $\frac{3}{10}$ of 40 (12)

5. $\frac{5}{6}$ of 42 (35)

6. $\frac{3}{4}$ of 60 (45)

Lesson Quiz

Draw a picture to solve each problem.

1. After Tina spent $\frac{1}{2}$ of all her money on a sketch pad, $\frac{1}{4}$ of it on pencils, and $2 on erasers, she had no money left. How much money did Tina spend altogether? ($8)

2. Cary used $\frac{1}{2}$ of a piece of ribbon to make a large bow and $\frac{3}{8}$ of it to make a smaller bow. He had 3 inches of ribbon left over. How many inches of ribbon did Cary start with? (24 in.)

NCTM Standards

Problem Solving: Build new mathematical knowledge through problem solving; apply and adapt a variety of appropriate strategies to solve problems.

Getting Started

Building Math Vocabulary

Students should be familiar with the vocabulary in this lesson.

Use a Drawing to Visualize the Problem

Whole Class	10 minutes
Objective	Draw a picture to solve a problem.
Materials	Blank transparency
Visual, Auditory	

- Write the following problem on the board or overhead: *Four friends are standing in line. Max is ahead of Julie. Ellen is behind Julie, and Max is behind Dan. In what order are they standing?* **What strategy will you use to solve this problem?**
- Discuss students' suggested strategies. Then tell them that drawing a picture is an effective strategy to apply. Elicit from students that drawing a picture can help them organize and display the information in the problem. Talk about how using the strategy can help them to visualize and solve this particular problem.
- Point out that the lesson in the book will give them additional practice using this problem solving strategy.

Differentiated Instruction

English Learners

Pairs	15 minutes
Objective	Draw a picture to solve a problem.
Materials	None
Auditory, Visual	

Early Production

- Some students may need help working through ***Guided Practice.***
- Do the first problem with students, using the ***Ask Yourself*** questions to help students make a drawing. Allow students to work together to solve the problem.
- Ask student pairs to complete the second problem, independently, verbalizing the ***Ask Yourself*** section to their partners.

Intermediate/Advanced

- English Learner Resource 19.6
- English Learner Handbook

Intervention

Whole Class	15 minutes
Objective	Draw a picture to solve a problem.
Materials	None
Auditory, Visual	

Help students move from a detailed drawing to a more abstract drawing:

- Write the following problem on the board: *Ariana has 16 plastic ducks. She gives $\frac{1}{4}$ to David, $\frac{1}{4}$ to Kate, and keeps 8. How many ducks did Ariana give to David? to Kate?*
- Have a student volunteer draw 16 ducks on the board in any configuration. Circle 8 of the ducks and label them "Ariana". Guide students to find how many David and Kate were given, then circle and label them.
- Do the same problem, this time using rectangles as shown on page 504 of the student text. Discuss the differences and similarities between the two types of drawings with students.

Other Resources

- *Ways to Success* CD-ROM 19.6

Gifted & Talented

Small Groups	10 minutes
Objective	Solve problems using skills and strategies.
Materials	None
Auditory, Visual	

Have students draw a picture or use any strategy to solve the following problem: **Omar, Sarah, Tom, Linda, and Nina are in line to see a movie. Omar is in front of Nina but behind Tom. Sarah is last. Linda is in front of two boys. Describe the order of the people in line.** (front to back: Linda, Tom, Omar, Nina, Sarah)

Real-World Connection

- Tell students that carpenters often make drawings in the course of doing their work. Discuss the idea that they make and use drawings to help know where to saw, nail, or glue things.
- Then present the following problem for students to solve by drawing a picture: A carpenter can cut a board into 4 pieces in 12 min. How long would it take her to cut the same board into 6 pieces? (20 min; 5 cuts at 4 min each)

❶ Introduce

Explain to students that one of the best ways to solve a problem is to draw a picture. The lesson in the book will describe how to use this strategy.

❷ Teach

Draw a Picture

Use the Four-Part Problem-Solving Transparency to guide students through the problem-solving process.

- For ***Understand,*** guide students to see that the number of ants Annie ate is the total of black ants, red ants, and brown ants. **How would you describe the full meal she ate?** (sum of red, black, and brown ants; $\frac{1}{2}$ were black, $\frac{1}{4}$ were red, 6 were brown)
- For ***Plan,*** guide students to understand that a plan can help them understand the situation.
- For ***Solve,*** ask: **How does the rectangle show the information?** (It is divided into 3 parts. The $\frac{1}{2}$ part is represented by half the rectangle and is twice the size of the $\frac{1}{4}$ part. The 6-ants part fills out the rest.)
- For ***Look Back,*** say: **Suppose the problem stated that Annie also ate some brown ants, but didn't tell how many. Could you answer the question?** (No; you wouldn't have enough information.)

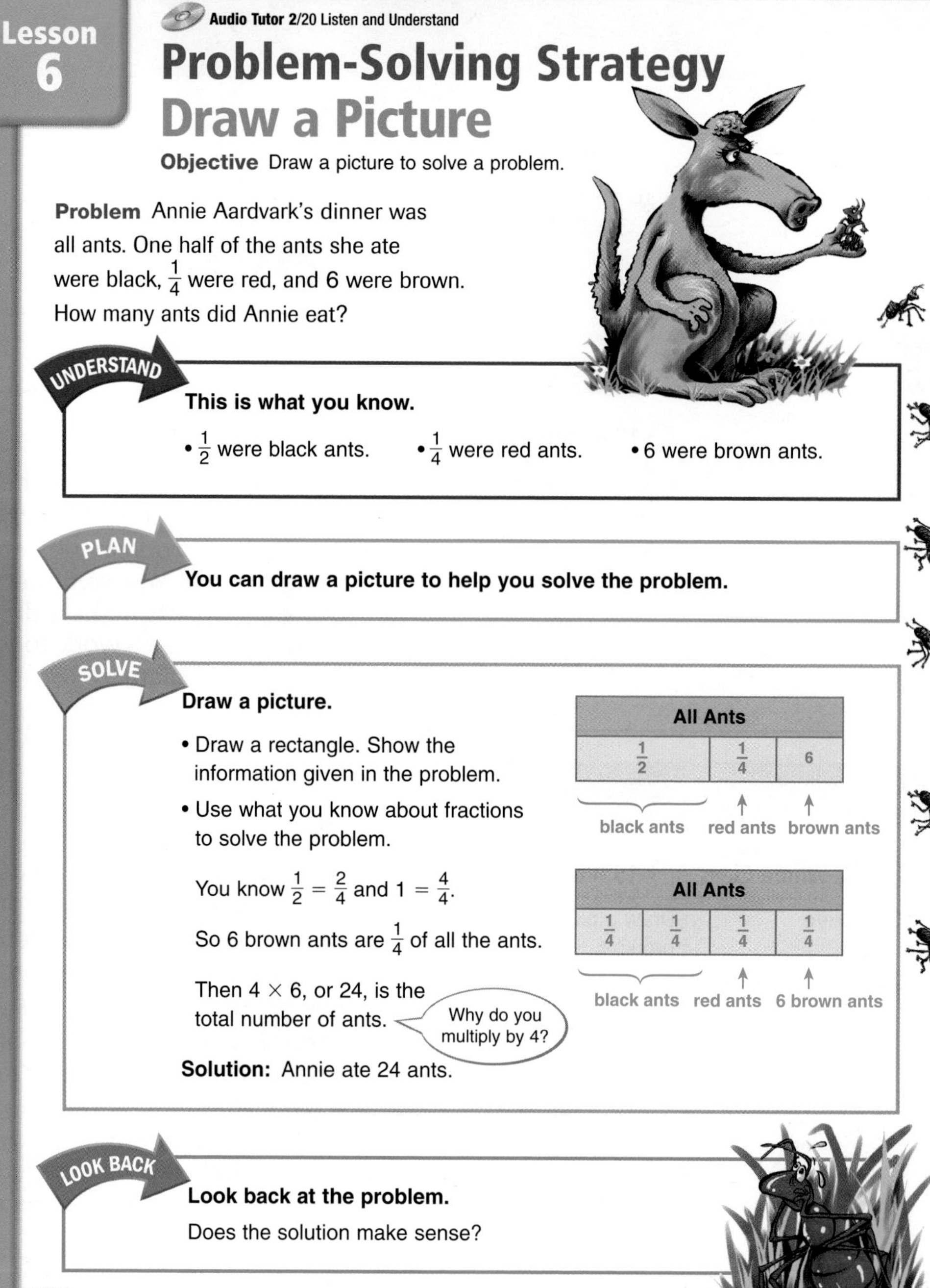
Lesson 6

Audio Tutor 2/20 Listen and Understand

Problem-Solving Strategy
Draw a Picture

Objective Draw a picture to solve a problem.

Problem Annie Aardvark's dinner was all ants. One half of the ants she ate were black, $\frac{1}{4}$ were red, and 6 were brown. How many ants did Annie eat?

UNDERSTAND

This is what you know.

- $\frac{1}{2}$ were black ants.
- $\frac{1}{4}$ were red ants.
- 6 were brown ants.

PLAN

You can draw a picture to help you solve the problem.

SOLVE

Draw a picture.

- Draw a rectangle. Show the information given in the problem.
- Use what you know about fractions to solve the problem.

You know $\frac{1}{2} = \frac{2}{4}$ and $1 = \frac{4}{4}$.

So 6 brown ants are $\frac{1}{4}$ of all the ants.

Then 4×6, or 24, is the total number of ants.

Solution: Annie ate 24 ants.

LOOK BACK

Look back at the problem.

Does the solution make sense?

504

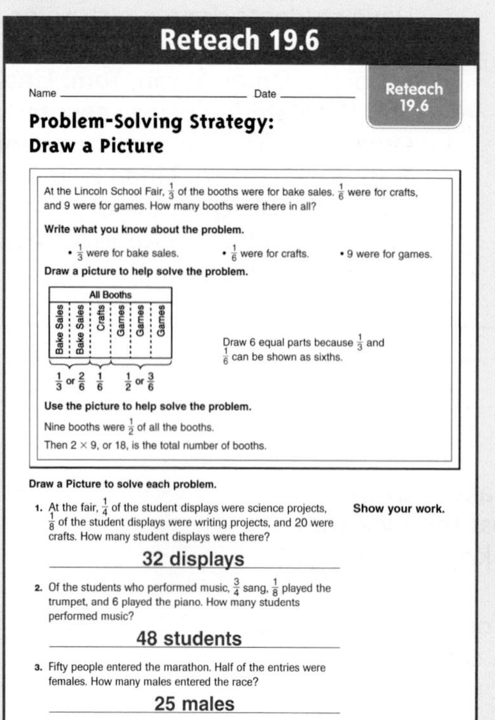
Reteach 19.6

Name ____________ Date ________

Reteach 19.6

Problem-Solving Strategy: Draw a Picture

At the Lincoln School Fair, $\frac{1}{3}$ of the booths were for bake sales. $\frac{1}{6}$ were for crafts, and 9 were for games. How many booths were there in all?

Write what you know about the problem.

- $\frac{1}{3}$ were for bake sales.
- $\frac{1}{6}$ were for crafts.
- 9 were for games.

Draw a picture to help solve the problem.

Draw 6 equal parts because $\frac{1}{3}$ and $\frac{1}{6}$ can be shown as sixths.

Use the picture to help solve the problem.

Nine booths were $\frac{1}{2}$ of all the booths.

Then 2×9, or 18, is the total number of booths.

Draw a Picture to solve each problem.

1. At the fair, $\frac{1}{4}$ of the student displays were science projects, $\frac{1}{8}$ of the student displays were writing projects, and 20 were crafts. How many student displays were there? **Show your work.**

   32 displays

2. Of the students who performed music, $\frac{3}{4}$ sang, $\frac{1}{8}$ played the trumpet, and 6 played the piano. How many students performed music?

   48 students

3. Fifty people entered the marathon. Half of the entries were females. How many males entered the race?

   25 males

Use with text pages 504–506.

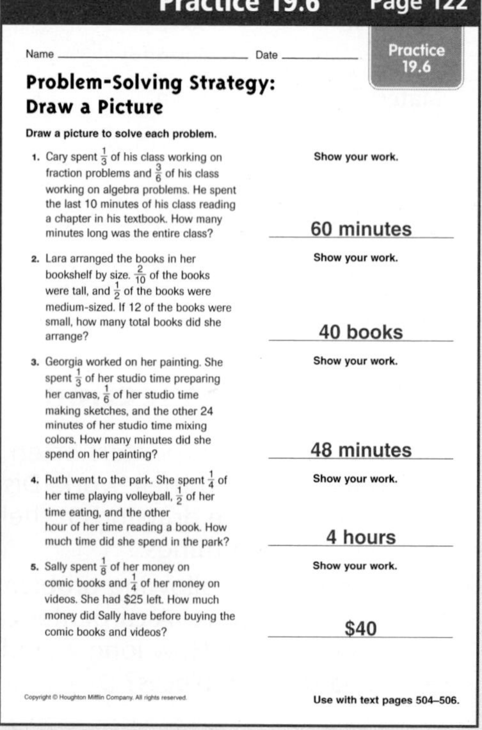
Practice 19.6 Page 122

Name ____________ Date ________

Practice 19.6

Problem-Solving Strategy: Draw a Picture

Draw a picture to solve each problem.

1. Cary spent $\frac{1}{3}$ of his class working on fraction problems and $\frac{3}{6}$ of his class working on algebra problems. He spent the last 10 minutes of his class reading a chapter in his textbook. How many minutes long was the entire class? **Show your work.**

   60 minutes

2. Lara arranged the books in her bookshelf by size. $\frac{2}{10}$ of the books were tall, and $\frac{1}{2}$ of the books were medium-sized. If 12 of the books were small, how many total books did she arrange? **Show your work.**

   40 books

3. Georgia worked on her painting. She spent $\frac{1}{3}$ of her studio time preparing her canvas, $\frac{1}{6}$ of her studio time making sketches, and the other 24 minutes of her studio time mixing colors. How many minutes did she spend on her painting? **Show your work.**

   48 minutes

4. Ruth went to the park. She spent $\frac{1}{4}$ of her time playing volleyball, $\frac{1}{2}$ of her time eating, and the other hour of her time reading a book. How much time did she spend in the park? **Show your work.**

   4 hours

5. Sally spent $\frac{1}{8}$ of her money on comic books and $\frac{1}{4}$ of her money on videos. She had $25 left. How much money did Sally have before buying the comic books and videos? **Show your work.**

   $40

Use with text pages 504–506.

Guided Practice

Use the Ask Yourself questions to help you solve each problem.

1. Spencer Spider bought insects. Two sixths were centipedes, $\frac{1}{2}$ were millipedes, and 12 were flies. How many insects did he buy? **72 insects**

2. Betty Bat has a bug collection. Two eighths are flies, $\frac{3}{8}$ are locusts, and 9 are moths. How many flies are in her collection? **6 flies**

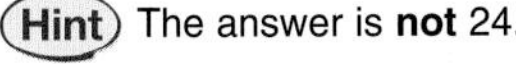
Hint The answer is **not** 24.

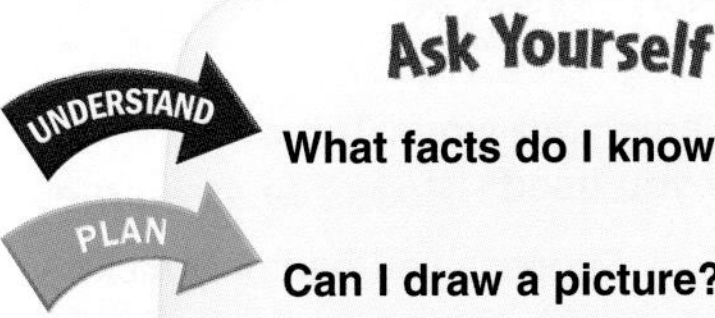
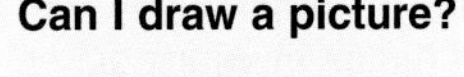

Ask Yourself

UNDERSTAND **What facts do I know?**

PLAN **Can I draw a picture?**

SOLVE
- **Did I separate the rectangle into equal parts?**
- **Did I label the parts?**
- **Did I find the number each part represents?**

LOOK BACK **Did I solve the problem?**

Independent Practice

Draw a picture to solve each problem.

3. Rodney spent half of his money on paint and $\frac{1}{6}$ on art paper. He had \$8 left. What was his starting amount? **\$24**

4. All the students in Ann's art class must complete one final project. Three eighths painted, $\frac{1}{4}$ drew charcoal sketches, and 12 made pottery. How many students are there in Ann's class? **32 students**

5. Tina collects colorful beads. Five twelfths are green, $\frac{1}{3}$ are red, and 9 are yellow. How many beads are red? **12 red beads**

6. Carl made fruit punch. Half of it was orange juice, $\frac{2}{6}$ was cranberry juice, and 12 ounces was ginger ale. How many ounces of punch did he make? **72 ounces**

Guided Practice

Have students complete **Problems 1–2** as you observe. Remind them to use the ***Ask Yourself*** question to help.

3 Practice

Independent Practice

Select from **Problems 3–13** as independent work.

- ***Problem 3*** Ask: **What fraction of your rectangle will you use to show how much Rodney spent on paint?** ($\frac{1}{2}$) **What common denominator will you use to find equivalent fractions?** (sixths) **What fraction of the whole does \$8 represent?** ($\frac{1}{3}$)
- ***Problem 4*** Ask: **What fraction represents the sum of the number of students who worked in charcoal and the number who made pottery?** ($\frac{5}{8}$) **How do you know?** ($\frac{3}{8}$ of the class painted; $\frac{3}{8} + \frac{5}{8} = \frac{8}{8}$.)

Enrichment 19.6

Name ______ Date ______ Enrichment 19.6

Problem-Solving Strategy: Draw a Picture

Draw a picture to solve each problem. Explain how you found your answer.

Ryan and Jodi went to the movies. They spent $\frac{1}{3}$ of their money on the tickets and $\frac{2}{5}$ of their money on food. The movie lasted 120 minutes. Previews for upcoming movies were shown for $\frac{1}{8}$ of that time. The theatre seats 300 people. At this showing, $\frac{1}{4}$ of the seats were empty.

Show your work.

1. After the movie, Ryan and Jodi had \$8 left. How much money did they bring to the movie? \$30
2. Ryan and Jodi each bought a ticket to the movie. Their tickets were the same price. What was the price of each ticket? \$5
3. Did Ryan and Jodi spend more on the tickets or on food? How much more? food; \$2 more (\$12 for food; \$10 for tickets)
4. How many minutes were previews of upcoming movies shown? 15 minutes
5. How many people were at this showing of the movie? 225 people

 Use with text pages 504–506.

Problem Solving 19.6

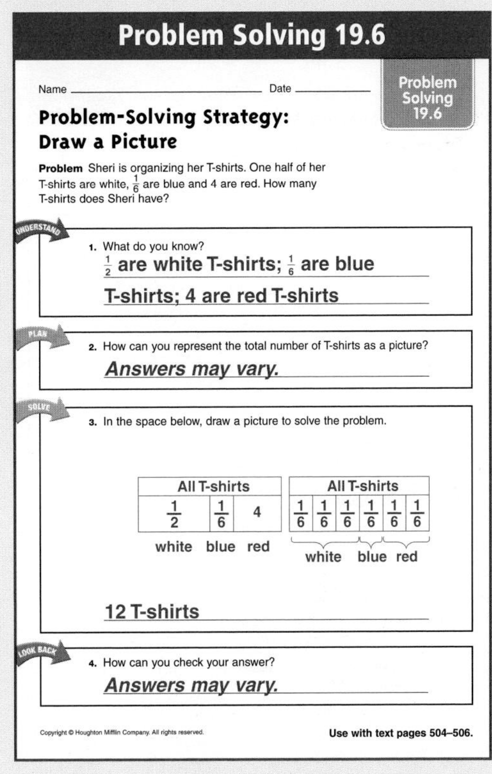
Name ______ Date ______ Problem Solving 19.6

Problem-Solving Strategy: Draw a Picture

Problem Sheri is organizing her T-shirts. One half of her T-shirts are white, $\frac{1}{6}$ are blue and 4 are red. How many T-shirts does Sheri have?

UNDERSTAND 1. What do you know? $\frac{1}{2}$ are white T-shirts; $\frac{1}{6}$ are blue T-shirts; 4 are red T-shirts

PLAN 2. How can you represent the total number of T-shirts as a picture? *Answers may vary.*

SOLVE 3. In the space below, draw a picture to solve the problem.

All T-shirts		
$\frac{1}{2}$	$\frac{1}{6}$	4
white	blue	red

All T-shirts					
$\frac{1}{6}$	$\frac{1}{6}$	$\frac{1}{6}$	$\frac{1}{6}$	$\frac{1}{6}$	$\frac{1}{6}$

white blue red

12 T-shirts

LOOK BACK 4. How can you check your answer? *Answers may vary.*

 Use with text pages 504–506.

Mixed Problem Solving

Select from **Problems 7–13** as independent work.

- ***Problems 7–9*** Make sure students know to use any strategy to solve these problems.
- ***Data*** Ask: **What other type of graph could we use to show this same data? Explain.** (Circle graph; it shows parts of a whole.)

Mixed Problem Solving

Solve. Show your work. Tell what strategy you used. ***Possible strategies given.***

You Choose

Strategy
- Draw a Picture
- Guess and Check
- Make a Table
- Write an Equation

Computation Method
- Mental Math
- Estimation
- Paper and Pencil
- Calculator

7. **Money** Suppose you had only nickels and dimes in your pocket. Then you lost 10 coins that totaled 85 cents. How many of each coin did you lose? **7 dimes, 3 nickels; Guess and Check**
8. Rico spent half of his money on admission to the museum and $\frac{1}{4}$ on lunch. He has $5 left. What was his starting amount? **$20; Draw a Picture**
9. Colleen wants a computer game that costs $64. She has $30. If she saves $5 a week, how many weeks will it take until she has enough money to buy the game? **7 weeks; Make a Table**

Data Use the graph to solve Problems 10–13.

Each week Steve earns money by helping in art classes for younger students. The graph shows what he does with his money each week.

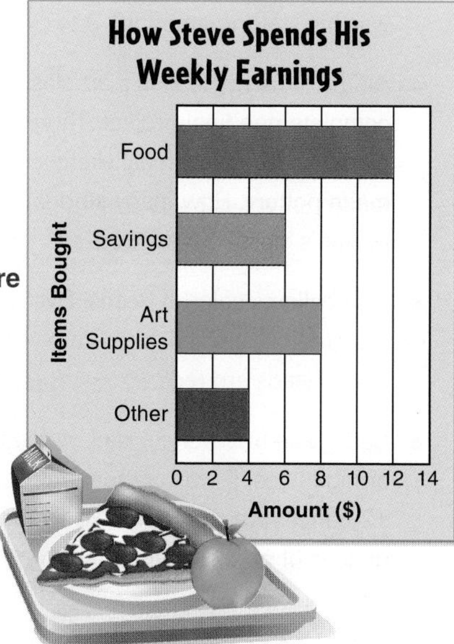

10. How much money does Steve earn each week? **$30**
11. How much more money does Steve spend on food than on art supplies? **$4 more**
12. Steve spends $\frac{1}{2}$ of his food money at school. How much does he spend on food at school? **$6**
13. After 9 weeks, how much money will Steve have earned? How much money will he have saved? **$270; $54**

506

Homework 19.6 Page 122

Name ______________ Date ________ Homework 19.6

Problem-Solving Strategy: Draw a Picture

Draw a picture to solve each problem.

Kacey painted several pieces of pottery. One third of the pieces were plates, $\frac{1}{6}$ of the pieces were bowls, and 10 of the pieces were cups. How many pieces of pottery did Kacey paint?

$\frac{1}{3} = \frac{2}{6}$; $\frac{2}{6}$ of the pieces were plates
$\frac{2}{6} + \frac{1}{6} = \frac{3}{6}$; $\frac{3}{6}$ of the pieces were plates or bowls
$\frac{6}{6} - \frac{3}{6} = \frac{3}{6}$; $\frac{3}{6}$ of the pieces were cups

Draw a picture using what you know.

$\frac{3}{6} = \frac{1}{2}$

Cups make up half of the total pieces painted.

$\frac{1}{2}$ of the total pieces painted = 10

1					
$\frac{1}{6}$	$\frac{1}{6}$	$\frac{1}{6}$	$\frac{1}{6}$	$\frac{1}{6}$	$\frac{1}{6}$
plates		bowls	cups		

Kacey painted 20 pieces of pottery.

Problem Solving

Show your work.

1. Beth spent $\frac{3}{8}$ of her money on guitar strings, $\frac{1}{8}$ of her money on guitar picks, and $15 on a guitar tuner. How much money did Beth have before buying guitar accessories? $30
2. Rusty arranged ornaments by color. One fourth of the ornaments were green, $\frac{3}{8}$ of the ornaments were yellow, and 24 of the ornaments were red. How many ornaments did Rusty arrange? 64

Use with text pages 504–506.

Problem Solving on Tests

Multiple Choice

Choose the letter of the correct answer.

1. Tina bought some bottled water for a bike trip. She drank 3 bottles. Then she bought 5 more. After drinking another 2 bottles, she had 4 bottles left. How many bottles of water did Tina start with?

   A 14 **C** 10

   B 12  4

   (Chapter 9, Lesson 5)

2. What is the next likely picture in this pattern?

   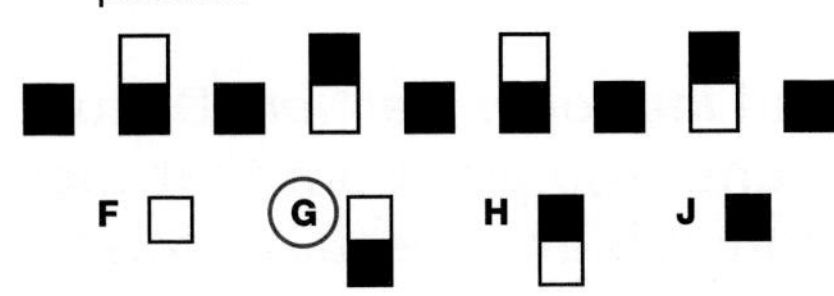

   (Chapter 16, Lesson 6)

Open Response

Solve each problem. *See Additional Answers.*

3. In a picture of turtles and parrots, there are 7 animals with 22 legs altogether. How many parrots are in the picture?

   Represent Support your solution with a picture or table.

   (Chapter 13, Lesson 3)

4. Tommy has 36 photos. He wants to put the photos in an album. He puts 4 photos on each page. How many pages will he use?

   Represent Write an equation that can be used to find the number of pages he will need.

   See Additional Answers. (Chapter 5, Lesson 5)

Extended Response

5. Josh is making a new habitat for his pet turtle. He has a glass aquarium that measures 6 in. deep by 12 in. wide by 8 in. high.

   a. One of the long sides of the aquarium was removed and replaced with a piece of screen. What is the area of the screen?

   b. Josh has a plastic dish that measures 4 in. long by 6 in. wide by 1 in. deep. He plans to put $\frac{1}{2}$ inch of water in it so the turtle can swim. What will the volume of the water in the dish be? Show how you know.

   c. After Josh places the dish in the aquarium, he plans to put a mixture of sand and soil around it to the top of the dish. The base of the aquarium will be completely covered. What is the volume of sand and soil that he will use? Explain.

   d. Decide what else Josh might add to the aquarium. Tell why he should add these things.

   See Additional Answers. (Chapter 18, Lesson 7)

Education Place

See **eduplace.com/map** for more Test-Taking Tips.

Problem Solving on Tests

Problem Solving on Tests provides an opportunity for students to apply previously learned skills in the types of problem contexts typically encountered in standardized tests. ***Problem Solving on Tests*** includes practice in a variety of formats: multiple choice, extended response, and open response.

Students will gain experience in writing about mathematics and using various representations to solve problems. Discuss students' solutions. Have several students explain the thinking behind their work.

More test prep practice is available on Houghton Mifflin's Web site, **Education Place**. Go to www.eduplace.com/map.

4 Assess & Close

Math Talk in Action

Have students refer to **Problems 1–6** to conclude the lesson. Have them explain how drawing a picture helped them to solve the problems.

Math Journal Prompt

Have students write an explanation of when to draw a picture to solve a problem. Have them write a problem that can be solved by drawing a picture.

Lesson Quiz

Use the quiz on Lesson Transparency 19.6.

Lesson 19.6 Transparency

Test Prep & Spiral Review

Use Test Prep Transparency 19.6.

Test Prep 19.6 Transparency

Lesson 19.7

Mixed Numbers and Improper Fractions

Planning

Lesson Objective Write mixed numbers and improper fractions.

Math Background

An improper fraction has a numerator greater than or equal to the denominator. There is nothing wrong with an improper fraction. Sometimes it is necessary and more convenient to compute with improper fractions. An improper fraction can be converted to a whole or mixed number by dividing the numerator by the denominator.

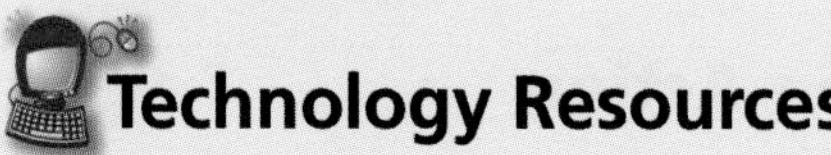

Technology Resources

- Audio Tutor **2**/21 Listen and Understand
- *Ways to Success* CD-ROM 19.7

Lesson 19.7 Transparency

Problem of the Day

Inez gave $\frac{1}{4}$ of her collection of coins to her brother. She gave him 12 coins. How many coins does Inez have left? (36; 48 − 12 = 36)

Spiral Review

Divide.

1. 25 ÷ 4 (6 R1)
2. 31 ÷ 8 (3 R7)
3. 42 ÷ 9 (4 R6)
4. 35 ÷ 6 (5 R5)

Lesson Quiz

Copy and complete the table

Division	Improper Fraction	Mixed Number
1. 17 ÷ 4	($\frac{17}{4}$)	($4\frac{1}{4}$)
2. 22 ÷ 5	($\frac{22}{5}$)	$4\frac{2}{5}$
3. (11 ÷ 3)	$\frac{11}{3}$	($3\frac{2}{3}$)

NCTM Standards

Number and Operations: Develop understanding of fractions as parts of unit wholes, as parts of a collection; use models, benchmarks, and equivalent forms to judge the size of fractions.

Getting Started

Building Math Vocabulary

mixed number a number containing a whole number part and a fraction part

improper fraction a fraction that is greater than or equal to 1; the numerator in an improper fraction is greater than or equal to the denominator

Use the vocabulary cards for ***mixed number*** and ***improper fraction.*** Discuss that these two forms can name the same amount. Also point out that there is nothing "improper" about an improper fraction; it is an acceptable form of expressing a fractional amount.

Naming Fractions

Whole Class	5 minutes
Objective	Write and identify fractional parts.
Materials	Blank transparency
	Visual, Auditory

- Draw these figures on a blank transparency or the board. Have students write a fraction for each of the parts.

1. ($\frac{2}{3}$) **2.** ($\frac{3}{5}$)

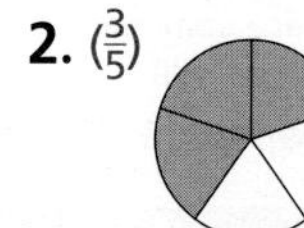

3. ($\frac{5}{6}$)

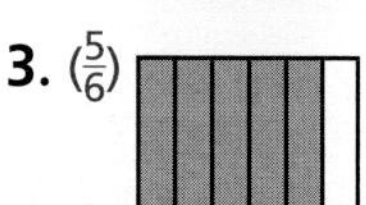

4. ($\frac{5}{8}$)

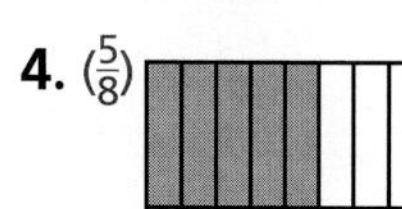

Ask students:

- **What does the numerator of each of your answers tell?** (how many of the parts are shaded) **What does the denominator tell?** (how many parts in the whole)
- Explain that the lesson will introduce fractions in which the numerator is greater than or equal to the denominator and numbers that combine whole numbers with fractions.

Differentiated Instruction

English Learners

Whole Class	15 minutes
Objective	Practice reading and writing mixed numbers and fractions.
Materials	None
Auditory, Visual	

Early Production

- Have students practice recognizing proper, improper, and mixed fractions.
- Write four examples of each type of fraction on the board.
- Point to different fractions and ask students to call out the type.
- Then call out a type of fraction and have students write an example.

Intermediate/Advanced

- English Learner Resource 19.7
- English Learner Handbook

Intervention

Small Groups	15 minutes
Objective	Interpret models of mixed numbers and improper fractions.
Materials	None
Auditory, Visual	

- Draw a 6-slice pizza on the board (or use a model of one). Then draw a second 6-slice pizza next to it. Discuss that there are 2 whole pies, or 12 sixths of pizza. Now draw one more slice. (Note: all slices should be the same size.)
- Discuss the idea that there are now $2\frac{1}{6}$ pizzas, or 13 sixths. Write $2\frac{1}{6} = \frac{13}{6}$. Repeat with pizzas with different numbers of slices.

Other Resources

- *Ways to Success* CD-ROM 19.6

Special Needs

Small Groups	10 minutes
Objective	Understand mixed numbers.
Materials	Fraction pieces (Learning Tool 34)
Auditory, Visual	

Have students work with fraction pieces to represent mixed numbers. For example, to show the mixed number $1\frac{3}{5}$, they would use two sets of $\frac{1}{5}$ fraction pieces. They arrange five $\frac{1}{5}$ pieces in a row to form 1 whole. Then they arrange three $\frac{1}{5}$ pieces in another row to show $\frac{3}{5}$. To change $1\frac{3}{5}$ to an improper fraction, they simply count all the $\frac{1}{5}$ pieces. ($\frac{8}{5}$)

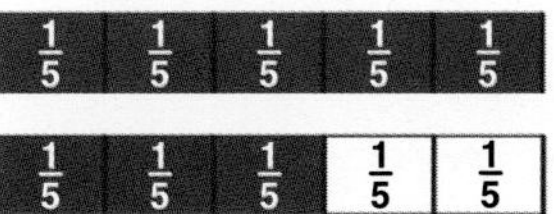

Real-World Connection

Discuss with students the fact that over time, things cost more to buy and people earn more money to pay for them. Tell them, for example, that a toll for crossing a bridge that was \$1 ten years ago costs $2\frac{1}{2}$ times as much today.

- **What is the cost of the toll today? Use mental math to figure it out.** (2 × \$1 = \$2; $\frac{1}{2}$ of \$1 is \$.50; \$2 + \$.50 = \$2.50)

Provide additional problems like this for students to solve mentally.

❶ Introduce

Explain to students that fractions get more complicated when the numerator is greater than the denominator.

❷ Teach

Learn About It

- Have students read the opening situation and look at the pictures. **As we have just seen, there are two forms for writing fractional numbers that are greater than or equal to 1—mixed numbers and improper fractions.** Refer students to the mixed number $2\frac{1}{4}$.
- **How many whole waffles? How many parts?** (2 wholes, 1 part) Have students use fraction strips to show that $\frac{9}{4}$ is equal to $2\frac{1}{4}$.
- **What is the difference between an improper fraction and a proper one?** (An improper fraction represents greater than or equal to a whole.)

Common Error

- **Incorrectly forming improper fractions** Students may incorrectly change a mixed number to an improper fraction.
- **Intervention** Students may make this mistake in several ways. For instance, they may multiply the whole number by the numerator and then add the denominator. Or they may simply add all three numbers. Remind them that they must *multiply* the whole-number part by the denominator and then *add* the numerator to the product.

Lesson 7

Audio Tutor 2/21 Listen and Understand

Mixed Numbers and Improper Fractions

Vocabulary
mixed number
improper fraction

Objective Write mixed numbers and improper fractions.

Learn About It

There are two whole waffles and one fourth of a waffle. There are nine fourths waffles.

You can write the amount of waffles as a mixed number or as an improper fraction.

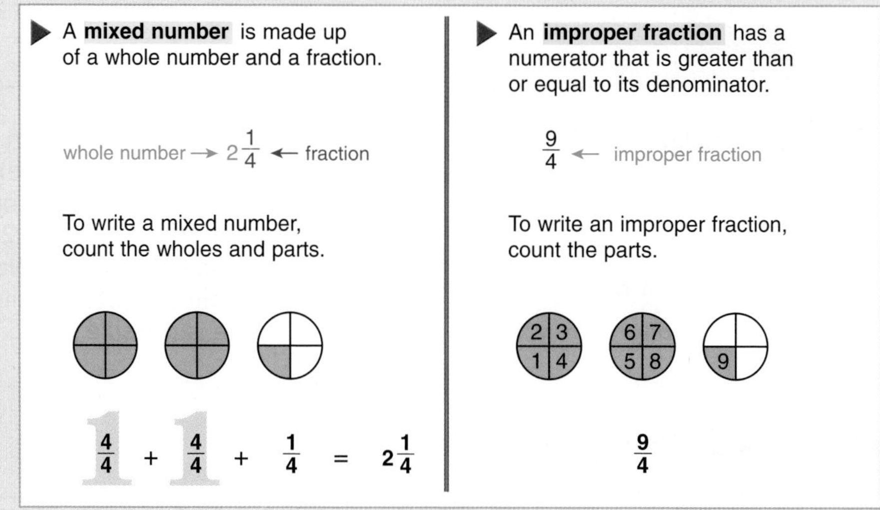

▶ A **mixed number** is made up of a whole number and a fraction.
whole number → $2\frac{1}{4}$ ← fraction
To write a mixed number, count the wholes and parts.
$\frac{4}{4} + \frac{4}{4} + \frac{1}{4} = 2\frac{1}{4}$
▶ An **improper fraction** has a numerator that is greater than or equal to its denominator.
$\frac{9}{4}$ ← improper fraction
To write an improper fraction, count the parts.
2 3 1 4
6 7 5 8
9
$\frac{9}{4}$

508

Reteach 19.7

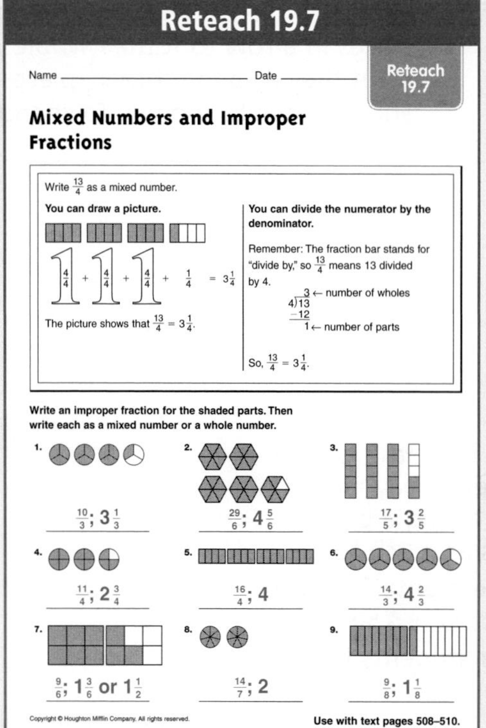

Name ______ Date ______ Reteach 19.7

Mixed Numbers and Improper Fractions

Write $\frac{13}{4}$ as a mixed number.

You can draw a picture.

$\frac{4}{4} + \frac{4}{4} + \frac{4}{4} + \frac{1}{4} = 3\frac{1}{4}$

The picture shows that $\frac{13}{4} = 3\frac{1}{4}$.

You can divide the numerator by the denominator.

Remember: The fraction bar stands for "divide by," so $\frac{13}{4}$ means 13 divided by 4.

$4\overline{)13}$ → 3 ← number of wholes; -12; 1 ← number of parts

So, $\frac{13}{4} = 3\frac{1}{4}$.

Write an improper fraction for the shaded parts. Then write each as a mixed number or a whole number.

1. $\frac{10}{3}$; $3\frac{1}{3}$
2. $\frac{29}{6}$; $4\frac{5}{6}$
3. $\frac{17}{5}$; $3\frac{2}{5}$
4. $\frac{11}{4}$; $2\frac{3}{4}$
5. $\frac{16}{4}$; 4
6. $\frac{14}{3}$; $4\frac{2}{3}$
7. $\frac{9}{6}$; $1\frac{3}{6}$ or $1\frac{1}{2}$
8. $\frac{14}{7}$; 2
9. $\frac{9}{8}$; $1\frac{1}{8}$

Use with text pages 508–510.

Practice 19.7 Page 123

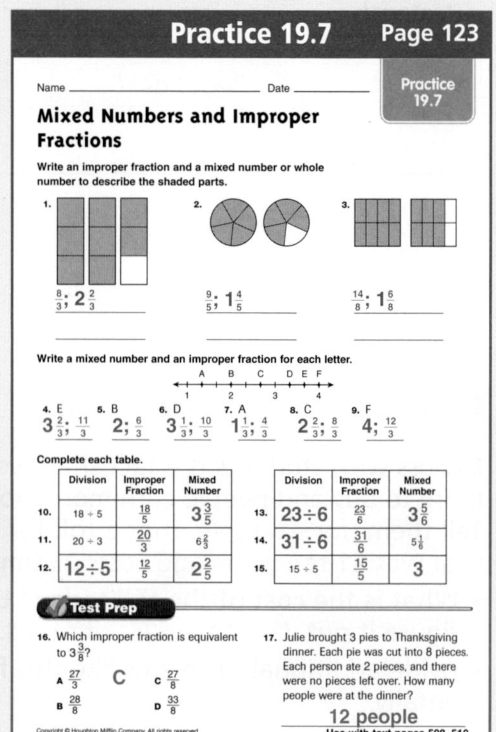

Name ______ Date ______ Practice 19.7

Mixed Numbers and Improper Fractions

Write an improper fraction and a mixed number or whole number to describe the shaded parts.

1. $\frac{8}{3}$; $2\frac{2}{3}$
2. $\frac{9}{5}$; $1\frac{4}{5}$
3. $\frac{14}{8}$; $1\frac{6}{8}$

Write a mixed number and an improper fraction for each letter.

4. E $3\frac{2}{3}$; $\frac{11}{3}$
5. B 2; $\frac{6}{3}$
6. D $3\frac{1}{3}$; $\frac{10}{3}$
7. A $1\frac{1}{3}$; $\frac{4}{3}$
8. C $2\frac{2}{3}$; $\frac{8}{3}$
9. F 4; $\frac{12}{3}$

Complete each table.

	Division	Improper Fraction	Mixed Number
10.	18 ÷ 5	$\frac{18}{5}$	$3\frac{3}{5}$
11.	20 ÷ 3	$\frac{20}{3}$	$6\frac{2}{3}$
12.	12÷5	$\frac{12}{5}$	$2\frac{2}{5}$

	Division	Improper Fraction	Mixed Number
13.	23÷6	$\frac{23}{6}$	$3\frac{5}{6}$
14.	31÷6	$\frac{31}{6}$	$5\frac{1}{6}$
15.	15 ÷ 5	$\frac{15}{5}$	3

Test Prep

16. Which improper fraction is equivalent to $3\frac{3}{8}$?
   A $\frac{27}{3}$ B $\frac{28}{8}$ C $\frac{27}{8}$ D $\frac{33}{8}$
   C

17. Julie brought 3 pies to Thanksgiving dinner. Each pie was cut into 8 pieces. Each person ate 2 pieces, and there were no pieces left over. How many people were at the dinner?
   12 people

Use with text pages 508–510.

Here's how to change from one form to another.

To change an improper fraction to a mixed number, you can divide.	To change a mixed number to an improper fraction, you can multiply and add, as shown below.
The fraction bar stands for "divided by." So $\frac{9}{4}$ means "9 divided by 4."	
$4\overline{)9}$ → 2 ← number of wholes; -8; 1 ← number of fourths	$2\frac{1}{4} = \frac{9}{4}$ ← $(4 \times 2) + 1$; 4 ← denominator stays the same
So $\frac{9}{4}$ is equal to $2\frac{1}{4}$.	So $2\frac{1}{4} = \frac{9}{4}$.

Work through the steps for changing an improper fraction to a mixed number. Emphasize that mixed numbers and improper fractions name the same amount—the only change is in the way they express that amount.

Then work through the steps for changing a mixed number to an improper fraction. Invite students to change another mixed number to an improper fraction.

Other Examples Work through the examples. Then write $\frac{12}{4}$ on the board. Guide students to see that when the numerator is a multiple of the denominator, the quotient will be a whole number. Invite students to suggest other examples of fractions like $\frac{12}{4}$.

Other Examples

Improper Fractions Equal to Whole Numbers

A.

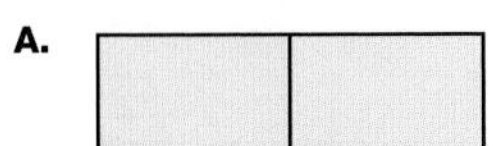

$\frac{2}{2} = 1$, because $2 \div 2 = 1$

B.

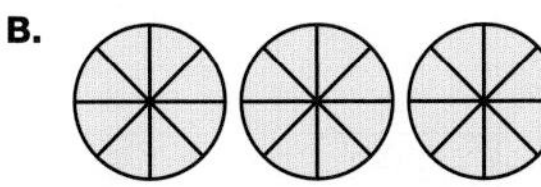

$\frac{24}{8} = 3$, because $24 \div 8 = 3$

Guided Practice

Have students complete **Exercises 1–4** as you observe. Remind them to use the *Ask Yourself* questions to help. Give students the oppor-tunity to talk about the question in *Explain Your Thinking*.

Ask Yourself

- Into how many equal parts is each figure divided?
- How many wholes are represented?

Write an improper fraction for the shaded parts. Then write each as a mixed number or as a whole number.

1.

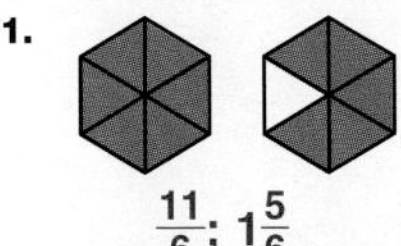

$\frac{11}{6}$; $1\frac{5}{6}$

2.

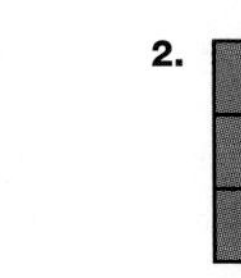

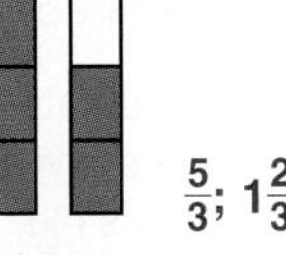

$\frac{5}{3}$; $1\frac{2}{3}$

3.

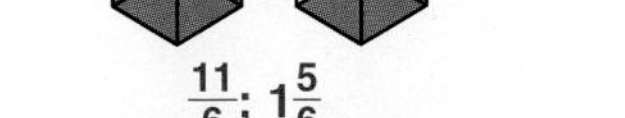

$\frac{12}{4}$; 3

4.

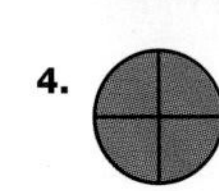

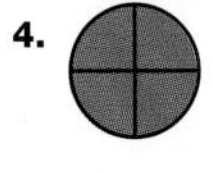

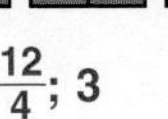

$\frac{4}{4}$; 1

Explain Your Thinking ▶ How can you tell whether a fraction can be rewritten as a mixed number or as a whole number?

If the numerator of the improper fraction is a multiple of the denominator, it will be rewritten as a whole number.

Go On

Enrichment 19.7

Name ____ Date ____ Enrichment 19.7

The Town of Mixed Up and Improper

The citizens of the town of Mixed Up and Improper have written descriptions of themselves. Read each description below. Write the mixed number or improper fraction described. There may be more than one correct answer.

1. I am greater than 3 but less than 4. My brother and I both have 3 as the denominator of our fractional part. I am greater than my brother. $3\frac{2}{3}$ or $\frac{11}{3}$
2. I am a mixed number greater than 2 and less than 3. The denominator of my fractional part is 2. $2\frac{1}{2}$
3. I am an improper fraction with a value greater than 5 and less than 6. My denominator is 12. My numerator is less than 62. $\frac{61}{12}$
4. I am a mixed number with a value greater than $1\frac{1}{3}$ and less than $1\frac{1}{2}$. As an improper fraction, I am written as $\frac{7}{5}$. $1\frac{2}{5}$
5. I am an improper fraction. As a mixed number, I have 2 as my whole number and 100 as my denominator. If you add the digits in my numerator, you get 3. $\frac{201}{100}$ or $\frac{210}{100}$
6. I am a mixed number with a value greater than $2\frac{1}{4}$ and less than $2\frac{1}{2}$. The denominator of my fractional part is 6. $2\frac{2}{6}$

 Use with text pages 508–510.

Problem Solving 19.7

Name ____ Date ____ Problem Solving 19.7

Mixed Numbers and Improper Fractions

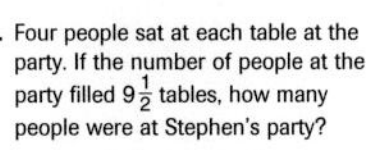

Show your work.

1. Stephen had pizza at his birthday party. The picture shows how much pizza was eaten. Write the amount of pizza eaten as a mixed number and an improper fraction. $4\frac{3}{8}$; $\frac{35}{8}$
2. If each person who had pizza ate $\frac{1}{8}$ of the pizza, how many people ate pizza at Stephen's birthday party? 35 people
3. Four people sat at each table at the party. If the number of people at the party filled $9\frac{1}{2}$ tables, how many people were at Stephen's party? 38 people
4. Stephen's mom made punch for the party. She made enough so that each person could drink $\frac{1}{6}$ of a gallon. If she planned for 42 people, how many gallons of punch did she make? 7 gallons
5. Stephen's party lasted for $2\frac{3}{4}$ hours. Write this as an improper fraction. Then find what time the party ended if it started at 1:00 P.M. $\frac{11}{4}$ hours; 3:45 P.M.

 Use with text pages 508–510.

❸ Practice

Practice and Problem Solving

Select from **Exercises 5–27** as independent work.

- ***Problem 22*** Elicit from students that the number of people that ate oranges needs to be a multiple of 5.
- ***Problem 24*** Guide students to make sure that Ms. Carter brings enough whole pies; there will be pieces of pie left over.

❹ Assess & Close

Math Talk in Action

- **How do you know a mixed number is between two whole numbers?** (Each whole number is 1 greater than the last, and the fraction part of a mixed number is always less than 1.)
- **What mixed number can we write for $\frac{11}{3}$?** ($3\frac{2}{3}$)

Math Journal Prompt

Have students write an improper fraction and then express it as a mixed number. Have them choose any mixed number and express it as an improper fraction.

Lesson Quiz

Use the quiz on Lesson Transparency 19.7.

Test Prep & Spiral Review

Use Test Prep Transparency 19.7.

Practice and Problem Solving

Write an improper fraction and a mixed number or whole number to describe the shaded parts.

5. 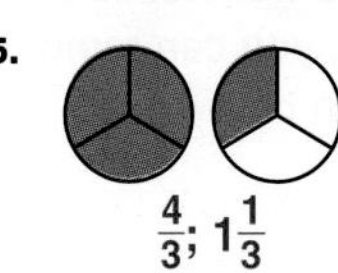 $\frac{4}{3}$; $1\frac{1}{3}$

6. 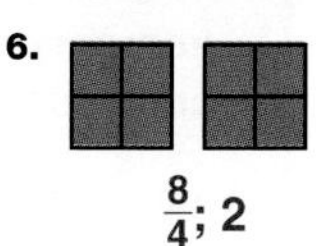 $\frac{8}{4}$; 2

7. 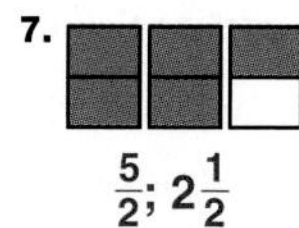 $\frac{5}{2}$; $2\frac{1}{2}$

Write a mixed number and an improper fraction for each letter.

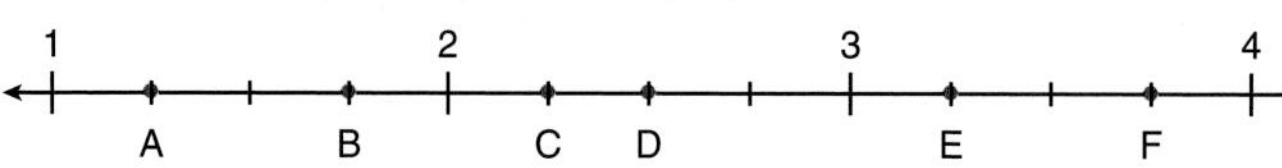

8. A $1\frac{1}{4}$; $\frac{5}{4}$
9. C $2\frac{1}{4}$; $\frac{9}{4}$
10. F $3\frac{3}{4}$; $\frac{15}{4}$
11. D $2\frac{1}{2}$; $\frac{5}{2}$
12. B $1\frac{3}{4}$; $\frac{7}{4}$
13. E $3\frac{1}{4}$; $\frac{13}{4}$

Copy and complete each table.

	Division	Improper Fraction	Mixed Numbers or Whole Numbers
14.	16 ÷ 3	$\frac{16}{3}$	$5\frac{1}{3}$
15.	19 ÷ 2	$\frac{19}{2}$	$9\frac{1}{2}$
16.	11 ÷ 9	$\frac{11}{9}$	$1\frac{2}{9}$
17.	15 ÷ 8	$\frac{15}{8}$	$1\frac{7}{8}$

	Division	Improper Fraction	Mixed Numbers or Whole Numbers
18.	28 ÷ 7	$\frac{28}{7}$	4
19.	24 ÷ 5	$\frac{24}{5}$	$4\frac{4}{5}$
20.	10 ÷ 2	$\frac{10}{2}$	5
21.	15 ÷ 6	$\frac{15}{6}$	$2\frac{1}{2}$

Solve.

22. Mr. Alvarez brought 5 oranges to a picnic. All the oranges were cut into halves. Each person ate one half of an orange, and there were no oranges left over. How many people ate oranges? **10 people**

23. Michael is 5 years older than Elizabeth. Elizabeth is 8 years younger than José. Meredith is 2 years younger than José. If Meredith is 12 years old, how old is Michael? **11 years old**

24. **Reasoning** Ms. Carter made pies for the picnic. She brought enough so that each person could have $\frac{1}{8}$ of a pie. What is the least number of pies she could have made if 20 people were at the picnic? **3 pies**

510

Extra Practice See page 513, Set E.

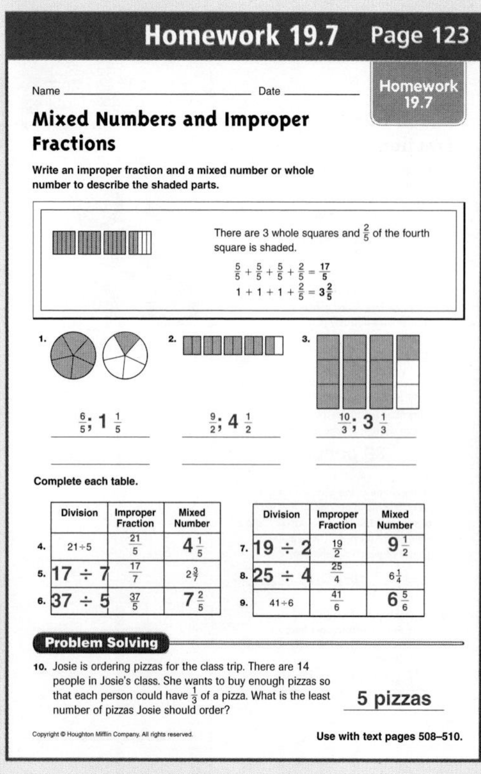

Homework 19.7 Page 123

Name ____________ Date ________

Homework 19.7

Mixed Numbers and Improper Fractions

Write an improper fraction and a mixed number or whole number to describe the shaded parts.

There are 3 whole squares and $\frac{2}{5}$ of the fourth square is shaded.

$\frac{5}{5} + \frac{5}{5} + \frac{5}{5} + \frac{2}{5} = \frac{17}{5}$

$1 + 1 + 1 + \frac{2}{5} = 3\frac{2}{5}$

1. $\frac{6}{5}$; $1\frac{1}{5}$
2. $\frac{9}{2}$; $4\frac{1}{2}$
3. $\frac{10}{3}$; $3\frac{1}{3}$

Complete each table.

	Division	Improper Fraction	Mixed Number
4.	21 ÷ 5	$\frac{21}{5}$	$4\frac{1}{5}$
5.	17 ÷ 7	$\frac{17}{7}$	$2\frac{3}{7}$
6.	37 ÷ 5	$\frac{37}{5}$	$7\frac{2}{5}$

	Division	Improper Fraction	Mixed Number
7.	19 ÷ 2	$\frac{19}{2}$	$9\frac{1}{2}$
8.	25 ÷ 4	$\frac{25}{4}$	$6\frac{1}{4}$
9.	41 ÷ 6	$\frac{41}{6}$	$6\frac{5}{6}$

Problem Solving

10. Josie is ordering pizzas for the class trip. There are 14 people in Josie's class. She wants to buy enough pizzas so that each person could have $\frac{1}{3}$ of a pizza. What is the least number of pizzas Josie should order? **5 pizzas**

Use with text pages 508–510.

Mixed Review and Test Prep

Open Response

Find the fractional part of each number.

25. $\frac{2}{3}$ of 15
10

☆☆☆☆☆
☆☆☆☆☆
☆☆☆☆☆

26. $\frac{5}{6}$ of 18
15

□□□□□□
□□□□□□
□□□□□□

(Ch. 19, Lesson 5)

Solve.

27. Mr. Cronin's class made 4 pecan pies for the school bake sale. Each of the pies is cut into 8 equal pieces. Mr. Cronin bought 10 pieces of pie for a party. What fraction of 1 pie did he buy? Write your answer as an improper fraction in simplest form and as a mixed number.

$\frac{5}{4}$; $1\frac{1}{4}$ (Ch. 19, Lesson 7)

Problem Solving

Math Reasoning
Pie Pieces

You can use these pies to help you round fractions.

$\frac{1}{8}$ is close to 0.
Round $\frac{1}{8}$ to 0.

$\frac{3}{8}$ is close to $\frac{1}{2}$.
Round $\frac{3}{8}$ to $\frac{1}{2}$.

$\frac{7}{8}$ is close to 1.
Round $\frac{7}{8}$ to 1.

Write whether the fraction rounds to 0, $\frac{1}{2}$, or 1.

1. $\frac{1}{10}$ 0 **2.** $\frac{5}{6}$ 1 **3.** $\frac{4}{5}$ 1 **4.** $\frac{2}{6}$ $\frac{1}{2}$

5. $\frac{3}{5}$ $\frac{1}{2}$ **6.** $\frac{9}{8}$ 1 **7.** $\frac{4}{6}$ $\frac{1}{2}$ **8.** $\frac{4}{10}$ $\frac{1}{2}$

Math Reasoning
Pie Pieces

In this activity, students use visual clues to estimate fractional parts of wholes. Compare the way we round fractions (0, $\frac{1}{2}$, 1) to the way we round whole numbers. Guide students, as a first step, to look to decide whether a fraction is greater than or less than $\frac{1}{2}$.

- **How can you tell just by reading a fraction whether it is greater than $\frac{1}{2}$?** (The numerator is more than half of the denominator.)
- **How can you tell just by reading a fraction whether it is close to 1?** (Its numerator and denominator are very close in value.)

Discuss with students what to do when a fraction is halfway between two benchmarks. You may also wish to have students use number lines or rulers to explore rounding fractions visually.

Monitoring Student Progress

Chapter Review/Test

Chapter Review/Test Items 1–20

To assign a numerical grade for this Chapter Test, use 5 points for each item.

Check Understanding

You can use the ***Write About It*** question to assess understanding of a key chapter concept.

Customize Your Instruction

The Chapter Review/Test is a formal evaluation of chapter objectives. For students who have not yet mastered these objectives, you can use the Reteaching Resources listed in the chart below.

Additional Assessment Resources

Alternate Chapter Test A Chapter Test is also provided in the Unit Resource folder. You might use the Review/Test in the student book as review and the test in the Unit Resource folder as a summary test for the chapter.

***Ways to Assess* CD-ROM** allows you to create your own lesson, chapter, or unit tests or practice and review worksheets.

Adequate Yearly Progress Guide helps familiarize your students with the format of standardized tests.

Chapter Review/Test

Vocabulary

denominator
simplest form
mixed number
improper fraction

VOCABULARY

Choose the best term to complete each sentence.

1. The number 7 in $\frac{4}{7}$ is the ____ of the fraction. **denominator**
2. If the only number that divides both the numerator and the denominator is 1, then the fraction is in ____. **simplest form**
3. If the denominator is less than the numerator, then the number is a(n) ____. **improper fraction**

CONCEPTS AND SKILLS

Draw a picture to show each. (Lesson 1, pp. 490–491; Lesson 7, pp. 508–510)
Check that student drawings match the fractions indicated.

4. $\frac{6}{7}$ 5. $\frac{8}{8}$ 6. $1\frac{1}{3}$ 7. $\frac{14}{5}$

Write each fraction in simplest form. Then write another equivalent fraction. (Lessons 2–3, pp. 492–497) ***Possible equivalent fractions given.***

8. $\frac{6}{8}$ $\frac{3}{4}$; $\frac{9}{12}$ 9. $\frac{3}{9}$ $\frac{1}{3}$; $\frac{2}{6}$ 10. $\frac{4}{10}$ $\frac{2}{5}$; $\frac{6}{15}$ 11. $\frac{12}{20}$ $\frac{3}{5}$; $\frac{6}{10}$

Compare. Write >, <, or = for each ●. (Lesson 4, pp. 498–500)

12. $\frac{3}{10}$ ● $\frac{7}{10}$ **<** 13. $\frac{5}{25}$ ● $\frac{1}{5}$ **=** 14. $\frac{5}{8}$ ● $\frac{6}{16}$ **>** 15. $\frac{2}{2}$ ● $\frac{5}{6}$ **>**

Find the fractional part of each number. (Lesson 5, pp. 502–503)

16. $\frac{3}{5}$ of 15 **9** 17. $\frac{1}{4}$ of 8 **2** 18. $\frac{1}{3}$ of 21 **7**

PROBLEM SOLVING

Solve. (Lesson 6, pp. 504–507)

19. Mari collects books. One third of her books are fiction, $\frac{1}{6}$ are nature books, and 12 are mysteries. How many books are in Mari's collection? **24 books**
20. Cody bought some sports cards. One half were baseball cards, 18 were soccer cards, and $\frac{1}{8}$ were football cards. How many sports cards did Cody buy? **48 cards**

Write About It

Show You Understand

Bob wrote $\frac{13}{5}$ as a mixed number.

Bob

$\frac{13}{5}$ means "13 ÷ 5".

$13 \div 5 = 2$ R3 (5)13, −10, 3)

So $\frac{13}{5} = 3\frac{2}{5}$.

Explain what Bob did wrong. Then solve the problem correctly.

See Additional Answers.

512 Chapter 19 Chapter Review/Test

Chapter Review/Test Items	Objectives	Covered On Teacher's Edition Pages	Use These Reteaching Resources
1, 4–5, 16–18	**19A** Represent a fraction of a region, of a set, and of a number.	490A–491, 502A–503	Reteach Resources 19.1, 19.5 *Ways to Success* CD-ROM 19.1, 19.5 *Ways to Success* Skillsheets 162, 164
2, 8–11	**19B** Find equivalent fractions.	492A–496	Reteach Resources 19.2, 19.3 *Ways to Success* CD-ROM 19.2, 19.3 *Ways to Success* Skillsheet 165
12–15	**19C** Compare and order fractions.	498A–500	Reteach Resources 19.4 *Ways to Success* CD-ROM 19.4 *Ways to Success* Skillsheet 166
3, 6–7	**19D** Write mixed numbers.	508A–510	Reteach Resources 19.7 *Ways to Success* CD-ROM 19.7 *Ways to Success* Skillsheet 167
19–20	**19D** Solve problems using skills and strategies.	504A–506	Reteach Resources 19.6 *Ways to Success* CD-ROM 19.6 *Ways to Success* Skillsheet 168

Extra Practice

Set A (Lesson 1, pp. 490–491)

Write the fraction for the shaded part.

1. 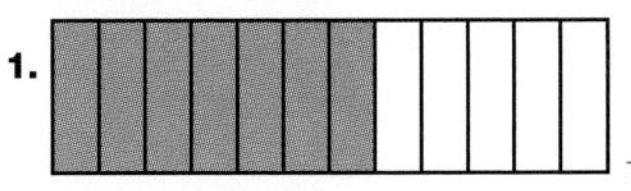 $\frac{7}{12}$

2. 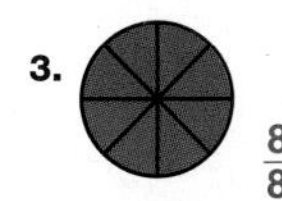 $\frac{5}{8}$

3. $\frac{8}{8}$

Set B (Lesson 3, pp. 494–497) *Possible equivalent fractions given.*

Write each fraction in simplest form. Then write another equivalent fraction.

1. $\frac{2}{16}$ $\frac{1}{8}$; $\frac{3}{24}$ 2. $\frac{6}{12}$ $\frac{1}{2}$; $\frac{2}{4}$ 3. $\frac{4}{20}$ $\frac{1}{5}$; $\frac{2}{10}$ 4. $\frac{3}{9}$ $\frac{1}{3}$; $\frac{2}{6}$ 5. $\frac{10}{15}$ $\frac{2}{3}$; $\frac{4}{6}$ 6. $\frac{2}{14}$ $\frac{1}{7}$; $\frac{3}{21}$

Set C (Lesson 4, pp. 498–500)

Compare. Write >, <, or = for each ⬭.

1. $\frac{2}{5} < \frac{3}{5}$ 2. $\frac{1}{2} > \frac{1}{6}$ 3. $\frac{5}{8} < \frac{3}{4}$ 4. $\frac{2}{3} > \frac{3}{9}$

Order the fractions from least to greatest.

5. $\frac{4}{10}$ $\frac{7}{10}$ $\frac{9}{10}$ $\frac{4}{10}$ $\frac{7}{10}$ $\frac{9}{10}$ 6. $\frac{3}{4}$ $\frac{2}{8}$ $\frac{2}{4}$ $\frac{2}{8}$ $\frac{2}{4}$ $\frac{3}{4}$ 7. $\frac{2}{5}$ $\frac{4}{15}$ $\frac{2}{3}$ $\frac{4}{15}$ $\frac{2}{5}$ $\frac{2}{3}$ 8. $\frac{1}{2}$ $\frac{3}{7}$ $\frac{5}{14}$ ($\frac{5}{14}$ $\frac{3}{7}$ $\frac{1}{2}$)

Set D (Lesson 5, pp. 502–503)

Find the fractional part of each number.

1. $\frac{2}{4}$ of 16 8 2. $\frac{2}{3}$ of 21 14 3. $\frac{1}{2}$ of 18 9 4. $\frac{3}{5}$ of 15 9 5. $\frac{3}{4}$ of 12 9

Set E (Lesson 7, pp. 508–510)

Write each as an improper fraction.

1. $3\frac{1}{5}$ $\frac{16}{5}$ 2. $4\frac{3}{4}$ $\frac{19}{4}$ 3. $2\frac{3}{7}$ $\frac{17}{7}$ 4. $5\frac{1}{2}$ $\frac{11}{2}$ 5. $1\frac{4}{9}$ $\frac{13}{9}$ 6. $3\frac{2}{3}$ $\frac{11}{3}$

Write a mixed number or a whole number for each improper fraction.

7. $\frac{11}{3}$ $3\frac{2}{3}$ 8. $\frac{9}{2}$ $4\frac{1}{2}$ 9. $\frac{21}{6}$ $3\frac{1}{2}$ 10. $\frac{20}{3}$ $6\frac{2}{3}$ 11. $\frac{8}{4}$ 2 12. $\frac{16}{5}$ $3\frac{1}{5}$

Extra Practice at **eduplace.com/map**

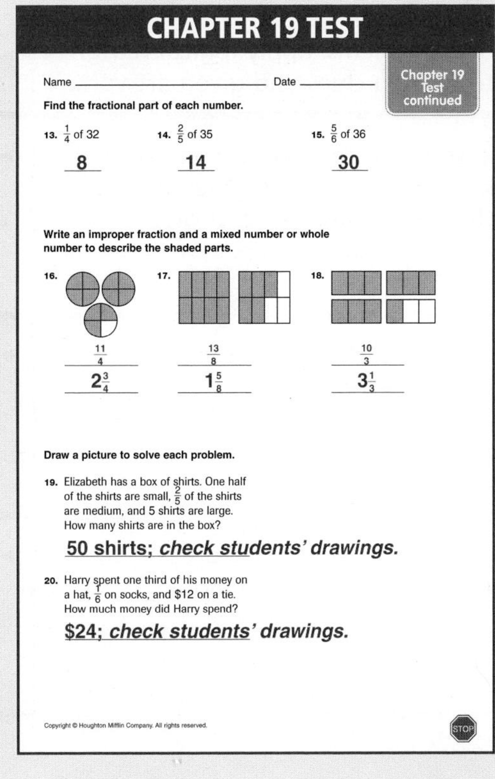

CHAPTER 19 TEST

Chapter 19 Test

Name ______ Date ______

Write a fraction for the shaded part. Then write a fraction for the part that is not shaded.

1. $\frac{5}{6}$; $\frac{1}{6}$ 2. $\frac{6}{10}$ or $\frac{3}{5}$; $\frac{4}{10}$ or $\frac{2}{5}$ 3. $\frac{0}{8}$ or 0; $\frac{8}{8}$ or 1

Decide whether the fractions are equivalent. Write *yes* or *no*.

4. $\frac{1}{3}$ and $\frac{5}{6}$ no 5. $\frac{2}{6}$ and $\frac{3}{9}$ yes 6. $\frac{4}{8}$ and $\frac{8}{16}$ yes

Possible equivalent fractions are given for Problems 7–9.

Write each fraction in simplest form. Then write another equivalent fraction.

7. $\frac{4}{6}$ $\frac{2}{3}$; $\frac{8}{12}$ 8. $\frac{12}{18}$ $\frac{2}{3}$; $\frac{24}{36}$ 9. $\frac{20}{60}$ $\frac{1}{3}$; $\frac{2}{6}$

Compare. Write >, <, or = for each ◯.

10. $\frac{3}{5} < \frac{5}{5}$ 11. $\frac{6}{8} > \frac{1}{4}$ 12. $\frac{5}{6} < \frac{8}{9}$

Go on

CHAPTER 19 TEST

Chapter 19 Test continued

Name ______ Date ______

Find the fractional part of each number.

13. $\frac{1}{4}$ of 32 8 14. $\frac{2}{5}$ of 35 14 15. $\frac{5}{6}$ of 36 30

Write an improper fraction and a mixed number or whole number to describe the shaded parts.

16. $\frac{11}{4}$; $2\frac{3}{4}$ 17. $\frac{13}{8}$; $1\frac{5}{8}$ 18. $\frac{10}{3}$; $3\frac{1}{3}$

Draw a picture to solve each problem.

19. Elizabeth has a box of shirts. One half of the shirts are small, $\frac{2}{5}$ of the shirts are medium, and 5 shirts are large. How many shirts are in the box?

50 shirts; *check students' drawings.*

20. Harry spent one third of his money on a hat, $\frac{1}{6}$ on socks, and \$12 on a tie. How much money did Harry spend?

\$24; *check students' drawings.*

STOP

CHAPTER 20

Planning Guide

Add and Subtract Fractions

Lesson	Overview	Objective/Vocabulary
1 Add and Subtract Fractions with Like Denominators p. 516A	► Use fraction strips to add and subtract fractions with like denominators. ► Write fraction sums and differences in simplest form.	► Add and subtract fractions that have the same denominators. like denominators
2 Add and Subtract Mixed Numbers p. 520A	► Add and subtract mixed numbers. ► Complete function tables and solve word problems to reinforce adding and subtracting mixed numbers.	► Add and subtract mixed numbers with like denominators.
3 Problem-Solving Application: Decide how to Write the Quotient p. 522A	► Decide how to write a quotient to solve a problem so that it makes sense. ► Depending on the situation and the remainder, learn to write the quotient as a mixed number.	► Decide how to write the quotient to solve a problem.
4 Estimate with Fractions p. 524A	► From the value of each term, estimate whether the sum of two fractions is less than or greater than 1.	► Estimate sums of fractions. estimate
5 Problem-Solving Decision: Choose a Method p. 526A	► Choose the most efficient way to solve a problem—mental math, paper and pencil, or calculator. ► To solve problems, apply logical reasoning to written clues and given artwork.	► Choose a method to solve a problem.
6 Hands On: Add Fractions with Unlike Denominators p. 528A	► Using fraction strips, add fractions with unlike denominators and match equivalent fraction strips to the original fraction strip to find the sum.	► Use models to add fractions that have different denominators. unlike denominator
7 Hands On: Subtract Fractions with Unlike Denominators p. 530A	► Using fraction strips, subtract fractions with unlike denominators.	► Use models to subtract fractions that have different denominators. unlike denominator
8 Problem-Solving Application: Use a Circle Graph p. 534A	► Solve problems with circle graphs, which resemble a fraction circle model.	► Use circle graphs to solve problems

Skills Trace: Add and Subtract Fractions		
Grade 3	**Grade 4**	**Grade 5**
• Add and subtract fractions with like denominators (ch. 19)	• Add and subtract fractions and mixed numbers with like denominators • Use models to add and subtract fractions with unlike denominators • Estimate fraction sums	• Add and subtract fractions and mixed numbers with like and unlike denominators (ch. 10) • Estimate fractions sums and differences (ch. 10)

Differentiated Instruction	Materials	NCTM Standards
▶ Differentiated Instruction activities, p. 516B ▶ *Chapter Challenges*, p. 115 *Ways to Success* CD-ROM 20.1 ▶ *Ways to Success* Skillsheet 172 Audio Tutor **2**/22 Listen and Understand	Fraction Pieces Transparency, blank transparency, Fraction pieces (Learning Tool 34)	**Number and Operations:** Use visual models, benchmarks, and equivalent forms to add and subtract commonly used fractions.
▶ Differentiated Instruction activities, p. 520B *Ways to Success* CD-ROM 20.2 ▶ *Ways to Success* Skillsheets 170, 173 Audio Tutor **2**/23 Listen and Understand		**Number and Operations:** Use visual models, benchmarks, and equivalent forms to add and subtract commonly used fractions.
▶ Differentiated Instruction activities, p. 522B ▶ *Chapter Challenges*, p. 117 *Ways to Success* CD-ROM 20.3 ▶ *Ways to Success* Skillsheet 177		**Problem Solving:** Solve problems that arise in mathematics and other contexts
▶ Differentiated Instruction activities, p. 524B *Ways to Success* CD-ROM 20.4 ▶ *Ways to Success* Skillsheet 174		**Number and Operations:** Develop and use strategies to estimate the results of computations involving fractions.
▶ Differentiated Instruction activities, p. 526B ▶ *Chapter Challenges*, p. 119 *Ways to Success* CD-ROM 20.5	Blank transparency	**Problem Solving:** Solve problems that arise in mathematics and other contexts.
▶ Differentiated Instruction activities, p. 528B *Ways to Success* CD-ROM 20.6 ▶ *Ways to Success* Skillsheet 175	Fraction Pieces Transparency, blank transparency, Fraction pieces (Learning Tool 34),	**Number and Operations:** Use visual models, benchmarks, and equivalent forms to add and subtract commonly used fractions.
▶ Differentiated Instruction activities, p. 530B *Ways to Success* CD-ROM 20.7 ▶ *Ways to Success* Skillsheet 176	Fraction pieces (Learning Tool 34), Fraction Pieces Transparency, blank transparency	**Number and Operations:** Use visual models, benchmarks, and equivalent forms to add and subtract commonly used fractions.
▶ Differentiated Instruction activities, p. 534B *Ways to Success* CD-ROM 20.8	Workmat 8	**Data Analysis and Probability:** Represent data using tables and graphs such as line plots, bar graphs, and line graphs.

Math Notes

Chapter Objectives

20A Add and subtract fractions and mixed numbers with like denominators.

20B Estimate sums of fractions.

20C Use models to add and subtract fractions with unlike denominators.

20D Solve problems using skills and strategies.

Mathematical Background

Add and Subtract Fractions

To add and subtract fractions that have the same denominator, find the sum or difference of the numerators and keep the same denominator. Then express the answer in simplest form.

To add or subtract fractions with unlike denominators, one must first find equivalent fractions with common denominators. At this level, students add and subtract with fraction pieces. Using fraction pieces provides students with the conceptual basis they will need in the future when they will add and subtract fractions using the least common denominator (LCD).

The following model can be helpful.

Find $\frac{2}{3} + \frac{1}{2}$.

Always use a 1-whole fraction piece as a reference.

Use fraction pieces to model $\frac{2}{3} + \frac{1}{2}$.

Find fraction pieces that fit exactly $\frac{2}{3} + \frac{1}{2}$.

Count the number of these fraction pieces. There are seven $\frac{1}{6}$ fraction pieces, so $\frac{2}{3} + \frac{1}{2} = \frac{7}{6}$, or $1\frac{1}{6}$.

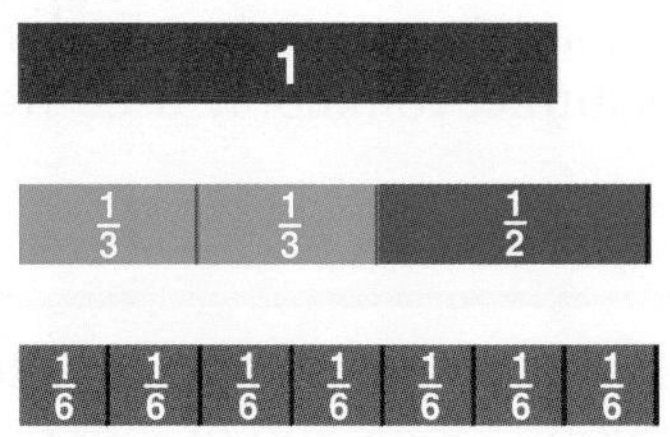

Research-Based Teaching

Research, Mathematics Content, and Language Intervention

Research supports the belief that students are better able to develop meaning for symbols and procedures when they draw on referents that are meaningful for them. It is not enough to teach concepts and procedures. We need to understand how students are internalizing what is being taught and develop ways to help them use their conceptual knowledge when working through the problems. See *Professional Resources Handbook, Grade 4,* Unit 7.

For more ideas relating to Unit 7, see the Teacher Support Handbook at the back of this Teacher's Edition.

Language Intervention

In East Asian countries, children learn that just as numbers can be composed and decomposed as sets and subsets, fractions can be composed and decomposed as well. For further explanation, see "Mathematical Language and Fractions" in the Professional Resources Handbook, Grade 4.

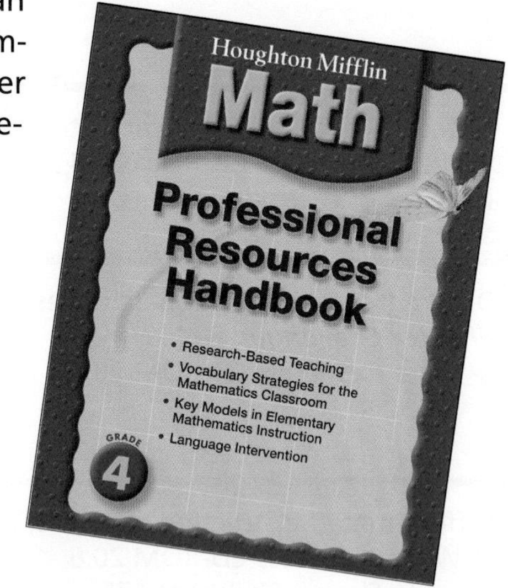

Chapter Activities

Assesing Prior Knowledge

Pairs	15 minutes
Objective	Reinforce vocabulary related to fractions.
Materials	None
Visual, Tactual	

Fraction Words

- Write some fraction words on the board with the letters mixed up. Tell students these are fraction words.

dixme (mixed)

roppimer (improper)

ratenumor (numerator)

acfronit (fraction)

- Have students work in pairs or small groups to figure out the correct spelling for each fraction word.
- Then have them write a definition and give an example for each word. Call on students to say the fraction words and give their definitions.

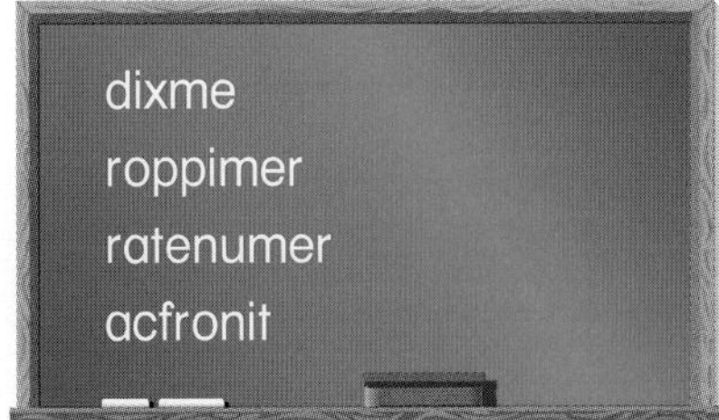

Ongoing Skill Activity

Small Groups	45 minutes
Objective	Add fractions and mixed numbers.
Materials	12 index cards
Visual, Auditory	

Mixed-Number Measurements

- Tell students to use inch rulers to measure the dimensions of a small square or rectangular object in the classroom to the nearest $\frac{1}{2}$, $\frac{1}{4}$, or $\frac{1}{8}$ inch.
- Record the dimensions of the four sides and then add them to find the perimeter.
- Measure around the object again, going around it in a continuous fashion, to see how near the measurement is to the calculated sum.

Math Expressions

Pairs	25 minutes
Objective	Use unit fractions to estimate fractions and fraction sums.
Materials	Work with Unit Fractions Copymaster, scissors
Tactual, Visual	

Estimate Fractions and Fraction Sums

This activity uses instructional practices from *Math Expressions* with the content of this chapter.

- Distribute a copy of Working with Unit Fractions Copymaster to pairs. Have them cut out each strip and the dashed lines within the strips.
- Have students line up in one column one each of: 1, $\frac{1}{2}$, $\frac{1}{3}$, $\frac{1}{4}$, $\frac{1}{5}$, $\frac{1}{6}$, $\frac{1}{7}$, $\frac{1}{8}$, $\frac{1}{9}$, $\frac{1}{10}$. Have students compare the sizes of the unit fractions.
- Have students compare each of the following to $\frac{1}{2}$ by forming a row of multiple unit fractions beneath the $\frac{1}{2}$ piece: $\frac{3}{5}$, $\frac{3}{4}$, $\frac{5}{6}$, $\frac{2}{7}$, $\frac{3}{8}$, $\frac{5}{10}$. Have them record statements using $>$, $<$, or $=$.
- Display this exercise for students to estimate whether the sum is greater or less than 1: $\frac{3}{8} + \frac{2}{5}$. Model how to compare each fraction to $\frac{1}{2}$ and decide if adding each fraction will give a total of less than or greater than 1 whole.

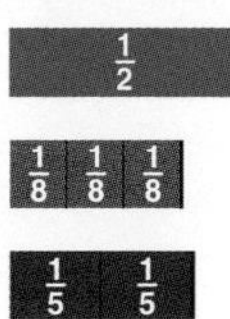

- Have pairs work to estimate whether other sums are greater or less than 1.

Starting Chapter 20

Investigation

Using Data

Have students work in small groups to do the activity on page 514.

- To extend the investigation, provide the following problem.
- Use the table on page 514. How long is Family Fun day, from the beginning of the hike to the river until the arrival at camp? ($5\frac{3}{4}$ hours). If the families begin the hike to the river at 10:30 A.M. and they participate in all the activities, at what time should they arrive at camp? (4:15 P.M.)

For more information about projects and investigations,

Visit **Education Place**® **www.eduplace.com/mat**

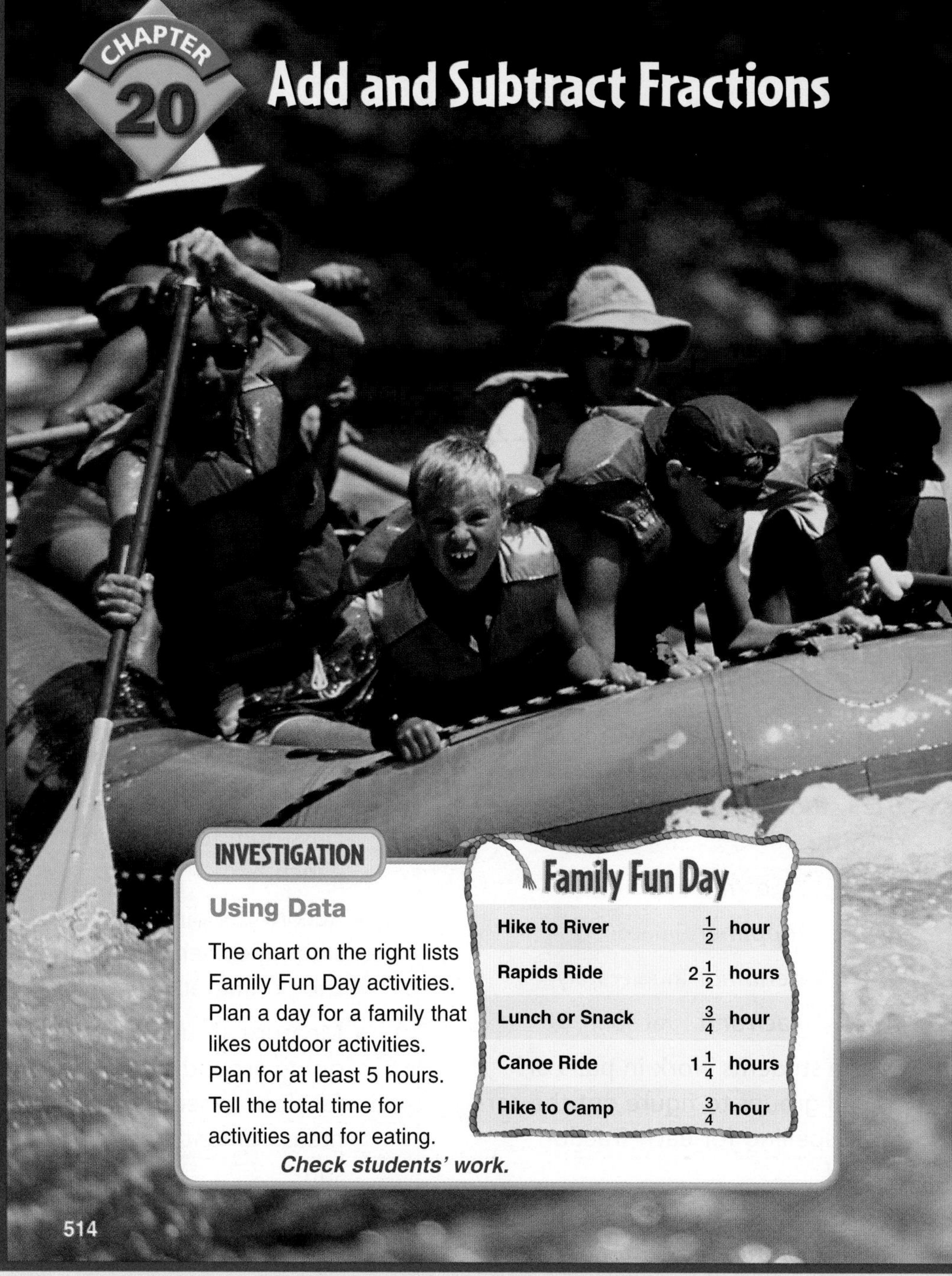

CHAPTER 20
Add and Subtract Fractions
INVESTIGATION
Using Data
The chart on the right lists Family Fun Day activities. Plan a day for a family that likes outdoor activities. Plan for at least 5 hours. Tell the total time for activities and for eating.
Check students' work.
Family Fun Day
Hike to River $\frac{1}{2}$ hour
Rapids Ride $2\frac{1}{2}$ hours
Lunch or Snack $\frac{3}{4}$ hour
Canoe Ride $1\frac{1}{4}$ hours
Hike to Camp $\frac{3}{4}$ hour
514

Chapter 20 Prerequisite Skills Pretest

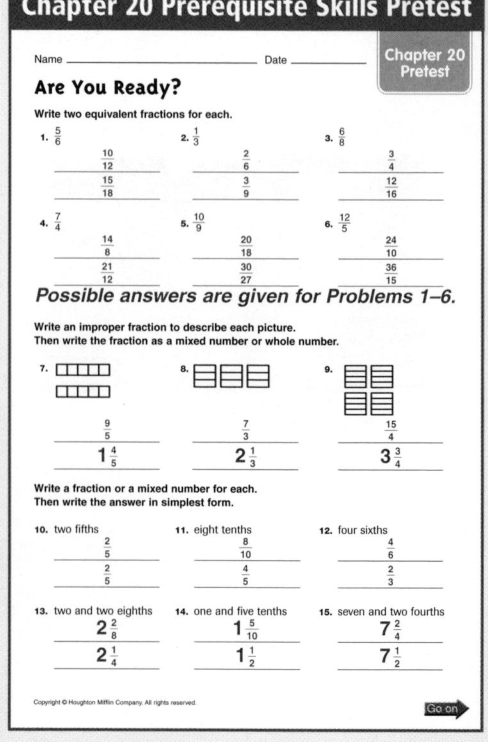

Name ______ Date ______ Chapter 20 Pretest

Are You Ready?

Write two equivalent fractions for each.

1. $\frac{5}{6}$ $\frac{10}{12}$, $\frac{15}{18}$
2. $\frac{1}{3}$ $\frac{2}{6}$, $\frac{3}{9}$
3. $\frac{6}{8}$ $\frac{3}{4}$, $\frac{12}{16}$
4. $\frac{7}{4}$ $\frac{14}{8}$, $\frac{21}{12}$
5. $\frac{10}{9}$ $\frac{20}{18}$, $\frac{30}{27}$
6. $\frac{12}{5}$ $\frac{24}{10}$, $\frac{36}{15}$

Possible answers are given for Problems 1–6.

Write an improper fraction to describe each picture. Then write the fraction as a mixed number or whole number.

7. $\frac{9}{5}$, $1\frac{4}{5}$
8. $\frac{7}{3}$, $2\frac{1}{3}$
9. $\frac{15}{4}$, $3\frac{3}{4}$

Write a fraction or a mixed number for each. Then write the answer in simplest form.

10. two fifths $\frac{2}{5}$, $\frac{2}{5}$
11. eight tenths $\frac{8}{10}$, $\frac{4}{5}$
12. four sixths $\frac{4}{6}$, $\frac{2}{3}$
13. two and two eighths $2\frac{2}{8}$, $2\frac{1}{4}$
14. one and five tenths $1\frac{5}{10}$, $1\frac{1}{2}$
15. seven and two fourths $7\frac{2}{4}$, $7\frac{1}{2}$

Go on

✓ Use What You Know

Use this page to review and remember what you need to know for this chapter.

VOCABULARY

Vocabulary
mixed number
simplest form
whole number
equivalent fractions

Choose the best term to complete each sentence.

1. The fraction $\frac{1}{3}$ is in ____. **simplest form**
2. A number made up of a whole number and a fraction is called a ____. **mixed number**
3. Fractions that name the same amount are ____. **equivalent fractions**

CONCEPTS AND SKILLS

Write two equivalent fractions for each. *Possible answers given.*

4. $\frac{3}{4}$ $\frac{6}{8}, \frac{9}{12}$
5. $\frac{1}{3}$ $\frac{2}{6}, \frac{3}{9}$
6. $\frac{4}{8}$ $\frac{1}{2}, \frac{2}{4}$
7. $\frac{2}{5}$ $\frac{4}{10}, \frac{6}{15}$
8. $\frac{1}{8}$ $\frac{2}{16}, \frac{3}{24}$
9. $\frac{4}{6}$ $\frac{2}{3}, \frac{8}{12}$
10. $\frac{8}{8}$ $\frac{1}{1}, \frac{2}{2}$
11. $\frac{4}{14}$ $\frac{2}{7}, \frac{8}{28}$
12. $\frac{5}{9}$ $\frac{10}{18}, \frac{15}{27}$
13. $\frac{2}{9}$ $\frac{4}{18}, \frac{8}{36}$

Write an improper fraction to describe each picture. Then write the fraction as a mixed number or whole number.

14. 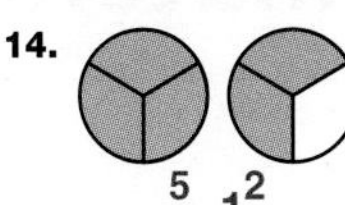 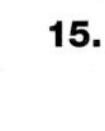 $\frac{5}{3}, 1\frac{2}{3}$

15. 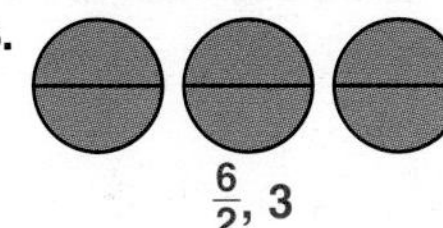 $\frac{6}{2}, 3$

16. 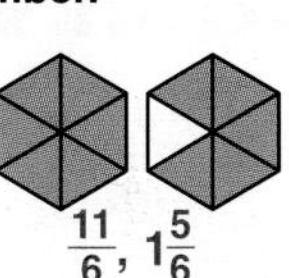 $\frac{11}{6}, 1\frac{5}{6}$

Write a fraction or mixed number for each. Then write the answer in simplest form.

17. six eighths $\frac{6}{8}, \frac{3}{4}$
18. ten fourths $\frac{10}{4}$ or $2\frac{2}{4}$; $2\frac{1}{2}$
19. one and three sixths $1\frac{3}{6}, 1\frac{1}{2}$

Write About It

20. Which is greater, $\frac{1}{3}$ of 12 or $\frac{1}{4}$ of 20? Use pictures, symbols, or words to explain your answer.

$\frac{1}{4}$ of 20; Explanations should include 4 parts in $\frac{1}{3}$ of 12 and 5 parts in $\frac{1}{4}$ of 20.

Facts Practice, See Page 668.

Chapter 20 New Content Pretest

Name ______________ Date ________ Chapter 20 Pretest continued

Check What You Know

Add or subtract. Write your answer in simplest form.

1. $\frac{3}{8} + \frac{3}{8}$ = $\frac{3}{4}$
2. $\frac{10}{12} - \frac{5}{12}$ = $\frac{5}{12}$
3. $2\frac{10}{12} + 1\frac{1}{6}$ = **4**
4. $6\frac{3}{4} - 2\frac{1}{4} =$ **$4\frac{1}{2}$**
5. $3\frac{5}{7} + 2\frac{2}{7} =$ **6**
6. $1\frac{1}{8} + 2\frac{3}{8} =$ **$3\frac{1}{2}$**

Estimate each sum. Write *greater than 1* or *less than 1*.

7. $\frac{1}{5} + \frac{2}{9}$ **less than 1**
8. $\frac{4}{7} + \frac{3}{5}$ **greater than 1**
9. $\frac{1}{4} + \frac{1}{8}$ **less than 1**

Find each sum. Draw fraction pieces to help you.

10. $\frac{3}{4} + \frac{1}{2} =$ **$1\frac{1}{4}$**
11. $\frac{7}{12} + \frac{1}{4} =$ $\frac{5}{6}$
12. $\frac{2}{3} + \frac{1}{4} =$ $\frac{11}{12}$

Draw fraction pieces to help you find each difference.

13. $\frac{9}{10} - \frac{3}{5} =$ $\frac{3}{10}$
14. $\frac{1}{2} - \frac{1}{8} =$ $\frac{3}{8}$
15. $\frac{5}{6} - \frac{3}{4} =$ $\frac{1}{12}$

Go on

Chapter 20 New Content Pretest

Name ______________ Date ________ Chapter 20 Pretest continued

Mark makes $48 each day. The circle graph shows how Mark spends that money. Use the graph to solve Problems 16–18.

Money Spent

Savings	$\frac{1}{8}$
Entertainment	$\frac{1}{8}$
Food	$\frac{1}{4}$
Bills	$\frac{1}{2}$

16. How much does Mark spend on entertainment each day? **$6**
17. In a day, how much does Mark spend on bills and food combined? **$36**
18. In a day, how much more does Mark spend on food than he puts in savings? **$6**

Solve. Explain how you decided to write each quotient.

19. There are 80 students going on a field trip. Seven students will ride in each van. The remaining students will ride in cars. How many students will ride in cars? **3 students; explanations will vary.**

Solve. Explain which method you chose.

20. Elizabeth bought $1\frac{2}{5}$ pounds of oranges, $2\frac{1}{5}$ pounds of apples, and $2\frac{2}{5}$ pounds of bananas. How many pounds of fruit did Elizabeth buy? **6 pounds; methods will vary.**

STOP

Use What You Know

Use this page for informal assessment and review of prerequisite skills.

- Items 1–3: Use math vocabulary
- Items 4–13: Write equivalent fractions
- Items 14–16: Write improper fractions
- Items 17–19: Write fractions or mixed numbers in simplest form
- Item 20: Find a fractional part of a number

Customize Your Instruction

Use the Chapter Pretest in the Unit Resource folder to help customize and pace instruction.

Objectives and Resources

► Prerequisite Skills Pretest

- Items 1–6: Write equivalent fractions.
- Items 7–9: Write improper fractions or mixed numbers.
- Items 10–15: Write fractions or mixed numbers in simplest form.

► New Content Pretest

- Items 1–6: Add and subtract fractions and mixed numbers with like denominators.
- Items 7–9: Estimate fraction sums.
- Items 10–15: Use models to add and subtract fractions with unlike denominators.
- Items 16–20: Solve problems.

► For Students Having Difficulty

- *Ways to Success* CD-ROM 19F, 20C
- *Ways to Success* Skillsheets 169–171

► For Students Having Success

- Enrichment 20.1–20.8

► For Mathematically Promising Students

Explore: Fraction Patterns page 115, after Lesson 1

Extend: Fraction Sums page 117, after Lesson 3

Connect: Building a Garden page 119, after Lesson 5

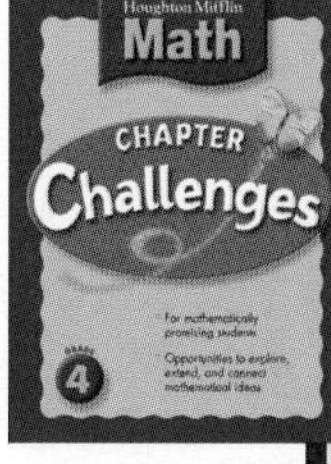

Lesson 20.1

Add and Subtract Fractions With Like Denominators

Planning

Lesson Objective Add and subtract fractions that have the same denominators.

Math Background

When fractions have like denominators, students can use skills they learned when adding whole numbers. In this case, they add the numerators, while keeping the denominators the same.

Technology Resources

- Audio Tutor **2**/22 Listen and Understand
- *Ways to Success* CD-ROM 20.1
- Education Place: Extra Practice, eGlossary, eManipulatives, eGames www.eduplace.com/map

Problem of the Day

Place the digits 0, 2, 4, and 5 into the squares below to make the greatest possible product.

□□□ × □ = ___

(420 × 5 = 2,100)

Spiral Review

Write each improper fraction as a whole number or mixed number.

1. $\frac{6}{5}$ ($1\frac{1}{5}$)	**2.** $\frac{8}{3}$ ($2\frac{2}{3}$)
3. $\frac{20}{5}$ (4)	**4.** $\frac{7}{4}$ ($1\frac{3}{4}$)
5. $\frac{12}{7}$ ($1\frac{5}{7}$)	**6.** $\frac{9}{3}$ (3)

Lesson Quiz

Add or subtract. Write your answer in simplest form.

1. $\frac{3}{10} + \frac{4}{10}$ ($\frac{7}{10}$)	**2.** $\frac{1}{3} + \frac{1}{3}$ ($\frac{2}{3}$)
3. $\frac{5}{9} + \frac{5}{9}$ ($1\frac{1}{9}$)	**4.** $\frac{5}{8} + \frac{7}{8}$ ($1\frac{1}{2}$)

NCTM Standards

Number and Operations: Use visual models, benchmarks, and equivalent forms to add and subtract commonly used fractions.

Getting Started

Building Math Vocabulary

like denominators denominators in two or more fractions that are the same

Use the vocabulary card for ***like denominators.*** Say the fraction $\frac{2}{9}$. Ask students to suggest a fraction with a like denominator. ($\frac{1}{9}$, $\frac{4}{9}$, etc.) Ask them to suggest an improper fraction with a like denominator. ($\frac{10}{9}$, $\frac{13}{9}$, etc.) Repeat for fractions with other denominators.

Model Addition With Like Denominators

Whole Class	15 minutes
Objective	Add fractions with like denominators.
Materials	Fraction Pieces Transparency, blank transparency
Auditory, Visual	

- Use the 1 fraction piece and the $\frac{1}{8}$ fraction pieces cut out from the Fraction Pieces Transparency.
- Place the 1 fraction piece at the top of a blank transparency. Place three $\frac{1}{8}$ fraction pieces beneath it, with the first one aligned at the left. **What fraction names this amount?** ($\frac{3}{8}$)
- Place two $\frac{1}{8}$ fraction pieces to the right of the three $\frac{1}{8}$ fraction pieces. **What have I added?** ($\frac{2}{8}$) Write $\frac{3}{8} + \frac{2}{8}$ under the fraction pieces. **When we add fractions with like denominators, we just add the numerators. What is the sum?** ($\frac{5}{8}$) Write $= \frac{5}{8}$.
- Model $\frac{5}{8} - \frac{2}{8}$ with a similar process. Show the subtraction by crossing out two $\frac{1}{8}$ fraction pieces. Write $\frac{5}{8} - \frac{2}{8} = \frac{3}{8}$. **When we subtract fractions with like denominators, we just subtract the numerators.**
- Tell students that the lesson will explain several different ways to add and subtract fractions with the same denominators.

Differentiated Instruction

English Learners

Small Groups	10 minutes
Objective	Use fraction models to practice addition and subtraction with like denominators.
Materials	Index cards
Visual	

Early Production

- Before ***Guided Practice,*** have students practice addition and subtraction with fraction models.
- Do the ***Intervention*** activity found below. Students should find the sums and differences and write them on the index cards. Ask students to verbalize each written equation.

Intermediate/Advanced

- English Learner Resource 20.1
- English Learner Handbook

Intervention

Small Groups	10 minutes
Objective	Model adding and subracting fractions with like denominators.
Materials	Index cards
Tactual, Visual	

Have students model adding and subtracting fractions with like denominators using a different model, a fraction circle divided into fifths.

- Have students write problems like these on index cards: $\frac{2}{5} + \frac{1}{5}$, $\frac{3}{5} + \frac{2}{5}$, $\frac{4}{5} - \frac{2}{5}$, $\frac{3}{5} - \frac{1}{5}$, and $\frac{5}{5} - \frac{5}{5}$.
- Have students work together to model each subtraction or addition using a fraction circle.
- Vary the activity by having students find sums and differences with fraction circles in sixths, eighths, and tenths.

Other Resources

- *Ways to Success* CD-ROM 20.1

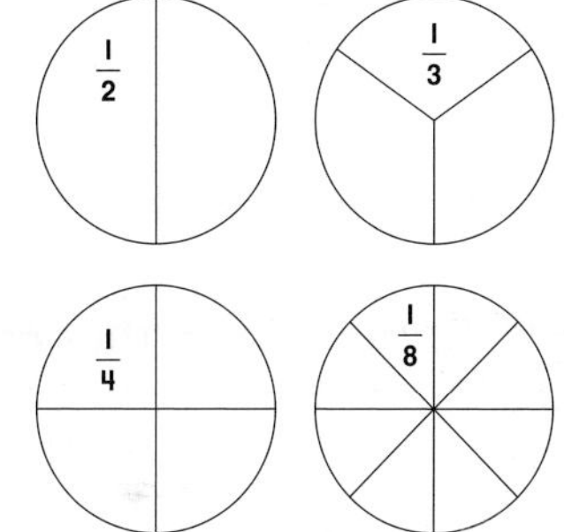

Special Needs

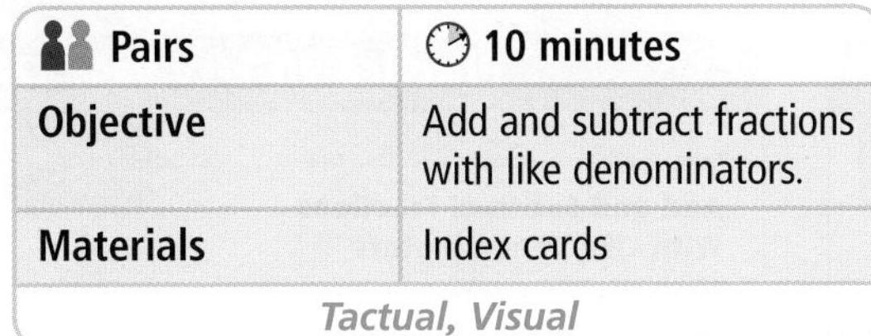

Pairs	10 minutes
Objective	Add and subtract fractions with like denominators.
Materials	Index cards
Tactual, Visual	

- Have pairs prepare several 3-card sets (fraction, fraction, sum). Tell them that all fractions in a set must have like denominators. Have them also make a "−" card and a "+" card.
- Have pairs keep their "−" and "+" cards, but shuffle their deck of other cards and swap decks with another pair. Pairs must use the cards to make true equations.

Music Connection

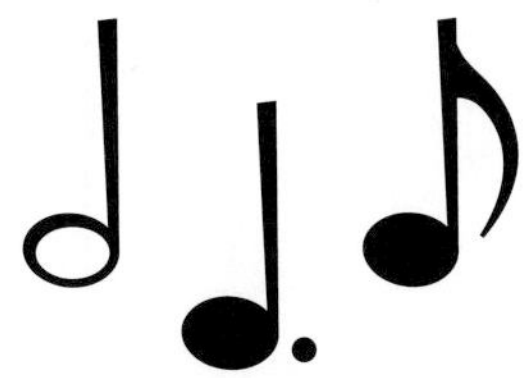

Tell students that fraction concepts are at the heart of Western musical notation. Invite the music teacher or a student who can read music to present a brief lesson on whole notes, half notes, quarter notes, and eighth notes. More musically advanced students can explore the value of the dot that may appear after some notes. (The dot increases the value of that note by half.)

Facts Practice

Have students review their whole-number addition facts with a partner: Have each pair write the numbers 1 through 20 on index cards or squares of paper. Have students take turns drawing a number, then writing two addends that have that number as their sum.

❶ Introduce

Read the objective to students and tell them that in this lesson they will add and subtract fractions with like denominators using fraction pieces and they will also write fraction sums and differences in simplest form. Have students discuss the meaning of *simplest form*.

❷ Teach

Learn About It

Begin by having a volunteer read aloud the opening problem.

- **How do we know that the problem can be solved by adding?** (Possible answer: The question asks "how far did they row together?")
- For ***Step 1***, work through how to add $\frac{4}{8} + \frac{2}{8}$. **When adding fractions with like denominators, why don't we find the sum of the denominators?** (The denominator shows the parts into which the whole is divided, 8. The whole has 8 parts, not 16.)
- For ***Step 2***, work through how to simplify the sum. **How do we know that $\frac{6}{8}$ can be simplified?** (Possible answer: Even numbers are divisible by 2.)
- Work through the ***Other Examples*** with students. Invite a volunteer to model these on the overhead, using the fraction pieces.

Common Error

- **Adding or subtracting denominators**
- **Intervention** Help students avoid this error by thinking of, for example, $\frac{3}{4}$ as 3 fourths, $\frac{2}{5}$ as 2 fifths, $\frac{5}{6}$ as 5 sixths, and so on.
- **Not expressing answers in simplest form**
- **Intervention** Remind students that if any number other than 1 can divide both the numerator and the denominator with a remainder of 0, the fraction is not in simplest form.

Lesson 1

Audio Tutor 2/22 Listen and Understand

Add and Subtract Fractions With Like Denominators

Vocabulary
like denominators

Objective Add and subtract fractions that have the same denominators.

Learn About It

Adam and Josh took turns rowing their boat around the pond. Adam rowed $\frac{4}{8}$ of a mile, and Josh rowed $\frac{2}{8}$ of a mile. How far did they row together?

You can add the fractions with **like denominators** to find the distance they rowed.

Add. $\frac{4}{8} + \frac{2}{8} = ■$

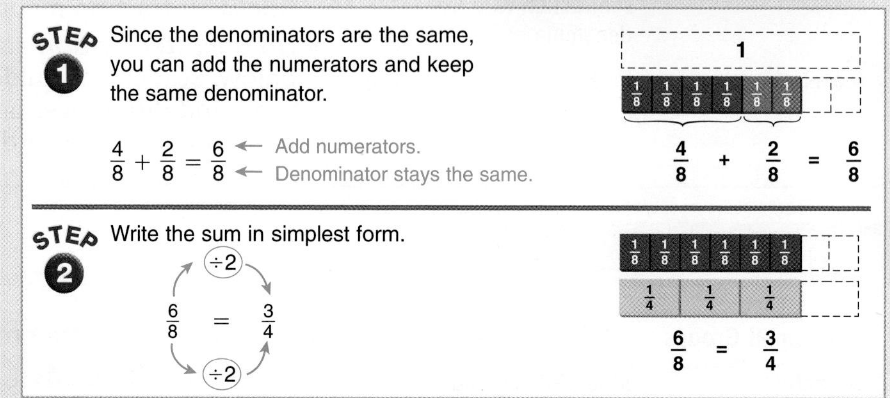

STEP 1 Since the denominators are the same, you can add the numerators and keep the same denominator.

$\frac{4}{8} + \frac{2}{8} = \frac{6}{8}$ ← Add numerators. ← Denominator stays the same.

STEP 2 Write the sum in simplest form.

$\frac{6}{8} = \frac{3}{4}$ (÷2, ÷2)

Solution: Together they rowed $\frac{3}{4}$ of a mile.

Other Examples

A. Sum equal to 1

$\frac{2}{6} + \frac{4}{6} = \frac{6}{6} = 1$

1
1/6 1/6 1/6 1/6 1/6 1/6
2/6 4/6

B. Sum greater than 1

$\frac{2}{5} + \frac{4}{5} = \frac{6}{5} = 1\frac{1}{5}$

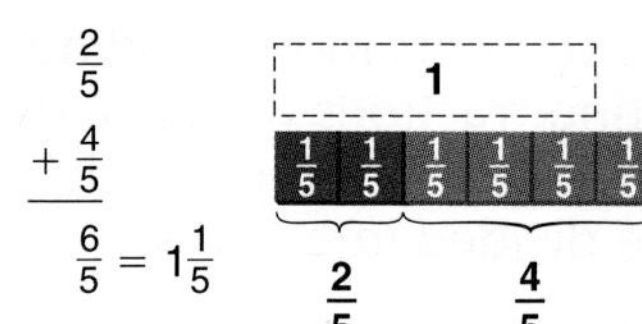

516

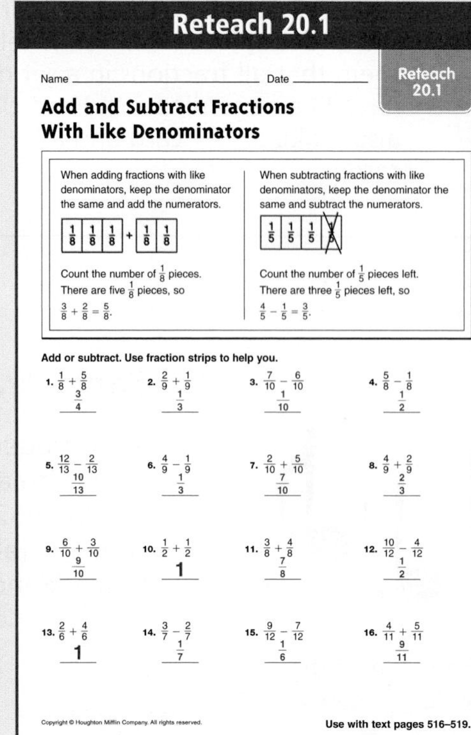

Reteach 20.1

Name ________ Date ________ Reteach 20.1

Add and Subtract Fractions With Like Denominators

When adding fractions with like denominators, keep the denominator the same and add the numerators.

1/8 1/8 1/8 + 1/8 1/8

Count the number of $\frac{1}{8}$ pieces. There are five $\frac{1}{8}$ pieces, so $\frac{3}{8} + \frac{2}{8} = \frac{5}{8}$.

When subtracting fractions with like denominators, keep the denominator the same and subtract the numerators.

1/5 1/5 1/5 1/5

Count the number of $\frac{1}{5}$ pieces left. There are three $\frac{1}{5}$ pieces left, so $\frac{4}{5} - \frac{1}{5} = \frac{3}{5}$.

Add or subtract. Use fraction strips to help you.

1. $\frac{1}{8} + \frac{5}{8}$ $\frac{3}{4}$
2. $\frac{2}{9} + \frac{1}{9}$ $\frac{1}{3}$
3. $\frac{7}{10} - \frac{6}{10}$ $\frac{1}{10}$
4. $\frac{5}{8} - \frac{1}{8}$ $\frac{1}{2}$
5. $\frac{12}{13} - \frac{2}{13}$ $\frac{10}{13}$
6. $\frac{4}{9} - \frac{1}{9}$ $\frac{1}{3}$
7. $\frac{2}{10} + \frac{5}{10}$ $\frac{7}{10}$
8. $\frac{4}{9} + \frac{2}{9}$ $\frac{2}{3}$
9. $\frac{6}{10} + \frac{3}{10}$ $\frac{9}{10}$
10. $\frac{1}{2} + \frac{1}{2}$ 1
11. $\frac{3}{8} + \frac{4}{8}$ $\frac{7}{8}$
12. $\frac{10}{12} - \frac{4}{12}$ $\frac{1}{2}$
13. $\frac{2}{6} + \frac{4}{6}$ 1
14. $\frac{3}{7} - \frac{2}{7}$ $\frac{1}{7}$
15. $\frac{9}{12} - \frac{7}{12}$ $\frac{1}{6}$
16. $\frac{4}{11} + \frac{5}{11}$ $\frac{9}{11}$

Use with text pages 516–519.

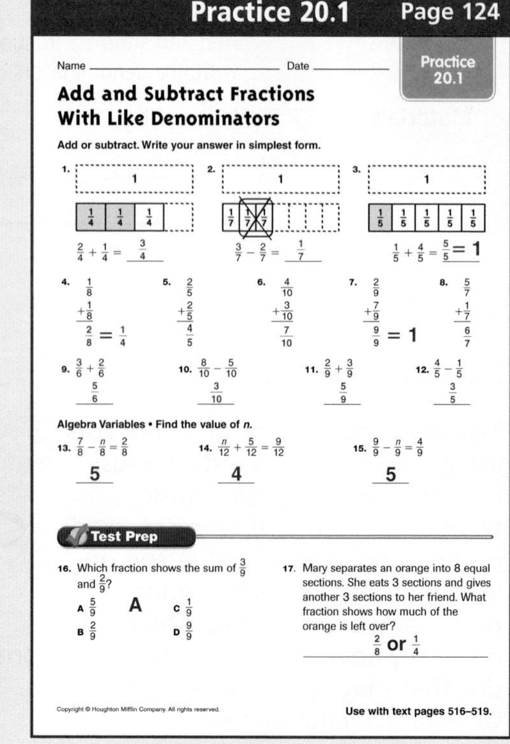

Practice 20.1 Page 124

Name ________ Date ________ Practice 20.1

Add and Subtract Fractions With Like Denominators

Add or subtract. Write your answer in simplest form.

1. $\frac{2}{4} + \frac{1}{4} = \frac{3}{4}$
2. $\frac{3}{7} - \frac{2}{7} = \frac{1}{7}$
3. $\frac{1}{5} + \frac{4}{5} = \frac{5}{5} = 1$
4. $\frac{1}{8} + \frac{1}{8} = \frac{2}{8} = \frac{1}{4}$
5. $\frac{2}{5} + \frac{2}{5} = \frac{4}{5}$
6. $\frac{4}{10} + \frac{3}{10} = \frac{7}{10}$
7. $\frac{2}{9} + \frac{7}{9} = \frac{9}{9} = 1$
8. $\frac{5}{7} + \frac{1}{7} = \frac{6}{7}$
9. $\frac{3}{6} + \frac{2}{6}$ $\frac{5}{6}$
10. $\frac{8}{10} - \frac{5}{10}$ $\frac{3}{10}$
11. $\frac{2}{9} + \frac{3}{9}$ $\frac{5}{9}$
12. $\frac{4}{5} - \frac{1}{5}$ $\frac{3}{5}$

Algebra Variables • Find the value of *n*.

13. $\frac{7}{8} - \frac{n}{8} = \frac{2}{8}$ 5
14. $\frac{n}{12} + \frac{5}{12} = \frac{9}{12}$ 4
15. $\frac{9}{9} - \frac{n}{9} = \frac{4}{9}$ 5

Test Prep

16. Which fraction shows the sum of $\frac{3}{9}$ and $\frac{2}{9}$?
A $\frac{5}{9}$ B $\frac{2}{9}$ C $\frac{1}{9}$ D $\frac{9}{9}$
A

17. Mary separates an orange into 8 equal sections. She eats 3 sections and gives another 3 sections to her friend. What fraction shows how much of the orange is left over?
$\frac{2}{8}$ or $\frac{1}{4}$

Use with text pages 516–519.

▶ You can also subtract fractions with **like denominators**.

Subtract. $\frac{4}{8} - \frac{2}{8} = \blacksquare$

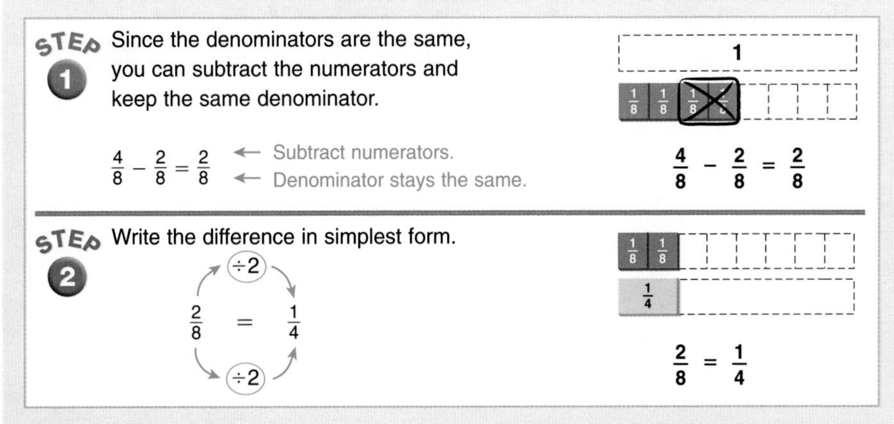

STEP 1 Since the denominators are the same, you can subtract the numerators and keep the same denominator.

$\frac{4}{8} - \frac{2}{8} = \frac{2}{8}$ ← Subtract numerators. ← Denominator stays the same.

$\frac{4}{8} - \frac{2}{8} = \frac{2}{8}$

STEP 2 Write the difference in simplest form.

$\frac{2}{8} = \frac{1}{4}$ (÷2 numerator and denominator)

$\frac{2}{8} = \frac{1}{4}$

Solution: $\frac{4}{8} - \frac{2}{8} = \frac{1}{4}$

Guided Practice

Add or subtract. Use the fraction pieces to help you.

1. 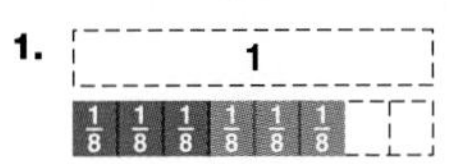 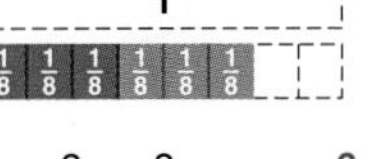

$\frac{3}{8} + \frac{3}{8} = \blacksquare$ **$\frac{6}{8}$ or $\frac{3}{4}$**

2. 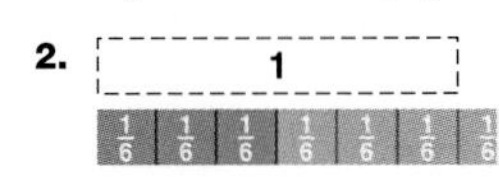 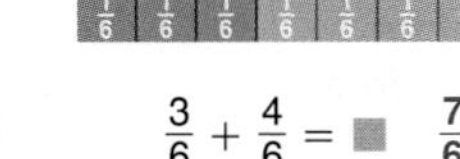

$\frac{3}{6} + \frac{4}{6} = \blacksquare$ **$\frac{7}{6}$ or $1\frac{1}{6}$**

Ask Yourself

- Should I add or subtract the numerators?
- Do I need to simplify the answer?

3. 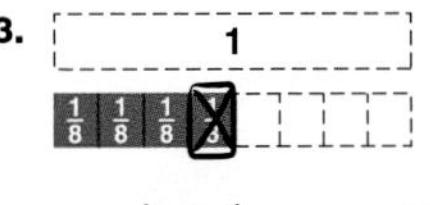

$\frac{4}{8} - \frac{1}{8} = \blacksquare$ **$\frac{3}{8}$**

4. 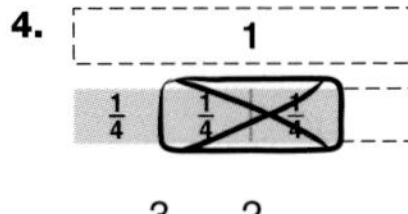 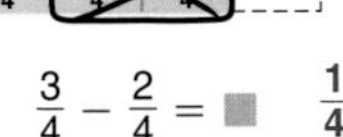

$\frac{3}{4} - \frac{2}{4} = \blacksquare$ **$\frac{1}{4}$**

5. 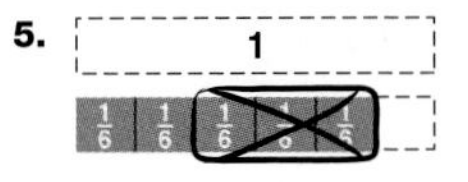

$\frac{5}{6} - \frac{3}{6} = \blacksquare$ **$\frac{2}{6}$ or $\frac{1}{3}$**

Add or subtract. Write your answer in simplest form.

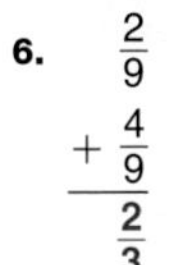

6. $\frac{2}{9} + \frac{4}{9}$ **$\frac{2}{3}$**

7. $\frac{4}{6} - \frac{2}{6}$ **$\frac{1}{3}$**

8. $\frac{8}{10} + \frac{9}{10}$ **$1\frac{7}{10}$**

9. $\frac{10}{11} - \frac{5}{11}$ **$\frac{5}{11}$**

10. $\frac{10}{12} - \frac{4}{12}$ **$\frac{1}{2}$**

Explain Your Thinking ▶ For like fractions, why can you add or subtract the numerators and keep the same denominator? **Like fractions have the same number of equal parts.**

- For ***Steps 1 and 2*** on page 517, work through how to subtract $\frac{2}{8}$ from $\frac{4}{8}$ and express the difference in simplest form. **How do we use fraction pieces to model finding the difference?** (by crossing out the number of fraction pieces we are subtracting and then counting how many pieces remain)
- You may wish to provide another subtraction example for students to work through.

Guided Practice

Have students complete **Exercises 1–10** as you observe. Remind them to use the ***Ask Yourself*** questions to help. Give students the opportunity to talk about the question in ***Explain Your Thinking***.

Enrichment 20.1

Name ____________ Date ________ Enrichment 20.1

Mystery Code

Solve. Write each sum or difference in simplest form. Write the letter of the problem on the blank with the correct answer. Read the mystery message.

A. $1 - \frac{7}{10}$ = $\frac{3}{10}$ C. $\frac{1}{8} + \frac{1}{8}$ = $\frac{1}{4}$ F. $\frac{5}{12} + \frac{1}{12}$ = $\frac{1}{2}$

I. $\frac{11}{16} - \frac{5}{16}$ = $\frac{3}{8}$ N. $\frac{2}{3} + \frac{2}{3}$ = $1\frac{1}{3}$ O. $\frac{9}{10} - \frac{7}{10}$ = $\frac{1}{5}$

R. $\frac{2}{9} + \frac{3}{9}$ = $\frac{5}{9}$ S. $\frac{7}{8} + \frac{5}{8}$ = $1\frac{1}{2}$ T. $\frac{1}{9} + \frac{2}{9}$ = $\frac{1}{3}$

F	A	N	T	A	S	T	I	C
$\frac{1}{2}$	$\frac{3}{10}$	$1\frac{1}{3}$	$\frac{1}{3}$	$\frac{3}{10}$	$1\frac{1}{2}$	$\frac{1}{3}$	$\frac{3}{8}$	$\frac{1}{4}$

F	R	A	C	T	I	O	N	S
$\frac{1}{2}$	$\frac{5}{9}$	$\frac{3}{10}$	$\frac{1}{4}$	$\frac{1}{3}$	$\frac{3}{8}$	$\frac{1}{5}$	$1\frac{1}{3}$	$1\frac{1}{2}$

Use with text pages 516–519.

Problem Solving 20.1

Name ____________ Date ________ Problem Solving 20.1

Add and Subtract Fractions With Like Denominators

Show your work.

1. Max served pizza at his birthday party. Max ate $\frac{3}{6}$ of a pizza and Becky ate $\frac{1}{6}$ of the same pizza. How much more did Max eat than Becky?
 $\frac{2}{6}$ or $\frac{1}{3}$ pizza
2. At the party, $\frac{1}{8}$ of the guests were 9 years old, $\frac{3}{8}$ of the guests were 10 years old, and $\frac{1}{8}$ of the guests were 11 years old. What fraction of the guests were 9, 10 or 11 years old?
 $\frac{5}{8}$
3. At Max's party, the children spent $\frac{3}{4}$ of an hour playing volleyball and $\frac{1}{4}$ of an hour playing darts. How much longer did the children play volleyball than darts?
 $\frac{2}{4}$ or $\frac{1}{2}$ hour
4. Max got two new computer games for his birthday. He spent $\frac{2}{6}$ of an hour playing *Space Adventure* and $\frac{5}{6}$ of an hour playing *Puzzles and Mazes*. How much total time did he spend playing the computer games? Which game did he play longer? How much longer?
 $\frac{7}{6}$ or $1\frac{1}{6}$ hours; Puzzles and Mazes; $\frac{1}{2}$ hour
5. Max's mom made 3 containers of punch. One container held $\frac{4}{8}$ gallon of punch. The second container held $\frac{7}{8}$ gallon of punch and the other container held $\frac{2}{8}$ gallon of punch. Did she make more than 1 gallon of punch? Explain.
 Yes; She made $1\frac{5}{8}$ gallons and $1\frac{5}{8} > 1$.

Use with text pages 516–519.

❸ Practice

Practice and Problem Solving

Select from **Exercises 11–56** as independent work. Emphasize that all answers need to be in simplest form,

- ***Problem 32*** Elicit from students that "either blue or yellow" means the sum of the blue and yellow parts.
- ***Problem 33*** Elicit from students that the fraction that is "neither blue nor green" is the sum of the other parts of the sail.

Practice and Problem Solving

Add or subtract. Write your answer in simplest form.

11. 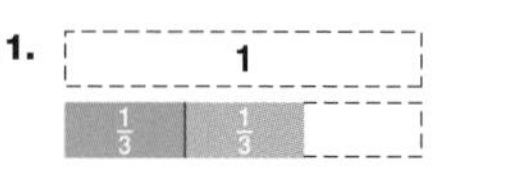

$\frac{1}{3} + \frac{1}{3} = \blacksquare$ $\frac{2}{3}$

12. 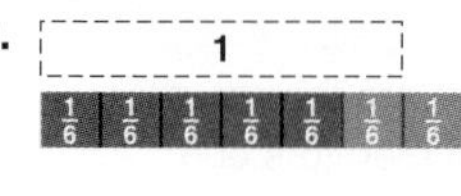

$\frac{5}{6} + \frac{2}{6} = \blacksquare$ $1\frac{1}{6}$

13. 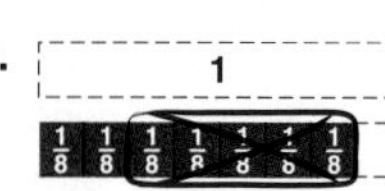

$\frac{7}{8} - \frac{5}{8} = \blacksquare$ $\frac{1}{4}$

14. $\frac{1}{4} + \frac{1}{4}$ $\frac{1}{2}$

15. $\frac{3}{8} + \frac{4}{8}$ $\frac{7}{8}$

16. $\frac{1}{3} + \frac{2}{3}$ 1

17. $\frac{2}{5} + \frac{4}{5}$ $1\frac{1}{5}$

18. $\frac{2}{10} + \frac{4}{10}$ $\frac{3}{5}$

19. $\frac{5}{6} - \frac{1}{6}$ $\frac{2}{3}$

20. $\frac{2}{3} - \frac{1}{3}$ $\frac{1}{3}$

21. $\frac{7}{8} - \frac{3}{8}$ $\frac{1}{2}$

22. $\frac{6}{10} - \frac{2}{10}$ $\frac{2}{5}$

23. $\frac{4}{9} - \frac{1}{9}$ $\frac{1}{3}$

24. $\frac{3}{7} + \frac{2}{7}$ $\frac{5}{7}$

25. $\frac{8}{9} - \frac{5}{9}$ $\frac{1}{3}$

26. $\frac{7}{10} + \frac{3}{10}$ 1

27. $\frac{6}{12} - \frac{3}{12}$ $\frac{1}{4}$

28. $\frac{9}{10} - \frac{3}{10}$ $\frac{3}{5}$

29. $\frac{7}{12} + \frac{4}{12}$ $\frac{11}{12}$

30. $\frac{8}{7} - \frac{3}{7}$ $\frac{5}{7}$

31. $\frac{9}{11} + \frac{2}{11}$ 1

Use the triangular sail on the right for Problems 32–36. Show your work. Write each answer in simplest form.

32. What fraction of the sail is either blue or yellow? $\frac{3}{8}$

33. What fraction of the sail is neither blue nor green? $\frac{1}{2}$

34. What is the difference between the fraction of the sail that is red and the fraction that is blue? $\frac{1}{8}$

35. Which colors make up $\frac{7}{8}$ of the sail? **red, green, blue**

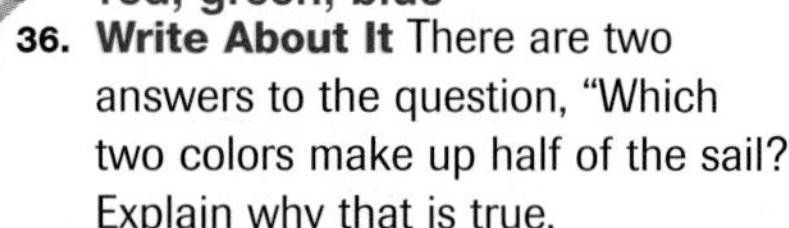

36. Write About It There are two answers to the question, "Which two colors make up half of the sail?" Explain why that is true.

Red and yellow: $\frac{3}{8} + \frac{1}{8} = \frac{4}{8}$ or $\frac{1}{2}$

Blue and green: $\frac{2}{8} + \frac{2}{8} = \frac{4}{8}$ or $\frac{1}{2}$

518

Homework 20.1 Page 124

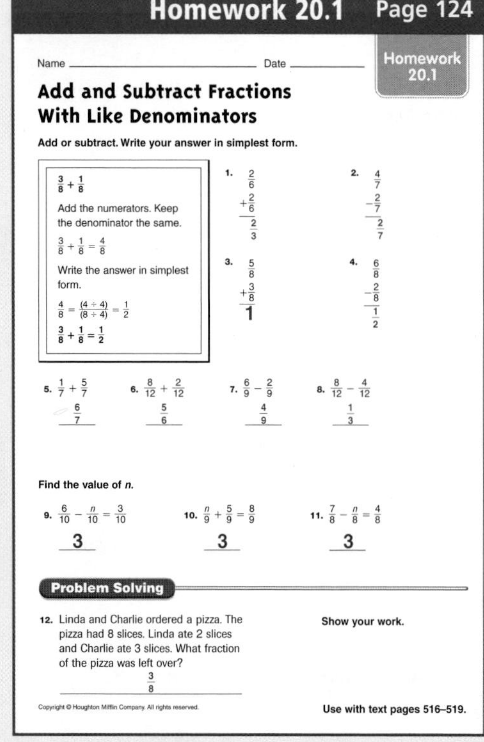

Name ______ Date ______

Homework 20.1

Add and Subtract Fractions With Like Denominators

Add or subtract. Write your answer in simplest form.

$\frac{3}{8} + \frac{1}{8}$

Add the numerators. Keep the denominator the same.

$\frac{3}{8} + \frac{1}{8} = \frac{4}{8}$

Write the answer in simplest form.

$\frac{4}{8} = \frac{(4 \div 4)}{(8 \div 4)} = \frac{1}{2}$

$\frac{3}{8} + \frac{1}{8} = \frac{1}{2}$

1. $\frac{2}{6} + \frac{2}{6}$ $\frac{2}{3}$

2. $\frac{4}{7} - \frac{2}{7}$ $\frac{2}{7}$

3. $\frac{5}{8} + \frac{3}{8}$ 1

4. $\frac{6}{8} - \frac{2}{8}$ $\frac{1}{2}$

5. $\frac{1}{7} + \frac{5}{7}$ $\frac{6}{7}$

6. $\frac{8}{12} + \frac{2}{12}$ $\frac{5}{6}$

7. $\frac{6}{9} - \frac{2}{9}$ $\frac{4}{9}$

8. $\frac{8}{12} - \frac{4}{12}$ $\frac{1}{3}$

Find the value of *n*.

9. $\frac{6}{10} - \frac{n}{10} = \frac{3}{10}$ 3

10. $\frac{n}{9} + \frac{5}{9} = \frac{8}{9}$ 3

11. $\frac{7}{8} - \frac{n}{8} = \frac{4}{8}$ 3

Problem Solving

12. Linda and Charlie ordered a pizza. The pizza had 8 slices. Linda ate 2 slices and Charlie ate 3 slices. What fraction of the pizza was left over? $\frac{3}{8}$

Show your work.

Use with text pages 516–519.

Algebra • Variables Find the value of n.

37. $\frac{5}{10} + \frac{n}{10} = \frac{8}{10}$ **3**

38. $\frac{n}{5} - \frac{4}{5} = \frac{1}{5}$ **5**

39. $\frac{8}{3} - \frac{n}{3} = \frac{3}{3}$ **5**

40. $\frac{5}{9} - \frac{n}{9} = \frac{0}{9}$ **5**

41. $\frac{n}{11} + \frac{6}{11} = \frac{11}{11}$ **5**

42. $\frac{4}{9} + \frac{n}{9} = \frac{7}{9}$ **3**

43. $\frac{n}{8} + \frac{3}{8} = 1$ **5**

44. $1 - \frac{n}{6} = \frac{5}{6}$ **1**

45. $\frac{n}{5} + \frac{3}{5} = \frac{11}{5}$ **8**

46. $1 - \frac{n}{10} = \frac{7}{10}$ **3**

47. $\frac{9}{12} + \frac{n}{12} = 1$ **3**

48. $\frac{6}{7} + \frac{n}{7} = \frac{6}{7}$ **0**

Data Use the table for Problems 49–51.

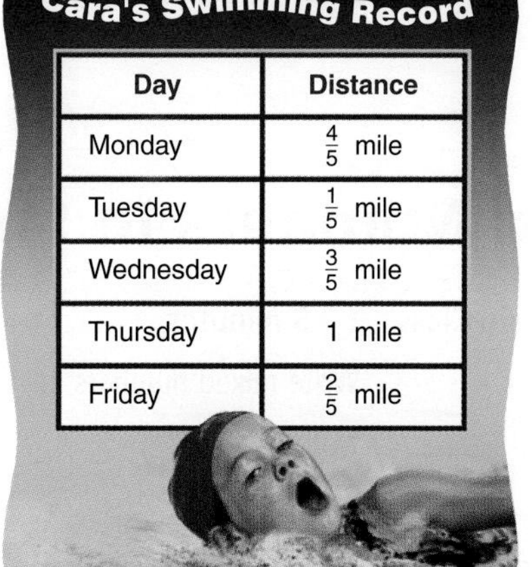

Cara's Swimming Record

Day	Distance
Monday	$\frac{4}{5}$ mile
Tuesday	$\frac{1}{5}$ mile
Wednesday	$\frac{3}{5}$ mile
Thursday	1 mile
Friday	$\frac{2}{5}$ mile

49. How many miles did Cara swim altogether during the 5 days? **3 miles**

50. Twelve people each donated \$1.25 for every fifth of a mile Cara swam. How much money did Cara raise on Monday? **\$60.00**

51. **Write About It** How much farther did Cara swim on Thursday than on Wednesday? Explain how you know. ***See below.***

52. Tina has saved \$45 to buy binoculars. The 13 bills she has are \$1 bills and \$5 bills. How many of each kind of bill has she saved? **Five \$1 bills; Eight \$5 bills**

51. $\frac{2}{5}$ mile; *Possible answer:* I subtracted $\frac{3}{5}$ from 1 mile to find the difference. Since $1 = \frac{5}{5}$, the answer is $\frac{2}{5}$.

Mixed Review and Test Prep

Open Response

Match each road sign with the name of its shape. (Ch. 16, Lesson 4)

53. octagon **B**   54. triangle **C**   55. pentagon **A**

A   B    C 

Explanations may vary.

56. Kimberly and her 2 friends ate an entire pizza that was cut into 6 equal slices. They each ate an equal amount. What fraction of the pizza did her friends eat?

Explain how you got your answer.
$\frac{4}{6}$ or $\frac{2}{3}$ of the pizza (Ch. 20, Lesson 1)

Extra Practice See page 539, Set A.

- ***Algebra • Variables*** Emphasize that the variable n has a different value in each exercise.
- ***Data*** Have students explain how they solved **Problem 50.** Make sure they are reading the problem correctly: *each* of the people contributed \$1.25 for every fifth of a mile, not all of them together. Allow students to use a calculator.

4 Assess & Close

Math Talk in Action

Have students refer to **Exercises 26–27** to conclude the lesson.

- **How can you find each answer using fraction pieces?** (Accept reasonable explanations.)
- **How can you find each answer without using fraction pieces?** (Accept reasonable explanations.)
- **How can you express each answer in simplest form?** (Accept reasonable explanations.)

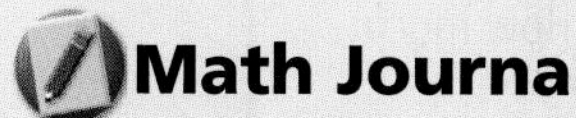

Math Journal

Have students write an explanation of how adding and subtracting fractions with the same denominator is like adding and subtracting measures, like inches or feet.

Lesson Quiz

Use the quiz on Lesson Transparency 20.1.

Test Prep & Spiral Review

Use Test Prep Transparency 20.1.

Lesson 20.2

Add and Subtract Mixed Numbers

Planning

Lesson Objective Add and subtract mixed numbers with like denominators.

Technology Resources

- Audio Tutor **2**/23 Listen and Understand
- *Ways to Success* CD-ROM 20.2
- Education Place: Extra Practice, Extra Help www.eduplace.com/map

Lesson 20.2 Transparency

Problem of the Day

Jack found $\frac{7}{10}$ of a dollar under the cushions of the couch. Irina found $\frac{4}{10}$ of a dollar under the cushions of another couch. How much money did the two find in all? ($1.10)

Spiral Review

Add or subtract. Write the answer in simplest form.

1. $\frac{3}{5} + \frac{4}{5}$ $(1\frac{2}{5})$ **2.** $\frac{1}{6} + \frac{5}{6}$ (1)

3. $\frac{2}{9} + \frac{4}{9}$ $(\frac{2}{3})$ **4.** $\frac{5}{12} + \frac{5}{12}$ $(\frac{5}{6})$

Lesson Quiz

Add or subtract. Write your answer in simplest form.

1. $1\frac{3}{4} + 2\frac{1}{4}$ (4) **2.** $5\frac{5}{6} - 2\frac{1}{6}$ $(3\frac{2}{3})$

3. $4\frac{2}{9} - 3$ $(1\frac{2}{9})$ **4.** $6\frac{7}{12} + 2\frac{1}{12}$ $(8\frac{2}{3})$

NCTM Standards

Number and Operations: Use visual models, benchmarks, and equivalent forms to add and subtract commonly used fractions.

Getting Started

Building Math Vocabulary

Students should be familiar with the mathematical vocabulary in this lesson.

Mixed Numbers in Simplest Form

Whole Class	5 minutes
Objective	Write mixed numbers in simplest form.
Materials	None
Visual, Auditory	

- Introduce the lesson by saying: *Today we are going to add and subtract mixed numbers with like denominators.*
- Explain that when we find these sums and differences, we need to express our answers as mixed numbers in simplest form.
- Help students recall how to write mixed numbers by asking students to write the following improper fractions as mixed numbers in simplest form.

  1. $\frac{2}{1}$ (2) **2.** $\frac{4}{3}$ $(1\frac{1}{3})$ **3.** $\frac{8}{5}$ $(1\frac{3}{5})$

  4. $\frac{9}{6}$ $(1\frac{1}{2})$ **5.** $\frac{8}{4}$ (2) **6.** $\frac{9}{2}$ $(4\frac{1}{2})$
- Tell students that the lesson will explain how to add and subtract mixed numbers.

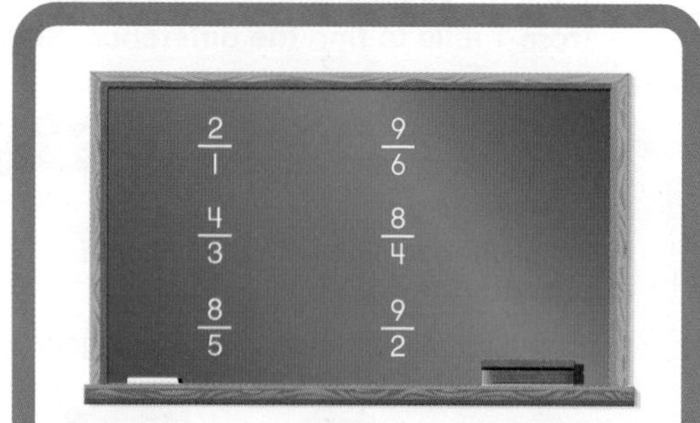

Differentiated Instruction

English Learners

Small Groups	10 minutes
Objective	Review fraction vocabulary.
Materials	None
Auditory, Visual	

Early Production

- Go over lesson vocabulary with students. Write a completed mixed-number addition or subtraction problem on the board and have students point to or describe the following: *numerator, denominator, like fractions, mixed number, like denominators.*

Intermediate/Advanced

- English Learner Resource 20.2
- English Learner Handbook

Intervention

Small Groups	10 minutes
Objective	Model addition of mixed numbers.
Materials	None
Tactual, Visual	

- An approach you can use to model adding mixed numbers is to have students shade divided rectangles. Use the denominator of the mixed numbers to determine how many equal sections to make in the divided rectangles.
- For the problem $1\frac{3}{4} + 1\frac{1}{4}$, use rectangles divided into fourths. To show the addition, students shade 1 whole rectangle and 3 parts of a second one to model the first addend. They shade 1 whole rectangle and 1 part of another to model the second addend. Students count shaded sections to find the sum $\frac{4}{4} + \frac{3}{4} + \frac{4}{4} + \frac{1}{4}$.

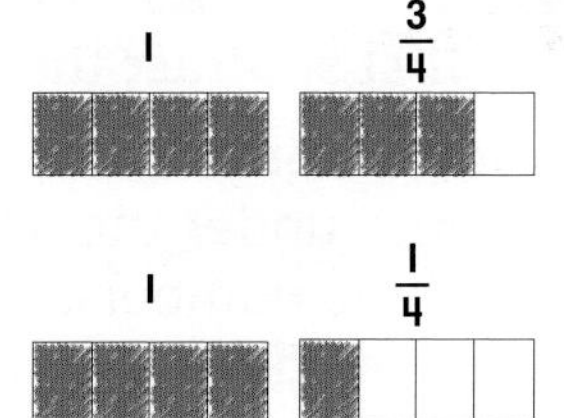

Other Resources

- *Ways to Success* CD-ROM 20.2

Inclusion

Pairs	10 minutes
Objective	Use fraction pieces to model addition and subtraction of mixed numbers.
Materials	Fraction pieces (Learning Tool 34)
Tactual, Visual	

Provide fraction pieces. Have students use the fraction pieces to model addition and subtraction. Then work through the ***Guided Practice*** together.

Real-World Connection

Materials: TV listings

- Have pairs of students create a list of imaginary TV programs. Have them include dramas, sitcoms, news, sports, game shows, cartoons, and so on. For each program have students choose a running time in hours and fractions of hours. Suggest 1 h, $1\frac{1}{2}$ h, 2 h, $\frac{1}{2}$ h, $\frac{1}{3}$ h, etc.
- Have pairs use their list to create a 4-hour TV schedule. They can refer to actual TV listings for ideas on how to format their schedule.

❶ Introduce

Tell students that in this lesson they will put two known skills together—adding and subtracting fractions with adding and subtracting whole numbers.

❷ Teach

Learn About It

Cut the $\frac{1}{4}$ circle pieces from the Mixed Numbers Transparency. Place a blank transparency on the overhead.

- Arrange six of the $\frac{1}{4}$ circle pieces to model $1\frac{2}{4}$. **What mixed number names this amount?** ($1\frac{2}{4}$) Write *$1\frac{2}{4}$* on the transparency.
- **Suppose we want to add $2\frac{1}{4}$ to $1\frac{2}{4}$.** Write *$+2\frac{1}{4}$* beneath $1\frac{2}{4}$ and draw a line under it. Have a volunteer model $2\frac{1}{4}$ with $\frac{1}{4}$ circle pieces and then move the $\frac{1}{4}$ circle pieces together to model the sum, *$3\frac{3}{4}$*.
- Write the subtraction *$3\frac{3}{4} - 2\frac{1}{4}$* with a line under it but no answer. **To subtract mixed numbers, first subtract the fractions.**
- Invite a volunteer to find $\frac{3}{4} - \frac{1}{4}$ and write the difference under the line. ($\frac{2}{4}$) Then subtract the whole numbers. Write *1* under the line. **So the difference is $1\frac{2}{4}$.**
- Continue to work through the *$3\frac{3}{4} - 2\frac{1}{4}$* problem, focusing on expressing the answer in simplest form. **Is the difference in simplest form?** (no) **By what number should we divide the numerator and denominator of the difference?** (2) **What is the difference in simplest form?** ($1\frac{1}{2}$)
- Then guide students through the examples in the ***Learn About It*** section. Discuss how to determine what operation is called for in each problem.

Guided Practice

Have students complete **Exercises 1–4** as you observe. Remind them to use the ***Ask Yourself*** questions to help. Give students the opportunity to talk about the question in ***Explain Your Thinking***.

Common Error

- **Not expressing answers in simplest form**
- **Intervention** Remind students that if any number other than 1 can divide both the numerator and the denominator with a remainder of 0, the fraction is not in simplest form.

Lesson 2

Audio Tutor 2/23 Listen and Understand

Add and Subtract Mixed Numbers

Objective Add and subtract mixed numbers with like denominators.

Learn About It

Steve and Aliya used this recipe to make trail mix for a hike. How many cups of peanuts and raisins did they use in all?

Add. $1\frac{3}{4} + 1\frac{1}{4} = ■$

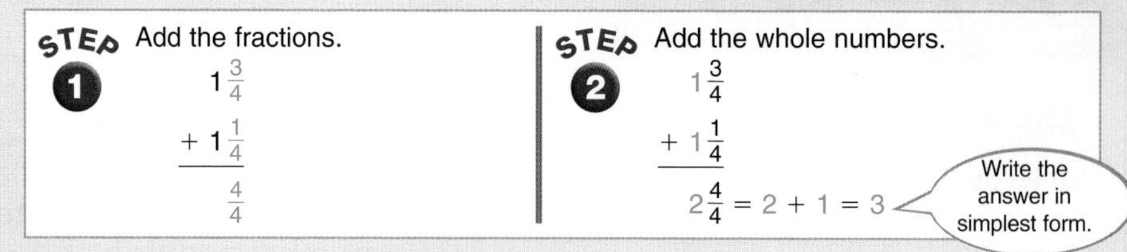

STEP 1 Add the fractions.
1 3/4
+ 1 1/4
4/4
STEP 2 Add the whole numbers.
1 3/4
+ 1 1/4
2 4/4 = 2 + 1 = 3
Write the answer in simplest form.

Solution: They used 3 cups of peanuts and raisins.

▶ How many more cups of peanuts than chocolate chips did they use?

Subtract. $1\frac{3}{4} - \frac{1}{4} = ■$

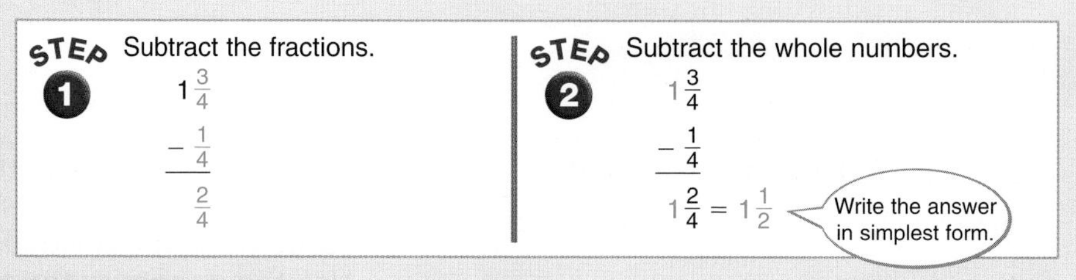

STEP 1 Subtract the fractions.
1 3/4
− 1/4
2/4
STEP 2 Subtract the whole numbers.
1 3/4
− 1/4
1 2/4 = 1 1/2
Write the answer in simplest form.

Solution: They used $1\frac{1}{2}$ more cups of peanuts.

Guided Practice

Add or subtract. Write your answer in simplest form.

1. $2\frac{1}{2} + 1$ $3\frac{1}{2}$
2. $3\frac{7}{8} - \frac{3}{8}$ $3\frac{1}{2}$
3. $5\frac{2}{3} - 4\frac{1}{3}$ $1\frac{1}{3}$
4. $4\frac{3}{4} + 2\frac{3}{4}$ $7\frac{1}{2}$

Ask Yourself

- Did I add or subtract the fractions first?
- Is my answer in simplest form?

Explain Your Thinking ▶ Look back at Exercise 4. Describe how you found the sum in simplest form.

See Additional Answers.

Extra Help at **eduplace.com/map**

Reteach 20.2

Name ______________ Date ________ Reteach 20.2

Add and Subtract Mixed Numbers

$1\frac{1}{3} + 2\frac{1}{3}$

Find $1\frac{1}{3}$ on the number line.

Add the fraction $\frac{1}{3}$.

Then add the whole number 2.

$1\frac{1}{3} + 2\frac{1}{3} = 3\frac{2}{3}$

$3\frac{3}{4} - 1\frac{1}{4}$

Find $3\frac{3}{4}$ on the number line.

Subtract the fraction $\frac{1}{4}$.

Then subtract the whole number 1.

$3\frac{3}{4} - 1\frac{1}{4} = 2\frac{2}{4} = 2\frac{1}{2}$

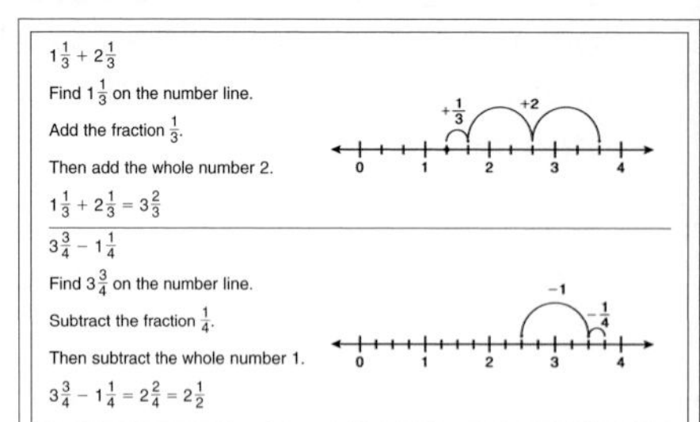

Add or subtract. Write your answer in simplest form.

1. $3\frac{1}{4} + 5\frac{2}{4}$ **$8\frac{3}{4}$**
2. $4\frac{5}{10} + 4\frac{3}{10}$ **$8\frac{4}{5}$**
3. $2\frac{2}{6} - 1\frac{1}{6}$ **$1\frac{1}{6}$**
4. $3\frac{3}{7} - 1\frac{1}{7}$ **$2\frac{2}{7}$**
5. $8\frac{7}{10} - 3\frac{2}{10}$ **$5\frac{1}{2}$**
6. $3\frac{4}{9} - 2\frac{1}{9}$ **$1\frac{1}{3}$**
7. $2\frac{5}{8} + 1\frac{3}{8}$ **4**
8. $2\frac{1}{7} + 9\frac{2}{7}$ **$11\frac{3}{7}$**
9. $6\frac{7}{15} + 2\frac{3}{15}$ **$8\frac{2}{3}$**
10. $3\frac{1}{3} - 2\frac{1}{3}$ **1**
11. $3\frac{5}{6} - 1\frac{1}{6}$ **$2\frac{2}{3}$**
12. $8\frac{5}{12} + 1\frac{4}{12}$ **$9\frac{3}{4}$**

Use with text pages 520–521.

Practice 20.2 Page 125

Name ______________ Date ________ Practice 20.2

Add and Subtract Mixed Numbers

Add or subtract. Write your answer in simplest form.

1. $3\frac{1}{7} + 4\frac{3}{7}$ **$7\frac{4}{7}$**
2. $2\frac{4}{6} - 1\frac{2}{6}$ **$1\frac{1}{3}$**
3. $5\frac{4}{8} + 4\frac{3}{8}$ **$9\frac{7}{8}$**
4. $4\frac{6}{8} - 2\frac{2}{8}$ **$2\frac{1}{2}$**
5. $3\frac{5}{10} + 3\frac{3}{10}$ **$6\frac{4}{5}$**
6. $3\frac{2}{10} + 5\frac{3}{10}$ **$8\frac{1}{2}$**
7. $5\frac{5}{6} - 1\frac{2}{6}$ **$4\frac{1}{2}$**
8. $3\frac{3}{8} + 2\frac{3}{8}$ **$5\frac{3}{4}$**
9. $5\frac{8}{9} - 2\frac{5}{9}$ **$3\frac{1}{3}$**
10. $7\frac{1}{4} + 3\frac{3}{4}$ **11**

Algebra Functions • Follow the rule to complete each table.

	Rule: Add $2\frac{2}{7}$	
	Input	Output
11.	$4\frac{3}{7}$	$6\frac{5}{7}$
12.	$3\frac{4}{7}$	$5\frac{6}{7}$
13.	$1\frac{3}{7}$	$3\frac{5}{7}$

	Rule: Subtract $1\frac{1}{4}$	
	Input	Output
14.	$2\frac{3}{4}$	$1\frac{1}{2}$
15.	$3\frac{2}{4}$	$2\frac{1}{4}$
16.	$6\frac{1}{4}$	5

	Rule: Add $\frac{3}{12}$	
	Input	Output
17.	$2\frac{5}{12}$	$2\frac{2}{3}$
18.	$4\frac{6}{12}$	$4\frac{3}{4}$
19.	$5\frac{3}{4}$	6

Test Prep

20. Harry's teakettle holds $6\frac{4}{8}$ cups of water. He fills the kettle, then pours $3\frac{1}{8}$ cups of water to make tea for himself and a friend. How much water is left in the kettle?

    A $3\frac{5}{8}$ cups
    B $9\frac{5}{8}$ cups
    C $6\frac{3}{8}$ cups
    D $3\frac{3}{8}$ cups

    D

21. Jake made 2 standing long jumps. The first jump was $4\frac{3}{12}$ feet long. The second jump was $5\frac{7}{12}$ feet long. How much longer was his second jump than his first jump?

    $1\frac{1}{3}$ feet

Use with text pages 520–521.

Practice and Problem Solving

Add or subtract. Write your answer in simplest form.

5. $3\frac{1}{3} + 1\frac{2}{3}$ = **5**

6. $1\frac{5}{9} - \frac{3}{9}$ = **$1\frac{2}{9}$**

7. $4\frac{1}{6} + 3\frac{2}{6}$ = **$7\frac{1}{2}$**

8. $6\frac{1}{2} - 5$ = **$1\frac{1}{2}$**

9. $4\frac{2}{7} + 2\frac{5}{7}$ = **7**

10. $6\frac{3}{4} - 3\frac{1}{4}$ = **$3\frac{1}{2}$**

11. $5\frac{1}{9} + 3\frac{2}{9}$ = **$8\frac{1}{3}$**

12. $7\frac{5}{6} - 2\frac{1}{6}$ = **$5\frac{2}{3}$**

13. $3\frac{3}{5} + \frac{1}{5}$ = **$3\frac{4}{5}$**

14. $2\frac{7}{8} - 1\frac{7}{8}$ = **1**

Algebra • Functions Follow the rule to complete each table.

	Rule: Add $1\frac{2}{5}$.		
	Input	Output	
15.	$4\frac{4}{5}$	■	$6\frac{1}{5}$
16.	■	$5\frac{2}{5}$	4

	Rule: Subtract $2\frac{1}{6}$.		
	Input	Output	
17.	$6\frac{4}{6}$	■	$4\frac{3}{6}$
18.	■	$5\frac{2}{6}$	$7\frac{3}{6}$

	Rule: Subtract $\frac{2}{3}$.		
	Input	Output	
19.	■	5	$5\frac{2}{3}$
20.	$3\frac{2}{3}$	■	3

21. How many cups of trail mix does the recipe on page 520 make? If it is doubled, how many cups will be made?
$3\frac{1}{4}$ cups, $6\frac{1}{2}$ cups

22. Pete's water bottle holds $4\frac{3}{4}$ cups of water. He drinks $3\frac{1}{4}$ cups of water while hiking. How much water is left?
$1\frac{1}{2}$ cups

23. Write About It Use words and diagrams to explain how to subtract $2\frac{4}{8}$ from $4\frac{6}{8}$. Write the difference in simplest form.
See Additional Answers.

24. Mary made $4\frac{3}{4}$ cups of a snack. She used 2 cups of nuts, $1\frac{1}{4}$ cups of granola, and some raisins. How many cups of raisins did she use? **$1\frac{1}{2}$ cups**

Mixed Review and Test Prep

Open Response

Solve. (Ch. 7, Lesson 4; Ch. 8, Lesson 2)

25. 25×19 **475**

26. 16×23 **368**

27. 64×41 **2,624**

28. $35 \div 3$ **11 R2**

29. $67 \div 2$ **33 R1**

30. $48 \div 4$ **12**

31. $85 \div 5$ **17**

32. 36×28 **1,008**

33. 15×27 **405**

34. $84 \div 4$ **21**

Multiple Choice

35. Joey took 2 plane trips. The first lasted $5\frac{2}{3}$ hours. The second lasted $2\frac{2}{3}$ hours. How much longer was his first trip? (Ch. 20, Lesson 2)

A 2 hours
(B) 3 hours
C $3\frac{1}{3}$ hours
D $8\frac{1}{3}$ hours

Extra Practice See page 539, Set B.

3 Practice

Practice and Problem Solving

Select from **Exercises 5–35** as independent work.

- ***Algebra* • *Functions*** Point out that each function table has an addition or subtraction rule. **If the output number is given, how do we find the input number?** (Use the inverse operation.)
- ***Problem 24*** Ask a volunteer to make a drawing to model the solution.

4 Assess & Close

Math Talk in Action

Have students explain how to add and subtract mixed numbers.

Math Journal Prompt

Have students write about the similarities between adding and subtracting with mixed numbers and operations with fractions.

Lesson Quiz

Use the quiz on Lesson Transparency 20.2.

Lesson 20.2 Transparency

Test Prep & Spiral Review

Use Test Prep Transparency 20.2.

Test Prep 20.2 Transparency

Enrichment 20.2

Name ______ Date ______ Enrichment 20.2

Anyone for Tic-Tac-Toe?

Solve. Write the answer in simplest form. Check to see whether each answer is an X or an O. Place an X or O over each problem.

$4\frac{5}{6} - 2\frac{1}{6}$ **$2\frac{2}{3}$; X**	$2\frac{5}{12} + 1\frac{1}{12}$ **$3\frac{1}{2}$; O**	$12\frac{9}{14} - 9\frac{1}{14}$ **$3\frac{4}{7}$; O**
$5\frac{5}{6} + 3\frac{5}{6}$ **$9\frac{2}{3}$; O**	$10\frac{7}{16} - 8\frac{5}{16}$ **$2\frac{1}{8}$; X**	$2\frac{2}{7} + 1\frac{1}{7}$ **$3\frac{3}{7}$; O**
$9\frac{12}{15} - 7\frac{7}{15}$ **$2\frac{1}{3}$; O**	$3\frac{5}{12} + 1\frac{11}{12}$ **$5\frac{1}{3}$; X**	$2\frac{9}{15} + 1\frac{8}{15}$ **$4\frac{2}{15}$; X**

Do the X's or the O's win?
X's win diagonally.

X
$2\frac{2}{3}$ $2\frac{1}{8}$ $5\frac{1}{3}$ $4\frac{2}{15}$

O
$9\frac{2}{3}$ $2\frac{1}{3}$ $3\frac{1}{2}$ $3\frac{4}{7}$ $3\frac{3}{7}$

Use with text pages 520–521.

Problem Solving 20.2

Name ______ Date ______ Problem Solving 20.2

Add and Subtract Mixed Numbers

Use the punch recipe for Problems 1–3.

Citrus Punch Recipe
$1\frac{2}{4}$ gallon of orange juice
$2\frac{3}{4}$ gallon of pineapple juice
$\frac{3}{4}$ gallon of grapefruit juice

1. How many total gallons of punch does the recipe make?
$3\frac{8}{4}$ or 5 gallons

2. How much more pineapple juice is used than orange juice?
$1\frac{1}{4}$ gallons

3. Mrs. Tisdale decides to double the Citrus Punch Recipe. How much of each type of juice will she need? How much punch will the recipe make?
3 gal orange juice; $5\frac{1}{2}$ gal of pineapple juice and $1\frac{1}{2}$ gal grapefruit juice; Total of 10 gallons

4. There is a rectangular walking trail around the school grounds. One side of the rectangle measures $2\frac{1}{4}$ miles. The other side measures $1\frac{3}{4}$ miles. What is the total length of the walking trail?
8 miles

5. **Write About It** Jessica is $4\frac{7}{12}$ feet tall. Her younger sister Marcia is $3\frac{5}{12}$ feet tall. How much taller is Jessica than her sister Marcia? Explain how to find the answer and write it in simplest form.
$1\frac{1}{6}$ feet; First I subtract $4\frac{7}{12} - 3\frac{5}{12} = 1\frac{2}{12}$. $\frac{2}{12}$ can be simplified. 2 can be divided into the numerator and denominator. $1\frac{2}{12} = 1\frac{1}{6}$.

Use with text pages 520–521.

Homework 20.2 Page 125

Name ______ Date ______ Homework 20.2

Add and Subtract Mixed Numbers

Add or subtract. Write your answer in simplest form.

$3\frac{4}{6} + 2\frac{2}{6}$	**Step 1:** Add the fractions.	**Step 2:** Add the whole numbers. Then simplify.
	$3\frac{4}{6} + 2\frac{2}{6}$ = $\frac{6}{6}$	$3\frac{4}{6} + 2\frac{2}{6}$ = $5\frac{6}{6} = 5 + 1 = 6$ **$3\frac{4}{6} + 2\frac{2}{6} = 6$**

1. $2\frac{2}{5} + 3\frac{3}{5}$ = **6**
2. $3\frac{5}{8} - 2\frac{3}{8}$ = **$1\frac{1}{4}$**
3. $2\frac{4}{10} + 4\frac{1}{10}$ = **$6\frac{1}{2}$**
4. $5\frac{8}{12} - 1\frac{2}{12}$ = **$4\frac{1}{2}$**
5. $1\frac{5}{6} + 3\frac{1}{6}$ = **5**
6. $3\frac{2}{7} + 1\frac{2}{7}$ = **$4\frac{4}{7}$**
7. $5\frac{7}{8} - 2\frac{7}{8}$ = **3**
8. $3\frac{3}{5} + 5\frac{2}{5}$ = **9**
9. $6\frac{3}{4} - 2\frac{1}{4}$ = **$4\frac{1}{2}$**
10. $8\frac{7}{12} - 2\frac{4}{12}$ = **$6\frac{1}{4}$**

Problem Solving

Show your work.

11. Ursula started with a jar that contained $4\frac{7}{8}$ cups of flour. She used $2\frac{3}{8}$ cups for a recipe. How much flour was left in the jar?
$2\frac{1}{2}$ cups

Use with text pages 520–521.

Lesson 20.3

Problem-Solving Application: Decide How to Write the Quotient

Planning

Lesson Objective Decide how to write the quotient to solve a problem.

Math Background

When deciding how to write the solution of a division problem, students will consider the different possibilities, such as using a remainder or a mixed number. Then they will decide which way best answers the question.

Technology Resources

- *Ways to Success* CD-ROM 20.3
- Education Place: Extra Practice www.eduplace.com/map

Problem of the Day

Suppose you can fit 12 rows of chairs in a room. You can fit 8 or 9 chairs in each row. How could you set up exactly 100 chairs? (Possible answer: 8 chairs in 8 rows and 9 chairs in 4 rows)

Spiral Review

Divide.

1. 36 ÷ 9 (4) **2.** 16 ÷ 8 (2)
3. 42 ÷ 7 (6) **4.** 56 ÷ 8 (7)
5. 32 ÷ 4 (8) **6.** 40 ÷ 10 (4)

Lesson Quiz

Solve.

1. Boxes of crayons cost $4 at the shop. How many boxes can you buy with $15? How much change is left? (3; $3)
2. For lunch at the zoo, 6 students shared 9 sandwiches equally. How many sandwiches did each student eat? ($1\frac{1}{2}$)

NCTM Standards

Problem Solving: Solve problems that arise in mathematics and other contexts.
Number and Operations: Recognize equivalent representations for the same number.

Getting Started

Building Math Vocabulary

Students should be familiar with the mathematical vocabulary in this lesson.

Working with Remainders

Whole Class	5 minutes
Objective	Review division with remainders.
Materials	None
Auditory, Visual	

- Provide the following exercises in which the quotients include remainders.
  1. 50 ÷ 6 (8 R2)
  2. 41 ÷ 7 (5 R6)
  3. 35 ÷ 8 (4 R3)
  4. 28 ÷ 5 (5 R3)
- Discuss students' answers. Then tell them that in real life, they may need to interpret remainders in different ways depending on the circumstances.
- Explain that deciding how to write a quotient is the topic of today's lesson.

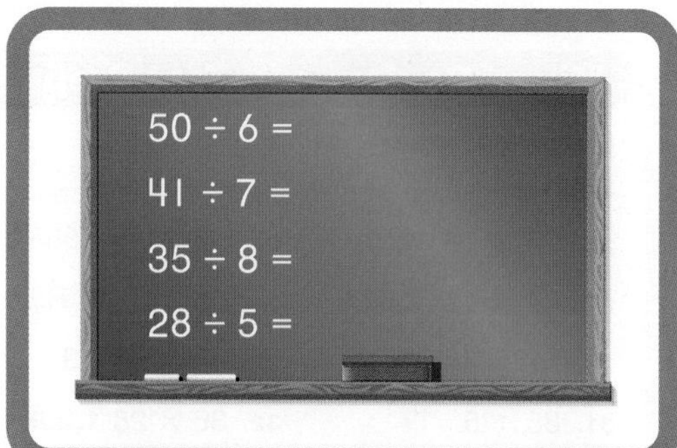

Differentiated Instruction

English Learners

Small Groups	10 minutes
Objective	Use models to divide.
Materials	Student page 523, play money, fraction pieces
Auditory, Visual, Tactual	

Early Production

- Have students act out the ***Guided Practice*** problems.
- Divide students into two groups. Give the first group play money to model the first problem.
- Give the second group 1 fraction pieces and $\frac{1}{2}$ fraction pieces to model the second problem.
- Have groups explain their solutions to each other.

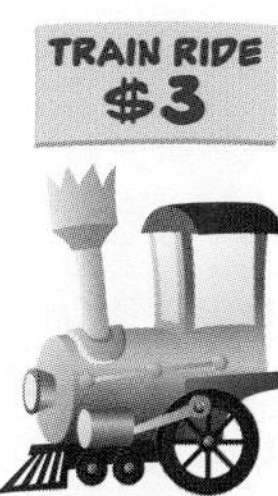

Intermediate/Advanced

- English Learner Resource 20.3
- English Learner Handbook

Intervention

Small Groups	10 minutes
Objective	Model division problems.
Materials	None
Kinesthetic	

- Have students act out the two problems on page 522. (You may wish to use simpler numbers for the first problem to match the number of students who use this approach.)
- For the second problem, you can demonstrate the solution by actually having four students share an orange or other food that is easily divided into its fractional parts.

Other Resources

- *Ways to Success* CD-ROM 20.3

Gifted & Talented

Individuals	30 minutes
Objective	Write division problems.
Materials	None
Tactual, Visual	

- Have students write two real-life division problems with remainders. For example, Henry and his two brothers went fishing and caught 7 fish. Could they each have caught the same number of fish?
- Ask them to write a problem that can be best answered by writing a remainder.
- Then challenge students to write a second problem that can be best answered by a mixed-number answer.

Alternate Teaching Strategy

- Have students work in groups of three or four.
- Have students refer to the problems in the ***Independent Practice*** section of the lesson. For each problem, have the groups identify the "key" words in the problem—the words that help them decide on the best way to write the solution.
- Allow each group to share their key words as well as the reasoning behind their choices.
- If students wrote their own word problems, compile these and allow groups to repeat the exercise. Alternatively, have each group collaborate to write a word problem, then have the groups swap problems and repeat the exercise.

❶ Introduce

Read the objective to students and tell them that in this lesson they will learn how to write the quotient so it makes the most sense in response to the problem. Depending on the situation and the remainder, students will learn to write the quotient as a mixed number.

❷ Teach

Decide How to Write the Quotient

- Have a volunteer read aloud the first problem. **What is the greatest number of students who would go with the teacher on this trip? Why?** (3; if the remainder were 4, 1 more group could be made to go with a parent.) Guide students to see that a remainder makes sense in this problem situation because we can't have fractions of students!
- Have a student read aloud the second problem. **How many oranges would each student get if there were two of them sharing the oranges?** ($2\frac{1}{2}$)
- Have students contrast these two situations. Have them discuss the way we interpret the remainder in each so that the answer makes sense.

Guided Practice

Have students complete **Exercises 1–2** as you observe. Remind them to use the ***Ask Yourself*** questions to help.

Lesson 3

Problem-Solving Application

Decide How to Write the Quotient

Objective Decide how to write the quotient to solve a problem.

You can write the solution to a division problem in different ways. You should choose the way that makes the most sense.

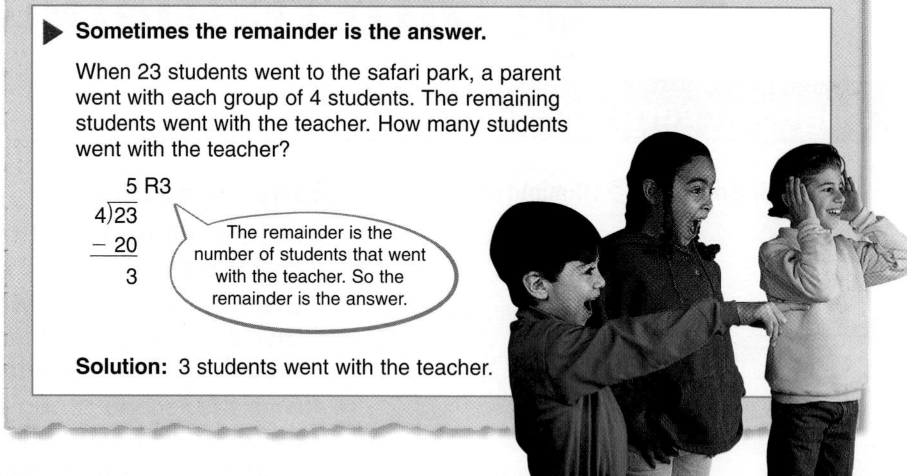

▶ Sometimes the remainder is the answer.

When 23 students went to the safari park, a parent went with each group of 4 students. The remaining students went with the teacher. How many students went with the teacher?

$$\begin{array}{r} 5 \text{ R}3 \\ 4\overline{)23} \\ -\,20 \\ \hline 3 \end{array}$$

The remainder is the number of students that went with the teacher. So the remainder is the answer.

Solution: 3 students went with the teacher.

▶ Sometimes you need to write the quotient as a mixed number.

A parent gave 5 oranges to the 4 students in his group. If the students shared the oranges equally, what did each student receive?

$$\begin{array}{r} 1\frac{1}{4} \\ 4\overline{)5} \\ -\,4 \\ \hline 1 \end{array}$$

It is possible to split an orange into parts. So write the quotient as a mixed number.

Solution: Each student received $1\frac{1}{4}$ oranges.

Look Back Why couldn't you write the quotient in the first problem as a mixed number? **The first problem is asking only for the remainder.**

522

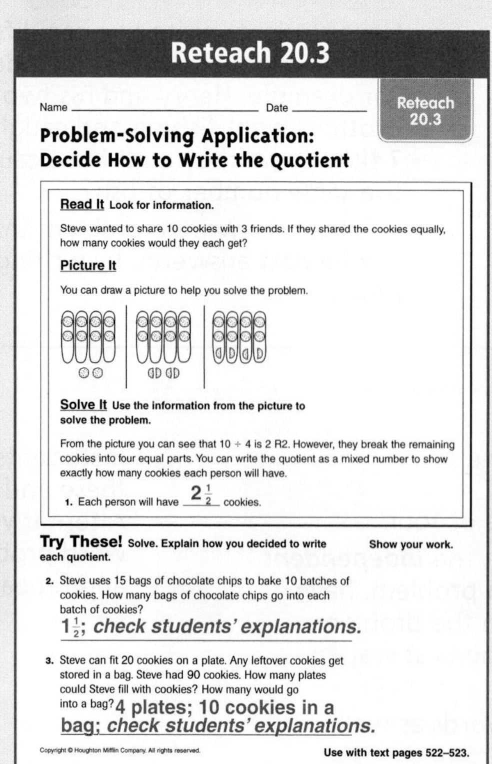

Reteach 20.3

Name ____________ Date ________ Reteach 20.3

Problem-Solving Application: Decide How to Write the Quotient

Read It Look for information.

Steve wanted to share 10 cookies with 3 friends. If they shared the cookies equally, how many cookies would they each get?

Picture It

You can draw a picture to help you solve the problem.

Solve It Use the information from the picture to solve the problem.

From the picture you can see that 10 ÷ 4 is 2 R2. However, they break the remaining cookies into four equal parts. You can write the quotient as a mixed number to show exactly how many cookies each person will have.

1. Each person will have $2\frac{1}{2}$ cookies.

Try These! Solve. Explain how you decided to write each quotient. **Show your work.**

2. Steve uses 15 bags of chocolate chips to bake 10 batches of cookies. How many bags of chocolate chips go into each batch of cookies? $1\frac{1}{2}$; *check students' explanations.*
3. Steve can fit 20 cookies on a plate. Any leftover cookies get stored in a bag. Steve had 90 cookies. How many plates could Steve fill with cookies? How many would go into a bag? 4 plates; 10 cookies in a bag; *check students' explanations.*

Use with text pages 522–523.

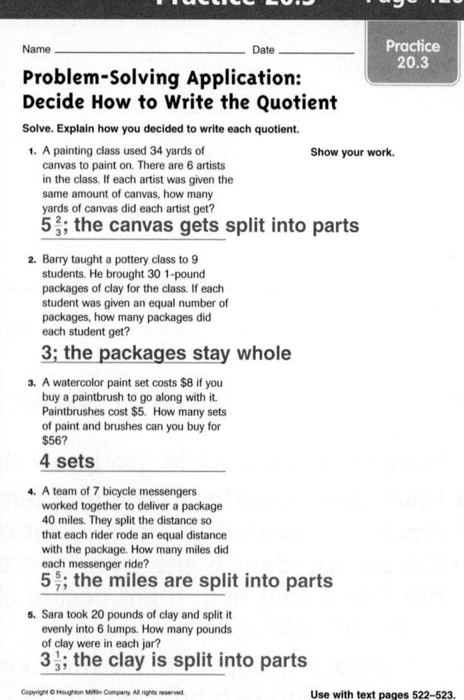

Practice 20.3 Page 126

Name ____________ Date ________ Practice 20.3

Problem-Solving Application: Decide How to Write the Quotient

Solve. Explain how you decided to write each quotient. **Show your work.**

1. A painting class used 34 yards of canvas to paint on. There are 6 artists in the class. If each artist was given the same amount of canvas, how many yards of canvas did each artist get? $5\frac{2}{3}$; the canvas gets split into parts
2. Barry taught a pottery class to 9 students. He brought 30 1-pound packages of clay for the class. If each student was given an equal number of packages, how many packages did each student get? 3; the packages stay whole
3. A watercolor paint set costs $8 if you buy a paintbrush to go along with it. Paintbrushes cost $5. How many sets of paint and brushes can you buy for $56? 4 sets
4. A team of 7 bicycle messengers worked together to deliver a package 40 miles. They split the distance so that each rider rode an equal distance with the package. How many miles did each messenger ride? $5\frac{5}{7}$; the miles are split into parts
5. Sara took 20 pounds of clay and split it evenly into 6 lumps. How many pounds of clay were in each jar? $3\frac{1}{3}$; the clay is split into parts

Use with text pages 522–523.

Guided Practice

Use the Ask Yourself questions to help you solve each problem.

Ask Yourself

- What does the question ask me to find?
- What does the remainder represent?
- Does my answer make sense?

1. Fred has $10 to ride the jungle train at the zoo. Each ride costs $3. How many rides can he take? How much money will he have left? **3 rides; $1 left**
2. For lunch at the park, 8 students shared 12 sandwiches. Each student ate the same amount. If all of the sandwiches were eaten, how many sandwiches did each student eat? **$1\frac{1}{2}$ sandwiches**

Hint Can you eat a fractional part of a sandwich?

Independent Practice

Check students' explanations.

Solve. Explain how you decided to write each quotient.

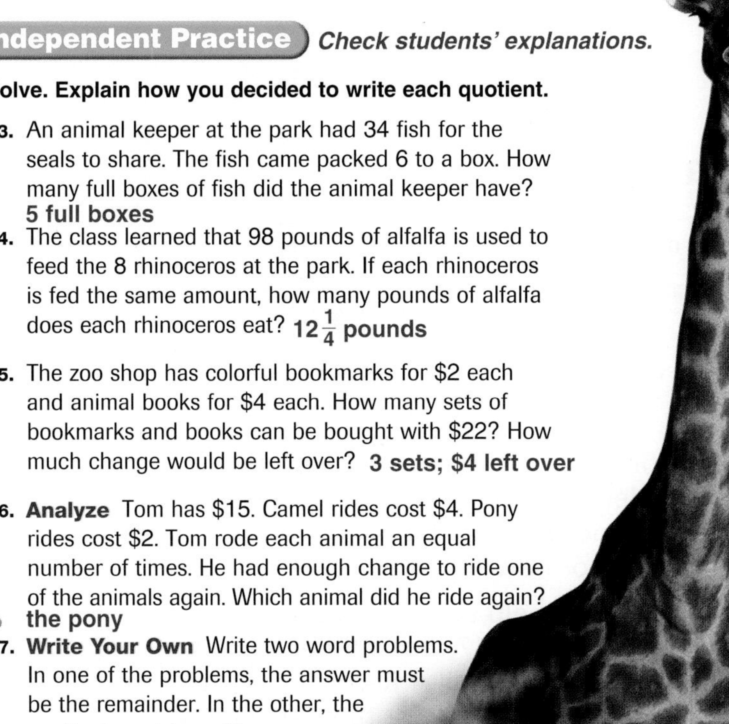

3. An animal keeper at the park had 34 fish for the seals to share. The fish came packed 6 to a box. How many full boxes of fish did the animal keeper have? **5 full boxes**
4. The class learned that 98 pounds of alfalfa is used to feed the 8 rhinoceros at the park. If each rhinoceros is fed the same amount, how many pounds of alfalfa does each rhinoceros eat? **$12\frac{1}{4}$ pounds**
5. The zoo shop has colorful bookmarks for $2 each and animal books for $4 each. How many sets of bookmarks and books can be bought with $22? How much change would be left over? **3 sets; $4 left over**
6. **Analyze** Tom has $15. Camel rides cost $4. Pony rides cost $2. Tom rode each animal an equal number of times. He had enough change to ride one of the animals again. Which animal did he ride again? **the pony**
7. **Write Your Own** Write two word problems. In one of the problems, the answer must be the remainder. In the other, the quotient must be written as a mixed number. ***Check students' work.***

3 Practice

Independent Practice

Select from **Exercises 3–7** as independent work. Emphasize the importance of reading the problems carefully.

Have students review their answers to make sure they have done the following:

- expressed the solution clearly
- used appropriate mathematical notation and terms
- supported their solution with verbal and symbolic work.

4 Assess & Close

Math Talk in Action

To conclude the lesson, ask questions about decisions that must be made when a division problem has a remainder.

Math Journal Prompt

Ask students to describe real-life situations that may involve remainders—one for which the remainder is the answer and one for which the answer can be a mixed number.

Lesson Quiz

Use the quiz on Lesson Transparency 20.3.

Lesson 20.3 Transparency

Test Prep & Spiral Review

Use Test Prep Transparency 20.3

Test Prep 20.3 Transparency

Enrichment 20.3

Name ______ Date ______ Enrichment 20.3

Problem-Solving Application: Decide How to Write the Quotient

There are 34 boys in Chad's Boy Scout troop. The troop recently went on a camping trip. They drove 136 miles to the campground. Then the boys set up their tents. It took a total of 55 minutes to set up all the tents. The boys were divided into groups of 5 and assigned tents. In the morning, the boys went on a 5-mile hike.

1. If you wanted to find how many tents there were, how would you need to write the quotient? Explain your choice then divide to find the answer. **I would write the quotient and remainder. A tent can't be divided into fractional parts. There were 7 tents**
2. The average speed on the drive to the campground was 60 miles per hour. How long did it take them to drive to the campground? Find the answer and explain how you wrote the quotient. **$2\frac{4}{15}$ hours; I wrote the quotient as a mixed number. An hour can be divided into fractional parts.**
3. Use the data from the problem to write a question that can be solved using division, writing the quotient as a number and a remainder. **Answers may vary.**
4. Use the data from the problem to write a question that can be solved using division, writing the quotient as a mixed number. **Answers may vary.**

Use with text pages 522–523.

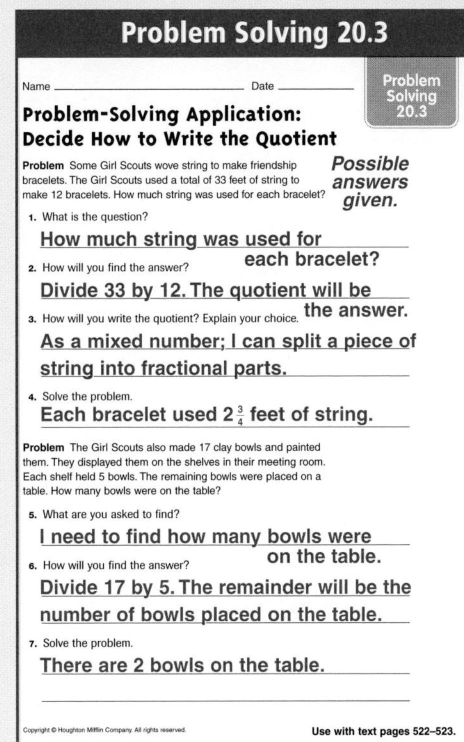

Problem Solving 20.3

Name ______ Date ______ Problem Solving 20.3

Problem-Solving Application: Decide How to Write the Quotient

Possible answers given.

Problem Some Girl Scouts wove string to make friendship bracelets. The Girl Scouts used a total of 33 feet of string to make 12 bracelets. How much string was used for each bracelet?

1. What is the question? **How much string was used for each bracelet?**
2. How will you find the answer? **Divide 33 by 12. The quotient will be the answer.**
3. How will you write the quotient? Explain your choice. **As a mixed number; I can split a piece of string into fractional parts.**
4. Solve the problem. **Each bracelet used $2\frac{3}{4}$ feet of string.**

Problem The Girl Scouts also made 17 clay bowls and painted them. They displayed them on the shelves in their meeting room. Each shelf held 5 bowls. The remaining bowls were placed on a table. How many bowls were on the table?

5. What are you asked to find? **I need to find how many bowls were on the table.**
6. How will you find the answer? **Divide 17 by 5. The remainder will be the number of bowls placed on the table.**
7. Solve the problem. **There are 2 bowls on the table.**

Use with text pages 522–523.

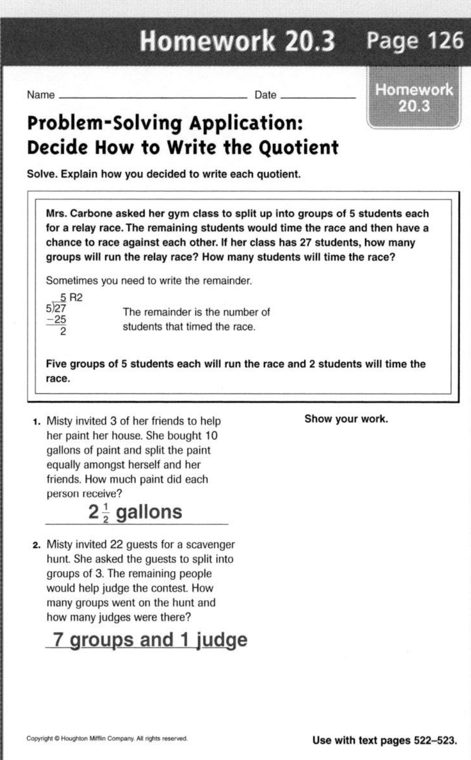

Homework 20.3 Page 126

Name ______ Date ______ Homework 20.3

Problem-Solving Application: Decide How to Write the Quotient

Solve. Explain how you decided to write each quotient.

Mrs. Carbone asked her gym class to split up into groups of 5 students each for a relay race. The remaining students would time the race and then have a chance to race against each other. If her class has 27 students, how many groups will run the relay race? How many students will time the race?

Sometimes you need to write the remainder.

$$\begin{array}{r} 5\text{ R2} \\ 5\overline{)27} \\ -25 \\ \hline 2 \end{array}$$

The remainder is the number of students that timed the race.

Five groups of 5 students each will run the race and 2 students will time the race.

Show your work.

1. Misty invited 3 of her friends to help her paint her house. She bought 10 gallons of paint and split the paint equally amongst herself and her friends. How much paint did each person receive? **$2\frac{1}{2}$ gallons**
2. Misty invited 22 guests for a scavenger hunt. She asked the guests to split into groups of 3. The remaining people would help judge the contest. How many groups went on the hunt and how many judges were there? **7 groups and 1 judge**

Use with text pages 522–523.

Lesson 20.4

Estimate with Fractions

Planning

Lesson Objective Estimate sums of fractions.

Technology Resources

- *Ways to Success* CD-ROM 20.4
- Education Place: Extra Practice, eManipulatives, eGames www.eduplace.com/map

Lesson 20.4 Transparency

Problem of the Day

Of the students in Tony's class, $\frac{17}{23}$ have dogs and $\frac{2}{23}$ have cats. None of the other students have pets. What fraction of the students in the group does not have pets? ($\frac{4}{23}$)

Spiral Review

Round to 0, $\frac{1}{2}$, or 1.

1. $\frac{3}{8}$ ($\frac{1}{2}$) **2.** $\frac{9}{10}$ (1)

3. $\frac{1}{8}$ (0) **4.** $\frac{4}{10}$ ($\frac{1}{2}$)

Lesson Quiz

Estimate each sum. Write > 1 or < 1.

1. $\frac{5}{6} + \frac{3}{4}$ (> 1) **2.** $\frac{1}{3} + \frac{1}{5}$(< 1)

3. $\frac{1}{2} + \frac{4}{5}$ (> 1) **4.** $\frac{5}{8} + \frac{1}{2}$ (> 1)

5. $\frac{4}{9} + \frac{2}{7}$ (< 1)

NCTM Standards

Number and Operations: Use visual models, benchmarks, and equivalent forms to add and subtract commonly used fractions; develop and use strategies to estimate the results of computations involving fractions.

Getting Started

Building Math Vocabulary

You may wish to review this word with students.

estimate a number close to an exact amount; an estimate tells about how much or about how many

Daily Estimating

Whole Class	5 minutes
Objective	Estimate sums of fractions.
Materials	None
	Visual, Auditory

- Discuss the fact that estimating is something we do in daily life. Elicit from students that we estimate, for example, how long an event or activity may take, how much we will need of something, or how far away something is.
- Discuss familiar benchmarks to help students consider how far a mile is, 20 city blocks or about 17 football fields. **How long do you think it takes to walk a mile?** Record students' responses. Invite interested students to test their estimates and report their findings.
- Explain that this lesson will give them practice estimating with fractions.

Differentiated Instruction

English Learners

Small Groups	10 minutes
Objective	Estimate with fractions.
Materials	Student page 525, fraction pieces
Visual, Tactual	

Early Production

- Give students fraction pieces for visually comparing each fraction to one half.
- Ask students to write and verbalize each step to solve the exercises in the ***Guided Practice.*** For example:

One-third is less than one-half, one-fourth is less than one-half, so one-third plus one-half is less than one.

Intermediate/Advanced

- English Learner Resource 20.4
- English Learner Handbook

Intervention

Small Groups	10 minutes
Objective	Compare fractions to $\frac{1}{2}$.
Materials	None
Auditory, Visual	

- Work through the following approach for determining whether a fraction is greater than, equal to, or less than $\frac{1}{2}$.
- Write the fraction $\frac{3}{4}$ on the board. **For $\frac{1}{2}$ and every fraction equivalent to $\frac{1}{2}$, the numerator is *half* the denominator.** Write several examples that show this.
- **What can you say about a fraction whose numerator is more than half its denominator?** ($> \frac{1}{2}$) **So, $\frac{2}{4} = \frac{1}{2}$. Is $\frac{3}{4}$ greater than, equal to, or less than $\frac{1}{2}$? Why?** (greater than, because 3 is more than half of 4)
- Provide other examples. Ask students to explain the comparison.

Other Resources

- *Ways to Success* CD-ROM 20.4

Early Finishers

Small Groups	30 minutes
Objective	Model fraction problems.
Materials	Fraction pieces
Visual, Tactual	

- Have students use fraction pieces to estimate the following sums to the nearest whole number:

1. $4\frac{1}{8} + 3\frac{2}{9}$ (7) **2.** $3\frac{7}{8} + 5\frac{5}{9}$ (10)

3. $2\frac{9}{10} + 5\frac{3}{8}$ (8) **4.** $5\frac{5}{6} + \frac{9}{10}$ (7)

- Have students compare answers with a classmate. Have them explain whether their estimate will be greater or less than the actual answer.

Real-World Connection

Material: Cookbook

- Discuss with students that chefs constantly adjust the amounts of ingredients in their recipes to make new flavors.
- Have pairs of students use a cookbook to find a recipe for something they would like to eat and list its ingredients. Have them round each fractional amount to the nearest whole number.

Grandma's Favorite Cookies

$\frac{1}{2}$ pound butter
2 eggs
2 cups flour
1 cup brown sugar
1 tsp vanilla
$\frac{1}{2}$ tsp salt
$\frac{1}{2}$ cup peanuts

Mix ingredients well.
Refrigerate for 2 hours.
Bake in a 375° F oven.

❶ Introduce

Read the objective to students. By looking at the value of each addend, students will be able to estimate whether the sum of two fractions is less than or greater than 1.

❷ Teach

Learn About It

- Work through the first problem together. **How do you know that these fractions are less than $\frac{1}{2}$?** ($\frac{3}{8} < \frac{4}{8}$; $\frac{1}{6} < \frac{3}{6}$)
- Work through the second problem. **How do you know that these fractions are greater than $\frac{1}{2}$?** ($\frac{7}{8} > \frac{4}{8}$; $\frac{5}{6} > \frac{3}{6}$)
- **By classifying addends as greater than or less than $\frac{1}{2}$, our estimates have been either < 1 or > 1. What might our estimate be for $\frac{1}{3} + \frac{5}{8}$? Why?** (About 1; $\frac{1}{3}$ is less than $\frac{1}{2}$, $\frac{5}{8}$ is greater than $\frac{1}{2}$.)

Guided Practice

Have students complete **Exercises 1–4** as you observe. Remind them to use the ***Ask Yourself*** questions to help. Give students the opportunity to talk about the question in ***Explain Your Thinking***.

Common Error

- **Incorrectly comparing a fraction to $\frac{1}{2}$**
- **Intervention** Remind students how to compare fractions: find a common denominator, then compare numerators. Elicit that a fraction equivalent to $\frac{1}{2}$ will have a numerator that is half its denominator. Alternatively, have students use fraction pieces or an inch ruler to visually compare fractions to $\frac{1}{2}$.

Lesson 4

Estimate With Fractions

Objective Estimate sums of fractions.

Learn About It

Carlos wants to hike at least a mile. Should he take Falls Trail or Mine Trail?

Falls Trail
$\frac{1}{6}$ mile
$\frac{3}{8}$ mile
$\frac{5}{6}$ mile
Start of Trails
$\frac{7}{8}$ mile
Mine Trail

You can estimate to solve this problem. One way to estimate the sum of two fractions is by comparing each addend to $\frac{1}{2}$.

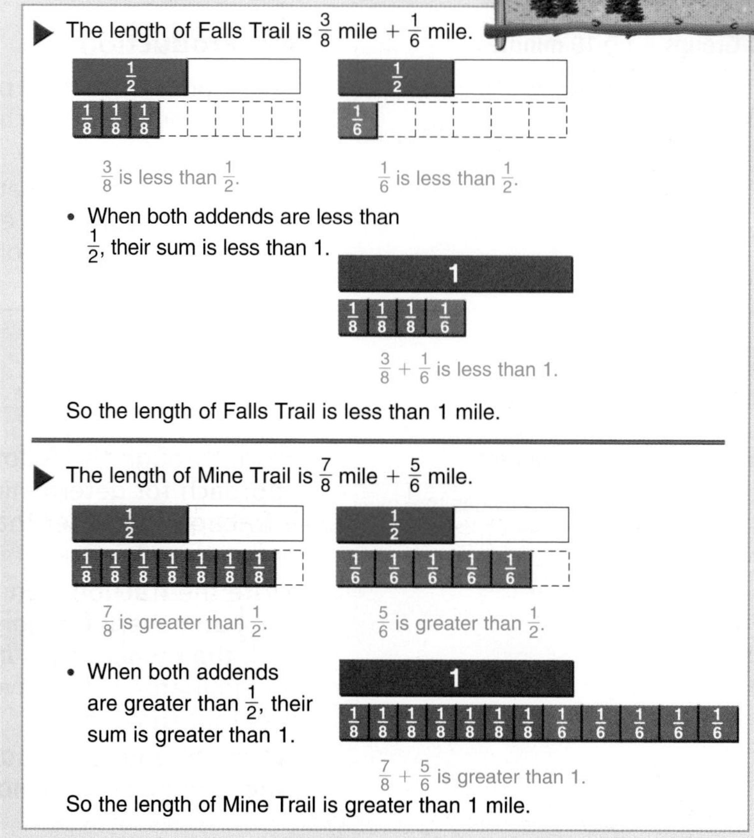

▶ The length of Falls Trail is $\frac{3}{8}$ mile + $\frac{1}{6}$ mile.

$\frac{3}{8}$ is less than $\frac{1}{2}$. $\frac{1}{6}$ is less than $\frac{1}{2}$.

- When both addends are less than $\frac{1}{2}$, their sum is less than 1.

$\frac{3}{8} + \frac{1}{6}$ is less than 1.

So the length of Falls Trail is less than 1 mile.

▶ The length of Mine Trail is $\frac{7}{8}$ mile + $\frac{5}{6}$ mile.

$\frac{7}{8}$ is greater than $\frac{1}{2}$. $\frac{5}{6}$ is greater than $\frac{1}{2}$.

- When both addends are greater than $\frac{1}{2}$, their sum is greater than 1.

$\frac{7}{8} + \frac{5}{6}$ is greater than 1.

So the length of Mine Trail is greater than 1 mile.

Solution: Carlos should hike Mine Trail.

524

Reteach 20.4

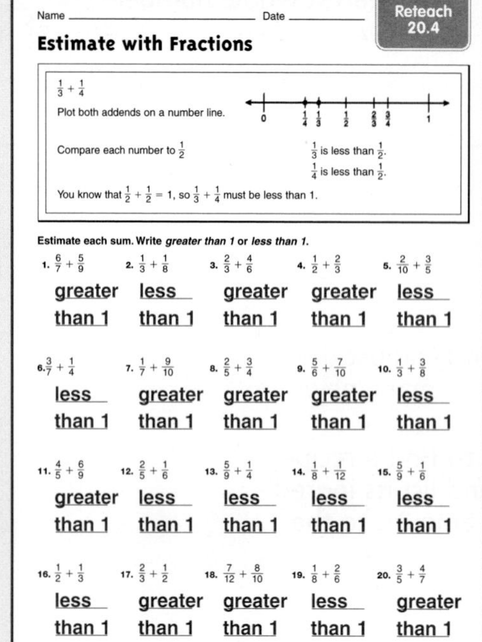

Name ____________ Date ________ Reteach 20.4

Estimate with Fractions

$\frac{1}{3} + \frac{1}{4}$

Plot both addends on a number line.

Compare each number to $\frac{1}{2}$

$\frac{1}{3}$ is less than $\frac{1}{2}$.
$\frac{1}{4}$ is less than $\frac{1}{2}$.

You know that $\frac{1}{2} + \frac{1}{2} = 1$, so $\frac{1}{3} + \frac{1}{4}$ must be less than 1.

Estimate each sum. Write *greater than 1* or *less than 1*.

1. $\frac{6}{7} + \frac{5}{9}$ greater than 1
2. $\frac{1}{3} + \frac{1}{8}$ less than 1
3. $\frac{2}{3} + \frac{4}{6}$ greater than 1
4. $\frac{1}{2} + \frac{2}{3}$ greater than 1
5. $\frac{2}{10} + \frac{3}{5}$ less than 1
6. $\frac{3}{7} + \frac{1}{4}$ less than 1
7. $\frac{1}{7} + \frac{9}{10}$ greater than 1
8. $\frac{2}{5} + \frac{3}{4}$ greater than 1
9. $\frac{5}{6} + \frac{7}{10}$ greater than 1
10. $\frac{1}{3} + \frac{3}{8}$ less than 1
11. $\frac{4}{5} + \frac{6}{9}$ greater than 1
12. $\frac{2}{5} + \frac{1}{6}$ less than 1
13. $\frac{5}{9} + \frac{1}{4}$ less than 1
14. $\frac{1}{8} + \frac{1}{12}$ less than 1
15. $\frac{5}{9} + \frac{1}{6}$ less than 1
16. $\frac{1}{2} + \frac{1}{3}$ less than 1
17. $\frac{2}{3} + \frac{1}{2}$ greater than 1
18. $\frac{7}{12} + \frac{8}{10}$ greater than 1
19. $\frac{1}{8} + \frac{2}{6}$ less than 1
20. $\frac{3}{5} + \frac{4}{7}$ greater than 1

Use with text pages 524–525.

Practice 20.4 Page 127

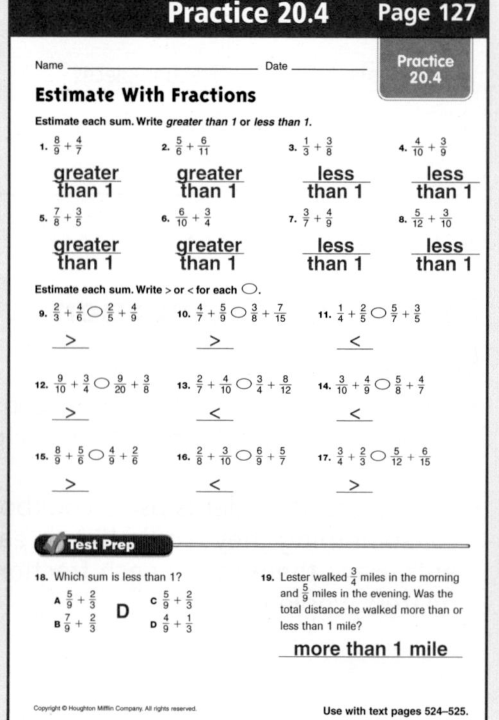

Name ____________ Date ________ Practice 20.4

Estimate With Fractions

Estimate each sum. Write *greater than 1* or *less than 1*.

1. $\frac{8}{9} + \frac{4}{7}$ greater than 1
2. $\frac{5}{6} + \frac{6}{11}$ greater than 1
3. $\frac{1}{3} + \frac{3}{8}$ less than 1
4. $\frac{4}{10} + \frac{3}{9}$ less than 1
5. $\frac{7}{8} + \frac{3}{5}$ greater than 1
6. $\frac{6}{10} + \frac{3}{4}$ greater than 1
7. $\frac{3}{7} + \frac{4}{9}$ less than 1
8. $\frac{5}{12} + \frac{3}{10}$ less than 1

Estimate each sum. Write > or < for each ◯.

9. $\frac{2}{3} + \frac{4}{6}$ ◯ $\frac{2}{5} + \frac{4}{9}$ >
10. $\frac{4}{7} + \frac{5}{9}$ ◯ $\frac{3}{8} + \frac{7}{15}$ >
11. $\frac{1}{4} + \frac{2}{5}$ ◯ $\frac{5}{7} + \frac{3}{5}$ <
12. $\frac{9}{10} + \frac{3}{4}$ ◯ $\frac{9}{20} + \frac{3}{8}$ >
13. $\frac{2}{7} + \frac{4}{10}$ ◯ $\frac{3}{4} + \frac{8}{12}$ <
14. $\frac{3}{10} + \frac{4}{9}$ ◯ $\frac{5}{8} + \frac{4}{7}$ <
15. $\frac{8}{9} + \frac{5}{6}$ ◯ $\frac{4}{9} + \frac{2}{6}$ >
16. $\frac{2}{8} + \frac{3}{10}$ ◯ $\frac{6}{9} + \frac{5}{7}$ <
17. $\frac{3}{4} + \frac{2}{3}$ ◯ $\frac{5}{12} + \frac{6}{15}$ >

Test Prep

18. Which sum is less than 1? D
    A $\frac{5}{9} + \frac{2}{3}$
    B $\frac{7}{9} + \frac{2}{3}$
    C $\frac{5}{9} + \frac{2}{3}$
    D $\frac{4}{9} + \frac{1}{3}$

19. Lester walked $\frac{3}{4}$ miles in the morning and $\frac{5}{9}$ miles in the evening. Was the total distance he walked more than or less than 1 mile?
    more than 1 mile

Use with text pages 524–525.

Guided Practice

Estimate each sum. Write *greater than 1* or *less than 1*.

1. $\frac{1}{3} + \frac{1}{4}$ less than 1
2. $\frac{3}{4} + \frac{5}{8}$ greater than 1
3. $\frac{1}{8} + \frac{3}{10}$ less than 1
4. $\frac{5}{9} + \frac{2}{3}$ greater than 1

Ask Yourself

- Are both fractions less than $\frac{1}{2}$?
- Are both fractions greater than $\frac{1}{2}$?

Explain Your Thinking ▶ What can you say about the sum of $\frac{3}{4}$ and $\frac{2}{5}$? **The sum is greater than one because if you write the fractions as $\frac{15}{20}$ and $\frac{8}{20}$, the sum is greater than 1.**

Practice and Problem Solving

Estimate each sum. Write *greater than 1* or *less than 1*.

5. $\frac{5}{8} + \frac{7}{10}$ *greater than 1*
6. $\frac{3}{8} + \frac{3}{9}$ *less than 1*
7. $\frac{1}{8} + \frac{1}{3}$ *less than 1*
8. $\frac{2}{5} + \frac{2}{5}$ *less than 1*
9. $\frac{4}{5} + \frac{8}{9}$ *greater than 1*
10. $\frac{4}{9} + \frac{2}{5}$ *less than 1*
11. $\frac{5}{6} + \frac{7}{8}$ *greater than 1*
12. $\frac{3}{10} + \frac{3}{8}$ *less than 1*
13. $\frac{1}{2} + \frac{3}{4}$ *greater than 1*
14. $\frac{1}{2} + \frac{1}{3}$ *less than 1*

Estimate each sum. Write > or < for each ⬬.

15. $\frac{1}{3} + \frac{3}{8}$ < $\frac{3}{4} + \frac{5}{8}$
16. $\frac{3}{8} + \frac{4}{9}$ < $\frac{2}{3} + \frac{4}{6}$
17. $\frac{5}{6} + \frac{5}{8}$ > $\frac{5}{12} + \frac{5}{15}$
18. $\frac{5}{6} + \frac{7}{10}$ > $\frac{5}{12} + \frac{1}{3}$
19. $\frac{5}{8} + \frac{3}{4}$ > $\frac{1}{5} + \frac{2}{10}$
20. $\frac{2}{5} + \frac{1}{6}$ < $\frac{4}{5} + \frac{6}{9}$

Data Use the table at the right to solve Problems 21–24.

21. On what day did Jen run less than 1 mile? **Day 1**
22. On what day did Jen run more than a mile? **Day 2**
23. How many miles did Jen run on Day 3? **1 mile**
24. On Day 3, how much farther did Jen run in the evening than in the morning? **$\frac{1}{3}$ mile**

Jen's Running Log

	Morning	Evening
Day 1	$\frac{1}{4}$ mile	$\frac{3}{8}$ mile
Day 2	$\frac{4}{5}$ mile	$\frac{7}{10}$ mile
Day 3	$\frac{1}{3}$ mile	$\frac{2}{3}$ mile

Mixed Review and Test Prep

Open Response

Find each product or quotient.
(Ch. 7, Lesson 4; Ch. 8, Lesson 2)

25. 21 × 31 **651**
26. 84 × 42 **3,528**
27. 78 ÷ 7 **11 R1**
28. 37 ÷ 3 **12 R1**

Multiple Choice

29. Which sum is greater than 1? (Ch. 20, Lesson 4)

A $\frac{1}{3} + \frac{2}{5}$
B $\frac{2}{7} + \frac{4}{10}$
C $\frac{3}{8} + \frac{1}{9}$
(D) $\frac{4}{5} + \frac{7}{8}$

Extra Practice See page 539, Set C.

3 Practice

Practice and Problem Solving

Select from **Exercises 5–29** as independent work. Allow students to work with fraction pieces, as needed, to help make their estimates.

- ***Data*** For **Problems 21–24**, ask: **On which day did Jen run for exactly 1 mile?** (Day 3) **On which day did Jen run farther in the morning than in the evening?** (Day 2; $\frac{4}{5} > \frac{7}{10}$)

4 Assess & Close

Math Talk in Action

Have students refer to **Exercises 5 and 7** to conclude the lesson. Have them explain how to estimate each sum.

Math Journal Prompt

Have students write an explanation of how to estimate the sum of two fractions. Have them explain how estimating sums of fractions is similar to estimating sums of whole numbers. Ask them to explain how the process is different.

Lesson Quiz

Use the quiz on Lesson Transparency 20.4.

Test Prep & Spiral Review

Use Test Prep Transparency 20.4.

Enrichment 20.4

Name ______ Date ______ **Enrichment 20.4**

Fitness Mile

As part of a fitness plan, the fourth-graders at Mathville Middle School agreed to walk at least 1 mile each day. The students made charts showing the distance they walked in the morning and the distance they walked in the evening. Look at the charts below. For each chart, place a circle around the days in which the student walked at least 1 mile.

1. *Sean*	Morning	Evening
Monday	$\frac{1}{4}$ mile	$\frac{3}{8}$ mile
(Tuesday)	$\frac{1}{2}$ mile	$\frac{5}{8}$ mile
(Wednesday)	$\frac{2}{3}$ mile	$\frac{7}{10}$ mile
(Thursday)	$\frac{5}{6}$ mile	$\frac{7}{12}$ mile
Friday	$\frac{1}{5}$ mile	$\frac{5}{12}$ mile

2. *Charles*	Morning	Evening
(Monday)	$\frac{5}{8}$ mile	$\frac{3}{4}$ mile
Tuesday	$\frac{3}{10}$ mile	$\frac{1}{3}$ mile
Wednesday	$\frac{3}{8}$ mile	$\frac{4}{9}$ mile
(Thursday)	$\frac{7}{12}$ mile	$\frac{3}{4}$ mile
(Friday)	$\frac{4}{6}$ mile	$\frac{2}{3}$ mile

3. *Courtney*	Morning	Evening
(Monday)	$\frac{5}{9}$ mile	$\frac{7}{10}$ mile
(Tuesday)	$\frac{2}{3}$ mile	$\frac{3}{5}$ mile
Wednesday	$\frac{3}{8}$ mile	$\frac{1}{2}$ mile
Thursday	$\frac{1}{4}$ mile	$\frac{1}{3}$ mile
(Friday)	$\frac{3}{5}$ mile	$\frac{7}{8}$ mile

4. *Tamara*	Morning	Evening
(Monday)	$\frac{8}{12}$ mile	$\frac{3}{4}$ mile
(Tuesday)	$\frac{3}{5}$ mile	$\frac{1}{2}$ mile
(Wednesday)	$\frac{7}{10}$ mile	$\frac{5}{8}$ mile
(Thursday)	$\frac{7}{8}$ mile	$\frac{3}{6}$ mile
(Friday)	$\frac{5}{9}$ mile	$\frac{2}{3}$ mile

5. *Heidi*	Morning	Evening
(Monday)	$\frac{3}{5}$ mile	$\frac{3}{4}$ mile
Tuesday	$\frac{2}{7}$ mile	$\frac{3}{8}$ mile
Wednesday	$\frac{4}{9}$ mile	$\frac{1}{2}$ mile
(Thursday)	$\frac{7}{10}$ mile	$\frac{3}{5}$ mile
(Friday)	$\frac{9}{12}$ mile	$\frac{5}{6}$ mile

6. *Curtis*	Morning	Evening
(Monday)	$\frac{8}{9}$ mile	$\frac{1}{2}$ mile
(Tuesday)	$\frac{7}{10}$ mile	$\frac{4}{7}$ mile
Wednesday	$\frac{5}{16}$ mile	$\frac{1}{2}$ mile
(Thursday)	$\frac{9}{10}$ mile	$\frac{3}{5}$ mile
Friday	$\frac{7}{16}$ mile	$\frac{4}{9}$ mile

 Use with text pages 524–525.

Problem Solving 20.4

Name ______ Date ______ **Problem Solving 20.4**

Estimate With Fractions

Solve. ***Possible explanations given.*** Show your work.

1. Mrs. Unger is making pudding. The recipe calls for a quart of milk. She has $\frac{5}{6}$ quart of milk in one container and $\frac{3}{4}$ quart of milk in another container. Does she have enough milk? Explain.
Yes; $\frac{5}{6} + \frac{3}{4}$ is greater than 1.
2. Lita has $\frac{1}{3}$ cup of almonds and $\frac{2}{5}$ cup of walnuts. She wants to combine the nuts in a 1-cup container. Will the nuts fit in the container? Explain.
Yes; $\frac{1}{3} + \frac{2}{5}$ is less than 1.
3. Mick takes a karate class. First the class spends $\frac{1}{2}$ hour doing stretches and strength exercises. Then they spend $\frac{3}{4}$ hour doing karate moves. Is Mick's class greater than or less than 1 hour long? Explain.
greater than 1 hour; *Possible explanation:* $\frac{1}{2} + \frac{3}{5}$ is greater than 1.
4. **You Decide** The Sharp family ordered pizzas for dinner. They ate $\frac{5}{12}$ of the pepperoni pizza and $\frac{5}{8}$ of the plain pizza. Did they eat more or less than 1 whole pizza?
More than 1 pizza.

 Use with text pages 524–525.

Homework 20.4 Page 127

Name ______ Date ______ **Homework 20.4**

Estimate With Fractions

Estimate each sum. Write *greater than 1* or *less than 1*.

$\frac{7}{12} + \frac{2}{3}$

$\frac{7}{12}$ is greater than $\frac{1}{2}$
$\frac{2}{3}$ is greater than $\frac{1}{2}$
When both addends are greater than $\frac{1}{2}$, their sum is greater than 1.
$\frac{7}{12} + \frac{2}{3}$ is *greater than 1.*

1. $\frac{7}{8} + \frac{8}{10}$ **greater than 1**
2. $\frac{4}{9} + \frac{3}{8}$ **less than 1**
3. $\frac{3}{4} + \frac{8}{12}$ **greater than 1**
4. $\frac{3}{5} + \frac{4}{7}$ **greater than 1**

Estimate each sum. Write > or < for each ◯.

5. $\frac{1}{4} + \frac{2}{7}$ < $\frac{6}{8} + \frac{7}{11}$
6. $\frac{5}{9} + \frac{12}{15}$ > $\frac{9}{20} + \frac{6}{14}$
7. $\frac{2}{3} + \frac{7}{9}$ > $\frac{4}{10} + \frac{1}{8}$
8. $\frac{5}{12} + \frac{7}{15}$ < $\frac{11}{16} + \frac{5}{7}$

Problem Solving

9. Willow decorated $\frac{4}{6}$ of a square yard of fabric in the morning and $\frac{3}{4}$ of a square yard in the evening. Her sister Jessica decorated 1 whole square yard of fabric on the same day. Which sister decorated more fabric that day? Show your work.
Willow

 Use with text pages 524–525.

Lesson 20.5

Problem-Solving Decision: Choose a Method

Planning

Lesson Objective Choose a method to solve a problem.

Technology Resources

- *Ways to Success* CD-ROM 20.5
- *Ways to Assess* CD-ROM
- Education Place: Extra Practice, Weekly Reader www.eduplace.com/map

Lesson 20.5 Transparency

Problem of the Day

The Chen family brought cookies to a bake sale. Anna brought $\frac{3}{12}$ of the cookies they baked, Nelson brought $\frac{2}{12}$, and Louise brought $\frac{5}{12}$. What fraction of the cookies did the Chen children bring to the bake sale? Give your answer in simplest form. $(\frac{5}{6})$

Spiral Review

Find each sum or difference. Write your answer in simplest form.

1. $\frac{9}{10} - \frac{4}{10}$ $(\frac{1}{2})$

2. $2\frac{1}{3} + 4\frac{2}{3}$ (7)

Lesson Quiz

Solve. Explain which method you chose.

1. Every seat was filled in the stadium. The stadium has 32 sections. Each section has 1,588 seats. How many fans were in the stands? (50,816; calculator)

2. A jogger ran $5\frac{3}{5}$ miles one day, $3\frac{1}{5}$ miles the next day, and $4\frac{2}{5}$ miles the third day. How many more miles did she run the first day than the third? ($1\frac{1}{5}$; mental math)

NCTM Standards

Problem Solving: Solve problems that arise in mathematics and other contexts.
Number and Operations: Recognize equivalent representations for the same number.

Getting Started

Building Math Vocabulary

Students should be familiar with the mathematical vocabulary in this lesson.

Using Mental Math

Whole Class	25 minutes
Objective	Describe mental math techniques.
Materials	Blank transparency
Visual, Auditory	

- Write $\frac{7}{8} - \frac{2}{8}$ on the transparency. Ask a volunteer to solve the problem using mental math.
- Ask the student to explain why this problem can be done easily using mental math.
- Write 21 − 9 on the transparency. Ask: **Can we use mental math to find the solution?** Allow students to discuss possible strategies.
- Write $3\frac{3}{4} + 4\frac{1}{4} + 7\frac{3}{4}$ on the transparency. Ask **Can we use mental math to find the solution? What other methods of finding the solution could we use?**
- Direct students' attention to page 526 of their book. Explain that there are many methods for solving problems—including mental math. In this lesson they will have to decide on the best method for each problem.

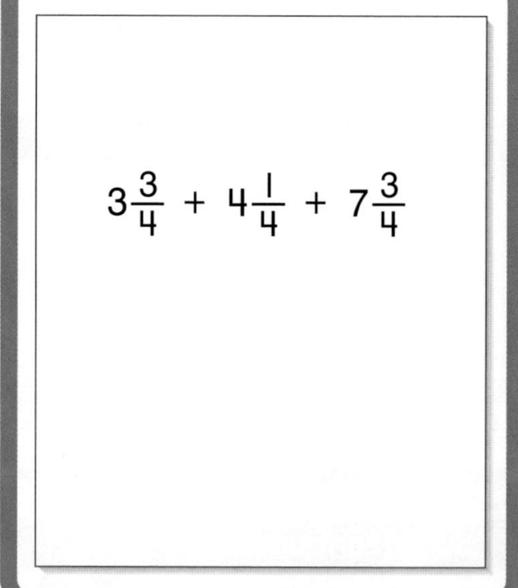

Differentiated Instruction

English Learners

Small Groups	15 minutes
Objective	Choose a method to solve a problem.
Materials	Student page 526
Auditory, Visual	

Early Production

- Have students follow these directions with ***Try These*** problems.
- Read the problem aloud. Write the phrase that tells what operation to use and the symbol of the operation needed to solve it.
- Then use the ***Ask Yourself*** questions to find the answer.

Intermediate/Advanced

- English Learner Resource 20.5
- English Learner Handbook

Intervention

Small Groups	10 minutes
Objective	Choose a method to solve a problem.
Materials	Calculators
Auditory, Visual	

- Tell students that in today's lesson they are going to focus on different computation methods they can use to solve a problem. Write $4\frac{3}{4} + 1\frac{1}{4}$ on the board. **Would you use paper and pencil or mental math to find the sum? Why?** Discuss students' explanations.
- Then write $4 \times (523 + 477)$. **Would you use mental math, paper and pencil, or a calculator to find this answer? Explain.** Again discuss students' responses and explanations.

Other Resources

- *Ways to Success* CD-ROM 20.5

Special Needs

Small Groups	30 minutes
Objective	Use a calculator to add and subtract fractions.
Materials	Calculator
Tactual, Auditory	

- Spend time helping students to understand and use the calculator. Give them time to examine the keys and see what each does.
- Work together through the steps in the process for adding and subtracting fractions.
- Have students solve the following computations in simplest form:

1. $\frac{1}{3} + \frac{2}{3}$ (1)
2. $\frac{5}{6} + \frac{5}{6}$ ($1\frac{2}{3}$)
3. $\frac{11}{12} - \frac{5}{12}$ ($\frac{1}{2}$)
4. $\frac{7}{8} - \frac{3}{8}$ ($\frac{1}{2}$)

Social Studies Connection

Materials: Bicycle magazines

- Have students learn more about bicycle racing. They can research local races or famous ones such as the *Tour de France*. Students can learn about the courses, riders, rules, and so on.
- Have students use information they gather to write questions about the race. They can, for instance, write map-distance questions. Questions can require solvers to choose a solution method.

1 Introduce

Read the objective with students. Explain to students that they will learn to choose the most efficient way to solve a problem—mental math, paper and pencil, or calculator.

2 Teach

Choose a Method

Materials: Calculators

- Have a volunteer read aloud the opening problem. Then have students show how to solve it using each method.
- **When would you use mental math to solve a problem involving adding or subtracting fractions?** Discuss students' answers.
- **When would you use a calculator?** Guide students to see that they should use mental math if the fractions involved are easy for them to compute. Suggest they use a calculator when the fractions are not so easy to compute mentally and when computing quickly is important.

3 Practice

Try These

Select from **Problems 1–4** as independent work. Have students explain their strategies. Ask, **How would you use mental math to solve Problem 3?** (Use division fact: 20 ÷ 4.)

4 Assess & Close

Math Talk in Action

Have students explain how they would decide whether to estimate, use mental math, or use a calculator. Allow them to use examples from the lesson.

Math Journal Prompt

Have students write a problem involving fractions or mixed numbers that can be solved using mental math.

Lesson Quiz

Use the quiz on Lesson Transparency 20.5.

Lesson 20.5 Transparency

Test Prep & Spiral Review

Use Test Prep Transparency 20.5

Test Prep 20.5 Transparency

Lesson 5

Problem-Solving Decision

Choose a Method

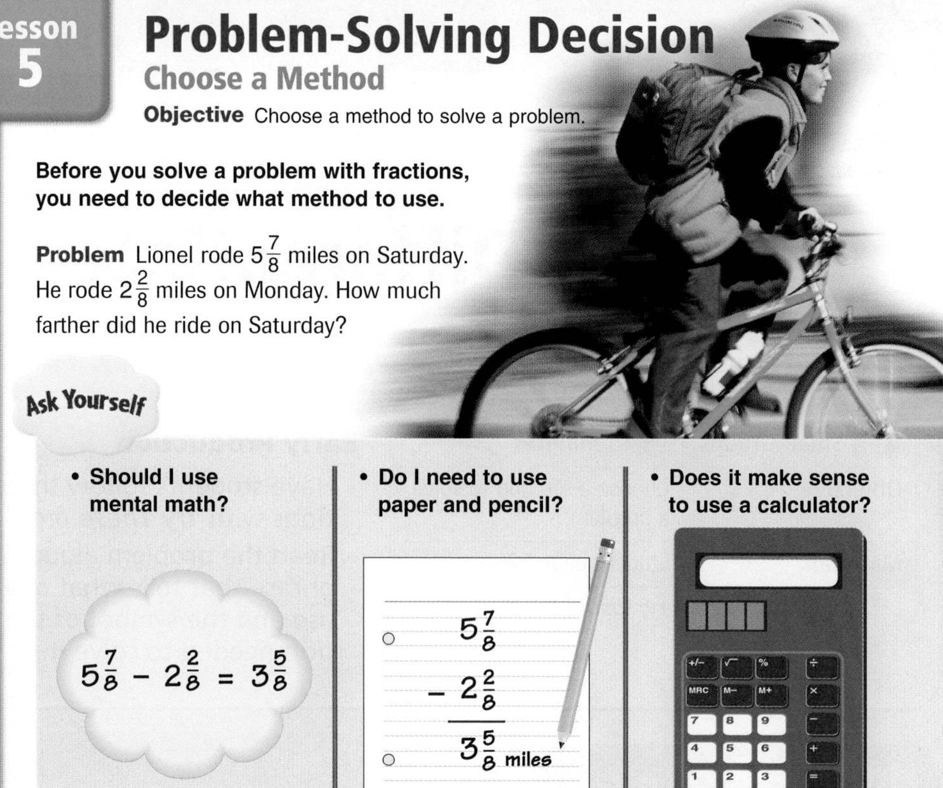

Objective Choose a method to solve a problem.

Before you solve a problem with fractions, you need to decide what method to use.

Problem Lionel rode $5\frac{7}{8}$ miles on Saturday. He rode $2\frac{2}{8}$ miles on Monday. How much farther did he ride on Saturday?

Ask Yourself

- Should I use mental math?
- Do I need to use paper and pencil?
- Does it make sense to use a calculator?

$5\frac{7}{8} - 2\frac{2}{8} = 3\frac{5}{8}$

$$\begin{array}{r} 5\frac{7}{8} \\ -\ 2\frac{2}{8} \\ \hline 3\frac{5}{8} \text{ miles} \end{array}$$

Solution: Lionel rode $3\frac{5}{8}$ miles farther on Saturday. Which method would you have chosen to solve?

Try These

Solve. Explain which method you chose and why. ***Possible methods given.***

1. A group of bicyclists rode $\frac{7}{10}$ mile before lunch and $\frac{2}{10}$ mile after lunch. How much farther did they ride before lunch? **$\frac{1}{2}$ mile; Mental Math**
2. In three days a cyclist rode $4\frac{1}{5}$ miles, $3\frac{3}{5}$ miles, and $2\frac{1}{5}$ miles. How many miles did she ride in those three days? **10 miles; Paper and Pencil**
3. Helen won $\frac{1}{4}$ of her bicycle races last year. If she competed in 20 races, how many races did she win? **5 races; Mental Math**
4. Four professional bicyclists rode 3,280 miles in 41 days. What was the mean number of miles that they rode each day? **80 miles; Calculator**

526

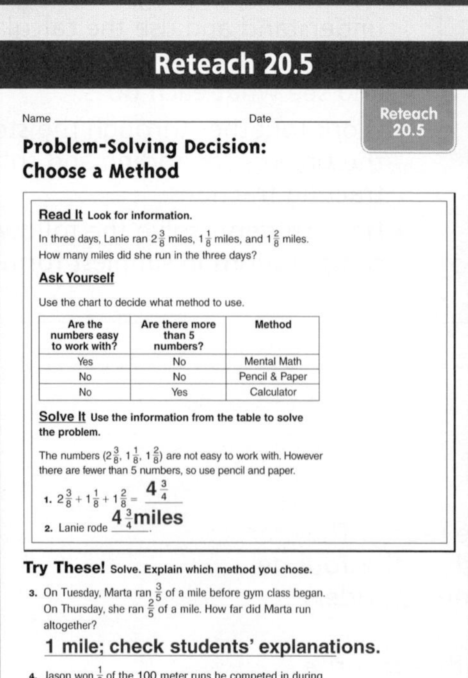

Reteach 20.5

Name ______________ Date ________

Reteach 20.5

Problem-Solving Decision: Choose a Method

Read It Look for information.

In three days, Lanie ran $2\frac{3}{8}$ miles, $1\frac{1}{8}$ miles, and $1\frac{2}{8}$ miles. How many miles did she run in the three days?

Ask Yourself

Use the chart to decide what method to use.

Are the numbers easy to work with?	Are there more than 5 numbers?	Method
Yes	No	Mental Math
No	No	Pencil & Paper
No	Yes	Calculator

Solve It Use the information from the table to solve the problem.

The numbers ($2\frac{3}{8}$, $1\frac{1}{8}$, $1\frac{2}{8}$) are not easy to work with. However there are fewer than 5 numbers, so use pencil and paper.

1. $2\frac{3}{8} + 1\frac{1}{8} + 1\frac{2}{8} =$ **$4\frac{3}{4}$**
2. Lanie rode **$4\frac{3}{4}$ miles**.

Try These! Solve. Explain which method you chose.

3. On Tuesday, Marta ran $\frac{3}{5}$ of a mile before gym class began. On Thursday, she ran $\frac{2}{5}$ of a mile. How far did Marta run altogether? **1 mile; check students' explanations.**
4. Jason won $\frac{1}{3}$ of the 100 meter runs he competed in during track season. If he competed in 15 races, how many did he win? **5 races; check students' explanations.**

Use with text page 526.

Practice 20.5 Page 128

Name ______________ Date ________

Practice 20.5

Problem-Solving Decision: Choose a Method

Solve. Explain which method you chose. **Show your work.**

1. Byron painted $\frac{3}{12}$ of his painting before lunch and $\frac{8}{12}$ of his painting after lunch. How much more of his painting did he work on after lunch? **$\frac{5}{12}$; mental math**
2. Joan recorded $\frac{1}{3}$ of the songs on her record in January. If the record has 18 songs total, how many did she record in January? **6; mental math**
3. In three days David drove $4\frac{2}{10}$ miles, $8\frac{3}{10}$ miles, and $5\frac{4}{10}$ miles. How many miles did he drive in the three days? **$17\frac{9}{10}$; pencil and paper**
4. Xavier ran 798 miles in 95 days while training for the marathon. How many miles did he average per day? **$8\frac{2}{5}$; calculator**
5. The band Skywriter played 234 shows in 52 weeks. How many shows did they average per week? **$4\frac{1}{2}$; calculator**

Use with text page 526.

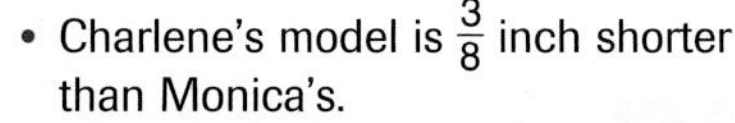

Art Connection

Pet Projects

In art class, five students made models of their pets. Match each model with the student who created it.

- Earl's model is $1\frac{5}{8}$ inches taller than Monica's.
- Bob's model is 2 inches taller than Marla's.
- Charlene's model is $\frac{3}{8}$ inch shorter than Monica's.
- Monica's model is $2\frac{3}{8}$ inches tall.

Marla: bird
Monica: small dog
Earl: large dog
Charlene: rabbit
Bob: cat

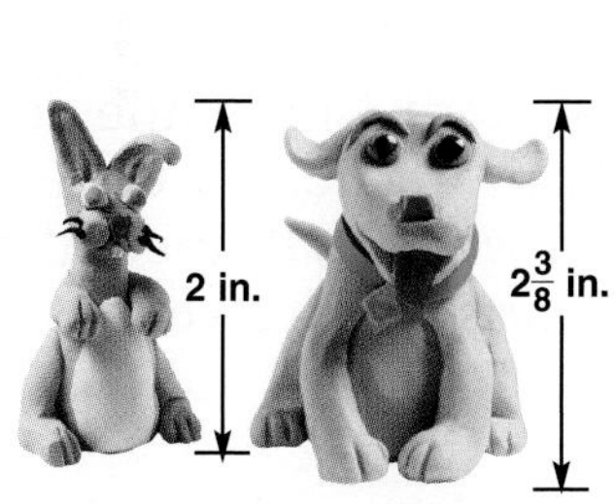

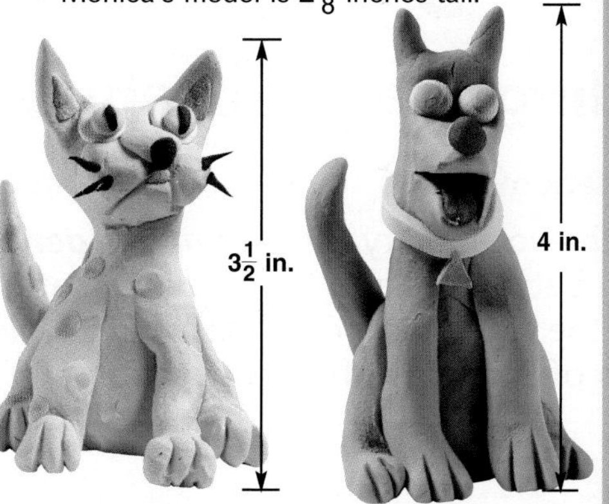

WEEKLY WR READER eduplace.com/map

Quick Check

Check your understanding of Lessons 1–5.

Find each sum or difference in simplest form. (Lessons 1–2)

1. $\frac{2}{6} + \frac{4}{6}$ **1**

2. $\frac{7}{12} - \frac{5}{12}$ **$\frac{1}{6}$**

3. $3\frac{1}{6} + 5\frac{1}{6}$ **$8\frac{1}{3}$**

4. $4\frac{5}{6} - 1\frac{2}{6}$ **$3\frac{1}{2}$**

Estimate each sum. Write *greater than 1* or *less than 1*. (Lesson 4)

5. $\frac{7}{8} + \frac{3}{4}$ *greater than 1*

6. $\frac{1}{6} + \frac{1}{4}$ *less than 1*

7. $\frac{2}{5} + \frac{3}{10}$ *less than 1*

8. $\frac{8}{9} + \frac{3}{5}$ *greater than 1*

Solve. (Lessons 3, 5)

9. Sarah has \$30 to buy books. Each book costs \$4. How many books can she buy? **7 books**

10. An express train leaves at 5:30 P.M. and arrives $1\frac{1}{2}$ hours later. What time does the train arrive? **7:00 P.M.**

Extra Practice at **eduplace.com/map**

Art Connection

Pet Projects

Remind students that all clues they need are provided. **Which piece of information can you use to begin to solve the problem?**
(height of Monica's model)

Quick Check

The *Quick Check* allows you to assess the students' understanding of the concepts presented in Lessons 1–5.

Item	Lesson Objectives	Pages	Intervention
1–2	Add and subtract fractions with like denominators.	516–519	Reteach Resources 20.1 *Ways to Success* CD 20.1
3–4	Add and subtract mixed numbers with like denominators.	520–521	Reteach Resources 20.2 *Ways to Success* CD 20.2
5–8	Estimate sums of fractions.	524–525	Reteach Resources 20.4 *Ways to Success* CD 20.4
9	Decide how to write the quotient to solve a problem.	522–523	Reteach Resources 20.3 *Ways to Success* CD 20.3
10	Choose a method to solve a problem.	526	Reteach Resources 20.5 *Ways to Success* CD 20.5

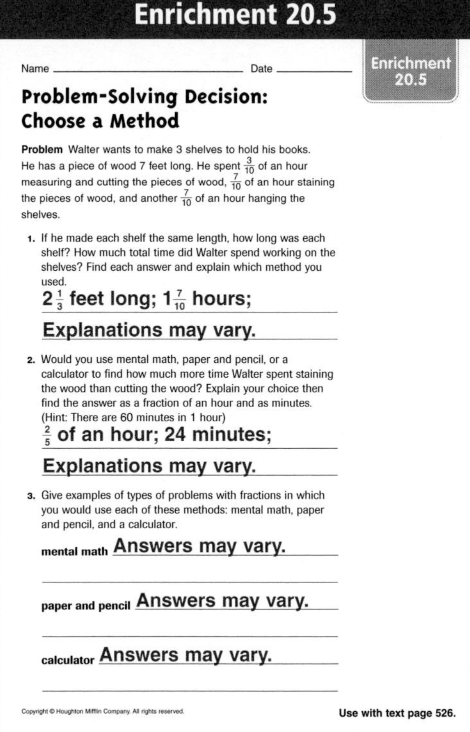

Enrichment 20.5

Name ______________ Date ________

Enrichment 20.5

Problem-Solving Decision: Choose a Method

Problem Walter wants to make 3 shelves to hold his books. He has a piece of wood 7 feet long. He spent $\frac{3}{10}$ of an hour measuring and cutting the pieces of wood, $\frac{7}{10}$ of an hour staining the pieces of wood, and another $\frac{7}{10}$ of an hour hanging the shelves.

1. If he made each shelf the same length, how long was each shelf? How much total time did Walter spend working on the shelves? Find each answer and explain which method you used.
$2\frac{1}{3}$ feet long; $1\frac{7}{10}$ hours;
Explanations may vary.

2. Would you use mental math, paper and pencil, or a calculator to find how much more time Walter spent staining the wood than cutting the wood? Explain your choice then find the answer as a fraction of an hour and as minutes. (Hint: There are 60 minutes in 1 hour)
$\frac{2}{5}$ of an hour; 24 minutes;
Explanations may vary.

3. Give examples of types of problems with fractions in which you would use each of these methods: mental math, paper and pencil, and a calculator.
mental math **Answers may vary.**
paper and pencil **Answers may vary.**
calculator **Answers may vary.**

Use with text page 526.

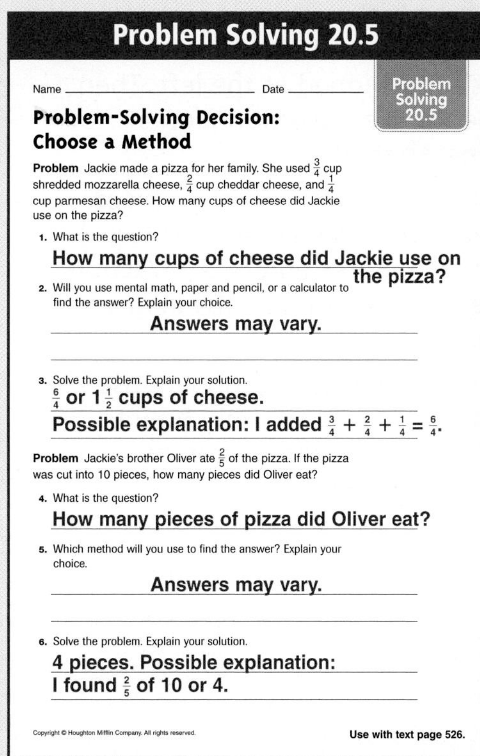

Problem Solving 20.5

Name ______________ Date ________

Problem Solving 20.5

Problem-Solving Decision: Choose a Method

Problem Jackie made a pizza for her family. She used $\frac{3}{4}$ cup shredded mozzarella cheese, $\frac{2}{4}$ cup cheddar cheese, and $\frac{1}{4}$ cup parmesan cheese. How many cups of cheese did Jackie use on the pizza?

1. What is the question?
How many cups of cheese did Jackie use on the pizza?

2. Will you use mental math, paper and pencil, or a calculator to find the answer? Explain your choice.
Answers may vary.

3. Solve the problem. Explain your solution.
$\frac{6}{4}$ or $1\frac{1}{2}$ cups of cheese.
Possible explanation: I added $\frac{3}{4} + \frac{2}{4} + \frac{1}{4} = \frac{6}{4}$.

Problem Jackie's brother Oliver ate $\frac{2}{5}$ of the pizza. If the pizza was cut into 10 pieces, how many pieces did Oliver eat?

4. What is the question?
How many pieces of pizza did Oliver eat?

5. Which method will you use to find the answer? Explain your choice.
Answers may vary.

6. Solve the problem. Explain your solution.
4 pieces. Possible explanation: I found $\frac{2}{5}$ of 10 or 4.

Use with text page 526.

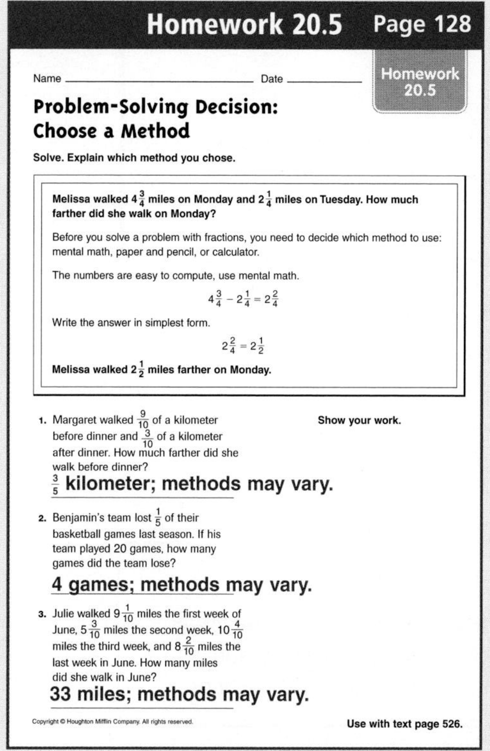

Homework 20.5 Page 128

Name ______________ Date ________

Homework 20.5

Problem-Solving Decision: Choose a Method

Solve. Explain which method you chose.

Melissa walked $4\frac{3}{4}$ miles on Monday and $2\frac{1}{4}$ miles on Tuesday. How much farther did she walk on Monday?

Before you solve a problem with fractions, you need to decide which method to use: mental math, paper and pencil, or calculator.

The numbers are easy to compute, use mental math.

$$4\frac{3}{4} - 2\frac{1}{4} = 2\frac{2}{4}$$

Write the answer in simplest form.

$$2\frac{2}{4} = 2\frac{1}{2}$$

Melissa walked $2\frac{1}{2}$ miles farther on Monday.

Show your work.

1. Margaret walked $\frac{9}{10}$ of a kilometer before dinner and $\frac{3}{10}$ of a kilometer after dinner. How much farther did she walk before dinner?
$\frac{3}{5}$ kilometer; methods may vary.

2. Benjamin's team lost $\frac{1}{5}$ of their basketball games last season. If his team played 20 games, how many games did the team lose?
4 games; methods may vary.

3. Julie walked $9\frac{1}{10}$ miles the first week of June, $5\frac{3}{10}$ miles the second week, $10\frac{4}{10}$ miles the third week, and $8\frac{2}{10}$ miles the last week in June. How many miles did she walk in June?
33 miles; methods may vary.

Use with text page 526.

Hands On Lesson 20.6

Add Fractions with Unlike Denominators

Planning

Lesson Objective Use models to add fractions that have different denominators.

Technology Resources

- *Ways to Success* CD-ROM 20.6
- Education Place: Extra Practice, eGlossary, eManipulatives, eGames www.eduplace.com/map

Lesson 20.6 Transparency

Problem of the Day

A leap year has 366 days because February has 29 days during this kind of year. On what date are we exactly $\frac{1}{6}$ of the way through a leap year? (March 1)

Spiral Review

Write two equivalent fractions for each.
(Sample answers are given.)

1. $\frac{4}{5}$ ($\frac{8}{10}$, $\frac{16}{20}$)
2. $\frac{9}{12}$ ($\frac{3}{4}$, $\frac{18}{24}$)
3. $\frac{14}{28}$ ($\frac{1}{2}$, $\frac{7}{14}$)
4. $\frac{12}{8}$ ($\frac{3}{2}$, $\frac{6}{4}$)

Lesson Quiz

Find each sum. Use fraction pieces to help you.

1. $\frac{3}{10} + \frac{2}{5}$ ($\frac{7}{10}$)
2. $\frac{1}{3} + \frac{5}{6}$ ($1\frac{1}{6}$)
3. $\frac{5}{9} + \frac{2}{3}$ ($1\frac{2}{9}$)
4. $\frac{5}{8} + \frac{1}{6}$ ($\frac{19}{24}$)
5. $\frac{3}{8} + \frac{3}{4}$ ($1\frac{1}{8}$)
6. $\frac{5}{6} + \frac{1}{4}$ ($1\frac{1}{12}$)

NCTM Standards

Number and Operations: Use visual models, benchmarks, and equivalent forms to add and subtract commonly used fractions.

Getting Started

Building Math Vocabulary

unlike denominators denominators that are not equal

Review the vocabulary card for ***unlike denominators.*** Discuss the difference in meaning between $\frac{2}{3}$ and $\frac{2}{7}$. Point out that in both fractions, we are considering 2 of the total number of parts into which a whole is divided; the whole is made up of 3 parts in the first fraction and 7 parts in the second.

Model Addition with Unlike Denominators

Whole Class	15 minutes
Objective	Add fractions with unlike denominators.
Materials	Fraction Pieces Transparency, blank transparency
Visual, Auditory	

- Use the 1 fraction piece, $\frac{1}{6}$ fraction pieces, and $\frac{1}{3}$ fraction pieces cut out from the Fraction Pieces Transparency.
- Model $\frac{2}{3} + \frac{1}{6}$ on the overhead using the fraction pieces. **How can I use the fraction pieces to model $\frac{2}{3}$?** (Use two $\frac{1}{3}$ fraction pieces.)
- Place the 1 fraction piece at the top of a blank transparency. Place two $\frac{1}{3}$ fraction pieces and one $\frac{1}{6}$ fraction piece beneath it, with the first one aligned at the left. Then line up five $\frac{1}{6}$ fraction pieces beneath them.
- Ask: **How many $\frac{1}{6}$ fraction pieces show the same amount as two $\frac{1}{3}$ fraction pieces and one $\frac{1}{6}$ fraction piece?** (5) **So what is the sum of $\frac{2}{3}$ and $\frac{1}{6}$?** ($\frac{5}{6}$)
- Explain that the lesson will use fraction pieces to show how to add fractions with different denominators.

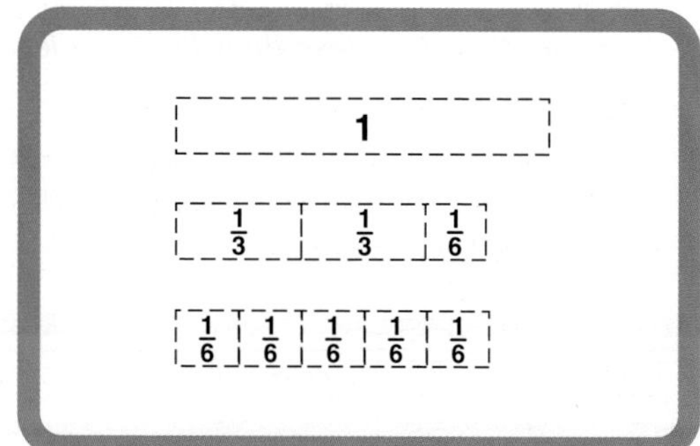

Differentiated Instruction

English Learners

Small Groups	10 minutes
Objective	Add fractions with unlike denominators.
Materials	Student page 529, fraction pieces (Learning Tool 34)
Auditory, Visual	

Early Production

- Students may need help finding the correct size of the fraction pieces that will fit exactly under the sum.
- Model the first two exercises in ***On Your Own.*** Ask students: **Can we use $\frac{1}{3}$ pieces? $\frac{1}{4}$ pieces? $\frac{1}{6}$ pieces? Why or why not?**
- Ask them to do **Exercise 3** independently using the fraction pieces to help.

Intermediate/Advanced

- English Learner Resource 20.6
- English Learner Handbook

Intervention

Small Groups	10 minutes
Objective	Review equivalent fractions.
Materials	Egg carton and beads or counters
Tactual, Visual	

- Reinforce students' understanding of equivalent fractions. Provide small groups with an egg carton and beads or counters.
- Have students put a counter in each of 6 cups. Elicit that they have filled $\frac{6}{12}$ of the carton. Students can see that $\frac{6}{12}$ of the carton is $\frac{1}{2}$ of it. Repeat with $\frac{2}{12}$, $\frac{3}{12}$, $\frac{4}{12}$, and other twelfths equivalent to simpler fractions. You can have students delineate the fractional parts of the carton they form by using yarn or pipe cleaners.

Other Resources

- *Ways to Success* CD-ROM 20.6

Early Finishers

Small Groups	10 minutes
Objective	Add fractions with unlike denominators.
Materials	Fraction pieces (Learning Tool 34)
Auditory, Tactual	

- Have students formulate additional exercises they can try with or without looking at the fraction pieces.
- Have them check their answers using the models.
- Invite them to discuss their methods and progress.

Science Connection

Materials: Rain gauge

- Provide a simple rain gauge, graduated in fractions of inches. Place it in an unobstructed location outside.
- Have students keep track of rainfall for one week and record the data in a table. (As an alternative, gather rainfall data for a longer period of time and provide it to students.)
- Have students use the data to formulate and solve problems involving sums and differences with amounts of rainfall.

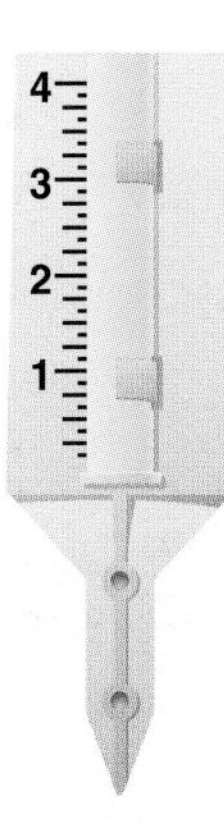

❶ Introduce

Read the objective with students. Tell students that they will learn to add fractions with unlike denominators using fraction pieces.

❷ Teach

Work Together

- For **Step 1** of the first addition, guide students to align the fraction pieces at the left.
- For **Step 2**, Ask: **Why do we choose $\frac{1}{4}$ fraction pieces to place under $\frac{1}{2} + \frac{1}{4}$?** (Fourths are a common denominator of halves and fourths.)
- Repeat these steps for $\frac{2}{3} + \frac{3}{4}$.
- Show students another way to model addition: For $\frac{1}{2} + \frac{1}{4}$, say: **We need like denominators, so rewrite $\frac{1}{2}$ as $\frac{2}{4}$. We will use two $\frac{1}{4}$ fraction pieces to model $\frac{2}{4}$ and one $\frac{1}{4}$ fraction piece to model $\frac{1}{4}$.** Then place the fraction pieces in a row and count them to see that $\frac{1}{2} + \frac{1}{4} = \frac{3}{4}$.
- Have students try this approach to model $\frac{2}{3} + \frac{3}{4}$.

Add Fractions With Unlike Denominators

Vocabulary
unlike denominators

Objective Use models to add fractions that have different denominators.

Materials
Fraction Pieces
(Learning Tool 34)

Work Together

You can use fraction pieces to add fractions with different denominators, or **unlike denominators**.

Find $\frac{1}{2} + \frac{1}{4}$.

STEP 1 Use fraction pieces. Place $\frac{1}{2}$ and $\frac{1}{4}$ under 1 whole.

STEP 2 Find like fraction pieces that fit exactly under $\frac{1}{2} + \frac{1}{4}$.

- How many $\frac{1}{4}$ pieces fit exactly under $\frac{1}{2} + \frac{1}{4}$? **3**
- What is $\frac{1}{2} + \frac{1}{4}$? $\mathbf{\frac{3}{4}}$

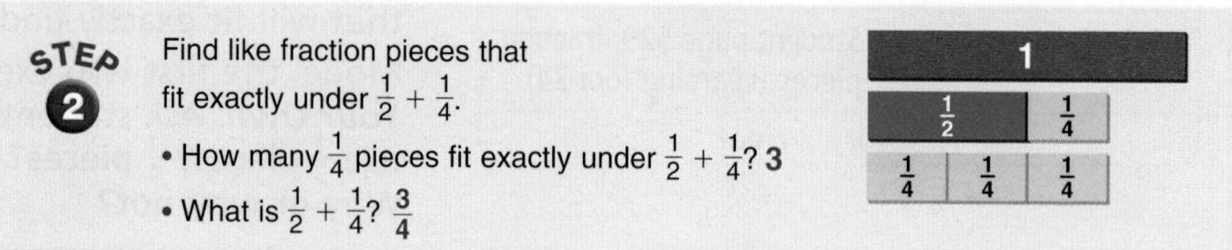

Now find $\frac{2}{3} + \frac{3}{4}$.

STEP 1 Use fraction pieces to model $\frac{2}{3} + \frac{3}{4}$.

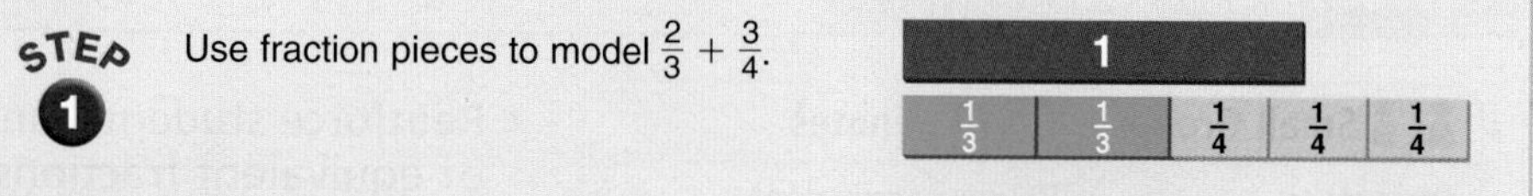

STEP 2 Find like fraction pieces that fit exactly under $\frac{2}{3} + \frac{3}{4}$.

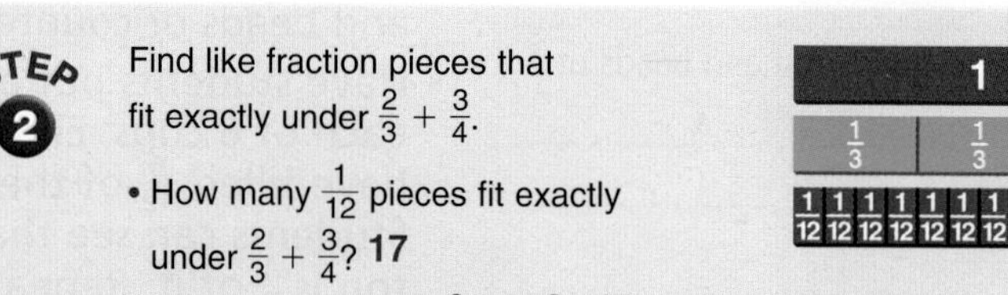

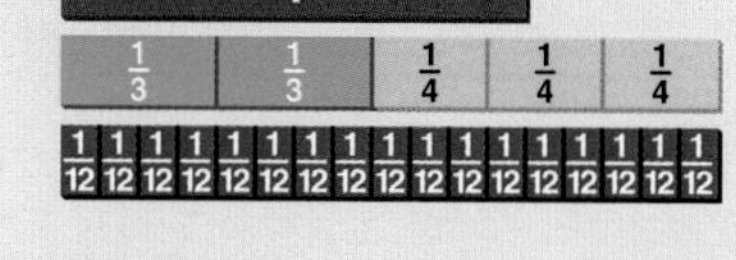

- How many $\frac{1}{12}$ pieces fit exactly under $\frac{2}{3} + \frac{3}{4}$? **17**
- What is the sum of $\frac{2}{3}$ and $\frac{3}{4}$? $\mathbf{\frac{17}{12}}$
- How do you know that the sum is greater than 1? **17 is greater than 12**
- How can you write the sum as a mixed number? $\mathbf{1\frac{5}{12}}$

528

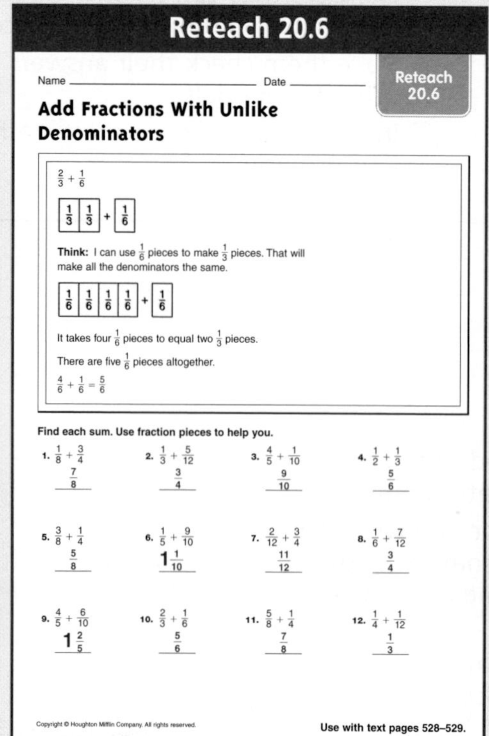

Reteach 20.6

Name ____________ Date ________

Reteach 20.6

Add Fractions With Unlike Denominators

$\frac{2}{3} + \frac{1}{6}$

$\frac{1}{3}$ $\frac{1}{3}$ + $\frac{1}{6}$

Think: I can use $\frac{1}{6}$ pieces to make $\frac{1}{3}$ pieces. That will make all the denominators the same.

$\frac{1}{6}$ $\frac{1}{6}$ $\frac{1}{6}$ $\frac{1}{6}$ + $\frac{1}{6}$

It takes four $\frac{1}{6}$ pieces to equal two $\frac{1}{3}$ pieces.

There are five $\frac{1}{6}$ pieces altogether.

$\frac{4}{6} + \frac{1}{6} = \frac{5}{6}$

Find each sum. Use fraction pieces to help you.

1. $\frac{1}{8} + \frac{3}{4}$ $\frac{7}{8}$
2. $\frac{1}{3} + \frac{5}{12}$ $\frac{3}{4}$
3. $\frac{4}{5} + \frac{1}{10}$ $\frac{9}{10}$
4. $\frac{1}{2} + \frac{1}{3}$ $\frac{5}{6}$
5. $\frac{3}{8} + \frac{1}{4}$ $\frac{5}{8}$
6. $\frac{1}{5} + \frac{9}{10}$ $1\frac{1}{10}$
7. $\frac{2}{12} + \frac{3}{4}$ $\frac{11}{12}$
8. $\frac{1}{6} + \frac{7}{12}$ $\frac{3}{4}$
9. $\frac{4}{5} + \frac{6}{10}$ $1\frac{2}{5}$
10. $\frac{2}{3} + \frac{1}{6}$ $\frac{5}{6}$
11. $\frac{5}{8} + \frac{1}{4}$ $\frac{7}{8}$
12. $\frac{1}{4} + \frac{1}{12}$ $\frac{1}{3}$

Use with text pages 528–529.

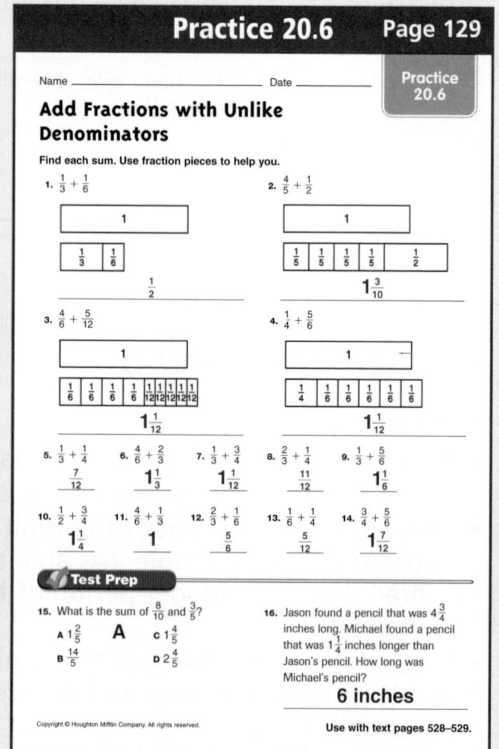

Practice 20.6 **Page 129**

Name ____________ Date ________

Practice 20.6

Add Fractions with Unlike Denominators

Find each sum. Use fraction pieces to help you.

1. $\frac{1}{3} + \frac{1}{6}$
   1
   $\frac{1}{3}$ $\frac{1}{6}$
   $\frac{1}{2}$
2. $\frac{4}{5} + \frac{1}{2}$
   1
   $\frac{1}{5}$ $\frac{1}{5}$ $\frac{1}{5}$ $\frac{1}{5}$ $\frac{1}{2}$
   $1\frac{3}{10}$
3. $\frac{4}{6} + \frac{5}{12}$
   1
   $\frac{1}{6}$ $\frac{1}{6}$ $\frac{1}{6}$ $\frac{1}{6}$ $\frac{1}{12}$ $\frac{1}{12}$ $\frac{1}{12}$ $\frac{1}{12}$ $\frac{1}{12}$
   $1\frac{1}{12}$
4. $\frac{1}{4} + \frac{5}{6}$
   1
   $\frac{1}{4}$ $\frac{1}{6}$ $\frac{1}{6}$ $\frac{1}{6}$ $\frac{1}{6}$ $\frac{1}{6}$
   $1\frac{1}{12}$
5. $\frac{1}{3} + \frac{1}{4}$ $\frac{7}{12}$
6. $\frac{4}{6} + \frac{2}{3}$ $1\frac{1}{3}$
7. $\frac{1}{3} + \frac{3}{4}$ $1\frac{1}{12}$
8. $\frac{2}{3} + \frac{1}{4}$ $\frac{11}{12}$
9. $\frac{1}{3} + \frac{5}{6}$ $1\frac{1}{6}$
10. $\frac{1}{2} + \frac{3}{4}$ $1\frac{1}{4}$
11. $\frac{4}{6} + \frac{1}{3}$ 1
12. $\frac{2}{3} + \frac{1}{6}$ $\frac{5}{6}$
13. $\frac{1}{6} + \frac{1}{4}$ $\frac{5}{12}$
14. $\frac{3}{4} + \frac{5}{6}$ $1\frac{7}{12}$

Test Prep

15. What is the sum of $\frac{8}{10}$ and $\frac{3}{5}$? **A**
    A $1\frac{2}{5}$
    B $\frac{14}{5}$
    C $1\frac{4}{5}$
    D $2\frac{4}{5}$
16. Jason found a pencil that was $4\frac{3}{4}$ inches long. Michael found a pencil that was $1\frac{1}{4}$ inches longer than Jason's pencil. How long was Michael's pencil? **6 inches**

Use with text pages 528–529.

On Your Own

Find each sum. Use fraction pieces to help you.

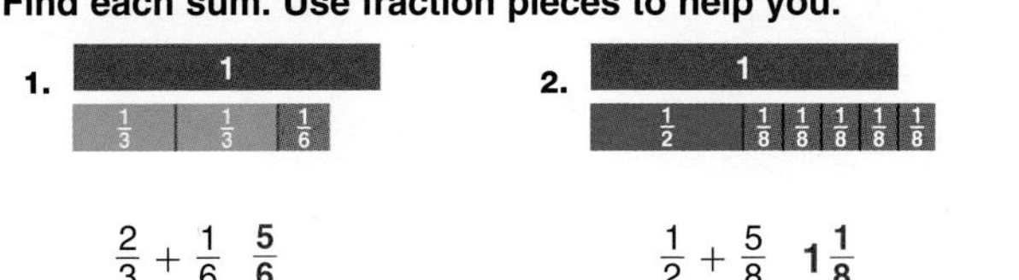
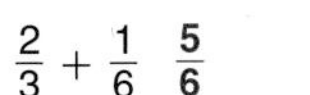

1. $\frac{2}{3} + \frac{1}{6}$ $\frac{5}{6}$
2. $\frac{1}{2} + \frac{5}{8}$ $1\frac{1}{8}$
3. $\frac{2}{5} + \frac{1}{2}$ $\frac{9}{10}$
4. $\frac{3}{4} + \frac{1}{6}$ $\frac{11}{12}$
5. $\frac{1}{3} + \frac{3}{6}$ $\frac{5}{6}$
6. $\frac{3}{8} + \frac{1}{4}$ $\frac{5}{8}$
7. $\frac{5}{12} + \frac{1}{4}$ $\frac{2}{3}$
8. $\frac{5}{6} + \frac{1}{3}$ $1\frac{1}{6}$
9. $\frac{2}{3} + \frac{1}{2}$ $1\frac{1}{6}$
10. $\frac{1}{3} + \frac{3}{4}$ $1\frac{1}{12}$
11. $\frac{3}{5} + \frac{1}{2}$ $1\frac{1}{10}$
12. $\frac{5}{6} + \frac{3}{4}$ $1\frac{7}{12}$
13. $\frac{3}{4} + \frac{5}{8}$ $1\frac{3}{8}$

Measurement Jan, Erin, and Devin found some arrowheads while hiking. Jan measured her arrowhead. It was $1\frac{1}{4}$ inches long.

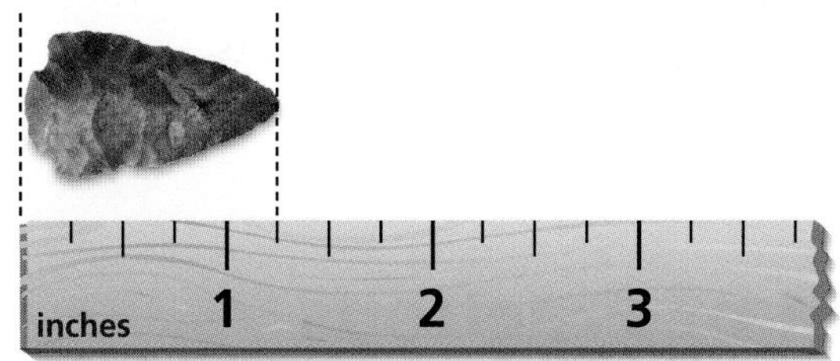

14. Devin found an arrowhead that was $\frac{1}{2}$ inch longer than Jan's. How long was the arrowhead that Devin found? $1\frac{3}{4}$ **inches**
15. Erin found an arrowhead that was $1\frac{1}{12}$ inches longer than Jan's. How long was the arrowhead that Erin found? $2\frac{1}{3}$ **inches**

Talk About It • Write About It

You learned how to use models to add fractions with unlike denominators.

16. Explain how adding fractions with unlike denominators is different from adding fractions with like denominators.

16. *Possible explanation:* You need to find equivalent fractions before you can add fractions with unlike denominators.

17. Explain how you can add $\frac{3}{4}$ and $\frac{1}{3}$. Use words and a picture.

***Check students' drawings.* Explanations should show that $\frac{3}{4} + \frac{1}{3} = 1\frac{1}{12}$.**

3 Practice

On Your Own

Select from **Exercises 1–17** as independent work. Invite more capable students to work the problems without the fraction pieces. They can use the strips to check their answers.

Measurement Guide students to see that the ruler is calibrated in fourths. Make sure they read it correctly. Ask them, for instance, to identify $1\frac{1}{4}$ or $2\frac{1}{2}$.

4 Assess & Close

Math Talk in Action

Have students discuss their responses to the ***Talk About It • Write About It*** section to conclude the lesson. Have them explain how to use fraction pieces to find sums of fractions with unlike denominators.

Math Journal Prompt

Have students write an explanation of how to find the sum of $\frac{2}{3}$ and $\frac{5}{8}$ using fraction pieces.

Lesson Quiz

Use the quiz on Lesson Transparency 20.6.

Lesson 20.6 Transparency

Test Prep & Spiral Review

Use Test Prep Transparency 20.6.

Test Prep 20.6 Transparency

Enrichment 20.6

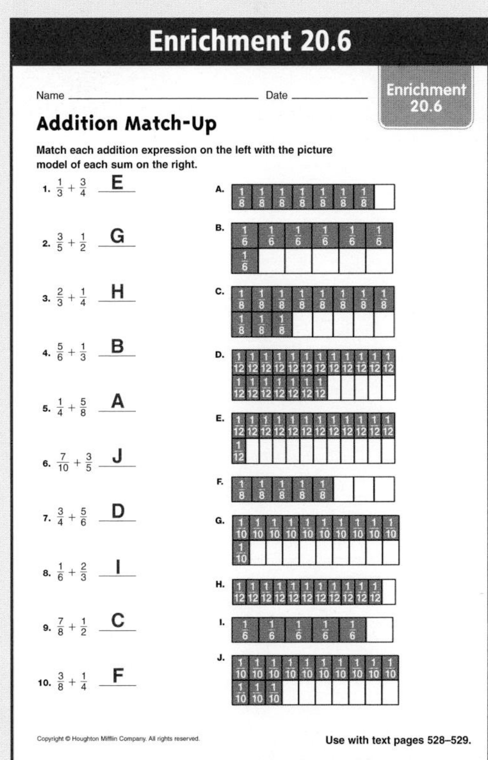

Name ______ Date ______ Enrichment 20.6

Addition Match-Up

Match each addition expression on the left with the picture model of each sum on the right.

1. $\frac{1}{3} + \frac{3}{4}$ E
2. $\frac{3}{5} + \frac{1}{2}$ G
3. $\frac{2}{3} + \frac{1}{4}$ H
4. $\frac{5}{6} + \frac{1}{3}$ B
5. $\frac{1}{4} + \frac{5}{8}$ A
6. $\frac{7}{10} + \frac{3}{5}$ J
7. $\frac{3}{4} + \frac{5}{6}$ D
8. $\frac{1}{6} + \frac{2}{3}$ I
9. $\frac{7}{8} + \frac{1}{2}$ C
10. $\frac{3}{8} + \frac{1}{4}$ F

Use with text pages 528–529.

Problem Solving 20.6

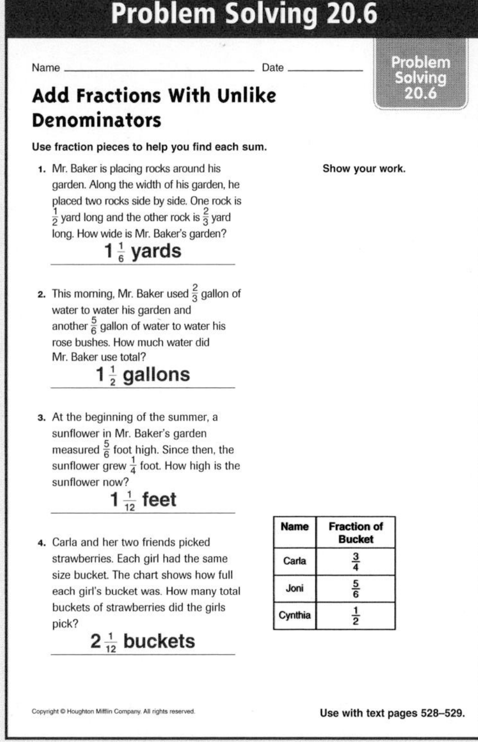

Name ______ Date ______ Problem Solving 20.6

Add Fractions With Unlike Denominators

Use fraction pieces to help you find each sum. Show your work.

1. Mr. Baker is placing rocks around his garden. Along the width of his garden, he placed two rocks side by side. One rock is $\frac{1}{2}$ yard long and the other rock is $\frac{2}{3}$ yard long. How wide is Mr. Baker's garden? **$1\frac{1}{6}$ yards**
2. This morning, Mr. Baker used $\frac{2}{3}$ gallon of water to water his garden and another $\frac{5}{6}$ gallon of water to water his rose bushes. How much water did Mr. Baker use total? **$1\frac{1}{2}$ gallons**
3. At the beginning of the summer, a sunflower in Mr. Baker's garden measured $\frac{5}{6}$ foot high. Since then, the sunflower grew $\frac{1}{4}$ foot. How high is the sunflower now? **$1\frac{1}{12}$ feet**
4. Carla and her two friends picked strawberries. Each girl had the same size bucket. The chart shows how full each girl's bucket was. How many total buckets of strawberries did the girls pick? **$2\frac{1}{12}$ buckets**

Name	Fraction of Bucket
Carla	$\frac{3}{4}$
Joni	$\frac{5}{6}$
Cynthia	$\frac{1}{2}$

Use with text pages 528–529.

Homework 20.6 Page 129

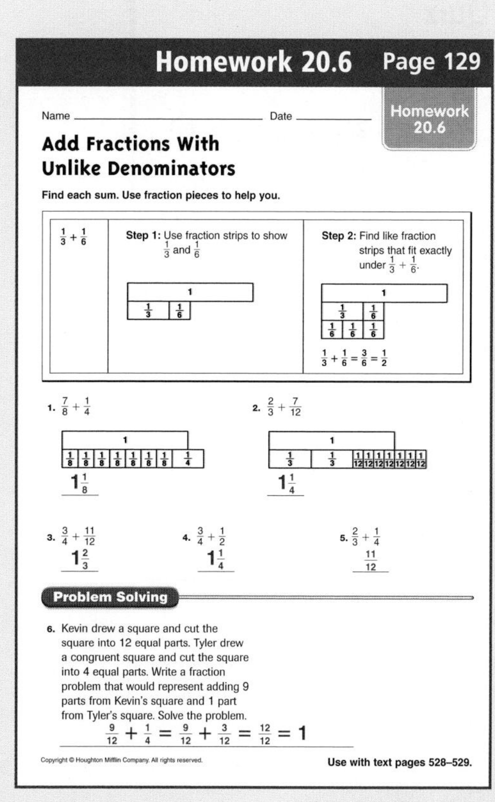

Name ______ Date ______ Homework 20.6

Add Fractions With Unlike Denominators

Find each sum. Use fraction pieces to help you.

$\frac{1}{3} + \frac{1}{6}$ — Step 1: Use fraction strips to show $\frac{1}{3}$ and $\frac{1}{6}$. Step 2: Find like fraction strips that fit exactly under $\frac{1}{3} + \frac{1}{6}$. $\frac{1}{3} + \frac{1}{6} = \frac{3}{6} = \frac{1}{2}$

1. $\frac{7}{8} + \frac{1}{4}$ $1\frac{1}{8}$
2. $\frac{2}{3} + \frac{7}{12}$ $1\frac{1}{4}$
3. $\frac{3}{4} + \frac{11}{12}$ $1\frac{2}{3}$
4. $\frac{3}{4} + \frac{1}{2}$ $1\frac{1}{4}$
5. $\frac{2}{3} + \frac{1}{4}$ $\frac{11}{12}$

Problem Solving

6. Kevin drew a square and cut the square into 12 equal parts. Tyler drew a congruent square and cut the square into 4 equal parts. Write a fraction problem that would represent adding 9 parts from Kevin's square and 1 part from Tyler's square. Solve the problem.

$\frac{9}{12} + \frac{1}{4} = \frac{9}{12} + \frac{3}{12} = \frac{12}{12} = 1$

Use with text pages 528–529.

Hands On Lesson 20.7

Subtract Fractions with Unlike Denominators

Planning

Lesson Objective Use models to subtract fractions that have different denominators.

Technology Resources

- *Ways to Success* CD-ROM 20.7
- Education Place: Extra Practice, eGlossary, eManipulatives, eGames, Brain Teasers www.eduplace.com/map

Problem of the Day

Miguel bought $\frac{7}{8}$ yard of white ribbon, $\frac{3}{4}$ yard of black ribbon, and $\frac{5}{6}$ yard of blue ribbon. Did he buy enough ribbon for a costume that requires 2 yards of ribbon? Explain how you know. (Yes; possible response: Each amount is nearly 1 yd, for a total of more than 2 yd, but less than 3 yd.)

Spiral Review

Find each sum. Use fraction pieces to help you.

1. $\frac{3}{5} + \frac{7}{10}$ = ___ ($1\frac{3}{10}$) **2.** $\frac{2}{3} + \frac{5}{6}$ = ___ ($1\frac{1}{2}$)

3. $\frac{5}{9} + \frac{1}{3}$ = ___ ($\frac{8}{9}$) **4.** $\frac{5}{8} + \frac{3}{4}$ = ___ ($1\frac{3}{8}$)

Lesson Quiz

Use fraction pieces to help you find each difference.

1. $\frac{1}{2} - \frac{1}{4}$ = ___ ($\frac{1}{4}$) **2.** $\frac{5}{12} - \frac{1}{6}$ = ___ ($\frac{1}{4}$)

3. $\frac{4}{9} - \frac{1}{3}$ = ___ ($\frac{1}{9}$) **4.** $\frac{5}{8} - \frac{1}{4}$ = ___ ($\frac{3}{8}$)

NCTM Standards

Number and Operations: Use visual models, benchmarks, and equivalent forms to add and subtract commonly used fractions.

Getting Started

Building Math Vocabulary

unlike denominators denominators that are not equal

Help students recall the meaning of ***unlike denominators.*** Elicit from students that the denominator of a fraction tells the total number of parts into which the whole is divided, and that "unlike denominators" refers to fractions in which the wholes are made up of different numbers of parts.

Modeling Addition of Fractions

Whole Class	15 minutes
Objective	Use fraction models to model addition.
Materials	Fraction Pieces (Learning Tool 34), Fraction Pieces Transparency, blank transparency
Visual, Auditory	

- Provide fraction pieces to students. Ask them to use the fraction pieces to model $\frac{5}{6} + \frac{2}{3}$. As they do, have a volunteer model the same addition at the overhead, using fraction pieces cut out from the Fraction Pieces Transparency.
- Tell students that today they are going to use the fraction pieces to model subtraction of fractions with unlike denominators.

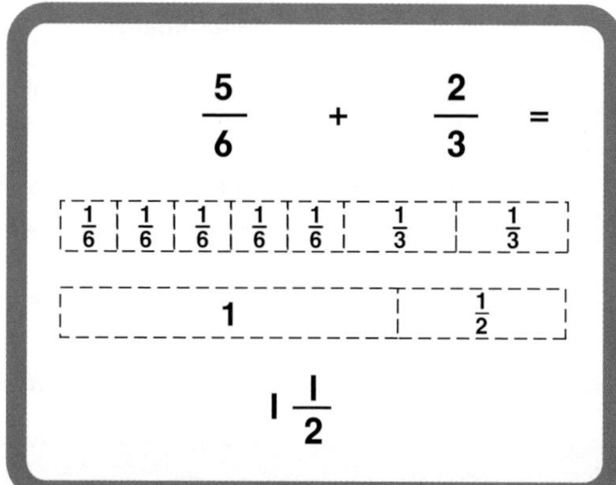

Differentiated Instruction

English Learners

Pairs	10 minutes
Objective	Subtract fractions with unlike denominators.
Materials	Fraction pieces (Learning Tool 34)
Auditory, Visual	

Early Production

- Before doing ***On Your Own***, write this problem on the board: $\frac{3}{5} - \frac{1}{2} = \frac{2}{3}$. Ask: **Is the answer correct? What did I do wrong? Can you find the correct answer?**
- Pair students. Give them fraction pieces to find the correct answer. Ask students to explain their work.

Intermediate/Advanced

- English Learner Resource 20.7
- English Learner Handbook

Intervention

Small Groups	10 minutes
Objective	Model subtracting fractions with like denominators.
Materials	Index cards
Kinesthetic, Visual	

- Use a game to review subtracting with like denominators. Write $\frac{4}{5} - \frac{2}{5}$ on the board. Have 5 students represent fifths. Each one holds an index card that reads $\frac{1}{5}$.
- Ask how $\frac{4}{5}$ can be shown. Have 4 students, each holding $\frac{1}{5}$, stand.
- Ask students to tell how many should sit to show subtracting $\frac{2}{5}$. (2) Have a volunteer write the difference: $\frac{4}{5} - \frac{2}{5} = \frac{2}{5}$.
- Repeat with other subtractions of fractions with like denominators.

Other Resources

- *Ways to Success* CD-ROM 20.7

Gifted & Talented

Small Groups	10 minutes
Objective	Find patterns in subtraction with unlike denominators.
Materials	Fraction pieces (Learning Tool 34)
Visual, Auditory	

- Write the following subtraction expressions on the board: $1 - \frac{1}{4}$, $1 - \frac{1}{5}$, $1 - \frac{1}{10}$, $1 - \frac{1}{8}$, and $1 - \frac{1}{3}$.
- Have students find each difference and look for a pattern among the answers. If they need to, they may use fraction pieces to solve the subtractions.
- Invite students to share their work and describe the patterns they discovered.

Music Connection

Materials: Recordings of waltzes and marches

- Tell students that musical notation usually includes a time signature at the beginning of a written score. $\frac{3}{4}$ *Time* means that each full measure has 3 quarter notes. Music in $\frac{3}{4}$ time is often called *waltz time*. Music in $\frac{2}{4}$ time is called *march time*.
- Ask the music teacher to supply examples of music in $\frac{2}{4}$ and $\frac{3}{4}$ time. Play excerpts to allow students to feel the different beats.

❶ Introduce

Read the objective to the students and tell them that in this lesson they will subtract fractions with unlike denominators using fraction pieces as they did in the lesson on adding fractions with unlike denominators.

❷ Teach

Work Together

- For **Step 1** of the first subtraction problem, guide students to align the fraction pieces.
- For **Step 2,** ask: **Why do we choose $\frac{1}{6}$ fraction pieces to place under the two $\frac{1}{3}$ fraction pieces?** (Because $\frac{4}{6}$ and $\frac{2}{3}$ are equivalent fractions)

Subtract Fractions With Unlike Denominators

Objective Use models to subtract fractions that have different denominators.

Vocabulary
unlike denominators

Materials
Fraction Pieces
(Learning Tool 34)

Work Together

You can use fraction pieces to subtract fractions that have **unlike denominators**.

Find $\frac{2}{3} - \frac{1}{6}$.

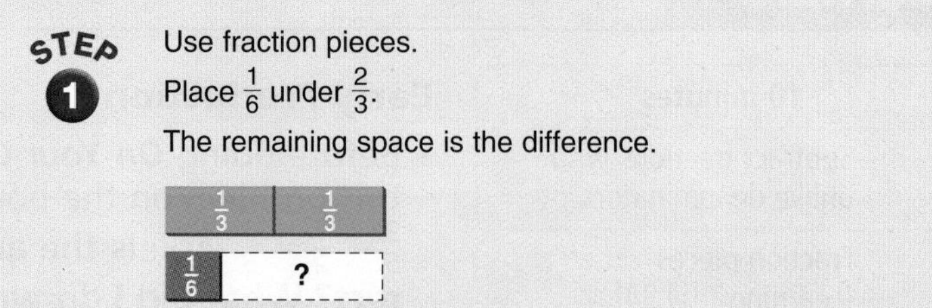

STEP 1 Use fraction pieces.
Place $\frac{1}{6}$ under $\frac{2}{3}$.
The remaining space is the difference.

STEP 2 Find like fraction pieces that fit exactly in the remaining space.

- How many $\frac{1}{6}$ pieces fill the remaining space? **3**
- What is $\frac{2}{3} - \frac{1}{6}$? **$\frac{3}{6}$ or $\frac{1}{2}$**

530

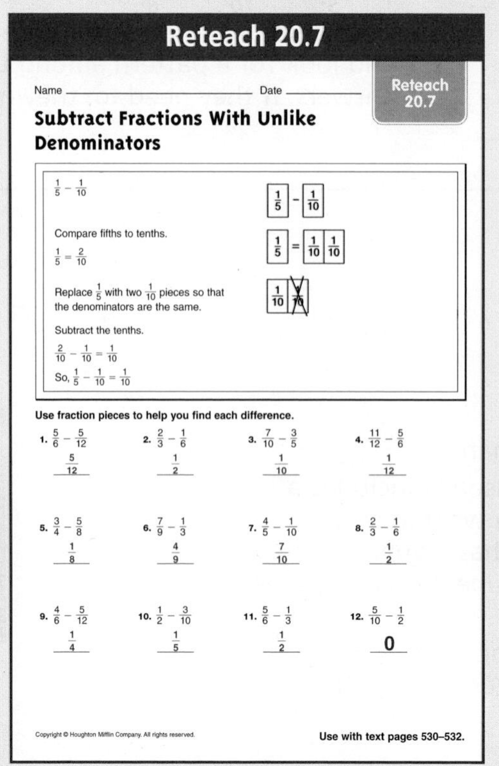

Reteach 20.7

Name ______ Date ______ Reteach 20.7

Subtract Fractions With Unlike Denominators

$\frac{1}{5} - \frac{1}{10}$

Compare fifths to tenths.

$\frac{1}{5} = \frac{2}{10}$

Replace $\frac{1}{5}$ with two $\frac{1}{10}$ pieces so that the denominators are the same.

Subtract the tenths.

$\frac{2}{10} - \frac{1}{10} = \frac{1}{10}$

So, $\frac{1}{5} - \frac{1}{10} = \frac{1}{10}$

Use fraction pieces to help you find each difference.

1. $\frac{5}{6} - \frac{5}{12}$ $\frac{5}{12}$
2. $\frac{2}{3} - \frac{1}{6}$ $\frac{1}{2}$
3. $\frac{7}{10} - \frac{3}{5}$ $\frac{1}{10}$
4. $\frac{11}{12} - \frac{5}{6}$ $\frac{1}{12}$
5. $\frac{3}{4} - \frac{5}{8}$ $\frac{1}{8}$
6. $\frac{7}{9} - \frac{1}{3}$ $\frac{4}{9}$
7. $\frac{4}{5} - \frac{1}{10}$ $\frac{7}{10}$
8. $\frac{2}{3} - \frac{1}{6}$ $\frac{1}{2}$
9. $\frac{4}{6} - \frac{5}{12}$ $\frac{1}{4}$
10. $\frac{1}{2} - \frac{3}{10}$ $\frac{1}{5}$
11. $\frac{5}{6} - \frac{1}{3}$ $\frac{1}{2}$
12. $\frac{5}{10} - \frac{1}{2}$ 0

Use with text pages 530–532.

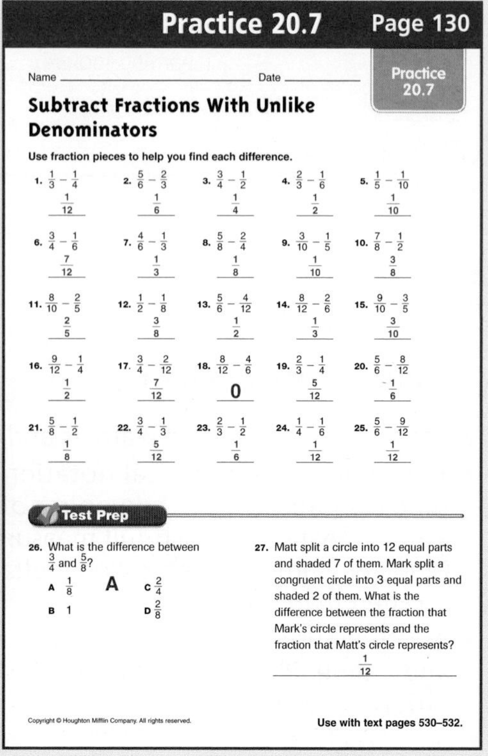

Practice 20.7 **Page 130**

Name ______ Date ______ Practice 20.7

Subtract Fractions With Unlike Denominators

Use fraction pieces to help you find each difference.

1. $\frac{1}{3} - \frac{1}{4}$ $\frac{1}{12}$
2. $\frac{5}{6} - \frac{2}{3}$ $\frac{1}{6}$
3. $\frac{3}{4} - \frac{1}{2}$ $\frac{1}{4}$
4. $\frac{2}{3} - \frac{1}{6}$ $\frac{1}{2}$
5. $\frac{1}{5} - \frac{1}{10}$ $\frac{1}{10}$
6. $\frac{3}{4} - \frac{1}{6}$ $\frac{7}{12}$
7. $\frac{4}{6} - \frac{1}{3}$ $\frac{1}{3}$
8. $\frac{5}{8} - \frac{2}{4}$ $\frac{1}{8}$
9. $\frac{3}{10} - \frac{1}{5}$ $\frac{1}{10}$
10. $\frac{7}{8} - \frac{1}{2}$ $\frac{3}{8}$
11. $\frac{8}{10} - \frac{2}{5}$ $\frac{2}{5}$
12. $\frac{1}{2} - \frac{1}{8}$ $\frac{3}{8}$
13. $\frac{5}{6} - \frac{4}{12}$ $\frac{1}{2}$
14. $\frac{8}{12} - \frac{2}{6}$ $\frac{1}{3}$
15. $\frac{9}{10} - \frac{3}{5}$ $\frac{3}{10}$
16. $\frac{9}{12} - \frac{1}{4}$ $\frac{1}{2}$
17. $\frac{3}{4} - \frac{2}{12}$ $\frac{7}{12}$
18. $\frac{8}{12} - \frac{4}{6}$ 0
19. $\frac{2}{3} - \frac{1}{4}$ $\frac{5}{12}$
20. $\frac{5}{6} - \frac{8}{12}$ $\frac{1}{6}$
21. $\frac{5}{8} - \frac{1}{2}$ $\frac{1}{8}$
22. $\frac{3}{4} - \frac{1}{3}$ $\frac{5}{12}$
23. $\frac{2}{3} - \frac{1}{2}$ $\frac{1}{6}$
24. $\frac{1}{4} - \frac{1}{6}$ $\frac{1}{12}$
25. $\frac{5}{6} - \frac{9}{12}$ $\frac{1}{12}$

Test Prep

26. What is the difference between $\frac{3}{4}$ and $\frac{5}{8}$?
 A $\frac{1}{8}$ **A** C $\frac{2}{4}$
 B 1 D $\frac{2}{8}$

27. Matt split a circle into 12 equal parts and shaded 7 of them. Mark split a congruent circle into 3 equal parts and shaded 2 of them. What is the difference between the fraction that Mark's circle represents and the fraction that Matt's circle represents? $\frac{1}{12}$

Use with text pages 530–532.

Now find $\frac{3}{4} - \frac{2}{3}$.

STEP 1 Use fraction pieces. Place $\frac{2}{3}$ under $\frac{3}{4}$. The remaining space is the difference.

STEP 2 Use fraction pieces to find equivalent fractions for $\frac{3}{4}$ and $\frac{2}{3}$ that have the same denominators.

$\frac{3}{4} = \frac{9}{12}$ $\frac{2}{3} = \frac{8}{12}$

STEP 3 Replace the $\frac{1}{4}$ pieces and the $\frac{1}{3}$ pieces with the equivalent fraction pieces.

$\frac{3}{4} = \frac{9}{12}$ →

$\frac{2}{3} = \frac{8}{12}$ →

STEP 4 Find like fraction pieces that fit exactly in the remaining space.

- How many $\frac{1}{12}$ pieces fill the space? 1
- What is $\frac{3}{4} - \frac{2}{3}$? $\frac{1}{12}$

On Your Own

Use the pictures to help you find each difference.

1. 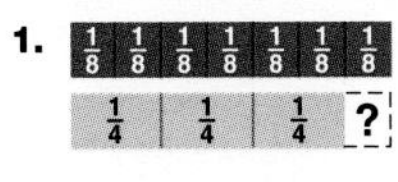

$\frac{7}{8} - \frac{3}{4}$ $\frac{1}{8}$

2. 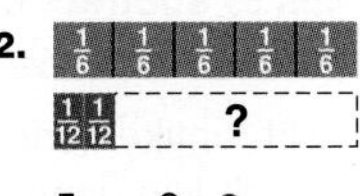

$\frac{5}{6} - \frac{2}{12}$ $\frac{2}{3}$

3. 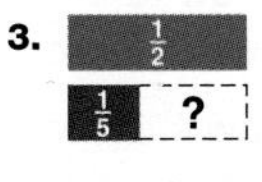

$\frac{1}{2} - \frac{1}{5}$ $\frac{3}{10}$

- Now focus on $\frac{3}{4} - \frac{2}{3}$. For **Step 1,** model the problem on the overhead. Have students do the same at their desks. **Is the difference between $\frac{3}{4}$ and $\frac{2}{3}$ more or less than $\frac{1}{4}$?** (less than $\frac{1}{4}$)
- For **Step 2,** guide students to see that they can find equivalent fractions using $\frac{1}{12}$ fraction pieces. Have them model $\frac{3}{4}$ as $\frac{9}{12}$ and $\frac{2}{3}$ as $\frac{8}{12}$, as you do the same on the overhead. **Why are the fraction pieces using twelfths the same lengths as the fraction pieces with fourths and thirds?** (equivalent fractions)
- For **Step 4,** students can see that adding $\frac{1}{12}$ makes the bottom fraction piece exactly the same length as the top fraction piece. **So, what is the difference between $\frac{3}{4}$ and $\frac{2}{3}$?** ($\frac{1}{12}$)

3 Practice

On Your Own

- Select from **Exercises 1–24** as independent work. Invite more capable students to work the problems without the fraction pieces. They can use the fraction pieces to check their answers.

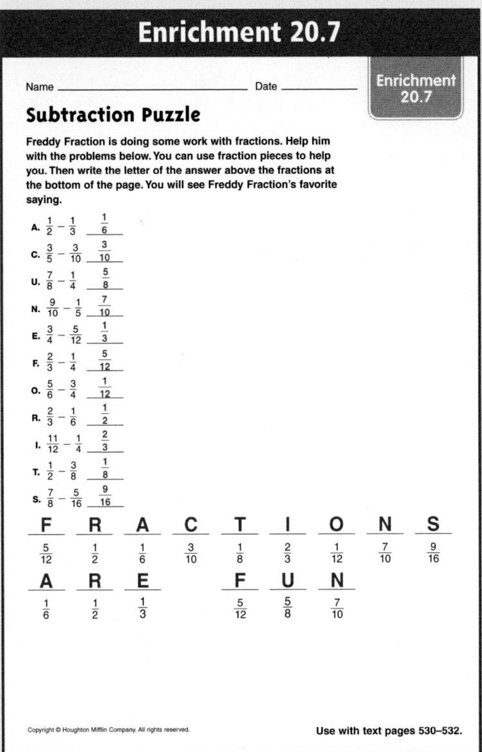

Enrichment 20.7

Name ______________ Date ________

Enrichment 20.7

Subtraction Puzzle

Freddy Fraction is doing some work with fractions. Help him with the problems below. You can use fraction pieces to help you. Then write the letter of the answer above the fractions at the bottom of the page. You will see Freddy Fraction's favorite saying.

A. $\frac{1}{2} - \frac{1}{3}$ $\frac{1}{6}$
C. $\frac{3}{5} - \frac{3}{10}$ $\frac{3}{10}$
U. $\frac{7}{8} - \frac{1}{4}$ $\frac{5}{8}$
N. $\frac{9}{10} - \frac{1}{5}$ $\frac{7}{10}$
E. $\frac{3}{4} - \frac{5}{12}$ $\frac{1}{3}$
F. $\frac{2}{3} - \frac{1}{4}$ $\frac{5}{12}$
O. $\frac{5}{6} - \frac{3}{4}$ $\frac{1}{12}$
R. $\frac{2}{3} - \frac{1}{6}$ $\frac{1}{2}$
I. $\frac{11}{12} - \frac{1}{4}$ $\frac{2}{3}$
T. $\frac{1}{2} - \frac{3}{8}$ $\frac{1}{8}$
S. $\frac{7}{8} - \frac{5}{16}$ $\frac{9}{16}$

F	R	A	C	T	I	O	N	S
$\frac{5}{12}$	$\frac{1}{2}$	$\frac{1}{6}$	$\frac{3}{10}$	$\frac{1}{8}$	$\frac{2}{3}$	$\frac{1}{12}$	$\frac{7}{10}$	$\frac{9}{16}$
A	R	E		F	U	N		
$\frac{1}{6}$	$\frac{1}{2}$	$\frac{1}{3}$		$\frac{5}{12}$	$\frac{5}{8}$	$\frac{7}{10}$		

Use with text pages 530–532.

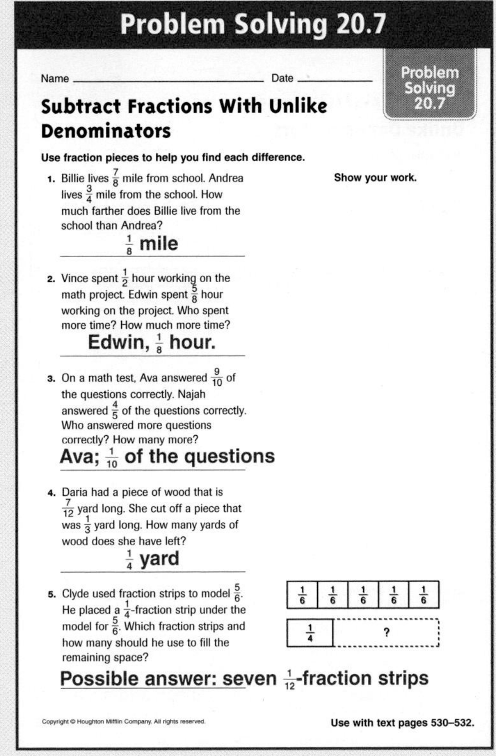

Problem Solving 20.7

Name ______________ Date ________

Problem Solving 20.7

Subtract Fractions With Unlike Denominators

Use fraction pieces to help you find each difference.

Show your work.

1. Billie lives $\frac{7}{8}$ mile from school. Andrea lives $\frac{3}{4}$ mile from the school. How much farther does Billie live from the school than Andrea?
   $\frac{1}{8}$ mile
2. Vince spent $\frac{1}{2}$ hour working on the math project. Edwin spent $\frac{5}{8}$ hour working on the project. Who spent more time? How much more time?
   Edwin, $\frac{1}{8}$ hour.
3. On a math test, Ava answered $\frac{9}{10}$ of the questions correctly. Najah answered $\frac{4}{5}$ of the questions correctly. Who answered more questions correctly? How many more?
   Ava; $\frac{1}{10}$ of the questions
4. Daria had a piece of wood that is $\frac{7}{12}$ yard long. She cut off a piece that was $\frac{1}{3}$ yard long. How many yards of wood does she have left?
   $\frac{1}{4}$ yard
5. Clyde used fraction strips to model $\frac{5}{6}$. He placed a $\frac{1}{4}$-fraction strip under the model for $\frac{5}{6}$. Which fraction strips and how many should he use to fill the remaining space?
   Possible answer: seven $\frac{1}{12}$-fraction strips

Use with text pages 530–532.

- Elicit from students how to check answers to subtraction problems. (Add the difference to the number being subtracted; the answer should be the number you are subtracting from.)
- ***Problems 19–22*** Remind students to align the fraction pieces carefully in order to see the exact difference between the two fractions.

4 Assess & Close

Math Talk in Action

Have students discuss their responses to the ***Talk About It • Write About It*** section to conclude the lesson. Ask them to explain how to use fraction pieces to find differences between two fractions with unlike denominators.

Math Journal Prompt

Have students write a step-by-step explanation of how to use fraction pieces to model $\frac{3}{4} - \frac{1}{6}$.

Lesson Quiz

Use the quiz on Lesson Transparency 20.7.

Test Prep & Spiral Review

Use Test Prep Transparency 20.7.

Use fraction pieces to help you find each difference.

4. $\frac{1}{2} - \frac{1}{3}$ $\frac{1}{6}$ **5.** $\frac{7}{8} - \frac{3}{4}$ $\frac{1}{8}$ **6.** $\frac{5}{6} - \frac{1}{3}$ $\frac{3}{6}$ or $\frac{1}{2}$ **7.** $\frac{1}{2} - \frac{1}{4}$ $\frac{1}{4}$ **8.** $\frac{2}{3} - \frac{1}{2}$ $\frac{1}{6}$

9. $\frac{3}{4} - \frac{1}{2}$ $\frac{1}{4}$ **10.** $\frac{3}{8} - \frac{1}{4}$ $\frac{1}{8}$ **11.** $\frac{1}{2} - \frac{1}{6}$ $\frac{2}{6}$ or $\frac{1}{3}$ **12.** $\frac{4}{6} - \frac{1}{4}$ $\frac{5}{12}$ **13.** $\frac{5}{6} - \frac{7}{12}$ $\frac{3}{12}$ or $\frac{1}{4}$

14. $\frac{5}{8} - \frac{1}{4}$ $\frac{3}{8}$ **15.** $\frac{1}{2} - \frac{3}{8}$ $\frac{1}{8}$ **16.** $\frac{3}{4} - \frac{1}{3}$ $\frac{5}{12}$ **17.** $\frac{7}{8} - \frac{1}{4}$ $\frac{5}{8}$ **18.** $\frac{5}{6} - \frac{3}{4}$ $\frac{1}{12}$

19. $\frac{2}{12}$ and $\frac{1}{6}$ are equivalent fractions.

Solve.

19. Analyze Jamie and Ray each used fraction pieces to find $\frac{1}{2} - \frac{1}{3}$. Jamie's answer was $\frac{1}{6}$. Ray's answer was $\frac{2}{12}$. They are both correct. Explain why. *See above.*

20. Reasoning Jay lined up three fraction pieces to fit exactly under $\frac{7}{10}$. One of the fraction pieces is a $\frac{1}{2}$ piece. What are the other two fraction pieces? $\frac{1}{10}$, $\frac{1}{10}$

21. What's Wrong? Look at Amy's work below. It shows how Amy subtracted $\frac{1}{3}$ from $\frac{2}{4}$. What did she do wrong? Use words and fraction pieces to explain your answer.

22. Evan lined up fraction pieces that showed $\frac{5}{8}$. Lily lined up fraction pieces that showed $\frac{3}{4}$. They want to make the two rows the same length. What fraction piece should be added? $\frac{1}{8}$

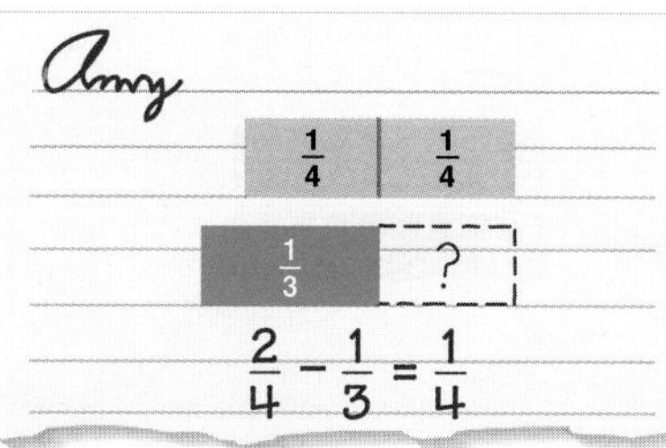

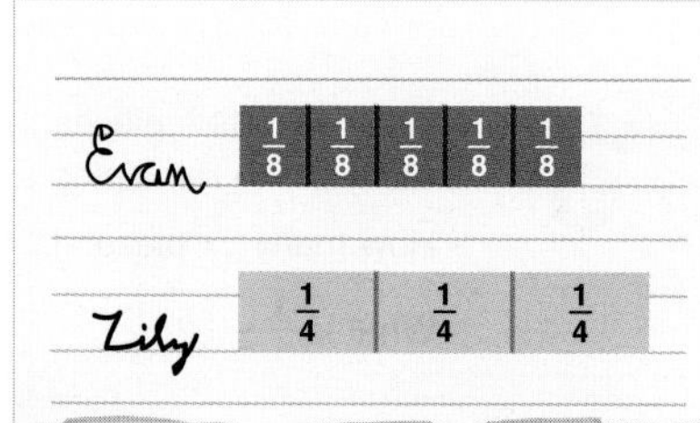

Possible answer: Amy did not line up the fraction pieces. She should use twelfth pieces.

Talk About It • Write About It

You learned how to use fraction pieces to subtract fractions with unlike denominators. *See Additional Answers.*

23. Explain how subtracting fractions with unlike denominators is different from subtracting fractions with like denominators.

24. Explain how to find $\frac{1}{2} - \frac{1}{3}$. Use words or a picture.

532

Homework 20.7 Page 130

Name ______ Date ______ Homework 20.7

Subtract Fractions With Unlike Denominators

Use fraction pieces to help you find each difference.

$\frac{3}{4} - \frac{1}{6}$	**Step 1:** Make fraction pieces using equivalent fractions.	**Step 2:** Find like fraction pieces that fit exactly in the remaining space.
	$\frac{3}{4} = \frac{9}{12}$ and $\frac{1}{6} = \frac{2}{12}$	$\frac{9}{12} - \frac{2}{12} = \frac{7}{12}$ $\frac{3}{4} - \frac{1}{6} = \frac{7}{12}$

1. $\frac{11}{12} - \frac{1}{4}$ $\frac{2}{3}$ 2. $\frac{1}{4} - \frac{1}{6}$ $\frac{1}{12}$ 3. $\frac{9}{12} - \frac{2}{3}$ $\frac{1}{12}$ 4. $\frac{1}{3} - \frac{1}{12}$ $\frac{1}{4}$ 5. $\frac{4}{5} - \frac{5}{10}$ $\frac{3}{10}$

6. $\frac{9}{10} - \frac{1}{2}$ $\frac{2}{5}$ 7. $\frac{2}{4} - \frac{2}{6}$ $\frac{1}{6}$ 8. $\frac{7}{8} - \frac{1}{4}$ $\frac{5}{8}$ 9. $\frac{2}{10} - \frac{1}{5}$ 0 10. $\frac{5}{8} - \frac{1}{2}$ $\frac{1}{8}$

Problem Solving

11. Betty lined up three different fraction pieces to fit exactly under $\frac{11}{12}$. One of the fraction pieces is a $\frac{1}{2}$ piece. What are the other two fraction pieces?
a $\frac{1}{3}$ piece and a $\frac{1}{12}$ piece or a $\frac{1}{6}$ piece and a $\frac{1}{4}$ piece.

Use with text pages 530–532.

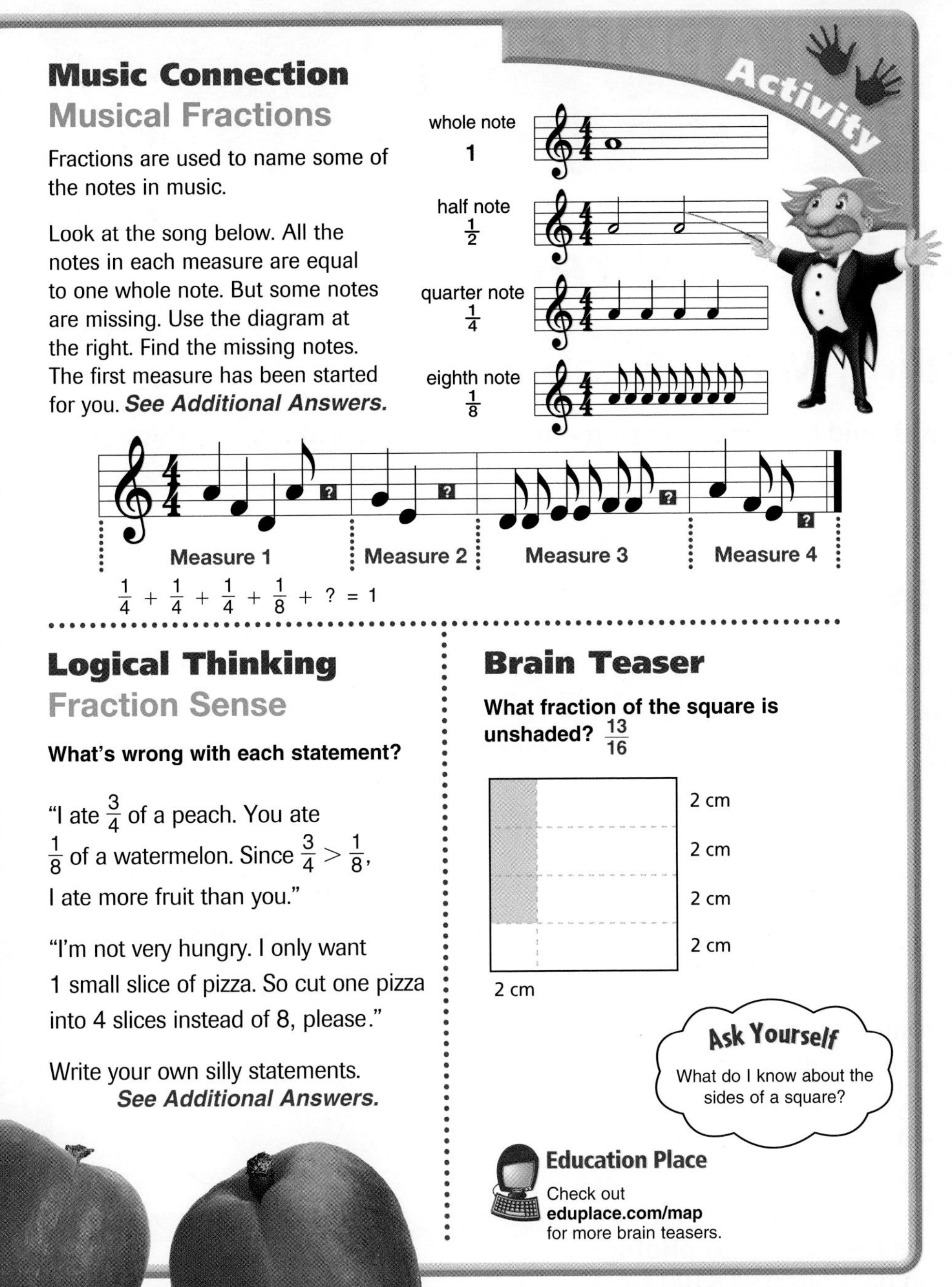

Activity

Music Connection

Musical Fractions

Fractions are used to name some of the notes in music.

Look at the song below. All the notes in each measure are equal to one whole note. But some notes are missing. Use the diagram at the right. Find the missing notes. The first measure has been started for you. ***See Additional Answers.***

$\frac{1}{4} + \frac{1}{4} + \frac{1}{4} + \frac{1}{8} + ? = 1$

Logical Thinking

Fraction Sense

What's wrong with each statement?

"I ate $\frac{3}{4}$ of a peach. You ate $\frac{1}{8}$ of a watermelon. Since $\frac{3}{4} > \frac{1}{8}$, I ate more fruit than you."

"I'm not very hungry. I only want 1 small slice of pizza. So cut one pizza into 4 slices instead of 8, please."

Write your own silly statements. ***See Additional Answers.***

Brain Teaser

What fraction of the square is unshaded? $\frac{13}{16}$

Ask Yourself

What do I know about the sides of a square?

Education Place

Check out **eduplace.com/map** for more brain teasers.

Chapter 20 Lesson 7 **533**

Music Connection

Musical Fractions

- Help students think of a $\frac{4}{4}$ measure as a unit similar to a whole. The time signature $\frac{4}{4}$ means that to be complete, each measure must have 4 quarter notes, or their equivalent.
- Help students "read" the notes in each measure by identifying whole notes, half notes, quarter notes, or eighth notes and counting up their total value. When they find how many beats are already in the measure, they can determine the value of the missing note.

Logical Thinking

Fraction Sense

- Have students discuss these nonsense statements in small groups. You may wish to create a file of silly statements that you could use later as logic questions to provide as problems of the day.
- For the first statement, elicit from students that half of a greater amount is a greater number.
- For the second statement, ask: **How might you slice the pie if you really did wish to have a smaller slice?** (Use any denominator greater than 8; 10ths or 12ths, for example, would give smaller slices.)

Brain Teaser

- Remind students to use the ***Ask Yourself*** question to help answer the Brain Teaser.

Lesson 20.8 Problem-Solving Application: Use a Circle Graph

Planning

Lesson Objective Use circle graphs to solve problems.

Technology Resources

- *Ways to Success* CD-ROM 20.8
- Education Place: Extra Practice www.eduplace.com/map

Lesson 20.8 Transparency

Problem of the Day

For the last half hour of a race, a runner ran at a rate of $\frac{3}{4}$ mile every 5 minutes. How far did she run in that half hour? *Hint:* How many minutes are in half an hour? ($4\frac{1}{2}$ miles)

Spiral Review

Find each amount.

1. $\frac{1}{2}$ of 30 (15) **2.** $\frac{5}{6}$ of 12 (10)
3. $\frac{2}{3}$ of 21 (14) **4.** $\frac{2}{5}$ of 40 (16)
5. $\frac{1}{4}$ of 24 (6) **6.** $\frac{3}{8}$ of 32 (12)

Lesson Quiz

The graph shows how many of each kind of fish Greg has in his aquarium. He has 16 fish in all.

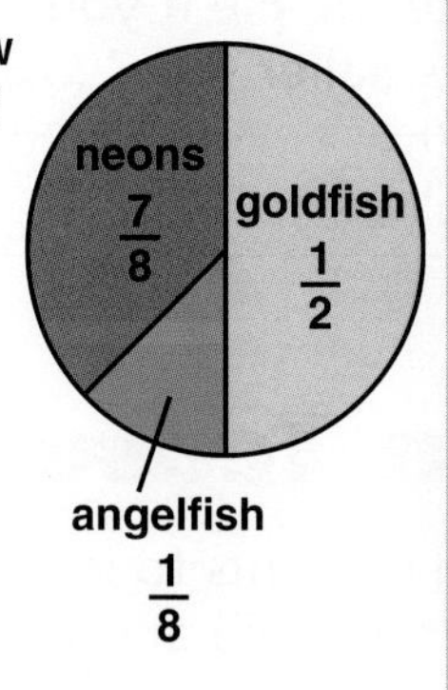

1. How many more goldfish does he have than angelfish (6)
2. How many fewer angelfish does he have than neons? (4)

NCTM Standards
Data Analysis and Probability: Represent data using tables and graphs such as line plots, bar graphs, and line graphs.

Getting Started

Building Math Vocabulary

Students should be familiar with the mathematical vocabulary in this lesson.

Finding Parts of Numbers

Whole Class	15 minutes
Objective	Use a circle graph.
Materials	Workmat 8
Auditory, Visual	

- Have a class discussion about the graphs students have studied and worked with and what each is most useful for showing.
- Have volunteers explain how to find the following: $\frac{1}{8}$ of 24, $\frac{1}{6}$ of 30, $\frac{2}{3}$ of 18, $\frac{3}{5}$ of 25, and $\frac{7}{8}$ of 48. (3; 5; 12; 15; 42)
- Have students make a circle graph with the following information using their workmats: A photography club has collected \$100 from sales at an exhibit. They spent \$25 to pay for the booth. The rest of the money was profit.
- Then tell students that today they are going to use similar circle graphs to solve problems. Discuss that to do this, they will draw upon both their prior understanding of circle graphs and of how to find a part of a number.

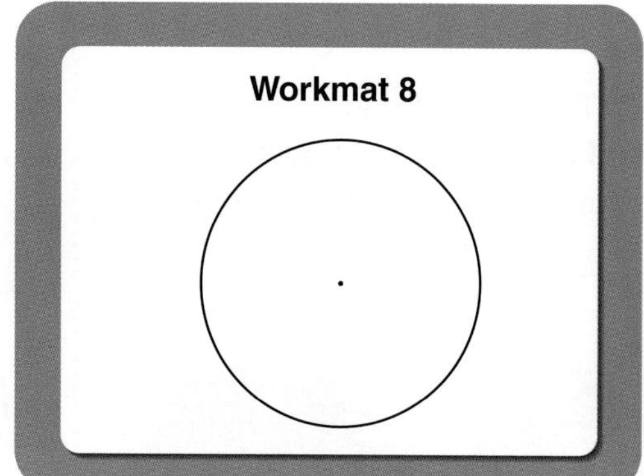

Differentiated Instruction

English Learners

Pairs	20 minutes
Objective	Use a circle graph.
Materials	Fraction pieces (Learning Tool 34)
Visual, Tactual	

Early Production

- Before doing ***Guided Practice,*** give students practice working with circle graphs.
- Distribute eight $\frac{1}{8}$ fraction pieces to represent their school day. Ask students to assign fractions for times spent on various activities.
- Then have them make a graph using the simplest form of each fraction.

Intermediate/Advanced

- English Learner Resource 20.8
- English Learner Handbook

Intervention

Small Groups	5–10 minutes
Objective	Use a circle graph.
Materials	A handout with a circle divided into 12 equal parts
Tactual, Auditory	

- Tell students to suppose that the circle represents 12 hours of the day when they are awake. Instruct them to figure out how many of these hours are spent on various activities, such as eating, school, homework, watching TV, etc. Then have students color in the circle, using one color per activity.
- Pair students. Have them describe their graphs to each other.

Other Resources

- *Ways to Success* CD-ROM 20.8

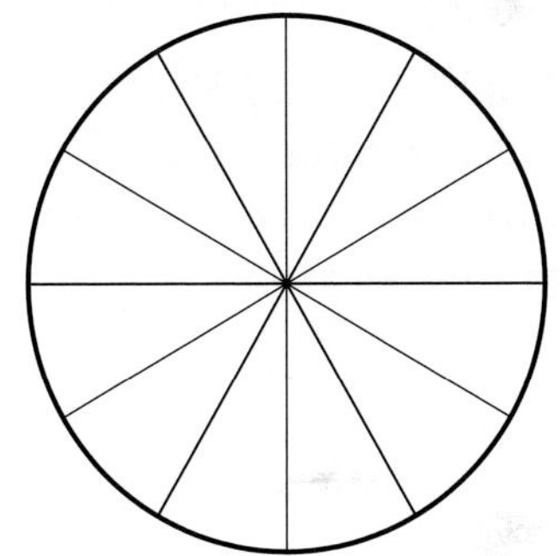

Inclusion

Small Groups	10 minutes
Objective	Use fraction models to model addition.
Materials	Fraction circles (Learning Tool 35)
Tactual, Visual	

- Students can use fraction circles to compare fractional parts to the whole and to one another. For instance, they can model $\frac{1}{2} + \frac{1}{2} = 1$, and $\frac{3}{8} + \frac{1}{8} = \frac{1}{2}$. Have them use the circles to show that $\frac{1}{2} > \frac{3}{8} > \frac{1}{8}$.

Literature Connection

Material: *Circles* by Catherine Sheldrick Ross

This cheerfully illustrated, reader-friendly book provides interesting and useful information about circles, as well as many hands-on activities for students to do.

One activity students can try is to make a sundial. They will draw upon their understanding of parallel lines, midpoints, and degrees to do so. They follow clear instructions to make and use the instrument.

❶ Introduce

Read the objective with students. Explain to students that circle graphs resemble fraction circles and that they will use them to solve problems.

❷ Teach

Use a Circle Graph

- Have a volunteer read aloud the opening information. Guide the students through the problem-solving steps.
- For the ***Understand*** step, ask: **How many students are represented?** (16) **Into how many parts is the circle divided?** (3) **What is the sum of the parts, in simplest form?** (1 whole)
- For the ***Plan*** step, ask: **What must you do before you can compare the number of paints and colored pencils?** (Find the number of each.)
- Work through the ***Solve*** step with students. **What do you divide a number by to find $\frac{1}{8}$ of it?** (8) **$\frac{1}{2}$ of it?** (2)
- For the ***Look Back*** step, guide students to see that the answer makes sense. **How can we find how many students chose markers?** (Find $\frac{3}{8}$ of 16.)

Common Error

- **Making a circle graph incorrectly**
- **Intervention** Emphasize that students should record their fractional parts in a table before making their graphs. Have them make sure that the fractional parts add up to 1, and that the sizes of the parts of the circle they draw accurately represent the relationship among those parts.

Lesson 8

Problem-Solving Application

Use a Circle Graph

Objective Use circle graphs to solve problems.

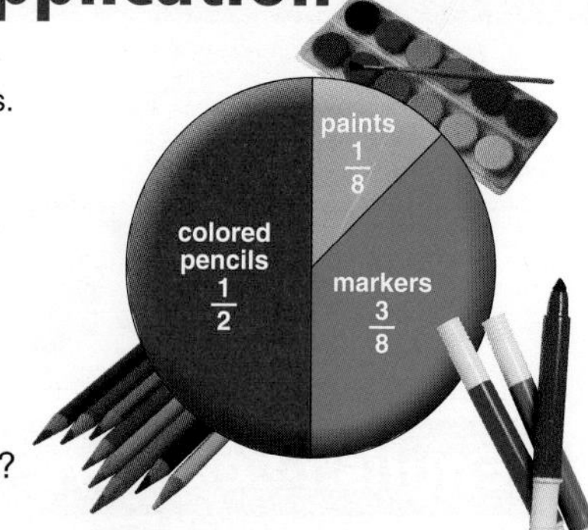

You can use fractions and a circle graph to show a total amount divided into parts.

Problem There are 16 students in one art class. The circle graph shows what fractions of the students chose to use paints, markers, and colored pencils to complete their projects. How many more students chose colored pencils than paints?

UNDERSTAND

This is what the question asks you to find.

How many more students chose colored pencils than paints?

This is what you know.

- There are 16 students.
- $\frac{1}{8}$ chose paints.
- $\frac{1}{2}$ chose colored pencils.
- $\frac{3}{8}$ chose markers.

PLAN

You can use the information in the graph.

Use the fractions on the circle graph to find how many students chose colored pencils and how many chose paints. Then subtract to find the difference.

SOLVE

Find the fractional parts of the whole.

- Find how many students chose colored pencils and how many chose paints.

  $\frac{1}{2}$ of 16 = 8 ← chose colored pencils $\frac{1}{8}$ of 16 = 2 ← chose paints

- Then subtract. 8 − 2 = 6

Solution: Six more students chose colored pencils than chose paints.

LOOK BACK

Look back at the circle graph.

Does your answer seem reasonable?

534

Reteach 20.8

Name ______________ Date ________

Reteach 20.8

Problem-Solving Application: Use a Circle Graph

Read It Look for information.

Fourth-grade students are collecting data for a recycling project. They made a circle graph of the waste in the lunchroom trash cans. There were 100 pieces of trash. How many more pieces of plastic waste than paper waste were there?

Types of Waste: $\frac{1}{2}$ plastic, $\frac{2}{10}$ glass, $\frac{3}{10}$ paper

Organize It

You can organize the information from the circle graph in a table.

Number of Pieces of Waste: 100		
$\frac{1}{2}$ plastic	$\frac{2}{10}$ glass	$\frac{3}{10}$ paper

Solve It Use the information from the table to solve the problem.

1. $\frac{1}{2}$ of 100 = **50** pieces of plastic waste.
2. $\frac{3}{10}$ of 100 = **30** pieces of paper waste.

Use the information from 1 and 2 to help you solve 3.

3. **50** pieces of plastic waste − **30** pieces of paper waste = **20**

   There were **20** more pieces of plastic waste than paper waste.

Try These! Use the circle graph above to solve these questions. **Show your work.**

4. How many pieces of paper and plastic waste were there? **80**
5. How many more pieces of paper waste than glass waste were there? **10**

Use with text pages 534–536.

Practice 20.8 Page 131

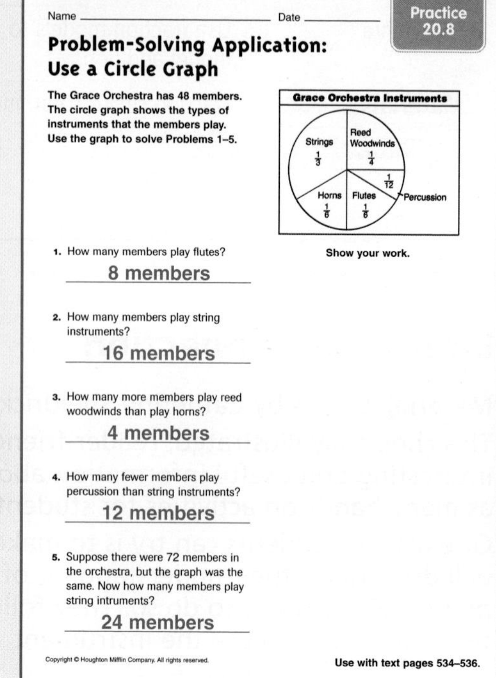

Name ______________ Date ________

Practice 20.8

Problem-Solving Application: Use a Circle Graph

The Grace Orchestra has 48 members. The circle graph shows the types of instruments that the members play. Use the graph to solve Problems 1–5.

Show your work.

1. How many members play flutes? **8 members**
2. How many members play string instruments? **16 members**
3. How many more members play reed woodwinds than play horns? **4 members**
4. How many fewer members play percussion than string instruments? **12 members**
5. Suppose there were 72 members in the orchestra, but the graph was the same. Now how many members play string intruments? **24 members**

Use with text pages 534–536.

Guided Practice

Use the circle graph on Page 534 to solve each problem.

1. How many more students chose markers than chose paints? **4 more students**

   Hint What part of the circle graph shows markers?

2. Suppose the art class has 8 more students, but the circle graph remains the same. Now how many students chose markers? **9 students**

Ask Yourself

UNDERSTAND **What does the question ask me to find?**

PLAN **Did I use the correct information from the graph?**

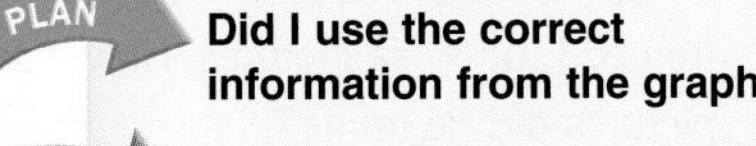

SOLVE
- **Did I find the fractional parts of the whole?**
- **Did I decide what operation to use?**

LOOK BACK **Does my answer make sense?**

Independent Practice

An art club has 36 members. The circle graph shows the types of projects the students chose to do for an art show.

Use the graph to solve Problems 3–6.

3. How many members chose woodworking projects? **3 members**
4. How many more students chose pottery than chose drawing? **9 more students**
5. How many more students chose drawing and pottery than chose woodworking and weaving? **18 more students**
6. Suppose there are 72 members, but the graph is the same. Now how many students chose weaving? **12 students**
7. **Create and Solve** Use real or made-up data to create a circle graph of your own. Then write and solve a problem about the graph you drew. ***Check students' work.***

Art Projects

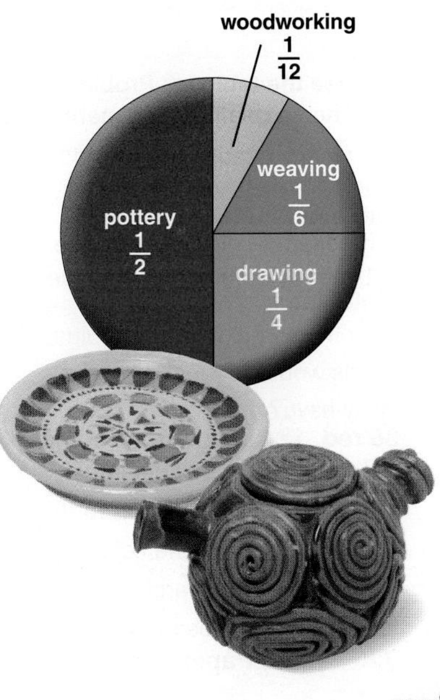

Go On

Guided Practice

Have students complete **Problems 1–2** as you observe. Remind them to use the *Ask Yourself* questions to help.

3 Practice

Independent Practice

Select from **Exercises 3–15** as independent work.

Enrichment 20.8

Name ______ Date ______ Enrichment 20.8

Problem-Solving Application: Use a Circle Graph

Jonathan works at a shoe store. Last week, he sold 64 shoes. He made a table that lists the types of shoes he sold as fractions of the total number sold. Make a circle graph using the data in the table. Be sure to label each section of the graph with the type of shoe and the fraction. Then use the circle graph to find how many sneakers Jonathan sold. Explain how you found your answer.

Shoe Sales

Type of Shoe	Fraction of Sales
Boots	$\frac{1}{8}$
Dress Shoes	$\frac{1}{4}$
Sneakers	?
Slippers	$\frac{1}{4}$

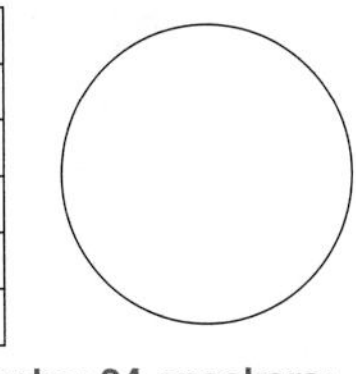

Check students' graphs; 24 sneakers; explanations may vary.

 Use with text pages 534–536.

Problem Solving 20.8

Name ______ Date ______ Problem Solving 20.8

Problem-Solving Application: Use a Circle Graph

Problem Josephine ordered 12 carnations for her mom for her birthday. The circle graph shows what fraction of the flowers were pink, red, and white.

How many more pink carnations were there than red carnations?

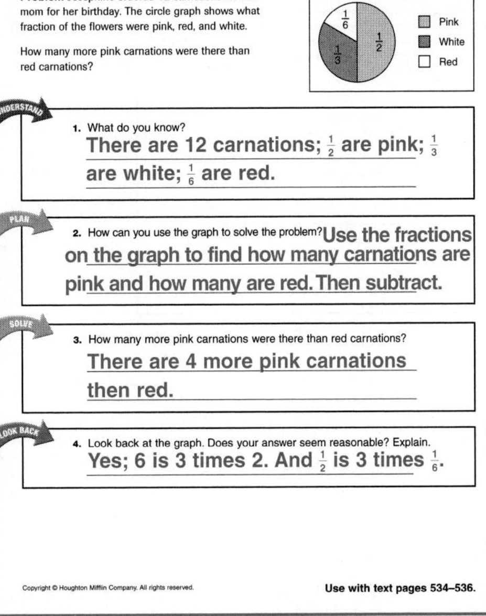

1. What do you know? There are 12 carnations; $\frac{1}{2}$ are pink; $\frac{1}{3}$ are white; $\frac{1}{6}$ are red.
2. How can you use the graph to solve the problem? Use the fractions on the graph to find how many carnations are pink and how many are red. Then subtract.
3. How many more pink carnations were there than red carnations? There are 4 more pink carnations then red.
4. Look back at the graph. Does your answer seem reasonable? Explain. Yes; 6 is 3 times 2. And $\frac{1}{2}$ is 3 times $\frac{1}{6}$.

 Use with text pages 534–536.

Mixed Problem Solving

Have students review their answers to make sure they have:

- expressed the solution clearly
- used appropriate mathematical notation and terms
- supported their solution with verbal and symbolic work

4 Assess & Close

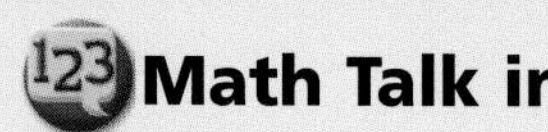

Math Talk in Action

Have students suppose that the following data about student preferences was represented in a circle graph: $\frac{1}{2}$ of the students chose oil paint; $\frac{1}{3}$ chose charcoal; $\frac{1}{4}$ chose colored pencil. Discuss why these data cannot be correct.

Math Journal Prompt

Have students write an explanation of how to use a circle graph to show how to solve problems involving fractional parts of a whole.

Lesson Quiz

Use the quiz on Lesson Transparency 20.8.

Test Prep & Spiral Review

Use Test Prep Transparency 20.8.

Mixed Problem Solving

Solve. Show your work. Tell what strategy you used. ***Possible strategies given.***

You Choose

Strategy
- Act It Out
- Draw a Picture
- Use Logical Reasoning
- Write an Equation

Computation Method
- Mental Math
- Estimation
- Paper and Pencil
- Calculator

8. Lin painted 6 pictures in art class. He framed $\frac{2}{3}$ of those pictures. How many pictures did he frame?
4 pictures; Draw a Picture

9. Clemence used red, white, and blue stripes to make a flag. The red stripe is not on the top. The white stripe is not next to the red stripe. In what order from top to bottom are the stripes?
white, blue, red; Use Logical Reasoning

10. Marlena bought apples and oranges. She bought twice as many apples as oranges. Together, she bought 18 pieces of fruit. How many of each type of fruit did she buy?
12 apples, 6 oranges; Write an Equation

Data **Use the table for Problems 11–15.** ***Possible methods given.*** **Then explain which method you chose.**

Beads Needed For 8-Inch Long Bracelets			
Bracelet Width	**Red**	**White**	**Blue**
$\frac{1}{2}$ inch	60	24	36
1 inch	120	48	72
2 inches	240	96	144

11. How many beads are needed to make a 2-inch-wide bracelet?
480 beads; Mental Math

12. What fraction of the beads needed for a 1-inch-wide bracelet are blue?
$\frac{3}{10}$; Calculator

13. How many red, white, and blue beads would a $\frac{1}{4}$ inch bracelet likely have?
30 red, 12 white, 18 blue; Mental Math

14. Robert wants to make a larger bracelet to use as a collar for his dog. Robert wants the collar to be $1\frac{1}{2}$ inches wide and 16 inches long. How many beads will he need?
720 beads; Paper and Pencil

15. **You Decide** Each color bead comes in a bag of 60 or 200. You want to make 3 bracelets. Decide which size bracelets to make. Then decide how many bags of beads to buy. Explain your thinking.
Check students' work.

536

Homework 20.8 Page 131

Name ______________________ Date __________

Homework 20.8

Problem-Solving Application: Use a Circle Graph

Mrs. Lucille gave 60 students the choice of four different activities during recess time. The circle graph shows what fractions of the students chose to play racing, dodge ball, kick ball, or hide and seek. Use the circle graph to solve each problem.

Recess Activities
racing $\frac{1}{2}$
kick ball $\frac{1}{4}$
hide and seek $\frac{1}{12}$
dodge ball $\frac{1}{6}$

How many more students chose kick ball than dodge ball?

Find out how many students chose kick ball and how many students chose dodge ball.

kick ball = $\frac{1}{4}$ of 60 = 15 students

dodge ball = $\frac{1}{6}$ of 60 = 10 students

Find the difference.
15 − 10 = 5

Five more students chose kick ball than dodge ball.

Show your work.

1. How many students chose either racing or hide and seek?
35 students

2. Suppose that there are 96 students instead of 60, but the graph is the same. How many students chose dodge ball?
16 students

Use with text pages 534–536.

Social Studies Connection

Egyptian Fractions

Problem Solving

A **unit fraction** is a fraction that has 1 as its numerator. All ancient Egyptian fractions were written as unit fractions or as the sum of more than one unit fraction.

Look at the examples below.

- $\frac{1}{4}$ is a unit fraction, because its numerator is 1.

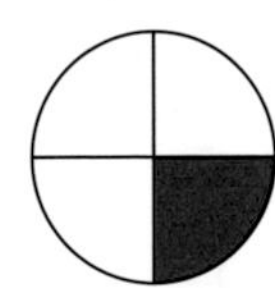

- $\frac{3}{4}$ is not a unit fraction, because its numerator is 3, not 1.

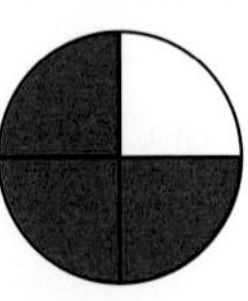

- In ancient Egypt, $\frac{3}{4}$ was written as the sum of unit fractions: $\frac{1}{2} + \frac{1}{4}$.

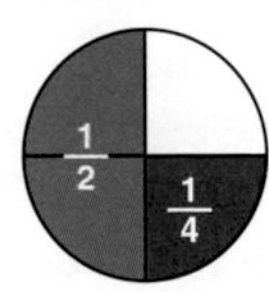

Write each of these fractions as sums of unit fractions.

1. $\frac{5}{8}$ 2. $\frac{8}{15}$ 3. $\frac{7}{12}$ 4. $\frac{7}{8}$

5. $\frac{5}{6}$ 6. $\frac{3}{8}$ 7. $\frac{3}{5}$ 8. $\frac{5}{12}$

Answers may vary.

1. $\frac{1}{2} + \frac{1}{8}$
2. $\frac{1}{3} + \frac{1}{5}$
3. $\frac{1}{2} + \frac{1}{12}$
4. $\frac{1}{2} + \frac{1}{4} + \frac{1}{8}$
5. $\frac{1}{2} + \frac{1}{3}$
6. $\frac{1}{4} + \frac{1}{8}$
7. $\frac{1}{5} + \frac{1}{5} + \frac{1}{5}$
8. $\frac{1}{3} + \frac{1}{12}$

WEEKLY WR READER eduplace.com/map

Social Studies Connection

Egyptian Fractions

- Discuss that the ancient Egyptians and other ancient cultures developed mathematical systems to suit their needs. Invite students to learn more about ways fractional amounts were represented long ago and in different places.
- Invite interested students to do research to find out about the Rosetta Stone. Have students share their findings, in both cases, with classmates.
- Work through the first exercise with students. Elicit that the solution to each exercise relies on understanding equivalent fractions. Point out that they will need to use *more* than two unit fractions to write some of these Egyptian fractions.

Chapter Review/Test

Chapter Review/Test

Items 1–20 To assign a numerical grade for this Chapter Review/Test, use 5 points for each item.

Check Understanding

You can use the ***Write About It*** question to assess student understanding of a key chapter concept.

Customize Your Instruction

The Chapter Review/Test is a formal evaluation of chapter objectives. For students who have not yet mastered these objectives, you can use the Reteaching Resources listed in the chart below.

Additional Assessment Resources

Alternate Chapter Test A Chapter Test is also provided in the Unit Resource folder. You might use the Review/Test in the student book as review and the test in the Unit Resource folder as a summary test for the chapter.

***Ways to Assess* CD-ROM** allows you to create your own lesson, chapter, or unit tests or practice and review worksheets.

Adequate Yearly Progress Guide helps familiarize your students with the format of standardized tests.

Chapter Review/Test

VOCABULARY

Choose the best term to complete each sentence.

Vocabulary
- estimate
- like denominators
- mixed number
- unlike denominators

1. When you do not need an exact answer, you can ___. **estimate**
2. The fractions $\frac{4}{6}$ and $\frac{3}{6}$ have ___. **like denominators**
3. The fractions $\frac{2}{7}$ and $\frac{1}{3}$ have ___. **unlike denominators**

CONCEPTS AND SKILLS

Add or subtract. Use fraction pieces if you wish. Write your answer in simplest form. (Lessons 1, 2, 6, 7, pp. 516–521, 524–525)

4. $\frac{1}{3} + \frac{1}{3}$ **$\frac{2}{3}$**
5. $\frac{4}{6} + \frac{2}{6}$ **1**
6. $\frac{10}{12} - \frac{5}{12}$ **$\frac{5}{12}$**
7. $\frac{18}{24} - \frac{12}{24}$ **$\frac{1}{4}$**
8. $1\frac{1}{4} + 2\frac{1}{4}$ **$3\frac{1}{2}$**
9. $5\frac{3}{5} + 4\frac{2}{5}$ **10**
10. $3\frac{2}{6} - 1\frac{1}{6}$ **$2\frac{1}{6}$**
11. $7\frac{1}{9} - 4\frac{1}{9}$ **3**
12. $\frac{3}{5} + \frac{1}{10}$ **$\frac{7}{10}$**
13. $\frac{1}{4} + \frac{3}{8}$ **$\frac{5}{8}$**
14. $\frac{5}{6} - \frac{1}{2}$ **$\frac{1}{3}$**
15. $\frac{1}{3} - \frac{2}{12}$ **$\frac{1}{6}$**

Estimate each sum. Write *greater than 1* or *less than 1*. (Lesson 4, pp. 524–525)

16. $\frac{1}{4} + \frac{3}{8}$ ***less than 1***
17. $\frac{4}{5} + \frac{3}{4}$ ***greater than 1***
18. $\frac{2}{9} + \frac{4}{12}$ ***less than 1***

PROBLEM SOLVING

Solve. (Lessons 3, 8, pp. 522–523, 534–536)

19. At an arcade, four friends shared 25 tokens. If each person got the same number of tokens, how many tokens were left? **1 token**
20. The circle graph shows the different coins Carl has. If Carl has 18 coins, how many of them are pennies? **12 pennies**

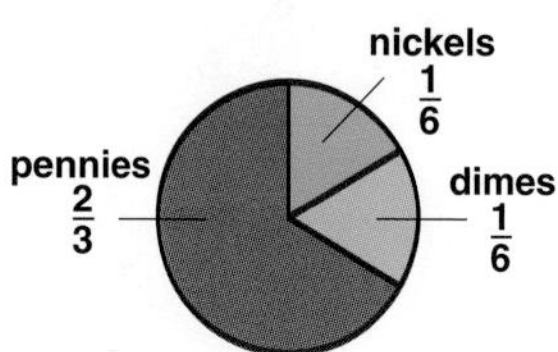

Write About It: Jim solved $\frac{5}{8} - \frac{1}{2}$; *Possible explanation:* I worked backwards. I know that $\frac{1}{2}$ is equivalent to $\frac{4}{8}$ and that $\frac{4}{8} + \frac{1}{8} = \frac{5}{8}$.

Write About It

Show You Understand

Jim used these fraction strips to solve a subtraction problem.

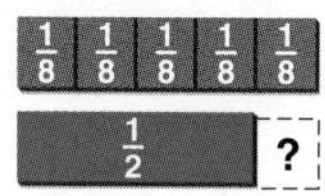

Jim's answer was $\frac{1}{8}$. What problem did he solve? Explain how you found your answer.
See above.

Chapter Review/Test Items	Objectives	Covered On Teacher's Edition Pages	Use These Reteaching Resources
2, 4–11	**20A** Add and subtract fractions and mixed numbers with like denominators.	516A–521	Reteach Resources 20.1, 20.2 *Ways to Success* CD-ROM 20.1, 20.2 *Ways to Success* Skillsheets 172, 173
1, 16–18	**20B** Estimate sums of fractions.	524A–525	Reteach Resources 20.4 *Ways to Success* CD-ROM 20.4 *Ways to Success* Skillsheet 174
3, 12–15	**20C** Use models to add and subtract fractions with unlike denominators.	528A–532	Reteach Resources 20.6, 20.7 *Ways to Success* CD-ROM 20.6, 20.7 *Ways to Success* Skillsheets 175, 176
19–20	**20D** Solve problems using skills and strategies.	522A–523 526A–526 534A–536	Reteach Resources 20.3, 20.5, 20.8 *Ways to Success* CD-ROM 20.3, 20.5, 20.8 *Ways to Success* Skillsheet 177

Extra Practice

Set A (Lesson 1, pp. 516–519)

Add or subtract. Write your answer in simplest form.

1. $\frac{3}{5} + \frac{2}{5}$ **1**
2. $\frac{2}{9} + \frac{4}{9}$ **$\frac{2}{3}$**
3. $\frac{3}{4} + \frac{1}{4}$ **1**
4. $\frac{6}{7} - \frac{5}{7}$ **$\frac{1}{7}$**
5. $\frac{2}{3} - \frac{2}{3}$ **0**
6. $\frac{4}{5} - \frac{1}{5}$ **$\frac{3}{5}$**
7. $\frac{4}{8} - \frac{2}{8}$ **$\frac{1}{4}$**
8. $\frac{4}{5} + \frac{4}{5}$ **$1\frac{3}{5}$**
9. $\frac{5}{6} - \frac{2}{6}$ **$\frac{1}{2}$**
10. $\frac{7}{8} + \frac{5}{8}$ **$1\frac{1}{2}$**
11. $\frac{3}{4} + \frac{3}{4}$ **$1\frac{1}{2}$**
12. $\frac{7}{8} - \frac{1}{8}$ **$\frac{3}{4}$**
13. $\frac{2}{3} - \frac{1}{3}$ **$\frac{1}{3}$**
14. $\frac{5}{7} + \frac{4}{7}$ **$1\frac{2}{7}$**

Set B (Lesson 2, pp. 520–521)

Add or subtract. Write your answer in simplest form.

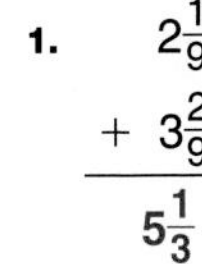

1. $2\frac{1}{9} + 3\frac{2}{9}$ **$5\frac{1}{3}$**
2. $5\frac{4}{6} + 3\frac{2}{6}$ **9**
3. $4\frac{5}{12} - 3\frac{1}{12}$ **$1\frac{1}{3}$**
4. $7\frac{8}{10} - 5\frac{3}{10}$ **$2\frac{1}{2}$**
5. $2\frac{7}{8} + 4\frac{5}{8}$ **$7\frac{1}{2}$**
6. $9\frac{5}{6} - 6\frac{4}{6}$ **$3\frac{1}{6}$**
7. $6\frac{2}{4} - 4\frac{1}{4}$ **$2\frac{1}{4}$**
8. $8\frac{3}{5} + 2\frac{4}{5}$ **$11\frac{2}{5}$**
9. $5\frac{5}{7} - 2\frac{3}{7}$ **$3\frac{2}{7}$**
10. $9\frac{3}{10} + 6\frac{7}{10}$ **16**
11. $2\frac{9}{10} - 2\frac{7}{10}$ **$\frac{1}{5}$**
12. $4\frac{1}{8} + 3\frac{5}{8}$ **$7\frac{3}{4}$**
13. $1\frac{2}{3} + 2\frac{2}{3}$ **$4\frac{1}{3}$**
14. $5\frac{5}{8} - 3\frac{3}{8}$ **$2\frac{1}{4}$**

Set C (Lesson 4, pp. 524–525)

Estimate each sum. Write *greater than 1* or *less than 1*.

1. $\frac{6}{8} + \frac{7}{8}$ ***greater than 1***
2. $\frac{3}{8} + \frac{2}{5}$ ***less than 1***
3. $\frac{3}{10} + \frac{1}{3}$ ***less than 1***
4. $\frac{3}{4} + \frac{2}{3}$ ***greater than 1***
5. $\frac{3}{5} + \frac{7}{10}$ ***greater than 1***
6. $\frac{1}{5} + \frac{3}{12}$ ***less than 1***
7. $\frac{2}{3} + \frac{9}{10}$ ***greater than 1***
8. $\frac{5}{8} + \frac{4}{7}$ ***greater than 1***
9. $\frac{6}{10} + \frac{8}{15}$ ***greater than 1***
10. $\frac{2}{3} + \frac{1}{2}$ ***greater than 1***

Estimate each sum. Write > or < for each ⬬.

11. $\frac{1}{5} + \frac{3}{8}$ ⬬ $\frac{5}{8} + \frac{2}{3}$ **<**
12. $\frac{6}{8} + \frac{3}{5}$ ⬬ $\frac{7}{18} + \frac{4}{10}$ **>**
13. $\frac{1}{2} + \frac{3}{5}$ ⬬ $\frac{2}{5} + \frac{1}{8}$ **>**
14. $\frac{3}{4} + \frac{4}{5}$ ⬬ $\frac{1}{3} + \frac{3}{8}$ **>**
15. $\frac{1}{4} + \frac{2}{5}$ ⬬ $\frac{4}{5} + \frac{7}{10}$ **<**
16. $\frac{3}{9} + \frac{1}{3}$ ⬬ $\frac{2}{3} + \frac{7}{9}$ **<**

Extra Practice at **eduplace.com/map**

CHAPTER 20 TEST

Chapter 20 Test

Name ____________________ Date __________

Add or subtract. Write your answer in simplest form.

1. $\frac{7}{8} - \frac{5}{8}$ **$\frac{1}{4}$**
2. $\frac{2}{9} + \frac{4}{9}$ **$\frac{2}{3}$**
3. $1\frac{1}{5} + 2\frac{3}{5}$ **$3\frac{4}{5}$**
4. $2\frac{9}{10} - 1\frac{5}{10} =$ **$1\frac{2}{5}$**
5. $3\frac{1}{6} + 2\frac{3}{6} =$ **$5\frac{2}{3}$**
6. $4\frac{4}{7} + 3\frac{1}{7} =$ **$7\frac{5}{7}$**

Estimate each sum. Write *greater than 1* or *less than 1*.

7. $\frac{2}{9} + \frac{3}{6}$ **less than 1**
8. $\frac{7}{8} + \frac{3}{5}$ **greater than 1**
9. $\frac{1}{5} + \frac{4}{12}$ **less than 1**

Find each sum. Draw fraction pieces to help you.

10. $\frac{3}{4} + \frac{1}{6} =$ **$\frac{11}{12}$**
11. $\frac{1}{6} + \frac{2}{3} =$ **$\frac{5}{6}$**
12. $\frac{1}{5} + \frac{3}{10} =$ **$\frac{1}{2}$**

Draw fraction pieces to help you find each difference.

13. $\frac{2}{3} - \frac{1}{4} =$ **$\frac{5}{12}$**
14. $\frac{11}{12} - \frac{2}{6} =$ **$\frac{7}{12}$**
15. $\frac{3}{8} - \frac{1}{4} =$ **$\frac{1}{8}$**

Go on

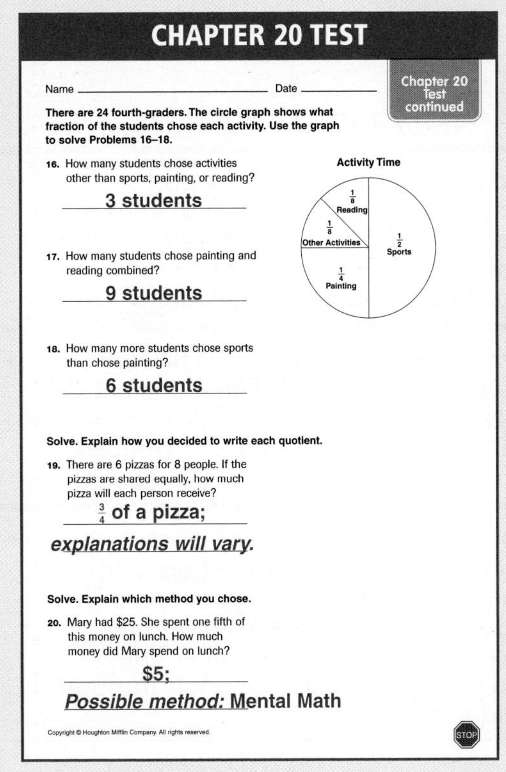

CHAPTER 20 TEST

Chapter 20 Test continued

Name ____________________ Date __________

There are 24 fourth-graders. The circle graph shows what fraction of the students chose each activity. Use the graph to solve Problems 16–18.

Activity Time

16. How many students chose activities other than sports, painting, or reading? **3 students**
17. How many students chose painting and reading combined? **9 students**
18. How many more students chose sports than chose painting? **6 students**

Solve. Explain how you decided to write each quotient.

19. There are 6 pizzas for 8 people. If the pizzas are shared equally, how much pizza will each person receive? **$\frac{3}{4}$ of a pizza; *explanations will vary.***

Solve. Explain which method you chose.

20. Mary had $25. She spent one fifth of this money on lunch. How much money did Mary spend on lunch? **$5; *Possible method:* Mental Math**

STOP

CHAPTER 21 Planning Guide

Understand Decimals

Lesson	Overview	Objective/Vocabulary
1 Hands On: Tenths and Hundredths p. 542A	▶ Relate shaded models of tenths and hundredths grids with fractions and decimals in tenths and hundredths. ▶ Discover similarities and differences among decimals such as 0.3, 0.30, and 0.03.	▶ Use models to show tenths and hundredths. decimal decimal point tenth hundredth
2 Hands On: Thousandths p. 544A	▶ Introduce thousandths through models and place-value charts. ▶ Learn to name the same amount using equivalent decimals in tenths, hundredths, and thousandths.	▶ Write decimals for thousandths. thousandths equivalent decimals
3 Mixed Numbers and Decimals p. 546A	▶ Learn three different ways to show decimal values greater than 1: shaded tenths or hundredths models, mixed numbers, and place-value charts. ▶ Express decimals greater than one in standard form, word form, and expanded form similar to whole numbers.	▶ Read, write, and model amounts greater than 1. mixed number
4 Fractions and Decimal Equivalents p. 550A	▶ Using shaded tenths and hundredths models and a number line in tenths scales, write a fraction for the same amount.	▶ Write fractions and decimals that name the same amount. decimal equivalent
5 Problem-Solving Strategy: Find a Pattern p. 554A	▶ Find patterns to solve problems. ▶ Some patterns require more than one operation to show a sequence of numbers. ▶ Choose a problem-solving strategy.	▶ Use patterns to solve problems.
6 Compare and Order Decimals p. 558A	▶ Compare and order decimals through thousandths, using a number line and place-value charts. ▶ Use the symbols <, =, and > to compare decimals.	▶ Compare and order decimals and recognize equivalent decimals. compare
7 Compare and Order Decimals and Mixed Numbers p. 560A	▶ Expand on previous lessons presenting equivalent decimals for fractions and mixed numbers, and compare and order these decimal equivalents. ▶ Place-value charts and number lines help student compare decimals through hundredths.	▶ Compare and order decimals and mixed numbers.

Skills Trace: Understand Decimals		
Grade 3	**Grade 4**	**Grade 5**
• Read and write decimals through hundredths (ch. 20) • Read and write decimals greater than 1 (ch. 20) • Compare and order decimals and fractions (ch. 20) • Relate decimals, fractions, and money (ch. 20) • Solve problems by finding a number pattern (ch. 1)	• Read and write decimals through thousandths • Relate fractions, mixed numbers, and decimals • Compare and order decimals, fractions, and mixed numbers • Use patterns to solve problems	• Read and write decimals through thousandths (ch. 1) • Compare, order, and round decimals (ch. 1) • Relate, compare, and order fractions, mixed numbers, and decimals (ch. 9) • Use patterns to solve problems (ch. 1)

Differentiated Instruction	Materials	NCTM Standards
▸ Differentiated Instruction activities, p. 542B ▸ *Chapter Challenges,* p. 121 *Ways to Success* CD-ROM 21.1 ▸ *Ways to Success* Skillsheet 178	Decimal Grids or Learning Tools 38 and 39, colored pencils	**Number and Operations:** Understand the place-value structure of the base-ten number system and be able to represent and compare whole numbers and decimals; recognize and generate equivalent forms of commonly used fractions, decimals, and percent. **Representation:** Create and use representations to organize, record, and communicate mathematical ideas.
▸ Differentiated Instruction activities, p. 544B *Ways to Success* CD-ROM 21.2 ▸ *Ways to Success* Skillsheet 181 Audio Tutor **2**/24 Listen and Understand	Decimal Grids or Learning Tools 38, 39, and 40, colored pencils	**Number and Operations:** Understand the place-value structure of the base-ten number system and be able to represent and compare whole numbers and decimals; recognize and generate equivalent forms of commonly used fractions, decimals, and percent.
▸ Differentiated Instruction activities, p. 546B ▸ *Chapter Challenges,* p. 123 *Ways to Success* CD-ROM 21.3 ▸ *Ways to Success* Skillsheet 184	Tenths and Hundredths Grid Transparency, blank transparency	**Number and Operations:** Recognize equivalent representations for the same number and generate them by decomposing and composing numbers.
▸ Differentiated Instruction activities, p. 550B *Ways to Success* CD-ROM 21.4 ▸ *Ways to Success* Skillsheet 182 Audio Tutor **2**/25 Listen and Understand	Tenths and Hundredths Grid Transparency, blank transparency, Workmat 6	**Number and Operations:** Recognize equivalent representations for the same number and generate them by decomposing and composing numbers; recognize and generate equivalent forms of commonly used fractions, decimals, and percents. **Connections:** Recognize and use connections among mathematical ideas.
▸ Differentiated Instruction activities, p. 554B ▸ *Chapter Challenges,* p. 125 *Ways to Success* CD-ROM 21.5 ▸ *Ways to Success* Skillsheet 186	Hundred Chart (Learning Tool 14)	**Algebra:** Describe, extend, and make generalizations abut geometric and numeric patterns. **Problem Solving:** Apply and adapt a variety of appropriate strategies to solve problems.
▸ Differentiated Instruction activities, p. 558B *Ways to Success* CD-ROM 21.6 ▸ *Ways to Success* Skillsheet 183	Grid paper	**Number and Operations:** Understand the place-value structure of the base-ten number system and be able to represent and compare whole numbers and decimals.
▸ Differentiated Instruction activities, p. 560B *Ways to Success* CD-ROM 21.7 ▸ *Ways to Success* Skillsheet 185 Audio Tutor **2**/26 Listen and Understand	Decimal Place-Value Chart Transparency, calculator	**Number and Operations:** Recognize and generate equivalent forms of commonly used fractions, decimals, and percents. **Connections:** Recognize and use connections among mathematical ideas.

Math Notes

Chapter Objectives

21A Read, write, and identify place value of a digit in a decimal through thousandths.

21B Write fractions and mixed numbers as decimals and vice versa.

21C Compare and order decimals and mixed numbers.

21D Solve problem using skills and strategies.

Mathematical Background

Decimals

Whole numbers and fractions belong to the set of rational numbers. The decimal notation for whole numbers can be extended to represent rational numbers.

The key to such an extension is the use of a decimal point to the right of the digit in the ones place. The place-value rule that states that each digit has a place value 10 times that of the digit to the right can be extended to digits to the right of the decimal point.

tens	ones	.	tenths	hundredths	thousandths
10×1 or 10	1 or 1		$\frac{1}{10} \times 1$ or $\frac{1}{10}$ or 0.1	$\frac{1}{10} \times \frac{1}{10}$ or $\frac{1}{100}$ or 0.01	$\frac{1}{10} \times \frac{1}{100}$ or $\frac{1}{1,000}$ or 0.001
4	6	.	1	9	7

The decimal 46.197 is read *forty-six and one hundred ninety-seven thousandths.*

Students should also realize that a decimal can be written as a fraction.

For example: $0.37 = \frac{37}{100}$

Comparing decimals is similar to comparing whole numbers. Begin by comparing digits in each place, starting at the left until different digits appear. The number with the greater of these digits is the greater number.

Research-Based Teaching

Much research has been done on how students understand connections between fractions and decimals. As a result, specific strategies for better developing intuitive relationships between fractions and decimals have been noted. They include proper use of technology, manipulative models, and the use of contextual problems (Irwin, 2001; Middleton et al., 1998; Nickson, 2000). A study by Oppenheimer and Hunting (1999) supported the idea of using a "100s scheme" in which students thought of the fractions and decimals as being parts of 100. See *Professional Resources Handbook, Grade 4,* Unit 7.

For more ideas relating to Unit 7, see the Teacher Support Handbook at the back of this Teacher's Edition.

Language Intervention

When students are working together on hands-on activities, encourage them to verbalize what they are doing and why. This will help them build their own understanding and math vocabulary. It will also benefit the other students in the group.

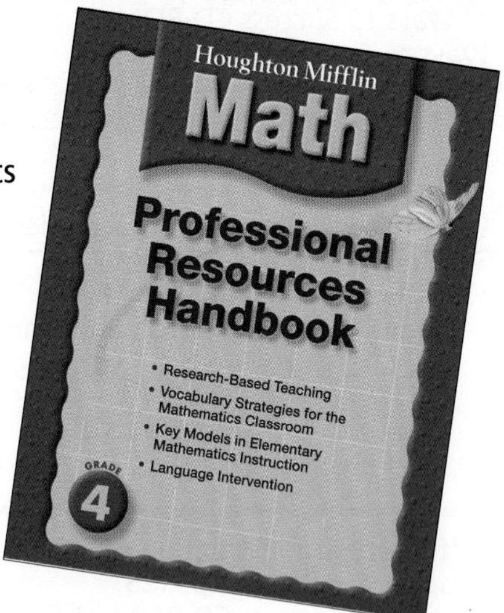

Chapter Activities

Connecting to the Unit Project

Whole Class	30 minutes
Objective	Use decimals.
Materials	None
Visual, Auditory	

Use Decimals

- Some students might research the price of the uniform or equipment for an Olympic event or the price of tickets to attend an event.
- Have them figure out the cost of an athlete's uniform. Or have them calculate the cost of taking a family of four to an event, complete with snacks and souvenirs.

Assessing Prior Knowledge

Pairs	30 minutes
Objective	Recognize equivalent fractions and decimals.
Materials	Two sets of cards
Tactual, Visual	

Equivalent Fractions and Decimals

- Make two sets of cards, one with fractions and the other with decimals.

  Fractions: $\frac{1}{10}$, $\frac{3}{10}$, $\frac{7}{10}$, $\frac{1}{100}$, $\frac{3}{100}$, $\frac{7}{100}$

  Decimals: 0.1, 0.3, 0.7, 0.01, 0.03, 0.07
- Shuffle the cards in each set and lay them facedown in two piles. Ask students to take turns choosing a card from each pile and stand in front of the room displaying their card.
- Ask the students who choose the cards to find a partner with an equivalent fraction or decimal, such as 0.3 and $\frac{3}{10}$. Or, ask students at their desks to match up pairs of students as partners to show fraction/decimal equivalents.

$\frac{1}{10}$ 0.1

Math Expressions

Small Groups	20 minutes
Objective	Compare and order decimals.
Materials	None
Visual	

Compare and Order Decimals

This activity uses instructional practices from *Math Expressions* with the content of this chapter.

- Display these decimal numbers:

  0.35 0.318 0.4
- Ask students which number they think is greatest and which is least.
- Explain that it can be easier to compare decimal numbers if the numbers each have the same number of decimal places. We can put in extra zeros to help us see all the decimal places aligned. Model how to put extra zeros in the decimal numbers:

  0.35**0** 0.318 0.4**00**
- Write the numbers in a column, lining up the decimal points of the numbers.

  0.350

  0.318

  0.400
- Have students write comparison statements using $>$ or $<$.
- Have students work in pairs to compare other decimal numbers.

Starting Chapter 21

Investigation

Using Data

Have students work in small groups to answer the question posed on page 540.

- To extend the investigation, provide the following problem.
- Use the table on page 540. Suppose a soccer game for players over 17 years of age is divided into 2 time periods. Would this game last for more or less than 1 hour? Explain. (More. 0.75 is 3/4 of an hour, so 2 sections of 0.75 hours would have to be more than 1 hour.)

For more information about projects and investigations,

Visit **Education Place**®
www.eduplace.com/mat

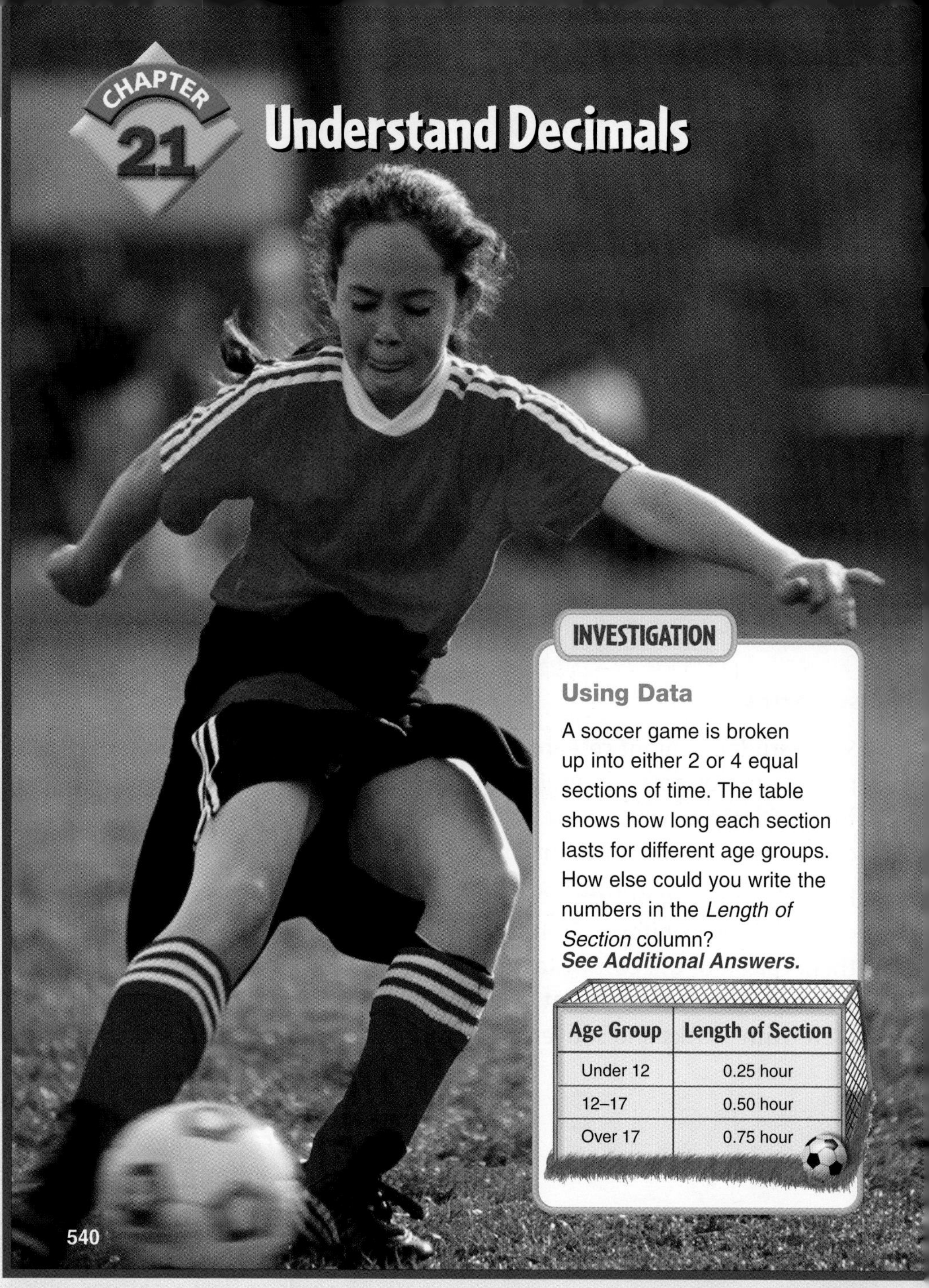

CHAPTER 21

Understand Decimals

INVESTIGATION

Using Data

A soccer game is broken up into either 2 or 4 equal sections of time. The table shows how long each section lasts for different age groups. How else could you write the numbers in the *Length of Section* column?
See Additional Answers.

Age Group	Length of Section
Under 12	0.25 hour
12–17	0.50 hour
Over 17	0.75 hour

540

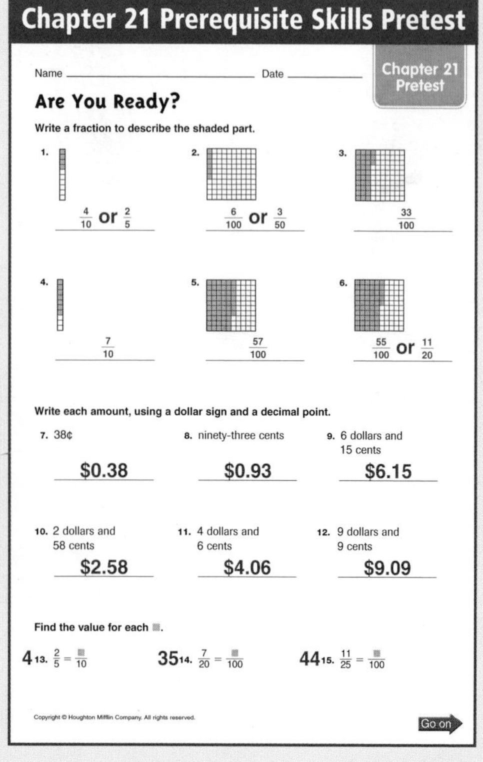

Chapter 21 Prerequisite Skills Pretest

Name ______ Date ______

Chapter 21 Pretest

Are You Ready?

Write a fraction to describe the shaded part.

1. $\frac{4}{10}$ or $\frac{2}{5}$
2. $\frac{6}{100}$ or $\frac{3}{50}$
3. $\frac{33}{100}$
4. $\frac{7}{10}$
5. $\frac{57}{100}$
6. $\frac{55}{100}$ or $\frac{11}{20}$

Write each amount, using a dollar sign and a decimal point.

7. 38¢ **$0.38**
8. ninety-three cents **$0.93**
9. 6 dollars and 15 cents **$6.15**
10. 2 dollars and 58 cents **$2.58**
11. 4 dollars and 6 cents **$4.06**
12. 9 dollars and 9 cents **$9.09**

Find the value for each ■.

13. $\frac{2}{5} = \frac{■}{10}$ **4**
14. $\frac{7}{20} = \frac{■}{100}$ **35**
15. $\frac{11}{25} = \frac{■}{100}$ **44**

Go on

Use this page to review and remember what you need to know for this chapter.

VOCABULARY

Choose the best word to complete each sentence.

Vocabulary
tenths
improper
equivalent
hundredths

1. A whole can be divided into 100 equal parts called _____. **hundredths**
2. If two fractions name the same amount, they are called _____ fractions. **equivalent**
3. A whole can be divided into 10 equal parts called _____. **tenths**

CONCEPTS AND SKILLS

Write a fraction to describe the shaded part.

4. 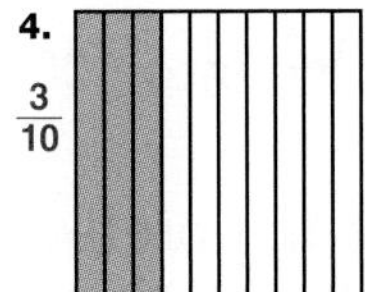 $\frac{3}{10}$
5. 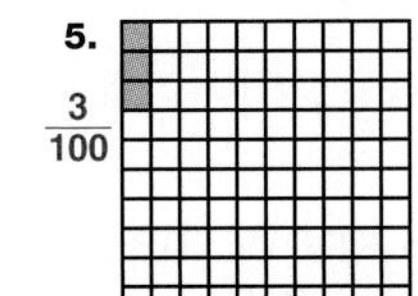 $\frac{3}{100}$
6. 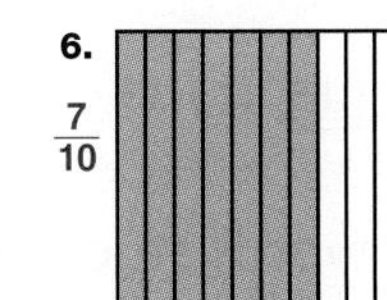 $\frac{7}{10}$
7. 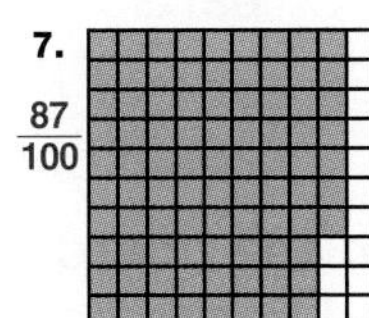 $\frac{87}{100}$

Write each amount, using a dollar sign and a decimal point.

8. 75¢ **$0.75**
9. 2 dollars and 53 cents **$2.53**
10. 3 dollars and 4 cents **$3.04**
11. 10 dollars and 1 cent **$10.01**

Find the value for each ■.

12. $\frac{1}{2} = \frac{■}{10}$ **5**
13. $\frac{1}{5} = \frac{■}{10}$ **2**
14. $\frac{3}{5} = \frac{■}{10}$ **6**
15. $\frac{4}{5} = \frac{■}{10}$ **8**
16. $\frac{1}{4} = \frac{■}{100}$ **25**
17. $\frac{1}{2} = \frac{■}{100}$ **50**
18. $\frac{1}{25} = \frac{■}{100}$ **4**
19. $\frac{2}{5} = \frac{■}{100}$ **40**

Write About It

20. Draw pictures to show $\frac{5}{10}$ and $\frac{50}{100}$. How are these fractions alike? How are they different? ***See above.***

20. Drawings may vary. *Possible answer:* The two fractions represent the same amount. They have different numerators and different denominators.

Facts Practice, See Page 669.

Use What You Know

Use this page for informal assessment and review of prerequisite skills.

- Items 1–3: Use math vocabulary
- Items 4–7: Write a fraction for a model
- Items 8–11: Write money amounts
- Items 12–19: Write equivalent fractions
- Item 20: Describe how equivalent fractions are alike and different

Customize Your Instruction

Use the Chapter Pretest in the Unit Resource folder to help customize and pace instruction.

Objectives and Resources

► Prerequisite Skills Pretest

- Items 1–6: Write a fraction for the shaded part of a picture.
- Items 7–12: Write money amounts.
- Items 13–15: Find equivalent fractions.

► New Content Pretest

- Items 1–6: Read and write decimals.
- Items 7–12: Write fractions and mixed numbers as decimals and vice versa.
- Items 13–18: Compare and order decimals and mixed numbers.
- Items 19–20: Solve problems using skills and strategies.

► For Students Having Difficulty

- *Ways to Success* 20C, 21A
- *Ways to Success* Skillsheets 178–180

► For Students Having Success

- Enrichment 21.1–21.5

► For Mathematically Promising Students

Explore: Fraction and Decimal Models, page 121, after Lesson 1

Extend: Fraction and Decimal Patterns, page 123, after Lesson 3

Connect: Math Analogies, page 125, after Lesson 5

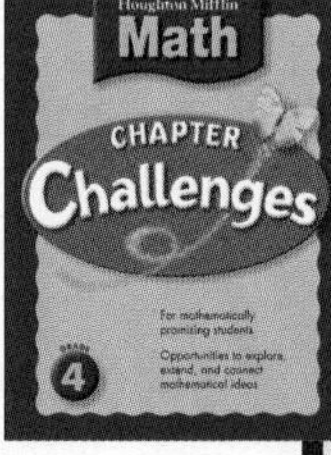

Chapter 21 New Content Pretest

Name __________ Date ______ Chapter 21 Pretest continued

Check What You Know

Write a fraction and a decimal to describe each model.

1. $\frac{9}{10}$ **0.9**
2. $\frac{38}{100}$ **0.38**
3. $\frac{40}{100}$ **0.40**

Write each as a decimal.

4. $\frac{7}{1,000}$ **0.007**
5. $\frac{93}{1,000}$ **0.093**
6. $\frac{380}{1,000}$ **0.380**

Write each mixed number as a decimal.

7. $3\frac{7}{10}$ **3.7**
8. $6\frac{48}{100}$ **6.48**
9. $93\frac{6}{1,000}$ **93.006**

Write each decimal as an equivalent fraction.

10. 0.55 $\frac{55}{100}$ **or** $\frac{11}{20}$
11. 0.078 $\frac{78}{1,000}$ **or** $\frac{39}{500}$
12. 0.29 $\frac{29}{100}$

Go on

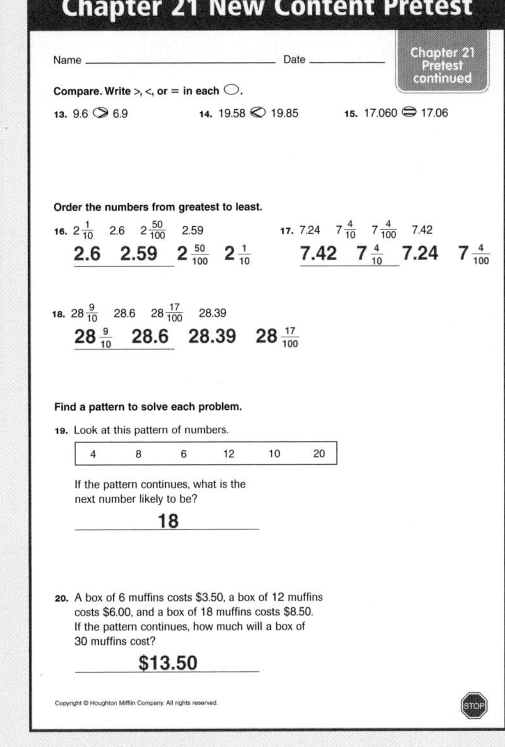

Chapter 21 New Content Pretest

Name __________ Date ______ Chapter 21 Pretest continued

Compare. Write >, <, or = in each ○.

13. 9.6 > 6.9
14. 19.58 < 19.85
15. 17.060 = 17.06

Order the numbers from greatest to least.

16. $2\frac{1}{10}$ 2.6 $2\frac{50}{100}$ 2.59
2.6 2.59 $2\frac{50}{100}$ $2\frac{1}{10}$

17. 7.24 $7\frac{4}{10}$ $7\frac{4}{100}$ 7.42
7.42 $7\frac{4}{10}$ 7.24 $7\frac{4}{100}$

18. $28\frac{9}{10}$ 28.6 $28\frac{17}{100}$ 28.39
$28\frac{9}{10}$ 28.6 28.39 $28\frac{17}{100}$

Find a pattern to solve each problem.

19. Look at this pattern of numbers.

4	8	6	12	10	20

If the pattern continues, what is the next number likely to be?

18

20. A box of 6 muffins costs $3.50, a box of 12 muffins costs $6.00, and a box of 18 muffins costs $8.50. If the pattern continues, how much will a box of 30 muffins cost?

$13.50

STOP

Hands On Lesson 21.1

Tenths and Hundredths

Planning

Lesson Objective Use models to show tenths and hundredths.

Math Background

A digit in any place has a value 10 times the value of the digit one place to the right. In the ones place, 1 has a value of 1, which is 10 times the value of 1 in the tenths place (0.1 or $\frac{1}{10}$).

Technology Resources

- *Ways to Success* CD-ROM 21.1
- Education Place: Extra Practice www.eduplace.com/map

Lesson 21.1 Transparency

Problem of the Day

Continue each pattern:

- 1.2, 1.0, 0.8, __, __, __...
- 0.09, 0.18, 0.27, __, __, __...
- 0.92, 0.95, 0.98, __, __, __...

(0.6, 0.4, 0.2; 0.36, 0.45, 0.54; 1.01, 1.04, 1.07)

Spiral Review

Write each fraction in simplest form.

1. $\frac{7}{3}$ ($2\frac{1}{3}$) **2.** $\frac{9}{18}$ ($\frac{1}{2}$)

3. $\frac{11}{4}$ ($2\frac{3}{4}$)

Lesson Quiz

Use grid paper. Draw a model to show each fraction. Then write each fraction as a decimal. (Check students' drawings.)

1. $\frac{7}{10}$ (0.7) **2.** $\frac{30}{100}$ (0.30)

Use grid paper. Draw a model to show each decimal. Then write each decimal as a fraction. (Check students' drawings.)

3. 0.9 ($\frac{9}{10}$) **4.** 0.44 ($\frac{44}{100}$)

NCTM Standards

Number and Operations: Understand the place-value structure of the base-ten number system and be able to represent and compare whole numbers and decimals; recognize and generate equivalent forms of commonly used fractions, decimals, and percents.

Representation: Create and use representations to organize, record, and communicate mathematical ideas.

Getting Started

Building Math Vocabulary

decimal a number with one or more digits to the right of a decimal point

decimal point a symbol used to separate dollars and cents in monetary amounts or to separate ones and tenths in decimals

tenth one of the equal parts when a whole is divided into 10 equal parts

hundredth one of the equal parts when a whole is divided into 100 equal parts

Write *dec-* on the board. List words students know that have this prefix, such as *decade* and *decimeter.* **What does *dec-* mean?** (10) **What do you think decimals are?** Accept answers that mention 10. Define *decimals* as numbers that include fractional parts using denominators that are powers of ten. Introduce the terms *decimal point, tenth,* and *hundredth* and explain their relationship to the term *decimal.*

Real-Life Decimals

Whole Class	5 minutes
Objective	Identify decimals.
Materials	None
Auditory	

- **Where have you seen or used decimals in real life?** (Accept all reasonable answers, which may include sports statistics, money amounts, and some measurements.)
- **What do all decimals have that other numbers don't have?** (decimal point) **What does a decimal point look like?** (a dot)
- Tell students that in this lesson, they will explore decimal numbers using tenths and hundredths.

Differentiated Instruction

English Learners

Small Groups	10 minutes
Objective	Identify decimals.
Materials	Coin set
Auditory, Visual	

Early Production

- Before doing ***On Your Own,*** show students how to use coins to make decimal numbers, and then convert them into fractions.
- Give students coins and say the amount of money as a decimal and a fraction.

Intermediate/Advanced

- English Learner Resource 21.1
- English Learner Handbook

Intervention

Small Groups	15 minutes
Objective	Write fractions as decimals, and vice versa.
Materials	Coin set
Auditory, Visual, Tactual	

- Display the pennies and dimes.
- **Which coin is $\frac{1}{10}$ of a dollar? $\frac{1}{100}$ of a dollar?** (dime; penny) **Can you write these money amounts with a dollar sign and a decimal point?** (\$0.10; \$0.01) **How can you use pennies and dimes to explain how hundredths relates to $\frac{1}{10}$?** (10 pennies = 1 dime, so 10 hundredths = 1 tenth)
- Show amounts of pennies and dimes. Have students write each value with a dollar sign and decimal point. Compare these to the models of non-money decimals.

Other Resources

- *Ways to Success* CD-ROM 21.1

Early Finishers

Pairs	15 minutes
Objective	Write fractions as decimals, and vice versa.
Materials	Learning Tools 38 and 39
Visual, Tactual	

- Have students model each decimal, then write it as a fraction.

0.2 ($\frac{2}{10}$)
0.67 ($\frac{67}{100}$)

- Have students model each fraction, then write it as a decimal.

$\frac{91}{100}$ (0.91)
$\frac{8}{100}$ (0.08)

Science Connection

Materials: Daily newspapers

- Ask students to explain *precipitation* in weather. (a deposit of moisture from air to ground, such as rain, snow, or dew)
- Tell students that amounts of precipitation are usually measured in tenths or hundredths of an inch.
- Have students record daily or weekly precipitation in U.S. cities and display the data in a table.

WEEKLY PRECIPITATION IN U.S. CITIES

	SUN	MON	TUES	WED	THURS	FRI	SAT
#1							
#2							
#3							
#4							
#5							

❶ Introduce

Read the lesson objective aloud. Tell students that they will use models to understand fractions and decimals.

❷ Teach

Work Together

- **In what way are fractions and decimals alike?** (Both show parts of a whole.) **How are they different?** (Fractions can show a whole divided into any number of parts; decimals can describe a whole divided into parts that are multiples of 10.)
- **Look at the model of 1 whole. How many tenths make 1 whole?** (10) **How many hundredths?** (100)
- **Decimal numbers have place value. How can we label the place to the right of the decimal point?** (tenths place) **To the right of that?** (hundredths place)
- Have pairs do the activity as you circulate, asking questions and guiding work.

Tenths and Hundredths

Objective Use models to show tenths and hundredths.

Vocabulary
decimal
decimal point
tenth
hundredth

Materials
Decimal Grids or Learning Tools 38 and 39

Work Together

One way to show parts of a whole is to use fractions. Another way is to use decimals.

A **decimal** is a number with one or more digits to the right of the **decimal point**.

Look at the models below.

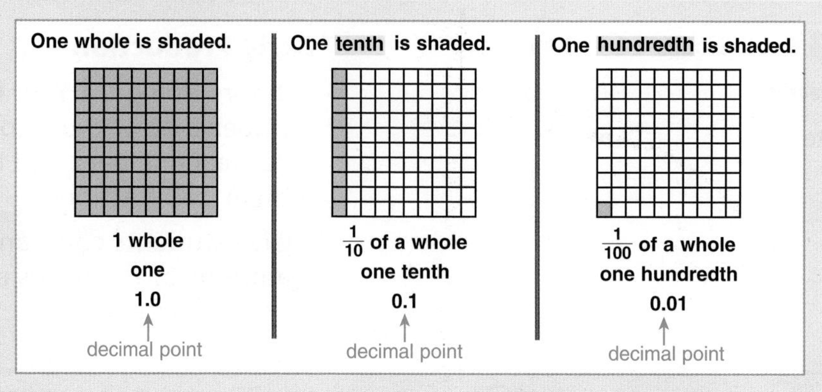

Work with a partner to model decimals.

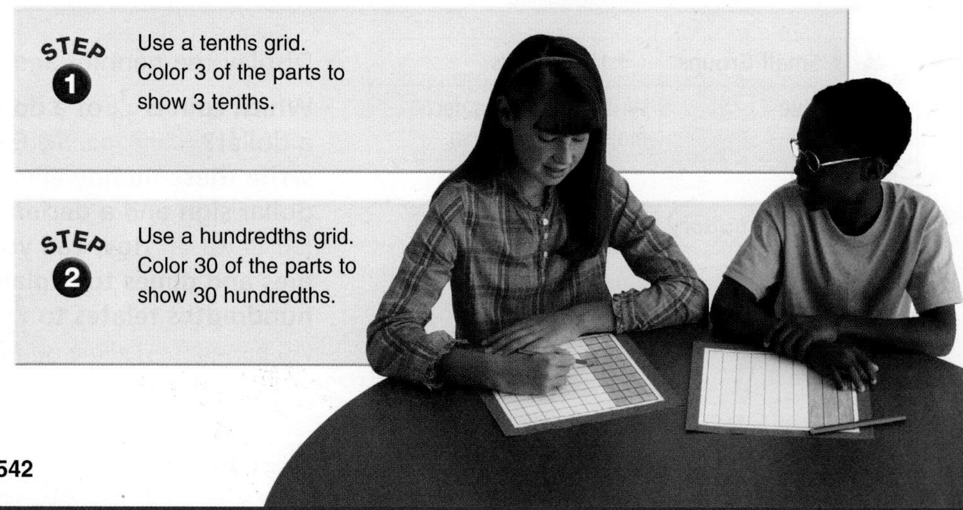

STEP 1
Use a tenths grid.
Color 3 of the parts to show 3 tenths.
STEP 2
Use a hundredths grid.
Color 30 of the parts to show 30 hundredths.

542

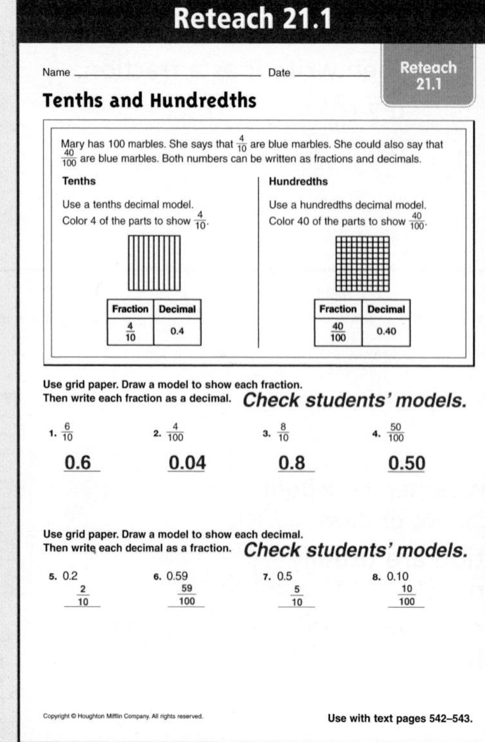

Reteach 21.1

Name ______________ Date ________

Reteach 21.1

Tenths and Hundredths

Mary has 100 marbles. She says that $\frac{4}{10}$ are blue marbles. She could also say that $\frac{40}{100}$ are blue marbles. Both numbers can be written as fractions and decimals.

Tenths

Use a tenths decimal model.
Color 4 of the parts to show $\frac{4}{10}$.

Fraction	Decimal
$\frac{4}{10}$	0.4

Hundredths

Use a hundredths decimal model.
Color 40 of the parts to show $\frac{40}{100}$.

Fraction	Decimal
$\frac{40}{100}$	0.40

Use grid paper. Draw a model to show each fraction. Then write each fraction as a decimal. *Check students' models.*

1. $\frac{6}{10}$ 0.6
2. $\frac{4}{100}$ 0.04
3. $\frac{8}{10}$ 0.8
4. $\frac{50}{100}$ 0.50

Use grid paper. Draw a model to show each decimal. Then write each decimal as a fraction. *Check students' models.*

5. 0.2 $\frac{2}{10}$
6. 0.59 $\frac{59}{100}$
7. 0.5 $\frac{5}{10}$
8. 0.10 $\frac{10}{100}$

Use with text pages 542–543.

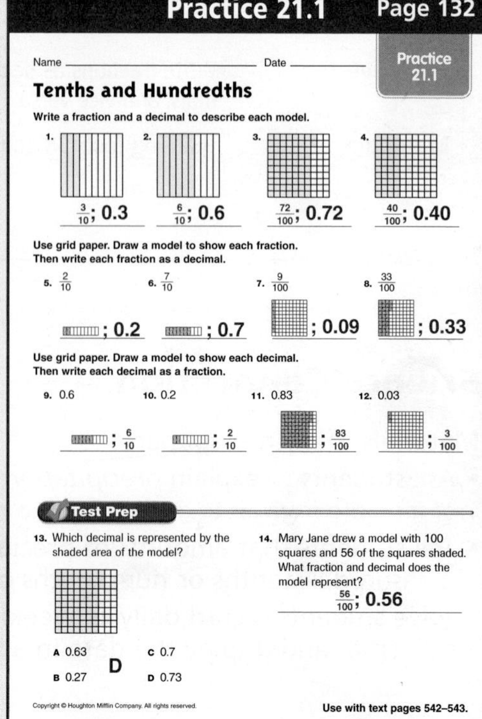

Practice 21.1 Page 132

Name ______________ Date ________

Practice 21.1

Tenths and Hundredths

Write a fraction and a decimal to describe each model.

1. $\frac{3}{10}$; 0.3
2. $\frac{6}{10}$; 0.6
3. $\frac{72}{100}$; 0.72
4. $\frac{40}{100}$; 0.40

Use grid paper. Draw a model to show each fraction. Then write each fraction as a decimal.

5. $\frac{2}{10}$; 0.2
6. $\frac{7}{10}$; 0.7
7. $\frac{9}{100}$; 0.09
8. $\frac{33}{100}$; 0.33

Use grid paper. Draw a model to show each decimal. Then write each decimal as a fraction.

9. 0.6 ; $\frac{6}{10}$
10. 0.2 ; $\frac{2}{10}$
11. 0.83 ; $\frac{83}{100}$
12. 0.03 ; $\frac{3}{100}$

Test Prep

13. Which decimal is represented by the shaded area of the model?
   A 0.63
   B 0.27
   C 0.7
   D 0.73
   D
14. Mary Jane drew a model with 100 squares and 56 of the squares shaded. What fraction and decimal does the model represent?
   $\frac{56}{100}$; 0.56

Use with text pages 542–543.

Compare your models.

- Is the same area colored in both models? yes
- How do you write 3 tenths as a decimal? 0.3
- How do you write 30 hundredths as a decimal? 0.30

Repeat Steps 1–3. This time show 0.6 and 0.60. Is the same area colored on both models? yes

On Your Own

Write a fraction and a decimal to describe each model.

1. $\frac{6}{10}$ 0.6 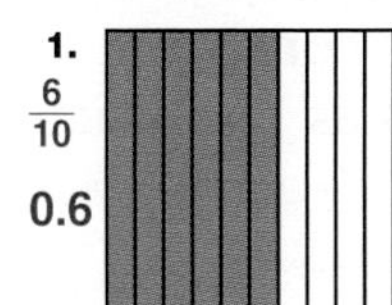
2. $\frac{2}{10}$ 0.2 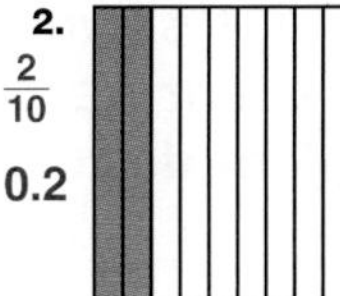
3. $\frac{97}{100}$ 0.97 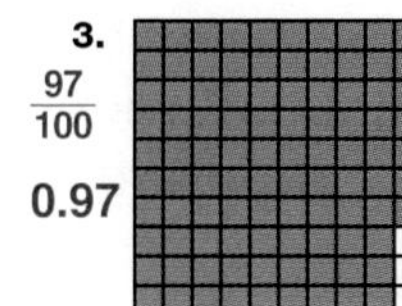
4. $\frac{20}{100}$ 0.20 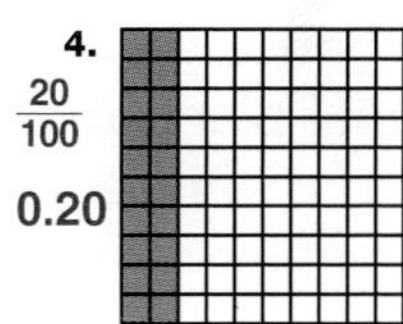

Use grid paper. Draw a model to show each fraction. Then write each fraction as a decimal. *Check students' drawings.*

5. $\frac{9}{10}$ 0.9
6. $\frac{1}{10}$ 0.1
7. $\frac{99}{100}$ 0.99
8. $\frac{7}{100}$ 0.07
9. $\frac{70}{100}$ 0.70

Use grid paper. Draw a model to show each decimal. Then write each decimal as a fraction. *Check students' drawings.*

10. 0.3 $\frac{3}{10}$
11. 0.5 $\frac{5}{10}$
12. 0.01 $\frac{1}{100}$
13. 0.76 $\frac{76}{100}$
14. 0.54 $\frac{54}{100}$

Talk About It • Write About It

You learned how to represent fractions and decimals.

15. How are 0.9 and 0.90 alike? How are they different? *See right.*
16. Why is 0.1 greater than 0.01? *See below.*

15. They represent equal amounts. 0.9 is written as tenths, and 0.90 is written as hundredths.

16. 0.1 is greater because 0.1 represents 1 of 10 equal parts; 0.01 represents 1 of 100 equal parts.

3 Practice

On Your Own

- Select from **Exercises 1–16** as independent work.

4 Assess & Close

Math Talk in Action

Invite students to share their responses to the ***Talk About It • Write About It*** section.

- **What does a decimal number look like?** (a number with a decimal point and digits to its right)
- **When do we use decimals?** (to describe amounts between 0 and 1, expressed as tenths and/or hundredths)

Math Journal Prompt

Have students write the decimals and fractions for each quantity: three tenths; sixty-two hundredths; nine hundredths.

Lesson Quiz

Use the quiz on Lesson Transparency 21.1.

Test Prep & Spiral Review

Use Test Prep Transparency 21.1.

Enrichment 21.1

Name ______ Date ______ Enrichment 21.1

Twins

Each citizen of Decimal Town knows someone in Fractionville that looks the same as him or her in pictures. Look at the table below. In the left column is a citizen of Decimal Town. The middle column is a picture of that citizen and the third column is a citizen of Fractionville that looks the same as the citizen of Decimal Town. Complete the table by filling in the decimal, the picture, or the fraction. Each row should show three equal amounts.

Decimal Town	Picture	Fractionville
0.1		$\frac{1}{10}$
0.3		$\frac{3}{10}$
0.2		$\frac{2}{10}$
0.75		$\frac{75}{100}$
0.08		$\frac{8}{100}$
0.38		$\frac{38}{100}$

Use with text pages 542–543.

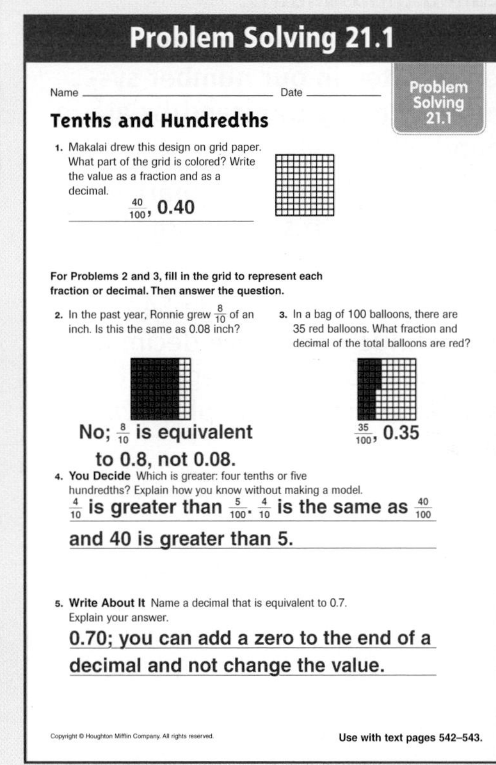

Problem Solving 21.1

Name ______ Date ______ Problem Solving 21.1

Tenths and Hundredths

1. Makalai drew this design on grid paper. What part of the grid is colored? Write the value as a fraction and as a decimal. $\frac{40}{100}$, 0.40

For Problems 2 and 3, fill in the grid to represent each fraction or decimal. Then answer the question.

2. In the past year, Ronnie grew $\frac{8}{10}$ of an inch. Is this the same as 0.08 inch? No; $\frac{8}{10}$ is equivalent to 0.8, not 0.08.
3. In a bag of 100 balloons, there are 35 red balloons. What fraction and decimal of the total balloons are red? $\frac{35}{100}$, 0.35
4. **You Decide** Which is greater: four tenths or five hundredths? Explain how you know without making a model. $\frac{4}{10}$ is greater than $\frac{5}{100}$. $\frac{4}{10}$ is the same as $\frac{40}{100}$ and 40 is greater than 5.
5. **Write About It** Name a decimal that is equivalent to 0.7. Explain your answer. 0.70; you can add a zero to the end of a decimal and not change the value.

Use with text pages 542–543.

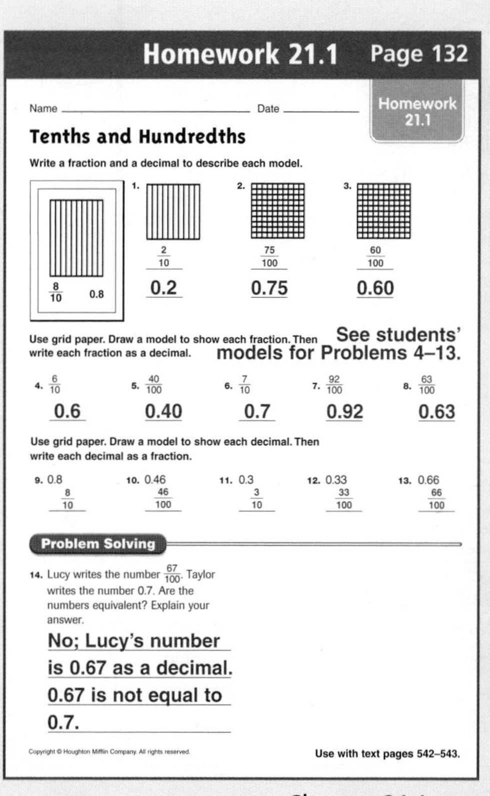

Homework 21.1 Page 132

Name ______ Date ______ Homework 21.1

Tenths and Hundredths

Write a fraction and a decimal to describe each model.

Example: $\frac{8}{10}$ 0.8

1. $\frac{2}{10}$ 0.2
2. $\frac{75}{100}$ 0.75
3. $\frac{60}{100}$ 0.60

Use grid paper. Draw a model to show each fraction. Then write each fraction as a decimal. See students' models for Problems 4–13.

4. $\frac{6}{10}$ 0.6
5. $\frac{40}{100}$ 0.40
6. $\frac{7}{10}$ 0.7
7. $\frac{92}{100}$ 0.92
8. $\frac{63}{100}$ 0.63

Use grid paper. Draw a model to show each decimal. Then write each decimal as a fraction.

9. 0.8 $\frac{8}{10}$
10. 0.46 $\frac{46}{100}$
11. 0.3 $\frac{3}{10}$
12. 0.33 $\frac{33}{100}$
13. 0.66 $\frac{66}{100}$

Problem Solving

14. Lucy writes the number $\frac{67}{100}$. Taylor writes the number 0.7. Are the numbers equivalent? Explain your answer. No; Lucy's number is 0.67 as a decimal. 0.67 is not equal to 0.7.

Use with text pages 542–543.

Hands On Lesson 21.2

Thousandths

Planning

Lesson Objective Write decimals for thousandths.

Technology Resources

- Audio Tutor **2**/24 Listen and Understand
- *Ways to Success* CD-ROM 21.2
- Education Place: Extra Practice, eGlossary, eGames www.eduplace.com/map

Lesson 21.2 Transparency

Problem of the Day

Lulu says that there are many decimals greater than 0.65 but less than 0.66, and she can prove it! What decimals does Lulu have in mind? Possible answer: (0.651–0.659)

Spiral Review

Write each fraction as a decimal.

1. $\frac{7}{10}$ (0.7)
2. $\frac{5}{10}$ (0.5)
3. $\frac{41}{100}$ (0.41)
4. $\frac{30}{100}$ (0.30 or 0.3)

Lesson Quiz

Write each as a decimal.

1. $\frac{212}{1,000}$ (0.212)
2. 943 thousandths (0.943)
3. $\frac{11}{1,000}$ (0.011)
4. 75 thousandths (0.075)
5. 8 thousandths (0.008)

NCTM Standards

Number and Operations: Understand the place-value structure of the base-ten number system and be able to represent and compare whole numbers and decimals; recognize and generate equivalent forms of commonly used fractions, decimals, and percent.

Getting Started

Building Math Vocabulary

thousandths	one of the equal parts when a whole is divided into 1,000 equal parts
equivalent decimals	decimals that name the same amount

As you introduce *thousandths,* stress the ending *-ths,* which is consistent with other decimal place-value names. Review *equivalent fractions* as two fractions that name the same amount. **What are equivalent decimals?** (decimals that name the same amount)

Modeling Decimals

Whole Class	15 minutes
Objective	Model decimals through thousandths.
Materials	Learning Tool 39
Auditory, Visual	

- Distribute Learning Tool 39 to students. **What decimals could you model with this chart?** (tenths, hundredths less than or equal to 1)
- **How many tenths are in 1 whole?** (10) **How many hundredths are in 1 tenth?** (10) **The next decimal place is called thousandths.**
- **Think about the pattern you've seen so often in our number system. How many thousandths are in 1 hundredth?** (10)
- **How would you draw a chart to show thousandths?** (Cut each $\frac{1}{100}$ in 10 parts; 100 x 10 = 1,000.)
- Tell students that on page 544 they will continue to practice decimal modeling and pattern-recognition while beginning to use place-value charts.

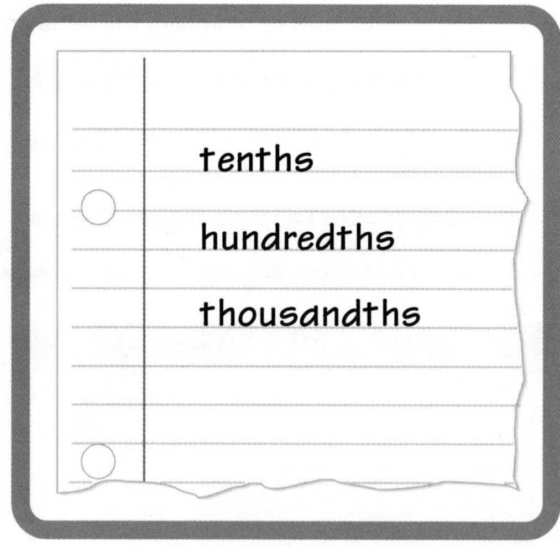

Differentiated Instruction

English Learners

Whole Class	20 minutes
Objective	Read, write, and identify place value through thousandths.
Materials	Student pages 544 and 545
Visual	

Early Production

- Give students practice writing and saying decimals.
- For ***Guided Practice,*** ask students to make a table with three columns: *Fraction, Decimal,* and *Words,* as found on Student page 544.
- Have them fill in the columns for each exercise and then verbalize the answers.

Intermediate/Advanced

- English Learner Resource 21.2
- English Learner Handbook

Intervention

Pairs	15 minutes
Objective	Write a decimal through thousandths.
Materials	Place-value models
Visual	

- Write *thousandths* on the board. Underline *ths* and emphasize to students that the *ths* indicates that the number is a decimal. Guide students to understand that for a thousandths number, there are three digits after the decimal point. On the board write 0. ____ ____ ____.
- Write *twenty-three thousandths* on the board. Work with students to fill in the digits. Remind students to be sure to write a 0 in the tenths place.
- Continue using the 0. ____ ____ ____ template for students to practice writing other thousandths.

Other Resources

- *Ways to Success* CD-ROM 21.2

Gifted & Talented

Whole Class	20 minutes
Objective	Write a decimal through thousandths.
Materials	Number cube, decimal place-value chart to 1000ths
Tactual	

- Have students play a game in which the goal is to make the least decimal.
- Players roll a number cube and write the digit in any place from tenths to thousandths. Once written, a digit cannot be moved. They roll and write to fill the decimal. The student with the least decimal gets 1 point.

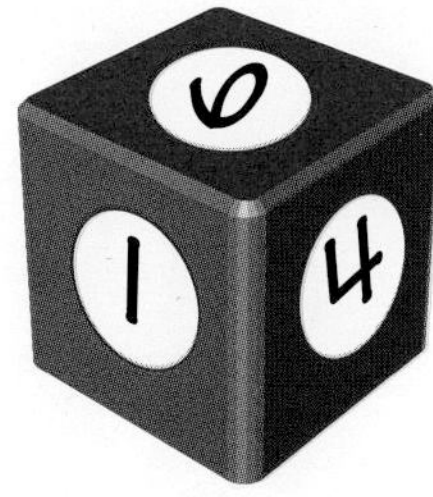

Alternate Teaching Strategy

- Show students a "big prism" place-value model. Tell students that the big cube represents one whole and 1,000 of the unit place-value models make the big prism.
- As you show each type of place-value model, tell students that each unit cube has a value of 0.001, each rod has a value of 0.01, and each flat has a value of 0.1 compared to the big prism.
- Have pairs of students use place-value models to show 0.245, 0.409, and 0.009. Discuss with students their representations for each decimal.

Facts Practice

Have a volunteer write a decimal on the board with a zero in the tenths, hundredths, or thousandths place. Have another volunteer identify the place value of the zero. Repeat as time allows.

❶ Introduce

The rationale and purpose should be to underscore students' thinking about using modeled fractions and decimals in a practical way. Relate these principles to real-life applications that can be demonstrated to have significant relevance to the students' experience, such as sports statistics.

❷ Teach

Learn About It

- **How many places to the right of the decimal point is the digit that represents thousandths?** (3)
- After students do the activity, ask: **When are decimals equivalent?** (when they name the same amount)
- **In *Other Example A*, why is there a 0 in the tenths place?** (There are no tenths.) **In *Other Example B*, why are there 2 zeros between the decimal point and 9?** (to show that there are no tenths and hundredths)

Guided Practice

Have students complete **Exercises 1–6** as you observe. Remind them to use the ***Ask Yourself*** questions to help. Give students the opportunity to talk about the question in ***Explain Your Thinking***.

Common Error

- **Omitting place-holding zeros** Many students can grasp the concept of thousandths, yet they forget to use place-holding zeros when writing decimals in the thousandths place.
- **Intervention** Suggest that students use lined paper with the lines going vertically, and label columns to indicate each decimal place to thousandths. Then they write the decimal making sure the place-holding zeros are included. The students should then write the number on another paper without the labeled columns.

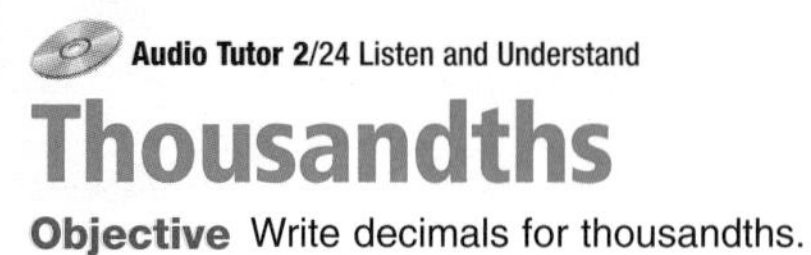

Audio Tutor 2/24 Listen and Understand

Thousandths

Objective Write decimals for thousandths.

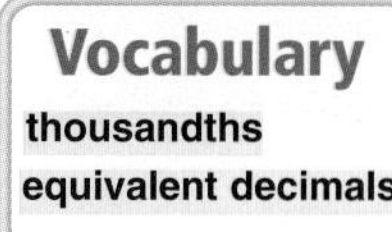

Vocabulary
thousandths
equivalent decimals

Materials
Decimal Grids or Learning Tools 38, 39 and 40

Learn About It

A whole can be divided into 1,000 equal parts called **thousandths**. Thousandths are even smaller than hundredths.

Look at these models and place-value charts.

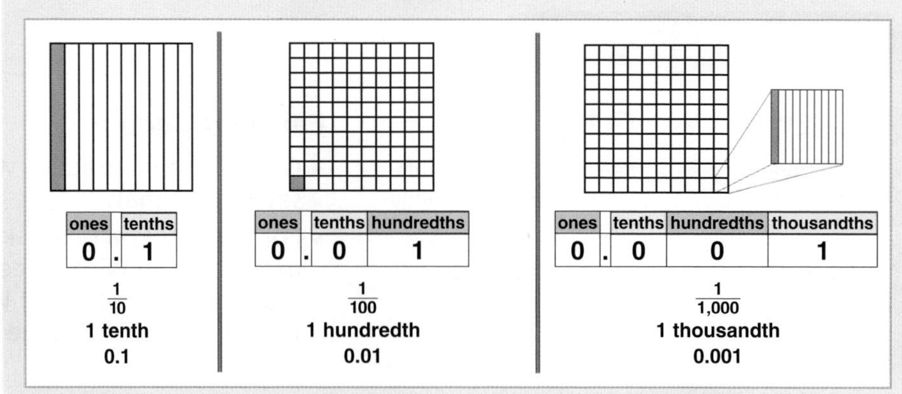

Try this activity to explore thousandths.

STEP 1 Color 5 tenths on the tenths grid.
Color 50 hundredths on the hundredths grid.
Color 500 thousandths on the thousandths grid.

STEP 2 Compare the 3 models that you colored.
- Do they all cover the same area? yes

▶ Decimals that name the same amount are called **equivalent decimals**.

0.5, 0.50, and 0.500 are equivalent decimals.

Other Examples

A. Zero in Tenths Place

Fraction	Decimal	Words
$\frac{21}{1,000}$	0.021	twenty-one thousandths

B. Zero in Tenths and Hundredths Places

Fraction	Decimal	Words
$\frac{9}{1,000}$	0.009	nine thousandths

544

Reteach 21.2

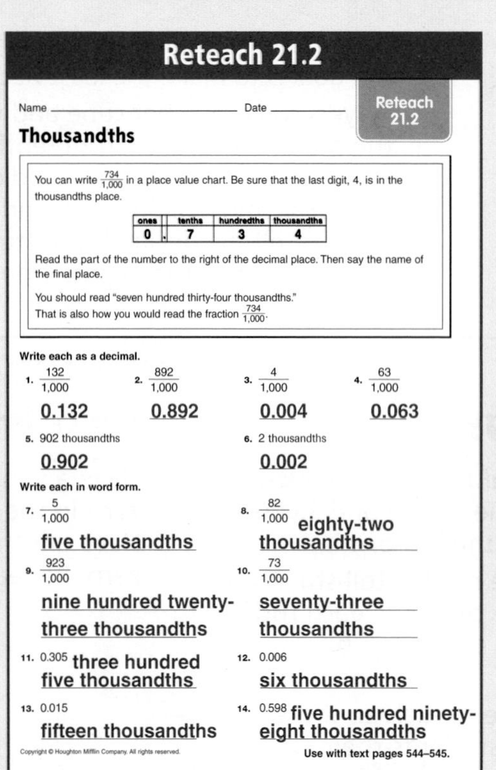

Name ____ Date ____

Reteach 21.2

Thousandths

You can write $\frac{734}{1,000}$ in a place value chart. Be sure that the last digit, 4, is in the thousandths place.

ones		tenths	hundredths	thousandths
0	.	7	3	4

Read the part of the number to the right of the decimal place. Then say the name of the final place.

You should read "seven hundred thirty-four thousandths."
That is also how you would read the fraction $\frac{734}{1,000}$.

Write each as a decimal.

1. $\frac{132}{1,000}$ 0.132
2. $\frac{892}{1,000}$ 0.892
3. $\frac{4}{1,000}$ 0.004
4. $\frac{63}{1,000}$ 0.063
5. 902 thousandths 0.902
6. 2 thousandths 0.002

Write each in word form.

7. $\frac{5}{1,000}$ five thousandths
8. $\frac{82}{1,000}$ eighty-two thousandths
9. $\frac{923}{1,000}$ nine hundred twenty-three thousandths
10. $\frac{73}{1,000}$ seventy-three thousandths
11. 0.305 three hundred five thousandths
12. 0.006 six thousandths
13. 0.015 fifteen thousandths
14. 0.598 five hundred ninety-eight thousandths

Use with text pages 544–545.

Practice 21.2 Page 133

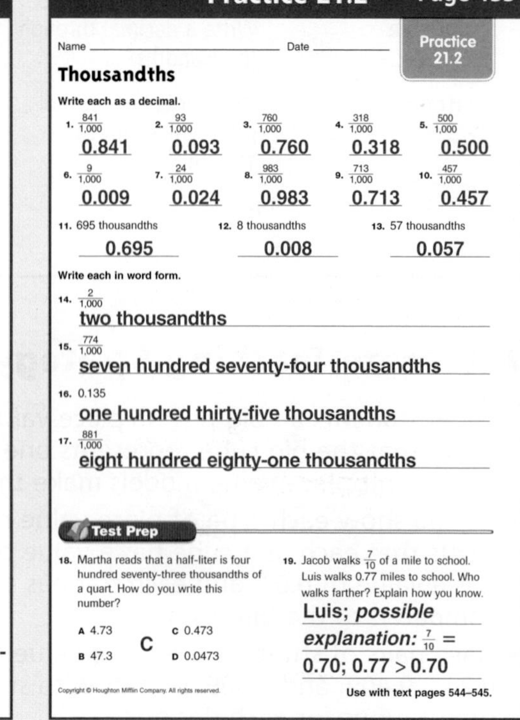

Name ____ Date ____

Practice 21.2

Thousandths

Write each as a decimal.

1. $\frac{841}{1,000}$ 0.841
2. $\frac{93}{1,000}$ 0.093
3. $\frac{760}{1,000}$ 0.760
4. $\frac{318}{1,000}$ 0.318
5. $\frac{500}{1,000}$ 0.500
6. $\frac{9}{1,000}$ 0.009
7. $\frac{24}{1,000}$ 0.024
8. $\frac{983}{1,000}$ 0.983
9. $\frac{713}{1,000}$ 0.713
10. $\frac{457}{1,000}$ 0.457
11. 695 thousandths 0.695
12. 8 thousandths 0.008
13. 57 thousandths 0.057

Write each in word form.

14. $\frac{2}{1,000}$ two thousandths
15. $\frac{774}{1,000}$ seven hundred seventy-four thousandths
16. 0.135 one hundred thirty-five thousandths
17. $\frac{881}{1,000}$ eight hundred eighty-one thousandths

Test Prep

18. Martha reads that a half-liter is four hundred seventy-three thousandths of a quart. How do you write this number? C
A 4.73
B 47.3
C 0.473
D 0.0473

19. Jacob walks $\frac{7}{10}$ of a mile to school. Luis walks 0.77 miles to school. Who walks farther? Explain how you know.
Luis; *possible explanation:* $\frac{7}{10}$ = 0.70; 0.77 > 0.70

Use with text pages 544–545.

Guided Practice

Write each as a decimal.

1. $\frac{782}{1,000}$ **0.782**
2. $\frac{206}{1,000}$ **0.206**
3. $\frac{45}{1,000}$ **0.045**
4. $\frac{3}{1,000}$ **0.003**
5. 37 thousandths **0.037**
6. 222 thousandths **0.222**

Ask Yourself

- How many equal parts are there?
- How many digits do I put after the decimal point to show thousandths?

Explain Your Thinking ▶ Look at the place-value charts on Page 544. How does the value of the digit change as you move from left to right?
Possible answer: **The value gets smaller.**

Practice and Problem Solving

Write each as a decimal.

7. $\frac{356}{1,000}$ **0.356**
8. $\frac{350}{1,000}$ **0.350**
9. $\frac{49}{1,000}$ **0.049**
10. $\frac{70}{1,000}$ **0.070**
11. $\frac{3}{1,000}$ **0.003**
12. 450 thousandths **0.450**
13. 6 thousandths **0.006**
14. 15 thousandths **0.015**

Write each in word form.

15. 0.005 **five thousandths**
16. 0.023 **16. twenty-three thousandths**
17. $\frac{455}{1,000}$ **17. four hundred fifty-five thousandths**
18. 0.302 **18. three hundred two thousandths**
19. $\frac{300}{1,000}$ **three hundred thousandths**

20. Mark walks $\frac{4}{10}$ mile to school. Carla walks 0.450 miles to school. Who walks farther? Explain how you know.
Carla walks farther. 0.45 > 0.4

21. Cho Yia and her mother drive 0.7 kilometers to the store. Write an equivalent decimal for this distance.
Possible answers: **0.70 or 0.700**

22. **What's Wrong?** Look at Brian's work on the right. What's wrong with his reasoning?
Possible answer: **Both have the three in the tenths column.**

Brian
300 > 30 so
0.300 > 0.30

Mixed Review and Test Prep

Open Response

Write all the factors of each number.
(Ch. 10, Lesson 1) ***See Additional Answers.***

23. 6
24. 24
25. 18
26. 25
27. 14
28. 27
29. 30
30. 20
31. 42

Multiple Choice

32. Marcia's mother tells her that a liter is nine hundred forty-six thousandths of a quart. How do you write this number?
(Ch. 21, Lesson 2)

(A) 0.946
B 900.046
C 940.006
D 946,000

Extra Practice See page 565, Set A.

3 Practice

Practice and Problem Solving

Select from **Exercises 7–32** as independent work.

- ***Problem 22*** Use discussion of this problem as a chance to discuss decimal place value versus whole-number place value.

4 Assess & Close

Math Talk in Action

Discuss students' work to conclude the lesson.

- **Name the 3 decimal places, in order, moving right from the decimal point.** (tenths, hundredths, thousandths)
- **Name 2 decimals that are equivalent to 0.7.** Possible answers: (0.70 and 0.700)

Math Journal Prompt

Have students compare 1 thousandth to 1 hundredth.

Lesson Quiz

Use the quiz on Lesson Transparency 21.2.

Test Prep & Spiral Review

Use Test Prep Transparency 21.2.

Enrichment 21.2

Name ____ Date ____ Enrichment 21.2

Decimal Description

Read each paragraph below. Write the decimal that is described. Each decimal is less than 1. None of the decimals have values that go beyond the thousandths place (such as ten-thousandths).

1. I am a decimal with a value in the thousandths place. In my tenths place, you'll find a digit one less than the digit in my hundredths place and three less than my other digit. My last digit is a 3. What decimal am I? **0.013**
2. You could write me using three decimal places, but you only need two. Find the sum of 1 and 3 and you have my tenths digit. My hundredths digit is twice my tenths digit. What decimal am I? **0.480 or 0.48**
3. My digits are 4, 7, and 9 in some order. My hundredths digit is greater than either of my other digits. I am greater than 0.4 but less than 0.7. What decimal am I? **0.497**
4. I have three decimal places. You can model me by shading 56 squares on a 10 by 10 grid. What decimal am I? **0.560**
5. Write my name in word form, and you'll see the word thirty-three. In my tenths place, you'll find a zero. What decimal am I? **0.033**
6. All my digits are even numbers greater than 2. My thousandths digit is 2 more than my tenths digit and 4 more than my hundredths digit. What decimal am I? **0.648**
7. Find the product of 3 and 2 and you have my hundredths digit. This number is the same as my thousandths digit but 5 more than my tenths digit. What decimal am I? **0.166**
8. My digits are in order from least to greatest. My tenths digit is a 2. My thousandths digit is a 5. What decimals could I be? **0.235 or 0.245**

 Use with text pages 544–545.

Problem Solving 21.2

Name ____ Date ____ Problem Solving 21.2

Thousandths

Solve. Show your work.

1. The density of butter is 0.860 g/cm³. The density of ice is 0.92 g/cm³. Which item has the greater density? Explain.
ice; 0.920 is greater than 0.860.
2. In science class, Tara weighed two different marbles. The red marble weighed 0.058 kg and the blue marble weighed 0.580 kg. Which marble weighed more?
the blue marble; 58 hundredths is greater than 58 thousandths.
3. **What's Wrong?** A student wrote 0.328 in word form as three hundred twenty-eight hundredths. What did the student do wrong? What is the correct answer?
The last digit is in the thousandth place, not the hundredths place. The correct answer is three hundred twenty-eight thousandths.
4. **You Decide** Are 0.04 and 0.040 equivalent? Explain.
Yes; 4 hundredths is the same as 40 thousandths.

 Use with text pages 544–545.

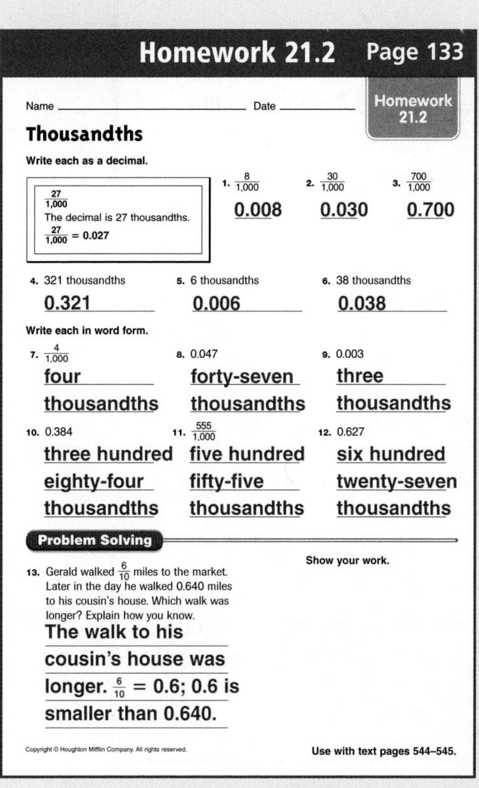

Homework 21.2 Page 133

Name ____ Date ____ Homework 21.2

Thousandths

Write each as a decimal.

$\frac{27}{1,000}$
The decimal is 27 thousandths.
$\frac{27}{1,000} = 0.027$

1. $\frac{8}{1,000}$ **0.008**
2. $\frac{30}{1,000}$ **0.030**
3. $\frac{700}{1,000}$ **0.700**
4. 321 thousandths **0.321**
5. 6 thousandths **0.006**
6. 38 thousandths **0.038**

Write each in word form.

7. $\frac{4}{1,000}$ **four thousandths**
8. 0.047 **forty-seven thousandths**
9. 0.003 **three thousandths**
10. 0.384 **three hundred eighty-four thousandths**
11. $\frac{555}{1,000}$ **five hundred fifty-five thousandths**
12. 0.627 **six hundred twenty-seven thousandths**

Problem Solving Show your work.

13. Gerald walked $\frac{6}{10}$ miles to the market. Later in the day he walked 0.640 miles to his cousin's house. Which walk was longer? Explain how you know.
The walk to his cousin's house was longer. $\frac{6}{10}$ = 0.6; 0.6 is smaller than 0.640.

 Use with text pages 544–545.

Lesson 21.3

Mixed Numbers and Decimals

Planning

Lesson Objective Read, write, and model amounts greater than 1.

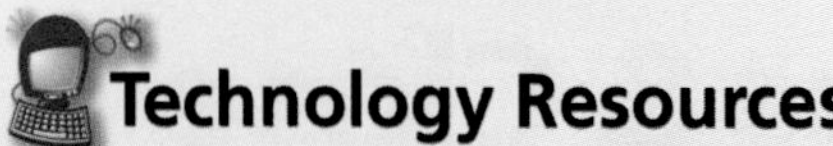

Technology Resources

- *Ways to Success* CD-ROM 21.3
- *Ways to Assess* CD-ROM
- Education Place: Extra Practice, eGlossary, eGames, Weekly Reader www.eduplace.com/map

Lesson 21.3 Transparency

Problem of the Day

Using the digits 6, 5, 4, and 3, create a mixed number that is between 3.5 and 3.6. (3.546 or 3.564)

Spiral Review

Write each decimal in standard form.

1. six tenths (0.6)
2. seventeen hundredths (0.17)
3. ninety-eight thousandths (0.098)

Lesson Quiz

Write each decimal in standard form.

1. one and eight tenths (1.8)
2. five and twelve hundredths (5.12)
3. ninety-nine and forty-four hundredths (99.44)
4. seventy and seventy-six thousandths (70.076)
5. six and two hundred five thousandths (6.205)

NCTM Standards

Number and Operations: Recognize equivalent representations for the same number and generate them by decomposing and composing numbers.

Getting Started

Building Math Vocabulary

You may wish to review this term with students.

mixed number a whole number containing a whole-number part and a fraction part.

Mixing Up Decimals and Fractions

Whole Class	20 minutes
Objective	Write mixed numbers as decimals and vice versa.
Materials	Tenths and Hundredths Grid Transparency, blank transparency
Auditory, Visual	

- Display 2 Tenths Grids. Shade all of one grid and 3 tenths of the second grid. Ask, **What mixed number describes the shaded amount?** ($1\frac{3}{10}$) **We can write this same amount as a decimal. Can you guess how?** (1.3) Write this decimal beneath the mixed number. **We read both of these as "one and three tenths."**
- Put 2 Hundredths Grids on the transparency. Write $1\frac{25}{100}$ below them. Ask a volunteer to shade the grids to show $1\frac{25}{100}$. **How can we write this mixed number as a decimal?** (1.25)
- Repeat for $1\frac{9}{100}$ and for $\frac{200}{100}$. (1.09 and 2.0)
- **How would we write a decimal for the mixed number $25\frac{4}{100}$?** (25.04)

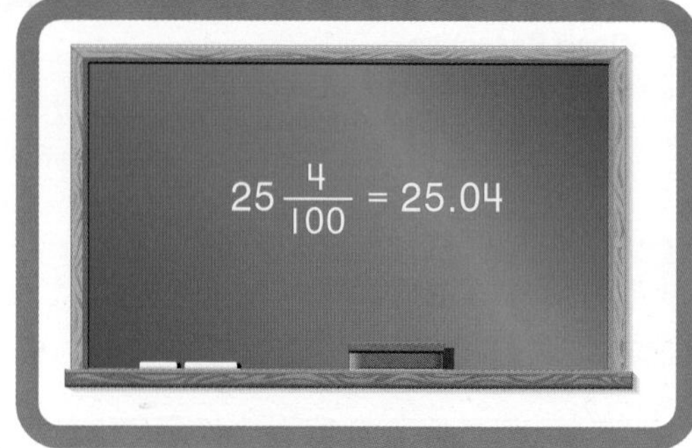

Explain to students that on page 546 they will continue learning how to express mixed numbers and decimals in different ways.

Differentiated Instruction

English Learners

Whole Class	20 minutes
Objective	Write mixed numbers and decimals.
Materials	Student page 547
Visual	

Early Production

- For ***Guided Practice*** problems, ask students to make a place-value chart like those shown in ***Learn About It***.
- Have them fill in each section with the numbers from the ***Guided Practice***. Encourage students to read aloud each form name and number.

Intermediate/Advanced

- English Learner Resource 21.3
- English Learner Handbook

Intervention

Small Groups	10 minutes
Objective	Write mixed numbers as decimals.
Materials	Place-value chart
Visual, Auditory	

- Prepare a decimal place-value chart for tens, ones, tenths, hundredths, and thousandths places. Include an oversized decimal point between ones and tenths.
- Help students use this chart as a point of reference as they write mixed numbers as decimals and rewrite decimals from word or expanded form into standard form.

Other Resources

- *Ways to Success* CD-ROM 21.3

tens	ones		tenths	hundredths	thousandths
		•			

Special Needs

Small Groups	10 minutes
Objective	Read decimals.
Materials	None
Auditory	

- Write *six and three-tenths* on the board. Tell students that the word *and* tells the spot for the decimal point that separates the number of wholes from the parts.
- Have students read decimals in word form, clapping when they say *and*. Have them write what they said up to *and,* then write a decimal point. Everything after *and* is the decimal part.

Real-World Connection

Materials: Almanac

- Since 1911, Indianapolis has hosted the Indy 500 auto race. Average speeds (in miles per hour) are given to the thousandths of a mile.
- Help students find the almanac page listing the winners. Assign each student a different year. Have them record that winner's speed in standard form, word form, and expanded form.

1 Introduce

The students should be guided toward fitting their knowledge of mixed numbers, fractions, and decimals to real-life applications; moving more easily between various forms; and becoming adept at modeling those applications.

2 Teach

Learn About It

- **Which path is 2.8 km long?** (Red Path) **What are the different ways to show the decimal "two and eight tenths"?** (use models; write in standard form; write a mixed number; write in word form; use a place-value chart; write in expanded form) **What does the 2 stand for in each case?** (2 wholes) **How is the 8 shown in a place-value chart?** (8 in tenths place) **What does the expanded form show?** (sum of the whole and decimal parts by places)
- **What is the length of the Blue Path?** (2.45 km) **How is the place-value chart different for this example?** (has hundredths place) **How is the expanded form different?** (3 addends: wholes, tenths, hundredths)

Common Error

- **Place-value mistakes** Students may omit a zero as a placeholder or confuse decimal and whole-number places when they write mixed numbers as decimals.
- **Intervention** Have them use a decimal place-value chart to help them correctly write equivalent decimals for mixed numbers or decimals given in word form or expanded notation.

Lesson 3

Mixed Numbers and Decimals

Objective Read, write, and model amounts greater than 1.

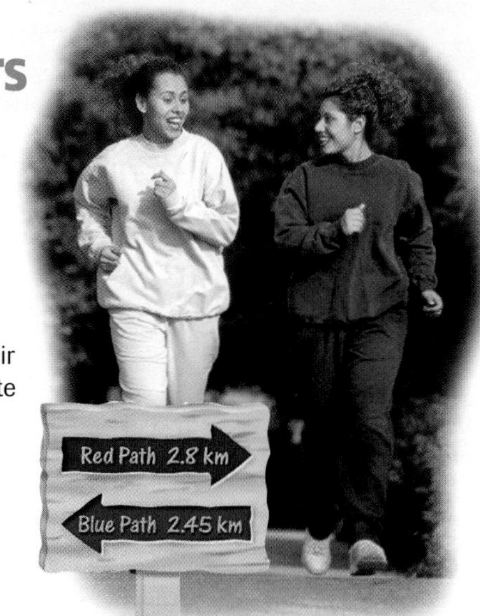

Learn About It

Melanie and Elena like to jog every day at their local park. There are two paths. Elena's favorite is the Blue Path. Melanie's favorite is the Red Path. The Red Path is two and eight tenths kilometers long.

Here are different ways to show two and eight tenths.

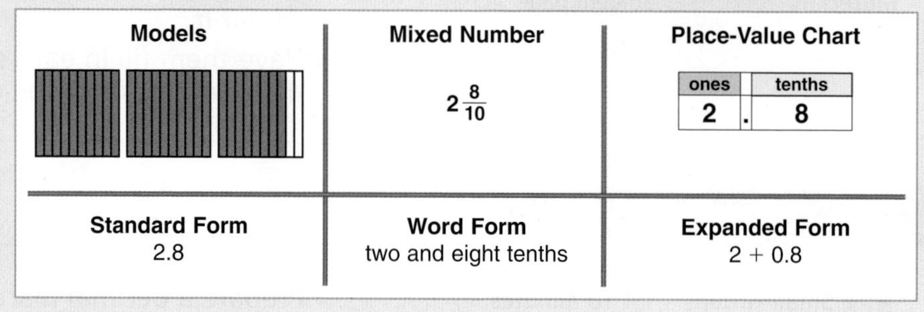

Models	Mixed Number	Place-Value Chart
	$2\frac{8}{10}$	ones: 2 . tenths: 8
Standard Form 2.8	**Word Form** two and eight tenths	**Expanded Form** 2 + 0.8

Here are different ways to show two and forty-five hundredths.

Models	Mixed Number	Place-Value Chart
	$2\frac{45}{100}$	ones: 2 . tenths: 4 hundredths: 5
Standard Form 2.45	**Word Form** two and forty-five hundredths	**Expanded Form** 2 + 0.4 + 0.05

546

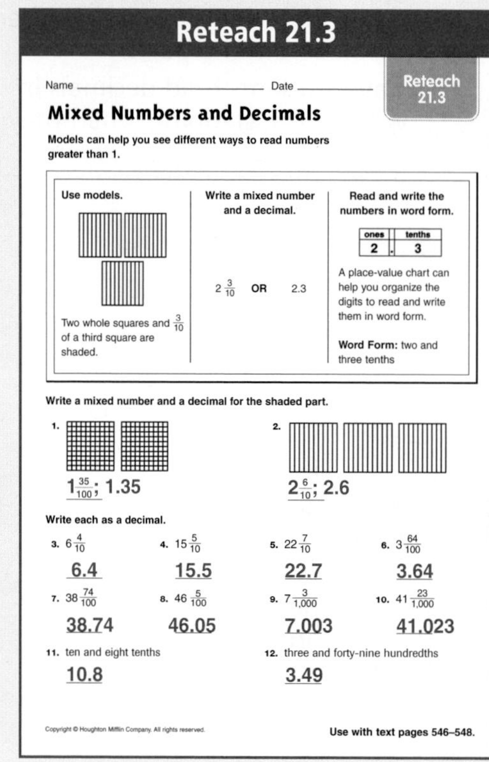

Reteach 21.3

Name ______________ Date ________ Reteach 21.3

Mixed Numbers and Decimals

Models can help you see different ways to read numbers greater than 1.

Use models.	Write a mixed number and a decimal.	Read and write the numbers in word form.
Two whole squares and $\frac{3}{10}$ of a third square are shaded.	$2\frac{3}{10}$ OR 2.3	ones: 2 . tenths: 3 A place-value chart can help you organize the digits to read and write them in word form. **Word Form:** two and three tenths

Write a mixed number and a decimal for the shaded part.

1. $1\frac{35}{100}$; 1.35
2. $2\frac{6}{10}$; 2.6

Write each as a decimal.

3. $6\frac{4}{10}$ 6.4
4. $15\frac{5}{10}$ 15.5
5. $22\frac{7}{10}$ 22.7
6. $3\frac{64}{100}$ 3.64
7. $38\frac{74}{100}$ 38.74
8. $46\frac{5}{100}$ 46.05
9. $7\frac{3}{1,000}$ 7.003
10. $41\frac{23}{1,000}$ 41.023
11. ten and eight tenths 10.8
12. three and forty-nine hundredths 3.49

Use with text pages 546–548.

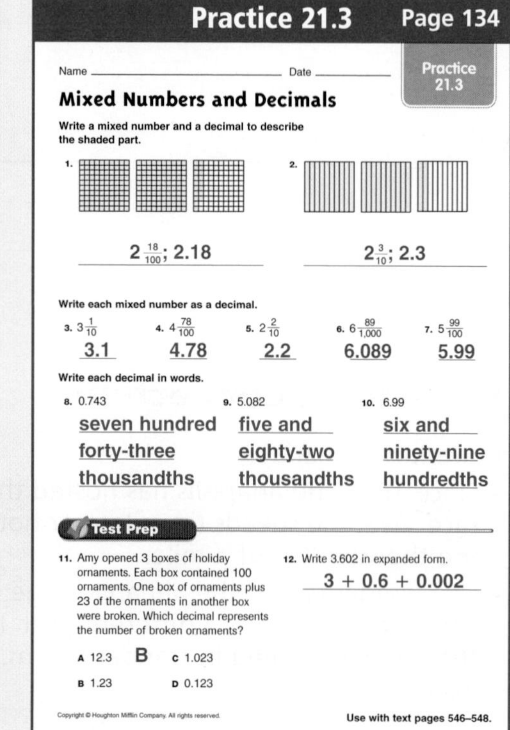

Practice 21.3 Page 134

Name ______________ Date ________ Practice 21.3

Mixed Numbers and Decimals

Write a mixed number and a decimal to describe the shaded part.

1. $2\frac{18}{100}$; 2.18
2. $2\frac{3}{10}$; 2.3

Write each mixed number as a decimal.

3. $3\frac{1}{10}$ 3.1
4. $4\frac{78}{100}$ 4.78
5. $2\frac{2}{10}$ 2.2
6. $6\frac{89}{1,000}$ 6.089
7. $5\frac{99}{100}$ 5.99

Write each decimal in words.

8. 0.743 seven hundred forty-three thousandths
9. 5.082 five and eighty-two thousandths
10. 6.99 six and ninety-nine hundredths

Test Prep

11. Amy opened 3 boxes of holiday ornaments. Each box contained 100 ornaments. One box of ornaments plus 23 of the ornaments in another box were broken. Which decimal represents the number of broken ornaments? B
    A 12.3
    B 1.23
    C 1.023
    D 0.123
12. Write 3.602 in expanded form. 3 + 0.6 + 0.002

Use with text pages 546–548.

▶ Thinking about money can help you understand decimals.

Here are different ways to show $1.49.

Models	Mixed Number	Place Value Chart
(one dollar bill and coins)	$1\frac{49}{100}$	dollars (ones) 1 . dimes (tenths) 4, pennies (hundredths) 9
Standard Form	**Word Form**	**Expanded Form**
$1.49	one dollar and forty-nine cents	$1 + $0.4 + $0.09

Guided Practice

Write a mixed number and a decimal to describe the shaded part in each model.

Ask Yourself

- What part is the whole number?
- What should the numerator be? What should the denominator be?

1. 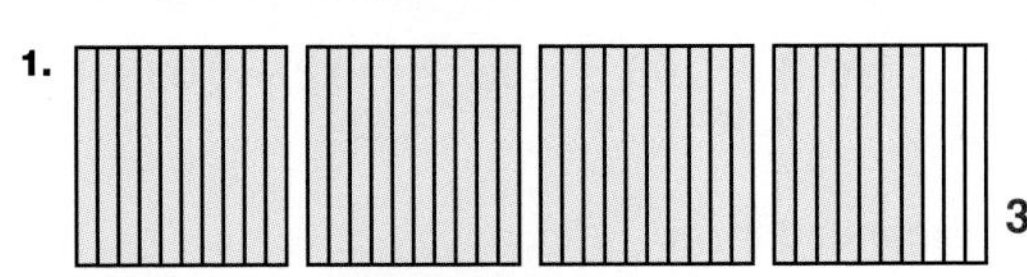 $3\frac{7}{10}$; 3.7

2. 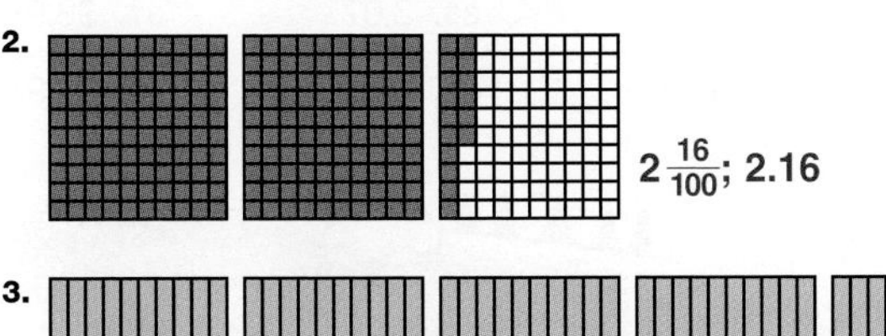 $2\frac{16}{100}$; 2.16

3. 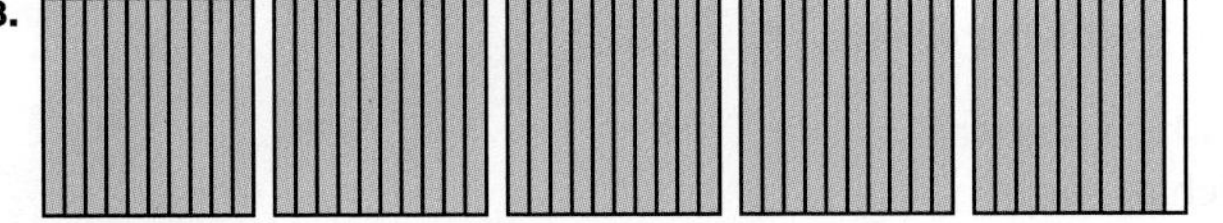 $4\frac{9}{10}$; 4.9

Write each as a decimal.

4. $5\frac{3}{10}$ 5.3
5. $9\frac{9}{10}$ 9.9
6. $26\frac{7}{10}$ 26.7
7. $15\frac{55}{100}$ 15.55
8. $12\frac{5}{100}$ 12.05
9. $2\frac{17}{1,000}$ 2.017
10. seven tenths 0.7
11. twenty-two hundredths 0.22
12. one and 5 thousandths 1.005

Explain Your Thinking ▶ Look back at Exercise 7. Why is the value of each 5 different?

Possible explanation: **The first 5 is in the ones place and has a value of 5. The second 5 is in the tenths place and has a value of 0.5. The third 5 is in the hundredths place and has a value of 0.05.**

- **Look at ways to write the money amount $1.49. What other models could you use?** (bills and coins) **What would you show?** (one $1 bill, 4 dimes, 9 pennies)

Guided Practice

Have students complete **Exercises 1–12** as you observe. Remind them to use the ***Ask Yourself*** questions to help. Give students the opportunity to talk about the question in ***Explain Your Thinking***.

Enrichment 21.3

Name ____________ Date ________ Enrichment 21.3

Name Tag Match Up

Martin Math is having a party. He made name tags for all his guests. Help Martin by matching the decimals in the left-hand column with the name tags in the right hand column.

Decimal		Name Tag
1. 1.457 C	A	five and six tenths
2. 5.06 E	B	two and eight thousandths
3. 2.18 G	C	one and four hundred fifty-seven thousandths
4. 4.006 H	D	two and twenty-five hundredths
5. 2.25 D	E	five and six hundredths
6. 5.6 A	F	three and forty-five thousandths
7. 3.045 F	G	two and eighteen hundredths
8. 2.008 B	H	four and six thousandths

 Use with text pages 546–548.

Problem Solving 21.3

Name ____________ Date ________ Problem Solving 21.3

Mixed Numbers and Decimals

Did you know that an adult human has 206 bones? Did you know the longest bone in the human body is the femur? Use the table about some of the longest bones in the body for Problems 1–4.

Name of Bone	Average Length (inches)
Femur	19.88
Humerus	14.35
Innominate Bone	7.28
Fibula	15.94
Ulna	11.10
Tibia	16.94
Radius	10.40

1. The femur is the bone in your upper leg. What is the length of the femur written in word form? nineteen and eighty-eight hundredths
2. The bone with a length of fifteen and ninety-four hundredths is found in the outer lower leg. What is the name of this bone? fibula
3. Which bone or bones are less than 10 inches long? innominate bone
4. Which bone length in the table has the digit 4 in the ones place? Write this length in word form and expanded form. Humerus; fourteen and thirty-five hundredths; 10 + 4 + 0.3 + 0.05
5. **You Decide** The seventh rib has an average length of nine and forty-five hundredth inches. The sternum, which connects the ribs in front, has an average length of 6 + 0.6 + 0.09 inches. Which bone is longer? Explain your reasoning. The seventh rib bone is longer. The whole number is greater: 9 > 6.

 Use with text pages 546–548.

3 Practice

Practice and Problem Solving

Select fom **Exercises 13–45** as independent work.

- Review the number of decimal places needed to show tenths, hundredths, and thousandths to help students write decimals correctly. (1, 2, 3)

4 Assess & Close

Math Talk in Action

- **How do all mixed numbers compare with 1?** (They are all greater than 1.)
- **Write the decimal four and fifty-six thousandths in standard form and in expanded form.** (4.056; 4 + 0.05 + 0.006)

Math Journal Prompt

Have students show the quantity five and twelve hundredths in six different ways.

Lesson Quiz

Use the quiz on Lesson Transparency 21.3.

Test Prep & Spiral Review

Use Test Prep Transparency 21.3.

Practice and Problem Solving

Write a mixed number and a decimal to describe the shaded part.

13.

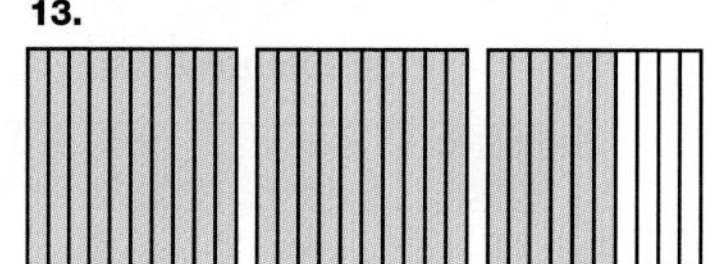

$2\frac{6}{10}$; 2.6

14.

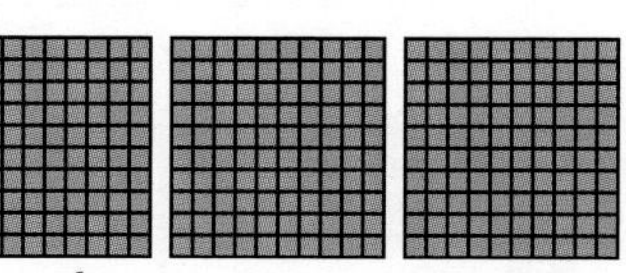

$3\frac{4}{100}$; 3.04

Write each mixed number as a decimal.

15. $1\frac{2}{10}$ **1.2**	**16.** $7\frac{7}{100}$ **7.07**	**17.** $4\frac{54}{100}$ **4.54**	**18.** $4\frac{7}{10}$ **4.7**	**19.** $34\frac{17}{100}$ **34.17**
20. $158\frac{85}{100}$ **158.85**	**21.** $175\frac{8}{100}$ **175.08**	**22.** $19\frac{38}{100}$ **19.38**	**23.** $45\frac{26}{1,000}$ **45.026**	**24.** $56\frac{3}{1,000}$ **56.003**

Write each as a decimal in standard form.

25. sixty-four hundredths **0.64**

26. five and seven tenths **5.7**

27. forty and four hundredths **40.04**

28. three and sixteen thousandths **3.016**

29. 7 + 0.5 **7.5**

30. 3 + 0.9 + 0.07 **3.97**

31. 4 + 0.06 **4.06**

32. 2 + 0.2 + 0.03 + 0.004 **2.234**

Write each decimal in words and in expanded form.
See Additional Answers.

33. 0.4	**34.** 0.65	**35.** 5.03	**36.** 3.07	**37.** $3.98
38. 4.3	**39.** 5.67	**40.** 4.876	**41.** 0.005	**42.** 3.098

Data Use the table for Problems 43–45.

43. Measurement On which day was there less than 1 inch of snow?
Wednesday

44. Represent Use a ruler to draw a line segment that shows the height of the snow that fell on Tuesday.
Line segments should be $3\frac{1}{2}$ in.

45. Analyze Melanie decided not to jog one day because eight and five tenths inches of snow fell on the day before. On which day of the week didn't she jog?
Saturday

Day	Inches of Snow
Monday	3.0 inches
Tuesday	3.5 inches
Wednesday	0.5 inches
Thursday	4.0 inches
Friday	8.5 inches

548

Extra Practice See page 565, Set B

Homework 21.3 Page 134

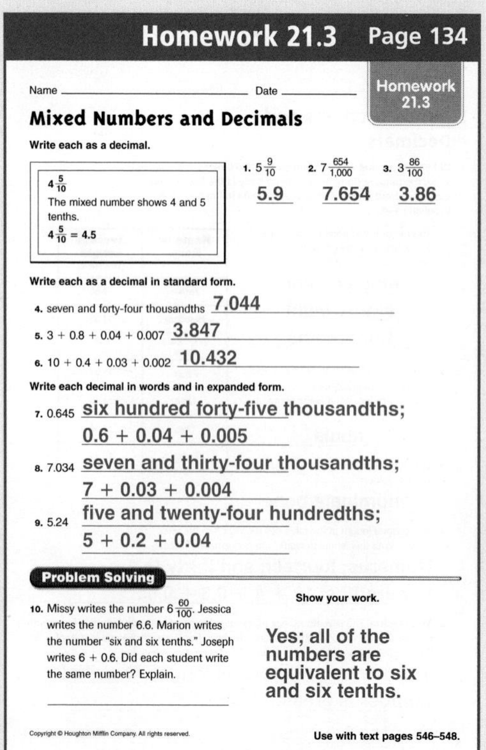

Name ______ Date ______

Homework 21.3

Mixed Numbers and Decimals

Write each as a decimal.

$4\frac{5}{10}$
The mixed number shows 4 and 5 tenths.
$4\frac{5}{10} = 4.5$

1. $5\frac{9}{10}$ **5.9**   **2.** $7\frac{654}{1,000}$ **7.654**   **3.** $3\frac{86}{100}$ **3.86**

Write each as a decimal in standard form.

4. seven and forty-four thousandths **7.044**

5. 3 + 0.8 + 0.04 + 0.007 **3.847**

6. 10 + 0.4 + 0.03 + 0.002 **10.432**

Write each decimal in words and in expanded form.

7. 0.645 **six hundred forty-five thousandths; 0.6 + 0.04 + 0.005**

8. 7.034 **seven and thirty-four thousandths; 7 + 0.03 + 0.004**

9. 5.24 **five and twenty-four hundredths; 5 + 0.2 + 0.04**

Problem Solving

10. Missy writes the number $6\frac{60}{100}$. Jessica writes the number 6.6. Marion writes the number "six and six tenths." Joseph writes 6 + 0.6. Did each student write the same number? Explain.

Show your work.

Yes; all of the numbers are equivalent to six and six tenths.

Use with text pages 546–548.

Real World Connection
Batting Averages

Problem Solving

Did you know that baseball statistics use decimals? Jackie Robinson was the first African-American player in major league baseball. His batting average in 1949 was .342.

A batting average is the number of hits divided by the number of times at bat. It is shown as a decimal in thousandths. Jackie Robinson's .342 means that he made 342 hits out of 1,000 times at bat, on average.

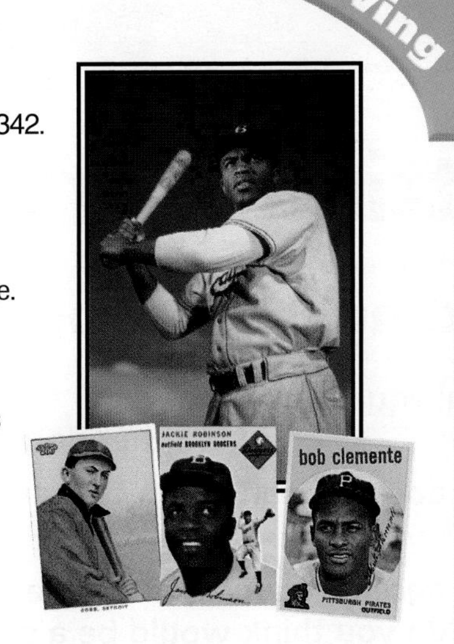

- Roberto Clemente was the first Latin American player to be inducted into baseball's Hall of Fame. He averaged 357 hits out of 1,000 times at bat in 1967. Write his batting average as a decimal. **0.357**
- Ty Cobb had a batting average of .377. What does that mean?

Possible answer: **It means that he averaged 377 hits out of 1,000 times at bat.**

WEEKLY WR READER eduplace.com/map

Quick Check

Check your understanding of Lessons 1–3.

Write a fraction and a decimal to describe each model. (Lesson 1)

1. $\frac{5}{10}$, or $\frac{1}{2}$; 0.5
2. $\frac{75}{100}$, or $\frac{3}{4}$; 0.75

Write each fraction as a decimal. (Lesson 2)

3. $\frac{8}{1,000}$ 0.008
4. $\frac{11}{1,000}$ 0.011
5. $\frac{139}{1,000}$ 0.139
6. $\frac{500}{1,000}$ 0.500 or 0.5

Write each decimal in words. (Lesson 3)

7. 1.2 one and two tenths
8. 3.03 three and three hundredths
9. 9.016 nine and sixteen thousandths
10. 5.179 five and one hundred seventy-nine thousandths

Real World Connection
Batting Averages

Batting average is a measure of how well a player hits. Tell students that a player need not be at bat 1,000 times before having a batting average. To find a batting average, we divide the number of hits by the number of times at bat, whatever those numbers may be. For example, if Ruthie bats 17 times and gets 3 hits, we divide 3 by 17 to find her average. We read the quotient to the thousandths place: 0.176.

By convention, when batting average is stated, we say that her batting average is 176.

Quick Check

The ***Quick Check*** allows you to assess the students' understanding of the concepts presented in Lessons 1–3.

Items	Objectives Tested	Pages	Intervention
1–2	Use models to show tenths and hundredths.	542–543	Reteaching Resource 21.1 *Ways to Success* CD-ROM 21.1
3–6	Write decimals for thousandths.	544–545	Reteaching Resource 21.2 *Ways to Success* CD-ROM 21.2
7–10	Read, write, and model amounts greater than 1.	546–548	Reteaching Resource 21.3 *Ways to Success* CD-ROM 21.3

Lesson 21.4

Fractions and Decimal Equivalents

Planning

Lesson Objective Write fractions and decimals that name the same amount.

Technology Resources

- Audio Tutor 2/25 Listen and Understand
- *Ways to Success* CD-ROM 21.4
- Education Place: Extra Practice, eGlossary, Extra Help, eGames www.eduplace.com/map

Lesson 21.4 Transparency

Problem of the Day

Damian recorded $\frac{68}{100}$ inches of rain. Nola recorded 0.68 inches of rain. Who recorded a greater amount? (Neither; scores are equivalent.)

Spiral Review

Are the fractions equivalent? Write *yes* or *no*.

1. $\frac{3}{4}$ and $\frac{5}{8}$ (no) **2.** $\frac{4}{12}$ and $\frac{1}{3}$ (yes)
3. $\frac{1}{6}$ and $\frac{3}{12}$ (no) **4.** $\frac{8}{10}$ and $\frac{4}{5}$ (yes)
5. $\frac{3}{5}$ and $\frac{60}{100}$ (yes)

Lesson Quiz

Write each decimal as a fraction.

1. 0.8 ($\frac{8}{10}$) **2.** 0.68 ($\frac{68}{100}$)
3. 0.20 ($\frac{2}{10}$ or $\frac{20}{100}$)

Write each fraction as a decimal.

4. $\frac{3}{10}$ (0.3) **5.** $\frac{25}{100}$ (0.25)
6. $\frac{7}{20}$ (0.35)

NCTM Standards

Number and Operations: Recognize equivalent representations for the same number and generate them by decomposing and composing numbers; recognize and generate equivalent forms of commonly used fractions, decimals, and percents.
Connections: Recognize and use connections among mathematical ideas.

Getting Started

Building Math Vocabulary

decimal equivalent a decimal that is equal to a whole number, a fraction, or another decimal

- **What does it mean when two amounts are equivalent?** (They express the same value even if written different ways.)
- Write *decimal equivalent* on the board. **Think about fractions and decimals. What do you think would be a decimal equivalent of $\frac{1}{2}$?** (0.5; 0.50; 0.500)

Decimal Equivalents

Whole Class	25 minutes
Objective	Write fractions as decimals and vice versa.
Materials	Workmat 6, Tenths and Hundredths Grid Transparencies, blank transparency
Auditory, Visual	

- Display a tenths grid. Write $\frac{1}{5}$ below it. **To write $\frac{1}{5}$ as a decimal, first we find an equivalent fraction with a denominator of 10.** Help students solve $\frac{1}{5} = \frac{■}{10}$. (Multiply both terms of $\frac{1}{5}$ by 2; ■ = 2.) **The fraction $\frac{2}{10}$ is equivalent to $\frac{1}{5}$.**
- **How do we write $\frac{2}{10}$ as a decimal?** (0.2) Have a student shade 0.2 on either the tenths grid or the Workmat 6 centimeter grid. **A decimal that names the same amount as a fraction is the fraction's decimal equivalent. So, 0.2 is a decimal equivalent of $\frac{1}{5}$.**
- Repeat with a hundredths grid to find the decimal equivalent of $\frac{1}{5}$. ($\frac{1}{5}$ = 0.20)
- Tell students that the lesson also uses number lines to find equivalent decimals and fractions.

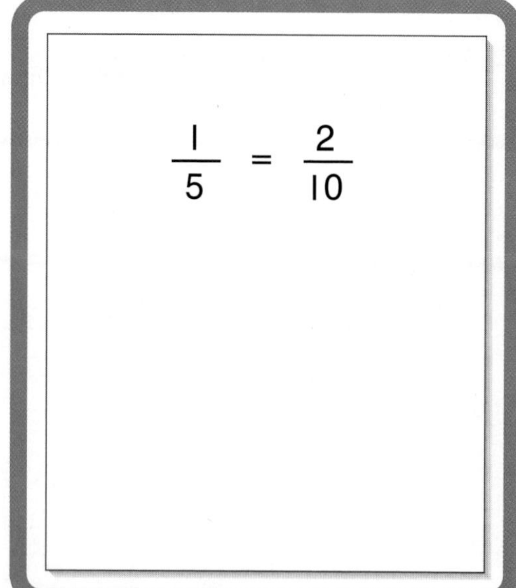

Differentiated Instruction

English Learners

Whole Class	10 minutes
Objective	Find equivalent fractions.
Materials	Student page 551
Auditory, Visual	

Early Production

- Students may need help making equivalent fractions before they do the ***Guided Practice.***
- Write the following on the board:
  $\frac{1}{4} = \frac{25}{100}$ $\frac{1}{2} = \frac{?}{10}$ $\frac{2}{25} = \frac{?}{100}$
- Have students discuss how they know the first two fractions are equivalent and explain how to find equivalent fractions for the other two.

Intermediate/Advanced

- English Learner Resource 21.4
- English Learner Handbook

Intervention

Small Groups	15 minutes
Objective	Write fractions as decimals and vice versa.
Materials	None
Visual, Auditory	

- **What makes fractions equivalent?** (if they name the same part of a whole)
- **What are some other fractions you can name that are equivalent to $\frac{1}{2}$?** List all correct responses on the board.
- **What are some pairs of fractions and decimals that name the same quantity?** (Accept all reasonable responses, such as $\frac{1}{10} = 0.1$ and $\frac{2}{100} = 0.02$, etc.)
- Tell students that in this lesson they will learn to write more fractions and decimals that name the same amount.

Other Resources

- *Ways to Success* CD-ROM 21.4

Gifted & Talented

Whole Class	15 minutes
Objective	Write fractions as decimals.
Materials	Calculators
Visual, Tactual	

- All fractions have an equivalent decimal. Have students divide on a calculator to find a decimal equivalent to $\frac{3}{4}$: $3 \div 4 = 0.75$. Decimal equivalents with more decimal places can be shown by writing the first three decimal places.
- Have students find decimal equivalents to $\frac{2}{5}, \frac{4}{9}, \frac{7}{11}, \frac{12}{40}, \frac{15}{48}, \frac{12}{60}, \frac{16}{80}$, and $\frac{3}{120}$.

Literature Connection

Materials: *The Phantom Tollbooth* by Norton Juster

- Read aloud the section of this children's classic in which Milo, the main character, meets half a child—or, more accurately, 0.58 of a boy (Chapter 16, "A Very Dirty Bird").
- Invite students to discuss the humor of the accompanying illustration and the absurdity of this scene, despite its mathematical accuracy.

❶ Introduce

Have a student volunteer read the lesson objective. Tell students that they will use different ways, such as number lines and models, to show equivalent amounts.

❷ Teach

Learn About It

- Read the opening problem. **What fractions did the girls use to describe the shaded part of the grid?** ($\frac{1}{2}$, $\frac{5}{10}$) **How are these two fractions alike?** (Both name the same part of the grid.)
- **What decimals did the girls use to describe the shaded part of the grid?** (0.5, 0.50) **How are these two decimals alike?** (The digits in the ones and tenths places are the same.)
- **To change a fraction to a decimal, why do we start by finding an equivalent fraction with a denominator like 10, 100, or 1,000?** (The place values of decimals are tenths, hundredths, and thousandths.)
- **Look at *Way 1*. How do the shaded models show that the four expressions are equivalent?** (All shade the same amount of the whole.)
- **Look at *Way 2*. How do the number lines show equivalence among the expressions?** (0.5, $\frac{1}{2}$, $\frac{5}{10}$, and 0.50 all line up at the same place on the number lines.)

Common Error

- **Equivalent fraction errors** Students sometimes make errors in computing equivalent fractions.
- **Intervention** Remind students that whenever they compute to write an equivalent fraction for a given fraction, they must always multiply both the numerator and denominator by the same factor in order to maintain equivalence.

Lesson 4

Audio Tutor 2/25 Listen and Understand

Fractions and Decimal Equivalents

Vocabulary
decimal equivalent

Objective Write fractions and decimals that name the same amount.

Learn About It

A decimal that names the same amount as a fraction is the fraction's **decimal equivalent**.

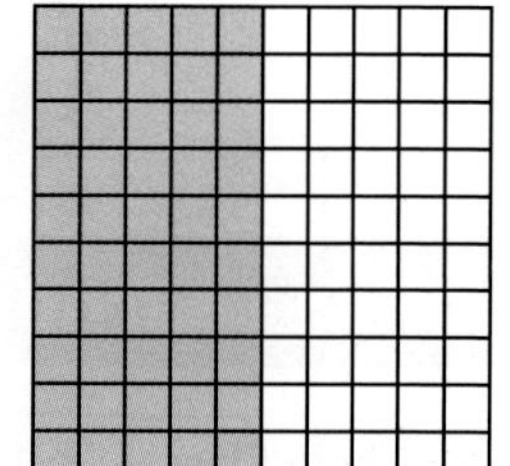

Carrie says that $\frac{1}{2}$ of the grid is orange. Jenny says that $\frac{5}{10}$ is orange. Rosa says that 0.5 is orange, and Marla says that 0.50 of the grid is orange. Which of the girls is correct?

To change a fraction to a decimal, find an equivalent fraction with a denominator of 10, 100, or 1,000.

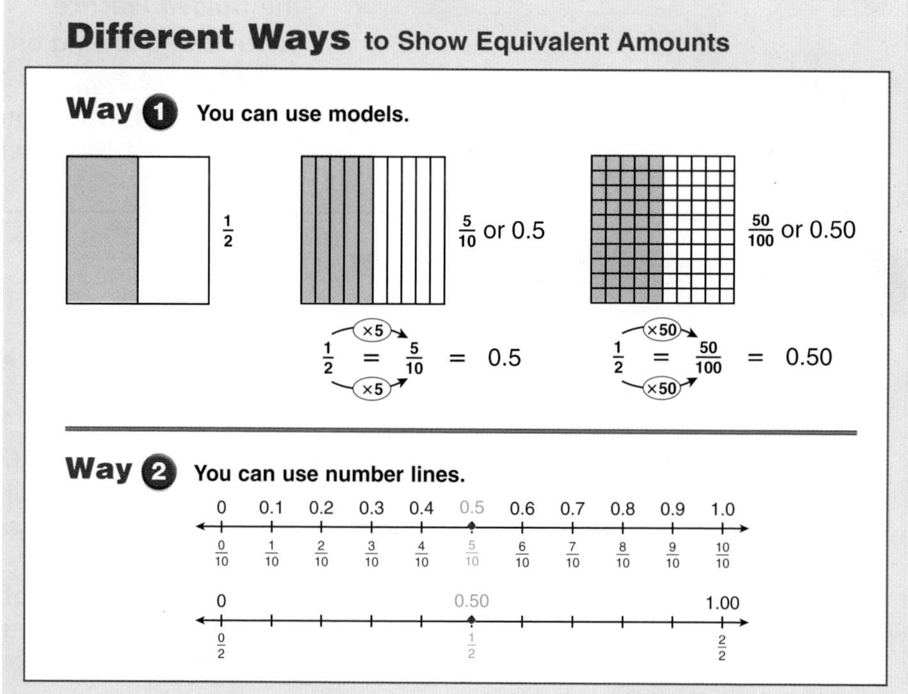

Different Ways to Show Equivalent Amounts
Way 1 You can use models.
1/2
5/10 or 0.5
50/100 or 0.50
×5
1/2 = 5/10 = 0.5
×5
×50
1/2 = 50/100 = 0.50
×50
Way 2 You can use number lines.
0 0.1 0.2 0.3 0.4 0.5 0.6 0.7 0.8 0.9 1.0
0/10 1/10 2/10 3/10 4/10 5/10 6/10 7/10 8/10 9/10 10/10
0 0.50 1.00
0/2 1/2 2/2

Solution: All four girls are correct.

Extra Help at eduplace.com/map

Reteach 21.4

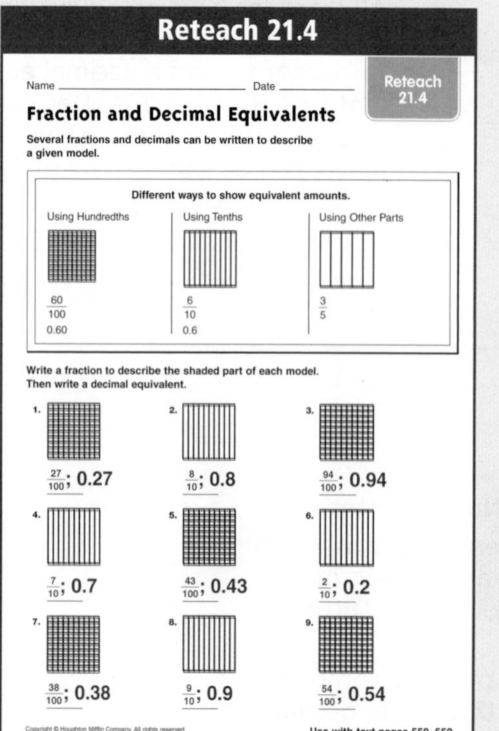

Name ______ Date ______

Reteach 21.4

Fraction and Decimal Equivalents

Several fractions and decimals can be written to describe a given model.

Different ways to show equivalent amounts.

Using Hundredths	Using Tenths	Using Other Parts
$\frac{60}{100}$ 0.60	$\frac{6}{10}$ 0.6	$\frac{3}{5}$

Write a fraction to describe the shaded part of each model. Then write a decimal equivalent.

1. $\frac{27}{100}$; 0.27
2. $\frac{8}{10}$; 0.8
3. $\frac{94}{100}$; 0.94
4. $\frac{7}{10}$; 0.7
5. $\frac{43}{100}$; 0.43
6. $\frac{2}{10}$; 0.2
7. $\frac{38}{100}$; 0.38
8. $\frac{9}{10}$; 0.9
9. $\frac{54}{100}$; 0.54

Use with text pages 550–552.

Practice 21.4 Page 135

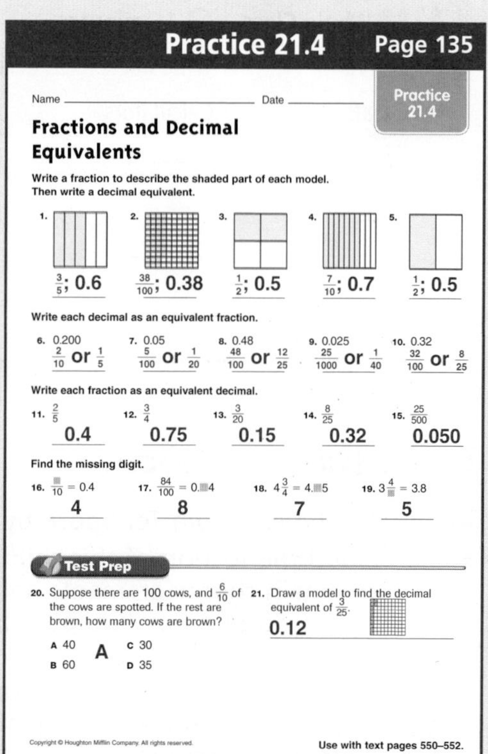

Name ______ Date ______

Practice 21.4

Fractions and Decimal Equivalents

Write a fraction to describe the shaded part of each model. Then write a decimal equivalent.

1. $\frac{3}{5}$; 0.6
2. $\frac{38}{100}$; 0.38
3. $\frac{1}{2}$; 0.5
4. $\frac{7}{10}$; 0.7
5. $\frac{1}{2}$; 0.5

Write each decimal as an equivalent fraction.

6. 0.200 $\frac{2}{10}$ or $\frac{1}{5}$
7. 0.05 $\frac{5}{100}$ or $\frac{1}{20}$
8. 0.48 $\frac{48}{100}$ or $\frac{12}{25}$
9. 0.025 $\frac{25}{1000}$ or $\frac{1}{40}$
10. 0.32 $\frac{32}{100}$ or $\frac{8}{25}$

Write each fraction as an equivalent decimal.

11. $\frac{2}{5}$ 0.4
12. $\frac{3}{4}$ 0.75
13. $\frac{3}{20}$ 0.15
14. $\frac{8}{25}$ 0.32
15. $\frac{25}{500}$ 0.050

Find the missing digit.

16. $\frac{■}{10}$ = 0.4 4
17. $\frac{84}{100}$ = 0.■4 8
18. $4\frac{3}{4}$ = 4.■5 7
19. $3\frac{4}{■}$ = 3.8 5

Test Prep

20. Suppose there are 100 cows, and $\frac{6}{10}$ of the cows are spotted. If the rest are brown, how many cows are brown?
A 40 B 60 C 30 D 35 — A

21. Draw a model to find the decimal equivalent of $\frac{3}{25}$. 0.12

Use with text pages 550–552.

Other Examples

A. Denominator of 100

$\frac{3}{4} = \frac{75}{100} = 0.75$ (×25 on numerator and denominator)

B. Denominator of 1,000

$\frac{7}{500} = \frac{14}{1000} = 0.014$ (×2 on numerator and denominator)

Guided Practice

Ask Yourself

- What part of the square is shaded?
- How do I write that amount as a fraction? as a decimal?

Write a fraction to describe the shaded part of each model. Then write a decimal equivalent.

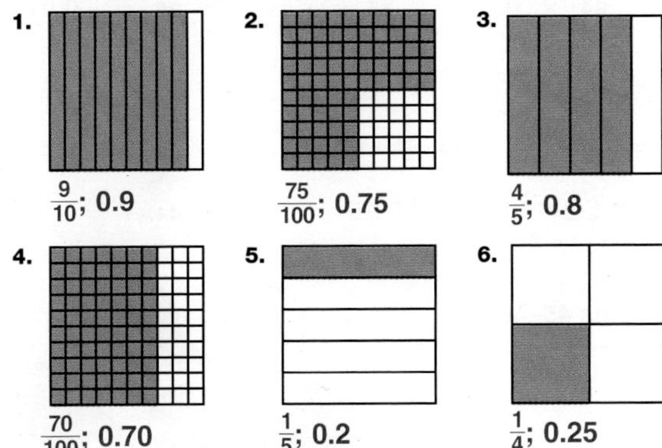

1. $\frac{9}{10}$; 0.9
2. $\frac{75}{100}$; 0.75
3. $\frac{4}{5}$; 0.8
4. $\frac{70}{100}$; 0.70
5. $\frac{1}{5}$; 0.2
6. $\frac{1}{4}$; 0.25

Explain Your Thinking ▶ Describe how you would find the decimal equivalent for $\frac{7}{20}$. ***Possible answer:*** **Multiply both the numerator and the denominator by 5 to get $\frac{35}{100}$ which equals 0.35.**

Practice and Problem Solving

Write a fraction to describe the shaded part of each model. Then write a decimal equivalent.

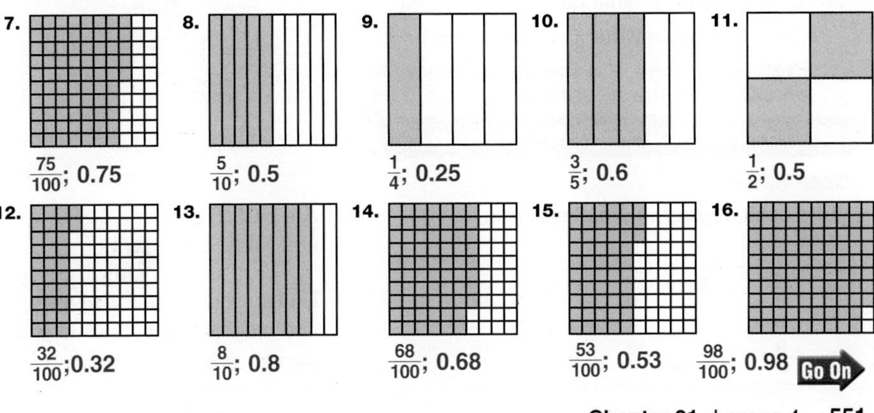

7. $\frac{75}{100}$; 0.75
8. $\frac{5}{10}$; 0.5
9. $\frac{1}{4}$; 0.25
10. $\frac{3}{5}$; 0.6
11. $\frac{1}{2}$; 0.5
12. $\frac{32}{100}$; 0.32
13. $\frac{8}{10}$; 0.8
14. $\frac{68}{100}$; 0.68
15. $\frac{53}{100}$; 0.53
16. $\frac{98}{100}$; 0.98

Go On

- **Look at Other Example A. Why do we change $\frac{3}{4}$ to a decimal in hundredths rather than tenths?** (We can't make an equivalent fraction in tenths.) **Why do we multiply both terms by 25?** ($4 \times 25 = 100$, so multiply the numerator by that same factor to maintain equivalence.)

Guided Practice

Have students complete **Exercises 1–6** as you observe. Remind them to use the *Ask Yourself* questions to help. Give students the opportunity to talk about the question in *Explain Your Thinking*.

3 Practice

Practice and Problem Solving

Select from **Exercises 7–52** as independent work.

Enrichment 21.4

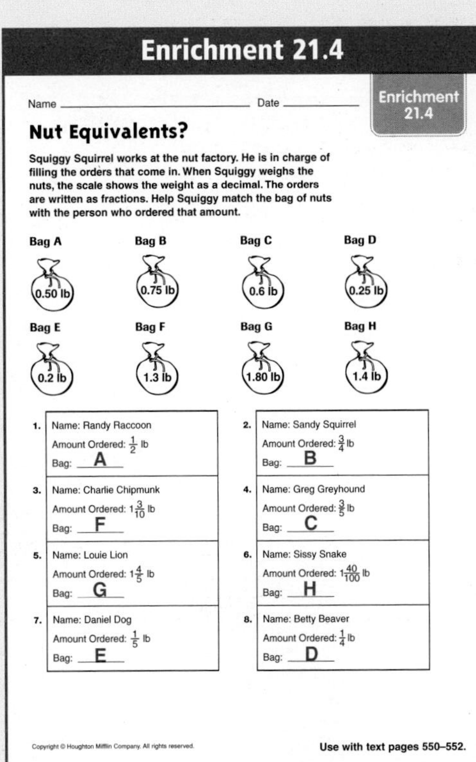

Name ______ Date ______ Enrichment 21.4

Nut Equivalents?

Squiggy Squirrel works at the nut factory. He is in charge of filling the orders that come in. When Squiggy weighs the nuts, the scale shows the weight as a decimal. The orders are written as fractions. Help Squiggy match the bag of nuts with the person who ordered that amount.

Bag A (0.50 lb) Bag B (0.75 lb) Bag C (0.6 lb) Bag D (0.25 lb)
Bag E (0.2 lb) Bag F (1.3 lb) Bag G (1.80 lb) Bag H (1.4 lb)

1. Name: Randy Raccoon; Amount Ordered: $\frac{1}{2}$ lb; Bag: A
2. Name: Sandy Squirrel; Amount Ordered: $\frac{3}{4}$ lb; Bag: B
3. Name: Charlie Chipmunk; Amount Ordered: $1\frac{3}{10}$ lb; Bag: F
4. Name: Greg Greyhound; Amount Ordered: $\frac{3}{5}$ lb; Bag: C
5. Name: Louie Lion; Amount Ordered: $1\frac{4}{5}$ lb; Bag: G
6. Name: Sissy Snake; Amount Ordered: $1\frac{40}{100}$ lb; Bag: H
7. Name: Daniel Dog; Amount Ordered: $\frac{1}{5}$ lb; Bag: E
8. Name: Betty Beaver; Amount Ordered: $\frac{1}{4}$ lb; Bag: D

 Use with text pages 550–552.

Problem Solving 21.4

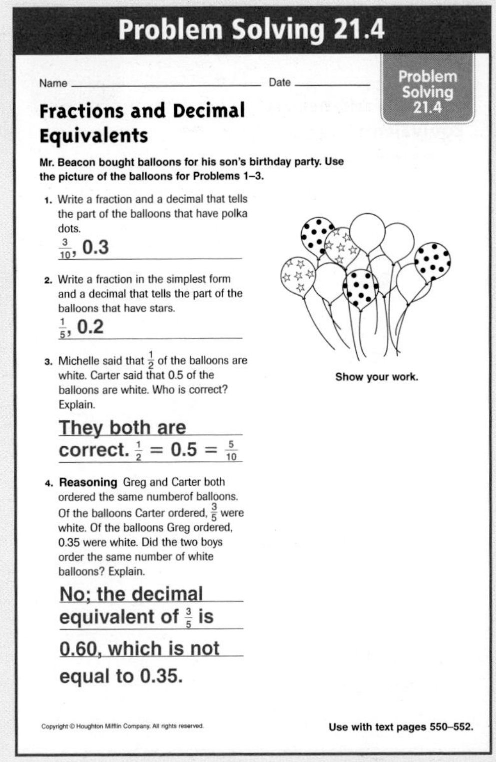

Name ______ Date ______ Problem Solving 21.4

Fractions and Decimal Equivalents

Mr. Beacon bought balloons for his son's birthday party. Use the picture of the balloons for Problems 1–3.

1. Write a fraction and a decimal that tells the part of the balloons that have polka dots. $\frac{3}{10}$, 0.3
2. Write a fraction in the simplest form and a decimal that tells the part of the balloons that have stars. $\frac{1}{5}$, 0.2
3. Michelle said that $\frac{1}{2}$ of the balloons are white. Carter said that 0.5 of the balloons are white. Who is correct? Explain. They both are correct. $\frac{1}{2} = 0.5 = \frac{5}{10}$
4. **Reasoning** Greg and Carter both ordered the same numberof balloons. Of the balloons Carter ordered, $\frac{3}{5}$ were white. Of the balloons Greg ordered, 0.35 were white. Did the two boys order the same number of white balloons? Explain. No; the decimal equivalent of $\frac{3}{5}$ is 0.60, which is not equal to 0.35.

Show your work.

 Use with text pages 550–552.

- For **Exercises 37–44,** have students rewrite all decimals as fractions. Have them rewrite mixed numbers as fractions in 10ths, 100ths, or 1,000ths.
- ***Problem 48*** Invite students to share how they found Brett's error.

4 Assess & Close

Math Talk in Action

- **What does it mean that a fraction or mixed number has a decimal equivalent?** (You can express the value of the fraction or mixed number as a decimal for that same quantity.)
- **Explain how to find an equivalent decimal for $\frac{7}{25}$.**

Listen for responses that describe multiplying $\frac{7}{25}$ by $\frac{4}{4}$; $\frac{7}{25} = \frac{28}{100} = 0.28$.

Math Journal Prompt

Have students write the fraction and its decimal equivalent for the number of states whose names begin with M. ($\frac{8}{50}$, 0.16)

Lesson Quiz

Use the quiz on Lesson Transparency 21.4.

Test Prep & Spiral Review

Use Test Prep Transparency 21.4.

Practice and Problem Solving

Write each decimal as an equivalent fraction.

17. 0.4 **$\frac{4}{10}$ or $\frac{2}{5}$** **18.** 0.04 **$\frac{4}{100}$ or $\frac{1}{25}$** **19.** 0.75 **$\frac{75}{100}$ or $\frac{3}{4}$** **20.** 0.67 **$\frac{67}{100}$** **21.** 0.25 **$\frac{25}{100}$ or $\frac{1}{4}$**

22. 0.34 **$\frac{34}{100}$** **23.** 0.98 **$\frac{98}{100}$** **24.** 0.30 **$\frac{3}{10}$** **25.** 0.500 **$\frac{5}{10}$** **26.** 0.005 **$\frac{5}{1,000}$**

Write each fraction as an equivalent decimal.

27. $\frac{3}{5}$ **0.6** **28.** $\frac{4}{50}$ **0.08** **29.** $\frac{2}{25}$ **0.08** **30.** $\frac{1}{20}$ **0.05** **31.** $\frac{1}{25}$ **0.04**

32. $\frac{9}{10}$ **0.9** **33.** $\frac{27}{100}$ **0.27** **34.** $\frac{4}{5}$ **0.8** **35.** $\frac{643}{1,000}$ **0.643** **36.** $\frac{9}{500}$ **0.018**

Find the missing digit.

37. $\frac{■}{10} = 0.30$ **3** **38.** $\frac{42}{100} = 0.■2$ **4** **39.** $\frac{3}{5} = 0.■0$ **6** **40.** $\frac{1}{5} = 0.■$ **2**

41. $4\frac{4}{5} = 4.■$ **8** **42.** $3\frac{1}{2} = ■.5$ **3** **43.** $10.■5 = 10\frac{1}{20}$ **0** **44.** $7\frac{2}{■} = 7.4$ **5**

Data Use the picture for Problems 45–46.

45. Write a decimal that tells the part of the hats that is blue. **0.4**

46. Write a decimal that tells the part of the hats that is not blue. **0.6**

47. Analyze Suppose there are 100 hats, and $\frac{4}{10}$ of them are not red. If the rest are red, how many hats are red? **60 hats**

48. What's Wrong? What did Brett do wrong when he tried to write $\frac{1}{25}$ as a decimal?
Brett placed the 4 in the tenths place. It should be in the hundredths place. 0.04

Brett
$\frac{1}{25} = \frac{1 \times 4}{25 \times 4} = \frac{4}{100} = 0.4$

Mixed Review and Test Prep

Open Response

Write each answer in simplest form. (Ch. 20, Lesson 1)

49. $\frac{2}{9} + \frac{4}{9}$ **$\frac{2}{3}$** **50.** $\frac{9}{10} + \frac{7}{10}$ **$1\frac{3}{5}$** **51.** $\frac{5}{12} + \frac{7}{12}$ **1**

52. Are 5.05, 5.005, and 5.500 equivalent decimals? (Ch. 21, Lesson 4)

Explain your answer using words and models or place-value charts. ***See above.***

52. Possible answer: **No. 5.500 is the greatest because 0.5 means 5 tenths. 0.05 means 5 hundredths and 0.005 means 5 thousandths.**

552

Extra Practice See page 565, Set C.

Homework 21.4 Page 135

Name ______ Date ______

Homework 21.4

Fractions and Decimal Equivalents

Write each decimal as an equivalent fraction.

0.4
You can use number lines.

$0.4 = \frac{2}{5}$ or $\frac{4}{10}$ or $\frac{40}{100}$

1. 0.74 **$\frac{74}{100}$ or $\frac{37}{50}$** **2.** 0.31 **$\frac{31}{100}$**

3. 0.062 **$\frac{62}{1,000}$ or $\frac{31}{500}$** **4.** 0.59 **$\frac{59}{100}$**

Write each fraction as an equivalent decimal.

5. $\frac{3}{5}$ **0.6** **6.** $\frac{1}{4}$ **0.25** **7.** $\frac{13}{20}$ **0.65** **8.** $\frac{19}{25}$ **0.76** **9.** $\frac{450}{1,000}$ **0.45**

Find the missing digit.

10. $\frac{74}{1000} = .0■4$ **7** **11.** $\frac{■5}{100} = .15$ **1** **12.** $4\frac{7}{■0} = 4.7$ **1**

Problem Solving

13. Suppose there are 1,000 marbles and $\frac{3}{4}$ of the marbles are colors other than black. If the rest of them are black, how many marbles are black? Explain how you found your answer.
250 marbles; ***explanations may vary.***

Use with text pages 550–552.

Math Challenge
Percent

Did you ever get 100% on a test? Congratulations! That means that all your answers were correct!

Problem Solving

Vocabulary
percent

The symbol **%** is read as "**percent**".
Percent means per hundred.

100% means 100 out of 100. It means all.
50% means 50 out of 100.
25% means 25 out of 100.

Look at these examples.

6. ***Possible answer:* Because a dollar is divided into 100 cents, it can represent a whole of 100%. Half of a dollar is 50¢ or 50%.**

7. **10% means 10 parts out of 100 parts; $\frac{10}{100}$ or $\frac{1}{10}$; 0.1; $\frac{75}{100}$ or $\frac{3}{4}$; 0.75**

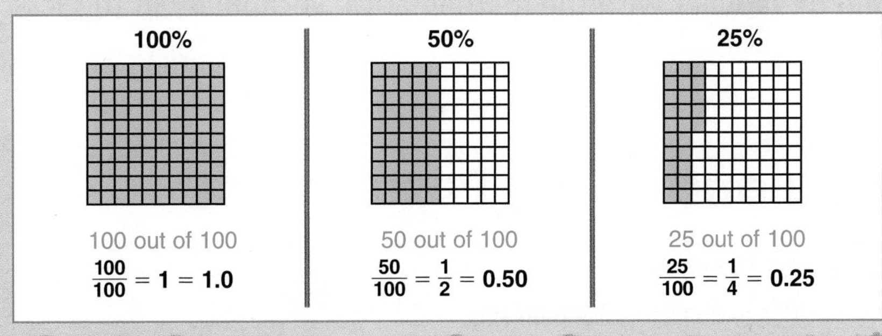

Copy and complete this chart.

1.	**Fraction**	$\frac{25}{100}$	$\frac{50}{100}$	**$\frac{75}{100}$**	$\frac{100}{100}$
2.	**Decimal**	0.25	**0.5**	0.75	**1.0**
3.	**Percent**	**25%**	50%	75%	**100%**

4. A basketball team won $\frac{1}{2}$ of the games it played last season. What percent of the games did it win? **50%**
5. Suppose 25% of the students in Amy's class bought lunch today. What fraction of the students bought lunch? **One fourth of the students**

6. **Write About It** How can thinking about a fractional part of a dollar help you change a fraction to a percent? Give an example. ***See above.***
7. What do you think 10% means? How would you show 10% as a fraction and as a decimal? How would you show 75% as a fraction and as a decimal? ***See above.***

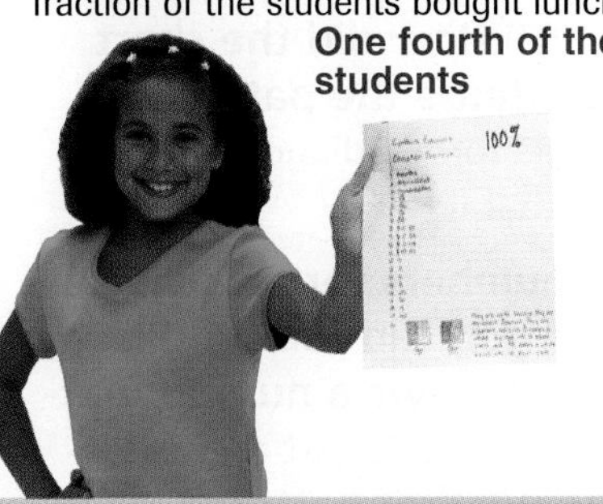

Math Challenge
Percent

Point out that *cent* comes from the same word root students know in *cent*imeter or *cent*ury; *cent* means 100.

Students may have seen percents in stores. They may have seen signs advertising 50% off or discounts of 25%. Help them understand these expressions in terms of the cost of simple items, such as a $10 book on sale for 50% off its usual cost.

Reaching All Learners

Number Sense

Fractions and Decimals Write the following fractions and decimals on the board.

$\frac{2}{10}$	$\frac{1}{2}$	$\frac{3}{5}$	$\frac{15}{100}$	$\frac{42}{100}$
0.9	0.15	0.5	0.2	0.75

1. Have students match any fractions and decimals that are equivalent and use grid paper to explain.
2. Have students write an equivalent decimal for each fraction and an equivalent fraction for each decimal in the list. Have students use grid paper to help, if needed.
3. Have students write each decimal in the list as a fraction in simplest form. Then have them write a decimal for each of the fractions.

Answers:

1. $\frac{2}{10} = 0.2$; $\frac{1}{2} = 0.5$; $\frac{15}{100} = 0.15$; Check grids.
2. Check equivalent fractions and decimals.
3. $0.9 = \frac{9}{10}$; $0.15 = \frac{3}{20}$; $0.5 = \frac{1}{2}$; $0.2 = \frac{1}{5}$; $0.75 = \frac{3}{4}$; $\frac{2}{10} = 0.2$; $\frac{1}{2} = 0.5$; $\frac{3}{5} = 0.6$; $\frac{15}{100} = 0.15$; $\frac{42}{100} = 0.42$

Differentiated Assignments		
At Risk	**Average**	**Advanced**
Exercise 1	Exercise 2	Exercise 3

Lesson 21.5

Problem-Solving Strategy: Find a Pattern

Planning

Lesson Objective Use patterns to solve problems.

Technology Resources

- *Ways to Success* CD-ROM 21.5
- Education Place: Extra Practice www.eduplace.com/map

Lesson 21.5 Transparency

Problem of the Day

The house numbers on Margie's side of her block are even numbers from 538 to 562. How many houses are there on her side of the block? (13)

Spiral Review

Complete each pattern.

1. □ ■ ○ ● □ ■ ___ ___ (○ ●)

2. Δ ■ Δ ■ ■ Δ ■ ___ ___ ___ (■ ■ Δ)

3. $< = > = \leq \neq \geq = < = > =$ ___ ___ ___ ($\leq \neq \geq$)

4. $\frac{1}{3}$ $\frac{1}{9}$ $\frac{1}{27}$ $\frac{1}{81}$ ___ ___ ($\frac{1}{243}$, $\frac{1}{729}$)

Lesson Quiz

Look at each pattern of numbers. If the pattern continues, what is the next number likely to be?

1. 7 11 15 19 23 27 31 35 (39)

2. 3 8 14 21 29 38 48 59 (71)

NCTM Standards

Algebra: Describe, extend, and make generalizations about geometric and numeric patterns.
Problem Solving: Apply and adapt a variety of appropriate strategies to solve problems.

Getting Started

Building Math Vocabulary

Students should be familiar with the mathematical vocabulary in this lesson.

Visualizing and Using Patterns

Whole Class	15 minutes
Objective	Use patterns to solve problems.
Materials	Hundred Chart (Learning Tool 14)
Auditory, Visual	

- Display the Hundred Chart. Ask students to use it to figure out the next number in this series: 2, 13, 24, 35, 46. (57) **How did the chart help you continue the pattern?** (Those numbers form a diagonal line; 57 is next along that line.)
- **This set of numbers forms a visual pattern that you can see on the chart. It also follows a number pattern that works without a chart. What is the number pattern?** (add 11) **If the pattern continues, what will the 10th number be?** (101) **Is this number on the chart?** (no) **Then how do you know it's right?** (It follows the addition pattern.)
- Tell students that the problem on page 554 shows how to use patterns with money.

1	2	3	4	5	6	7	8	9	10
11	12	13	14	15	16	17	18	19	20
21	22	23	24	25	26	27	28	29	30
31	32	33	34	35	36	37	38	39	40
41	42	43	44	45	46	47	48	49	50
51	52	53	54	55	56	57	58	59	60
61	62	63	64	65	66	67	68	69	70
71	72	73	74	75	76	77	78	79	80
81	82	83	84	85	86	87	88	89	90
91	92	93	94	95	96	97	98	99	100

Differentiated Instruction

English Learners

Pairs	20 minutes
Objective	Use patterns to solve problems.
Materials	Index cards
Auditory, Visual	

Early Production

- Students may need help recognizing patterns.
- Give each pair of students an index card with a number pattern on it. Ask them to find the pattern and add three more numbers to it.
- Encourage student pairs to share their answers with the other students.

Intermediate/Advanced

- English Learner Resource 21.5
- English Learner Handbook

Intervention

Whole Class	20 minutes
Objective	Use patterns to solve problems.
Materials	None
Visual, Auditory	

- Talk about patterns by writing this set of numbers on the board: 37, 42, 47, 52, 57, . . . **What is the pattern of this list of numbers?** (+5) **How can we figure out the eighth number in the list?** (Count on by 5s until you reach the 8th number, 72.)
- Invite a volunteer to create and write another number pattern on the board for classmates to solve and complete. Have students discuss what the pattern is and how they figured it out.

Other Resources

- *Ways to Success* CD-ROM 21.5

Special Needs

Whole Class	25 minutes
Objective	Use patterns to solve problems.
Materials	Calculators
Visual, Tactual	

- Allow students to use a calculator to find number patterns.
- Model how students can use a calculator to determine the relationship between adjacent numbers in a given pattern.
- When they figure out the pattern, they should record it, then apply it to extend the pattern to as many numbers as required.

Art Connection

Materials: A book of flags

- Instruct students to look though different flag books that feature flags from different countries, organizations, schools, states, etc.
- Have them describe the types of patterns they see. These could describe geometric or color patterns.
- Challenge students to create personal flags by using interesting and unusual patterns.

❶ Introduce

Have students develop pattern-finding and pattern-recognition abilities with respect to practical solutions. Ensure that they can reasonably and clearly explain how they use patterns to solve problems.

❷ Teach

Find a Pattern

Read the opening problem together.

- **Look at the *Understand* step. What question is asked?** (How much do 6 photo packages cost?) **What data is given?** (the cost of 1, 2, 3, and 4 photo packages)
- **Look at the *Plan* step. Do 2 photos cost twice as much as 1?** (no) **Then how can you decide whether there is a pattern?** (Figure out by how much each cost changes when you compare it to the previous one.)
- **Look at the *Solve* step. What operation is used to describe the pattern?** (addition) **Is the same number added each time?** (no) **How would you describe the pattern of addends?** (Add $14 to the price of 1 photo package; then add $1 less than that each time the pattern increases.) **How can we apply the pattern to solve the problem?** (Find the cost of 5 photo packages first, then apply the pattern again to find the cost of 6.)
- **Look at the *Look Back* step. Why can't we multiply the cost of 1 package by 6 to check whether the answer makes sense?** (because the pattern does not use multiples of $15)

Common Error

- **Not continuing a pattern far enough** Some students may correctly determine a numerical pattern, but give the next number as their answer rather than a number later in the pattern sequence.
- **Intervention** Suggest that these students present their solution in a simple table with enough rows to show *all* the intermediate steps in the pattern until they reach the target position.

Lesson 5

Problem-Solving Strategy

Find a Pattern

Objective Use patterns to solve problems.

Problem An ice-skating club orders photos of the year's skating highlights. The sign on the right shows the prices for photo packages. If the pattern continues, how much do 6 packages of photos cost?

Photo Prices

Number of Packages	Price
1	$15.00
2	$29.00
3	$42.00
4	$54.00
5	
6	

UNDERSTAND

These are the facts that you know.

- 1 package costs $15.00.
- 2 packages cost $29.00.
- 3 packages cost $42.00.
- 4 packages cost $54.00.

PLAN

You can find a pattern to help you solve the problem.

SOLVE

Find the pattern.

$15.00 → + $14.00 → $29.00 → + $13.00 → $42.00 → + $12.00 → $54.00

The pattern is: Add $14.00 to the first amount and $1.00 less to each amount after that.

Now use the pattern to solve the problem.

- First, find the cost of 5 packages.
  Add $11.00 to the cost of 4 packages.
  $54.00 + $11.00 = $65.00
- Then find the cost of 6 packages.
  Add $10.00 to the cost of 5 packages.
  $65.00 + $10.00 = $75.00

Solution: It will cost $75.00 for 6 packages.

LOOK BACK

Look back at the problem.

Is your answer reasonable? Tell why.

Yes. The cost for the packages is decreased by $1.00 for each additional package.

PHOTOGRAPHS

554

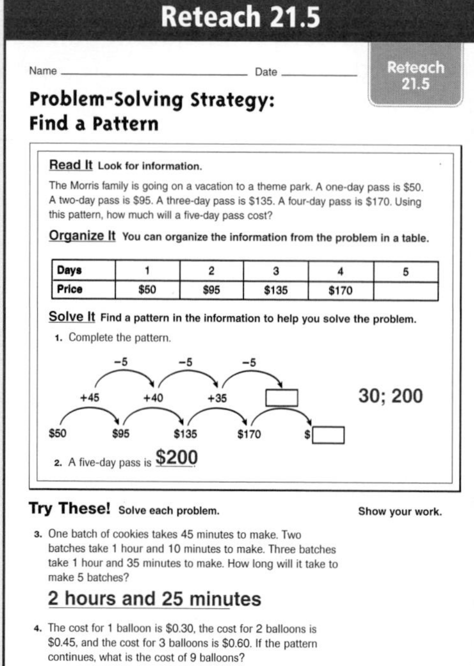

Reteach 21.5

Name ______ Date ______ Reteach 21.5

Problem-Solving Strategy: Find a Pattern

Read It Look for information.

The Morris family is going on a vacation to a theme park. A one-day pass is $50. A two-day pass is $95. A three-day pass is $135. A four-day pass is $170. Using this pattern, how much will a five-day pass cost?

Organize It You can organize the information from the problem in a table.

Days	1	2	3	4	5
Price	$50	$95	$135	$170	

Solve It Find a pattern in the information to help you solve the problem.

1. Complete the pattern.

−5, −5, −5

+45, +40, +35, [ ]

$50, $95, $135, $170, $[ ]

30; 200

2. A five-day pass is $200.

Try These! Solve each problem. **Show your work.**

3. One batch of cookies takes 45 minutes to make. Two batches take 1 hour and 10 minutes to make. Three batches take 1 hour and 35 minutes to make. How long will it take to make 5 batches?
   2 hours and 25 minutes
4. The cost for 1 balloon is $0.30, the cost for 2 balloons is $0.45, and the cost for 3 balloons is $0.60. If the pattern continues, what is the cost of 9 balloons?
   $1.50

Use with text pages 554–556.

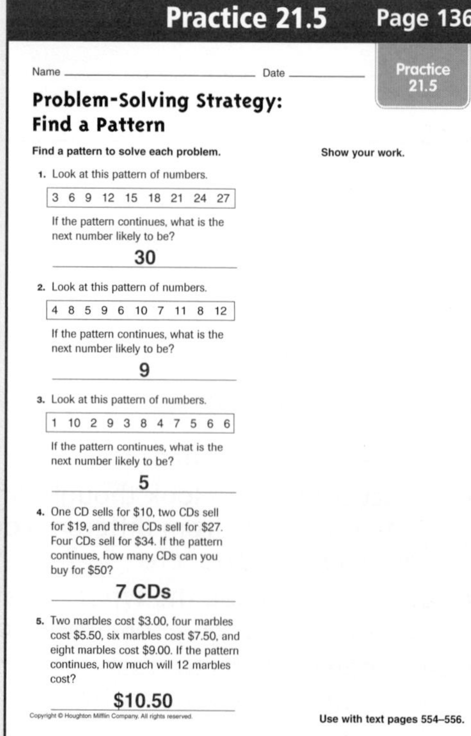

Practice 21.5 Page 136

Name ______ Date ______ Practice 21.5

Problem-Solving Strategy: Find a Pattern

Find a pattern to solve each problem. **Show your work.**

1. Look at this pattern of numbers.
   3 6 9 12 15 18 21 24 27
   If the pattern continues, what is the next number likely to be?
   30
2. Look at this pattern of numbers.
   4 8 5 9 6 10 7 11 8 12
   If the pattern continues, what is the next number likely to be?
   9
3. Look at this pattern of numbers.
   1 10 2 9 3 8 4 7 5 6 6
   If the pattern continues, what is the next number likely to be?
   5
4. One CD sells for $10, two CDs sell for $19, and three CDs sell for $27. Four CDs sell for $34. If the pattern continues, how many CDs can you buy for $50?
   7 CDs
5. Two marbles cost $3.00, four marbles cost $5.50, six marbles cost $7.50, and eight marbles cost $9.00. If the pattern continues, how much will 12 marbles cost?
   $10.50

Use with text pages 554–556.

Guided Practice

Use the Ask Yourself questions to help you solve each problem.

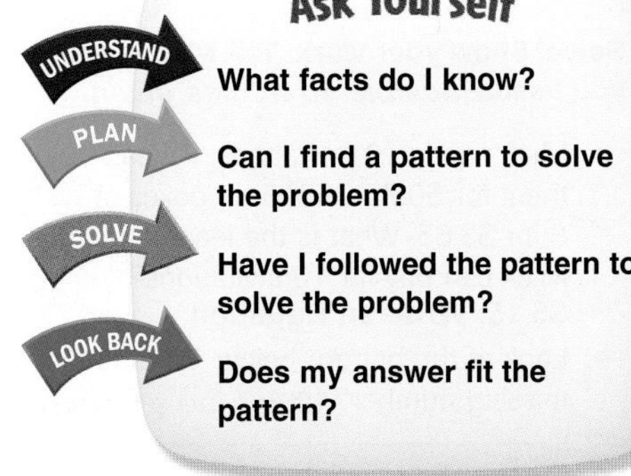

Ask Yourself
UNDERSTAND
What facts do I know?
PLAN
Can I find a pattern to solve the problem?
SOLVE
Have I followed the pattern to solve the problem?
LOOK BACK
Does my answer fit the pattern?

1. Look at this pattern of numbers.

4	7	6	9	8	11	10	13	12

   If the pattern continues, what is the next number likely to be? **15**

   Hint The pattern is: +■, −■.

2. One skating photo enlargement costs \$3.50, two cost \$5.75, three cost \$8.00, and four cost \$10.25. If the pattern continues, what is likely to be the cost of seven enlargements? **\$17.00**

Independent Practice

Find a pattern to solve each problem.

3. Look at this pattern of numbers.

4	8	12	16	20	24	28	32

   If the pattern continues, what is the next number likely to be? **36**

4. Look at this pattern of numbers.

2	6	4	12	10	30	28

   If the pattern continues, what is the next number likely to be? **84**

5. One wallet-sized photo sells for \$1.00, two wallet-sized photos sell for \$1.75, and three sell for \$2.50. If this pattern continues, how many wallet-sized photos can you buy for \$5.00? **6 wallet-sized photos**

6. One pair of skate laces costs \$5.75, two pairs cost \$10.00, three pairs cost \$14.25, and four pairs cost \$18.50. If the pattern continues, how much will eight pairs cost? **\$35.50**

7. **Create and Solve** Make up your own number pattern. Have a classmate find the rule and name the next number in the pattern. ***Check students' problems.***

Go On

Guided Practice

Have students complete **Problems 1–2** as you observe. Remind them to use the *Ask Yourself* questions to help.

❸ Practice

Independent Practice

Select from **Problems 3–15** as independent work.

Enrichment 21.5

Name ______________ Date ________ Enrichment 21.5

Problem-Solving Strategy: Find a Pattern

Problem Look at the pattern below.

1.2 2.4 3.7 5.1 6.6 ____ 9.9

1. Describe the pattern and find the missing number. **Add 1.2 to the first number, 1.3 to the next, 1.4 to the next, etc.; 8.2.**
2. Continue the pattern to find the next three numbers. **11.7, 13.6, 15.6**
3. If the pattern represents the height of a plant in inches over a 7-week period, how tall was the plant the third week? Explain how you found your answer. **3.7 inches; explanations may vary.**

Problem Jerome made a pattern with numbers. He started with the number 4. He added 3.5 to get the next number. He subtracted 1.5 to get the next number. Then, he repeated the pattern.

4. Write the first ten numbers of the pattern. **4.0, 7.5, 6.0, 9.5, 8.0, 11.5, 10.0, 13.5, 12.0, 15.5**
5. Make up your own number pattern that involves addition. Explain your pattern and write the first 6 numbers. **Answers may vary. Check students' patterns.**
6. Make up your own number pattern that involves subtraction. Explain your pattern and write the first 6 numbers. **Answers may vary. Check students' patterns.**

Use with text pages 554–556.

Problem Solving 21.5

Name ______________ Date ________ Problem Solving 21.5

Problem-Solving Strategy: Find a Pattern

Problem The dance team is ordering costumes from a catalog. The catalog charges a shipping and handling fee depending on the number of costumes ordered. The chart shows the shipping and handling fee. If the pattern continues, what will be the shipping and handling fee for 7 costumes?

Number of Costumes	Fee
1	\$8.00
2	\$15.50
3	\$22.50
4	\$29.00
5	\$35.00
6	
7	

UNDERSTAND

1. How many patterns do you need to find? What quanties are in the patterns? **Two; the number of costumes and the fee**

PLAN

2. Does the pattern involve addition or subtraction? How can you tell? **Addition; the fee increases with each costume ordered.**

SOLVE

3. What is the shipping and handling fee for 6 costumes? 7 costumes? **\$40.50; \$45.50**

LOOK BACK

4. Tell why your answer is reasonable. **Possible answer: The cost for shipping and handling decreases by \$0.50 for each additional costume.**

Use with text pages 554–556.

Mixed Problem Solving

Problems 8–10 Remind students that they can use any strategy listed in the box, or a combination of them, to solve.

- ***Problem 10*** Have students share and discuss their work.

Data In **Problem 15,** ask students what they think Antonia meant by using *C* to begin her equation. (cost)

Have students review their answers to make sure they have

- Expressed the solution clearly.
- Used appropriate mathematical notation and terms.
- Supported their solution with verbal and symbolic work.
- Determined the reasonableness of the solution in the context of the original problem.

Mixed Problem Solving

Solve. Show your work. Tell what strategy you used. ***Possible strategies given.***

8. Mick needs 10 invitations. He can buy them for $0.75 each or in boxes of 8 for $3.65. What is the least amount Mick can pay for 10 invitations?
$5.15; Write an Equation

9. Look at the pattern below. What is the missing number? **12.4; Find a Pattern**

3.1	6.2	9.3	____	15.5

10. John cut a 12 foot board into 3 pieces. The first piece is as long as the second and third pieces together. The third piece is half as long as the second piece. How long is each piece?
first piece is 6 ft; second piece is 4 ft; third piece is 2 ft; Draw a Picture

You Choose

Strategy
- Draw a Picture
- Find a Pattern
- Solve a Simpler Problem
- Write an Equation

Computation Method
- Mental Math
- Estimation
- Paper and Pencil
- Calculator

Data **The sign shows the prices for renting a bike. Use the sign to solve Problems 11–15.**

11. What is the cost of renting a bike for 3 hours? **$10**

12. What is the cost of renting a bike for 2 weeks and 1 day? **$137**

13. Marcy rents a bike for 7 hours. How much less is the daily rate than the hourly rate? **$1**

14. Manuel rents a bike at 10:30 A.M. and returns it the same day at 2:30 P.M. How much does he pay? **$12**

15. **Analyze** Antonia used this equation to find her cost of renting a bike.

$$C = 6 + (4 \times 2)$$

How long did she rent the bike? **5 hours**

Bob's Bike Shop
Rental Rates
First hour $ 6
Each additional hour $ 2
All day $17
Three days $35
Weekly $60

556

Homework 21.5 **Page 136**

Name ________________ Date ________

Homework 21.5

Problem-Solving Strategy: Find a Pattern

Find a pattern to solve each problem.

Look at this pattern of numbers.

7 12 18 25 33 42 52 63

If the pattern continues, what is the next number likely to be?

What is the difference between each number and the following number?

7 + **5** = 12
12 + **6** = 18
18 + **7** = 25
25 + **8** = 33
33 + **9** = 42
42 + **10** = 52
52 + **11** = 63

Use the pattern to find the next number.

63 + **12** = 75

The next number is 75.

1. One book sells for $8, two books sell for $15.50, and three books sell for $22.50. If the pattern continues, how many books can you buy for $35?
5 books

2. Look at this pattern of numbers.

91 82 73 64 55 46 37

If the pattern continues, what is the next number likely to be?
28

Show your work.

Use with text pages 554–556.

Problem Solving on Tests

Multiple Choice

Choose the letter of the correct answer. If the correct answer is not here, choose NH.

1. Ethan mixes $\frac{3}{4}$ gallon of orange juice with $\frac{1}{4}$ gallon of cranberry juice. How much juice does he now have?

   A $\frac{2}{8}$ gallon **C** $\frac{4}{8}$ gallon

   B $\frac{3}{8}$ gallon **(D)** 1 gallon

   (Chapter 20, Lesson 1)

2. A piece of cardboard is 0.015 inch thick. Which shows 0.015 in word form?

   F fifteen thousand

   G fifteen hundredths

   (H) fifteen thousandths

   J NH

   (Chapter 21, Lesson 2)

See Additional Answers.

Open Response

Solve each problem.

3. What is the area of a room that is 12 ft by 14 ft? **168 ft²**

   (Chapter 18, Lesson 4)

4. Gloria collected 3 kinds of toys for a toy drive. Of the toys, $\frac{2}{5}$ were cars, $\frac{1}{5}$ were puppets, and 10 were dolls. How many toys did Gloria collect?

   Represent Support your solution with pictures.

   (Chapter 19, Lesson 6)

Extended Response

5. Mrs. Stewart has $40 to buy food and party supplies for 28 people.

Food and Party Supplies	
Ice Cream ($\frac{1}{2}$ gal)	$3.89
Lemonade (1 gal)	$1.98 (serves 16)
Chips	$2.85
Napkins	$3.49
Plastic Spoons	$0.89 (package of 12)
Paper Plates	$2.99 (package of 15)
Plastic Cups	$0.69 (package of 8)

   a. Mrs. Stewart wants to buy 4 half gallons of ice cream, 3 bags of chips, 1 package of napkins, and enough lemonade, plastic spoons, paper plates, and cups for 28 people. Does she have enough money? How do you know?

   b. Plan a party for your class using the table above as a guide for your purchases. If each person is served 1 cup of ice cream, how many $\frac{1}{2}$ gallon containers of ice cream will you need to buy? Decide what you will buy and how much it will cost.

See Additional Answers. (Chapter 7)

Education Place

Check out **eduplace.com/map** for more test prep practice.

Chapter 21 Lesson 5 **557**

Problem Solving on Tests

Problem Solving on Tests provides an opportunity for students to apply previously learned skills in the types of problem contexts typically encountered in standardized tests. ***Problem Solving on Tests*** includes practice in a variety of formats: multiple choice, extended response, and open response.

Students will gain experience in writing about mathematics and using various representations to solve problems. Discuss students' solutions. Have several students explain the thinking behind their work.

More test prep practice is available on Houghton Mifflin's web site, **Education Place**. Go to www.eduplace.com/map.

4 Assess & Close

Math Talk in Action

- **Compare and contrast number patterns and geometric patterns.** (In both, something changes in a regular way. In number patterns, you look for operations that cause the changes; in geometric patterns, you look for changes in shape, color, orientation, or other visual features.)
- **What can you do to help recognize a pattern in a series of numbers?** Listen for responses that show a need to compare adjacent numbers in the pattern to decide how addition, subtraction, multiplication, or division is used to change the numbers.

Math Journal Prompt

Have students create an original number pattern and a story problem that involves applying it.

Lesson Quiz

Use the quiz on Lesson Transparency 21.5.

Test Prep & Spiral Review

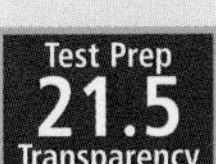

Use Test Prep Transparency 21.5.

Lesson 21.6

Compare and Order Decimals

Planning

Lesson Objective Compare and order decimals and recognize equivalent decimals.

Technology Resources

- *Ways to Success* CD-ROM: 21.6
- Education Place: Extra Practice, eGames www.eduplace.com/map

Lesson 21.6 Transparency

Problem of the Day

Add a decimal point to both numbers to make each statement true.

- 25 = 250 (2.5 = 2.50)
- 678 < 678 (6.78 < 67.8)
- 409 > 409 (40.9 > 4.09)

Spiral Review

Order the numbers from greatest to least.

1. 889 898 888 890 (898, 890, 889, 888)
2. \$4.30 \$4 \$4.27 \$4.32 (\$4.32, \$4.30, \$4.27, \$4)
3. $1\frac{1}{2}$ $2\frac{1}{8}$ 2 $2\frac{1}{4}$ ($2\frac{1}{4}$, $2\frac{1}{8}$, 2, $1\frac{1}{2}$)
4. 5,864 5,871 5,846 (5,871; 5,864; 5,846)

Lesson Quiz

Order the numbers from greatest to least.

1. 3.14 3.16 3.61 3.46 (3.61, 3.46, 3.16, 3.14)
2. 7.03 7.3 7.0 7.12 (7.3, 7.12, 7.03, 7.0)
3. 4.15 5.01 15.04 5 (15.04, 5.01, 5, 4.15)

NCTM Standards

Number and Operations: Understand the place-value structure of the base-ten number system and be able to represent and compare whole numbers and decimals.

Getting Started

Building Math Vocabulary

You may wish to review this word with students.

compare to decide if one number is greater then, less than, or equal to another number

Decimals Greater or Less Than One

Whole Class	15 minutes
Objective	Compare decimals.
Materials	Grid paper
Visual	

- Review decimals greater and less than 1 by having volunteers contribute to a table like the one shown. Have them write decimals to tenths, hundredths, and thousandths in both columns.

Decimals < 1	*Decimals > 1*

- **How could we tell which is the greatest decimal listed? The least decimal?** (Compare them by place.) Tell students that in this lesson they will learn to compare and order decimals. Also, remind them that they can put zeros in all the empty decimal places.
- Students will compare and order decimals using number lines and place-value charts on page 558.

Differentiated Instruction

English Learners

Pairs	20 minutes
Objective	Compare and order decimals.
Materials	Student page 559
Auditory, Visual	

Early Production

- Changing decimals into dollar amounts can help students better understand their value.
- For ***Guided Practice,*** have students use one of the ways explained in ***Learn About It*** to find the answer. They can check their work by saying the decimals as dollar amounts and then comparing.

Intermediate/Advanced

- English Learner Resource 21.6
- English Learner Handbook

Intervention

Small Groups	10 minutes
Objective	Compare and order decimals.
Materials	Decimal place-value chart, number cards 0–9
Visual	

- Students have compared and ordered whole numbers of varying magnitude by aligning like places and looking at the greatest place first. Point out that to compare and order decimals, they use the same method, but they should be careful to align at the decimal point, not the leftmost place value.
- Have students use a decimal place-value chart and number cards to build the decimals they must compare and order to solve **Exercises 1–14.**

Other Resources

- *Ways to Success* CD-ROM 21.6

Inclusion

Whole Class	30 minutes
Objective	Compare and order decimals.
Materials	Masking tape
Visual, Auditory	

- Make a decimal number line on the floor by marking a long piece of masking tape into tenths. Label it from 0.0 to 2.0.
- As students compare decimals, have two of them stand at the values on the number line to see which number is farther to the right (greater).

Social Studies Connection

Materials: Almanac

- The U.S. Department of Education collects data on America's schools, including the rate of graduation from high schools, listed by state.
- Help students find data about graduation rates, given as a decimal, in an almanac. Have them list the rate for your state and three others, and rank them in order from the greatest percent of graduates to the least.

Pattern Practice

On the board, write a fraction pattern such as: $\frac{1}{3}$, _, $\frac{2}{3}$, $\frac{5}{6}$, 1. Ask students to identify the pattern rule and name the missing fraction in the pattern. ($+\frac{1}{6}$, $\frac{1}{2}$) If time permits, have students continue the pattern.

❶ Introduce

Explain to students that by using the number lines and place-value charts on page 558, they will learn about ordering and comparing decimals greater and less than one.

❷ Teach

Learn About It

- **Look at *Way 1*. When we compare these decimals, why does it help to line up the decimal points?** (to be sure to compare digits in the same places) **Why do we begin in the ones place?** (it is the greatest place)
- **Look at *Way 2*. How does the number line help us?** (the farther right, the greater the number)
- **Look at *Another Example*. How do we compare decimals that have different numbers of places?** (Line up the decimal points, begin in the greatest place, and then compare.)

Guided Practice

Have students complete **Exercises 1–5** as you observe. Remind them to use the ***Ask Yourself*** questions to help. Give students the opportunity to talk about the question in ***Explain Your Thinking.***

Common Error

- **Misaligning places** Sometimes students fail to align decimal points when they compare and order decimals.
- **Intervention** Suggest that they write the decimals in a decimal place-value chart, on grid paper, or on lined paper turned sideways.

Lesson 6

Compare and Order Decimals

Objective Compare and order decimals and recognize equivalent decimals.

3.9

4.0

4.6

4.8

Learn About It

At a diving meet, Sue earned these scores. What are her highest and lowest scores? What is the order of the scores from least to greatest?

Different Ways to Compare and Order Decimals

Way 1 Use a place-value chart.

- Line up the decimal points.
- Start comparing in the ones place. 3 < 4. So, 3.9 is the least.
- Continue comparing in the tenths place. 8 > 6 > 0. So, 4.8 is the greatest.

ones		tenths
4	.	6
3	.	9
4	.	8
4	.	0

4.8 > 4.6 > 4.0 > 3.9

Way 2 Use a number line.

- Locate all the scores on a number line.

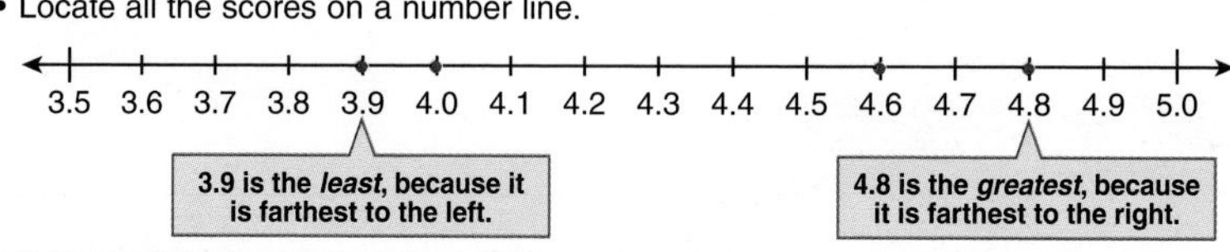

3.5 3.6 3.7 3.8 3.9 4.0 4.1 4.2 4.3 4.4 4.5 4.6 4.7 4.8 4.9 5.0
3.9 is the least, because it is farthest to the left.
4.8 is the greatest, because it is farthest to the right.

Solution: 4.8 is Sue's highest score and 3.9 is her lowest score.
The order of her scores is: 3.9 4.0 4.6 4.8.

Another Example

Order 2.59, 2.5, 2.067, and 2.12 from least to greatest.

- Line up the decimal points.
- Start comparing in the ones place.
- Continue until all are ordered.

ones		tenths	hundredths	thousandths	
2	.	5	9	0	
2	.	5	0	0	2.5 = 2.500
2	.	0	6	7	
2	.	1	2	0	2.12 = 2.120

same | 0 < 1, so 2.067 is the least | 0 < 9 so, 2.500 < 2.590

2.067 < 2.120 < 2.5 < 2.59

558

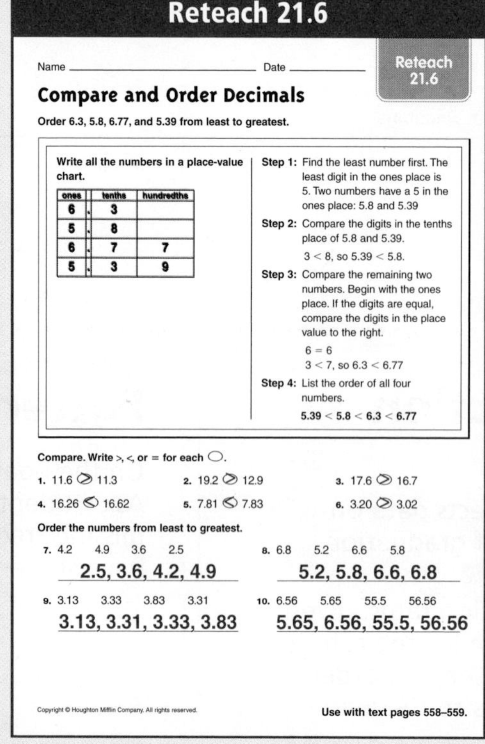

Reteach 21.6

Name ______ Date ______

Reteach 21.6

Compare and Order Decimals

Order 6.3, 5.8, 6.77, and 5.39 from least to greatest.

Write all the numbers in a place-value chart.

ones		tenths	hundredths
6	.	3	
5	.	8	
6	.	7	7
5	.	3	9

Step 1: Find the least number first. The least digit in the ones place is 5. Two numbers have a 5 in the ones place: 5.8 and 5.39

Step 2: Compare the digits in the tenths place of 5.8 and 5.39.
3 < 8, so 5.39 < 5.8.

Step 3: Compare the remaining two numbers. Begin with the ones place. If the digits are equal, compare the digits in the place value to the right.
6 = 6
3 < 7, so 6.3 < 6.77

Step 4: List the order of all four numbers.
5.39 < 5.8 < 6.3 < 6.77

Compare. Write >, <, or = for each ○.

1. 11.6 (>) 11.3
2. 19.2 (>) 12.9
3. 17.6 (>) 16.7
4. 16.26 (<) 16.62
5. 7.81 (<) 7.83
6. 3.20 (>) 3.02

Order the numbers from least to greatest.

7. 4.2 4.9 3.6 2.5
2.5, 3.6, 4.2, 4.9
8. 6.8 5.2 6.6 5.8
5.2, 5.8, 6.6, 6.8
9. 3.13 3.33 3.83 3.31
3.13, 3.31, 3.33, 3.83
10. 6.56 5.65 55.5 56.56
5.65, 6.56, 55.5, 56.56

Use with text pages 558–559.

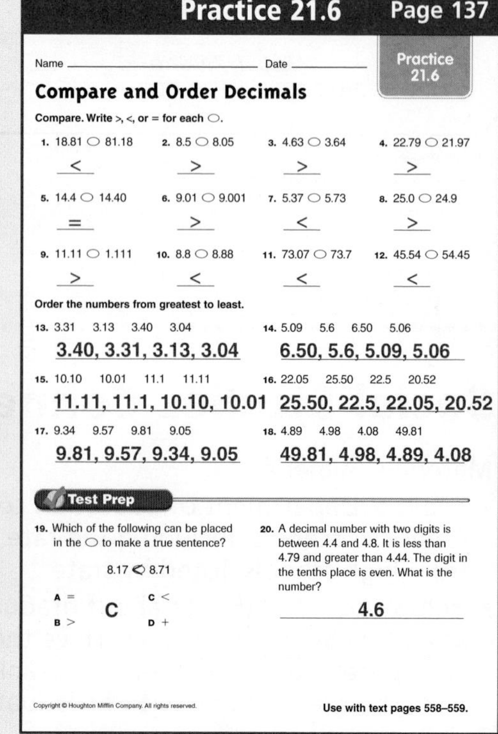

Practice 21.6 Page 137

Name ______ Date ______

Practice 21.6

Compare and Order Decimals

Compare. Write >, <, or = for each ○.

1. 18.81 ○ 81.18 <
2. 8.5 ○ 8.05 >
3. 4.63 ○ 3.64 >
4. 22.79 ○ 21.97 >
5. 14.4 ○ 14.40 =
6. 9.01 ○ 9.001 >
7. 5.37 ○ 5.73 <
8. 25.0 ○ 24.9 >
9. 11.11 ○ 1.111 >
10. 8.8 ○ 8.88 <
11. 73.07 ○ 73.7 <
12. 45.54 ○ 54.45 <

Order the numbers from greatest to least.

13. 3.31 3.13 3.40 3.04
3.40, 3.31, 3.13, 3.04
14. 5.09 5.6 6.50 5.06
6.50, 5.6, 5.09, 5.06
15. 10.10 10.01 11.1 11.11
11.11, 11.1, 10.10, 10.01
16. 22.05 25.50 22.5 20.52
25.50, 22.5, 22.05, 20.52
17. 9.34 9.57 9.81 9.05
9.81, 9.57, 9.34, 9.05
18. 4.89 4.98 4.08 49.81
49.81, 4.98, 4.89, 4.08

Test Prep

19. Which of the following can be placed in the ○ to make a true sentence?
8.17 (<) 8.71
A = B > C < D +
C

20. A decimal number with two digits is between 4.4 and 4.8. It is less than 4.79 and greater than 4.44. The digit in the tenths place is even. What is the number?
4.6

Use with text pages 558–559.

Guided Practice

Compare. Write >, <, or = for each ●.

1. 3.6 ● 3.8 **<**
2. 9.25 ● 8.93 **>**
3. 12.5 ● 12.50 **=**

Order the numbers from least to greatest.

4. 2.9 3.5 3.2 2.3 **2.3 2.9 3.2 3.5**
5. 4.7 4.78 4.73 4.67 **4.67 4.7 4.73 4.78**

Ask Yourself

- Where would each decimal be on a number line?
- What if the numbers do not have the same number of decimal places?

Explain Your Thinking ▶ How is comparing decimals like comparing whole numbers? ***Possible answer:*** **You work from left to right, comparing the value of each digit.**

Practice and Problem Solving

Algebra • Symbols **Compare. Write >, <, or = for each ●.**

6. 7.8 ● 8.7 **<**
7. 24.6 ● 24.58 **>**
8. 6.9 ● 6.90 **=**
9. 21.003 ● 21.300 **<**

Order the numbers from greatest to least.

10. 2.13 2.14 2.24 2.42 **2.42 2.24 2.14 2.13**
11. 9.8 6.9 8.299 9.85 **9.85 9.8 8.299 6.9**
12. 6.24 6.2 6.09 6.9 **6.9 6.24 6.2 6.09**
13. 3.76 3.07 3.7 3.762 **3.762 3.76 3.7 3.07**
14. Four swim teams have scores of 49.5, 50.0, 47.6, and 47.8. What is the order of the scores from least to greatest? **47.6 47.8 49.5 50.0**
15. At a diving meet, Alina's mean score was 4.2 and Carmine's mean score was 3.8. Which girl had the greater average score? **Alina**

16. **Analyze** A decimal number with two digits is between 7.3 and 7.9. It is less than 7.89 and greater than 7.58. The digit in the tenths place is odd. What is the number? **7.7**

Mixed Review and Test Prep

Open Response

Write all the factors of each number.
(Ch. 10, Lesson 1) ***See Additional Answers.***

17. 81
18. 35
19. 18
20. 24
21. 20
22. 15
23. 42
24. 36

Multiple Choice

25. Which of the following can be placed in the ● to make a true sentence? (Ch. 21, Lesson 6)

4.56 ● 4.7

(A) < B > C = D +

Extra Practice See page 565, Set D.

❸ Practice

Practice and Problem Solving

Select from **Exercises 6–25** as independent work.

- ***Problem 16*** Invite students to share their solution strategies.

❹ Assess & Close

Math Talk in Action

- **Explain how to compare 1.4 and 1.43.** Listen for responses that describe locating both numbers on a number line, or comparing them by place values beginning with ones.
- **Which method do you prefer? Explain.** (Accept all reasonable responses.)

Math Journal Prompt

Have students draw a place-value chart to compare and order 27.34, 27.43, 27, and 27.4.

Lesson Quiz

Use the quiz on Lesson Transparency 21.6.

Lesson 21.6 Transparency

Test Prep & Spiral Review

Use Test Prep Transparency 21.6.

Enrichment 21.6

Name ______________ Date ________

Enrichment 21.6

Greatest Decimal Game

Rules:

- **Copy and cut out the digit cards and place them in a bag or face down on a table.**
- **Player 1 draws a card and records the digit on his or her game card. Once a digit is placed, it can not be changed. The card is returned to the bag or table.**
- **Players take turns drawing a card and recording the digit on their game cards until all the spaces are filled in.**
- **The winner is the player with the greatest decimal.**

Note: You can also play the *Least Decimal Game.* The winner is the player with the least decimal.

0	1	2	3	4
5	6	7	8	9

Game Card

0 . ___ ___ ___

1. In this game, what is the greatest possible decimal? What is the least possible decimal?
0.999; 0.000

2. Explain what strategy you used to try to form the greatest decimal number.
Possible answers: I tried to place the greater digit in the tenths place. When I drew a digit greater than 5, I placed it in the tenths place.

Use with text pages 558–559.

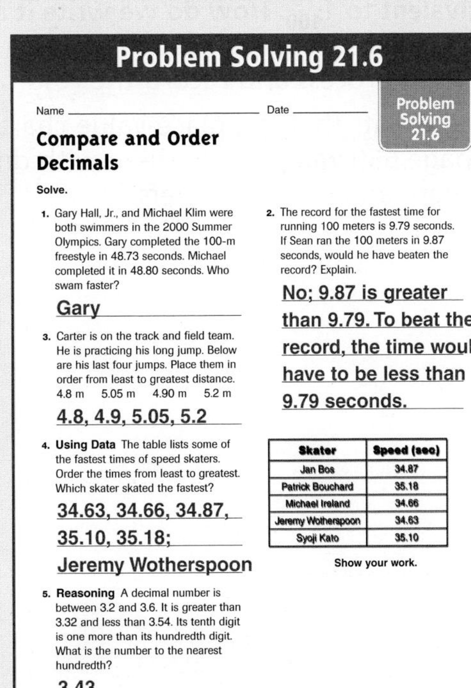

Problem Solving 21.6

Name ______________ Date ________

Problem Solving 21.6

Compare and Order Decimals

Solve.

1. Gary Hall, Jr., and Michael Klim were both swimmers in the 2000 Summer Olympics. Gary completed the 100-m freestyle in 48.73 seconds. Michael completed it in 48.80 seconds. Who swam faster?
Gary

2. The record for the fastest time for running 100 meters is 9.79 seconds. If Sean ran the 100 meters in 9.87 seconds, would he have beaten the record? Explain.
No; 9.87 is greater than 9.79. To beat the record, the time would have to be less than 9.79 seconds.

3. Carter is on the track and field team. He is practicing his long jump. Below are his last four jumps. Place them in order from least to greatest distance.
4.8 m 5.05 m 4.90 m 5.2 m
4.8, 4.9, 5.05, 5.2

4. **Using Data** The table lists some of the fastest times of speed skaters. Order the times from least to greatest. Which skater skated the fastest?
34.63, 34.66, 34.87, 35.10, 35.18; Jeremy Wotherspoon

Skater	Speed (sec)
Jan Bos	34.87
Patrick Bouchard	35.18
Michael Ireland	34.66
Jeremy Wotherspoon	34.63
Syoji Kato	35.10

Show your work.

5. **Reasoning** A decimal number is between 3.2 and 3.6. It is greater than 3.32 and less than 3.54. Its tenth digit is one more than its hundredth digit. What is the number to the nearest hundredth?
3.43

Use with text pages 558–559.

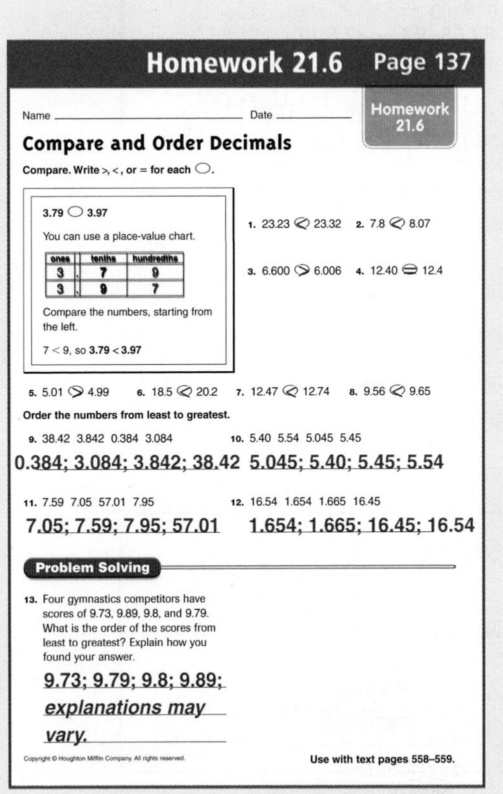

Homework 21.6 Page 137

Name ______________ Date ________

Homework 21.6

Compare and Order Decimals

Compare. Write >, <, or = for each ○.

3.79 ○ 3.97

You can use a place-value chart.

ones	tenths	hundredths
3 .	7	9
3 .	9	7

Compare the numbers, starting from the left.

7 < 9, so **3.79 < 3.97**

1. 23.23 **<** 23.32
2. 7.8 **<** 8.07
3. 6.600 **>** 6.006
4. 12.40 **=** 12.4
5. 5.01 **>** 4.99
6. 18.5 **<** 20.2
7. 12.47 **<** 12.74
8. 9.56 **<** 9.65

Order the numbers from least to greatest.

9. 38.42 3.842 0.384 3.084
0.384; 3.084; 3.842; 38.42

10. 5.40 5.54 5.045 5.45
5.045; 5.40; 5.45; 5.54

11. 7.59 7.05 57.01 7.95
7.05; 7.59; 7.95; 57.01

12. 16.54 1.654 1.665 16.45
1.654; 1.665; 16.45; 16.54

Problem Solving

13. Four gymnastics competitors have scores of 9.73, 9.89, 9.8, and 9.79. What is the order of the scores from least to greatest? Explain how you found your answer.
9.73; 9.79; 9.8; 9.89; *explanations may vary.*

Use with text pages 558–559.

Lesson 21.7

Compare and Order Decimals and Mixed Numbers

Planning

Lesson Objective Compare and order decimals and mixed numbers.

Technology Resources

- Audio Tutor **2**/26 Listen and Understand
- *Ways to Success* CD-ROM 21.7
- Education Place: Extra Practice, eGames www.eduplace.com/map

Lesson 21.7 Transparency

Problem of the Day

Bud was in bed with the flu. When he woke up, his temperature was 100.8 degrees. By noon, the thermometer said 100.5 degrees. Did Bud's fever go up or down? (down)

Spiral Review

Order the numbers from greatest to least.

1. 4.25 4.27 4.72 4.57 (4.72; 4.57; 4.27; 4.25)
2. 8.02 8.2 8.0 8.01 (8.2; 8.02; 8.01; 8.0)
3. 7.39, 8.01, 16.4, 8 (16.4; 8.01; 8; 7.39)

Lesson Quiz

Order the numbers from greatest to least.

1. 3.5 $3\frac{6}{10}$ $3\frac{57}{100}$ 3.9 (3.9; $3\frac{6}{10}$; $3\frac{57}{100}$; 3.5)
2. $87\frac{9}{100}$ 87.65 $87\frac{6}{10}$ 87.5 (87.65; $87\frac{6}{10}$; 87.5; $87\frac{9}{100}$)
3. 111.01 110.11 $111\frac{1}{10}$ $111\frac{11}{100}$ ($111\frac{11}{100}$; $111\frac{1}{10}$; 111.01; 110.11)

NCTM Standards

Number and Operations: Recognize and generate equivalent forms of commonly used fractions, decimals, and percents.
Connections: Recognize and use connections among mathematical ideas.

Getting Started

Building Math Vocabulary

Students should be familiar with the mathematical vocabulary in this lesson.

Ordering Difficult Numbers

Whole Class	20 minutes
Objective	Compare and order decimals and mixed numbers.
Materials	Decimal Place-Value Chart Transparency
Auditory, Visual	

- Display the Decimal Place-Value Chart as shown. Write $1\frac{3}{4}$, 1.45, 1.5, and $1\frac{2}{5}$ to be compared and ordered.

	tens	ones		tenths	hundredths
$1\frac{3}{4}$			.		
1.45			.		
1.5			.		
$1\frac{2}{5}$			.		

- **What makes these numbers difficult to order?** (2 mixed numbers, 2 decimals) **Let's change them all to decimals to compare and order them more easily.**
- Review changing $\frac{3}{4}$ and $\frac{2}{5}$ to decimals; multiply both terms to get a fraction whose denominator is 100 (or 10). **$1\frac{3}{4}$ is equivalent to $1\frac{75}{100}$. How do we write it as a decimal?** (1.75) **What is the decimal equivalent of $1\frac{2}{5}$?** (1.4) Complete the ordering process and record the result.
- Tell students that the place-value chart and number line on page 560 will provide them with different ways to compare and order numbers.

Differentiated Instruction

English Learners

Pairs	20 minutes
Objective	Recognize equilavent fractions and decimals.
Materials	Index cards
Visual, Auditory	

Early Production

- Give students practice converting simple fractions to decimals and memorizing more commonly used equivalent fractions and decimals.
- Write common fractions and their equivalent decimals on the board.
- Have students copy each value on an index card. Students mix the cards and match them, reading the values aloud.

Intermediate/Advanced

- English Learner Resource 21.7
- English Learner Handbook

Intervention

Small Groups	10 minutes
Objective	Write fractions and mixed numbers as decimals and vice versa.
Materials	Learning Tool 36 (Decimal Place-Value Charts)
Visual, Auditory	

- Some students may be unsure whether to change mixed numbers to decimals or decimals to mixed numbers to compare and order a set that includes numbers of each kind.
- Stress that either way works because they are equivalent. Students should use the way they prefer.
- Suggest that students start to memorize common decimal equivalents so they can do some of the conversions mentally.
- Encourage students to draw a decimal place-value chart to help them work.

Other Resources

- *Ways to Success* CD-ROM 21.7

Early Finishers

Small Groups	15 minutes
Objective	Compare and order decimals and mixed numbers.
Materials	None
Visual, Auditory, Tactual	

- Have students solve the following problems.
- Order from least to greatest: 5.05, 5.55, $5\frac{1}{2}$, 5.49, $5\frac{1}{10}$. (5.05; $5\frac{1}{10}$; 5.49; $5\frac{1}{2}$; 5.55)
- Write any three decimals that are between 3.1 and 3.41. (Possible answers: 3.24; 3.2; 3.15)
- Write three decimals greater than $1\frac{9}{10}$ but less than 2.01. (Possible answers: 1.91; 1.92; 2.001)

Alternate Teaching Strategy

- Make two sets of cards for small groups of students. One set has various decimal numbers written and the other set has various fractions and mixed numbers written. All decimals and fractions should have values from 1.0 to 2.0.
- Have one student in each group choose a card from each pile and compare the numbers using a number line or a place-value chart. If the student correctly identifies the greater value, he or she earns 1 point. The next player then has a turn.
- Play continues until all of the cards are used. The player with the greatest number of points wins.

❶ Introduce

Continue to help students develop their proficiency in comparing and ordering decimals and mixed numbers, using place-value charts and number lines.

❷ Teach

Learn About It

- **Have a volunteer read the opening problem aloud. What do you notice about the distances given?** (Some are mixed numbers; some are decimals.)
- **Look at Way 1. How do we use a place-value chart for the mixed numbers?** (Change them to decimals.) **How do we change $\frac{1}{2}$ to a decimal?** (Multiply both terms by 5 for the equivalent fraction $\frac{5}{10}$; then change to the decimal 0.5.) **Compare 1.5 and 1.50.** (They are equivalent.) **When we use a place-value chart to compare decimals, where do we look first?** (in the greatest place, which is ones)
- **Look at Way 2. What do you notice about the way the number line is labeled?** (mixed numbers above each mark, decimals below) **How do numbers on a number line change as you move from left to right?** (Their value increases.) **How do we know where to place $1\frac{1}{4}$?** (Use its decimal equivalents, 1.25.)

Lesson 7

Audio Tutor 2/26 Listen and Understand

Compare and Order Decimals and Mixed Numbers

Objective Compare and order decimals and mixed numbers.

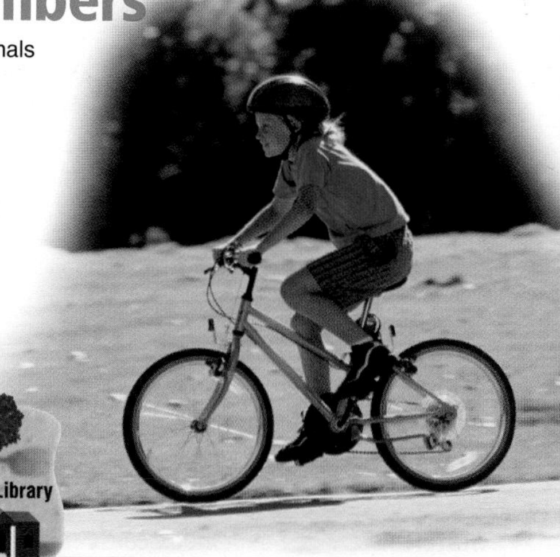

Learn About It

Diane rode her bike $1\frac{1}{2}$ miles to school. Then she rode 1.75 miles to the library. She then rode 1.6 miles to visit her aunt. Her ride home was $1\frac{1}{4}$ miles. What is the order of all the distances from least to greatest?

Different Ways to Compare and Order $1\frac{1}{2}$, 1.75, 1.6, and $1\frac{1}{4}$

Way ❶ Use a place-value chart.

- Change the fractions to decimals.
- Write the decimals in hundredths.
- Compare.

	ones		tenths	hundredths
$1\frac{1}{2}$ mi	1	.	5	0
1.75 mi	1	.	7	5
1.6 mi	1	.	6	0
$1\frac{1}{4}$ mi	1	.	2	5

Way ❷ Use a number line.

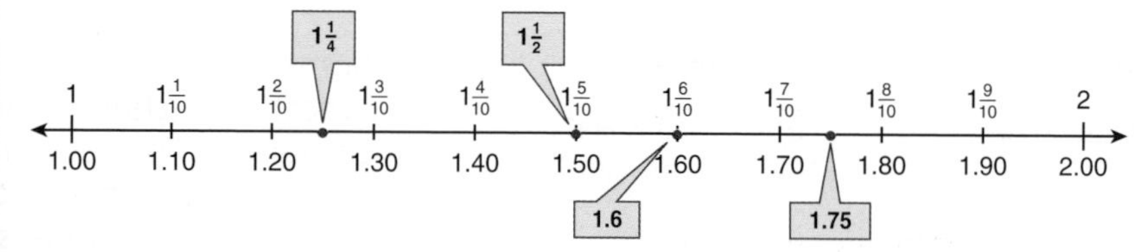

Solution: The order of the distances from least to greatest is:
$1\frac{1}{4}$ miles $1\frac{1}{2}$ miles 1.6 miles 1.75 miles

560

Common Error

- **Comparing fractions incorrectly** Remind students that to compare fractions, the fractions must have like denominators.
- **Intervention** When comparing fractions with decimals, it is easier to convert if the denominators are written as tenths or hundredths.

Reteach 21.7

Name ______________ Date ________ Reteach 21.7

Compare and Order Decimals and Mixed Numbers

Order the numbers from least to greatest: 5.33, 4.89, $6\frac{3}{10}$, $5\frac{88}{100}$.

Number lines can be used to compare and order decimals and mixed numbers.

Place each number on the number line. It helps to label the points with the value.

4.89 5.33 $5\frac{88}{100}$ $6\frac{3}{10}$ — 4 5 6 7

On a number line, numbers increase in value as you move from left to right.

So the order in which the numbers are located on the number line from left to right is their order from least to greatest.

$4.89 < 5.33 < 5\frac{88}{100} < 6\frac{3}{10}$

Compare. Write >, <, or = for each ◯.

1. 7.2 (<) $7\frac{4}{10}$
2. 5.54 (>) $5\frac{4}{10}$
3. 4.33 (<) $43\frac{3}{10}$
4. 1.9 (>) $1\frac{9}{100}$

Order the numbers from least to greatest.

5. $\frac{3}{10}$ 3.3 $\frac{33}{100}$ 3.33 — **$\frac{3}{10}$, $\frac{33}{100}$, 3.3, 3.33**
6. 7.4 $7\frac{44}{100}$ 7.74 $7\frac{4}{100}$ — **$7\frac{4}{100}$, 7.4, $7\frac{44}{100}$, 7.74**
7. 9.6 $9\frac{6}{100}$ 9.61 $9\frac{66}{100}$ — **$9\frac{6}{100}$, 9.6, 9.61, $9\frac{66}{100}$**
8. 2.8 $2\frac{8}{100}$ 2.89 $2\frac{98}{100}$ — **$2\frac{8}{100}$, 2.8, 2.89, $2\frac{98}{100}$**
9. 3.7 $3\frac{7}{100}$ $33\frac{7}{100}$ 3.89 — **$3\frac{7}{100}$, 3.7, 3.89, $33\frac{7}{100}$**
10. 1.54 2.05 $11\frac{5}{100}$ $12\frac{5}{10}$ — **1.54, 2.05, $11\frac{5}{100}$, $12\frac{5}{10}$**

Use with text pages 560–562.

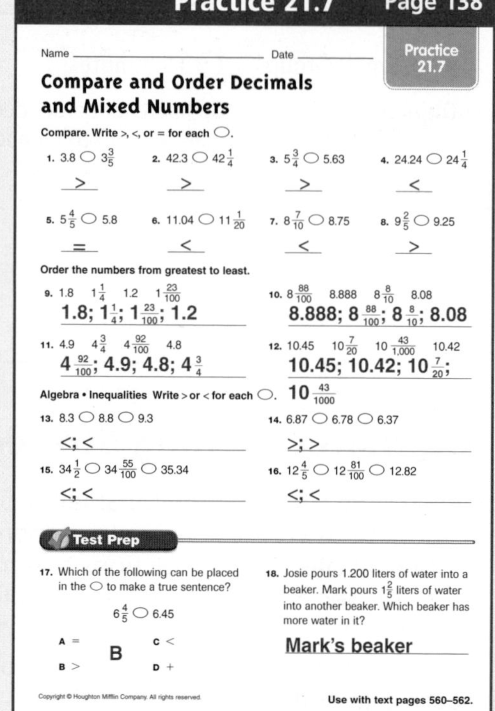

Practice 21.7 Page 138

Name ______________ Date ________ Practice 21.7

Compare and Order Decimals and Mixed Numbers

Compare. Write >, <, or = for each ◯.

1. 3.8 ◯ $3\frac{3}{5}$ **>**
2. 42.3 ◯ $42\frac{1}{4}$ **>**
3. $5\frac{3}{4}$ ◯ 5.63 **>**
4. 24.24 ◯ $24\frac{1}{4}$ **<**
5. $5\frac{4}{5}$ ◯ 5.8 **=**
6. 11.04 ◯ $11\frac{1}{20}$ **<**
7. $8\frac{7}{10}$ ◯ 8.75 **<**
8. $9\frac{2}{5}$ ◯ 9.25 **>**

Order the numbers from greatest to least.

9. 1.8 $1\frac{1}{4}$ 1.2 $1\frac{23}{100}$ — **1.8; $1\frac{1}{4}$; $1\frac{23}{100}$; 1.2**
10. $8\frac{88}{100}$ 8.888 $8\frac{8}{10}$ 8.08 — **8.888; $8\frac{88}{100}$; $8\frac{8}{10}$; 8.08**
11. 4.9 $4\frac{3}{4}$ $4\frac{92}{100}$ 4.8 — **$4\frac{92}{100}$; 4.9; 4.8; $4\frac{3}{4}$**
12. 10.45 $10\frac{7}{20}$ $10\frac{43}{1,000}$ 10.42 — **10.45; 10.42; $10\frac{7}{20}$; $10\frac{43}{1000}$**

Algebra • Inequalities Write > or < for each ◯.

13. 8.3 ◯ 8.8 ◯ 9.3 **<; <**
14. 6.87 ◯ 6.78 ◯ 6.37 **>; >**
15. $34\frac{1}{2}$ ◯ $34\frac{55}{100}$ ◯ 35.34 **<; <**
16. $12\frac{4}{5}$ ◯ $12\frac{81}{100}$ ◯ 12.82 **<; <**

Test Prep

17. Which of the following can be placed in the ◯ to make a true sentence?

    $6\frac{4}{5}$ ◯ 6.45

    A = B > C < D + **B**

18. Josie pours 1.200 liters of water into a beaker. Mark pours $1\frac{2}{5}$ liters of water into another beaker. Which beaker has more water in it? **Mark's beaker**

Use with text pages 560–562.

Guided Practice

Compare. Write >, <, or = for each ⬬.

1. $1\frac{3}{4}$ ⬬ 1.8 <
2. $3\frac{1}{2}$ ⬬ 3.21 >
3. $1\frac{1}{4}$ ⬬ 1.25 =

Order the numbers from least to greatest.

4. 1.4 $1\frac{9}{10}$ 1.05 $1\frac{15}{100}$
   1.05 $1\frac{15}{100}$ 1.4 $1\frac{9}{10}$
5. $\frac{25}{100}$ 6.1 4.26 $5\frac{8}{10}$
   $\frac{25}{100}$ 4.26 $5\frac{8}{10}$ 6.1

Ask Yourself

- Do I use a number line or place value?
- Do I start with the digit in the least place or in the greatest place?

Explain Your Thinking ▶ In Exercise 4, did you use a number line or a place-value chart? Explain your choice.
Possible answer: **A number line, because the numbers were between 1 and 2.**

Practice and Problem Solving

Compare. Write >, <, or = for each ⬬.

6. 2.9 ⬬ $2\frac{3}{4}$ >
7. 46.7 ⬬ $46\frac{1}{2}$ >
8. 35.7 ⬬ $53\frac{1}{5}$ <
9. 34.5 ⬬ 34.26 >
10. 8.6 ⬬ $8\frac{2}{5}$ >
11. $3\frac{1}{10}$ ⬬ 3.18 <
12. 4.5 ⬬ $4\frac{1}{2}$ =
13. 3.7 ⬬ 3.70 =

Order the numbers from greatest to least.

14. $1\frac{5}{10}$ 1.9 $1\frac{36}{100}$ 1.63
    1.9 1.63 $1\frac{5}{10}$ $1\frac{36}{100}$
15. $15\frac{3}{100}$ 18.05 12.9 $19\frac{1}{10}$
    $19\frac{1}{10}$ 18.05 $15\frac{3}{100}$ 12.9
16. 23.4 $23\frac{4}{100}$ $24\frac{3}{10}$ 23.34
    $24\frac{3}{10}$ 23.4 23.34 $23\frac{4}{100}$
17. 352.02 293.2 $352\frac{2}{10}$ $293\frac{2}{100}$
    $352\frac{2}{10}$ 352.02 293.2 $293\frac{2}{100}$

Algebra • Symbols Write >, <, or = for each ⬬.

18. 5.2 ⬬ 5.9 ⬬ 7.8 < <
19. 6.5 ⬬ $6\frac{1}{2}$ ⬬ 6.05 = >
20. 5.95 ⬬ 5.29 ⬬ 4.22 > >
21. 3.1 ⬬ $3\frac{1}{2}$ ⬬ $2\frac{1}{2}$ < >
22. 4.6 ⬬ $4\frac{3}{4}$ ⬬ 4.1 < >
23. 2.09 ⬬ 2.25 ⬬ $2\frac{1}{10}$ < >

24. **You Decide** Choose any four numbers from below. Then order them from least to greatest. ***Check students' work.***

Go On

Guided Practice

Have students complete **Exercises 1–5** as you observe. Remind them to use the ***Ask Yourself*** question to help. Give students an opportunity to talk about the question in ***Explain Your Thinking***.

3 Practice

Practice and Problem Solving

Select from **Exercises 6–39** as independent work.

- ***Algebra • Symbols*** Review the inequality symbols as needed. Point out to students that they must write two symbols to complete Exercises 18–23.
- ***Problem 24*** Extend by having students order all the given numbers from least to greatest. (6.02, 6.09, 6.2, $6\frac{1}{4}$, 6.3, $6\frac{1}{2}$, 6.75)

Enrichment 21.7

Name ____________ Date ________ Enrichment 21.7

Doll Repairs

Doreen's Doll Shop has to fix 5 sets of dolls. Each of the sets has 8 dolls that look the same except that each doll is slightly larger than the one before. Doreen has to list the dolls in order by height so that she can order the proper parts to fix each one. The dolls are grouped by their colors. Help Doreen put the dolls in each group in order from shortest to tallest. List the height of each doll in the table.

Group	1	2	3	4	5	6	7	8
Red	0.8 dm	$\frac{82}{100}$ dm	$\frac{7}{10}$ dm	0.9 dm	$\frac{1}{2}$ dm	0.85 dm	$\frac{93}{100}$ dm	1.0 dm
Blue	$\frac{1}{2}$ dm	0.4 dm	$\frac{66}{100}$ dm	0.37 dm	$\frac{3}{10}$ dm	0.55 dm	$\frac{6}{10}$ dm	$\frac{59}{100}$ dm
Green	$\frac{9}{10}$ dm	0.6 dm	1.0 dm	0.4 dm	$\frac{75}{100}$ dm	0.8 dm	$\frac{7}{10}$ dm	$\frac{68}{100}$ dm
Violet	0.1 dm	$\frac{25}{100}$ dm	0.16 dm	$\frac{2}{10}$ dm	$\frac{15}{100}$ dm	0.01 dm	0.3 dm	0.21 dm
Orange	1.0 dm	$1\frac{3}{4}$ dm	1.6 dm	0.95 dm	0.99 dm	0.87 dm	1.1 dm	$1\frac{1}{2}$ dm

Group	shortest	next tallest	next tallest	next tallest	next tallest	next tallest	next tallest	tallest
Red	$\frac{1}{2}$ dm	$\frac{7}{10}$ dm	0.8 dm	$\frac{82}{100}$ dm	0.85 dm	0.9 dm	$\frac{93}{100}$ dm	1.0 dm
Blue	$\frac{3}{10}$ dm	0.37 dm	0.4 dm	$\frac{1}{2}$ dm	0.55 dm	$\frac{59}{100}$ dm	$\frac{6}{10}$ dm	$\frac{66}{100}$ dm
Green	0.4 dm	0.6 dm	$\frac{68}{100}$ dm	$\frac{7}{10}$ dm	$\frac{75}{100}$ dm	0.8 dm	$\frac{9}{10}$ dm	1.0 dm
Violet	0.01 dm	0.1 dm	$\frac{15}{100}$ dm	0.16 dm	$\frac{2}{10}$ dm	0.21 dm	$\frac{25}{100}$ dm	0.3 dm
Orange	0.87 dm	0.95 dm	0.99 dm	1.0 dm	1.1 dm	$1\frac{1}{2}$ dm	1.6 dm	$1\frac{3}{4}$ dm

Use with text pages 560–562.

Problem Solving 21.7

Name ____________ Date ________ Problem Solving 21.7

Compare and Order Decimals and Mixed Numbers

Solve. **Show your work.**

1. Ciera walked $3\frac{1}{4}$ miles on Saturday. She walked 3.4 miles on Sunday. Did Ciera walk farther on Saturday or Sunday?
   Sunday
2. Joel's family is planning a hiking trip. There are four different trails they can hike. The first day, they want to hike the shortest trail. The last day, they want to hike the longest trail. Which trail should they hike the first day? The last day?
   Big Tree; Rocky Hills

Trail	Distance
Rocky Hills	6.85 miles
Pepperback	$6\frac{3}{4}$ miles
Big Tree	6.7 miles
Moonriser	$6\frac{4}{5}$ miles

3. Benjamin is $4\frac{3}{4}$ feet tall. His brother is 4.67 feet tall. Who is taller?
   Benjamin
4. Last night, Rachel slept $8\frac{13}{20}$ hours. Her sister slept 8.5 hours. Her brother slept $8\frac{3}{4}$ hours. Who slept the longest?
   Rachel's brother
5. **Reasoning** How can you quickly order these numbers from least to greatest without changing them all to fractions or decimals?
   $2\frac{5}{6}$ 1.98 3.25 $\frac{7}{8}$ $4\frac{1}{4}$
   Look at the whole number. All the numbers have different ones digits, so you can order them as you would whole numbers.

Use with text pages 560–562.

- ***Problem 28*** Ask: **What makes this a multi-step problem?** (First you multiply to find the total number of seats; then you multiply that number by the cost of entrance.)
- ***Data*** Ask: **What interval is used to mark the bar graph?** (0.04) **Why is there a jagged line at the bottom of the scale?** (to show that part of the scale has been omitted)

4 Assess & Close

Math Talk in Action

- **Explain how to compare and order $3\frac{43}{100}$, 3.62, and 3.5.** Listen for responses that describe how to change the mixed numbers to equivalent decimals (or vice versa) and locate them on a number line, or convert all to decimals and use a place-value chart to compare and order.

Math Journal Prompt

Have students explain which method of comparing and ordering fractions, mixed numbers, and decimals they prefer—the number line or the place-value chart. Have them explain their preference using an example.

Lesson Quiz

Use the quiz on Lesson Transparency 21.7.

Test Prep & Spiral Review

Use Test Prep Transparency 21.7.

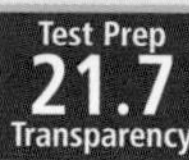

Solve.

25. **Mental Math** Bob can ride a mile in 8 minutes. If he rides at the same speed, how long will it take to ride $1\frac{1}{2}$ miles? **12 minutes**
26. Suppose Sasha starts riding her bike at 10:30 A.M. and ends at 2:00 P.M. How long does she ride her bike? **$3\frac{1}{2}$ hours**
27. **Measurement** A bicycle rally was held at a town park. The park measures 450 feet long and 700 feet wide. What is the area of the park? **315,000 square feet**
28. **Money** The entrance fee to the bleachers at the bike race is \$5.00. There are 10 rows of seats and each row has 14 seats. If all the seats are filled, how much money is collected? **\$700.00**

Data **The bar graph shows the best standing long jumps for five students. Use the graph for Problems 29–34.**

29. Which of the five students jumped the farthest? How far did he jump? **David; 1.79 meters**
30. Which student's farthest jump was 1.68 meters? **Kyle**
31. Which student's farthest jump was 1.58 meters? **Luke**
32. Which student jumped closest to 2 meters? **David**
33. Which student jumped closest to $1\frac{1}{2}$ meters? **Luke**
34. **Analyze** David says that the graph shows that he jumped about twice as far as Jim. Do you agree? Why or why not? ***Possible answer:*** **No. David's jump was under 2 meters and each boy jumped more than $1\frac{1}{2}$ meter. No one jumped less than one meter.**

562

Homework 21.7 **Page 138**

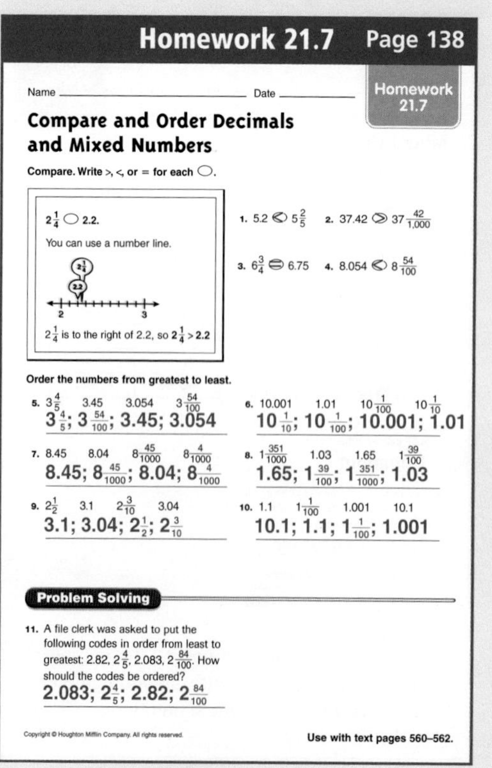

Name ______________ Date ______________

Homework 21.7

Compare and Order Decimals and Mixed Numbers

Compare. Write >, <, or = for each ◯.

$2\frac{1}{4}$ ◯ 2.2.

You can use a number line.

$2\frac{1}{4}$ is to the right of 2.2, so $2\frac{1}{4} > 2.2$

1. 5.2 $<$ $5\frac{2}{5}$
2. 37.42 $>$ $37\frac{42}{1,000}$
3. $6\frac{3}{4}$ $=$ 6.75
4. 8.054 $<$ $8\frac{54}{100}$

Order the numbers from greatest to least.

5. $3\frac{4}{5}$ 3.45 3.054 $3\frac{54}{100}$
   $3\frac{4}{5}$; $3\frac{54}{100}$; 3.45; 3.054
6. 10.001 1.01 $10\frac{1}{100}$ $10\frac{1}{10}$
   $10\frac{1}{10}$; $10\frac{1}{100}$; 10.001; 1.01
7. 8.45 8.04 $8\frac{45}{1000}$ $8\frac{4}{1000}$
   8.45; $8\frac{45}{1000}$; 8.04; $8\frac{4}{1000}$
8. $1\frac{351}{1000}$ 1.03 1.65 $1\frac{39}{100}$
   1.65; $1\frac{39}{100}$; $1\frac{351}{1000}$; 1.03
9. $2\frac{1}{2}$ 3.1 $2\frac{3}{10}$ 3.04
   3.1; 3.04; $2\frac{1}{2}$; $2\frac{3}{10}$
10. 1.1 $1\frac{1}{100}$ 1.001 10.1
   10.1; 1.1; $1\frac{1}{100}$; 1.001

Problem Solving

11. A file clerk was asked to put the following codes in order from least to greatest: 2.82, $2\frac{4}{5}$, 2.083, $2\frac{84}{100}$. How should the codes be ordered?
   2.083; $2\frac{4}{5}$; 2.82; $2\frac{84}{100}$

Use with text pages 560–562.

39. 52.04°F 52.12°F 52.121°F 52.211°F 54.006°F 54.024°F

Mixed Review and Test Prep 

Open Response

Compare. Write >, <, or = for each ●.
(Chapter 21, Lesson 6)

35. 0.9 ● 0.90 =

36. 0.071 ● 0.7 <

37. 0.03 ● 0.30 <

38. 0.45 ● 0.067 >

Solve.

39. Karen measured the temperature in her backyard with a digital thermometer 5 times during one day. The temperatures she recorded were: 52.04°F, 52.12°F, 54.006°F, 54.024°F, 52.121°F, and 52.211°F. How could Karen list the temperatures in order from least to greatest?
See above. (Chapter 21, Lesson 7)

Calculator Connection

Changing Fractions to Decimals

Activity

You can use a calculator to find decimal equivalents. The fraction $\frac{1}{2}$ means 1 divided by 2.

To find the decimal equivalent for $\frac{1}{2}$:

- Enter the numerator, 1. Press 
- Enter the denominator 2. Press 

The calculator display should show 0.5.

Find the decimal equivalent for each fraction.

1. $\frac{4}{5}$ 0.8	**2.** $\frac{15}{20}$ 0.75	**3.** $\frac{6}{24}$ 0.25	**4.** $\frac{9}{36}$ 0.25	**5.** $\frac{6}{30}$ 0.2
6. $\frac{14}{28}$ 0.5	**7.** $\frac{7}{35}$ 0.2	**8.** $\frac{3}{10}$ 0.3	**9.** $\frac{43}{100}$ 0.43	**10.** $\frac{77}{100}$ 0.77

Extra Practice, See page 565, Set E.

Calculator Connection

Changing Fractions to Decimals

To extend the activity, work with the class to create a reference table of decimal equivalents for commonly used fractions, such as halves, thirds, fourths, fifths, sixths, and eighths. When students encounter repeating decimals, such as 0.333333 for $\frac{1}{3}$, explain that by convention we often round such decimals.

Monitoring Student Progress

Chapter Review/Test

Chapter Review/Test Items 1–25

To assign a numerical grade for this Chapter Review/Test, use 4 points for each item.

Check Understanding

You can use the ***Write About It*** question to assess understanding of a key chapter concept.

Customize Your Instruction

The Chapter Review/Test is a formal evaluation of chapter objectives. For students who have not yet mastered these objectives, you can use the Reteaching Resources listed in the chart below.

Additional Assessment Resources

Alternate Chapter Test A Chapter Test is also provided in the Unit Resource folder. You might use the Review/Test in the student book as review and the test in the Unit Resource folder as a summary test for the chapter.

***Ways to Assess* CD-ROM** allows you to create your own lesson, chapter, or unit tests or practice and review worksheets.

Adequate Yearly Progress Guide helps familiarize your students with the format of standardized tests.

Chapter Review/Test

Write About It: The decimal is 1.354. John should not have added the tenths, hundredths, and thousandths together.

VOCABULARY

Choose the best term to complete each sentence.

Vocabulary
tenths
decimal
equivalent
hundredths

1. The decimals 0.5 and 0.50 are ____ decimals. **equivalent**
2. In the decimal 3.075, the 0 is in the ____ place. **tenths**
3. A number with one or more digits to the right of a decimal point is a ____. **decimal**

CONCEPTS AND SKILLS

Write each fraction as a decimal. (Lessons 1–2, pp. 542–545)

4. $\frac{3}{10}$ **0.3**
5. $\frac{9}{10}$ **0.9**
6. $\frac{37}{100}$ **0.37**
7. $\frac{99}{100}$ **0.99**
8. $\frac{6}{100}$ **0.06**
9. $\frac{426}{1,000}$ **0.426**
10. $\frac{22}{1,000}$ **0.022**
11. $\frac{306}{1,000}$ **0.306**

Write each mixed number as a decimal. (Lesson 3, pp.546–548)

12. $12\frac{6}{10}$ **12.6**
13. $3\frac{5}{100}$ **3.05**
14. $7\frac{566}{1,000}$ **7.566**
15. three and five tenths **3.5**
16. four and twenty-six hundredths **4.26**

Write each fraction as an equivalent decimal. (Lesson 4, pp. 550–552)

17. $\frac{1}{2}$ **0.5**
18. $\frac{3}{4}$ **0.75**
19. $\frac{77}{100}$ **0.77**
20. $\frac{14}{1,000}$ **0.014**

Compare. Write >, <, or = for each ⬬. (Lessons 6–7, pp. 558–562)

21. 3 ⬬ 3.2 **<**
22. $5\frac{1}{2}$ ⬬ 5.2 **>**
23. 4.71 ⬬ 4.071 **>**
24. $6\frac{1}{4}$ ⬬ 6.025 **>**

PROBLEM SOLVING

Solve. (Lesson 5, pp. 554–556)

25. One yard of velvet fabric sells for $3.00, two yards sell for $5.00, and three yards sell for $7.00. If this pattern continues, how many yards of velvet fabric can Jo buy for $15.00? **7 yards**

Write About It

Show You Understand

The following number is in expanded form.

1 + 0.3 + 0.05 + 0.004

John wrote the number in standard form as 1.12.

Explain what he did wrong. What should the decimal be? ***See above.***

564 **Chapter 21** Chapter Review/Test

Chapter Review/Test Items	Objectives	Covered On Teacher's Edition Pages	Use These Reteaching Resources
1–11, 1–6	**21A** Read, write, and identify place value of a digit in a decimal through thousandths.	542A–545	Reteaching Resources 21.1, 21.2 *Ways to Success* CD-ROM 21.1, 21.2 *Ways to Success* Skillsheets 178, 181
12–20, 7–12	**21B** Write fractions and mixed numbers as decimals and vice versa.	546A–548, 550A–552	Reteaching Resources 21.3, 21.4 *Ways to Success* CD-ROM 21.3, 21.4 *Ways to Success* Skillsheets 182, 184
21–24, 13–18	**21C** Compare and order decimals and mixed numbers.	558A–562	Reteaching Resources 21.6, 21.7 *Ways to Success* CD-ROM 21.6, 21.7 *Ways to Success* Skillsheets 183, 185
25, 19, 20	**21D** Solve problems using skills and strategies.	554A–556	Reteaching Resources 21.5 *Ways to Success* CD-ROM 21.5 *Ways to Success* Skillsheet 186

Extra Practice

Set B
6. three and eight tenths; 3 + 0.8
7. nine and twelve hundredths; 9 + 0.1 + 0.02
8. six and seven hundredths; 6 + 0.07
9. fifteen and three thousandths; 15 + 0.003
10. two and fifty-five thousandths; 2 + 0.05 + 0.005

Set A (Lesson 2, pp. 544–545)

Write each fraction as a decimal.

1. $\frac{9}{10}$ 0.9 2. $\frac{6}{10}$ 0.6 3. $\frac{4}{100}$ 0.04 4. $\frac{16}{100}$ 0.16 5. $\frac{125}{1,000}$ 0.125

6. thirteen thousandths 0.013 7. one hundred seven thousandths 0.107

Set B (Lesson 3, pp. 546–548)

Write each mixed number as a decimal. *See above.*

1. $3\frac{8}{10}$ 3.8 2. $1\frac{30}{100}$ 1.30 3. $16\frac{1}{100}$ 16.01 4. $2\frac{35}{1,000}$ 2.035 5. $9\frac{6}{1,000}$ 9.006

Write each decimal in words and in expanded form.

6. 3.8 7. 9.12 8. 6.07 9. 15.003 10. 2.055

Set C (Lesson 4, pp. 550–552)

Write a fraction to describe the shaded part.
Then write a decimal equivalent.

1.  $\frac{4}{5}$; 0.8
2. 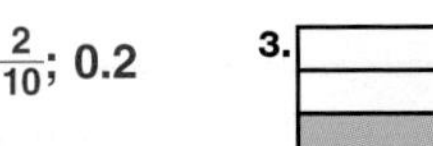 $\frac{2}{10}$; 0.2
3. $\frac{1}{2}$; 0.5
4. 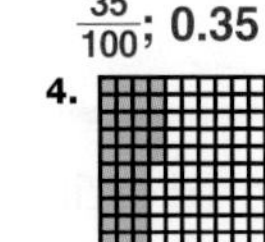 $\frac{35}{100}$; 0.35

Set D (Lessons 6, pp. 558–559)

Compare. Write >, <, or = for each ⬭.

1. 0.7 ⬭ 0.3 > 2. 5.65 ⬭ 5.065 > 3. 1.7 ⬭ 1.17 > 4. 1.05 ⬭ 1.5 <

5. 6.65 ⬭ 6.56 > 6. 8.08 ⬭ 8.80 < 7. 22.9 ⬭ 22.90 = 8. 13.03 ⬭ 13.30 <

Set E (Lesson 7, pp. (560–562)

Order the numbers from least to greatest.

1. 0.2 $\frac{1}{2}$ $\frac{1}{4}$ 0.6 — 0.2 $\frac{1}{4}$ $\frac{1}{2}$ 0.6
2. $1\frac{1}{2}$ 1.05 1.005 1.55 — 1.005 1.05 $1\frac{1}{2}$ 1.55
3. $2\frac{3}{4}$ $1\frac{2}{5}$ 1.3 2.09 — 1.3 $1\frac{2}{5}$ 2.09 $2\frac{3}{4}$
4. 0.67 1.5 0.007 $2\frac{1}{4}$ — 0.007 0.67 1.5 $2\frac{1}{4}$
5. 4.1 $4\frac{1}{5}$ 4.07 $4\frac{1}{2}$ — 4.07 4.1 $4\frac{1}{5}$ $4\frac{1}{2}$
6. 6.007 6.070 $6\frac{3}{4}$ 6 — 6 6.007 6.070 $6\frac{3}{4}$

Extra Practice at eduplace.com/map

CHAPTER 21 TEST

Name ______ Date ______ Chapter 21 Test

Write a fraction and a decimal to describe each model.

1. $\frac{6}{10}$ 0.6 2. $\frac{80}{100}$ 0.80 3. $\frac{46}{100}$ 0.46

Write each as a decimal.

4. $\frac{19}{1,000}$ 0.019 5. $\frac{4}{1,000}$ 0.004 6. $\frac{280}{1,000}$ 0.280

Write each mixed number as a decimal.

7. $13\frac{22}{100}$ 13.22 8. $6\frac{9}{10}$ 6.9 9. $26\frac{13}{1,000}$ 26.013

Write each decimal as an equivalent fraction.

10. 0.17 $\frac{17}{100}$ 11. 0.330 $\frac{330}{1,000}$ or $\frac{33}{100}$ 12. 0.065 $\frac{65}{1,000}$ or $\frac{13}{200}$

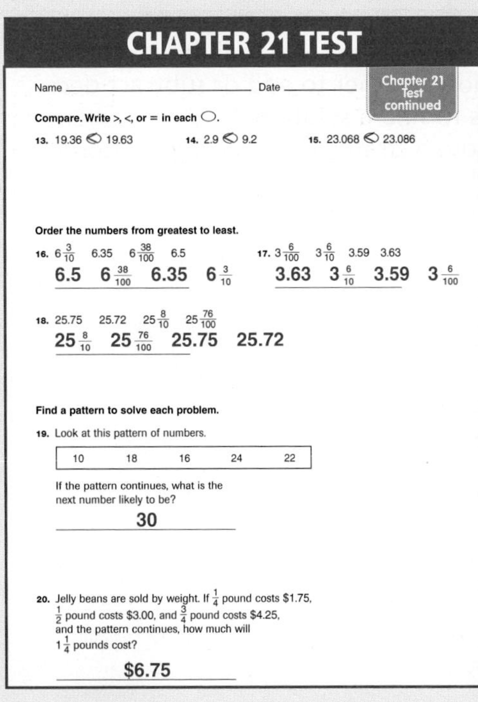

CHAPTER 21 TEST

Name ______ Date ______ Chapter 21 Test continued

Compare. Write >, <, or = in each ◯.

13. 19.36 ◯ 19.63 14. 2.9 ◯ 9.2 15. 23.068 ◯ 23.086

Order the numbers from greatest to least.

16. $6\frac{3}{10}$ 6.35 $6\frac{38}{100}$ 6.5 — 6.5 $6\frac{38}{100}$ 6.35 $6\frac{3}{10}$
17. $3\frac{6}{100}$ $3\frac{6}{10}$ 3.59 3.63 — 3.63 $3\frac{6}{10}$ 3.59 $3\frac{6}{100}$
18. 25.75 25.72 $25\frac{8}{10}$ $25\frac{76}{100}$ — $25\frac{8}{10}$ $25\frac{76}{100}$ 25.75 25.72

Find a pattern to solve each problem.

19. Look at this pattern of numbers.

10	18	16	24	22

If the pattern continues, what is the next number likely to be? 30

20. Jelly beans are sold by weight. If $\frac{1}{4}$ pound costs \$1.75, $\frac{1}{2}$ pound costs \$3.00, and $\frac{3}{4}$ pound costs \$4.25, and the pattern continues, how much will $1\frac{1}{4}$ pounds cost? \$6.75

CHAPTER 22

Planning Guide

Add and Subtract Decimals

Lesson	Overview	Objective/Vocabulary
1 Round Decimals p. 568A	► Use a number line or rounding rules to round decimals to a given place value. ► Round decimals to the nearest whole number, tenth, or hundredth.	► Use rules or a number line to round decimals. rounding
2 Estimate Decimal Sums and Differences p. 570A	► Use rounding to estimate sums and differences of decimals and money. ► Estimate by rounding numbers to the nearest whole number or to the nearest $1, $10, or $100.	► Use rounding to estimate sums and differences. decimal
3 Hands On: Explore Addition and Subtraction of Decimals p. 572A	► Add and subtract decimals through hundredths, using decimal models or decimal grids. ► Add and subtract decimals and money amounts.	► Use models to add and subtract decimals.
4 Add and Subtract Decimals p. 574A	► Add and subtract decimals. ► Align decimal points and include a decimal point in the answer. ► Estimate to check addition problem answers, and add to check subtraction problems.	► Add and subtract decimals.
5 Problem-Solving Application: Use Decimals p. 576A	► Use decimals to solve real-life problems. ► Decide whether to add or subtract decimals to find a solution. ► Choose a strategy and a computational method.	► Use decimals to solve problems.

Skills Trace: Number Theory and Fractions		
Grade 3	**Grade 4**	**Grade 5**
• Add and subtract decimals through hundredths (ch. 20)	• Round decimals • Estimate decimal sums and differences • Add and subtract decimals through thousandths	• Round decimals (ch. 1) • Estimate decimal sums and differences (ch. 11) • Add and subtract decimals (ch. 11)

Differentiated Instruction	Materials	NCTM Standards
▶ Differentiated Instruction activities, p. 568B ▶ *Chapter Challenges,* p. 127 *Ways to Success* CD-ROM 22.1 ▶ *Ways to Success* Skillsheets 189–190 Audio Tutor **2**/27 Listen and Understand	Number Line Transparency, Workmat 5	**Number and Operations:** Understand the place-value structure of the base-ten number system and be able to represent and compare whole numbers and decimals.
▶ Differentiated Instruction activities, p. 570B *Ways to Success* CD-ROM 22.2 ▶ *Ways to Success* Skillsheet 191		**Number and Operations:** Develop and use strategies to estimate computations involving fractions and decimals in situations relevant to students' experience.
▶ Differentiated Instruction activities, p. 572B ▶ *Chapter Challenges,* p. 129 *Ways to Success* CD-ROM 22.3 ▶ *Ways to Success* Skillsheet 187	Tenths and Hundredths Grids Transparency, blank transparency, markers in two colors, Decimal Models (Learning Tool 41), colored pencils in red and blue	**Number and Operations:** Use visual models, benchmarks, and equivalent forms to add and subtract commonly used fractions and decimals. **Representations:** Select, apply, and translate among mathematical representations to solve problems.
▶ Differentiated Instruction activities, p. 574B *Ways to Success* CD-ROM 22.4 ▶ *Ways to Success* Skillsheets 188, 192 Audio Tutor **2**/28 Listen and Understand	Blank transparency	**Number and Operations:** Use visual models, benchmarks, and equivalent forms to add and subtract commonly used fractions and decimals.
▶ Differentiated Instruction activities, p. 576B ▶ Chapter Challenges, p. 131 *Ways to Success* CD-ROM 22.5 ▶ *Ways to Success* Skillsheet 193	Blank transparency, calculators	**Number and Operations:** Compute fluently and make reasonable estimates. **Problem Solving:** Apply and adapt a variety of appropriate strategies to solve problems.

Math Notes

Chapter Objectives

22A Round decimals.

22B Estimate decimal sums and differences.

22C Add and subtract decimals to thousandths.

22D Solve problems using skills and strategies.

Mathematical Background

Add and Subtract Decimals

The algorithms that were used to add and subtract whole numbers can be used to add and subtract decimals. To add decimals, align the digits according to place value, so the decimal points align. Complete the computation from right to left and put the decimal point in the answer.

When subtracting decimals, often the numbers do not have the same number of digits. In this case, affixing one or more zeros after the decimal point helps to keep the place values aligned.

Example: 7.3 − 1.43 = ■

210 7.30 −1.43 7	Affix a zero so that both numbers have 2 digits to the right of the decimal point. Rename. 3 tenths = 2 tenths + 10 hundredths. Subtract the hundredths.
6 1210 7.30 −1.43 87	Rename. 7 ones = 6 ones + 10 tenths 10 tenths + 2 tenths = 12 tenths. Subtract the tenths.
6 1210 7.30 −1.43 5.87	Subtract the ones. Place the decimal point in the answer.

So, 7.3 − 1.43 = 5.87

Research-Based Teaching

It is important to build students' understanding of decimals by connecting to their everyday knowledge of decimals. A study by Irwin (2001) revealed that students who worked on contextual problems made more progress in their knowledge of decimals than students who worked on noncontextual problems. Using money as a model for decimals can help. Undoubtedly, fourth-grade students have had real-world experiences with money. Drawing on students' prior knowledge will help them connect the idea that the expressions \$0.25 and $\frac{1}{4}$ of a dollar are equivalent. See *Professional Resources Handbook, Grade 4,* Unit 7.

For more ideas relating to Unit 7, see the Teacher Support Handbook at the back of this Teacher's Edition.

Language Intervention

When students are working together on hands-on activities, encourage them to verbalize what they are doing and why. This will help them build their own understanding and math vocabulary. It will also benefit the other students in the group.

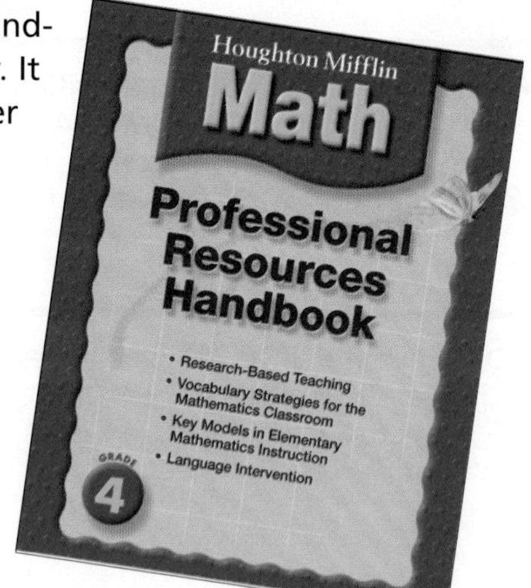

Chapter Activities

Connecting to the Unit Project

Whole Class	20 minutes
Objective	Use fractions and decimals in real-world contexts.
Materials	Pencils, paper, scissors, old magazines or newspapers, construction paper or tag board
Visual, Tactual	

Use Fractions and Decimals

- As students write their scripts for the television program, encourage them to use fractions and decimals to describe times, distances, prices, and other quantities.
- Also encourage students to cut out pictures of Olympic athletes from old magazines or newspapers. Display them on a sheet of construction paper or tag board along with their name, height, weight, Olympic event, and their distance or times for the event.

Ongoing Skill Activity

Whole Class	15–20 minutes
Objective	Add and subtract decimals.
Materials	None
Visual, Auditory	

Add and Subtract Decimals

- Start out by giving students two decimals and having them find the difference. Have students record the problem in the back of their math notebooks.
- Tell students that you are going to give them another decimal and operation each day of the week. Write the decimal and operation in the same place on a corner of the blackboard each day. For example, *add 1.52* or *subtract 0.09*.
- At the end of one or two weeks, ask students for the final answer. Did all of the students get the same answer? Discuss the results.

Math Expressions

Whole Class	20 minutes
Objective	Add decimal numbers using a number line.
Materials	None
Visual	

Add Whole Numbers and Decimals

This activity uses instructional practices from *Math Expressions* with content from this unit.

A number line can help show how larger and smaller decimal numbers are added.

- Display this exercise: $4 + 0.8 =$.
- Have students describe how they might go about adding the numbers.
- Discuss the idea that a number line can help us see the value of each number, how they are added together, and what the total looks like. Model, or have a student volunteer model, how to place a mark on the number line to show the number 4. Demonstrate how to begin from the number 4 and add the decimal number 8 tenths. Count by tenths and point to each tick mark that comes after the 4 on the number line, until you reach 8 tenths. Mark the position 4.8 and read the decimal number aloud.
- Discuss why the answer was 4.8 rather than 12, 1.2, or 0.12. Then have students work in pairs to draw number lines and find the sums of various whole numbers and decimal numbers.

Starting Chapter 22

Investigation

Using Data

Have students work in small groups to answer the questions posed on page 566.

To extend the investigation, have students do the following activity.

Research currency exchange rates for 3 countries that are not shown on page 566. For each, calculate the amount of currency you would receive for $2.00.

For more information about projects and investigations,

Visit **Education Place**®
www.eduplace.com/mat

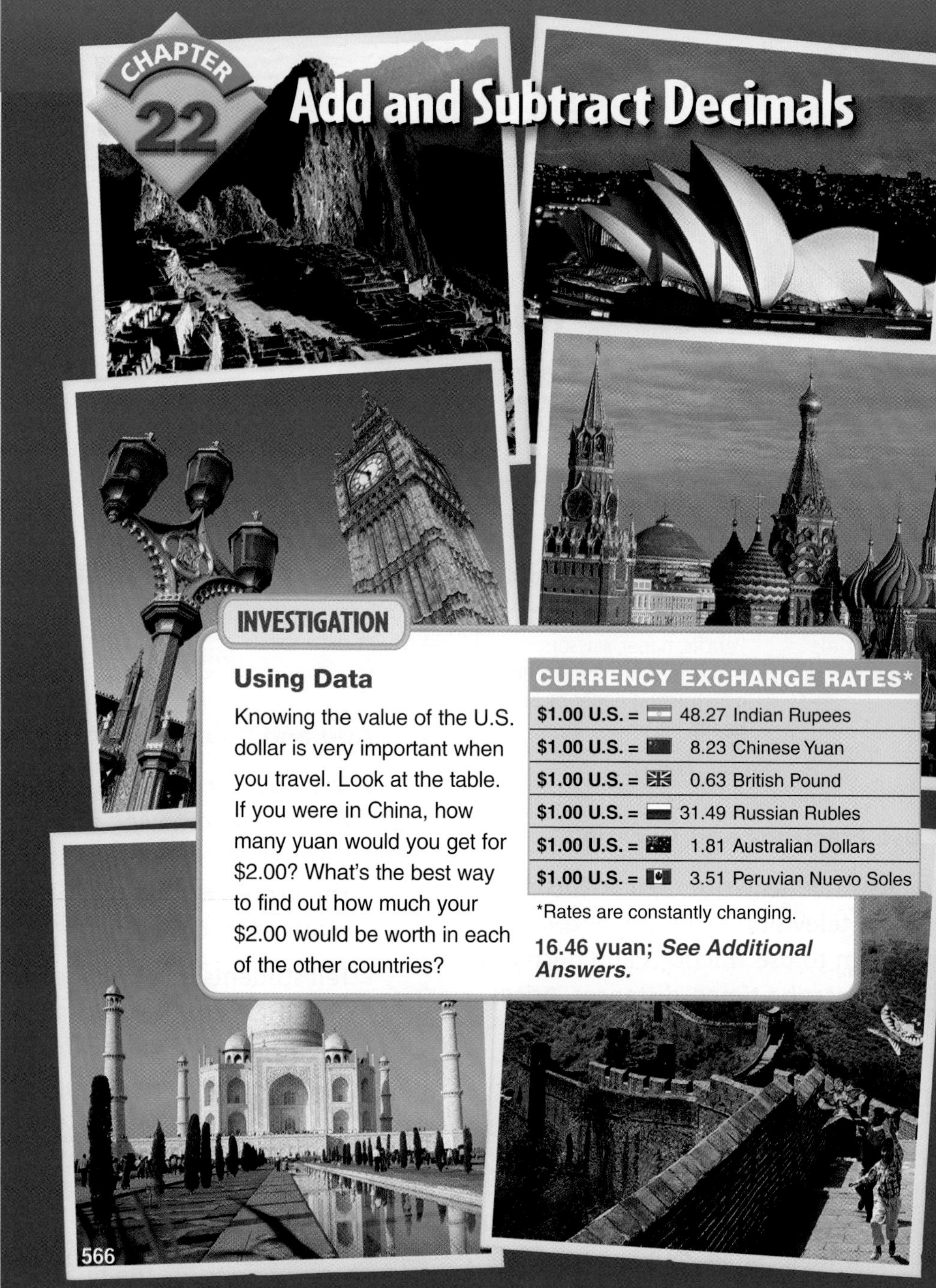

CHAPTER 22
Add and Subtract Decimals
INVESTIGATION
Using Data
Knowing the value of the U.S. dollar is very important when you travel. Look at the table. If you were in China, how many yuan would you get for $2.00? What's the best way to find out how much your $2.00 would be worth in each of the other countries?

CURRENCY EXCHANGE RATES*
$1.00 U.S. = 48.27 Indian Rupees
$1.00 U.S. = 8.23 Chinese Yuan
$1.00 U.S. = 0.63 British Pound
$1.00 U.S. = 31.49 Russian Rubles
$1.00 U.S. = 1.81 Australian Dollars
$1.00 U.S. = 3.51 Peruvian Nuevo Soles

*Rates are constantly changing.

16.46 yuan; *See Additional Answers.*

566

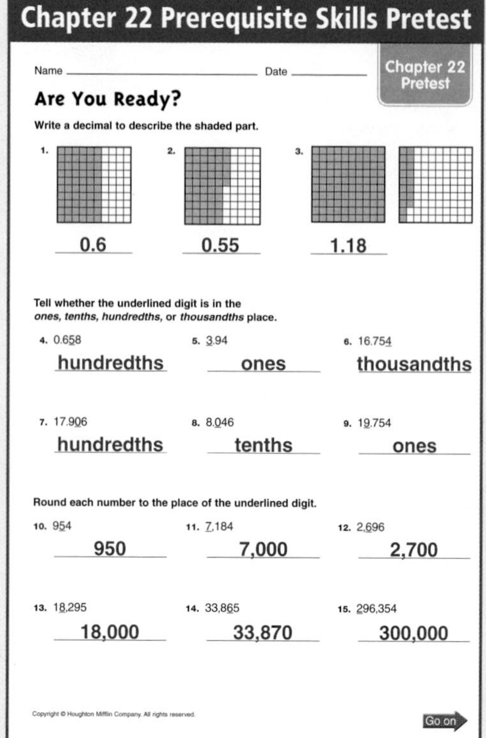

Chapter 22 Prerequisite Skills Pretest

Name ______ Date ______ Chapter 22 Pretest

Are You Ready?

Write a decimal to describe the shaded part.

1. 0.6 2. 0.55 3. 1.18

Tell whether the underlined digit is in the *ones, tenths, hundredths,* or *thousandths* place.

4. 0.658 hundredths 5. 3.94 ones 6. 16.754 thousandths

7. 17.906 hundredths 8. 8.046 tenths 9. 19.754 ones

Round each number to the place of the underlined digit.

10. 954 950 11. 7,184 7,000 12. 2,696 2,700

13. 18,295 18,000 14. 33,865 33,870 15. 296,354 300,000

Go on

Use What You Know

Use this page to review and remember what you need to know for this chapter.

VOCABULARY

Choose the best term to complete each sentence.

Vocabulary
- tenth
- round
- estimate
- hundredth
- decimal point

1. When you find an approximate answer, you are making an ____. **estimate**
2. One of ten equal parts of a whole is a ____. **tenth**
3. The symbol that separates ones and tenths in a decimal is a ____. **decimal point**
4. You write $3.59 as $4.00 when you ____ to the nearest dollar. **round**

CONCEPTS AND SKILLS

Write a decimal to describe the shaded part.

5. 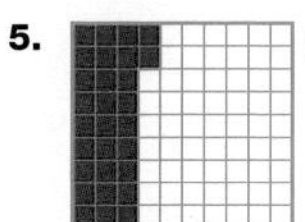 0.32
6. 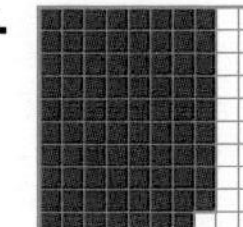 0.79
7. 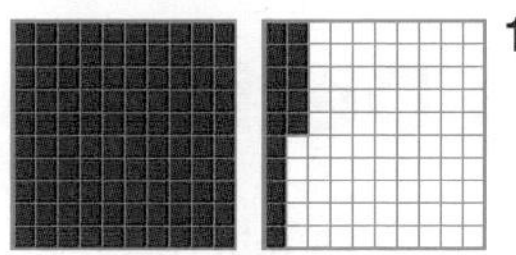 1.15

Tell whether the underlined digit is in the *ones, tenths, hundredths,* or *thousandths* place.

8. 0.421 **tenths**
9. 5.618 **thousandths**
10. 1.276 **hundredths**
11. 2.015 **ones**

Round each number to the place of the underlined digit.

12. 43 **40**
13. 257 **260**
14. 298 **300**
15. 3,139 **3,100**
16. 4,622 **5,000**
17. 14,372 **14,000**
18. 61,315 **60,000**
19. 309,897 **310,000**

Write About It

20. Why is 0.4 greater than 0.04? Use pictures, symbols, or words to explain your answer. ***See above.***

20. *Possible answer:* 0.4 is greater because 0.4 represents 4 of 10 equal parts; 0.04 represents 4 of 100 equal parts.

Facts Practice, See Page 669.

Chapter 22 New Content Pretest

Name ____ Date ____ Chapter 22 Pretest continued

Check What You Know

Round each decimal to the nearest whole number.

1. 17.56 **18**
2. 674.2 **674**
3. 6,745.84 **6,746**

Round each decimal to the place of the underlined digit

4. 38.7 **39**
5. 4.252 **4.25**
6. 18.74 **18.7**

Estimate by rounding to the nearest whole number.

7. 7.4 + 3.6 **11**
8. 19.564 − 5.205 **15**
9. $759.15 + 30.25 **$789**

Find the sum or difference. Draw models if you wish.

10. 2.8 − 1.7 = **1.1**
11. 8.54 + 3.92 = **12.46**
12. $6.27 − $3.66 = **$2.61**

Go on

Chapter 22 New Content Pretest

Name ____ Date ____ Chapter 22 Pretest continued

Add or subtract. Check your work.

13. 13.56 + 17.09 **30.65** **13 + 17 = 30**
14. $37.56 − 24.70 **$12.86** **$12.86 + $24.70 = $37.56**
15. 9.542 + 3.704 **13.246** **10 + 4 = 14**
16. 15.69 − 11.84 = **3.85** **11.84 + 3.85 = 15.69**
17. $6.94 + $8.55 = **$15.49** **$7 + $9 = $16**
18. 7.542 − 4.305 = **3.237** **3.237 + 4.305 = 7.542**

Solve.

19. Mary had 34.6 square feet of linen. She used 26.9 square feet of it to make placemats. How much linen does Mary have left? **7.7 square feet**

20. Admission to an amusement park is $29.55. A souvenir cup is $3.68. How much will Neil spend if he pays for admission and a souvenir cup? **$33.23**

STOP

Use What You Know

Use this page for informal assessment and review of prerequisite skills.

- Items 1–4: Use math vocabulary
- Items 5–7: Write a decimal for the shaded part of a grid
- Items 8–11: Identify place value
- Items 12–19: Round whole numbers
- Item 20: Compare decimals

Customize Your Instruction

Use the Chapter Pretest in the Unit Resource folder to help customize and pace instruction.

Objectives and Resources

Prerequisite Skills Pretest

- Items 1–3: Write a decimal for the shaded part of a grid.
- Items 4–9: Identify place value.
- Items 10–15: Round numbers.

New Content Pretest

- Items 1–6: Round decimals.
- Items 7–9: Estimate decimal sums and differences.
- Items 10–18: Add and subtract decimals to thousandths.
- Items 19–20: Solve Problems.

For Students Having Difficulty

- *Ways to Success* CD-ROM 21.1, 22.2
- *Ways to Success* Skillsheets 187–189

For Students Having Success

- Enrichment 22.1–22.5

For Mathematically Promising Students

Explore: Round Rule, p. 127, after Lesson 1

Extend: Time Capsule Map, p. 129, after Lesson 3

Connect: Patterns, Sums, and Differences, p. 131, after Lesson 5

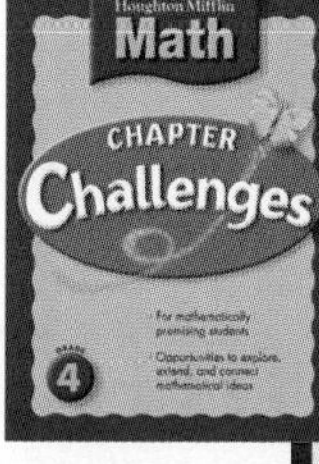

Lesson 22.1

Round Decimals

Planning

Lesson Objective Use rules or a number line to round decimals.

Math Background

Rounding decimals is similar to rounding whole numbers. Round up if the digit to the right is 5 or greater. Round down if the digit to the right is 4 or less.

Technology Resources

- Audio Tutor **2**/27 Listen and Understand
- *Ways to Success* CD-ROM 22.1
- Education Place: Extra Practice, eManipulatives, eGames www.eduplace.com/map

Lesson 22.1 Transparency

Problem of the Day

Figure out a three-digit mystery decimal.
HINT: There is more than one answer!

- To the nearest ten, it rounds to the number of days in November.
- To the nearest whole, it rounds to a multiple of 9.
- The digit sum is a prime number.
  (26.5, 26.9, 27.2, or 27.4)

Spiral Review

Round to the nearest dollar.

1. $0.83 ($1) **2.** $7.25 ($7)
3. $3.50 ($4) **4.** $16.68 ($17)
5. $904.07 ($904)

Lesson Quiz

Round each decimal to the place of the underlined digit.

1. 4.6 (5) **2.** 518.96 (520)
3. 61.52 (61.5) **4.** 20.071 (20.1)
5. 876.543 (876.54)

NCTM Standards

Number and Operations: Understand the place-value structure of the base-ten number system and be able to represent and compare whole numbers and decimals.

Getting Started

Building Math Vocabulary

You may wish to review this word with students.

rounding a method of finding *about how many* or *about how much* by expressing a number to the nearest ten, hundred, thousand, and so on

Rounding Decimals

Whole Class	15 minutes
Objective	Round decimals.
Materials	Number Line Transparency, Workmat 5
Visual, Tactual	

- Have students work the problems on their workmats.
- Show Number Line 2 marked from 11 to 12 by tenths.
- Write *11.45* on the board. **What is this decimal?** (11 and 45 hundredths) **Let's use the number line to round it. Where would it go?** (between 11.4 and 11.5) **Is 11.45 closer to 11 or to 12?** (11) **So, 11.45 rounded to the nearest whole number is 11.**
- Renumber the number line 311–312 for rounding 311.82. **Where would we position 311.82 on the number line?** (between 311.8 and 311.9) **If we rounded this number to the nearest whole, what would it be?** (312) **To the nearest tenth?** (311.8)
- Tell students that this lesson shows different ways to round decimals.

Differentiated Instruction

English Learners

Whole Class	20 minutes
Objective	Round decimals.
Materials	None
Auditory, Visual	

Early Production

- Before ***Guided Practice,*** do the Intervention activity below to help students understand how to use zeros when rounding.
- Have students practice saying the same value with different numbers of zeros. For example: *3.4 (three and four tenths), 3.40 (three and forty hundredths), etc.*

Intermediate/Advanced

- English Learner Resource 22.1
- English Learner Handbook

Intervention

Small Groups	15 minutes
Objective	Round decimals.
Materials	None
Visual, Tactual	

- When students round decimals, they may not know how many decimal places to indicate.
- Review the equivalence of decimals such as 5.6, 5.60, and 5.600.
- To round 2.35 to the nearest tenth, students need only write 2.4, not 2.40.
- Remind students that when they round to the nearest whole number, they don't need decimal places because 4.0 = 4.
- Repeat with other examples.

Other Resources

- *Ways to Success* CD-ROM 22.1

Inclusion

Small Groups	15 minutes
Objective	Round decimals.
Materials	Masking tape, number cards 28–31, number cube labeled 1–6
Kinesthetic	

- Make a floor number line with 28.0–31.6 on masking tape marked in tenths.
- Have students draw a card for the whole number, roll the number cube for tenths, and position the decimal on the number line.
- Help students round to the nearest ten and whole number.

Alternate Teaching Strategy

Provide students with a newspaper. Ask students to find an article which has a decimal. Ask students to decide whether the decimal was rounded or not. Students should explain their reasoning.

❶ Introduce

Read the objective to students and explain that in this lesson they will use a number line or rounding rules to round decimals to a given place value.

❷ Teach

Learn About It

- Read the opening problem. **Where is the ones place in any decimal?** (to the left of the decimal point)
- **Look at *Way 1.* How is the number line labeled?** (by tenths) **Where does 1.35 go?** (halfway between 1.30 and 1.40)
- **Look at *Way 2.* To what place do we round 1.35?** (ones place or whole kg) **What does the 3 mean?** (3 tenths) **How does 0.3 kilogram compare to a whole kilogram?** (less) **Why do we round 1.35 to 1, not 2?** (The digit to the right of ones is less than 5, so the ones digit does not change.)

Guided Practice

Have students complete **Exercises 1–9** as you observe. Remind them to use the ***Ask Yourself*** questions to help. Give students the opportunity to talk about the question in ***Explain Your Thinking.***

Common Error

- **Choosing an incorrect rounding place**
- **Intervention** Have students make a simple place-value chart in pen. To help them determine the rounding place, have them write on the chart in pencil the number to be rounded. Then have them circle the key place and look to its right to decide which way to round.

Lesson 1

Audio Tutor 2/27 Listen and Understand

Round Decimals

Objective Use rules or a number line to round decimals.

Learn About It

Ami sells nuts and vegetables at an outdoor market in Ghana. She has 1.35 kilograms of kola nuts to sell. What is the weight of the kola nuts to the nearest whole kilogram?

Here are some different ways to round decimals.

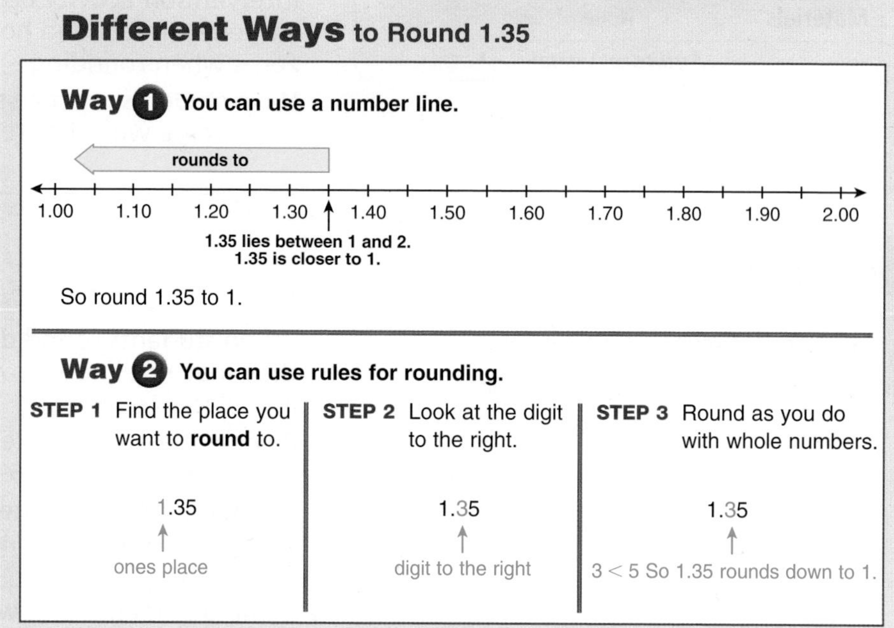

Different Ways to Round 1.35
Way 1 You can use a number line.
rounds to
1.00 1.10 1.20 1.30 1.40 1.50 1.60 1.70 1.80 1.90 2.00
1.35 lies between 1 and 2.
1.35 is closer to 1.
So round 1.35 to 1.
Way 2 You can use rules for rounding.
STEP 1 Find the place you want to round to.
1.35
ones place
STEP 2 Look at the digit to the right.
1.35
digit to the right
STEP 3 Round as you do with whole numbers.
1.35
3 < 5 So 1.35 rounds down to 1.

Solution: The weight of the kola nuts to the nearest whole kilogram is 1 kilogram.

568

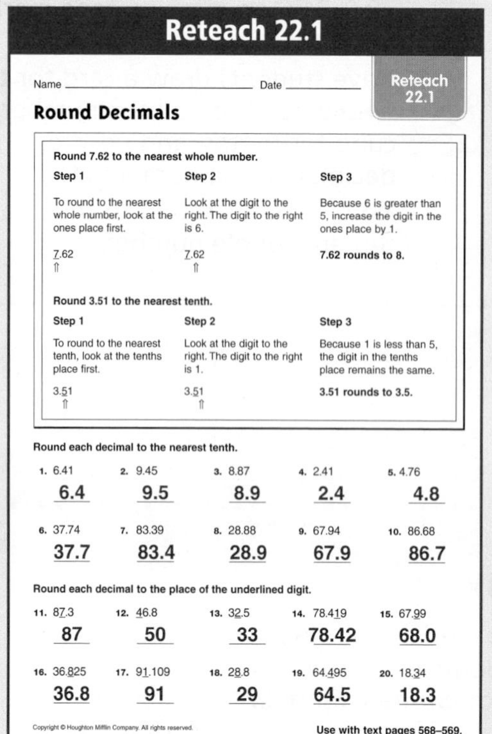

Reteach 22.1

Name ______________ Date ________ Reteach 22.1

Round Decimals

Round 7.62 to the nearest whole number.

Step 1	Step 2	Step 3
To round to the nearest whole number, look at the ones place first.	Look at the digit to the right. The digit to the right is 6.	Because 6 is greater than 5, increase the digit in the ones place by 1.
7.62 ⇑	7.62 ⇑	**7.62 rounds to 8.**

Round 3.51 to the nearest tenth.

Step 1	Step 2	Step 3
To round to the nearest tenth, look at the tenths place first.	Look at the digit to the right. The digit to the right is 1.	Because 1 is less than 5, the digit in the tenths place remains the same.
3.51 ⇑	3.51 ⇑	**3.51 rounds to 3.5.**

Round each decimal to the nearest tenth.

1. 6.41 **6.4**
2. 9.45 **9.5**
3. 8.87 **8.9**
4. 2.41 **2.4**
5. 4.76 **4.8**
6. 37.74 **37.7**
7. 83.39 **83.4**
8. 28.88 **28.9**
9. 67.94 **67.9**
10. 86.68 **86.7**

Round each decimal to the place of the underlined digit.

11. 87.3 **87**
12. 46.8 **50**
13. 32.5 **33**
14. 78.419 **78.42**
15. 67.99 **68.0**
16. 36.825 **36.8**
17. 91.109 **91**
18. 28.8 **29**
19. 64.495 **64.5**
20. 18.34 **18.3**

Use with text pages 568–569.

Practice 22.1 Page 139

Name ______________ Date ________ Practice 22.1

Round Decimals

Round each decimal to the nearest whole number.

1. 32.87 **33**
2. 9.481 **9**
3. 57.224 **57**
4. 5.247 **5**
5. 351.58 **352**
6. 865.12 **865**
7. 45.512 **46**
8. 1.238 **1**
9. 54.579 **55**
10. 17.54 **18**
11. 1,235.84 **1,236**
12. 542.23 **542**
13. 42.325 **42**
14. 78.953 **79**
15. 42.336 **42**

Round each decimal to the place of the underlined digit.

16. 75.6 **76**
17. 5.3 **5**
18. 6.71 **6.7**
19. 1,482.23 **1,482**
20. 67.54 **68**
21. 81.246 **81.25**
22. 172.34 **172**
23. 8.95 **9**
24. 237.354 **237.4**
25. 87.321 **87.32**
26. 15.87 **16**
27. 56.37 **56.4**
28. 89.324 **89.32**
29. 750.158 **750.16**
30. 57.339 **57.34**

Test Prep

31. Aaron has 8.39 kg of apples. What is the weight of the apples to the nearest whole kilogram?
    A 8.3 B 8 C 8.30 D 9 **B**
32. Julia lives $3\frac{1}{4}$ km from the market. What is this distance to the nearest tenth kilometer? **3.3 kilometers**

Use with text pages 568–569.

Guided Practice

Use the number line to round each decimal to the nearest tenth.

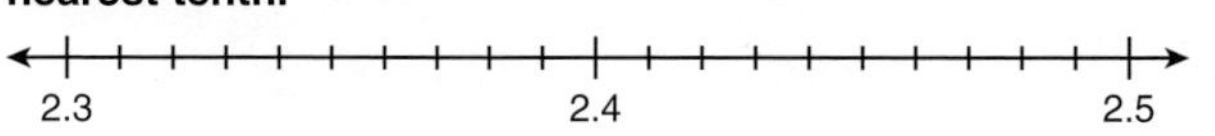

1. 2.31 **2.3** 2. 2.38 **2.4** 3. 2.46 **2.5** 4. 2.43 **2.4**

Ask Yourself

- Which digit do I need to look at in order to round the decimal?
- Should the rounding-place digit change or stay the same?

Round each decimal to the place of the underlined digit.

5. 38.6 **39** 6. 95.05 **95** 7. 7.37 **7.4** 8. 6.194 **6.19** 9. 5.704 **5.70**

Explain Your Thinking ▶ Compare rounding decimals to rounding whole numbers. ***See Additional Answers.***

Practice and Problem Solving

Round each decimal to the nearest whole number.

10. 10.01 **10**	11. 680.46 **680**	12. 501.79 **502**	13. 12.536 **13**	14. 14.376 **14**	15. 19.62 **20**
16. 238.49 **238**	17. 302.63 **303**	18. 5.989 **6**	19. 199.08 **199**	20. 498.57 **499**	21. 5,679.91 **5,680**

Round each decimal to the place of the underlined digit.

22. 2.8 **3**	23. 9.4 **9**	24. 118.16 **118**	25. 89.98 **90**	26. 7.86 **7.9**	27. 73.57 **73.6**
28. 6.51 **6.5**	29. 236.437 **236.4**	30. 9.054 **9.05**	31. 10.427 **10.43**	32. 9.132 **9.13**	33. 125.096 **125.10**

Solve.

34. Ami has 15.47 kg of yams. What is the weight of the yams to the nearest whole kilogram? **15 kilograms**

35. Ami lives $1\frac{3}{4}$ km from the market. What is this distance to the nearest tenth of a kilometer? **1.8 kilometers**

36. **Analyze** What is the greatest decimal in tenths that rounds to 83? **83.4**

37. **Explain** What is a reasonable rounded estimate for 35.27? ***See Additional Answers.***

Mixed Review and Test Prep

Open Response

Write a mixed number for each. (Ch. 19, Lesson 7)

38. $\frac{9}{7}$ $1\frac{2}{7}$ 39. $\frac{7}{3}$ $2\frac{1}{3}$ 40. $\frac{8}{5}$ $1\frac{3}{5}$

41. $\frac{5}{4}$ $1\frac{1}{4}$ 42. $\frac{10}{6}$ $1\frac{2}{3}$ 43. $\frac{7}{2}$ $3\frac{1}{2}$

Multiple Choice

44. Which is 18.26 rounded to the nearest tenth? (Ch. 22, Lesson 1)

A 18 C 18.2

B 19 **(D) 18.3**

Extra Practice See page 581, Set A.

3 Practice

Practice and Problem Solving

Select from **Exercises 10–44** as independent work.

- ***Problem 35*** Ask: **How do we round a mixed number to tenths?** (Change it to a decimal.)

4 Assess & Close

Math Talk in Action

- **How is rounding decimals like rounding whole numbers?** (Follow the same rounding rules, or use a number line as you would with whole numbers.)
- **Explain how to round 79.26 to the nearest tenth.** (Responses should show that students can find the tenths place and know to round to 79.3 because the hundredths digit is 5 or higher.)

Math Journal

Have students write a set of steps to follow in order to round 23.47 to the nearest tenth.

Lesson Quiz

Use the quiz on Lesson Transparency 22.1.

Lesson 22.1 Transparency

Test Prep & Spiral Review

Use Test Prep Transparency 22.1.

Enrichment 22.1

Name ______ Date ______ Enrichment 22.1

Around and Around We Go

June and Joe are rounding the numbers to the place of the underlined digit. Your job is to find who is right about each number. Put a check in the column by that number if the answer is right.

June is Right	How June Rounds	The Number	How Joe Rounds	Joe is Right
✓	5	5.25	6	
	9.0	8.94	8.9	✓
	6	6.77	7	✓
✓	9.37	9.365	9.36	
	21	21.82	22	✓
	44.5	44.44	44.4	✓
✓	57	56.65	56	
	73.10	73.197	73.20	✓
✓	100	99.51	99	

1. Choose three numbers that were rounded wrong. List them and explain why June or Joe was wrong in how they rounded the numbers. **Answers may vary.**

2. June rounded a 5-digit number to 62.5 and Joe rounded the number to 62. They are both right. What number could they have possibly rounded? **Possible answers are any decimal between 62.450 and 62.499**

Use with text pages 568–569.

Problem Solving 22.1

Name ______ Date ______ Problem Solving 22.1

Round Decimals

The table lists the density of some elements. Use the table for Problems 1–4.

Element	Density (g/cm³)
Gold	19.32
Potassium	0.862
Sulfur	2.070
Sodium	0.97
Platinum	21.45
Magnesium	1.74
Calcium	1.54

1. What is the density of potassium to the nearest tenth? **0.9**

2. What is the density of gold to the nearest whole number? **19**

3. What is the density of calcium to the nearest whole number? The nearest tenth? **2; 1.5**

4. If you round all the densities to the nearest whole number, which elements would have the same densities? Explain. **Potassium and sodium would both have densities of 1. Sulfur, magnesium, and calcium would all have densities of 2.**

5. **Reasoning** Rachel recorded the density of beryllium to the nearest tenth. She wrote 1.8 g/cm^3. Bobby recorded the density of beryllium to the nearest hundredth. He wrote 1.85 g/cm^3. What is the density of beryllium? Choose from the list below and explain your reasoning.

1.844 g/cm^3 1.855 g/cm^3 1.854 g/cm^3
1.846 g/cm^3 1.756 g/cm^3

1.846 g/cm^3; This is the only number listed that is 1.85 when rounded to the nearest hundredth and 1.8 when rounded to the nearest tenth.

Use with text pages 568–569.

Homework 22.1 Page 139

Name ______ Date ______ Homework 22.1

Round Decimals

Round each decimal to the nearest tenth.

9.75

Use rounding rules to round 9.75 to the nearest tenth.

Step 1: Find the place you want to round to. 9.75

Step 2: Look at the digit to the right. 9.75

Step 3: Round as you do with whole numbers. 5 is greater than or equal to 5. So increase the tenths digit by one. **9.75 rounds to 9.8.**

Round each decimal to the nearest tenth.

1. 4.812 **4.8**	2. 7.234 **7.2**	3. 53.327 **53.3**	4. 20.481 **20.5**	5. 19.937 **19.9**
6. 35.781 **35.8**	7. 401.87 **401.9**	8. 48.614 **48.6**	9. 1,687.12 **1,687.1**	10. 9.187 **9.2**

Round each decimal to the place of the underlined digit.

11. 47.81 **48**	12. 8.8 **9**	13. 7.81 **7.8**	14. 67.18 **67**	15. 51.90 **51.9**
16. 45.83 **46**	17. 958.66 **959**	18. 14.621 **14.62**	19. 578.196 **578.20**	20. 64.749 **64.75**

Problem Solving

21. Kim filled her car with 7.38 gallons of gasoline. How much gas did she buy to the nearest whole gallon? **7 gallons**

Use with text pages 568–569.

Lesson 22.2

Estimate Decimal Sums and Differences

Planning

Lesson Objective Use rounding to estimate sums and differences.

Math Background

Rounding can be used to estimate sums and differences. Estimating an answer before doing a calculation can make sure an answer is reasonable. Sometimes, an estimate is all that is needed.

Technology Resources

- *Ways to Success* CD-ROM 22.2
- Education Place: Extra Practice, eGlossary, eGames www.eduplace.com/map

Lesson 22.2 Transparency

Problem of the Day

Find the value of K and P. (P = 8; K = 3)

$54.KP
+1K.97
$6P.K5

Spiral Review

Round each decimal to the place of the underlined digit.

1. 8.09 (8) **2.** 326.85 (326.9)
3. 25.59 (25.6) **4.** 60.083 (60.1)
5. 913.544 (913.54)

Lesson Quiz

Estimate by rounding to the nearest whole number or dollar.

1. 7.3 + 5.7 (13)
2. 8.2 − 1.6 (6)
3. 29.501 + 64.006 (94)
4. $5.67 + $9.08 ($15)
5. $510.47 − 9.84 ($500)

NCTM Standards

Number and Operations: Develop and use strategies to estimate computations involving fractions and decimals in situations relevant to students' experience.

Getting Started

Building Math Vocabulary

decimal a number with one or more digits to the right of a decimal point

Display the vocabulary card for **decimal.** Have students give examples of where they've seen or used decimals before.

Rounding and Estimating

Whole Class	15 minutes
Objective	Estimate decimal sums and differences.
Materials	None
Auditory	

- Lead students in a discussion about rounding and estimating.
- **Why do we sometimes estimate sums and differences instead of finding exact answers?** (so we can compute mentally; to get an approximate answer)
- **When have you used estimation in real life?** (Accept all reasonable responses.)
- Tell students that in this lesson they will use rounding to estimate sums and differences with decimals and money amounts.

Differentiated Instruction

English Learners

Small Groups	10 minutes
Objective	Round decimals.
Materials	None
Auditory, Visual	

Early Production

- Students may need additional practice rounding decimals to whole numbers.
- Write some decimals and whole numbers with decimals on the board (tenths and hundredths). Write an incorrectly rounded number for each decimal.
- Ask students to explain the error and give the correct answer.

Intermediate/Advanced

- English Learner Resource 22.2
- English Learner Handbook

Intervention

Pairs	20 minutes
Objective	Estimate decimal sums.
Materials	Menus or circulars
Tactual	

- Provide students with menus from local restaurants or circulars from a local grocery store.
- Have pairs of students use these to plan a meal.
- Ask students to estimate the cost of their combined meal.

Other Resources

- *Ways to Success* CD-ROM 22.2

Special Needs

Small Groups	20 minutes
Objective	Round decimals.
Materials	Highlighter pen
Visual, Auditory	

- Have students write each number in **Exercises 1–6** on page 571 and use a highlighter pen to mark the place to which they are asked to round.
- Ask them to circle the place directly to the right of the highlighted place. This is the digit that will help them know whether to leave the highlighted digit as-is or to round to the next greater number.

Real-World Connection

Materials: Almanac

- Tell students that the discus is a heavy plate thrown by athletes since ancient times.
- Have students use an almanac to find the Olympic records since 1896 for the discus throw. Have them find the greatest and least winning distances, round measures to the nearest meter, and estimate the difference between them.

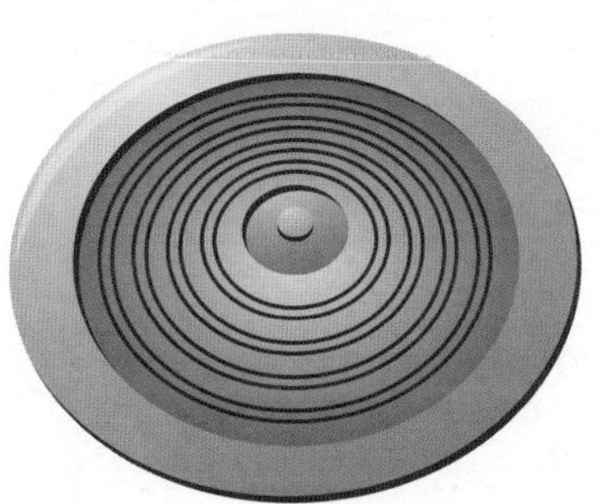

❶ Introduce

Read the objective to students and explain that in this lesson they will use rounding to estimate sums and differences of decimals and money. Explain that estimates are found by rounding numbers to the nearest whole number or to the nearest $1, $10, or $100.

❷ Teach

Learn About It

- **Look at *Step 1.* Why is 2.3 rounded to 2?** (because of the 3 in the tenths place) **Why is 2.5 rounded to 3?** (because of the 5 in the tenths place)
- **Look at *Step 2.* Why do we compare 7 meters and 6 meters?** (to decide which kite needs less bamboo)
- **Look at *Other Example A.* Why do we round to the nearest $10?** (for easier mental addition)
- **Look at *Other Example B.* Why does it make sense to round these amounts to the nearest $100?** ($97.25 is almost $100; makes mental math easy.)

Guided Practice

Have students complete **Exercises 1–6** as you observe. Remind them to use the *Ask Yourself* questions to help. Give students the opportunity to talk about the question in ***Explain Your Thinking.***

Common Error

- **Rounding to the wrong place**
- **Intervention** Have students read each direction line carefully to know the place to which they should round. Point out that for **Exercises 12–17,** they must round to the nearest $10 *and* $100.

Lesson 2

Estimate Decimal Sums and Differences

Vocabulary
decimal

Objective Use rounding to estimate sums and differences.

Learn About It

Liang is making a kite with his grandfather. He wants to make the kite that uses the least amount of bamboo. Should he pick the butterfly kite or the hawk kite?

You do not need an exact answer. You can solve the problem with an estimate.

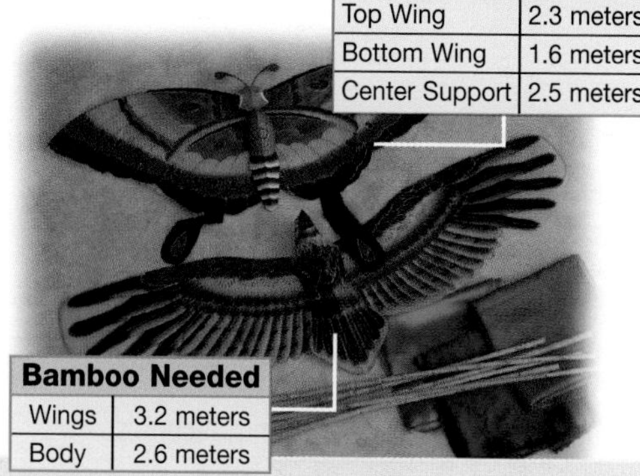

Bamboo Needed	
Top Wing	2.3 meters
Bottom Wing	1.6 meters
Center Support	2.5 meters

Bamboo Needed	
Wings	3.2 meters
Body	2.6 meters

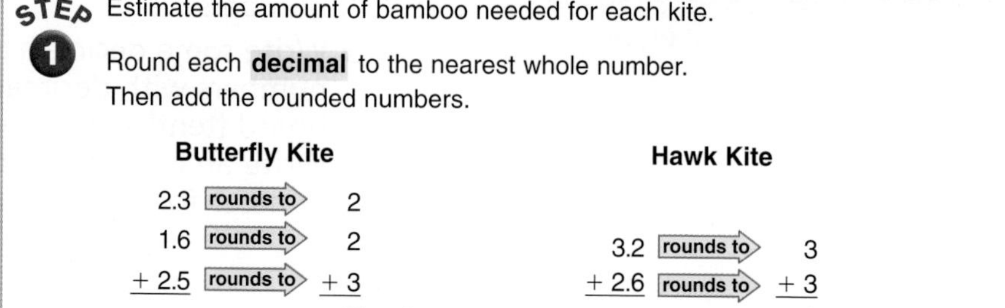

STEP 1 Estimate the amount of bamboo needed for each kite.

Round each **decimal** to the nearest whole number.
Then add the rounded numbers.

Butterfly Kite

2.3	rounds to	2
1.6	rounds to	2
+ 2.5	rounds to	+ 3
		7 meters

Hawk Kite

3.2	rounds to	3
+ 2.6	rounds to	+ 3
		6 meters

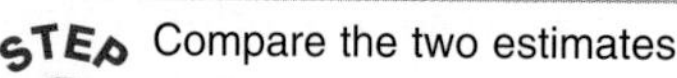

STEP 2 Compare the two estimates.

7 meters > 6 meters

The butterfly kite needs more bamboo than the hawk kite.

Solution: Liang should pick the hawk kite.

Other Examples

A. Round to the Nearest $10.

$16.25	rounds to	$20
+ 12.35	rounds to	+ 10
		$30

B. Round to the Nearest $100.

$306.75	rounds to	$300
− 97.25	rounds to	− 100
		$200

570

Reteach 22.2

Name ______________ Date ________

Reteach 22.2

Estimate Decimal Sums and Differences

Mr. Smith drives 3.7 miles and 15.4 miles to get to the mall. Ms. Lang drives 12.8 miles and 4.3 miles to get to the mall. Who drives the greater distance to the mall?

Step 1
Estimate the length of each route.

Mr. Smith: 3.7 → 4; +15.4 → 15; 19 miles
Ms. Lang: 12.8 → 13; + 4.3 → 4; 17 miles

Step 2
Compare the two estimates.
19 miles > 17 miles

Solution: Mr. Smith drives the greater distance to the mall.

Estimate by rounding to the nearest whole number.

1. 6.3 + 5.7 — 12
2. 22.9 + 17.1 — 40
3. 8.9 − 4.3 — 5
4. 14.6 − 10.3 — 5
5. 43.72 + 7.88 — 52
6. 24.14 − 15.63 — 8
7. 86.224 + 9.831 — 96
8. 37.09 − 24.63 — 12
9. $43.72 + 15.88 — $60
10. $527.65 − 260.85 — $267
11. $300.25 − 65.75 — $234
12. $506.02 + 423.75 — $930

Use with text pages 570–571.

Practice 22.2 Page 140

Name ______________ Date ________

Practice 22.2

Estimate Decimal Sums and Differences

Estimate by rounding to the nearest whole number.

1. 9.3 + 6.1 — 15
2. 7.3 − 4.7 — 2
3. $83.82 + 24.13 — $108
4. $45.38 − 18.77 — $26
5. 38.872 + 25.913 — 65
6. $8.92 − 4.23 — $5
7. 48.32 + 68.37 — 116
8. 73.253 − 45.892 — 27
9. $46.22 + 89.79 — $136
10. 64.327 − 32.781 — 31

Estimate by rounding to the nearest $10 and $100.

11. $832.34 + $243.98 — $1,070; $1,000
12. $581.48 − $293.98 — $290; $300
13. $184.33 + $284.79 — $460; $500
14. $465.81 − $368.54 — $100; $100
15. $346.55 + $784.15 — $1,130; $1,100
16. $412.84 − $335.71 — $70; $100
17. $584.35 + $953.51 — $1,530; $1,600
18. $334.58 − $227.49 — $100; $100
19. $848.84 − $484.48 — $370; $300

Test Prep

20. Brian has 12 meters of canvas for his paintings. He uses 4.78 m for one painting and 5.87 m for another. About how much canvas does he have left?
   A 12 meters B 1 meter C 2 meters D 11 meters
   B

21. Jeffrey is making a chair. He spent $14.87 on wood and $18.48 on other supplies. About how much did he spend in all?
   $33

Use with text pages 570–571.

21. *Possible explanation:* I rounded to the greatest place, or the nearest million. $4,000,000 + $10,000,000 = $14,000,000.

Guided Practice

Ask Yourself
- How do I round each decimal to the nearest whole number?
- Should I add or subtract?

Estimate by rounding to the nearest whole number.

1. 5.1 − 1.7 = **3**
2. $44.63 + 14.35 = **$59**
3. 349.29 + 34.516 = **384**
4. 4.7 + 2.5 + 3.1 **11**
5. 21.73 − 19.959 **2**
6. $157.93 + $104.52 **$263**

Explain Your Thinking ▶ Would rounding to the nearest $10 or $100 give the most reasonable estimate for Exercise 6? ***See Additional Answers.***

Practice and Problem Solving

Estimate by rounding to the nearest whole number.

7. 8.6 + 5.2 = **14**
8. 8.2 − 3.9 = **4**
9. $23.82 − 20.49 = **$4**
10. 13.534 + 15.972 = **30**
11. $349.59 + 34.25 = **$384**

Make two estimates for each exercise. First round to the nearest $10, then to the nearest $100.

12. $139.24 + $406.37 **$550; $500**
13. $274.85 + $135.40 **$410; $400**
14. $527.49 − $248.21 **$280; $300**
15. $902.55 − $383.72 **$520; $500**
16. $727.33 + $91.89 **$820; $800**
17. $563.50 − $329.90 **$230; $300**

Solve.

18. **Money** Tom spent $18.96 on fabric and $15.37 on other supplies to make a kite. About how much did he spend? **about $34**
19. Kaya has 15 m of silk. She uses 7.15 m for one kite and 5.76 m for another. About how much does she have left? **about 2 meters**
20. Buses taking people to a kite-flying competition leave every 7 minutes, starting at 9:05 A.M. At what time will the sixth bus leave for the show? **9:40 A.M.**
21. **Explain** Give a reasonable estimate for the sum of $4,109,384.75 and $9,834,523.78. What place did you round to? ***See above.***

Mixed Review and Test Prep

Open Response

Write each decimal as a fraction. (Ch. 21, Lesson 4)

22. 0.1 $\frac{1}{10}$
23. 0.48 $\frac{48}{100}$
24. 0.125 $\frac{125}{1,000}$
25. 0.70 $\frac{70}{100}$
26. 0.6 $\frac{6}{10}$
27. 0.08 $\frac{8}{100}$

28. Miguel rode his bike 3.3 km, 1.5 km, and 2.8 km. About how much farther does he need to ride to reach 10 km? Explain how you got your answer. ***See Additional Answers.*** (Ch.22, Lesson 2)

Extra Practice See page 581, Set B.

❸ Practice

Practice and Problem Solving

Select from **Exercises 7–28** as independent work.

- Have students share their answers and explain how they made their estimates.
- ***Problem 18*** Ask: **What word suggests that you can estimate the sum?** (about)

❹ Assess & Close

Math Talk in Action

Conclude the lesson by having volunteers share their work.

- **Why do we sometimes find estimated sums and differences?** (to be able to solve problems mentally; to get approximate answers)
- **Tell how to estimate the difference of 87.39 − 46.71.** (Round each decimal to the nearest whole number or ten. Then subtract the rounded numbers; 87 − 47 = 40; or 90 − 50 = 40.)

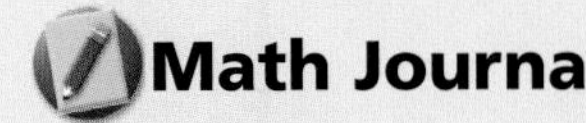

Math Journal

Have students describe some situations in which they might estimate with decimals.

Lesson Quiz

Use the quiz on Lesson Transparency 22.2. (Lesson 22.2 Transparency)

Test Prep & Spiral Review

Use Test Prep Transparency 22.2. (Test Prep 22.2 Transparency)

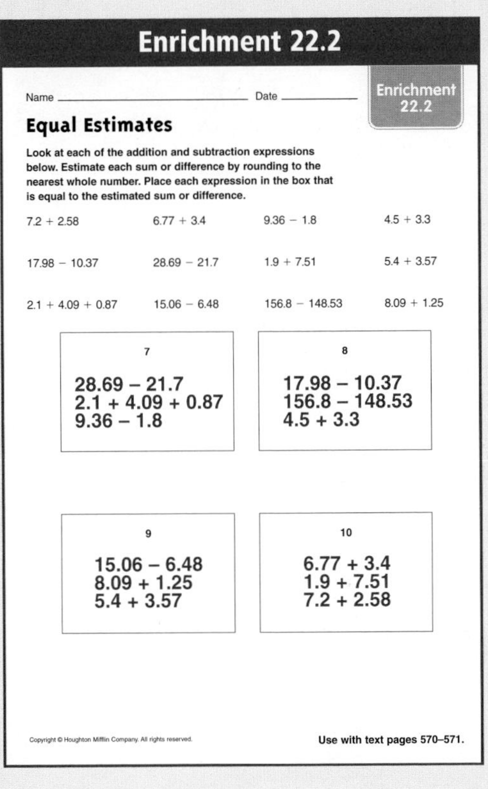

Enrichment 22.2

Name ____ Date ____ Enrichment 22.2

Equal Estimates

Look at each of the addition and subtraction expressions below. Estimate each sum or difference by rounding to the nearest whole number. Place each expression in the box that is equal to the estimated sum or difference.

7.2 + 2.58	6.77 + 3.4	9.36 − 1.8	4.5 + 3.3
17.98 − 10.37	28.69 − 21.7	1.9 + 7.51	5.4 + 3.57
2.1 + 4.09 + 0.87	15.06 − 6.48	156.8 − 148.53	8.09 + 1.25

7	8
28.69 − 21.7 2.1 + 4.09 + 0.87 9.36 − 1.8	17.98 − 10.37 156.8 − 148.53 4.5 + 3.3

9	10
15.06 − 6.48 8.09 + 1.25 5.4 + 3.57	6.77 + 3.4 1.9 + 7.51 7.2 + 2.58

Use with text pages 570–571.

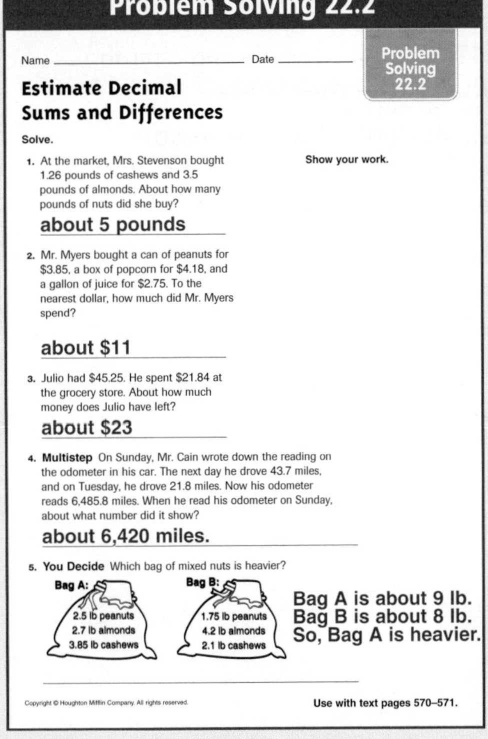

Problem Solving 22.2

Name ____ Date ____ Problem Solving 22.2

Estimate Decimal Sums and Differences

Solve. Show your work.

1. At the market, Mrs. Stevenson bought 1.26 pounds of cashews and 3.5 pounds of almonds. About how many pounds of nuts did she buy? **about 5 pounds**
2. Mr. Myers bought a can of peanuts for $3.85, a box of popcorn for $4.18, and a gallon of juice for $2.75. To the nearest dollar, how much did Mr. Myers spend? **about $11**
3. Julio had $45.25. He spent $21.84 at the grocery store. About how much money does Julio have left? **about $23**
4. **Multistep** On Sunday, Mr. Cain wrote down the reading on the odometer in his car. The next day he drove 43.7 miles, and on Tuesday, he drove 21.8 miles. Now his odometer reads 6,485.8 miles. When he read his odometer on Sunday, about what number did it show? **about 6,420 miles.**
5. **You Decide** Which bag of mixed nuts is heavier?

Bag A is about 9 lb. Bag B is about 8 lb. So, Bag A is heavier.

Use with text pages 570–571.

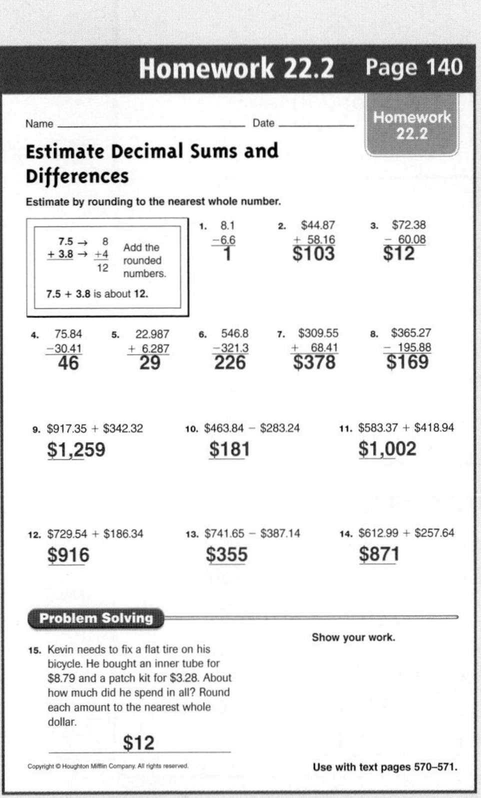

Homework 22.2 Page 140

Name ____ Date ____ Homework 22.2

Estimate Decimal Sums and Differences

Estimate by rounding to the nearest whole number.

7.5 → 8; + 3.8 → +4; 12. Add the rounded numbers.
7.5 + 3.8 is about **12.**

1. 8.1 − 6.6 = **1**
2. $44.87 + 58.16 = **$103**
3. $72.38 − 60.08 = **$12**
4. 75.84 − 30.41 = **46**
5. 22.987 + 6.287 = **29**
6. 546.8 − 321.3 = **226**
7. $309.55 + 68.41 = **$378**
8. $365.27 − 195.88 = **$169**
9. $917.35 + $342.32 **$1,259**
10. $463.84 − $283.24 **$181**
11. $583.37 + $418.94 **$1,002**
12. $729.54 + $186.34 **$916**
13. $741.65 − $387.14 **$355**
14. $612.99 + $257.64 **$871**

Problem Solving Show your work.

15. Kevin needs to fix a flat tire on his bicycle. He bought an inner tube for $8.79 and a patch kit for $3.28. About how much did he spend in all? Round each amount to the nearest whole dollar. **$12**

Use with text pages 570–571.

Hands On Lesson 22.3

Explore Addition and Subtraction of Decimals

Planning

Lesson Objective Use models to add and subtract decimals.

Technology Resources

- *Ways to Success* CD-ROM 22.3
- Education Place: Extra Practice, eGames www.eduplace.com/map

Lesson 22.3 Transparency

Problem of the Day

Describe the pattern. Then extend it.

2.00 2.14 2.28 2.42 ____ ____ ____

(Pattern is to add 0.14; 2.56, 2.70, 2.84)

Spiral Review

Add or subtract.

1. $5.67 + 3.24 ($8.91)
2. $6.01 − 2.78 ($3.23)
3. $47.98 + 88.75 ($136.73)
4. $20.80 − 15.29 ($5.51)

Lesson Quiz

Find the sum or difference. Use models if you wish.

1. 4.3 − 1.7 (2.6)
2. 1.4 + 1.8 (3.2)
3. 2.47 − 1.24 (1.23)
4. 1.06 + 1.24 (2.30 or 2.3)
5. 2.08 − 1.34 (0.74)

NCTM Standards

Number and Operations: Use visual models, benchmarks, and equivalent forms to add and subtract commonly used fractions and decimals.

Representation: Select, apply, and translate among mathematical representations to solve problems.

Getting Started

Building Math Vocabulary

Students should be familiar with the mathematical vocabulary in this lesson.

Using Models

Whole Class	15 minutes
Objective	Add and subtract decimals.
Materials	Tenths and Hundredths Grids Transparency, blank transparency, markers in two colors
Visual	

- Write *1.1 + 0.7* on the board as students read it aloud. **How can I model this problem?** (Show 1 whole + 1 tenth, then 7 tenths more.)
- Invite one student to shade 1 whole and 1 tenth in one color and another student to shade 7 tenths in the second color. **What is the total amount shaded?** (1.8) Erase the transparency and repeat for 1.26 + 1.08. (2.34)
- **How could we show subtraction?** (Shade a total, cross out the amount to subtract.) Shade 2.35. **How much is shaded?** (2.35) **How can we subtract 1.1?** (Cross off 1 whole and 1 tenth.) **What is the difference?** (1.24)
- Tell students that this lesson explains how to add and subtract decimals by using models.

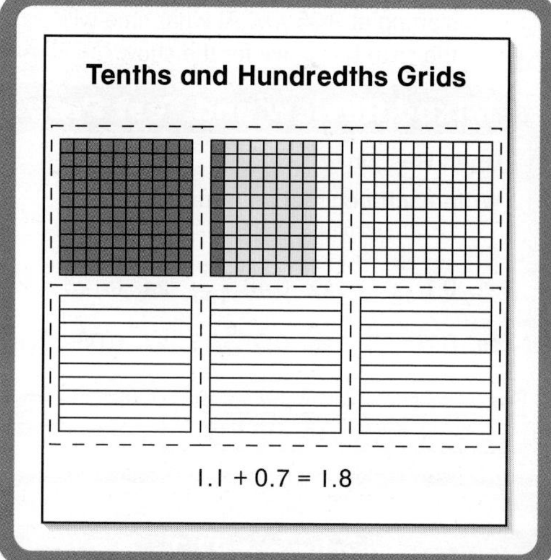

Differentiated Instruction

English Learners

Small Groups	10 minutes
Objective	Add and subtract decimals.
Materials	Student page 573, grid paper
Auditory, Visual	

Early Production

- To practice aligning decimals, have students use grid paper for ***On Your Own,*** placing each digit and decimal point in separate boxes.
- Suggest that they ask themselves: *Did I line up the all of the decimals in the problem and my answer?*

Intermediate/Advanced

- English Learner Resource 22.3
- English Learner Handbook

Intervention

Small Groups	15 minutes
Objective	Add and subtract decimals.
Materials	Decimal Models (Learning Tool 41)
Visual, Auditory	

- Point out to students that when they use decimal models, they need not count the boxes in a row or column individually. Because of our base-ten system, the grid for hundredths has 10 rows of 10 boxes.
- Remind students that the word *decimal* means "based on 10." Encourage students to count by 10s as they do the exercises in this lesson. Also have them repeat the decimal relationships they know: 100 hundredths = 1 whole, 10 tenths = 1 whole, 1,000 thousandths = 1 whole, 10 hundredths = 1 tenth, and so on.

Other Resources

- *Ways to Success* CD-ROM 22.3

Early Finishers

Small Groups	15 minutes
Objective	Add and subtract decimals to thousandths.
Materials	None
Visual, Auditory	

- Challenge early finishers to extend their ability to add and subtract decimals by including decimals to the thousandths place. Although students don't have thousandths models, they can apply their understanding of place value to find decimal sums and differences.
- Have students complete the following problems:
  3.427 + 2.139 (5.566)
  2.864 − 1.357 (1.507)
  0.593 + 1.748 (2.341)
  1.042 − 0.506 (0.536)

Art Connection

Materials: Decimal Models (Learning Tool 41), color pencils or markers

Have students use decimal models to show decimal addition as a design that represents the values. To show 1.32 + 0.64, students could color 132 hundredths in any position in one color and 64 hundredths in another color to form a pleasing image. Display completed works with mathematical expressions to match.

❶ Introduce

Read the objective to students and explain that in this lesson they will use decimal grids to add and subtract decimals though hundredths. Students will add and subtract decimals and money amounts.

❷ Teach

Work Together

Materials: Learning Tool 41, red and blue colored pencils

- **Look at *Step 1* for adding 1.5 + 0.75. Why must we use 2 grids to show 1.5?** (1.5 = 1 whole + 5 tenths of the next whole.)
- **Look at *Step 2.* Why do we use a second color?** (to ensure that we shade 0.75 correctly)
- **Look at *Step 3.* How does the chart relate to the grid?** (The top number shows the parts of the grids that are shaded red. The bottom number shows the parts that are shaded blue.)
- **Look at the steps to subtract 2.1 − 1.4. In *Step 2,* why do we outline 1.4?** (to ensure we subtract the amount in the problem) **Would we get the same answer if we outlined a total of 1.4 in some other arrangement?** (yes)

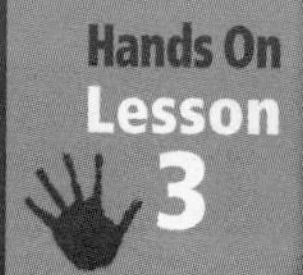

Explore Addition and Subtraction of Decimals

Objective Use models to add and subtract decimals.

Materials
Decimal Models
(Learning Tool 41)
colored pencils in red and blue

Work Together

You can use models to add and subtract decimals.

Work with a partner.
Use models to add.

Find 1.5 + 0.75.

Shade 1.5 decimal grids red.

STEP 2 Shade an additional 0.75 decimal grids blue.

- How many decimal grids do you need? Why?

3 grids; because there is more to shade than fits in 2 squares

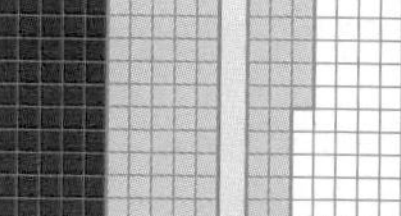

STEP 3 Record your work in a chart like the one on the right.

	ones	.	tenths	hundredths
	1	.	5	0
+	0	.	7	5

- How should you line up the numbers?

You should align the decimal points.

- Why do you record 0 in the hundredths place for 1.5?

to show that there are no hundredths

- What is the sum? **2.25**

572

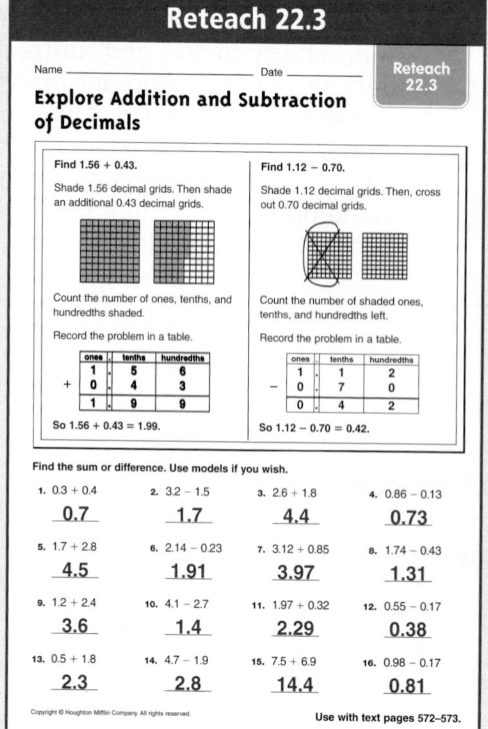

Reteach 22.3

Name ______________ Date ________ Reteach 22.3

Explore Addition and Subtraction of Decimals

Find 1.56 + 0.43.

Shade 1.56 decimal grids. Then shade an additional 0.43 decimal grids.

Count the number of ones, tenths, and hundredths shaded.

Record the problem in a table.

	ones	.	tenths	hundredths
	1	.	5	6
+	0	.	4	3
	1	.	9	9

So 1.56 + 0.43 = 1.99.

Find 1.12 − 0.70.

Shade 1.12 decimal grids. Then, cross out 0.70 decimal grids.

Count the number of shaded ones, tenths, and hundredths left.

Record the problem in a table.

	ones	.	tenths	hundredths
	1	.	1	2
−	0	.	7	0
	0	.	4	2

So 1.12 − 0.70 = 0.42.

Find the sum or difference. Use models if you wish.

1. 0.3 + 0.4 **0.7**
2. 3.2 − 1.5 **1.7**
3. 2.6 + 1.8 **4.4**
4. 0.86 − 0.13 **0.73**
5. 1.7 + 2.8 **4.5**
6. 2.14 − 0.23 **1.91**
7. 3.12 + 0.85 **3.97**
8. 1.74 − 0.43 **1.31**
9. 1.2 + 2.4 **3.6**
10. 4.1 − 2.7 **1.4**
11. 1.97 + 0.32 **2.29**
12. 0.55 − 0.17 **0.38**
13. 0.5 + 1.8 **2.3**
14. 4.7 − 1.9 **2.8**
15. 7.5 + 6.9 **14.4**
16. 0.98 − 0.17 **0.81**

Use with text pages 572–573.

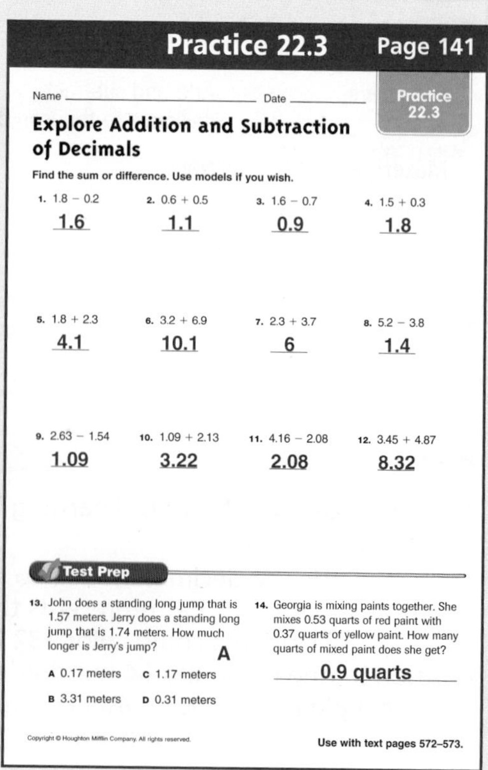

Practice 22.3 Page 141

Name ______________ Date ________ Practice 22.3

Explore Addition and Subtraction of Decimals

Find the sum or difference. Use models if you wish.

1. 1.8 − 0.2 **1.6**
2. 0.6 + 0.5 **1.1**
3. 1.6 − 0.7 **0.9**
4. 1.5 + 0.3 **1.8**
5. 1.8 + 2.3 **4.1**
6. 3.2 + 6.9 **10.1**
7. 2.3 + 3.7 **6**
8. 5.2 − 3.8 **1.4**
9. 2.63 − 1.54 **1.09**
10. 1.09 + 2.13 **3.22**
11. 4.16 − 2.08 **2.08**
12. 3.45 + 4.87 **8.32**

Test Prep

13. John does a standing long jump that is 1.57 meters. Jerry does a standing long jump that is 1.74 meters. How much longer is Jerry's jump? **A**

 A 0.17 meters C 1.17 meters
 B 3.31 meters D 0.31 meters

14. Georgia is mixing paints together. She mixes 0.53 quarts of red paint with 0.37 quarts of yellow paint. How many quarts of mixed paint does she get? **0.9 quarts**

Use with text pages 572–573.

Find 2.1 − 1.4.

Shade 2.1 decimal grids red.

Outline 1.4 on the shaded part of the grids and cross it out.

- Why do you cross out part of your model? **to show the part taken away**
- How many tenths are not crossed out? **7**

STEP 3

Record your work in a chart like the one on the right.

- What is the difference? **0.7**

	ones		tenths
	2	.	1
−	1	.	4

On Your Own

Find the sum or difference. Use models if you wish.

1. 1.3 + 1.7 **3**
2. 3.2 − 1.4 **1.8**
3. 2.9 + 3.5 **6.4**
4. 4.5 − 2.9 **1.60**
5. 3.71 − 1.47 **2.24**
6. 1.04 + 1.18 **2.22**
7. 2.36 − 1.12 **1.24**
8. 3.27 + 4.96 **8.23**

Talk About It • Write About It

You learned how to use models to add and subtract decimals.

9. What does the decimal point in a number tell you? ***See below.***
10. Look at how the decimals are lined up in the addition chart. What would happen if the decimal points were not lined up? **You would add digits with different place values and your answer would be incorrect.**

9. It separates the ones and the tenths and determines the value of the digits.

3 Practice

On Your Own

Select from **Exercises 1–10** as independent work. Provide extra models as needed.

4 Assess & Close

Math Talk in Action

Discuss the ***Talk About It • Write About It*** feature. Invite students to share their responses.

How is adding and subtracting decimals like adding and subtracting whole numbers? In what way is it different? (Use the same base-ten relationships for regrouping with decimals as with whole numbers; the main difference is the need for a decimal point.)

Math Journal

Have students describe how they would add and subtract decimals without using models.

Lesson Quiz

Use the quiz on Lesson Transparency 22.3.

Test Prep & Spiral Review

Use Test Prep Transparency 22.3.

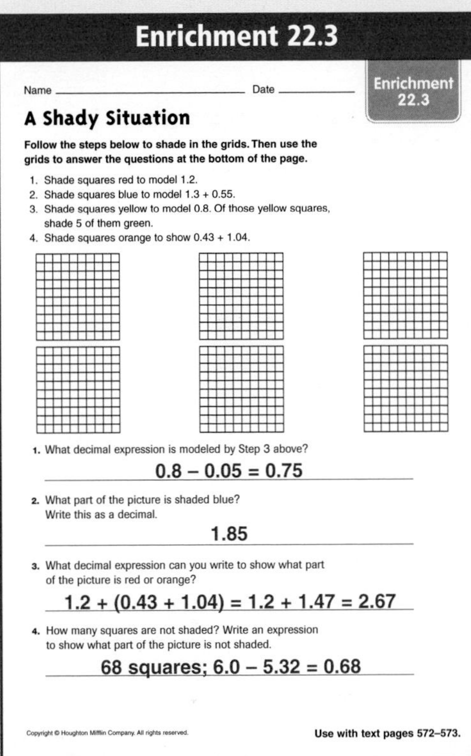

Enrichment 22.3

Name ______ Date ______ Enrichment 22.3

A Shady Situation

Follow the steps below to shade in the grids. Then use the grids to answer the questions at the bottom of the page.

1. Shade squares red to model 1.2.
2. Shade squares blue to model 1.3 + 0.55.
3. Shade squares yellow to model 0.8. Of those yellow squares, shade 5 of them green.
4. Shade squares orange to show 0.43 + 1.04.

1. What decimal expression is modeled by Step 3 above? **0.8 – 0.05 = 0.75**
2. What part of the picture is shaded blue? Write this as a decimal. **1.85**
3. What decimal expression can you write to show what part of the picture is red or orange? **1.2 + (0.43 + 1.04) = 1.2 + 1.47 = 2.67**
4. How many squares are not shaded? Write an expression to show what part of the picture is not shaded. **68 squares; 6.0 – 5.32 = 0.68**

Use with text pages 572–573.

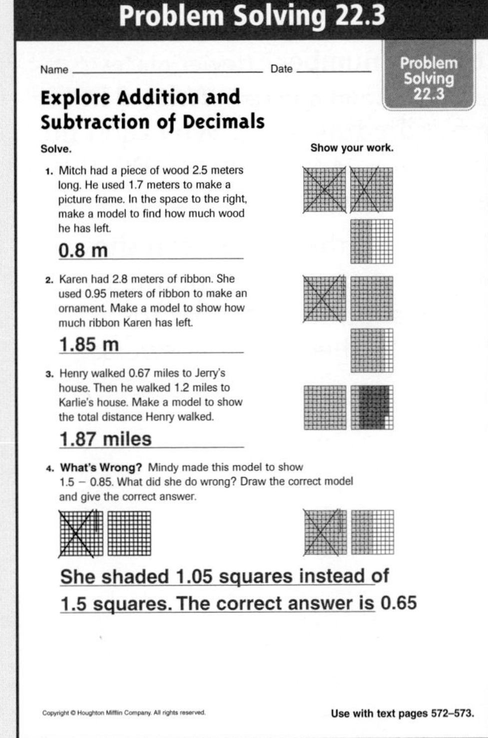

Problem Solving 22.3

Name ______ Date ______ Problem Solving 22.3

Explore Addition and Subtraction of Decimals

Solve. **Show your work.**

1. Mitch had a piece of wood 2.5 meters long. He used 1.7 meters to make a picture frame. In the space to the right, make a model to find how much wood he has left. **0.8 m**
2. Karen had 2.8 meters of ribbon. She used 0.95 meters of ribbon to make an ornament. Make a model to show how much ribbon Karen has left. **1.85 m**
3. Henry walked 0.67 miles to Jerry's house. Then he walked 1.2 miles to Karlie's house. Make a model to show the total distance Henry walked. **1.87 miles**
4. **What's Wrong?** Mindy made this model to show 1.5 − 0.85. What did she do wrong? Draw the correct model and give the correct answer. **She shaded 1.05 squares instead of 1.5 squares. The correct answer is 0.65**

Use with text pages 572–573.

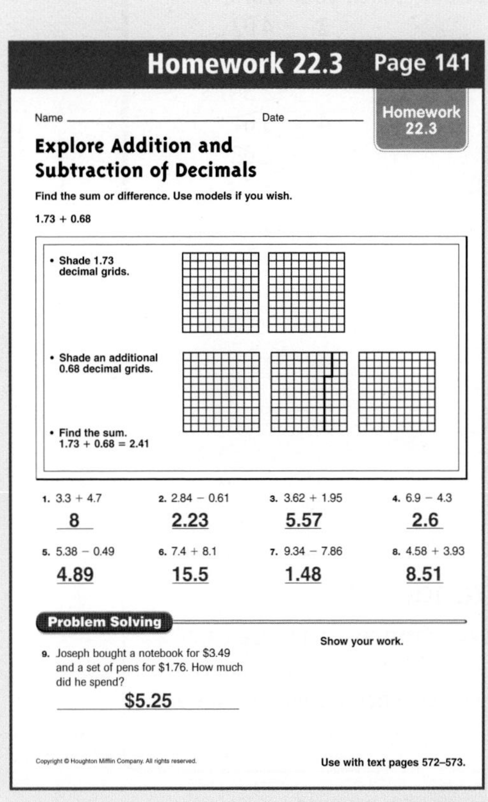

Homework 22.3 **Page 141**

Name ______ Date ______ Homework 22.3

Explore Addition and Subtraction of Decimals

Find the sum or difference. Use models if you wish.

1.73 + 0.68

- **Shade 1.73 decimal grids.**
- **Shade an additional 0.68 decimal grids.**
- **Find the sum. 1.73 + 0.68 = 2.41**

1. 3.3 + 4.7 **8**
2. 2.84 − 0.61 **2.23**
3. 3.62 + 1.95 **5.57**
4. 6.9 − 4.3 **2.6**
5. 5.38 − 0.49 **4.89**
6. 7.4 + 8.1 **15.5**
7. 9.34 − 7.86 **1.48**
8. 4.58 + 3.93 **8.51**

Problem Solving

Show your work.

9. Joseph bought a notebook for $3.49 and a set of pens for $1.76. How much did he spend? **$5.25**

Use with text pages 572–573.

Lesson 22.4

Add and Subtract Decimals

Planning

Lesson Objective Add and subtract decimals.

Technology Resources

- Audio Tutor 2/28 Listen and Understand
- *Ways to Success* CD-ROM 22.4
- *Ways to Assess* CD-ROM
- Education Place: Extra Practice, Extra Help, eGames www.eduplace.com/map

Lesson 22.4 Transparency

Problem of the Day

Describe the pattern. Then continue it.
(Pattern is to add 5.79; 33.18; 38.97; 44.76)
10.02 15.81 21.6 27.39 _____ _____ _____

Spiral Review

Write each decimal in standard form.

1. two hundred fifty-six thousandths (0.256)
2. 40 + 7 + 0.9 + 0.006 (47.906)
3. nine and eighteen hundredths (9.18)
4. 7 + 3 tenths + 8 thousandths (7.308)
5. ten and sixty-one thousandths (10.061)

Lesson Quiz

Add or subtract. Check your work.

1. 5.7 + 9.4 (15.1)
2. 4.02 − 1.63 (2.39)
3. 7.918 + 1.375 (9.293)
4. 5.61 − 2.08 (3.53)

NCTM Standards

Number and Operations: Use visual models, benchmarks, and equivalent forms to add and subtract commonly used fractions and decimals.

Getting Started

Building Math Vocabulary

Students should be familiar with the mathematical vocabulary in this lesson.

Adding and Subtracting Decimals

Whole Class	15 minutes
Objective	Add and subtract decimals.
Materials	Blank transparency
Visual, Auditory	

- Write *9.42 + 7.60* horizontally. Have students read the decimals. **How do we write decimals vertically to add them?** (Line up decimal points.) **Adding decimals is like adding whole numbers. Where do we begin?** (in the place farthest right, which is hundredths) **Ask a student to do the addition. Where does the decimal point go?** (between ones and tenths) **What is the sum?** (17.02)

- Now write *34.4 − 27.41* horizontally. Have students read the decimals. **How do we write decimals vertically to subtract them?** (Line up decimal points.) **What do you notice in the top number?** (fewer places than the bottom number) **Write *0* in the hundredths place. Why can I do this?** (34.4 = 34.40) **Subtract. What is the difference?** (6.99)
- Tell students that this lesson shows how to line up decimal points to add and subtract and how to estimate to check their answers.

Differentiated Instruction

English Learners

Small Groups	10 minutes
Objective	Add and subtract decimals.
Materials	Student page 575, grid paper
Visual, Tactual	

Early Production

- Students may need help setting up problems in ***Guided Practice.***
- Using grid paper, have them write the three decimal points first. Then, looking at the first decimal point, copy the numbers first to the left and then to the right. Repeat for the second decimal point, and then add or subtract.

Intermediate/Advanced

- English Learner Resource 22.4
- English Learner Handbook

Intervention

Small Groups	5–10 minutes
Objective	Compare decimals.
Materials	Decimal place-value chart
Visual, Auditory	

- Help students see why we may affix zeros to the right of a decimal without changing its value.
- Write *4.5* and *4.50* in the decimal place-value chart as students read them. **Why are these decimals equivalent?** (They both mean "4 wholes + half," either as $\frac{5}{10}$ or $\frac{50}{100}$.) Affix another zero onto each decimal: 4.50, 4.500. **Has either decimal changed its value?** (no)
- **Why would we ever want to add a zero to a decimal?** (so both addends have the same number of places)

Other Resources

- *Ways to Success* CD-ROM 22.4

Gifted & Talented

Small Groups	15 minutes
Objective	Order decimals.
Materials	None
Visual, Tactual	

Present this data from *Guinness World Records 2002* on car speed records (in miles per hour):

- regular: 240.25
- electric: 245.951
- rocket: 631.366
- solar: 48.71
- diesel: 235.756

Have students order the test car speeds from fastest to slowest. Then have them write three word problems using the given data.

Literature Connection

- Read excerpts from *Olympic Math: Gold Medal Activities and Projects* by Sharon Vogt with students.
- Challenge them to use their knowledge of adding and subtracting decimals to create and solve problems based on the data given in the book.

❶ Introduce

Read the objective to students and explain that in this lesson they will follow step-by-step procedures to add and subtract decimals. Encourage students to use estimation to check answers to addition problems and use addition to check answers to subtraction problems.

❷ Teach

Learn About It

- **Look at *Step 1.* Why must we line up decimal points?** (to add ones to ones, tenths to tenths, etc.) **Why is it okay to write a *0* in the hundredths place in the second addend?** (7.5 = 7.50)
- **Look at *Step 2.* Would 875 be a correct answer? Explain.** (No, there must be a decimal point.)
- **Look at *Step 3.* Why do we add to check?** (Adding and subtracting are opposites.)

Guided Practice

Have students complete **Exercises 1–7** as you observe. Remind them to use the *Ask Yourself* questions to help. Give students the opportunity to talk about the question in *Explain Your Thinking*.

❸ Practice

Practice and Problem Solving

Select from **Exercises 8–20** as independent work.

- ***Mental Math*** Ask: **How can you decide where the missing decimal points belong?** (Use number sense and work backward.)

Common Error

- **Omitting decimal points**
- **Intervention** Remind students that although they may align numbers properly and compute correctly, decimal answers are incorrect if they lack the decimal point. Suggest that students write the decimal point where it belongs *before* they compute.

Lesson 4

Audio Tutor 2/28 Listen and Understand

Add and Subtract Decimals

Objective Add and subtract decimals.

Learn About It

Inez is visiting the Mayan ruins at Uxmal. The Governor's Palace stands on a series of four platforms. One of the platforms is 1.25 meters high. Another is 7.5 meters high. What is the total height of the two platforms?

Add. $1.25 + 7.5 = n$

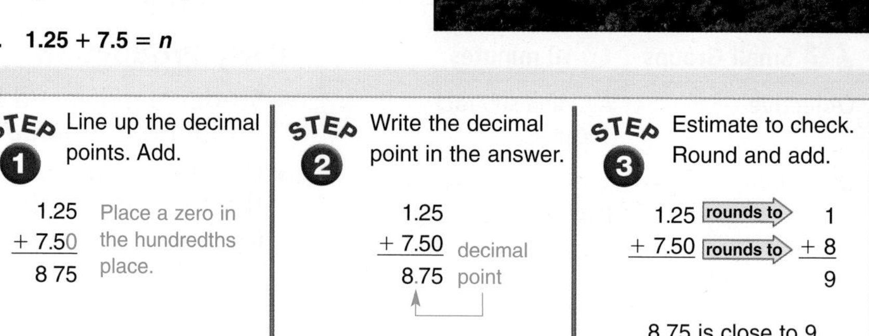

STEP 1 Line up the decimal points. Add.
1.25
+ 7.50
8 75
Place a zero in the hundredths place.
STEP 2 Write the decimal point in the answer.
1.25
+ 7.50
8.75
decimal point
STEP 3 Estimate to check. Round and add.
1.25 rounds to 1
+ 7.50 rounds to + 8
9
8.75 is close to 9.

Solution: The total height of the two platforms is 8.75 meters.

If the height of all four platforms is 18.05 meters, what is the combined height of the remaining two platforms?

Subtract. $18.05 - 8.75 = n$

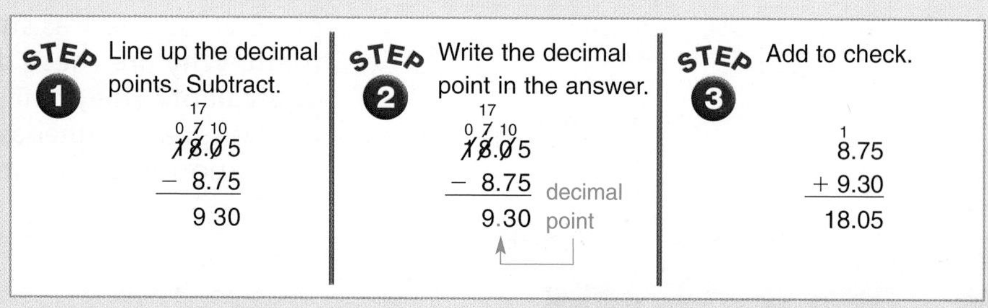

STEP 1 Line up the decimal points. Subtract.
17
0 7 10
18.05
− 8.75
9 30
STEP 2 Write the decimal point in the answer.
17
0 7 10
18.05
− 8.75
9.30
decimal point
STEP 3 Add to check.
1
8.75
+ 9.30
18.05

Solution: The combined height of the remaining two platforms is 9.3 meters.

574

Extra Help, See page 581, Set C.

Extra Help at **eduplace.com/map**

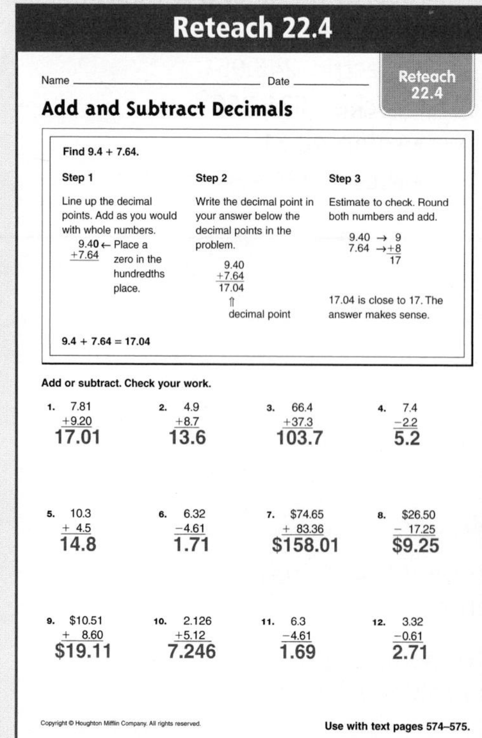

Reteach 22.4

Name ______________ Date __________ Reteach 22.4

Add and Subtract Decimals

Find 9.4 + 7.64.

Step 1 Line up the decimal points. Add as you would with whole numbers.
9.40 ← Place a zero in the hundredths place.
+7.64

Step 2 Write the decimal point in your answer below the decimal points in the problem.
9.40
+7.64
17.04
⇑ decimal point

Step 3 Estimate to check. Round both numbers and add.
9.40 → 9
7.64 → +8
17
17.04 is close to 17. The answer makes sense.

9.4 + 7.64 = 17.04

Add or subtract. Check your work.

1. 7.81 + 9.20 = **17.01**
2. 4.9 + 8.7 = **13.6**
3. 66.4 + 37.3 = **103.7**
4. 7.4 − 2.2 = **5.2**
5. 10.3 + 4.5 = **14.8**
6. 6.32 − 4.61 = **1.71**
7. \$74.65 + 83.36 = **\$158.01**
8. \$26.50 − 17.25 = **\$9.25**
9. \$10.51 + 8.60 = **\$19.11**
10. 2.126 + 5.12 = **7.246**
11. 6.3 − 4.61 = **1.69**
12. 3.32 − 0.61 = **2.71**

Use with text pages 574–575.

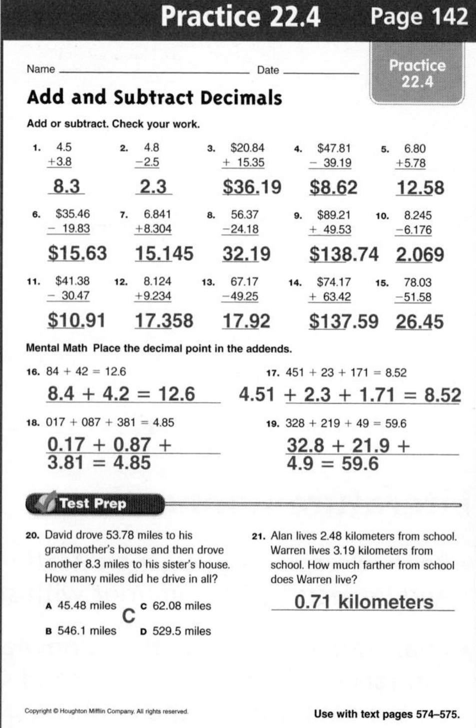

Practice 22.4 **Page 142**

Name ______________ Date __________ Practice 22.4

Add and Subtract Decimals

Add or subtract. Check your work.

1. 4.5 + 3.8 = **8.3**
2. 4.8 − 2.5 = **2.3**
3. \$20.84 + 15.35 = **\$36.19**
4. \$47.81 − 39.19 = **\$8.62**
5. 6.80 + 5.78 = **12.58**
6. \$35.46 − 19.83 = **\$15.63**
7. 6.841 + 8.304 = **15.145**
8. 56.37 − 24.18 = **32.19**
9. \$89.21 + 49.53 = **\$138.74**
10. 8.245 − 6.176 = **2.069**
11. \$41.38 − 30.47 = **\$10.91**
12. 8.124 + 9.234 = **17.358**
13. 67.17 − 49.25 = **17.92**
14. \$74.17 + 63.42 = **\$137.59**
15. 78.03 − 51.58 = **26.45**

Mental Math Place the decimal point in the addends.

16. 84 + 42 = 12.6 **8.4 + 4.2 = 12.6**
17. 451 + 23 + 171 = 8.52 **4.51 + 2.3 + 1.71 = 8.52**
18. 017 + 087 + 381 = 4.85 **0.17 + 0.87 + 3.81 = 4.85**
19. 328 + 219 + 49 = 59.6 **32.8 + 21.9 + 4.9 = 59.6**

Test Prep

20. David drove 53.78 miles to his grandmother's house and then drove another 8.3 miles to his sister's house. How many miles did he drive in all?
A 45.48 miles
B 546.1 miles
C 62.08 miles
D 529.5 miles
C

21. Alan lives 2.48 kilometers from school. Warren lives 3.19 kilometers from school. How much farther from school does Warren live? **0.71 kilometers**

Use with text pages 574–575.

Guided Practice

Add or subtract. Check your work.

1. 8.2 + 2.5 = **10.7**　**2.** \$2.32 + 1.71 = **\$4.03**　**3.** 12.34 − 10.125 = **2.215**

4. \$83.35 − \$20.67 **\$62.68**　**5.** 24.31 + 2.579 **26.889**　**6.** 9.31 − 3.4 **5.91**　**7.** 76.41 − 8.15 **68.26**

Ask Yourself
- Should I add or subtract?
- Where do I put the decimal point?

Explain Your Thinking ▶ Compare adding and subtracting decimals to adding and subtracting whole numbers. ***See Additional Answers.***

Practice and Problem Solving

Add or subtract. Check your work.

8. 2.4 + 7.1 = **9.5**　**9.** 3.25 + 3.49 = **6.74**　**10.** \$91.42 − 35.21 = **\$56.21**　**11.** 5.38 − 0.67 = **4.71**　**12.** 5.384 − 1.921 = **3.463**

Mental Math Place the decimal points in the addends to make the sentences correct.

13. 14 + 32 = 4.6 **1.4 + 3.2**
14. 47 + 189 = 23.6 **4.7 + 18.9**
15. 12 + 258 + 101 = 13.88 **1.2 + 2.58 + 10.1**
16. 451 + 109 = 5.6 **4.51 + 1.09**
17. 237 + 374 = 39.77 **2.37 + 37.4**
18. 12 + 295 + 41 = 45.15 **1.2 + 2.95 + 41**

19. When Emilio was on vacation last summer, his family drove 8.25 km to Merida and 78.4 km to Uxmal. How many kilometers did they drive? **86.65 kilometers**

20. Create and Solve Write a problem that requires adding or subtracting decimals. Give your problem to a classmate to solve. ***Check students' work.***

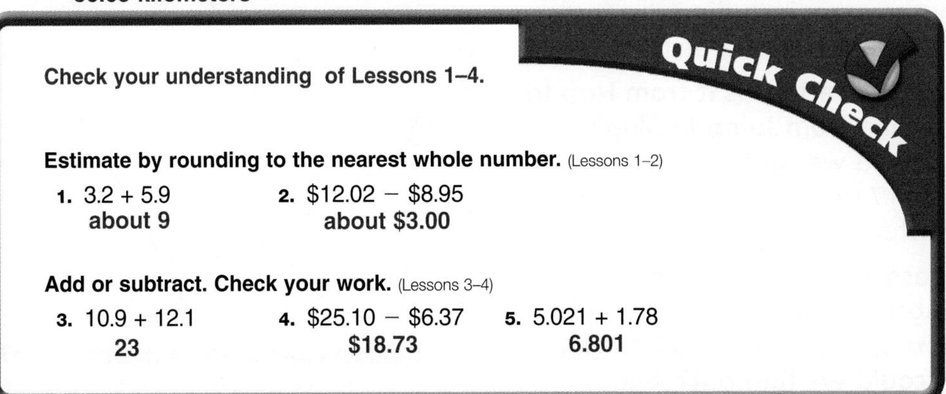
Quick Check

Check your understanding of Lessons 1–4.

Estimate by rounding to the nearest whole number. (Lessons 1–2)

1. 3.2 + 5.9 **about 9**　**2.** \$12.02 − \$8.95 **about \$3.00**

Add or subtract. Check your work. (Lessons 3–4)

3. 10.9 + 12.1 **23**　**4.** \$25.10 − \$6.37 **\$18.73**　**5.** 5.021 + 1.78 **6.801**

Extra Practice at eduplace.com/map

4 Assess & Close

Math Talk in Action

- **Why is it acceptable to write a zero at the end of a decimal?** (Zeros to the right of the given places won't change the value of the decimal.)

Math Journal

Have students show all work to add 30.8 + 43.26. Have them explain how to check their answers.

Lesson Quiz

Use the quiz on Lesson Transparency 22.4.

Test Prep & Spiral Review

Use Test Prep Transparency 22.4.

Quick Check

The *Quick Check* allows you to assess students' understanding of the concepts presented in **Lessons 1–4.**

Items	Objectives Tested	Pages	Intervention
1–2	Use rounding to estimate sums and differences.	568–571	Reteach Resources 22.1, 22.2 *Ways to Success* 22.1, 22.2
3–5	Add and subtract decimals.	572–575	Reteach Resources 22.3, 22.4 *Ways to Success* 22.3, 22.4

Enrichment 22.4

Name ______ Date ______ Enrichment 22.4

Pathways

Wacky Wally walked to Wendy's house. He doesn't like to take the straight road, but rather weaves along the paths to Wendy's house. Wally said he took the path that when he added the signs he saw along the way, the sum was 16.4. Find which path Wally took.

The path is shown below.

START　1.5　2.8　1.6　2.3　4.75　4.5　2.45　3.5　3.4　6.1　3.82　4.25　1.7　5.1　3.75　1.2　6.4　Wendy's House

1.6 + 2.3 + 2.45 + 3.4 + 1.7 + 3.75 + 1.2 = 16.4

　Use with text pages 574–575.

Problem Solving 22.4

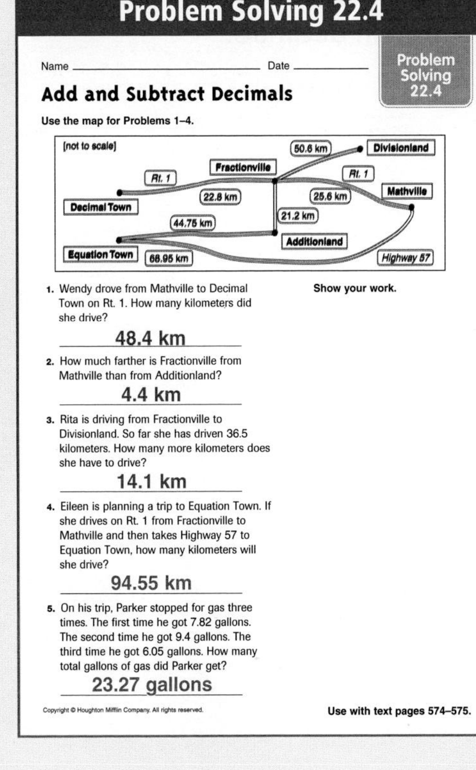
Name ______ Date ______ Problem Solving 22.4

Add and Subtract Decimals

Use the map for Problems 1–4.

1. Wendy drove from Mathville to Decimal Town on Rt. 1. How many kilometers did she drive? **48.4 km**
2. How much farther is Fractionville from Mathville than from Additionland? **4.4 km**
3. Rita is driving from Fractionville to Divisionland. So far she has driven 36.5 kilometers. How many more kilometers does she have to drive? **14.1 km**
4. Eileen is planning a trip to Equation Town. If she drives on Rt. 1 from Fractionville to Mathville and then takes Highway 57 to Equation Town, how many kilometers will she drive? **94.55 km**
5. On his trip, Parker stopped for gas three times. The first time he got 7.82 gallons. The second time he got 9.4 gallons. The third time he got 6.05 gallons. How many total gallons of gas did Parker get? **23.27 gallons**

Show your work.

　Use with text pages 574–575.

Homework 22.4 Page 142

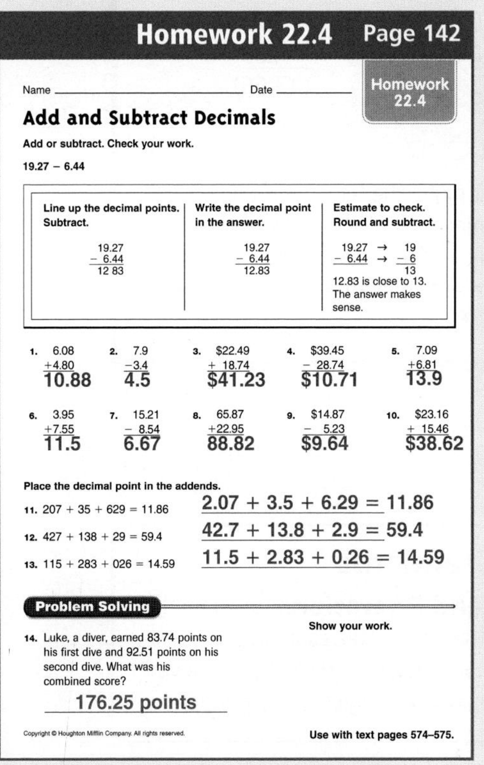
Name ______ Date ______ Homework 22.4

Add and Subtract Decimals

Add or subtract. Check your work.

19.27 − 6.44

Line up the decimal points. Subtract.	Write the decimal point in the answer.	Estimate to check. Round and subtract.
19.27 − 6.44 = 12 83	19.27 − 6.44 = 12.83	19.27 → 19; − 6.44 → − 6; 13. 12.83 is close to 13. The answer makes sense.

1. 6.08 + 4.80 = **10.88**　2. 7.9 − 3.4 = **4.5**　3. \$22.49 + 18.74 = **\$41.23**　4. \$39.45 − 28.74 = **\$10.71**　5. 7.09 + 6.81 = **13.9**

6. 3.95 + 7.55 = **11.5**　7. 15.21 − 8.54 = **6.67**　8. 65.87 + 22.95 = **88.82**　9. \$14.87 − 5.23 = **\$9.64**　10. \$23.16 + 15.46 = **\$38.62**

Place the decimal point in the addends.

11. 207 + 35 + 629 = 11.86 **2.07 + 3.5 + 6.29 = 11.86**
12. 427 + 138 + 29 = 59.4 **42.7 + 13.8 + 2.9 = 59.4**
13. 115 + 283 + 026 = 14.59 **11.5 + 2.83 + 0.26 = 14.59**

Problem Solving

14. Luke, a diver, earned 83.74 points on his first dive and 92.51 points on his second dive. What was his combined score? **176.25 points**

Show your work.

　Use with text pages 574–575.

Lesson 22.5

Problem-Solving Application: Use Decimals

Planning

Lesson Objective Use decimals to solve problems.

Math Background

There are many everyday examples of math problems students have to solve using decimals. Cooking, painting, and sewing all involve the use of decimals. Ask students to find examples of their own.

Technology Resources

- *Ways to Success* CD-ROM 22.5
- Education Place: Extra Practice www.eduplace.com/map

Lesson 22.5 Transparency

Problem of the Day

A marker costs $0.88 and a pad of paper costs $1.29. Reba needs 2 markers and 3 pads of paper. She has $5.00. Is this enough money? If yes, how much change will she get? If not, how much more money does she need? (No; Reba needs $0.63 more.)

Spiral Review

Add or subtract. Check your work.

1. 6.8 + 7.3 (14.1)

2. 5.06 − 3.57 (1.49)

3. 6.095 + 2.446 (8.541)

4. 7.72 − 4.06 (3.66)

Lesson Quiz

One winter night, the temperature fell 0.2°F every 15 minutes for 2 hours. When the temperature hit 15.6°F, it stayed there until dawn. What was the temperature when it began to fall? (17.2°F)

NCTM Standards

Number and Operations: Compute fluently and make reasonable estimates.

Problem Solving: Apply and adapt a variety of appropriate strategies to solve problems.

Getting Started

Building Math Vocabulary

Students should be familiar with the mathematical vocabulary in this lesson.

Adding and Subtracting Decimals

Whole Class	15 minutes
Objective	Use decimals to solve problems.
Materials	Blank transparency
Visual, Auditory	

- Copy the map, including distances, onto a blank transparency.
- **How much farther is it from Hop to Jump than from Jump to Skip? How could we find out?** (Subtract 31.6 − 28.7.) Have students compute the difference. (2.9 mi)
- **Suppose we wondered how far we'd go starting at Hop, going to Skip, then Jump, and back to Hop. How could we find out?** (Add 37 + 28.7 + 31.6) Have students compute the sum. (97.3 mi)
- Tell students that this lesson shows the steps to use to solve problems that contain decimals.

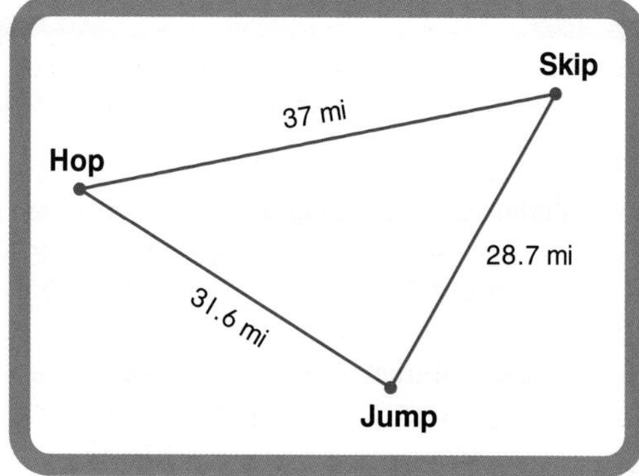

Differentiated Instruction

English Learners

Small Groups	10 minutes
Objective	Use decimals to solve problems.
Materials	Student page 577
Auditory, Visual	

Early Production

- Ask students to read the problems in ***Guided Practice*** aloud. Have them write the word or phrase that helps them decide which operation to use.
- Suggest that they add the following to ***Look Back:*** *Did I write the unit of measure in my answer?*

Intermediate/Advanced

- English Learner Resource 22.5
- English Learner Handbook

Intervention

Whole Class	5 minutes
Objective	Understand the problem.
Materials	None
Visual, Auditory	

- For some students, the greatest challenge in a problem-solving lesson is to comprehend the problem itself.
- Have students read for meaning. Stop them after each sentence and ask them to restate the details in their own words.

Answer questions or clarify as needed. Before they compute, ask students to justify why they should add or subtract.

Other Resources

- *Ways to Success* CD-ROM 22.5

Special Needs

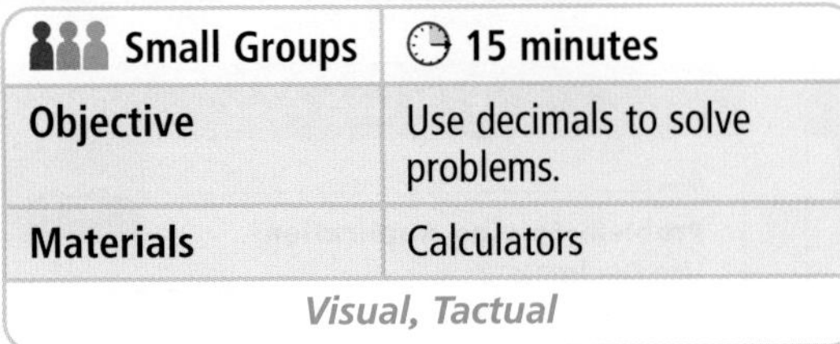

Small Groups	15 minutes
Objective	Use decimals to solve problems.
Materials	Calculators
Visual, Tactual	

- Students must solve problems involving decimals and decide which operation to use in each case. You might allow them to use calculators to compute so they can focus on the decision-making parts of the lesson.
- Have students state the operation they would use for each problem *before* they solve it.

Alternate Teaching Strategies

Explain to students that their neighbor will pay them $0.03 per linear foot for trimming the edge of a lawn 62 feet long and 38 feet wide. Ask students to figure out what the perimeter of the lawn is and how much they will be paid.

❶ Introduce

Read the objective to students and explain that in this lesson they will use decimals to solve real-life problems, decide whether to add or subtract decimals to find a solution, and choose a strategy and a computational method.

❷ Teach

Use Decimals

Work through the *Four-Step Problem Solving* section.

- Read the opening problem together. If needed, explain that London is the capital of England.
- **Look at the *Understand* step. What question will you try to answer?** (total number of passengers at Victoria and Oxford Circus stations in 2001) **What data does the problem give?** (number of millions of passengers at each station, in decimals)
- **Look at the *Plan* step. How do you know that this problem requires adding?** (Add for a total.)
- **Look at the *Solve* step. Why is it important to line up the decimal points before you add?** (to ensure that you add tens to tens, ones to ones, and tenths to tenths) **Why isn't the answer 142.6 people?** (It's 142.6 million people.)
- **Look at the *Look Back* step. How could you determine whether the answer is reasonable?** (Round and estimate: 80 + 70 = 150, which is close to 142.6.)

Guided Practice

Have students complete **Problems 1–2** as you observe. Remind them to use the ***Ask Yourself*** questions to help.

Common Error

- **Omitting decimal points**
- **Intervention** Remind students that although they may align numbers properly and compute correctly, decimal answers are incorrect if they lack the decimal point. Suggest that students write the decimal point where it belongs *before* they compute.

Lesson 5

Problem-Solving Application

Use Decimals

Objective Use decimals to solve problems.

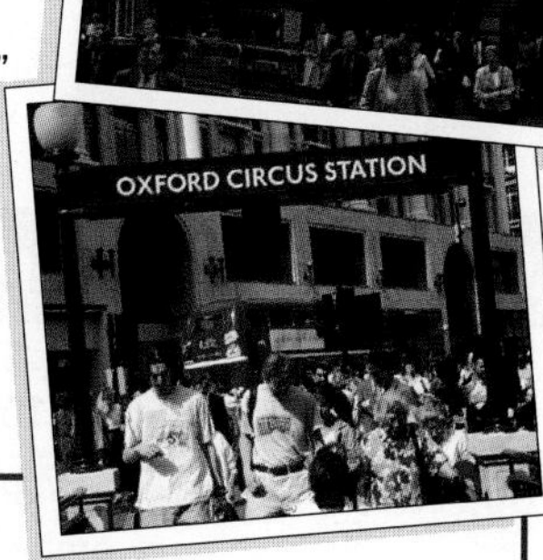

You can add or subtract decimals to solve problems.

Problem The London subway system is called "The Tube." Victoria and Oxford Circus are two busy Tube stations. In the year 2001, Victoria had 76.5 million passengers and Oxford Circus had 66.1 million passengers.

How many passengers did the two stations have in 2001?

UNDERSTAND

This is what the question asks.

How many passengers did Victoria Station and Oxford Circus Station have in the year 2001?

This is what you know.

- Victoria Station had 76.5 million passengers.
- Oxford Circus Station had 66.1 million passengers.

PLAN

Choose an operation.

Add the number of people who used Victoria Station and the number who used Oxford Circus Station.

SOLVE

Line up the decimal points and add.

$$\begin{array}{r} \overset{1}{7}6.5 \leftarrow \text{Victoria Station} \\ +\ 66.1 \leftarrow \text{Oxford Circus Station} \\ \hline 142.6 \end{array}$$

Solution: The two stations had 142.6 million passengers in the year 2001.

LOOK BACK

Look back at the problem.

Is your answer reasonable? Explain. **76.5 rounds to 80; 66.1 rounds to 70. 80 + 70 = 150. 150 is close to 142.6, so the answer is reasonable.**

576

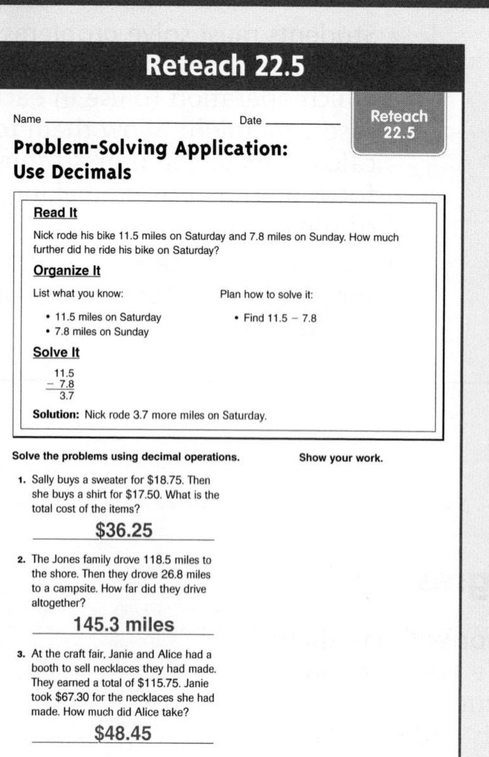

Reteach 22.5

Name ______________ Date ________ Reteach 22.5

Problem-Solving Application: Use Decimals

Read It

Nick rode his bike 11.5 miles on Saturday and 7.8 miles on Sunday. How much further did he ride his bike on Saturday?

Organize It

List what you know:

- 11.5 miles on Saturday
- 7.8 miles on Sunday

Plan how to solve it:

- Find 11.5 − 7.8

Solve It

$$\begin{array}{r} 11.5 \\ -\ 7.8 \\ \hline 3.7 \end{array}$$

Solution: Nick rode 3.7 more miles on Saturday.

Solve the problems using decimal operations. **Show your work.**

1. Sally buys a sweater for $18.75. Then she buys a shirt for $17.50. What is the total cost of the items?
   $36.25
2. The Jones family drove 118.5 miles to the shore. Then they drove 26.8 miles to a campsite. How far did they drive altogether?
   145.3 miles
3. At the craft fair, Janie and Alice had a booth to sell necklaces they had made. They earned a total of $115.75. Janie took $67.30 for the necklaces she had made. How much did Alice take?
   $48.45

Use with text pages 576–578.

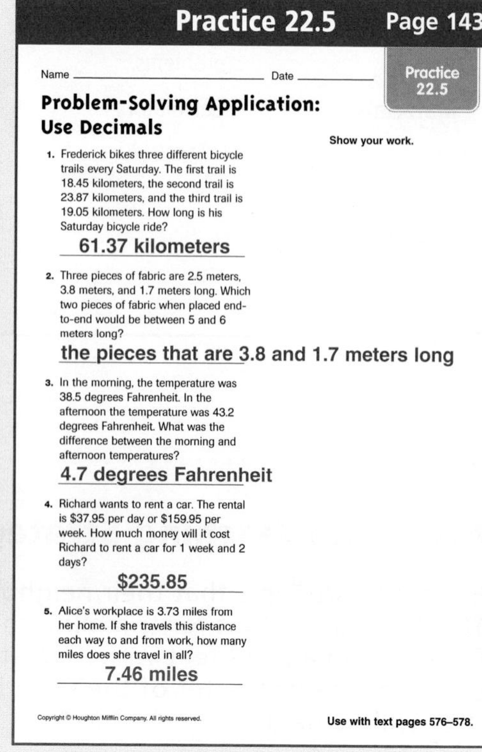

Practice 22.5 Page 143

Name ______________ Date ________ Practice 22.5

Problem-Solving Application: Use Decimals

Show your work.

1. Frederick bikes three different bicycle trails every Saturday. The first trail is 18.45 kilometers, the second trail is 23.87 kilometers, and the third trail is 19.05 kilometers. How long is his Saturday bicycle ride?
   61.37 kilometers
2. Three pieces of fabric are 2.5 meters, 3.8 meters, and 1.7 meters long. Which two pieces of fabric when placed end-to-end would be between 5 and 6 meters long?
   the pieces that are 3.8 and 1.7 meters long
3. In the morning, the temperature was 38.5 degrees Fahrenheit. In the afternoon the temperature was 43.2 degrees Fahrenheit. What was the difference between the morning and afternoon temperatures?
   4.7 degrees Fahrenheit
4. Richard wants to rent a car. The rental is $37.95 per day or $159.95 per week. How much money will it cost Richard to rent a car for 1 week and 2 days?
   $235.85
5. Alice's workplace is 3.73 miles from her home. If she travels this distance each way to and from work, how many miles does she travel in all?
   7.46 miles

Use with text pages 576–578.

Guided Practice

Use the Ask Yourself questions to help you solve each problem.

1. The average depth below ground of the deep-level Tube lines is 24.4 meters. The maximum depth is 43 meters more. What is the maximum depth? **67.4 meters**

   Hint: Are the numbers lined up correctly?

2. The Seikan Tunnel in Japan is 53.9 km long. It is the world's longest rail tunnel. The Tube's longest tunnel is 26.1 km shorter than the Seikan. What is its length? **27.8 km**

Ask Yourself

- UNDERSTAND: What facts do I know?
- PLAN: What operation should I use?
- SOLVE: Are the decimal points lined up?
- LOOK BACK: Does my answer make sense?

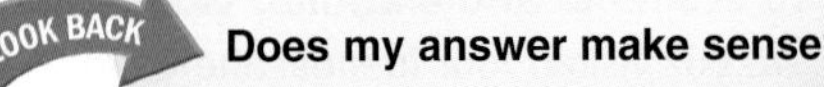

Independent Practice

3. Inside Gloucester Road Station, one art display measures 2.4 ft across. Another display measures 0.7 ft. What is the difference? **1.7 ft**

4. The longest trip Bill can make by Tube without changing trains is 54.9 km. If he travels this distance to and from his house, how many kilometers does he travel? **109.8 kilometers**

5. **Measurement** A subway has three tunnels that are 1.9 km, 2.7 km, and 1.6 km long. Which two tunnels when placed end-to-end would be between 3 and 4 kilometers long? **1.9 km and 1.6 km**

6. **Money** Barry needs a Tube pass for 6 days. Suppose a one-day pass costs $8.24 and a week pass costs $29.99. How much money will Barry save if he buys the week pass? **$19.45**

This elephant is part of the Underground Safari Art Exhibition at Gloucester Road Station.

3 Practice

Independent Practice

Select from **Exercises 3–6** as independent work.

Problem-Solving Reminders

Have students review their answers to make sure they have:

- Expressed the solution clearly
- Used appropriate mathematical notation and terms
- Supported their solution with verbal and symbolic work
- Determined the reasonableness of the solution in the context of the original problem

Enrichment 22.5

Name ____________ Date ________ Enrichment 22.5

Problem-Solving Application Use Decimals

Problem The table shows the estimated populations of the 10 most populated states in 2025. The estimates are based on the current population in each state and the rate of growth. Answer the following questions.

Most Populated States in 2025	
State	**Estimated Population (millions)**
California	49.285
Florida	20.71
Michigan	10.078
Texas	27.183
Pennsylvania	12.683
New Jersey	9.558
Georgia	9.869
New York	19.83
Ohio	11.744
Illinois	13.44

1. In the year 2025, which state will have the greater population, Georgia or New Jersey? How much greater? **Georgia; 0.311 million**

2. If you round all the populations to the nearest whole number, will any of the states have the same population in 2025? Explain. **Yes; Michigan, New Jersey, and Georgia all round to 10 million. Pennsylvania and Illinois both round to 13 million.**

3. Pennsylvania, New Jersey, and New York border each other. What is the estimated total population of these three states to the nearest tenth? Explain how you found your answer. **42.1 million; I rounded each population and then added the populations.**

Use with text pages 576–578.

Problem Solving 22.5

Name ____________ Date ________ Problem Solving 22.5

Problem-Solving Application: Use Decimals

Problem The estimated population of New York City for the year 2015 is about 17.9 million people. The estimated population of Los Angeles for the year 2015 is about 14.5 million people. In the year 2015, about how many people will live in New York City and Los Angeles?

UNDERSTAND
1. What do you know? **17.9 million people will live in New York City and 14.5 million people will live in Los Angeles in 2015.**

PLAN
2. How can you solve the problem? **Add the number of people who will be living in New York City and Los Angeles.**

SOLVE
3. What is the estimated total number of people that will be living in New York and Los Angeles in 2015? **Show your work.** **32.4 million people**

   $$\begin{array}{r} 17.9 \\ +14.5 \\ \hline 32.4 \end{array}$$

LOOK BACK
4. How can you check that your answer is reasonable? **Round both decimals to a whole number and add. 18 + 15 = 33. 32.4 is close to 33, so my answer is reasonable.**

Use with text pages 576–578.

Mixed Problem Solving

- Remind students that they may use any of the strategies in the box to solve **Problems 7–9.**
- ***Data*** Remind students to indicate which computation method they used to solve each problem. You might suggest that students use a second method to check the answer they found.

4 Assess & Close

Math Talk in Action

Have students share their solutions to conclude the lesson.

- **What four steps can you follow to help you solve problems?** (Understand, Plan, Solve, Look Back)
- **When you compute with decimals, what must you always remember?** (Align decimals by place and by decimal point; write a decimal point in the answer.)

Math Journal

Have students use any of the data given in this lesson to write an original problem that involves decimal addition or subtraction.

Lesson Quiz

Use the quiz on Lesson Transparency 22.5.

Test Prep & Spiral Review

Use Test Prep Transparency 22.5.

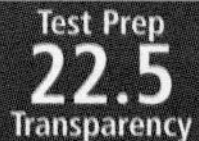

Mixed Problem Solving

Solve. Show your work. Tell what strategy you used. *Possible strategies given.*

You Choose

Strategy
- Guess and Check
- Use Logical Reasoning
- Work Backward
- Write an Equation

Computation Method
- Mental Math
- Estimation
- Paper and Pencil
- Calculator

7. For a trip, each student pays $10.00 and each adult pays $18.50. A 10-seat minibus costs $117.00 to rent. How many students and adults must go to pay for exactly 2 buses?
16 students and 4 adults; Guess and Check
8. Luz visited four friends. She visited Earl second. She visited Nicki before Joe. She visited Mary right after Earl. In what order did Luz visit her friends?
Nicki, Earl, Mary, Joe; Use Logical Reasoning
9. One night in November, the temperature dropped 0.2 degrees every 15 minutes for 2 hours. Then the temperature stayed at 15.6°F. What was the temperature when it began to drop? **17.2°F; Work Backward**

Data **Use the table for Problems 10–13. Then tell which method you chose and why.** *Possible methods given. Explanations may vary.*

10. What would it cost for 2 adults and 2 children to visit the water park?
$72; Mental Math
11. **Analyze** Lita and her dad have $65. If they pay one adult fee and one child's fee at the amusement park, will they have enough money left to visit the state park? Explain your reasoning.
See Additional Answers.
12. How much more would it cost for 1 adult and 2 children to visit the animal park than to visit the state park?
$12.15; Paper and Pencil
13. **You Decide** Your family has $100 to spend on any of the attractions. Decide which you would visit and find the total cost for your family.
***Check students' work;* Calculator**

Attraction	Adult Fee	Child Fee
Amusement Park	$28.99	$19.99
Animal Park	$12.00	$ 7.00
Water Park	$20.50	$15.50
State Park	$ 5.95	$ 3.95

578

Homework 22.5 **Page 143**

Name ____________ Date ____________ Homework 22.5

Problem-Solving Application: Use Decimals

Solve.

There are two different ways Karl can walk to school. The first way is 2.08 kilometers long and the second way is 2.42 kilometers long. If he takes the first way to school and then the second way back home, how many kilometers will he walk?

Plan how to solve the problem: Add the 2 amounts.

$$\begin{array}{r} 2.08 \\ +2.42 \\ \hline 4.50 \end{array}$$

Karl will walk 4.5 kilometers.

Show your work.

1. On Monday the average temperature was 29.7 degrees Fahrenheit. On Tuesday the average temperature was 37.64 degrees Fahrenheit. What is the difference between the temperatures on Monday and Tuesday?
7.94 degrees
2. Leslie wants to buy 5 donuts. The donuts cost $0.65 each. Leslie can buy a box of six donuts for $3.00. How much money will Leslie save if she buys the box of 6 instead of 5 individual donuts?
$0.25

Use with text pages 576–578.

Problem Solving

Calculator Connection

Place Value Pathways

Use your calculator to get from each Start Number to each End Number.

1. 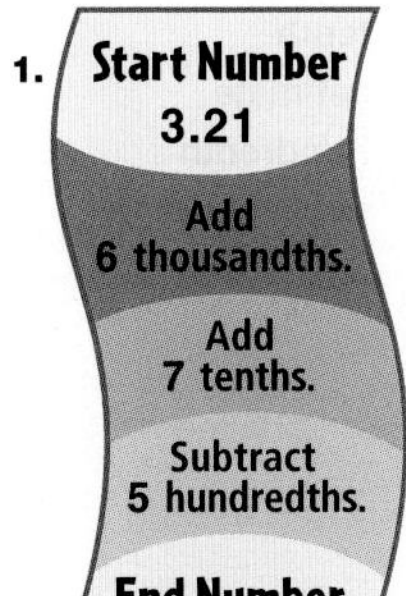

2. 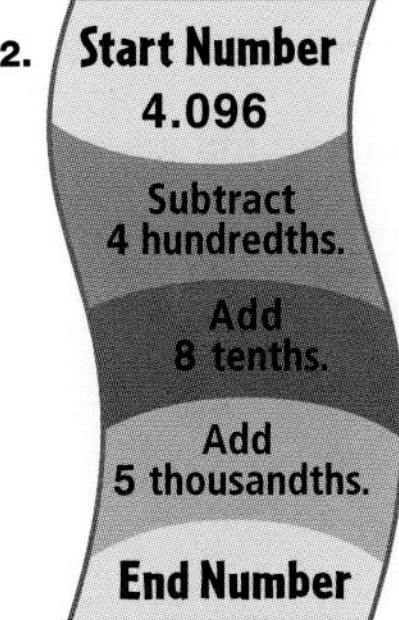

3. 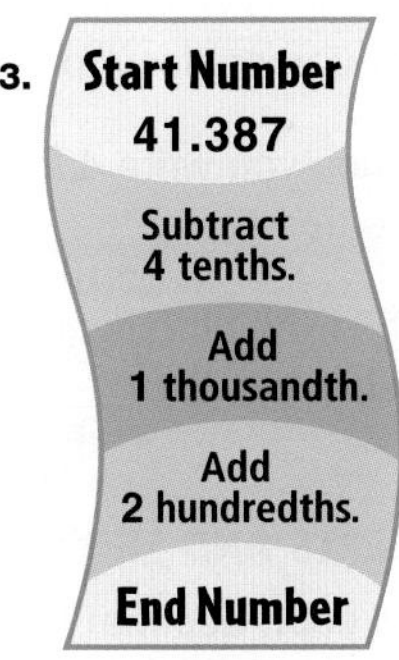

4. 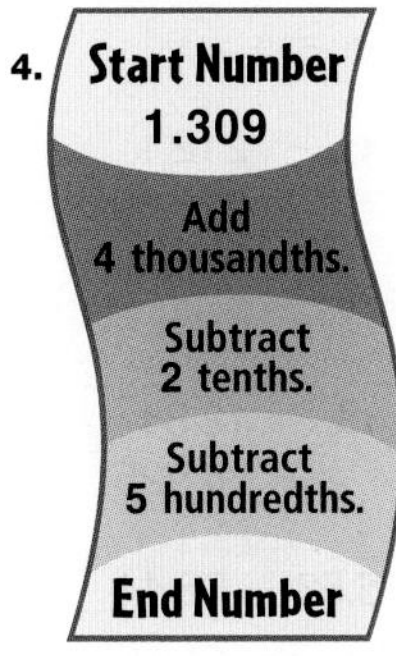

5. 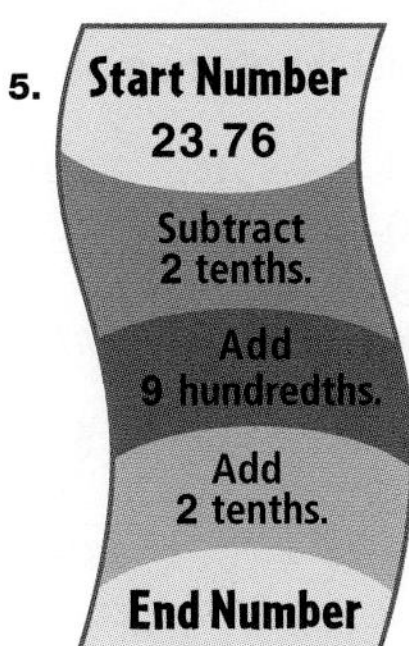

6. 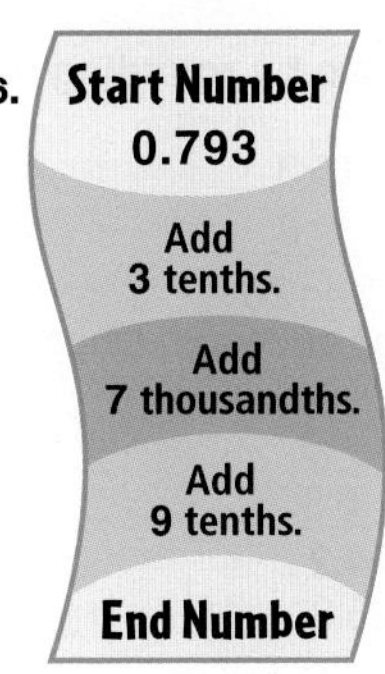

7. **Challenge** Compare each Start Number with its End Number. Decide which is greater. Then use your calculator to find how much greater.
   Check students' work.

8. Create your own Place Value Pathway. Start by choosing a decimal number as a Start Number. Then add and subtract tenths, hundredths, and thousandths as in the examples above. What End Number do you end up with? Challenge a classmate to solve your Place Value Pathway and compare your results.
   Check students' work.

Calculator Connection

Place-Value Pathways

Before students begin, ask them how they would "add four thousandths" with a calculator. (Press +, enter 0.004, press =.) Stress the importance of reading each quantity carefully. Students might make themselves a simple decimal place-value chart as a reminder.

Chapter Review/Test

Chapter Review/Test Items 1–20

To assign a numerical grade for this Chapter Review/Test, use 5 points for each item.

Check Understanding

You can use the ***Write About It*** question to assess student understanding of a key chapter concept.

Customize Your Instruction

The Chapter Review/Test is a formal evaluation of chapter objectives. For students who have not yet mastered these objectives, you can use the Reteaching Resources listed in the chart below.

Additional Assessment Resources

Alternate Chapter Test A Chapter Test is also provided in the Unit Resource folder. You might use the Review/Test in the student book as review and the test in the Unit Resource folder as a summary test for the chapter.

***Ways to Assess* CD-ROM** allows you to create your own lesson, chapter, or unit tests or practice and review worksheets.

Adequate Yearly Progress Guide helps familiarize your students with the format of standardized tests.

Chapter Review/Test

VOCABULARY

Choose the best term to complete each sentence.

1. A number close to the exact amount is an ____. **estimate**
2. When you write 4.237 as 4.2 you are rounding to the nearest ____. **tenth**
3. The symbol between the ones and tenths in a decimal is the ____. **decimal point**

Vocabulary
- tenth
- estimate
- hundredth
- decimal point

CONCEPTS AND SKILLS

Round each decimal to the place of the underlined digit. (Lesson 1, pp. 568–569)

4. 1.55 **2**
5. 4.92 **4.9**
6. 3.189 **3.19**
7. 16.39 **16**

Estimate by rounding to the nearest whole number. (Lesson 2, pp. 570–571)

8. 16.3 + 9.8 **26**
9. \$25.83 − 6.70 **\$19**
10. 199.7 − 30.32 **170**
11. 212.1 + 318.59 **531**

Add or subtract. Check your work. (Lessons 3–4, pp. 572–575)

12. 7.3 + 6.9 **14.2**
13. 6.5 − 3.2 **3.3**
14. \$6.17 − 3.53 **\$2.64**
15. 12.84 + 6.925 **19.765**
16. 125.3 + 12.7 **138**
17. 2.9 − 1.64 **1.26**
18. \$15.53 − \$6.44 **\$9.09**

PROBLEM SOLVING

Solve. (Lesson 5, pp. 576–579)

19. Ella's family drove 26.7 miles to visit her grandparents. Then they drove 15.9 miles to visit her cousins. How many miles did they drive? **42.6 miles**
20. Mr. Jacob's grocery bill is \$58.76. He gives the clerk \$100. How much change will he get back? **\$41.24**

Write About It

Show You Understand

The teacher asked the class to round to estimate.

Rich
6.81 → 6
5.76 → 5
+ 7.53 → + 7
18

Explain what Rich did wrong. Then estimate the answer correctly.

See Additional Answers.

580 **Chapter 22** Chapter Review/Test

Chapter Review/Test Items	Objectives	Covered On Teacher's Edition Pages	Use These Reteaching Resources
2, 4–7	**22A** Round decimals.	568A–569	Reteach Resources 22.1 *Ways to Success* CD-ROM 22.1 *Ways to Success* Skillsheet 190
1, 3, 8–11	**22B** Estimate decimal sums and differences.	570A–571	Reteach Resources 22.2 *Ways to Success* CD-ROM 22.2 *Ways to Success* Skillsheet 191
12–18	**22C** Add and subtract decimals to thousandths.	572A–575	Reteach Resources 22.3, 22.4 *Ways to Success* CD-ROM 22.3, 22.4 *Ways to Success* Skillsheet 192
19–20	**22D** Solve problems using skills and strategies.	576A–578	Reteach Resources 22.5 *Ways to Success* CD-ROM 22.5 *Ways to Success* Skillsheet 193

Extra Practice

Set A (Lesson 1, pp. 568–569)

Round each decimal to the place of the underlined digit.

1. 3.4 **3**	2. 9.7 **10**	3. 13.5 **14**	4. 21.91 **22**	5. 73.15 **73**	6. 126.09 **126**
7. 4.76 **4.8**	8. 8.31 **8.3**	9. 11.67 **11.7**	10. 35.92 **35.9**	11. 57.98 **58.00**	12. 98.54 **98.5**
13. 2.122 **2.12**	14. 5.109 **5.11**	15. 33.189 **33.19**	16. 42.271 **42.27**	17. 61.993 **61.99**	18. 23.017 **23.02**

Set B (Lesson 2, pp. 570–571)

Estimate by rounding to the nearest whole number.

1. 2.7 + 3.2 **6**
2. 16.5 − 9.8 **7**
3. 35.1 − 10.6 **24**
4. 52.9 + 9.6 **63**
5. $23.56 + 13.10 **$37**
6. 3.98 − 0.75 **3**
7. 4.29 − 1.52 **2**
8. $49.91 + 25.27 **$75**
9. 100.3 + 99.98 **200**
10. 119.18 − 87.04 **32**
11. 5.6 + 2.3 **8**
12. 18.27 − 9.5 **8**
13. $215.20 − $14.95 **$200**

Make two estimates for each exercise. First round to the nearest $10, then to the nearest $100.

14. $267.39 + $361.22 **$630; $700**
15. $807.13 − $698.79 **$110; $100**
16. $316.55 + $628.31 **$950; $900**
17. $435.17 − $287.29 **$150; $100**
18. $534.78 + $645.35 **$1,180; $1,100**
19. $211.21 − $171.89 **$40; $0**
20. $793.25 + $129.56 **$920; $900**
21. $638.48 + $382.71 **$1,020; $1,000**
22. $441.98 + $219.24 **$660; $600**

Set C (Lesson 4, pp. 574–575)

Add or subtract. Check your work.

1. 9.1 + 5.6 **14.7**
2. 10.7 + 9.3 **20**
3. 18.3 − 7.2 **11.1**
4. 21.3 − 10.7 **10.6**
5. $49.21 + 13.96 **$63.17**
6. 7.25 + 6.98 **14.23**
7. 32.67 − 14.25 **18.42**
8. 16.7 + 9.851 **26.551**
9. 13.5 − 11.98 **1.52**
10. $176.51 − 49.28 **$127.23**
11. 16.5 − 10 **6.5**
12. 37.2 − 9.85 **27.35**
13. 100 − 2.588 **97.412**
14. $3.15 + $6.98 **$10.13**
15. $10.19 − $7.00 **$3.19**
16. $200.00 − $17.25 **$182.75**

Extra Practice at **eduplace.com/map**

Chapter 22 Extra Practice 581

CHAPTER 22 TEST

Chapter 22 Test

Name ____________ Date ________

Round each decimal to the nearest whole number.

1. 29.63 **30**
2. 504.33 **504**
3. 1,789.09 **1,789**

Round each decimal to the place of the underlined digit

4. 18.9 **19**
5. 56.38 **56**
6. 38.046 **38.05**

Estimate by rounding to the nearest whole number.

7. 9.4 − 3.8 **5**
8. 17.856 + 3.904 **22**
9. $105.35 + 46.90 **$152**

Find the sum or difference. Draw models if you wish.

10. 3.5 + 6.4 = **9.9**
11. 6.84 − 3.66 = **3.18**
12. $8.64 + $1.39 = **$10.03**

Go on

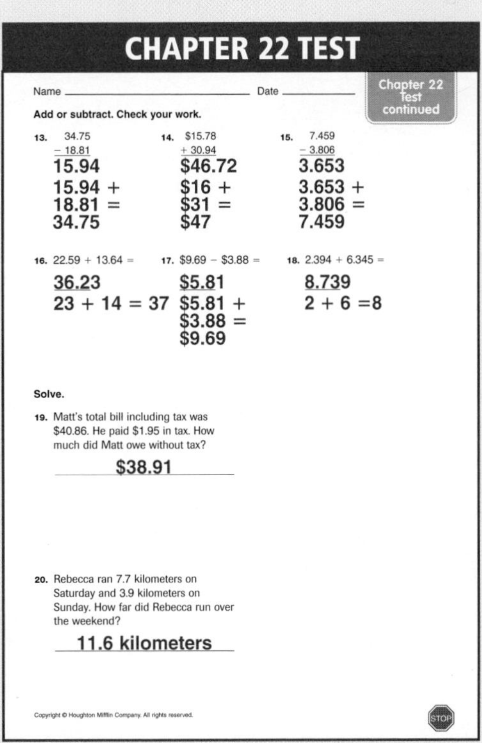

CHAPTER 22 TEST

Chapter 22 Test continued

Name ____________ Date ________

Add or subtract. Check your work.

13. 34.75 − 18.81 **15.94**; 15.94 + 18.81 = 34.75
14. $15.78 + 30.94 **$46.72**; $16 + $31 = $47
15. 7.459 − 3.806 **3.653**; 3.653 + 3.806 = 7.459
16. 22.59 + 13.64 = **36.23**; 23 + 14 = 37
17. $9.69 − $3.88 = **$5.81**; $5.81 + $3.88 = $9.69
18. 2.394 + 6.345 = **8.739**; 2 + 6 = 8

Solve.

19. Matt's total bill including tax was $40.86. He paid $1.95 in tax. How much did Matt owe without tax? **$38.91**

20. Rebecca ran 7.7 kilometers on Saturday and 3.9 kilometers on Sunday. How far did Rebecca run over the weekend? **11.6 kilometers**

STOP

Science Connection

PURPOSE

To read, write, estimate, compare, and order fractions and mixed numbers.

- Ask students to estimate the depths of all the different fish shown in the graphic on the right side of page 583 and explain their answers.
- Remind students that the number of feet of water increases as you go down to the bottom, not as you go up to the surface. The surface is at 0 feet; the coral is 80 feet below the surface.
- Have students draw a picture for **Exercise 4** to help them explain how to solve the problem. Ask questions like **What fraction of the fish were stingrays?** ($\frac{1}{6}$) and **How many grunts and snappers are there?** (12; 8)
- Challenge students to give the lengths of the fish in **Exercise 5** in *feet and inches* to the nearest half-inch. Remind them to find a fraction of a foot using 12 inches. For example, the length of the chub can be found this way:

$2\frac{1}{3}$ ft = 2 + $\frac{1}{3}$ of 12 in. = 2 ft 4 in.
(moray eel: 2 ft $10\frac{1}{2}$ in.; snapper: 2 ft 5 in.; stingray: 2 ft $1\frac{1}{2}$ in.)

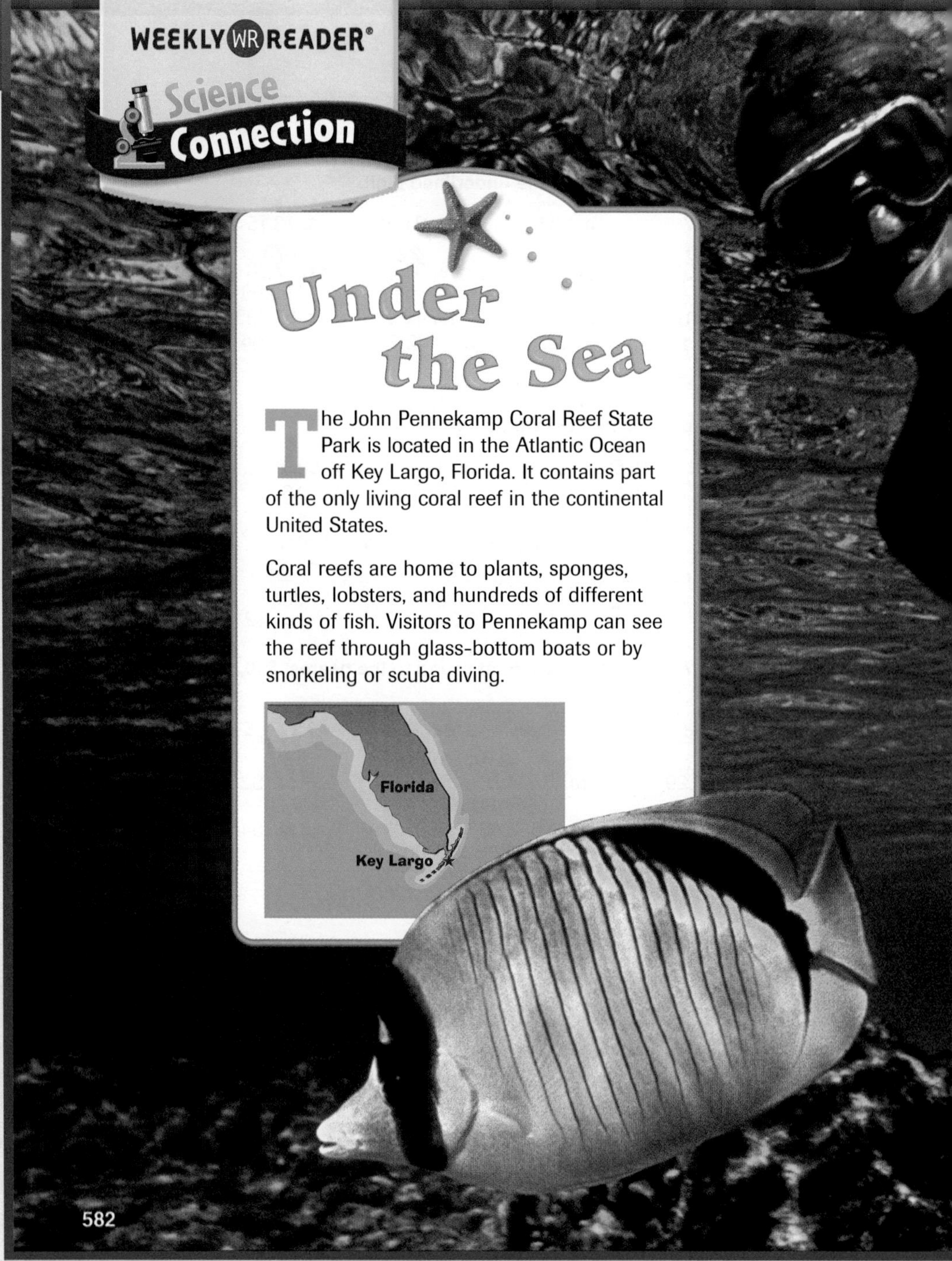

WEEKLY WR READER®
Science Connection
Under the Sea
The John Pennekamp Coral Reef State Park is located in the Atlantic Ocean off Key Largo, Florida. It contains part of the only living coral reef in the continental United States.
Coral reefs are home to plants, sponges, turtles, lobsters, and hundreds of different kinds of fish. Visitors to Pennekamp can see the reef through glass-bottom boats or by snorkeling or scuba diving.
Florida
Key Largo
582

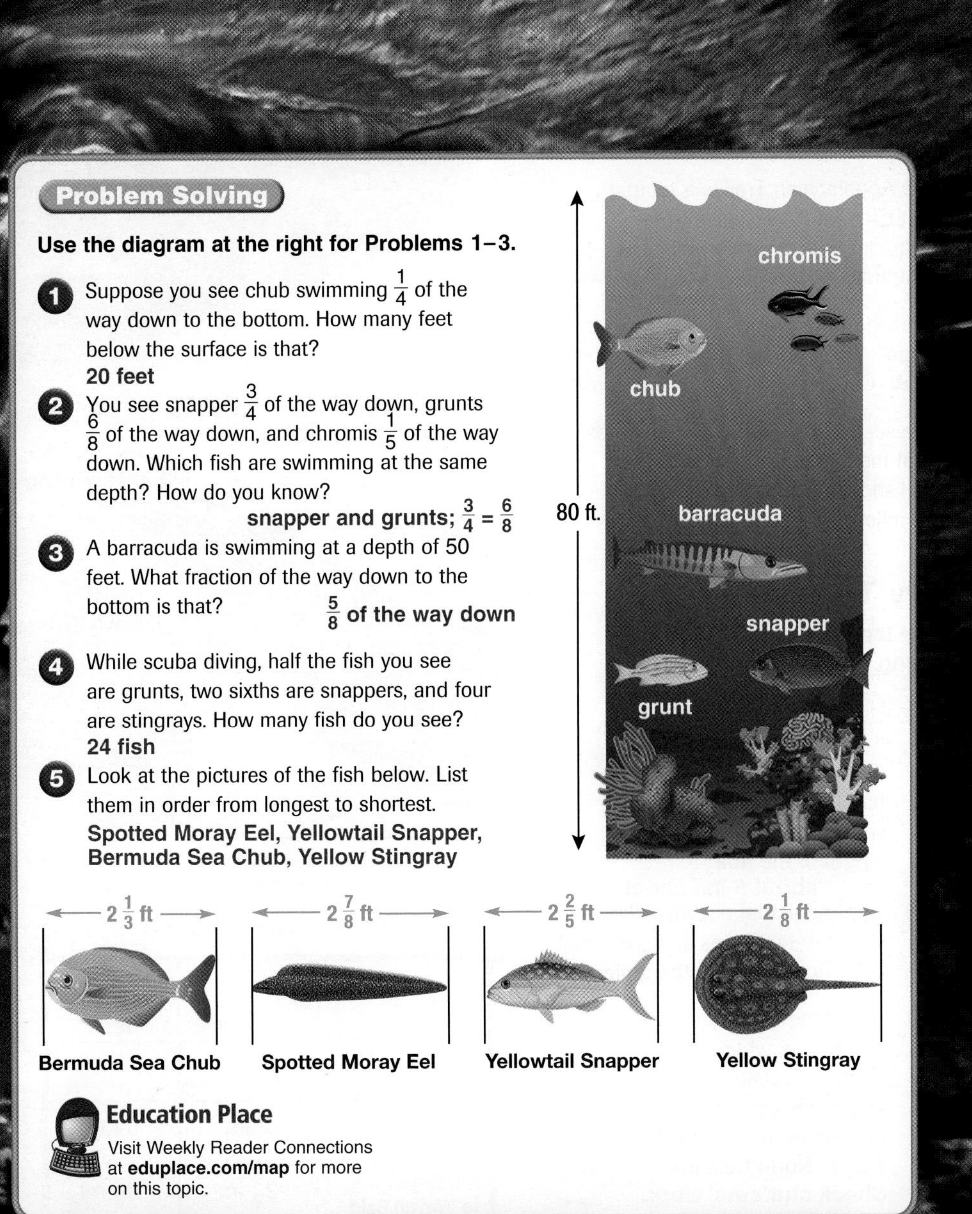

Problem Solving

Use the diagram at the right for Problems 1–3.

1. Suppose you see chub swimming $\frac{1}{4}$ of the way down to the bottom. How many feet below the surface is that?
20 feet
2. You see snapper $\frac{3}{4}$ of the way down, grunts $\frac{6}{8}$ of the way down, and chromis $\frac{1}{5}$ of the way down. Which fish are swimming at the same depth? How do you know?
snapper and grunts; $\frac{3}{4} = \frac{6}{8}$
3. A barracuda is swimming at a depth of 50 feet. What fraction of the way down to the bottom is that?
$\frac{5}{8}$ of the way down
4. While scuba diving, half the fish you see are grunts, two sixths are snappers, and four are stingrays. How many fish do you see?
24 fish
5. Look at the pictures of the fish below. List them in order from longest to shortest.
Spotted Moray Eel, Yellowtail Snapper, Bermuda Sea Chub, Yellow Stingray

Education Place

Visit Weekly Reader Connections at **eduplace.com/map** for more on this topic.

Enrichment

PURPOSE

This page provides an opportunity for students to learn about using scales on a map.

- This lesson utilizes the concepts and skills learned in Chapters 6, 7, 12, and 19, and applies these skills to finding actual distances shown on a map using a scale model.
- Ask students how to use an inch ruler to measure to the nearest half-inch. Encourage students to be as careful and accurate as possible using the string and ruler to find the measurements on the map.
- As you work through the page, ask students the following questions: **How do you use the string and ruler to find the length of the trail shown on the map?** (Lay the string along the outline of the trail on the map, carefully noting the beginning and end points. Then straighten the string and measure with a ruler.) **How do you find the actual distance between two places on the map if the measured length is 4 inches? $\frac{1}{2}$ inch? $2\frac{1}{2}$ inches?** (Multiply each map distance by 32: $4 \times 32 = 128$; $\frac{1}{2} \times 32 = 16$; $2\frac{1}{2} \times 32 = 2 \times 32 + \frac{1}{2} \times 32 = 64 + 16 = 80$.)

Enrichment: Use a Scale

A LONG WALK!

The Appalachian Trail is a footpath that runs for 2,167 miles from Katahdin, Maine, to Springer Mountain in Georgia.

The map at the right shows the Appalachian Trail as it passes through North Carolina and parts of Tennessee.

The scale shows 1 inch = 32 miles. That means that every inch of the trail shown on the map represents 32 miles of the actual trail.

APPALACHIAN TRAIL (NORTH CAROLINA)

Try These!

Use the map, a piece of string, and a ruler.

1. Use the string to find the length of the trail on the map to the nearest half inch. Then use the scale to find the actual length of the trail.
   about 6 in., about 192 mi
2. Find the actual distances between some of the places along the trail. Copy and complete the table.
3. If a hiking trail started in your hometown, where would it end? Use a U.S. road map and plan a route that has about the same total miles as the Appalachian Trail in North Carolina.
   Check students' work.

Possible answers given.

Places	Distance on Map (to nearest half inch)	Approximate Distance (in miles)
Roan High Knob to Big Bald	1 in.	32 mi
Big Bald to Mt. Guyot	2 in.	64 mi
Mt. Guyot to Wayah Bald	$2\frac{1}{2}$ in.	80 mi

584 Unit 7 Enrichment

Fun With Fractions!

$\frac{7}{4}+\frac{1}{4}=?$

You can use the fraction models found on Education Place at **eduplace.com/map** to add and subtract fractions.

Find $\frac{7}{8}+\frac{1}{4}$.	Find $\frac{4}{5}-\frac{3}{10}$.
• At **Change Mat,** choose **Circles.** To divide into eighths, put pointer over the scissors. Choose $\frac{1}{8}$ and click the first circle. • To show $\frac{7}{8}$, click **Fill.** Then click on 7 of the 8 sections. • Repeat with the second circle. Divide it into fourths and fill 1 section. • To make common denominators, put pointer over the scissors, choose $\frac{1}{8}$, and click the second circle. • Click the **Hand Tool.** Drag 2 sections from the second circle to the first. $\frac{7}{8}+\frac{1}{4}=1\frac{1}{8}$	• To divide into fifths, put pointer over the scissors. Choose $\frac{1}{5}$ and click the first circle. • To show $\frac{4}{5}$, click **Fill.** Then click on 4 of the 5 sections. • To subtract, first make common denominators. Put pointer over the scissors and choose $\frac{1}{10}$. Click the circle showing $\frac{4}{5}$. • Click **Fill.** Click on 3 out of the 10 filled sections to empty them. $\frac{4}{5}-\frac{3}{10}=\frac{1}{2}$

Use the fraction models. Write each answer in simplest form.

1. $\frac{1}{3}+\frac{5}{6}$ $1\frac{1}{6}$
2. $\frac{7}{8}-\frac{1}{4}$ $\frac{5}{8}$
3. $\frac{10}{12}+\frac{5}{6}$ $1\frac{2}{3}$
4. $\frac{5}{6}-\frac{1}{2}$ $\frac{1}{3}$
5. $\frac{1}{2}-\frac{1}{4}$ $\frac{1}{4}$
6. $\frac{2}{3}+\frac{1}{6}$ $\frac{5}{6}$
7. $\frac{3}{4}+\frac{1}{2}$ $1\frac{1}{4}$
8. $\frac{7}{10}-\frac{1}{5}$ $\frac{1}{2}$
9. $\frac{2}{3}+\frac{5}{6}$ $1\frac{1}{2}$
10. $\frac{1}{2}+\frac{1}{4}$ $\frac{3}{4}$

Fun With Fractions!

Technology Time

PURPOSE

Use a computer program to add and subtract fractions using fraction models.

- This page gives students practice adding and subtracting fractions with unlike denominators. Review with students how to find equivalent fractions for a pair of fractions, especially when one of the denominators is a multiple of the other.
- Work through both examples with the students. Guide them in how to show a model for each fraction. When making common denominators in the fourth step of the addition example, students must have some idea about what the common denominator is before they choose $\frac{1}{8}$.
- Students can work in pairs to complete this page. They can take turns solving the exercises. One student can model the problem on the computer and the other student can read the directions and check the answer using pencil and paper or modeling the problem with hands-on fraction models.
- Remind students to write each answer in simplest form.

Unit 7 Test

PURPOSE

This test provides an informal assessment of the Unit 7 objectives.

Unit Test Items 1–33

To assign a numerical grade for this Unit Test, use 3 points for each test item.

Customize Your Instruction

For students who have not yet mastered these objectives, use the **Reteaching Resources** listed in the chart below. ***Ways to Success*** is Houghton Mifflin's Intervention program, available in CD-ROM and blackline master formats.

Assessment Options

Formal Tests for this unit are also provided in the Unit Resource folder.

Unit 7 Form A (Open Response Test)

Unit 7 Form B (Multiple Choice Test)

Unit 7 Test

VOCABULARY Open Response

Choose the correct term to complete each sentence.

Vocabulary
decimal
mixed number
improper fraction
equivalent fractions

1. A fraction with a numerator greater than or equal to its denominator is a(n) ____. **improper fraction**
2. Fractions that show equal parts using different numbers are called ____. **equivalent fractions**
3. A number that is made up of a whole number and a fraction is called a(n) ____. **mixed number**

CONCEPTS AND SKILLS Open Response ***Possible equivalent fractions given.***

Write each fraction in simplest form. Then write another equivalent fraction. (Chapter 19)

4. $\frac{6}{8}$ **$\frac{3}{4}$, $\frac{9}{12}$**
5. $\frac{10}{15}$ **$\frac{2}{3}$, $\frac{4}{6}$**
6. $\frac{8}{12}$ **$\frac{2}{3}$, $\frac{10}{15}$**
7. $\frac{3}{9}$ **$\frac{1}{3}$, $\frac{4}{12}$**

Write each improper fraction as a mixed number or whole number. (Chapter 19)

8. $\frac{15}{4}$ **$3\frac{3}{4}$**
9. $\frac{10}{3}$ **$3\frac{1}{3}$**
10. $\frac{16}{2}$ **8**
11. $\frac{21}{5}$ **$4\frac{1}{5}$**

Add or subtract. Write your answer in simplest form. (Chapter 20)

12. $\frac{4}{6} + \frac{1}{6}$ **$\frac{5}{6}$**
13. $\frac{5}{12} - \frac{4}{12}$ **$\frac{1}{12}$**
14. $6\frac{2}{8} + 1\frac{3}{8}$ **$7\frac{5}{8}$**
15. $4\frac{3}{5} - 2\frac{2}{5}$ **$2\frac{1}{5}$**
16. $\frac{3}{8} - \frac{1}{4}$ **$\frac{1}{8}$**
17. $\frac{5}{6} - \frac{1}{2}$ **$\frac{1}{3}$**
18. $\frac{3}{5} + \frac{3}{10}$ **$\frac{9}{10}$**
19. $\frac{7}{12} + \frac{5}{6}$ **$1\frac{5}{12}$**

Write a fraction and a decimal to describe the shaded part. (Chapter 21)

20. 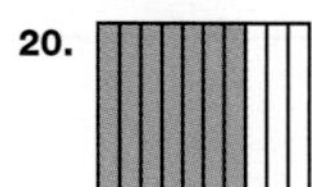 **$\frac{7}{10}$, 0.7**
21. 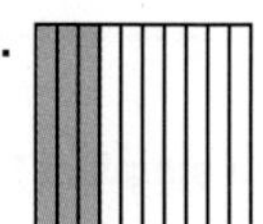 **$\frac{3}{10}$, 0.3**
22. 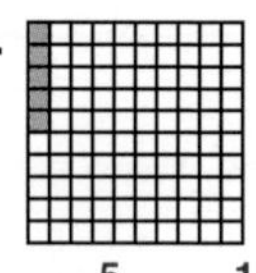 **$\frac{5}{100}$ or $\frac{1}{20}$, 0.05**
23. **$\frac{25}{100}$ or $\frac{1}{4}$, 0.25**

Order the numbers from greatest to least. (Chapter 21)

24. 1.3 $1\frac{8}{10}$ 1.05 $\frac{11}{10}$ **$1\frac{8}{10}$, 1.3, $\frac{11}{10}$, 1.05**
25. $1\frac{25}{100}$ 1.1 $1\frac{5}{10}$ $1\frac{3}{5}$ **$1\frac{3}{5}$, $1\frac{5}{10}$, $1\frac{25}{100}$, 1.1**

586

Reteaching Support

Unit Test Item	Unit Objectives Tested	Covered On Teacher's Edition Pages	Use These Reteaching Resources
2, 4–7	**7A** Identify parts of groups; find fractional parts; find equivalent fractions.	494A–496	Reteach Resources and *Ways to Success* CD-ROM, 19.3
1, 3, 8–11	**7B** Identify and write mixed numbers.	508A–510	Reteach Resources and *Ways to Success* CD-ROM, 19.7
24–25	**7C** Compare and order fractions.	498A–500	Reteach Resources and *Ways to Success* CD-ROM, 19.4
12–19	**7D** Add and subtract fractions and mixed numbers.	516A–521, 528A–532	Reteach Resources and *Ways to Success* CD-ROM, 20.1, 20.2, 20.6, 20.7
20–23	**7E** Write fractions and mixed numbers as decimals, and vice versa.	5424A–543, 550A–552	Reteach Resources and *Ways to Success* CD-ROM, 21.1, 21.4
24–25	**7F** Identify, compare, order, and round decimals.	558A–562	Reteach Resources and *Ways to Success* CD-ROM, 21.6, 21.7
26–29	**7G** Estimate, add, and subtract decimals to thousandths.	568A–575	Reteach Resources and *Ways to Success* CD-ROM, 22.1–22.4
30–33	**7H** Solve problems using skills and strategies.	504A–506, 522A–523, 526A–526, 534A–536, 554A–556, 576A–578	Reteach Resources and *Ways to Success* CD-ROM, 19.6, 20.3, 20.5, 20.8, 21.5, 22.5

33. Yes; *Possible explanation:* The food is less than \$5. The treat and toy are about \$3 + \$1, which is also less than \$5. If two numbers less than 5 are

Estimate each answer by rounding. Then find the exact answer. (Chapter 22)

26. $2.81 + 3.75$ — **7; 6.56**

27. $4.381 + 7.987$ — **12; 12.368**

28. $16.53 - 14.82$ — **2; 1.71**

29. $\$27.87 - 12.19$ — **\$16; \$15.68**

PROBLEM SOLVING Open Response

30. After Kim spent $\frac{1}{2}$ of her money on a sandwich, $\frac{1}{6}$ of her money on juice, and \$2 for a salad, she had no money left. How much money did Kim spend? **\$6**

31. A store manager ordered five sizes of bottles: 1.2 oz, 2.4 oz, ? oz, 4.8 oz, and 6.0 oz. She knows the sizes follow a pattern, but forgot one size. What is that size likely to be? **3.6 oz**

32. Raj has 7 liters of water to share equally with 3 friends. If each person receives the same amount, how much water will each of the four people receive? **1,750 mL or $1\frac{3}{4}$ liters**

33. Write About It Pedro has \$10.00. Does he have enough money to buy dog food for \$4.89, a dog treat for \$2.48, and a dog toy for \$1.29? Explain how you solved the problem. ***See above.***

Performance Assessment

Extended Response

PIZZA LAND

SMALL PIZZA - 4 slices	
Cheese	\$3.99
Pepperoni	\$5.99
Vegetable	\$4.99
MEDIUM PIZZA - 6 slices	
Cheese	\$5.99
Pepperoni	\$7.99
Vegetable	\$6.99
LARGE PIZZA - 8 slices	
Cheese	\$9.99
Pepperoni	\$11.99
Vegetable	\$10.99
DRINKS - medium/large	
Soft Drink	\$0.75/\$0.95
Juice	\$1.00/\$1.25

Task A class-trip leader has \$45 to buy food for himself and 9 students. Use the menu above and the information at the right. How should the leader spend the money so that everyone gets at least 2 slices of pizza and a drink they like? Explain your thinking.

See Additional Answers.

Information You Need

- Two thirds of the students like pepperoni.
- The leader and two of the students like vegetable pizza.
- All the students would be willing to eat cheese pizza.
- Half of the group prefer juice to soft drinks.
- The leader wants a large juice.

Performance Assessment & Scoring Rubric

4 EXEMPLARY

Compares, adds, and subtracts fractions or decimals. Applies skills and strategies to solve the problem correctly.

3 PROFICIENT

Compares, adds, and subtracts fractions or decimals to solve the problem. Reasoning or decision making is faulty.

2 ACCEPTABLE

Compares, adds, and subtracts fractions or decimals. Shows little or no understanding of strategies or skills to solve the problem completely.

1 LIMITED

The task is completed incorrectly or not at all.

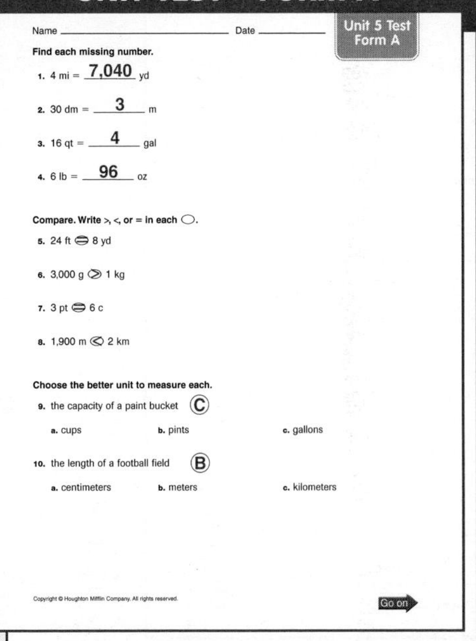

UNIT TEST – FORM A

Name ______ Date ______ Unit 5 Test Form A

Find each missing number.

1. 4 mi = 7,040 yd
2. 30 dm = 3 m
3. 16 qt = 4 gal
4. 6 lb = 96 oz

Compare. Write >, <, or = in each ◯.

5. 24 ft = 8 yd
6. 3,000 g > 1 kg
7. 3 pt = 6 c
8. 1,900 m < 2 km

Choose the better unit to measure each.

9. the capacity of a paint bucket (C)
   a. cups b. pints c. gallons
10. the length of a football field (B)
   a. centimeters b. meters c. kilometers

Go on

UNIT TEST – FORM B

Name ______ Date ______ Unit 5 Test Form B

Choose the letter of the correct answer.
Find each missing number.

1. 2 L = (D) mL — A 2 B 20 C 200 D 2,000
2. (H) lb = 6 T — F 2,000 G 6,000 H 12,000 J 18,000
3. 8,000 g = (C) kg — A 1 B 40 C 8 D 80
4. 16 pt = (G) gal — F 1 G 2 H 4 J 8

Compare. Choose the correct symbol for each ◯.

5. 25 in. ◯ 1 yd — A > B < C = D + (B)
6. 6 c ◯ 2 pt — F > G < H = J + (F)
7. 30 cm ◯ 3 m — A > B < C = D + (B)
8. 6 L ◯ 60,000 mL — F > G < H = J + (G)

Choose the better unit to measure each.

9. the weight of a whale
   A pounds B tons C ounces D liters (B)
10. the mass of a truck
   F grams G pints H quarts J kilograms (J)

Go on

Unit 7 Test Answers: Form A

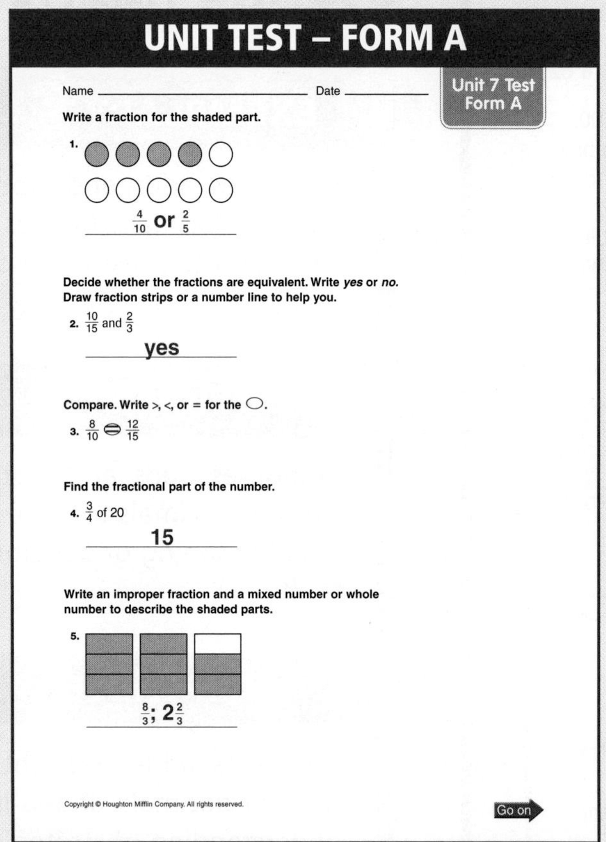

UNIT TEST – FORM A

Unit 7 Test Form A

Name ______________ Date ______

Write a fraction for the shaded part.

1. $\frac{4}{10}$ or $\frac{2}{5}$

Decide whether the fractions are equivalent. Write *yes* or *no*. Draw fraction strips or a number line to help you.

2. $\frac{10}{15}$ and $\frac{2}{3}$ yes

Compare. Write >, <, or = for the ◯.

3. $\frac{8}{10} = \frac{12}{15}$

Find the fractional part of the number.

4. $\frac{3}{4}$ of 20 15

Write an improper fraction and a mixed number or whole number to describe the shaded parts.

5. $\frac{8}{3}$; $2\frac{2}{3}$

Go on

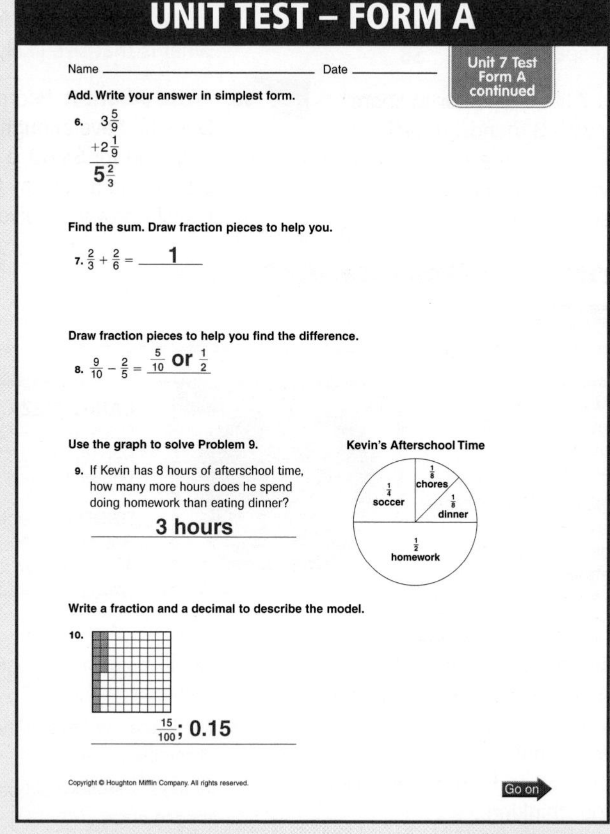

UNIT TEST – FORM A

Unit 7 Test Form A continued

Name ______________ Date ______

Add. Write your answer in simplest form.

6. $3\frac{5}{9} + 2\frac{1}{9} = 5\frac{2}{3}$

Find the sum. Draw fraction pieces to help you.

7. $\frac{2}{3} + \frac{2}{6} =$ 1

Draw fraction pieces to help you find the difference.

8. $\frac{9}{10} - \frac{2}{5} = \frac{5}{10}$ or $\frac{1}{2}$

Use the graph to solve Problem 9.

9. If Kevin has 8 hours of afterschool time, how many more hours does he spend doing homework than eating dinner? 3 hours

Kevin's Afterschool Time

Write a fraction and a decimal to describe the model.

10. $\frac{15}{100}$; 0.15

Go on

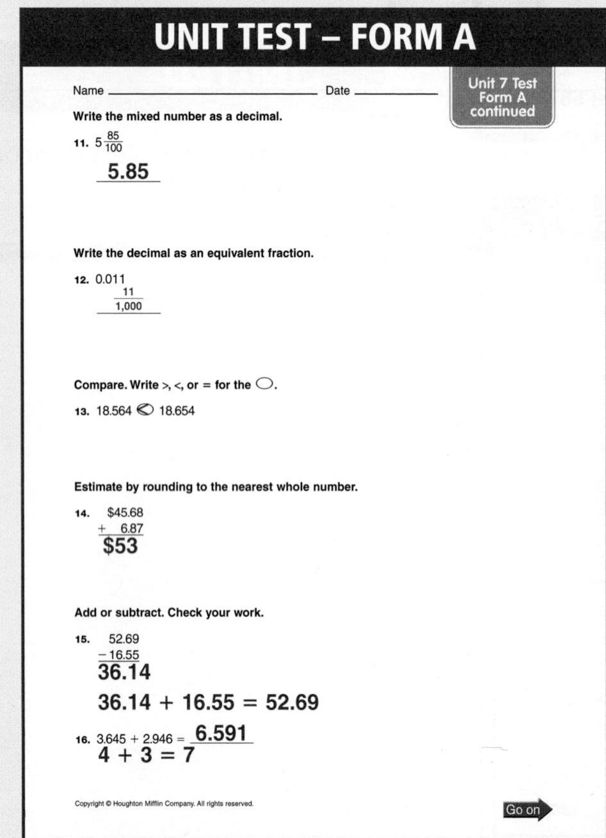

UNIT TEST – FORM A

Unit 7 Test Form A continued

Name ______________ Date ______

Write the mixed number as a decimal.

11. $5\frac{85}{100}$ 5.85

Write the decimal as an equivalent fraction.

12. 0.011 $\frac{11}{1,000}$

Compare. Write >, <, or = for the ◯.

13. 18.564 < 18.654

Estimate by rounding to the nearest whole number.

14. \$45.68 + 6.87 = \$53

Add or subtract. Check your work.

15. 52.69 − 16.55 = 36.14

36.14 + 16.55 = 52.69

16. 3.645 + 2.946 = 6.591

4 + 3 = 7

Go on

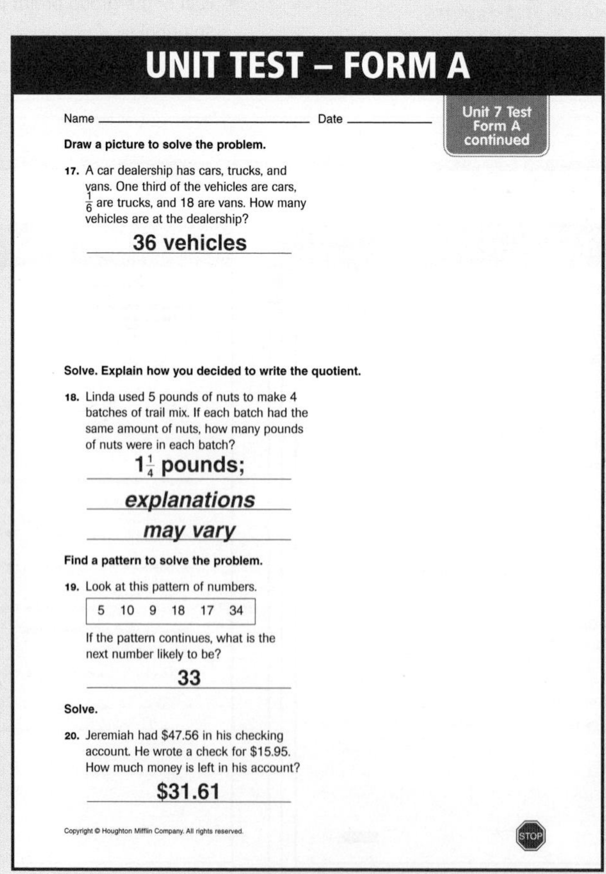

UNIT TEST – FORM A

Unit 7 Test Form A continued

Name ______________ Date ______

Draw a picture to solve the problem.

17. A car dealership has cars, trucks, and vans. One third of the vehicles are cars, $\frac{1}{6}$ are trucks, and 18 are vans. How many vehicles are at the dealership? 36 vehicles

Solve. Explain how you decided to write the quotient.

18. Linda used 5 pounds of nuts to make 4 batches of trail mix. If each batch had the same amount of nuts, how many pounds of nuts were in each batch? $1\frac{1}{4}$ pounds; *explanations may vary*

Find a pattern to solve the problem.

19. Look at this pattern of numbers.

5	10	9	18	17	34

If the pattern continues, what is the next number likely to be? 33

Solve.

20. Jeremiah had \$47.56 in his checking account. He wrote a check for \$15.95. How much money is left in his account? \$31.61

STOP

Unit 7 Test Answers: Form B

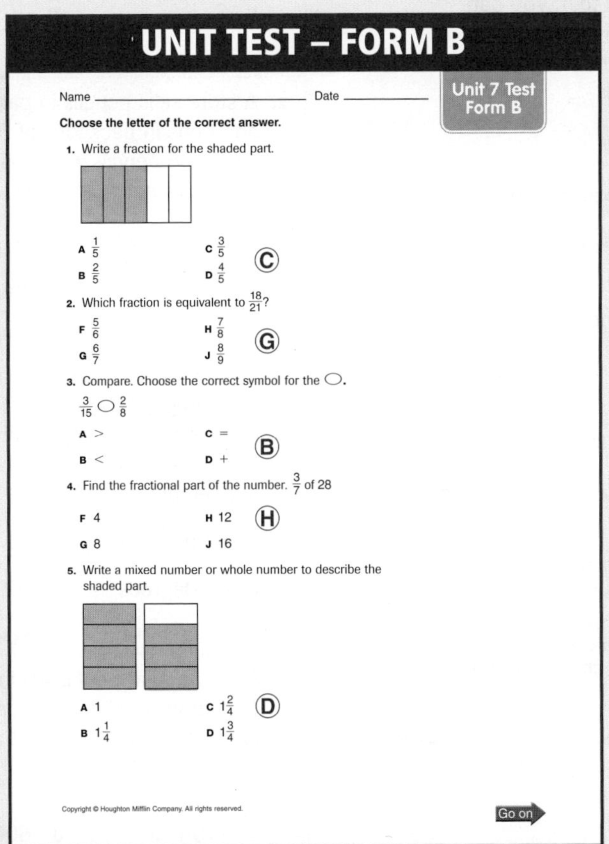

UNIT TEST – FORM B

Name ______________________ Date __________ **Unit 7 Test Form B**

Choose the letter of the correct answer.

1. Write a fraction for the shaded part.

   A $\frac{1}{5}$ C $\frac{3}{5}$
   B $\frac{2}{5}$ D $\frac{4}{5}$ (C)

2. Which fraction is equivalent to $\frac{18}{21}$?

   F $\frac{5}{6}$ H $\frac{7}{8}$
   G $\frac{6}{7}$ J $\frac{8}{9}$ (G)

3. Compare. Choose the correct symbol for the ◯.

   $\frac{3}{15}$ ◯ $\frac{2}{8}$

   A > C =
   B < D + (B)

4. Find the fractional part of the number. $\frac{3}{7}$ of 28

   F 4 H 12 (H)
   G 8 J 16

5. Write a mixed number or whole number to describe the shaded part.

   A 1 C $1\frac{2}{4}$ (D)
   B $1\frac{1}{4}$ D $1\frac{3}{4}$

Go on

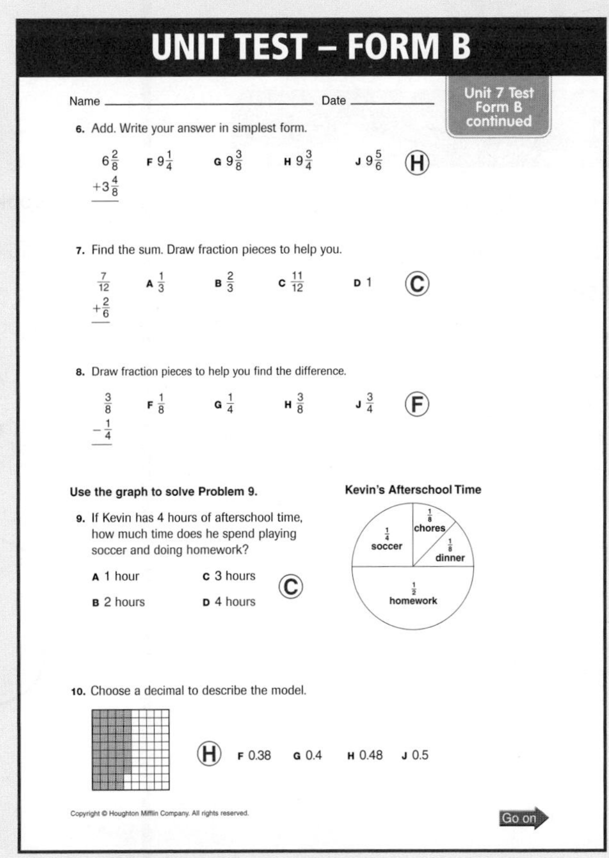

UNIT TEST – FORM B

Name ______________________ Date __________ **Unit 7 Test Form B continued**

6. Add. Write your answer in simplest form.

   $6\frac{2}{8} + 3\frac{4}{8}$ F $9\frac{1}{4}$ G $9\frac{3}{8}$ H $9\frac{3}{4}$ J $9\frac{5}{6}$ (H)

7. Find the sum. Draw fraction pieces to help you.

   $\frac{7}{12} + \frac{2}{6}$ A $\frac{1}{3}$ B $\frac{2}{3}$ C $\frac{11}{12}$ D 1 (C)

8. Draw fraction pieces to help you find the difference.

   $\frac{3}{8} - \frac{1}{4}$ F $\frac{1}{8}$ G $\frac{1}{4}$ H $\frac{3}{8}$ J $\frac{3}{4}$ (F)

Use the graph to solve Problem 9.

Kevin's Afterschool Time

9. If Kevin has 4 hours of afterschool time, how much time does he spend playing soccer and doing homework?

   A 1 hour C 3 hours (C)
   B 2 hours D 4 hours

10. Choose a decimal to describe the model.

    (H) F 0.38 G 0.4 H 0.48 J 0.5

Go on

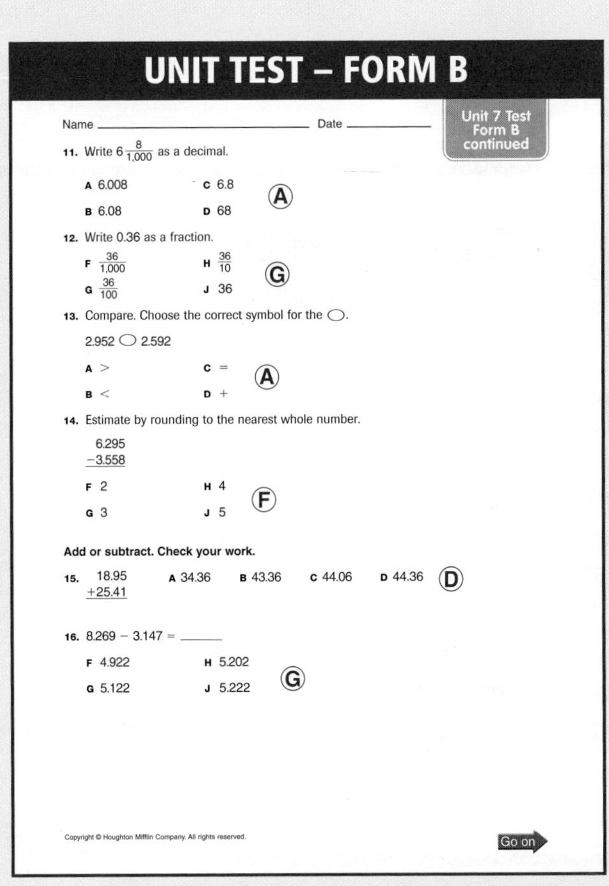

UNIT TEST – FORM B

Name ______________________ Date __________ **Unit 7 Test Form B continued**

11. Write $6\frac{8}{1,000}$ as a decimal.

    A 6.008 C 6.8 (A)
    B 6.08 D 68

12. Write 0.36 as a fraction.

    F $\frac{36}{1,000}$ H $\frac{36}{10}$ (G)
    G $\frac{36}{100}$ J 36

13. Compare. Choose the correct symbol for the ◯.

    2.952 ◯ 2.592

    A > C = (A)
    B < D +

14. Estimate by rounding to the nearest whole number.

    6.295 − 3.558

    F 2 H 4
    G 3 J 5 (F)

Add or subtract. Check your work.

15. 18.95 + 25.41 A 34.36 B 43.36 C 44.06 D 44.36 (D)

16. 8.269 − 3.147 = ______

    F 4.922 H 5.202
    G 5.122 J 5.222 (G)

Go on

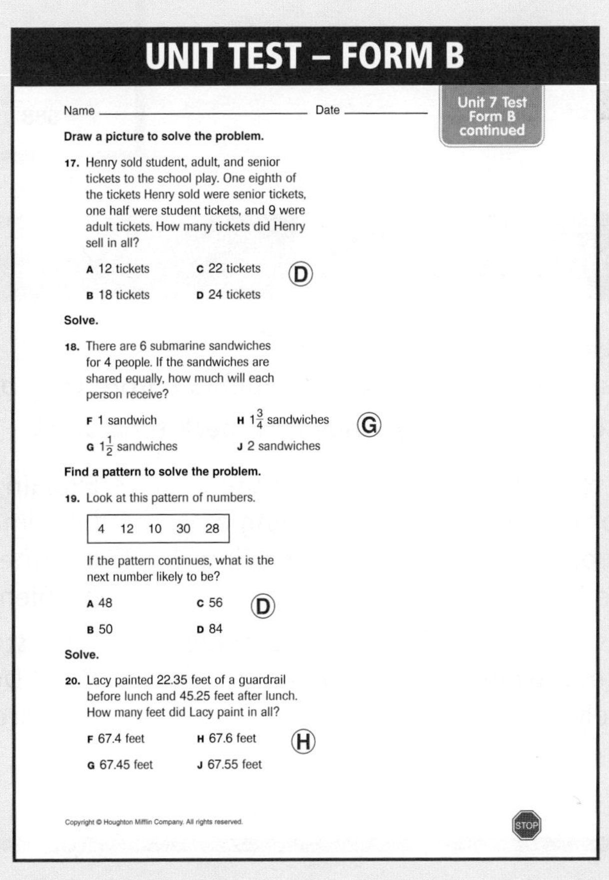

UNIT TEST – FORM B

Name ______________________ Date __________ **Unit 7 Test Form B continued**

Draw a picture to solve the problem.

17. Henry sold student, adult, and senior tickets to the school play. One eighth of the tickets Henry sold were senior tickets, one half were student tickets, and 9 were adult tickets. How many tickets did Henry sell in all?

    A 12 tickets C 22 tickets (D)
    B 18 tickets D 24 tickets

Solve.

18. There are 6 submarine sandwiches for 4 people. If the sandwiches are shared equally, how much will each person receive?

    F 1 sandwich H $1\frac{3}{4}$ sandwiches (G)
    G $1\frac{1}{2}$ sandwiches J 2 sandwiches

Find a pattern to solve the problem.

19. Look at this pattern of numbers.

4	12	10	30	28

    If the pattern continues, what is the next number likely to be?

    A 48 C 56 (D)
    B 50 D 84

Solve.

20. Lacy painted 22.35 feet of a guardrail before lunch and 45.25 feet after lunch. How many feet did Lacy paint in all?

    F 67.4 feet H 67.6 feet (H)
    G 67.45 feet J 67.55 feet

STOP

Cumulative Test Prep

PURPOSE

This page will familiarize students with the multiple-choice and open-response formats of many standardized state tests.

Cumulative Test Prep

Solve Problems 1–10.

Test-Taking Tip

Sometimes when you take a test, you can eliminate answer choices that are clearly wrong.

Look at the example below.

Kim has $2\frac{1}{4}$ yards of red ribbon and $1\frac{3}{4}$ yards of blue ribbon. How much ribbon does she have?

A $3\frac{1}{8}$ yards **C** $4\frac{1}{8}$ yards

(B) 4 yards **D** 10 yards

THINK

You know that $1\frac{3}{4}$ is a little less than 2 and $2\frac{1}{4}$ is a little more than 2. So the answer will be about 4 yards. Therefore, you can eliminate choices A and D.

Multiple Choice

1. What is the remainder when you divide 38 by 4?

A 0 **C** 9

(B) 2 **D** 10

(Chapter 4, Lesson 8)

2. A store sells pencils in packages of 7 and pens in packages of 8. Mrs. Ruíz needs 56 pencils. How many packages of pencils must she buy?

F 0 **(H)** 8

G 7 **J** 56

(Chapter 12, Lesson 5)

3. In January, the normal temperature in Anchorage, Alaska, is 15°F. The normal temperature in Miami, Florida, is 67°F. What is the difference between these two temperatures?

(A) 52 degrees **C** 72 degrees

B 60 degrees **D** 82 degrees

(Chapter 13, Lesson 4)

4. A rectangular pool is 40 feet long, 15 feet wide, and 8 feet deep. What is the perimeter of the pool?

F 8 feet **H** 126 feet

(G) 110 feet **J** 600 feet

(Chapter 18, Lesson 2)

For Test-Taking Tips, See Page 658.

Test-Taking TIPS

Review the test-taking tips with students before they begin the test. Discuss with students some of the ways they can check their work.

- Suggest to students that they can use a variety of methods, such as drawing a diagram or making a list, when solving a complex problem.
- Remind students that if they have made a mistake, they must erase the mark completely.
- Explain that unreasonable choices may be eliminated using what they know and the information given in the problem.
- Have students ask themselves the question "Does my answer make sense?" as they are checking each problem.

Open Response

5. Bob collected 48 cans of food. Sue collected $\frac{2}{3}$ as many cans as Bob. How many cans of food did Sue collect? **32 cans**

(Chapter 19, Lesson 5)

6. Emily wrote this number pattern.

7, 14, 28, 56

If Emily continues the pattern, what will the sixth number be? **224**

(Chapter 21, Lesson 5)

7. Vern gave a clerk $20.00 to pay for a $15.95 shirt. The tax was $0.76. How much change should Vern get? **$3.29**

(Chapter 22, Lesson 4)

8. Travis had a board that was $4\frac{3}{4}$ feet long. He used the board to make a shelf that was $2\frac{1}{4}$ feet long. How much of the board does Travis have left? **$2\frac{1}{2}$ feet**

(Chapter 20, Lesson 2)

9. How much money will a family of 2 adults, 3 teenagers, and a 10-year-old girl save by buying their tickets to the state fair in advance? **$16**

State Fair Admission Prices		
Ages	**Bought in Advance**	**Bought at the Gate**
12 years or older	$5	$8
6–11 years	$3	$4
Under 6	Free	Free

(Chapter 11, Lesson 7)

Extended Response

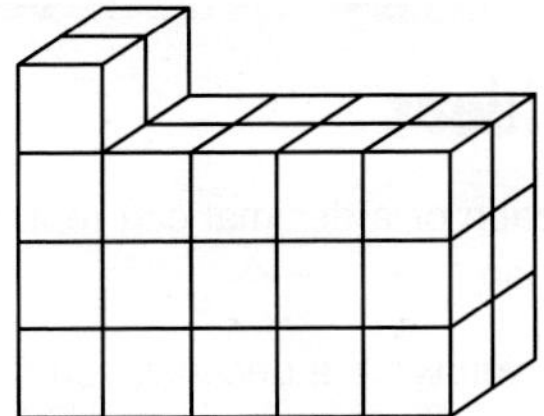

10. Each cube in the drawing above represents 5 tons of trash.

A How many cubes are represented in the drawing? **32 cubes**

B How many tons of trash are represented in the drawing? **160 tons**

C Central City produces 230 tons of trash. Make a drawing of cubes to show how to represent that amount. Tell how much each cube represents. Explain how you decided how many cubes to use in your drawing. ***Check work.***

D Suppose the amount of trash Central City produces is cut in half. How would your answer to Question C change? Make a new drawing to help you explain your answer.

Answers should include representation of 115 tons.

(Chapter 18, Lesson 6)

Education Place

Look for Cumulative Test Prep at **eduplace.com/map** for more practice.

Test-Taking Vocabulary

- Caution students to read **Item 2** very carefully. The numbers used in the problem and the choices can be confusing. Find the key word in the question that is being asked. In this case, the word is *pencils*.
- For **Item 9,** ask students how adults, teenagers, and a 10-year-old girl match the age categories in the table. Also ask them which price column to use if tickets are purchased in advance.
- For **Item 10,** remind students to include the hidden cubes in the figure to answer part A. Ask students how parts A and B are different.

National and state tests may also use these words to indicate fractions.

- portion
- part
- How many equal parts. . . ?
- half, thirds, quarter

Vocabulary Wrap-Up

PURPOSE

Use this page to encourage students to use math vocabulary to talk about the important concepts they have learned in this unit.

Big Ideas and Key Vocabulary

Review and discuss with students the Big Ideas of this unit using the Key Vocabulary terms *fraction, decimal,* and *place value.*

Math Conversations

Have students work together in small groups to discuss **Exercises 1–4.** Check to see whether individual students understand the key concepts and are able to use the math vocabulary correctly. Clear up any misunderstandings students may have. After students have discussed the exercises in small groups, continue the conversation as a whole class. Have volunteers from each group share what their group talked about.

Write About It Students should include specific examples of the fractions and decimals they found as well as general descriptions of where they found them.

Vocabulary Wrap-Up for Unit 7

Look back at the big ideas and vocabulary in this unit.

Big Ideas

A fraction or a decimal can represent a number less than 1.

When you write a decimal, you use place-value notation.

You can name the same amount as a fraction or decimal.

Key Vocabulary

fraction
decimal
place-value

2. They are all equal to $1\frac{1}{2}$. **3. Find the common denominator of 8; $\frac{3}{8} + \frac{4}{8} = \frac{7}{8}$**

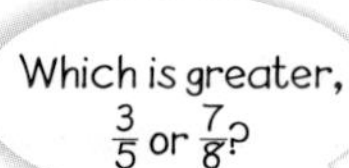

Use your new vocabulary to discuss these big ideas.

1. Explain how the fraction $\frac{4}{8}$ is different from the fraction $\frac{8}{4}$. **$\frac{4}{8}$ is $\frac{1}{2}$, $\frac{8}{4}$ is 2.**
2. Explain the relationship between $\frac{3}{2}$, 1.5, and 1.50. ***See above.***
3. Explain how to add $\frac{3}{8}$ and $\frac{1}{2}$. ***See above.***
4. Explain how to subtract 0.31 from 0.9. ***See below.***
5. **Write About It** Search for decimals and fractions in a newspaper or magazine. List the different ways that fractions and decimals are used. ***Check students' work.***

Which is greater, $\frac{3}{5}$ or $\frac{7}{8}$?
We can use a picture or fraction pieces to find out.
MATH

4. Place a 0 place holder in the hundredths place of 0.9. Subtract 0.90 − 0.31, regrouping the 9 to subtract; 0.59.

Wrap Up the Unit Project

- As students or groups present their segments of the Olympics program, have other students in the studio audience listen for fractions and decimals being used to tell about distances, quantities, costs, and so on. Allow students to pose questions to the sportscasters.
- You may wish to have students put all their scripts into a collection and "publish" all the data about the Olympics in a classroom "sports magazine," or you may wish to videotape the mock television program.
- Invite a local radio or television sportscaster to speak to the class about gathering and displaying information about sports events and athletes for a broadcast.

UNIT 8

Probability/ Algebra and Graphing

Probability

page 594A

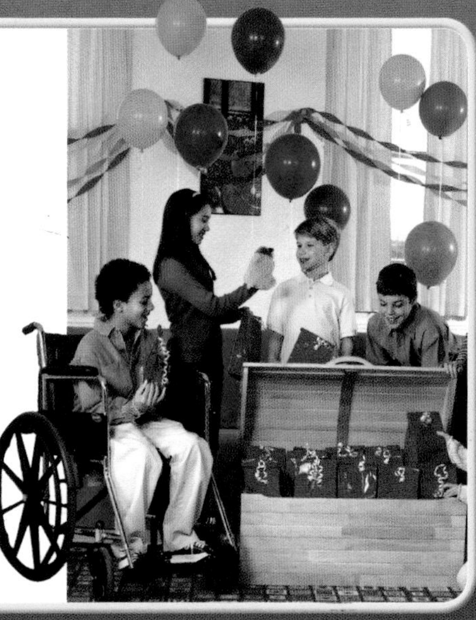

Algebra and Graphing

page 614A

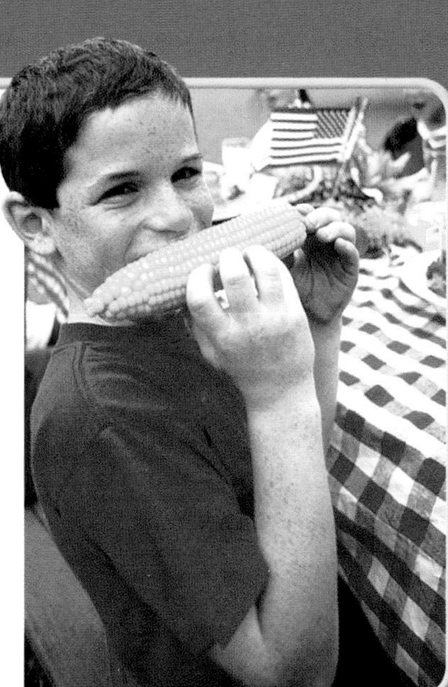

Standards

Unit 8 Objectives	Lessons	NCTM Standards	Your State's Standards
8A Describe the probability of an event and determine the number of possible outcomes in an experiment.	23.1, 23.2	**Data Analysis and Probability:** Describe certain events as likely or unlikely and discuss the degree of likelihood using such words as *certain, equally likely,* and *impossible*. Understand that the measure of the likelihood of an event can be represented by a number from 0 to 1.	
8B Use probability to make predictions.	23.3	**Data Analysis and Probability:** Predict the probability of outcomes of simple experiments and test the predictions. Propose and justify conclusions and predictions that are based on data and design studies to further investigate the conclusions or predictions.	
8C Use tables, graphs, and tree diagrams to represent probability outcomes.	23.5	**Data Analysis and Probability:** Understand and apply basic concepts of probability.	
8D Locate, identify, and graph points on a coordinate plane; graph lines.	24.1, 24.2, 24.3	**Geometry:** Describe location and movement using common language and geometric vocabulary. Make and use coordinate systems to specify locations and to describe paths. Find the distance between points along horizontal and vertical lines of a coordinate system.	
8E Write integers.	24.4	**Number and Operations:** Explore numbers less than 0 by extending the number line and through familiar applications.	
8F Solve problems using skills and strategies.	23.4, 24.5	**Problem Solving:** Apply and adapt a variety of appropriate strategies to solve problems. **Data Analysis and Probability:** Represent data using tables and graphs.	

NCTM Process Standards	Sample Lessons or Features	Your State's Standards
Reasoning and Proof: Use various levels and types of reasoning, including formulating proofs, patterns, conjectures, and rules.	Reasoning, Problem Solving, and Algebra Readiness features. For example, see **Lessons 23.2, 23.4, 24.3, 24.4, 24.5.**	
Communication: Understand vocabulary, organization of processes, and how to communicate and comprehend mathematical concepts and justifications with accuracy.	Hands-On and Problem-Solving lessons, Explain Your Thinking questions, games, and Reading Mathematics. For example, see **23.3, 23.4, 24.3, 24.5.**	
Connections: Relate mathematics to real-life situations and other subject areas and make connections from one mathematical idea to another.	Connections features, skills lessons, and Problem Solving. For example, see **Lessons 23.4, 23.5, 24.3, 24.5.**	
Representation: Represent mathematical ideas using concrete objects, pictures, and symbols.	Occurs throughout as students use manipulatives, workmats, number lines, drawings, tables, symbols, and equations to model or explain. For example, see **Lessons 23.1, 23.2, 23.3, 24.1, 24.4.**	

Assessment System

Monitoring Student Progress

Objectives

8A	Describe the probability of an event and determine the number of possible outcomes in an experiment.
8B	Use probability to make predictions.
8C	Use tables, graphs, and tree diagrams to represent probability outcomes.
8D	Locate, identify, and graph points on a coordinate plane; graph lines.
8E	Write integers.
8F	Solve problems using skills and strategies.

Classroom-Based Assessment

Prior Knowledge

Use What You Know, PE pp. 595, 615
Chapters 23 and 24 Pretests, Unit Resources
Unit 8 Reading Mathematics, PE pp. 592–593

Ongoing Assessment

Student Self-Assessment

Explain Your Thinking, PE pp. 597, 599, 608, 617, 618, 621, 625
Mixed Review & Test Prep, PE pp. 597, 617, 622, 626
Quick Check, PE pp. 601, 619
Vocabulary Wrap-Up, PE p. 642

Informal Assessment by Teachers

Problem of the Day, First page of every TE lesson
Spiral Review, First page of every TE lesson
Common Error/Intervention, TE pp. 596, 598, 604, 608, 616, 618, 620, 624, 628
Lesson Quiz, First page of every TE lesson

Diagnostic/Intervention

Quick Check, PE pp. 601, 619
Common Error/Intervention, TE pp. 596, 598, 604, 608, 616, 618, 620, 624, 628
Chapter Review/Test PE pp. 612, 632
Unit 8 Test, PE pp. 638–639

Formal Evaluation

Chapter & Unit Assessment

Chapter Review/Test, PE pp. 612, 632
Chapter 23 Test, Unit Resources
Chapter 24 Test, Unit Resources
***Unit Test, Form A and Form B,** Unit Resources
Unit 8 Test, PE pp. 638–639

Performance Assessment & Rubric

Performance Assessment, PE p. 639
Scoring Rubric, TE p. 639

Test Prep

***Problem Solving on Tests,** PE pp. 607
***Cumulative Test Prep,** PE pp. 640–641
Test Prep on the Net, on Education Place
www.eduplace.com/map

(Starred tests use standardized test formats.)

Test Generator 

The ***Ways to Assess*** **CD-ROM** allows you to create and score customized tests or review pages. You can select items that assess your state standards, NCTM standards, or lesson objectives of your choosing. The CD-ROM also includes program, chapter, and unit tests for online administration and scoring or for printing.

Intervention 

Ways to Success **CD-ROM** Reteach the lesson objective, provide extra practice, or reteach a key prerequisite skill. **Lessons** 23.1–23.5, 24.1–24.5

Audio Tutor For students who need extra support, who were absent, or who have reading difficulties. **Lessons** 23.1, 23.4, 23.5, 24.1, 24.2

Unit Activities

Unit Project

Individuals	30 minutes
Objective	Locate, identify, and graph points on a coordinate grid; graph lines.
Materials	10×10 grid paper (Learning Tool 26)
Tactual	

Use a Coordinate Grid

- Ask students about the types of board games they like to play or puzzles they like to solve. Tell students that in this Unit Project, they will design a game or a puzzle on a coordinate grid. Have students focus on making a fair game.
- Students who are designing a game should put an attractive game box together to include rules, scorecards, and materials.
- Use the activity found on page 642 to wrap up the Unit Project.

Spiral Review

Pairs	20 minutes
Objective	Model fractions.
Materials	Paper, colored pencils
Visual, Tactual	

Fraction Models

- Write the following on the board: *Choices:* $\frac{1}{4}, \frac{1}{2}, \frac{1}{3}, \frac{3}{4}, \frac{5}{5}, 0$
- Students play in pairs. The first student chooses a fraction and shades a circle to show the fraction. The partner guesses which fraction the drawing represents. Both partners discuss if the answer is correct and why or why not. Then partners switch roles and play until all fractions are used.

Vocabulary Activity

Pairs	20 minutes
Objective	Locate, identify, and graph points on a coordinate grid.
Materials	Poster board, ruler, markers, sticky notes
Tactual, Visual	

Coordinate Grids

Each student draws a grid with examples of each of the following vocabulary words on the grid: *ordered pair, coordinate, origin, x-axis, y-axis.* Students also write each word on a sticky note. Students exchange grids and stick vocabulary words beneath the appropriate examples.

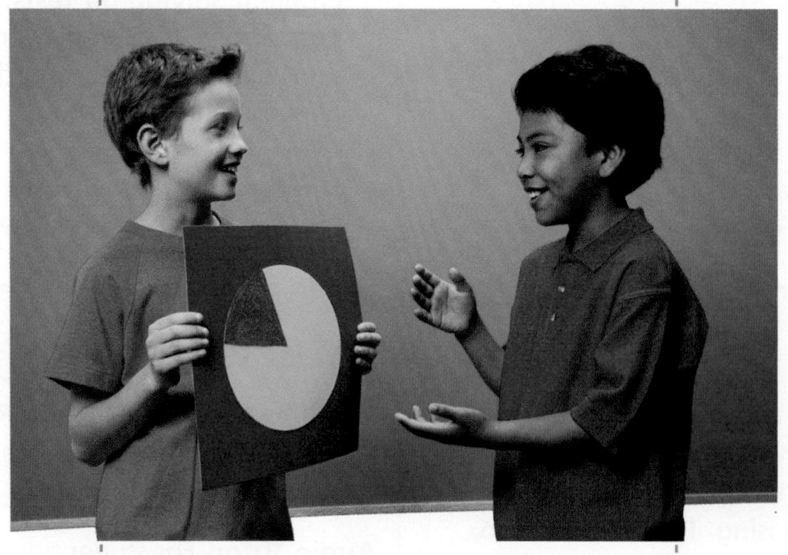

Take-Home Game

Individuals	15 minutes
Objective	Make an organized list.
Materials	None
Tactual	

Make an Organized List

Students pretend to plan a picnic lunch. They write down five food items they can use to make sandwiches, not including the bread. Students then make an organized list of different kinds of sandwiches they can make using any two of these items and tally the total. There should be 10 different combinations.

Repeatable Unit Game

Pairs	15 minutes
Objective	Locate, identify, and graph points on a coordinate grid.
Materials	10×10 number grids
Auditory, Visual	

Locate Points on a Grid

Have students work in pairs. Each student has a grid labeled 0–10 on both the *x*- and *y*-axis. Have them write each of the letters *H, O, M,* and *E* on four different points on the grid. Partners take turns guessing the points where the other player's letters are located, such as (1, 3). Play ends when one player locates all the other player's letters.

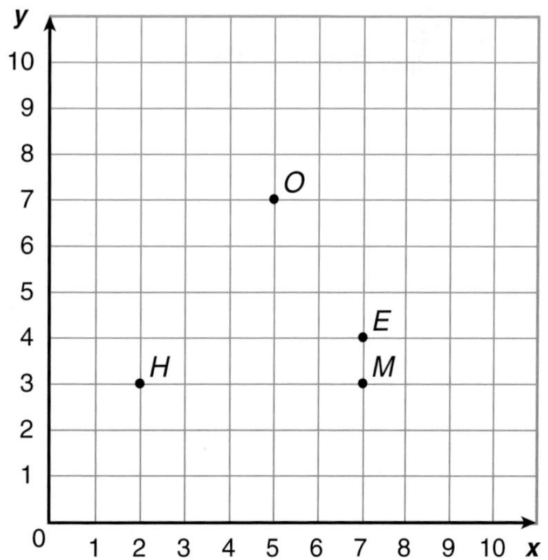

Math Expressions

Small Groups	30 minutes
Objective	Conduct probability experiments.
Materials	Paper bags, blocks or squares of paper in red and blue, blank spinner
Visual, Kinesthetic	

Probability Experiments

This activity uses instructional practices from *Math Expressions* with the content of this unit.

Students choose from the following:

- **Choose Without Looking:** Students imagine putting 6 objects in a bag, so that when one object is chosen without looking, one of the given events likely occurs: A) Certain to choose red B) Likely to choose red C) Equally likely to choose red and blue D) Unlikely to choose red
- **What's in the Bag?:** Student A puts 5 objects (some of each of 2 colors) in a bag. Student B picks an object from the bag without looking, tallies the color, and returns the object to the bag. Student B continues picking, then makes a prediction of how many objects of each color are in the bag.
- **Predicting Spins:** Students make a spinner with 6 equal sections, colored: 1 red, 2 blue, 3 yellow. They predict what fraction of each color will be spun if they spin 100 times. Students take turns spinning and recording the result. They compare the outcome with their prediction.

Starting Unit 8

Reading Mathematics

Use the *Reading Mathematics* pages to be sure that students have adequate understanding and fluency with the unit vocabulary. This provides the key foundation for developing the unit concepts and skills.

Reviewing Vocabulary

- Discuss the term *ordered pair* with students first, and then talk about the three probability terms.
- Use the First-Quadrant Grid Transparency. Draw a large dot at (2, 3). Point out the numbers along two sides of the grid. Ask students to recall how to name the point using an ordered pair of numbers. Also ask them how the points located at (2, 3) and (3, 2) are the same and different. Remind students that the first number in the pair refers to a horizontal move and the second number refers to a vertical move.
- Explain to students that *probability* is a mathematical way to describe how likely it is for something to happen. Ask students about the likelihood of getting a head or a tail when tossing a coin. If the coin is fair, the chances are *equally likely.* The usual *outcomes* for this probability experiment are heads and tails.

Reading Words and Symbols

- Write the following on the board to show how fractions and probability are related, based on the example on page 592.

Chances of landing on blue:

3 ← number of blue parts on spinner
8 ← number of parts on spinner

Reading Mathematics

Reviewing Vocabulary

Here are some math vocabulary words that you should know.

equally likely	having the same chance of occurring
ordered pair	a pair of numbers in which one number is named as the first and the other number is named as the second
outcome	a result in a probability experiment
probability	the chance that an event will occur

Reading Words and Symbols

You can find the probability that something will happen by looking at the possible results. Look at the spinner.

The spinner has 8 parts altogether. 3 parts are blue.

The chance of landing on blue is 3 out of 8.

- You can write this in words: three out of eight.
- You can write this as a fraction: $\frac{3}{8}$

Use the spinner to answer these questions.

1. What is the chance that a spin will land on red? **2 out of 8 or 1 out of 4**
2. What is the chance that a spin will land on yellow? **1 out of 8**

592

Reading Test Questions

Choose the correct answer for each.

3. Which statement describes the location of Point *A*?

a. 2 units right and 3 units up

b. 3 units right and 2 units up

(c.) 1 unit right and 4 units up

d. 4 units right and 1 unit up

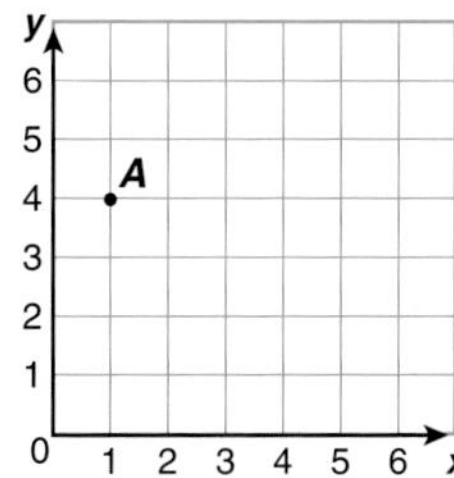

Location means "place" or "position."

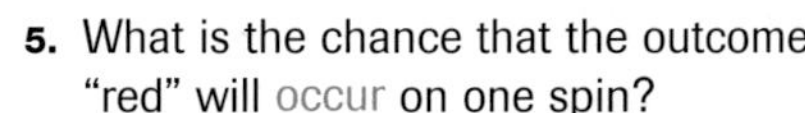

4. On which spinner is the arrow most likely to land on blue?

a.

(c.)

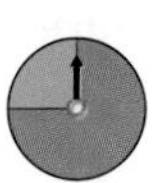

b.

d.

Most likely means "having the greatest chance."

5. What is the chance that the outcome "red" will occur on one spin?

a. 4 out of 5

b. 3 out of 5

c. 2 out of 5

(d.) 1 out of 5

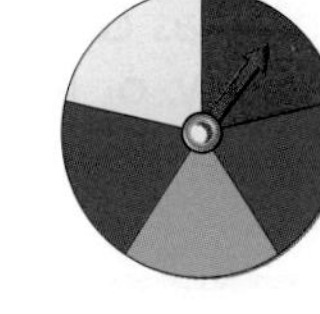

Occur means "happen."

Learning Vocabulary

Watch for these words in this unit. Write their definitions in your journal.

coordinates
integers
tree diagram
***x*-axis**
***y*-axis**

Education Place
At **eduplace.com/map** see eGlossary and eGames–Math Lingo.

Literature Connection

Read "The Perfect Present" on Pages 654–655. Then work with a partner to answer the questions about the story.

Reading Test Questions

- Tell students to think of other words for *location* and *occur* in **Items 3 and 5.** Elicit words or phrases like *place* or *site* and *show up* or *turn up.*
- For **Item 4,** remind students to think of comparing fractional parts of circles. The arrow will *most likely* land on blue if the spinner has lots of blue sections or a very large blue section.

Learning Vocabulary

- Go over the list of new words with the class. Help students pronounce the words correctly and explain that they will learn about these words as they work on this unit. If students are keeping Math Journals, be sure that they enter the words and their definitions as they find them in the unit.
- The *Building Vocabulary Kit* includes vocabulary cards and additional teaching strategies for unit vocabulary.

Writing in Mathematics

Writing helps students learn and remember. Throughout the unit, students have opportunities to write for different purposes:

- explaining their thinking or solution strategies
- creating new problems
- recording what they have learned
- listing questions they still have.

Look for *Explain Your Thinking* questions in the student text and *Math Journal Prompts* in this Teacher's Edition.

Literature Connection

Student Book List Selection

You may use the ***Literature Connection*** (Student Book pages 654–655, Teacher's Edition page T55) at any time during this unit.

Other Literature Connections

Jumanji
by Chris Van Allsburg

Do You Wanna Bet?: Your Chance to Find Out About Probability
by Jean Cushman

A Place for Zero: A Math Adventure
by Angeline Sparagna Lopresti

CHAPTER 23

Planning Guide

Probability

Lesson	Overview	Objective/Vocabulary
1 Probability p. 596A	► Describe the likelihood of an occurrence. ► Spinners are used to model the probability of an outcome as certain, likely, equally likely, unlikely, or impossible. ► Predict the likelihood of an outcome, using a tally board.	► Decide the probability that something will happen. probability outcome
2 Probability as a Fraction p. 598A	► Learn to write the probability of a favorable outcome in words and as a fraction. ► Practice determining and writing probabilities for situations involving spinners and number cubes.	► Write probabilities in words and as fractions. favorable outcome
3 Hands On: Make Predictions p. 602A	► In this hands-on exploration lesson, probability experiments teach how to predict outcomes. ► Experiments include picking cards from a bag and tossing labeled cubes.	► Predict outcomes in a probability experiment. prediction
4 Problem-Solving Strategy: Make an Organized List p. 604A	► Using an organized list, practice all the ways to arrange a set of objects. ► Listing arrangements methodically helps students find all possible arrangements of a set of objects. ► Additional problem-solving practice involves choosing a strategy and interpreting a line plot.	► Use an organized list to solve a problem. prediction
5 Find Probability p. 608A	► Use two or more organizational devices, such as grids and tree diagrams, to list all outcomes of probability experiments. ► Experiments include tossing coins, spinning spinners, and tossing number cubes.	► Find the probability of outcomes, using a grid or a tree diagram. grid tree diagram

Skills Trace: Probability		
Grade 3	**Grade 4**	**Grade 5**
• Identify outcomes (ch. 7) • Determine the likelihood of an occurrence (ch. 7) • Make predictions (ch. 7)	• Describe the probability of an event; identify outcomes • Make predictions • Use grids and tree diagrams to find the probability of outcomes • Use an organized list to solve a problem	• Determine combinations (ch. 20) • Find the theoretical probability of single and compound events (ch. 20)

Differentiated Instruction	Materials	NCTM Standards
▶ Differentiated Instruction activities, p. 596B ▶ *Chapter Challenges,* p. 133 *Ways to Success* CD-ROM 23.1 ▶ *Ways to Success* Skillsheet 194 Audio Tutor **2**/29 Listen and Understand	Workmat 8, blank transparency, 3 colors of markers, protractors	**Data Analysis and Probability:** Describe certain events as likely or unlikely and discuss the degree of likelihood using such words as *certain*, *equally likely*, and *impossible*.
▶ Differentiated Instruction activities, p. 598B *Ways to Success* CD-ROM 23.2 ▶ *Ways to Success* Skillsheets 195, 196	Blank transparency, protractor, red and blue markers, playing board (Learning Tool 43), spinners (Learning Tools 44–47), 1 red counter, 1 yellow counter	**Data Analysis and Probability:** Understand that the measure of the likelihood of an event can be represented by a number from 0 to 1.
▶ Differentiated Instruction activities, p. 602B ▶ *Chapter Challenges,* p. 135 *Ways to Success* CD-ROM 23.3 ▶ *Ways to Success* Skillsheet 197	Transparent Spinner, Table II Transparency, protractor, markers, paper bag, Probability Cards (Learning Tool 48), number cube	**Data Analysis and Probability:** Predict the probability of outcomes of simple experiments and test the predictions; propose and justify conclusions and predictions that are based on data and design studies to further investigate the conclusions or predictions.
▶ Differentiated Instruction activities, p. 604B *Ways to Success* CD-ROM 23.4 ▶ *Ways to Success* Skillsheet 199 Audio Tutor **2**/30 Listen and Understand	Color tiles or pattern blocks	**Problem Solving:** Apply and adapt a variety of appropriate strategies to solve problems.
▶ Differentiated Instruction activities, p. 608B ▶ *Chapter Challenges,* p. 137 *Ways to Success* CD-ROM 23.5 ▶ *Ways to Success* Skillsheet 198 Audio Tutor **2**/31 Listen and Understand	Newspapers or magazines, colored pens or pencils	**Data Analysis and Probability:** Understand and apply basic concepts of probability.

Math Notes

Chapter Objectives

23A Describe the probability of an event and determine the number of possible outcomes in an experiment.

23B Use probability to make predictions.

23C Use tables, graphs, and tree diagrams to represent probability outcomes.

23D Solve problems using skills and strategies.

Mathematical Background

Probability

Probability is a measure of the likelihood that an event will occur. Probabilities are numbers from 0 to 1. A probability of 1 means that an event is certain, while a probability of 0 means an event is impossible.

Probability experiments are useful in helping students understand probability. The result of an experiment is called an *outcome*. When a number cube is tossed, there are six possible outcomes, one for each face of the cube.

Students at this level begin to build an understanding of theoretical probability and experimental probability.

The theoretical probability of landing on the red section of this spinner can be written as a ratio of favorable outcomes (1 red) to total possible outcomes (4 sections). This probability can be written $\frac{1}{4}$.

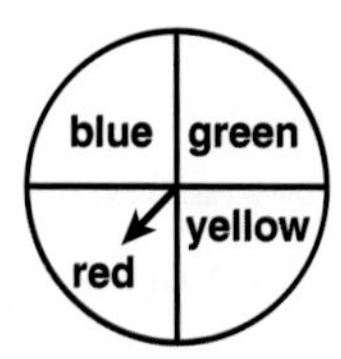

As probability experiments are performed, the experimental and theoretical probabilities are not always equal. As the experiment is repeated, however, the experimental probability approaches the theoretical probability.

Research-Based Teaching

Van de Walle (1994) believes that an experimental approach is important for students learning the rudiments of probability. It is more intuitive; the results make sense and do not come from abstract rules. It provides experimental background for further examining theoretical probability. As students increase the number of trials, they can see that the experimental probability comes closer to the theoretical probability. See *Professional Resources Handbook, Grade 4,* Unit 8.

For more ideas relating to Unit 8, see the Teacher Support Handbook at the back of this Teacher's Edition.

Language Intervention

When new vocabulary words (for example, *probability, outcome, favorable outcome*) are introduced in a lesson, have students write their own definitions. Use the students' definitions to help you identify misconceptions students may have.

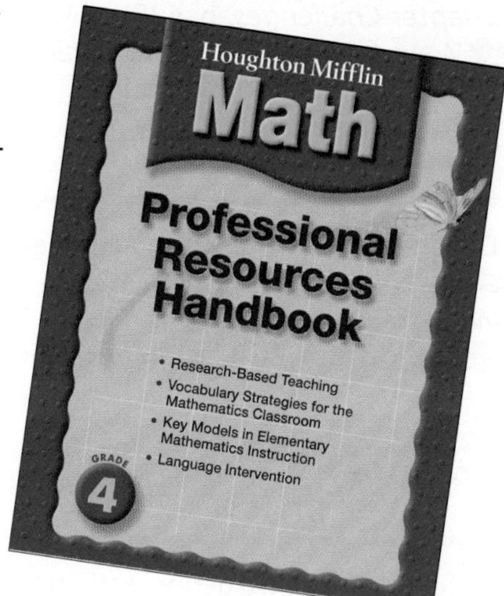

Chapter Activities

Connecting to the Unit Project

Individuals	30 minutes
Objective	Connect to the Unit Project.
Materials	Number cubes, spinners, coins, cards, and game boards (as needed)
Tactual	

Games and Probability

- Students who are designing a game involving number cubes, spinners, coins, or cards should be preparing a rough draft of the game rules.
- Have them include the name of the game, the number of players, the materials needed (including game board, if needed), the rules for playing the game, and how to win.
- Then students should play the game themselves to see if the game makes sense. This is called Quality Assurance, or QA. Students should perform QA and rewrite the rules as many times as needed until the game works.

Ongoing Skill Activity

Whole Class	15 minutes
Objective	Describe the probability of an event.
Materials	None
Visual, Auditory	

Weather and Probability

- Ask students to look out the window at the weather. Ask them if it is likely to rain (or snow). Have them respond with likelihood terms such as "more likely" or "impossible."
- Based on their predictions, ask them other questions like these: **What are the chances for going outside for recess? What is the probability that an afternoon or evening event will be canceled or postponed? Do you think many people would vote on a day like today?**

Math Expressions

Whole Class	20 minutes
Objective	Order likelihood of events on a number line.
Materials	None
Visual	

Probabilities on a Number Line

This activity uses instructional practices from *Math Expressions* with the content of this chapter.

- Discuss with students how a number line can help show how events compare to one another in terms of likelihood of occurring.
- As a class, generate a list of events. Use a letter to itemize each event.
  A. I will play outside after school.
  B. I will call someone on the telephone tonight.
  C. It will rain tomorrow.
- Draw a number line on the board with the following numbers labeled:
  0: impossible
  $\frac{1}{2}$: 50–50 chance
  1: certain
- Then have volunteers label the number line to show how likely he or she thinks each event is.

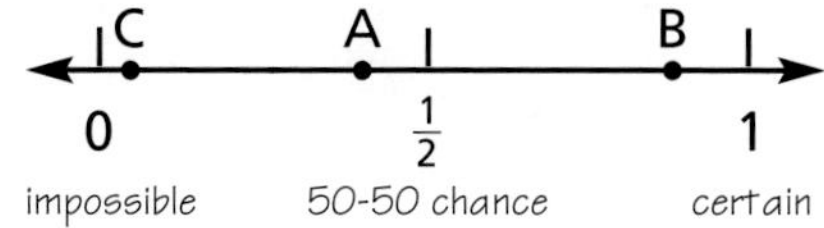

- Continue the activity by extending the lettered list of events.

Starting Chapter 23

Investigation

Using Data

Have students work in small groups to answer the questions posed on page 594.

- To extend the investigation, provide the following problem.
- Use the bar graph on page 594. Suppose that before anyone picked a bag from the treasure chest, 3 bags were removed. How could this affect the type of item you are most likely to pick? How could it affect the type of item you are least likely to pick? (Answers will vary. Possible answer: It depends on which bags are removed. If 3 bags of action figures are removed, then there would be an equal number of bags of action figures and bags of stuffed animals, making the probability that they are picked equally likely.)

For more information about projects and investigations,

Visit **Education Place**®
www.eduplace.com/mat

CHAPTER 23

Probability

INVESTIGATION

Using Data

Gabrielle just picked a bag from the treasure chest. Look at the graph. Suppose you were to pick a bag. What type of item are you most likely to pick? How would the graph change if all picks were equally likely?

Action Figure; The bars would all be the same height.

594

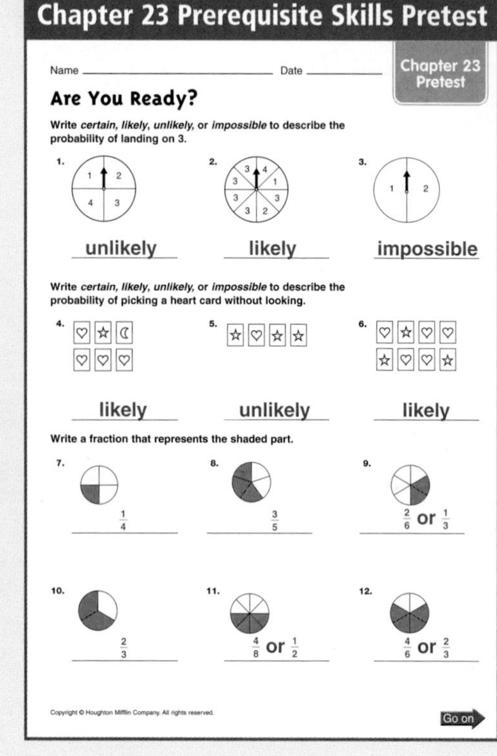
Chapter 23 Prerequisite Skills Pretest

Name ______ Date ______

Chapter 23 Pretest

Are You Ready?

Write *certain, likely, unlikely,* or *impossible* to describe the probability of landing on 3.

1. unlikely
2. likely
3. impossible

Write *certain, likely, unlikely,* or *impossible* to describe the probability of picking a heart card without looking.

4. likely
5. unlikely
6. likely

Write a fraction that represents the shaded part.

7. $\frac{1}{4}$
8. $\frac{3}{5}$
9. $\frac{2}{6}$ or $\frac{1}{3}$
10. $\frac{2}{3}$
11. $\frac{4}{8}$ or $\frac{1}{2}$
12. $\frac{4}{6}$ or $\frac{2}{3}$

Go on

Use What You Know

Use this page to review and remember what you need to know for this chapter.

VOCABULARY

Choose the best word to complete each sentence.

Vocabulary
certain
fraction
impossible
denominator

1. If an event will definitely happen, it is ____ certain
2. A ____ names a part of a whole. fraction
3. In a fraction, the number that tells how many equal parts are in a whole is the ____. denominator

CONCEPTS AND SKILLS

Write *likely, equally likely,* or *unlikely* to describe the probability of picking a red tile without looking.

4.  unlikely

5.   equally likely
6.  likely

Write a fraction that represents the red part.

7. $\frac{1}{6}$ 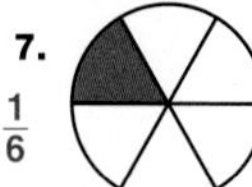
8. $\frac{5}{8}$ 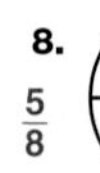 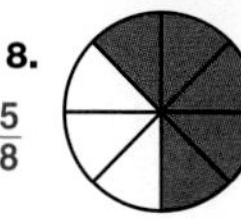
9. $\frac{3}{4}$ 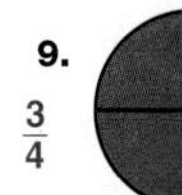

Write About It

10. If you pick one cube from the bag on the right, are you likely to pick a blue cube? Why or why not? Which two colors have the same probablility of being picked?
No; there is only one blue cube in the bag; red and green

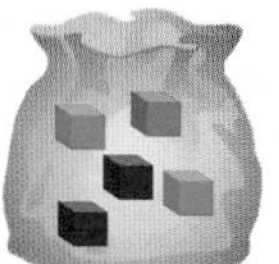

Facts Practice, See page 670.

Chapter 23 New Content Pretest

Name ________ Date ________

Chapter 23 Pretest continued

Check What You Know

Write *certain, likely, unlikely,* or *impossible* to describe the probability of landing on 2.

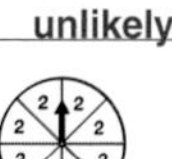

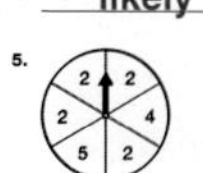

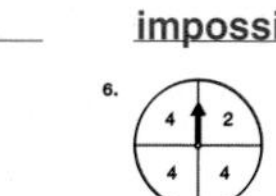

1. unlikely
2. likely
3. impossible
4. certain
5. likely
6. unlikely

For each set of tiles, write the probability that you will pick a 4 if you pick one tile without looking. Write the probability in both words and fraction form.

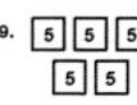
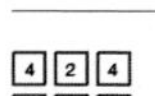

7. 1 2 3 4 — 1 out of 4; $\frac{1}{4}$
8. 1 4 5 / 4 3 1 — 2 out of 6 or 1 out of 3; $\frac{2}{6}$ or $\frac{1}{3}$
9. 5 5 5 / 5 5 — 0 out of 5; $\frac{0}{5}$
10. 2 2 4 4 / 3 3 4 4 — 4 out of 8 or 1 out of 2; $\frac{4}{8}$ or $\frac{1}{2}$
11. 4 4 4 — 3 out of 3 or 1 out of 1; $\frac{3}{3}$ or 1
12. 4 2 4 / 2 4 4 — 4 out of 6 or 2 out of 3; $\frac{4}{6}$ or $\frac{2}{3}$

Go on

Chapter 23 New Content Pretest

Name ________ Date ________

Chapter 23 Pretest continued

The faces of a cube are labeled with the letters *A, B, C, A, B,* and *A*. Think about the cube for Problems 13–14.

13. Predict how many times the cube will land on *A* if the cube is tossed 30 times.
15 times
14. Predict how many times the cube will land on *C* if the cube is tossed 60 times.
10 times

Make an organized list to solve each problem.

15. Nick is writing the 4 letters in his name in different orders. How many different ways can he write his name?
24 ways
16. Joseph is making a sandwich. He can choose white or wheat bread. He can choose turkey, ham, or peanut butter. How many different combinations of bread and filling can Joseph choose from?
6 combinations
17. Keith, Annie, Elizabeth, and Marcus are taking a picture. How many different ways can the friends stand in a horizontal line for the picture?
24 ways

Use the spinners for Problems 18–20.

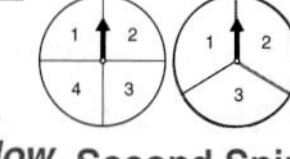

18. You spin both spinners at the same time. Draw a grid on a separate page to show all the possible outcomes.
Check students' grids. See below.
19. How many outcomes show one spinner landing on 4?
3 outcomes
20. Find the probability of both spinners landing on 2. Write your answer in fraction form.
$\frac{1}{12}$

First Spin \ Second Spin	1	2	3
1	1, 1	1, 2	1, 3
2	2, 1	2, 2	2, 3
3	3, 1	3, 2	3, 3
4	4, 1	4, 2	4, 3

STOP

Monitoring Student Progress

Use What You Know

Use this page for informal assessment and review of prerequisite skills.

- Items 1–3: Use math vocabulary
- Items 4–6, 10: Determine the likelihood of an event
- Items 7–9: Write a fraction for the shaded portion of the circle
- Item 10: Explain probabilities

Customize Your Instruction

Use the Chapter Pretest in the Unit Resource folder to help customize and pace instruction.

Objectives and Resources

Prerequisite Skills Pretest

- Items 1–6: Determine the likelihood of an event.
- Items 7–12: Write a fraction for the shaded part of a circle.

New Content Pretest

- Items 1–6: Determine the likelihood of an event.
- Items 7–12: Write the probability in words and as fractions.
- Items 13–20: Use probability to make predictions.

For Students Having Difficulty

- *Ways to Success* CD-ROM: 19A, 23A
- *Ways to Success* Skillsheets: 194, 195

For Students Having Success

- Enrichment 23.1–23.5

For Mathematically Promising Students

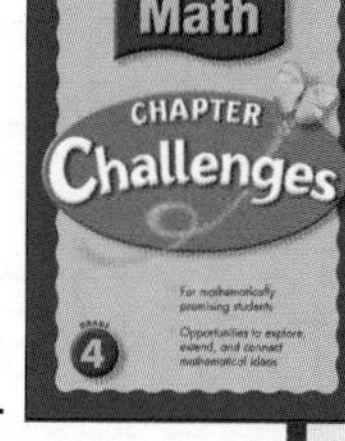

Explore: Surveys and Samples, page 133, after Lesson 1

Extend: Probability and Replacement, page 135, after Lesson 3

Connect: Card Experiment, page 137, after Lesson 5

Lesson 23.1 Probability

Planning

Lesson Objective Decide the probability that something will happen.

Technology Resources

- Audio Tutor **2**/29 Listen and Understand
- *Ways to Success* CD-ROM 23.1
- Education Place: Extra Practice, eGlossary, eGames www.eduplace.com/map

Lesson 23.1 Transparency

Problem of the Day

Kevin has only blue socks and white socks. He never pairs them, but just stuffs them in a drawer. One morning, without looking, he grabs 2 socks. What socks might he have? (2 blues, 2 whites, or 1 of each)

Spiral Review

What comes next?

1. $\frac{1}{2}, \frac{2}{4}, \frac{3}{6}, \frac{4}{8}, \frac{5}{10}$, ___ $(\frac{6}{12})$

2. $\frac{3}{5}, \frac{6}{10}, \frac{9}{15}, \frac{12}{20}$, ___ $(\frac{15}{25})$

3. 2.3, 4.6, 9.2, 18.4, ___ (36.8)

4. 7, 0.7, 0.07, 0.007, ___ (0.0007)

Lesson Quiz

Look at the bag of cubes. Write *certain, likely, equally likely, unlikely,* or *impossible* to describe the probability of picking the color.

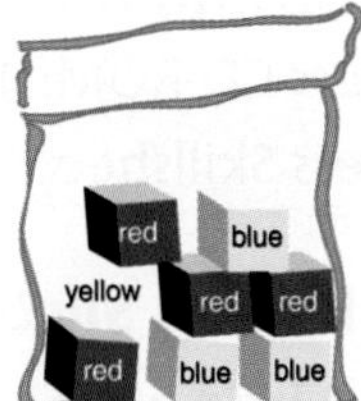

1. yellow (unlikely)

3. red or blue (likely)

2. green (impossible)

NCTM Standards

Data Analysis and Probability: Describe certain events as likely or unlikely and discuss the degree of likelihood using such words as *certain, equally likely,* and *impossible.*

Getting Started

Building Math Vocabulary

probability a mathematical way of describing how likely it is that something will happen

outcome a result in a probability experiment

Spinner Probability

Whole Class	15 minutes
Objective	Describe the probability of an event and determine the number of possible outcomes.
Materials	Workmat 8, blank transparency, 3 colors of markers, protractors
Visual, Tactual	

- Make 2-part, 3-part, and 8-part spinners using blank transparencies. Color the 2-part spinner $\frac{1}{2}$ blue, $\frac{1}{2}$ green. Color the 3-part spinner all green. Color the 8-part spinner $\frac{6}{8}$ blue, $\frac{2}{8}$ red.
- Display the 2-part spinner. **Probability is a way to describe how likely it is that an outcome will happen. We can use the terms *certain, likely, equally likely, unlikely,* and *impossible* to describe probability.** Write these words on the blank transparency.
- **Which term would we use to describe the probability that the spinner will land on blue?** (equally likely) **Why?** (equal parts of blue and green)
- Repeat this activity with the other spinners.
- Have students use Workmat 8 and their protractors to make 6-part spinners with 2 parts colored red, 4 parts green. **Which term best describes the probability that the spinner will land on blue?** (impossible) **How many possible outcomes are there?** (2) **Which term best describes that the spinner will land on green? Explain.** (Likely; there are 4 green parts out of 6 possible, which is more than half.)
- Tell students that they will learn more about the probability of different outcomes in the lesson in their book.

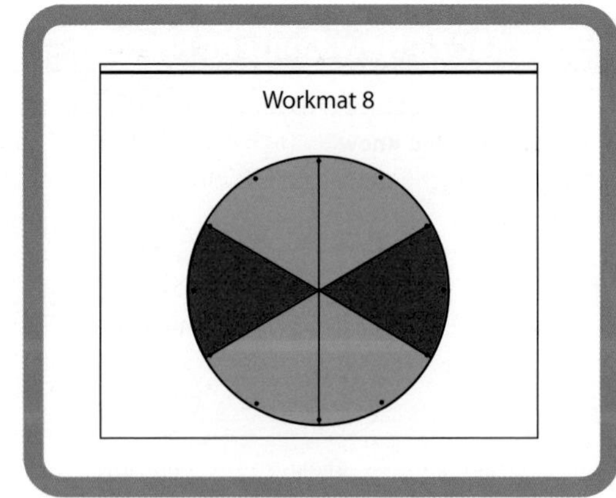

Differentiated Instruction

English Learners

Individuals	5 minutes
Objective	Describe the probability of an event.
Materials	Student page 597
Tactual	

Early Production

- For ***Guided Practice,*** have students make a chart using vocabulary words and percents to help them remember what the words mean: *certain* = 100%, *likely* > 50%, *equally likely* = all possibilities same, *unlikely* < 50%, and *impossible* = 0%.
- Ask them to read their answers aloud.

Intermediate/Advanced

- English Learner Resource 23.1
- English Learner Handbook

Intervention

Pairs	10 minutes
Objective	Describe the probability of an event.
Materials	Bag, colored cubes
Tactual, Visual	

- Students may better grasp the concepts of probability if they experiment. Form pairs and give each pair a bag with colored cubes. (Use any mix of colors to start; for example, 6 red cubes, or 3 red cubes and 2 blue cubes.) Have students see and count the contents of the bag.
- Have one student hold the bag and name a color. The other student should say whether it would be certain, likely, equally likely, unlikely, or impossible to pick that color without looking.
- Have students reverse roles. The student with the bag should vary the mix in the bag by changing the colors or numbers of cubes or both.

Other Resources

- *Ways to Success* CD-ROM 23.1

Gifted & Talented

Individuals	20 minutes
Objective	Determine the number of possible outcomes of an experiment.
Materials	Spinners (Learning Tool 42), markers or crayons, protractors
Visual, Tactual	

- Give students 6-part spinner cutouts (LT 42). Tell students to color each of the equal parts either red or blue so that it is equally likely that either red or blue would be the outcome.
- Repeat the activity. Have students create a spinner with 12 equal parts and use red, blue, and orange. Challenge the students to color the spinner so that no part may be next to a part with the same color.

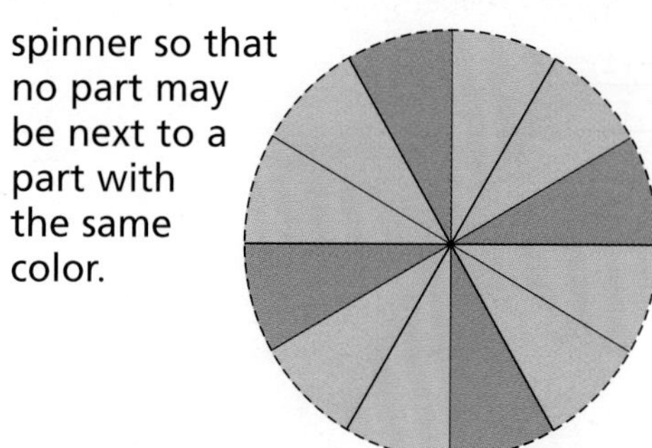

Literature Connection

Materials: *Do You Wanna Bet?: Your Chance to Find Out About Probability* by Jean Cushman

- This book examines probability, using scenes from two boys' lives.
- Read one of the stories to students. Stop frequently to discuss probability and outcomes. Then talk about the given solution.

Pattern Practice

Have each student make up a pattern based on simple addition or subtraction, such as 40, 31, 22, 13... . Have students take turns writing their patterns on the board, leaving out one number, for example, 40, 31, ___, 13. Have the class figure out the missing number.

❶ Introduce

What are the chances that you will see a live elephant today? (not too likely, but not impossible) **What could make it happen?** (if a circus came to town) Tell students that the lesson will examine mathematical ways to explain how likely things are to happen.

❷ Teach

Learn About It

- **What is an outcome?** (something that happens in a probability experiment) **Is picking a pink cube a possible outcome? Explain.** (no; no pink cube in bag)
- **Look at the spinners. If you were playing a game that gave points for spinning red, which spinner would you want to use? Explain.** (first one; you will always spin red)
- **Look at *Another Example.* Why is the probability of landing on red the same in the first two spinners?** ($\frac{1}{2} = \frac{2}{4}$) **Why is the probability of landing on green, red, and yellow equally likely in the third spinner?** (All sections are thirds, and yellow, orange, and green are each $\frac{1}{3}$.)

Guided Practice

Have students complete **Exercises 1–4** as you observe. Remind them to use the ***Ask Yourself*** questions to help. Give students the opportunity to talk about the question in ***Explain Your Thinking.***

Common Error

- **Confusing probability terms**
- **Intervention** Work with students to list examples of everyday events that are certain, likely, equally likely, unlikely, or impossible. Post the lists where students can refer to them as they work.

Lesson 1

Audio Tutor 2/29 Listen and Understand

Probability

Objective Decide the probability that something will happen.

Vocabulary
probability
outcome

Learn About It

Probability is a mathematical way of describing how likely it is that something will happen. An **outcome** is a result of a probability experiment.

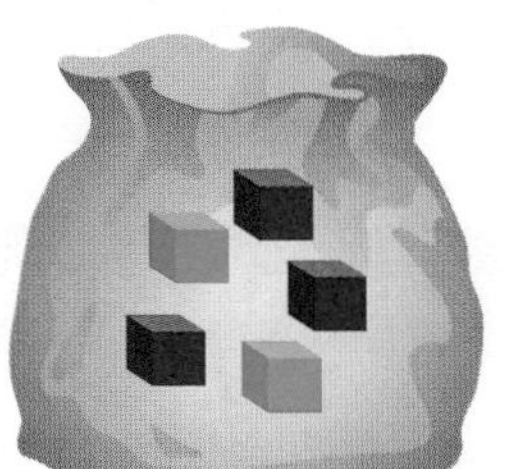

If you pick one cube from the bag at the right without looking, the outcome will be either a red cube or a green cube.

You are more likely to pick a red cube than a green cube, because there are more red cubes than green cubes.

▶ **Look at the spinners below.**

- What are the possible outcomes for each spinner?
- What words can be used to describe the probability that the spinner will land on red?

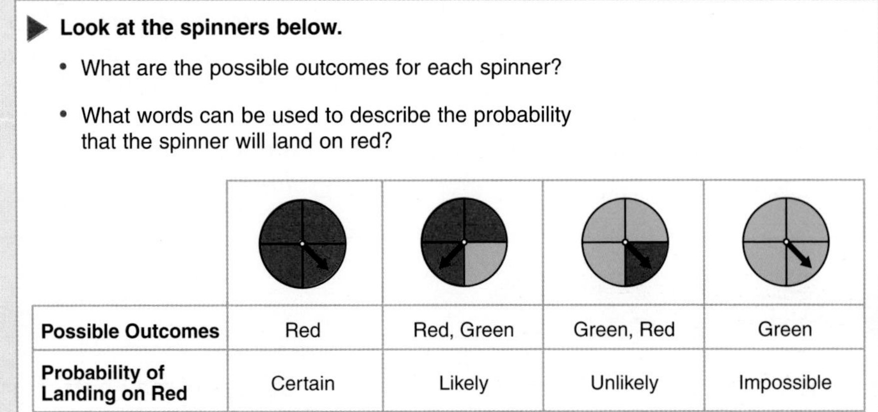

Possible Outcomes	Red	Red, Green	Green, Red	Green
Probability of Landing on Red	Certain	Likely	Unlikely	Impossible

Another Example

Equally Likely Outcomes

Each of the spinners on the right is divided into congruent regions. On each spinner, the number of regions of each color is equal. So the probability of the arrow landing on each color is equally likely.

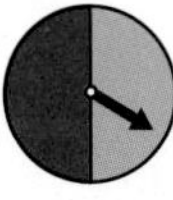 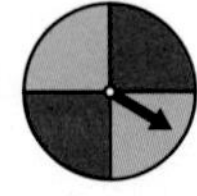 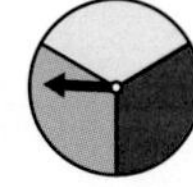 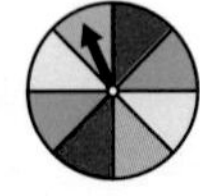

596

Reteach 23.1

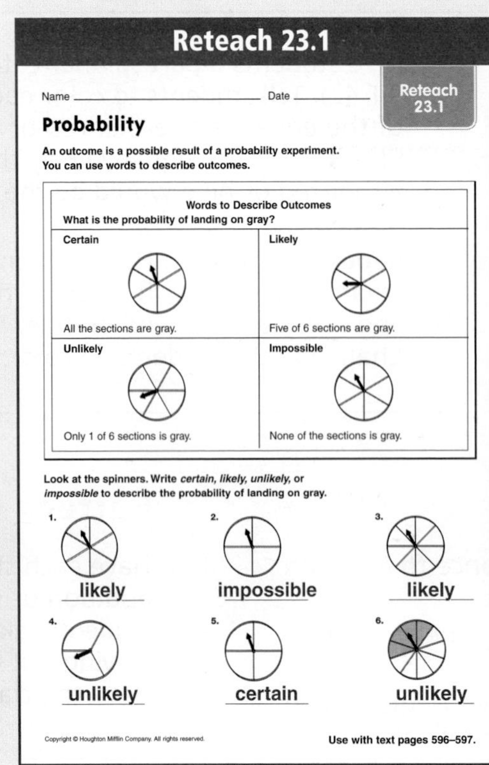

Name ______ Date ______ Reteach 23.1

Probability

An outcome is a possible result of a probability experiment. You can use words to describe outcomes.

Words to Describe Outcomes
What is the probability of landing on gray?

Certain	Likely
All the sections are gray.	Five of 6 sections are gray.
Unlikely	**Impossible**
Only 1 of 6 sections is gray.	None of the sections is gray.

Look at the spinners. Write *certain, likely, unlikely,* or *impossible* to describe the probability of landing on gray.

1. likely
2. impossible
3. likely
4. unlikely
5. certain
6. unlikely

Use with text pages 596–597.

Practice 23.1 Page 144

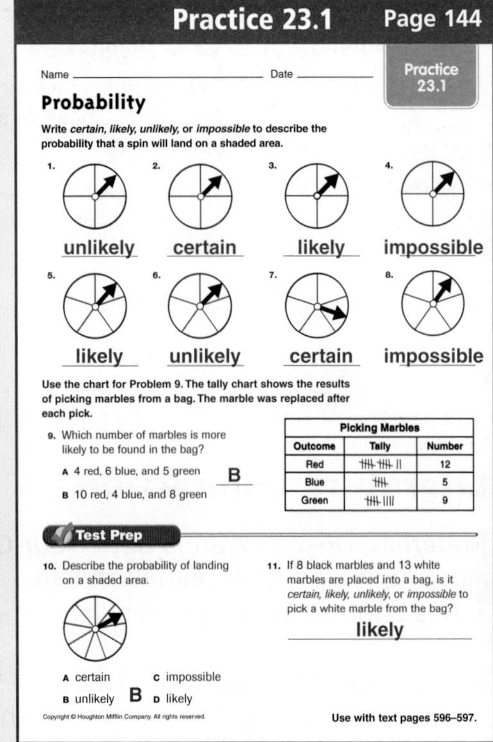

Name ______ Date ______ Practice 23.1

Probability

Write *certain, likely, unlikely,* or *impossible* to describe the probability that a spin will land on a shaded area.

1. unlikely
2. certain
3. likely
4. impossible
5. likely
6. unlikely
7. certain
8. impossible

Use the chart for Problem 9. The tally chart shows the results of picking marbles from a bag. The marble was replaced after each pick.

9. Which number of marbles is more likely to be found in the bag? B
   A 4 red, 6 blue, and 5 green
   B 10 red, 4 blue, and 8 green

Picking Marbles		
Outcome	**Tally**	**Number**
Red	|||| |||| ||	12
Blue	||||	5
Green	|||| ||||	9

Test Prep

10. Describe the probability of landing on a shaded area.
    A certain C impossible
    B unlikely D likely
    B

11. If 8 black marbles and 13 white marbles are placed into a bag, is it *certain, likely, unlikely,* or *impossible* to pick a white marble from the bag? likely

Use with text pages 596–597.

Guided Practice

Look at the bag of marbles. Write *certain, likely, equally likely, unlikely,* or *impossible* to describe the probability of picking each color without looking.

1. blue **likely**
2. yellow **impossible**
3. red **unlikely**
4. blue or red **certain**

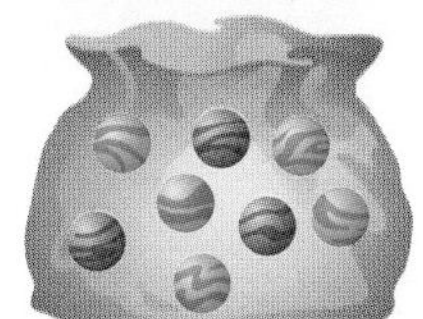

Ask Yourself

- How many marbles of each color are there?
- Are there more marbles of one color than another?

Explain Your Thinking ▶ How would you change the colors in the bag above to make it likely that red would be picked?

Possible answer: **Change two marbles from blue to red.**

Practice and Problem Solving

Write *certain, likely, equally likely, unlikely,* or *impossible* to describe the probability of landing on blue.

5. 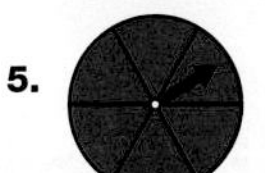 **impossible**
6. 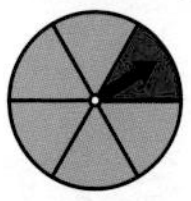 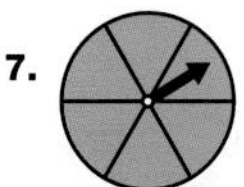 **likely**
7. 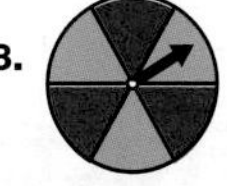 **certain**
8. **equally likely**

Data Use the chart for Problems 9 and 10.

9. **Predict** Which number of tiles is more likely to be found in the bag?
   - 5 yellow, 5 orange, and 5 brown
   - 10 yellow, 10 orange, and 5 brown

   10 yellow, 10 orange, and 5 brown
10. **Write About It** Is it likely that exactly 6 brown tiles, 11 orange tiles, and 13 yellow tiles are in the bag? Explain.
    See Additional Answers.

Picking Tiles

Outcome	Tally	Number
Brown	卌 I	6
Orange	卌 卌 I	11
Yellow	卌 卌 III	13

The tally chart shows the results of picking tiles from a bag. The chosen tile was replaced after each pick.

Mixed Review and Test Prep

Open Response

Divide. (Ch. 11, Lessons 4 and 5)

11. 25)178 **7 R3**
12. 13)247 **19**
13. 19)182 **9 R11**
14. 32)384 **12**
15. 770 ÷ 35 **22**
16. 729 ÷ 81 **9**
17. 145 ÷ 11 **13 R2**
18. 468 ÷ 26 **18**
19. On which two colors is the arrow equally likely to land? Explain. (Ch. 23, Lesson 1)

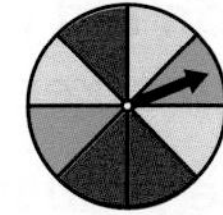

yellow and red; there are 3 yellow sections and 3 red sections.

Extra Practice See page 613, Set A.

3 Practice

Practice and Problem Solving

Select from **Exercises 5–19** as independent work.

- ***Data*** Review the use of tallies as needed.
- ***Problem 10*** Invite students to share their responses and explain how they determined their answers.

4 Assess & Close

Math Talk in Action

Suppose you roll a number cube with the digits 1–6 on its faces. Are outcomes *odd* and *even* equally likely? Explain. (Students should see that 3 odd and 3 even outcomes are possible, so either outcome is equally likely.)

Math Journal Prompt

Have students describe a simple probability experiment with eight colored marbles. Have them list three different outcomes and describe the probability of each.

Lesson Quiz

Use the quiz on Lesson Transparency 23.1.

Test Prep & Spiral Review

Use Test Prep Transparency 23.1.

Enrichment 23.1

Name ______ Date ______ Enrichment 23.1

Bag of Numbers

Place the numbers into the bags below so that the events described below each bag are true. Some of the numbers may be placed in more than one bag.

Check students' responses.

1	1	2	2	2	3	3	3
4	4	5	5	5	6	8	8
9	10	10	12	12	14	15	16
16	18	20	20	21	22	24	24

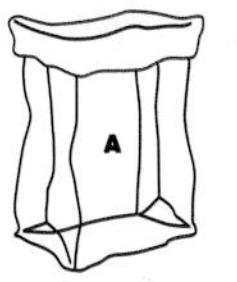

A
- Picking an even number is likely.
- Picking a multiple of 3 is unlikely.
- Picking a number less than 10 is impossible.

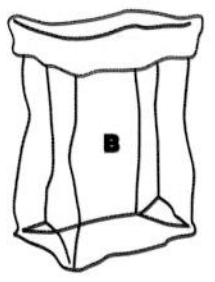

B
- Picking a 3 or a 2 is equally likely.
- Picking a multiple of 5 is impossible.
- Picking a factor of 24 is certain.

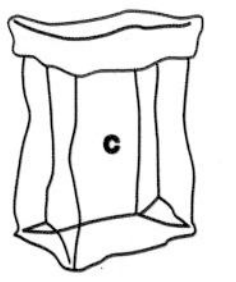

C
- Picking a multiple of 5 is likely.
- Picking a number less than 10 is unlikely.

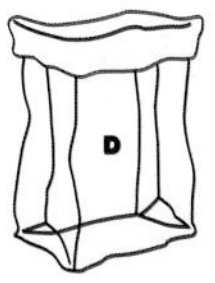

D
- Picking an odd number is impossible.
- Picking a number with the digit 4 is certain.

Use with text pages 596–597.

Problem Solving 23.1

Name ______ Date ______ Problem Solving 23.1

Probability

Use the spinners for Problems 1–4.

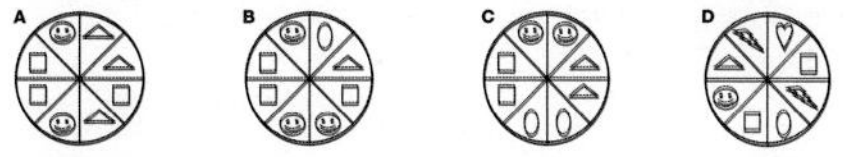

A B C D

1. On which spinner or spinners is it unlikely to land on a triangle? **Spinners A, B, C, and D**
2. On which spinner is it impossible to land on an oval? **Spinner A**
3. Carlos wants to use a spinner in which landing on each shape is equally likely. Which spinner should he use? **Spinner C**
4. Patty is playing a game in which she earns a point when the spinner lands on a smiley face. Which spinner should Patty use? **Spinner B**
5. **Write About It** In a bag of 25 marbles, 15 marbles are black, 7 are clear, and 3 are blue. You pick a marble from the bag without looking. Explain which colors, if any, are certain, likely, unlikely, and impossible to pick.

It is likely that you will pick a black marble. It is unlikely that you will pick a blue marble. It is impossible to pick any color other than black, clear, or blue. Explanations may vary.

Use with text pages 596–597.

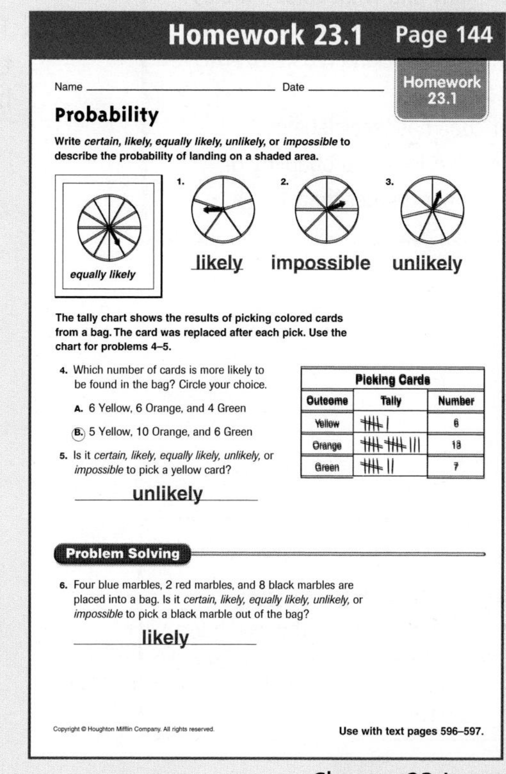

Homework 23.1 Page 144

Name ______ Date ______ Homework 23.1

Probability

Write *certain, likely, equally likely, unlikely,* or *impossible* to describe the probability of landing on a shaded area.

equally likely

1. **likely**
2. **impossible**
3. **unlikely**

The tally chart shows the results of picking colored cards from a bag. The card was replaced after each pick. Use the chart for problems 4–5.

Picking Cards

Outcome	Tally	Number
Yellow	卌 I	6
Orange	卌 卌 III	13
Green	卌 II	7

4. Which number of cards is more likely to be found in the bag? Circle your choice.
   A. 6 Yellow, 6 Orange, and 4 Green
   (B.) 5 Yellow, 10 Orange, and 6 Green
5. Is it *certain, likely, equally likely, unlikely,* or *impossible* to pick a yellow card? **unlikely**

Problem Solving

6. Four blue marbles, 2 red marbles, and 8 black marbles are placed into a bag. Is it *certain, likely, equally likely, unlikely,* or *impossible* to pick a black marble out of the bag? **likely**

Use with text pages 596–597.

Lesson 23.2

Probability as a Fraction

Planning

Lesson Objective Write probabilities in words and as fractions.

Technology Resources

- *Ways to Success* CD-ROM 23.2
- *Ways to Assess* CD-ROM
- Education Place: Extra Practice, eGlossary, eManipulatives, eGames www.eduplace.com/map

Lesson 23.2 Transparency

Problem of the Day

LeVar loves to read. He got 11 books for his birthday. Five of them were biographies. What fraction of the gift books were on other topics? ($\frac{6}{11}$)

Spiral Review

Write each as a fraction or whole number in simplest form.

1. 3 out of 9 ($\frac{1}{3}$) **2.** 5 out of 10 ($\frac{1}{2}$)
3. 6 out of 7 ($\frac{6}{7}$) **4.** 5 out of 9 ($\frac{5}{9}$)
5. 8 out of 8 (1)

Lesson Quiz

Solve.

1. A box holds 2 blue marbles and 6 red marbles. How many and what color marbles would you remove from the bag to make the probability of picking red $\frac{1}{2}$? (Remove 4 red marbles.)

2. A number cube has faces labeled 1–6. Write a fraction for the probability of rolling a number greater than 1. ($\frac{5}{6}$)

NCTM Standards

Data Analysis and Probability: Understand that the measure of the likelihood of an event can be represented by a number from 0 to 1.

Getting Started

Building Math Vocabulary

favorable outcome a desired result in a probability experiment

Using Fractions to Describe Probability of Outcomes

Whole Class	15 minutes
Objective	Describe the probability of an event and determine the number of possible outcomes of an experiment.
Materials	Blank transparency, protractor, red and blue markers
Visual, Tactual	

- Use the blank transparency to make an 8-part spinner for this activity. Shade the spinner $\frac{3}{8}$ red and $\frac{5}{8}$ blue. **We can use a fraction to describe the probability of an outcome. If we spin this spinner, what are the possible outcomes?** (blue or red) **Since 3 of the 8 parts are red, the probability that the spinner will land on red is 3 out of 8, or $\frac{3}{8}$.** Write $\frac{3}{8}$ below the spinner in red marker.
- **What fraction describes the probability that the spinner will land on blue? Explain.** ($\frac{5}{8}$; 5 out of 8 parts are blue) **Which is a more likely outcome, red or blue?** (blue) **How do the fractions support this?** ($\frac{5}{8} > \frac{3}{8}$)
- Tell students that they will learn more about using fractions to describe probable outcomes in the lesson in their book.

Differentiated Instruction

English Learners

Pair	15 minutes
Objective	Describe the probability of an event.
Materials	Student page 599
Auditory	

Early Production

- Have students practice saying the word *probability*.
- Pair students. After completing each problem in the ***Guided Practice***, ask them to take turns saying their answers in complete sentences. *The probability of picking a T is two-elevenths, or two out of eleven times.*

Intermediate/Advanced

- English Learner Resource 23.2
- English Learner Handbook

Intervention

Small Groups	5–10 minutes
Objective	Use probability to make a prediction.
Materials	Pennies
Visual, Tactual	

- Help students gain a sense of *theoretical* and *experimental* probabilities without introducing the terms or definitions.
- Show a penny. **If I flip this penny, what is the probability of getting heads?** ($\frac{1}{2}$) **tails?** ($\frac{1}{2}$) **So, if we flipped a penny 10 times, what might we expect to see?** (5 heads, 5 tails)
- Have students flip a penny 10 times. Discuss the results. Explain that the probability expressed in the fractions is correct based on many flips of the coin. Still, what actually happens in real life may differ, especially with a small number of tries.

Other Resources

- *Ways to Success* CD-ROM 23.2

Early Finishers

Individuals	15 minutes
Objective	Describe the probability of an event in words and in fraction form.
Materials	Student page 599
Visual, Tactual	

- Have students answer the same questions that appear in ***Guided Practice 1–5,*** but use each of the following place names instead of the word *mathematics:* Connecticut, South Dakota, Atlantic Ocean, District of Columbia.

Real-World Connection

- Ask students to express the probability of guessing a person's birthday. ($\frac{1}{366}$) Tell students that mathematicians have found that in a group of at least 23 people, the probability is more than $\frac{1}{2}$ that at least two will share a birthday.
- Find out if this is true in your class. If you have fewer than 23 students, add birthdays for the teacher, principal, class pet, etc.

❶ Introduce

Review the names of the parts of fractions and what they each describe. (numerator: how many parts to consider; denominator: how many parts in all) Tell students that in this lesson they will learn to write fractions to describe probabilities.

❷ Teach

Learn About It

- **In any probability experiment, what is a favorable outcome?** (the result you want) **How many sections does the spinner have?** (8) **What are the possible outcomes?** (numbers 1–8) **Why are these outcomes equally likely?** (sections all the same size)
- **How do we know how to express the probability of getting any number greater than 3?** (We decide which numbers fit this rule, count them, and then write a fraction for the expression.)
- **What does it mean for an outcome to have a probability of 0?** (impossible) **What is the probability of landing on 9?** (0)
- **What does it mean for an outcome to have a probability of 1?** (It is certain to happen.)
- **Can a probability ever be greater than 1? Explain.** (No. 1 means certain; there is nothing greater than certain.)

Common Error

- **Miswriting fractions** Some students mix up the terms of the fraction when trying to describe a probability.
- **Intervention** Remind them that the denominator is always the total number of possible outcomes. The numerator represents the number of desired outcomes.

Lesson 2

Probability as a Fraction

Objective Write probabilities in words and as fractions.

Vocabulary
favorable outcome

Learn About It

You can use words or fractions when you describe probability.

The spinner on the right has eight equally likely outcomes: 1, 2, 3, 4, 5, 6, 7, and 8. A **favorable outcome** is a result that you are looking to find. When you use a fraction to describe a probability, it is written as:

$$\frac{\text{favorable outcomes}}{\text{total possible outcomes}}$$

Favorable Outcome	Explanation
3	The probability of landing on 3 is 1 out of 8. Probability = $\frac{1}{8}$ ← favorable outcome (3) / ← total possible outcomes (1, 2, 3, 4, 5, 6, 7, 8) It is **unlikely** that a spin will land on 3.
a number greater than 3	The probability of landing on a number greater than 3 is 5 out of 8. Probability = $\frac{5}{8}$ ← favorable outcomes (4, 5, 6, 7, 8) / ← total possible outcomes (1, 2, 3, 4, 5, 6, 7, 8) It is **likely** that a spin will land on a number greater than 3.
9	The probability of landing on 9 is 0 out of 8. Probability = $\frac{0}{8}$ ← favorable outcome (none, 9 is not possible) / ← total possible outcomes (1, 2, 3, 4, 5, 6, 7, 8) It is **impossible** that a spin will land on 9.
1 or greater	The probability of landing on 1 or greater is 8 out of 8. Probability = $\frac{8}{8}$ ← favorable outcomes (1, 2, 3, 4, 5, 6, 7, 8) / ← total possible outcomes (1, 2, 3, 4, 5, 6, 7, 8) It is **certain** that a spin will land on 1 or greater.

598

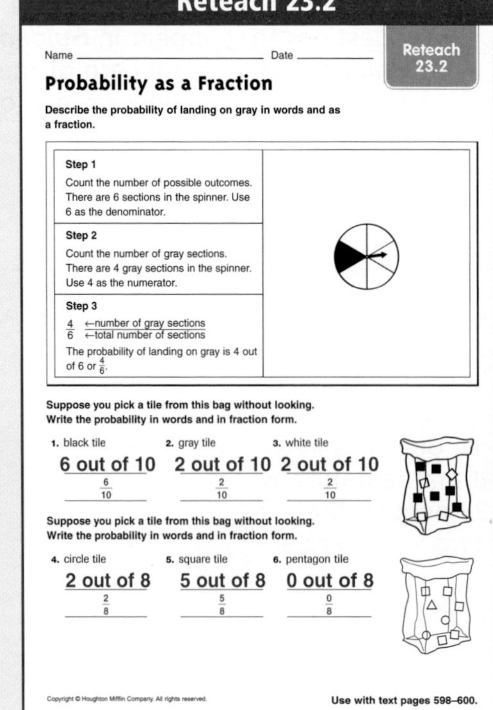

Reteach 23.2

Name ______ Date ______

Reteach 23.2

Probability as a Fraction

Describe the probability of landing on gray in words and as a fraction.

Step 1
Count the number of possible outcomes. There are 6 sections in the spinner. Use 6 as the denominator.

Step 2
Count the number of gray sections. There are 4 gray sections in the spinner. Use 4 as the numerator.

Step 3
$\frac{4}{6}$ ←number of gray sections / ←total number of sections
The probability of landing on gray is 4 out of 6 or $\frac{4}{6}$.

Suppose you pick a tile from this bag without looking. Write the probability in words and in fraction form.

1. black tile 6 out of 10; $\frac{6}{10}$
2. gray tile 2 out of 10; $\frac{2}{10}$
3. white tile 2 out of 10; $\frac{2}{10}$

Suppose you pick a tile from this bag without looking. Write the probability in words and in fraction form.

4. circle tile 2 out of 8; $\frac{2}{8}$
5. square tile 5 out of 8; $\frac{5}{8}$
6. pentagon tile 0 out of 8; $\frac{0}{8}$

Use with text pages 598–600.

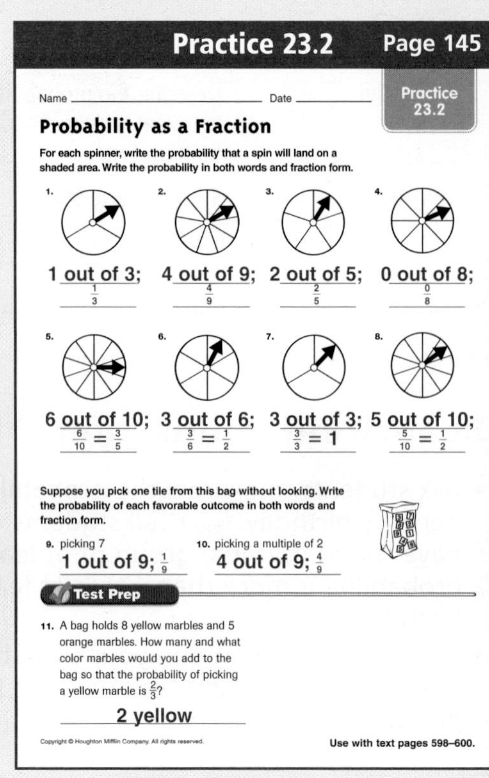

Practice 23.2 Page 145

Name ______ Date ______

Practice 23.2

Probability as a Fraction

For each spinner, write the probability that a spin will land on a shaded area. Write the probability in both words and fraction form.

1. 1 out of 3; $\frac{1}{3}$
2. 4 out of 9; $\frac{4}{9}$
3. 2 out of 5; $\frac{2}{5}$
4. 0 out of 8; $\frac{0}{8}$
5. 6 out of 10; $\frac{6}{10} = \frac{3}{5}$
6. 3 out of 6; $\frac{3}{6} = \frac{1}{2}$
7. 3 out of 3; $\frac{3}{3} = 1$
8. 5 out of 10; $\frac{5}{10} = \frac{1}{2}$

Suppose you pick one tile from this bag without looking. Write the probability of each favorable outcome in both words and fraction form.

9. picking 7 1 out of 9; $\frac{1}{9}$
10. picking a multiple of 2 4 out of 9; $\frac{4}{9}$

Test Prep

11. A bag holds 8 yellow marbles and 5 orange marbles. How many and what color marbles would you add to the bag so that the probability of picking a yellow marble is $\frac{2}{3}$?
2 yellow

Use with text pages 598–600.

▶ The number line below shows that the probability of an outcome ranges from 0 (impossible) to 1 (certain).

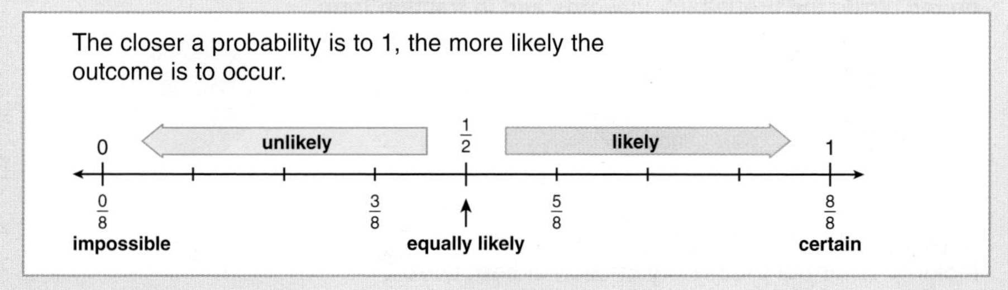

Guided Practice

Suppose you pick a tile in the word below without looking. Write the probability of each favorable outcome in words and in fraction form.

Ask Yourself

- How many tiles are there altogether?
- How many tiles have the letter or letters I am looking for?

M A T H E M A T I C S

1. T $\frac{2}{11}$, unlikely **2.** C $\frac{1}{11}$, unlikely **3.** H or A $\frac{3}{11}$, unlikely **4.** a vowel $\frac{4}{11}$, unlikely **5.** a consonant $\frac{7}{11}$, likely

For each spinner, write the probability that a spin will land on blue. Write the probability in both words and fraction form.

6. 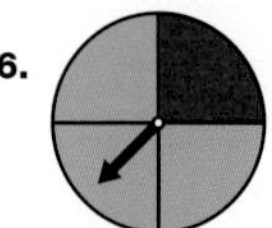 $\frac{3}{4}$, likely

7. 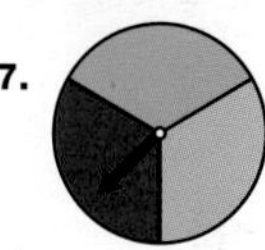 $\frac{1}{3}$, unlikely

8. 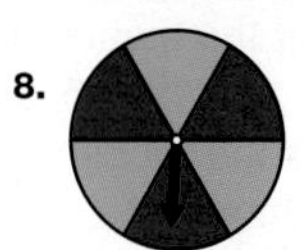 $\frac{3}{6}$ or $\frac{1}{2}$, equally likely

9. 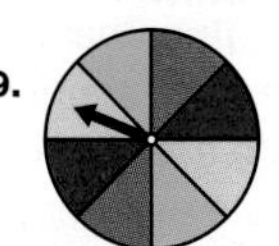 $\frac{0}{8}$, impossible

Explain Your Thinking ▶ If the probability of spinning blue is $\frac{3}{8}$, does this mean that you will always spin blue 3 out of 8 times? Explain why or why not. ***Possible answer:*** **No; a probability is a prediction. In an experiment, the actual results may differ from the prediction.**

- **How does the number line summarize probability?** (The closer a probability is to 1, the more likely that outcome is; the closer a probability is to 0, the less likely the outcome is.)

Guided Practice

Have students complete **Exercises 1–9** as you observe. Remind them to use the *Ask Yourself* questions to help. Give students the opportunity to talk about the question in *Explain Your Thinking*.

Enrichment 23.2

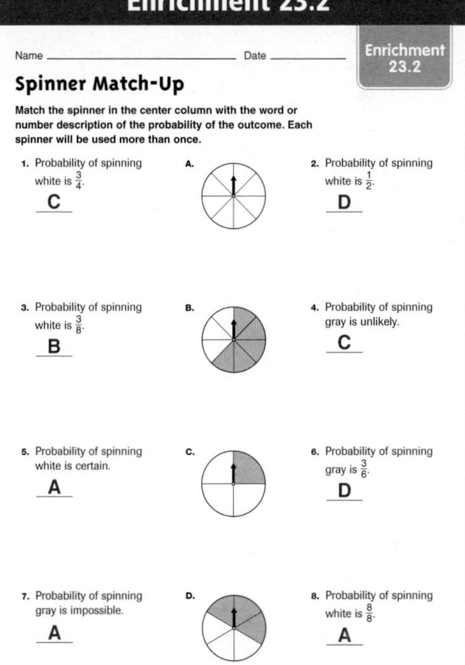

Name ______ Date ______ Enrichment 23.2

Spinner Match-Up

Match the spinner in the center column with the word or number description of the probability of the outcome. Each spinner will be used more than once.

1. Probability of spinning white is $\frac{3}{4}$. C
2. Probability of spinning white is $\frac{1}{2}$. D
3. Probability of spinning white is $\frac{3}{8}$. B
4. Probability of spinning gray is unlikely. C
5. Probability of spinning white is certain. A
6. Probability of spinning gray is $\frac{3}{6}$. D
7. Probability of spinning gray is impossible. A
8. Probability of spinning white is $\frac{8}{8}$. A

A. B. C. D.

Use with text pages 598–600.

Problem Solving 23.2

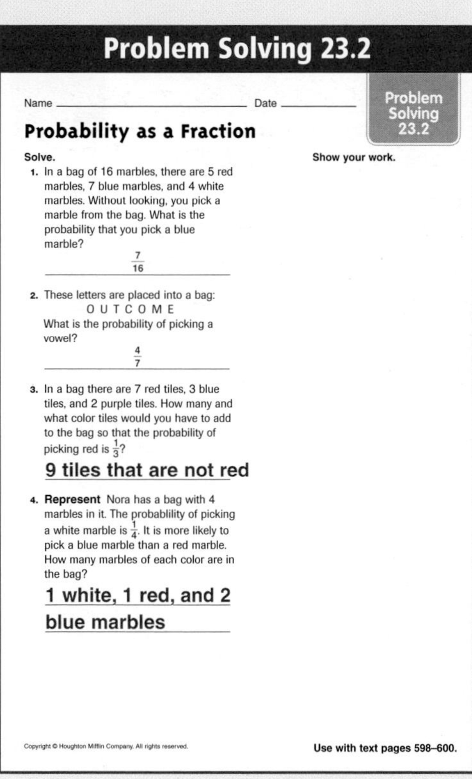

Name ______ Date ______ Problem Solving 23.2

Probability as a Fraction

Solve. **Show your work.**

1. In a bag of 16 marbles, there are 5 red marbles, 7 blue marbles, and 4 white marbles. Without looking, you pick a marble from the bag. What is the probability that you pick a blue marble? $\frac{7}{16}$
2. These letters are placed into a bag: O U T C O M E What is the probability of picking a vowel? $\frac{4}{7}$
3. In a bag there are 7 red tiles, 3 blue tiles, and 2 purple tiles. How many and what color tiles would you have to add to the bag so that the probability of picking red is $\frac{1}{3}$? **9 tiles that are not red**
4. **Represent** Nora has a bag with 4 marbles in it. The probability of picking a white marble is $\frac{1}{4}$. It is more likely to pick a blue marble than a red marble. How many marbles of each color are in the bag? **1 white, 1 red, and 2 blue marbles**

Use with text pages 598–600.

3 Practice

Practice and Problem Solving

Select from **Exercises 10–22** as independent work.

- ***Problem 18*** Suggest that students model the problem, or draw a picture of it, to help them find the solution.

4 Assess & Close

Math Talk in Action

If the probability of an outcome is $\frac{1}{8}$, how would you describe that outcome? (unlikely) **Would the fraction for the probability of a highly unlikely outcome be closer to 0 or 1?** (0)

Math Journal Prompt

Have each student write a fraction that describes the probability of picking the first letter of his or her first name out of a bag that has letter tiles for all the letters of his or her first name. Have them explain their answers.

Lesson Quiz

Use the quiz on Lesson Transparency 23.2.

Test Prep & Spiral Review

Use Test Prep Transparency 23.2.

Practice and Problem Solving

For each spinner, write the probability that a spin will land on red. Write the probability in words and in fraction form.

10. 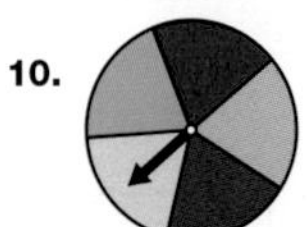 **$\frac{1}{5}$, 1 out of 5**

11. 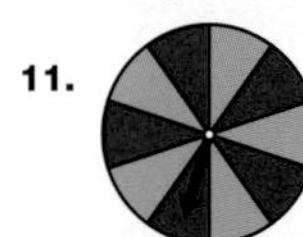 **$\frac{5}{10}$ or $\frac{1}{2}$, 5 out of 10 or 1 out of 2**

12. 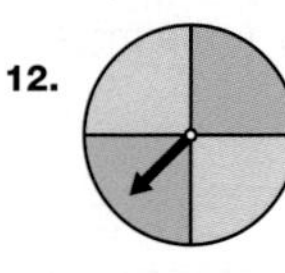 **$\frac{0}{4}$, 0 out of 4**

13. 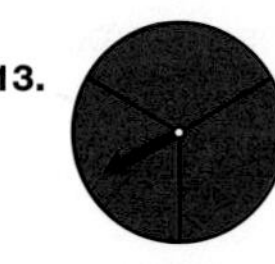 **$\frac{3}{3}$ or 1, 3 out of 3 or 1 out of 1**

Suppose you pick one tile from this bag without looking. Write the probability of each in both words and fraction form.

14. picking 1 **$\frac{1}{9}$, 1 out of 9**
15. picking a multiple of 3 **$\frac{3}{9}$ or $\frac{1}{3}$, 3 out of 9 or 1 out of 3**
16. picking 3 or 5 **$\frac{2}{9}$, 2 out of 9**
17. picking a number greater than 4 **$\frac{5}{9}$, 5 out of 9**

Solve.

18. A bag holds 5 red marbles and 3 blue marbles. How many and what color marbles would you add to the bag so that the probability of picking a blue marble is $\frac{1}{2}$? **Add 2 blue marbles.**
19. **Represent** Draw a spinner for which the probability of spinning yellow is $\frac{1}{6}$ and it is more likely to spin red than blue. ***See Additional Answers.***
20. **Reasoning** The six sides of the number cube on the right are numbered 1, 2, 3, 4, 5, and 6. Write a fraction that tells the probability of tossing a number greater than 4 **$\frac{2}{6}$ or $\frac{1}{3}$**
21. After winning the class spelling bee, Natalia picks from a bag of prizes. The bag contains 4 pencil sets, 3 notepads, and 3 magnet sets. If Natalia picks from the bag without looking, what is the probability that she will pick a pencil set? Write the probability in simplest form. **$\frac{2}{5}$ or 2 out of 5**
22. **Write Your Own** Imagine that you were to pick your classmates' names from a hat. Write 2 probability problems and solve them. Write your solutions as a fraction. ***Check students' problems.***

600

Extra Practice See page 613, Set B.

Homework 23.2 Page 145

Name ______ Date ______ Homework 23.2

Probability as a Fraction

For each spinner, write the probability that a spin will land on a shaded region. Write the probability in both words and fraction form.

The probability is 5 out of 5 or 1 out of 1. As a fraction, it is $\frac{5}{5}$ or 1.

1. $\frac{7}{12}$; 7 out of 12
2. $\frac{2}{7}$; 2 out of 7
3. $\frac{0}{4}$; 0 out of 4

Write the probability of each favorable outcome in both words and fraction form.

4. spinning 7, 3, or 2 — $\frac{3}{8}$; 3 out of 8
5. spinning a multiple of 2 — $\frac{4}{8}$ or $\frac{1}{2}$; 4 out of 8 or 1 out of 2

Problem Solving

6. A bag holds 3 yellow marbles and 7 blue marbles. How many and what color marbles could you add to the bag so that the probability of picking a yellow marble is $\frac{1}{4}$? **Show your work.**
Possible answer: 2 blue marbles

Use with text pages 598–600.

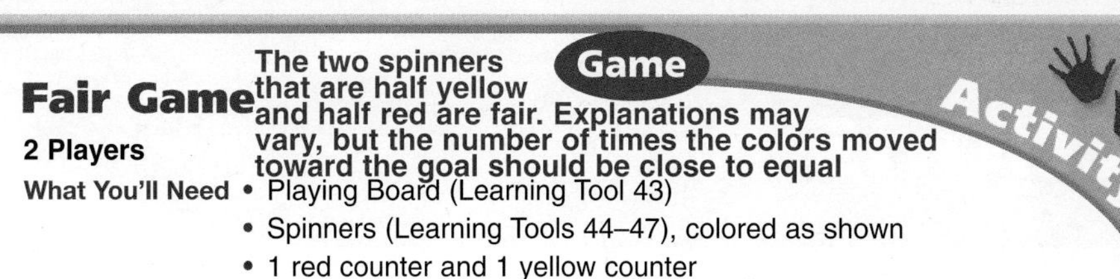

Fair Game

The two spinners that are half yellow and half red are fair. Explanations may vary, but the number of times the colors moved toward the goal should be close to equal

2 Players

What You'll Need
- Playing Board (Learning Tool 43)
- Spinners (Learning Tools 44–47), colored as shown
- 1 red counter and 1 yellow counter

How to Play

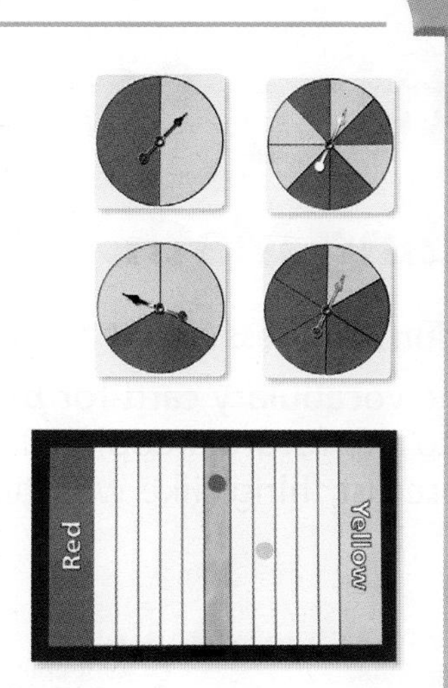

1. Players pick a color and place their counters in the center section of the board. The first player picks the spinner for the first game.
2. Players take turns spinning. If the spinner lands on yellow, the player who chose yellow moves the yellow counter 1 space toward the yellow goal. If the spinner lands on red, the player who chose red moves 1 space toward the red goal.
3. The game continues until a player reaches his or her goal. That player wins.
4. Repeat Steps 2 and 3 to play the game three more times. Use a different spinner each time.

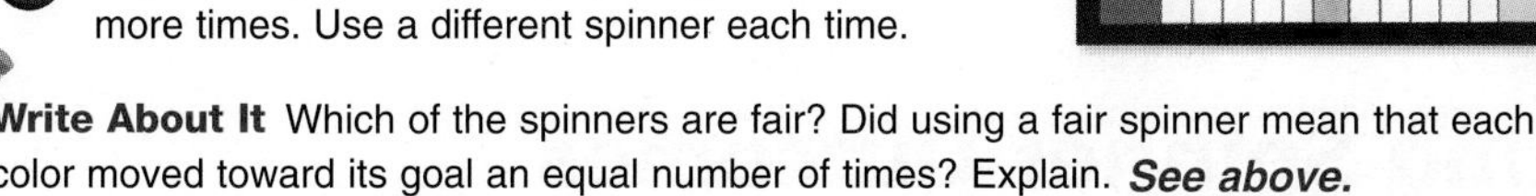

Write About It Which of the spinners are fair? Did using a fair spinner mean that each color moved toward its goal an equal number of times? Explain. ***See above.***

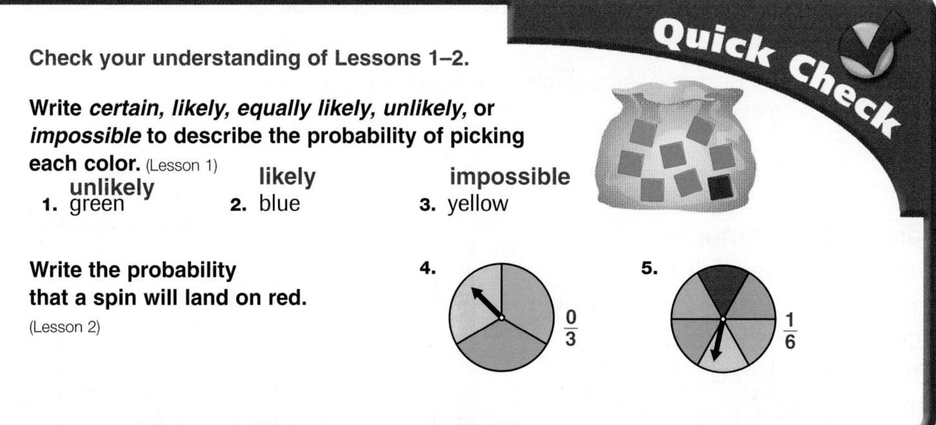

Check your understanding of Lessons 1–2.

Write *certain, likely, equally likely, unlikely,* or *impossible* to describe the probability of picking each color. (Lesson 1)

1. green **unlikely**
2. blue **likely**
3. yellow **impossible**

Write the probability that a spin will land on red. (Lesson 2)

4. **0/3**
5. **1/6**

Extra Practice at **eduplace.com/map**

Game

Fair Game

Materials: Playing Board (Learning Tool 43), 4 spinners (Learning Tools 44–47), 1 red counter, 1 yellow counter

You might have students play as pairs against pairs so that each player has a partner with whom to discuss strategies.

To extend the game, ask which spinners might be called "unfair." (the 2 spinners in the second row) Discuss how the "unfair" spinners are necessary if you want to be able to plan strategies.

Quick Check

The *Quick Check* allows you to assess students' understanding of the concepts presented in Lessons 1–2.

Items	Objectives Tested	Pages	Intervention
1–3	Decide the probability that something will happen.	596–597	Reteach Resources 23.1 *Ways to Success* CD-ROM 23.1
4–5	Write probabilities in words and as fractions.	598–600	Reteach Resources 23.2 *Ways to Success* CD-ROM 23.2

Reaching All Learners

Data Sense

Collecting Data Have students create a spinner with 4 equal parts, labeling the parts 1, 2, 3, and 4.

1. Have students create a tally chart and record the outcomes of 20 spins. (Check students' charts. Each tally chart should list four outcomes (1, 2, 3, and 4) and 20 tallies in total.)
2. After completing **Exercise 1**, students decide if the next spin is more likely to be a number greater than 3 or a number less than 3. (a number less than 3)
3. Students complete **Exercise 2** and then describe how to change the spinner so that spinning an odd number is less likely. (Possible answer: Change 1 or 3 to an even number.)

Differentiated Assignments		
At Risk	**Average**	**Advanced**
Exercise 1	Exercise 2	Exercise 3

Hands On Lesson 23.3

Make Predictions

Planning

Lesson Objective Predict outcomes in a probability experiment.

Technology Resources

- *Ways to Success* CD-ROM 23.3
- Education Place: Extra Practice, eGlossary, eGames www.eduplace.com/map

Lesson 23.3 Transparency

Problem of the Day

A bag holds 3 red, 7 green, and 5 purple beads. Without looking, you reach in and pick 1 bead. What is the probability that you will pick a purple bead? ($\frac{5}{15}$, or $\frac{1}{3}$)

Spiral Review

Name each polygon.

1. It has 6 sides. (hexagon)
2. It has 3 sides, 2 of which are equal. (isosceles triangle)
3. It has 4 sides, but only one pair of sides is parallel. (trapezoid)
4. It has 5 sides of equal length and 5 angles of equal measure. (regular pentagon)

Lesson Quiz

You put 10 marbles in a pouch. 4 are red, 3 are blue, 2 are pink, and 1 is gray. Each time you pick a marble, you record its color and put it back in the bag. You try this 100 times. Predict how many times you will pick—

1. red (40) **2.** gray (10) **3.** black (0)

NCTM Standards

Data Analysis and Probability:
Predict the probability of outcomes of simple experiments and test the predictions; propose and justify conclusions and predictions that are based on data and design studies to further investigate the conclusions or predictions.

Getting Started

Building Math Vocabulary

prediction a guess about the likelihood that an event will occur

Show the vocabulary card for ***prediction***. Explain that a prediction is like a peek into the future. People who make predictions rely on data and probability to forecast things like weather, traffic patterns, or shopping trends.

Predicting Spinner Outcomes

Whole Class	20 minutes
Objective	Use probability to make predictions; use tables to represent probability outcomes.
Materials	Transparent Spinner, Table II Transparency, protractor, markers
Visual	

- Make an 8-part spinner on the Transparent Spinner. Fill the 8 sections with 1 square, 2 triangles, and 5 circles, one shape per section. On the overhead, stack the Table II Transparency and the spinner.
- **Suppose we spin this spinner. Using fractions, give the probability of spinning a square, a triangle, and a circle.** ($\frac{1}{8}$, $\frac{2}{8}$ or $\frac{1}{4}$, $\frac{5}{8}$) Record this data beside the spinner.
- **Suppose we spin the spinner 40 times. Let's predict how many squares we'll spin. Think of $\frac{1}{8}$ of 40. What number is that?** (5) Repeat for the triangle and circle. (10, 25)
- Do the experiment. Record the outcomes as tallies on Table II. Compare the results with the predictions.

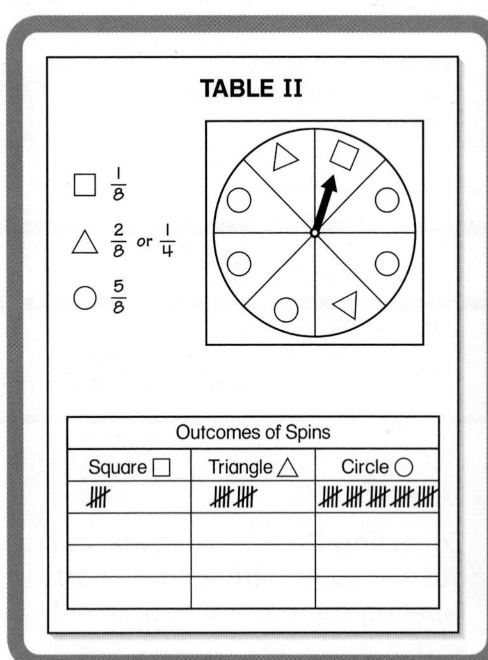

Differentiated Instruction

English Learners

Individuals	15 minutes
Objective	Use probability to make predictions.
Materials	Student page 603
Auditory, Visual	

Early Production

- Students may need help finding probabilities in ***On Your Own.*** Model **Problem 1a** by asking: **How many sides does a cube have?** (6) **What is the probability of rolling an *R*?** ($\frac{1}{6}$) **How do I find the number of times?** (multiply 30 times $\frac{1}{6}$)
- Have them complete the problem independently using these questions.

Intermediate/Advanced

- English Learner Resource 23.3
- English Learner Handbook

Intervention

Whole Class	10 minutes
Objective	Use probability to make predictions; use tables to represent probability outcomes.
Materials	Table II Transparency, 3-part spinner (Learning Tool 42), brass fasteners
Tactual, Visual	

- On the spinner, draw 1 star and 2 hearts. **What fraction describes the probability of spinning a star?** ($\frac{1}{3}$) **a heart?** ($\frac{2}{3}$) **Suppose we spin 60 times. Let's predict what will happen.** (20 stars, 40 hearts) Record the possible outcomes and predictions in Table II.
- Help students do the experiment. They can take turns spinning and tallying. **How will we know when we have made 60 spins?** (Count the tallies.)
- Discuss the results. Remind students that predictions are estimates of what may actually occur.

Other Resources

- *Ways to Success* CD-ROM 23.3

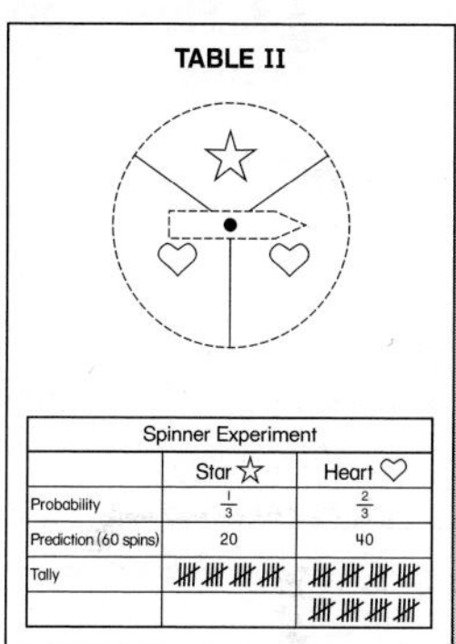

Inclusion

Individuals	20 minutes
Objective	Conduct a probability experiment.
Materials	Workmat 2
Visual, Tactual	

- Students who have organizational or attention deficits may have trouble tracking how many tries they have made during an experiment.
- Have students use Workmat 2 as they do the ***Work Together*** experiment. Each time they draw a card, they cross off a number on the hundred chart. This tells them when they reach 48 tries.

Alternate Teaching Strategy

- Have students design a probability experiment using colored candies or colored chips by choosing a certain number of each color and placing them in a cup.
- Have them find the probability of drawing red.
- Then, keeping the number of reds the same, have students reduce the total number of candies or chips by half.
- Invite students to discuss how reducing the number of items will affect the probability of drawing red.
- Have students find the probability of drawing red with the reduced number of items.

❶ Introduce

Write *prediction* on the board. **What is the difference between a prediction and a guess?** (A prediction is based on data; a guess can be wild.) **If I predict rain and it rains, can I read the future?** (Probably not; you might have based your prediction on data, or maybe you just made a lucky guess.) Tell students that they are going to use their understanding of probability to predict outcomes in an experiment.

❷ Teach

Work Together

- **Look at *Step 1*. Why should we all have the same cards for the experiment?** (to compare results)
- **Look at *Step 2*. Why is it important not to look when you pick a card?** (for fairness) **Why must you return the card each time?** (so that the bag always has the same possible outcomes)
- **Look at *Step 3*. How can you be sure that you pick 48 times in all?** (count tallies)

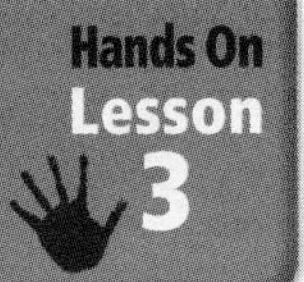

Hands On Lesson 3

Make Predictions

Objective Predict outcomes in a probability experiment.

Vocabulary
prediction

Materials
paper bag
Probability Cards (Learning Tool 48)
number cube

Work Together

Sometimes you can use probability to make a **prediction** about what may happen.

STEP 1

Work with a partner. Make 12 cards like the ones shown and put them in a bag.

Step 2: triangle: $\frac{2}{12}$ or $\frac{1}{6}$; circle: $\frac{6}{12}$ or $\frac{1}{2}$; square: $\frac{4}{12}$ or $\frac{1}{3}$

STEP 2

Predict what may happen if you pick one card from the bag without looking.

- What is the probability of picking each kind of card? ***See above.***
- Suppose you pick from the bag 48 times and put the card back each time. Predict how many times you will pick each shape. Put your predictions in a chart like the one below. ***See below.***

Card Experiment

Outcome	Prediction	Tally	Number
Circle			
Square			
Triangle			

STEP 3

Pick a card without looking. Make a tally mark to record the result in your chart. Put the card back in the bag. Do this 47 more times.

- How did your predictions compare to your actual results? ***Check students' work.***

Possible predictions:
circle: 24 times;
square: 16 times;
triangle: 8 times

602

Reteach 23.3

Name ______ Date ______ Reteach 23.3

Make Predictions

You can use probability to make predictions about outcomes.

In a bag there are 10 cards: 3 red, 5 green, and 2 yellow cards. If you pick a card from the bag 30 times and put it back, how many times will you pick a yellow card?

Outcome	Prediction	Tally	Number
Red			
Green			
Yellow	6	卌 II	7

Think:

- In a set of 10 cards, there are 2 yellow cards.
- There are 3 groups of 10 cards in 30 cards.

Predict:

You can predict that you will pick a yellow card 6 times because $3 \times 2 = 6$. The actual number may match the prediction, or it may be close to the prediction.

Choose three colors. Make 15 cards, with at least 1 card of each color.

1. Complete the table below. Record the colors and the number of each color.
2. Make predictions about how many times you will pull each color from the bag if you pull a card and put it back 30 times.
3. Choose a card and put it back 30 times. Complete the tally table.

Answers will vary.

Color	Number in bag	Prediction	Tally	Number

Use with text pages 602–603.

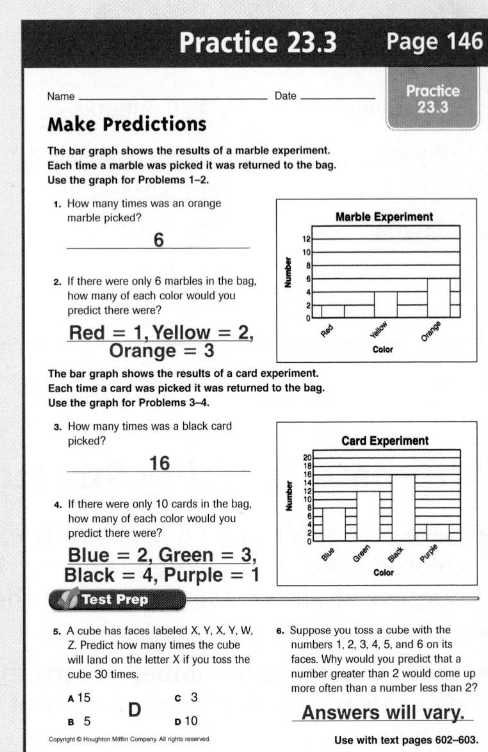

Practice 23.3 Page 146

Name ______ Date ______ Practice 23.3

Make Predictions

The bar graph shows the results of a marble experiment. Each time a marble was picked it was returned to the bag. Use the graph for Problems 1–2.

1. How many times was an orange marble picked? **6**
2. If there were only 6 marbles in the bag, how many of each color would you predict there were? **Red = 1, Yellow = 2, Orange = 3**

The bar graph shows the results of a card experiment. Each time a card was picked it was returned to the bag. Use the graph for Problems 3–4.

3. How many times was a black card picked? **16**
4. If there were only 10 cards in the bag, how many of each color would you predict there were? **Blue = 2, Green = 3, Black = 4, Purple = 1**

Test Prep

5. A cube has faces labeled X, Y, X, Y, W, Z. Predict how many times the cube will land on the letter X if you toss the cube 30 times.
   A 15
   B 5
   C 3
   D 10
   D
6. Suppose you toss a cube with the numbers 1, 2, 3, 4, 5, and 6 on its faces. Why would you predict that a number greater than 2 would come up more often than a number less than 2? **Answers will vary.**

Use with text pages 602–603.

You can use the results of an experiment to make predictions.

The bar graph shows the results of a card experiment. Each time a card was picked, it was returned to the bag.

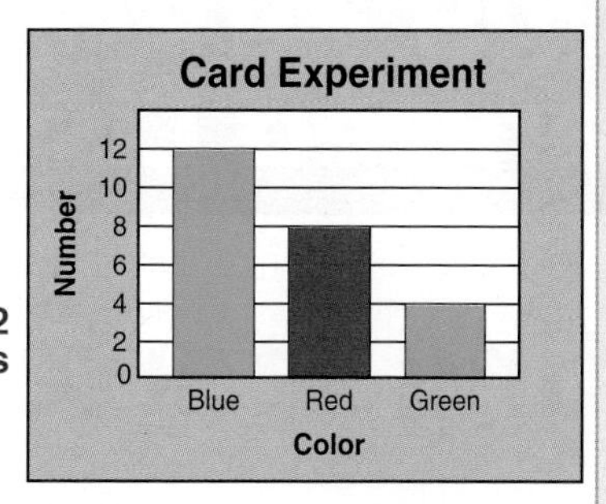

- How many times was a blue card picked? a red card? a green card? **blue card: 12 times; red card: 8 times; green card: 4 times**
- If 12 cards were in the bag, how many of each color would you predict there were?
  Based on the probabilities, the predictions would be: **blue: 6; red: 4; green: 2.**

On Your Own

Follow these steps for a probability experiment.

1. Label the faces of a cube with the letters *R, E, C, E, S,* and *S.*
   a. Predict how many times the cube will land on each letter if you toss the cube 30 times. ***R,* 5 times; *E,* 10 times; *C,* 5 times; *S,* 10 times**
   b. Toss the cube. Record the result on a line plot like the one at the right. Do this 29 more times.

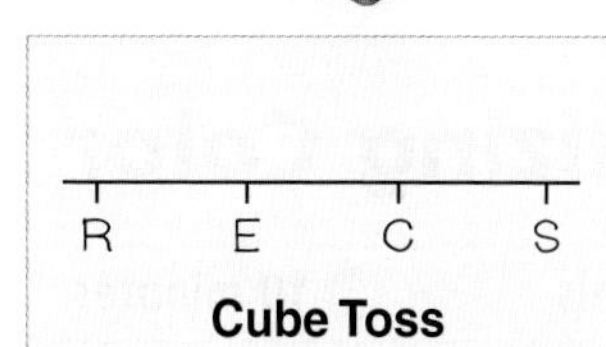

2. Compare your prediction with your results. Was your prediction accurate? Explain your thinking. ***Answers will vary with experiment results.***
3. If you tossed the cube 600 times, about how many times do you think you would toss an *S*? Explain.
   About 200 times; for 6 tries, the probability is $\frac{2}{6}$, or $\frac{1}{3}$. The probability in 600 tries is $\frac{1}{3}$ of 600, or 200.

You learned how to predict outcomes in a probability experiment.

4. Suppose you toss a cube with the numbers 1, 2, 3, 4, 5, and 6. Why would you predict that you would toss a number less than 4 more often than a number greater than 4?
   There are three numbers less than 4 and only two numbers greater than 4.

- **Look at the graph on page 603. Without knowing the exact count, for which color would you expect to find the fewest cards?** (green)

3 Practice

On Your Own

Select from **Exercises 1–4** as independent work. Provide number cubes that students can label to do the experiment described.

- ***Problems 2–3*** Discuss why it is possible to make accurate predictions based on the math, yet have the actual outcomes be different. (Probability is what *ought* to happen; with a small number of trials, actual results may vary.)

4 Assess & Close

Math Talk in Action

How does knowing about probability help us make predictions? (If you know what *should* happen, you can make reasonable predictions.)

Have students give their opinions of doing probability experiments, including what they like, what they don't like, and what they can learn from doing hands-on experiments.

Lesson Quiz

Use the quiz on Lesson Transparency 23.3.

Lesson 23.3 Transparency

Test Prep & Spiral Review

Use Test Prep Transparency 23.3

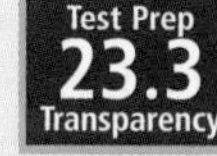

Enrichment 23.3

Name ______ Date ______ Enrichment 23.3

Pick a Color

The following cards are placed in a bag.

Yellow	Red	Green	Red	Blue	Green	Yellow	Red
Red	Blue	Green	Yellow	Red	Red	Blue	Green

1. Suppose you were to pick a card from the bag 80 times. Each time you pick a card, you return it to the bag. Predict how many times you will pick each color.
   Students should predict yellow 15 times, red 30 times, green 20 times, and blue 15 times.
2. Do the experiment and record your results in the tally chart below.

Outcome	Tally	Number

3. Make a line plot that shows your results. Then compare your predictions with your results.
   Check students' line plots. Comparisons will vary depending upon experiment results.

Use with text pages 602–603.

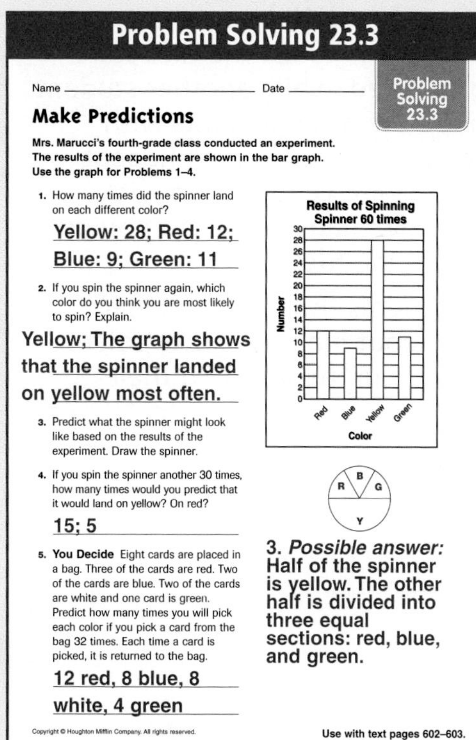

Problem Solving 23.3

Name ______ Date ______ Problem Solving 23.3

Make Predictions

Mrs. Marucci's fourth-grade class conducted an experiment. The results of the experiment are shown in the bar graph. Use the graph for Problems 1–4.

Results of Spinning Spinner 60 times (bar graph: Number 0–30; Color: Red, Blue, Yellow, Green)

1. How many times did the spinner land on each different color?
   Yellow: 28; Red: 12; Blue: 9; Green: 11
2. If you spin the spinner again, which color do you think you are most likely to spin? Explain.
   Yellow; The graph shows that the spinner landed on yellow most often.
3. Predict what the spinner might look like based on the results of the experiment. Draw the spinner.
   3. *Possible answer:* Half of the spinner is yellow. The other half is divided into three equal sections: red, blue, and green. (Spinner: R, B, G, Y)
4. If you spin the spinner another 30 times, how many times would you predict that it would land on yellow? On red?
   15; 5
5. **You Decide** Eight cards are placed in a bag. Three of the cards are red. Two of the cards are blue. Two of the cards are white and one card is green. Predict how many times you will pick each color if you pick a card from the bag 32 times. Each time a card is picked, it is returned to the bag.
   12 red, 8 blue, 8 white, 4 green

Use with text pages 602–603.

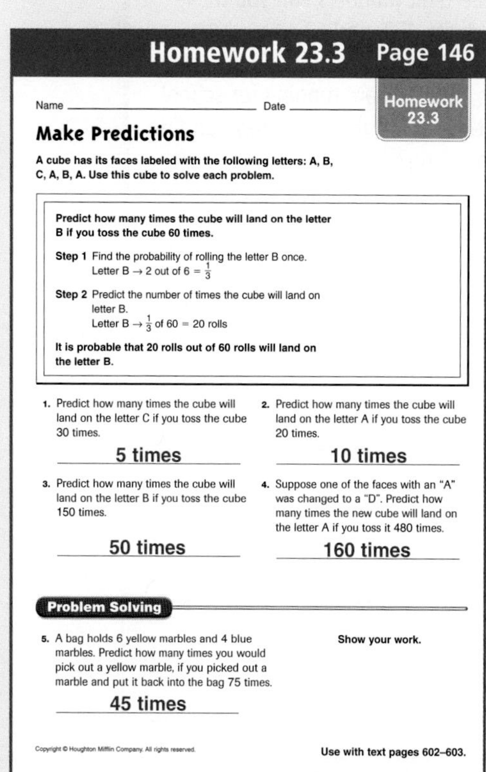

Homework 23.3 Page 146

Name ______ Date ______ Homework 23.3

Make Predictions

A cube has its faces labeled with the following letters: A, B, C, A, B, A. Use this cube to solve each problem.

Predict how many times the cube will land on the letter B if you toss the cube 60 times.

Step 1 Find the probability of rolling the letter B once.
Letter B → 2 out of 6 = $\frac{1}{3}$

Step 2 Predict the number of times the cube will land on letter B.
Letter B → $\frac{1}{3}$ of 60 = 20 rolls

It is probable that 20 rolls out of 60 rolls will land on the letter B.

1. Predict how many times the cube will land on the letter C if you toss the cube 30 times. **5 times**
2. Predict how many times the cube will land on the letter A if you toss the cube 20 times. **10 times**
3. Predict how many times the cube will land on the letter B if you toss the cube 150 times. **50 times**
4. Suppose one of the faces with an "A" was changed to a "D". Predict how many times the new cube will land on the letter A if you toss it 480 times. **160 times**

Problem Solving

5. A bag holds 6 yellow marbles and 4 blue marbles. Predict how many times you would pick out a yellow marble, if you picked out a marble and put it back into the bag 75 times. **45 times**

Show your work.

Use with text pages 602–603.

Lesson 23.4

Problem-Solving Strategy: Make an Organized List

Planning

Lesson Objective Use an organized list to solve a problem.

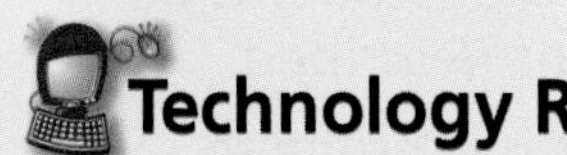

Technology Resources

- Audio Tutor **2**/30 Listen and Understand
- *Ways to Success* CD-ROM 23.4
- Education Place: Extra Practice, Extra Help, eGames www.eduplace.com/map

Lesson 23.4 Transparency

Problem of the Day

Dawn sleeps 9 hours a day and walks her dog for 30 minutes twice a day. If Dawn is in school for 7 hours a day, how much time is left in her day for doing other things? (7 hours)

Spiral Review

Write the numbers in order from least to greatest.

1. 205; 250; 25; 2.5 (2.5, 25, 205, 250)

2. $3\frac{1}{2}; \frac{5}{2}; \frac{3}{2}$ ($\frac{3}{2}, \frac{5}{2}, 3\frac{1}{2}$)

Lesson Quiz

Make an organized list to solve each problem.

1. What three-digit numbers can you make with the digits 4, 3, and 6? (436; 463; 346; 364; 634; 643)

2. Amy, Tess, and Luis are running for school president. What are the ways they can finish in the voting? (ATL, ALT, TAL, TLA, LAT, and LTA)

NCTM Standards

Problem Solving: Apply and adapt a variety of appropriate strategies to solve problems.

Getting Started

Building Math Vocabulary

You may wish to review this word with students.

prediction a guess about the likelihood that an event will occur

Organizing Color Tiles

Individuals	10 minutes
Objective	Solve problems using skills and strategies.
Materials	Color tiles or pattern blocks
Auditory, Tactual	

- **You have 3 tiles—1 red, 1 yellow, and 1 blue. You wish to know the number of ways you can put the tiles in order. You can count the number of ways by making a list. How many colors are there?** (3) **Think of one way to put the tiles in order. Then think of another.**
- Tell students that it makes good sense to organize the list to make sure that they do not miss any arrangements. Explain that one way is to choose one color and list all ways that start with that color.
- Start with red. Have a volunteer tell the ways to list the tiles starting with red, while another student models the arrangements with color counters. (RYB; RBY) Repeat starting with yellow, then with blue. **How many ways can you put the tiles in order?** (6)
- Tell students that they will learn more about making lists to solve problems in the lesson in their book.

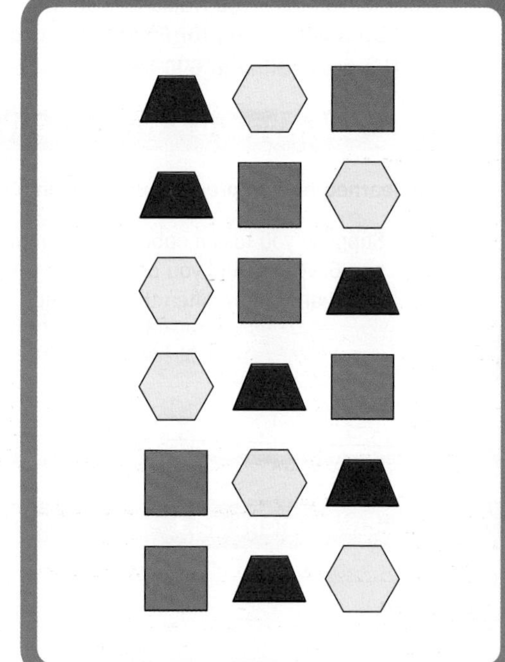

Differentiated Instruction

English Learners

Individuals	5 minutes
Objective	Use an organized list to solve a problem.
Materials	Student page 604
Visual	

Early Production

- Suggest that students use the first letter in the words they are listing instead of writing out the words. This way they can focus on organizing and not on writing.
- Have them use the example in ***Solve*** on Student page 604 to help them organize their lists.

Intermediate/Advanced

- English Learner Resource 23.4
- English Learner Handbook

Intervention

Whole Class	5–10 minutes
Objective	Discuss listing as a problem-solving strategy.
Materials	None
Auditory	

- Tell students: **Suppose your parents asked you to thoroughly clean your room. This is a big job. You think it's a good idea to list all the tasks and check them off as you complete each one. Once you make your list, how will you use it?**
- Discuss students' ideas. Talk about the value of making lists and then using them to set priorities. Have students suggest the best order in which to do some tasks when cleaning their rooms.
- Explain: **Today we are gong to use the strategy of making a special kind of list to solve problems.**

Other Resources

- *Ways to Success* CD-ROM 23.4

Special Needs

Individuals	10 minutes
Objective	Model an organized list.
Materials	Connecting cubes, Student page 604
Visual, Tactual	

- Students can use connecting cubes to help them solve problems like the opening problem on Student page 604. Guide them to let each color represent one of the people in the problem (or any particular person, digit, coin, etc., in other problems like it.)
- Have Peggy Smith be represented with a green cube, Janet Chan with a red cube, and Pete Tobias with a blue cube. Create 3-cube combinations for all 6 variations. Start with red in the first position and conclude that the only possible arrangements are R, G, B and R, B, G. Repeat with blue and then with green cubes in the first position. Students can use their models to help them make their organized lists.

Social Studies Connection

Materials: Road atlas

Provide pairs of students with a road atlas. Have them choose two towns or cities in their state. Challenge them to find and list as many different *reasonable* driving routes from one place to the other. Tell them to avoid routes that involve retracing steps or driving too far out of the way.

As needed, have classroom map-reading experts help others to read the maps.

❶ Introduce

List *ABC, CBA, ACB, BAC, CAB*, and *BCA* on the board. **Is it easy to tell if all the possible combinations of the three letters are listed?** Then write a second list: *ABC, ACB, BAC, BCA, CBA, CAB*. **Is it easier now?** Tell students that the lesson will explore organizing a list to help solve problems.

❷ Teach

Tell students that making an organized list is a good strategy to use when you need to keep track of different ways of doing things. Then have a volunteer read aloud the opening problem on page 604. Use the Four-Part Problem-Solving Transparency to guide students through the steps of the problem-solving process to figure out the number of arrangements of the names.

- For the ***Understand*** step, discuss what is known and what you have to find out.
- For the ***Plan*** step, emphasize the usefulness of choosing one name to list first and then finding the set of all possible arrangements that begin with that name. **What is another way to list the names?** (by first name)
- Suggest to students that they can use a letter to represent a name if only one name begins with that letter. **What letters might we use for our list?** (S, C, T) **Why wouldn't we use the first letters of the first names in this case?** (Both Peggy and Pete begin with *P*.)
- For the ***Solve*** step, discuss the arrangements shown. You may wish to have a volunteer model the arrangements with connecting cubes or color counters to verify the number of them.
- For the ***Look Back*** step, ask: **How do you know that you did not repeat or leave any arrangement out?** (The list is organized with one name in the first position two times to show the ways the other two names can be listed.)

Common Error

- **Omitting an arrangement**
- **Intervention** Emphasize the importance of organizing lists with the same element first, such as writing all orders beginning with red, then all beginning with blue, and so on. Guide students to follow the same order within each set.

Lesson 4

Audio Tutor 2/30 Listen and Understand

Problem-Solving Strategy

Make an Organized List

Objective: Use an organized list to solve a problem.

Problem Peggy Smith, Janet Chan, and Pete Tobias have invented a game. They plan to use their last names to identify themselves as the makers of the game. How many different ways can the names be arranged?

UNDERSTAND

This is what you know.

- The last names are *Smith, Chan,* and *Tobias.*

PLAN

You can make an organized list to help you solve the problem.

SOLVE

List all the items.

Begin with one name.

- There are two ways to arrange the names when *Smith* is first.
- There are two ways to arrange the names when *Chan* is first.
- There are two ways to arrange the names when *Tobias* is first.

Smith, Chan, Tobias
Smith, Tobias, Chan
Chan, Smith, Tobias
Chan, Tobias, Smith
Tobias, Smith, Chan
Tobias, Chan, Smith

Solution: There are six ways to arrange the names.

Look back at the problem. Is your answer reasonable?

Extra Help at **eduplace.com/map**

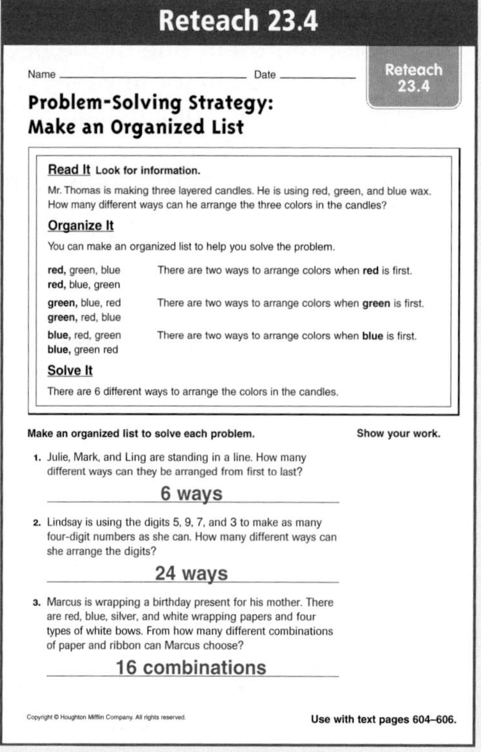

Reteach 23.4

Name ________________ Date ________

Reteach 23.4

Problem-Solving Strategy: Make an Organized List

Read It Look for information.

Mr. Thomas is making three layered candles. He is using red, green, and blue wax. How many different ways can he arrange the three colors in the candles?

Organize It

You can make an organized list to help you solve the problem.

red, green, blue **red,** blue, green	There are two ways to arrange colors when **red** is first.
green, blue, red **green,** red, blue	There are two ways to arrange colors when **green** is first.
blue, red, green **blue,** green red	There are two ways to arrange colors when **blue** is first.

Solve It

There are 6 different ways to arrange the colors in the candles.

Make an organized list to solve each problem. **Show your work.**

1. Julie, Mark, and Ling are standing in a line. How many different ways can they be arranged from first to last?
   6 ways
2. Lindsay is using the digits 5, 9, 7, and 3 to make as many four-digit numbers as she can. How many different ways can she arrange the digits?
   24 ways
3. Marcus is wrapping a birthday present for his mother. There are red, blue, silver, and white wrapping papers and four types of white bows. From how many different combinations of paper and ribbon can Marcus choose?
   16 combinations

Use with text pages 604–606.

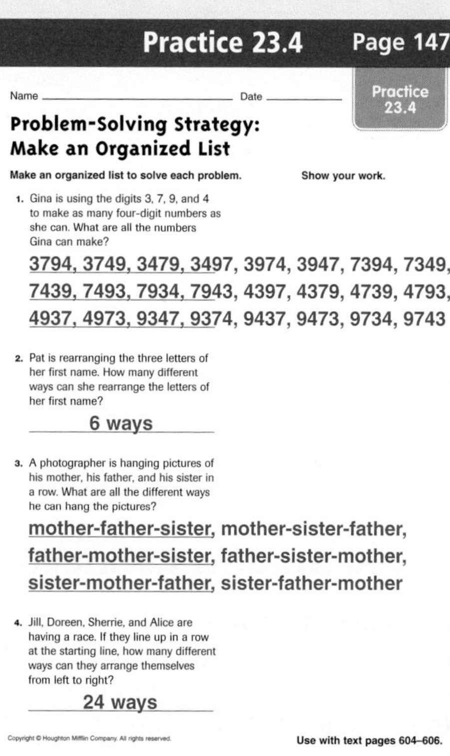

Practice 23.4 **Page 147**

Name ________________ Date ________

Practice 23.4

Problem-Solving Strategy: Make an Organized List

Make an organized list to solve each problem. **Show your work.**

1. Gina is using the digits 3, 7, 9, and 4 to make as many four-digit numbers as she can. What are all the numbers Gina can make?
   3794, 3749, 3479, 3497, 3974, 3947, 7394, 7349, 7439, 7493, 7934, 7943, 4397, 4379, 4739, 4793, 4937, 4973, 9347, 9374, 9437, 9473, 9734, 9743
2. Pat is rearranging the three letters of her first name. How many different ways can she rearrange the letters of her first name?
   6 ways
3. A photographer is hanging pictures of his mother, his father, and his sister in a row. What are all the different ways he can hang the pictures?
   mother-father-sister, mother-sister-father, father-mother-sister, father-sister-mother, sister-mother-father, sister-father-mother
4. Jill, Doreen, Sherrie, and Alice are having a race. If they line up in a row at the starting line, how many different ways can they arrange themselves from left to right?
   24 ways

Use with text pages 604–606.

Guided Practice

Use the Ask Yourself questions to help you solve each problem.

Ask Yourself

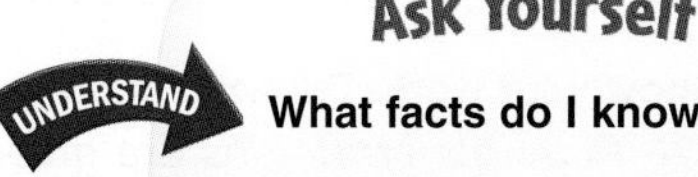

What facts do I know?

Can I make an organized list?

SOLVE

- **Did I list all the items?**
- **Did I try every possible arrangement?**

Did I solve the problem?

1. A gardener is planting tulip, daffodil, lily, and hyacinth bulbs in clusters along a sidewalk. How many different ways can he arrange the four kinds of bulbs? **24 ways**
2. Ann, Sue, Jo, and Nina are in line. How many ways can the girls be arranged if Ann has to be first in line? **6 ways**

   (Hint) Which names cannot be first?

3. portrait, landscape, still life; portrait, still life, landscape; landscape, portrait, still life; landscape, still life, portrait; still life, portrait, landscape; still life, landscape, portrait

Independent Practice

Make an organized list to solve each problem.

3. A painter is hanging a portrait, a landscape, and a still life in a row. What are all the different arrangements he can make? ***See above.***
4. Lena wants to use the four letters of her name as part of an e-mail address. How many different ways can she arrange the letters of her name? **24 ways**
5. Nick is using the digits 5, 6, 7, and 8 to make as many four-digit numbers as he can. What are all the numbers Nick can make? ***See below.***
6. A conductor is organizing players in a row.
   - He has people who play violins, cellos, flutes, saxophones, and drums.
   - The violins have to be on the left end.
   - The cellos have to be on the right end.

   How many ways can the conductor arrange the players? **6 ways**

5. 5,678; 5,687; 5,768; 5,786; 5,867; 5,876; 6,578; 6,587; 6,758; 6,785; 6,875; 6,857; 7,568; 7,586; 7,658; 7,685; 7,865; 7,856; 8,567; 8,576; 8,657; 8,675; 8,756; 8,765

Go On

Guided Practice

Have students complete **Problems 1–2** as you observe. Remind them to use the ***Ask Yourself*** questions to help.

❸ Practice

Independent Practice

- Select from **Problems 3–14** as independent work. Remind students to use letters to represent names or things, as it will lessen the amount of writing they will need to do. For example, for **Problem 6**, ask: **Which letters will you use to represent the different instruments?** (V, C, F, S, and D)

Have students review their answers to make sure they have done the following:

- expressed the solution clearly
- used appropriate mathematical notation and terms
- supported their solution with verbal and symbolic work.

Enrichment 23.4

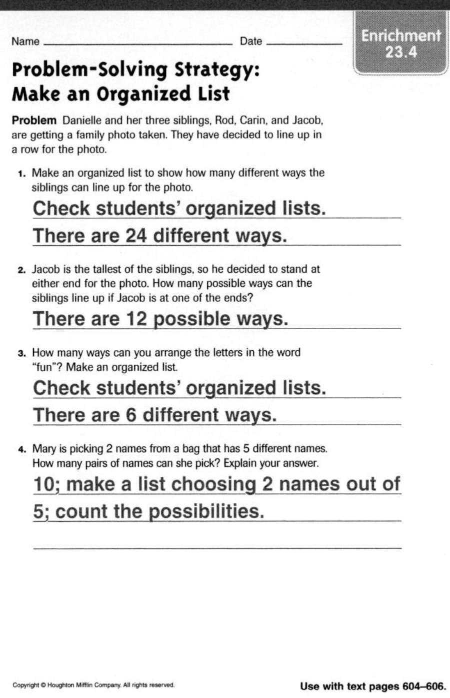

Name ______________ Date ________ Enrichment 23.4

Problem-Solving Strategy: Make an Organized List

Problem Danielle and her three siblings, Rod, Carin, and Jacob, are getting a family photo taken. They have decided to line up in a row for the photo.

1. Make an organized list to show how many different ways the siblings can line up for the photo.
   Check students' organized lists.
   There are 24 different ways.
2. Jacob is the tallest of the siblings, so he decided to stand at either end for the photo. How many possible ways can the siblings line up if Jacob is at one of the ends?
   There are 12 possible ways.
3. How many ways can you arrange the letters in the word "fun"? Make an organized list.
   Check students' organized lists.
   There are 6 different ways.
4. Mary is picking 2 names from a bag that has 5 different names. How many pairs of names can she pick? Explain your answer.
   10; make a list choosing 2 names out of 5; count the possibilities.

 Use with text pages 604–606.

Problem Solving 23.4

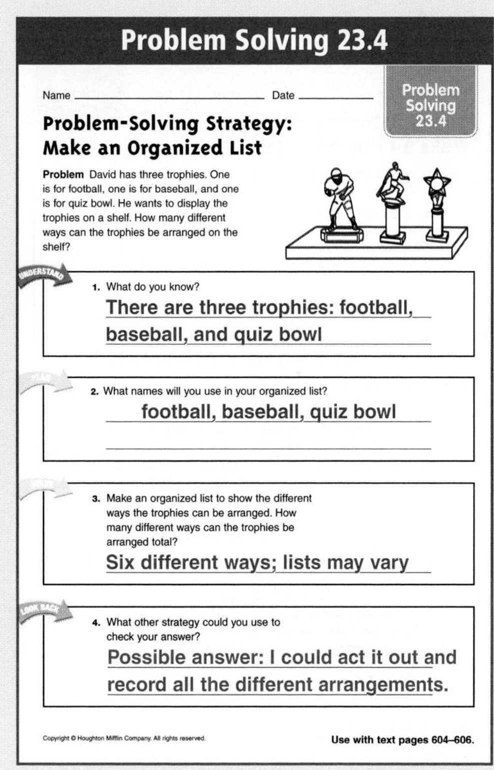

Name ______________ Date ________ Problem Solving 23.4

Problem-Solving Strategy: Make an Organized List

Problem David has three trophies. One is for football, one is for baseball, and one is for quiz bowl. He wants to display the trophies on a shelf. How many different ways can the trophies be arranged on the shelf?

1. What do you know?
   There are three trophies: football, baseball, and quiz bowl
2. What names will you use in your organized list?
   football, baseball, quiz bowl
3. Make an organized list to show the different ways the trophies can be arranged. How many different ways can the trophies be arranged total?
   Six different ways; lists may vary
4. What other strategy could you use to check your answer?
   Possible answer: I could act it out and record all the different arrangements.

 Use with text pages 604–606.

Mixed Problem Solving

For **Problems 7–10** tell students that they may use any of the strategies listed in the table, or a combination of strategies, to solve the problems. Encourage them to look back at their work to be sure they have answered the question that was asked.

Data Have students summarize the information shown in the line plot about medal winners.

Mixed Problem Solving

Solve. Show your work. Tell what strategy you used. ***Possible strategies are given.***

You Choose

Strategy
- Draw a Picture
- Make an Organized List
- Make a Table
- Work Backward
- Write an Equation

Computation Method
- Mental Math
- Estimation
- Paper and Pencil
- Calculator

7. Mr. Rios is 31 years old. His son Luis is 7 years old. How old will each of them be when Mr. Rios's age is three times Luis's age? **Mr. Rios: 36 years old; Luis: 12 years old; Make a Table**
8. Half of Sal's hats are red, $\frac{1}{6}$ are blue, and 4 are black. How many hats does Sal have? **12 hats; Draw a Picture**
9. Luz has post cards from New Jersey, Delaware, North Carolina, and Connecticut. How many different ways can she arrange them in a row? **24 ways; Make an Organized List**
10. Mark has saved $131. He has saved the same amount for four months. If he started with $15, how much did he save each month? **$29; Work Backward**

Data Use the line plot for Problems 11–14.

The line plot at the right shows the number of gold medals won by 11 countries during the 2002 Winter Olympic Games.

11. What do the three X's above the number 4 tell you? **Three countries won 4 gold medals each.**
12. What are the range, median, and mode of the data? **range: 9; median: 4; modes: 3, 4**
13. What is the mean of the data? What does the mean tell you? ***See below.***
14. Why are there no X's above the numbers 5, 7, 8, and 9? **There were no countries that won a total of exactly 5, 7, 8, or 9 gold medals.**

3	4	5	6	7	8	9	10	11	12
X X X	X X X		X X				X	X	X

Gold Medals in 2002 Winter Olympic Games

13. mean: 6; The mean tells how many of the 66 gold medals each of the 11 countries would have won if they each had won the same number.

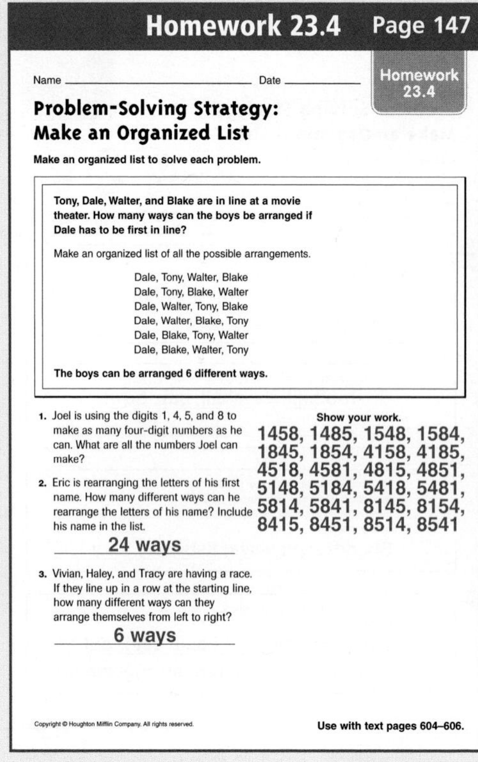

Homework 23.4 Page 147

Name ______ Date ______ Homework 23.4

Problem-Solving Strategy: Make an Organized List

Make an organized list to solve each problem.

Tony, Dale, Walter, and Blake are in line at a movie theater. How many ways can the boys be arranged if Dale has to be first in line?

Make an organized list of all the possible arrangements.

Dale, Tony, Walter, Blake
Dale, Tony, Blake, Walter
Dale, Walter, Tony, Blake
Dale, Walter, Blake, Tony
Dale, Blake, Tony, Walter
Dale, Blake, Walter, Tony

The boys can be arranged 6 different ways.

Show your work.

1. Joel is using the digits 1, 4, 5, and 8 to make as many four-digit numbers as he can. What are all the numbers Joel can make? **1458, 1485, 1548, 1584, 1845, 1854, 4158, 4185, 4518, 4581, 4815, 4851, 5148, 5184, 5418, 5481, 5814, 5841, 8145, 8154, 8415, 8451, 8514, 8541**
2. Eric is rearranging the letters of his first name. How many different ways can he rearrange the letters of his name? Include his name in the list. **24 ways**
3. Vivian, Haley, and Tracy are having a race. If they line up in a row at the starting line, how many different ways can they arrange themselves from left to right? **6 ways**

 Use with text pages 604–606.

Problem Solving on Tests

Multiple Choice

Choose the letter of the correct answer.

1. How many 100-gram weights are needed to balance the scale?

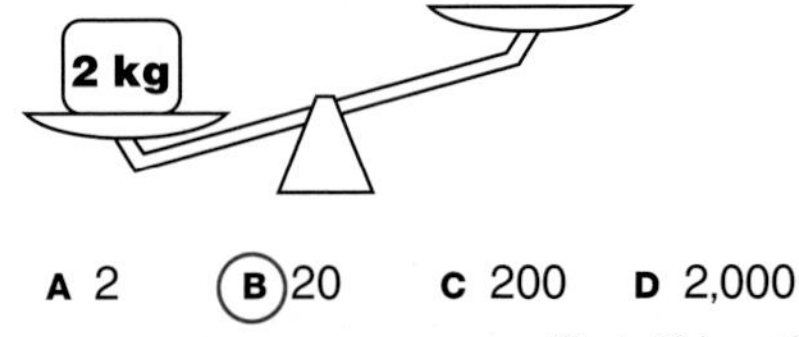

A 2 (B) 20 C 200 D 2,000

(Chapter 12, Lesson 9)

2. Look at this pattern of numbers.

5, 10, 6, 12, 8, 16, 12, 24

If the pattern continues, what is the next number likely to be?

F 16 (G) 20 H 28 J 48

(Chapter 21, Lesson 5)

Open Response

Solve each problem.

3. Look at the spinner below. What is the probability that the arrow will land on the shaded area? $\frac{5}{8}$

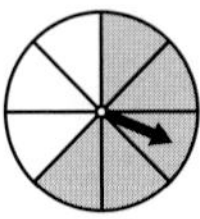

(Chapter 23, Lesson 2)

4. A spinner is divided into more than 4 equal sections. The colors on the spinner are red, yellow, and blue.

Represent Draw a spinner so that the probability of spinning blue is $\frac{1}{4}$ and it is more likely to spin red than yellow.

See Additional Answers. (Chapter 23, Lesson 2)

Extended Response

5. At the National Storytelling Festival in Tennessee, people from all over the world come to hear great stories.

National Storytelling Festival

	1-day ticket	3-day ticket
Child 6–12	$80.00	$115.00
Adult	$90.00	$135.00
Senior Citizen	$85.00	$120.00

a. Mr. and Mrs. Peterson and their two young sons plan to attend for three days. How much will it cost for their tickets?

b. Mr. and Mrs. Nguyen are both senior citizens. They will be able to attend only 2 days. Should they buy 2 one-day tickets each, or 1 three-day ticket each? Which would be the better buy? How do you know?

c. Mr. and Mrs. Patel will go to the festival for 3 days. They will stay at a motel for 4 nights. The motel will cost them $119 each night. How much will they spend for tickets and their motel room? Show your work.

(Chapter 7)

See Additional Answers.

Education Place

See **eduplace.com/map** for more Test-Taking Tips.

Problem Solving on Tests

Problem Solving on Tests provides an opportunity for students to apply previously learned skills in the types of problem contexts typically encountered in standardized tests. ***Problem Solving on Tests*** includes practice in a variety of formats: multiple choice, open response, and extended response.

Students will gain experience in writing about mathematics and using various representations to solve problems. Discuss students' solutions. Have several students explain the thinking behind their work.

More test prep practice is available on Houghton Mifflin's Web site, **Education Place**. Go to www.eduplace.com/map

4 Assess & Close

Math Talk in Action

What real-life situations can you think of in which we might use the strategy of making an organized list? (Accept all reasonable responses.)

Math Journal Prompt

Have students write an explanation of what an organized list is and how to use one to solve a particular kind of problem.

Lesson Quiz

Use the quiz on Lesson Transparency 23.4.

Lesson 23.4 Transparency

Test Prep & Spiral Review

Use Test Prep Transparency 23.4.

Test Prep 23.4 Transparency

Helping Students Become Learners

Students' thinking about probability is limited by their ability to list **all possible outcomes** of a situation.

It becomes even more difficult for students when events are not equally likely; for example, when a spinner is divided into 3 equal sections with 2 sections red and 1 section blue. Their reasoning about events that are not equally likely is tied to how well they understand and work with rational numbers.

As in other domains of mathematics, solving problems helps students become better learners. One way to facilitate this is to give students opportunities to **solve problems by conducting their own probability experiments.** As students count and record outcomes and discuss results, teachers can listen for ways to encourage thinking about rational numbers.

Lesson 23.5

Find Probability

Planning

Lesson Objective Find the probability of outcomes, using a grid or a tree diagram.

Technology Resources

- Audio Tutor **2**/31 Listen and Understand
- *Ways to Success* CD-ROM 23.5
- Education Place: Extra Practice, eGames, Weekly Reader www.eduplace.com/map

Lesson 23.5 Transparency

Problem of the Day

If Aisha answers a True or False question by guessing, what is the probability that she will answer it correctly? ($\frac{1}{2}$)

Spiral Review

You pick a letter from the word below without looking. Write the probability in the simplest form.

D I A G R A M

1. I ($\frac{1}{7}$)
2. A ($\frac{2}{7}$)
3. a vowel ($\frac{3}{7}$)
4. a letter that comes before T in the alphabet (1)

Lesson Quiz

You spin a spinner that is divided into thirds and labeled A, B, C, and you flip a coin. Use a tree diagram to answer the questions.

1. How many outcomes show heads and B? (1)
2. What is the probability of tails and C? ($\frac{1}{6}$)
3. What is the probability of tails and B or heads and C? ($\frac{1}{3}$)

NCTM Standards
Data Analysis and Probability: Understand and apply basic concepts of probability.

Getting Started

Building Math Vocabulary

grid a chart that shows combinations of outcomes of an event
tree diagram a diagram that lists the outcome of an event

Use the vocabulary card for ***tree diagram.*** Link the meaning of the term to students' experiences, such as the factor trees they have used to find prime factors or the diagrams in newspapers that show games in tournaments, such as the NCAA basketball tournament.

Using Tree Diagrams

Whole Class	5 minutes
Objective	Use tree diagrams to represent probability outcomes.
Materials	None
Visual, Auditory	

- Write *48* on the board. Invite a volunteer to demonstrate how to use a factor tree to write the prime factorization of the number. ($2 \times 2 \times 2 \times 2 \times 3$) Discuss that the outcome will be the same no matter how we list and find factors.
- Then tell students that in today's lesson we will again use a tree diagram, this time to show all possible outcomes in a probability experiment, as well as to find the probability of an event.

Differentiated Instruction

English Learners

Pairs	5 minutes
Objective	Use grids and tree diagrams to represent probability outcomes.
Materials	Student page 608
Auditory, Visual	

Early Production

- Pair students for ***Guided Practice.*** Have them make a tree diagram and a grid for the problems. They should verbalize their work and the ***Ask Yourself*** questions and answers as they write.
- Have students discuss which way they prefer to represent outcomes and why.

Intermediate/Advanced

- English Learner Resource 23.5
- English Learner Handbook

Intervention

Whole Class	5–10 minutes
Objective	Use tree diagrams to represent probability outcomes.
Materials	None
Visual, Tactual	

- To help students understand the idea of tree diagrams, have them imagine that they are riding their bikes along a road. Ask them to draw the road they are riding on.
- Then have students imagine that the road comes to a fork where they can turn left or turn right. Have them draw this fork and extend each road.
- Then tell them that a little farther along each of the forks there is an intersection where, again, they can go left or right. Have students draw these roads, too. **Look at the ends of your map. How many destinations are there?** (4: left, left; left, right; right, left; right, right)

Other Resources

- *Ways to Success* CD-ROM 23.5

Gifted & Talented

Individuals	10 minutes
Objective	Use tree diagrams to represent probability outcomes.
Materials	None
Visual, Tactual	

- Ask students to explain and show how to use a tree diagram to find all possible outcomes for tossing one number cube labeled 1–6 and one number cube labeled 7–12. (36)

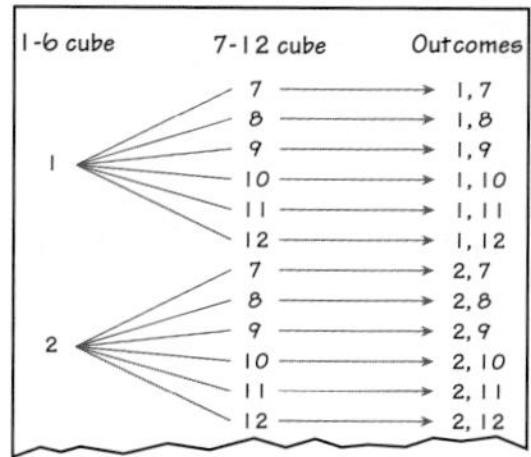

Literature Connection

Materials: *Jumanji* by Chris Van Allsburg, number cubes labeled 1–6

- When the children in this story play a board game using dice, the creatures and events in the game come to life. Use this book and number cubes labeled 1–6 to explore probability concepts.
- For example, you can explore the difference between certain, likely, unlikely, and impossible outcomes. Students can learn, for example, that, when the cube is rolled twice, rolling a 12 is less likely than rolling an 8.

Facts Practice

Have students work in pairs to quiz each other on multiplication facts, using flash cards or a multiplication table. Have them keep a list of facts that were missed or that presented difficulty. Then plan a strategy for remembering them, such as limericks, colorful flash cards, or skits.

❶ Introduce

Read the objective statement with students and explain that the lesson shows two ways to represent the outcomes of a probability problem: grids and tree diagrams.

❷ Teach

Learn About It

- Guide students through the two ways presented in the ***Learn About It*** section for representing all outcomes. Tell them that the grid and the tree diagram show the same information.
- First, help students read the grid. Discuss that the area *outside* the grid shows the possible ways the coins can land in each toss. Elicit that each pair *within* the grid represents an outcome for the two tosses. Then focus on the tree diagram. Ask: **In the tree diagram, what do the branches represent?** (the different ways the coin can land) **When a coin is tossed two times, how many outcomes are possible?** (4)
- Next, focus students on the probabilities of the outcomes, as shown by the grid and the tree diagram. Ask: **How many outcomes show two heads?** (1) **What is the probability of tossing two coins and having them both land on heads?** ($\frac{1}{4}$)

Guided Practice

Have students complete **Exercises 1–2** as you observe. Remind them to use the ***Ask Yourself*** questions to help. Give students the opportunity to talk about the question in ***Explain Your Thinking.***

Common Error

- **Miscounting possible outcomes**
- **Intervention** To avoid this error, guide students to number the ends of the branches of their tree diagrams.

Lesson 5

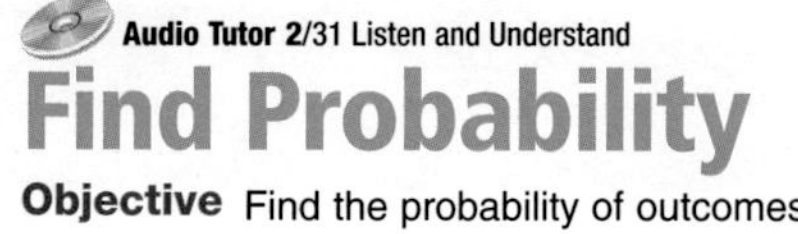

Find Probability

Objective Find the probability of outcomes, using a grid or a tree diagram.

Vocabulary
grid
tree diagram

Learn About It

A coin is tossed twice. What is the probability that it will land heads-up once and tails-up once?

Here are two ways you can represent all the outcomes.

▶ You can use a grid.

- Write the possible outcomes for the first toss at the left.
- Write the possible outcomes for the second toss at the top.
- Put the possible outcomes for both tosses in each part of the grid.

		Second Toss	
		heads	**tails**
First Toss	**heads**	heads, heads	heads, tails
	tails	tails, heads	tails, tails

▶ You can use a tree diagram.

- Use branches to show the possible outcomes for the first toss.
- Show the possible outcomes for the second toss.
- List the possible outcomes for both tosses.

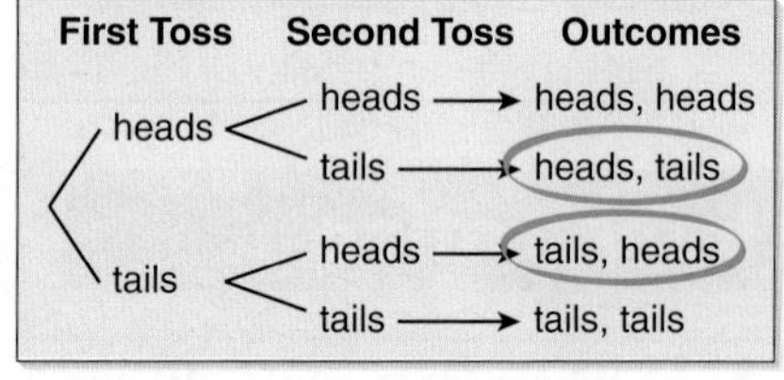

Solution: The probability is 2 out of 4, or $\frac{2}{4}$.

Guided Practice

A bag holds two cards, one with the letter *T* and one with the letter *Y*. A card is picked and put back each time.

1. Make a tree diagram or a grid to show all possible outcomes when a card is picked twice. ***See Additional Answers.***
2. What is the probability of spelling the name TY? $\frac{1}{4}$

Ask Yourself
- What are all the possible outcomes?
- How many ways can the outcome I want occur?

Explain Your Thinking ▶ Why is it helpful to use a tree diagram or a grid? **It makes it easy to see what the outcomes are.**

Reteach 23.5

Name ____________ Date ______ **Reteach 23.5**

Find Probability

Rosa is going to do a book report. She can chose a fiction book or a non-fiction book. She can illustrate her report by hand or make computer art. How can you show all the types of reports Rosa can do? What is the probability that she will choose a fiction book and handmade drawings?

You can use a **grid.**

	handmade drawings	computer art
non-fiction	non-fiction, handmade drawings	non-fiction, computer art
fiction	fiction, handmade drawings	fiction, computer art

All of the possible outcomes are in the center of the grid.

You can use a **tree diagram.**

book report
- non-fiction — handmade drawings / computer art
- fiction — handmade drawings / computer art

All of the possible outcomes are shown in the branches on the right.

There are four types of reports that Rosa can do. One of the choices is fiction and handmade art.

Solution: The probability that Rosa will choose fiction and handmade drawings is 1 out of 4 or $\frac{1}{4}$.

Campers may choose between swimming and hiking in the morning. They may choose between crafts and games in the afternoon.

1. Make a tree diagram or grid to show all possible outcomes. How many different outcomes are there? **4 outcomes**
2. What is the probability that a camper will choose hiking and crafts? $\frac{1}{4}$

Michelle has a red shirt and a white shirt. She has a blue cap, a black cap, and a green cap.

3. Make a tree diagram or grid to show all possible outcomes. How many outcomes are there? **6 outcomes**
4. What is the probability that Michelle will choose to wear a white shirt and green cap? $\frac{1}{6}$

Use with text pages 608–610.

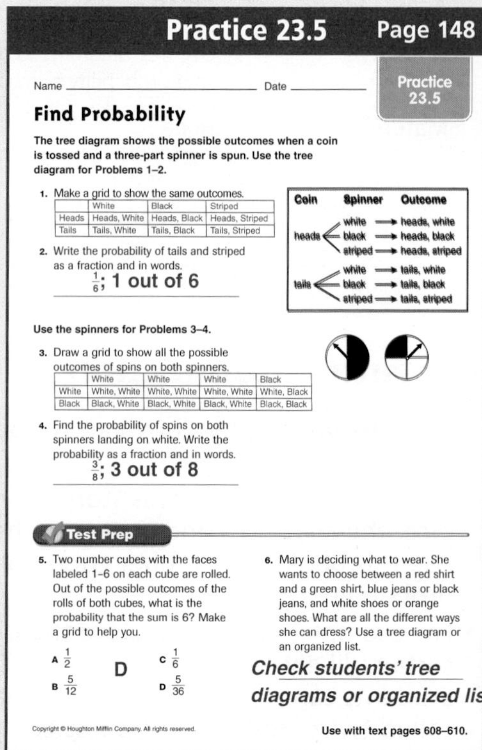

Practice 23.5 Page 148

Name ____________ Date ______ **Practice 23.5**

Find Probability

The tree diagram shows the possible outcomes when a coin is tossed and a three-part spinner is spun. Use the tree diagram for Problems 1–2.

1. Make a grid to show the same outcomes.

	White	Black	Striped
Heads	Heads, White	Heads, Black	Heads, Striped
Tails	Tails, White	Tails, Black	Tails, Striped

Coin	Spinner	Outcome
heads	white	heads, white
	black	heads, black
	striped	heads, striped
tails	white	tails, white
	black	tails, black
	striped	tails, striped

2. Write the probability of tails and striped as a fraction and in words. $\frac{1}{6}$; **1 out of 6**

Use the spinners for Problems 3–4.

3. Draw a grid to show all the possible outcomes of spins on both spinners.

	White	White	White	Black
White	White, White	White, White	White, White	White, Black
Black	Black, White	Black, White	Black, White	Black, Black

4. Find the probability of spins on both spinners landing on white. Write the probability as a fraction and in words. $\frac{3}{8}$; **3 out of 8**

Test Prep

5. Two number cubes with the faces labeled 1–6 on each cube are rolled. Out of the possible outcomes of the rolls of both cubes, what is the probability that the sum is 6? Make a grid to help you.

   A $\frac{1}{2}$ B $\frac{5}{12}$ C $\frac{1}{6}$ D $\frac{5}{36}$ **D**

6. Mary is deciding what to wear. She wants to choose between a red shirt and a green shirt, blue jeans or black jeans, and white shoes or orange shoes. What are all the different ways she can dress? Use a tree diagram or an organized list. ***Check students' tree diagrams or organized lis***

Use with text pages 608–610.

Practice and Problem Solving

The tree diagram shows the possible outcomes when a coin is tossed and a four-part spinner is spun.

Coin	Spinner	Outcome
heads	blue →	heads, blue
	red →	heads, red
	yellow →	heads, yellow
	green →	heads, green
tails	blue →	tails, blue
	red →	tails, red
	yellow →	tails, yellow
	green →	tails, green

3. Make a grid to show the same outcomes.
   See Additional Answers.
4. How many outcomes show heads and red or heads and blue? **2 outcomes**
5. Write the probability of tails and blue as a fraction and in words. **$\frac{1}{8}$, 1 out of 8**
6. What is the probability of heads and yellow or heads and green? **$\frac{2}{8}$ or $\frac{1}{4}$**

Use Spinners A and B for Problems 7–9.

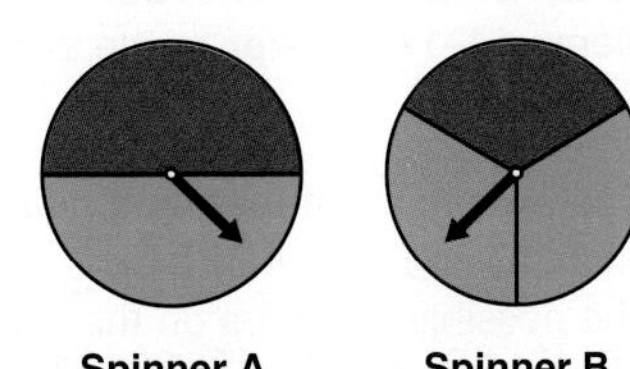

7. Make a grid to show all the possible outcomes of spins on both spinners.
   See Additional Answers.
8. Find the probability of spins on both spinners landing on red. Write the probability as a fraction and in words.
   $\frac{1}{6}$, 1 out of 6
9. What is the probability of Spinner A landing on blue and Spinner B landing on green or red? **$\frac{2}{6}$ or $\frac{1}{3}$**
10. Ed and Kim will each glaze the inside of a mug red or yellow, the outside green or blue, and the handle black or white. What are all the ways the mug can be glazed? Use a tree diagram or an organized list. ***See Additional Answers.***

❸ Practice

Practice and Problem Solving

- Select from **Exercises 3–18** as independent work. For **Problems 3–6**, point out that the spinner is divided into 4 equal parts. Ask: **How is using a tree diagram like using an organized list?** (Members of the set are listed in an organized way so that all outcomes are represented.)
- Help students set up their grids for **Problems 7–10**. Ask: **How many outcomes are possible for Spinner A?** (2) **For Spinner B?** (3) **Are they equally likely?** (yes)

Enrichment 23.5

Name ______________ Date ________ Enrichment 23.5

Party Possibilities

Christina is having a party. She is planning the menu and the location of the party. For the menu, she will serve pizza, burgers, or hot dogs and have either punch or orange juice for drinks. She also can't decide if she wants to have the party inside and play board games or outside and go swimming.

1. Make a tree diagram to show all the different combinations Christina can have for her party. Include both the menu and location choices.

   Check students' work; 12 different combinations

2. How would the tree diagram you drew be adjusted to show the possible outcomes if it rains and the party must be held inside? Show or explain the difference. How many possible outcomes are there?

   Check students' work; 6 possible outcomes

3. Christina's mom offered Christina a choice of 4 desserts if the party is held outside. She could have cake, cupcakes, ice cream, or fruit cocktail. How many possible combinations are there if Christina chooses 1 food item, 1 drink item, and 1 dessert?

   24 possible outcomes

 Use with text pages 608–610.

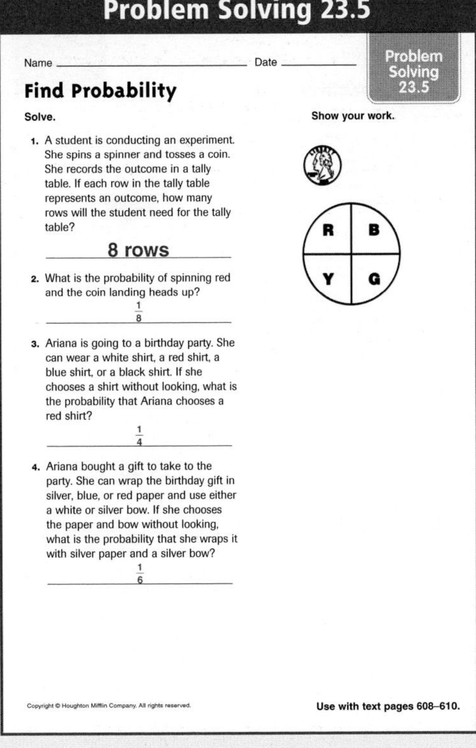

Problem Solving 23.5

Name ______________ Date ________ Problem Solving 23.5

Find Probability

Solve. Show your work.

1. A student is conducting an experiment. She spins a spinner and tosses a coin. She records the outcome in a tally table. If each row in the tally table represents an outcome, how many rows will the student need for the tally table?
   8 rows
2. What is the probability of spinning red and the coin landing heads up?
   $\frac{1}{8}$
3. Ariana is going to a birthday party. She can wear a white shirt, a red shirt, a blue shirt, or a black shirt. If she chooses a shirt without looking, what is the probability that Ariana chooses a red shirt?
   $\frac{1}{4}$
4. Ariana bought a gift to take to the party. She can wrap the birthday gift in silver, blue, or red paper and use either a white or silver bow. If she chooses the paper and bow without looking, what is the probability that she wraps it with silver paper and a silver bow?
   $\frac{1}{6}$

 Use with text pages 608–610.

- For **Problems 11–13**, ask: **How can you find the total number of outcomes for each without using a tree diagram or grid?** (One way: multiply the number of choices for one part by the number of choices for the other.)
- You may wish to have students work in pairs on **Problems 14–18**.

4 Assess & Close

Math Talk in Action

How would you decide when to use a grid and when to use a tree diagram to represent all the outcomes and then solve a probability problem? (Accept all reasonable answers, including personal preference.) Discuss whether students find it easier to represent a larger number of possible outcomes using one method or the other.

Math Journal Prompt

Have students explain how to use a tree diagram to find the probability of two equally likely events. Have them provide an example using spinners.

Lesson Quiz

Use the quiz on Lesson Transparency 23.5.

Test Prep & Spiral Review

Use Test Prep Transparency 23.5.

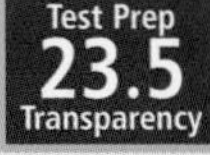

For Problems 11–13, make a grid or a tree diagram to show the total number of possible outcomes when one of each is chosen.
See Additional Answers.

11. Ice Cream
Flavors: vanilla, chocolate, strawberry
Way of serving: cup, cone

12. Sandwiches
Bread: white, wheat, rye
Filling: cheese, peanut butter, tuna, ham

13. Outfits
Shirts: white, red, blue
Pants: black, green, brown

Tina and a friend are playing a game with a six-sided number cube. Problems 14–17 all refer to the same number cube.

14. The probability of tossing a number greater than 13 and less than 24 is $\frac{6}{6}$, or 1. What are the possible numbers on the cube?
14, 15, 16, 17, 18, 19, 20, 21, 22, 23

15. The probability of tossing a number that is divisible by 5 is $\frac{2}{6}$, or $\frac{1}{3}$. What does this tell you about the numbers on the cube?
Two of the numbers are 15 and 20.

16. The probability of tossing an odd number greater than 17 is $\frac{3}{6}$, or $\frac{1}{2}$. What additional information does this give you about the numbers on the cube?
Three of the numbers are 19, 21, and 23.

17. The probability of tossing a number that can be divided evenly by 3 is $\frac{3}{6}$, or $\frac{1}{2}$. What information does this give you about the numbers? **See above.**

17. The numbers are 15, 18, and 21. The numbers 15 and 21 are already used.

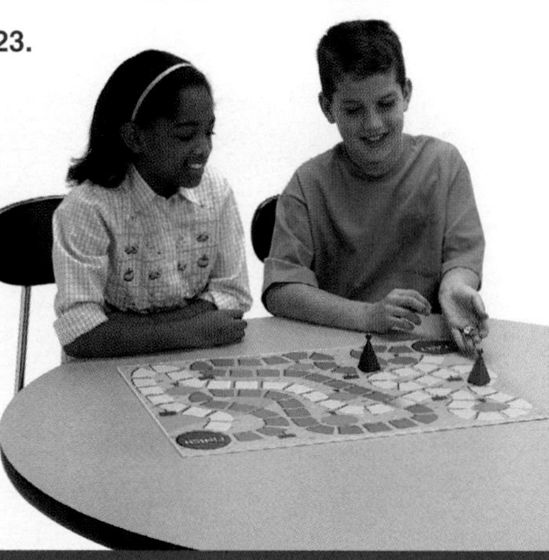

18. Create and Solve Design a probability experiment that uses a fair spinner, a number cube, or both. Work with a partner to list all the possible outcomes and the probability of each. Then do the experiment.
Check students' experiments.

 Extra Practice, See page 613, Set C.

Homework 23.5 Page 148

Name ____________ Date ________ Homework 23.5

Find Probability

Use the spinner to solve each problem.

If you spin the spinner two times, what is the probability that the spinner will land on the black region twice?

You can use a grid.

Second Spin

First Spin		black	white	striped
	black	black, black	black, white	black, striped
	white	white, black	white, white	white, striped
	striped	striped, black	striped, white	striped, striped

Count the number of outcomes that have black two times.

The probability of landing on black twice is $\frac{1}{9}$.

1. What is the probability of one spin landing on the white area and one spin landing on the black area?
$\frac{2}{9}$; 2 out of 9

2. What is the probability that one of the spins will land on the white area and that the other will not land on the white area?
$\frac{4}{9}$; 4 out of 9

Problem Solving

3. Make a tree diagram or a grid to show the possible outcomes of two consecutive spins if the spinner had 4 equal parts that are red, blue, yellow, and green.

Possible grid shown.

Second Spin

First Spin		red	blue	yellow	green
	red	red, red	blue, red	yellow, red	green, red
	blue	red, blue	blue, blue	yellow, blue	green, blue
	yellow	red, yellow	blue, yellow	yellow, yellow	green, yellow
	green	red, green	blue, green	yellow, green	green, green

Use with text pages 608–610.

Reading Connection

Give Me an E!

Materials: newspapers or magazines, colored pens or pencils

It is said that the letter *e* is the vowel that is used most often. Is this true? Do your own test to find out.

1. Choose a paragraph in a newspaper or magazine and cut it out.
2. Use colored pencils to circle each of the vowels (*a, e, i, o,* and *u*). Use a different color for each vowel.
3. Make a tally chart showing how many times each of the vowels is used.
4. Try again, using other paragraphs.

Dominoes

Old Game, New Uses

Domino games have been played all over the world for centuries. No one knows who invented dominoes, but a set of tiles like dominoes was found in the tomb of Tutankhamen, the king of Egypt in 1355 B.C. That's more than 3,300 years ago. Today dominoes are used for many games, but they also are used to build mazes that fall in intricate patterns when one domino is knocked over.

Number of Vowels	
E	卌 卌 卌 卌 卌 卌 卌 ||
A	
O	
U	
I	

5. **Write About It** Is the letter *e* the most frequently used vowel? Why do you think so? ***Answers may vary.***
6. Which vowel is used least, according to your tally? Did this result surprise you? Explain. ***Answers may vary.***

Reading Connection

Give Me an E!

- Have students compare and discuss their findings. Then ask them to guess which is the most frequently used *consonant* and then to do experiments to see what they find out. Similarly, have students experiment to see which letters show up with the least frequency in their paragraphs. Have them make predictions first.
- As needed, remind students how to make tally marks.

Chapter Review/Test

Chapter Review/Test Items 1–15

To assign a numerical grade for this Chapter Review/Test, use 6 points for items 1–10 and 8 points for items 11–15.

Check Understanding

You can use the ***Write About It*** question to assess understanding of a key chapter concept.

Customize Your Instruction

The Chapter Review/Test is a formal evaluation of chapter objectives. For students who have not yet mastered these objectives, you can use the Reteaching Resources listed in the chart below.

Additional Assessment Resources

Alternate Chapter Test A Chapter Test is also provided in the Unit Resource folder. You might use the Review/Test in the student book as review and the test in the Unit Resource folder as a summary test for the chapter.

***Ways to Assess* CD-ROM** allows you to create your own lesson, chapter, or unit tests or practice and review worksheets.

Adequate Yearly Progress Guide helps familiarize your students with the format of

Chapter Review/Test

VOCABULARY

Vocabulary
- outcome
- prediction
- probability
- tree diagram

1. A ____ is the chance of an event occurring. **probability**
2. A result in a probability experiment is an ____. **outcome**
3. Combinations of outcomes can be shown on a ____. **tree diagram**

CONCEPTS AND SKILLS

Write *certain, likely, equally likely, unlikely,* or *impossible* to describe the probability of landing on blue. (Lesson 1, pp. 596–597)

4. 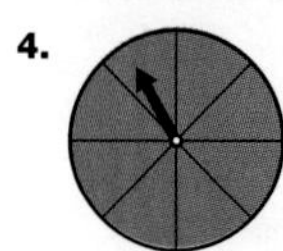 **certain**
5. **likely**
6.  **impossible**
7. 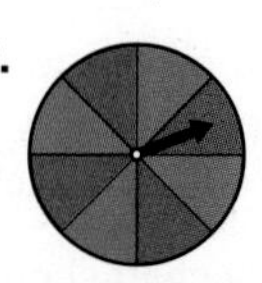 **equally likely**

Suppose you pick one tile from this bag without looking. Write the probability of each. (Lesson 2, pp. 598–600)

8. picking 11 or 15 **2 out of 8 or 1 out of 4; $\frac{2}{8}$ or $\frac{1}{4}$**
9. picking an odd number **8 out of 8 or 1 out of 1, $\frac{8}{8}$ or 1**
10. picking a multiple of 10 **0 out of 8, $\frac{0}{8}$ or 0**

Use the tree diagram for Problems 11–13. (Lesson 5, pp. 608–610)

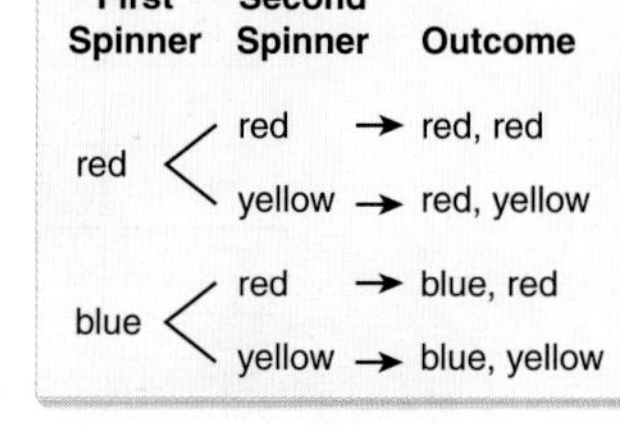

11. What are the possible outcomes for the second spinner? **red, yellow**
12. What are the possible outcomes for both spinners? **red, red; red, yellow; blue, red; blue, yellow**
13. What is the probability of landing on two different colors for both spins? **$\frac{3}{4}$**

PROBLEM SOLVING

Solve. (Lesson 4, pp. 604–606)

14. How many different ways can Joe, Beth, and Chad be arranged in a line? **6 ways**
15. How many different ways can four people be arranged in a line? **24 ways**

Write About It

Show You Understand

The probability of tossing 2 on a number cube is $\frac{1}{6}$. If the cube is tossed 48 times, can you predict how many times a 2 will be tossed? Explain your thinking.

See Additional Answers.

612 **Chapter 23** Chapter Review/Test

Chapter Review/Test Items	Objectives	Covered On Teacher's Edition Pages	Use These Reteaching Resources
1–2, 4–10	**23A** Describe the probability of an event and determine the number of possible outcomes in an experiment.	596A–600	Reteach Resources 23.1, 23.2 *Ways to Success* CD-ROM 23.1, 23.2 *Ways to Success* Skillsheets 194–196
Write About It	**23B** Use probability to make predictions.	602A–603	Reteach Resources 23.3 *Ways to Success* CD-ROM 23.3 *Ways to Success* Skillsheet 197
3, 11–13	**23C** Use tables, graphs, and tree diagrams to represent probability outcomes.	608A–610	Reteach Resources 23.5 *Ways to Success* CD-ROM 23.5 *Ways to Success* Skillsheet 198
14–15	**23D** Solve problems using skills and strategies.	604A–606	Reteach Resources 23.4 *Ways to Success* CD-ROM 23.4 *Ways to Success* Skillsheet 199

Extra Practice

Set A (Lesson 1, pp. 596–597)

Write *certain*, *likely*, *equally likely*, *unlikely*, or *impossible* to describe the probability of landing on red.

1. 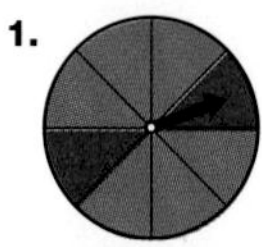
unlikely

2. 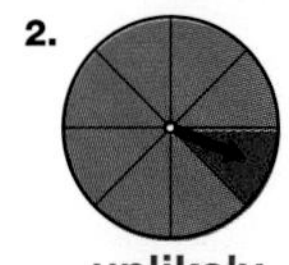
unlikely

3. 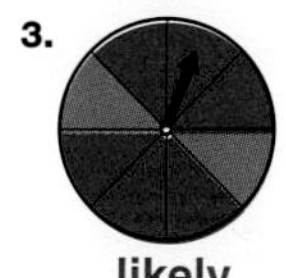
likely

4. 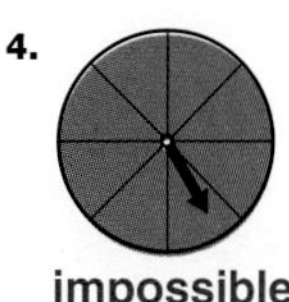
impossible

Set B (Lesson 2, pp. 598–600)

See Additional Answers.

Look at the spinner on the right. Write the probability of each outcome in both words and fraction form.

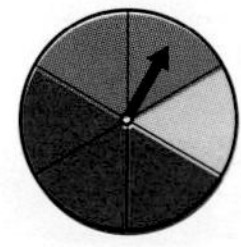

1. purple
2. red
3. yellow
4. yellow or red
5. purple or red
6. green

Set C (Lesson 5, pp. 608–610)

Use the tree diagram on the right for Problems 1–4.

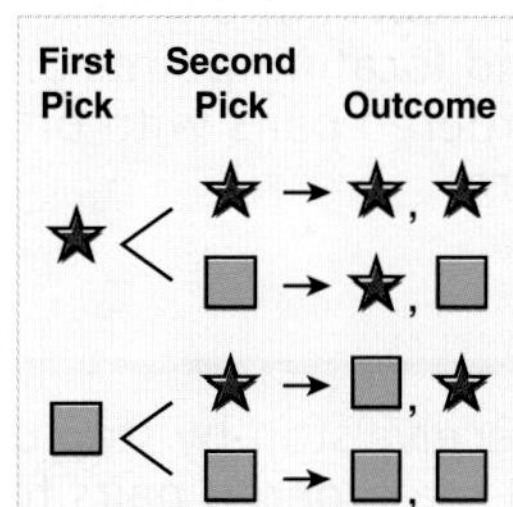

1. Write all the possible outcomes for two picks.
star, star; star, square; square, star; square, square
2. What is the probability of picking the star twice? $\frac{1}{4}$
3. What is the probability of picking a star and a square? $\frac{2}{4}$ or $\frac{1}{2}$
4. What is the probability of picking the square first and the star second? $\frac{1}{4}$

Use the grid on the right for Problems 5–7.

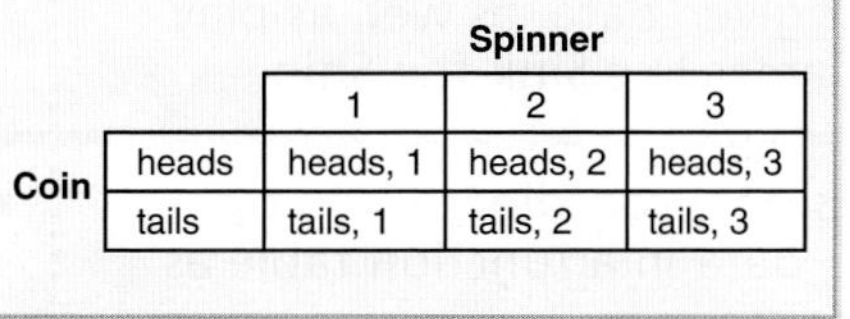

Coin \ Spinner	1	2	3
heads	heads, 1	heads, 2	heads, 3
tails	tails, 1	tails, 2	tails, 3

5. What is the probability of the coin landing heads up and the spinner landing on 3? $\frac{1}{6}$
6. What is the probability of the coin landing tails up and the spinner landing on 1, 2, or 3? $\frac{3}{6}$ or $\frac{1}{2}$
7. What is the probability of the coin landing heads up or tails up and the spinner landing on 1? $\frac{2}{6}$ or $\frac{1}{3}$

Extra Practice at **eduplace.com/map**

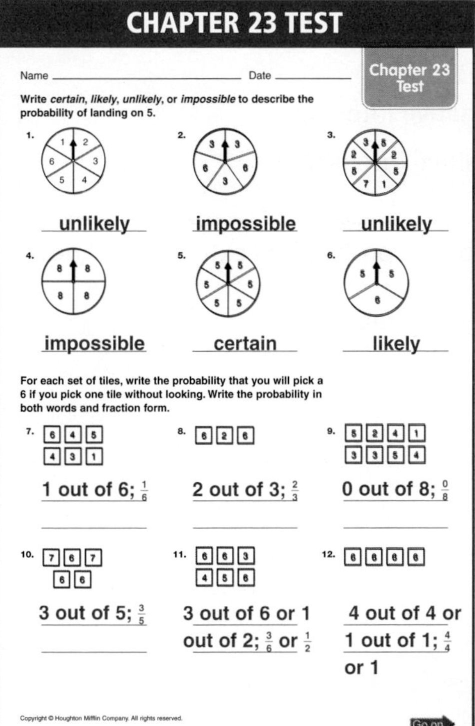

CHAPTER 23 TEST

Chapter 23 Test

Name ________ Date ________

Write *certain*, *likely*, *unlikely*, or *impossible* to describe the probability of landing on 5.

1. unlikely
2. impossible
3. unlikely
4. impossible
5. certain
6. likely

For each set of tiles, write the probability that you will pick a 6 if you pick one tile without looking. Write the probability in both words and fraction form.

7. 1 out of 6; $\frac{1}{6}$
8. 2 out of 3; $\frac{2}{3}$
9. 0 out of 8; $\frac{0}{8}$
10. 3 out of 5; $\frac{3}{5}$
11. 3 out of 6 or 1 out of 2; $\frac{3}{6}$ or $\frac{1}{2}$
12. 4 out of 4 or 1 out of 1; $\frac{4}{4}$ or 1

Go on

CHAPTER 23 TEST

Chapter 23 Test continued

Name ________ Date ________

The faces of a cube are labeled with the letters *L, E, T, T, E,* and *R*. Think about the cube for Problems 13–14.

13. Predict how many times the cube will land on *L* if the cube is tossed 48 times.
8 times
14. Predict how many times the cube will land on *T* if the cube is tossed 30 times.
10 times

Make an organized list to solve each problem.

15. Lionel, Henry, Felicia, and Deb are lining up. How many different ways can the 4 line up if Deb has to be first?
6 ways
16. Ben has brown pants and black pants. He has a red shirt, a green shirt, a purple shirt, and a black shirt. How many different combinations of pants and a shirt can Ben wear?
8 combinations
17. Gary is making numbers with the digits 2, 5, 3, and 4. How many 4-digit whole numbers can he make?
24 numbers

Use the spinners for Problems 18–20.

18. You spin both spinners at the same time. Draw a grid on a separate page to show all the possible outcomes.
Check students' grids. *See below.*
19. How many outcomes show one spinner landing on 2?
5 outcomes
20. Find the probability of both spinners landing on 1. Write your answer in fraction form.
$\frac{1}{9}$

First Spin \ Second Spin	1	2	3
1	1, 1	1, 2	1, 3
2	2, 1	2, 2	2, 3
3	3, 1	3, 2	3, 3

STOP

CHAPTER 24

Planning Guide

Algebra and Graphing

Lesson	Overview	Objective/Vocabulary
1 Locate Points on a Grid p. 616A	► Use ordered pairs to name and locate points on a coordinate grid. ► Naming and locating points on a grid includes ordered pairs with one coordinate of zero.	► Use ordered pairs to name points on a grid. coordinate ordered pair
2 Graph Ordered Pairs p. 618A	► Students receive step-by-step directions on how to use ordered pairs to plot points on a coordinate grid. ► Knowing how to plot points on a coordinate grid helps students make line graphs for given data, as well as play strategy games like Sink the Ship.	► Use ordered pairs to plot points on a grid. plot
3 Algebra: Graph Functions p. 620A	► Plot points on a coordinate grid by expressing data in a function table as ordered pairs. ► After plotting all points for the function, draw a line to show the pattern.	► Plot ordered pairs from a function table and draw a line to help you solve problems. origin x-axis axes y-axis
4 Algebra: Integers p. 624A	► Introduce integers. ► Use integers to describe temperatures, land elevations, and such real-life situations as writing $^-8$ for "spending $8." ► Expand the coordinate grid to include four quadrants.	► Learn about integers. integers opposites negative integers positive integers
5 Problem-Solving Application: Use a Graph p.628A	► Solve a problem by extending a line graph. ► The Real World Connection feature shows how chess players use ordered pairs with a letter and number to tell the location of any piece.	► Solve a problem by extending a line graph. function table

Skills Trace: Algebra and Graphing		
Grade 3	**Grade 4**	**Grade 5**
• Read and make graphs with ordered pairs (ch. 6)	• Identify and graph ordered pairs on a coordinate plane • Learn about integers (opposites, positive and negative numbers) • Use ordered pairs to graph functions • Solve problems by graphing a function	• Graph ordered pairs in four quadrants (ch. 23) • Identify transformations on a coordinate plane (ch. 23) • Use functions and function tables to solve problems (ch. 21) • Find absolute value of integers (ch. 22) • Compare, order, add, and subtract integers (ch. 22) • Write and solve equations using equity properties (ch. 21)

Differentiated Instruction	Materials	NCTM Standards
▶ Differentiated Instruction activities, p. 616B ▶ *Chapter Challenges*, p. 139 *Ways to Success* CD-ROM: 24.1 ▶ *Ways to Success* Skillsheet 200 Audio Tutor: **2**/32 Listen and Understand		**Geometry:** Describe location and movement using common language and geometric vocabulary; make and use coordinate systems to specify locations and to describe paths; find the distance between points along horizontal and vertical lines of a coordinate system.
▶ Differentiated Instruction activities, p. 618B *Ways to Success* CD-ROM: 24.2 ▶ *Ways to Success* Skillsheets 203, 204 Audio Tutor: **2**/33 Listen and Understand	First-Quadrant Grid transparency	**Geometry:** Describe location and movement using common language and geometric vocabulary; make and use coordinate systems to specify locations and to describe paths; find the distance between points along horizontal and vertical lines of a coordinate system.
▶ Differentiated Instruction activities, p. 620B ▶ *Chapter Challenges*, p. 141 *Ways to Success* CD-ROM: 24.3 ▶ *Ways to Success* Skillsheets 201, 204	Table II transparency, First-Quadrant Grid transparency	**Geometry:** Describe location and movement using common language and geometric vocabulary; make and use coordinate systems to specify locations and to describe paths; find the distance between points along horizontal and vertical lines of a coordinate system.
▶ Differentiated Instruction activities, p. 624B *Ways to Success* CD-ROM: 24.4 ▶ *Ways to Success* Skillsheet 205	Number Lines transparency, Blank transparency	**Number and Operations:** Explore numbers less than 0 by extending the number line and through familiar applications.
▶ Differentiated Instruction activities, p. 628B ▶ *Chapter Challenges*, p. 143 *Ways to Success* CD-ROM: 24.5 ▶ *Ways to Success* Skillsheet 206	Centimeter Grid Workmat	**Problem Solving:** Apply and adapt a variety of appropriate strategies to solve problems. **Data Analysis and Probability:** Represent data using tables and graphs.

Math Notes

Chapter Objectives

24A Locate, identify, and graph points on a coordinate plane; graph lines.

24B Write integers.

24C Solve problems using skills and strategies.

Mathematical Background

Functions and Integers

Points can be located and plotted on a coordinate grid. In an ordered pair, such as (3, 2), the first number is the *x*-coordinate. It tells how far to the right of 0 the point is. The second number is the *y*-coordinate. It tells how far up from 0 the point is. Notice that the point (3, 2) is not the same as the point (2, 3).

4
3 (2,3)
2 (3,2)
1
0 1 2 3 4

Students will revisit equations in this chapter as they graph linear functions on a grid. A function is a rule that pairs each input *x* with one and only one output *y*. To graph a function, use a function table to generate *x*- and *y*-values, plot these values as ordered pairs on the grid, and then connect them with a straight line.

Integers are the counting numbers 1, 2, 3, . . . , their opposites, $^{-}1$, $^{-}2$, $^{-}3$, . . . , and 0. Negative integers are used to record numbers such as temperature below 0°, the distance below sea level, and how much is owed. Numbers such as $^{-}3$ and $^{+}3$ are opposites. They are the same distance from zero.

Research-Based Teaching

Van de Walle (1994) suggested that the "related topics of probability and statistics represent two of the most prominent uses of mathematics in our lives." Knowledge of algebra and graphing is closely linked to understanding probability and statistics. See *Professional Resources Handbook, Grade 4*, Unit 8.

For more ideas relating to Unit 8, see the Teacher Support Handbook at the back of this Teacher's Edition.

Language Intervention

Be sure students are correctly reading mathematical notation as they work in this chapter. The pair (4, 6) is read as "four, six." Numbers less than 0 are negative numbers, so $^{-}4$ is read as "negative four," not "minus four." Be sure students understand the meaning of the word *integers*. Integers include 0, all positive whole numbers, and their opposites. The numbers $5\frac{1}{2}$ and $^{-}5\frac{1}{2}$ are not integers.

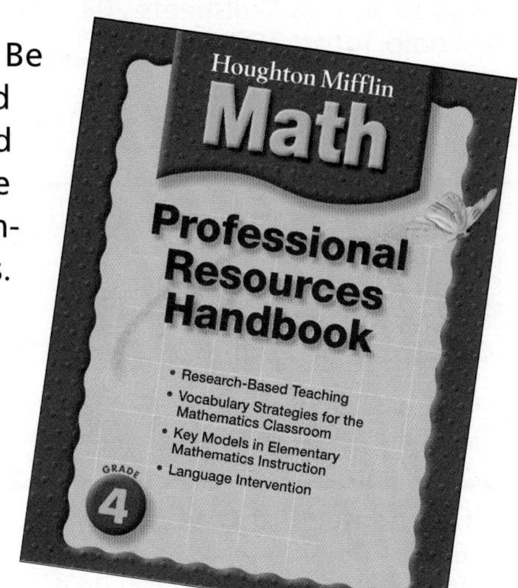

Chapter Activities

Assessing Prior Knowledge

Individuals	15 minutes
Objective	Identify points on a grid.
Materials	First-Quadrant Grid Transparency
Visual, Tactual	

Identifying Points on a Grid

- Show students a first-quadrant grid on the overhead. Label 4 or 5 points on the grid using polygon-shaped symbols. For example, put a square at (2, 5), a triangle at (5, 2), and a rectangle at (8, 6).
- Talk about ordered pairs.
- Ask students to identify the shape located at (2, 5). Then ask about the shape located at (5, 2). Talk about the location of these shapes.
- Ask students to use an ordered pair to name the location of the rectangle.

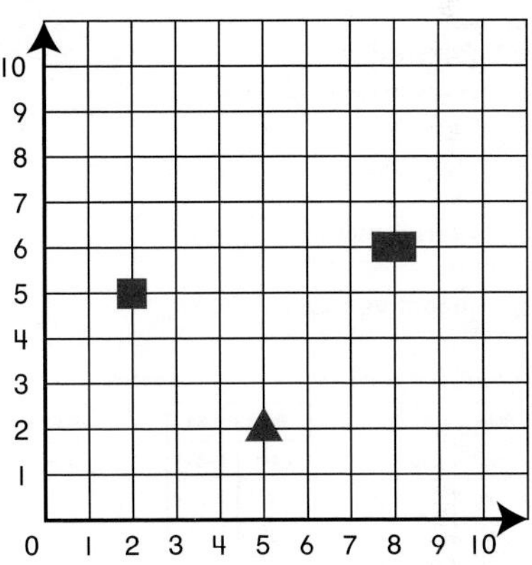

Ongoing Skill Activity

Whole Class	10 minutes
Objective	Play games to practice problem-solving.
Materials	Games such as sink the ship, chess, checkers, tick-tack-toe
Visual, Tactual	

Moves on a Grid

- Have games such as sink the ship, tick-tack-toe, checkers, and chess available in a recreational corner of the classroom.
- Encourage students to play the games using lateral moves and logic to win them. Have them explain how to win the games.

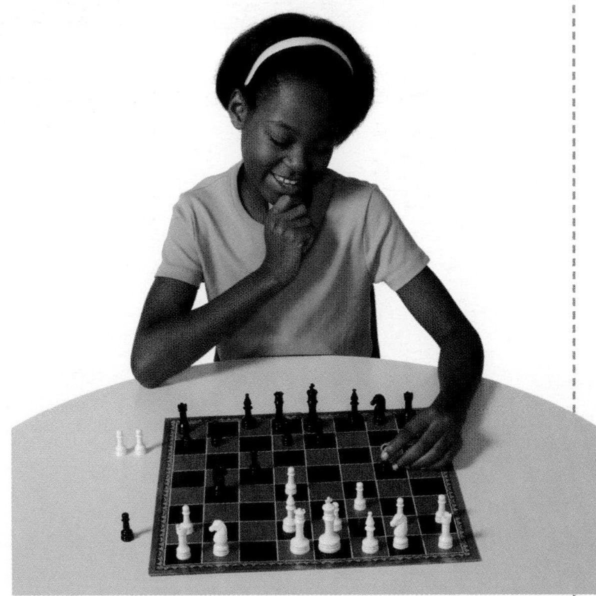

Math Expressions

Small Groups	25 minutes
Objective	Name and plot points on a coordinate grid.
Materials	First Quadrant Grids (LT 50), straightedge
Tactual, Visual	

Shapes on a Grid

This activity uses instructional practices from *Math Expressions* with content from this unit.

- Provide each pair of students with a copy of the First Quadrant Grids Learning Tool and a straightedge.
- Have students plot and label these points on the grid: *A*(4,3), *B*(4,1), *C*(5,1), *D*(5,4), *E*(9,6), *F*(9,3), *G*(3,7), *H*(7,9), *S*(1,4), *T*(1,1), *R*(2,3), *N*(2,1).
- Then students should connect the following vertices to make a polygon. Have them record the name of each polygon as they draw it.

DEFC (parallelogram)

DEHG (parallelogram)

GDS (triangle)

DCTS (rectangle)

BARN (square)

- Have students quiz each other on naming the letters at different points. For example, "Which point is located at (9,3)?" (F)

Starting Chapter 24

Investigation

Using Data

Have students work in small groups to follow the directions on page 614.

To extend the investigation, have students do the following activity.

- Think about a place in your community—for example, a playground, park, or shopping center. Use grid paper to make a map similar to the one on page 614. Use ordered pairs to describe each location on your map.

For more information about projects and investigations,

Visit **Education Place®**
www.eduplace.com/mat

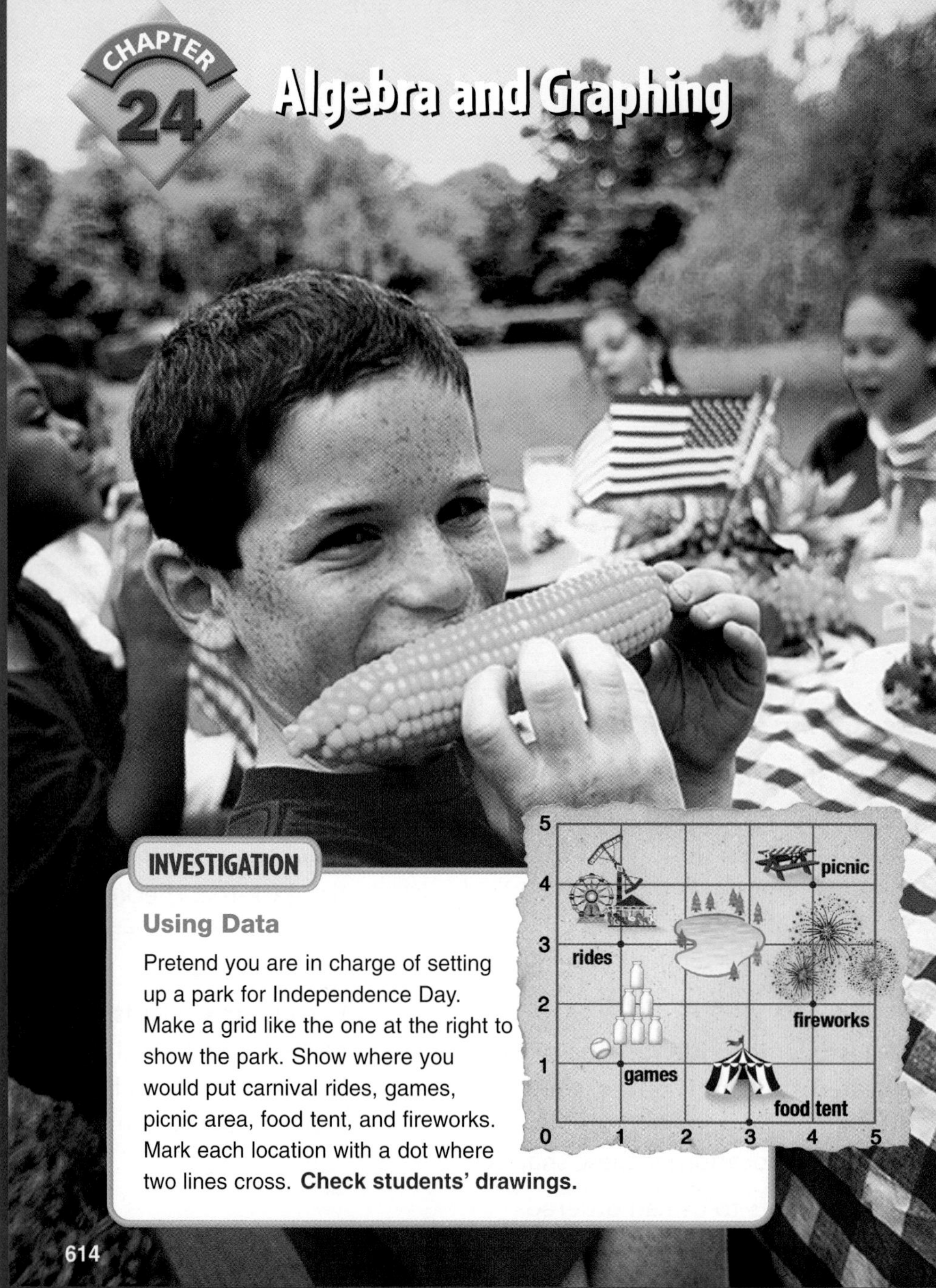

CHAPTER 24 **Algebra and Graphing**

INVESTIGATION

Using Data

Pretend you are in charge of setting up a park for Independence Day. Make a grid like the one at the right to show the park. Show where you would put carnival rides, games, picnic area, food tent, and fireworks. Mark each location with a dot where two lines cross. **Check students' drawings.**

614

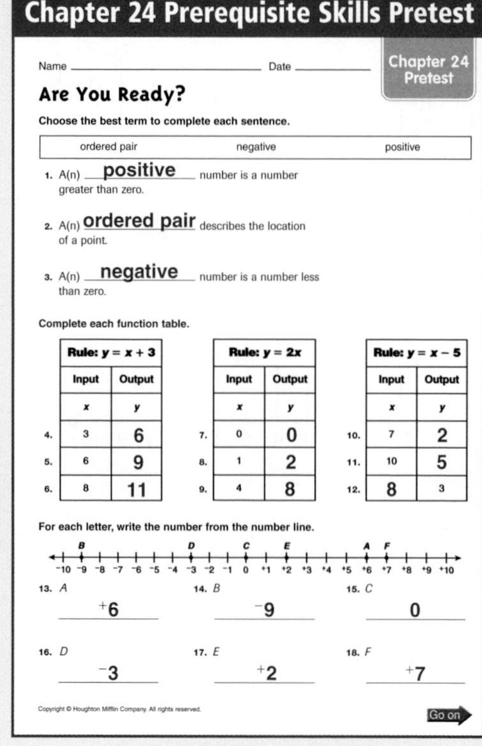

Chapter 24 Prerequisite Skills Pretest

Name ______ Date ______ Chapter 24 Pretest

Are You Ready?

Choose the best term to complete each sentence.

ordered pair | negative | positive

1. A(n) **positive** number is a number greater than zero.
2. A(n) **ordered pair** describes the location of a point.
3. A(n) **negative** number is a number less than zero.

Complete each function table.

	Rule: $y = x + 3$	
	Input	Output
	x	y
4.	3	**6**
5.	6	**9**
6.	8	**11**

	Rule: $y = 2x$	
	Input	Output
	x	y
7.	0	**0**
8.	1	**2**
9.	4	**8**

	Rule: $y = x - 5$	
	Input	Output
	x	y
10.	7	**2**
11.	10	**5**
12.	**8**	3

For each letter, write the number from the number line.

13. A **$^{+}6$**
14. B **$^{-}9$**
15. C **0**
16. D **$^{-}3$**
17. E **$^{+}2$**
18. F **$^{+}7$**

Go on

✓ Use What You Know

Use this page to review and remember what you need to know for this chapter.

VOCABULARY

Choose the best term to complete each sentence.

1. A table of pairs that follows a rule is a ____. **function table**
2. A number greater than zero is ____. **positive**
3. A number less than zero is ____. **negative**

Vocabulary
- positive
- negative
- ordered pair
- function table

CONCEPTS AND SKILLS

Copy and complete each function table.

	Rule: $y = 7 + x$		
	Input x	Output y	
4.	4	■	11
5.	19	■	26
6.	33	■	40

	Rule: $y = x - 3$		
	Input x	Output y	
7.	10	■	7
8.	17	■	14
9.	45	■	42

	Rule: $y = 3x$		
	Input x	Output y	
10.	2	■	6
11.	5	■	15
12.	■	24	8

Write the number for each letter.

J K L M N O P

⁻10 ⁻9 ⁻8 ⁻7 ⁻6 ⁻5 ⁻4 ⁻3 ⁻2 ⁻1 0 ⁺1 ⁺2 ⁺3 ⁺4 ⁺5 ⁺6 ⁺7 ⁺8 ⁺9 ⁺10

13. *M* ⁻1
14. *L* ⁻5
15. *K* ⁻7
16. *O* ⁺8
17. *N* ⁺4
18. *P* ⁺10
19. *J* ⁻10

20. *Possible answer:* 3 is positive so it is greater than 0. ⁻3 is negative so it is less than 0.

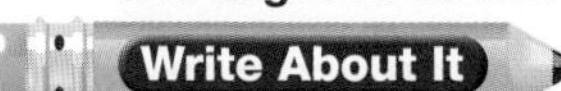

20. How are 3 and ⁻3 different? Use a number line, symbols, or words to explain your answer. ***See above.***

Facts Practice, See page 671.

Chapter 24 New Content Pretest

Name ______________ Date ________

Chapter 24 Pretest continued

Check What You Know

Use the graph on the right for Exercises 1–3. Write the letter of the point for each ordered pair.

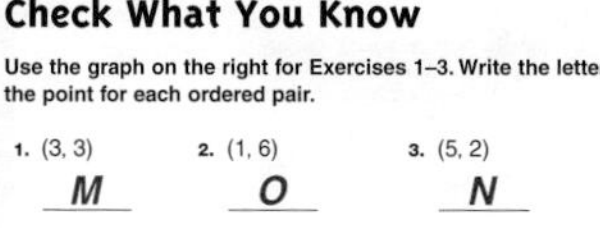

1. (3, 3) **M**
2. (1, 6) **O**
3. (5, 2) **N**

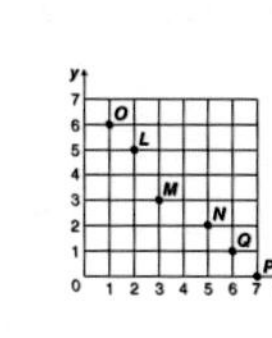

Use the graph on the right for Exercises 4–6. Write the ordered pair for each point.

4. *W* **(2, 6)**
5. *T* **(4, 3)**
6. *R* **(3, 4)**

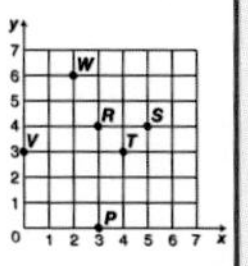

Plot each point and label it with the correct letter.

7. *E* (2, 6)
8. *F* (6, 2)
9. *G* (0, 5)

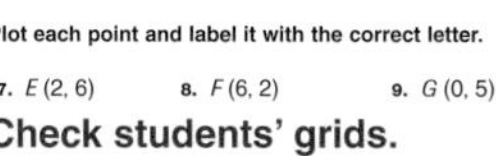

Check students' grids.

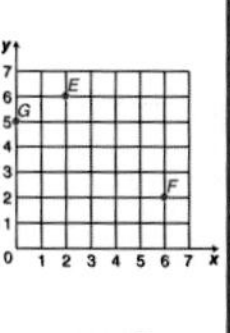

Go on

Chapter 24 New Content Pretest

Name ______________ Date ________

Chapter 24 Pretest continued

Use the table for Problems 10–12. **Check students' tables.**

10. Extend the table to 6 boxes.
11. Write the pairs of data as ordered pairs. Use the number of boxes as the first coordinate and the number of shirts as the second coordinate.

(1, 3) **(2, 6)** **(3, 9)**
(4, 12) **(5, 15)** **(6, 18)**

Boxes of Shirts $y = 3x$	
Number of Boxes (x)	Number of Shirts (y)
1	3
2	6
3	9
4	12
5	15
6	18

12. Make a grid on a separate sheet of paper. Number the x-axis to 10 and the y-axis to 20. Plot the points and connect the points with a line. Extend the line to find the number of shirts in 8 boxes.

Check students' graphs; 24 shirts

For each letter, write the integer from the number line.

K J N M O L

−8 −7 −6 −5 −4 −3 −2 −1 0 1 2 3 4 5 6 7 8

13. *K* **⁻7**
14. *N* **⁻3**
15. *L* **⁺8**

Write the integer for each situation.

16. 7 degrees below zero **⁻7**
17. \$5 earned **⁺5**
18. 9 feet below sea level **⁻9**

Use the graph for Problems 19–20.

19. How much will Hank make if he works 5 hours? **\$25**
20. How much will Hank make if he works 7 hours? **\$35**

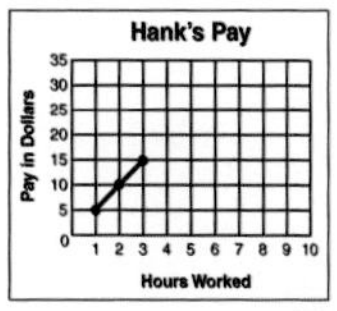

Hank's Pay

Pay in Dollars: 0 5 10 15 20 25 30 35

Hours Worked: 1 2 3 4 5 6 7 8 9 10

STOP

Monitoring Student Progress

Use What You Know

Use this page for informal assessment and review of prerequisite skills.

- Item 1–3: Use math vocabulary
- Items 4–12: Complete function tables
- Items 13–19: Identify integers on a number line
- Item 20: Understand integers

Customize Your Instruction

Use the Chapter Pretest in the Unit Resource folder to help customize and pace instruction.

Objectives and Resources

▶ Prerequisite Skills Pretest
- Items 1–3: Review vocabulary.
- Items 4–12: Complete function tables.
- Items 13–18: Identify integers on a number line.

▶ New Content Pretest
- Items 1–12: Locate, identify, and graph points on a coordinate plane; graph lines.
- Items 13–18: Write integers.
- Items 19–20: Solve problems using skills and strategies.

▶ For Students Having Difficulty
- *Ways to Success* CD-ROM: 13.4, 5.6
- *Ways to Success* Skillsheet: 200

▶ For Students Having Success
- Enrichment 24.1–24.5

▶ For Mathematically Promising Students

Explore: Distance Between Points, page 139, after Lesson 1

Extend: Graphing Shapes, page 141, after Lesson 3

Connect: Graph and Compare Functions, page 143, after Lesson 5

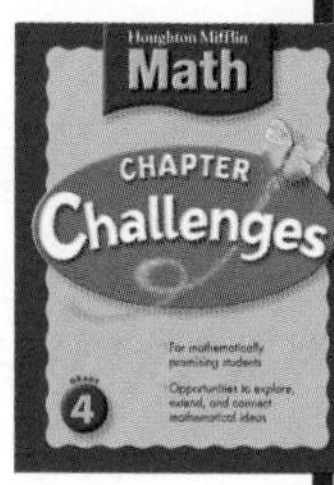

Lesson 24.1 Locate Points on a Grid

Planning

Lesson Objective Use ordered pairs to name points on a grid.

Technology Resources

- Audio Tutor **2**/32 Listen and Understand
- *Ways to Success* CD-ROM 24.1
- Education Place: Extra Practice, eGlossary, Extra Help, eGames www.eduplace.com/map

Lesson 24.1 Transparency

Problem of the Day

A ladybug landed at 0 on a number line. First the ladybug moved right 8 units. Then it moved left 6 units. Then it moved left again 2 units. Where on the number line was the lady bug then? (at 0)

Spiral Review

Complete the function table for the rule *add 2, subtract 3.*

6	(5)
4	(3)
(10)	9
8	(7)

Lesson Quiz

Use the graph.
Write the letter of the ordered pair.

1. (0, 5) (*B*)
2. (3, 1) (*A*)
3. (2, 4) (*C*)

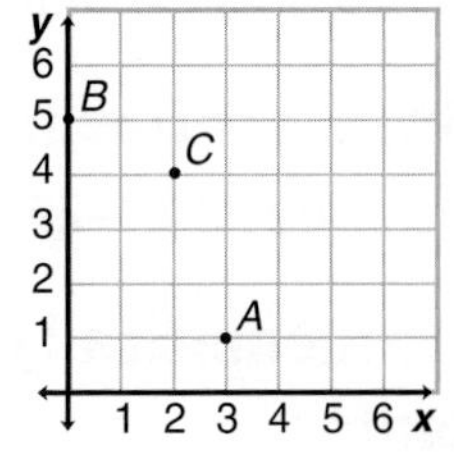

NCTM Standards

Geometry: Describe location and movement using common language and geometric vocabulary; make and use coordinate systems to specify locations and to describe paths; find the distance between points along horizontal and vertical lines of a coordinate system.

Getting Started

Building Math Vocabulary

coordinates ordered pair of numbers—for example (⁻4, 4)—that locates a point in the coordinate plane with reference to the *x*-axis and *y*-axis

ordered pair a pair of numbers used to locate a point on a grid

Use the vocabulary cards for *ordered pair* and *coordinates.* Compare the mathematical meaning of coordinates with the real-world use of the term as a means of locating things such as small islands, ships in the ocean, or airplanes in the sky.

Grids All Around Us

Whole Class	5 minutes
Objective	Identify grids in everyday life.
Materials	None
Auditory, Visual	

- Have students discuss the grids around them in their daily lives—the grids of streets in the neighborhood or the rows of seats in movie theaters, for example. Invite students to suggest other examples.
- Have them explain how these grids work to pinpoint locations. For example, students can describe how to find the person in the fourth row, third seat, or the store at the corner of 12th Street and Main Street.
- Tell students that in the lesson they will use ordered pairs to name and locate points on a grid.

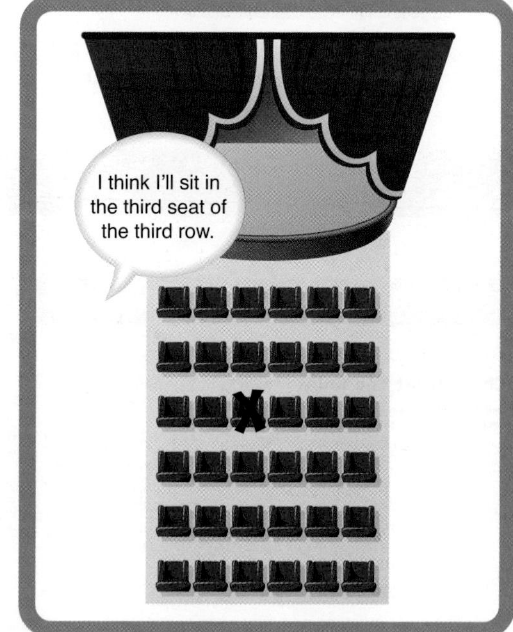

I think I'll sit in the third seat of the third row.

Differentiated Instruction

English Learners

Whole Class	5 minutes
Objective	Locate points on a grid.
Materials	None
Visual, Tactual	

Early Production

- Before ***Guided Practice,*** have students work with a grid.
- Say: **Start at 0. Move right 3 units. Move up 4 units. What are the coordinates?** (3, 4)
- Have students follow the procedure with a partner. Encourage them to alternate roles and start at points other than the origin.

Intermediate/Advanced

- English Learner Resource 24.1
- English Learner Handbook

Intervention

Small Groups	5–10 minutes
Objective	Investigate points on a grid.
Materials	Masking tape
Visual, Kinesthetic	

- Make a large grid on the floor. Tape grid lines and numbers along the axes, with zero as the origin. You can also use a shower curtain and markers to make a more permanent grid.
- Have students move around on the grid to appreciate, in a practical way, the orderly sequence and patterns of coordinate geometry. Moving about on the grid can help students distinguish left from right and horizontal from vertical.

Other Resources

- *Ways to Success* CD-ROM 24.1

Special Needs

Individuals	5 minutes
Objective	Locate points on a grid.
Materials	Desks in rows
Visual, Kinesthetic	

- Use rows of desks to model coordinates. For instance, ask students in the second row to raise their right hands. Ask students in the third seat of each row to raise their left hands. Ask: **What is the location of the student with both hands raised?** (row 2, seat 3)
- Repeat with other seats and rows.

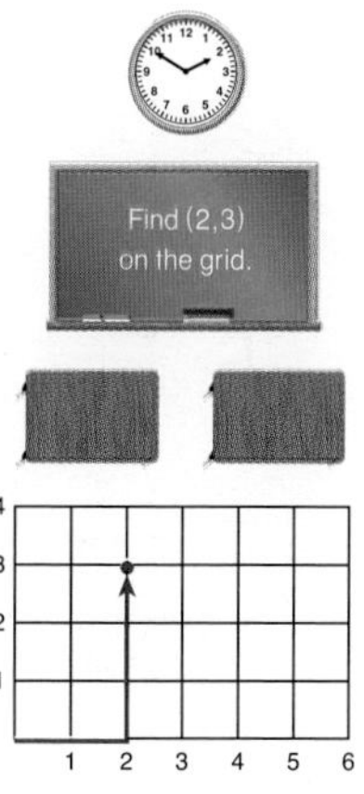

Social Studies Connection

Materials: Globe, maps

- You can use this opportunity to introduce the concepts of latitude and longitude, guiding students to appreciate the importance of the grid system we use to identify locations on a map.
- Guide students to understand lines of longitude (vertical lines that measure distances east and west) and latitude (horizontal lines measuring distances north and south). Provide examples of activities that use longitude and latitude.

❶ Introduce

Explain to students that in an ordered pair, the first number is the *x*-coordinate and the second number is the *y*-coordinate. The lesson will show how to use ordered pairs to name and locate points on a grid.

❷ Teach

Learn About It

- Emphasize that in an ordered pair, the two coordinates must always be written or read in a specific order. **What does the first coordinate in the pair name?** (distance to the right of 0 on the grid) **What does the second coordinate name?** (distance up from 0 on the grid)
- Discuss the ***Other Examples.*** **What can you say about the location of any point whose first coordinate is 0?** (It is on the vertical axis.) **Whose second coordinate is 0?** (It is on the horizontal axis.)

Guided Practice

Have students complete **Exercises 1–2** as you observe. Remind them to use the ***Ask Yourself*** questions to help. Give students the opportunity to talk about the question posed in ***Explain Your Thinking.***

Common Error

- **Transposing coordinates**
- **Intervention** Have students associate the first coordinate of an ordered pair with "right" and the second coordinate with "up."

Lesson 1

Audio Tutor 2/32 Listen and Understand

Locate Points on a Grid

Objective Use ordered pairs to name points on a grid.

Vocabulary
coordinate
ordered pair

Learn About It

Jana is having a treasure hunt at her birthday party. She made a map of her backyard. Guests will use the map to locate the prizes.

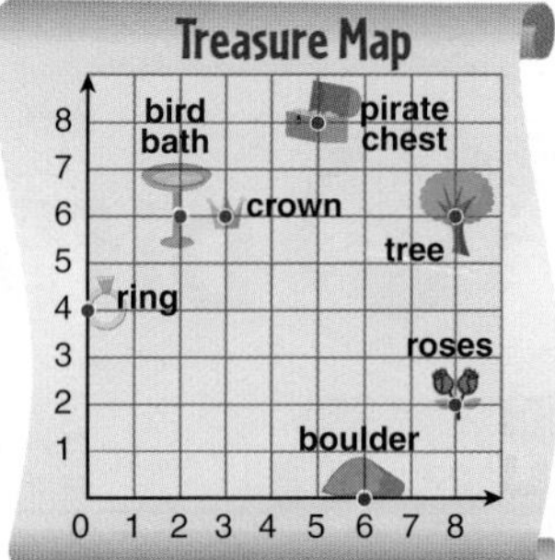

How can you use the map to locate the crown?

Different Ways to Locate the Crown

Way 1 Use directions.

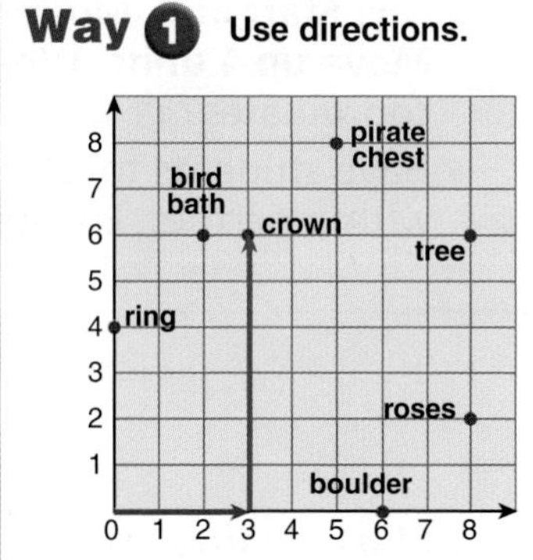

- Start at 0.
- Move right 3 units.
- Then move up 6 units.

Way 2 Use an ordered pair.

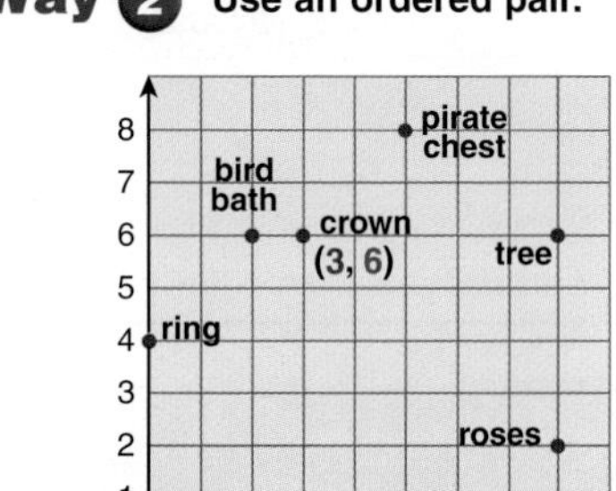

- The **ordered pair** for the crown is (3, 6).
  right up
- The numbers in an ordered pair are called **coordinates**.

Solution: You can use directions or an ordered pair. (3, 6) is the ordered pair that names the location of the crown.

Other Examples

A. Zero as the First Coordinate
The location of the ring is (0, 4).
- Start at 0. Move right 0 units. Then move up 4 units.

B. Zero as the Second Coordinate
The location of the boulder is (6, 0).
- Start at 0. Move right 6 units. Then move up 0 units.

616

Extra Help at eduplace.com/map

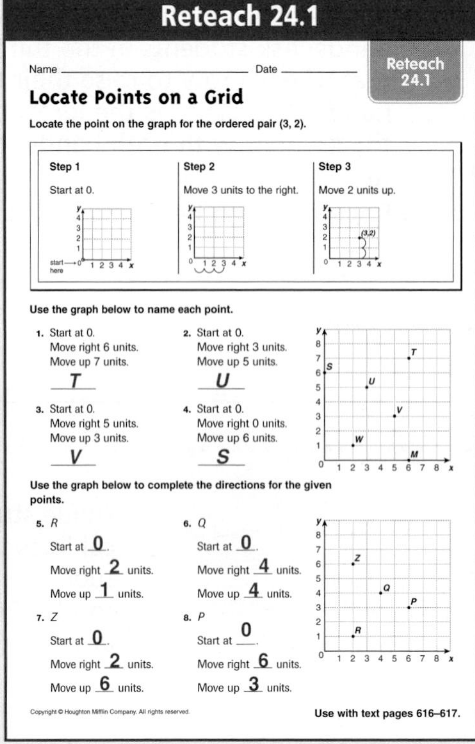

Reteach 24.1

Name ______________ Date ________ Reteach 24.1

Locate Points on a Grid

Locate the point on the graph for the ordered pair (3, 2).

Step 1	Step 2	Step 3
Start at 0.	Move 3 units to the right.	Move 2 units up.

Use the graph below to name each point.

1. Start at 0. Move right 6 units. Move up 7 units. __T__
2. Start at 0. Move right 3 units. Move up 5 units. __U__
3. Start at 0. Move right 5 units. Move up 3 units. __V__
4. Start at 0. Move right 0 units. Move up 6 units. __S__

Use the graph below to complete the directions for the given points.

5. *R* Start at __0__. Move right __2__ units. Move up __1__ units.
6. *Q* Start at __0__. Move right __4__ units. Move up __4__ units.
7. *Z* Start at __0__. Move right __2__ units. Move up __6__ units.
8. *P* Start at __0__. Move right __6__ units. Move up __3__ units.

Use with text pages 616–617.

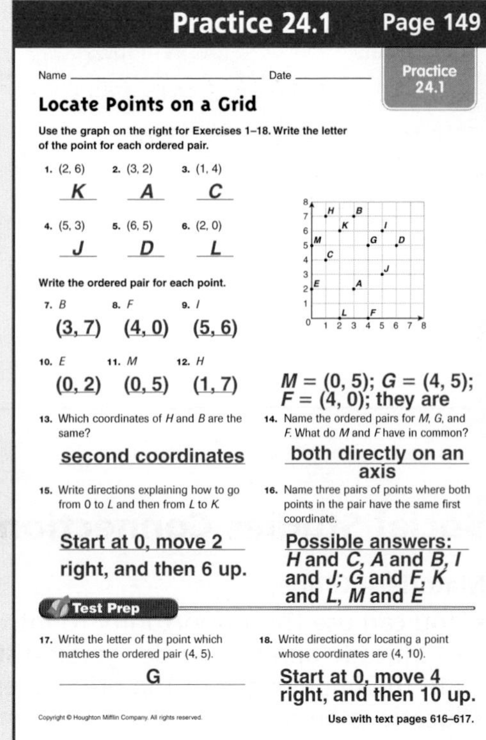

Practice 24.1 Page 149

Name ______________ Date ________ Practice 24.1

Locate Points on a Grid

Use the graph on the right for Exercises 1–18. Write the letter of the point for each ordered pair.

1. (2, 6) __K__
2. (3, 2) __A__
3. (1, 4) __C__
4. (5, 3) __J__
5. (6, 5) __D__
6. (2, 0) __L__

Write the ordered pair for each point.

7. *B* __(3, 7)__
8. *F* __(4, 0)__
9. *I* __(5, 6)__
10. *E* __(0, 2)__
11. *M* __(0, 5)__
12. *H* __(1, 7)__
13. Which coordinates of *H* and *B* are the same? __second coordinates__
14. Name the ordered pairs for *M*, *G*, and *F*. What do *M* and *F* have in common? __*M* = (0, 5); *G* = (4, 5); *F* = (4, 0); they are both directly on an axis__
15. Write directions explaining how to go from 0 to *L* and then from *L* to *K*. __Start at 0, move 2 right, and then 6 up.__
16. Name three pairs of points where both points in the pair have the same first coordinate. __Possible answers: *H* and *C*, *A* and *B*, *I* and *J*; *G* and *F*, *K* and *L*, *M* and *E*__

Test Prep

17. Write the letter of the point which matches the ordered pair (4, 5). __G__
18. Write directions for locating a point whose coordinates are (4, 10). __Start at 0, move 4 right, and then 10 up.__

Use with text pages 616–617.

Guided Practice

Use the treasure map on Page 616 to solve.

Ask Yourself
- Did I start at zero?
- Did I move to the right first?

1. What is described by the following directions?
   - Start at 0.
   - Move right 5 units.
   - Then move up 8 units.

   pirate chest

2. Complete the directions for the tree.
   - Start at ■. **0**
   - Move right ■ units. **8**
   - Then move up ■ units. **6**

Explain Your Thinking ▶ Why does knowing both coordinates of an ordered pair help you locate a point?
The first coordinate tells you how many units to the right to move. The second coordinate tells you how many units up to move.

Practice and Problem Solving

Use the graph on the right for Exercises 3–12. Write the letter of the point for each ordered pair.

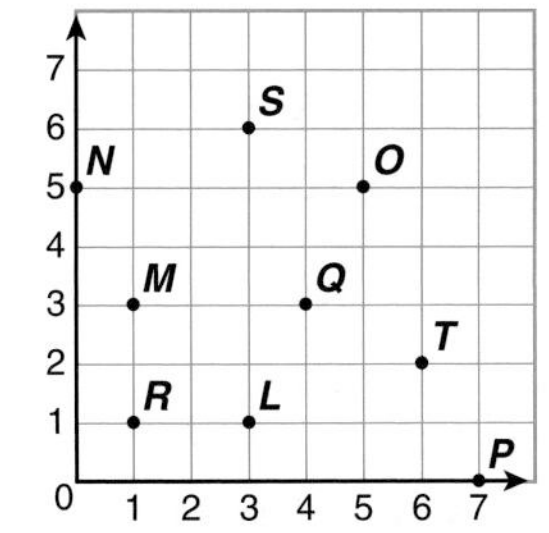

3. (1, 1) ***R***
4. (3, 6) ***S***
5. (6, 2) ***T***

Write the ordered pair for each point.

6. *Q* **(4, 3)**
7. *M* **(1, 3)**
8. *L* **(3, 1)**
9. Which coordinates of *M* and *Q* are the same? Which are different?
   second coordinates; first coordinates
10. Name the ordered pairs for *N, O,* and *P.* What do *N* and *P* have in common?
   (0, 5), (5, 5), and (7, 0); zero is a coordinate for both *N* and *P*
11. Write directions explaining how to go from (0, 0) to *R* and then from *R* to *L.*
   Start at (0, 0). Move right 1 unit. Then move up 1 unit. Finally, move right 2 units.
12. **Write About It** Does the ordered pair (3, 4) name point *Q*? Explain.
   No. *Q* is named by the ordered pair (4, 3).

Mixed Review and Test Prep

Open Response

Use order of operations to evaluate each expression. (Ch. 5, Lesson 1)

13. 3 × (6 + 2) **24**
14. 19 − (7 × 2) **5**
15. 24 ÷ (7 − 3) **6**
16. 48 + (8 × 4) **80**
17. Write directions for locating a point whose coordinates are (9, 7). (Ch. 24, Lesson 1)
   Start at 0. Move right 9 units. Then move up 7 units.

Extra Practice See page 633, Set A.

3 Practice

Practice and Problem Solving

Select from **Exercises 3–17** as independent work. Emphasize that the grids students are working on are two-dimensional grids and that the two distances—horizontal and vertical—are required to name a location. Guide students to use capital letters to name the points.

4 Assess & Close

Math Talk in Action

Have students refer to the grid on page 617 to conclude the lesson. Ask them to explain how to locate point (5, 2) on the grid. Then have them give directions explaining how to go from (5, 2) to any other point graphed on the grid.

Math Journal Prompt

Have students write an explanation of how to name a point on a grid using an ordered pair. Encourage them to use illustrations.

Lesson Quiz

Use the quiz on Lesson Transparency 24.1.

Lesson 24.1 Transparency

Test Prep & Spiral Review

Use Test Prep Transparency 24.1.

Test Prep 24.1 Transparency

Enrichment 24.1

Name ______________ Date ________ Enrichment 24.1

The Fairground Theft

Below is a part of a map of the county fairgrounds. Someone has stolen a valuable piece of art from the art exhibit. Your job is to go to the various areas and gather clues about who stole the art and where it is hidden. Cut six small pieces of paper the same size. Number them 1, 2, 3, 4, 5, and 6. Fold them and mix them up. Then choose one. Go to the coordinates listed by the number you chose. Find the coordinates on the map to find out which exhibit is there. Then go to the clue list and look under the coordinates of the exhibit. After you have the clue, draw the next piece of paper.

Number	Coordinates	Number	Coordinates
1	(1, 6)	4	(5, 4)
2	(8, 6)	5	(3, 2)
3	(2, 4)	6	(9, 3)

County Fairgrounds

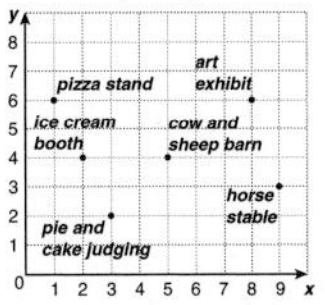

1. Who stole the art?
   Gaston
2. Where is the art hidden?
   The painting is hidden in a pizza box behind a display at the pie and cake judging exhibit.
3. Which clues helped you solve the mystery?
   (3, 2); (5, 4); (1, 6); (9, 3)

Clue List

(3, 2) A man came in with a pizza. He left the pizza behind a display. He was wearing a dark shirt.

(5, 4) I saw Gaston. He was wearing a purple shirt.

(2, 4) I saw Julietta. She was wearing a white shirt and had an umbrella. I thought it was odd because it wasn't raining.

(1, 6) A man in a purple shirt came in and asked for a large empty pizza box.

(8, 6) A painting is missing, but I saw nothing unusual. I talked with Nikolai and Julietta. They were both wearing light colored shirts.

(9, 3) I saw a man with a purple shirt carrying a pizza box. It looked very heavy – too heavy for pizza.

Use with text pages 616–617.

Problem Solving 24.1

Name ______________ Date ________ Problem Solving 24.1

Locate Points on a Grid

The map shows the location of the houses of several friends. Use the map for Problems 1–5.

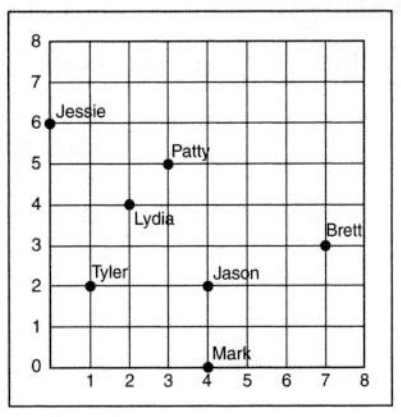

1. Describe how to find Patty's house on the map.
   Start at 0. Move right 3 units. Then move up 5 units.
2. What are the coordinates for Brett's house?
   (7, 3)
3. Name the ordered pairs for Mark's house and Jason's house. What relationship do you see?
   Mark (4, 0); Jason (4, 2). Possible answer: Mark and Jason are both 4 units to the right of 0.
4. Nicole decides to walk to Jessie's house and then go to Patty's house. Write directions explaining how to get to Jessie's house and then from Jessie's house to Patty's house.
   To get to Jessie's house, start at 0 and move 6 units up. Then to get to Patty's house from Jessie's, move 3 units right and 1 unit down.
5. Is the ordered pair for Jessie's house (6, 0)? Explain.
   No; The coordinates are (0, 6). From (0, 0) her house is located 0 units to the right and 6 units up.

Use with text pages 616–617.

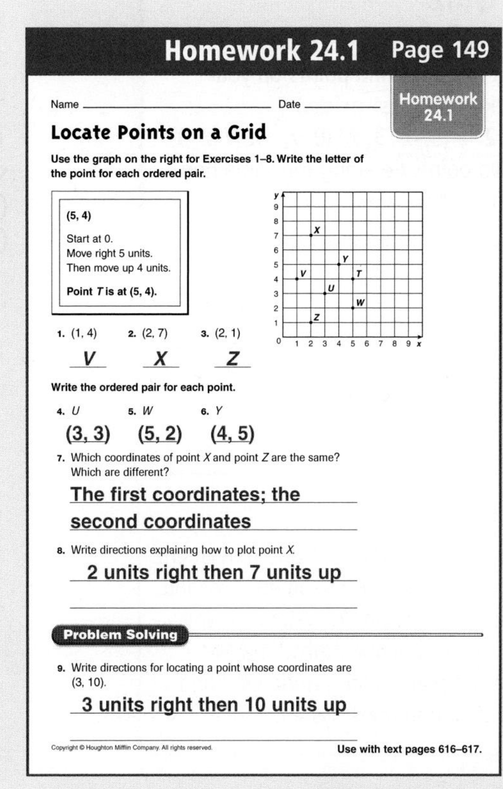

Homework 24.1 Page 149

Name ______________ Date ________ Homework 24.1

Locate Points on a Grid

Use the graph on the right for Exercises 1–8. Write the letter of the point for each ordered pair.

(5, 4)
Start at 0.
Move right 5 units.
Then move up 4 units.
Point *T* is at (5, 4).

1. (1, 4) ***V***
2. (2, 7) ***X***
3. (2, 1) ***Z***

Write the ordered pair for each point.

4. *U* **(3, 3)**
5. *W* **(5, 2)**
6. *Y* **(4, 5)**
7. Which coordinates of point *X* and point *Z* are the same? Which are different?
   The first coordinates; the second coordinates
8. Write directions explaining how to plot point *X.*
   2 units right then 7 units up

Problem Solving

9. Write directions for locating a point whose coordinates are (3, 10).
   3 units right then 10 units up

Use with text pages 616–617.

Lesson 24.2

Algebra: Graph Ordered Pairs

Planning

Lesson Objective Use ordered pairs to plot points on a grid.

Technology Resources

- Audio Tutor **2**/33 Listen and Understand
- *Ways to Success* CD-ROM 24.2
- *Ways to Assess* CD-ROM
- Education Place: Extra Practice, eGlossary, eGames www.eduplace.com/map

Lesson 24.2 Transparency

Problem of the Day

Carmen entered a stairwell on the 5th floor. She climbed 8 floors of stairs, delivered a message, and then walked down 3 flights to the cafeteria. What floor of the building is the cafeteria on? (10th floor)

Spiral Review

1. **What can you say about points with the same first coordinate?** (They are all the same number of spaces to the right [horizontal distance] from 0.)
2. **Where is the point (0, 3) located?** (3 spaces up along the vertical axis)

Lesson Quiz

Make a grid labeled from 0–10 on each axis. Plot each of the following points on your grid. (Check students' grids.)

1. *A* (5, 7) **2.** *B* (3, 0) **3.** *M* (0, 7) **4.** *N* (2, 3)

5. Which two points lie along the same horizontal line? (*A* and *M*)

NCTM Standards

Geometry: Describe location and movement using common language and geometric vocabulary; make and use coordinate systems to specify locations and to describe paths; find the distance between points along horizontal and vertical lines of a coordinate system.

Getting Started

Building Math Vocabulary

plot to place points in the coordinate plane

Introduce the term ***plot*** using the vocabulary card. Discuss the similarities between the mathematical meaning of *plot* and its everyday meaning: to mark the position of something on a map, diagram, or chart. Discuss other familiar meanings of the word.

Identifying Points on a Grid

Whole Class	5 minutes
Objective	Identify and locate points on a grid.
Materials	First-Quadrant Grid Transparency
Tactual, Visual	

- Students have learned that ordered pairs represent points on a grid. Now they will learn that the points represent horizontal and vertical movements on the grid.
- Use the First-Quadrant Grid Transparency. Mark several points with capital letters. Have volunteers identify the coordinates of the points you name. Then name the coordinates of different points and have students identify the letters located at those points.
- To summarize students' understanding, ask: **Is the ordered pair (3, 4) the same as the ordered pair (4, 3)?** (No; the first point is 3 to the right and 4 up, while the second is 4 to the right and 3 up.)
- Tell students that the lesson will show how to plot points on a grid.

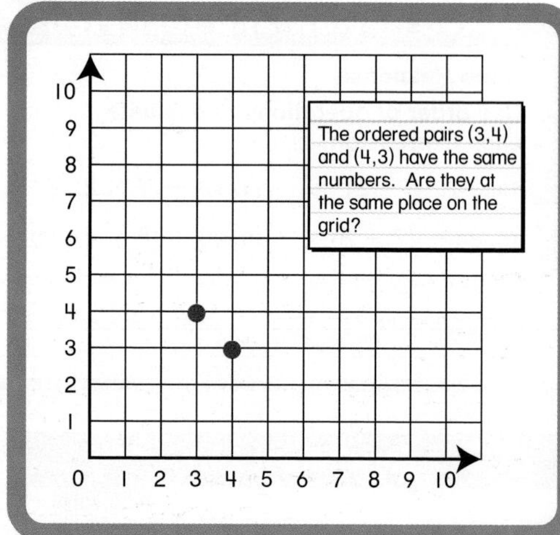

The ordered pairs (3,4) and (4,3) have the same numbers. Are they at the same place on the grid?
0 1 2 3 4 5 6 7 8 9 10
1 2 3 4 5 6 7 8 9 10

Differentiated Instruction

English Learners

Pairs	5 minutes
Objective	Plot points on a grid.
Materials	Coordinate grid
Visual, Auditory	

Early Production

- Have student pairs practice plotting points verbally. Model the problem below, and then have students complete the ***Guided Practice.***
- Student A says: *Plot the point five, two.* While finding the point, Student B says: *Move five units to the right, move two units up. Coordinates are five, two.*

Intermediate/Advanced

- English Learner Resource 24.2
- English Learner Handbook

Intervention

Small Groups	5–10 minutes
Objective	Plot points on a grid.
Materials	Workmat 6
Visual, Tactual	

- Distribute workmats. Guide students to draw a simple 10 × 10 coordinate map of the neighborhood around their school. Have them draw an upward arrow along the vertical scale.
- Use estimation to help students place local landmarks on the grid.

Ask questions such as: **What are the coordinates here at the bank? I am at the grocery store. How do I walk to the school?**

Other Resources

- *Ways to Success* CD-ROM 24.2

Gifted & Talented

Individuals	5 minutes
Objective	Identify points on a coordinate grid.
Materials	Coordinate grid
Visual, Tactual	

- Have students play a version of tick-tack-toe called "Four in a Row." In this game, the goal is to be the first to mark 4 points in a row horizontally, vertically, or diagonally.
- One student marks Xs, the other marks Os. Players take turns naming ordered pairs to mark with a point.

Four in a Row

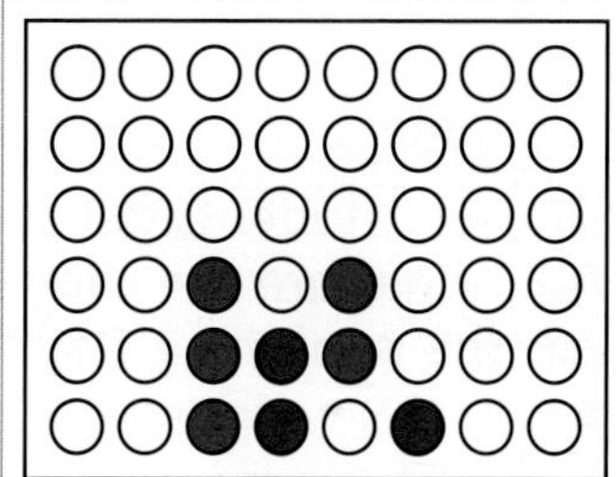

First player to get four in a row wins.

Soical Studies Connection

Materials: Coordinate grid

- Codes are systems of secret writing.
- Have pairs make up a secret word or message by placing letters on the grid in code.
- Once students have placed the letters at different points, they list in order the points that spell their messages.

❶ Introduce

Write the ordered pair (5, 7) on the board. Explain that the first coordinate, 5, represents the distance to the right of 0. The second coordinate, 7, represents the distance up from 0. Explain that the lesson shows how to use ordered pairs to plot points.

❷ Teach

Learn About It

Have students read aloud the opening paragraph. Then work through plotting the point (5, 7) to show that it falls within the ship. **Is the point named by (7, 4) inside the ship?** (no)

Then use the overhead transparency to plot points (1, 8), (3, 8), and (7, 8) with students' help. Draw a line connecting the points. **What can we say about this line? Why?** (parallel to horizontal axis; second coordinate in each point on the line is same direction up from 0)

Guided Practice

Have students complete **Exercises 1–6** as you observe. Remind them to use the ***Ask Yourself*** questions to help. Give students the opportunity to talk about the questions posed in ***Explain Your Thinking.***

❸ Practice

Practice and Problem Solving

Select from **Exercises 7–17** as independent work. Check students' points and labels.

- ***Problem 17*** Help students get started as needed. Ask: **What are the coordinates of the data for the rainfall on Day 1? How do you know?** [(1, 2); days are plotted by distances to the right of 0, while rainfall is plotted by distances up from 0]
- Guide students to use a straightedge to draw a line segment that connects the points.

Common Error

- **Not starting at 0**
- **Intervention** To help students avoid this mistake, guide them to highlight 0 with a marker or to write *Start* at 0.

Lesson 2

Audio Tutor 2/33 Listen and Understand

Algebra

Graph Ordered Pairs

Objective Use ordered pairs to plot points on a grid.

Vocabulary
plot

Learn About It

Mia and Luis are playing *Sink the Ship* at a party. They each color 4 rectangles on a grid. Then they take turns naming coordinates of a point. If the point is inside a rectangle, they have hit a ship.

To check, players **plot** the points on their grid. The first coordinate tells the horizontal distance from 0. The second coordinate tells the vertical distance from 0.

Mia names (5, 7). Did she hit one of Luis's ships?

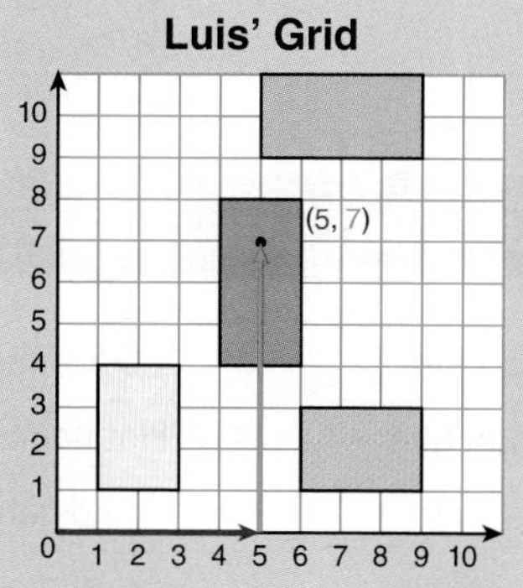

▶ **Plot the point named by (5, 7).**

- Start at 0. Move 5 units to the right.
- Next, move 7 units up.
- Then make a dot on the point.
- Label the point (5, 7).

Solution: Yes, Mia hit a ship. The point named by (5, 7) is inside a rectangle.

Guided Practice

Is the point named by each ordered pair in a rectangle?

1. (5, 2) **No**
2. (9, 4) **No**
3. (2, 3) **Yes**
4. (9, 8) **No**
5. (5, 5) **Yes**
6. (7, 10) **Yes**

Ask Yourself

- Did I move the correct number of units horizontally?
- Did I move the correct number of units vertically?

Explain Your Thinking ▶ Do (3, 5) and (5, 3) name the same point? Why or why not? **No. (3, 5) names a point that is 3 units to the right and 5 units up. (5, 3) names a point that is 5 units to the right and 3 units up.**

618

Extra Practice, See page 633, Set A.

Reteach 24.2

Name ______________ Date ________ Reteach 24.2

Algebra: Graph Ordered Pairs

Plot the point named by (2, 3). Label the point W.

Step 1	Step 2	Step 3
Start at 0.	The first number in the ordered pair tells you to move 2 units to the right.	The second number in the ordered pair tells you to move 3 units up. Make a dot and label it *W*.

Plot each point and label it with the correct letter.

1. *A* (3, 4)
2. *B* (5, 2)
3. *C* (6, 7)
4. *D* (2, 2)
5. *E* (8, 7)
6. *F* (4, 0)
7. *G* (4, 6)
8. *H* (0, 3)
9. *I* (3, 8)
10. *J* (5, 5)

Use with text pages 618–619.

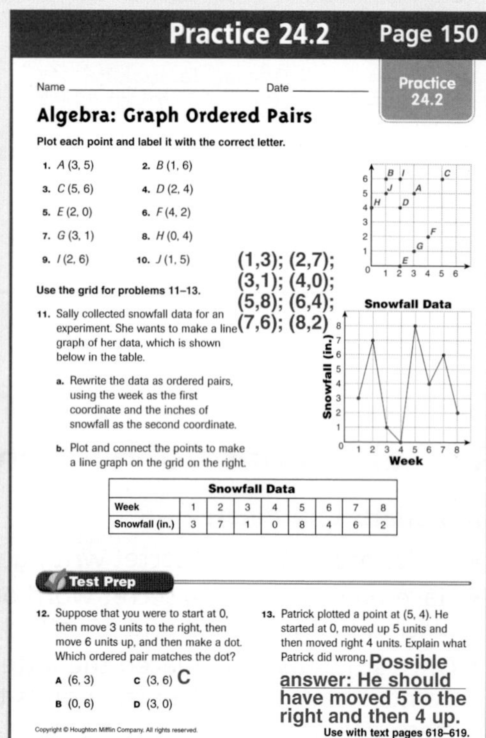

Practice 24.2 Page 150

Name ______________ Date ________ Practice 24.2

Algebra: Graph Ordered Pairs

Plot each point and label it with the correct letter.

1. *A* (3, 5)
2. *B* (1, 6)
3. *C* (5, 6)
4. *D* (2, 4)
5. *E* (2, 0)
6. *F* (4, 2)
7. *G* (3, 1)
8. *H* (0, 4)
9. *I* (2, 6)
10. *J* (1, 5)

Use the grid for problems 11–13.

11. Sally collected snowfall data for an experiment. She wants to make a line graph of her data, which is shown below in the table.
    a. Rewrite the data as ordered pairs, using the week as the first coordinate and the inches of snowfall as the second coordinate. **(1,3); (2,7); (3,1); (4,0); (5,8); (6,4); (7,6); (8,2)**
    b. Plot and connect the points to make a line graph on the grid on the right.

Snowfall Data

Week	1	2	3	4	5	6	7	8
Snowfall (in.)	3	7	1	0	8	4	6	2

Test Prep

12. Suppose that you were to start at 0, then move 3 units to the right, then move 6 units up, and then make a dot. Which ordered pair matches the dot?
    A (6, 3)
    B (0, 6)
    C (3, 6) **C**
    D (3, 0)
13. Patrick plotted a point at (5, 4). He started at 0, moved up 5 units and then moved right 4 units. Explain what Patrick did wrong. **Possible answer: He should have moved 5 to the right and then 4 up.**

Use with text pages 618–619.

Practice and Problem Solving

Copy the grid. Plot each point and label it with the correct letter.
See Additional Answers.

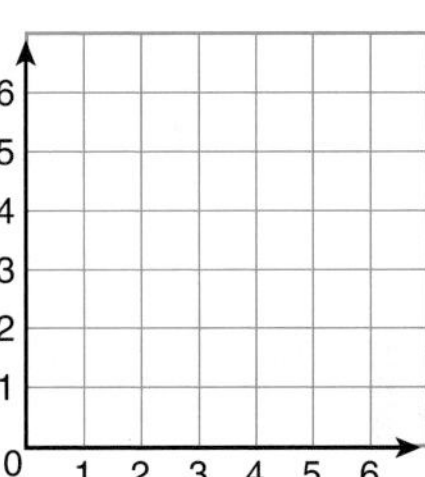

7. *E* (1, 4) **8.** *R* (6, 6)

9. *W* (0, 1) **10.** *L* (6, 1)

11. *T* (4, 3) **12.** *M* (1, 6)

13. *X* (4, 1) **14.** *S* (6, 4)

15. *Z* (6, 3) **16.** *P* (3, 1)

17. Karen collected rainfall data for a science experiment. She wants to make a line graph of her data, which is shown at the right.

a. Rewrite the data as ordered pairs. Use the day as the first coordinate and the inches of rainfall as the second coordinate.
(1, 2), (2, 0), (3, 0), (4, 3), (5, 4), (6, 1)

b. Copy the grid below. Then plot and connect the points to make a line graph.
See Additional Answers.

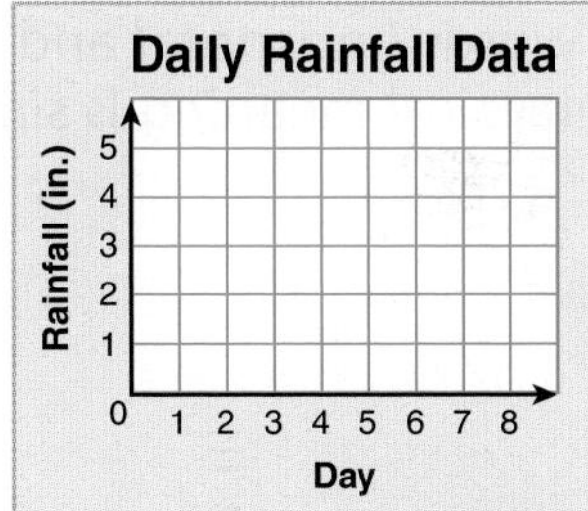

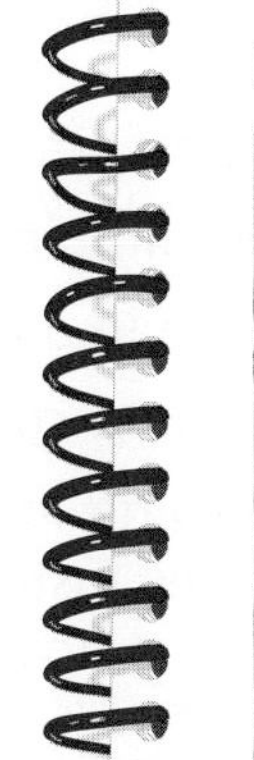

Karen

Rainfall Data	
Day	Rainfall (in.)
1	2
2	0
3	0
4	3
5	4
6	1

Quick Check

Check your understanding of Lessons 1–2.

Use the table for Problems 1–2. (Lessons 1–2)
See Additional Answers.

1. Write the pairs of data as ordered pairs. Use the number of bags as the first coordinate. Then plot and connect the points named by the ordered pairs.
(1, 3), (2, 6), (3, 9)

2. How many toys would be in 5 bags?
15 toys

Grab Bags	
Number of Bags	Number of Toys
1	3
2	6
3	9

Extra Practice at **eduplace.com/map**

4 Assess & Close

Math Talk in Action

Have students refer to the grid on page 618 to conclude the lesson. Ask them to name and plot 3 points that are not inside any of the ships.

Math Journal Prompt

Have students write an illustrated explanation of how to name a point on a grid using an ordered pair.

Lesson Quiz

Use the quiz on Lesson Transparency 24.2.

Lesson 24.2 Transparency

Test Prep & Spiral Review

Use Test Prep Transparency 24.2.

Quick Check

The *Quick Check* allows you to assess the students' understanding of the concepts presented in Lessons 1–2.

Items	Objectives Tested	Pages	Intervention
1–2	Use ordered pairs to name points on a grid; use ordered pairs to plot points on a grid.	616–619	Reteach Resources 24.1, 24.2 *Ways to Success* CD-ROM 24.1, 24.2

Enrichment 24.2

Name ______________ Date ________

Enrichment 24.2

Coordinate Hide-and-Seek

Here is a game you can play with another student.

- Out of sight of the other player, circle 5 different points on the first coordinate graph below. Then write the ordered pair that names each point. These are the points you are hiding. The other player should do the same.
- Each player should keep his or her graphs hidden from the other player.
- Take turns guessing a coordinate—for example, (5, 3). Mark the coordinate you guess on the second coordinate graph below so that you have a record of your guesses.
- If the other player guesses one of the coordinates you have circled, say "Found One" and he/she can circle that point on his/her second graph.
- The game is over when the first person finds all five of the other player's hidden coordinates.

Answers will vary.

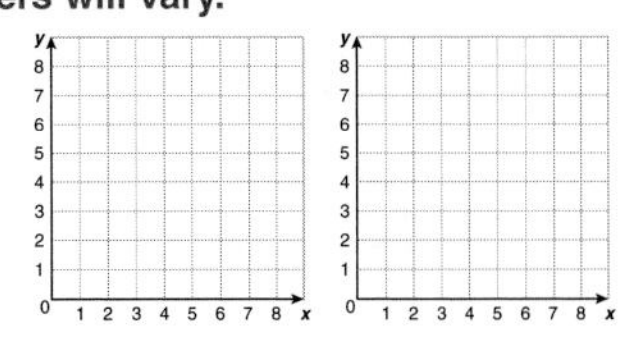

Use with text pages 618–619.

Problem Solving 24.2

Name ______________ Date ________

Problem Solving 24.2

Graph Ordered Pairs

Copy the grid. Use the grid for Problems 1–4.

1. Plot the points in the table below on the grid.

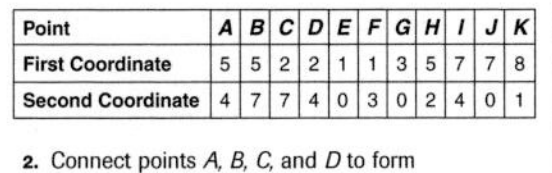

Point	A	B	C	D	E	F	G	H	I	J	K
First Coordinate	5	5	2	2	1	1	3	5	7	7	8
Second Coordinate	4	7	7	4	0	3	0	2	4	0	1

2. Connect points *A, B, C,* and *D* to form a quadrilateral. What type of quadrilateral is *ABCD*?
square

3. Connect points *E, F,* and *G* to form a triangle. What type of triangle is triangle *EFG*?
right

4. Connect points *H, I, K,* and *J* to form a quadrilateral. What type of quadrilateral is *HIKJ*?
trapezoid

5. **What's Wrong?** A student plotted the point (4, 3) on the grid and labeled it *S*. What did the student do wrong? Plot the correct answer.
The student plotted (3, 4) not (4, 3). The student plotted the point that is 3 units to the right and 4 units up. The correct point should be 4 units to the right and 3 units up.

Use with text pages 618–619.

Homework 24.2 Page 150

Name ______________ Date ________

Homework 24.2

Algebra: Graph Ordered Pairs

Plot each point and label it with the correct letter on the grid.

***Z* (3, 5)**

- Start at 0.
- Move right 3 units.
- Then move up 5 units.
- Then make a dot on the point.
- Label the point *Z*.

1. *A* (1, 3) 2. *B* (3, 2)
3. *C* (4, 4) 4. *D* (2, 5)
5. *E* (0, 6) 6. *F* (6, 3)
7. *G* (5, 0) 8. *H* (2, 1)
9. *I* (4, 1) 10. *J* (2, 2)

Problem Solving

11. Beth collected data on how many hours she spent on chores each day. She made a line graph of the data. Complete the table, using the day as the first coordinate and the number of hours as the second coordinate.

Chores	
Day	Hours
1	2
2	3
3	1
4	4
5	2

Chores

Use with text pages 618–619.

Lesson 24.3

Algebra: Graph Functions

Planning

Lesson Objective Plot ordered pairs from a function table and draw a line to help you solve problems.

Technology Resources

- *Ways to Success* CD-ROM 24.3
- Education Place: Extra Practice, eGlossary, eGames, Brain Teasers www.eduplace.com/map

Problem of the Day

A local recycling company will pay 2 cents for each aluminum can. How much will Jed earn if he sells 60 aluminum cans? ($1.20)

Spiral Review

Write each money amount.

1. 3 quarters ($0.75)
2. 5 quarters ($1.25)
3. 8 quarters ($2.00)
4. 16 quarters ($4.00)

Lesson Quiz

Solve.

1. Juice cans come in packages of 4. What function could you write to show how many cans of juice (y) are in x packages ($y = 4x$)
2. Let y stand for a number of turkey hot dogs. Let x stand for how many are in a package. What function could you write to show how many turkey hot dogs you would get if you bought 5 packages? ($y = 5x$)

NCTM Standards

Geometry: Describe location and movement using common language and geometric vocabulary; make and use coordinate systems to specify locations and to describe paths; find the distance between points along horizontal and vertical lines of a coordinate system.

Getting Started

Building Math Vocabulary

origin a point where the *x*- and *y*-axes intersect in a coordinate plane

***x*-axis** the horizontal number line in a coordinate system

***y*-axis** the vertical number line in a coordinate system

axes the number lines used in a coordinate plane

Display a grid on the overhead and identify the ***x*-axis** and ***y*-axis**. Guide students to use these terms for **axes** instead of the words *horizontal* and *vertical*. Introduce the term **origin**. Discuss how its mathematical meaning is similar to its ordinary meaning.

Graphing Functions

Whole Class	10 minutes
Objective	Write ordered pairs for a function rule.
Materials	Table II Transparency, First-Quadrant Grid Transparency
Visual, Auditory	

- Fill in the Table II Transparency as shown.
- Place the First-Quadrant Grid Transparency on top. Label the *y*-axis *Number of Pens* and the *x*-axis *Number of Packages*.
- Tell students that data in a function table can be expressed as ordered pairs, represented on the *x*- and *y*-axes. ((1, 2), (2, 4), (3, 6))

Packages of Pens		Equation: y = 2x
x (no. of packages)	y (no. of pens)	Ordered Pair
1	2	
2	4	
3	6	

Differentiated Instruction

English Learners

Pairs	5–10 minutes
Objective	Identify and label a coordinate grid.
Materials	Student page 621
Visual, Tactual	

Early Production

- Before ***Guided Practice,*** have students practice identifying and labeling a grid. Give students a grid with the *x*-axis, *y*-axis, and origin mislabeled. Label 3 points with coordinates in reversed order.
- In pairs, students find mistakes, explain what was done wrong, and make a new graph with corrections.

Intermediate/Advanced

- English Learner Resource 24.3
- English Learner Handbook

Intervention

Small Groups	10–15 minutes
Objective	Plot ordered pairs.
Materials	Workmat 6, straightedges
Visual, Tactual	

- Distribute workmats and have students plot and connect the points as described in these problems. Review and discuss their answers.
- **What figure will you get if you plot the following points and connect them with line segments in the order (2, 2), (5, 2), (5, 5), (2, 5)?** (square)
- **What figure will you get if you plot the points (1, 3), (5, 3), and (5, 8) and connect them?** (right triangle)

Other Resources

- *Ways to Success* CD-ROM 24.3

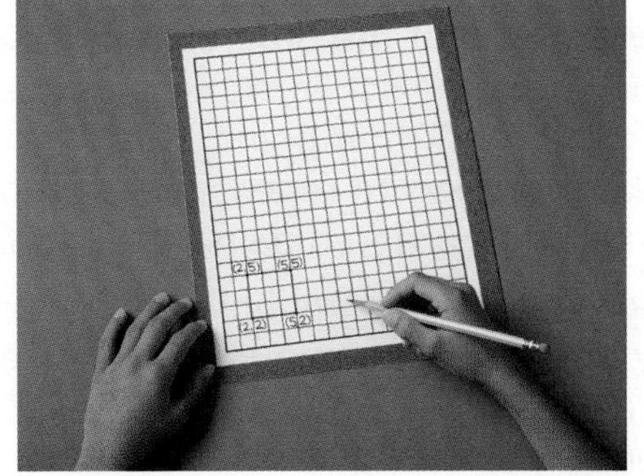

Early Finishers

Individuals	5 minutes
Objective	Plot ordered pairs from a function table.
Materials	Grid paper, straightedge
Visual, Tactual	

- Ask students to extend one of the graphs in the lesson to find greater numbers of fans, rings, or noisemakers.
- Alternatively, challenge students to make up their own function tables of data about party favors, and then graph the data by plotting and connecting ordered pairs representing the data.

Real-World Connection

- Discuss with students that functions abound in real life, which is full of patterns. Provide examples, such as $y = x \div 2$, to find how much comic books cost if you and your friend always share equally the price of every one you buy.
- Have pairs of students work together to come up with some everyday functions. Ask them to list their data in a function table first and then use that data to make a graph. Display students' tables and graphs.

Facts Practice

- Group students into pairs, and give each pair 24 index cards. Have each pair use half the cards to write 12 multiplication facts they find difficult to remember. On the other half, have them write the products.
- Have students play *Memory* with their decks: Students place the cards face-down in a 6×4 grid and take turns turning over two cards. If the cards match (one card contains the factors and the other the product) the student keeps the cards and takes another turn. If they do not match, they are turned face-down again and play passes to the other student.
- Have pairs trade decks with other pairs and play again.

❶ Introduce

Explain to students that the data in a function table can be expressed as ordered pairs, which can then be plotted as points on a grid. When all points are plotted, they can be connected by a line to show a pattern.

❷ Teach

Learn About It

- **Fans are sold in packages of 2. To find how many fans are in 4 packages, we can graph the points from the table. Before plotting the ordered pairs from the function table, let's first write the data in the table as ordered pairs. What ordered pair can we write for the first pair of numbers?** (1, 2) Then invite volunteers to give the ordered pairs for the other pairs of numbers. (2, 4); (3, 6)
- **How do we plot the ordered pair (1, 2)?** (Start at 0. Move 1 unit to the right and then move 2 units up.) Mark that point (1, 2) with a dot. Invite volunteers to repeat the procedure for the other ordered pairs in the table.
- **Look at the points we have plotted. Do they appear to lie on a line?** (yes) Use a straightedge to connect the dots. Then extend the line segment. Draw an arrow at its end to indicate that the line goes on indefinitely. **How can we use the line to find the number of fans in 4 packages?** (Start at 0. Move 4 units to the right and then move up to meet the line.) **Where did we cross the line?** (at y 5 8) **So, how many fans are in 4 packages?** (8) **What ordered pair names this point on the line?** (4, 8)
- Guide students through ***Step 3*** to find the number of fans in 5 packages.

Common Error

- **Graphing mistakes**
- **Intervention** Guide students to make sure to plot at least 3 sets of ordered pairs before they draw or extend a line to solve a problem.

Lesson 3

Algebra

Graph Functions

Objective Plot ordered pairs from a function table and draw a line to help you solve problems.

Vocabulary
origin
x-axis
y-axis
axes

Learn About It

Hiroko is buying fans to use as party favors. Each package has 2 fans. She wants to know how many fans are in 5 packages.

Hiroko could find the answer by extending the table on the right or by solving the equation $y = 2x$. She could also find the answer by graphing points.

Packages of Fans $y = 2x$

Number of Packages (x)	Number of Fans (y)
1	2
2	4
3	6

Here's how to graph points to find the number of fans in 5 packages.

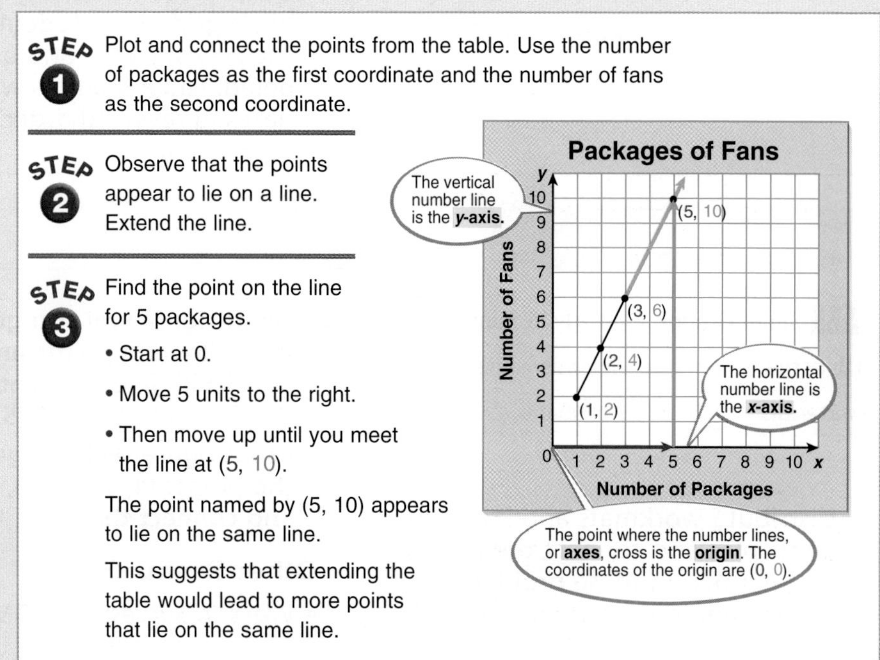

STEP 1 Plot and connect the points from the table. Use the number of packages as the first coordinate and the number of fans as the second coordinate.

STEP 2 Observe that the points appear to lie on a line. Extend the line.

STEP 3 Find the point on the line for 5 packages.

- Start at 0.
- Move 5 units to the right.
- Then move up until you meet the line at (5, 10).

The point named by (5, 10) appears to lie on the same line.

This suggests that extending the table would lead to more points that lie on the same line.

Packages of Fans
The vertical number line is the *y*-axis.
(1, 2)
(2, 4)
(3, 6)
(5, 10)
Number of Fans
Number of Packages
The horizontal number line is the *x*-axis.
The point where the number lines, or **axes**, cross is the **origin**. The coordinates of the origin are (0, 0).

Solution: There are 10 fans in 5 packages.

620

Reteach 24.3

Name ______ Date ______ Reteach 24.3

Graph Functions

Megan is making bags of apples. Each bag contains 3 apples. She wants to know how many apples she will need for 4 bags.

Bags of Apples $y = 3x$

x (number of bags)	y (number of apples)
1	3
2	6
3	9

Use the pairs of data in the table to write the ordered pairs: (1, 3), (2, 6), (3, 9)

Plot the ordered pairs and connect the points with a line. Extend the line.

Find the point on the line for 4 bags. Start at 0. Move 4 units to the right. Move up to meet the point (4, 12).

Megan will need 12 apples for 4 bags.

Use the grid and the table for Problems 1–3.

Jill's and Roy's Ages $y = x + 2$

x (Jill's age)	y (Roy's age)
1	3
2	4
3	5

1. Write the pairs of data in the table as ordered pairs. (1, 3); (2, 4); (3, 5)
2. Plot the points and connect them. Extend the line segment.
3. Use the graph to decide how old Roy will be when Jill is 6 years old. 8 years old

Use with text pages 620–622.

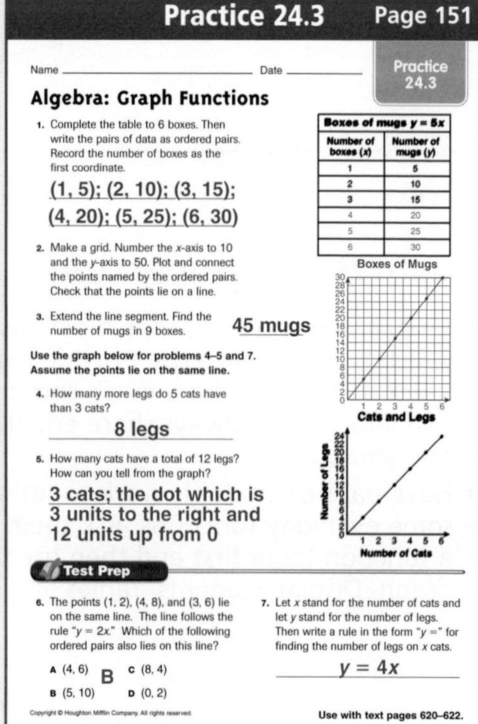

Practice 24.3 Page 151

Name ______ Date ______ Practice 24.3

Algebra: Graph Functions

1. Complete the table to 6 boxes. Then write the pairs of data as ordered pairs. Record the number of boxes as the first coordinate. (1, 5); (2, 10); (3, 15); (4, 20); (5, 25); (6, 30)

Boxes of mugs $y = 5x$

Number of boxes (x)	Number of mugs (y)
1	5
2	10
3	15
4	20
5	25
6	30

2. Make a grid. Number the x-axis to 10 and the y-axis to 50. Plot and connect the points named by the ordered pairs. Check that the points lie on a line.
3. Extend the line segment. Find the number of mugs in 9 boxes. 45 mugs

Use the graph below for problems 4–5 and 7. Assume the points lie on the same line.

4. How many more legs do 5 cats have than 3 cats? 8 legs
5. How many cats have a total of 12 legs? How can you tell from the graph? 3 cats; the dot which is 3 units to the right and 12 units up from 0

Boxes of Mugs
Cats and Legs
Number of Legs
Number of Cats

Test Prep

6. The points (1, 2), (4, 8), and (3, 6) lie on the same line. The line follows the rule "$y = 2x$." Which of the following ordered pairs also lies on this line? B
   A (4, 6) C (8, 4)
   B (5, 10) D (0, 2)
7. Let x stand for the number of cats and let y stand for the number of legs. Then write a rule in the form "$y =$" for finding the number of legs on x cats. $y = 4x$

Use with text pages 620–622.

Guided Practice

Use the grid and the table below for Problems 1–3.

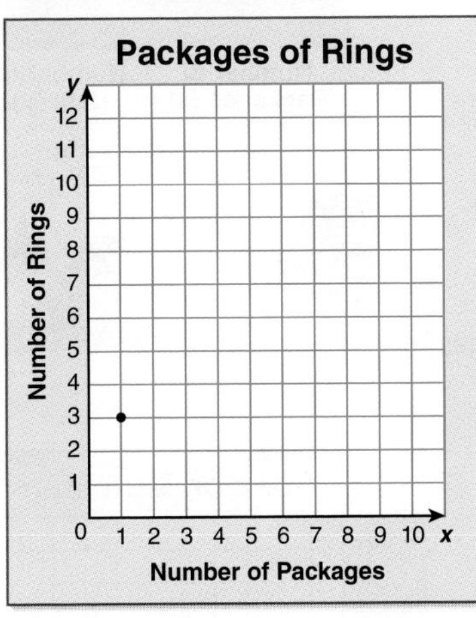

Ask Yourself

- Did I record ordered pairs in the correct order?
- Are all points on a line?

Packages of Rings $y = 3x$	
Number of Packages (x)	Number of Rings (y)
1	3
2	6
3	9

1. Write the data in the table as ordered pairs. Use the number of packages as the first coordinate. Use the number of rings as the second coordinate. **(1, 3), (2, 6), (3, 9)**
2. Copy the grid and the point named by the first ordered pair. Plot and connect the other points. Extend the line. Check that the points lie on a line. ***See Additional Answers.***
3. Use the graph to find the number of rings in 4 packages. **12 rings**

Explain Your Thinking ▶ Do you think the point named by (6, 16) lies on the line? **No. For each point on the line, the second coordinate is three times the first coordinate. Since 16 is not 3 × 6, (6, 16) does not lie on the line.**

Practice and Problem Solving

Packages of Noisemakers $y = 4x$	
Number of Packages (x)	Number of Noisemakers (y)
1	4
2	8
3	12

4. Copy the table at the right and extend it to 6 packages. Then write the pairs of data as ordered pairs. Use the number of packages as the first coordinate. **(1, 4), (2, 8), (3, 12), (4, 16), (5, 20), (6, 24)**
5. Make a grid. Label the x-axis to 10 and the y-axis to 34. Plot and connect the points named by the ordered pairs. Check that the points lie on a line. ***See Additional Answers.***
6. Extend the line. Find the number of noisemakers in 8 packages. ***See Additional Answers;* 32 noisemakers**

Guided Practice

Have students complete **Exercises 1–3** as you observe. Remind them to use the ***Ask Yourself*** question to help. Give students the opportunity to talk about the question in ***Explain Your Thinking.***

3 Practice

Practice and Problem Solving

Select from **Problems 4–17** as independent work, or have students work in pairs to check each other's graphs and answers. Ask: **What is the relationship between the ordered pairs in a function table and the graph of that same function?** (They show the identical information.)

- Circulate as students work. Guide them to double-check that they have plotted points correctly before they connect them. **What might be wrong if you are unable to draw a line segment to connect all your points?** (ordered pairs plotted incorrectly)
- You may wish to write *(x, y): (horizontal, vertical)* on the board. Students can refer to it as a reminder as they work.
- ***Problem 11*** **What number sentences can you write for this problem?** ((3 × 5) − (1 × 5) = 10, or 15 − 5 = 10))

Enrichment 24.3

Name ______________ Date ________ Enrichment 24.3

Party Graphs

Melia is planning a party. She graphed the cost of items she needs for her party. She forgot to label the graphs. Match each graph with the items she has priced. Then label the graphs for her. Next to each graph, write the function each graph shows.

Price List	Labels
Pizza – 1 medium pizza for $6.00	Number of Pizzas; Cost of Pizzas
Balloons – 3 balloons for $1.00	Number of Balloons; Cost of Balloons
Streamers – 4 packages for $2.00	Number of Packages; Cost of Streamers
Frozen Yogurt – $5.00 for a gallon	Number of Gallons; Cost of Frozen Yogurt

Number of Gallons — $5y = x$ — Cost of Frozen Yogurt

Number of Packages — $y = 2x$ — Cost of Streamers

Number of Balloons — $y = 3x$ — Cost of Balloons

Number of Pizzas — $6y = x$ — Cost of Pizzas

Use with text pages 620–622.

Problem Solving 24.3

Name ______________ Date ________ Problem Solving 24.3

Graph Functions

1. Brandy is making muffins. She can make 6 muffins using one tray. Complete the table. Write the pairs of data as ordered pairs. Record the number of trays as the first coordinate. Then plot the points on a grid. Do all the points lie on a line?
   yes

Muffin Trays	
Number of Trays	Total Number of Muffins
1	6
2	**12**
3	**18**
4	**24**

2. Extend the line on the grid. How many muffins can Brandy make if she uses 8 muffin trays?
   48 muffins
3. Explain how to use the grid to find how many muffin trays are needed to make 42 muffins. **Look for 42 on the y-axis. Follow across the line. Find the x-coordinate of this point. 7 muffin trays.**
4. **Reasoning** Look at the graph. Let y stand for the number of muffins. Let x stand for the number of trays. Write a rule in the form "$y =$" for calculating the number of muffins in x trays.
   $y = 6x$
5. **Represent** Joyce wants to make a graph to find how many inches are in 5 feet. She knows that 1 foot = 12 inches. Write 4 points that could be on Joyce's graph.
   Possible answers: **(1,12), (2,24), (3,36), (4,48), (5,60) etc.**

Number of Muffins — Muffin Trays

Use with text pages 620–622.

Math Talk in Action

Have students refer to the graphs they have drawn to conclude the lesson.

- **Why is the graph of the points (1, 5), (2, 10), and (3, 15) a straight line?** (The second number in each ordered pair is always twice the first.)
- **What can you say about ordered pairs that lie along the same line?** (The relationship between the numbers in the ordered pairs is the same.)

Math Journal Prompt

Have students write an explanation of how to use ordered pairs from a function to plot a line in order to solve a problem. Have them include a simple table and a graph that shows the same data.

Lesson Quiz

Use the quiz on Lesson Transparency 24.3.

Test Prep & Spiral Review

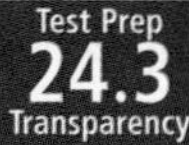

Use Test Prep Transparency 24.3.

Practice and Problem Solving

Use the table to complete Exercises 7–9.

7. There are 6 party hats in a package. Copy and complete the table. ***See answers at right.***
8. Make a grid. Label the x-axis to 7 and the y-axis to 38. Plot ordered pairs from the table. Use the number of packages as the first coordinate and the number of hats as the second coordinate. ***See Additional Answers.***
9. Check that the ordered pairs lie on the same line. Extend the line. How many hats are in 6 packages? ***See Additional Answers;* 36 hats**

Packages of Party Hats $y = 6x$

Number of Packages (x)	Number of Hats (y)
1	6
2	
3	

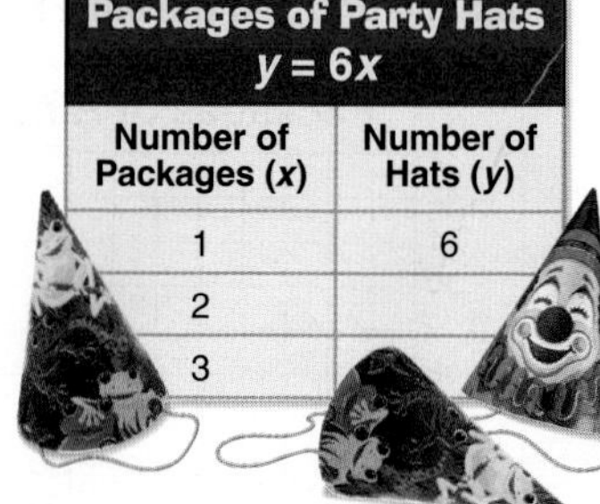

 **Data** **Use the graph for Problems 10–13. Assume the points lie on the same line.**

10. One mud star has 5 arms. How many arms do 3 mud stars have? **15 arms**
11. How many more arms do 3 mud stars have than 1 mud star? **10 more arms**
12. How many mud stars have a total of 10 arms? How can you tell from the graph? ***See Additional Answers.***
13. **Analyze** Let x stand for the number of mud stars. Let y stand for the number of arms. Write a rule for calculating the number of arms on x number of mud stars. $y = 5x$
14. Research the number of arms on a squid. Make a table showing the number of arms on up to 3 squids. Graph the data in the table. Then extend the line to find the number of arms on 4 squids. ***Check students' graphs.***

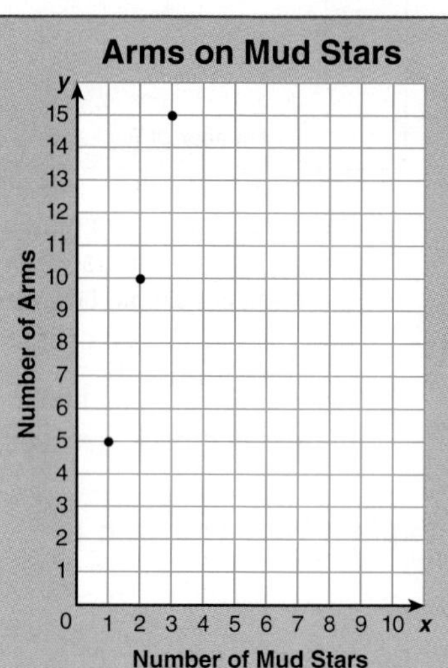

Mixed Review and Test Prep

Open Response

Write the probability of spinning blue as a fraction. (Ch. 23, Lesson 2)

15. 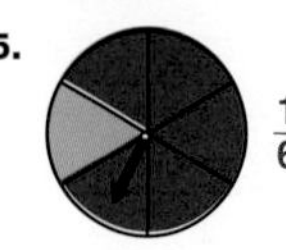 $\frac{1}{6}$

16. 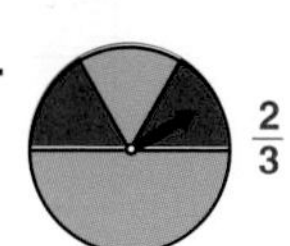 $\frac{2}{3}$

Multiple Choice

17. The points (1, 6), (2, 12), and (3, 18) lie on the same line. Which of the following ordered pairs also lies on this line? (Ch. 24, Lesson 3)

A (24, 4) C (6, 30)
B (6, 35) **D** (6, 36)

622

Extra Practice See page 633, Set B.

Homework 24.3 Page 151

Name ______ Date ______ Homework 24.3

Algebra: Graph Functions

Sarah is packing plates into boxes. Each box can fit 3 plates. She wants to know how many plates are in 6 boxes.

Find the number of plates by graphing the function $y = 3x$.

Step 1: Plot and **connect** the points from the table. Use the number of boxes as the x-coordinate and the number of plates as the y-coordinate.

Step 2: Extend the line segment to see how many plates will fit into larger numbers of boxes. The points should lie on a line.

Step 3: Find the point on the line for 6 boxes. Start at 0 and move 6 units to the right to match the number of boxes. Then move up to the meet the line at (6,18).

There are 18 plates in 6 boxes.

Boxes of Plates $y = 3x$

Number of boxes (x)	Number of plates (y)
1	3
2	6
3	9
4	12
5	15
6	18

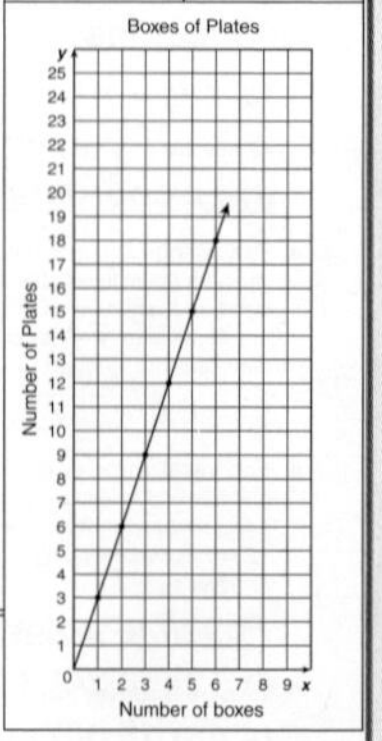

Boxes of Plates (graph: Number of Plates vs. Number of boxes)

1. Extend the graph. Find the number of plates in 8 boxes. **24 plates**
2. Thirty-six plates are in boxes. How many boxes were used. **12 boxes**

Problem Solving

3. Name three points that would lie on the line graphed by the function $y = 8x$. **Possible answers: (1, 8), (2, 16), (3, 24)**

Use with text pages 620–622.

Problem Solving

Visual Thinking
Research at Sea

A group of scientists are working at a research station. Use ordered pairs to describe the location of each of the following.

1. Research station (10,5)
2. Sea lions (11,1)
3. Research boat (0,0)
4. Killer whales (7,2)
5. Bottle-nosed dolphins (1, 6)
6. **Challenge** The shortest distance between two points on a flat surface is a straight line. Draw a straight line between the research boat and the research station. What 4 ordered pairs lie on this line? **(2, 1), (4, 2), (6, 3), (8, 4)**

Bottle-nosed Dolphins
Research Station
Killer Whales
Sea Lions
Research Boat

Algebraic Thinking
What's My Rule?

Choose the equation that shows the rule for the graph. Let *x* stand for the first coordinate. Let *y* stand for the second coordinate.

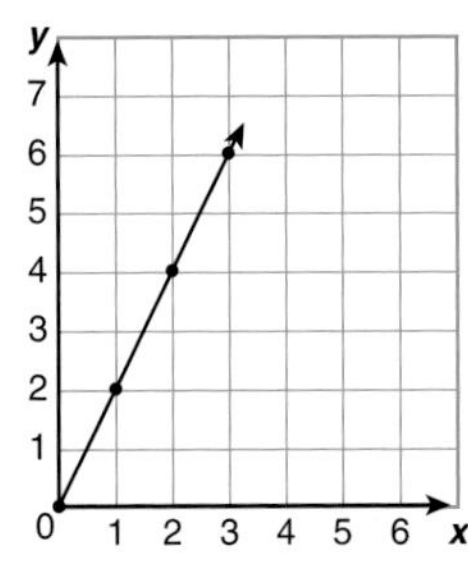

a. $y = x + 2$ (b.) $y = 2x$

Brain Teaser

Use the clues to find each ordered pair.

- The first coordinate is 8 times the only even prime number. The second coordinate is 3 more than the first. **(16, 19)**
- The first coordinate is 4 more than the second coordinate. The sum of the coordinates is the product of 2 and 7. **(9, 5)**

Education Place
Check out **eduplace.com/map** for more brain teasers.

Chapter 24 Lesson 3 623

Visual Thinking
Research at Sea

Tell students that to track animals in the wild, scientists tag them and keep a record of where they go. They use coordinates to describe the locations of the animals, much like we use ordered pairs to locate points on a grid.

Have students work in pairs on the activity. Invite them to share their findings with other pairs.

Algebraic Thinking
What's My Rule?

Have students explain how they figured out the equation for the rule. Challenge students to make a function table and from it graph a line based on the function rule. Have them ask each other to write the equation for their rule.

Brain Teaser

Review what prime numbers are (numbers with only two factors—themselves and 1). As needed, discuss the meaning of *even, sum,* and *product*. Then invite students to create their own brain teasers.

Technology Connection

Have students use Easy Sheet for the activity below.

- The table at the right shows the number of calories in *x* grams of protein. Have students input the data.
- Highlight cells A1 to B4. Click **Line Graph**. Double click the graph. In **Data**, put checks in the bottom 2 boxes. In **Labels**, check **Label Data;** label the axis.

Calories per Gram of Protein $y = 4x$	
Grams (x)	Calories (y)
1	4
2	8
3	12

Have students answer the following questions.

1. How could you use Easy Sheet to extend the graph to find the number of calories in 4 grams of protein?
2. How many calories are in 6 grams of protein?

Algebra: Integers

Planning

Lesson Objective Learn about integers.

Math Background

- A number line can be used to display integers—the set of positive whole numbers, their opposites, and zero. It is important to remember that the number line goes on forever in both directions.

Technology Resources

- *Ways to Success* CD-ROM 24.4
- Education Place: Extra Practice, eGlossary, eManipulatives, eGames www.eduplace.com/map

Lesson 24.4 Transparency

Problem of the Day

When Letitia woke up, the temperature was 71°F. Three hours later, she heard that the temperature had fallen 12°F. What was the temperature at that time? (59°F)

Spiral Review

Write a decimal equivalent to each fraction.

1. $\frac{4}{5}$ (0.8)	**2.** $\frac{3}{10}$ (0.3)
3. $2\frac{1}{4}$ (2.25)	**4.** $\frac{3}{4}$ (0.75)
5. $\frac{1}{5}$ (0.2)	**6.** $4\frac{9}{10}$ (4.9)

Lesson Quiz

Write the integer for each situation.

1. $6 earned ($^{+}6$)
2. 9 feet below sea level ($^{-}9$)
3. 12 yards lost running the football ($^{-}12$)
4. 24 stories above street level ($^{+}24$)

NCTM Standards

Number and Operations: Explore numbers less than 0 by extending the number line and through familiar applications.

Getting Started

Building Math Vocabulary

integers	the set of positive whole numbers, their opposites, and 0
opposite	an integer's opposite is the same distance from 0 as the integer, but in the opposite direction
negative integer	the opposite of a positive integer
positive integer	a whole number that is greater than 0

Discuss with students that **integers** can represent both positive and negative amounts, such as temperatures above and below 0. Guide students to read the numbers as *integers* rather than *minus;* they should say **negative 6** for $^{-}6$, not **minus 6.** Explain that all integers have an **opposite** and that 0 is its own opposite.

Identifying Integers

Whole Class	10 minutes
Objective	Learn about integers.
Materials	Number Lines Transparency, blank transparency
Visual, Tactual	

- Students have worked with positive integers as ordered pairs when graphing linear functions. Now they will consider the placement of negative integers on a number line.
- Use Number Line 1 from the Number Lines Transparency. Label it from $^{-}10$ to $^{+}10$. Mark and label points *A* ($^{-}3$), *B* ($^{-}1$), *C* (2), and *D* (6).
- Say: **Integers include positive whole numbers, their opposites, and 0. They can be shown on a number line. All negative integers are less than 0. All positive integers are greater than 0. How can you describe the location of point *A*?** (3 units left of 0) Draw an arrow below the number line from 0 to $^{-}3$. **What integer corresponds to point *A*?** ($^{-}3$) Then wipe off the arrow and repeat for the other three points.
- Relate integers on a number line to temperatures on a thermometer.

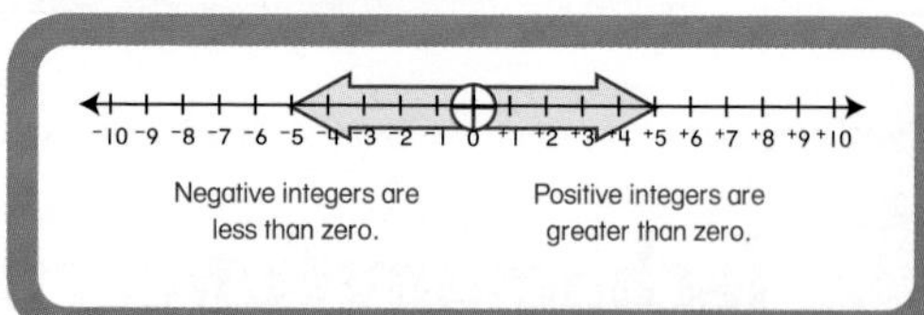
Negative integers are less than zero.
Positive integers are greater than zero.

Differentiated Instruction

English Learners

Whole Class	5–10 minutes
Objective	Learn about integers.
Materials	None
Visual, Tactual	

Early Production

- After discussing ***Learn About It,*** give students additional practice working with integers.
- Write ⁻5, ⁻2, 0, ⁺3, and ⁺4 on the board, and have students say the numbers and plot them on a number line. Then ask them to plot and say the opposites for each number.

Intermediate/Advanced

- English Learner Resource 24.4
- English Learner Handbook

Intervention

Small Groups	5 minutes
Objective	Learn about integers.
Materials	None
Auditory, Visual	

- To introduce the terms *positive* and *negative* as they relate to numbers, have students talk about familiar situations in which negative numbers are used. For example, they can suggest yardage in football games and temperatures below 0 degrees.
- To prepare students for writing integers to describe situations, have them tell whether situations such as the following indicate an increase or a decrease:
  - gaining weight (increase)
  - withdrawing money from a bank (decrease)
- Have students suggest other examples.

Other Resources

- *Ways to Success* CD-ROM 24.4

Early Finishers

Individuals	5 minutes
Objective	Model integers.
Materials	Number Lines Transparency, two-color counters
Visual, Tactual	

- Guide students to use yellow counters for positive numbers and red counters for negative numbers.
- Model how to show 4 degrees below zero: Show 4 red counters on Number Line 1. Write *negative 4* and ⁻*4* underneath them. Do the same with ⁺3. Repeat for other integers. Then ask students to name and model other situations.

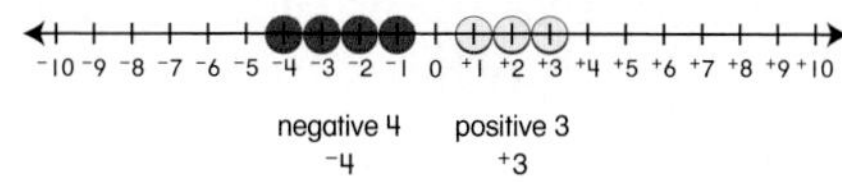

Alternate Teaching Strategy

- Display a large integer number line that includes integers from ⁻15 to 15. You may want to have a student volunteer draw this on the chalkboard.
- Begin at 0. Have students take turns rolling a number cube labeled 1–6. The student counts on from 0 to the number that is rolled. When the student lands on a number, ask, **Is it an integer? Is it positive or negative?**
- Have another student roll the number cube. This time, begin where the previous student left off and count back the number rolled. Ask if the number is an integer, and if it is positive or negative.
- Try the activity using a pair of number cubes, counting on or back the sum of both number cubes.

❶ Introduce

Explain to students that integers are simply the positive whole numbers 1, 2, 3 . . . , their opposites $^{-}1$, $^{-}2$, $^{-}3$ . . . , and 0. The lesson uses integers to describe temperatures, land elevations, and other real-world situations.

❷ Teach

Learn About It

Use Number Line 1 on the overhead to guide students through the *Learn About It* section.

- **Negative integers are the opposites of positive integers. Positive integers are the opposites of negative integers. Zero is neither positive nor negative. What is the opposite of negative 7?** (positive 7) Draw arrows to both integers. **What is the opposite of positive 9?** (negative 9) Wipe off the arrows and draw arrows to $^{-}9$ and 9. Then wipe off these arrows and repeat the question for other integers. **Why do you think these pairs of numbers are called opposites?** (same distance from 0 but on opposite sides of 0) **Negative 4 and positive 4 are opposites. How far apart are they on the number line?** (8 units)
- Have students focus on the number line on page 625, which they use to compare integers. Ask: **Why is every positive integer greater than every negative integer?** (Any positive integer is farther to the right than the negative integers.) **How is comparing two positive integers different from comparing two negative integers?** (For positive integers, the greater one is farther from 0; for two negative integers, the greater one is closer to 0.)
- Discuss *Other Examples* with students. Ask them to suggest other situations to add to both lists.

Common Error

- **Comparing integers incorrectly**
- **Intervention** Students may incorrectly compare integers by focusing on the numbers but not on their signs. Have students graph these integers on a number line. When comparing them, the integer to the right is always the greater one. Emphasize that any positive integer is greater than any negative integer.

Lesson 4

Algebra

Integers

Objective Learn about integers.

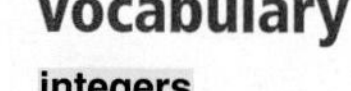

Vocabulary

integers
opposite
negative integer
positive integer

Learn About It

Carlos and Sara are playing a game at a party. In the first round, Carlos lost 4 points and Sara won 5 points. How will they record their scores?

To show he lost 4 points, Carlos writes $^{-}4$. To show she gained 5 points, Sara writes $^{+}5$.

The numbers $^{-}4$ and $^{+}5$ are **integers**.
$^{-}4$ is a **negative integer**.
$^{+}5$ is a **positive integer**. Positive 5 can be written either as $^{+}5$ or as 5.

▶ Integers include 0, the positive whole numbers, and the negative whole numbers.

Integers can be shown on a number line.

Negative integers are less than 0. | **Positive integers** are greater than 0.

$^{-}10$ $^{-}9$ $^{-}8$ $^{-}7$ $^{-}6$ $^{-}5$ $^{-}4$ $^{-}3$ $^{-}2$ $^{-}1$ 0 $^{+}1$ $^{+}2$ $^{+}3$ $^{+}4$ $^{+}5$ $^{+}6$ $^{+}7$ $^{+}8$ $^{+}9$ $^{+}10$

Zero is neither positive nor negative.

▶ All integers have an **opposite**. An integer's opposite is the same distance from 0 as the integer, but in the opposite direction. Zero is its own opposite.

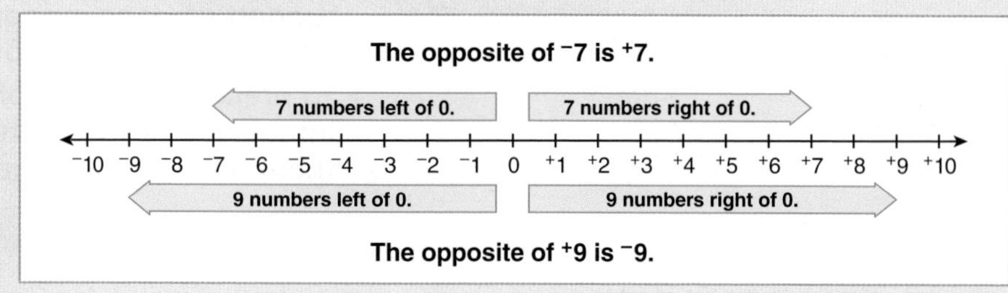

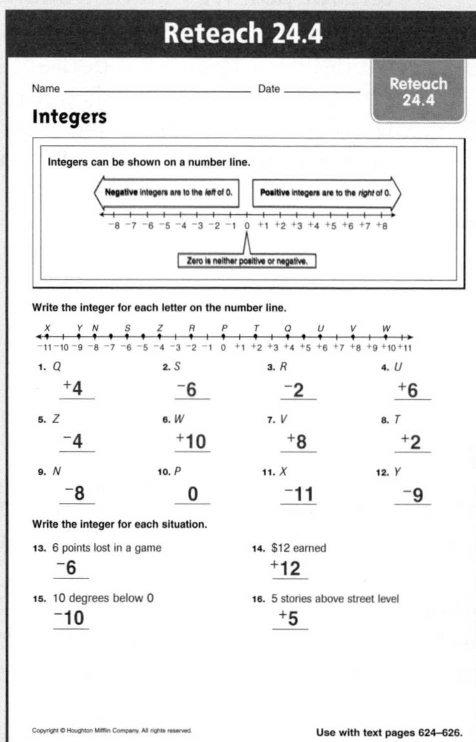

Reteach 24.4

Name ______________ Date ________ Reteach 24.4

Integers

Integers can be shown on a number line.

Negative integers are to the *left* of 0. | **Positive** integers are to the *right* of 0.

$^{-}8$ $^{-}7$ $^{-}6$ $^{-}5$ $^{-}4$ $^{-}3$ $^{-}2$ $^{-}1$ 0 $^{+}1$ $^{+}2$ $^{+}3$ $^{+}4$ $^{+}5$ $^{+}6$ $^{+}7$ $^{+}8$

Zero is neither positive or negative.

Write the integer for each letter on the number line.

X Y N S Z R P T Q U V W

$^{-}11$ $^{-}10$ $^{-}9$ $^{-}8$ $^{-}7$ $^{-}6$ $^{-}5$ $^{-}4$ $^{-}3$ $^{-}2$ $^{-}1$ 0 $^{+}1$ $^{+}2$ $^{+}3$ $^{+}4$ $^{+}5$ $^{+}6$ $^{+}7$ $^{+}8$ $^{+}9$ $^{+}10$ $^{+}11$

1. *Q* $^{+}4$
2. *S* $^{-}6$
3. *R* $^{-}2$
4. *U* $^{+}6$
5. *Z* $^{-}4$
6. *W* $^{+}10$
7. *V* $^{+}8$
8. *T* $^{+}2$
9. *N* $^{-}8$
10. *P* 0
11. *X* $^{-}11$
12. *Y* $^{-}9$

Write the integer for each situation.

13. 6 points lost in a game $^{-}6$
14. $12 earned $^{+}12$
15. 10 degrees below 0 $^{-}10$
16. 5 stories above street level $^{+}5$

Use with text pages 624–626.

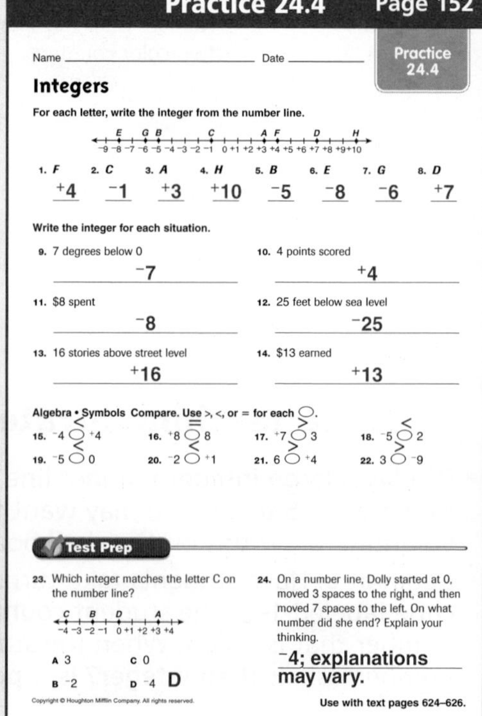

Practice 24.4 **Page 152**

Name ______________ Date ________ Practice 24.4

Integers

For each letter, write the integer from the number line.

E G B C A F D H

$^{-}9$ $^{-}8$ $^{-}7$ $^{-}6$ $^{-}5$ $^{-}4$ $^{-}3$ $^{-}2$ $^{-}1$ 0 $^{+}1$ $^{+}2$ $^{+}3$ $^{+}4$ $^{+}5$ $^{+}6$ $^{+}7$ $^{+}8$ $^{+}9$ $^{+}10$

1. *F* $^{+}4$
2. *C* $^{-}1$
3. *A* $^{+}3$
4. *H* $^{+}10$
5. *B* $^{-}5$
6. *E* $^{-}8$
7. *G* $^{-}6$
8. *D* $^{+}7$

Write the integer for each situation.

9. 7 degrees below 0 $^{-}7$
10. 4 points scored $^{+}4$
11. $8 spent $^{-}8$
12. 25 feet below sea level $^{-}25$
13. 16 stories above street level $^{+}16$
14. $13 earned $^{+}13$

Algebra • Symbols Compare. Use >, <, or = for each ◯.

15. $^{-}4$ < $^{+}4$
16. $^{+}8$ = 8
17. $^{+}7$ > 3
18. $^{-}5$ < 2
19. $^{-}5$ < 0
20. $^{-}2$ < $^{+}1$
21. 6 > $^{+}4$
22. 3 > $^{-}9$

Test Prep

23. Which integer matches the letter C on the number line?

C B D A

$^{-}4$ $^{-}3$ $^{-}2$ $^{-}1$ 0 $^{+}1$ $^{+}2$ $^{+}3$ $^{+}4$

A 3
B $^{-}2$
C 0
D $^{-}4$ **D**

24. On a number line, Dolly started at 0, moved 3 spaces to the right, and then moved 7 spaces to the left. On what number did she end? Explain your thinking.

$^{-}4$; explanations may vary.

Use with text pages 624–626.

▶ You can use a number line to compare integers. When comparing integers, the number farther to the right is greater.

Which is greater, $^{-}5$ or $^{-}2$?

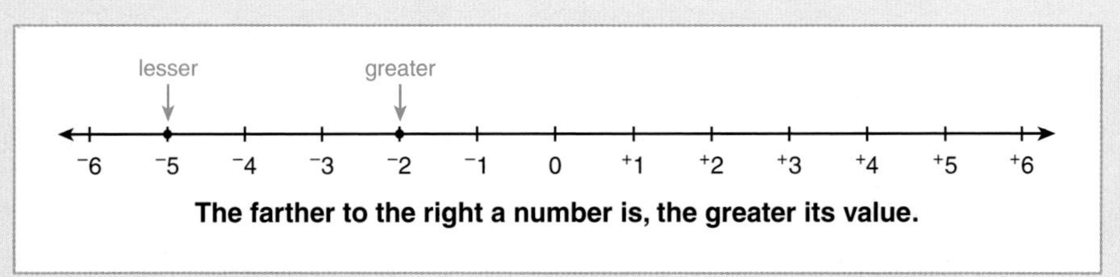

The farther to the right a number is, the greater its value.

Solution: $^{-}2$ is greater than $^{-}5$.

Other Examples

A. Positive Integers

- 17 feet above sea level is $^{+}17$.
- 50 degrees above zero is $^{+}50$.
- 4 floors above street level is $^{+}4$.
- $12 earned is $^{+}12$.

B. Negative Integers

- 5 feet below sea level is $^{-}5$.
- 14 degrees below zero is $^{-}14$.
- 3 floors below street level is $^{-}3$.
- $2 owed is $^{-}2$.

Guided Practice

Ask Yourself
- Is the number greater than 0?
- Is the number less than 0?

Write the integer for each letter on the number line.

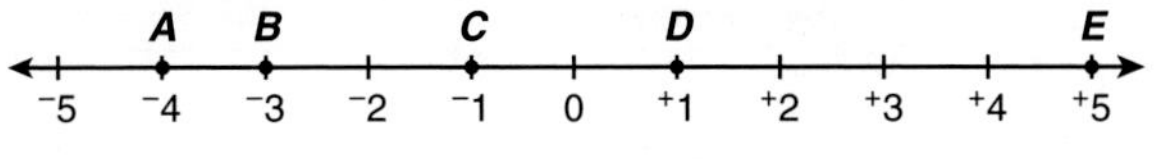

1. *A* $^{-}4$ **2.** *B* $^{-}3$ **3.** *C* $^{-}1$ **4.** *D* $^{+}1$ **5.** *E* $^{+}5$

Explain Your Thinking ▶ Locate $^{+}3$ and $^{-}3$ on a number line. Why are these numbers called opposites? **They are the same distance away from zero, but in opposite directions.**

Practice and Problem Solving

For each letter, write the integer from the number line.

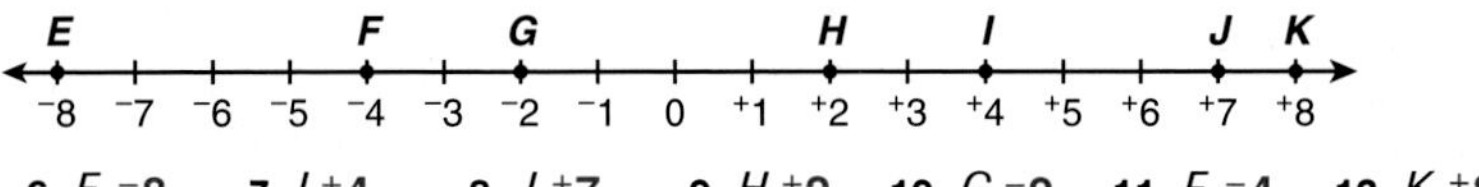

6. *E* $^{-}8$ **7.** *I* $^{+}4$ **8.** *J* $^{+}7$ **9.** *H* $^{+}2$ **10.** *G* $^{-}2$ **11.** *F* $^{-}4$ **12.** *K* $^{+}8$

Guided Practice

Have students complete **Exercises 1–5** as you observe. Remind them to use the ***Ask Yourself*** questions to help. Give students the opportunity to talk about the question in ***Explain Your Thinking.***

❸ Practice

Practice and Problem Solving

Select from **Exercises 6–35** as independent work.

- For ***Exercises 6–12,*** you may wish to ask students to list these letters from least to greatest integer.

Enrichment 24.4

Name ____________ Date ________ Enrichment 24.4

Number Line Game

- This game can be played by 1 or more players.
- Copy and cut out the cards below. Mix them up and place them face down.
- Each player begins at 0 on his or her number line. Players take turns picking a card. Each card has a value on it. Move the correct number of spaces and the correct direction on the number line.
- The number you land on is the number you begin with when you draw the next card.
- Play continues until all the cards have been used. Players circle the last number they landed on and compare it with the other players' numbers. The winner is the player with the greatest number.

2 feet lower	Gained 3 pounds	2 degrees below zero	opposite of $^{-}4$
Behind 4 points	1 step forward	Owes $3	3 degrees warmer
2 pages shorter	$5 more	3 days ago	earned $3
lost 3 yards	1 foot wider	opposite of $^{+}1$	adding 2 people

$^{-}10$ $^{-}9$ $^{-}8$ $^{-}7$ $^{-}6$ $^{-}5$ $^{-}4$ $^{-}3$ $^{-}2$ $^{-}1$ 0 $^{+}1$ $^{+}2$ $^{+}3$ $^{+}4$ $^{+}5$ $^{+}6$ $^{+}7$ $^{+}8$ $^{+}9$ $^{+}10$

$^{-}10$ $^{-}9$ $^{-}8$ $^{-}7$ $^{-}6$ $^{-}5$ $^{-}4$ $^{-}3$ $^{-}2$ $^{-}1$ 0 $^{+}1$ $^{+}2$ $^{+}3$ $^{+}4$ $^{+}5$ $^{+}6$ $^{+}7$ $^{+}8$ $^{+}9$ $^{+}10$

Use with text pages 624–626.

Problem Solving 24.4

Name ____________ Date ________ Problem Solving 24.4

Integers

Show your work.

1. Phyllis went to the movies last night. She spent $5 for a movie ticket. Write an integer for this situation.
   $^{-}5$
2. In the football game, the home team lost 7 yards and then gained 8 yards. Write integers for these situations.
   $^{-}7$; $^{+}8$
3. The low temperature on Tuesday was $^{-}3$°F. On Wednesday, the low temperature was 2°F. Was it colder on Tuesday or Wednesday?
   Tuesday; $^{-}3 < 2$
4. At 6:00 A.M., the temperature was $^{-}6$°F. The temperature rose to 4°F by noon. How many degrees did the temperature rise?
   10°F

Use the table for Problem 5.

5. The table shows the daily low temperatures for five days. Order the temperatures from least to greatest. On which day was it the coldest? The warmest?
   $^{-}8$°, $^{-}5$°, $^{-}3$°, 0, 1; It was the coldest on Wednesday and the warmest on Friday.

Daily Low Temperatures

Day	Low Temperature
Monday	0°F
Tuesday	$^{-}5$°F
Wednesday	$^{-}8$°F
Thursday	$^{-}3$°F
Friday	1°F

Use with text pages 624–626.

- ***Algebra* • *Inequalities*** Review the meaning and use of the inequality symbols. Remind students that the point of the symbol always aims at the smaller number.
- ***Data*** Elicit from students that these elevations are distances measured from sea level, which is how all elevations are measured. Tell students the elevation, in feet above or below sea level, of your town.

4 Assess & Close

Math Talk in Action

Have students choose any integer. Ask them to first describe where to find it on a number line, and then mark it on a number line. Ask them to name its opposite integer. Next, have them name one integer that is greater than and one that is less than the integer they have identified.

Math Journal Prompt

Have students write an explanation of what an integer is and how it differs from the kinds of numbers they have been working with thus far.

Have them describe how to locate an integer on a number line and how to compare two integers using a number line.

Lesson Quiz

Use the quiz on Lesson Transparency 24.4.

Test Prep & Spiral Review

Use Test Prep Transparency 24.4.

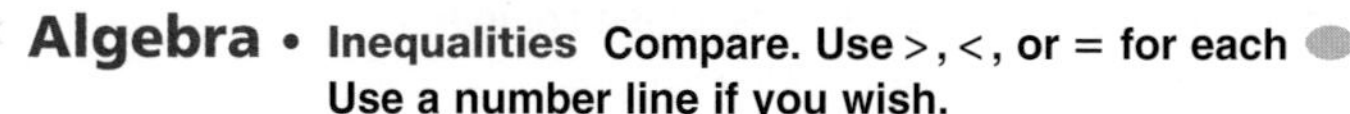

Algebra • Inequalities **Compare. Use >, <, or = for each ⬭. Use a number line if you wish.**

13. $^{-}3$ ⬭ $^{+}3$ **<**
14. 7 ⬭ $^{+}7$ **=**
15. $^{-}2$ ⬭ $^{-}5$ **>**
16. $^{-}8$ ⬭ $^{-}4$ **<**
17. $^{+}6$ ⬭ 3 **>**
18. $^{+}5$ ⬭ $^{-}4$ **>**
19. $^{-}1$ ⬭ 0 **<**
20. $^{-}3$ ⬭ $^{+}2$ **<**

Write the integer for each situation.

21. $3 earned **$^{+}3$**
22. 9 degrees below zero **$^{-}9$**
23. 2 stories above street level **$^{+}2$**
24. $4 spent **$^{-}4$**
25. 7 feet below sea level **$^{-}7$**
26. 6 points won in a game **$^{+}6$**

27. Analyze One day the temperature ranged from $^{-}3$ to $^{-}15$. Which was the low temperature for the day? How far from 0 was the high temperature?
$^{-}15$; 3 degrees

28. Write About It On a number line, Mavis started at 0, moved 4 spaces to the right, and then moved 9 spaces to the left. On what number did she end?
$^{-}5$

Data **Use the table for Problems 29–32. The elevation at sea level is 0 feet.**

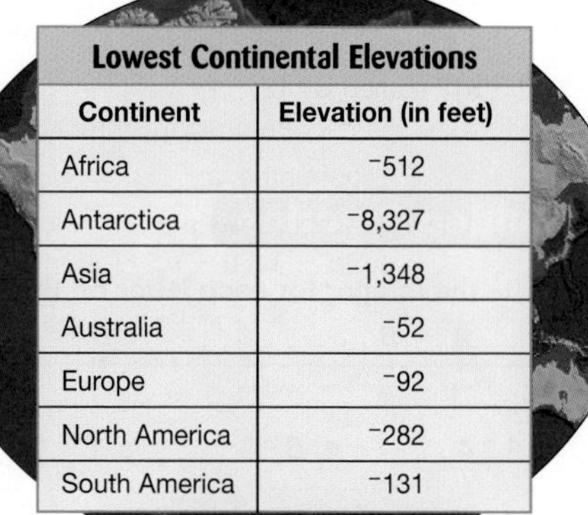

Lowest Continental Elevations

Continent	Elevation (in feet)
Africa	$^{-}512$
Antarctica	$^{-}8,327$
Asia	$^{-}1,348$
Australia	$^{-}52$
Europe	$^{-}92$
North America	$^{-}282$
South America	$^{-}131$

29. On which continent is the lowest elevation closest to sea level?
Australia

30. On which continent is the lowest elevation farthest from sea level?
Antarctica

31. Order the elevations from least to greatest. **$^{-}8,327$, $^{-}1,348$, $^{-}512$, $^{-}282$, $^{-}131$, $^{-}92$, $^{-}52$**

32. Write the integer that is the opposite of the lowest elevation in Europe. **$^{+}92$**

Mixed Review and Test Prep

Open Response

Find the total number of outcomes when one of each is chosen. (Ch. 23, Lesson 5)

33. Pants: tan, black, white
Shirt: red, blue
6 outcomes

34. Meal: chicken, fish, beef
Drink: milk, orange juice, water, soda
12 outcomes

35. Joe said that $^{-}6$ is greater than 2, because 6 is greater than 2.
(Ch. 24, Lesson 4)

Explain why he is right or wrong.
He is wrong. Negative numbers are always less than positive numbers.

626

Extra Practice See page 633, Set C.

Homework 24.4 Page 152

Name ______________ Date ________

Homework 24.4

Integers

For each letter, write the integer from the number line.

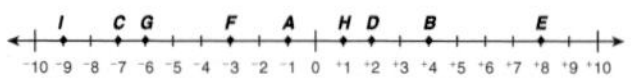

(Number line from $^{-}10$ to $^{+}10$ with points labeled I, C, G, F, A, H, D, B, E)

H
Point *H* is located 1 unit to the right of 0. It is a positive integer.
H = $^{+}1$

1. *E* **$^{+}8$**
2. *D* **$^{+}2$**
3. *C* **$^{-}7$**
4. *I* **$^{-}9$**
5. *F* **$^{-}3$**
6. *A* **$^{-}1$**
7. *G* **$^{-}6$**
8. *B* **$^{+}4$**

Compare. Use >, <, or = for each ◯.

9. $^{+}1$ = 1
10. $^{-}7$ < 4
11. 3 > $^{+}2$
12. $^{-}3$ < 1
13. 0 > $^{-}9$
14. 5 = $^{+}5$
15. $^{-}7$ < $^{-}1$
16. $^{-}3$ < 3

Problem Solving

17. One day in Burlington, Vermont, the temperature ranged from $^{-}12$ to $^{-}4$. Which was the low temperature for the day? How far from 0 was the high temperature?
$^{-}12$; 4 units

Show your work.

Use with text pages 624–626.

Math Reasoning
Coordinate Plane

The coordinate plane is formed by two perpendicular number lines.

- Points are located and plotted using ordered pairs of integers.
- When plotting a point in a coordinate grid, always start at the **origin** (0, 0).

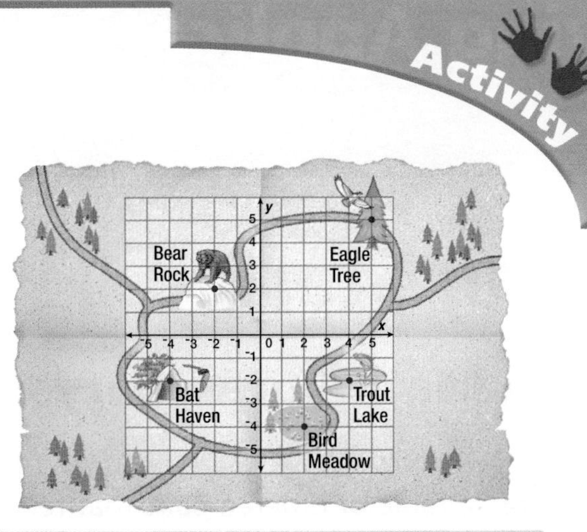

Activity

▶ **The sign of the integers in an ordered pair tells you in what direction to move.**

The first number in an ordered pair is called the ***x*-coordinate**.
If the *x*-coordinate is:
- **positive,** move **right**.
- **negative,** move **left**.

The second number in an ordered pair is called the ***y*-coordinate**.
If the *y*-coordinate is:
- **positive,** move **up**.
- **negative,** move **down**.

▶ **Here's how to locate and plot points on a coordinate plane.**

To locate Bat Haven:
- Start at the origin (0, 0).
- Move **left** 4 units.
- Move **down** 2 units.

To plot the point (3, $^-1$):
- Start at the origin (0, 0).
- Move **right** 3 units.
- Move **down** 1 unit.

Write the ordered pair for each location.

1. Eagle Tree **(5, 5)**
2. Bear Rock **($^-2$, 2)**
3. Trout Lake **(4, $^-2$)**
4. Bird Meadow **(2, $^-4$)**

Draw an *x*-axis and a *y*-axis on graph paper. Label each axis from $^-10$ to 10. Then plot and label the points below. ***See Additional Answers.***

5. M ($^-8$, 4)
6. S (0, $^-6$)
7. A (5, $^-7$)
8. Q ($^-3$, $^-1$)

Math Reasoning
Coordinate Plane

- Review the features of a coordinate plane, including how the numbers of the quadrants go in a counterclockwise direction from Quadrant I to Quadrant IV. Emphasize that the axes go on indefinitely and that there are an infinite number of positive and negative integers in the coordinate plane.
- Review and practice how to locate ordered pairs of integers in the coordinate plane. Ask: **In which quadrant will we find ordered pairs with coordinates that are both positive integers?** (Quadrant I) **In which quadrant will we find ordered pairs with coordinates that are both negative integers?** (Quadrant III) **Where do we find (0, 0) on the coordinate plane?** (at the origin)
- Demonstrate how to plot several ordered pairs on the coordinate plane. Emphasize that the first coordinate in an ordered pair is the *x*-coordinate and that it indicates a distance left or right of the *y*-axis. Emphasize that the second coordinate in each ordered pair is the *y*-coordinate, which indicates a distance up or down from the *x*-axis.

Reaching All Learners

Number Sense

Counting Integers Tell students that they can count integers the same way they count whole numbers.

Have students write the numbers for each counting sequence described below. Encourage students to draw a number line from $^-16$ to $^+16$ if they need help.

1. Count by ones from $^-5$ to $^+5$.
2. Count by twos from $^-10$ to $^+10$.
3. Count by fives from $^-15$ to $^+15$.
4. Count by fours from $^-16$ to $^+16$.
5. Count by threes from $^-12$ to $^+12$.
6. Write two counting exercises of your own and give them to a classmate to solve.

Answers:
Check students' responses.

Differentiated Assignments		
At Risk	**Average**	**Advanced**
Exercises 1, 2	Exercises 3–5	Exercises 4–6

Lesson 24.5

Problem-Solving Application: Use a Graph

Planning

Lesson Objective Solve a problem by extending a line graph.

Technology Resources

- *Ways to Success* CD-ROM 24.5
- Education Place: Extra Practice, eGames www.eduplace.com/map

Lesson 24.5 Transparency

Problem of the Day

A canoe rents for $6 an hour. Two people will share the cost of renting the canoe for $3\frac{1}{2}$ hours. What does each person pay? ($10.50)

Spiral Review

Complete each pattern.

1. 4, 8, 12, 16, __, 24 (20)

2. 2, 6, 18, __, 162, __ (54; 486)

Lesson Quiz

Use the table to answer the questions.

Bicycle Rental Fees	
Time	**Cost**
1 hr	$7
2 hr	$9
3 hr	$11

1. What will it cost to rent a bicycle for 4 hours? ($13)

2. What will it cost to rent a bicycle for 7 hours? ($19) What ordered pair on a graph would show this? (7, 19)

NCTM Standards

Problem Solving: Apply and adapt a variety of appropriate strategies to solve problems.

Data Analysis and Probability: Represent data using tables and graphs.

Getting Started

Building Math Vocabulary

You may wish to review the following term with students.

function table a table of ordered pairs that follows a rule

Functions and Graphs of Functions

Whole Class	5 minutes
Objective	Plot ordered pairs from a function table and draw a line to show the pattern.
Materials	Workmat 6
Visual, Tactual	

Students have worked with functions as ordered pairs that can be plotted as a line on a graph. Now they will learn to extend the line graphs.

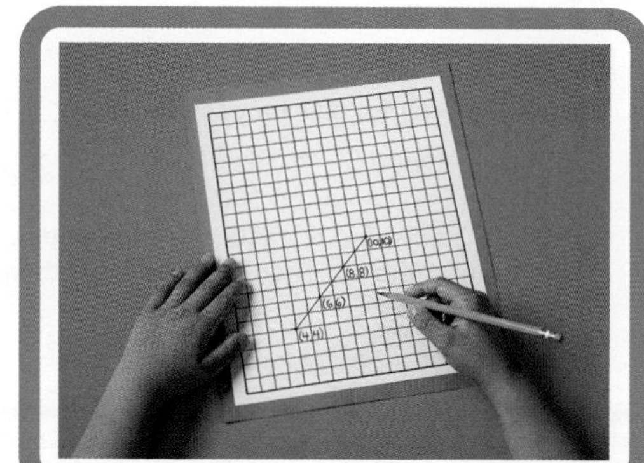

- Revisit the concept of functions with students. Then have them explain how to use ordered pairs from a function to plot a line to solve a problem. Have a volunteer suggest a simple rule for a table. Use the rule to fill the table. Have a student volunteer make a graph that shows the same data.
- Tell students that they will explore solving problems by extending line graphs.

Differentiated Instruction

English Learners

Whole Class	5–10 minutes
Objective	Solve a problem by extending a line graph.
Materials	Student page 629
Visual, Tactual	

Early Production

- Before ***Independent Practice,*** have students make a function table using the coordinates from the graph on Student page 629. Ask them to extend the function table to include the cost for 4 people.
- Students complete the ***Independent Practice,*** reading the problems and their answers aloud.

Intermediate/Advanced

- English Learner Resource 24.5
- English Learner Handbook

Intervention

Small Groups	5–10 minutes
Objective	Interpret a function table.
Materials	Student page 628
Auditory, Visual	

- You may wish to have students focus solely on the table on Student page 628 to spot and continue a pattern to solve problems.
- Together, look at the table of prices for miniature golf. Ask: **What does 1 person pay to play?** ($5) **How do you know?** (Move up the column for 1 player.) Say: **Look at *Number of Players.* How do the numbers change each time?** (increase by 1) **Now look at the amount of cash. How do these numbers change with each additional player?** (increase by $2)

Other Resources

- *Ways to Success* CD-ROM 24.5

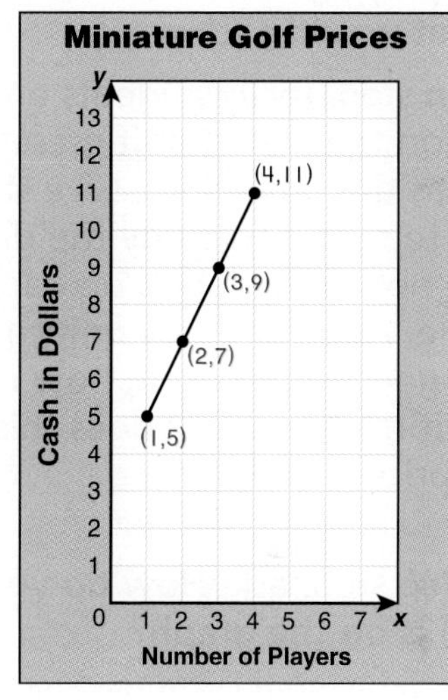

Special Needs

Individuals	5 minutes
Objective	Identify ordered pairs.
Materials	Student page 628
Visual, Tactual	

- Provide students with practice reading and interpreting a line graph. Start with the graph on student page 628. Help students identify the coordinates of each point. [(1, 5), (2, 7), (3, 9), (4, 11)]
- Elicit from students what each number in an ordered pair indicates. (distance to the right of 0; distance up from 0) Have students plot and read additional points along a line.

Alternate Teaching Strategy

- Divide students into groups of three to four. Have each group create a graph using coordinate pairs that fall in a straight line, such as the graphs on pages 628 and 629. (The graphs should not contain a heading or axis labels.)
- Have groups switch graphs. Then have each group use the new graph to write three story problems that the graph could represent

Facts Practice

- Distribute multiplication and division fact flashcards, one to each student. Have students wear their cards like name tags, with the answers hidden.
- Set a time limit, such as 1 hour, until lunch, etc. Within this limit, students must address classmates by their product or quotient (depending on whether the student has a multiplication or division fact).

❶ Introduce

Explain to students the concept of extending a line graph to solve a problem. Tell them that they can use a ruler to extend the line.

❷ Teach

Use a Graph

- Have a volunteer read aloud the opening information and the problems asked. Then guide students through the steps in the problem-solving process.
- For the ***Understand*** step, discuss the information the table presents. Ask: **Is the change in price from 1 to 2 hours the same as it is from 2 to 3 hours?** (yes) **What is it?** ($2) **What can you say about what it costs to play miniature golf?** (One person pays $5; for every additional person, the price goes up $2.) **If two people are playing and they share the cost evenly, what would each pay?** ($3.50)
- For the ***Plan*** step, focus students on the graph and on the idea that it presents the same data as the table does. Give students a moment to read and study the graph. Have them notice the labels on each axis and the title. Ask: **For every unit the graph of the line goes to the right, how many units does it rise?** (2) **What does this tell you about the price to play?** (For every additional player the price of a round of golf goes up $2.)
- For the ***Solve*** step, ask: **How do you know that (4, 11) is on the graph?** (To go from (3, 9) to (4, 11), the graph continues its pattern by rising 2 units for every 1 unit it goes across.)
- For the ***Look Back*** step, ask: **If we had continued the table, what data would we write in the next row down?** (4 for *Number of Players,* $11 for *Price*) **in the row beneath that?** (5, $13)

Common Error

- **Misreading the graph**
- **Intervention** Have students align strips of colored paper to help them make sure they are reading the correct scale numbers for the intersection of the line graph and the grid lines.

Lesson 5

Problem-Solving Application

Use a Graph

Objective Solve a problem by extending a line graph.

When data can be represented by points that lie on a line, you can sometimes solve a problem by extending the line.

Problem Lee had a party at a miniature-golf course. The table shows the price for different numbers of players. The graph shows the relationship between the number of players and the price. How much does it cost for 4 players to play golf?

UNDERSTAND

This is what the question asks.

What is the price for 4 players?

This is what the graph shows.

The blue line shows the price for 1 to 3 players.

Miniature Golf Prices	
Number of Players	**Price**
1	$5
2	$7
3	$9

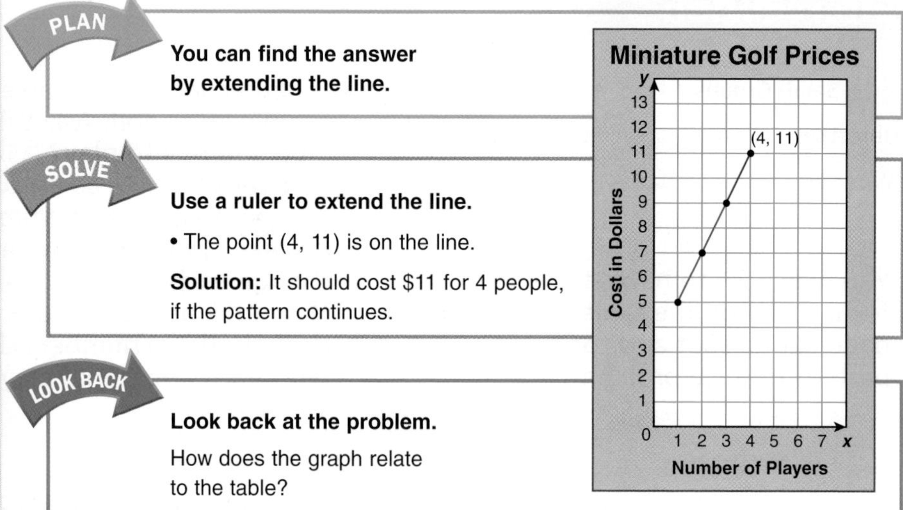

PLAN

You can find the answer by extending the line.

SOLVE

Use a ruler to extend the line.

- The point (4, 11) is on the line.

Solution: It should cost $11 for 4 people, if the pattern continues.

LOOK BACK

Look back at the problem.

How does the graph relate to the table?

628

Reteach 24.5

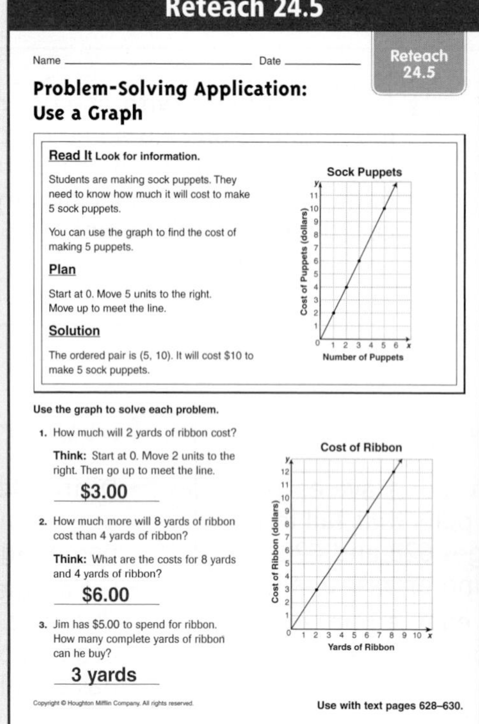

Name ______________ Date ________ Reteach 24.5

Problem-Solving Application: Use a Graph

Read It Look for information.

Students are making sock puppets. They need to know how much it will cost to make 5 sock puppets.

You can use the graph to find the cost of making 5 puppets.

Plan

Start at 0. Move 5 units to the right. Move up to meet the line.

Solution

The ordered pair is (5, 10). It will cost $10 to make 5 sock puppets.

Use the graph to solve each problem.

1. How much will 2 yards of ribbon cost?

   Think: Start at 0. Move 2 units to the right. Then go up to meet the line.

   $3.00

2. How much more will 8 yards of ribbon cost than 4 yards of ribbon?

   Think: What are the costs for 8 yards and 4 yards of ribbon?

   $6.00

3. Jim has $5.00 to spend for ribbon. How many complete yards of ribbon can he buy?

   3 yards

Use with text pages 628–630.

Practice 24.5 Page 153

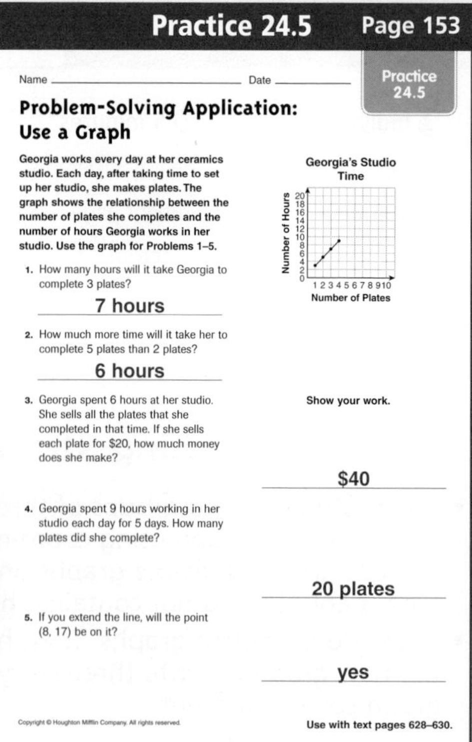

Name ______________ Date ________ Practice 24.5

Problem-Solving Application: Use a Graph

Georgia works every day at her ceramics studio. Each day, after taking time to set up her studio, she makes plates. The graph shows the relationship between the number of plates she completes and the number of hours Georgia works in her studio. Use the graph for Problems 1–5.

1. How many hours will it take Georgia to complete 3 plates?

   7 hours

2. How much more time will it take her to complete 5 plates than 2 plates?

   6 hours

Show your work.

3. Georgia spent 6 hours at her studio. She sells all the plates that she completed in that time. If she sells each plate for $20, how much money does she make?

   $40

4. Georgia spent 9 hours working in her studio each day for 5 days. How many plates did she complete?

   20 plates

5. If you extend the line, will the point (8, 17) be on it?

   yes

Use with text pages 628–630.

Guided Practice

Use the graph on Page 628 for Problems 1–2.

1. How much does it cost for 5 people to play miniature golf? **$13**
2. Lee has $10 to spend on his party. What is the greatest number of players he can afford? **3 players**

Hint Where on the line is the *y*-coordinate 10? Is the other point a whole number?

Ask Yourself

UNDERSTAND
- What does the question ask?
- What does the graph represent?

PLAN
Do I need to extend the line?

SOLVE
Do the points lie on the line?

LOOK BACK
Does my answer make sense?

Independent Practice

Alta has a party at a science museum. The museum offers a craft activity for an additional fee. The graph shows the relationship between the number of people and the cost.

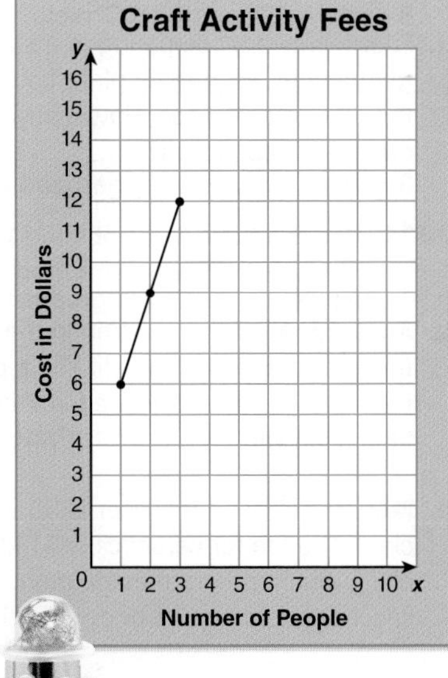

Use the graph for Problems 3–7.

3. What would a craft activity for Alta and 3 of her friends cost? **$15**
4. **Money** How much more would it cost for 4 people to do a craft than for 2 people to do a craft? **$6**
5. Alta's parents spent $15 on the craft activities for the party. They spent $4 per person on goody bags. How much did they spend on goody bags? **$16**
6. Tom is also having a party at the museum. He has $16 to spend on crafts. What is the greatest number of people that can do a craft, including himself? **4 people**
7. **Predict** If you extend the line, will the point (10, 35) be on it? **No**

Go On

Guided Practice

Have students complete **Problems 1–2** as you observe. Remind them to use the ***Ask Yourself*** questions to help.

3 Practice

Independent Practice

Select from **Problems 3–15** as independent work.

Have students review their answers to make sure they have done the following:

- expressed the solution clearly
- used appropriate mathematical notation and terms
- supported the solution with verbal and symbolic work

Enrichment 24.5

Name ______ Date ______ Enrichment 24.5

Problem-Solving Application: Use a Graph

The Super Sock Store is having a sale on socks. You can buy 2 pairs of socks for $3. The table shows the price of buying 2, 4, and 6 pairs of socks. Rewrite the data as ordered pairs using the pairs of socks as the *x*-coordinate and the price as the *y*-coordinate.

Number of Pairs of Socks	Price
2	$3
4	$6
6	$9

1. On the grid, plot and connect the points to make a line graph. **Check students' graphs.**
2. Coach Smith is buying socks for the volleyball team. Explain how to use the graph to find how much it will cost Coach Smith to buy 12 pairs of socks. **Extend the line and find the point that has the *x*-coordinate of 12. The *y*-coordinate tells me the price: $18.**
3. Frankie says that 10 pairs of socks cost $14. Explain how to use the graph to see if Frankie is correct. **Find the *x*-coordinate of 10 and follow it up until you hit the line. Then find the *y*-coordinate of the point on the line that has the *x*-coordinate of 10. The cost of 10 pairs is $15, not $14. Frankie was not correct.**

Price; Number of Pairs of Socks

 Use with text pages 628–630.

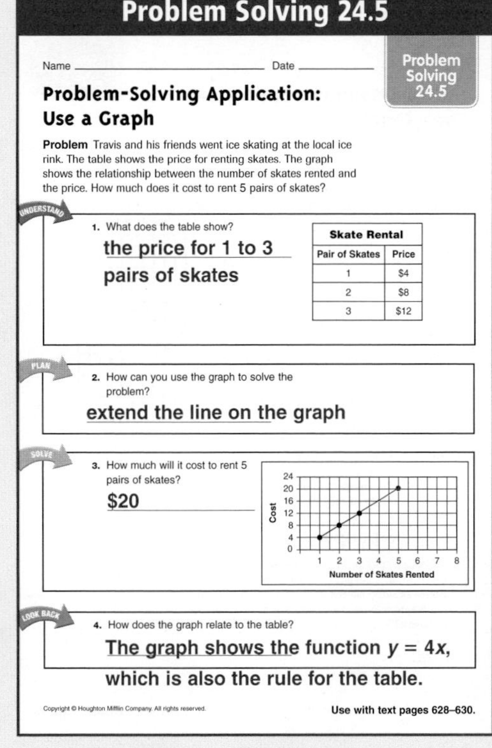

Problem Solving 24.5

Name ______ Date ______ Problem Solving 24.5

Problem-Solving Application: Use a Graph

Problem Travis and his friends went ice skating at the local ice rink. The table shows the price for renting skates. The graph shows the relationship between the number of skates rented and the price. How much does it cost to rent 5 pairs of skates?

UNDERSTAND

1. What does the table show? **the price for 1 to 3 pairs of skates**

Skate Rental	
Pair of Skates	Price
1	$4
2	$8
3	$12

PLAN

2. How can you use the graph to solve the problem? **extend the line on the graph**

SOLVE

3. How much will it cost to rent 5 pairs of skates? **$20**

Cost; Number of Skates Rented

LOOK BACK

4. How does the graph relate to the table? **The graph shows the function $y = 4x$, which is also the rule for the table.**

 Use with text pages 628–630.

Mixed Problem Solving

Problems 8–11 Have students identify and explain the strategies they used to solve the problems. Have them identify the problems that required an exact answer and the ones for which estimation was sufficient.

4 Assess & Close

Math Talk in Action

Have students refer to the Craft Activity Fees graph on page 629 to conclude the lesson. Ask: **If you were to extend the line to include more people in an activity, what effect would it have on the cost?** (The cost would increase.) **What would the cost be if 4 people participated in the activity?** ($15)

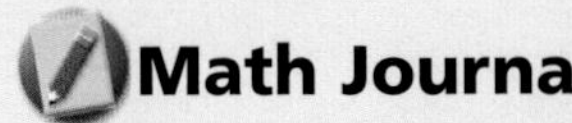

Math Journal Prompt

Have students describe a real-world situation where the graph is not a straight line. Have them explain if they can still extend this graph to solve problems.

Lesson Quiz

Use the quiz on Lesson Transparency 24.5.

Test Prep & Spiral Review

Use Test Prep Transparency 24.5.

Mixed Problem Solving

Solve. Show your work. Tell what strategy you used. ***Possible strategies given.***

You Choose

Strategy
- Guess and Check
- Make an Organized List
- Use Logical Reasoning
- Work Backward
- Write an Equation

Computation Method
- Mental Math
- Estimation
- Paper and Pencil
- Calculator

8. Al's used bike costs $3 more than Rosa's. Ed's bike costs $2 less than Rosa's. If Ed's bike costs $24, how much does Al's bike cost?
$29; Write an Equation
9. Leon is arranging 3 model cars on a shelf. The cars are red, silver, and blue. How many different ways can the cars be arranged in a line?
6 different ways; Make an Organized List
10. The product of two numbers is 128. One factor is half the other factor. What are the factors?
8 and 16; Guess and Check
11. Four teams are competing in a soccer tournament. Each team plays each of the other teams once. How many games will be played?
6 games; Make an Organized List

Data **Use the table for Problems 12–15. Then explain which method you chose.** ***Possible methods given.***

Town Recreation Center

Program	Number of Children
Basketball	89
Ceramics	32
Computers	25
Drama	60
Gymnastics	40
Soccer	58

12. **Analyze** All of the children in the basketball program are taking vans to see a game. How many vans are needed, if 7 children fit in each van? **13 vans; Paper and Pencil**
13. **Money** The fee for soccer is $8.95 per child. The fee for ceramics is $14.95 per child. Which program made more money, soccer or ceramics? **soccer; Estimation**
14. What is the total number of children signed up for programs at the Town Recreation Center? **304 children; Calculator**
15. How many more children signed up for drama and computers than for gymnastics? **45 more children; Mental Math**

630

Homework 24.5 Page 153

Name ______________________ Date ____________

Homework 24.5

Problem-Solving Application: Use a Graph

The local movie theater is having a deal for matinee movies. The first person in a group pays full price, and each other person in the group gets a discount. The graph shows the relationship between the number of people in a group and the cost of their tickets. Use the graph to solve each problem.

How much will it cost for 3 people to see the matinee movie?

Find 3 on the *x*-axis and then draw an arrow up to meet the graphed line.

It will cost $14 for 3 people to see the matinee movie.

Movie Prices

Cost of Tickets: 0, 2, 4, 6, 8, 10, 12, 14, 16, 18, 20, 22, 24, 26, 28 (y)
Number of People: 1, 2, 3, 4, 5, 6, 7, 8, 9 (x)

1. How much more would it cost for 6 people to see the matinee movie than for 4 people to see the matinee movie?
$8
2. A group of people spent a total of $22 on tickets and snacks for the matinee movie. If the group spent $8 on snacks, how many people were in the group?
3 people
3. John has $30 to spend on matinee tickets. What is the greatest number of people including himself that he can buy tickets for? How much money will he have left?
7; $0

Show your work.

Use with text pages 628–630.

Real World Connection
Chess Challenge

Problem Solving

Chess players use a set of ordered pairs with a letter and a number to tell the location of any piece.

Each chess piece moves differently. Knights make L-shaped moves. They move 2 squares in one row and then 1 square in a perpendicular row.

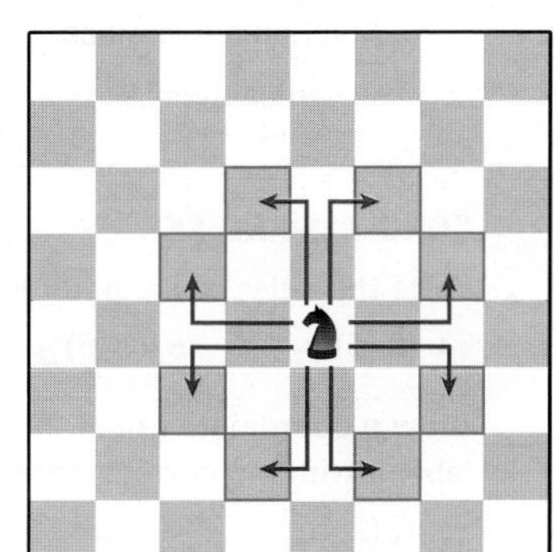

Here are some examples of a move that a knight might make.

At the start of the game, the 4 knights are located at b1, g1, b8, and g8.

The knight at b1 moves forward 2 spaces and then left 1 space to a3.

Use the chessboard on the right. Decide if each describes a move that a knight could make.

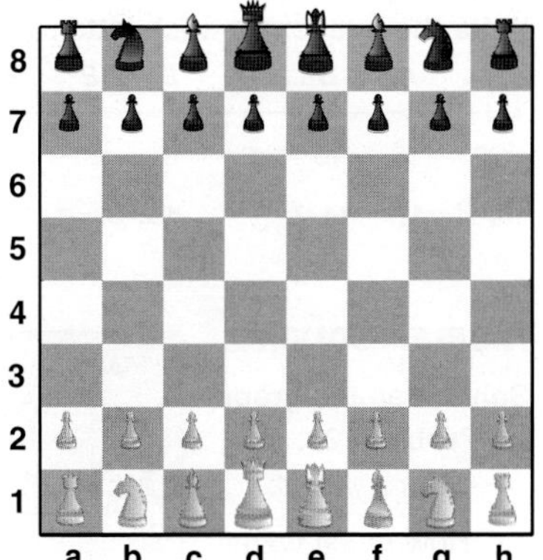

1. d5 to f6 **yes**
2. c3 to b5 **yes**
3. c5 to f4 **no**
4. h3 to g5 **yes**
5. f6 to f3 **no**
6. b1 to e1 **no**
7. Write three moves that a knight might make, using ordered pairs.

WEEKLY WR READER eduplace.com/map

Real World Connection

Chess Challenge

- Have volunteers show small groups of classmates what each chess piece looks like and how each moves about the board. Ask: **Which piece has the greatest freedom of movement?** (queen) **Which pieces are the most limited?** (pawn, king) **Which piece makes the most unusual movements?** (knight)
- Then focus on the chessboard itself. Guide students to see that a chessboard is the same grid as a checkerboard. To help them read the grid using the scales of numbers and letters, provide practice identifying various squares by letter and number. Ask students, for example, to find c5 or f6.

Monitoring Student Progress

Chapter Review/Test

Chapter Review Test Items 1–20

To assign a numerical grade for this Chapter Review/Test, use 5 points for each item.

Check Understanding

You can use the ***Write About It*** question to assess student understanding of a key chapter concept.

Customize Your Instruction

The Chapter Review/Test is a formal evaluation of chapter objectives. For students who have not yet mastered these objectives, you can use the Reteaching Resources listed in the chart below.

Additional Assessment Resources

Alternate Chapter Test A Chapter Test is also provided in the Unit Resource folder. You might use the Review/Test in the student book as review and the test in the Unit Resource folder as a summary test for the chapter.

***Ways to Assess* CD-ROM** allows you to create your own lesson, chapter, or unit tests or practice and review worksheets.

Adequate Yearly Progress Guide helps familiarize your students with the format of standardized tests.

Chapter Review/Test

Vocabulary
x-axis
y-axis
integers
coordinates

VOCABULARY

1. The set of positive whole numbers, their opposites, and 0 are called ____. **integers**
2. An ordered pair of numbers that locate a point on a coordinate grid are called ____. **coordinates**
3. The vertical number line on a coordinate grid is the ____. ***y*-axis**

CONCEPTS AND SKILLS

Write the letter of the point for each. (Lesson 1, pp. 616–617)

4. (5, 5) *H* 5. (3, 6) *J* 6. (4, 2) *D* 7. (1, 1) *B*

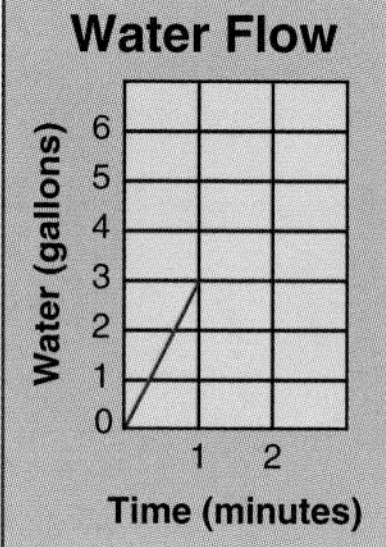

Draw a coordinate grid. Plot each point and label it with the correct letter. (Lesson 2, pp. 618–619)

8. *Q* (2, 5) 9. *R* (3, 7) 10. *S* (4, 4) 11. *T* (0, 6)

For exercises 8–11, see Additional Answers.

Use the table to answer Exersise 12. (Lesson 3, pp. 620–623)

12. If *x* stands for the number of packages, and *y* stands for the number of cards, what is the rule for calculating the number of cards in *x* packages? $y = 5x$

Packages of Game Cards			
Number of Packages	3	4	5
Number of Cards	15	20	25

Write the integer for each letter. (Lesson 4, pp. 624–627)

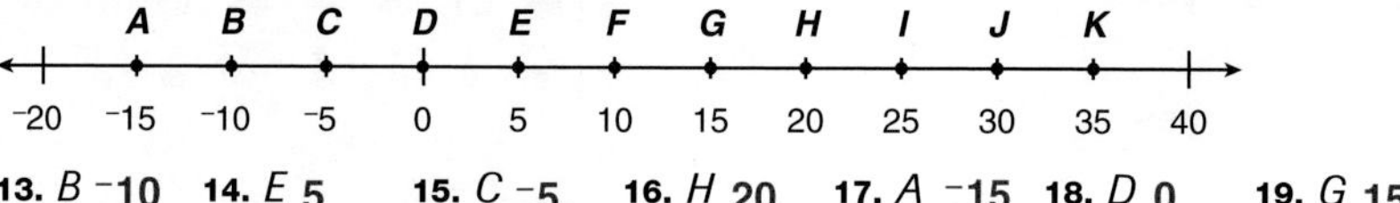

13. *B* ⁻10 14. *E* 5 15. *C* ⁻5 16. *H* 20 17. *A* ⁻15 18. *D* 0 19. *G* 15

PROBLEM SOLVING

Solve. Use the graph for Problem 20. (Lesson 5, pp. 628–631)

20. How much water flows out of the pipe in 1 minute? **3 gal** 2 minutes? **6 gal**

Water Flow
Water (gallons) 0 1 2 3 4 5 6
Time (minutes) 1 2

Write About It

Show You Understand

At sunrise, the temperature was 10°F. At noon, it rose 5°. At sunset, it went down 19°. Draw a number line to determine the temperature at sunset.

⁻4°; Check students' number lines.

632 **Chapter 24** Chapter Review/Test

Chapter Review/Test Items	Objectives	Covered On Teacher's Edition Pages	Use These Reteaching Resources
2–12	**24A** Locate, identify, and graph points on a coordinate plane; graph lines.	616A–622	Reteach Resources 24.1, 24.2, 24.3 *Ways to Success* CD-ROM 24.1, 24.2, 24.3 *Ways to Success* Skillsheets 200, 201, 203, 204
1, 13–19	**24B** Write integers.	624A–626	Reteach Resources 24.4 *Ways to Success* CD-ROM 24.4 *Ways to Success* Skillsheet 205
20	**24C** Solve problems using skills and strategies.	628A–630	Reteach Resources 24.5 *Ways to Success* CD-ROM 24.5 *Ways to Success* Skillsheet 206

Extra Practice

Set A (Lessons 1–2, pp. 616–619)

Use the grid at the right for Exercises 1–8. Write the ordered pair for each point.

1. *E* **(3, 5)**
2. *F* **(1, 7)**
3. *D* **(6, 7)**
4. *A* **(2, 2)**

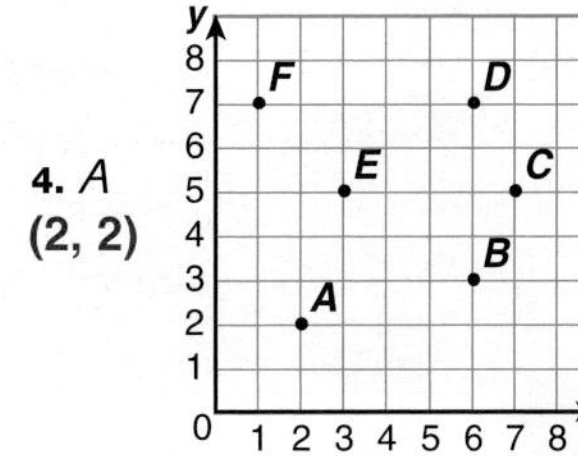

Copy the grid. Plot and label each point.

5. *G* (5, 0)
6. *H* (3, 4)
7. *I* (8, 3)
8. *J* (5, 5)

For exercises 5–8, see Additional Answers.

Set B (Lesson 3, pp. 620–623)

Use the table to complete Exercises 1–3.

1. Write the data in the table as ordered pairs. Use the number of packages as the first coordinate.
(1, 3), (2, 6), (3, 9), (4, 12), (5, 15)

Packages of Tomatoes					
Number of Packages	1	2	3	4	5
Number of Tomatoes	3	6	9	12	15

2. Copy the grid. Plot the coordinates from Exercise 1. Then connect the points.
See Additional Answers.
3. Extend your grid. Label the *x*-axis to 10 and the *y*-axis to 30. How many tomatoes would be in 7 packages? in 9 packages?
21 tomatoes; 27 tomatoes

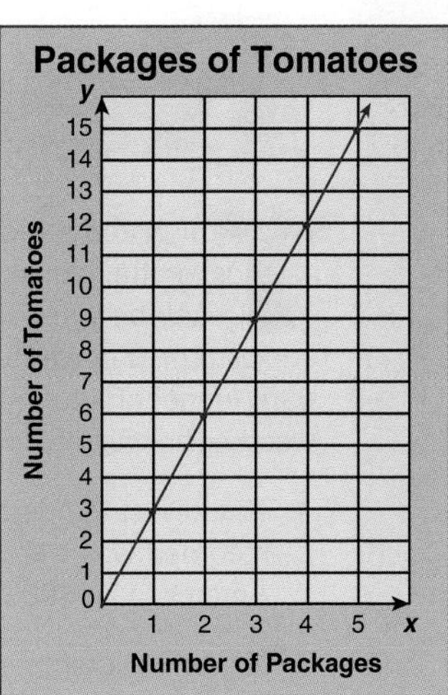

Set C (Lesson 4, pp. 624–627)

Write an integer for each situation.

1. sea level **0**
2. \$15 owed **$^{-}15$**
3. 14 floors above street level **$^{+}14$**
4. 89 feet below sea level **$^{-}89$**
5. \$25 won **$^{+}25$**
6. 75° above zero **$^{+}75$**

Extra Practice at **eduplace.com/map**

CHAPTER 24 TEST

Chapter 24 Test

Name ____________ Date ________

Use the graph on the right for Exercises 1–3. Write the letter of the point for each ordered pair.

1. (0, 4) **A**
2. (2, 3) **F**
3. (1, 6) **E**

Use the graph on the right for Exercises 4–6. Write the ordered pair for each point.

4. *J* **(5, 2)**
5. *M* **(2, 5)**
6. *O* **(0, 7)**

Plot each point and label it with the correct letter.

7. *R* (3, 0)
8. *S* (1, 5)
9. *T* (4, 3)

Check students' grids.

Go on

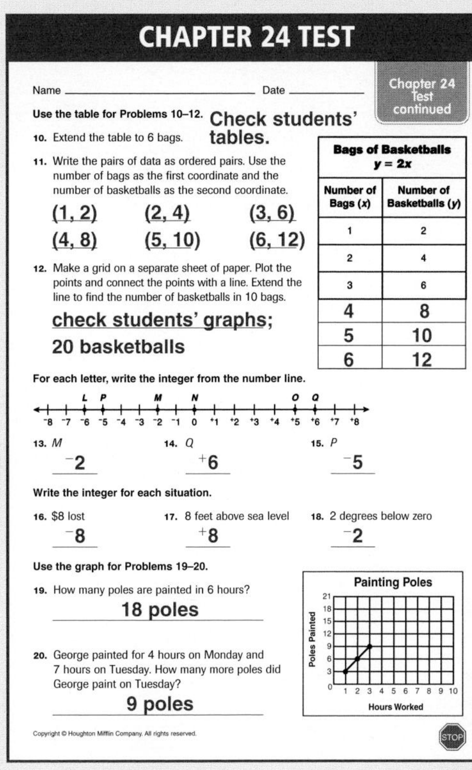

CHAPTER 24 TEST

Chapter 24 Test continued

Name ____________ Date ________

Use the table for Problems 10–12. **Check students' tables.**

10. Extend the table to 6 bags.
11. Write the pairs of data as ordered pairs. Use the number of bags as the first coordinate and the number of basketballs as the second coordinate.
(1, 2) (2, 4) (3, 6) (4, 8) (5, 10) (6, 12)
12. Make a grid on a separate sheet of paper. Plot the points and connect the points with a line. Extend the line to find the number of basketballs in 10 bags.
check students' graphs; 20 basketballs

Bags of Basketballs $y = 2x$	
Number of Bags (*x*)	Number of Basketballs (*y*)
1	2
2	4
3	6
4	8
5	10
6	12

For each letter, write the integer from the number line.

13. *M* **$^{-}2$**
14. *Q* **$^{+}6$**
15. *P* **$^{-}5$**

Write the integer for each situation.

16. \$8 lost **$^{-}8$**
17. 8 feet above sea level **$^{+}8$**
18. 2 degrees below zero **$^{-}2$**

Use the graph for Problems 19–20.

19. How many poles are painted in 6 hours?
18 poles
20. George painted for 4 hours on Monday and 7 hours on Tuesday. How many more poles did George paint on Tuesday?
9 poles

Painting Poles

Poles Painted

Hours Worked

STOP

Science Connection

PURPOSE

To solve problems using a coordinate grid.

- A branch of science dealing with the atmosphere and its phenomena is **meteorology.** It especially focuses on variations of heat, moisture, and wind. A **meteorologist** is a scientist who specializes in weather conditions.
- Many weatherpersons on television are meteorologists. These weather analysts try to give the most accurate forecasts of the weather. Sometimes they have to issue storm watches or warnings if there will be a tornado, hurricane, or thunderstorm.
- Suggest that students learn about weather conditions every day by watching television, listening to the radio, or reading the newspaper.
- Have students find out more about meteorology from reference books. Suggest that students learn more about climate phenomena, such as El Niño. They can use an almanac to look up extremes in temperature and precipitation on each continent and for major cities in the world. Students can also look up hurricane and tornado classifications.
- **Exercises 3–5** illustrate the impact of weather conditions on umbrella sales. Ask students to think of other ways good or bad weather conditions affect our lives.

WEEKLY WR READER®

Science Connection

Weather Records

Think about the most extreme weather you've ever seen. Maybe you remember a blinding snowstorm, a powerful hurricane, or the dark funnel of a tornado. Some extreme weather has set records.

- The lowest temperature ever recorded was $^-128.6$°F in Vostok, Antarctica, in 1983.
- The highest temperature ever recorded was 136°F on the Sahara Desert in Libya, in 1922.
- The fastest wind speed ever recorded was 231 miles per hour on Mount Washington, New Hampshire, in 1934.

634

Problem Solving

Use the coordinate grid for Problems 1–2.

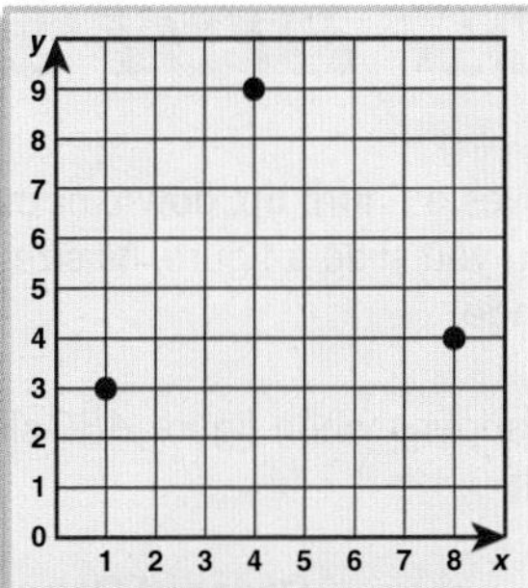

1. The coordinate grid shows the location of three tornado strikes. Write an ordered pair for each of the locations. **(1, 3), (4, 9), (8, 4)**
2. Suppose another tornado struck at (6, 7). Describe how you would graph the location of this tornado on the grid. **Plot a point at 6 on the *x*-axis and 7 on the *y*-axis.**

Use the table for Problems 3–5.

Umbrella Sales	
Number of Umbrellas (x)	Money Store Takes In (y)
1	$3
2	$6
3	$9
4	$12

3. An unexpected rainstorm sends people rushing to buy umbrellas. The table shows the number of umbrellas one store sells and the amount of money the store takes in. Write an equation for the values of x and y in the table. **$y = 3x$**
4. Write the pairs of data from the table as ordered pairs. Use the number of umbrellas as the first coordinate. Then graph the ordered pairs on a grid. Connect all the points. ***See Additional Answers.***
5. Extend the line on your graph. How much money will the store take in if 6 people buy umbrellas? **$18**

Education Place

Visit Weekly Reader Connections at **eduplace.com/map** for more on this topic.

Enrichment

PURPOSE

This page shows how to graph a translation of a figure.

This lesson utilizes the concepts and skills used in Chapters 16, 17, and 24 and applies them to graphing a translation of a figure. As you work through the page, ask students the following questions:

- **What happens to the numerical value of the coordinates of the original figure after it slides 3 units up?** (The first coordinate does not change. The second coordinate increases by 3.) **After it slides 3 units down?** (The first coordinate does not change. The second coordinate decreases by 3.)
- **What happens to the numerical value of the coordinates of the original figure after it slides 2 units right?** (The first coordinate does not change. The second coordinate increases by 2.) **After it slides 2 units left?** (The first coordinate does not change. The second coordinate decreases by 2.)
- **Why do you have to move all points of the original figure for a slide?** (to keep the figure's size and shape the same)

Enrichment: Transformations

Slips and Slides

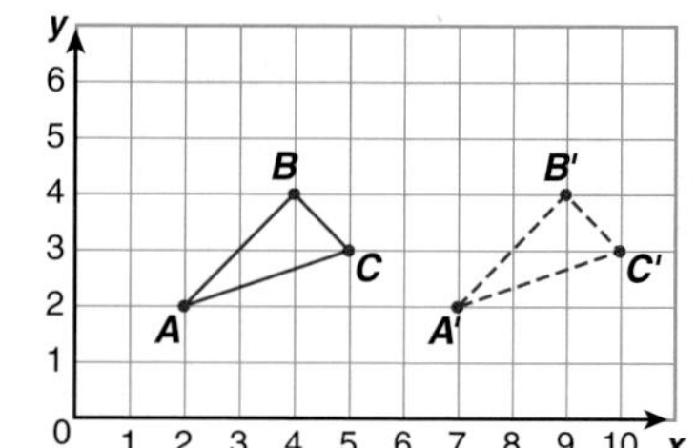

A **slide** moves a figure up, down, or over along a line. When you slide a figure, its size and shape do not change.

See what happens when figure *ABC* slides 5 units right.

	Ordered Pairs
Original Figure	*A* (2, 2) *B* (4, 4) *C* (5, 3)
Image	*A′* (7, 2) *B′* (9, 4) *C′* (10, 3)

After you slide *ABC* to the right:

- *A* becomes *A′*, *B* becomes *B′*, and *C* becomes *C′*.
- The first coordinate of each point increases by 5.
- The second coordinate of each point does not change.

The numbers in the coordinate change depending on how you slide.

When you slide right or left,

- The first coordinate increases or decreases.
- The second coordinate stays the same.

When you slide up or down,

- The first coordinate stays the same.
- The second coordinate increases or decreases.

Try These!

Graph triangle *ABC* on grid paper. Slide triangle *ABC* the number of units given. Write the ordered pairs for the Points *A′*, *B′*, and *C′*. ***See Additional Answers.***

1. 1 unit left
2. 2 units down
3. 2 units up
4. 4 units right

Get On Line!

Qwan was playing a game on the computer. In Round 1 he won 6 points. In Round 2 he lost 9 points. In Round 3 he won 4 points. How many points did Qwan have at the end of Round 3?

You can use the number line found on Education Place at eduplace.com/kids/map to work with integers.

- Click on 0 on the number line to start.
- To show Qwan's points at the end of Round 1, at **Choose Jump Size,** click on 6. Then click the **Jump Right** arrow.
- To show Qwan's points at the end of Round 2, change **Choose Jump Size.** Since Qwan lost 9 points, choose 9. Click the **Jump Left** arrow.
- To show Qwan's points at the end of Round 3, change **Choose Jump Size.** Since Qwan won 4 points, choose 4. Click the **Jump Right** arrow.

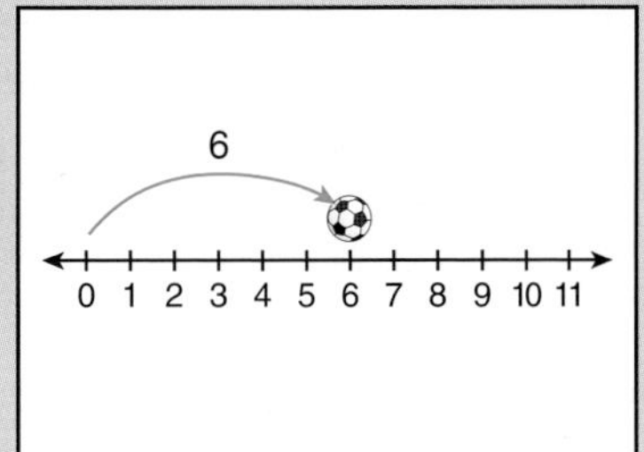

Solution: At the end of Round 3, Qwan had 1 point.

Use the number line to help you solve each problem.

1. Mia owes her brother \$3. She earns \$9. After paying her brother back, she spends \$5 on a book. How much money does Mia have left? **\$1**
2. A scuba diver dove 9 feet below sea level. She swam up 6 feet. Next she dove down 2 feet. How many feet below sea level was the scuba diver? **5 feet**
3. One day, the temperature at 10 A.M. was 83°F. By 3 P.M. it had risen 9°. At 8 P.M. the temperature was 7° lower than it was at 3 P.M. What was the temperature at 8 P.M? **85°F**
4. One day, the elevator in a building starts on the ground floor. It goes up 9 floors, down 3 and then up 2. How many floors above or below ground is the elevator? **8 floors above ground**

Get On Line!

PURPOSE

To provide an opportunity for students to use the Internet to model the addition of integers using number lines.

- This page uses the number line to model addition of integers. You may want to remind students that a number line includes negative integers.
- Work through **Exercise 1** with children. Encourage them to read the problem carefully, and point out that the first jump size will be 9, representing Mia earning \$9. The second jump size will be −3, representing Mia paying her brother back.
- For **Exercise 3,** help children see that only the temperatures are needed to determine jump sizes. The times will not be jump sizes.

Unit 8 Test

PURPOSE

This test provides an informal assessment of the Unit 8 objectives.

Unit Test Items 1–20

To assign a numerical grade for this Unit Test, use 5 points for each test item.

Customize Your Instruction

For students who have not yet mastered these objectives, you can use the **Reteaching Resources** listed in the chart below. ***Ways to Success*** is Houghton Mifflin's Intervention program, available in CD-ROM and blackline master formats.

Assessment Options

Formal Tests for this unit are also provided in the Unit Resource Folder.

- **Unit 8 Open Response Test (Form A)**
- **Unit 8 Multiple Choice Test (Form B)**

VOCABULARY Open Response

Choose the best term to complete each sentence.

Vocabulary
x-axis
y-axis
origin
outcome
tree diagram

1. You can use a ____ to show all the possible combinations of outcomes for an event. **tree diagram**
2. The point with the coordinates (0, 0) is called the ____. **origin**
3. A result of a probability experiment is an ____. **outcome**
4. The horizontal number line on a coordinate grid is the ____. ***x*-axis**

CONCEPTS AND SKILLS Open Response

For each spinner, write the probability that a spin will land on green, in both words and fraction form. (Chapter 23)

5. 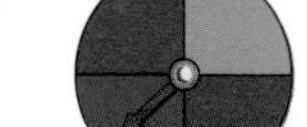 **1 out of 4, $\frac{1}{4}$**

6. 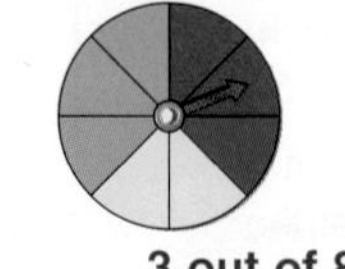 **3 out of 8, $\frac{3}{8}$**

7. 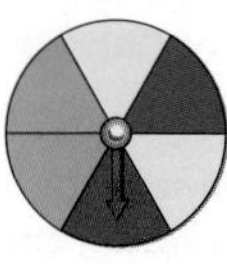 **2 out of 6 or 1 out of 3; $\frac{2}{6}$ or $\frac{1}{3}$**

Suppose you have a cube with sides numbered 1, 2, 3, 4, 5, and 6. If the cube is tossed 30 times, predict how many times you will toss each. (Chapter 23)

8. an even number **15 times**
9. 3 or 4 **10 times**
10. a number less than 5 **20 times**

Make a grid or tree diagram to show the total number of outcomes when one of each is chosen. (Chapter 23) ***See Additional Answers.***

11. **Lunches**
    Drink: juice, milk
    Sandwich: cheese, egg salad, hot dog
12. **Outfits**
    Dress: pink, blue, yellow
    Shoes: black, blue, white

Write the integer for each situation. (Chapter 24)

13. 5 floors up **$^+5$**
14. $10 spent **$^-10$**
15. 6 degrees below zero **$^-6$**

638

Reteaching Support

Unit Test Item	Unit Objectives Tested	Covered on Teacher's Edition Pages	Use These Reteaching Resources
3, 5–7	8A Describe the probability of an event and determine the number of possible outcomes in an experiment.	596A–600	Reteach Resources and *Ways to Success* CD-ROM 23.1, 23.2
8–10	8B Use probability to make predictions.	602A–603	Reteach Resources and *Ways to Success* CD-ROM 23.3
1, 11–12	8C Use tables, graphs, and tree diagrams to represent probability outcomes.	608A–610	Reteach Resources and *Ways to Success* CD-ROM 23.5
2, 4, 16–18	8D Locate, identify, and graph points on a coordinate plane; graph lines.	616A–622	Reteach Resources and *Ways to Success* CD-ROM 24.1, 24.2, 24.3
13–15	8E Write integers.	624A–626	Reteach Resources and *Ways to Success* CD-ROM 24.4
19–20	8F Solve problems using skills and strategies.	604A–606, 628A–630	Reteach Resources and *Ways to Success* CD-ROM 23.4, 24.5

Use the table and grid paper for Problems 16–18.

16. Write pairs of data in the table as ordered pairs. Use the number of hours as the first coordinate. **(1, 4) (2, 8) (3, 12)**

17. Plot the ordered pairs on a coordinate graph. ***See Additional Answers.***

18. How many hours does Carla have to work to earn $12? **3 hours**

Carla's Baby-sitting Earnings	
Hours Worked	**Dollars Earned**
1	4
2	8
3	12

PROBLEM SOLVING Open Response

19. Use the digits 2, 4, and 8 to make as many three-digit numbers as you can. What are all the numbers? **248, 284, 428, 482, 824, 842**

20. Extend the graph you made for Problem 17. How much will Carla earn if she baby-sits for 4 hours? **$16**

Performance Assessment

Constructed Response ***See Additional Answers.***

Task Trisha has invented a game that will use a spinner. The information at the right describes the kind of spinner that she wants for her game.

Use the information above and at the right to design a spinner for Trisha's game.

What is the probability of spinning each of the six colors on your spinner?

Information You Need

- The spinner should have 6 or 8 equal sections.
- The probability of landing on red must be more likely than the probability of landing on blue.
- The probability of landing on at least one of the colors is impossible.
- The probability of landing on two of the colors must be the same.

Spinner Section Colors		
Must Use	**May Use**	
red	green	orange
blue	yellow	purple

Performance Assessment & Scoring Rubric

4 EXEMPLARY

Fully completes the task, showing an understanding of probability. Describes the probabilities of events and determines the possible outcomes in the experiment.

3 PROFICIENT

Completes the task, correctly describing the probability of events. Students may require help in demonstrating how the probability of landing on one of the colors is impossible.

2 ACCEPTABLE

Completes part of the task, correctly describing the probability of events and determining their outcomes. May require help on the rest of the task.

1 LIMITED

Student is unable to complete the task or incorrectly describes the probability of events. Student is unable to determine possible outcomes in the task.

UNIT TEST – FORM A

Unit 8 Test Form A

Name ______ Date ______

Write *certain, likely, unlikely* or *impossible* to describe the probability of landing on 3.

1. likely

2. impossible

For each set of tiles, write the probability that you will pick a star if you pick one tile without looking. Write the probability in both words and fraction form.

3. $\frac{2}{4}$ or $\frac{1}{2}$; 2 out of 4 or 1 out of 2

4. $\frac{3}{5}$; 3 out of 5

Go on

UNIT TEST – FORM B

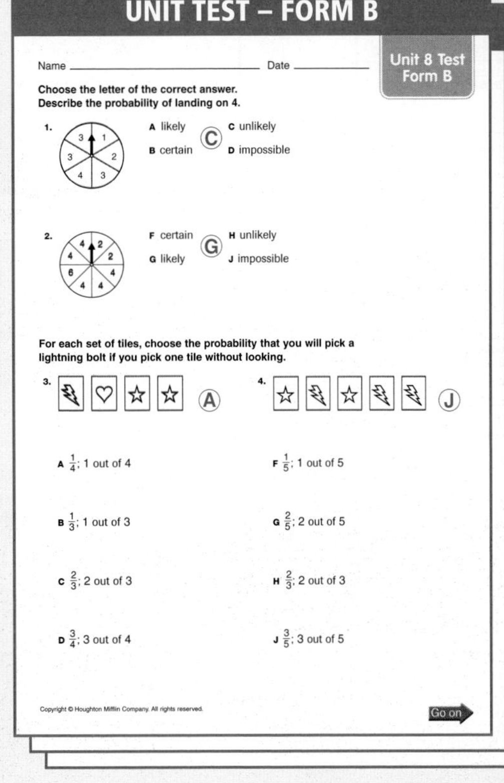

Unit 8 Test Form B

Name ______ Date ______

Choose the letter of the correct answer. Describe the probability of landing on 4.

1. A likely B certain (C) unlikely D impossible

2. F certain G likely (G) H unlikely J impossible

For each set of tiles, choose the probability that you will pick a lightning bolt if you pick one tile without looking.

3. (A)

A $\frac{1}{4}$; 1 out of 4

B $\frac{1}{3}$; 1 out of 3

C $\frac{2}{3}$; 2 out of 3

D $\frac{3}{4}$; 3 out of 4

4. (J)

F $\frac{1}{5}$; 1 out of 5

G $\frac{2}{5}$; 2 out of 5

H $\frac{2}{3}$; 2 out of 3

J $\frac{3}{5}$; 3 out of 5

Go on

Unit 8 Test Answers: Form A

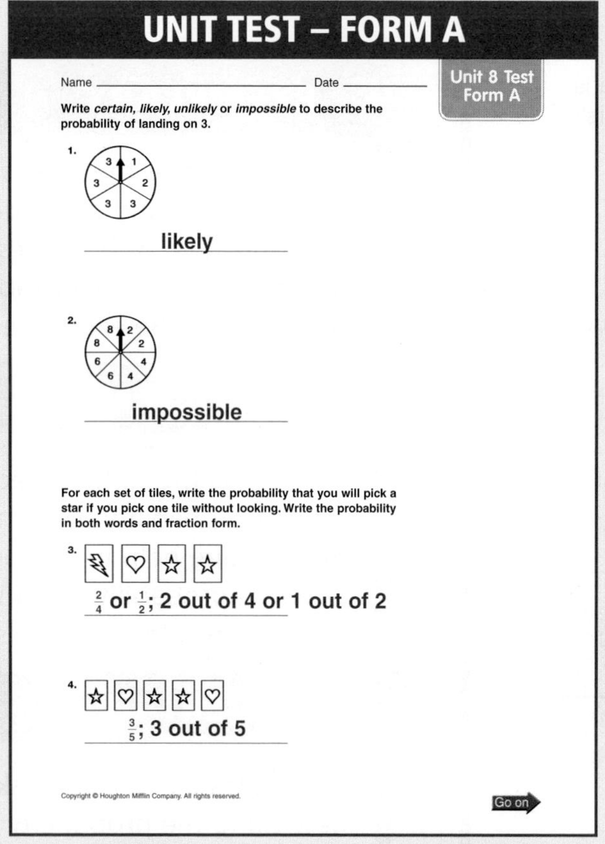

UNIT TEST – FORM A

Unit 8 Test Form A

Name ______________ Date ______

Write *certain, likely, unlikely* or *impossible* to describe the probability of landing on 3.

1. likely

2. impossible

For each set of tiles, write the probability that you will pick a star if you pick one tile without looking. Write the probability in both words and fraction form.

3. $\frac{2}{4}$ or $\frac{1}{2}$; 2 out of 4 or 1 out of 2

4. $\frac{3}{5}$; 3 out of 5

Go on

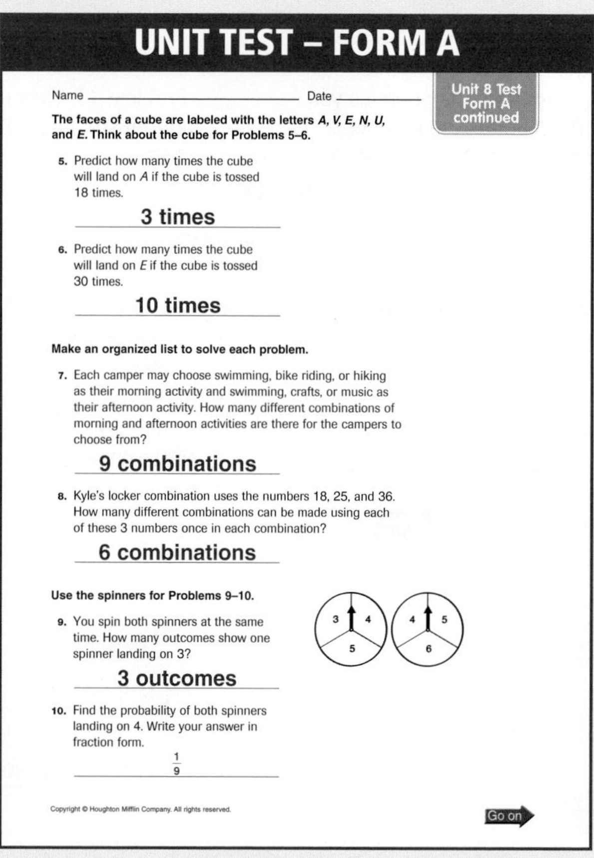

UNIT TEST – FORM A

Unit 8 Test Form A continued

Name ______________ Date ______

The faces of a cube are labeled with the letters *A, V, E, N, U,* and *E*. Think about the cube for Problems 5–6.

5. Predict how many times the cube will land on *A* if the cube is tossed 18 times.
3 times

6. Predict how many times the cube will land on *E* if the cube is tossed 30 times.
10 times

Make an organized list to solve each problem.

7. Each camper may choose swimming, bike riding, or hiking as their morning activity and swimming, crafts, or music as their afternoon activity. How many different combinations of morning and afternoon activities are there for the campers to choose from?
9 combinations

8. Kyle's locker combination uses the numbers 18, 25, and 36. How many different combinations can be made using each of these 3 numbers once in each combination?
6 combinations

Use the spinners for Problems 9–10.

9. You spin both spinners at the same time. How many outcomes show one spinner landing on 3?
3 outcomes

10. Find the probability of both spinners landing on 4. Write your answer in fraction form.
$\frac{1}{9}$

Go on

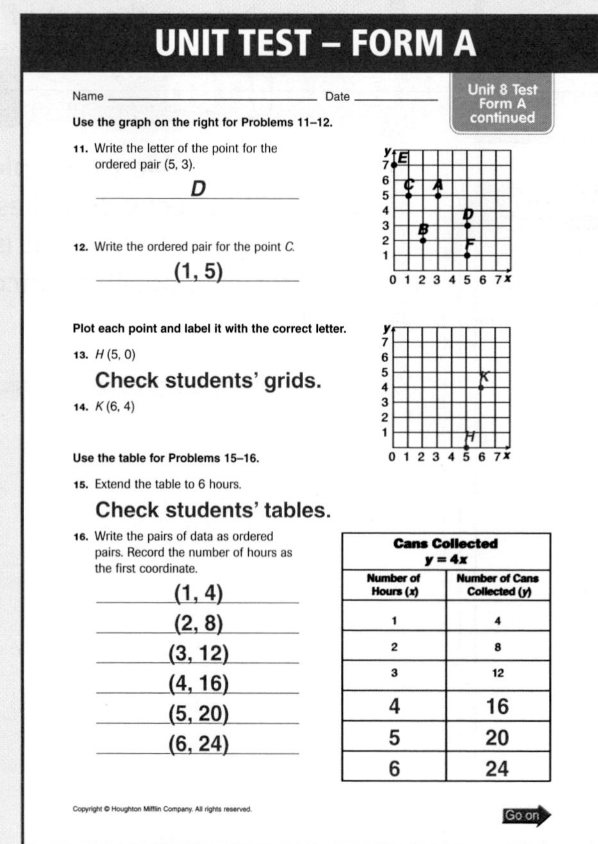

UNIT TEST – FORM A

Unit 8 Test Form A continued

Name ______________ Date ______

Use the graph on the right for Problems 11–12.

11. Write the letter of the point for the ordered pair (5, 3).
D

12. Write the ordered pair for the point *C*.
(1, 5)

Plot each point and label it with the correct letter.

13. *H* (5, 0)
Check students' grids.

14. *K* (6, 4)

Use the table for Problems 15–16.

15. Extend the table to 6 hours.
Check students' tables.

16. Write the pairs of data as ordered pairs. Record the number of hours as the first coordinate.
(1, 4)
(2, 8)
(3, 12)
(4, 16)
(5, 20)
(6, 24)

Cans Collected
$y = 4x$

Number of Hours (x)	Number of Cans Collected (y)
1	4
2	8
3	12
4	16
5	20
6	24

Go on

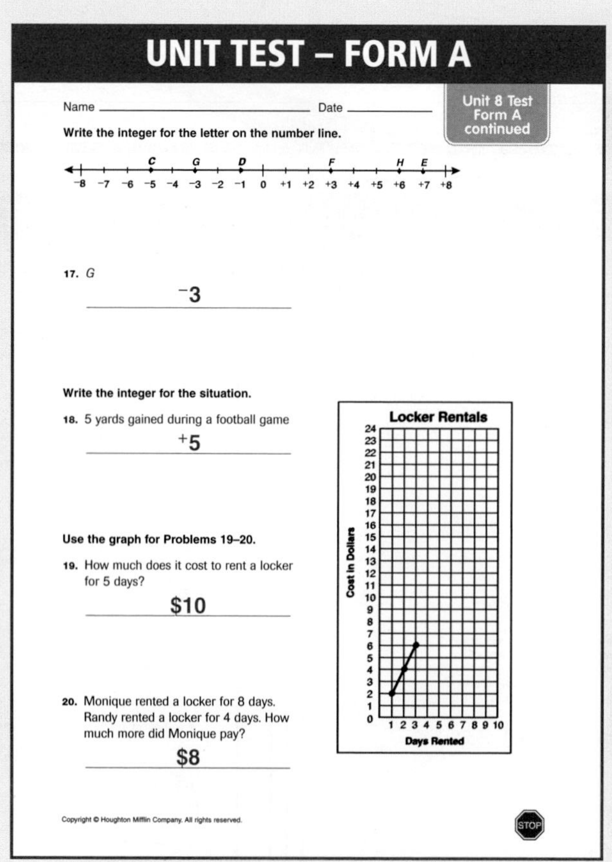

UNIT TEST – FORM A

Unit 8 Test Form A continued

Name ______________ Date ______

Write the integer for the letter on the number line.

17. *G*
$^-3$

Write the integer for the situation.

18. 5 yards gained during a football game
$^+5$

Use the graph for Problems 19–20.

Locker Rentals

19. How much does it cost to rent a locker for 5 days?
$10

20. Monique rented a locker for 8 days. Randy rented a locker for 4 days. How much more did Monique pay?
$8

STOP

Unit 8 Test Answers: Form B

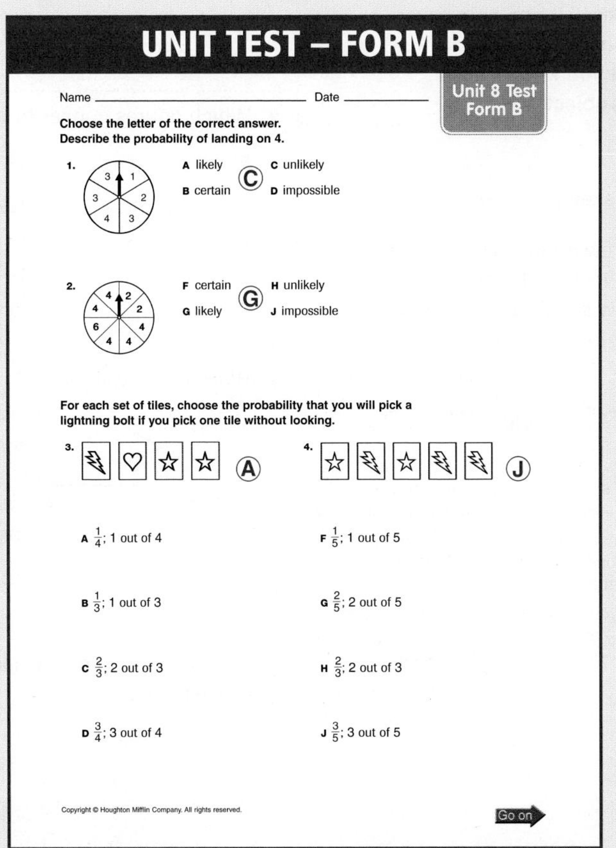

UNIT TEST – FORM B

Name ______________ Date __________ **Unit 8 Test Form B**

Choose the letter of the correct answer.
Describe the probability of landing on 4.

1. A likely B certain (C) C unlikely D impossible

2. F certain (G) G likely H unlikely J impossible

For each set of tiles, choose the probability that you will pick a lightning bolt if you pick one tile without looking.

3. (A)

4. (J)

A $\frac{1}{4}$; 1 out of 4
B $\frac{1}{3}$; 1 out of 3
C $\frac{2}{3}$; 2 out of 3
D $\frac{3}{4}$; 3 out of 4

F $\frac{1}{5}$; 1 out of 5
G $\frac{2}{5}$; 2 out of 5
H $\frac{2}{3}$; 2 out of 3
J $\frac{3}{5}$; 3 out of 5

Go on

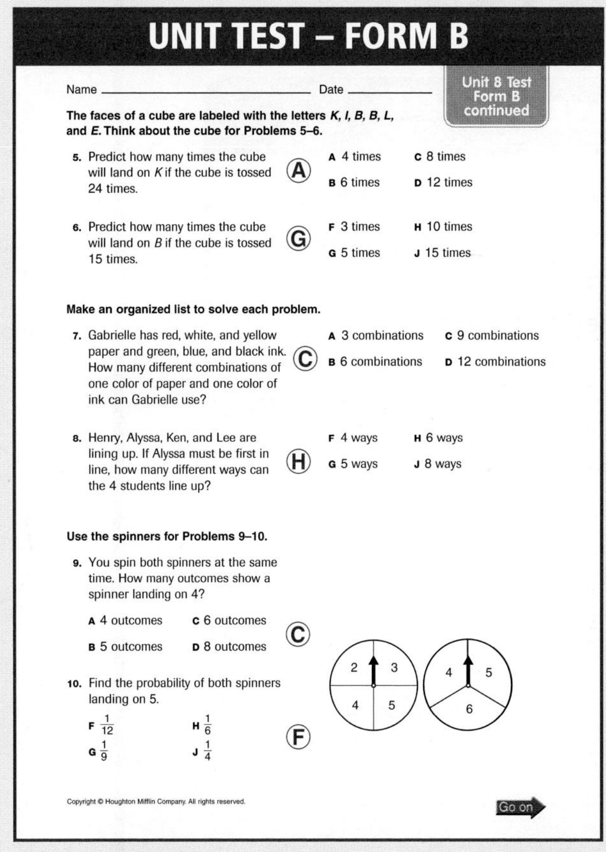

UNIT TEST – FORM B

Name ______________ Date __________ **Unit 8 Test Form B continued**

The faces of a cube are labeled with the letters *K, I, B, B, L,* and *E*. Think about the cube for Problems 5–6.

5. Predict how many times the cube will land on *K* if the cube is tossed 24 times. (A)
A 4 times B 6 times C 8 times D 12 times

6. Predict how many times the cube will land on *B* if the cube is tossed 15 times. (G)
F 3 times G 5 times H 10 times J 15 times

Make an organized list to solve each problem.

7. Gabrielle has red, white, and yellow paper and green, blue, and black ink. How many different combinations of one color of paper and one color of ink can Gabrielle use? (C)
A 3 combinations B 6 combinations C 9 combinations D 12 combinations

8. Henry, Alyssa, Ken, and Lee are lining up. If Alyssa must be first in line, how many different ways can the 4 students line up? (H)
F 4 ways G 5 ways H 6 ways J 8 ways

Use the spinners for Problems 9–10.

9. You spin both spinners at the same time. How many outcomes show a spinner landing on 4? (C)
A 4 outcomes B 5 outcomes C 6 outcomes D 8 outcomes

10. Find the probability of both spinners landing on 5. (F)
F $\frac{1}{12}$ G $\frac{1}{9}$ H $\frac{1}{6}$ J $\frac{1}{4}$

Go on

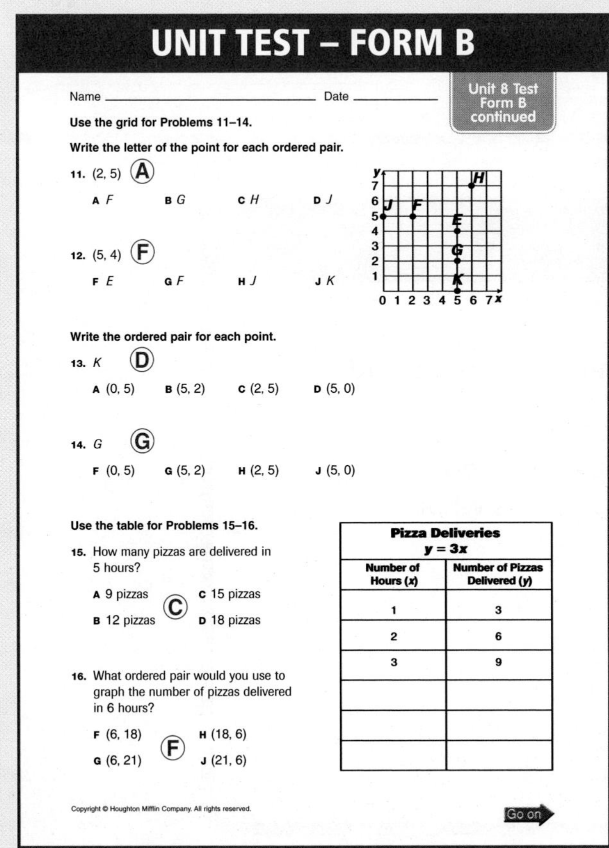

UNIT TEST – FORM B

Name ______________ Date __________ **Unit 8 Test Form B continued**

Use the grid for Problems 11–14.

Write the letter of the point for each ordered pair.

11. (2, 5) (A)
A *F* B *G* C *H* D *J*

12. (5, 4) (F)
F *E* G *F* H *J* J *K*

Write the ordered pair for each point.

13. *K* (D)
A (0, 5) B (5, 2) C (2, 5) D (5, 0)

14. *G* (G)
F (0, 5) G (5, 2) H (2, 5) J (5, 0)

Use the table for Problems 15–16.

Pizza Deliveries $y = 3x$	
Number of Hours (x)	Number of Pizzas Delivered (y)
1	3
2	6
3	9

15. How many pizzas are delivered in 5 hours? (C)
A 9 pizzas B 12 pizzas C 15 pizzas D 18 pizzas

16. What ordered pair would you use to graph the number of pizzas delivered in 6 hours? (F)
F (6, 18) G (6, 21) H (18, 6) J (21, 6)

Go on

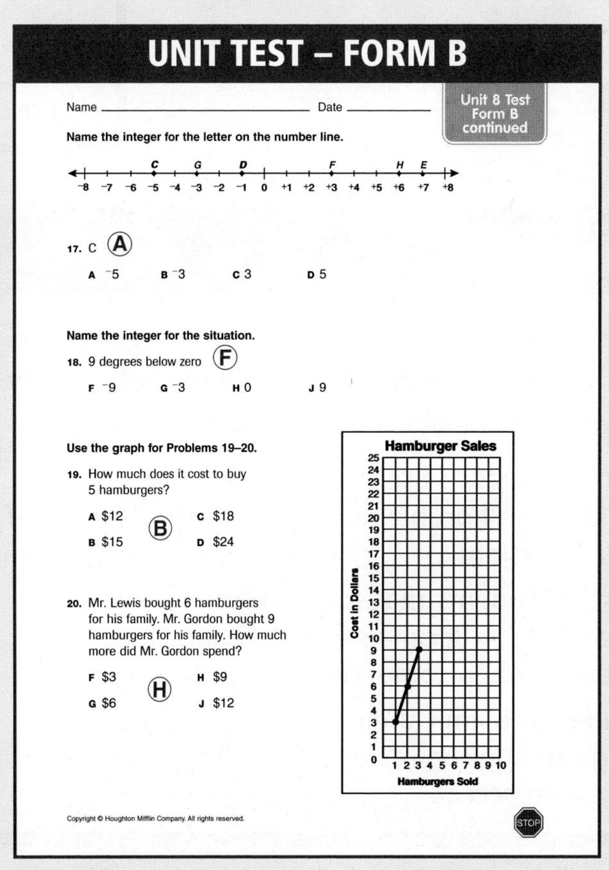

UNIT TEST – FORM B

Name ______________ Date __________ **Unit 8 Test Form B continued**

Name the integer for the letter on the number line.

17. C (A)
A $^-5$ B $^-3$ C 3 D 5

Name the integer for the situation.

18. 9 degrees below zero (F)
F $^-9$ G $^-3$ H 0 J 9

Use the graph for Problems 19–20.

19. How much does it cost to buy 5 hamburgers? (B)
A $12 B $15 C $18 D $24

20. Mr. Lewis bought 6 hamburgers for his family. Mr. Gordon bought 9 hamburgers for his family. How much more did Mr. Gordon spend? (H)
F $3 G $6 H $9 J $12

STOP

Monitoring Student Progress

Cumulative Test Prep

PURPOSE

This page will familiarize students with the multiple-choice and open-response formats of many standardized state tests.

Cumulative Test Prep

Solve Problems 1–10.

Test-Taking Tip

Sometimes a problem asks you to explain your thinking. It can help to remind yourself about what you know about the subject.

Look at the example below.

Samantha drew a triangle with sides measuring 3 inches, 4 inches, and 3 inches. How should she classify the triangle? Explain your thinking.

THINK

You know that an isosceles triangle has two equal sides. You also know that all the angles in an acute triangle are less than 90°.

Draw a triangle with two sides that are 3 units long and one side that is 4 units long. You can see that all the angles are less than 90°.

So, you can classify the triangle as acute isosceles.

Multiple Choice

1. What is the value of this expression?

$$4 + (14 - 6) \div 4$$

A 3 **(C)** 6

B 4 **D** 8

(Chapter 5, Lesson 1)

2. Which figures appear to be congruent?

F 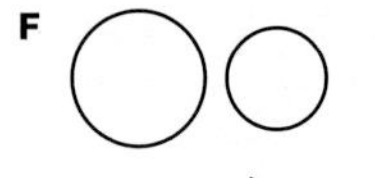

(H)  

G 

J 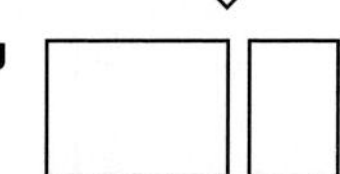

(Chapter 17, Lesson 1)

3. What shape will this net create?

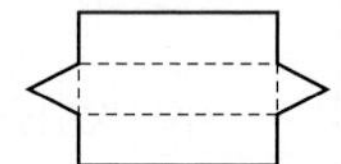

A cube **C** rectangular prism

B cone **(D)** triangular prism

(Chapter 18, Lesson 5)

4. Which set of numbers is listed from greatest to least?

F 0.09 $5\frac{2}{5}$ $3\frac{1}{4}$

(G) 2.3 $2\frac{1}{8}$ $1\frac{1}{8}$

H 0.75 $4\frac{5}{6}$ $1\frac{1}{2}$

J 0.2 $1\frac{1}{2}$ $1\frac{3}{4}$

(Chapter 21, Lesson 7)

640

For Test-Taking Tips, See page 658.

Test-Taking TIPS

Review the test-taking tips with students before they begin the test. Discuss with students some of the ways they can check their work.

- Remind students to use the order of operations in all problems with expressions or equations.
- Suggest to students that they can convert fractions to decimals and decimals to fractions when comparing numbers.
- Tell students to limit their choices by crossing out any choices that they are sure are incorrect.
- Encourage students to look back and see if their answer fits what the problem asks.

5. **milliliters; *Possible explanation:* A liter is close to the size of a quart. A dropper is much smaller than a quart, so milliliters are the better units of measure.**

Open Response

5. Which unit of measure, milliliters or liters, would be better to measure the capacity of a dropper full of vitamins for a cat? Explain your thinking.

See above. (Chapter 12, Lesson 8)

6. What fraction can be used to represent the shaded part of the figure below?

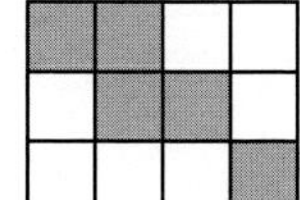

$\frac{5}{12}$

(Chapter 19, Lesson 1)

7. Which of the following factors of 48 are composite numbers? Explain how you know.

1, 2, 3, 4, 6, 8, 12, 16, 24, 48

4, 6, 8, 12, 16, 24, 48;
Each has factors other than 1 and itself. (Chapter 10, Lesson 2)

8. Neal and Joe paid a total of $10 for lunch. They each had 2 slices of pizza and 1 can of juice. Each can of juice cost $1. Write and solve an equation to find the cost of each slice of pizza.

Let p = the cost of 1 slice of pizza;
$4p + (2 \times 1) = 10$; $p = \$2$. (Chapter 5, Lesson 5)

9. Write the coordinates for Point *A*.

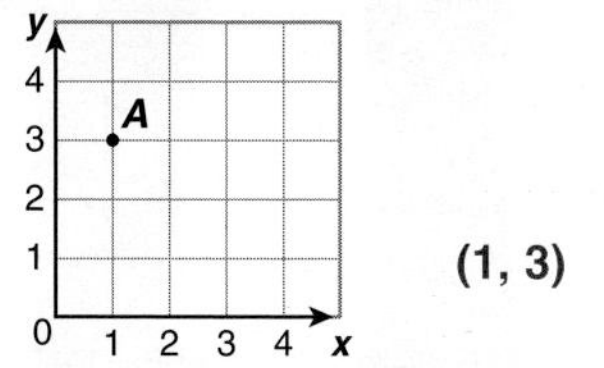

(1, 3)

(Chapter 24, Lesson 2)

10C. blue: $\frac{3}{10}$, green: $\frac{1}{10}$, orange: $\frac{1}{10}$, red: $\frac{2}{10}$ or $\frac{1}{5}$, yellow: $\frac{3}{10}$

10B. blue: 3, green: 1, orange: 1, red: 2, yellow: 3; *Possible explanation:* Since there were 10 marbles and 30 picks, I divided the number of times each color was picked by 3.

Extended Response

10. Rashad puts 10 marbles in a bag. He picks 1 marble without looking, records its color, and puts it back in the bag. He does this 30 times. His results are shown in the line plot.

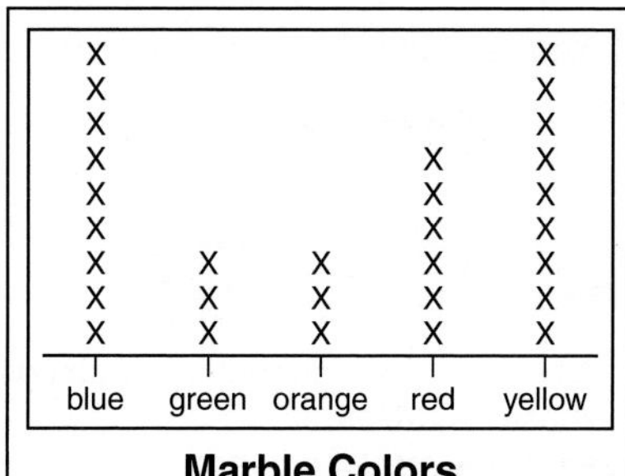

A How many times was a blue marble picked? a red marble? **blue: 9, red: 6**

B Predict how many marbles of each color are in the bag. Explain your thinking. ***See above.***

C Based on your prediction, what is the probability of choosing each color marble? ***See below.***

D Suppose Rashad does the same experiment 40 times. Predict how many times each color marble will be picked.

blue: 12, green: 4, orange: 4, red: 8, yellow: 12 (Chapter 23, Lesson 3)

Education Place
Look for Cumulative Test Prep at **eduplace.com/map** for more practice

Test-Taking Vocabulary

- Several mathematical terms are used in this test. Write the following words on the board and review them with students: *expression, congruent, cube, cone, rectangular prism, triangular prism, milliliters, liters, composite numbers, coordinates, line plot,* and *prediction.*
- For **Problem 1,** review how to perform order of operations on an expression. Encourage students to read the expression aloud to help them figure out which operation to do first.

National and state tests may also use these words with problems that deal with integers.

- above
- below
- sea level
- ground level
- higher
- lower

Vocabulary Wrap-Up

PURPOSE

Use this page to encourage students to use math vocabulary to talk about the important concepts they have learned in this unit.

Big Ideas and Key Vocabulary

Review and discuss with students the Big Ideas of this unit using the Key Vocabulary terms *probability, outcome*, and *coordinates.*

Math Conversations

Have students work together in small groups to discuss **Exercises 1–4.** Check to see whether individual students understand the key concepts and are able to use the math vocabulary correctly. Clear up any misunderstandings students may have. After students have discussed the exercises in small groups, continue the conversation as a whole class. Have volunteers from each group share what their group talked about.

Write About It Have volunteers share how they displayed their data. Then list on the chalkboard the different data displays that were used.

Vocabulary Wrap-Up for Unit 8

Look back at the big ideas and vocabulary in this unit.

Big Ideas

You can use a fraction to represent the probability of an outcome.

You can use coordinates to locate points on a grid.

Key Vocabulary

probability
outcome
coordinates

Math Conversations

Use your new vocabulary to discuss these big ideas.

See Additional Answers.

1. Explain how you know whether a probability is certain or impossible.
2. Suppose you put all of the letters in the word HAWAII in a bag. Explain how to describe the probability of picking each letter without looking.
3. Explain how to find the opposite of 7 on a number line.
4. Explain how to plot the ordered pairs in the table on the right to form a line.

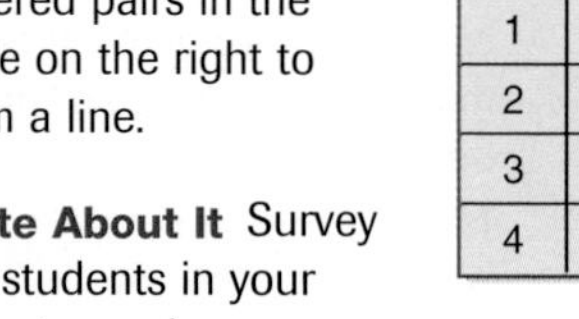

x	*y*
1	1
2	3
3	5
4	7

5. **Write About It** Survey the students in your class to see how many students are wearing blue socks. Show your data and write how you would find the probability that a student is wearing blue socks.

Check students' work.

I surveyed 20 students. Now how should I show my data?

Think about making a bar graph.

Wrap Up the Unit Project

- Before students place their games and puzzles in the Great Games Center in the classroom, have them report on their creations to the whole class in the form of a sales presentation.
- Have students or groups exchange the games and puzzles to see how they work. Then place them in a designated section of the classroom. Students may use the games and puzzles after they finish an assignment or during recess.
- After a designated time in the classroom, students may donate their games and puzzles to a local library, hospital, or senior center.

Student Resources

Literature Connections

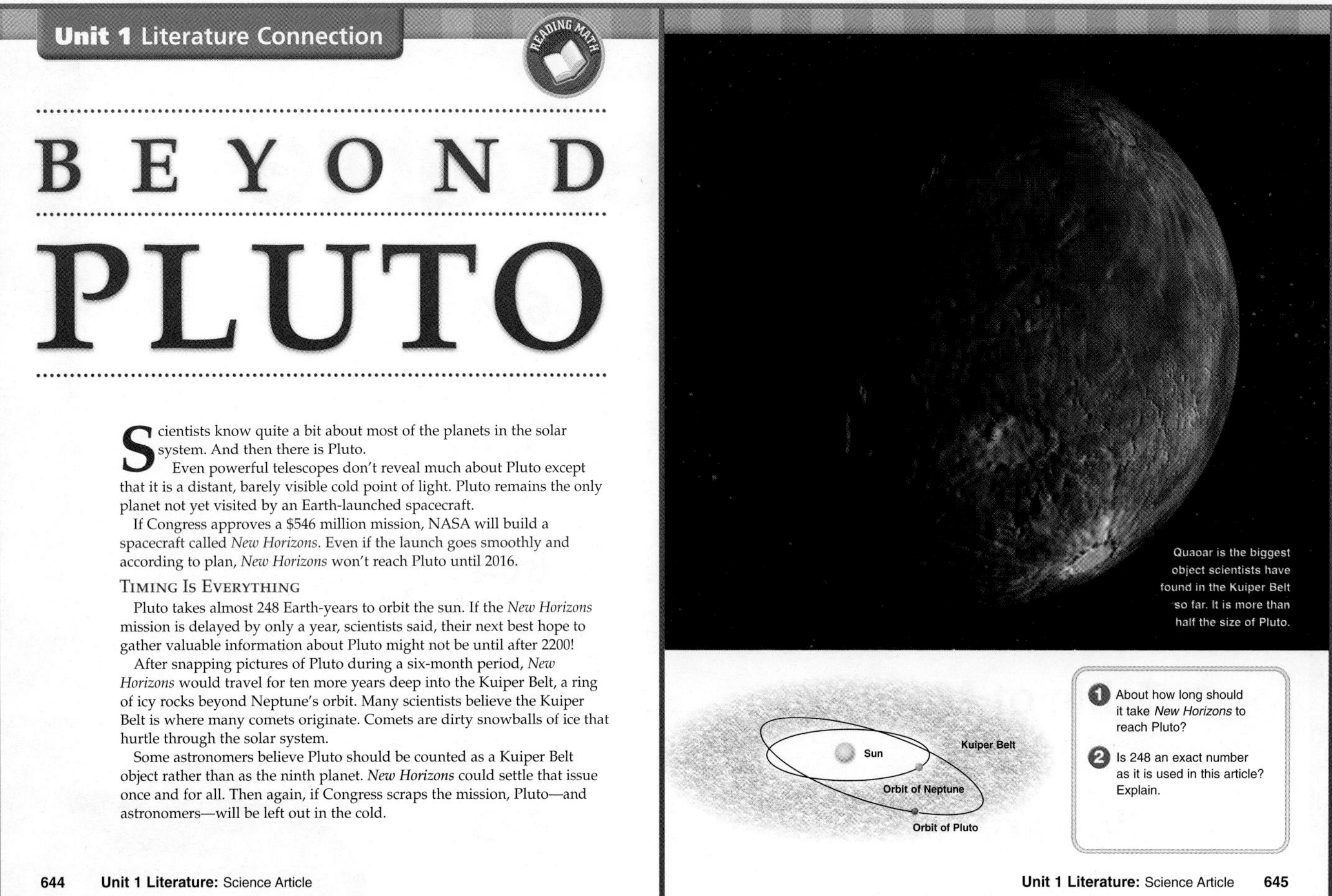

Unit 1 Literature Connection

READING MATH

BEYOND PLUTO

Scientists know quite a bit about most of the planets in the solar system. And then there is Pluto.

Even powerful telescopes don't reveal much about Pluto except that it is a distant, barely visible cold point of light. Pluto remains the only planet not yet visited by an Earth-launched spacecraft.

If Congress approves a $546 million mission, NASA will build a spacecraft called *New Horizons*. Even if the launch goes smoothly and according to plan, *New Horizons* won't reach Pluto until 2016.

TIMING IS EVERYTHING

Pluto takes almost 248 Earth-years to orbit the sun. If the *New Horizons* mission is delayed by only a year, scientists said, their next best hope to gather valuable information about Pluto might not be until after 2200!

After snapping pictures of Pluto during a six-month period, *New Horizons* would travel for ten more years deep into the Kuiper Belt, a ring of icy rocks beyond Neptune's orbit. Many scientists believe the Kuiper Belt is where many comets originate. Comets are dirty snowballs of ice that hurtle through the solar system.

Some astronomers believe Pluto should be counted as a Kuiper Belt object rather than as the ninth planet. *New Horizons* could settle that issue once and for all. Then again, if Congress scraps the mission, Pluto—and astronomers—will be left out in the cold.

Quaoar is the biggest object scientists have found in the Kuiper Belt so far. It is more than half the size of Pluto.

1. About how long should it take *New Horizons* to reach Pluto?
2. Is 248 an exact number as it is used in this article? Explain.

644 Unit 1 Literature: Science Article

Unit 1 Literature: Science Article 645

Unit 1
Reading the Selection

Read the selection aloud to the class or ask students to read it themselves. Then have them work independently, in small groups, or as a whole class to answer the questions.

Answers to Questions

1. about 200 years
2. No; *Possible explanation:* The word *almost* tells us that the number 248 is not an exact number.

Literature Connections

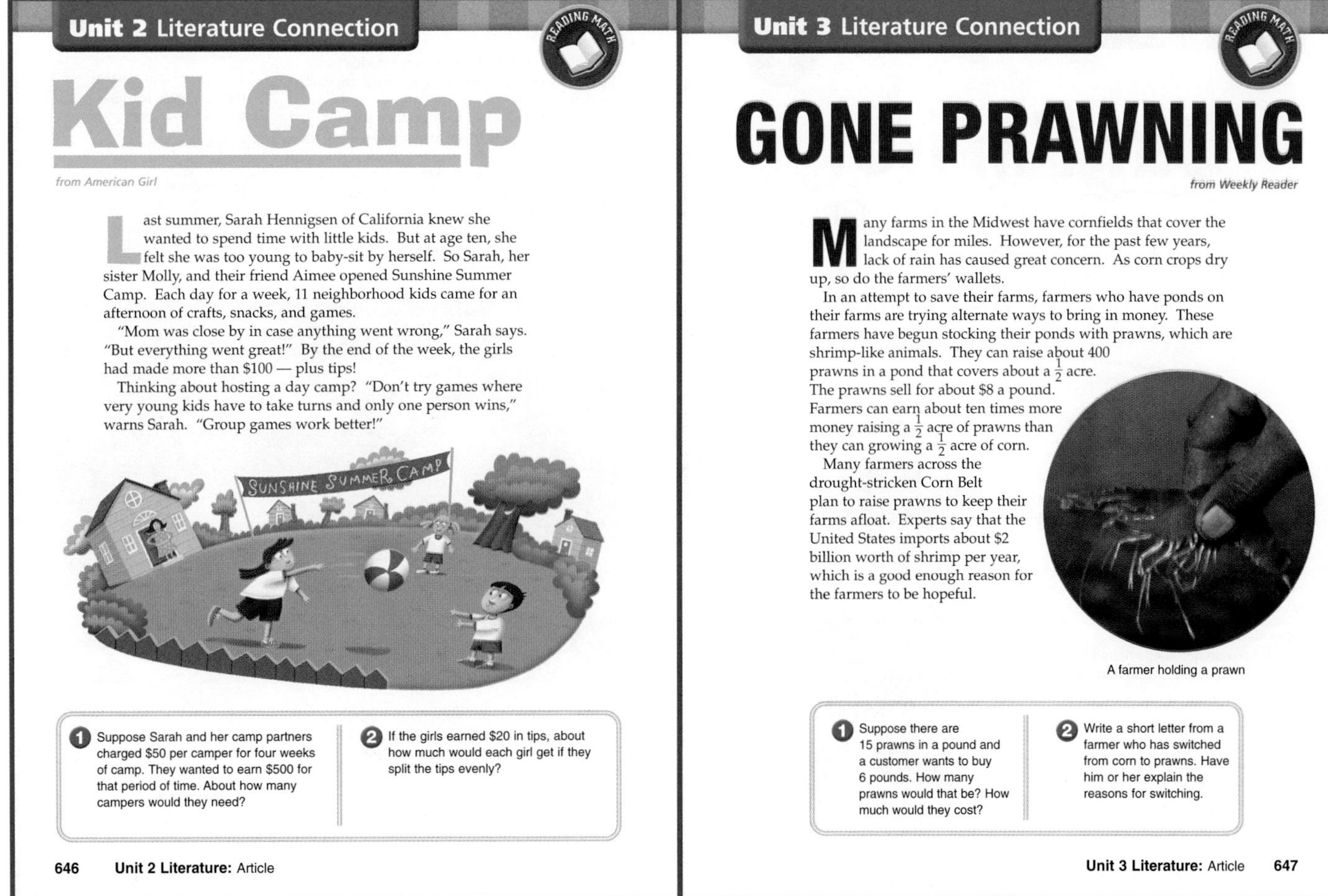

Unit 2 Literature Connection

READING MATH

Kid Camp

from American Girl

Last summer, Sarah Hennigsen of California knew she wanted to spend time with little kids. But at age ten, she felt she was too young to baby-sit by herself. So Sarah, her sister Molly, and their friend Aimee opened Sunshine Summer Camp. Each day for a week, 11 neighborhood kids came for an afternoon of crafts, snacks, and games.

"Mom was close by in case anything went wrong," Sarah says. "But everything went great!" By the end of the week, the girls had made more than $100 — plus tips!

Thinking about hosting a day camp? "Don't try games where very young kids have to take turns and only one person wins," warns Sarah. "Group games work better!"

1. Suppose Sarah and her camp partners charged $50 per camper for four weeks of camp. They wanted to earn $500 for that period of time. About how many campers would they need?
2. If the girls earned $20 in tips, about how much would each girl get if they split the tips evenly?

646 **Unit 2 Literature:** Article

Unit 3 Literature Connection

READING MATH

GONE PRAWNING

from Weekly Reader

Many farms in the Midwest have cornfields that cover the landscape for miles. However, for the past few years, lack of rain has caused great concern. As corn crops dry up, so do the farmers' wallets.

In an attempt to save their farms, farmers who have ponds on their farms are trying alternate ways to bring in money. These farmers have begun stocking their ponds with prawns, which are shrimp-like animals. They can raise about 400 prawns in a pond that covers about a $\frac{1}{2}$ acre. The prawns sell for about $8 a pound. Farmers can earn about ten times more money raising a $\frac{1}{2}$ acre of prawns than they can growing a $\frac{1}{2}$ acre of corn.

Many farmers across the drought-stricken Corn Belt plan to raise prawns to keep their farms afloat. Experts say that the United States imports about $2 billion worth of shrimp per year, which is a good enough reason for the farmers to be hopeful.

A farmer holding a prawn

1. Suppose there are 15 prawns in a pound and a customer wants to buy 6 pounds. How many prawns would that be? How much would they cost?
2. Write a short letter from a farmer who has switched from corn to prawns. Have him or her explain the reasons for switching.

Unit 3 Literature: Article 647

Unit 2
Reading the Selection

Read the article aloud to the class or ask students to read it themselves. Then have them work independently, in small groups, or as a whole class to answer the questions.

Answers to Questions

1. about 10 campers
2. about $7 each

Unit 3
Reading the Selection

Read the article aloud to the class or ask students to read it themselves. Then have them work independently, in small groups, or as a whole class to answer the questions.

Answers to Questions

1. 15 × 6 = 90 prawns; 6 × $8 = $48
2. Have students share their work.

Literature Connections

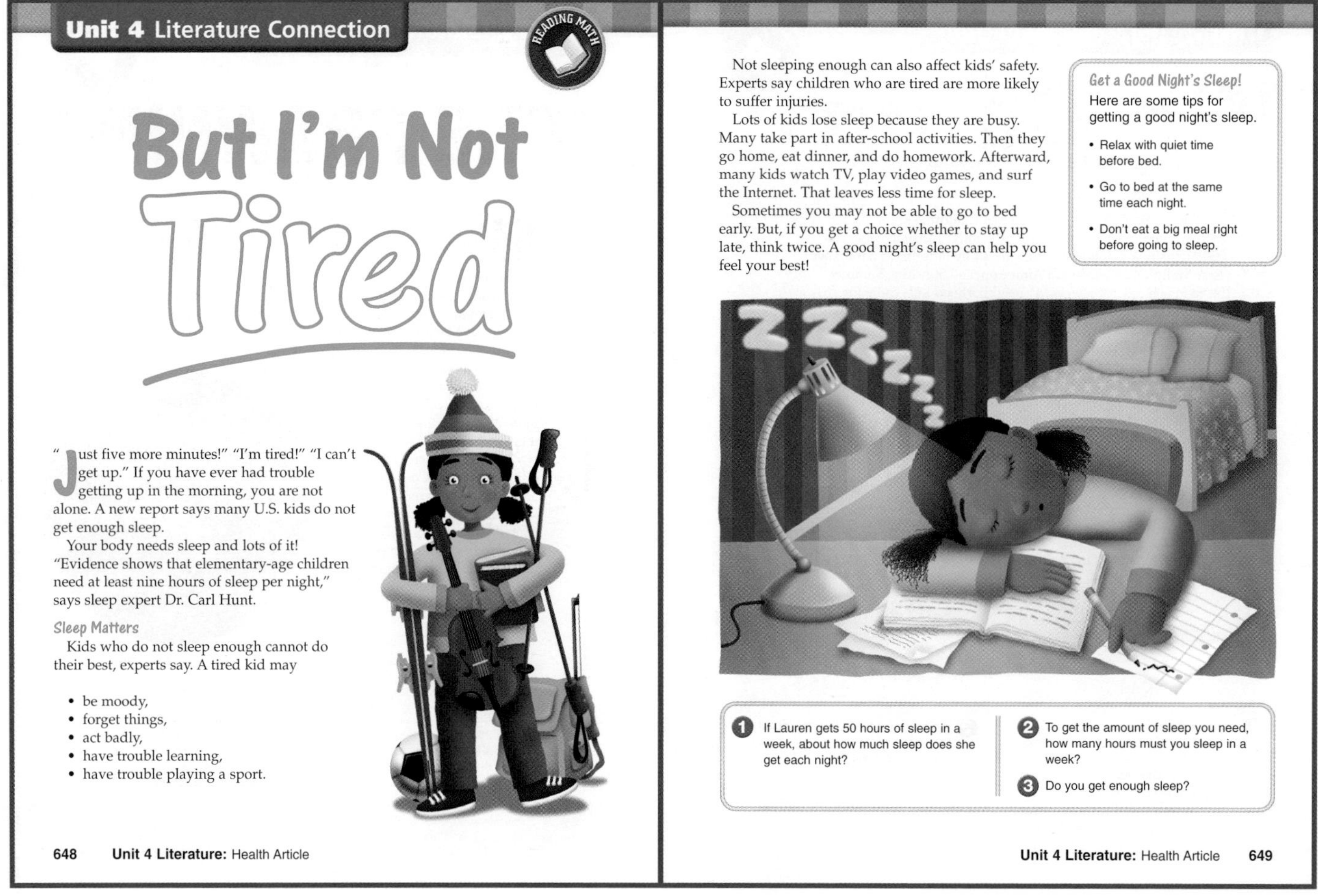

Unit 4 Literature Connection

READING MATH

But I'm Not Tired

"Just five more minutes!" "I'm tired!" "I can't get up." If you have ever had trouble getting up in the morning, you are not alone. A new report says many U.S. kids do not get enough sleep.

Your body needs sleep and lots of it! "Evidence shows that elementary-age children need at least nine hours of sleep per night," says sleep expert Dr. Carl Hunt.

Sleep Matters

Kids who do not sleep enough cannot do their best, experts say. A tired kid may

- be moody,
- forget things,
- act badly,
- have trouble learning,
- have trouble playing a sport.

Not sleeping enough can also affect kids' safety. Experts say children who are tired are more likely to suffer injuries.

Lots of kids lose sleep because they are busy. Many take part in after-school activities. Then they go home, eat dinner, and do homework. Afterward, many kids watch TV, play video games, and surf the Internet. That leaves less time for sleep.

Sometimes you may not be able to go to bed early. But, if you get a choice whether to stay up late, think twice. A good night's sleep can help you feel your best!

Get a Good Night's Sleep!

Here are some tips for getting a good night's sleep.

- Relax with quiet time before bed.
- Go to bed at the same time each night.
- Don't eat a big meal right before going to sleep.

1. If Lauren gets 50 hours of sleep in a week, about how much sleep does she get each night?
2. To get the amount of sleep you need, how many hours must you sleep in a week?
3. Do you get enough sleep?

648 Unit 4 Literature: Health Article

Unit 4 Literature: Health Article 649

Unit 4
Reading the Selection

Read the article aloud to the class or ask students to read it themselves. Then have them work independently, in small groups, or as a whole class to answer the questions.

Answers to Questions

1. Lauren gets about 7 hours of sleep per night.
2. 63 hours of sleep
3. Answers may vary.

Literature Connections

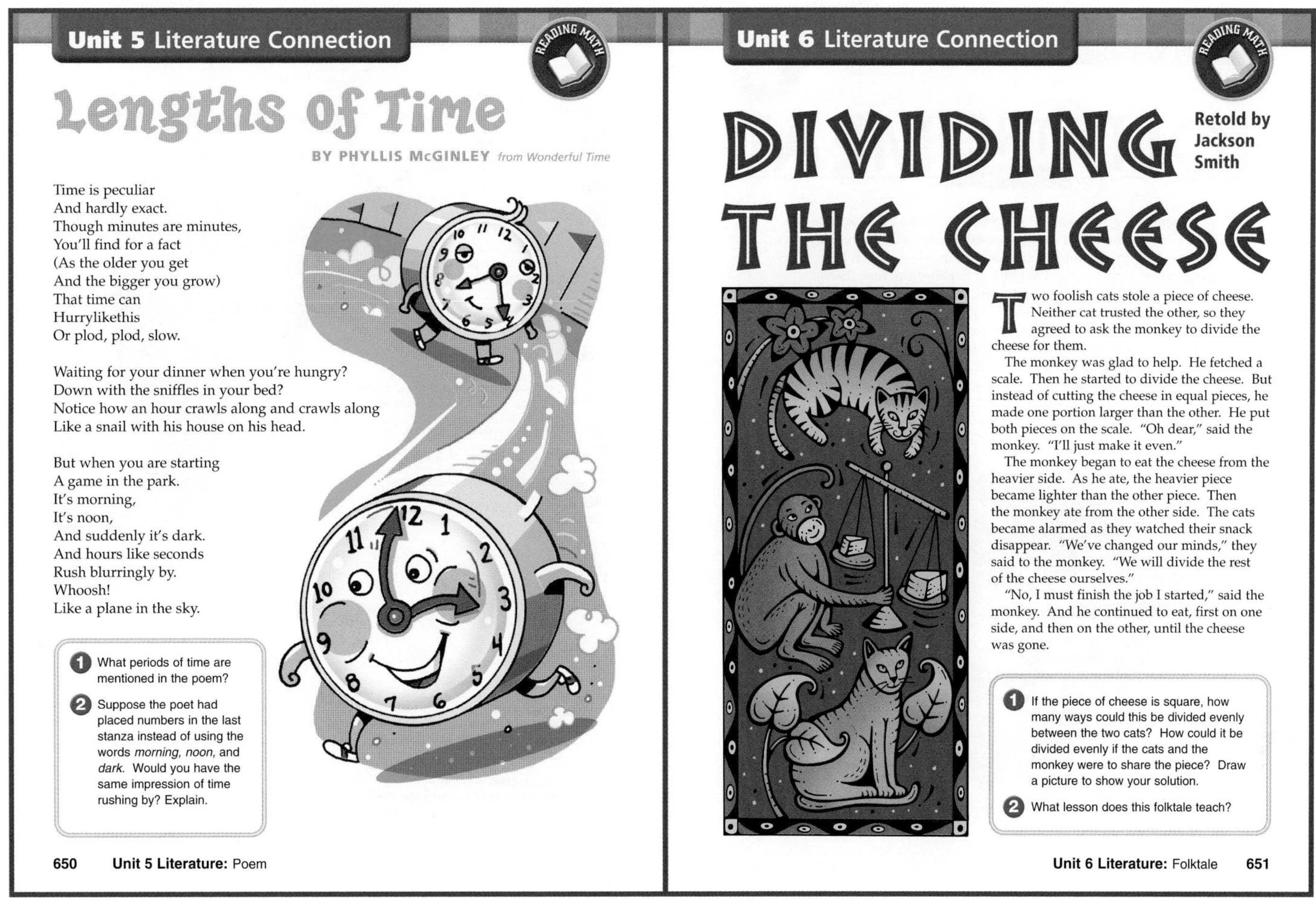

Unit 5 Literature Connection

READING MATH

Lengths of Time

BY PHYLLIS McGINLEY *from Wonderful Time*

Time is peculiar
And hardly exact.
Though minutes are minutes,
You'll find for a fact
(As the older you get
And the bigger you grow)
That time can
Hurrylikethis
Or plod, plod, slow.

Waiting for your dinner when you're hungry?
Down with the sniffles in your bed?
Notice how an hour crawls along and crawls along
Like a snail with his house on his head.

But when you are starting
A game in the park.
It's morning,
It's noon,
And suddenly it's dark.
And hours like seconds
Rush blurringly by.
Whoosh!
Like a plane in the sky.

1. What periods of time are mentioned in the poem?
2. Suppose the poet had placed numbers in the last stanza instead of using the words *morning, noon,* and *dark.* Would you have the same impression of time rushing by? Explain.

650 Unit 5 Literature: Poem

Unit 6 Literature Connection

READING MATH

DIVIDING THE CHEESE

Retold by Jackson Smith

Two foolish cats stole a piece of cheese. Neither cat trusted the other, so they agreed to ask the monkey to divide the cheese for them.

The monkey was glad to help. He fetched a scale. Then he started to divide the cheese. But instead of cutting the cheese in equal pieces, he made one portion larger than the other. He put both pieces on the scale. "Oh dear," said the monkey. "I'll just make it even."

The monkey began to eat the cheese from the heavier side. As he ate, the heavier piece became lighter than the other piece. Then the monkey ate from the other side. The cats became alarmed as they watched their snack disappear. "We've changed our minds," they said to the monkey. "We will divide the rest of the cheese ourselves."

"No, I must finish the job I started," said the monkey. And he continued to eat, first on one side, and then on the other, until the cheese was gone.

1. If the piece of cheese is square, how many ways could this be divided evenly between the two cats? How could it be divided evenly if the cats and the monkey were to share the piece? Draw a picture to show your solution.
2. What lesson does this folktale teach?

Unit 6 Literature: Folktale 651

Unit 5
Reading the Selection

Read the poem aloud to the class or ask students to read it themselves. Then have them work independently, in small groups, or as a whole class to answer the questions.

Answers to Questions

1. minutes, an hour, seconds
2. Accept reasonable answers.

Unit 6
Reading the Selection

Read the story aloud to the class or ask students to read it themselves. Then have them work independently, in small groups, or as a whole class to answer the questions.

Answers to Questions

1. Accept all drawings of a square cut into 2 equal pieces; Accept all drawings of a square cut into 3 equal pieces.
2. Accept reasonable responses.

Literature Connections

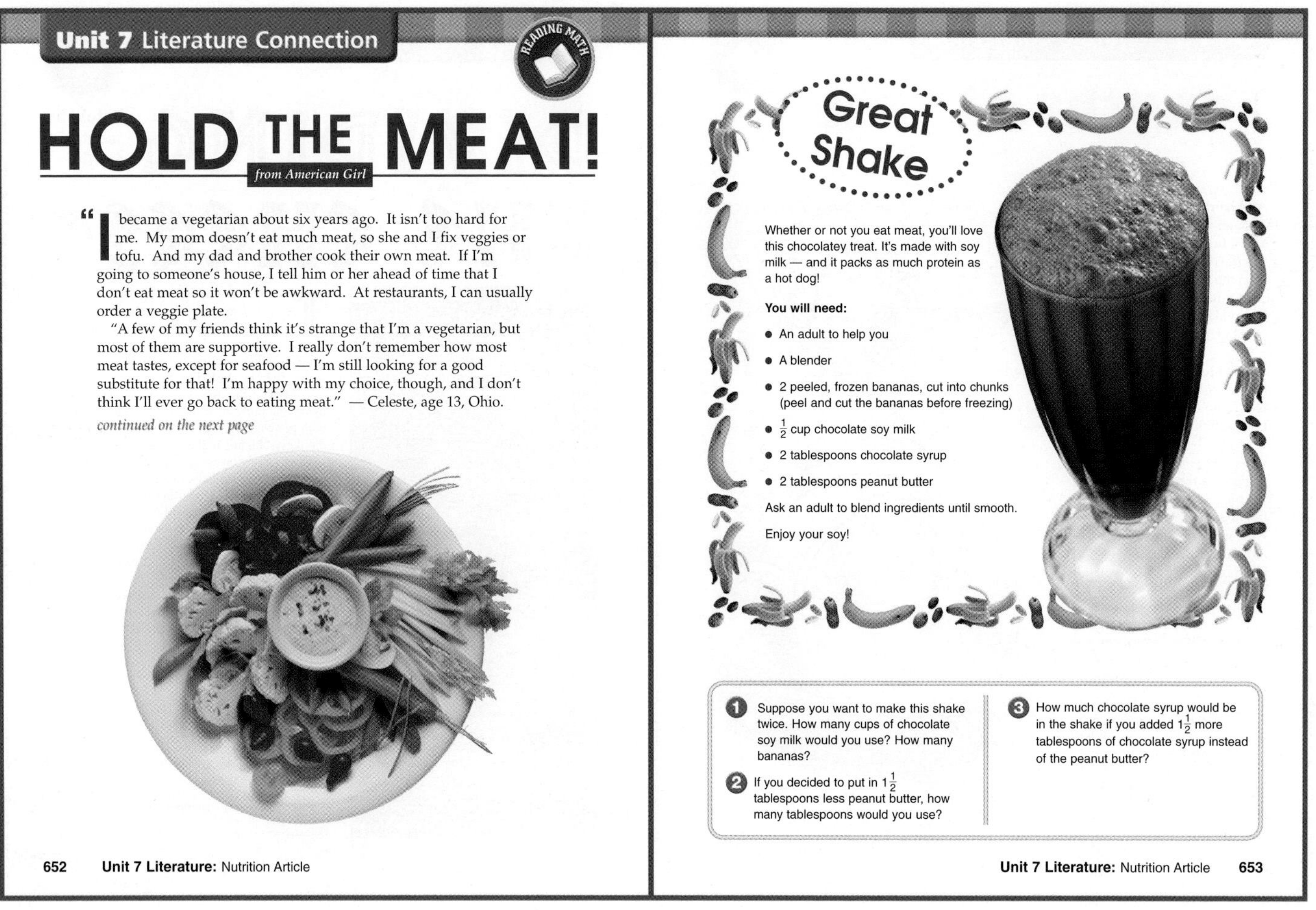

Unit 7 Literature Connection

READING MATH

HOLD THE MEAT!

from American Girl

"I became a vegetarian about six years ago. It isn't too hard for me. My mom doesn't eat much meat, so she and I fix veggies or tofu. And my dad and brother cook their own meat. If I'm going to someone's house, I tell him or her ahead of time that I don't eat meat so it won't be awkward. At restaurants, I can usually order a veggie plate.

"A few of my friends think it's strange that I'm a vegetarian, but most of them are supportive. I really don't remember how most meat tastes, except for seafood — I'm still looking for a good substitute for that! I'm happy with my choice, though, and I don't think I'll ever go back to eating meat." — Celeste, age 13, Ohio.

continued on the next page

652 **Unit 7 Literature:** Nutrition Article

Great Shake

Whether or not you eat meat, you'll love this chocolatey treat. It's made with soy milk — and it packs as much protein as a hot dog!

You will need:

- An adult to help you
- A blender
- 2 peeled, frozen bananas, cut into chunks (peel and cut the bananas before freezing)
- $\frac{1}{2}$ cup chocolate soy milk
- 2 tablespoons chocolate syrup
- 2 tablespoons peanut butter

Ask an adult to blend ingredients until smooth.

Enjoy your soy!

1. Suppose you want to make this shake twice. How many cups of chocolate soy milk would you use? How many bananas?
2. If you decided to put in $1\frac{1}{2}$ tablespoons less peanut butter, how many tablespoons would you use?
3. How much chocolate syrup would be in the shake if you added $1\frac{1}{2}$ more tablespoons of chocolate syrup instead of the peanut butter?

Unit 7 Literature: Nutrition Article 653

Unit 7
Reading the Selection

Read the article aloud to the class or ask students to read it themselves. Then have them work independently, in small groups, or as a whole class to answer the questions.

Answers to Questions

1. 1 cup of chocolate soy milk, 4 bananas
2. $\frac{1}{2}$ tablespoon
3. $3\frac{1}{2}$ tablespoons

Literature Connections

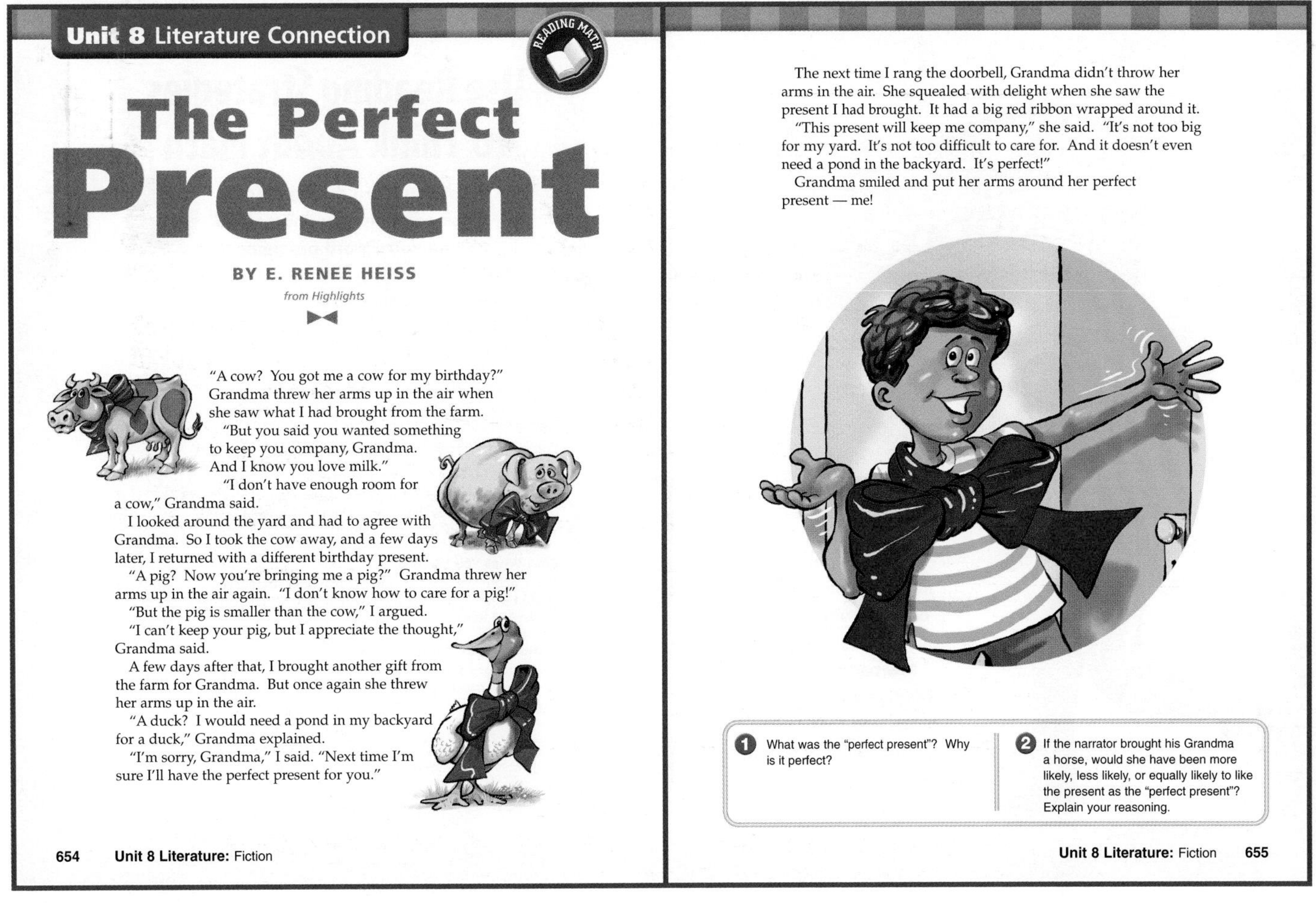

Unit 8 Literature Connection

READING MATH

The Perfect Present

BY E. RENEE HEISS

from Highlights

"A cow? You got me a cow for my birthday?" Grandma threw her arms up in the air when she saw what I had brought from the farm.

"But you said you wanted something to keep you company, Grandma. And I know you love milk."

"I don't have enough room for a cow," Grandma said.

I looked around the yard and had to agree with Grandma. So I took the cow away, and a few days later, I returned with a different birthday present.

"A pig? Now you're bringing me a pig?" Grandma threw her arms up in the air again. "I don't know how to care for a pig!"

"But the pig is smaller than the cow," I argued.

"I can't keep your pig, but I appreciate the thought," Grandma said.

A few days after that, I brought another gift from the farm for Grandma. But once again she threw her arms up in the air.

"A duck? I would need a pond in my backyard for a duck," Grandma explained.

"I'm sorry, Grandma," I said. "Next time I'm sure I'll have the perfect present for you."

654 **Unit 8 Literature:** Fiction

The next time I rang the doorbell, Grandma didn't throw her arms in the air. She squealed with delight when she saw the present I had brought. It had a big red ribbon wrapped around it.

"This present will keep me company," she said. "It's not too big for my yard. It's not too difficult to care for. And it doesn't even need a pond in the backyard. It's perfect!"

Grandma smiled and put her arms around her perfect present — me!

1. What was the "perfect present"? Why is it perfect?
2. If the narrator brought his Grandma a horse, would she have been more likely, less likely, or equally likely to like the present as the "perfect present"? Explain your reasoning.

Unit 8 Literature: Fiction 655

Unit 8
Reading the Selection

Read the story aloud to the class or ask students to read it themselves. Then have them work independently, in small groups, or as a whole class to answer the questions.

Answers to Questions

1. The perfect present was the boy in the story. Accept reasonable responses.
2. She would be less likely to like the horse. Accept reasonable explanations.

Student Handbook

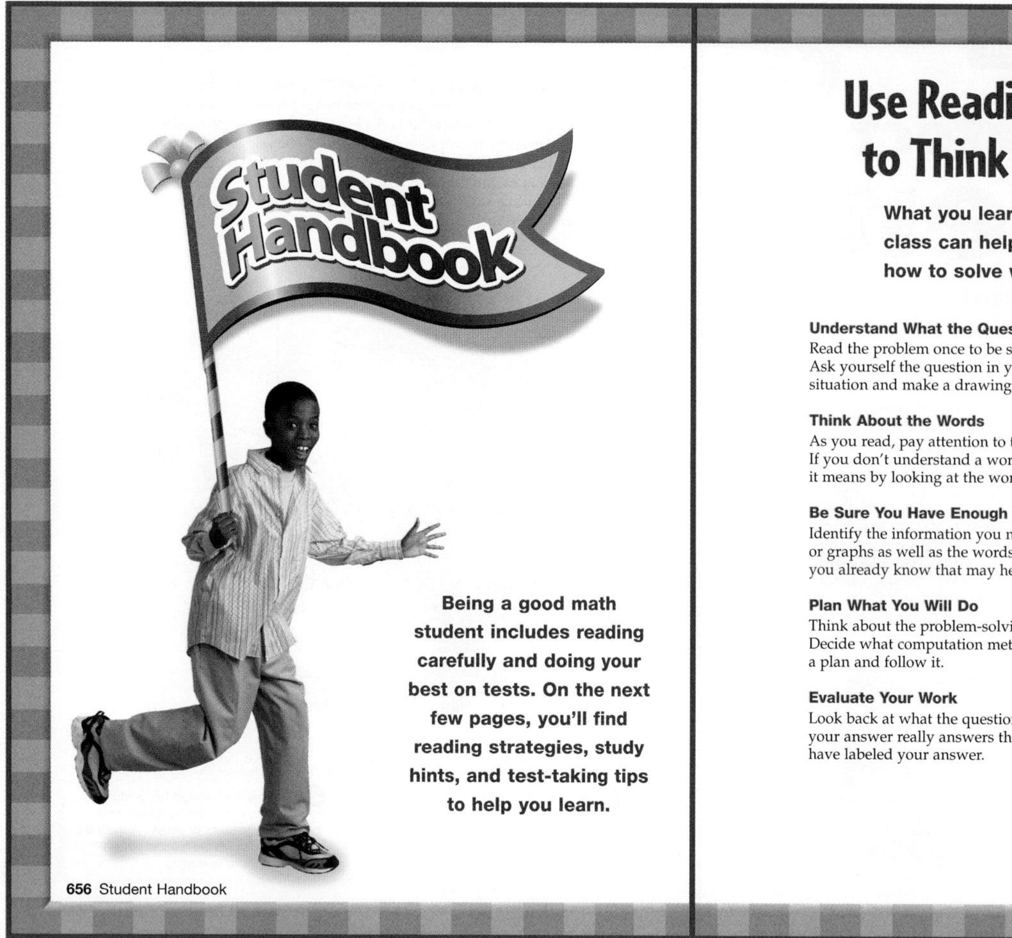

Being a good math student includes reading carefully and doing your best on tests. On the next few pages, you'll find reading strategies, study hints, and test-taking tips to help you learn.

656 Student Handbook

Use Reading Strategies to Think About Math

What you learn during reading class can help you understand how to solve word problems.

Understand What the Question Is
Read the problem once to be sure it makes sense to you. Ask yourself the question in your own words. Picture the situation and make a drawing if it helps.

Think About the Words
As you read, pay attention to the mathematical terms. If you don't understand a word, try to decide what it means by looking at the words around it.

Be Sure You Have Enough Information
Identify the information you need. Look at tables or graphs as well as the words. Think about what you already know that may help.

Plan What You Will Do
Think about the problem-solving plan and strategies. Decide what computation method is needed. Then make a plan and follow it.

Evaluate Your Work
Look back at what the question asked, and check that your answer really answers that question. Be sure you have labeled your answer.

Student Handbook 657

Strategies for Taking Tests

You need to think differently about how to answer various kinds of questions.

All Questions
If you can't answer a question, go on to the next question. You can return to it if there is time.

Always check your computation.

Multiple-Choice Questions
Estimate the answer. This can help eliminate any unreasonable choices.

On bubble sheets, be sure you mark the bubble for the right question and for the right letter.

Short-Answer Questions
Follow the directions carefully. You may need to show your work, write an explanation, or make a drawing.

If you can't give a complete answer, show what you do know. You may get credit for part of an answer.

Long-Answer Questions
Take time to think about these questions because you often need to explain your answer.

When you finish, reread the question and answer to be sure you have answered the question correctly.

Student Scoring Rubric
Your teacher may use a scoring rubric to evaluate your work. An example is on the next page. Not all rubrics are the same, so your teacher may use a different one.

658 Student Handbook

Scoring Rubric

Rating	My work on this problem
Exemplary (full credit)	• has no errors, has the correct answer, and shows that I checked my answer. • is explained carefully and completely. • shows all needed diagrams, tables, or graphs.
Proficient (some credit)	• has small errors, has a close answer, and shows that I checked only the math. • is explained but may have missing parts. • shows most needed diagrams, tables, or graphs.
Acceptable (little credit)	• has some errors, has an answer, and shows that I did not check my answer. • is not explained carefully and completely. • shows few needed diagrams, tables, or graphs.
Limited (very little credit)	• has many errors and may not have an answer. • is not explained at all. • shows no needed diagrams, tables, or graphs.

Two Important Things You Can Do Before a Test

- Get plenty of sleep the night before.
- Eat a good breakfast in the morning.

Student Handbook 659

Student Handbook

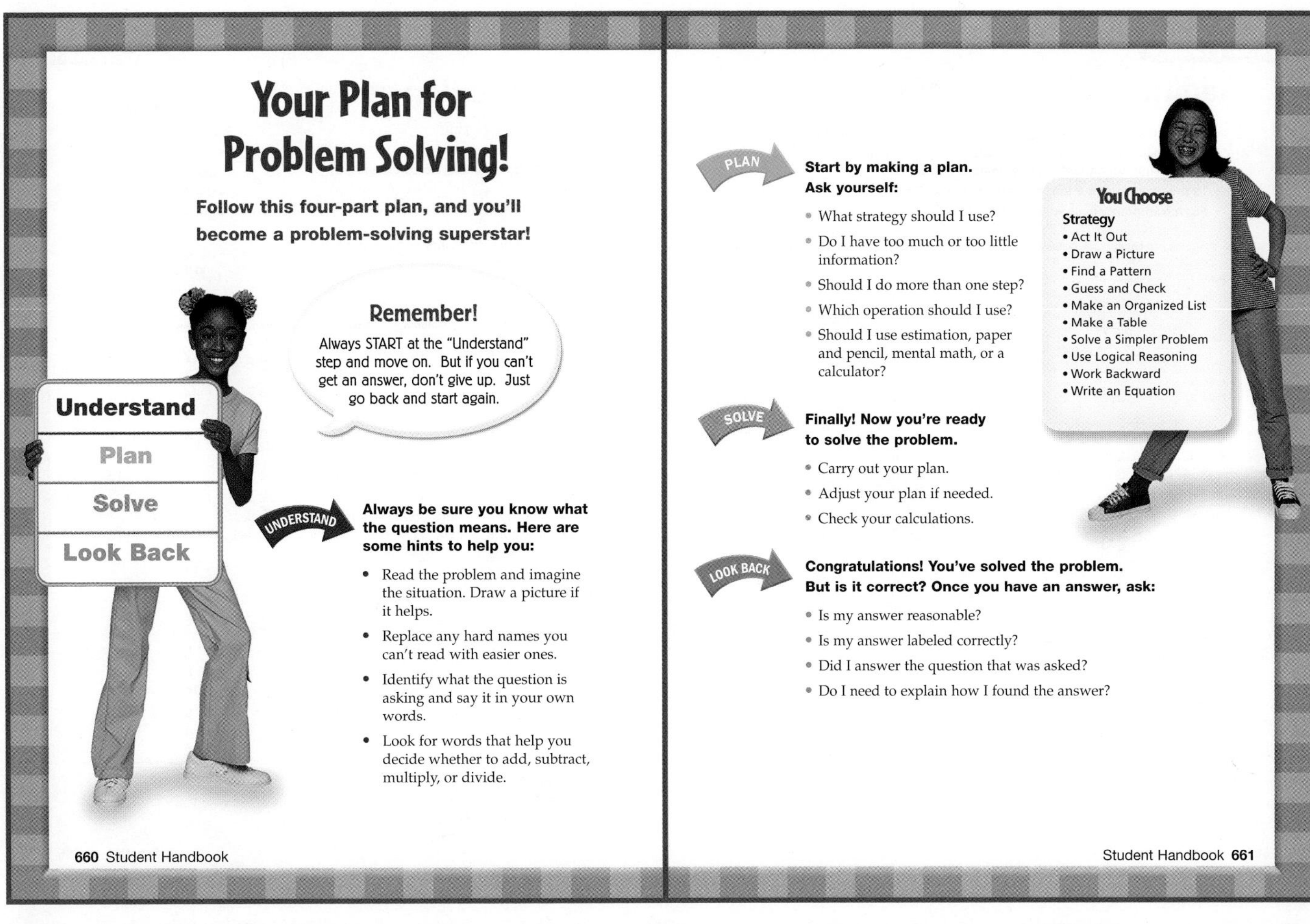

Your Plan for Problem Solving!
Follow this four-part plan, and you'll become a problem-solving superstar!
Remember!
Always START at the "Understand" step and move on. But if you can't get an answer, don't give up. Just go back and start again.
Understand
Plan
Solve
Look Back
UNDERSTAND
Always be sure you know what the question means. Here are some hints to help you:
• Read the problem and imagine the situation. Draw a picture if it helps.
• Replace any hard names you can't read with easier ones.
• Identify what the question is asking and say it in your own words.
• Look for words that help you decide whether to add, subtract, multiply, or divide.
660 Student Handbook
PLAN
Start by making a plan. Ask yourself:
• What strategy should I use?
• Do I have too much or too little information?
• Should I do more than one step?
• Which operation should I use?
• Should I use estimation, paper and pencil, mental math, or a calculator?
You Choose
Strategy
• Act It Out
• Draw a Picture
• Find a Pattern
• Guess and Check
• Make an Organized List
• Make a Table
• Solve a Simpler Problem
• Use Logical Reasoning
• Work Backward
• Write an Equation
SOLVE
Finally! Now you're ready to solve the problem.
• Carry out your plan.
• Adjust your plan if needed.
• Check your calculations.
LOOK BACK
Congratulations! You've solved the problem. But is it correct? Once you have an answer, ask:
• Is my answer reasonable?
• Is my answer labeled correctly?
• Did I answer the question that was asked?
• Do I need to explain how I found the answer?
Student Handbook 661

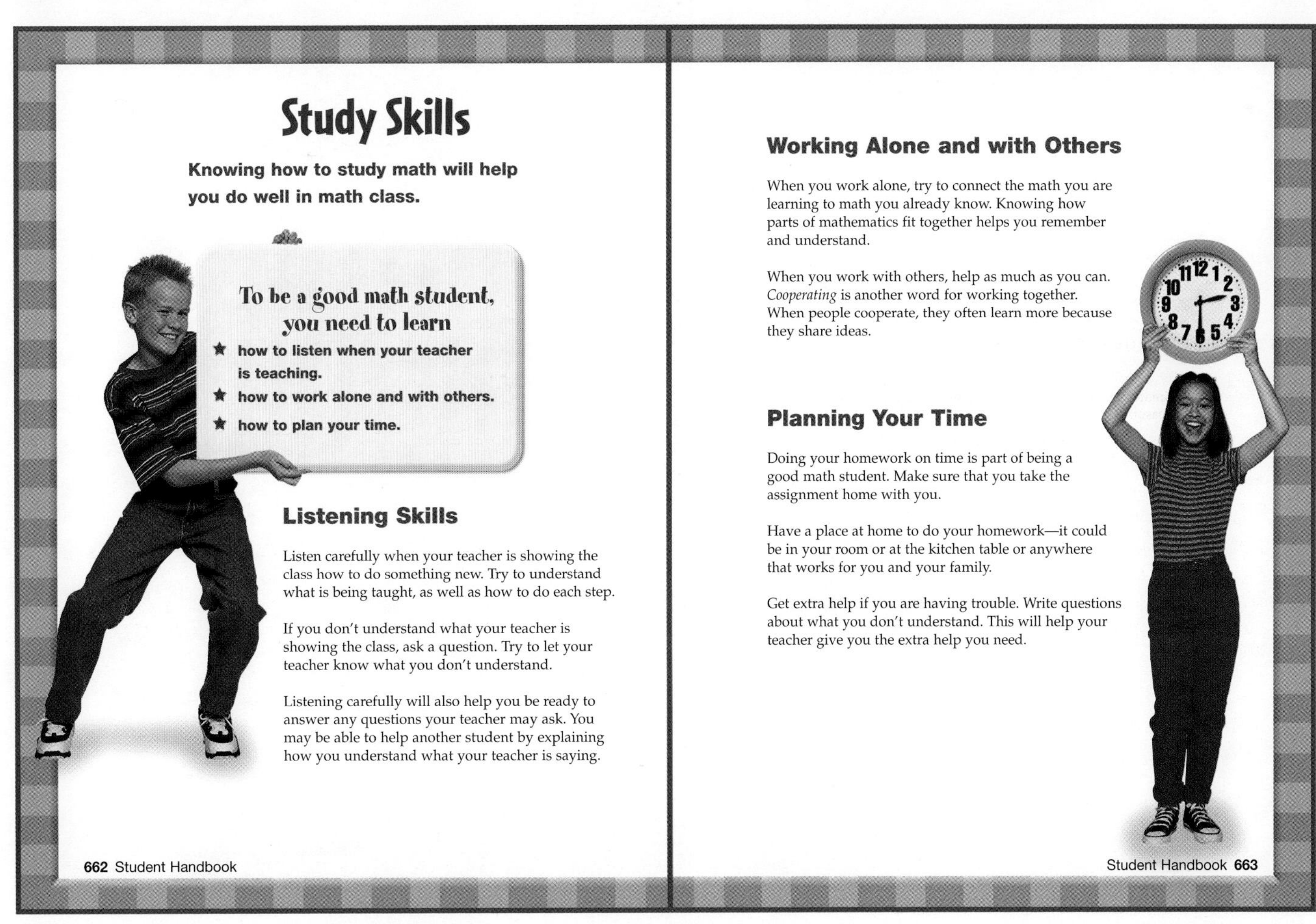

Study Skills
Knowing how to study math will help you do well in math class.
To be a good math student, you need to learn
★ how to listen when your teacher is teaching.
★ how to work alone and with others.
★ how to plan your time.
Listening Skills
Listen carefully when your teacher is showing the class how to do something new. Try to understand what is being taught, as well as how to do each step.
If you don't understand what your teacher is showing the class, ask a question. Try to let your teacher know what you don't understand.
Listening carefully will also help you be ready to answer any questions your teacher may ask. You may be able to help another student by explaining how you understand what your teacher is saying.
662 Student Handbook
Working Alone and with Others
When you work alone, try to connect the math you are learning to math you already know. Knowing how parts of mathematics fit together helps you remember and understand.
When you work with others, help as much as you can. Cooperating is another word for working together. When people cooperate, they often learn more because they share ideas.
Planning Your Time
Doing your homework on time is part of being a good math student. Make sure that you take the assignment home with you.
Have a place at home to do your homework—it could be in your room or at the kitchen table or anywhere that works for you and your family.
Get extra help if you are having trouble. Write questions about what you don't understand. This will help your teacher give you the extra help you need.
Student Handbook 663

Student Handbook Pages 660, 661, 662, 663

Facts Practice

Facts Practice

Addition and Subtraction

- **To practice counting on or counting back, do columns A and B.**
- **To practice adding doubles or doubles plus one and the related subtraction facts, do columns C and D.**
- **To practice making a ten, do columns E and F.**
- **For mixed practice, choose rows to do.**

	Column A	Column B	Column C	Column D	Column E	Column F
Row 1.	4 + 2 6	6 − 2 4	0 + 0 0	9 − 4 5	7 + 5 12	11 − 4 7
Row 2.	7 + 1 8	5 − 1 4	3 + 4 7	4 − 2 2	3 + 8 11	15 − 6 9
Row 3.	3 + 6 9	9 − 2 7	5 + 5 10	11 − 6 5	4 + 6 10	14 − 8 6
Row 4.	2 + 5 7	8 − 3 5	9 + 9 18	16 − 8 8	5 + 8 13	13 − 9 4
Row 5.	1 + 8 9	10 − 3 7	7 + 6 13	15 − 7 8	9 + 6 15	10 − 3 7
Row 6.	9 + 3 12	7 − 1 6	8 + 9 17	17 − 8 9	8 + 4 12	16 − 9 7
Row 7.	8 + 2 10	11 − 2 9	6 + 6 12	14 − 7 7	7 + 9 16	14 − 5 9

More Practice

Work with a partner. Make flash cards for the facts that give you trouble. Practice your facts by quizzing each other with the flash cards.

Facts Practice

More Addition and Subtraction

You Choose

Strategy
- Count on.
- Count back.
- Use doubles.
- Use doubles plus one.
- Make a ten.
- Use related addition and subtraction facts.

- **For addition practice, do columns A, C, and E.**
- **For subtraction practice, do columns B, D, and F.**
- **For mixed practice, choose rows to do.**

	Column A	Column B	Column C	Column D	Column E	Column F
Row 1.	5 + 5 10	13 − 4 9	7 + 2 9	15 − 7 8	7 + 7 14	12 − 3 9
Row 2.	4 + 3 7	14 − 6 8	5 + 8 13	10 − 9 1	7 + 9 16	16 − 8 8
Row 3.	7 + 8 15	15 − 9 6	6 + 6 12	14 − 9 5	8 + 1 9	13 − 9 4
Row 4.	8 + 9 17	11 − 4 7	9 + 5 14	17 − 8 9	6 + 7 13	12 − 8 4
Row 5.	7 + 5 12	16 − 7 9	4 + 7 11	12 − 6 6	3 + 3 6	18 − 9 9
Row 6.	9 + 4 13	12 − 9 3	2 + 2 4	10 − 4 6	8 + 8 16	11 − 6 5
Row 7.	6 + 8 14	14 − 7 7	9 + 2 11	13 − 5 8	9 + 6 15	15 − 8 7

More Practice

See how many fact families you can write in 3 minutes.

Facts Practice

Addition and Subtraction Facts

- To practice adding, do columns A, B, and C of rows 1–5.
- To practice subtracting, do columns D, E, and F of rows 1–5.
- For mixed practice, choose rows to do.

	Column A	Column B	Column C	Column D	Column E	Column F
Row 1.	5 + 9 14	6 + 6 12	8 + 7 15	14 − 8 6	13 − 4 9	15 − 6 9
Row 2.	4 + 6 10	7 + 9 16	9 + 1 10	16 − 8 8	9 − 9 0	12 − 5 7
Row 3.	6 + 8 14	3 + 0 3	4 + 4 8	7 − 0 7	14 − 7 7	11 − 6 5
Row 4.	4 + 7 11	3 + 9 12	6 + 9 15	11 − 8 3	17 − 9 8	10 − 5 5
Row 5.	9 + 8 17	6 + 7 13	2 + 9 11	15 − 7 8	13 − 5 8	16 − 9 7
Row 6.	6 + 0 6	8 + 3 11	0 + 0 0	9 − 9 0	7 + 7 14	12 − 3 9
Row 7.	5 + 7 12	13 − 8 5	9 + 7 16	11 − 2 9	4 + 9 13	9 + 6 15
Row 8.	18 − 9 9	8 + 5 13	14 − 9 5	2 + 2 4	6 − 0 6	15 − 8 7
Row 9.	7 + 8 15	8 − 8 0	12 − 4 8	8 + 8 16	17 − 8 9	14 − 6 8
Row 10.	13 − 7 6	16 − 7 9	11 − 7 4	15 − 9 6	9 + 0 9	13 − 9 4

More Practice

Make 20 pairs of practice facts on index cards. Write an addition or subtraction fact on a card. Write the answer on another card. Arrange the cards face down in an array. Have players take turns turning over 2 cards. If the cards match, the player collects the cards. If the cards do not match, they are turned back over. Play continues until no cards remain. The player with the most cards wins.

Multiplication Facts

- To practice skip counting by 2 and 3, do column A.
- To practice multiplying by 0 and 1, do column B.
- To practice skip counting by 5 and 10, do column C.
- To practice using doubles, do columns D and E.
- To practice multiplying by 7 and 9, do column F.
- For mixed practice, choose rows to do.

	Column A	Column B	Column C	Column D	Column E	Column F
Row 1.	2 × 3 6	0 × 0 0	5 × 3 15	3 × 3 9	3 × 4 12	7 × 7 49
Row 2.	5 × 3 15	1 × 1 1	10 × 8 80	6 × 6 36	6 × 7 42	2 × 9 18
Row 3.	2 × 4 8	1 × 0 0	7 × 5 35	4 × 4 16	4 × 5 20	7 × 3 21
Row 4.	6 × 3 18	9 × 1 9	10 × 1 10	8 × 8 64	8 × 9 72	9 × 5 45
Row 5.	8 × 2 16	0 × 8 0	5 × 9 45	5 × 5 25	5 × 6 30	7 × 4 28
Row 6.	3 × 7 21	5 × 1 5	10 × 4 40	7 × 7 49	7 × 6 42	9 × 6 54
Row 7.	2 × 6 12	0 × 4 0	5 × 8 40	9 × 9 81	9 × 8 72	7 × 8 56

More Practice

Work with a partner. Make flash cards for the facts that give you trouble. Practice your facts by quizzing each other with the flash cards.

Facts Practice

Facts Practice

More Multiplication

- To practice with 0, 1, and 2, do column A.
- To practice with 3, 4, and 5, do column B.
- To practice with 6 and 7, do column C.
- To practice with 8 and 9, do column D.
- For mixed practice, choose columns E and F or choose rows to do.

You Choose

Strategy
- Use skip counting.
- Use doubles.
- Draw an array.

	Column A	Column B	Column C	Column D	Column E	Column F
Row 1.	2 × 2 4	4 × 7 28	7 × 6 42	8 × 8 64	3 × 7 21	6 × 8 48
Row 2.	5 × 0 0	9 × 3 27	6 × 6 36	0 × 9 0	0 × 0 0	5 × 9 45
Row 3.	1 × 8 8	5 × 6 30	6 × 9 54	8 × 5 40	3 × 8 24	1 × 1 1
Row 4.	4 × 1 4	8 × 4 32	3 × 6 18	9 × 4 36	7 × 9 63	8 × 5 40
Row 5.	2 × 9 18	3 × 5 15	7 × 7 49	9 × 8 72	3 × 6 18	0 × 7 0
Row 6.	7 × 2 14	4 × 4 16	4 × 6 24	8 × 6 48	9 × 7 63	6 × 4 24
Row 7.	0 × 6 0	5 × 5 25	8 × 7 56	9 × 9 81	7 × 5 35	4 × 8 32

More Practice

Make a multiplication table. See how fast you can complete all the multiplication facts.

Facts Practice

Division

- To practice dividing by 1, 2, and 3, do column A.
- To practice dividing by 4 and 5, do column B.
- To practice dividing by 6 and 7, do column C.
- To practice dividing by 8 and 9, do column D.
- For mixed practice, choose columns E and F or rows to do.

	Column A	Column B	Column C	Column D	Column E	Column F
Row 1.	8 2)16	1 4)4	4 6)24	0 9)0	2 5)10	7 3)21
Row 2.	1 3)3	6 5)30	1 7)7	3 8)24	1 1)1	3 4)12
Row 3.	0 2)0	9 5)45	8 6)48	4 9)36	7 7)49	7 2)14
Row 4.	2 1)2	9 4)36	1 6)6	4 8)32	5 4)20	6 9)54
Row 5.	4 3)12	1 5)5	8 7)56	1 8)8	9 6)54	7 5)35
Row 6.	7 1)7	2 4)8	2 7)14	1 9)9	9 2)18	7 9)63
Row 7.	2 2)4	8 5)40	7 6)42	8 9)72	8 8)64	5 7)35
Row 8.	9 3)27	8 4)32	9 7)63	7 8)56	6 6)36	9 9)81

More Practice

Work with a partner. Make flash cards for the facts that give you trouble. Practice your facts by quizzing each other with the flash cards.

Facts Practice

Facts Practice

More Division

- To practice with 1, 2, and 3 do column A.
- To practice with 4 and 5, do column B.
- To practice with 6 and 7, do column C.
- To practice with 8 and 9, do column D.
- For mixed practice, choose columns E and F or choose rows to do.

You Choose

Strategy
- Use related multiplication facts.
- Use doubles.
- Draw a picture.

	Column A	Column B	Column C	Column D	Column E	Column F
Row 1.	9 1)9	5 5)25	0 7)0	2 8)16	7 5)35	7 4)28
Row 2.	2 3)6	0 4)0	3 7)21	5 9)45	3 6)18	9 3)27
Row 3.	3 1)3	4 4)16	2 6)12	6 8)48	6 2)12	8 9)72
Row 4.	4 2)8	3 5)15	5 6)30	2 9)18	0 1)0	8 5)40
Row 5.	5 3)15	8 4)32	6 7)42	9 9)81	6 4)24	7 8)56
Row 6.	1 2)2	9 4)36	6 6)36	5 8)40	8 3)24	9 7)63
Row 7.	6 3)18	4 5)20	4 7)28	3 9)27	9 8)72	9 6)54
Row 8.	9 2)18	9 5)45	1 6)6	8 8)64	8 7)56	0 9)0

More Practice

Make triangular flash cards for multiplication and division fact families. Place all cards face down. Without looking at the numbers, pick up a card by a corner so that one number is covered up. Use the numbers you can see to decide what the unknown number is.

Facts Practice

Multiplication and Division

- For mixed multiplication and division practice, choose columns or rows to do.

	Column A	Column B	Column C	Column D	Column E	Column F
Row 1.	5 × 5 25	27 ÷ 3 9	6 × 7 42	8 × 3 24	0 ÷ 2 0	36 ÷ 9 4
Row 2.	48 ÷ 6 8	5 × 8 40	45 ÷ 5 9	7 × 5 35	21 ÷ 7 3	4 ÷ 4 1
Row 3.	8 × 2 16	7 × 7 49	32 ÷ 8 4	56 ÷ 7 8	18 ÷ 2 9	9 × 8 72
Row 4.	9 × 4 36	15 ÷ 5 3	9 × 7 63	16 ÷ 8 2	8 × 6 48	45 ÷ 9 5
Row 5.	64 ÷ 8 8	6 × 6 36	5 × 9 45	20 ÷ 4 5	72 ÷ 9 8	7 × 8 56
Row 6.	8 × 2 16	40 ÷ 8 5	8 ÷ 8 1	9 × 0 0	5 × 3 15	63 ÷ 7 9
Row 7.	54 ÷ 6 9	8 × 9 72	42 ÷ 6 7	25 ÷ 5 5	4 × 7 28	9 × 3 27
Row 8.	2 × 3 6	36 ÷ 4 9	63 ÷ 9 7	2 × 9 18	49 ÷ 7 7	9 × 9 81
Row 9.	56 ÷ 8 7	4 × 8 32	3 × 3 9	72 ÷ 8 9	8 × 5 40	48 ÷ 8 6
Row 10.	81 ÷ 9 9	35 ÷ 5 7	6 × 9 54	8 × 8 64	36 ÷ 6 6	7 × 9 63
Row 11.	4 × 4 16	0 ÷ 6 0	3 × 7 21	42 ÷ 7 6	7 × 0 0	24 ÷ 4 6
Row 12.	6 × 8 48	5 × 7 35	9 ÷ 9 1	7 × 4 28	54 ÷ 9 6	9 × 5 45

Table of Measures/Glossary

Table of Measures/Glossary

Table Of Measures

Customary Units of Measure			Metric Units of Measure		
Length					
1 foot (ft)	=	12 inches (in.)	1 centimeter (cm)	=	10 millimeters (mm)
1 yard (yd)	=	36 inches	1 decimeter (dm)	=	10 centimeters
1 yard	=	3 feet	1 meter (m)	=	100 centimeters
1 mile (mi)	=	5,280 feet	1 meter	=	10 decimeters
1 mile	=	1,760 yards	1 kilometer (km)	=	1,000 meters
Capacity					
1 pint (pt)	=	2 cups (c)	1 liter (L)	=	1,000 milliliters (mL)
1 quart (qt)	=	2 pints			
1 gallon (gal)	=	4 quarts			
Weight/Mass					
1 pound (lb)	=	16 ounces (oz)	1 gram (g)	=	1,000 milligrams (mg)
1 ton (T)	=	2,000 pounds	1 kilogram (kg)	=	1,000 grams

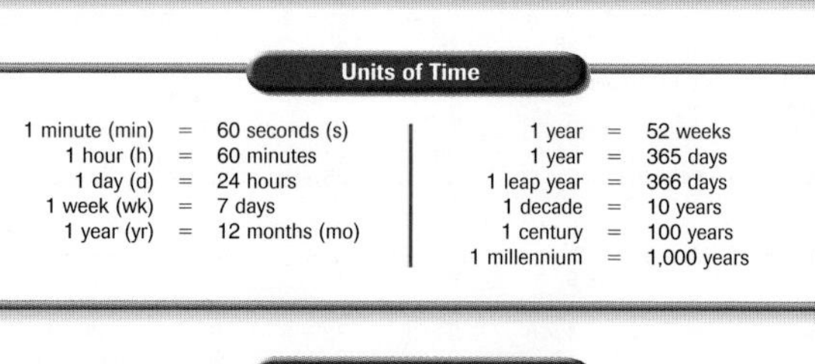

Units of Time

1 minute (min)	=	60 seconds (s)	1 year	=	52 weeks
1 hour (h)	=	60 minutes	1 year	=	365 days
1 day (d)	=	24 hours	1 leap year	=	366 days
1 week (wk)	=	7 days	1 decade	=	10 years
1 year (yr)	=	12 months (mo)	1 century	=	100 years
			1 millennium	=	1,000 years

Money

1 penny	=	1 cent (¢)	1 quarter	=	25 cents
1 nickel	=	5 cents	1 half-dollar	=	50 cents
1 dime	=	10 cents	1 dollar ($)	=	100 cents

672

Glossary

acute angle An angle that measures less than 90°.

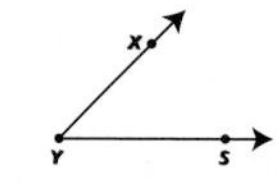

acute triangle A triangle in which each of the three angles is acute.

addend A number to be added in an addition problem.

Example: 5 + 8 = 13
↑ ↑
addends

A.M. The time between 12:00 midnight and 12:00 noon.

angle A figure that is formed by two rays with the same endpoint.

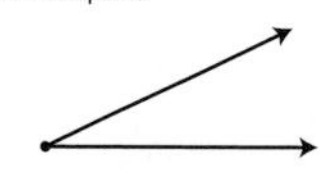

area The number of square units in a region.

array An arrangement of objects, pictures, or numbers in columns and rows.

Associative Property of Addition The property which states that the way in which addends are grouped does not change the sum. It is also called the *Grouping Property of Addition.*

Example: (3 + 4) + 5 = 3 + (4 + 5)

Associative Property of Multiplication The property which states that the way in which factors are grouped does not change the product. It is also called the *Grouping Property of Multiplication.*

Example: (6 × 7) × 9 = 6 × (7 × 9)

average *See mean.*

bar graph A graph in which information is shown by means of rectangular bars.

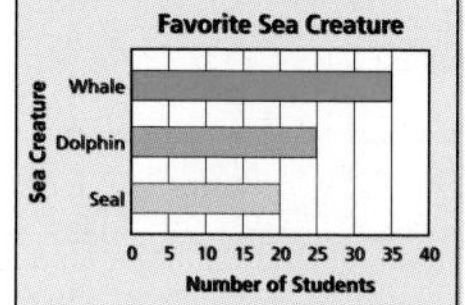

base ten A place-value system in which each digit has a value that is ten times greater than the digit to the right of it.

breaking apart A mental math strategy used to add and subtract.

Example: 28 = 20 + 8
+ 35 = 30 + 5
50 + 13 = 63

So, 28 + 35 = 63

Glossary 673

capacity The amount a container can hold.

certain An event that will always happen is certain.

chord A line segment that connects two points on a circle.

circle A closed figure in which every point is the same distance from a given point called the **center** of the circle.

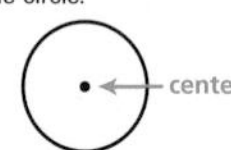

circle graph A graph that represents data as part of a circle. (sometimes called a **pie graph**)

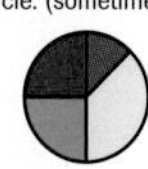

clustering An estimation strategy for finding sums.

Example:
Estimate 125 + 101 + 92
100 + 100 + 100 = 300

Commutative Property of Addition The property which states that the order of addends does not change the sum. It is also called the *Order Property of Addition.*

Example: 2 + 4 = 4 + 2

Commutative Property of Multiplication The property which states that the order of factors does not change the product. It is also called the *Order Property of Multiplication.*

Example: 3 × 5 = 5 × 3

compare To decide if one number is greater than, less than, or equal to another number.

compensation Adding one amount to an addend and subtracting an equal amount from another addend to add mentally.

composite number A whole number that has more than two factors.

cone A solid that has a circular face and comes to a point called the vertex.

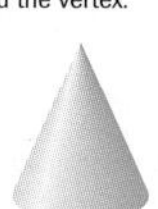

congruent figures Figures that have the same size and the same shape.

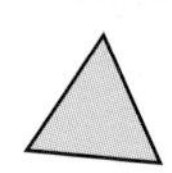

coordinates The numbers in an ordered pair.

cube A solid figure that has six square faces of equal size.

cubic unit A unit used to measure volume.

cylinder A solid that has parallel, congruent circular faces.

674 Glossary

data A set of information.

decimal A number with one or more digits to the right of a decimal point.

decimal equivalent A decimal that is equal to a whole number, a fraction, or another decimal.

decimal point (.) A symbol used to separate dollars and cents in money amounts or to separate ones and tenths in decimals.

Example: $1.55
↑
decimal point

degree (°) A unit for measuring angles or temperature.

degrees Celsius (°C) The metric temperature scale.

degrees Fahrenheit (°F) The customary temperature scale.

denominator The number below the bar in a fraction.

Example: $\frac{1}{3}$ ← denominator

diameter of a circle A line segment that connects two points on a circle and passes through the center.

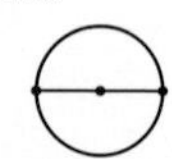

difference The answer in a subtraction problem.

Example: 12 − 5 = 7
↑
difference

digit Any one of the ten number symbols 0, 1, 2, 3, 4, 5, 6, 7, 8, and 9

Distributive Property of Multiplication The property which states that when two addends are multiplied by a factor, the product is the same as when each addend is multiplied by the factor and those products are added.

Example: (2 + 3) × 4 = (2 × 4) + (3 × 4)

dividend The number that is divided in a division problem.

Example: 35 ÷ 7 = 5
↑
dividend

divisible Describes a number that can be divided into equal parts and has no remainder.

divisor The number by which the dividend is divided in a division problem.

Example: 35 ÷ 7 = 5
↑
divisor

double bar graph A graph in which data is compared by means of pairs of rectangular bars drawn next to each other.

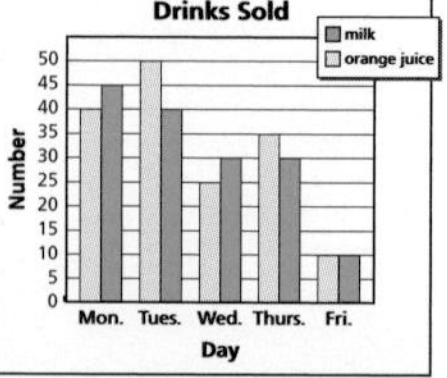

doubles A strategy for finding products.

Example: Since 2 × 3 = 6
Then 4 × 3 = 6 + 6
So 4 × 3 = 12

Glossary 675

Glossary

edge The line segment where two faces of a solid figure meet.

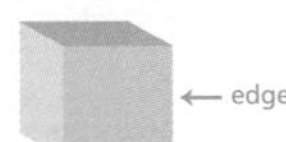

elapsed time The time that passes between the beginning and the end of an activity.

endpoint The point at either end of a line segment or the beginning point of a ray.

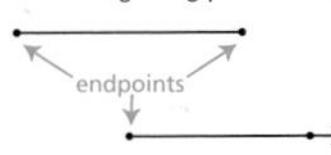

equal Having the same value.

equation A mathematical sentence with an equal sign.
Examples: $3 + 1 = 4$ and $2x + 5 = 9$

equilateral triangle A triangle that has three congruent sides.

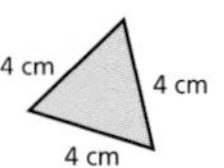

equivalent decimals Decimals that name the same amount.

equivalent fractions Fractions that name the same amount.
Example: $\frac{1}{2}$ and $\frac{3}{6}$

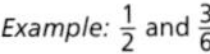

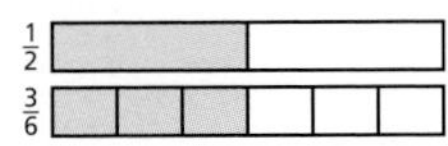

estimate A number close to an exact amount; to find about how many.

evaluate To find the value of an expression.

even number A whole number that is a multiple of 2. The ones digit in an even number is always 0, 2, 4, 6, or 8.

expanded form A number written to show the value of each digit.
Example: The expanded form of 2,345 is $2{,}000 + 300 + 40 + 5$.

expression A number or group of numbers with operation symbols. An expression may have a variable.
Example: $3 + n$

face A flat surface of a solid figure.

fact family Facts that are related, using the same numbers.
Examples: $1 + 4 = 5$; $4 + 1 = 5$
$5 - 4 = 1$; $5 - 1 = 4$
$3 \times 5 = 15$; $5 \times 3 = 15$
$15 \div 3 = 5$; $15 \div 5 = 3$

factor The numbers used in a multiplication problem.
Example: $7 \times 5 = 35$
factors

factor tree A visual representation of the prime factors of a number.

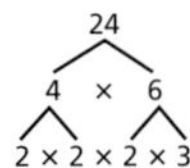

favorable outcome A desired result in a probability experiment.

formula An expression that shows a mathematical rule.

fraction A number that names a part of a whole, a part of a collection, or a part of a region.
Examples: $\frac{1}{2}$, $\frac{3}{4}$, and $\frac{2}{3}$

front-end estimation A method of estimating sums, differences, products, and quotients using front digits.

function table A table of ordered pairs that follows a rule.

Rule: $t = p \times 2$	
Input (p)	Output (t)
4	8
6	12
10	20

G

grid A chart that shows combinations of outcomes of an event.

		Second Toss	
		heads	tails
First Toss	heads	heads, heads	heads, tails
	tails	tails, heads	tails, tails

Grouping Property of Addition *See Associative Property of Addition*

Grouping Property of Multiplication *See Associative Property of Multiplication*

hexagon A polygon with six sides.

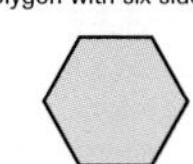

horizontal axis *See x-axis.*

horizontal line A line that lies straight across.
Example:

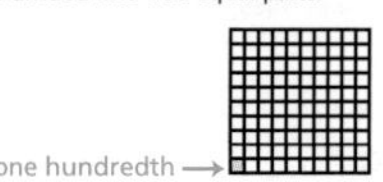

hundredth One of the equal parts when a whole is divided into 100 equal parts.

one hundredth

I

impossible An event that can not happen is impossible.

improper fraction A fraction that is greater than or equal to 1. The numerator in an improper fraction is greater than or equal to the denominator.

inequality Two expressions that are not equal. The symbols >, < and ≠ show an inequality.

integers The set of positive whole numbers, their opposites (negative numbers), and 0.

intersecting lines Lines that meet or cross at a common point.

interval The difference between two numbers on a scale.

inverse operations Opposite operations.
Examples: Addition and subtraction are inverse operations. Multiplication and division are inverse operations.

isosceles triangle A triangle that has two congruent sides and two congruent angles.

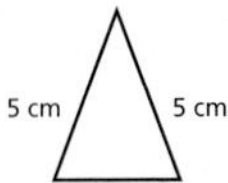

key A part of a map, graph, or chart that explains what symbols mean.

L

like denominators Denominators in two or more fractions that are the same.

line A straight path that extends in opposite directions with no endpoints.

line graph A graph that uses a line to show changes in data over time.

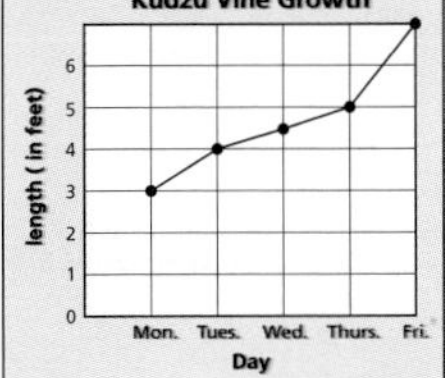

line plot A diagram that organizes data using a number line.

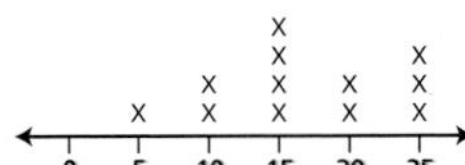

line segment A part of a line that has two endpoints.

line symmetry Describes whether a figure can be folded in half and its two parts match exactly.

line of symmetry The line along which a figure can be folded so that the two halves match exactly.

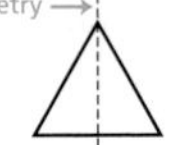

M

mass A measure of the amount of matter in an object.

mean The number found by dividing the sum of a group of numbers by the number of addends. Also called *average.*
Example:
$6 + 2 + 1 = 9$ $9 \div 3$ addends $= 3$
The average of 6, 2, and 1 is 3.

median The middle number when a set of numbers is arranged in order from least to greatest. For an even number of numbers, the median is the mean of the two middle numbers.
Examples: The median of 2, 5, 7, 9, and 10 is 7. The median of 2, 5, 7, and 12 is $(5 + 7) \div 2$, or 6.

mixed number A number containing a whole number part and a fraction part.
Example: $3\frac{1}{2}$

mode The number or numbers that occur most often in a set of data.
Example: The mode of 2, 3, 4, 4, and 6 is 4.

multiple A number that is the product of the given number and another number.

negative numbers Numbers that are less than 0.
Examples: $^-2$, $^-5$, and $^-26$

Negative numbers are less than 0.
$^-9$ $^-5$ $^-2$ 0

net A flat pattern that can be folded to make a solid.

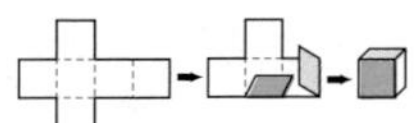

number sentence A mathematical sentence written in numerals and mathematical symbols. A number sentence always includes a greater than, less than, or equal sign.
Examples: $5 \times 5 = 19 + 6$
$2n \div 4 = 16$

numerator The number above the bar in a fraction.
Example: $\frac{1}{3}$ ← numerator

obtuse angle An angle that measures more than 90° and less than 180°.

obtuse triangle A triangle that has one obtuse angle.

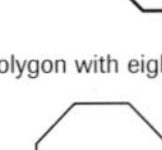

octagon A polygon with eight sides.

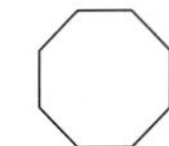

Glossary

Glossary Pages 680, 681, 682, 683

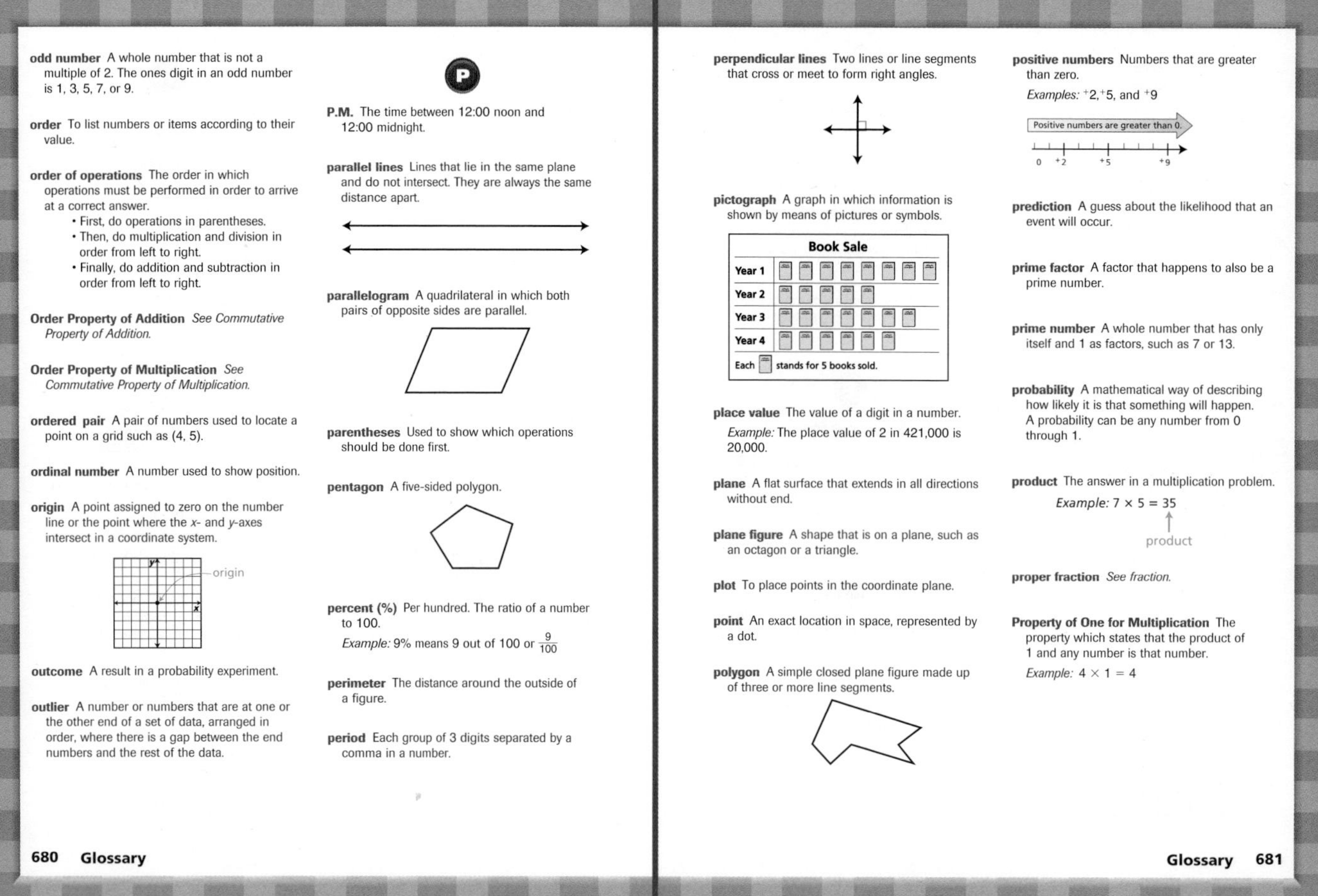

odd number A whole number that is not a multiple of 2. The ones digit in an odd number is 1, 3, 5, 7, or 9.

order To list numbers or items according to their value.

order of operations The order in which operations must be performed in order to arrive at a correct answer.
- First, do operations in parentheses.
- Then, do multiplication and division in order from left to right.
- Finally, do addition and subtraction in order from left to right.

Order Property of Addition *See Commutative Property of Addition.*

Order Property of Multiplication *See Commutative Property of Multiplication.*

ordered pair A pair of numbers used to locate a point on a grid such as (4, 5).

ordinal number A number used to show position.

origin A point assigned to zero on the number line or the point where the *x*- and *y*-axes intersect in a coordinate system.

outcome A result in a probability experiment.

outlier A number or numbers that are at one or the other end of a set of data, arranged in order, where there is a gap between the end numbers and the rest of the data.

P

P.M. The time between 12:00 noon and 12:00 midnight.

parallel lines Lines that lie in the same plane and do not intersect. They are always the same distance apart.

parallelogram A quadrilateral in which both pairs of opposite sides are parallel.

parentheses Used to show which operations should be done first.

pentagon A five-sided polygon.

percent (%) Per hundred. The ratio of a number to 100.

Example: 9% means 9 out of 100 or $\frac{9}{100}$

perimeter The distance around the outside of a figure.

period Each group of 3 digits separated by a comma in a number.

perpendicular lines Two lines or line segments that cross or meet to form right angles.

pictograph A graph in which information is shown by means of pictures or symbols.

place value The value of a digit in a number.

Example: The place value of 2 in 421,000 is 20,000.

plane A flat surface that extends in all directions without end.

plane figure A shape that is on a plane, such as an octagon or a triangle.

plot To place points in the coordinate plane.

point An exact location in space, represented by a dot.

polygon A simple closed plane figure made up of three or more line segments.

positive numbers Numbers that are greater than zero.

Examples: $^{+}2$, $^{+}5$, and $^{+}9$

prediction A guess about the likelihood that an event will occur.

prime factor A factor that happens to also be a prime number.

prime number A whole number that has only itself and 1 as factors, such as 7 or 13.

probability A mathematical way of describing how likely it is that something will happen. A probability can be any number from 0 through 1.

product The answer in a multiplication problem.

Example: 7 × 5 = 35

proper fraction *See fraction.*

Property of One for Multiplication The property which states that the product of 1 and any number is that number.

Example: 4 × 1 = 4

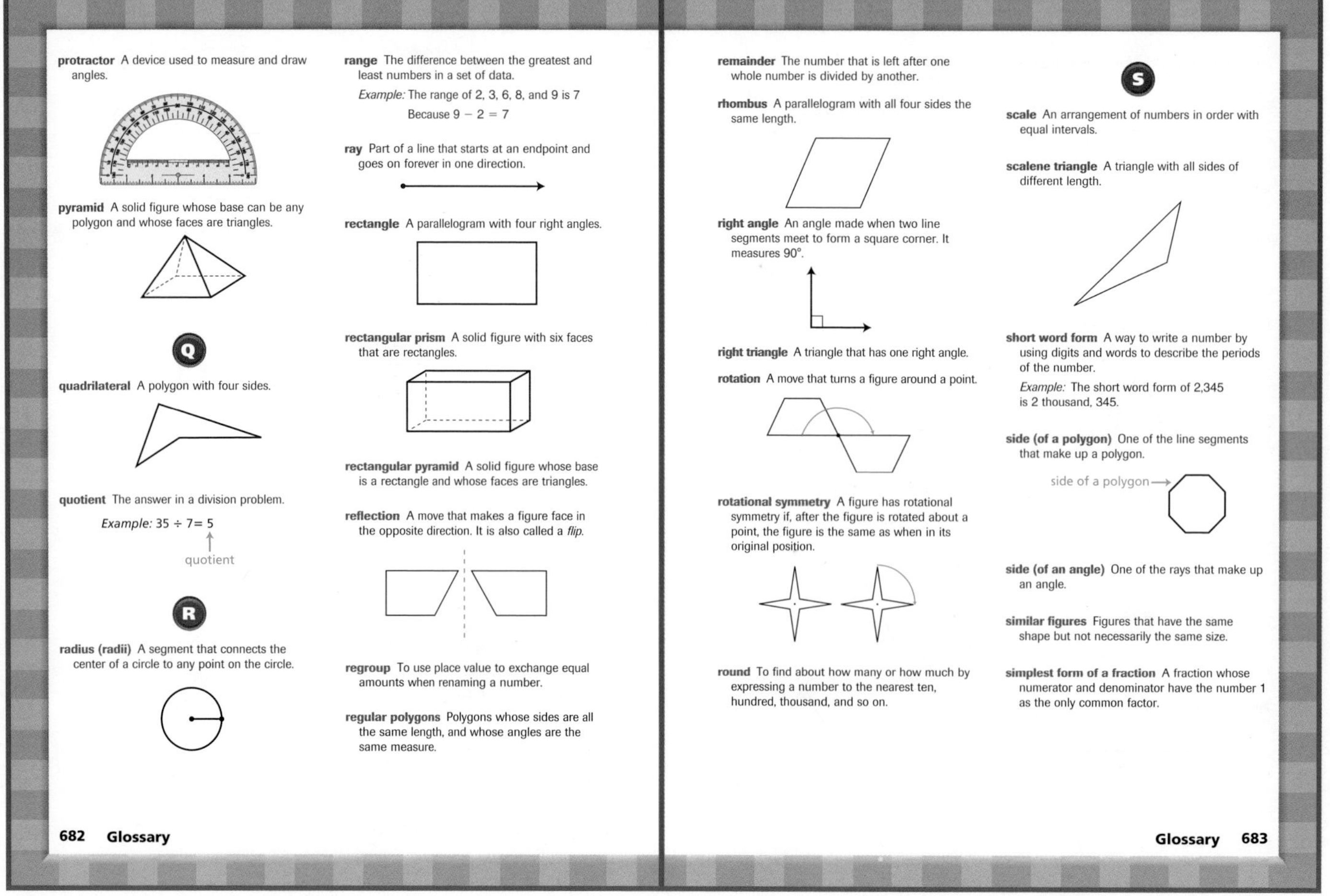

protractor A device used to measure and draw angles.

pyramid A solid figure whose base can be any polygon and whose faces are triangles.

Q

quadrilateral A polygon with four sides.

quotient The answer in a division problem.

Example: 35 ÷ 7 = 5

R

radius (radii) A segment that connects the center of a circle to any point on the circle.

range The difference between the greatest and least numbers in a set of data.

Example: The range of 2, 3, 6, 8, and 9 is 7
Because 9 − 2 = 7

ray Part of a line that starts at an endpoint and goes on forever in one direction.

rectangle A parallelogram with four right angles.

rectangular prism A solid figure with six faces that are rectangles.

rectangular pyramid A solid figure whose base is a rectangle and whose faces are triangles.

reflection A move that makes a figure face in the opposite direction. It is also called a *flip.*

regroup To use place value to exchange equal amounts when renaming a number.

regular polygons Polygons whose sides are all the same length, and whose angles are the same measure.

remainder The number that is left after one whole number is divided by another.

rhombus A parallelogram with all four sides the same length.

right angle An angle made when two line segments meet to form a square corner. It measures 90°.

right triangle A triangle that has one right angle.

rotation A move that turns a figure around a point.

rotational symmetry A figure has rotational symmetry if, after the figure is rotated about a point, the figure is the same as when in its original position.

round To find about how many or how much by expressing a number to the nearest ten, hundred, thousand, and so on.

S

scale An arrangement of numbers in order with equal intervals.

scalene triangle A triangle with all sides of different length.

short word form A way to write a number by using digits and words to describe the periods of the number.

Example: The short word form of 2,345 is 2 thousand, 345.

side (of a polygon) One of the line segments that make up a polygon.

side (of an angle) One of the rays that make up an angle.

similar figures Figures that have the same shape but not necessarily the same size.

simplest form of a fraction A fraction whose numerator and denominator have the number 1 as the only common factor.

Glossary

Glossary Pages 684, 685, 686

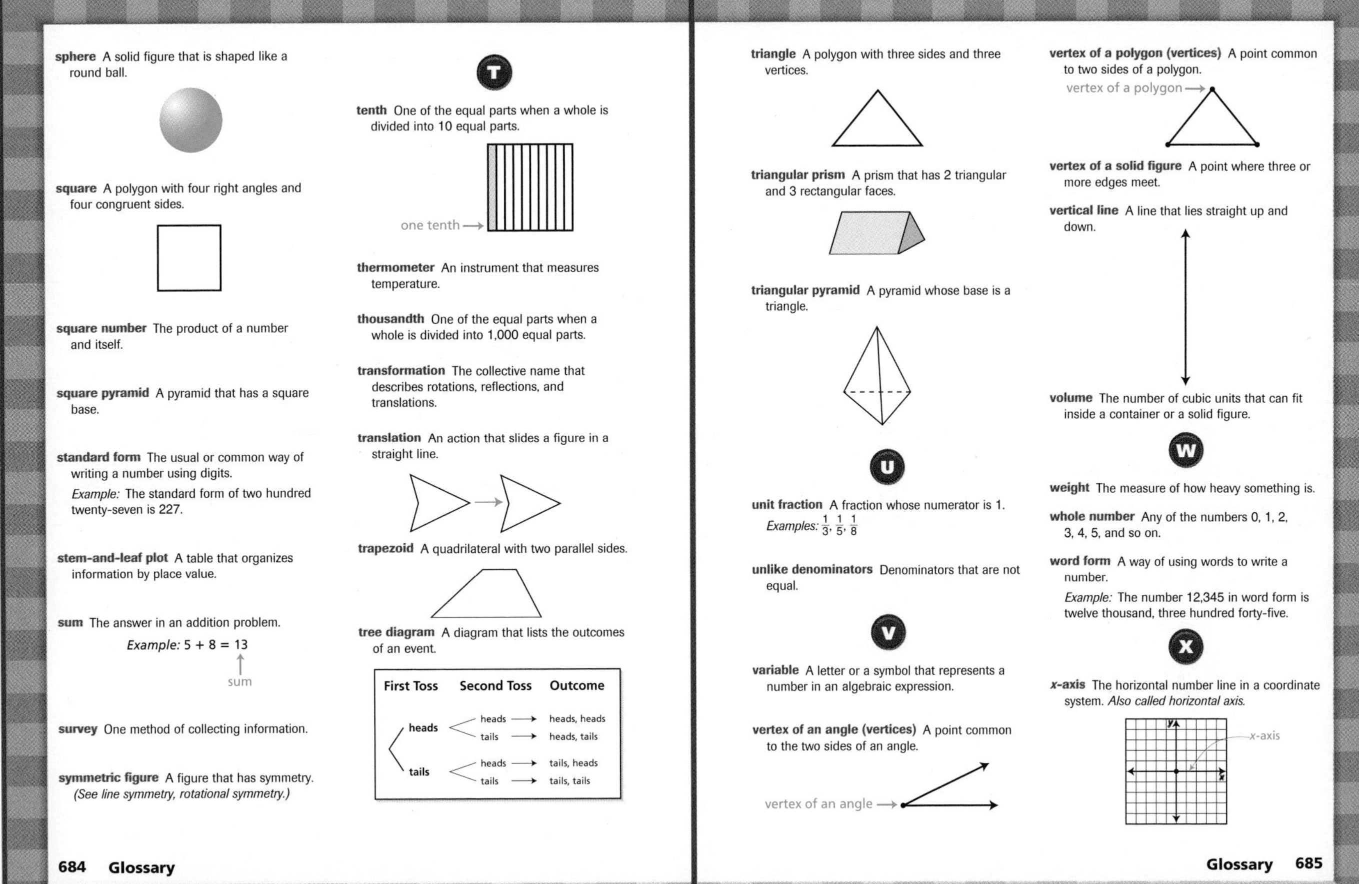

sphere A solid figure that is shaped like a round ball.

square A polygon with four right angles and four congruent sides.

square number The product of a number and itself.

square pyramid A pyramid that has a square base.

standard form The usual or common way of writing a number using digits.
Example: The standard form of two hundred twenty-seven is 227.

stem-and-leaf plot A table that organizes information by place value.

sum The answer in an addition problem.
Example: 5 + 8 = 13 (sum)

survey One method of collecting information.

symmetric figure A figure that has symmetry. *(See line symmetry, rotational symmetry.)*

T

tenth One of the equal parts when a whole is divided into 10 equal parts.

thermometer An instrument that measures temperature.

thousandth One of the equal parts when a whole is divided into 1,000 equal parts.

transformation The collective name that describes rotations, reflections, and translations.

translation An action that slides a figure in a straight line.

trapezoid A quadrilateral with two parallel sides.

tree diagram A diagram that lists the outcomes of an event.

First Toss	Second Toss	Outcome
heads	heads	heads, heads
	tails	heads, tails
tails	heads	tails, heads
	tails	tails, tails

684 Glossary

triangle A polygon with three sides and three vertices.

triangular prism A prism that has 2 triangular and 3 rectangular faces.

triangular pyramid A pyramid whose base is a triangle.

U

unit fraction A fraction whose numerator is 1.
Examples: $\frac{1}{3}, \frac{1}{5}, \frac{1}{8}$

unlike denominators Denominators that are not equal.

V

variable A letter or a symbol that represents a number in an algebraic expression.

vertex of an angle (vertices) A point common to the two sides of an angle.

vertex of a polygon (vertices) A point common to two sides of a polygon.

vertex of a solid figure A point where three or more edges meet.

vertical line A line that lies straight up and down.

volume The number of cubic units that can fit inside a container or a solid figure.

W

weight The measure of how heavy something is.

whole number Any of the numbers 0, 1, 2, 3, 4, 5, and so on.

word form A way of using words to write a number.
Example: The number 12,345 in word form is twelve thousand, three hundred forty-five.

X

***x*-axis** The horizontal number line in a coordinate system. *Also called horizontal axis.*

Glossary 685

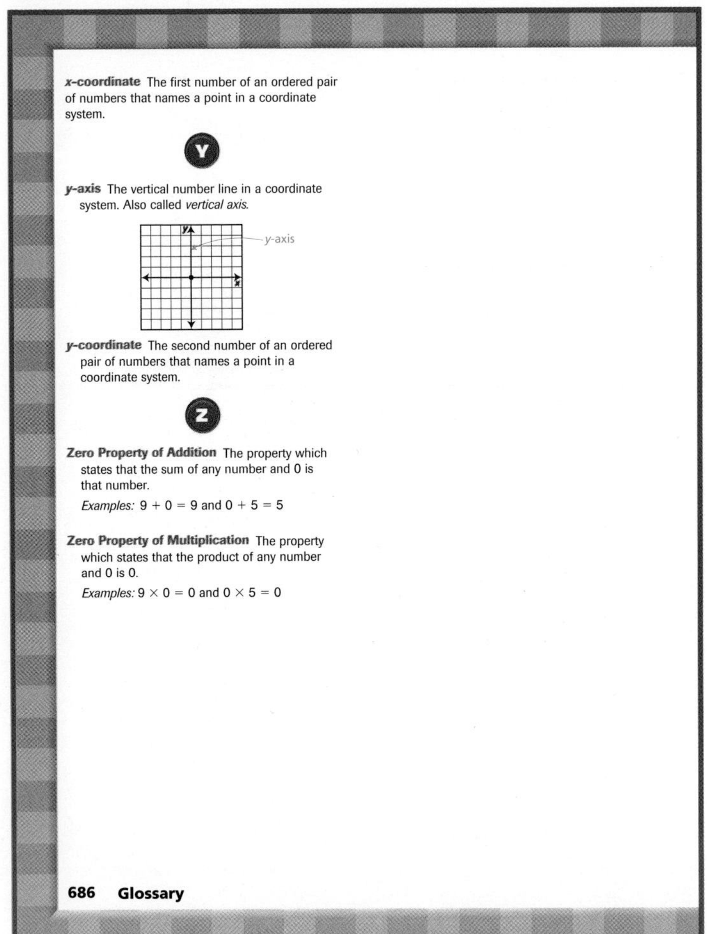

***x*-coordinate** The first number of an ordered pair of numbers that names a point in a coordinate system.

Y

***y*-axis** The vertical number line in a coordinate system. Also called *vertical axis.*

***y*-coordinate** The second number of an ordered pair of numbers that names a point in a coordinate system.

Z

Zero Property of Addition The property which states that the sum of any number and 0 is that number.
Examples: 9 + 0 = 9 and 0 + 5 = 5

Zero Property of Multiplication The property which states that the product of any number and 0 is 0.
Examples: 9 × 0 = 0 and 0 × 5 = 0

686 Glossary

Notes

Math and Literature Bibliography

Alice Ramsey's Grand Adventure
by Don Brown
This book chronicles the adventures of Alice Ramsay who, in 1909, drove out of New York City to do what no woman had ever done—drive across the United States! She reached San Francisco 59 days later.

Amanda Bean's Amazing Dream: A Mathematical Story
by Cindy Neuschwander and Marilyn Burns
Scholastic, 1998
The mysteries of multiplication are unraveled by young Amanda, who happily counts "anything and everything."

The Amazing Impossible Erie Canal
by Cheryl Harness
Before the completion of the Erie Canal in 1825, which this book recounts, it took a month to travel from Lake Erie to the Hudson River. The 524-mile long Erie Canal shortened the trip to seven days!

Anno's Mysterious Multiplying Jar
by Masaichiro and Mitsumasa Anno
Students will be delighted to see how quickly numbers grow in this imaginative story where the multiplication relationship known as factorials is used.

Arithme-Tickle: An Even Number of Odd Riddle-Rhymes
by J. Patick Lewis, Frank Remkiewicz
Silver Whistle, 2002
Eighteen clever and fun math riddles.

Arithmetricks
by Edward H. Julius
John Wiley & Sons, 1995
50 tips and tricks help make adding, subtracting, multiplying, and dividing easy and fun.

Bats on Parade
by Kathi Appelt
William Morrow, 1999
Interesting mathematical comparisons are made between human and animal behavior.

Can You Count to a Googol?
by Robert E. Wells
Albert Whitman & Co., 2000
The book helps students visualize greater and greater numbers.

A Cloak for the Dreamer
by Aileen Friedman
Scholastic, 1995
A story about a father, who is a tailor, and his three sons; each is asked to sew a cloak, and each uses a different pattern.

Counting On Frank
by Rod Clement
Counting on Frank follows a mathematical thinker through his day as he expands on facts he has discovered about everyday objects. Frank is the boy's dog, and he figures into the story by being a measure of volume!

Do You Wanna Bet? Your Chance to Find Out About Probability
by Jean Cushman
Houghton Mifflin, 1991
Two boys become involved in everyday situations that involve probability.

Einstein Anderson, Science Detective: On-line Spacemen and Other Cases
by Seymour Simon
Avon Books, 1998
Einstein Anderson, a whiz at science, investigates the mysteries of the universe.

Esio Trot
by Roald Dahl
Demco Media, 1992
Mr. Hoppy's plan to win Mrs. Silver's heart leads to thinking about measurement and division.

Fraction Fun
by David Adler
Holiday House, 1997
Hands-on activities, including "Pizza Math," help introduce fractions.

The Go-Around Dollar
by Barbara Johnston Adams
Simon & Schuster Children's, 1992
A picture book about the travels of a single dollar.

A Grain of Rice
by Helna C. Pittman Bantam
Doubleday Dell, 1995
A farmer teaches an emperor a math lesson and is rewarded by a single grain of rice, which doubles every day for 100 days.

Grandfather Tang's Story: A Tale Told with Tangrams
by Ann Tompert
Demco Media, 1997
A grandfather's story, told to his granddaughter, uses tangrams to show the shape of each animal in the tale.

How Much Is a Million?
by David M. Schwartz
William Morrow, 1993
One million, one billion, and one trillion are explained.

Math and Literature Bibliography

If You Made a Million
by David M. Schwartz
William Morrow, 1994
Ways to earn and spend a penny, a nickel, and a million dollars are explored.

The King's Commissioners
by Aileen Friedman
Scholastic, 1995
The concept of counting by grouping is introduced.

****The Life and Times of the Honeybee***
by Charles Micucci
The Life and Times of the Honeybee illustrates each phase of the workers', drones', and queen bee's lives.

****Little Oh***
by Laura Krauss Melmed
The story, with lovely illustrations, depicts how Little Oh, and Origami girl, finds her way back home and becomes a real little girl after being dropped under a marker stall.

Logic for Space Age Kids
by Lyn McClure Butrick
University Classics, 1984
Zeno, from the planet Zircon, tackles problems involving logical deduction.

Math Mysteries: Stories and Activities to Build Problem-Solving Skills
by Jack Silbert
Scholastic, 1996
The "Effective Detective Agency" introduces each reproducible story, presenting readers with engaging math problems to solve.

Math-Terpieces
by Greg Tang, Greg Paprocki
Scholastic, 2003
Tang explores basic problem solving through fun text and illustrations.

Measuring Penny
by Loreen Leedy
Henry Holt, 1998
A young girl, with the help of her dog, investigates various types of measurement.

Pigs at Odds: Fun With Math and Games
by Amy Axelrod, Sharon McGinley-Nally
Simon & Schuster, 2000
This book explores probability in the environment of a carnival complete with many games.

****The Real Thief***
by William Steig
Gawain is a trustworthy goose that is accused of stealing treasures from the royal vault. The real thief is a mouse who replaces the missing jewels to clear Gawain of the crime.

Sam Johnson and the Blue Ribbon Quilt
by Lisa Campbell Ernst
William Morrow, 1992
A tale about quilt-making, which introduces patterns and symmetry.

Sir Cumference and the First Round Table: A Math Adventure
by Cindy Neuschwander
Charlesbridge Publishing, 1997
The terms of geometry are brought to life, as problems with the Round Table force King Arthur and his knights to consider more suitable shapes.

Spaghetti and Meatballs for All: A Mathematical Story
by Marilyn Burns
Scholastic, 1997
This book is a real-life exploration of area and perimeter.

****The Story of Money***
by Betsy Maestro
This book explains how the money of today grew from a system of barter to the modern practice of trading money for goods and services. The history of coins and bills including wampum and "pieces of eight" is also explored.

Three Pigs, One Wolf, and Seven Magic Shapes
by Grace MacCarone, David Neuhaus, Marilyn Burns
Scholastic, 1998
The seven magic shapes, tangrams, form figures that help the pigs outsmart the wolf.

Tiger Math: Learning to Graph From a Baby Tiger
by Ann Whitehead Nagda, Cindy Bickel
Henry Holt & Company, 2000
The text and four different types of graphs (picture, circle, bar, and line) tell the story of how the tiger grows.

Time
by Henry Pluckrose
Children's Press, 1988
Units of time measurement, along with the importance of timekeeping, are explored.

*Also available for purchase

Math Trade Book Literature Library

Professional Resources Bibliography

Bresser, R., and C. Holtzman. ***Developing Number Sense –Grades 3-6.*** Math Solutions Publications, 1999.

Brodie, J. P. ***Constructing Ideas About Large Numbers.*** Creative Publications, 1995.

Burns, Marilyn. ***About Teaching Mathematics: A K–8 Resource,*** 2nd Ed. Sausalito, CA: Math Solutions Publications, 2000.

Butterworth, B. ***The Mathematical Brain.*** Macmillan, 1999.

Carpenter, Thomas P., Elizabeth Fennema, Megan Loef Franke, Linda Levi, and Susan P. Empson. ***Children's Mathematics: Cognitively Guided Instruction.*** Portsmouth, NH: Heinemann, 1999.

Cathcart. W., Y. Pothier, J. Vance, and N. Bezuk. ***Learning Mathematics in Elementary and Middle Schools.*** Merrill: Prentice-Hall, Inc., 2000.

Childs, L., and L Choate. ***Nimble with Numbers.*** Dale Seymour Publications, 1999.

Clapham, C. ***Concise Dictionary of Mathematics.*** Oxford University Press, 1996.

Coates, G., and J. Stenmark. ***Family Math for Young Children.*** Lawrence Hall of Science, 1997.

Cowan, T., and J. Maguire. ***Timelines of African-American History: 500 Years of Black Achievement.*** Berkley Publishing Group, 1994.

Crawford, M., and M. Witte. ***"Strategies for Mathematics: Teaching in Context."*** Educational Leadership, Vol. 57, ASCD, November 1999.

Eby, J., and E. Kujawa. ***Reflective Planning, Teaching and Evaluation: K-12.*** Merrill: Macmillan Publishing Company, 1994.

Flournoy, V., et al. ***The Patchwork Quilt.*** Scholastic, 1996.

Franco, B., et al. ***Understanding Geometry.*** Great Source Education Group, 1998.

Garland, T. Fibonacci ***Fun: Fascinating Activities with Intriguing Numbers.*** Dale Seymour Publications, 1998.

Geary, D. C. ***Children's Mathematical Development: Research and Practical Applications.*** Washington, D.C., 1994.

Gelfand, I., and A. Shen. ***Algebra.*** Birkhauser, 1993.

Ginsburg, H.P., Greenes, C., and Balfanz, R. ***Big Math for Little Kids.*** Dale Seymour Publications, 2003

Ginsburg, H. P., Greenes, C., Balfanz, R., Glassman, B., ed. ***Macmillan Visual Almanac.*** Blackbirch Press, 1996.

Greenes, C., and G. Immerzeel. ***Problem Solving Focus: Time and Money.*** Dale Seymour Publications, 1993.

Hiebert, J., T. Carpenter, E. Fennema, K. Fuson, D. Wearne, H. Murray, A. Olivier, and P. Humam. ***Making Sense: Teaching and Learning Mathematics with Understanding.*** Heinemann, 1997.

Hoffman, P. ***The Man Who Loved Only Numbers: The Story of Paul Erdos and the Search for Mathematical Truth.*** Hyperion, 1998.

Karp, Karen, E. Todd Brown, Linda Allen, and Candy Allen. ***Feisty Females: Inspiring Girls to Think Mathematically.*** Portsmouth, NH: Heinemann, 1998.

Kovalik, Susan J., and Karen D. Olsen. ***Exceeding Expectations: A User's Guide to Implementing Brain Research in the Classroom,*** 2nd Ed. Covington, WA: Books for Educators, Inc., 2001.

Lamon. Susan J. ***Teaching Fractions and Ratios for Understanding.*** Mahwah, NJ: Lawrence Erlbaum Associates, 1999.

Lee, M., and M. Miller. ***Great Graphing.*** Scholastic Professional Books, 1993.

Ma, Liping. ***Knowing and Teaching Elementary Mathematics.*** Lawrence Erlbaum Associates, 1999.

Mamchur, C. ***A Teacher's Guide to Cognitive Type Theory and Learning Style.*** ASCD, 1996.

The Math Learning Center. ***"Fractions on a Geoboard," in Opening Eyes to Mathematics,*** Volume 3. 1995.

McIntosh, A., B. Reys, R. Reys, and J. Hope. ***Number SENSE: Simple Effective Number Sense Experiences, Grades 4-6.*** Dale Seymour Publications, 1997.

Means, B., C. Chelener, and M. Knapp. ***Teaching Advanced Skills to At-Risk Students.*** Jossey-Bass Inc., 1991.

Mendlesohn, E. ***Teaching Primary Math with Music.*** Dale Seymour Publications, 1990.

Miller, D., and A. McKinnon. ***The Beginning School Mathematics Project.*** ASCD, 1995.

Miller, E. ***Read It! Draw It! Solve It! Problem Solving for Primary Grades.*** Dale Seymour Publications, 1997.

Myren, C. ***Posing Open-Ended Questions in the Primary Classroom.*** Teaching Resource Center, 1997.

Professional Resources Bibliography

Teacher's Resources

National Council of Teachers of Mathematics. Principles and Standards for School Mathematics (2000)

See also these NCTM products:

Addenda Series
Navigations Series
Yearbook

National Research Council. ***Adding It Up: Helping Children Learn Mathematics.*** Washington, DC, National Academy Press, 2001.

Newman, V. ***Math Journals, Grades K-5.*** Teaching Resource Center, 1994.

Norton-Wolf, S. ***Base-Ten Block Activities.*** Learning Resources, 1990.

Ohanian, S. ***Garbage, Pizza, Patchwork Quilts, and Math Magic.*** W. H. Freeman and Co., 1992.

Pappas, T. ***The Magic of Mathematics – Discovering the Spell of Mathematics.*** Wide World Publishing/Tetra, 1994.

Parker, M., ed. ***She Does Math! – Real-Life Problems from Women on the Job.*** The Mathematical Association of America, 1995.

Piccirilli, R. ***Mental Math: Computation Activities for Anytime.*** Scholastic Professional Books, 1996.

Rich, D. ***MegaSkills.*** Houghton Mifflin Company, 1992.

Salvin, R. E., N. L. Karweit, and B. A. Wasik, eds. ***Preventing Early School Failure: Research, Policy, and Practice.*** Boston: Allyn and Bacon. 1994.

Satariano, P. ***Storytime, Mathtime: Math Explorations in Children's Literature.*** Dale Seymour Publications, 1997.

Schechter, B. ***My Brain Is Open: The Mathematical Journeys of Paul Erdos.*** Simon & Schuster, 1998.

Schoenfeld, A. ***"When Good Teaching Leads to Bad Results: The Disasters of Well-Taught Mathematics Courses,"*** *Educational Psychologist,* Vol. 23, 145-66. 1998.

Schullman, D., and E. Rebeka. ***Growing Mathematical Ideas in Kindergarten.*** Math Solutions Publications, 1999.

Sheffield, Linda Jensen. ***Extending the Challenge in Mathematics: Developing Mathematical Promise in K–8 Students.*** Thousand Oaks, CA: Corwin Press, Inc., 2002.

Singer, Margie, et al. ***Between Never and Always.*** Dale Seymour Publications, 1997.

Skinner, P. ***It All Adds Up! Math Solutions Publications*** (Adapted by Permission of Addison-Wesley Longman, Australia), 1999.

Sparrow, Len, and Paul Swan. ***Learning Math with Calculators: Activities for Grades 3–8.*** Sausalito, CA: Math Solutions Publications, 2001.

Sternberg, R., and W. Williams. ***How to Develop Student Creativity.*** ASCD. 1996

Stewart, K., and K. Walker. ***20 Thinking Questions for Base-Ten Blocks, Grades 3-6.*** Creative Publications, 1995.

Tomlinson, Carol Ann. ***How to Differentiate Instruction in Mixed-Ability Classrooms.*** ASCD, 1995.

Trafton, P., and D. Thiesen. ***Learning Through Problems: Number Sense and Computational Strategies/A Resource for Teachers.*** Heinemann, 1999.

Van De Walle, J. ***Elementary and Middle School Mathematics: Teaching Developmentally,*** Fourth Edition. Dale Seymour Publications, 2000.

Wahl, Mark. ***Math for Humans: Teaching Math Through 8 Intelligences,*** 2nd Ed. Vernon Hills, IL: LivnLern Press, 1999.

Webb, N., and T. Romberg. ***Reforming Mathematics Education in America's Cities: The Urban Mathematics Collaborative Project.*** Teachers College Press, 1994.

Zaslavsky, C. ***Fear of Math – How to Get Over It and Get On with Your Life.*** Rutgers University Press, 1994.

Zemelman, S., H. Daniels, and A. Hyde. ***Best Practice: New Standards for Teaching and Learning in America's Schools.*** Heinemann, 1998.

Research Summary* for Unit 1

TO: **Fourth Grade Teachers**

SUBJECT: **Linking Money and Place Value**

A thorough knowledge of place value is an essential prerequisite for comparing, rounding, and operating with whole numbers and decimals. Despite its importance, Baroody (1990) reports that "many children in the United States have difficulty learning place-value skills and concepts." Although materials such as place-value charts, pockets, and manipulatives like base-ten blocks can serve as useful communication tools between teacher and student, these devices do not exploit students' informal out-of-school experience with place value.

The American monetary system surely is the most frequent instance of place value encountered outside of school. Money has the added advantage of representing both whole number place values and decimal place values when amounts involve cents. When place value and money are linked in the classroom, Baroody's criticism is seldom realized.

TRY IT OUT!

1. Represent $241 in terms of $100 bills, $10 bills, and $1 bills.
2. Order $182, $75, and $241 from least to greatest. Think in terms of $100, $10, and $5 bills.
3. Round to the nearest $100:

   $123

   $48

   $96

Think: If the number of $10 bills and $1 bills total $50 or more, replace them by $100.

CHECK IT OUT!

Baroody, A. J. (1990). How and when should place-value concepts and skills be taught? *Journal for Research in Mathematics Education*, 21(4), 281–286.

Griffin, Colleen (2005). Place value and money. *Professional Resources Handbook—Grade 4.* Boston: Houghton-Mifflin.

Ross, S. H. (1989). Parts, wholes, and place value: A developmental view. *Arithmetic Teacher, 36*(4), 47–51.

*** For more information about the research base for this unit of *Houghton Mifflin Math*, see *Professional Resources Handbook, Grade 4.***

Research Summary* for Unit 2

TO: **Fourth Grade Teachers**

SUBJECT: **"Guess My Rule"**

Pattern blocks or colored tiles can be used to bridge the gaps between arithmetic, algebra, and geometry in the intermediate grades. The use of these manipulatives provides opportunities for children to conjecture and confirm patterns and to represent arithmetic and geometric patterns algebraically. Algebraic thinking is extended by pattern games such as "Guess My Rule."

TRY IT OUT!

Begin by displaying geometric patterns on the overhead, chalkboard, work-table or floor. For example: circle, triangle, triangle, circle, triangle, triangle. Children should extend the pattern, then describe the rule in words. Other geometric patterns can be devised by the children challenging others to guess their rule!

Next, introduce sequences of numbers such as the following:

3, 6, 9, 12, ...

Then ask the children to extend the sequence and to explain the rule they used. Most children may see a simple "counting by threes pattern." Other children may write the rule using an algebraic expression involving n, the number of the term of the sequence. For example, in the following sequence,

3, 6, 9, 12, ...

the first term is 3, the second term is 2×3, the third term is 3×3, and so on. The rule used to find the nth term is $n \times 3$. Thus, the tenth term would be 10×3, or 30.

CHECK IT OUT!

Cai, J. (1998). Developing algebraic reasoning in the elementary grades. *Teaching Children Mathematics, 5*(4), 225–229.

Munakata, Mika (2005). Operations and algebraic reasoning. *Professional Resources Handbook—Grade 4.* Boston: Houghton-Mifflin.

Usiskin, Z. (1997). Doing algebra in grades K-4. *Teaching Children Mathematics, 3,* 346–356.

*** For more information about the research base for this unit of *Houghton Mifflin Math,* see *Professional Resources Handbook, Grade 4.***

Research Summary* for Unit 3

TO: **Fourth Grade Teachers**

SUBJECT: **A Mathematical "Recipe" for Multiplication**

The most important property of multiplication is the rule known as the distributive property. The distributive property states that for any numbers a, b, and c:

$$a \times (b + c) = a \times b + a \times c$$

Thus, there are two equally good ways to multiply a number and a sum—either add first and then multiply, or multiply each addend first and then add the products.

When combined with the expanded form of one factor, the distributive law reduces a difficult multiplication problem to several easier ones. For example:

$$7 \times 365 = 7 \times (300 + 60 + 5) =$$
$$(7 \times 300) + 7 \times 60) + (7 \times 5) =$$
$$2{,}100 + 420 + 35 = 2{,}555$$

To obtain the final answer, addition of the three products is required. When the use of the distributive property to multiply by a single digit is understood, multiplication by two-digit factors can be explained by a slightly longer but clearer "recipe."

TRY IT OUT!

$$17 \times 365 = (10 + 7) \times 365 = (10 \times 365) + (7 \times 365)$$

$$10 \times 365 = 3{,}650$$

$$7 \times 365 = 7 \times 300 + 7 \times 60 + 7 \times 5$$

$$= 2{,}100 + 420 + 35 = 2{,}555$$

and $3{,}650 + 2{,}555 = 6{,}205$

While not as compact as the customary algorithm, this procedure offers a more explicit rationale based upon place value and on the distributive law.

CHECK IT OUT!

Anghileri, J., & Johnson, D. (1992). Arithmetic operations on whole numbers. In T. Post (Ed.), *Teaching mathematics in grades K-8* (pp. 157–200). Needham Heights, MA: Allyn & Bacon.

Fischbein, E., Deri, M., Sainto Nello, M., & Sciolis, M. (1985). The role of implicit models in solving verbal problems in multiplication and division. *Journal for Research in Mathematics Education,* 16(1), 3–17.

Evered, Lisa (2005). Multiplication of whole numbers. *Professional Resources Handbook—Grade 4.* Boston: Houghton-Mifflin.

*** For more information about the research base for this unit of *Houghton Mifflin Math,* see *Professional Resources Handbook, Grade 4.***

Research Summary* for Unit 4

TO: **Fourth Grade Teachers**

SUBJECT: **Building "Scaffolds" to Divide**

The portrayal of division of whole numbers as the repeated subtraction of the divisor from the dividend is useful not only in clarifying aspects of the concept of division, but also in formulating an alternative algorithm for long division that is easier to understand than the customary procedure. Most children learn long division by imitation and memorization rather than with understanding.

One alternative procedure is called the "scaffolding method." In many cases, it takes more time to obtain a quotient than the customary method. Since scaffolding involves estimation, good estimators can find quotients using scaffolding as quickly as the best students using the customary procedure.

TRY IT OUT!

One model for division of whole numbers is repeated subtraction. Just subtract the divisor from the dividend repeatedly until the subtraction can no longer be repeated. For example:

$$36 \div 4 = 36 - 4 - 4 - 4 - 4 - 4 - 4 - 4 - 4 - 4 = 0$$

There are 9 subtractions.

The method can be abbreviated by subtracting multiples of 4 rather than just 4.

$$36 \div 4 = 36 - 12 = 24 - 12 = 12 - 12 = 0$$

Here, 3×4, or 12, was subtracted three times. Since $3 + 3 + 3 = 9$, the quotient is 9.

If you are a good estimator, possibly you can shorten your scaffold.

Divide the class into two teams—a "scaffold" team and a "long division team." Give each team the same division problem to do in class. See which team has the best success!

CHECK IT OUT!

Musser, G. L., Burger, W. F., & Peterson, B. E. (2003). *Mathematics for elementary teachers.* New York: John Wiley & Sons, Inc.

Parchesky, Michelle (2005). Division of whole numbers. In L. Esposito (Ed.), *Professional Resources Handbook—Grade 4.* Boston: Houghton-Mifflin.

Van de Walle, J. A. (2001). *Elementary and middle school mathematics.* New York: Addison-Wesley Longman, Inc.

*** For more information about the research base for this unit of *Houghton Mifflin Math*, see *Professional Resources Handbook, Grade 4.***

Research Summary* for Unit 5

TO: **Fourth Grade Teachers**

SUBJECT: **Are Students' Backpacks Too Heavy?**

Shaw and Cliett (1984) used the term "measurement sense" to describe a facility with measurement analogous to "number sense" and desirable for all students (p. 199). There are four bases for measurement sense:

1. An understanding of which units are appropriate for a measurement task.
2. An ability to carry out the measurement task.
3. A sense of when an estimate can be used instead of an actual measurement.
4. A knowledge of several strategies for obtaining good estimates.

These components of "measurement sense" are useful in planning instruction and developing measurement activities. Friel, Curcio, and Bright (2000) assert that the collection of data, often based upon measurements and the selection of the type of graph appropriate for displaying the data, are as important in understanding graphs as the ability to "read" a graph. Activities that involve measurement to obtain data to be displayed graphically lead simultaneously to "measurement sense" and "comfort" with graphs.

TRY IT OUT!

The PTA is concerned about the weight of textbooks—some parents complain that backpacks full of textbooks are too heavy for students to carry. Use a bathroom scale to weigh each student's backpack filled with the books usually carried home. What kinds of graphs could be used to display these data? Draw each type that seems appropriate. If the school physician says 15 pounds is the maximum healthy backpack weight, what do the graphs tell you about the PTA's complaint? Which type of graph answers the PTA's complaint best?

CHECK IT OUT!

Friel, S. N., Curcio, F. R., & Bright, G. W. (2001). Making sense of graphs: Critical factors influencing comprehension and instructional implications. *Journal for Research in Mathematics Education, 32*, 124–158.

Goldberg, Adam (2005). Measurement and graphing. *Professional Resources Handbook—Grade 4.* Boston: Houghton-Mifflin.

Shaw, J. M., & Puckett Cliatt, M. J. (1989). Developing measurement sense. In P. R. Trafton (Ed.), *New directions for elementary school mathematics: 1989 yearbook* (pp. 149–155). Reston, VA: National Council of Teachers of Mathematics.

*** For more information about the research base for this unit of *Houghton Mifflin Math*, see *Professional Resources Handbook, Grade 4.***

Research Summary* for Unit 6

TO: **Fourth Grade Teachers**

SUBJECT: **Estimating Areas of "Inconvenient" Figures**

Using manipulatives in geometry instruction is an excellent way to develop new concepts such as area. Although fourth grade students will have counted tiles used to "cover" geometric figures to determine the areas of standard figures, reliance upon manipulative materials that may not accurately cover non-standard figures is troublesome for some students.

All students must come to understand that every measurement is an approximation. Whether a simple ruler or beam balance or powerful microscope or analytic balance is used to measure something, the measurement is never exact.

Students are confronted with the approximate nature of measurement when they try to cover a non-standard geometric figure with tiles.

Even very tiny square tiles cannot cover a figure without overlapping the boundary. In such cases, grid paper rather than tiles can be used to estimate the area more closely.

TRY IT OUT!

After activities in which children use tiles to approximate the areas of convenient geometric figures like these, ask the class to use tiles to estimate the area of "inconvenient" figures.

Ask the boys to overestimate the area by always overlapping the boundary and ask the girls to underestimate by never overlapping the boundary. You and your students will be surprised at how large the difference between the underestimate and overestimate is!

To get a better estimate, have the class trace the figure on grid paper and obtain both an overestimate and an underestimate. One way to get an even better estimate is to average the overestimates and the underestimates.

CHECK IT OUT!

Clements, D. H., & Battista, M. T. (1992). Geometry and spatial reasoning. In D. A. Grouws (Ed.), *Handbook of research in mathematics teaching and learning* (pp. 420–464). New York: Macmillan Co.

Nickson, M. (2000). *Teaching and learning mathematics: A teacher's guide to recent research and its application.* New York: Cassell.

Walker, Erica (2005). Geometry and measurement. In L. Esposito (Ed.), *Professional Resources Handbook—Grade 4.* Boston: Houghton-Mifflin.

*** For more information about the research base for this unit of *Houghton Mifflin Math,* see *Professional Resources Handbook, Grade 4.***

Research Summary* for Unit 7

TO: **Fourth Grade Teachers**

SUBJECT: **Connecting Fractions and Decimals with Coins**

Difficulties in teaching rational numbers may be attributable to a repeated emphasis upon differences between their fraction and decimal form rather than their similarity (Middleton et al., 1998). The various ways of representing rational numbers have been taught as distinct topics, making it difficult for children to connect them conceptually.

Ways that children can make connections between fractions and decimals have been the focus of considerable research. Specific strategies for developing these connections have relied upon technology, manipulatives, and real-world problems. Among the most successful strategies are those that utilize bar models, popular in Singapore schools. Bar models of both fraction and decimal forms of rational numbers provide students who are visual thinkers with a basis for conceptualizing both the meaning of rational numbers and operations with them.

Another strategy that shows promise is the "100's scheme" of Oppenheimer and Hunting (1999). In that strategy, students think of both fractions and decimals as representing parts of 100. Money, especially coins, provides a real-world connection that exploits the students' out-of-school knowledge.

TRY IT OUT!

Begin by recalling that a dollar is equivalent to 100 cents. Then, 25c is $\frac{25}{100}$ of a dollar. Ask children if they know another name for $\frac{25}{100}$ of a dollar. Is there a coin that has that value? What is it called? Explain that $\frac{25}{100}$ is a complicated symbol. In fact, there are simpler symbols that mean the same thing: $\frac{1}{4}$ (read "one-fourth" or "one-quarter") and 0.25 (read 25 hundredths). The decimal point indicates that 0.25 is part of 100 cents and not 25 dollars. Repeat these activities with nickels, dimes, and half-dollars.

CHECK IT OUT!

DeBello, Joan and Esposito, Linda (2005). Fractions and decimals. In L. Esposito (Ed.), *Professional Resources Handbook—Grade 4.* Boston: Houghton-Mifflin.

Middleton, J. A., Heuvel-Panhuizen, M. V., & Shaw, J. A. (1998). Using bar representations as a model for connecting concepts of rational number. *Mathematics Teaching in the Middle School, 3,* 302–312.

Oppenheimer, L., & Hunting, R. P. (1999). Relating fractions and decimals: Listening to students talk. *Mathematics Teaching in the Middle School, 4(5),* 318–321.

*** For more information about the research base for this unit of *Houghton Mifflin Math,* see *Professional Resources Handbook, Grade 4.***

Research Summary* for Unit 8

TO: **Fourth Grade Teachers**

SUBJECT: **Fun with Food**

Probability and data collection and analysis have become key areas of the elementary school mathematics curriculum. These topics are relevant not only outside the classroom, but also for developing critical thinking and number sense. Further, they provide important links to other curricular areas such as social studies and science.

One way to convey the prevalence of probabilistic ideas in the real world is to have students keep a log of statements they hear, say, or see involving "chance" in books and magazines or on TV or the radio. Games and experiments are also excellent vehicles for teaching probability concepts. Fennel (1990) emphasizes that "classroom activities involving probability should be active...and furnish opportunities for questioning, problem solving and discussion," such as the use of spinners and number cubes.

Tables and graphs can be used to organize and display the data obtained from the activities.

TRY IT OUT!

Use packaged snacks that come in different colors or shapes to find the probability that a certain color or shape will be chosen from a bag. Have each child withdraw a single piece from the bag without looking. Have small squares matching colors or shapes available at the bulletin board. Children should build a bar graph showing the frequency that each color or shape is drawn.

Discuss the most likely and the least likely color to be drawn from the bag without looking.

CHECK IT OUT!

Han, Annie Yi (2005). Probability, algebra, and graphing. In L. Esposito (Ed.), *Professional Resources Handbook—Grade 4.* Boston: Houghton-Mifflin.

Hitch, C., & Armstrong, G. (1994). Daily activities for data analysis. *Arithmetic Teacher, 41*(5), 242–245.

Jones, G. A., Langrall, C. W., Thornton, C. A., & Mogill, A. T. (1997). A framework for assessing and nurturing young children's thinking in probability. *Educational Studies in Mathematics, 32,* 101–125.

*** For more information about the research base for this unit of *Houghton Mifflin Math,* see *Professional Resources Handbook, Grade 4.***

Additional Answers

Unit 5

Chapter 12

Lesson 1, p. 307

5. If the shorter green bean's length is between $4\frac{1}{2}$ inches and 5 inches, it is 5 inches long when measured to the nearest inch. If the longer green bean's length is between 5 and $5\frac{1}{2}$ inches, it is 5 inches long when measured to the nearest inch.

Lesson 3, p. 311

21. *Possible explanation:* 4 qts = 1 gal, so 1 gal costs $5.00; If $\frac{1}{2}$ gal costs $3, then 2 one-half gallon containers would cost $6.00; $5.00 < $6.00

27. *Possible explanation:* There are 2 pints in a quart and 2 quarts in one-half gallon, so multiply $2 \times 2 = 4$.

Art Connection, p. 317

Possible picture equation:

○ + ☆ + (fish) = △ + ☽ + ○ + ▯ + ▯

Chapter 13

Lesson 1, p. 335

24. four hundred six
25. seven hundred fifty-eight
26. ten thousand, two
27. four thousand, two hundred fifty
28. nine thousand, three hundred forty-five
29. sixteen thousand, four hundred
30. twenty thousand, two hundred fifty
31. nine hundred thousand, fifty
32. six hundred seven thousand, eight hundred forty-four

Math Reasoning, p. 339

Movie	Time	
	to the nearest quarter hour	to the nearest 5 minutes
The Eagle Soars	15 min	20 min
Owls of the Night	1 h 30 min	1 h 30 min
Hawks on High	1 h 15 min	1 h 15 min

Problem Solving on Tests, p. 343

3. 9 teams
   Possible explanation:
   First I divided 67 by 8. $67 \div 8 \rightarrow 8$ R3. There could be 8 teams of 8 and 1 team of 3.

4. 90 minutes
   Possible explanation:
   From quarter after 3 to quarter after 4 is 1 hour or 60 minutes. From quarter after 4 to quarter to 5 is 30 minutes. $60 + 30 = 90$ minutes

5. **a.** 21 tickets. You will not have any money left.
   b. *Answers may vary. Possible answer:* You could go on the Scrambler 3 times, the Hidden River 3 times, and the Crazy Cups 7 times.
   c. *Answers may vary. Possible answer:* You could go on the Scrambler 2 times, the Hidden River 1 time, and the Carousel 2 times.
   d. *Answers will vary. Possible answer:* You could go on the hot-air balloon ride, and then ride the Crazy Cups 1 time. I have never been on a hot-air balloon ride and I think it would be fun.

Chapter 14

Lesson 1, p. 357

Tally Chart

How Often Do You Bring Your Lunch to School?		
Answer	**Tally**	**Number**
Always	|||	3
Never	|	1
Sometimes	~~||||~~	5

Problem Solving on Tests, p. 363

3. 14 pins
   Possible explanation: Think of how many pins you need for 4 drawings, then for 5 drawings. Then look for a pattern to solve the problem.

4. Mike's estimate; check students' explanations.

5. **a.** *Answers may vary*. Possible answer: Georgia Peaches: 70¢; Delicious Apples: 35¢; Florida Oranges: 50¢; McIntosh Apples: 70¢; New York Pears: 60¢; Yellow Bananas: 45¢
   b. *Answers may vary. Possible answer:* Georgia Peaches: 73¢; Delicious Apples: 37¢; Florida Oranges: 52¢; McIntosh Apples: 71¢; New York Pears: 65¢; Yellow Bananas: 49¢
   c. *Answers may vary. Possible answer:* Georgia Peaches: 3¢; Delicious Apples: 2¢; Florida Oranges: 2¢; McIntosh Apples: 1¢; New York Pears: 5¢; Yellow Bananas: 4¢

Lesson 3, p. 365

6. *Possible explanation:* When the numbers are in order, the difference between the first number and the last number is the range. The median is the middle number in the list. The numbers that are the mode are clustered together.

Additional Answers

Chapter 14 (continued)

Lesson 5, p. 371

4.

Lionel's Piano Practice (minutes)	
Stem	Leaves
3	0
4	6 8
5	0 5 7
6	0 0 0 3 5

Mixed Review and Test Prep, p. 371

12.

My Miniature Golf Scores	
Stem	Leaves
3	2 5 8 9
4	0 1 4 5
5	7

Chapter 15

Chapter Investigation, p. 374

Possible answer: I find the number of seconds I counted on the left side of the graph and put my finger on it. Then I move my finger right until it hits the red line. I look at the bottom of the graph and read the number where my finger is. That is how far away the lightning struck.

Use What You Know, p. 375

Write About It:

10. A bar graph uses a scale and bars to represent the numbers for each item; a pictograph uses symbols and a key that tells what each symbol represents.

Lesson 1, p. 377

On Your Own

Graphs may vary. Sample:

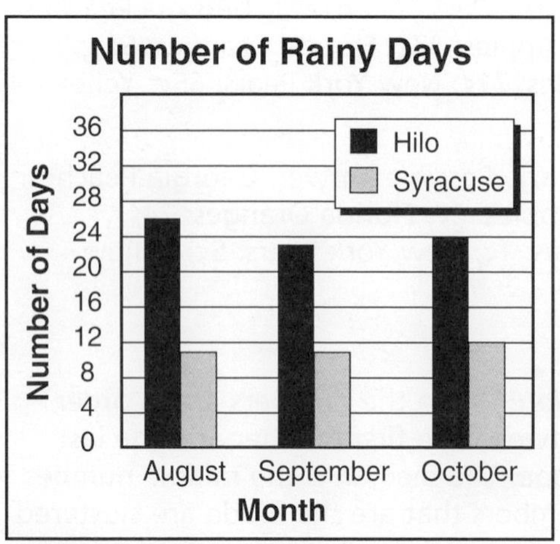

Lesson 3, p. 381

7. Climbers were climbing up faster here than during the rest of the climb because the graph indicates a greater increase in height between Point ***A*** and Point ***B*** than during any other similar time period.

Lesson 4, p. 382

Step 1–3

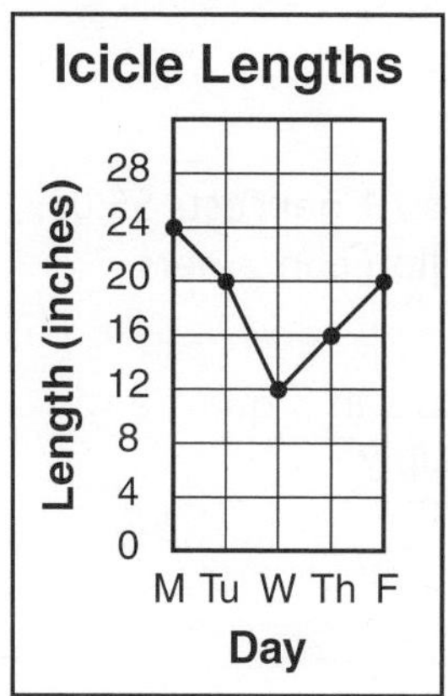

p. 383

4.

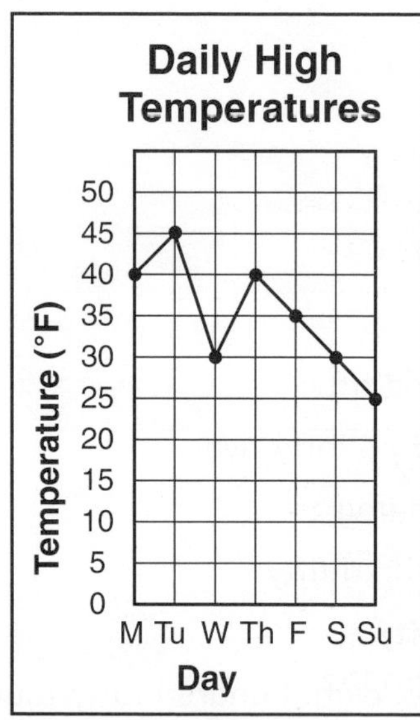

6. 20°F because the temperature was dropping 5°F per day since Thursday.

Lesson 5, p. 386

11. *Possible answer:*

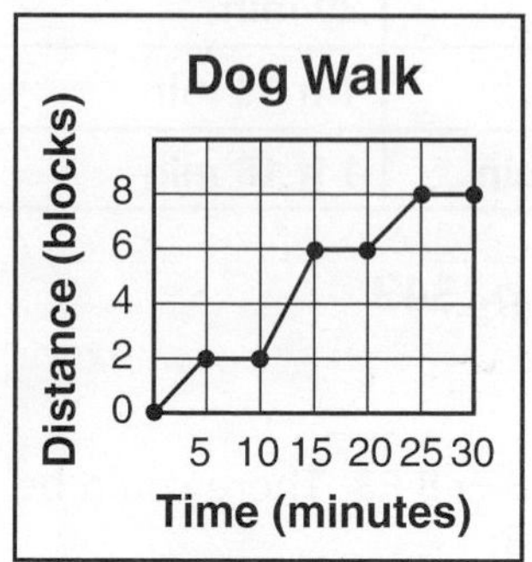

Additional Answers

Mixed Review and Test Prep, p. 387

12. mean: 8, median: 8, mode: 14, range: 13

13. mean: 7, median: 6, mode: 13, range: 12

14. mean: 9, median: 9, mode: 9, range: 6

15. mean: 6, median: 5, mode: 5, range: 8

16. mean: 30, median: 30, mode: 30, range: 20

17. mean: 20, median: 20, mode: none, range: 10

18. *Possible answer:* The bicyclist stopped to rest.

Unit 5 Test, p. 395

20.

Minutes Jacob Played in His Soccer Games

Stem	Leaves
0	1
1	3 3 3 4
2	0 0 5 5

Performance Assessment

Possible answer:

Day 1
9:00 A.M. – leave Campground
9:30 A.M. – arrive at Weather Station
11:30 A.M. – leave Weather Station
11:45 A.M. – arrive at Mini-Golf
2:45 P.M. – leave Mini-Golf
3:14 P.M. – arrive at Campground

Day 2
9:00 A.M. – leave Campground
9:14 A.M. – arrive at Nature Preserve
12:14 P.M. – leave Nature Preserve
12:22 P.M. – arrive at Colonial Village
2:22 P.M. – leave Colonial Village
2:44 P.M. – arrive at Campground

Vocabulary Wrap-Up, p. 398

Possible answers given.

1. Multiply 6 feet times 12, since there are 12 inches in 1 foot. The answer is 72 inches.
2. The mean is the average of all the numbers in the data set. The median is the middle number when the numbers are organized from least to greatest. The mode is the number listed most often.
3. Bar graphs and line graphs both show data. They both have titles and labels. They both have intervals. They are different because line graphs should be used to show data over time, while bar graphs show the number of counted items.

Unit 6

Building Vocabulary, p. 400

2. *Possible answers:* quadrilateral because it has 4 sides; rectangle because it has 4 right angles and opposite sides are parallel; rhombus because the lengths of the sides are equal; square because it has 4 right angles and 4 equal sides; parallelogram because it has two sets of parallel sides.

Chapter 16

Lesson 1, p. 406

17. *Sample:* J K

18. *Sample:* M N

19. W Y

20. *Sample:* E F G H

21. *Sample:*

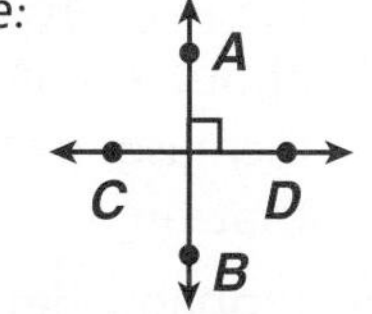

22. R P Q

23.

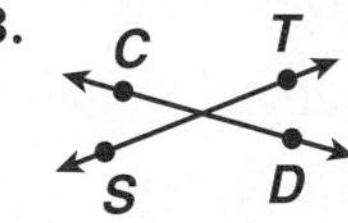

24. V W X Y

25.

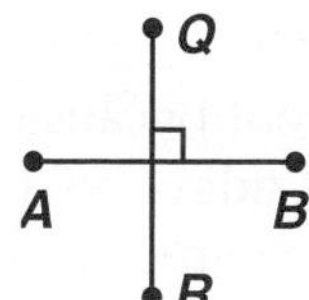

Lesson 3, p. 411

1.

2.

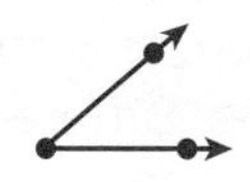

3.

4.

5.

Lesson 5, p. 417

12. *Drawings may vary. Sample:*

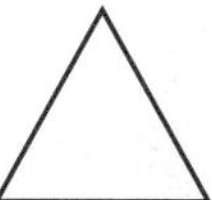

Additional Answers

13. *Drawings may vary. Sample:* 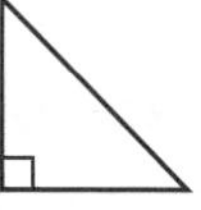

14. *Drawings may vary. Sample:* 

Problem Solving on Tests

Lesson 6, p. 421

3. There are 13. I counted the leaves on the plot.

4. The median; *Possible explanation:* The mean is $20. The $50 shirt makes the mean high. The median is $14. That seems to represent well the cost of a shirt. The mode, $10, gives the idea that shirts cost less than they actually did. The range, $40, tells little about the price of shirt.

5. *Possible answers:*

a. The Dunn family traveled the greatest distance between 10:00 A.M. and 11:00 A.M. They traveled about 75 miles. The graph has a scale showing increases of 50 miles and $1\frac{1}{2}$ spaces are crossed during that time.

b. Probably between 11:00 A.M. and 12:00 noon because they traveled the least distance during that time.

c. about $20.00; $5 \times 400 = 2{,}000$ or $20.00

Chapter Review/Test, p. 426

Write About It *Possible answer:* They are alike because they both have at least 2 equal sides and at least 2 equal angles. They are different because an equilateral triangle has exactly 3 equal sides and 3 equal angles and an isosceles triangle may have only 2 equal sides and 2 equal angles.

Chapter 17

Use What You Know, p. 429

10. *Possible answer:* They are the same because they all have four sides. Differences include: a square and a rhombus have congruent sides, the other figures don't. A trapezoid has only one pair of parallel sides, the other figures have both pairs of sides parallel. A square and a rhombus are parallelograms, a trapezoid is not. A square is a rhombus, the others are not.

Lesson 2, p. 435

6. 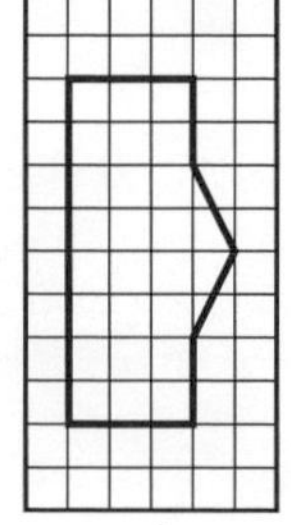

7. *Students should draw one of the following:*

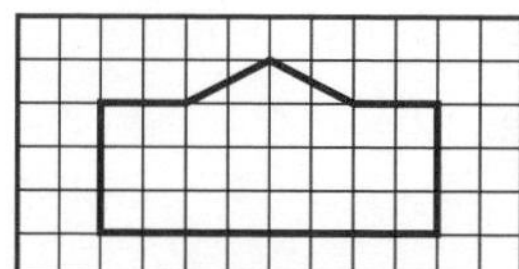 or 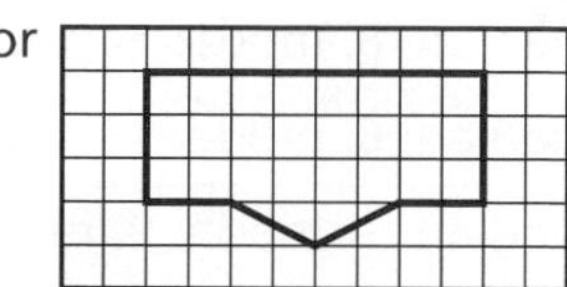

No. You can flip the figure horizontally or vertically.

Lesson 3, p. 437

1. **2.** 

3. 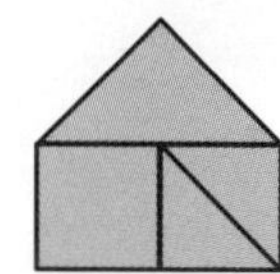

4. 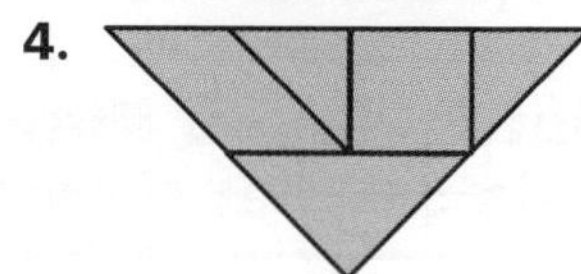

5. *Yes; Check students' drawings; possible answer shown:*

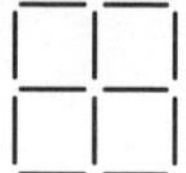

6. *Yes; Check students' drawings; possible answer shown:*

Problem Solving on Tests

Lesson 3, p. 439

3. Neither, they are the same. To find the mean, add all the values and get 39; then divide by 13, the number of values. The mean is 3 books. To find the median, find the 7th, or middle number when the numbers are in order; the median is also 3 books.

4. 2°C

Possible explanation: Start at 3 on the number line. Move 2 spaces to the right. You are at 5. Move 3 spaces to the left. You are at 2. The answer is 2°C.

5. a. *Possible explanation:*

They have 180 plants. They might use 12 rows of 15 plants.

$36 \times 5 = 180$; $180 \div 12 = 15$

b. Mr. Perez paid for 6 plants because the other 3 plants were free. He paid $29.34. 6 × $4.89 = $29.34

c.

84		?
42	42	42

About 42 plants were given away. 1 rounded the price of each plant to $5.00 and divided that into $420.00

$420 ÷ $5 = 84. About 84 plants were sold.

Additional Answers

Lesson 4

Step 3, p. 441: *Possible answer:* flip the trapezoid, slide or flip the rhombii; slide the square.

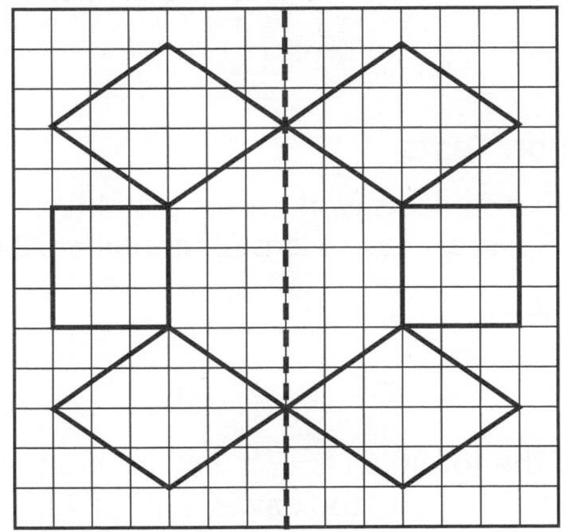

p. 442

14. 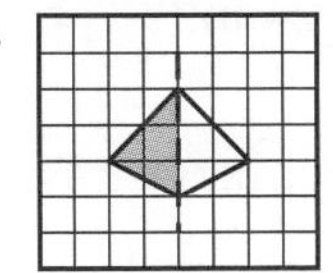

15. 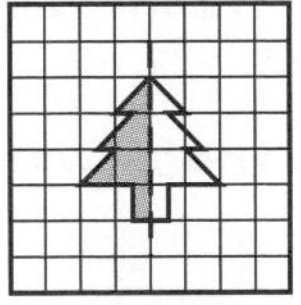

16. 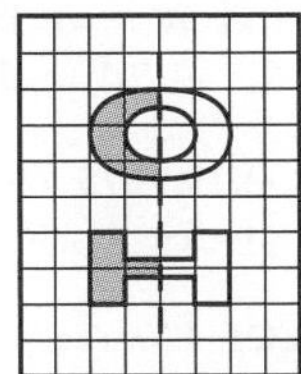

17. 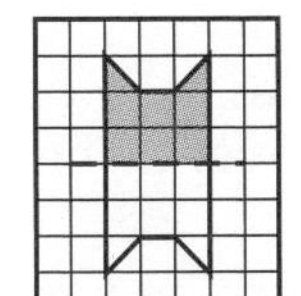

18. 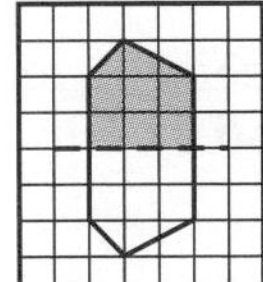

19. 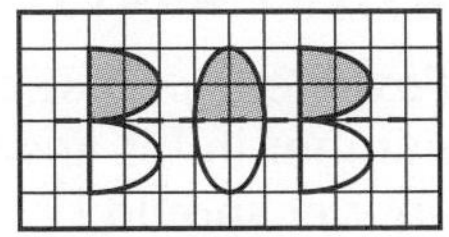

p. 443

28.   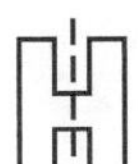

Lesson 5, p. 445

2. To find all 44 triangles, look for triangles in these sizes.

16  16 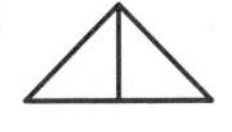

8 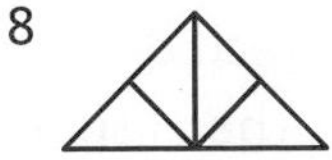 4 

Quick Check, p. 447

16. 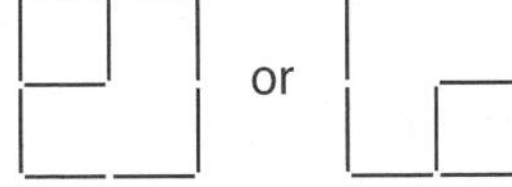

Chapter Review/Test, p. 448

9. 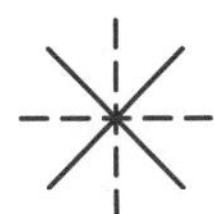

10. 

Chapter 18

Use What You Know, p. 451

20. *Possible answer:* Regular and irregular polygons are closed plane figures made up of three or more sides. The difference is that regular polygons have sides of equal length and angles of equal measure, and irregular polygons have sides of unequal lengths and can have angles of unequal measure.

Lesson 3, p. 458

25. If you double the perimeter of the living room, you are adding the length (19 ft) four times for a total of 112 ft. To find the total perimeter of the three rooms, you should add the length only twice:
19 ft + 19 ft + 18 ft + 18 ft = 74 ft.

Lesson 5, p. 465

Step 3

Shape	Number of Faces	Number of Edges	Number of Vertices
Cube	6	12	8
Rectangular Prism	6	12	8
Square Pyramid	5	8	5
Cone	1	0	1
Cylinder	2	0	0
Triangular Pyramid	4	6	4

Lesson 6, p. 469

15. $V = l \times h \times w$
$36 = 3 \times 2 \times l$
$36 = 6 \times l$
$36 \div 6 = 6 \times l \div 6$
$6 = l$

Lesson 7, p. 473

Math Reasoning

1. Yes, because there is an edge connecting Soccer and Lacrosse. No, because there is no edge connecting Soccer and Kickball.
2. Yes, because there are no students who are members of both teams.
3. *Possible answer:* I could write each activity and then draw lines between them to show which activities are shared by a student.

Art Connection, p. 477

1. square, rectangle, right triangle
2. translations, reflections, rotations
4. yes; 

Additional Answers

Enrichment, p. 478

Try These!

7. 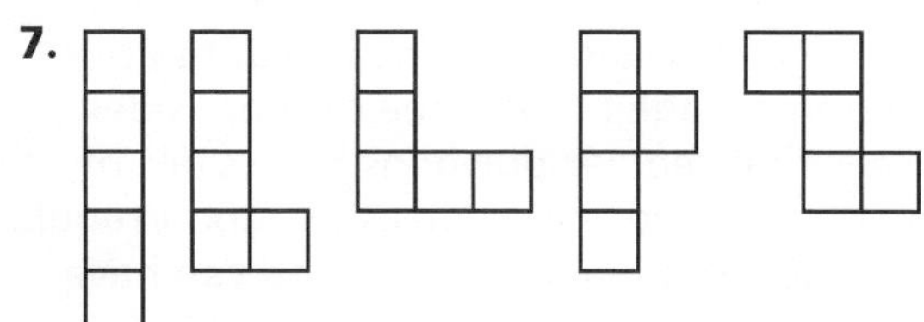

Unit Test, p. 480

22. square, hexagon, circle, square, hexagon, circle, square, hexagon

23. yes; 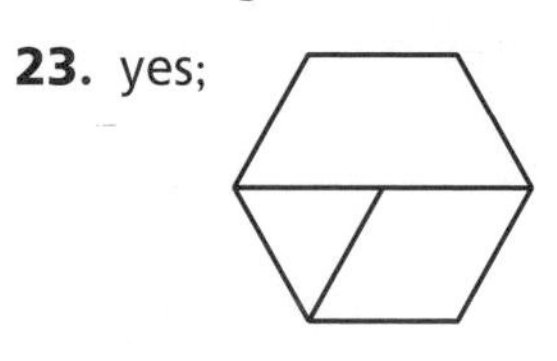

25. yes; 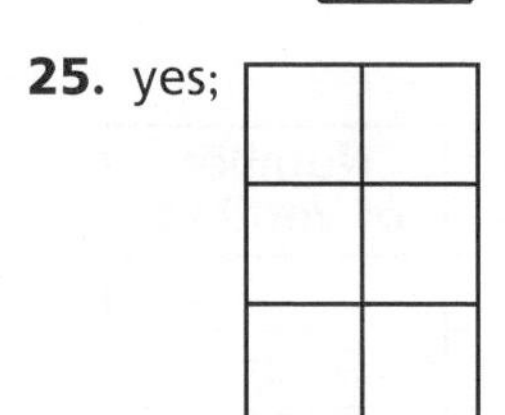

Performance Assessment

Possible answer: I started by making the display across the front. I chose 4 Rice Puffs (32 in.), 4 Oat Bran (24 in.), and 3 Coco Flakes (12 in.) for a total of 68 in. Then I found out how many boxes would fit front to back. There are 3 Rice Puffs (15 in.), 4 Oat Bran (16 in.) and 6 Coco Flakes (18 in.). So there are 12 Rice Puffs, 16 Oat Bran, and 18 Coco Flakes. There is enough room on the shelf to stack 2 Rice Puffs, 2 Oat Bran, and 3 Coco Flakes. So I can fit 24 Rice Puffs, 32 Oat Bran, and 54 Coco Flakes on the shelf.

Vocabulary Wrap-Up, p. 484

2. Area is the number of square units needed to cover a figure, $A = l \times w$; perimeter is the distance around a figure, $P = 2 \times l + 2 \times w$; volume is the amount of space inside a solid figure, $V = l \times w \times h$.

3. A figure has line symmetry if you can fold it in half so both halves match exactly. A figure has rotational symmetry if you can rotate it less than a full turn around a point and have it look the same as before you turned it.

Unit 7

Chapter 19

Chapter Investigation, p. 488

Possible answer: The school lunch staff could use the information to decide how many of each type of pizza to make in the future.

Lesson 4, p. 500

31. *Possible answer:* You can compare the numerators when the denominators are the same because you are comparing parts of the same number of total parts. When the denominators are different you need to find equivalent fractions with common denominators.

32. *Possible answer:* When you divide a whole into 12 parts, each part is bigger than a part of a whole divided into 16 parts.

Lesson 6, p. 507

Problem Solving on Tests

3. 3 parrots; check that students work shows that 4 turtles have 16 legs and 3 parrots have 6 legs for a total of 22 legs.

4. He will use 9 pages.
$36 \div 4 = 9$

5. a. 96 in.^{2}

b. 12 in.^{3}; I used the formula $l \times w \times h = v$. I multiplied $6 \times 4 \times 1$ in. $= 24$, then I took away half of 24, which I know is 12. So there is 12 in.^{3} water.

c. 48 in.^{2}; I found the area of the aquarium first. $l \times w = a$; $6 \times 12 = 72$ in.^{2}; $24 \times 6 = 24$ in.^{2}; $72 - 24 = 48$ in.^{2}; 48×1 in. $= 48$ in.^{3}

d. *Answers will vary. Possible answers*: pebbles, grass, sticks, food

Chapter Review/Test, p. 512

Write About It

Possible explanation: Bob used the remainder as the whole number in his answer instead of using the quotient. The answer should be $2\frac{3}{5}$.

Chapter 20

Lesson 2

Explain Your Thinking, p. 520

Possible answer: First I added the fractions to get $\frac{6}{4}$, which is equivalent to $\frac{3}{2}$. I rewrote the fraction as a mixed number, $1\frac{1}{2}$. Then I added the whole numbers to get 6. The answer is $1\frac{1}{2} + 6$ or $7\frac{1}{2}$.

p. 521

23. $2\frac{1}{6}$; *Possible explanation:* First I subtracted the fractions to get $\frac{2}{12}$, which is equivalent to $\frac{1}{6}$. Then I subtracted the whole numbers to get 2. The answer is $2 + \frac{1}{6}$ or $2\frac{1}{6}$.

Lesson 7, p. 532

23. *Possible answer:* To subtract fractions with unlike denominators, you need to find fractions with a common denominator.

24. *Possible answer:* Change $\frac{1}{2}$ to $\frac{3}{6}$ and $\frac{1}{3}$ to $\frac{2}{6}$.
$\frac{3}{6} - \frac{2}{6} = \frac{1}{6}$

Music Connection, p. 533

♪; 𝅗𝅥; ♩; 𝅗𝅥

Additional Answers

Fraction Sense, p. 533

Possible answer: A peach is much smaller than a watermelon, so you can't compare the parts. 1 piece of a 4-slice pizza would be bigger than 1 piece of an 8-slice pizza.

Chapter 21

Chapter Investigation, p. 540

Possible answer: I could write the numbers in the length column as fractions: $\frac{1}{4}$ hour, $\frac{1}{2}$ hour, $\frac{3}{4}$ hour

Lesson 2, p. 545

Mixed Review and Test Prep

23. 1, 2, 3, 6

24. 1, 2, 3, 4, 6, 8, 12, 24

25. 1, 2, 3, 6, 9, 18

26. 1, 5, 25

27. 1, 2, 7, 14

28. 1, 3, 9, 27

29. 1, 2, 3, 5, 6, 10, 15, 30

30. 1, 2, 4, 5, 10, 20

31. 1, 2, 3, 6, 7, 14, 21, 42

Lesson 3, p. 548

33. four tenths; 0.4

34. sixty-five hundredths; 0.6 + 0.05

35. five and three hundredths; 5 + 0.03

36. three and seven hundredths; 3 + 0.07

37. three dollars and ninety-eight cents; $3 + 0.9 + 0.08

38. four and three tenths; 4 + 0.3

39. five and sixty-seven hundredths; 5 + 0.6 + 0.07

40. four and eight hundred seventy-six thousandths; 4 + 0.8 + 0.07 + 0.006

41. five thousandths; 0.005

42. three and ninety-eight thousandths; 3 + 0.09 + 0.008

Lesson 5, p. 557

Problem Solving on Tests

4. 25 toys; Check pictures, which should show 10 dolls, 10 cars, and 5 puppets.

5. a. No, Mrs. Stewart does not have enough money.
4 × $3.89 = $15.56 for ice cream; 16 cups of lemonade per gallon, so 16 + 16 = 32 cups of lemonade
2 × $1.98 = $3.96 for lemonade;
3 × $2.85 = $8.55 for chips; $2.49 for napkins; 3 packages of spoons 3 × $0.89 = $2.67; 2 packages of paper plates 2 × $2.99 = $5.98; 4 packages of plastic cups 4 × $0.69 = $2.76;
$15.56 + $3.96 + $8.55 + $2.49 + $2.67 + $5.98 + $2.76 = $41.97; $41.97 > $40.00

b. *Answers will vary. Possible answer:* There are 23 students in my class and 1 teacher. I will need 24 cups of ice cream. There are 8 cups of ice cream in $\frac{1}{2}$ gallon, so I will need 3 half-gallon containers of ice cream.
3 × $3.89 = $11.67 for ice cream.
2 gallons of lemonade is plenty, so 2 × $1.98 = $3.96 for lemonade; 3 bags of chips 3 × $2.85 = $8.55;
1 package of napkins $3.49;
2 packages of plastic spoons 2 × $0.89 = $1.78;
2 packages of paper plates 2 × $2.99 = $5.98;
3 packages of plastic cups 3 × $0.69 = $2.07;
$11.67 + $3.96 + $8.55 + $3.49 + $1.78 + $5.98 + $2.07 = $37.50
It would cost $37.50 for a party for my class.

Lesson 6, p. 559

17. 1, 3, 9, 27, 81

18. 1, 5, 7, 35

19. 1, 2, 3, 6, 9, 18

20. 1, 2, 3, 4, 6, 8, 12, 24

21. 1, 2, 4, 5, 10, 20

22. 1, 3, 5,15

23. 1, 2, 3, 6, 7, 14, 21, 42

24. 1, 2, 3, 4, 6, 9, 12, 18, 36

Chapter 22

Chapter Investigation, p. 566

Multiply each foreign money amount by 2.

Lesson 1, p. 569

Explain Your Thinking:

Whether rounding decimals or whole numbers, you look at the digit to the right of the place you want to round to. You use the same rules whether rounding decimals or whole numbers.

37. *Possible answer:* Rounding to the nearest whole number would give a reasonable estimate of 35. Students should explain their choice of the rounding place.

Lesson 2, p. 571

Explain Your Thinking:

Rounding to the nearest $10 gives the most reasonable estimate. When you round to the nearest $10 you get an estimate of $260. When you round to the nearest $100, you get an estimate of $300. The actual answer of $262.45 is much closer to $260 than to $300.

Mixed Review and Test Prep:

28. Round each distance to the nearest whole number, then add: 3 + 2 + 3 = 8 kilometers. Subtract to find how much further he needs to ride: 10 − 8 = 2 kilometers.

Additional Answers

Lesson 4, p. 575

Explain Your Thinking:

When adding or subtracting either decimals or whole numbers, you work from right to left and regroup the same way. When adding and subtracting decimals, you have to line up the decimal points, add zeros when needed, and write the decimal point in the answer.

Lesson 5, p. 578

11. Yes; by rounding to the nearest dollar you find that Lita and her dad will spend about \$49 at the amusement park and have about \$16 left over. The state park will only cost about \$10; Estimation

Chapter Review/Test, p. 580

Write About It:

He did not use the rules of rounding. He just dropped the tenths and hundredths and added the whole numbers. He should have rounded 6.81 to 7, 5.76 to 6, and 7.53 to 8 and then added to get 21.

Unit Test, p. 587

Performance Assessment

Possible answer:
1 large cheese pizza (about \$10),
1 medium pepperoni pizza (about \$8),
1 medium vegetable pizza (about \$7),
4 small juices (\$4), 1 large juice (\$1.25),
5 small soft drinks (\$3.75);
\$10 + \$8 + \$7 + \$4 + \$1.25 + \$3.75 = \$34.00

Possible explanation:
Six students like pepperoni but are willing to eat cheese so I chose a large cheese pizza (8 slices) and a medium pepperoni pizza (6 slices) for them to share. The student who only likes cheese can have 2 slices of the large cheese pizza. The other 2 students and the leader can share the medium vegetable pizza (6 slices). Four students can each have a small juice, 5 students can have small soft drinks, and the leader can have a large juice.

Unit 8

Chapter 23

Lesson 1, p. 597

10. Answers may vary. Possible answer is: No; when you do a probability experiment, you usually do not pick exactly the number and type of tiles that are in the bag.

Lesson 2, p. 600

19.

Lesson 4, p. 607

Problem Solving on Tests

3. likely; The spinner has more shaded area than unshaded area.

4. *Answers may vary. Possible answer:* Spinner divided into 6 equal parts having 3 parts red, 2 parts blue and 1 part yellow.

5. a. \$500.00

b. They would save money by buying the 3 day ticket. Two 1-day tickets would cost \$170. One 3-day ticket costs \$120. \$170 − \$120 = \$50. They would each save \$50.

c. \$746.00; \$119 × 4 = \$476; \$135 × 2 = \$270; \$476 + \$270 = \$746

Lesson 5, p. 608

1.

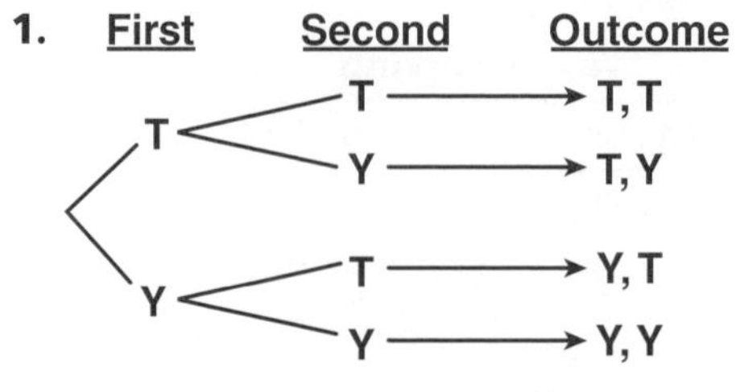

Second Draw

		T	Y
First Draw	T	T, T	T, Y
	Y	Y, T	Y, Y

Lesson 5, p. 609

3.

Spinner

		blue	red	yellow	green
Coin	heads	heads, blue	heads, red	heads, yellow	heads, green
	tails	tails, blue	tails, red	tails, yellow	tails, green

7.

Spinner B

		red	blue	green
Spinner A	red	red, red	red, blue	red, green
	blue	blue, red	blue, blue	blue, green

10. 8 ways:

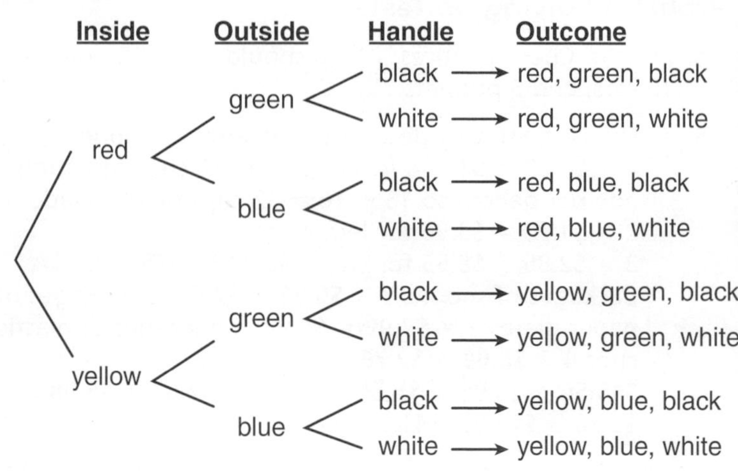

Additional Answers

p. 610

11. 6 outcomes:

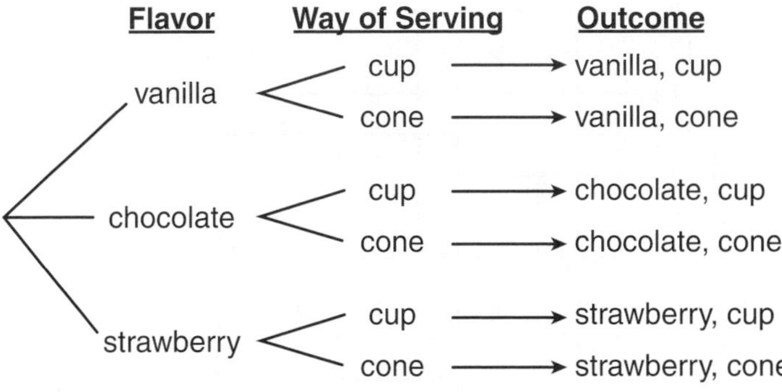

Way of Serving

Flavor		cup	cone
	vanilla	vanilla, cup	vanilla, cone
	chocolate	chocolate, cup	chocolate, cone
	strawberry	strawberry, cup	strawberry, cone

12. 12 outcomes;

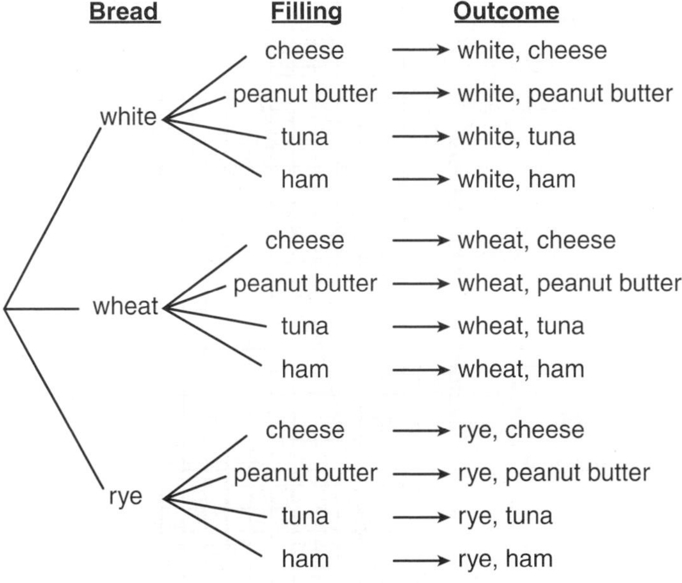

Filling

Bread		cheese	peanut butter	tuna	ham
	white	white, cheese	white, peanut butter	white, tuna	white, ham
	wheat	wheat, cheese	wheat, peanut butter	wheat, tuna	wheat, ham
	rye	rye, cheese	rye, peanut butter	rye, tuna	rye, ham

13. 9 outcomes;

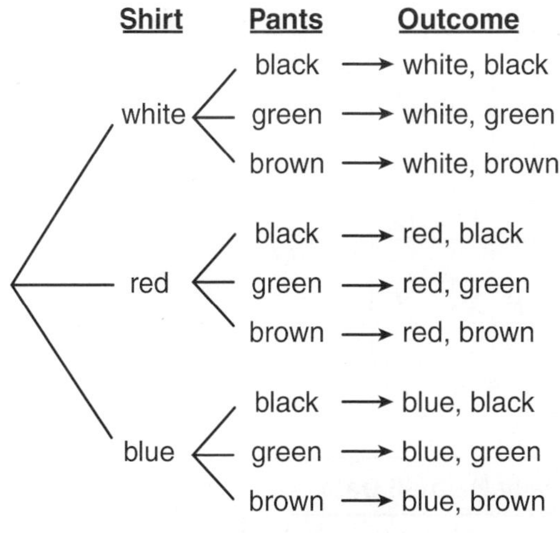

Pants

Shirt		black	green	brown
	white	white, black	white, green	white, brown
	red	red, black	red, green	red, brown
	blue	blue, black	blue, green	blue, brown

Chapter Review/Test, p. 612

Write About It

Possible explanation: Yes; 8 times. The probability that a 2 will be rolled is 1 out of 6. If the number cube is rolled 48 times, this is 8 times the number of rolls, so a 2 should be rolled 8 times as many.

Extra Practice, p. 613

Set B

1. 2 out of 6 or 1 out of 3; $\frac{2}{6}$ or $\frac{1}{3}$
2. 3 out of 6 or 1 out of 2; $\frac{3}{6}$ or $\frac{1}{2}$
3. 1 out of 6; $\frac{1}{6}$
4. 4 out of 6 or 2 out of 3; $\frac{4}{6}$ or $\frac{2}{3}$
5. 5 out of 6; $\frac{5}{6}$
6. 0 out of 6; $\frac{0}{6}$ or 0

Additional Answers

Chapter 24

Lesson 2, p. 619

7–16.

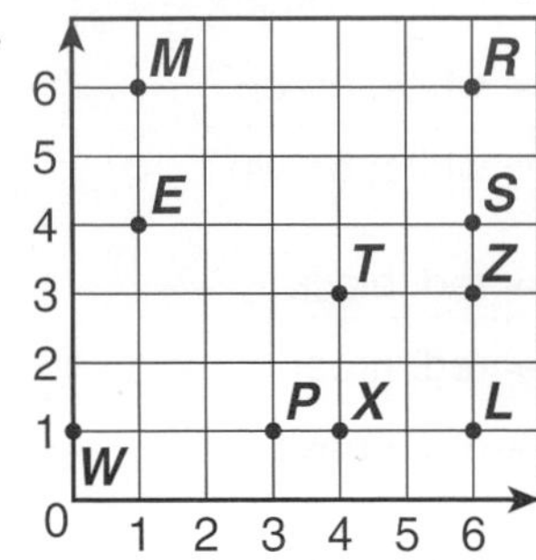

17b.

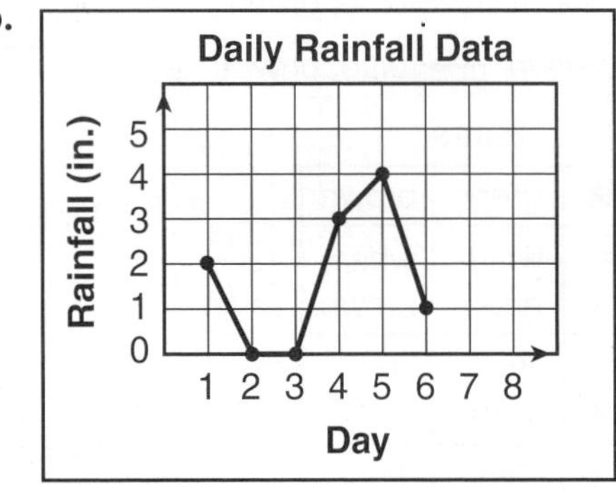

Quick Check

1. and 2.

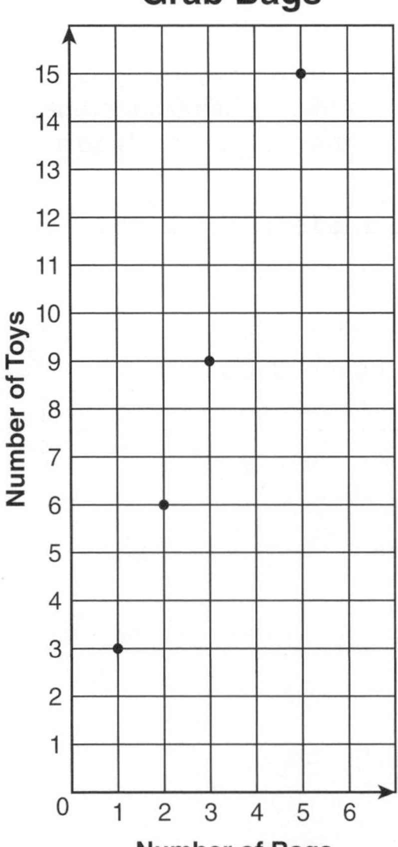

Lesson 3, p. 621

2.

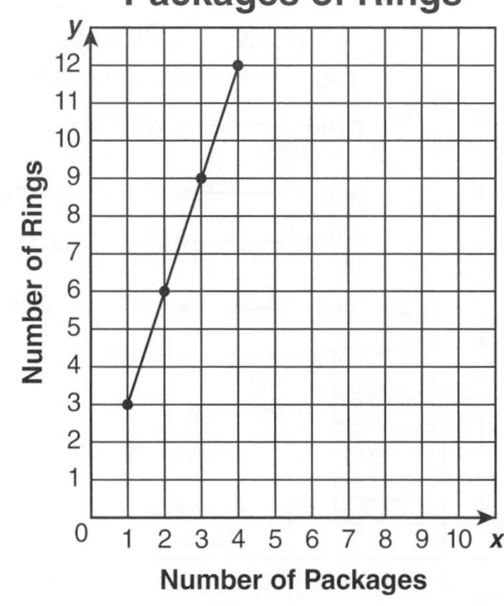

5. and 6.

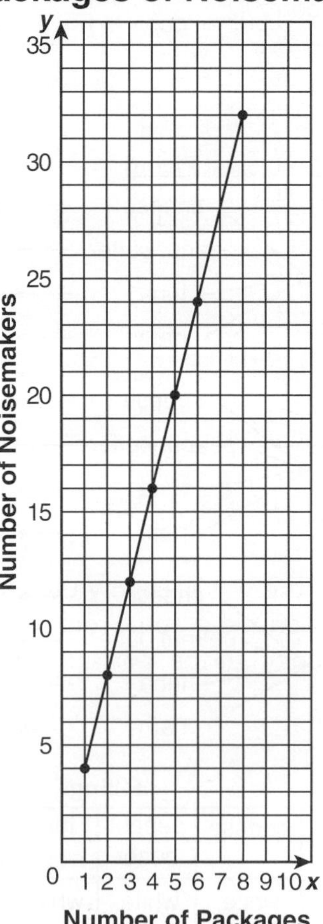

Additional Answers

p. 622

8. and 9.

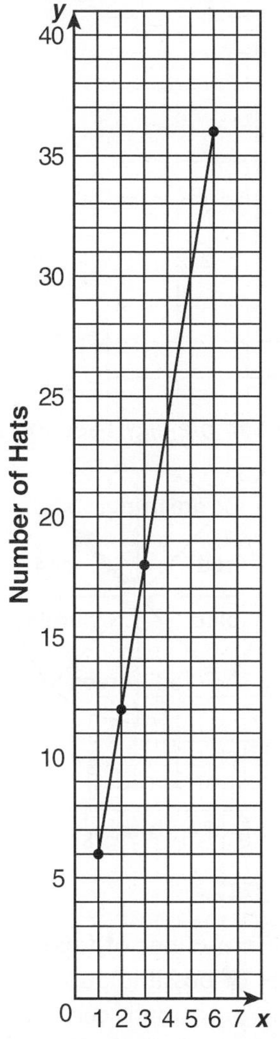

12. 2; Find 10 on the ***y***-axis. Follow the line across until you reach a point on the graph. From that point, follow the vertical line down to the ***x***-axis. Read the number of the *x*-axis: 2.

Math Reasoning, p. 627

5–8.

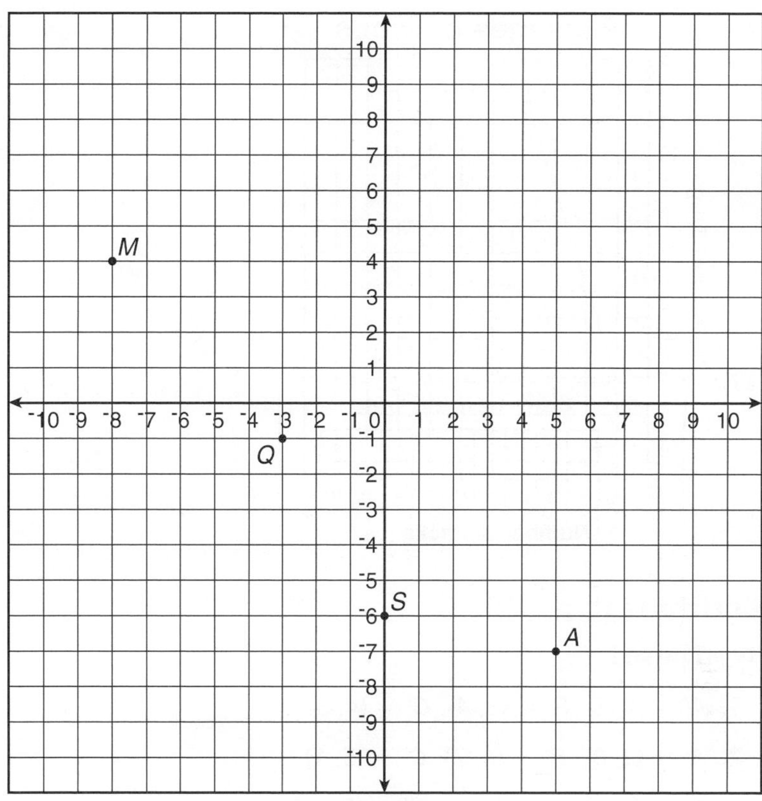

Chapter Review/Test, p. 632

8–11.

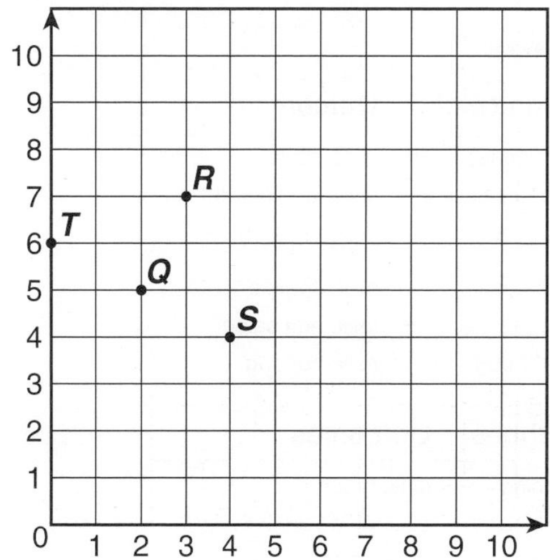

Extra Practice, p. 633

Set A, 5–8.

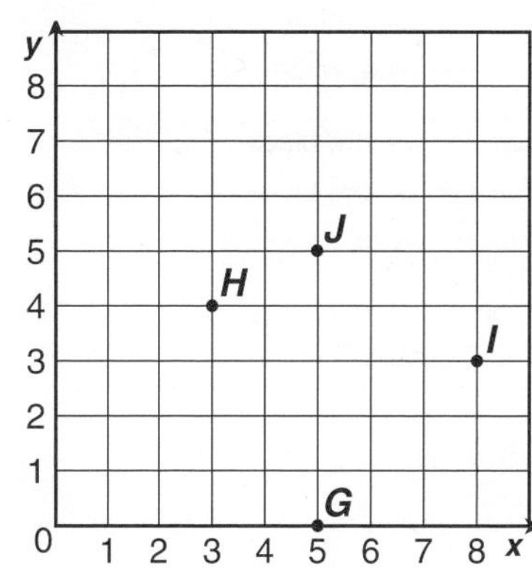

Additional Answers

Science Connection, p. 635

4. (1, 3), (2, 6), (3, 9), (4, 12)

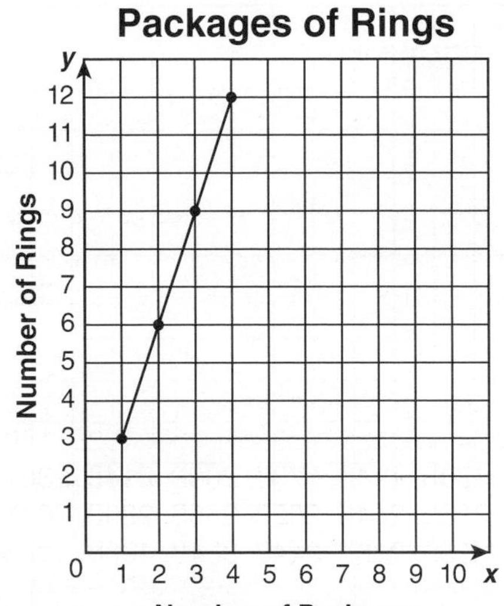

Enrichment, p. 636

Try These!

1. $A' = (1, 2)$; $B' = (3, 4)$; $C' = (4, 3)$
2. $A' = (2, 0)$; $B' = (4, 2)$; $C' = (5, 1)$
3. $A' = (2, 4)$; $B' = (4, 6)$; $C' = (5, 5)$
4. $A' = (6, 2)$; $B' = (8, 4)$; $C' = (9, 3)$

Unit Test, p. 638

11.

Drink	Sandwich	Outcomes
juice	cheese	juice, cheese
	egg salad	juice, egg salad
	hot dog	juice, hot dog
milk	cheese	milk, cheese
	egg salad	milk, egg salad
	hot dog	milk, hot dog

12. Dress Shoes Outcomes

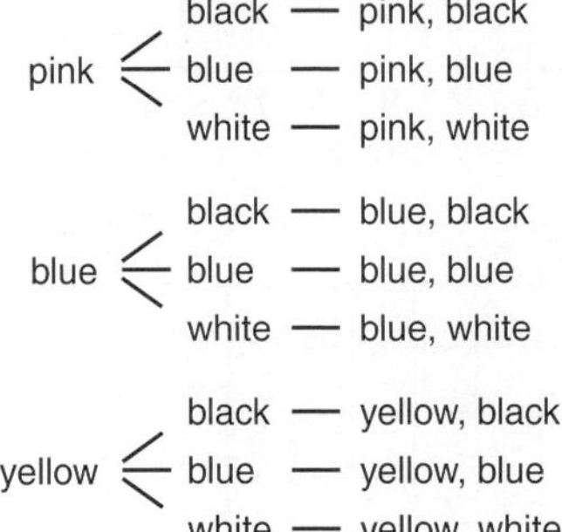

Unit Test, p. 639

17.

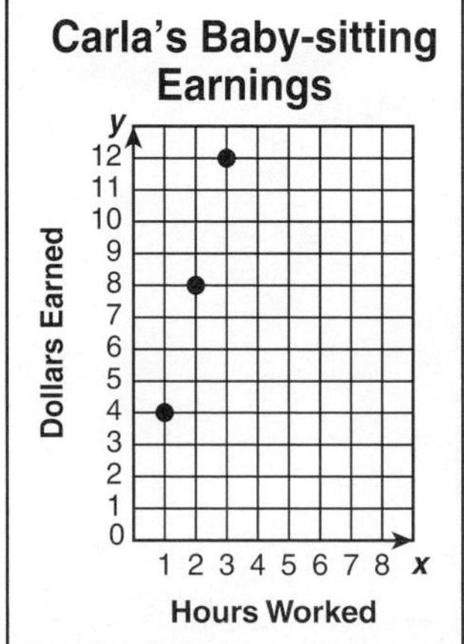

Performance Assessment

Sample six-section spinner: *Sample eight-section spinner:*

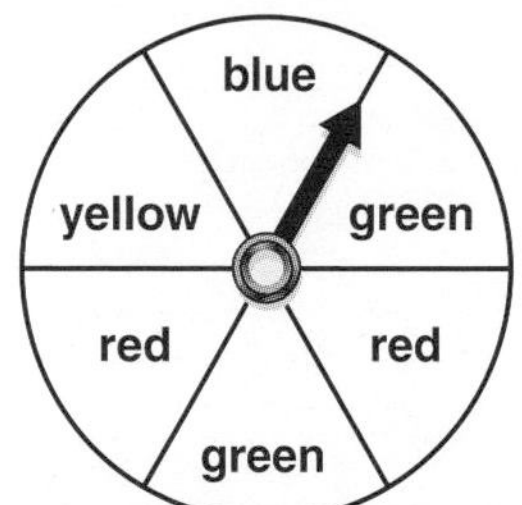

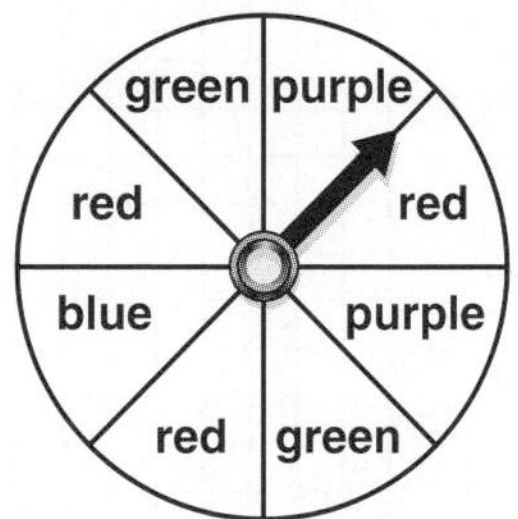

blue: $\frac{1}{6}$; green: $\frac{2}{6}$ or $\frac{1}{3}$; red: $\frac{2}{6}$ or $\frac{1}{3}$; yellow: $\frac{1}{6}$

purple: $\frac{2}{8}$ or $\frac{1}{4}$; red: $\frac{3}{8}$; green: $\frac{2}{8}$ or $\frac{1}{4}$; blue: $\frac{1}{8}$

Vocabulary Wrap-Up, p. 642

1. *Possible explanation:* If the number of favorable outcomes equals the number of possible outcomes, the probability of a favorable outcome is certain. If the number of favorable outcomes is 0, the probability of a favorable outcome is impossible.
2. H – 1 out of 6, or $\frac{1}{6}$
   A – 2 out of 6 or 1 out of 3; $\frac{2}{6}$ or $\frac{1}{3}$
   W – 1 out of 6, or $\frac{1}{6}$
   I – 2 out of 6 or 1 out of 3; $\frac{2}{6}$ or $\frac{1}{3}$.
3. *Possible explanation:* The opposite of 7 is $^{-}7$; both are the same distance from zero on the number line.
4. Use the first number to tell you how far to go to the right of the origin and the second number to tell you how far to go up. Use a straightedge to connect the points.

Index

Index

Index

Index

Index

U

Credits

Credits

PERMISSIONS ACKNOWLEDGMENTS

Houghton Mifflin Mathematics © 2005, Grade 4 PE/TE

"Beyond Pluto," by Michael D. Lemonick from *TIME For Kids*, World Report Edition, October 25, 2002 Issue. Copyright © 2002 by Time, Inc. Used with permission from TIME For Kids magazine.

"But I'm Not Tired!," by Alice Park from *TIME For Kids*, News Scoop Edition, April 28, 2000 Issue, Vol. 5, No. 25. Copyright © 2000 by Time, Inc. Used with permission from TIME For Kids magazine.

"Gone Prawning" from *Weekly Reader Magazine*, October 2, 2002 issue. Copyright © 2002 by Weekly Reader Corporation. Reprinted by permission of Weekly Reader Corporation. Weekly Reader is a federally registered trademark of Weekly Reader Corp.

"Hold the Meat!," from *American Girl Magazine*, March/April 2002. Copyright © 2002 by Pleasant Company. Reprinted by permission of Pleasant Company.

"Kid Camp" from *American Girl Magazine*, July/August 2001. Copyright © 2001 by Pleasant Company. Reprinted by permission of Pleasant Company.

"Lengths of Time," by Phyllis McGinley, originally appeared in *Wonderful Time*, originally published by J.P. Lippincott Co. Copyright © 1965, 1966 by Phyllis McGinley. Reprinted by permission of Curtis Brown, Ltd.

"The Perfect Present," by E. Renee Heiss from *Highlights for Children Magazine*, September 2002 Issue. Copyright © 2002 by Highlights for Children, Inc., Columbus, Ohio. Reprinted by permission of Highlights for Children.

Cover © HMCo./Bruton Stroube Studios.

PHOTOGRAPHY

vi © Gail Mooney/Masterfile. **vii** (t) Steve Vidler/SuperStock. (b) Image Ideas. **viii** (t) Artville. **ix** (l) PhotoDisc/Getty Images. (r) © Jeff Foott/Discovery Images/PictureQuest. **xiv** (b) Bob Elsdale/agefotostock. **xi** (t) DK Images. (b) Gary Mason/agefotostock. **xv** (t) © Tom Bean/CORBIS. (b) © Peter Barrett/Masterfile. **xvi** Image 100/Alamy. **xvii** © Coco McCoy/Rainbow/PictureQuest.
xvii (t) Artville. **xxi** © NRSC Ltd./Photo Researchers Inc.
2 © Gail Mooney/Masterfile. **4** (t) © Jim Pickerell/Stock Connection/PictureQuest. (tm) © James Lemass. (m) © Pictor International, Ltd./PictureQuest. (bm) © James Lemass. (b) © Joseph Nettis/ Stock, Boston Inc./PictureQuest. **8** © Chabruken/ Getty Images. **10** (b) © Janet Haas/Rainbow/PictureQuest. (mr) © Carol Christensen/Stock South/PictureQuest. (ml) Joyce Wilson/Earth Scenes. (t) © Lucy Ash/Rainbow/PictureQuest. **12** © Michael Newman/PhotoEdit. **18** Grant Heilman Photography.
22 © Tom Bean. **24** (r) Barbara von Hoffman/Earth Scenes. (l) Tim Fitzharris/Index Stock. **26** Jim Wark/Index Stock. **27** © Archive Photos/PictureQuest. **31** (r) Image Ideas. **33** © Garry Gay/Stock Connection/PictureQuest. **34** © David Muench/CORBIS. **36** ComstockKLIPS. **38** © Lester Lefkowitz/CORBIS. **46-7** Bob Thomas/Getty Images. **46** (b) Library of Congress. **51** (cr) Angelo Cavalli/Firstlight.ca. (cr) Heatons/Firstlight.ca. **58** Frank Siteman/Getty Images. **64** Artville. **65** PhotoSpin. **68** © Dorling Kindersley. **72** © Paul Hardy/CORBIS. **73** © Susan Van Etten/PhotoEdit. **74** © Natalie Fobes/CORBIS. **75** © James A. Sugar/CORBIS. **76** John Elk/Stock Boston. **78** © Tom Bean/CORBIS. **82** Shubroto Chattopadhyay/Index Stock. **94** Eulenspiegel Puppet Theatre Company. **100** © Jim Craigmyle/CORBIS. **102** Dave Bartruff/Stock Boston. **103** nowitz.com. **108** Jim Tuten. **110** Patricia Caufield/Animals Animals. **111** © Jeff Foott/Discovery Images/PictureQuest. **112** © Jeff Foott/Discovery Images/PictureQuest. **114** © Frank Krahmer/Pictor International, Ltd./PictureQuest. **116** Keren Su/Getty Images. **118** News Ltd. **119** PhotoDisc/Getty Images. **120** News Ltd. **123** © Kimball/Premium Stock/PictureQuest. **126** (b) Gary Griffen/Animals Animals. (t) ©Elena Rooraid/PhotoEdit. **128** (l) Gerry Ellis/Minden. (r) Manaj Shah/Animals Animals. **132-3** © Bettmann/CORBIS. **133** (t) © Bettmann/CORBIS. **144** © Layne Kennedy **172** Gary Mason/agefotostock. **174** Royalty-Free/CORBIS. **179** DK Images. **180** (l) © James L. Amos/CORBIS. (r) PhotoDisc/Getty Images. **183** © Bob Anderson/Masterfile. **184** Lawrence Migdale/Stock Boston. **192-3** Courtesy of NASA. **193** (b) © Denis Scott/CORBIS. **196** (tr) PhotoDisc/Getty Images. **204** © Mug Shots/CORBIS. **210** (t) © Lake County Museum/CORBIS. (b) Lake County (IL) Discovery Museum, Curt Teich Postcard Archives. Courtesy collection of Jonathan Yonan. **216** (r) PhotoDisc/Getty Images. (l) Royalty Free/CORBIS. **220** Ralph Krubner/Index Stock. **221** sedonawolf.com. **226** Mike Hill/agefotostock. **230** (ml) Essueve/agefotostock. **230** (bl) Martin Rugner/agefotostock. (t) Mark Moffett/Minden. (br) © Mark Tomalty/Masterfile. (mr) © John Serrao/Photo Researchers Inc. **231** © Syracuse Newspapers/Al Campanie/The Image Works. **232** Digital Vision/Getty Images. **234** © Kevin Dodge/Masterfile. **237** Spanish-American Dollars, (eight reales),18th-19th c. Mexico City mint. Cut pieces countermarked for Trinidad. Silver. Collection of The Newark Museum, Marcus L. Ward Bequest 1921. Inv.:TR.16985W. The Newark Museum/Art Resource, NY. **238** Michael S. Nolan/Seapics.com. **239** Michael S. Nolan/agefotostock. **240** David Hall/agefotostock. **245** Runk/Schoenberger/Grant Heilman Photography, Inc. **246** (t) © 2003 Calvin Hall/AlaskaStock.com. (b) Royalty-Free/CORBIS. **250** © Richard Cummins/CORBIS. **258** © Paul Barton/CORBIS. **260** PhotoDisc/Getty Images. **264** © Peter Beck/CORBIS. **266** (t) Royalty-Free/CORBIS. (b) Robin Smith/Getty Images. **267** Bernardo Strozzi, Eratosthenes Teaching in Alexandria. (detail) The Montreal Museum of Fine Arts, purchase, Horsley and Annie Townsend Bequest. Photo: The Montreal Museum of Fine Arts, Christine Guest. **270** © Jonathan Nourok/PhotoEdit. **272** David Madison Sports Images, Inc. **274** (t) Johann Schumacher. **275** Linda Raynsford, Link, made from discarded tool chests and shelves. **279** © B. Taylor/Robertstock.com. **281** AP Photo/Longview News-Journal, Kevin Green. **292-3** G. Brad Lewis/Getty Images. **304** © Tom Stewart/CORBIS. **306** PhotoDisc/Getty Images. **307** (mbl) Artville. (b) PhotoDisc/Getty Images. (mbr) PhotoDisc/Getty Images. **308** © Michael J. Doolittle/The Image Works. **310** © Tom Stewart/CORBIS. **312** (tl) (tm) FoodPix/Getty Images. (tr) DK Images. **315** (b) Karl Ammann/naturepl.com. **317** Lobster Trap and Fish Tail. 1939. Hanging mobile, painted steel wire and sheet aluminum, 8'6"" × 9'6"". Commissioned by the Advisory Committee for the stairwell of the Museum. (590.1939.a-d) The Museum of Modern Art. Digital Image ©The Museum of Modern Art/Licensed by SCALA/Art Resource, NY. **318** Dianne Huntress/Index Stock. **319** (tmr) (tml) (b) PhotoDisc/Getty Images. (m) Fred Whitehead/Earth Scenes. **323** (tl) (bl) Comstock. (tm) Artville. (bm) PhotoDisc/Getty Images. **326** Schmeul Thaler/Index Stock. **327** (bl) Artville. (br) DK Images. (tl) PhotoDisc/Getty Images. **332** (t) © Greg Stott/Masterfile. (b) Royalty Free/CORBIS. **336** Jim Brandenburg/Minden. **340** Frans Lanting/Minden. **341** (b) PhotoDisc/Getty Images. (t) Bob Elsdale/agefotostock. **342** (r) PhotoDisc/Getty Images. **345** Frans Lanting/Minden. **348** Johnny Johnson/Index Stock. **349** © 2003 Johnny Johnson/AlaskaStock.com. **350** National Academies Archives. **354** Daniel Pangbourne Media/Getty Images. **356** Mary Kate Denny/Getty Images. **357** (b) PhotoDisc/Getty Images. **359** (t) © Chris Hellier/CORBIS. **360** © Peter Barrett/Masterfile. **368** (l) Comstock KLIPS. (r) PhotoDisc/Getty Images. **370** PhotoDisc/Getty Images. **374** Gandee Vasan/Getty Images. **380** (t) Paul Harris/Getty Images. (b) PhotoDisc/Getty Images. **382** Wayne B. Bilenduke/Getty Images. **384** John Warden/Index Stock. **386** (l) Doug Wechsler/Earth Scenes. **386** (r) Robert Harding Picture Library Ltd/Alamy. **387** (l) © Tom Bean/CORBIS. (m) AP Photo/Brian Branch-Price. (r) © Andre Jenny/Focus Group/PictureQuest. **391** (b) Peter Lavery/Masterfile. **394** (tr) PhotoDisc/Getty Images. **402** © Mark E. Gibson. **404** BongoPhoto. **412** HMCo. Film Archive. **414** James M. Mejuto. **416** Frick Byers/Getty Images. **417** Image 100/Alamy. **424** Rubberball Productions. **425** Hermitage, St. Petersburg, Russia/Bridgeman Art Library. **428** ©1996 Lynda Richardson/www.lyndarichardson.com. **450** © Bryan F. Peterson/CORBIS. **466** (ml)(mr) PhotoDisc/Getty Images. (l) HMCo. Film Archive. **471** © Coco McCoy/Rainbow/PictureQuest. **472** Image Farm. **476-7** © Ralph A. Clevenger/CORBIS. **476** (m) "Symmetry Drawing E78 by M.C. Escher. © 2003 Cordon Art-Baarn-Holland. All rights reserved." **477** (b) © Scott T. Smith/CORBIS. **490** Artville. **496** PhotoDisc/Getty Images. **502** Patricia Barry Levy/Index Stock. **510** (t) Comstock. **514** Karl Weatherly/Getty Images. **516** © Ariel Skelley/CORBIS. **519** © David Madison/Getty Images. **523** © Robert Franz/Index Stock/PictureQuest. **526** Mike Brinson/Getty Images. **529** PhotoDisc/Getty Images. **533** Artville. **534** (bl) PhotoDisc/Getty Images. (tr) Artville. **537** (b) Artville. **537** (t) © Sasndro Vannini/CORBIS. **540** © Lynne Siler/Focus Group/PictureQuest. **546** Myrleen Cate/Index Stock. **549** (ml)(mr)(m) The Topps Company, Inc. (b) PhotoDisc/Getty Images. (t) © Bettman/CORBIS. **554** Copyright Kathy Goedeken. **555** (t) Copyright Kathy Goedeken. (b) Comstock. **559** © Rick Rickman/NewSport. **560** David Madison Sports Images, Inc. **566** (tl) Kevin Schafer/agefotostock. (tr) Peter Bowater/agefotostock. (ml) Kord.com/agefotostock. (mr) (bl) Jose Futse Raga/agefotostock. (br) David Allan Brandt/Getty Images. **574** (t) © Macduff Everton/CORBIS. (b) © Danny Lehman/CORBIS. **576** (t) Sea/Index Stock. (b) Pictures Colour Library. **577** Kendra Haste, Platform for Art-Gloucester Road

Credits

Tube Station, galvanized wire mesh sculptures. **582-3** © RO-MA Stock/ Index Stock Imagery/ PictureQuest. **582** (icon) © PhotoDisc/Getty Images. **586** (tr) Sean Justice /Image Bank/Getty Images. (bl) PhotoDisc/Getty Images. **587** (tr) Jane Faircloth/Transparencies, Inc. **605** Barros & Barros/Getty Images. **606** (t) © Reuters NewMedia Inc./CORBIS (b) © AFP/CORBIS. **614** Roger Tully/Getty Images. **622** (r) Stockbyte. **626** © NRSC Ltd./Photo Researchers Inc. **628** © Cleo Photography/PhotoEdit. **634-5** J.Leonard/WeatherStock. **634** (b) Adam Jones/Getty Images. **635** (b) Color Day Production/Getty Images. **647** NASA. **648** © Kevin R. Morris/CORBIS. **653** © PhotoDisc/Getty Images. **654** © Burke/Triolo Productions/FoodPix. **T3** © Jim Cummins/CORBIS. **T33** © Jose Luis Pelaez/CORBIS.

ASSIGNMENT PHOTOGRAPHY

xxi (b), **90, 146, 148, 157, 162, 252, 262** (b), **307** (t), **322, 324, 329, 376** (b), **436, 440** (r), **446, 465, 553, 604, 610** (b), **629** © HMCo./Greg Anthony.

xxii, xxviii, xxix © HMCo./Joel Benjamin.

297 (tr), **481** (tr) © HMCo./Ray Boudreau.

xxx (tr), **56, 142, 202, 302** (tr), **400, 486, 592** © HMCo./Dave Bradley.

15, 122, 186, 228, 454, 468, 594, 609, 624 © HMCo./Angela Coppola.

492, 530 © HMCo./Peter Fox.

xi (br), **xii** (b), **xii** (m), **xix** (b), **11, 37, 42, 55, 85, 98, 115, 124, 129, 141, 149-151, 160, 164, 181, 201, 206, 208, 209, 212, 217, 218, 233, 262** (t), **274** (b), **276, 280, 286, 287, 301, 312** (b), **316, 347, 359** (b), **399, 407, 433, 452, 467, 485, 494, 505, 542, 543, 556, 570, 572, 591, 599, 601** (b), **618, 643** © HMCo./Carol Kaplan.

vi (bl), **xx** (r), **14, 16, 87, 88, 152, 170, 211, 602, 610** (t) © HMCo./Michael Indresano.

xxiii, xxiv, xxv, 497 © HMCo./Allan Landau.

488 © HMCo./Tony Scarpetta.

196 (b), **295** (c), **296** (tr), **300** (tr) (cr), **303** (tr), **394** (bl), **480** (bl), **484** (tr), **637** (bl), **638** (tr)(cl)(bl), **639** (tr), **642** (tr) © HMCo./Dave Starrett.

54 (tr), **195** (c), **395** (br) © HMCo./Ron Tanaka.

522 © HMCo./Tracey Wheeler.

Additional Teacher Edition photography by Ed-Imaging LLC

ILLUSTRATION

22, 35 (t), **101, 158, 188, 189, 334, 335, 339, 362, 381, 382, 383, 455, 456, 463, 506, 540, 578, 579** Argosy. **135, 200, 393** (c) Steve Attoe. **5, 311, 320, 325, 424, 464, 468** Ken Batelman. **533** William Brinkley. **197** Scott Cameron. **251** Estelle Carol. **395** (cr) Michael Cho. **155** Chris Costello. **137** Claudia Davila. **xviii, 655-56** Eldon Doty. **562** Julie Durrell. **314, 318** Neverne Covington. **92, 93** John Edwards Inc. **504, 655-56** Eldon Doty. **375, 460, 462, 464, 498, 500, 568** Joel Dubin. **xiii, xv, xvii, 282, 285, 288, 361, 456, 548** Ruth Flanigan. **236** Patrick Gnan. **616, 631** Jim Gordon. **182** Mike Gordon. **xix, 2, 37, 144, 147, 163, 183, 204, 217, 222, 237** (t), **242, 250, 279, 289, 425, 490, 496, 497, 533** (tr), **563** Ken Hansen. **652** Eileen Hine. **35** (b) Rob Hynes. **25, 351, 649-50** Nathan Jarvis. **48** (b), **49** (tr)(c), **136, 140, 590** Kelly Kennedy. **vii, 40, 41, 70, 174, 175, 233, 265, 273, 313, 366, 377, 379, 651** Dave Klug. **54** (b), **398** Bernadette Lau. **315** Brian Lies. **13, 125, 159, 261, 343, 363, 421, 557** Ruth Linstromberg. **645** Ethan Long. **50** (cr)(br) Tadeusz Majewski. **587** (cr) Jack McMaster. **50** (tr) Dirk Michiels. **614, 627** Karen Minot. **244** Ortelius Design. **51** (tr), **142, 143, 296** (bl), **302** (br), **394** (tr) Jun Park. **165, 166, 329** Precision Graphics. **43, 178** Chris Reed. **479** (c) Francois Robert. **xvi, 430, 431** Brucie Rosch. **623** Patrice Rossi. **121, 150** Alfred Schrier. **28, 365, 369, 524, 525, 546, 552, 560 Rob** Schuster. **295** (c) Ted Sivell. **237** Steve Snider. **xiii, 104, 259, 263** George Ulrich. **328** David Wenzel.

Additional Teacher Edition illustrations by Timothy Johnson, Darcy Schwartz, Argosy Publishing

All tech art by Pronk & Associates